o the House of the God of Jacob and He will teach us
n shall go forth the Law and the word of the Lord from
lem...

ENCYCLOPAEDIA JUDAICA DECENNIAL BOOK

1983–1992

EVENTS OF 1982–1992

ENCYCLOPAEDIA JUDAICA JERUSALEM

EDITORIAL STAFF

Catalogue No. 502117
ISBN No.: 965-07-0396-9

Set, printed and bound by Keterpress Enterprises, Jerusalem, Israel

Contents

V Foreword by Chaim Herzog
Former President of Israel

VII Contributors

1 Diary of Events 1982–1992

33 Israel-PLO Mutual Recognition

The An-Sky Collections (color between pages 180 and 181)
Synagogues in Central and Southern Europe (color between pages 180 and 181)

FEATURE ARTICLES

36 1982–1992: Into a New Age of Uncertainty
William Frankel

46 Focus on Israel: Twenty-Five Years of Foreign Media Reporting
Yoel Cohen

57 Intermarriage in the United States
Mervin F. Verbit

65 A Fading Heritage: The Fate of Central and Southern European Synagogues
Rivka and Ben-Zion Dorfman

91 The An-Sky Collections: Jewish Collections of the State
Ethnographic Museum in St. Petersburg
Judith C. E. Belinfante and Ludmilla Uritskaya

1983–1992 NEW FACTS, NEW ENTRIES

97 New Facts, New Entries
397 Necrology
403 Glossary
407 Index

CHAIM HERZOG
حايم هرتصوغ

חיים הרצוג

March 3, 1994

The Encyclopedia Judaica has proved to be a landmark in Jewish encyclopedic endeavors in this century. Conceived, prepared and produced in the second half of this century, it is the first major Jewish encyclopedia to be published since the early years of this century.

I had the honor and privilege to be Chairman of the Keter Publishing House when the Encyclopedia was produced. Its contribution to Jewish scholarship and awareness has been incalculable. It is now a sine qua non in every Jewish, and many general libraries throughout the world. It was conceived to be a major element in sponsoring Jewish education and awareness. It is a monumental work of which all those associated with its production, the City of Jerusalem, and indeed the State of Israel, can be very proud.

Since the publication of the Encyclopedia, the world has changed dramatically, and with it, the Jewish world. It is right and appropriate, therefore, that we welcome the second Decennial volume of the Encyclopedia Judaica, which records the changes which have occurred, their implications for the Jewish People, and the realities of Jewish life.

The Encyclopedia Judaica was one of the important Jewish publications during the 20th century. It is right and fitting that the Decennial volume be published towards the end of the century and as the world and world Jewry move into a new century and face new challenges.

Chaim Herzog

Chaim Herzog

Contributors

Feature Articles

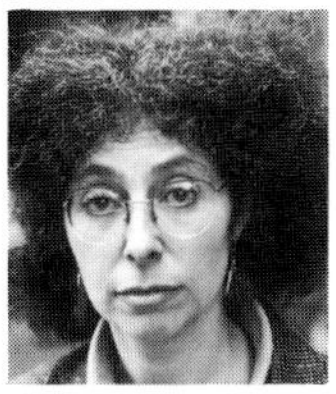
Judith Belinfante

JUDITH C.E. BELINFANTE was born in Voorburg, Holland, in 1943. She received her M.A. in history at the University of Amsterdam. In 1969 she became an assistant at the Jewish Historical Museum in Amsterdam and has been its director since 1976.

Yoel Cohen

YOEL COHEN was born in London in 1953 and emigrated to Israel in 1980. He is a graduate in International Relations from London University and has a doctorate in political sociology from City University London. Cohen, a research fellow at the Leonard Davis Institute for International Relations, The Hebrew University of Jerusalem, is a specialist in international communications. His publications include *Media Diplomacy* (1986). His research has included sociological aspects of the foreign press corps in Israel; military-media relations; and informational aspects of American Jewish-Israeli relations.

Rivka Dorfman

RIVKA and **BEN-ZION DORFMAN** were founding members of kibbutz Sasa in 1949. Rivka is a graduate of the Hebrew Teachers' College in Boston and earned an M.A. in ancient Semitic languages and Near Eastern art at Columbia University. After a career in early childhood education and special education, she studied art history and Jewish art informally at The Hebrew University of Jerusalem from 1979. Rivka and Ben-Zion, a geneticist, documented art and architecture of synagogues in central and southern Europe during the course of five summers, and are preparing their results for publication. Their project in synagogue art research was awarded the "Prize of the Minister of Education and Culture for Innovators in Jewish Culture, 5753–1993."

Ben-Zion Dorfman

WILLIAM FRANKEL, born in London in 1917, began his professional life as secretary of the British Mizrachi Federation. He was subsequently called to the Bar as a Member of the Middle Temple and practiced in London and on the South Eastern Circuit. In 1955 he was appointed general manager of the *Jewish Chronicle* and two years later became its editor, a post which he held until 1977. After his retirement he remained a member of the Board of Directors of the *Jewish Chronicle* and became chairman in 1991. In 1971 he was appointed by HM The Queen a Commander of the Order of the British Empire. He wrote *Israel Observed* (1980) and was the editor of the annual *Survey of Jewish Affairs* from 1982 through 1992.

William Frankel

LUDMILLA URITSKAYA is a curator at the State Ethnographic Museum in St. Petersburg and chief curator of the "Tracing An-Sky" exhibition.

MERVIN F. VERBIT was born in 1926 in Philadelphia, Penn., and received his Ph.D. from Columbia University in 1968. He is professor of sociology at Brooklyn College.

1983–1992 New Articles, Updating

A.F.L. **Asher Felix Landau**, B.A., LL.B.; Retired President of the District Court, Jerusalem

A.J.G. **Arden J. Geldman**, M.A.; Writer and researcher, Projects Administrator: Joint Program for Jewish Education, Jerusalem

Ak.Z. **Akiva Zimmerman**; Lecturer and Journalist on Hazzanut, Tel Aviv

Al.Gr. **Alice Greenwald**, M.A.; Museum Services Consultant

Al.Nar **Avram Alberto Nar**; Center of Historical Studies; Jewish Community of Thessalonika, Salonika, Greece

Am.E. **Amnon Einav**; Chief Scientist, Israel Ministry of Energy

Am.H. **Amnon Hadary**, Ph.D.; Writer and Researcher, Jerusalem

Am.N. **Amnon Netzer**, Ph.D.; Associate Professor of Iranian Studies, The Hebrew University of Jerusalem

An.Le. **Antony Lerman**; Director, Institute of Jewish Affairs, London

A. Ra. **Abraham Rabinovich**, B.A.; Journalist, Jerusalem

Ash. B. **Asher Benson**; Journalist, Dublin

Av.Ho. **Avner Holtzman**, Ph.D.; Lecturer, Dept. of Hebrew Literature, Tel Aviv University

Avi Be. **Avi Beker**; World Jewish Congress, Jerusalem

Aw.Hab. **Awni Habash**, Ph.D., LL.B.; Lawyer and sociologist, Bethlehem University

B.C. **Bryan Cheyette**, Ph.D.; Lecturer, Dept. of English, Queen Mary and Westfield College, University of London

Be.M. **Beverly Mizrachi**, M.A.; Sociologist, Jerusalem

Be.R. **Betty Roitman**, Ph.D.; Associate Professor of French and Comparative Literature, The Hebrew University of Jerusalem

B.Me. **Bent Melchior**, Chief Rabbi of Denmark, Copenhage

Da.B. **David Bellos**, Ph.D.; Professor of Literature, University of Manchester

Da.Dr. **Daniel Dratwa**, Ph.D., Curator of Musee Juif de Belgie, Brussels

Da.Ne. **David Newman**, Ph.D.; Senior Lecturer, Department of Geography and Environmental Development, Chaiman, Urban Studies Program, Ben Gurion University of the Negev, Beersheba

Da.P. **David Polish**, Rabbi; Emeritus Rabbi of the Free Synagogue, Evanston, Illinois

Da.Ru. **Daniel Rubinstein**; Journalist, Jerusalem

D.Ba. **Dan Barag**, Ph.D.; Professor of Archaeology, The Hebrew University of Jerusalem

D.B.-S. **Daniel Ben-Simhon**; Jerusalem

D.Bs. **Doris Bensimon-Donath**, D.esL.; Professor emerite, Institut National Langues et Civilisations, Paris

D.Ce. **David Cesearni**, D. Phil. (Oxon.); Director, Institute of Contemporary History and Wiener Library, London

D.J.L. **Daniel J. Lasker**, Ph.D.; Senior Lecturer, Jewish Thought Division, Ben-Gurion University of the Negev

D.Kh. **Dan Kharuv**, Ph.D.; Editor, The Shorter Jewish Encyclopaedia in Russian, Jerusalem

D.L.S. **Dora Leah Sowden**, M.A.; Critic and Journalist, Jerusalem

D.Ros. **Daniel Rossing**, M.T.S.; Director, Melitz Center for Christian Encounter with Israel, Jerusalem

D.Tr. **Daniel Tropper**, Ph.D.; Director, Gesher Foundation, Jerusalem

E.Ad. **Evelyn Adunka**, Ph.D.; Historian, Vienna

E.Ho. **Elaine Hoter**, M.A.; Materials developer for the Open University, Tel Aviv

El.C. **Eli Citonne**; businessman and photographer, Istanbul

El.Va. **Elaine Varady**; Israel Museum, Jerusalem

E.N.D. **Elliot N. Dorf**, M.H.L., Ph.D., Rabbi; Provost and Professor of Philosophy, University of Judaism, Los Angeles

E.Ra. **Emanuel Rackman**, Ph.D., Rabbi; Chancellor, Bar Ilan University, Ramat Gan

E.v.V. **Edward van Voolen**, Ph.D., Rabbi; Curator, Joods Historisch Museum, Amsterdam

E.We. **Eugen Werber**; Writer, Scholar, Lecturer on Judaica, Belgrade

Gi.Ko. **Gideon Kouts**; Israeli Correspondent and Journalist, Paris

Gl.M. **Gloria Mound**; Researcher, Ibiza

G.Ro. **Gerald Rosin**; Central African Jewish Board of Deputies, Harare, Zimbabwe

G.W. **Geoffrey Wigoder**; Editor in chief, Encyclopaedia Judaica, Jerusalem

H.Alt. **Hadas Altwarg**; Researcher, Institute of Jewish Affairs, London

Ha.Ro. **Harry L. Rosenfeld**, M.A., Rabbi; rabbi of Congregation Beth Sholom, Anchorage, Alaska

Ha.Sh. **Haim Shapiro**; Writer and Journalist, Jerusalem

H.Bo. **Henriette Boas**, Ph.D.; Journalist, Amsterdam

H.M.W. **Harold M. Waller**, Ph.D.; Associate Dean (Academic), Faculty of Arts, and Professor of Political Science, McGill University; Director, Canadian Centre for Jewish Studies

Ho.Sp. **Howard Spier**, Ph.D.; Researcher, Institute of Jewish Affairs, London

H.Try. **Hillel Tryster**; Film critic and journalist, Jerusalem

H.Y. **Hanri Yasova**; Writer, Istanbul

I.J.A. **Institute of Jewish Affairs**, London

Je.Ho. **Jerry Hochbaum**, Ph.D., MSW; Executive Director, Memorial Foundation for Jewish Culture, New York

J.F.C. **Judy Feld Carr**, Mus. M., Mus. Bac.; musicologist and music educator; Chairman, National Task Force for Syrian Jews, CJC; Chairman, Dr. Ronald Feld Fund for Jews in Arab Lands, housed in Beth Tzedec Congregation, Toronto

J.Fe. **John Felsteiner**, Ph.D.; Profesor of English, Stanford University, Stanford, California

J.H.S. **Jesse Harold Silver**; Sports writer, Surfside, Florida

Jo.Li. **Jonathan Licht**, B.A., M.F.A.; Writer, Jerusalem

Jo.Na. **Jose Luis Nachenson**, Ph.D.; Director of Research and Publications, Institute for Cultural Relations Israel-Latin America, Spain, and Portugal, Jerusalem

Ju.Ba. **Judith Barack**, M.A.; Writer, New York

Ju.Sch. **Julia Schopflin**; Researcher, Institute of Jewish Affairs, London

L.P.-B. **Lisa Palmieri-Billig**, M.A.; Writer and Journalist, ADL Representative in Italy, Rome

L.S.-C. **Lena Stanley-Clamp**, B.A.; Assistant Director, Institute of Jewish Affairs, London

Ma.Ki. **Mark Kipnis**, M.A.; Scientific Editor, Jewish Personalities Division of the Shorter Jewish Encyclopaedia in Russian, Jerusalem

Ma.Mar. **Marcel Marcus**, M.A., Rabbi; Communal Rabbi of Berne, lecturer at the University of Berne

M.Arb. **Mordechai Arbell**, B.A.; Writer, Researcher, Jerusalem

M.D.G. **M. David Gefffen**, Ph.D., Rabbi; Researcher and writer, Jerusalem

M.Fel. **Mary Lowenthal Felsteiner**, Ph.D.; Professor of History, San Francisco State University, San Francisco

M.Fri. **Mark Friedman**, Mhil.; Director of Cultural Affairs, World Jewish Congress, New York

Mi.Be. **Michael Beizer**, Ph.D.; Director, Centre for the Study and Documentation of East European Jewry, Jerusalem

Mi.Sh. **Milton Shain**, Ph.D.; Professor, Department of Hebrew and Jewish Studies, University of Cape Town

Mi.Z. **Michael Zand**, Ph.D.; Professor of Persian and Tajik Language and Literature, The Hebrew University of Jerusalem; chief scientific consultant to The Shorter Jewish Encyclopaedia in Russian, Jerusalem

M.J.Sh. **Michael J. Schudrich**, Rabbi; former rabbi of Jewish Community of Japan, Tokyo

M.Lit. **Meir Litvak**, Ph.D.; Department of Middle Eastern History and African Studies, Tel Aviv University

M.Me. **Meron Medzini**, Ph.D.; Author, Journalist, Senior Lecturer, School for Overseas Students, The Hebrew University of Jerusalem

M.R.K. **Milton Ridvas Konvitz**, Ph.D.; Professor Emeritus of Industrial and Labor Relations and Law, Cornell University, Ithica

M.Sic. **Moshe Sicron**, Ph.D.; Government statistician in the Central
Bureau of Statistics; professor, The Hebrew University of Jerusalem

M.V. **Max Vorspan**, D.H.L., Rabbi; Vice-President, University of Judaism, Los Angeles

N.H.dN. **Noemi Hervits de Najenson**, Ph.D.; Pedagogical Center, No'ar Vehalutz, Jerusalem

N.Kr. **Naftali Kraus**; Journalist, Tel Aviv

No.So. **Normon Solomon**, Ph.D., Rabbi; Founder-Director of the Centre for the Study of Judaism and Jewish/Christian Relations, Birmingham, England

O.M. **Oskar Mendelsohn** (*deceased*), M.A.; Historian, retired teacher, Oslo

P.M.-F. **Paul Mendes-Flohr**, Ph.D.; Professor, Department of Jewish Thought, The Hebrew University of Jerusalem

P.S.G. **Percy S. Gourgey**, M.B.E.; Journalist, Twickenham, Middlesex, England

R.E.G. **Ruth E. Gruber**, B.A.; Journalist, writer, photographer specializing on Jewish issues in East-Central Europe, Rome

Ri.Fe. **Ricardo Feierstein**; Director Editorial Mila, AMIA, Buenos Aires

Ri.Mi. **Richard Mitten**, Ph.D.; Historian, free-lance writer, Vienna

Ro.Re. **Ronny Reich**, Ph.D.; Director of Documentation, Israel Antiquities Authority, Jerusalem

Ro.Reb. **Roberta Rebold**, B.A.; Writer and Researcher, Jerusalem

Ro.Roz. **Robert Rozette**; Researcher and Writer, Jerusalem

Ro.Sa. **Rochelle G. Saidel**, Ph.D.; Writer and journalist, Sao Paulo

Sa.Wh. **Sally Whyte**; Member, International Association of Art Critics, Conseil International de la Danse (UNESCO), London

S.B.F. **Sylvia Barack Fishman**, Ph.D.; Asst. Prof. of Jewish Studies, Brandeis University, Waltham

S.Fa. **Salomon Faber**, Ph.D., Rabbi; New York

Shi.Ar. **Shimshon Arad**, Israel Diplomat, Jerusalem

S.J.E.R. *The Shorter Jewish Encyclopaedia in Russian*, Jerusalem

S.Kov. **Santiago Ezequiel Kovadloff**, Licenciado en Filosofia; Writer, Translator, Professor of Classical Philosophy, Buenos Aires

S.L. **Sol Liptzin**, Ph.D.; Emeritus Professor of Comparative Literature, City College of the City University of New York, Jerusalem

S.Lev. **Samuel Levin**; Writer, translator, Givat Savyon

S.Str. **Susan Strul**; Writer, Jerusalem

St.K. **Steven Kaplan**, Ph.D.; Harry S. Truman Research Center, The Hebrew University of Jerusalem

U.E. **Ury Eppstein**, Ph.D.; Lecturer, Musicology Dept., The Hebrew University of Jerusalem

Ur.R. **Uri Regev**, LL.B., Rabbi; Director, The Israel Religious Action Center, Jerusalem

U.S. **Uriel Simri**, Ed.D.; Former Scientific Director of the Wingate Institute for Physical Education and Sport, Netanyah

V.D.L. **Vivan David Lerman** (*deceased*), C.V.O., Ph.D.; Former Director of Ancient Monuments and Historic Buildings, London

W.D.R. **William D. Rubinstein**, Ph.D.; Professor of Social and Economic History, School of Australian and International Studies, Deakin University, Geelong, Victoria, Australia

Wi.M. **Will Maslow**, A.B., J.D.; General Counsel, American Jewish Congress, New York

Wi.W. **William Wollheim**; Writer, New York

Ya.So. **Yaakov Soroker**; Jerusalem Symphony Orchestra

Y.Ho. **Yehoshua Horowitz**, Dr. Phil.; Educator, Lecturer in Talmud and Rabbinic Literature, Ben-Gurion University of the Negev, Beersheba

Yi.K. **Yitzhak Kerem**, M.A.; Historian, Writer, Researcher, Jerusalem

Yi.Sh. **Yisrael Shrenzel**; Chess columnist, Tel Aviv

Y.J.T. **Yitchak Julius Taub**, B.A., M.Jur.; Jouranlist, Director of "The Bialik Institute," Jerusalem

Y.M.B. **Y. Michal Bodemann**, Ph.D.; Assoc. Professor of Sociology, University of Toronto

Yo.D. **Yonah David**, Ph.D.; Professor Emeritus of Medieval Hebrew Literature, Tel Aviv University

Yu.Ku. **Yuri Kulker**; Jerusalem

Using This Volume

The *Encyclopaedia Judaica Decennial Book 1983–1992* is a compendium of additional information, encompassing new entries as well as articles complementing those already in the *Encyclopaedia Judaica.* Complementary entries are a continuation of items which appeared in the original set or in the supplementary volume 17 / *Encyclopaedia Judaica Decennial Book 1973–1982* — as new entries or as complementary ones. They either take up where the original left off, such as the entry on Museums, or begin where the entry in the 17th volume closed, such as for the United States, or are a more detailed and up-do-date examination of the original entry or a facet of it, as in Talmud (Recent Research).

The references at the beginning of entries indicate where the initial material on the subject is located in the Encyclopaedia and / or volume 17/Decennial Book 1973–1982. The index also refers the reader to the 17-volume set. Moreover, the tone and format of the entries in this volume are more comprehensive than in a Year Book.

This supplementary volume covers in-depth the decade which has passed since the publication of the first Encyclopaedia Judaica Decennial Book. This volume incorporates material which appeared in the intervening Year Books along with a great deal of new material, all providing the owner of this encyclopaedia with an easily accessible means for keeping the set as up-to-date as possible as well as easy to use.

Additional useful features in this volume are the diary of events in the Jewish world 1982–1992 which allows the reader to follow events as they occurred, maintaining a chronological perspective. The feature entries cover topics of current as well as lasting interest, such as the article on intermarriage in the United States. The necrology list is current through 1992.

By using this volume together with the Encyclopaedia itself, the reader can learn of trends, for example, within the branches of Judaism — Orthodox, Conservative, and Reform — or of the situation in the various Jewish communities the world over. The biographical entries allow the reader to keep up with the continuing contribution of Jewish individuals to civilization in general and to fields of particular Jewish interest.

We hope that our readers will find that the concentration of this information into a single volume makes it easier for them to derive many hours of enjoyable, profitable use from the entire *Encyclopaedia Judaica.*

The dynamics of events, on-going scholarship, and new discoveries remind us that completeness is a claim few would make, but we must still follow "You are not obligated to complete the work (of the study of Torah), but you are not free to excuse yourself from it. If you have studied much Torah — your reward will be great" (Rabbi Tarfon, Ethics of the Fathers, 2:21).

Diary of Events 1982-1992

The Madrid Middle East peace conference: Flanked by U.S. president George Bush (left) and Soviet For. Min. Pankin and U.S. Sec. of State Baker (right), Pres. Mikhail Gorbachev of the U.S.S.R. addresses the conference, Oct. 30, 1991. Across the table are the Israeli (right) and Egyptian (left) delegations. (GPO, Jerusalem)

Just arrived! Two new young immigrants to Israel in September 1990, one from the U.S.S.R. and one from Ethiopia, represent one of the most compelling themes of the past decade in the Jewish world: mass emigration from the countries of the former U.S.S.R. and the airlift of Ethiopian Jewry to Israel. (GPO, Jerusalem)

Granite and steel Holocaust monument, by Imre Varga, in form of a tree in Budapest, dedicated July 1990. (Photo Ruth E. Gruber, Rome)

Protesters resist soldiers in Yammit during the final evacuation and dismantling of the city as part of the Israel-Egypt peace agreement, April 24, 1982. (GPO, Jerusalem)

Diary of Events 1982-1992

January 1982

4
Pres. Reagan warns Israel not to annex West Bank.

7
Israel Foreign Minister Shamir meets with Pope John Paul II in the Vatican.

Israel cabinet votes (5–4) a compensation package to settlers in northern Sinai of 4.4 billion shekel ($250 million)

15
Jewish restaurant in West Berlin bombed, a 14-month-old girl is killed, 24 wounded.

20
U.S. vetoes Jordanian resolution in UN Security Council calling for sanctions against Israel over annexation of Golan Heights.

21
Two Palestinians sentenced to life imprisonment for Aug. 21, 1981, attack on Vienna synagogue in which 2 were killed, 30 wounded.

28
Israel cabinet cancels planned visit of Egypt's President Mubarak unless he visits Jerusalem.

February

5
UN General Assembly votes for total international boycott of Israel, 86–21, as punishment for annexation of Golan Heights.

7–10
Egyptian Chief of Staff, Lt. Gen. Abed Rab el-Nabi Hafez, visits Israel.

Israel's Chief of Staff Raphael Eitan and Egyptian Chief of Staff Abed Rab el-Nabi Hafez in Tel Aviv. (GPO, Jerusalem)

9
A group of 28 Leningrad "refuseniks" send open letter to Helsinki accords review conference meeting in Madrid listing Soviet violations of the accords.

16
Bir Zeit University is closed for 2-month period within 6 weeks of re-opening. The move causes unrest and closure of municipalities.

21
Gershom Scholem, leading authority on Kabbalah and Jewish mysticism, dies.

March

3
IDF ordered to begin the removal of non-residents from the Yammit area.

3–5
French President Mitterrand on state visit to Israel.

French President François Mitterrand and Israel Prime Minister Menaḥem Begin during their joint press conference, Jerusalem, March 4. (GPO, Jerusalem)

7
Newspaper story in Nashville, Tennessee reveals that Leo Frank — Jew lynched in Georgia in 1915 after his scheduled execution as convicted murdered was commuted to life imprisonment — was innocent; key witness, now 83, changes story.

16
Settlers in four Yammit-area moshavim allow dismantling to begin — Sadot, Ugdah, Nir Avraham, and Pri'el.

Demonstration in protest against Sinai withdrawal attracts 25,000 to Western Wall.

25
Ida Nudel, Soviet Jewish activist, released after four-year imprisonment in Siberia.

31
Final day of Israeli civilian presence in Sinai

April

2
U.S. vetoes a Jordanian-sponsored Security Council resolution denouncing Israel's policies in the West Bank and calling on Israel to reinstate the ousted mayors of Nablus, Ramallah, and El-Bireh.

3
Yaacov Bar-Simantov, Israeli diplomat in Paris, murdered by female terrorist.

11
Gunman, later identified as Allen H. Goodman, attacks Arabs on Temple Mount, killing one, wounding 12. Arabs attack tourists in reprisal; West Bank swept by unrest.

18
Israeli cabinet votes to proceed with final withdrawal from Sinai on April 25 as scheduled.

Lynching of Leo Frank, Atlanta, Georgia, 1915. (HUC-JIR, American Jewish Archives, Cincinnati)

23
Yammit leveled in preparation for final Israeli withdrawal from Sinai.

One of the last quarters of Yammit to be razed. (GPO, Jerusalem)

25
ADL erects monument in Dag Hammarskjold Plaza adjoining UN building to Jewish Holocaust victims.

Israeli presence ended in Yammit area at midnight. Sinai transfer ceremonies held. New border goes into effect. Sinai returned in its entirety to the Egyptian government.

28
HIAS decides to terminate agreement with Jewish Agency not to assist Russian Jews who want to emigrate to the West.

29
Tel Aviv–Cairo bus route inaugurated.

May
13
Costa Rica announces it will move its embassy back to Jerusalem.

14
Zaire announces resumption of diplomatic relations with Israel.

Nimyaidika Ngimbi, Directort General of Zaire, with PM Begin, upon renewal of diplomatic relations, May 16. (Courtesy WZPS, Scoop 80)

25
Israeli airforce downs 2 Syrian MiGs near Beirut.

June
Austrian Jewish museum opens in Vienna.

3
Assassination attempt on Israel Ambassador to Britain, Shlomo Argov, in London; 3 Arabs charged with the shooting.

President Reagan warns Romania that it must improve emigration procedures for Jews or forfeit its "most-favored nation" trade status.

4
Israeli air strikes and artillery barrages on PLO targets in Beirut and 15 other PLO concentrations in Lebanon.

4–5
PLO terrorists fire between 500 to 700 rockets on northern border of Israel.

5
150th anniversary of legislation giving full civil rights to Jews in Canada. Week of celebration declared (in September) by Quebec Premier Rene Levesque.

6
Israel launches "Operation Peace for Galilee" with the stated objective of pushing the PLO units "forty kilometers to the north."

Israeli armored division assembled along the Israel-Lebanon border on June 6. (GPO, Jerusalem)

7
Tyre and Beaufort Castle taken by the IDF.

9
Israel aircraft and ground forces destroy SAM-6 missile batteries of the Syrians in Lebanon and down over 20 Syrian MiGs.

11
Israeli Merkavah tanks knock out 9 of the most advanced, modern Soviet tank, the T-72.

12
Israel announces unilateral cease-fire; PLO informs UN Secretary-General of decision to respond in the affirmative to the Security Council call for a cease-fire.

18
Two bombs explode outside offices with Israeli links in central Rome causing slight damage, but no casualties.

21
PM Begin meets with U.S. President Reagan to discuss joint American-Israeli strategy for "solving conflict in Lebanon."

30
World Zionist Executive closes Jewish Agency's immigrant transit center in Vienna because of low number of emigrants.

July
2
Bombs explode in Athens outside Israeli firm's factory. Greek Jewish community protests and asks government to condemn attacks against Greek Jews.

3
Peace Now demonstration against the war in Lebanon draws approximately 100,000 to Kikar Malkhei Yisrael in Tel Aviv.

4
Israel tightens military control around West Beirut.

5
Cease-fire in Beirut.

11
Cease-fire in Lebanon follows fierce military battle.

20
Israeli bank and import firm damaged by explosion in Paris. Three bombs explode in Rome: at the JDC, the Italy-Israel Chamber of Commerce, and American-Express.

24
Teḥiyyah joins Israel government.

Israel Air Force knocks out three SAM-8 missiles. Syria shoots down a Phantom, the two pilots are taken prisoner.

31
Seven people — four Israelis and three Germans — injured by bomb explosion near El Al terminal in Munich Airport.

August
1
IDF push in southwest Beirut; the airport is captured.

9
Terrorist attack on Paris Jewish restaurant killing 6, wounding 22.

10
French President Mitterrand and Interior Minister Deferre attend memorial for victims of attack on restaurant held at Rue des Rosiers synagogue in Paris.

12
U.S. Pres. Reagan expresses his anger over the heavy bombing raids on Beirut.

Israel cabinet decides to restrict further bombardment of Beirut — complete cease-fire in effect.

19
Israel cabinet approves plan for PLO withdrawal from West Beirut as presented by U.S. special envoy Philip Habib.

21
First group of 400 PLO terrorists leave Beirut for Cyprus on their way to Jordan and Iraq.

Expelled PLO terrorists embark from Beirut for Cyprus, supervised by French and Lebanese soldiers. (GPO, Jerusalem)

22
Israel cabinet tells El Al no Sabbath flights as of Sept. 1.

25
Israel agrees to American and Italian contingents of the multinational force taking up positions in Beirut as of Aug. 30.

29
Nahum Goldmann dies; he is buried on Sept. 2 on Mt. Herzl in the section reserved for leaders of the Zionist movement.

30
Arafat evacuated from Beirut.

September

1–3
U.S. Secretary of Defense Weinberger visits Israel for the first time.

2
Israel cabinet rejects U.S. President Reagan's proposed plan for advancing Mid-East negotiations — the Reagan "peace initiative."

5
Israeli government and the WZO decide to establish 8 more settlements in the West Bank and Gaza Strip, 5 of them in principle and 3 in actuality. U.S. Sec. of State Shultz states that it is "a very unwelcome development if it's so."

8
Israel Knesset rejects Pres. Reagan's Middle East peace initiative.

14
Lebanese president-elect Bashir Jemayel assassinated in large explosion in Beirut.

15
IDF moves into key positions in West Beirut following murder of Bashir Jemayel.

Pope John Paul II receives Yasser Arafat in private audience for 20 minutes — meeting condemned by Israel and Jewish leaders.

16
Attack on Jewish homes and stores in Tunisia.

17
Massacre of hundreds of Arab refugees by Phalange militiamen; men, women, and children killed in Sabra and Shatilla Palestinian refugee camps of West Beirut.

18
Four wounded in gunfire attack on worshipers at Brussels synagogue.

20
Protest in Paris against attacks by terrorists on Jewish institutions following bomb explosion near Carnot high school in Paris.

Huge mass demonstration in Tel Aviv demanding establishment of state inquiry commission into the massacres at Sabra and Shatilla, September 25. (GPO, Jerusalem)

26
Anatoly Shcharansky begins hunger strike in Siberian prison camp.

Jewish demonstration after the terrorist attack on the Carnot high school, Paris, September 20. (Photo Daniel Franck, Paris)

21
Israel cabinet rejects demands for establishing committee of inquiry into Beirut refugee camp massacres.

Red Cross personnel evacuate bodies at Shatilla refugee camp, September 21. (GPO, Jerusalem)

25
Hundreds of thousands — estimated between 200,000 and 400,000 — participate in demonstration sponsored by Labor Party, Mapai, Peace Now, Shinui, and Independent Liberals in demand for establishment of judicial commission to inquire into massacres at Sabra and Shatilla.

28
Israel cabinet decides to establish judicial commission of inquiry to look into Beirut massacre.

29
IDF withdraws from Beirut airport ending Israeli occupation of the city; first group of U.S. marines arrive.

30
Bill to bring back prayers in public schools defeated in U.S. Senate.

October

9
Four men attack Rome's main synagogue as people leave following Shabbat — Shemini Aẓeret services, one killed (a two-year-old boy), 34 wounded.

November

1
Soviet source reveals that Edgar Bronfman, president of the WJC, invited by Central Committee of Soviet Communist Party to visit Moscow as guest and meet members of Soviet leadership.

8
Jewish activist Yossif Begun is arrested by Soviets and faces trial on a charge of anti-Soviet agitation and propaganda.

8–14
Council of Jewish Federations celebrates 50th anniversary in Los Angeles.

Moshe Arens speaking at CJF 50th anniversary, L.A. (Courtesy CJF, N.Y.; photo R.A. Cumins, N.J.)

11
U.S. President Reagan appoints Philip Habib to "supervise U.S. efforts to achieve an overall peace in the (Mid-East) region."

12
PM Begin arrives in Los Angeles; meetings scheduled with Jewish leaders.

14
Aliza Begin dies in Israel; Prime Minister's trip cut short as he returns home.

28
Israel embassy in Quito, Ecuador hit by bomb.

December

1
Foreign Minister Shamir begins 3-day visit to Zaire to further the reestablished diplomatic relations. Technical and agricultural agreements signed.

7–16
30th Zionist Congress meets in Jerusalem.

12
Ceremonial transfer of books to the new Jewish Theological Seminary library in Manhattan, the first of the approximately 100,000 books stored since 1966 when fire destroyed the library.

17
Reconstruction of the historical synagogue of Worms, Germany, completed with the opening of the new Rashi House on Jews' Street in Worms.

23
First conference of Jewish leaders from Commonwealth countries meets in London: delegates from Jewish communities of Australia, Canada, Gibraltar, Hong Kong, Jamaica, Kenya, Malta, New Zealand, Singapore, the United Kingdom, Northern Ireland, Zambia, and Zimbabwe.

23
Bombs in Sydney, Australia, damage Israeli consulate and in Bondi, near Sydney, cars near Jewish recreation club.

28
Israel-Lebanon negotiations open at Khalde, Lebanon with U.S. special envoy Morris Draper in attendance.

Israel-Lebanon talks at Khalde. At the left of the triangular table are the Lebanese, in the center — Israel, on the right — U.S.A. (GPO, Jerusalem)

January 1983

3–14
Israel President Navon visits the U.S., meets with government and Jewish leaders.

8
Hand-grenade attack on Egged bus in Tel Aviv, 12 injured.

14
Anatoly Shcharansky ends hunger strike begun in Sept. 1982 after authorities banned exchange of letters with relatives. Receipt of note from his mother puts end to strike.

17–21
Defense Minister Ariel Sharon visits Zaire to discuss Israeli military training and equipment and agricultural projects: 5-year development and military aid agreement signed with Pres. Mobutu Sese Seko.

25
Klaus (Altman) Barbie, "the Butcher of Lyon," arrested in La Paz, Bolivia.

28
Italian union leaders meet with Jewish community leaders for the first time.

February

4
Jewish Daily Forward begins appearance as weekly.

5
Klaus Barbie brought to France from Bolivia to stand trial on charges of ordering the death of thousands of Jews and anti-Nazis in WWII.

6
Foreign Minister Shamir in Germany to meet with Foreign Minister Hans Dietrich Genscher.

8
Publication of results of Kahan Inquiry Commission.

10
Grenade thrown into crowd of Peace Now demonstrators gathered opposite the Prime Minister's Office, Jerusalem, one killed (Emil Grunzweig), 9 injured.

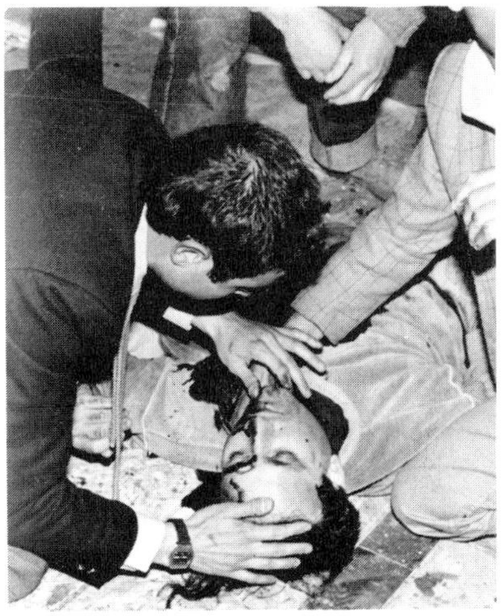
The Peace Now demonstration attacked, February 10. (GPO, Jerusalem)

Israel cabinet votes 16–1 to accept the report of the Kahan Commission and its recommendations. Lone dissenter is Ariel Sharon.

27
Moshe Arens replaces Ariel Sharon as minister of defense.

March

15–17
World Conference on Soviet Jewry convenes with 1,300 participants in Jerusalem.

18
Central Conference of American Rabbis convention in L.A. approves resolution that the child of a mixed marriage is to be considered — with the consent and cooperation of both parents — to be under the "presumption" of Jewish descent which will be validated by acts of identification with the Jewish people.

22
Chaim Herzog chosen 6th president of Israel 61–57 over Menachem Elon.

April

1
Formation of an "Anti-Zionist Committee of the Soviet Public" called for by eight Soviet Jews in Moscow.

7
Allen H. Goodman, the Temple Mount killer, sentenced to life imprisonment plus two terms of 20 years.

10
American gathering of Jewish Holocaust Survivors begins in Washington, D.C., with 15,000 participants.

15
40th anniversary of Warsaw Ghetto Uprising; eight days of commemorative events marked in Warsaw.

19
Moshe Levy becomes Israel Army Chief of Staff.

Chief of Staff Moshe Levy. (GPO, Jerusalem)

26
French Court of Appeals confirms sentence of Rene Faurisson of July 1981 "for insulting the memory of Nazi victims": one franc in damages to organization of former deportees and court costs.

May

16
Israel Knesset approves Israel-Lebanon accords, by vote of 56 to 6.

Chaim Herzog sworn in as the 6th president of Israel on May 5. (GPO, Jerusalem)

June

4
Moscow Chief Rabbi Fishman, 70, dies.

7
Satmar Rebbe arrives in Israel for 2-week visit.

27
Britain's first National Holocaust Memorial unveiled: a small garden in London's Hyde Park of "newly planted silver birch trees around a cluster of large boulders."

July

1
Beth-El synagogue of Baranquilla, Colombia, damaged by explosion shortly after Friday night services end.

20
Israel Cabinet decides to withdraw from the surrounding areas of Beirut, the road to Damascus, and the Shouf mountains to a base on Awali river.

25
WJC announces move of world headquarters from Geneva to New York City and establishment of European office in Paris.

26
Islamic University of Hebron attacked by 4 masked gunmen, 3 Arabs killed, 33 wounded; perpetrators found to be Jews.

August

6
Temple Israel of Johannesburg is site of bomb attack only hours before scheduled ceremonies in honor of 50th anniversary of Reform Judaism in South Africa.

13
Liberia announces decision to renew ties with Israel.

15–17
Minister of Foreign Affairs Shamir pays official visit to Romania as guest of Foreign Minister Stefan Andrez.

22–25
Liberian President Samuel Doe makes 4-day official visit to Israel a week after Liberia announces resumption of diplomatic relations with Israel.

The Israel-Lebanon accord is signed in Khalde, Lebanon, on May 17: on left — signing for Israel is David Kimche; on right — signing for Lebanon is Antoine Fattal. (Courtesy WZPS, Jerusalem)

28
Israel Prime Minister Menahem Begin announces intention of resigning.

September

1
Foreign Minister Shamir selected by Ḥerut party as nominee for prime minister in choice between himself and Housing Minister David Levy, 436–302.

David Levy (Deputy Prime Minister) and Yiẓḥak Shamir (Foreign Minister), candidates for prime minister. (GPO, Jerusalem)

3
IDF withdrawal from Shouf Mountains and Aley to new line of Awali river without incident.

12
Citibank, one of the U.S. largest banks, agrees to pay fine of $323,000 as penalty for violation of law forbidding U.S. firms from cooperating with the Arab boycott against Israel.

Likkud and coalition partners sign final agreement to reconstitute current coalition under Shamir.

20
Laying of cornerstone for first Jewish chapel at West Point, U.S. military academy.

October

10
Knesset gives approval to Shamir government, 60–53.

12
Trial of Yossif Begun, 51, begins in Vladimir; he is charged with violating Article 70 of Soviet Criminal Code against disseminating anti-Soviet propaganda. Begun dismisses state-appointed lawyer to defend self.

24
Faculty of Jewish Theological Seminary of America votes 34–8 to allow women to train as rabbis.

Jewish Movement for Human Rights holds march in Buenos Aires to call for government action in light of increase of anti-Semitic acts and violation of human rights.

26–28
Oldest Jewish cemetery in Vienna rededicated following restoration.

November

4

Suicide truck bomb explodes at Israeli military headquarters in Tyre — 28 members of Israeli security forces and 32 non-Israelis killed.

27

Meir Shamgar installed as president of Israel Supreme Court. Miriam Ben-Porat is deputy president.

Prime Minister Shamir and Defense Minister Arens visit America for talks with Pres. Reagan, Sec. of State George Shultz and Sec. of Defense Casper Weinberger.

Ruins of the destroyed IDF Headquarters in Tyre, blown up by an explosive-laden truck, November 4. (GPO, Jerusalem)

14–23

Israel president Herzog visits U.S. and addresses UN General Assembly.

15

National Conference of Soviet Jewry condemns "open letter" from 50 "Soviet citizens of Jewish nationality," distributed by Tass, which asks American Jews to reject reports of anti-Semitism in the U.S.S.R.

24

Six Israeli PoW's held by PLO released in exchange for 4,500 detainees of Ansar camp in southern Lebanon, 99 terrorists in Israeli jails and the return of the PLO archives captured during Operation Peace for Galilee.

Prime Minister Yiẓhak Shamir at his farewell address at the White House, November 29. (GPO, Jerusalem)

Jubilant terrorists, PLO members, flash the "V" sign as they board an Air France plane for Algeria, during an exchange of thousands of PLO for six Israeli PoW's in Tripoli, November 24. (GPO, Jerusalem)

December

3

Israel Embassy in Bangkok hit by rocket-propelled grenade, some damage caused to building.

6

Explosion on public bus caused by bomb in Jerusalem, 6 dead, 44 injured. PLO claims responsibility.

Sifting through the debris of a no. 18 bus after it exploded in Beit ha-Kerem, Jerusalem, killing four. (GPO, Jerusalem)

20

Arafat and 4,000 followers leave northern Lebanon undisturbed by Israeli forces.

28

Call for official protection of Syrian Jewry following murder of Mrs. Lillian Abadi, a pregnant mother, and her two children aged 6½ and 3½ in Aleppo, Syria.

January 1984

4

Israel Air Force bombs terrorist training bases in the area of Baalbek, Bekaa valley, Lebanon, 100 dead, 400 wounded.

17–25

Israel President Chaim Herzog visits Zaire and Liberia.

24–28

West German Chancellor Helmut Kohl visits Israel to advance relations between Israel and Germany.

West German Chancellor Helmut Kohl calls on Jerusalem mayor Teddy Kollek at his office in Jerusalem, January 25. (GPO, Jerusalem)

27

Discovery of explosives intended for attack against Islamic shrines on the Temple Mount in Jerusalem.

February

26

Rev. Jesse Jackson, contender for the U.S. Democratic presidential nomination, admits using derogatory terms (in private) about Jews. Widespread protests by U.S. Jewry.

March

4

Jewish group responsible for shooting attack on bus carrying Arab workers from the Administered Territories to work in Israel, 7 wounded.

Pres. Chaim Herzog visits with British Prime Minister Margaret Thatcher in 10 Downing St., March 30. (GPO, Jerusalem)

5

Lebanon formally cancels May 17, 1983, agreement with Israel.

6

Arrival of Ethiopian Jews in Israel via Sudan confirmed.

22

Knesset votes (61–58) to hold early elections. On March 28 election date is fixed for July 23, 1984.

April

2

Terrorist attack on bus in downtown Jerusalem, one dead, 47 wounded. Three perpetrators apprehended, one dies of wounds.

12

Bus traveling from Tel Aviv to Ashkelon hijacked by terrorists. Army action rescues bus, one passenger killed, one hijacker killed. Two other terrorists later reported as dead; circumstances are investigated.

13

El Salvador relocates embassy in Israel in Jerusalem — following 1980 move to Tel Aviv.

May

9

Investigation of alleged Jewish underground group in Israel leads to some 25 arrests, mostly Jewish residents of the West Bank.

27–29

First International Conference of Children of Holocaust Survivors meets in New York City with 1,700 participants; gathering organized by the International Network of Children of Jewish Holocaust Survivors.

June

11

Three "refuseniks," Boris Klotz, Victor Fulmacht, and Lev Tuka, hold unofficial press conference in Russia to negate claims by the authorities that few Jews wish to emigrate.

17

22 alleged members of Jewish underground go on trial in Jerusalem.

Defendants in the trial of the Jewish terrorist group are led out of the Jerusalem District Court at the end of a court session, June 17. (GPO, Jerusalem)

24

Louis Farrakhan, Nation of Islam leader, calls Judaism "gutter religion" on Chicago radio broadcast. His remarks draw sharp criticism from the Jewish community

28

Syria and Israel exchange prisoners-of-war, 291 Syrians and 20 others for 6 Israelis — first exchange in 10 years.

July

18

Jewish Agency publicly confirms that thousands of Ethiopian Jews are in Israel.

23

Elections for Eleventh Knesset held in Israel; Labor Alignment gains 44 seats, Likkud 41.

Likkud leaders cheering optimistic election results on TV screen at Metzudat Ze'ev, party headquarters in Tel Aviv, July 23, 1984. (GPO, Jerusalem)

Israel Elections for 11th Knesset — Results

Party	Seats	%
Labor Alignment	44	34.9
Likkud	41	31.9
Teḥiyyah	5	4.0
National Religious Party	4	3.5
Ḥadash (Communist)	4	3.4
Shas	4	3.1
Shinui	3	2.6
Citizens Rights Movement	3	2.4
Yaḥad	3	2.2
Progressive List for Peace	2	1.8
Agudat Israel	2	1.7
Morashah	2	1.6
Tami	1	1.5
Kach	1	1.2
Omeẓ	1	1.2

August

13

Eleventh Knesset sworn in.

Archbishop Valerian Trifa deported from the U.S. after being deprived of his American citizenship because of his activities in Rumania during WWII. Only country willing to accept him is Portugal.

September

4

Law published in Chile making Jewish religious education optional for primary and secondary school pupils; schools are to make provisions for organizing Jewish religious classes.

5

At the Jewish Theological Seminary in New York, 18 women begin studies leading to ordination as Conservative rabbis.

10–12

Representatives of the Asian and Pacific Jewish communities (Australia, New Zealand, India, Singapore, Hong Kong, Thailand, the Philippines, Japan, Taiwan, and Korea) convene in Singapore, the main topic of discussion being the improvement of Jewish educational facilities.

14

National Unity Government led by Labor Alignment party leader Shimon Peres begins functioning in Israel after several weeks of negotiations.

Alignment and Likkud leaders sign agreement on formation of National Unity Government in the Knesset, Jerusalem, Sept. 13, 1984; in the photo (left to right) are Moshe Nissim, Yizḥak Modai, David Levy, Yizḥak Shamir, Shimon Peres, and Itzhak Navon. (GPO, Jerusalem)

October

5
South African minister of foreign affairs Botha visits Israel.

7–12
Israel prime minister Peres visits the United States for official talks and meets with President Reagan.

24
UNESCO's executive council decides upon commemoration of 850th anniversary of birth of Maimonides in 1985.

25
JWB's Commission on Jewish Chaplaincy announces for the first time a unified Jewish prayer book for Orthodox, Conservative, and Reform U.S. servicemen has been published — combines traditional Hebrew text with freer, modern English translation.

28
Rocket attack on Arab bus in Jerusalem, perpetrated by a Jew — one killed, 10 injured.

November

6
Poll shows that in U.S. presidential elections nearly 70% of Jewish voters chose Walter Mondale over Pres. Reagan (nationwide 59% voted for Reagan and 41% for Mondale).

7
San Francisco dedicates monument to the Holocaust, "The Holocaust" by George Segal. Vandals desecrate it on the night of Nov. 10.

8
Military representatives of Israel and Lebanon open talks at Nakoura, Lebanon — negotiations towards Israeli withdrawal.

25
American Jewish Joint Distribution Committee announces receipt of permission to open feeding stations in Gondar, Ethiopia.

Announcement of agreement reached by the Polish government and the World Federation of Polish Jews to restore cemeteries in Poland desecrated in World War II.

December

5–8
Israel prime minister on official visit to France, meets with President Mitterrand and Premier Fabius.

PM Shimon Peres received by French Premier Laurent Fabius and a company of the presidential guard at Orly airport, Dec. 5. (GPO, Jerusalem)

18
Nadezhda Fradkova, a Leningrad refusenik, sentenced to two years in a Soviet labor camp for "parasitism"; she is one of the Jewish activists recently arrested for persisting in her desire to obtain exit visa to Israel.

January 1985

3
Israel government and the Jewish Agency confirm large immigration by Ethiopian Jews to Israel —probably over 50% of the community airlifted in Operation Moses.

6
Airlift of Ethiopian Jews through Sudan halted after operation made public.

14
Israel government votes 16–6 for a 3-stage withdrawal of the IDF from south Lebanon.

21
IDF begins first stage of withdrawal from south Lebanon — from the area of Sidon to the Litani river.

24
Military honors at reception in Austria for released Nazi war criminal, Walter Reder, after serving 40 years in an Italian prison, causes great consternation; Defense Min. Friedhelm Frischenschlager, who greeted Reder upon his return, is responsible. Apologizes for "miscalculating" (29th).

31
Austrian government promises to return objets d'art stolen by Nazis to their Jewish owners or heirs; items for which no owner will be found will become property of the international Jewish community.

February

5
Opposition to the sales of arms to Saudi Arabia by the U.S. is expressed in a letter to Pres. Reagan signed by 62 senators.

7
UJA collected a record $367.6 million in 1984 — highest sum for a peace year.

10
Canadian report that an independent commission has been appointed by Justice Minister John Crosbie to investigate Nazi war criminals living in Canada — conclusions due by end of Dec. 1985.

14
Rabbinical Assembly of America passes amendment to allow acceptance of women rabbis; all Jewish Theological Seminary ordainees automatically to become Rabbinical Assembly members.

16
IDF completes first stage of withdrawal from Lebanon.

18–19
Israel prime minister Peres goes to Rome for official visit and meetings with the prime minister of Italy, Bettino Craxi, and with Pope John Paul II.

Pope John Paul II receives Prime Minister Shimon Peres in the Vatican, Feb. 19. (GPO, Jerusalem)

19
Israeli chief rabbinate rules Ethiopian Jews must perform symbolic conversion by immersion in a *mikveh*.

March

3
Israel cabinet decides to begin second stage of Israeli withdrawal from Lebanon.

Second stage of evacuation of the IDF from Lebanon operation. (GPO, Jerusalem)

10
Suicide car-bomb explosion kills 12 Israeli soldiers and wounds 14 north of Metullah.

18
Anti-Zionist Committee of the Soviet Public reveals that it sent a telegram to U.S. Congress demanding end of anti-Semitism in America.

28
Marc Chagall dies and is buried (April 1) in Saint Paul de Vence with no religious service.

29
Announcement that Polish restoration of graves of leaders of Ḥasidic dynasties and rabbis of Ger, Belz, and Bobow is complete; financing came from $50,000 donation by American rabbis.

30
The 850th anniversary of the birth of Maimonides — 1985 is the International Year of the Rambam.

Paris cinema bombed during showing at Jewish film festival, 18 injured. On March 31 a protest march against racism and the bombing draws 6,000 including well-known cultural and political figures (Yves Montand, Simone Signoret, Rabbi Sirat, and Enrico Macias).

31
Fourth Beirut Jew in a week kidnapped by Arabs — Yitzḥak Sasson, head of the city's small remaining Jewish community.

April

12
First Jewish male astronaut, Jeffrey Hoffman, participates in mission of space shuttle Discovery; in his personal kit are four *mezuzot* and two *atarot*.

20
Israel Navy patrol boat sights and sinks craft carrying Arab terrorists attempting to infiltrate Israel — of the 28 aboard, one body recovered, 19 presumed drowned, 8 captured. The terrorists were acting on orders of Abu Jihad for the PLO.

May

Amy Eilberg first woman ordained as Conservative rabbi — also first female to be admitted to the Rabbinical Assembly.

5
U.S. president Reagan in Germany on official visit goes to Bitburg military cemetery where 47 Waffen S.S. are buried among the 2,000 German war dead. Scores of protests call for cancellation of visit. Stop at site of Bergen-Belsen concentration camp is added to itinerary.

Left to right: German Chancellor Helmut Kohl, retired general Johaness Steinhoff, U.S. Pres. Ronald Reagan, and retired general Matthew Ridgeway in military cemetery of Bitburg to pay tribute to World War II dead. (AFP, France)

12
Rabbinical Assembly decides to close its synagogues to the 51 Knesset members who voted to change the Law of Return so as to recognize only halakhic conversions.

President of Zaire, Mobutu Sese Seko, arrives in Israel for official visit.

20
Prisoner exchange — 3 Israelis held by Popular Front for the Liberation of Palestine-General Command traded for 1,100 Arab terrorists and others, including Kozo Okamoto; 600 allowed to return to homes in Judea and Samaria.

June

Report of panel investigating Arlosoroff murder clears the 3 suspects of all suspicion (they were tried and released in 1932 for lack of evidence).

Reports that Josef Mengele drowned in 1979 as Wolfgang Gerhard in Enbu, Brazil, 20 miles south of São Paulo.

5
President Zail Singh of India participates in centenary of Knesseth Elijah Synagogue in Bombay.

10
IDF completes final withdrawal of units from Lebanon — a number of officers remain as advisers.

12
South African Jewish Board of Deputies adopts resolution rejecting apartheid and denouncing racial discrimination at its biennial National Assembly.

17
Israel pres. Herzog begins state visit to Ireland.

July

12th Maccabiah opens in Ramat Gan — 4,000 athletes from 39 countries participate.

22
Two bombings in Copenhagen; at Northwest Orient Airlines and at synagogue near Jewish old age home where five are injured from splintered glass — in "retaliation for American-Zionist aggression" as claimed by Arab terrorists.

24
Superior Court of Los Angeles rules that the Institute for Historical Review must pay $50,000 reward it offered against proof that the Nazis actually killed Jews by gassing in concentration camps. Mel Mermelstein, 58, documented how he saw his mother and sister led to the gas chamber. The Institute settles out of court.

August

20
Albert Atrakchi, Israel embassy administrative attaché in Cairo, killed in attack on his way to work; his wife and another embassy worker are wounded.

31
Yacht taken by Israeli Navy off coast of Lebanon; on board 31 PLO terrorists of Force 17 with mission to infiltrate Israel and kill maximum possible.

September

First woman appointed military chaplain for the United States armed forces, Julie Schwartz, rabbinical student at the Hebrew Union College.

Chaplain LTJG Julie S. Schwartz

1
Queen Beatrix of the Netherlands and Prince Consort Claus attend synagogue service at the Sephardi Esnoga synagogue in celebration of 350th anniversary of Amsterdam Ashkenazi congregation.

8–11
International Maimonides Conference (Cordoba) is held as part of Spanish government's celebration of 850th anniversary of Maimonides's birth.

25
Three Israelis murdered aboard yacht in Cyprus by terrorists — two Arabs, one Englishman.

Body of Esther Palzur slumped over railings of the yacht where she was gunned down by terrorist in predawn attack, Larnaca, Sept. 25. (AFP, France)

October

1
Israel Air Force jets bomb PLO headquarters twenty miles outside of Tunis. Negative reaction by the UN and European countries.

2
Four-week sit-down strike by Ethiopian Jews in Jerusalem opposite Hekhal Shlomo, seat of the Chief Rabbinate, ends. Agreement that Ethiopian *qesim* (priests) would determine family history of couples registering for marriage.

Early morning blast at Buenos Aires Sholom Aleichem Jewish kindergarten, damage to property, no casualties.

5
Israel and Poland announce decisions to open liaison offices in Tel Aviv and Warsaw; decide (Oct. 20) to expand cultural ties too.

Egyptian policeman suddenly shoots Israelis vacationing at Ras Burka in the Sinai Desert. Egyptian authorities refuse to allow medical assistance to the wounded: 7 die — five of them bleeding to death; two others wounded. Four of the dead are children.

7
Two Israeli sailors killed in Barcelona, Spain, after being tortured; PLO is held responsible.

Terrorists seize Italian cruise ship, Achille Lauro, with crew of 350 and 70–80 passengers of the total 680 (others were on shore sightseeing); one passenger is shot, Leon Klinghoffer, an American Jew.

8–11
West German president Richard von Weizsaecker is in Israel on official visit, the first by German chief of state.

8
Tunisian policeman opens fire on Simḥat Torah services in Jerba, 4 killed (including a 4-year-old boy), 8 wounded.

10
U.S. plane intercepts plane carrying four hijackers who took the Achille Lauro and forces it to land in Italy. Muhammed Abbas, alleged planner of the hijacking, is freed (Oct. 12) despite U.S. warrant for his arrest.

16–17
Israel Prime Minister Peres in the U.S. meets with Pres. Reagan and Jewish leaders. He speaks at the UN General Assembly (Oct. 21) and presents a peace initiative calling for end of state of war between Israel and Jordan.

November

1
Premiere of previously unperformed anti-Semitic *Garbage, the City of Death*, which was written in 1975 by Rainer Werner Fassbinder, in Frankfurt arouses ire of Jewish community, 30 Jewish protesters disrupt performances.

19
Israeli jets down two Syrian MiGs over Lebanon as Syria attempts to interfere with Israel reconnaisance flight.

21
Jonathan Pollard, 31, a Naval Investigative Service counterintelligence analyst, arrested near Israel embassy in Washington, D.C., on suspicion of having provided Israel with secret defense documents. Anne Henderson-Pollard, 25, his wife, also arrested.

23
Egyptian airliner hijacked from Athens — 80 passengers plus crew. Two Israeli passengers, Nitzan Mendelsohn and Tamar Artzi, singled out by terrorists and shot, Nitzan dies of her wounds. Rescue attempt by Egyptian forces leaves 60 dead.

December

1
Israel apologizes to U.S. over spying incident of Jonathan Pollard.

18
Ivory Coast announces reestablishment of relations with Israel.

A few words between PM Peres and Ivory Coast Pres. Felix Houphouet-Boigny in Geneva, Dec. 18. (GPO, Jerusalem)

Egyptian police in front of the *Achille Lauro* after hijackers are gone. (AFP, France)

25
Body of slain Lebanese Jew discovered in Beirut; Haim Cohen Halala of west Beirut, kidnapped March 29, 1985.

27
Attacks on El-Al check-in counters at Vienna and Rome airports — 18 killed, over 110 wounded — by Palestinian terrorists.

Departure hall near El-Al check-in counter after terrorist attack, Shwechat Airport, Vienna, Dec. 27. (AFP, France; photo Votava GL)

January 1986

16
California court grants $2.25 million award in libel case to Mel Mermelstein, Holocaust survivor, who sued Dietlieb Felderer for calling him "racist and exterminationist" and for denying the historicity of the Holocaust.

17
Spain and Israel announce establishment of full diplomatic relations.

Prime Minister Peres and Prime Minister of Spain, Felipe Gonzalez, raise a toast after sealing establishment of diplomatic relations between Spain and Israel, The Hague, Jan. 19. (GPO, Jerusalem)

18–19
"Refusenik" scientists in Moscow convene 2-day seminar on subjects in physics, biology, and medicine.

26–29
Israel prime minister Peres in West Germany to meet German leaders.

February

11
Anatoly Shcharansky, 33-year-old Soviet and Jewish dissident, released in trade for Soviet spies, after eight years imprisonment in the U.S.S.R. Shcharansky immigrates to Israel.

Anatoly Shcharansky walks to freedom across Glienicke Bridge linking East and West Berlin, flanked by U.S. ambassador to Germany, Richard Burt (right), and State Secretary for Inter-German Affairs, Ludwig Rehlinger. (Bar-David, Tel Aviv)

27
John Demjanjuk, 66, alleged "Treblinka killer," extradited from U.S. to Israel to stand trial for crimes committed during World War II.

March

14
Israeli pavilion opens to public at the Cairo International Trade Fair.

Curious Egyptians mob Tourist Industry booth of the Israeli pavilion at the Cairo International Trade Fair, March 14. (AFP, France; photo Mike Nelson)

19
Israeli woman killed, 3 Israelis wounded in terrorist attack in Cairo.

April

13
Pope John Paul II visits Rome synagogue, first papal visit ever to Jewish house of worship; chief rabbi of Rome, Elio Toaff, welcomes him.

17
Attempt to smuggle bomb aboard El Al flight at London's Heathrow Airport foiled by El Al security. Nezar Hindawi tried to have his girl friend unknowingly carry it on board.

May

Canadian Jewish Congress, for the first time, elects a woman — Dorothy Reitman — as president.

19
U.S. Conservative Judaism's Rabbinical Assembly votes, 235–92, against "patrilineal descent."

June

8
Kurt Waldheim elected president of Austria. Israel recalls Ambassador Michael Elitzur for "urgent consultations." The source of friction is Waldheim's war time activities and alleged involvement with the deportation of Jews to death camps.

12
First new synagogue built in Hungary since World War II is dedicated in Siofolk; it is to be run by the Central Board of Jewish Community.

26
Bomb explodes at El Al check-in-counter at Baras Airport, Madrid — 8 injured.

July

1
United Jewish Appeal of Greater New York merges with the Federation of Jewish Philanthropies to become UJA-Federation.

21–24
Israel prime minister Peres in Morocco for talks with King Hassan at Efruna in search for solution to Middle East problems.

King Hassan II of Morocco and PM Peres at the king's summer palace, Ifrane, July 22. (GPO, Jerusalem)

23
The archibishop of Cracow, Franciszek Macharski, promises to halt building of Carmelite convent at Auschwitz concentration camp site.

August

6
East Germany publicizes the projected restoration of Orianienburger Str. synagogue destroyed in World War II and the reopening of the Adas Yisroel cemetery in Berlin.

September

6
Attack in Istanbul, Turkey on Sabbath

morning during synagogue services, 21 dead, 4 wounded — the perpetrators, Arab terrorists.

Windows reflected in a pool of blood after the terrorist attack on the worshipers of Neveh Shalom Synagogue, Istanbul, Sept. 6. (*Koteret Rashi*; photo Tom Segev)

10
Israel and Egypt reach formula for settling Taba dispute through arbitration.

11–12
Israel PM Peres and Egyptian president Mubarak meet in Alexandria.

14
Community center, including *kasher* restaurant, opens in Frankfurt — first secular center built by Frankfurt Jewish community.

15–22
PM Peres in U.S., meets, among others, with Pres. Reagan and with the Russian foreign minister.

23
U.S. Postal Service issues one-dollar stamp, a special commemorative, of Dr. Bernard Revel, Yeshiva University's first president.

Mohammed Bassiouny presents credentials as Egyptian ambassador to Israel after four years of absence of an Egyptian ambassador in Tel Aviv.

Egyptian Ambassador Extraordinary and Plenipotentiary Mohammed Bassiouny presents his credentials to President Herzog, President's Residence, Sept. 23. (GPO, Jerusalem)

29
In Jerusalem, John Demjanjuk, Ukrainian-born, former U.S. citizen, extradited to Israel in Feb. 1986, formally charged on four counts of war crimes.

October

5
London *Sunday Times* prints story claiming "Israel ... sixth most powerful nuclear reactor." Israel offers no comment. Lead to story is Mordechai Vanunu, former technician at Israel atomic installation; Vanunu later apprehended by Israel.

10
Israel PM Peres tenders resignation in order to allow Foreign Minister Shamir to assume role of prime minister in accordance with the 1984 Alignment-Likkud agreement on rotation.

14
Yiẓhak Shamir becomes prime minister of Israel.

Signing of rotation agreement by Israel PM Shimon Peres and Vice-PM Yiẓhak Shamir, Oct. 10. (GPO, Jerusalem)

16
Israel Air Force Phantom jet falls over Lebanon — pilot rescued, navigator apparently captured by terrorists.

24
Nezar Hindawi convicted of attempting to place bomb on El Al passenger flight in April 1986. British court sentences him to 45 years in prison and severs relations with Syria which was implicated in the plot.

November

9
Israel confirms that it is holding Mordechai Vanunu who is suspected of selling photos and information about Israel's nuclear reactor at Dimonah. He was located outside of Israel and brought back.

11
Romi Goldmuntz synagogue, Antwerp, damaged by bomb which explodes outside of entrance, no casualties.

15
Eliahu Amadi, 22, student at Jerusalem's Old City yeshivah Shuvu Banim, stabbed to death by 3 Arab terrorists who wanted "to spill Jewish blood." They were apprehended soon after the deed; at the end of Dec. 1986 they were sentenced to life imprisonment.

25
Israel denies it transferred funds from sales of U.S. arms to Iran on to the Contras in Nicaragua as alleged by U.S. officials.

December

The National Bishops' Conference of Brazil issues and disseminates 187-page *Guide for a Catholic-Jewish Dialogue in Brazil* to help "Catholics in Brazil to understand better the historical, religious, and national aspirations of the Jewish people."

2
Israel's High Court of Justice rules that the Ministry of the Interior must register Reform convert Shoshana Miller as a Jew.

31
Three Lebanese Jews held captive by extremist Shi'ite group reported killed — no bodies found.

Report only 914 Jews allowed to emigrate from Russia in 1986 — a 20% decrease over 1985 (1,140 emigres).

January 1987

4
Philadelphia, Penn., is site of First Zionist Assembly convened by the American Zionist Federation — some 1,000 delegates representing American Zionist organizations, youth groups, and *garinim* and *aliyah* support groups.

12
Report that Lebanese Jewish hostage killed by Shi'ites: Yehouda Benesti, 70 (father of two earlier victims — Ibrahim Benesti, 34, killed Feb. 15, 1986, and Yousouf Benesti, 33, killed Dec. 30, 1986).

21
Royal Court Theatre, London, announces cancellation of 5-week run of Jim Allen's *Perdition*, a play described as anti-Semitic — deals with role of Zionists depicted as collaborators with Nazis in fate of Hungarian Jewry during Holocaust.

27
Ontario Court of Appeals reverses on technical grounds conviction of Ernst Zundel, anti-Semitic propagandist, sentenced in 1985 to 15-month imprisonment for booklet "Did Six Million Really Die?" denying the Holocaust.

February

5
Jewish Theological Seminary announces decision to recognize women as authorized cantors for Conservative congregations.

10
India informs Israel that Israeli players will not be granted visas needed to participate in world table tennis championship tournament in New Delhi.

16
Extensive damage by vandals to Jewish community center at St. Germain en Laye near Paris.

Trial of John Demjanjuk, American immigrant from the Ukraine accused of being "Ivan the terrible" of Treblinka, opens in Jerusalem.

Prosecutor Michael Shaked interrogating John Demjanjuk. (GPO, Jerusalem)

20

U.S. citizenship of Meir Kahane, Brooklyn-born Knesset member and leader of the Kach party, restored as Federal District Judge Glasser rules that the State Department does not have the right to rescind the citizenship.

Yossif Begun, Soviet Jewish dissident freed and pardoned after being imprisoned since 1983 for allegedly slandering the Soviet state.

22

Meeting held in Geneva between Catholic and Jewish leaders — agreement reached whereby Carmelite convent at Auschwitz to be moved within two years.

25

Israel foreign minister Peres goes to Egypt to meet with Pres. Mubarak.

March

3

U.S. federal grand jury indicts Israeli Air Force colonel Aviem Sella on three counts of espionage, for conspiring with Jonathan Pollard, U.S. Navy analyst, to provide classified U.S. military information to Israel.

4

Jonathan Pollard sentenced to life imprisonment after being found guilty of spying for Israel; his wife Anne Henderson-Pollard given five-year sentence as accessory.

6–20

Seven "Prisoners of Zion" are released in the U.S.S.R., six prior to completion of serving sentence.

11

"David Ben-Gurion Place" — a square in New York City at the site of the Biltmore Hotel — dedicated by Mayor Koch.

18

Israel's "Inner Cabinet" decides to phase out Israel's links to South Africa with regard to trade in military equipment and technology.

23–24

Second biennial Asian-Jewish colloquium meets in Hong Kong; first participation of a Chinese scholar (Prof. Sha Boli [Sidney Shapiro]) at an international Jewish conference.

28

China makes official announcement that a high-level meeting has taken place between Chinese and Israel officials at UN headquarters.

29

Colonel Aviem Sella resigns as commander of Tel Nof air base; U.S. welcomes move (See March 3, 1987.)

April

1

Israel Pres. Herzog makes state visit to Switzerland.

6

Pres. Herzog recites mourner's *Kaddish* at Bergen Belsen, Germany, in memory of Holocaust victims.

Pres. Herzog speaking with Chancellor Kohl of Germany in Bonn, April 10, 1987. (GPO, Jerusalem)

9

One hundred pupils, Jews and non-Jews, plant memorial forest in outskirts of Vienna — there are to be 65,000 trees in memory of the 65,000 Austrian Jews killed in the Holocaust.

11

Firebomb thrown in Samaria at family car causes death of Ofra Moses and injuries to five other passengers (son Tal, 5, dies July 5 from his burns), all residents of Alfei Menashe.

13

U.S. Secretary of State Shultz attends a Passover *seder* for refuseniks at American embassy in Moscow while on official visit to Russia.

26

Hyde Park, London, memorial to Holocaust victims defaced.

27

Austrian president Kurt Waldheim barred from entering U.S. as private citizen — placed on watch list; he can enter in his official capacity.

30

Announcement in Israel media that Foreign Minister Peres and King Hussein of Jordan have reached an agreement towards convening an international conference for peace in the Middle East. Peres' office denies report.

May

Bejing University of the People's Republic of China offers course on Israel and Judaism for the first-time.

5

Official opening of Israel Interest Section in Warsaw.

6–7

Expanded Executive Committee of the WJC gathers in Budapest, first such meeting in Communist country.

6–17

In U.S.S.R. five visiting American Orthodox rabbis receive assurances from Chairman of Council for Religious Affairs and Foreign Ministry representative that six Russian Jews will be trained as rabbis in the United States on condition they serve as rabbis in Russia.

10

Announcement of agreement of Hungary for reprint by the Joint Distribution Committee of 5,000 copies of prayerbook, *Siddur Pollak*, first published 1924.

11

Opening in Lyons of trial of Klaus Barbie, the "Butcher of Lyons."

14

Jewish Theological Seminary of America ordains first Soviet-born Jew as Conservative rabbi, Leonid Feldman, 34.

Pope John Paul II meets with representatives of Polish Jewish community on visit to Poland.

14–19

Israel foreign minister Peres in America for projected 7-day visit which is cut short over Israeli political crisis concerning his proposals for the convening of an international conference for peace in the Middle East. On May 17 Peres meets with Soviet ambassador to the U.S., Yuri Dubinin, for 90 minutes in Washington, D.C.

20–23

First International Congress on the Inquisition held at the University of São Paulo with 700 participants from 15 countries to mark 450th anniversary of establishment of Inquisition in Portugal.

22

5,000 copies of Hebrew-Russian Pentateuch sent to U.S.S.R. from the U.S.A. with approval of Soviet authorities by Appeal of Conscience Foundation.

June

15
Israel Prime Minister Shamir in Togo on first stop of West African tour.

25
Pope John Paul II meets with Austrian pres. Waldheim in Vatican. World Jewish and Israeli criticism rejected by Vatican: visit was official, not personal.

July

For first time since Holocaust three books for Jewish youth published in Hungary, part of series; the works are an illustrated book on the Bible, for ages 3–6; *Shma Yisroel* on Jewish practices, for ages 8–12; and a book on Jewish history, for ages 12–18.

2
Budapest, Hungary: Center of Jewish Studies — first in Eastern bloc — dedicated at Hungarian Academy of Sciences under whose auspices it will function.

12
Three-member Soviet delegation comes to Israel to discuss Russian property — first official Soviet group since 1967.

20
Egyptian foreign minister, Abdel Meguid, visits Israel — first senior Egyptian to come since Lebanon War in 1982.

Egyptian FM Meguid mets with Israel PM Shamir in the Prime Minister's Office, Jerusalem, July 20, 1987. (GPO, Jerusalem)

August

Jewish Museum of Amsterdam inaugurates new premises.

Amsterdam Mayor Ed van Thijn affixing *mezuzah* at Jewish Historical Museum opening. (Courtesy Jewish Historical Museum, Amsterdam)

6
Deschenes Commission report on war criminals living in Canada has secret appendage which comes to conclusion that Canada accepted suspected Nazi war criminals after World War II, even up to 1983. Principal researcher criticizes Canadian government for censoring report.

30
Israel cabinet decides to end Lavi fighter aircraft project by vote of 13–12 after long public debate.

Demonstration by IAI workers against cancellation of Lavi project. (GPO, Jerusalem)

September

Pushkin Museum in Moscow holds Chagall exhibition for 100th anniversary of his birth.

1
Jewish representatives meet with Pope John Paul II at his summer home. Delegation's members are affiliated with International Jewish Committee for Interreligious Consultations. Pope promises to issue official document on anti-Semitism and the Holocaust.

Meeting of IJCIC representatives with Pope John Paul II in Castelgondolfo. (Courtesy G. Wigoder; photo Arturo Mari, Vatican)

8–14
Jewish Book Publishers participate in 6th Moscow International Book Fair and exhibit over 1,000 works from over 115 American publishers.

10
East German Jewish community has a rabbi for the first time in 25 years: Rabbi Isaac Neuman, 65, of Champaign, Ill. (He resigns after a few months.)

15
Final remaining Prisoner of Conscience, Alexei Magarik, 28-year-old Jewish activist, released from Siberian labor camp.

30
China's Foreign Minister Wu Xuegian has meeting with Israel foreign minister Shimon Peres in New York, a first for the two countries; further contacts to follow.

October

1
U.S. gives permission to Israel to sell 14 Kefir jet fighter planes to Colombia.

C-17 Kfir multi-mission fighter plane. (Courtesy Israel Aircraft Industries)

14
Vladimir and Maria Slepak notified they have permission to emigrate from the Soviet Union after 17-year wait; they arrive in Israel on Oct. 26.

Vladimir and Masha Slepak cutting cake with Pres. and Mrs. Herzog at combination reception and birthday party for Mr. Slepak. (GPO, Jerusalem)

15
Ida Nudel arrives in Israel from U.S.S.R..

Ida Nudel arriving in Israel — with her dog, Oct. 15. (GPO, Jerusalem)

16–19
U.S. Secretary of State Shultz in Israel, first time since 1985 — no breakthrough on peace talks. Palestinians invited to speak with him refuse to come.

November

6
UN Secretary General Javier Perez announces that files on 40,000 suspected Nazi war criminals will now be open to researchers as well as governments general access begins on Nov. 23.

7
200 refuseniks hold hunger strike to protest new Russian emigration procedures.

9
First state visit to Washington by Israel president: Pres. Chaim Herzog meets with Pres. Reagan at White House (Nov. 10).

14
Bomb blast at synagogue in old Jewish neighborhood of Once in Buenos Aires short time after arrest in Cordoba province of accused Nazi war criminal Josef Schwammberger.

15
Jerusalem district court rules that trial of accused spy Mordechai Vanunu will not be held in open session.

19
Report that over 70 Jews have registered for first officially authorized Hebrew courses in Russia; they will be held in Baku.

19–23
Israel prime minister Shamir in the U.S. for meetings with national leaders, including Pres. Reagan, and Jewish groups.

22
Moscow demonstration against anti-Semitism broken up by police.

25
Arab terrorist who enters northern Israel by hang-glider kills 6 IDF soldiers, wounds 7.

Demonstration by 30,000 Jews in Buenos Aires protesting increase in serious anti-Semitic incidents.

30
Greek Foreign Minister Karolos Papoulias in Israel on official visit Nov. 30–Dec. 3, first senior member of Greek cabinet to do so.

Greek foreign minister, Karolos Papoiulias, being welcomed at President's Residence by Pres. Herzog. (GPO, Jerusalem)

December

2
U.S. District Court rules State Department order to close PLO office in Washington, D.C., is valid.

4
Jewish personnel in U.S. armed forces to be allowed to wear *kippot* (skullcaps) following signature of Pres. Reagan on amendment 1988 Defense Authorization Law.

6
National Mall Sunday draws 200,000 to Washington, D.C., rally in support of Soviet Jewry one day before arrival of Soviet premier Gorbachev.

6–10
31st Zionist Congress meets in Jerusalem.

7
Simcha Dinitz is elected chairman of the World Zionist Organization Executive.

9
Violence spread in Gaza Strip after fatal shooting of a 17-year-old high school student and wounding of 10 others when fire bombs thrown at army patrol, and soldiers responded. Rumors of deliberate running over of Arabs by Jewish settlers spark unrest which turns into the *intifada*, uprising, among the Arabs of the Administered Territories.

14
Some 60,000 Arab workers from the Administered Territories remain away from work in Israel. Week of rioting.

17
Number of violent incidences and demonstrations by Arabs around and in Jerusalem. Weekend (Dec. 19) sees continued violence.

Arab unrest manifested by riots on Temple Mount. (GPO, Jerusalem)

21
Israeli Arabs call general strike in identification and solidarity with their brethren in the Administered Territories.

Arab youths standing behind roadblock of stones and burning tires in a Bir Zeit street, Jan. 1988. (GPO, Jerusalem)

22
UN Security Council condemns by 14-0 Israel's actions in handling the unrest in the Administered Territories. The U.S. abstains.

31
Report total of 8,153 Jews emigrate from U.S.S.R in 1987.

January 1988

20
Refusenik Yossif Begun arrives in Israel from U.S.S.R., accompanied by wife and family after 16-year wait for exit visa.

Yossif Begun, holding his granddaughter, and his wife deplane at Ben-Gurion Airport, Israel. (GPO, Jerusalem)

31
Israel Interior Ministry agrees to register three non-Orthodox converts as Jews.

February

13
Palestinian Uprising Committee distributes seventh leaflet — means of communi-

cation clandestinely printed and spread since start of disturbances; this one calls for attacks on Israeli settlements, a general strike, and violent demonstrations.

15
In Limassol, Cyprus, explosion below water line on the *Sol Phryne*, ship which was to bring Palestinian deportees and hundreds of supporters to Haifa; PLO cancels trip.

18
Trial of John Demjanjuk ends. Verdict to be given in April.

23
Israel pres. Herzog elected by Knesset to serve second term.

25
U.S. secretary of state Shultz in Israel begins 5-day Middle East shuttle mission. Palestinian delegation refuses to speak with him.

The Shamirs host U.S. Sec. of State George Shultz and his wife for dinner at their home in Jerusalem. (GPO, Jerusalem)

March

Conservative Judaism in U.S. publishes *Emet Ve-Emmunah*, the first common statement of principle of the movement.

7
Three PLO terrorists attack workers' bus in the Negev between Dimona and Beersheba, 3 Israelis killed, 8 wounded; the three terrorists are killed.

10
Parliament of Europe condemns Israel for its policy and treatment of Arabs in the Administered Territories.

13
U.S. Justice Department orders PLO observer mission at the UN to close by March 21, PLO refuses to do so.

13–22
Israel PM Shamir makes 10-day visit to the U.S., meets with Reagan administration officials and Jewish leaders.

14
Hungary and Israel open interest sections in Tel Aviv and Budapest, the lowest level of diplomatic representation but first between the two since the Six-Day War in 1967.

22
U.S. sues for closure of PLO UN observer mission.

24
Mordecai Vanunu, Israeli who sold details of Israel's nuclear reactor to English press, found guilty of treason and aggravated espionage by Israeli court sentenced to 18 years imprisonment.

April

Memorials for Warsaw Ghetto on 45th anniversary of uprising.

Floral tributes at Warsaw Ghetto memorial. (Photo G. Wigoder, Jerusalem)

11
Israel deports eight Palestinians from the Administered Territories to Lebanon and orders 12 others to be expelled. American, British, and UN officials censure Israel's move.

16
Khalil al-Wazir (Abu Jihad), the number two leader of the PLO, assassinated at home in suburb of Tunis.

18
John Demjanjuk convicted by Israeli court of war crimes; court accepts identification of Demjanjuk as "Ivan the Terrible" of Treblinka.

Frankfurt, Germany, Jewish Community Center suffers half million dollars worth of damage to building in bomb explosion, no casualties.

20
Polish government states that Carmelite convent will definitely be removed from grounds of Auschwitz.

The Great Synagogue of Essenwood Road and the Jewish Club, both in Durban, S.A., targets of anti-Jewish acts: pig's head placed at the door of the synagogue with Magen David on ears and swastika drawn on the forehead.

24–28
First Jewish-Christian dialogue in Poland between Polish bishop's committee for relations with Jews and delegation from Anti-Defamation League.

Prayer in front of ruins of Birkenau gas chamber with participation of Bishop Stefanek of Szczecin, Rabbi Leo Klenicki (ADL), Cardinal Macharski, archbishop of Cracow, and Bishop Henryk Muszynski of Wloclawek. (Photo G. Wigoder, Jerusalem)

25
Demjanjuk sentenced to death. Appeal filed.

27
World Court rules U.S.A. must submit its decision to close PLO observer mission at the UN to arbitration.

May

Istanbul synagogue, Neve Shalom, reopens following refurbishment after Sept. 1986 massacre of 22 Jews during Sabbath services.

2–4
IDF operation into Lebanon, target terrorist bases at Maidoun; on May 10 U.S. vetoes UN Security Council resolution condemning Israel.

3
Cantors Assembly (Conservative) rejects move to admit women.

11
Blast in Cyprus intended for Israel embassy kills 3, injures 20, less than 100 yards from target.

17
Revelation of alleged huge embezzlement (approximately $20 million) by late president of West German Jewish community, Werner Nachmann, from "hardship funds" for reparations to West German Jews.

19
Israel Supreme Court rules that a woman, Leah Shakdiel of Yeruḥam, may serve as a member of a local religious council, ending months of public and legal debate.

20
Conference of Italian Bishops condemns anti-Jewish incidents in Italy following Chief Rabbi Toaff's statements on subject.

23
Israel Supreme Court rules that women may participate in Tel Aviv election of chief Ashkenazi rabbi.

June

Statue of Alfred Dreyfus placed in gardens of the Tuileries, Paris — unveiled by Jacques Lang, minister of culture.

4
Alberta, Canada, Court of Appeals overturns conviction of former high school teacher and mayor of Eckville, Jim Keegstra, who denied the Holocaust and taught Jews plotting to seize the world.

9
Israel PM Shamir confers with Russian FM Shevardnadze in New York.

12
Spate of forest fires in Israel, destroying over 25,000 acres in five weeks, attributed

for the most part to Arabs, both within the pre-1967 border and the Administered Territories.

21
Direct El-Al weekly flight begins Tel-Aviv–Warsaw.

23
Pope John Paul II begins five-day visit to Austria, meets with Waldheim; meets with heads of Jewish community.

29
U.S. District Court rules PLO observer mission to the UN in New York cannot be closed. The government announces in August decision not to appeal.

July

3
Ground-breaking for Holocaust memorial in Budapest draws large crowd of Jews.

17
Dutch Prime Minister Ruud Lubbers and Foreign Minister Hans van der Broek pay official visit to Israel, a first for any Dutch premier.

24
Israeli consular mission leaves for Russia, first such delegation since 1967.

26
First four Israeli-trained Conservative rabbis ordained in Jerusalem.

First rabbinical ordination ceremony of the Seminary of Judaic Studies of the Masorti (Conservative) Movement in Israel. (Courtesy of the Seminary of Judaic Studies, Jerusalem)

28
Jordan cancels development plans for West Bank.

August

Congress of Uruguay takes stand against UN Resolution 3379, which declared Zionism is racism.

5
U.S. Court of Appeals for District of Columbia upholds order to close PLO office in Washington.

19
Hand grenade thrown at mall in Haifa, 27 injured. Israeli Arab perpetrators apprehended in November.

28
Rabbi Israel Lau elected chief Ashkenazi rabbi of Tel Aviv, for first time women participate in voting.

30
UN Secretary-General Perez de Cuellar asks non-governmental organizations to use international pressure on Israel to "promote an effective negotiating process and to help create the conditions necessary for it to succeed."

September

14–15
Israel prime minister Shamir in Hungary — meets with Premier Karoly Grosz and FM Peter Varkonyi.

Rabbi Joel Schoener, chief rabbi of Hungary, accompanies PM Shamir on visit to Great Synagogue in Budapest. (GPO, Jerusalem)

19
Israel launches satellite, Ofek One, to test its systems.

29
Arbitrators' decision on Taba by 4–1 gives it to Egypt.

October

5
The Kach party, led by Meir Kahane, barred from forthcoming Israeli elections by Central Election Committee as racist.

U.S. pres. Reagan lays cornerstone of the U.S. Holocaust Memorial Museum in Washington, D.C.

U.S. immigration judge orders deportation of former SS guard at Auschwitz, Josef Ecker, who did not note his service when applying for U.S. immigration in 1956.

8
Pope John Paul II meets with Jewish leaders in Strasbourg — offers no response to request to recognize Israel.

12
The Parliament of Europe ratifies three economic agreements with Israel (314–25) which had been rejected in March.

Jerusalem rabbi, Adin Steinsaltz, goes to Moscow to prepare opening of Judaic Studies center there with approval of Russian government.

14
U.S. Senate adopts law which will allow U.S. to ratify an international treaty outlawing genocide already adopted by 97 countries. The Congress approves the law on Oct. 19. Discussion began 40 years ago. Pres. Reagan signs the law in Chicago ceremony on Nov. 4.

19
Suicide car-bomb explodes in Lebanon close to Metullah: 7 Israeli soldiers killed, 8 wounded.

24
Maurice Sabatier, 91, and Maurice Papon 79, Vichy regime leaders in Bordeaux, indicted for their roles in deportation of French Jews from the area in 1942–44.

25
U.S. Lt.-Gen. James Abrahamson states in Israel that the $160 million research and development contract with the U.S. makes Israel largest foreign participant in "Star Wars" program.

30
Rachel Weiss, and her three children (aged 3½, 2½, and 10 months) die, 5 others wounded in firebomb attack on Israeli bus by Arab terrorists in Jericho. Soldier seriously injured in rescue attempt (David Delarosa, 19) dies Dec. 22 while awaiting heart-lung transplant in London.

November

1
Elections for 12th Knesset in Israel. Religious parties in Israel push for change in

Getting out the vote by phone for the Likkud, Nov. 1. (GPO, Jerusalem)

"Who is a Jew" ruling to have it conform to Orthodoxy. Non-Orthodox groups the world over call for rejection of the demand. Issue is dropped with the establishment of the National Unity Government in which the religious parties play a minor role.

Israel Elections for 12th Knesset — Results

Party	Seats	%
Likkud	40	31.1
Labor Alignment	39	30.0
Shas	6	4.7
Agudat Israel	5	4.5
Citizens Rights Movement	5	4.3
National Religious Party	5	3.9
Dem. List for Peace & Equality	4	3.7
Teḥiyyah	3	3.1
Mapam	3	2.5
Ẓomet	2	2.0
Moledet	2	1.9
Center-Shinui Movement	2	1.7
Degel ha-Torah	2	1.5
Progressive List for Peace	1	1.5
Arab Democratic Party	1	1.2

4
UN General Assembly's Economic and Financial Committee passes resolution (90–14) asking UN bodies to deny any form of assistance to Israel and condemns her for measures taken against Arab uprising.

8
Governors of all 50 U.S. states sign proclamations in commemoration of 50th anniversary of Kristallnacht.

U.S. elections — George Bush elected president. 3 Jews to join the 28 already in Congress, total number of Jewish senators remains 8.

9
50th anniversary of Kristallnacht. Worldwide commemorations. Synagogues leave lights on for 24 hours.

10
The Bundestag president Phillip Jenninger resigns following criticism of his speech in West German parliament at session commemorating Kristallnacht; some of the listeners felt his remarks praised the Hitler era.

14
Palestine National Council declares independent State of Palestine with Jerusalem as capital; no borders cited. Israeli reaction mostly negative. Many countries recognize the new state.

16
U.S. State Dept. review of Palestine National Council political statements after Algiers meeting does not yet allow America to talk to the PLO.

26
U.S. Secretary of State, George Shultz, announces decision to deny Yasser Arafat entry to U.S. as supporter of terror. The UN debate on Palestine is moved to Geneva to allow Arafat to address it.

December

1
U.S.S.R. ceases interference of radio broadcasts from Israel.

6
Five American Jews meet with Arafat in Stockholm. Mainstream American Jewish organizations' response is negative — group not representative.

General Assembly of UN adopts 19 anti-Israel resolutions.

7
Soviet premier Mikhail Gorbachev in speech to UN General Assembly says "the problem of so-called refuseniks" is no longer on the agenda after the reworking of U.S.S.R. "state secrecy" laws.

13
Arafat in 90-minute speech to UN General Assembly in Geneva stops short of recognizing Israel. At press conference following day makes statements which allows the U.S. to announce decision to open dialogue with the PLO.

15
UN General Assembly votes to recognize Palestinian state and upgrades PLO to "Palestine observer delegation."

17
Violent weekend in Administered Territories — 8 Palestinians killed, dozens wounded; a number of Jewish residents seriously injured.

20
National Unity Government in Israel after weeks of negotiations — Likkud and Alignment form the majority.

Government of National Unity formed December 1988. (GPO, Jerusalem)

23
Knesset approves government, 84–19.

January 1989

4
Statistics on Soviet Jewish emigration in 1988 show that close to 19,000 Jews emigrated, with 11.4% going to Israel.

7
In Vilnius a local radio station begins broadcasts in Yiddish on local cultural activities and the Maccabi sports organization opens a branch.

8
Meeting in Paris between Israel foreign minister Arens and Russian foreign minister Shevardnadze who announces Israel consular delegation to U.S.S.R. to be upgraded.

24
Opening of Cairo library, housed in synagogue, focusing on Jewish heritage in Egypt, 60,000 volumes from 12 synagogues.

February

JDC to stop accepting Soviet Jews at transit facilities near Rome for financial reasons.

3
Twenty-seven U.S. national Jewish organizations announce the establishment of the Coalition for Jewish Unity to promote religious pluralism in Israel.

6
A Committee for the Yiddish Language established in Moscow.

12
The Solomon Mikhoels Cultural Center is dedicated in Moscow. Many Jewish leaders and delegations from outside the U.S.S.R. attend, including a WJC delegation led by President Edgar Bronfman.

20
Israel foreign minister Arens talks with Russian foreign minister Shevardnadze in Cairo. A meeting with President Mubarak yields no progress on peace process.

22
First Moscow *yeshivah* in 60 years opens.

March

JDC includes Soviet Union in "Operation Passover" for first time in over 50 years.

3
The Italian Senate passes a law guaranteeing freedom of worship for Jews and defines new rules for relations between the government and the Jewish community.

15
Taba handed to Egyptians by Israel.

19
A Jewish Cultural Association is founded in Leningrad.

20
Prime Minister's Conference on Jewish Solidarity with Israel convenes in Jerusalem.

Ghetto uprising, says "Holocaust must never be forgotten."

May

1–10
The first international rabbinical delegation, all Orthodox, visits the Jewish communities and institutions of Moscow, Leningrad, and Kiev at the invitation of the chairman of the U.S.S.R. Council of Religious Affairs, K. Kharchev.

2
East Berlin Jewish community hold first Holocaust Day commemoration.

bombing attempt against Copenhagen synagogue and airline office in 1985.

22
U.S. sec. of state Baker calls on Israel to stop settlement of occupied territories.

22–23
PM Shamir in England, meets with PM Thatcher, who expresses understanding for Israel's peace plan but does not offer support for it.

Israel PM Shamir answering journalists' questions in London after meeting with British Prime Minister Thatcher (right) and British Foreign Minister Howe (center), May 1989. (GPO, Jerusalem)

Closing session, at Western Wall, of Prime Minister's Solidarity Conference: Seymour Reich, chairman, is flanked by Shimon Peres to his left and Yiẓhak Shamir to his right, March 1989. (GPO, Jerusalem)

24–25
Israel PM Shamir in Spain, meets with King Juan Carlos in Madrid, has session with Prime Minister Felipe Gonzalez.

King Juan Carlos of Spain (right) and his wife Queeen Sophia (left) host PM Shamir for lunch at La Zarazuela Royal Palace in Madrid, May 1989. (GPO, Jerusalem)

April

The Irkutsk *mazzah* factory, the only one in Siberia, is burned down by vandals.

3
PM Shamir goes to U.S. for talks, meets with U.S. president Bush (April 6) to discuss Shamir's proposal for elections in the Administered Territories.

7
Hundreds of Palestinians on Temple Mount throw rocks on Western Wall plaza, over 12 injured (police, journalists, and Jewish visitors), 34 Arabs arrested.

22
San Diego *Jewish Times* fire bombed.

23
Lech Walesa, Solidarity leader, lays wreath at monument to heroes of Warsaw

Arafat says PLO covenant *"caduque"* (passé); Israel is skeptical.

3
Arab terrorist kills 2 elderly Jews, injures three others, at bus stop in Jerusalem.

10
Some 40 Russian Jews demonstrate during first day of U.S. Sec. of State Baker's Moscow visit; they ask not to give the U.S.S.R. most-favored-nation status unless emigration made easier.

17–28
Union of Hebrew Teachers in the U.S.S.R. conducts seminar for Hebrew-teaching candidates, examinations from the Israel Academy of the Hebrew Language.

18
In Stockholm, 15 people of Arab descent held in connection with involvement in

June

5
Israeli consular delegation reoccupies 3-story Moscow building which housed the Israel embassy.

9
U.S. vetoes UN Security Council resolution condemning Israel policy on settlement in Administered Territories, a vote of 14–1.

9–10
94 of the 100 U.S. senators send letter to Sec. Baker expressing approval for PM Shamir's peace initiative.

15
The JDC office, ordered closed in 1953, allowed to reopen in Hungary.

21
Pres. Herzog on first state visit to Canada by an Israeli president.

27
El Al plane flies to Erevan and picks up 66

victims of the Armenian earthquake to take them to Israel for rehabilitation.

July

Sweden decides to rescind Sept. 1988 ban on *kasher* slaughtering of chickens.

3–13
13th Maccabiah held in Israel, 42 countries participating, including Russia, Lithuania, and Hungary.

From the opening ceremony of the 13th Maccabiah, July 1989. (Courtesy Maccabi World Union, Tel Aviv)

5
PM Shamir tells Likkud Central Committee: no East Jerusalem Arab in elections; no negotiations as long as violence continues; no foreign sovereignty over any part of the Land of Israel; settlement will continue in the Administered Territories; no negotiations with the PLO; no Palestine in the Land of Israel.

France and the U.S.S.R. reject Shamir's peace initiative.

6
Bus traveling from Tel Aviv to Jerusalem forced off road by Arab, 16 passengers killed, 25 injured.

Burnt-out shell of Egged bus forced off road near Jerusalem by Arab passenger, July 18, 1989. (Media, Jerusalem; photo G. Feinblatt)

13
Polish construction workers at Auschwitz convent site attack protesting American Jews; Poles say Jews provoked them.

24
Israel High Court of Justice decides that non-Orthodox converts must be registered as Israeli citizens under Law of Return by Interior Ministry.

29
Sheikh Obeid, Hizbullah leader, kidnapped by IDF in Lebanon, taken to Israel; Arab and U.S. protests.

August

Yeshivah opens in Tbilisi, Georgia; a third Ḥabad institution after Moscow and Leningrad.

5&12
London's Hyde Park Holocaust Memorial vandalized two weekends in a row.

8
The *Jewish Times* of San Diego, California, firebombed second time (see April 22).

27
5 Palestinians considered a security threat by Israel deported; U.S. scores the move.

31
Poland begins events marking 50th anniversary of start of WWII. Jews boycott the events following anti-Semitic remarks by Cardinal Glemp.

September

A record number 6,000 Soviet Jewish emigrés reach the U.S., including a one-day high of 1,500.

Announcement that U.S. Dept. of Education will fund innovative Holocaust educational program for junior and senior high school.

9
Great Synagogue of Szeged, Hungary, restored and dedicated; maintenance to be funded by anonymous donor.

18
Hungary resumes full diplomatic relations with Israel after break in 1967.

Israel Foreign Minister Arens (center, on right) seated opposite his Hungarian counterpart at the signing of the agreement reestablishing Israel-Hungary diplomatic relations, Sept. 1989. (GPO, Jerusalem)

Austria to remove envoy from Israel in response to Israel's not returning its ambassador over Waldheim affair.

October

First Talmud Torah in recent generations opens in U.S.S.R.

1
Dutch embassy in Moscow to issue Soviet Jews visas only for Israel; the U.S. embassy will now give the visas to those headed for America.

3
In Brussels, Prof. Joseph Wybran, president of the Coordinating Committee of Belgian Jewish Organizations, is murdered, perpetrators not apprehended.

8
U.S. sec. of state Baker proposes a 5-point plan for talks between Israel and a Palestinian delegation in Cairo.

11
Defecting Syrian pilot flies his MiG-23 to Israel.

November

Announcement that ORT is to resume operations in U.S.S.R. stopped in 1930; a

Moscow resource center will be set up to train teachers in advanced technology.

5

Ethiopia reestablishes diplomatic relations with Israel.

Israel's inner cabinet gives conditional approval to Baker's 5-point peace plan; the U.S. must provide assurances that there will be no negotiations with the PLO.

French government lifts 21-year embargo on military sales to Israel.

East German Jewish Community makes statement against official history books and school system for downplaying Nazi era, calls for diplomatic relations with Israel.

9

Agudat Israel withdraws from Israeli coalition government.

10–20

P.M. Shamir in U.S. meets with Jewish and political leaders, including Pres. Bush.

A session between President Bush (on left, seated third from front) and Israel PM Shamir (seated third, on right) and their working teams, Washington, D.C., Nov. 1989. (GPO, Jerusalem)

27

Agriculture Minister Katz-Oz, visits Moscow, first Israel cabinet member since 1967, agrees to send Israeli produce to U.S.S.R.

December

3

Gregor Gysi, a Jew, is chosen as chairman of the East German Communist Party.

"Feminist Judaism" Conference sponsored by American National Council for Jewish Women on ways feminist Jewish actions can be taken to empower women in the future.

12

British Parliament votes to allow prosecution of Nazi war criminals on British soil in British courts.

18

In Moscow, hundreds of Jews gather to form a Jewish Congress, called Va'ad, as umbrella body to coordinate activities of all Jewish organizations in the Soviet Union.

25

First shipment leaves, from Ben-Gurion Airport, for the U.S.S.R. with Israeli produce, agreement calls for 90,000 tons of produce (=$30 mil.) in 6 months.

30

Peace Now hand-in-hand chain around Old City walls with Israeli Jews and Arabs, Palestinians, and European visitors taking part, gathering marred by disturbances and arrests.

31

PM Shamir fires Science Minister Ezer Weizman for meeting with PLO leaders. Government crisis resolved with Min. Weizman still in government but no longer in Inner Cabinet.

January 1990

Passage of Canadian Amended Divorce Act, "Get Law," that "neither partner may get a civil divorce until the religious barriers to remarrying are removed."

21–22

Vice Premier Peres in Prague for first visit of Israeli official since 1967, meets with Pres. Havel and with Alexander Dubcek.

22

Israel reopens embassy in Ethiopia after 16-year closure.

23

420 Soviet Jews arrive in Israel on single flight from Budapest, largest group to come on one flight.

Children from Chernobyl at Ben-Gurion Airport upon arrival in Israel for medical treatment, Jan. 9, 1990. (GPO, Jerusalem)

Israel and U.S.S.R. sign trade pact after 23-year break in formal economic relations.

24

Shimon Peres meets with Pres. Mubarak to discuss ways to advance peace process, the Baker peace plans, and Israeli-Palestinian talks in Cairo on elections in the Administered Territories.

February

Work commences on interfaith center about 800 meters from present Auschwitz convent site.

Hadassah Org. decides to halt participation in future WZO elections.

An exhibition — the first of its kind in the U.S.S.R. — of over 300 books on Jewish history, culture, and religion, is held in the Moscow National Library for Foreign Literature.

Austria to pay some 300 million schilling (about $25 million) over 5 years to social welfare institutions and retirement homes in Israel, U.S., Austria, and elsewhere as compensation to Jewish victims of the Nazis.

4

Busload of Israeli tourists in Egypt attacked by terrorists, 15 dead, 17 wounded.

9

Israel and Czechoslovakia reestablish diplomatic relations.

Speaker of Czechoslovakian Parliament, Alexander Dubcek (left), receives Israel Foreign Minister Arens in Prague, Feb. 1990. (GPO, Jerusalem)

March

In U.S.S.R., first non-Orthodox Jewish congregation sponsored in Moscow by the World Union of Progressive Synagogues.

Unzer Kol ("Our Voice"), a Russian-Yiddish newspaper, begins to appear in Moldavia.

2

Bush administration agrees to loan of $400 million for housing immigrants to Israel as long as not used to settle Soviet Jews in the Administered Territories.

6
Israel admitted as founding member of European Bank for Reconstruction and Development of the EC which is to assist the economic integration and democratization of East European countries.

9
East German prime minister, Hans Modrow, in a letter to Israel prime minister, acknowledges the GDR's responsibility in Nazi persecution of Jews and expresses readiness to discuss compensation to Jewish Nazi victims. In June a framework for compensation negotiations is agreed upon by representatives of the Conference on Jewish Material Claims Against Germany.

13
Prime Minister Shamir fires Vice Premier Peres, Labor quits government, Shamir loses no-confidence votes on the 15th and government falls.

20
Israel pres. Herzog asks Shimon Peres to form a government. On April 26, Peres announces he cannot do it; Shamir puts together a new government without Labor.

21
Sri Lanka gives Israel 30 days to close its diplomatic mission.

The *intifada* continued through the year — above, some of the weapons seized by Israel Border Police in the Gaza Strip, 1990. (GPO, Jerusalem)

April

1
Reestablishment of Hungarian Zionist Federation in Budapest.

6
Arafat meets with the pope to speak against Soviet Jewish emigration.

10–11
Communal Passover *seders* held in the U.S.S.R. — including Siberia, Georgia, and Central Asia — for first time in 40 years.

11
Some 150 Jews in Jerusalem move into premises of St. John's Hospice near the Church of the Holy Sepulcher, building obtained from lessee. The Greek Church, owner of the property, goes to court. On April 26, the High Court of Justice orders the Jews to move out, leaving only 20 people for maintenance, pending final decision.

15
U.S.S.R. pres. Gorbachev makes first public statement against anti-Semitism.

24
U.S. House of Representatives passes a non-binding resolution, 378–34, that "Jerusalem is and must remain the capital of the State of Israel."

24
Poland and Israel renew diplomatic relations.

25–27
Czech President Havel visits Israel.

26
Daf Yomi *siyyum* (conclusion of Talmud reading cycle) held in New York's Madison Square Garden, 17,000 men and 3,000 women take part.

30
Hand grenade thrown into concert hall in Kielce injures two at performance of Jewish folk music from the Ukraine.

Union for Traditional (Conservative) Judaism, a breakaway from the Rabbinical Assembly, to train its own rabbis.

May

Announcement that YIVO and the Jewish Theological Seminary will build a joint Jewish Studies program with Moscow State Institute to begin Fall 1991.

Synagogues desecrated in European countries: Switzerland, Holland, and West Germany.

10
Jewish cemetery in Carpentras, France, desecrated; 34 graves damaged, one body removed from coffin. The following day protest marches take place throughout France, and on May 14 some 100,000 participate in Paris march, including Pres. Mitterrand.

16
At Rabbinical Assembly meeting Conservative rabbis endorse full civil equality for gay and lesbian Jews and say they should be welcome in the synagogue.

20
7 Arabs killed by Jewish gunman in Rishon le-Zion; rioting erupts.

30
In two assaults, 3 hours apart, Arab terrorists attempt landing on Israel beach (Niẓanim) during Shavuot holiday, 4 invaders killed, 12 captured.

June

At the end of the month Jean Marie Le-Pen is charged in France for slander and spreading racist propaganda after anti-Semitic remarks.

1
Sephardi Jews the world over awarded the 1990 Prince of Asturias Cooperation Prize as a group.

5
Lech Walesa statement against anti-Semitism appears in leading Polish newspapers.

7
List of alleged Nazi war criminals is presented to British Home Office officials.

10
Nelson Mandela meets in Geneva with representatives of American Jewish organizations and regrets having offended Jews.

11
Yiẓḥak Shamir's fourth government approved by Knesset, 62–57.

Prime Minister Shamir's fourth government, June 1990. (GPO, Jerusalem)

Four youths arrested for Carpentras cemetery desecration.

15
Israel opens academic liaison office in China.

20
Pres. Bush announces suspension of dialogue with the PLO because of its refusal to condemn the May 30 attempted attack on Israel.

21
First Israeli ambassador to Greece, Moshe Gilboa, presents credentials.

25
The Central Conference of American Rabbis decides to accept homosexual rabbis.

July

First East German Jewish day school opens in Prenzlauer Berg near East Berlin.

1
Bomb thrown at South Eastern Hebrew Center in Risettenville, Johannesburg.

8
Government-sponsored Holocaust memorial by sculptor Imre Varga dedicated in Budapest near Dohany synagogue, President Arpad Goncz and Prime Minister Josef Antall attend gathering.

19
Jewish Agency opens office in Warsaw for first time since WWII.

25

Jacob Hasson, Peruvian Jewish leader, shot 5 times by unknown assailants.

August

Some 10,000 people gather in the Leningrad central sports stadium for completion of Torah scrolls (writing began in the U.S.) to be distributed in the U.S.S.R.

17,484 Soviet Jews reach Israel during the month, the largest monthly total in 39 years.

2

Iraqi army invades Kuwait, with thousands more soldiers following on the 4th.

8

Iraq annexes Kuwait.

10

Iraq declares *jihad*, holy war, against the U.S. and Israel.

12

Saddam Hussein links resolving of crisis to Israeli withdrawal from Administered territories.

19

U.S. calls for UN Security Council meeting and asks Israel to maintain low profile.

25

Ihringen, West Germany, Jewish cemetery desecrated, about 175 headstones overturned or broken, swastikas and slogans written on walls.

30

Iraq threatens to attack Israel — Shamir says they will rue the day.

September

U.S.S.R. adopts law guaranteeing freedom of religion.

6

Vatican Commission for Religious Relations with Jews produces a statement condemning anti-Semitism as a sin after a 3-day meeting with IJCIC in Prague.

30

Israel FM David Levy and Soviet FM Shevardnadze meet at UN and agree on full consular relations.

October

7

Distribution of gas masks begins in Israel as threat of attack deemed real. Israel reserves the right to move against Iraq.

8

On Jerusalem Temple Mount some 3,000 Arabs hurl rocks onto Western Wall plaza where Jews are gathered for prayer on the Sukkot holiday; in police response to the riot 21 of the Arabs are killed and over 100 wounded. Israel is condemned by the UN for its actions, and the Security Council (on the 9th) discusses sending a delegation to Israel to examine the situation (rejected by Israel, Oct. 14).

Escaping rocks at the Western Wall, Oct. 8, 1990, a soldier and a visitor assist worshipers to leave the area. (Media, Jerusalem; photo Karine L. Quist)

21

A 19-year-old Arab from Ubeidaya, east of Bethlehem, stabs three Jews to death in Baka, a Jerusalem neighborhood.

24

A UN Security Council resolution censures Israel for refusing to cooperate with the UN investigation of the Temple Mount incident.

26

UN ultimatum to Iraq; withdraw by January or else...

November

1

Un Sec.-Gen. Perez de Cuellar submits report on October Temple Mount incident. Israel is criticized for violating Fourth Geneva Convention but no specific UN action is called for except for a meeting of the 1949 accord signatorees. Israel is disappointed by the "one-sidedness" of the report.

5

Report that 20,324 Soviet Jews arrived in Israel during October 1990, fifth record month in a row.

Rabbi Meir Kahane shot to death while speaking in N.Y. hotel.

16

Agudat Israel joins coalition with promise of religious legislation (on pork, Sabbath transportation, and indecent advertising).

21

Israel and the U.S.S.R. sign a 3-year agreement on the exchange of scientific and technical information; joint research programs; exchange visits; and sharing of equipment.

24

Desider Galsky, president of the Council of Czech Jewish communities, dies in car accident.

Desider Galsky (left) in Prague's Pinkas Synagogue. (Courtesy Geoffrey Wigoder, Jerusalem)

25

Infiltrator from Egypt attacks Israeli bus, 3 IDF soldiers and the bus driver are killed.

Israeli soldier helps civilian adjust gas mask at Jerusalem distribution point, Nov. 1, 1990. (GPO, Jerusalem)

December

3

Lod military court sentences the 12 terrorists responsible for the attempted attack on May 30 to 30 years in prison.

20
Polish Roman Catholic bishops produce document condemning anti-Semitism and acknowledging that some Poles did help to kill Jews in WWII.

Israel Prime Minister Shamir (right) with British Prime Minister John Major after meeting in London, Dec. 1990. (GPO, Jerusalem)

Jewish sailors on the USS *Saratoga*, in the Red Sea during Operation Desert Shield, light the *menorah* with chaplain, Rabbi Kaprow (second from left). (Courtesy United States Navy; photo PH2 Bruce L. Davis)

January 1991

Some 200,000 immigrants Jews arrived in Israel in 1990, 184,602 from the U.S.S.R.

3
Israel flag flies anew at Moscow consulate after 23-year break. Israel Consul-General Aryeh Levin calls for full U.S.S.R.-Israel diplomatic relations.

5
Patriot anti-missile batteries arrive in Israel, sent by U.S.

9
German government and the 16 federal states decide that number of Soviet Jews allowed to settle in Germany will be unlimited.

10
Israel Air Force on full alert — pilots sit in cockpits.

UJA solidarity mission of 600 U.S. Jews arrives in Israel.

17
1:30 A.M. (local time) U.S. coalition begins bombing of Baghdad. White House announces start of Operation Desert Storm. In Israel, Civil Defense controls the homefront, schools stay closed, adults are to stay close to home. Israelis are asked to take their gas masks wherever they go.

18
8 missiles with conventional warheads hit Israel; 30 injured.

19
Patriots positioned to cover Israel.

Residents of south Tel Aviv evacuated from homes following Iraqi Scud missile attack, en route to temporary housing, Jan. 19, 1991; their gas masks are in the boxes they are carrying. (GPO, Jerusalem)

20–21
In Rome, Paris, Amsterdam, rallies of solidarity with Israel after two missile attacks — offer support and money.

22
Scud missile scores direct hit on Tel Aviv area houses; 96 injured; 3 die of heart attacks.

23
Scud attack intercepted, not totally successfully, by Patriot missiles.

26
Scud attack hits Tel Aviv area — 5 Scuds destroyed by Patriots and 2 diverted. One killed in attack in Ramat Gan.

29
German cabinet agrees to send military equipment to Israel, including anti-aircraft missiles and systems for warning against gas attack; appropriates $65 million in humanitarian aid; on the 31st 300 tons of equipment begin to arrive.

February

3–4
Solidarity Mission arrives with 1,300 French Jews; Mayor Dinkins of New York visits Israel in support.

4
Letter from 50 U.S. governors to Israel ambassador Zalman Shoval expressing support and concern for Israel in face of ongoing attacks, praise Israel's restraint.

9
Missile attack on Saturday morning, 500 homes damaged (11 destroyed), 26 injured.

11–12
The 12th and 13th Scud attacks; total now 33 missiles, damaging 7,000 homes in Tel Aviv and Ramat Gan areas.

21
Agreement reached for ceasefire and withdrawal of Iraq from Kuwait.

Patriot missile launcher with Tel Aviv's Ramat Aviv neighborhood in the background, Feb. 7, 1991. (GPO, Jerusalem)

25
Last Scud attack.

27
Elhanan Atali, 25-year-old yeshivah student, stabbed to death in Old City Jerusalem by Arab terrorists.

28
U.S. President Bush declares the war is over; Gulf War state of emergency canceled in Israel.

March

Dead Sea Scrolls tested by Swiss laboratory — results: scrolls are as old and authentic as claimed.

10
Four Jewish women stabbed to death at Jerusalem bus stop by Arab from Gaza Region; Defense Minister Arens bars Arab entry from Administered Territories to Israel (ban gradually lifted by month's end).

Pres. Herzog speaking with reporters while surveying Scud damage in the center of Israel, Jan. 1991. (GPO, Jerusalem)

11
Gazan driver runs down two IDF soldiers killing them.

12–13
U.S. Sec. of State Baker in Israel to work toward Israel-Arab peace talks.

U.S. Sec. of State Baker (right) at the King David Hotel with Foreign Minister David Levy (center) and Binyamin Netanyahu (left), March 11, 1991. (GPO, Jerusalem)

17–21
U.S. National Council for Soviet Jewry arranges for emergency airlift of *mazzot* to the Ukraine due to shortage there.

22
Sec. Baker in testimony to congressional subcommittee says new settlements and expansion of existing ones in Israel-Administered Territories are largest obstacle to peace.

27
Patriarch of Russian Orthodox Church, Alexei II, of Moscow visits Israel — first visit of a patriarch of the Church since 1948.

April

1
Ehud Barak becomes Israel's 14th chief of staff

Ehud Barak, 14th IDF chief of staff. (GPO, Jerusalem)

8
U. S. Sec. of State Baker on unexpected trip to Mid-East to work towards regional peace conference.

In Budapest Jewish Agency opens transit camp for Soviet Jews on way to Israel.

11
Arrival in Israel of 13 Albanian Jews; all Albanian Jews (about 300) brought to Israel since Dec. 1990.

Jewish Chaplain, LT Jon Cutler, CHC, USN, serving with the Marines in Saudi Arabia and Kuwait during Operation Desert Storm, leads a field Passover *Seder* for 1st Marine Corps, American toops in Kuwait, April 1991. (Courtesy Jewish Chaplains Council, New York)

19
U.S. Sec. Baker in Jerusalem meets for 5 hours with Israeli officials over peace conference. On the 21st Israel says it looks favorably on many of the U.S. ideas.

20–30
Japanese prime minister visits Israel.

May

1
Anti-Jewish march with 3,000 participants in Leningrad accusing authorities of favoring Jews.

10
Soviet Foreign Minister Alexander Bessmertnykh begins Israel visit, first Soviet foreign minister to do so.

12
Israel's Rafael, state armament authority, reveals the advanced Popeye air-to-ground missile.

13–24
Hungarian Prime Minister, Jozef Antall, visits Israel.

Jozef Antall (right) and Yizḥak Shamir sign agreement renewing diplomatic relations between Israel and Hungary, May 13, 1991. (GPO, Jerusalem)

14
U.S. Dept. of Commerce fines three related biomedical companies $65,000 for complying with Arab Boycott of Israel (Flow International).

20–23
President of Poland, Lech Walesa, visits Israel.

Lech Walesa (front, center) during his visit to the Western Wall, Jerusalem, May 21, 1991. (GPO, Jerusalem)

21–22
Portuguese foreign minister, Joao Deus Pinheiro, visits Israel, highest ranking Portuguese visitor thus far.

25
"Operation Solomon" — 14,400 Ethiopian Jews airlifted from Addis Ababa in 24 hours.

May 1991, Operation Solomon, airlift of Ethiopian Jews to Israel. (GPO, Jerusalem)

June

Report of U.S. Council of Jewish Federation that intermarriage rate of U.S. Jews passes 50% mark.

11–21
Pres. Herzog of Israel visits Hungary (11–17) and Bulgaria (17–21).

17
Israel and the Republic of Georgia sign scientific cooperation agreement.

20
UJA representative states that $30 million were collected in one month for Operation Solomon immigrants to Israel from Ethiopia.

26
Bulgaria becomes transit station for Soviet Jews en route to Israel.

27
Kashmiri Muslim group attacks Israeli tourists in Srinigar, Kashmir, India: 1 killed, 3 wounded, 1 kidnapped (later released unharmed).

July

17
3 IDF soldiers killed, 4 wounded in Hizbullah ambush north of the security zone in Lebanon.

18
Court ruling in Jerusalem that there is "no cause to indict" any policemen or border policemen for the October 1990 Temple Mount riots.

August

1
U.S. President Bush visits Babi-Yar.

PM Shamir agrees to peace talks with Arabs.

4
Israel cabinet agrees to peace talks.

19
Israel and Albania establish relations for the first time; agreement signed by Albanian foreign minister, Mohammed Kaflani, in Israel.

Car accident in which Ḥasidic driver kills 7-year-old Black boy leads to four nights of racial rioting in New York's Crown Heights neighborhood between Ḥasidim and Blacks.

21–23
Congo foreign minister, Jean Blaise Kololo, in Israel to discuss renewal of ties, signs friendship agreement.

24
Kaddish said in Red Square for Ilya Krichevsky, 28, one of 3 killed during failed anti-Gorbachev coup.

25
Announce plan to protest razing of Hamburg Jewish cemetery with 4,000 graves, the earliest 1663.

27
Israel PM Shamir visits Bulgaria after renewal of relations.

28
70 Israelis go to the former U.S.S.R. to teach Hebrew, Judaism, and bar and bat mitzvah lessons.

September

1
Ukrainian delegation in Israel signs trade agreement with the Israel Chamber of Commerce.

2–4
First visit to Israel by a Romanian president — Ion Iliescu.

Sept. 2, 1991, Labor party chairman Shimon Peres greets Ion Iliescu, president of Romania, in Jerusalem. (GPO, Jerusalem)

4
U.S. sec. of state Baker urges Congress to delay loan guarantees to Israel — granting them might "undercut" the peace process.

5
Shamir rejects linking the loans to the Mid-East peace process.

11
Information that Rahamim Alsheikh, missing in action since 1986, is dead comes in exchange for release of 51 Arab prisoners and bodies of 9 Hizbullah terrorists killed in clashes with the IDF.

12
Pres. Bush says he will veto any call for loan guarantees to Israel in the next 120 days. Shamir says he wants the guarantees now and will not compromise.

13
Body of Samir Assad, IDF sergeant missing since April 1983, given to Israel in return for allowing Alki Abu Hill of Abu Dis, deported in Jan. 1986 for subversive activities, to return home.

18
U.S. admonishes — "no guarantees without freeze on settlements."

23
Bush in speech to UN General Assembly demands repeal of 1975 UN resolution equating Zionism with racism.

Aug. 28, 1991, on visit to Bulgaria, Shamir shakes hands with Chief Patriarch of the city of Kazanlik; behind Shamir is Prime Minister Popov. (GPO, Jerusalem)

October

1–3
Argentine president, Carlos Menem, in Israel on official trip — first time visit of Argentinian head of state.

2
Arab terrorist stabs 2 women, German tourists, in Old City of Jerusalem, one dies, other wounded.

4
Russian court orders 12,000-volume library of Jewish books in Lenin Library returned to Lubavich ḥasidim. Decision reversed later on appeal.

5
Gathering of some 50,000 in Babi Yar in commemoration of 50th anniversary of massacre (Sept. 29–30, 1941) — the first official memorial of the event by the U.S.S.R.

6
Israel peace activist Abie Nathan sentenced to 18 months prison and 18 months suspended sentence for meeting PLO leader Arafat.

8
First direct flight from Moscow of Soviet immigrants to Israel.

9
Jews enter Jewish-owned Silwan home (in Jerusalem's City of David) with intent to settle. Arab neighbors in turmoil. Police thwart plans for settlement of a sizeable number of Jews in the area.

13
Several thousand Jews plus leaders of other ethnic groups march in downtown Manhattan in protest of anti-Semitism in Crown Heights, Brooklyn, and elsewhere in U.S., after riots and killing of yeshivah student Yankel Rosenbaum.

President Herzog leaves for week's visit to Czechoslovakia.

16
U.S. sec. of state Baker in Israel to finish preparations toward peace conference.

17
Soviet foreign minister Boris Pankin visits Israel.

18
Israel and U.S.S.R. resume diplomatic ties broken in 1967.

Commemoration of 50th anniversary of deportation of Berlin Jews; a memorial to Berlin Jews murdered by Nazis unveiled at Grunewald station.

20
Israel appoints ambassador to the U.S.S.R., Arye Levin, who reopens embassy on Oct. 24.

24
Austrian student federation holds silent march in Vienna to protest anti-Semitism

after attacks on Jewish graves there. Poll results show one-third of Austrians would not want Jewish neighbors.

28

Terrorist attack on bus en route from Shilo to Tel Aviv leaves 2 dead, 6 wounded (5 of them children).

29

Soviet premier Mikhail Gorbachev and Israel prime minister Shamir meet in Madrid — first time discussion between Soviet and Israeli leader.

At the Madrid peace conference, members of the Israeli delegation look on as Mikhail Gorbachev, president of the U.S.S.R., and Yitzḥak Shamir, Israel prime minister, shake hands. (GPO, Jerusalem)

Oct. 30–Nov. 1

Madrid Peace conference on the Middle East convenes with participation of Israel and delegations representing Syria, Lebanon, Jordan and the Palestinians. At opening session Pres. Bush and Premier Gorbachev also take part. The success of the talks leads to the continuation of bilateral talks towards peace in the Middle East.

November

6

Berlin monument to Jewish victims of Nazis desecrated.

10

South Africa's president, F. W. de Klerk, and foreign minister, F. R. Botha, begin 4-day state visit to Israel.

18

Israel PM Shamir begins visit to the U.S.; meets with Pres. Bush on the 22nd.

27 & 29

Pro-Assad rallies by Syrian Jews — 2,000 out of 4,000 total march.

December

1

3-meter-tall menorah lit in Kremlin by Ḥabad; candlelighting ceremony inside the Palace of Congresses. Small protest by anti-Semites, 25 demonstrators.

2

Felipe Gonzalez, Spanish prime minister, in Israel to start commemorations for 500th year since the expulsion from Spain. Knesset marks the event.

16

UN rescinds Zionism = Racism resolution of 1975, 112–25.

16–19

Bilateral Israel-Arab talks resume in Washington; break for 3 weeks.

19

Turkey announces upgrading diplomatic relations with Israel to ambassadorial level.

21

NY jury acquits El Sayyid Nosair of murder of Meir Kahane shot Nov. 5, 1990.

23

Car bomb with 100 kilos of explosive explodes in Budapest as bus with Soviet immigrants in transit on way to Israel passes by, 1 policeman killed, 1 wounded, no immigrant hurt.

Demjanjuk appeal opens.

24

Yang Fu-chang, Chinese deputy foreign minister, is first senior Chinese official to visit Israel.

Spanish Prime Minister Felipe Gonzalez (third from left) listens to Pres. Herzog address a gathering in commemoration of 500 years of the expulsion from Spain, President's Residence, Jerusalem, Dec. 1991. (GPO, Jerusalem)

25

Zambia and Israel announce resumption of relations, severed in 1973.

January 1992

Sefarad 92 (year of events) opens in commemoration of 500 years since the expulsion of Jews from Spain.

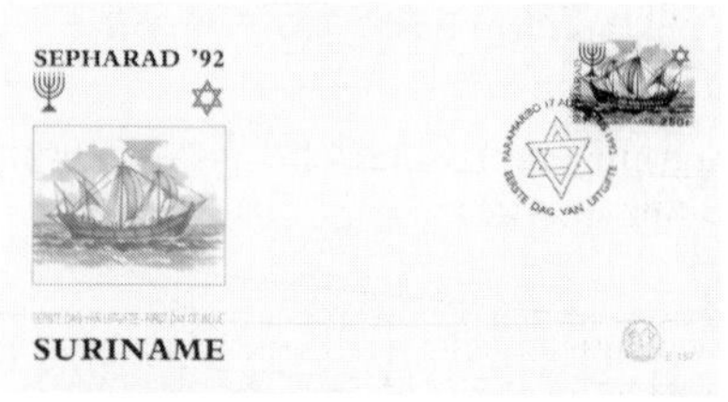

Sepharad '92 — First day cover of special Surinam stamp commemorating 500 years of Jews in America (380 years in Surinam). (Courtesy Mordechai Arbell Collection, Jerusalem)

50th anniversary of Wannsee Conference — opening of Germany's new memorial to Holocaust victims at the Wannsee Villa.

Bosque [Memory] Forest dedicated in Ben Shemen, Israel, in honor of the Jewish *desaparecidos* of Argentina (1,500 out of 9,000 were Jews).

Immigrant count for 1991 — 170,500 came to Israel, 147,292 of them Soviet Jews.

Israel population reaches 5.05 million — 4.1 million Jews and 900,000 Arabs.

5

All Arab delegations to the Mid-East peace talks delay departure for the discussions in protest of Israel's decision to expel 12 Arabs. UN Security Council unanimously condemns Israel move (Jan. 6).

13

After days of talks in Washington corridors, Israel and Jordanian-Palestinian delegations move into a room to conduct discussions; two tracks: Israel-Jordan-Palestine relations; Israel-Palestine issues, the interim five-year plan for autonomy.

16

Teḥiyyah party announces decision to withdraw from Israel government.

Prime Minister Shamir with Chinese Foreign Minister Yang Fuchang on a secret visit to Israel, Dec. 24, 1991. (GPO, Jerusalem)

17
Moledet party decides to leave Israel government making early elections inevitable.

24
Israel and China establish diplomatic relations.

26
Israel foreign minister David Levy arrives in Moscow — first visit by an Israeli foreign minister.

29
India announces decision to establish diplomatic relations with Israel.

31
Roman Catholic Church abolishes Bavarian pilgrimage connected to 1338 murder of Jews in Deggendorf who were later claimed to have desecrated the Holy Eucharist.

February

3
Argentina declassifies files on Nazis who immigrated there.

5
Two Israeli Arabs, a father and daughter, arrested in Egypt as spies for Israel. Son arrested on Feb. 10. On Feb. 12, a Jewish Israeli, David Ovitz is arrested. Feb. 18, Egypt claims all four have confessed.

6
Officials of German Jewish community report that 25,000 CIS Jews have applied to immigrate to Germany.

14
Three IDF soldiers axed to death in Galed training camp for new immigrant soldiers.

16
Hizbullah leader Sheikh Abbas Musawi killed in south Lebanon by Israel Air Force helicopter attack on a convoy of vehicles.

17
Katyusha attack on Galilee by Hizbullah in response to Musawi's death begins round of attacks and counter-attacks. On the 22nd Hizbullah signs agreement to desist from Katyusha attacks on Israel, but the following day its leader, Sheikh Hassan Nasrallah declares to carry on fighting.

17–19
First visit of an Icelandic prime minister to Israel, David Oddsson.

19
Israel Labor party primaries — Yitzḥak Rabin chosen leader.

20
Likkud selects candidate for prime minister — Yitzḥak Shamir.

22
Israel and Uzbekistan establish diplomatic relations.

March

1
Hand grenade thrown at Istanbul's Neve Shalom synagogue — one bystander hurt; one of the two assailants apprehended.

7
Ehud Sadan, 37, Ankara Israel Embassy security chief killed by car bomb.

9
Menahem Begin dies.

A glimpse at part of the masses of mourners at the funeral of Menaḥem Begin in Jerusalem, March 9, 1992. (GPO, Jerusalem)

16
Pres. Bush rejects compromise Senate proposal on the $10 billion loan guarantees for immigrant absorption in Israel. Israel must accept U.S. demands or face presidential veto.

17
Israel embassy in Buenos Aires destroyed by bomb, entire building collapses, 29 dead, some 240 injured.

Arab terrorist kills two in Jaffa, one Jew, one Arab, and injures 16 others, mostly schoolchildren.

18
Knesset approves bill for direct election of the Israel prime minister.

First public appearance by Yizḥak Rabin after Labor Party primaries in which he was elected Labor Party chairman and candidate for prime minister, March 1992. (GPO, Jerusalem)

18–20
First Israel visit by a Bulgarian prime minister; PM Filip Dimitrov spends three days in Israel.

March 30–April 2

Israel president Herzog visits Spain, welcomed by King Juan Carlos.

Parade in Madrid in honor of Israel president Herzog; on viewing stand Aura and Chaim Herzog, King Juan Carlos and Queen Sophia, March 30, 1992. (GPO, Jerusalem)

31
King Juan Carlos of Spain visits a synagogue for the first time in his 20-year reign.

April

11–13
350 Jewish refugees airlifted from Sarajevo to Belgrade.

12
Israel and Kazakhstan establish diplomatic relations.

20
Syria frees two Jewish brothers held as Israel spies.

21
Latvia opens consulate in Tel Aviv, the first Baltic diplomatic office in Israel.

23
Israel and Armenia establish relations.

27
U.S. State Dept. announces Syria lifting travel restrictions on Jews — but not to Israel. Syrian foreign minister states travel does not equal emigration.

April 29–May 1

Russian vice-president Alexander Ruskoi visits Israel.

May

CIS Jews found umbrella body, a council with 13 co-chairmen.

4
Israel and Nigeria renew diplomatic relations after 19 years.

10
8 Syrian Jews arrive in New York; by month's end 120 individuals come from Syria.

25th anniversary of unification of Jerusalem celebrated.

18–19
Greek prime minister Constantine Mitsotakis in Israel.

21
Jerusalem's chief Ashkenazi rabbi, Yitzhak Kolitz, rules Hamburg Jewish graves not to be moved, but mall built over them under Jewish supervision.

24
Helen Rapp, 15, stabbed to death in Bat Yam, Israel, by Arab terrorist from Gaza; anti-Arab riots ensue. Gaza Region ordered sealed for 3 days.

25
President Herzog makes 5-day trip to Poland, visits Warsaw memorials to Jews murdered by Nazis in World War II and tours Auschwitz.

Israel president Herzog (3rd from left) visiting site of Birkenau death camp, May 1992. (GPO, Jerusalem)

26
First visit by prime minister of a CIS republic to Israel, Belarus PM Baclav Kebich arrives for 3-day stay.

27
Rabbi Shimon Biran, 32, murdered by Arab at Kefar Darom.

28
Israel and Sierra Leone renew diplomatic ties.

30
Palestinians swim across from Jordan to Eilat, kill guard at Eilat marine station, one terrorist killed, one wounded.

31
Opening of congress in Istanbul commemorating 500th anniversary of Sephardi Jews in Turkey.

June

1
Official opening of Indian embassy in Tel Aviv.

Israel and Georgia establish diplomatic relations.

12
74 Yugoslavian Jewish youngsters ages 10–17 arrive in Israel after evacuation from Sarajevo.

14
Mikhail Gorbachev visits Israel to receive Harvey Prize of the Technion and other awards.

A gathering at the Western Wall marking the 25th anniversary of the unification of Jerusalem. (GPO, Jerusalem)

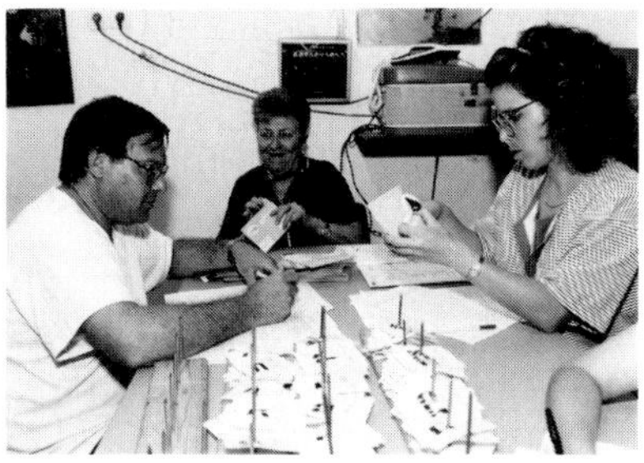
Counting the votes in the elections for the 13th Knesset, June 23, 1992. (GPO, Jerusalem)

18
Palestinian delegates to Mid-East peace conference meet in public with Arafat. Israel decides not to arrest the Palestinians.

23
Israel Labor Party wins elections to 13th Knesset — Labor 44 seats, Likkud 32.

Israel Elections for 13th Knesset — Results

Party	Seats	%
Labor	44	34.6
Likkud	32	24.9
Merez	12	9.6
Zomet	8	6.4
National Religious Party	6	5.0
Shas	6	4.9
Agudat Israel	4	3.3
Moledet	3	2.4
Dem. List for Peace & Equality	3	2.4
Arab Democratic Party	2	1.6

July

40 Jewish gravestones vandalized in Trier, Germany, cemetery.

2
Confirmation that the JDC has closed Ethiopia's Gondar region transit camps since *Aliyah* of Ethiopian Jewry is almost complete.

5
WJC opens "My Brother's Keeper: Antisemitism and Prejudice in a Changing World" in Brussels with 12,000 delegates from 72 countries.

9
Gerer rebbe, 96-year-old Simha Bunim Alter dies in Jerusalem, 70,000 attend funeral.

Israel Labor Party signs coalition agreement with left-wing Merez and Orthodox Shas.

13
Rabin government approved by 13th Knesset, 67–53.

Prime Minister Yizhak Rabin's government. (GPO, Jerusalem)

16
Pres. Herzog, in Turkey to participate in Jewish community's celebration of 500 years since the arrival of Jews in Ottoman Empire after expulsion from Spain, speaks in Istanbul's Neveh Shalom synagogue.

Pres. Mitterrand lays wreath at Drancy collection site where 50 years ago 16,000 Jews were deported to death camps.

17
Israel and Benin renew diplomatic ties broken in 1973.

21
Rabin and Mubarak meet for one-day summit in Cairo — first such meeting in six years.

23
First ordination in Israel of female Reform rabbi, Na'ama Kelman Ha-Ezrahi, 37.

Israel renews ambassadorial-level relations with Austria after six-year break over Waldheim affair.

26
32nd Zionist Congress opens in Jerusalem with some 700 delegates from Israel and 31 Diaspora communities.

August

Jewish Restitution Organization, union of 8 groups, established to seek return of communal property taken by Nazi and communist regimes (Albania, Bulgaria, Czechoslovakia, Hungary, Poland, Romania, and CIS republics)

1–2
First Israeli Olympic medals — both in Judo — silver for Yael Arad, 25, and bronze for Oren Smadga, 22.

8
Israel prime minister Rabin in U.S. During his stay meets with Butros-Ghali (Aug. 9), with Pres. Bush (Aug. 10 and 11). Bush and Rabin close summit at Kennebunkport, Maine, with agreement on $10 billion loan guarantees.

Talks at U.S. presidential summer residence in Kennebunkport, Maine: from right to left — U.S. president George Bush; U.S. sec. of state James Baker; Israel prime minister Yiẓhak Rabin; Israel government sec. Elyakim Rubinstein, Aug. 11, 1992. (GPO, Jerusalem)

12

Sempo Sugihara, only Japanese Righteous Gentile, honored in Japan with memorial park in his name (as Japanese consul in Kaunas, Lithuania, in 1940 he issued some 6,000 visas to Japan to Jews).

13

Bulgarian charge d'affaires in Israel announces that the Bulgarian government is donating $750,000, one-fifth of its cultural heritage budget, to restoring the Great Synagogue of Sofia.

17

Final group of Jewish children evacuated from Sarajevo to Split by the JDC.

20–24

Israel FM Peres on 4–day visit to Russia, meets with FM Andrei Kozarov.

24

Israel cancels expulsion order against 11 Palestinian terrorists issued in January and replaces them with detention for "security reasons."

800 security prisoners released by Israel as conciliatory measure as prelude to next round to peace talks in Washington.

Prime Minister Rabin meets in Cairo with President Hosni Mubarak of Egypt, Aug. 1992. (GPO, Jerusalem)

27

Zimbabwe president, Robert Mugabe, meets with Zimbabwe Jewish Board of Deputies to quiet row over his alleged anti-Semitic remarks, claims he referred to Shamir and his Palestinian policy and not to local Jews.

30

Berlin Holocaust memorial bombed.

Report 1/4 of Syria's Jews have left in the past 4 months, since Hafiz Assad has allowed Syrian Jews to travel; 2,900 remain.

September

Israel and Nicaragua resume diplomatic relations.

4

First 150 immigrants to Israel from Abkhazia arrive on special Jewish Agency flight from Sukhumi (in 1990–92 3,000 Georgian Jews came to Israel).

6

Visit of Kazakhstan prime minister Sergei Tereschenko to Israel results in agreement to set up joint committee of economists, businessmen, and manufacturers.

15

Chinese foreign minister Qian Qichen on official visit to Israel.

Rabin inspects Berlin Jewish Community memorial, Sept. 16, 1992. (GPO, Jerusalem)

20

Hungarian president, Arpad Goencz, visits Israel, first such visit by a president of Hungary.

25

"Jewish hut" at Sachsenhausen concentration camp site burnt.

October

Work begins on restoration of Czech Holocaust Memorial on the wall of the Pinkas Synagogue with the names of 80,000 Czech Jews who perished.

15

Yad Vashem inaugurates Valley of the Destroyed Communties in commemoration of the 5,000 annihilated ones.

27

Katyusha attack on Kiryat Shemona, kills one, 14-year-old Vadim Shuchman.

29

New York courts acquits Lemrick Nelson, 17, of killing visiting Australian yeshivah student Yankel Rosenbaum during 1991 Brooklyn riots. U.S. Dept. of Justice approves federal investigation into the acquittal.

November

7

Under sniper fire, American Joint Distribution Committee sets up communication links to the besieged Sarajevo Jewish community of 500.

Foreign Minister Peres welcomes China's Foreign Minister Qian Qichen, Sept. 17, 1992. (GPO, Jerusalem)

8–9
Polish FM Krysktof Skubiszewski visits Israel.

9
New Czech chief rabbi, Karl Sidon, 50, installed.

Rome march, 30,000 participants, against racism and anti-Semitism; 30 other rallies throughout Italy — activities follow rash of anti-Semitic incidents.

10
Israel Supreme Court building, funded by Rothschild family, officially inaugurated.

12
French Jews demonstrate at Velodrome d'Hiver, where Jews were interned in 1942, against presidential wreath on Petain's grave.

16
Over 50,000 demonstrate in Tel Aviv against relinquishing the Golan Heights.

18
German Foreign Minister Klaus Kinkel in Israel.

25
Francois Mitterrand, president of France, visits Israel; asks Israel to accept Palestinian state.

26
First Israel ambassador to India, Ephraim Dowek, presents credentials.

Israel embassy in South Korea reopens after 15 years.

30
Palestinians refuse Israel offer to administer 92% of the land, in whole or part, of Gaza and Judea and Samaria — want 100%.

December

Report Syria apparently halts travel of Syrian Jews; 1,200 Jews prevented from leaving.

2
Bill allowing Israeli contacts with PLO members passes first reading, 37–36.

Foreign Minister Peres in Austria — first official visit by and Israeli FM since 1973.

Pres. Herzog receives President Mitterrand of France at President's Residence, Jerusalem, Nov. 25, 1992. (GPO, Jerusalem)

3
Japan's foreign minister tells leading Japanese companies to desist from complying with Arab boycott of Israel.

7
3 IDF soldiers shot to death by Palestinian terrorists as they ride on main road near Beit Laḥiya.

13
Israel border policeman Nissim Toledano kidnapped by Hamas in Lod; Hamas want Sheikh Ahmad Yassin of Gaza, group's founder, released. Toledano's body is found on Dec. 15.

14
Israel FM Peres in Tokyo, calls for Japanese to help end Arab boycott of Israel.

17
Israel deports temporarily 415 Hamas and Islamic Jihad activists to Lebanon in response to Toledano killing. Israel High Court of Justice rules move is legal and rejects appeals. The U.S. protests the action.

18–19
8 Palestinians killed during violent disruptions in the Gaza Region and Judea and Samaria.

24
Israel pres. Herzog sets out on six-day visit to China, the first by an Israel president.

29–30
UN Envoy James Jonah shuttles between Israel trying to get Lebanon to accept deportees or to have Israel rescind the deportation — no success.

Israel Foreign Minister Peres signing the Declaration of Principles with the PLO with White House aide indicating where to sign. Standing behind them are (left to right) Russian Foreign Minister Kozyrev, Israel Prime Minister Yiẓhak Rabin, U.S. President Clinton, PLO chairman Arafat, U.S. Sec. of State Christopher, and PLO representative Mahmoud Abbas. (GPO, Jerusalem)

ISRAEL-PLO: MUTUAL RECOGNITION

A dramatic and unexpected development in the Middle East occurred in early September 1993 with the announcement that Israel and the Palestine Liberation Organization (the PLO) had been conducting secret negotiations and had reached the stage where they were prepared to recognize the legitimacy of the other and that Israel was willing to grant autonomy to the Gaza Strip and the town of Jericho. Previously each side had demonized the other. The PLO in its basic statement of principles, the "Covenant," had committed itself to the elimination of the State of Israel. Israel for its part had regarded the PLO as a constant threat and one of its deadliest enemies, responsible for a long string of terrorist attacks which had resulted in many deaths and casualties not only among Israelis but among Jewish targets throughout the world.

It was revealed that the negotiations had been going on for almost a year in Norway under the discreet auspices of the Norwegian foreign minister, Johan Jorgen Holst. They had begun, therefore, not long after Yiẓhak Rabin's government had come to power. A key figure in their conduct had been the Israeli foreign minister, Shimon Peres, for long a rival of Rabin but now the two men worked closely hand-in-hand.

Both sides had strong motivations for this development. PLO Chairman Yasser Arafat had made a fateful miscalculation during the Gulf War of 1990–1991 when he supported Saddam Hussein, as did many Palestinians. As a result his main backers, Saudi Arabia and the Gulf States, ceased their financial aid and he found himself in desperate financial straits — with insufficient money to support his military groups and to maintain his activities in the Administered Territories (into which he sent $350 million in 1988 but only $40 million in 1992). The break-up of the U.S.S.R., one of his important supporters, was also a blow. He had also made enemies within his Organization by his authoritarian style and his personal decision-making. Another challenge came with the emergence of an indigenous Palestinian leadership when Israel agreed to negotiate with Palestinians in the framework of the Peace Process but excluded members of the PLO. The Palestinian delegation, although nominally accepting Arafat's guidance, felt that they were closer to the grass-roots than he and resented some of his decisions.

In addition to all these factors, the PLO and Israel found they had a serious common enemy in the militant Islamic fundamentalist movement — Hamas in Palestine and its parallel body, Hizballah, in Lebanon. Both were financed and supported by Iran, and the PLO, a secular organization, was alarmed at the inroads being made by Hamas among the Palestinians. Israel, which initially had encouraged Hamas in order to counter the PLO, had come to realize that it had now become the more dangerous and extremist threat which could best be countered in cooperation with the PLO.

Israel for its part had long wondered how it could get rid of the Gaza Strip. This densely populated area with a population of over three-quarters of a million Arabs, most of them refugees, was a hotbed of hate, terror, intrigue and poverty. Even the Egyptians, when it was under their control from 1948 to 1967, had held it at arm's length. The Israeli army was unhappy with the responsibility for maintaining law and order in this hostile region, and Israelis were frequently being killed or wounded either inside the Strip or by its inhabitants working in Israel. Already during the Shamir government, members of the Likkud party were asking how to get rid of the Gaza Strip. It also emerged that in the late 1980s, Israel military intelligence had stated that the key to the future peace of the region was through dialogue with the PLO but this had been turned down by Yiẓhak Shamir.

Rabin and Peres originally proposed to the PLO that Israel would withdraw only from the Gaza Strip, but Arafat claimed that this would appear he was abandoning the West Bank Palestinians. He suggested adding the town of Jericho as a gesture towards them, and this was accepted by Israel.

On September 10, after Arafat had sent him a letter expressing his recognition of the State of Israel and its right to exist, Yiẓhak Rabin signed in Jerusalem a Declaration of Principles, consisting of 17 articles and four annexes. This provided for Israeli withdrawal from the Gaza Strip and Jericho which within four months would be handed over to Palestinian administration, with Israel retaining responsibility only for external security and for the protection of Jewish settlers within these areas. At the same time the rest of the West Bank would move towards self-rule in matters of education, health, social services, tourism, and taxation. Eventually a Palestinian Interim Self-Government Authority would be elected to govern all the Administered Territories. The possibility of a future Palestine State or any change in the status of Jerusalem was barred for discussion by the Israelis.

Three days later, on September 13, a ceremony was held on the lawn of the White House before several hundred guests and extensive media coverage. President Clinton stood between Rabin and Arafat as they signed the document and then encouraged them to shake hands. Both men faced intense opposition among their constituents. Members of Israeli opposition groups demonstrated massively and lengthily but the Agreement was ratified by the Knesset by a vote of 61 votes to 50. In the Arab world, Arafat faced the opposition of some of his colleagues, of the extremist bodies within the PLO, and of the Arab rejectionist states. However, he obtained a large majority when the matter was brought for confirmation to the Palestine National Council.

A few weeks after the signing, Rabin initiated a further meeting with Arafat, this time in Cairo. Arrangements were agreed for the implementation of the Agreement through the establishment of a series of groups discussing the various aspects. These began to meet in mid-October. However, the first stage of the Agreement proved impossible to implement within the projected timetable and protracted negotiations were held to seek solutions to the points of disagreement.

Feature Articles

1982–1992: Into a New Age of Uncertainty

William Frankel

On September 12, 1990, World War II officially came to a close when the four wartime allies, Britain, France, the Soviet Union, and the United States, signed a treaty handing back full sovereignty to a Germany on the verge of reunification. Among the many momentous events of the last ten years, this essentially symbolic occasion attracted little publicity. For many Jews who survived the Holocaust, World War II will never end: it lives on as a constant, harrowing memory. For others born after 1945, who have no personal memory of the war, the defeat of Hitler and the Nazi German surrender were as official an end to World War II as they ever needed. The treaty signed in 1990 may have been necessary as an act of bureaucratic or historical housekeeping, but among Jews from Seattle to Singapore, from Moscow to Melbourne, it had and has no resonance.

And yet, if it was necessary to choose an event which encapsulates a deep and significant truth about the last ten years, the official ending of the war serves very well. For most Jews, the pattern of international relations established as the war ended and the establishment of the state of Israel in 1948, have shaped Jewish existence during the last 47 years. When communism collapsed in 1989, allowing the reunification of Germany — and the event of September 12, 1990 — it irrevocably altered the world order. It then became fashionable to discuss a theory propounded by an American academic and former State Department official, Francis Fukuyama, that communism's collapse marked the end of history. This was proved completely wide of the mark — the demise of communist Eastern Europe meant a *return* to history for the world in general. While it would not be accurate to talk of a return to history for Jews — in many ways, the establishment of Israel signified that, or at least the emergence from powerlessness — the revolutions of 1989 brought about a radical shift in historical emphasis and direction, such that, in ways which are still not very widely understood, Jewish life was fundamentally transformed.

In 1982, the continuation of the bi-polar world, and everything that flowed from that, was largely taken for granted. There was a sense of permanence and stability — unwarranted in many respects, but people were resigned to operate within the status quo. By 1992, the certainties that had come to characterize the years to 1989 had almost all disappeared. What were those certainties for Jews and with what have they been replaced?

Nineteen-eighty-two was the year of Lebanon. Israel invaded the south of the country ostensibly to drive out the Palestine Liberation Organization (PLO) which had established a state within a state there, but in fact to implement the grand design of the then Defense Minister Ariel Sharon. The objectives were in the words of Abba Eban, "the destruction of the PLO as a military and political force; the establishment of a stable, sovereign government in Lebanon; the election of a Lebanese president who would sign a peace treaty with Israel; the creation of a 'belt of peace and free movement' in the Egypt-Lebanon-Israel 'triangle'; and the creation of an opportunity for the Palestinians in the West Bank and Gaza, liberated from PLO intimidation, to come forward and negotiate with Israel on the basis of Menachem Begin's interpretation of the Camp David agreements." Underlying this design was a desire to demonstrate that Israel, under Likkud leadership, was not bound by the fundamental constraints arising out of the political positions adopted by the Arab world (excluding Egypt) and the Soviet bloc. Israel acted as if she could impose a solution, no matter what others believed to be the fundamentals of world political realities.

The failure of Sharon's grand design proved just how far Arab and Soviet opposition to Israel and Zionism determined Israel's position in the world and the degree to which Israel's foreign policy was circumscribed by factors about which the country's leaders could do very little. The Arab and Soviet campaigns against Israel — indeed, the anti-democratic world's hostility to Jewish aspirations — had far-reaching implications for the Jewish people as a whole. It ensured that

Jewish energies on the external front were constantly directed towards combating the effects of hostility, with all that implies for the internal matters which were then perforce neglected or starved of attention. Not that there was anything insignificant about the dimensions of such hostility. In the early 1980s, Arab terrorism directed at Diaspora Jewish targets was at its height. The anti-Zionist campaign, waged at the United Nations and in the UN's specialized agencies, in international Third World forums, on university and college campuses, and in the media, produced an outpouring of propaganda funded and directed by Arab, Soviet, and far left sources. Much of that anti-Zionism comprised either thinly disguised anti-Semitism or was indistinguishable from anti-Semitism as far as its effects were concerned. For Jews outside Arab or Soviet bloc countries, the campaign against Israel did not become an excuse for discrimination and persecution. But communism's hostility to the assertion of Jewish identity, except in forms strictly controlled by the communist authorities, meant that a quarter to one-fifth of the Jewish people were denied the opportunity to be Jews in any meaningful sense.

Arab opposition to Israel and communist hostility to the expression of Jewish identity constituted the two fundamental negatives of Jewish life, the two most serious external challenges to Jewish self-expression, to the way Jews defined themselves in the modern world. There were always those who took a more optimistic view of the possibility of progress in the Middle East conflict — had not Egypt taken, and persevered with, the peaceful path? Others believed that change would come to the Soviet bloc — after all, large numbers of Jews had emigrated during the 1970s. But for most people the intractable nature of the two problems were part of the sine qua non of Jewish existence.

To define oneself continually in purely negative terms can have very serious consequences, and there is ample evidence to suggest that Israel's continual need to confront the enemy (even though deliberate demonization of that enemy was in many respects weaker than in many other conflicts between peoples) had disturbing consequences for the development of Israeli society during the period under review. Nevertheless, both campaigns — defending and expressing solidarity with Israel and working for Soviet Jewry — also produced a flowering of Jewish activity, ingenuity, and inventiveness. Activity directed towards supporting Israel — from UJA fundraisers in Tucson, Arizona, to political lobbying in Brussels, from sponsoring Israeli arts in London, to promoting Israeli bonds in Guatemala — and the place this occupied in Jewish life constituted a form of cultural activity that was important in its own right as a means of expressing Jewishness.

The 1982 Lebanon war was like no previous war fought by the state of Israel. Israel's image in the world was severely damaged when reports of tens of thousands killed and 600,000 made homeless gained wide currency, only to suffer even further following the massacre of Palestinians by Phalangists in the Sabra and Shatilla refugee camps. Israel's enemies, and anti-Semites everywhere, were able to make effective use of these events, irrespective of the accuracy of the reporting. It was a war which again demonstrated that, for good or ill, and whether wished for or not, the fate of Diaspora Jews was linked to the decisions of Israel's leaders.

Whatever the rights and wrongs of the decision to invade Lebanon, 1982 marked a low point in Israel's international position. Far from exerting control over events, Israel seemed only to have compounded its existing difficulties. Israeli society became increasingly polarized and Lebanon rapidly became a quagmire from which escape became ever more urgent.

The years which followed the Lebanon War indicated how Israel could become the beneficiary

(Left) Official visitors from Eastern Europe have become a common sight in Israel: Czech president Vaclav Havel (second from right) with Pres. Herzog (far right) at a ceremony at the close of his visit, April 1990 (GPO, Jerusalem); (right) Upon renewal of Cameroon-Israel relations Prime Minister Peres visited Cameroon and met with President Paul Biya in the Presidential Palace, Yaounde, August 1986 (GPO, Jerusalem).

of changing regional and world realities, irrespective of its government's hard-line position on the Administered Territories. First, Third-Worldist revolutionary rhetoric and ideology were rapidly becoming bankrupt. An increasing number of states which had broken off diplomatic relations with Israel came to realize that diplomatic ties with the Jewish state made sense in terms of a pragmatic realignment towards the West. Even before the advent of Mikhail Gorbachev, anti-Zionism had begun to lose its potency as a means of mobilization. The Arab oil money which many states believed would be the quid pro quo for anti-Israel and pro-Palestinian positions was never forthcoming to the degree expected. Secondly, the weakening of communism from the mid-1980s permitted more channels to be opened up to Eastern bloc countries. Thirdly, the European Community, whose 1981 Venice Declaration signaled a distinctly pro-Palestinian position, was unable to develop a concerted foreign policy and therefore pressure from what might have been a very influential source never fully materialized.

What had been incremental changes in the mid-1980s became fast and furious after the collapse of Communism in 1989. Over the next few years, the states of Eastern Europe and the former Soviet Union opened ties with Israel, the notorious UN General Assembly resolution equating Zionism with racism was rescinded, the colossal outpouring of anti-Zionist propaganda from communist sources ceased, and those Arab states, like Syria, which relied heavily on the communist bloc for financial and ideological support, were forced to rethink their stance vis-à-vis the U.S.A. and the Middle East conflict. As a result, Israel's position was transformed. The goal of much of Israel's foreign policy activity had been achieved, even if success came in spite of rather than because of the totality of Israel's international diplomacy. There was always a strand of Israel's foreign policy activity which worked assiduously and behind the scenes to improve relations with countries that publicly would have nothing to do with the Jewish state. But external factors created the environment for the radical changes that occurred.

Israel's international position during the years of Israel's most hard line government and prime minister had vastly improved. But there was a price to be paid. The cold war rules that had governed international affairs ceased to apply. Those rules put Israel at a great disadvantage regionally and globally but this situation was mitigated by the relationship with the U.S. Much of the world was hostile, but Israel had learnt to maneuver within that climate, navigating by certain fixed points which seemed immutable. With the end of the cold war, those fixed points melted away; certainty gave way to extreme uncertainty. Israel ceased to be of such great strategic importance to the U.S., especially following the 1991 Gulf War. Israel could not avoid participating in peace talks brokered by the Americans. Suddenly, Iran and the Central Asian republics with their predominantly Muslim populations, posed new questions and potential problems, and so too did Islamic fundamentalism.

The phrase which soon came to be attached to the post-cold war world was "the new world order" — at least that was how President George Bush wanted to see it, as if it was merely a matter of working out reasonable arrangements for maintaining stability among the emerging democracies in Eastern Europe, the Commonwealth of Independent States, Africa, and Latin America. But it rapidly became clear that the end of the bi-polar world had given way to a new world *disorder* which, for Israel, promised at least as many dangers as it did benefits.

By the end of 1992, there was little sign that the implications of the new uncertainties had been grasped either in Israel or in the Diaspora. Invalid though they now were, most of the old assumptions about Israel's position in the world still prevailed.

In 1982, Jewish emigration from the U.S.S.R. was practically at a standstill. Repression of the Jewish movement continued, and there seemed little likelihood of any change in the attitude of the Brezhnev regime. There was no let-up in activity, throughout the Jewish world on behalf of

(Left) Israel army camp with welcome greeting for Soviet immigrants to be housed there temporarily. September 1990 (GPO, Jerusalem); (right) Soviet Jewish immigrants arriving in Israel, on a direct flight from Moscow (GPO, Jerusalem)

Soviet Jewry despite the sense of despair as to the prospects of the gates opening once more. The heady days of mass emigration of the 1970s seemed destined never to return, although those who engaged in activity for Soviet Jewry did not give up hope.

As with the many forms of support for Israel, work on behalf of Soviet Jewry increasingly became an act of Jewish self-expression — something that may sometimes have been more beneficial to those who were involved than for those who were the object of the activity.

This was not a monolithic movement. Strategies for persuading the communists to let Jews leave were fiercely contested. Growing attempts to seek direct and secret discussions with the Soviet leadership were seen by many as futile at best and as supping with the devil at worst. Those who advocated working for cultural rights for Jews in the U.S.S.R. were often regarded as naive, and even as detracting from the principal aim of securing freedom to emigrate. However, nothing could detract from the fact that the movement for Soviet Jewry spanned the spectrum of Jewish life and was a genuinely common endeavor between Israel and the Diaspora.

When Mikhail Gorbachev became general secretary of the Communist Party of the Soviet Union, few had any idea what his appointment would come to mean for the Jews of the U.S.S.R., or, for that matter, for the entire U.S.S.R. population. With the first glimmerings of *glasnost* and *perestroika*, stories of the imminent commencement of mass exodus began to circulate. In retrospect, the changes that then took place were extraordinarily rapid, in view of the perceived rigidity of the Soviet system. But at the time, when months passed with practically no change in the very small numbers leaving, it all seemed wishful thinking. Eventually, with the release of Anatoly (as he was then) Shcharansky and the other Prisoners of Zion, and then with the increasingly apparent liberalization, emigration in large numbers no longer seemed a distant dream. During 1987–89, 100,000 Jews left the U.S.S.R. In 1990, over 200,000 emigrated. Between 1987 and the end of 1992, something close to 500,000 Jews emigrated from the U.S.S.R. (or former U.S. S.R.), and most of those had gone to Israel.

This huge migration was an event of major Jewish historical significance, altering the path of Jewish history definitively. It changed the face of Russian Jewry, of course, and despite the fact that the vast majority of emigrating Jews went to Israel, it has deeply affected Diaspora communities, including Germany, where up to 9,000 Jews had settled by the end of 1992. More important perhaps was the impact on Israel. Not only did former-U.S.S.R. Jews help to put Yitzḥak Rabin into power, thereby turning direct talks with the Arab states and the Palestinians into a process that could deliver peace, they also changed the entire character of Israeli society.

It may seem curious, but when it arrived, the Jewish world was unprepared for the mass emigration and its implications. Israel was slow to respond to the challenge and only belatedly began to take the kind of drastic action on housing and absorption which the situation demanded. The world economic recession did not make things any easier; neither did President George Bush's decision to withhold loan guarantees unless Israel agreed to freeze settlement activity in the Administered Territories. In the end, the practicalities of absorbing such immense numbers — immense both proportionately and absolutely — were taken in hand, if not as systematically as they should have been.

In 1982, the official suppression of Jewish religious life and culture in the Soviet Union was as strong as ever. With the coming of *perestroika* this suppression was relaxed and by 1989 the revival of Jewish life in the U.S.S.R. was in full, if somewhat haphazard, swing. When Jews began emigrating in large numbers, the scale and permanence of the Jewish revival was put in doubt. The exodus of hundreds of thousands could not but mean that in some places in the Soviet Union, Jewish life would come to a complete end. Some even predicted that the process of emigration would continue at such a rate that Jewish life as a whole was on a downward spiral. Israeli Sovietologist Theodore Friedgut wrote at the time: "The interlude of renaissance of Jewish communal activity was in fact the opening of the last act of modern Jewish life in Russia and the Soviet Union."

Such a scenario seemed eminently plausible when the emigration figures were set against a Jewish population of 1.7 million according to the last Soviet census in 1989. What no one seemed to anticipate was the possibility that large numbers of Jews who had hidden their Jewish origins from the census officials — to avoid the many problems Jews faced in Soviet Russia — would declare themselves when the opportunity to emigrate from the U.S.S.R. arose. As tens of thousands applied for emigration visas it soon became clear that there were many more Jews in the U.S.S.R. than the 1.7 million counted in the census. For the purposes of emigrating to Israel — since the Law of Return would allow a Jew to bring to Israel all of his immediate family even if he or she had married a non-Jew — the U.S.S.R. had a potential Jewish population in excess of three million (some estimates even put it as high as 12 million). As these realities began to impinge on the Jewish consciousness, the future for Jews in the former U.S.S.R. no longer looked so clear cut.

Many expected that emigration would continue at the high levels of 1991, especially in view of the virtual explosion of anti-Semitic propaganda since the liberalization of the press and politics and the increasingly difficult economic situation. But numbers fell sharply in 1992, partly because of the absorption problems in Israel and partly because anti-Semitism remained a potential rather than an actual threat. By the end of 1992, the notion that Jewish life in the U.S.S.R. would rapidly disappear seemed completely wide of the mark. Simplistic futurology seemed again to have taken hold — projections of decline took little account of the unpredictable.

Under the Soviets, one could be fairly certain of what was happening to Jews, despite the closed nature of Soviet society. The struggle for Soviet Jewry had a Manichean quality — the forces of good lined up against the forces of evil. Because Jewish life in the U.S.S.R was suppressed, it did not appear to suffer from the confusion, duplication of effort, pettiness and division of life in Jewish communities in the free world. Under post-communism, everything has been turned upside-down. Despite the now open access to almost all centers of Jewish life in the former U.S.S.R., the future is impossible to predict. The revival of Jewish communal activity has brought out into the open the same negative and contentious features of Jewish existence found elsewhere in the world.

Jewish communities west of Russia — in Poland, Romania, Bulgaria, Czechoslovakia, Hungary, Yugoslavia, and East Germany — were never quite so uniformly cut off from outside Jewish influences as were the Jews of the Soviet Union. Yet, in 1982, all were considered backwaters where Jewish life was in terminal decline. The very survival of any form of organized Jewish existence involved compromise with the regimes. Those willing to do this were mostly elderly. Since being Jewish was invariably a disadvantage in Communist Eastern Europe, younger Jews had little incentive to identify with the organized Jewish communities.

Liberalization in Eastern Europe proceeded at different speeds in different countries. In Yugoslavia, Hungary, and Poland, significant changes had taken place well before 1989, predating the coming to power of Mikhail Gorbachev. But the political revolutions in Romania, Bulgaria, Czechoslovakia, and East Germany were the direct result of Gorbachev's policies. For Jews, the collapse of communism led to a revival of Jewish communal activity, but given the small size of many of the communities, that revival was always likely to be limited. Nevertheless, any revival — given the dire predictions of the future of these communities — was remarkable.

Some Jews left for Israel or other destinations, but there was no wholesale exodus. On the contrary, Jews in these countries demonstrated a strong desire to remain where they were. Even in former Yugoslavia, during Sarajevo's worst period when Jewish relief efforts had succeeded in evacuating a sizeable part of the 500-strong Jewish community there, many Sarajevo Jews insisted that they did not want to leave and maintained that many who had gone would want to return as soon as circumstances allowed.

"Traditional Alternatives" conference at Jews' College, London, in May 1989 with 1,000 participants, discussed issues ranging from the rift between Orthodox and non-Orthodox Jews to women and Judaism and the future of Modern Orthodoxy. (Courtesy Jews' College Publications; photo Robert Aberman, London)

Fortunately, not all of Eastern Europe had degenerated into the blood bath that was former Yugoslavia, but elsewhere Jews had another problem with which to contend: anti-Semitism. Under the communist authorities, the free expression of anti-Semitism was either suppressed or carefully controlled and when it did manifest itself it was often in the form of anti-Zionism. Very little had been done to confront either the reality of anti-Semitism or the truth about Jewish life in the countries of Eastern Europe. The collapse of communism brought with it a wholesale revival of pre-Communist and pre-war political ideologies, with anti-Semitism playing a central part in many of them.

This anti-Semitism presented more of a danger than elsewhere — to Jews and to the societies themselves — precisely because of the extreme political, social, and economic instability that the collapse of communism had engendered. Politicians, many from mainstream parties which had developed ties with Western European conservative and Christian Democratic parties, proved themselves unscrupulous in their use of anti-Semitism to curry favor with their electorates. So Europe witnessed the entry of anti-Semitism into mainstream political processes, which purported to be democratic, for the first time since the end of World War II.

During the decade 1982–92, the Jewish communities of Eastern Europe moved from shriveling periphery to objects of great concern and attention on the part of Jews from the West; they were now able to take their places as authentic and free Jewish communities within the constellation of European Jewry. However, this posed a dilemma which, by the end of 1992, had not been resolved — again, a dilemma arising out of the shift from unwanted but convenient certainty, to a troubling and confusing uncertainty. These communities needed outside support but what kind of future should that support be directed towards creating? Many argued that *aliyah*, emigration to Israel, was the only answer; the communities had become too small and had been starved of Jewish educational, cultural, and religious input for too long. Others dreamed of and took active steps to work for Jewish revival. There was no mechanism for resolving the competing visions of post-communist Eastern Europe — not in itself a disaster. But since the barriers in Europe were coming down, a concerted policy for the development of Jewish life in Europe seemed a practical necessity.

The policy vacuum in Europe was made even more acute as a result of the reunification of Germany. Jewish attitudes to reunification demonstrated how unprepared Jews were for the changes Europe as a whole was undergoing. Jewish concern about the development of German society is a natural product of the Holocaust and there were good reasons during the decade under review why that concern should remain strong. The Hitler Diaries affair in 1983 showed just how far Germans were still in thrall to the fascination exerted by Nazism and to the need to find some way of proving that what had happened was somehow not quite as terrible as everyone believed. Apart from an exercise in sheer financial exploitation, the affair was also an exercise in humanizing Hitler: if Hitler wrote diaries and seemed somehow to be detached from the worst excesses of the Nazi regime, there was no doubt some solace to be found in that. The need for Germans to put the past behind them was particularly apparent when President Reagan visited a war cemetery at Bitburg where SS soldiers were buried. Chancellor Helmut Kohl had clearly signaled that a line had to be drawn under the past and that visiting Bitburg would be an act of reconciliation indicating that all were in some sense victims. Such incidents, coupled with signs that the far right in Germany were still able to win electoral support for their views, provided ample cause for Jews to remain cautious about modern Germany.

With the destruction of the Berlin Wall and Chancellor Kohl's rapid drive to reunification, old fears surfaced: fears about the revival of German nationalism, German domination of Europe, and the dredging up of German claims on such areas as the Sudetenland and parts of Poland. Many Jews opposed the reunification process and issued dire warnings about its consequences. When widespread neo-Nazi and skinhead violence against asylum-seekers and refugees erupted, and far right parties began to make significant gains in state (Land) elections, the worst Jewish fears seemed on the point of realization. There was talk in Israel, America, and elsewhere of a boycott of Germany unless the German government took decisive action to bring the violence to an end. Throughout the Jewish world, attention turned to Germany and Jews united in protest.

As 1992 drew to a close, the specifically Jewish outcry over Germany, which was clearly an expression of concern that Jews were the underlying targets of what was happening, had taken on the character of a moral panic. It was as if the enormous changes in Germany that had taken place since the war had been ignored, as if there existed no desire in Germany to maintain the stable democratic system that had been painstakingly established, as if the mass of the German population were ready, at the drop of a swastika, to abandon prosperity, price stability, and stable government for fascism.

The Jewish dimensions of the crisis in Germany had been grossly exaggerated. The problems of racism and neo-Nazi violence were acute but to turn them into a problem which principally affected Jews was symptomatic of deeper processes in Jewry during the period.

Once again, it seemed that it was easier to revert to outdated certainties about perceived external enemies than to confront the real dimensions of change and uncertainty. It was not German Jews who raised the moral panic: they were in the forefront of criticism of their government for not doing enough, but all along had a more realistic view of the seriousness of the problem than Jews elsewhere. Jewish reality in Germany had to take account of a significant number of former Soviet Jews who had gone to live in Germany (up to 9,000 by the end of 1992), and many more who apparently wished to do so.

There is a sense in which the organized Jewish world as a whole manifested a tendency during these years to act like a vaguely authoritarian nation state which, when confronted with insurmountable internal conflicts, chooses to export the internal crisis and to project that crisis onto external enemies. For Jews, these enemies were Arabs, Germans, the United Nations, anti-Semitism, Muslim fundamentalists, the Communist bloc, the third world and more. Not that Jews had no enemies during the last ten years, far from it. But by 1992, it often seemed that despite the very substantial diminution of general hostility to Jews and Israel, there was some innate need to make hostility to the Jewish people the main focus of Jewish life.

The Jewish communities of the free world — in Western Europe, North and South America, South Africa, and Australia — are all substantially different from each other, and their development during the last ten years is intimately related to local conditions. To generalize about them is therefore to risk ignoring each community's unique achievements and problems. But there are certain common themes and trends, the occurrence of which illuminates the central theme of this survey. For the nature of the principal internal developments during this period shows why focusing on the external enemy has loomed so large.

Across the Jewish world, increasing assimilation and apprehension about Jewish continuity proved the most perplexing of internal issues. Given the dispersed nature of Jewish communities, it was impossible to establish precisely the dimensions of assimilation, but the increased sophistication in Jewish demographic studies left no one in any doubt that some communities were shrinking at an alarming rate, mostly as a result of out-marriage. Discussion of this problem, even in the largest, most self-confident community — the United States — increasingly took on an apocalyptic character. With the rate of assimilation so high in the U.S. (a 1992 survey estimated the rate of intermarriage to be 57%), it was asked, how long would it be before terminal decline set in? The question of assimilation and what to do about it dominated the debate about Jewish education, religious observance, the relationship between Israel and the Diaspora. There was a widespread obsession with decline and survival.

Not everyone shared this obsession, however. During this period, Jewish Orthodoxy underwent a remarkable revival, the origins of which predated 1982. Orthodox groups claimed that not only were they increasing in number, they were also, and more importantly, the source of a strengthen-

Over the past decade large-scale Jewish efforts were devoted to gaining Freedom for Soviet Jews; above: Freedom Sunday for Soviet Jews, Washington, D.C., Dec. 12, 1987. (Photo Twins Lens Photo 1987)

(Left) One of the four Jewish men in Tokaj, Hungary, Lajos Lowy, who tries to preserve and document local Jewish history, opens prayer house door for Hungarian art historian putting together an exhibit on Jews (photo Ruth E. Gruber, Rome); (right) U.S. Jews have the opportunity to enjoy sophisticated Torah learning — above, a Stern College student delves into Talmud. (Photo courtesy Yeshiva University, N.Y.)

ing of religious observance. The Jewish people as a whole may be shrinking, it was argued, but that was of little consequence set against the growing strength of the core. The self-confidence of Orthodoxy stood in marked contrast to the increasing sense of uncertainty about the Jewish future felt by practically everyone else. The power of the religious parties in Israel increased, making secular Israelis wonder just how far towards a theocratic state Israel might go under such influence. What perhaps most epitomized the power of Orthodoxy was the remarkable influence exerted by the Lubavicher Rebbe, Menahem Mendel Schneerson, hailed by many of his followers as the messiah. Not only did the Rebbe exert influence over the Israeli political scene, it also became common for secular Jewish leaders to seek audiences with the Rebbe. In practical terms the growing self-confidence of Orthodoxy meant increasing demands for the tightening up of adherence to the strict letter of Jewish law, the alteration of Israel's Law of Return to accomodate a stricter definition of who is a Jew, and the continued denial of halakhic legitimacy to Progressive Judaism. Rabbinic law courts vied with each other in their adherence to ever stricter definitions of what was and what was not permissible.

The growing fundamentalism among the Orthodox mirrored the growth of fundamentalism in society at large, even to the extent of giving birth to a Jewish extremist movement linked to the ideology of a Greater Israel. Whatever the long-term prospects for the fundamentalist approach to Judaism, one of the most significant facets of its progress during the period was its ability to turn the paraphernalia of modernity to its own advantage. The image of the religious Jew with side curls and a mobile phone running extensive business interests became commonplace.

It is in the nature of fundamentalism and Orthodoxy to take the long view and to avoid seeking innovative solutions to the problems of the moment. But for other Jews who saw the flight from Jewishness as a catastrophe that demanded an immediate remedy, the search for new methods of ensuring Jewish continuity went on. There is no doubt that during the last ten years enormous strides have been taken in pioneering new forms of Jewish education, experimenting with alternative frameworks for preserving Jewish identity, encouraging Jews to return to their roots through adult education, the study of Yiddish, genealogy, and many other creative ways of being Jewish which by-passed organized religious Judaism. In some communities, this revival of Jewish culture constituted a positive ferment of activity.

Progressive Judaism, however, seemed to benefit little from this quest, even though Progressive Jews were at the forefront of the struggle to come to terms with the problems of assimilation. The number of adherents to organized Progressive Judaism did not increase significantly during the decade 1982–92. The pluralism they preached did not seem in accord with the tenor of the times, however eminently reasonable the concept. True, there were some in the Orthodox community who also spoke of pluralism, but this was pluralism on their terms, not a pluralism of equals. The fact is that, as the world moved towards the end of the second millennium, the irrational and the intuitive gained ground over the rational and the reasonable, and this did not augur well for Progressive Judaism.

The failure of the religious strands in Judaism to reach any agreement on questions relating to marriage, divorce, conversion, and Jewish identity in general led to increasing religious polarization both in Israel and among Diaspora communities.

Since the establishment of the State of Israel, Zionism has been a permanent contender for the role of prime promoter of Jewish unity and Jewish continuity. Despite the accomplishment of the principal task of Zionism, the Zionist movement, as an organizational and ideological entity, remained active, and indeed, with Soviet Jewry a reservoir of potential *aliyah* before the collapse of communism and a source of actual mass *aliyah* after 1989, Zionism appeared to have a genuine role to play in the 1980s. But the image of a humanitarian Zionism which prevailed during the first few decades of the state had given way to the more severe, hard-line Zionism of the Likkud and of Gush Emunim — those who wanted Jewish sovereignty over the entire biblical land of Israel. This development showed just how clearly the Zionist movement had become an arm of the state of Israel, existing by courtesy of the Israel-dominated Jewish Agency. In these circumstances it was extremely difficult for Zionism to appear as an authentic solution to the problems of Jewish identity in modern society, except where political and social pressures on Jews, *as Jews*, were acute, as in the U.S.S.R. and the former U.S.S.R. and in some Latin American countries. In the latter part of the period, the World Zionist Organization promoted the large immigrations from the former U.S.S.R. and Ethiopia, but this was essentially an organizational effort. The motives for emigrating to Israel on the part of the vast majority of former Soviet Jews had little to do with Zionism, and the fact that, after some hesitation, the process of absorbing these people seemed to be proceeding with a certain degree of success, further demonstrated the marginal importance of Zionism as a living ideology.

Part of the appeal of right-wing Zionism was its insistence on using the Holocaust as justification for its political actions. Despite the often expressed fear that the Holocaust was being forgotten and that anti-Semitism was being expressed more openly because the Holocaust was ceasing to be a current memory — both of which notions were exploited by right-wing Zionists and others — there was ample evidence to suggest that public awareness of the Holocaust reached new heights during this period. There was a massive growth in serious scholarship on the Holocaust; World War II came increasingly to be seen as a war whose aim was to destroy Nazi Germany principally because of anti-Semitism and the Holocaust; and Holocaust representations in popular culture became ubiquitous, although some were in questionable taste. Holocaust studies became a growth industry in the U.S.; many hundreds of Holocaust memorials, in all shapes and sizes, were erected; and as 1992 came to a close, the multi-million dollar National Holocaust Memorial Museum was about to open in Washington, D.C.

This explosion of interest in the Holocaust was more than just a matter of memorialization, of ensuring that the historical truth be preserved and continually retold. In the struggle for the preservation of Jewish identity, the Holocaust emerged as a factor of crucial importance — indeed, for increasing numbers of Jews it became the central determinant of their Jewish identity and the touchstone by which gentile attitudes to Jews were measured.

A sense of history is integral to Jewish identity, but however the significance of the Holocaust is measured, it is only a part of Jewish history, and inevitably a part that shows the Jew mostly as victim. That the Holocaust became so significant during this time had a great deal to do with the uncertainties afflicting Jewish life enumerated above. The Holocaust is a Jewish historical event about which there can be no doubt; it is a fixed reference point. For all that it is a tragedy of incalculable proportions, it serves as a haven for Jews — other than Orthodox Jews — seeking a reason to be Jewish in a world where other positive reasons were increasingly questioned.

Not that there was any lack of Jewish cultural, intellectual, scientific, philanthropic, and material achievement during these years, both in Israel and the Diaspora. But the temper of the age had taken its toll on Jews also. The economic miracles of the early 1980s had turned distinctly sour by 1992. The recession that still had most of the world in its grip in 1992 had affected the Jewish middle classes more than any other recession since the Second World War. Prominent Jewish businessmen in the U.S.A., Britain, and Australia had experienced some spectacular collapses and some were found in breach of the law. Concern for the environment increased dramatically among Jews as it did among people at large. The "greed is good" years gave way to an atmosphere in which questions about the fundamental nature of human existence came to the fore, engendered in great part by medical advances which prolonged life and scientific advances which made possible genetic engineering. There was no indication that Judaism was any less able to provide answers to these problems than any other religion, but that did not seem to be the point. The secular-leaning majority of Jews tended not to look to their Judaism for answers to contemporary social and moral questions; the Orthodox minority of Jews looked nowhere else, but did not view those contemporary questions as being of any particular importance.

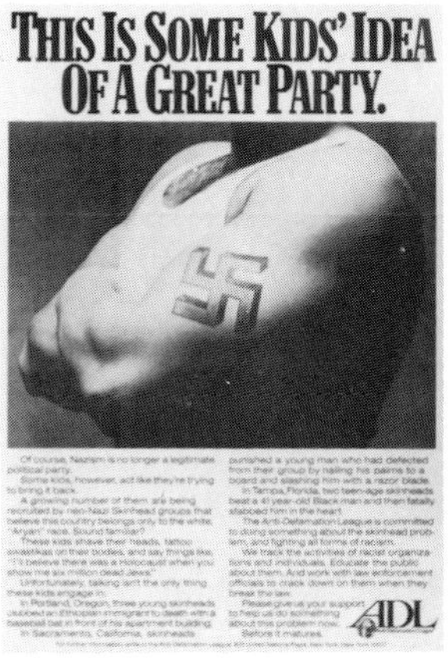

Anti-Semitism remains a threat; from an ADL advertisement. (Courtesy Anti-Defamation League)

In the years prior to 1989, the circumstances which shaped Jewish existence added up to a set of certainties, not all of which were considered as beneficial. The world was governed by the bi-polar U.S.-Soviet relationship; the Communist order and the cold war were assumed to be the status quo; despite cyclical downturns, continued prosperity in the free world was expected; no one expected any change in the implacable opposition of the Arab states and the Palestinians to Israel; the U.S.-Israel relationship was secure, if somewhat bumpy at times; America remained the principal defender of Jewish rights in the world; the two centers of Jewish gravity remained America and Israel, the essence of the Israel-Diaspora relationship; Jews in Eastern Europe were largely cut off from the rest of Jewry; anti-Semitism flared up from time to time, but most indices suggested a continual decline in anti-Jewish hostility.

The fundamentals of these circumstances of Jewish life had changed quite drastically by 1992. The world was no longer bi-polar; if anything, a tri-polar relationship was emerging: the U.S., the European Community and Japan (together with the other Asia-Pacific economic success stories), with the U.S. as the only superpower. Communism had collapsed, taking most people by surprise, and competing nationalisms rushed in to fill the vacuum. Economic prosperity no longer seemed assured. The disastrous state of most of the former communist economies and the intractable economic backwardness of the third world pressed in on a capitalist system that was no longer able to deliver ever rising standards of living even in the strongest economies of the western world.

The collapse of communism was the principal factor making possible a fundamental pragmatic change in the attitude of the Arab states to peace with Israel. Although the UN remained a hostile environment for Israel, anti-Zionism diminished and Israel's foreign relations were transformed. But the collapse of communism lessened the significance of the U.S.-Israel strategic relationship. With the new Democratic administration wishing to concentrate attention on the U.S. domestic agenda, Israel could no longer structure her position in the world on the basis of a special relationship with the U.S. Other regional crises and potential crises — in the Balkans, in Central Asia — confronted the Jewish state as problems and challenges which Israel would have to face without the U.S. as an intermediary.

While the Jewish communities of the U.S. and Israel remained the largest in the world, the collapse of communism and other world developments — in Latin America, South Africa, and Canada for example — meant greatly increased significance for Jewish communities previously considered on the periphery. In some cases — France and Australia for example — it was a case of unexpected communal growth and Jewish religious and intellectual ferment. In others, it was a matter of the pressure of external political forces — in South Africa, where the inevitable move to black majority rule brought turmoil to the Jewish community; in Canada, where the constitutional crisis raised fears for the future of Montreal's Jewish community. And finally, the rise in racism and intolerance towards foreigners which disfigured the European landscape in the latter part of the period under review brought with it an increase in anti-Semitism to levels not witnessed since the Second World War.

For Jews, the world seemed an increasingly uncertain place in 1992. Not that the uncertainties present were all negative by any means. The situation in Eastern Europe, for example, looked quite grim, with a war underway which could spread throughout the Balkans and with some of the fledgling democracies in the former communist states looking very fragile. But the very fact that attempts were being made to build democratic institutions in such societies was in itself a sign of great hope.

What seemed to be lacking in the Jewish world in 1992, was the will and determination to face up to the uncertainties. Instead, many appeared to be retreating into past certainties, acting as if nothing had changed.

Focus on Israel: Twenty-Five Years of Foreign Media Reporting

Yoel Cohen

The 1967 Six-Day War had wide-ranging repercussions for Israel and the Middle East across the politico-strategic sphere. The war was also a cornerstone for the projection of Israel's image and for generating foreign media interest in the country. True, earlier episodes in the Israel story — the War of Independence, and the allied operation at Suez in 1956 — aroused wide interest. Yet the 1967 war began a seemingly continuous chain of episodes which produced a momentum of media and public fascination with Israel. The series of episodes included Israeli military rule of the Administered Territories; spectacular terrorist incidents including the Munich Olympics and the Lod Airport massacre in 1972; the 1973 Yom Kippur War; the Israeli rescue at Entebbe in 1976; the Begin-Sadat peace initiative; the 1982 Lebanon War; the *intifada* which began in December 1987; the 1991 Gulf War and the 1993 Israel-PLO accord. Other stories, among them Russian and Ethiopian *aliyah*, also aroused interest. The dramatic elements in these events, including daring and military prowess, ensured continued high audience ratings for this best-selling story. Yet, media concentration raised serious questions about whether Israel's open society could cope with intensive foreign media interest.

THE MAKING OF THE ISRAELI NEWS STORY

A major increase in foreign media interest in Israel occurred in 1967 with the Six-Day War. Since then there have been ebbs and flows in this interest as the Arab-Israeli conflict developed into all-out war or incidents of terrorism. In the 1970s studies showed that Israel received greater foreign media coverage than many other foreign countries. The Arab-Israeli conflict continued to receive headline treatment in the 1980s, notably during the 1982 Lebanon War. There was also very considerable media treatment in the first months following the outbreak of the *intifada* in December 1987. Yet there remains a need for perspective. A poll of the most important stories of the 1980s, conducted by the Associated Press among 121 editors from 44 countries, found that the only Israel-related story to be listed was "Mid-East peace efforts" in tenth place. In a similar poll by Reuters, Israel was unplaced.

Wide foreign media interest in Israel is reflected in the relatively large foreign press corps in Israel; 270 foreign news organizations are represented in Israel full-time or part-time. It has the tenth largest foreign press corps in the world. Even more significant is that today Israel has the largest foreign press corps in the Middle East. In the past, Beirut, a Western-looking city, was a convenient base from which to follow events in the Arab world, it might have had the largest foreign press corps in the region. But the Lebanon civil war resulted in many foreign news organizations moving their operations either to Nicosia, to Cairo, or to Israel. While the growth in the size of the foreign press corps in Israel may largely be explained by the war story, even before the 1967 war the foreign press corps was not inconsiderable in size. Any suggestion of a lack of real growth in the foreign press corps between the pre-1967 and post-1967 periods is corrected by the lateral growth in the sizes of the bureaus of the major news agencies and major Western television networks and by the fact that before 1967 almost all correspondents were local Isrelis working part-time for particular foreign news organizations. Today, some thirty foreign TV stations are represented.

In terms of geographical breakdown, the foreign press corps in Israel has been consistently dominated by West European and North American news organizations; in 1992, some 185 news organizations from West Europe and 55 from North America were represented. In the early years West Germany and Britain constituted the largest country contingents, but by 1965 the U.S. was the lead country. U.S. media interest reflected a later growth in the importance of U.S.-Israeli bilateral relations. By contrast, only six, four, three, and two news organizations from Asia/Oceania, East Europe, South America and Africa respectively were represented. With the exceptions of *Al Ahram* and a London-based Middle East Arab satellite TV station, there are no correspondents from the Arab world.

The permanent foreign press corps is augmented at times of war and major crisis by 'firemen' or visiting reporters who fly in especially to cover the events as they unfold. In the 1973 war, 900 visiting reporters flew in to Israel in the first month; 1,500 reporters flew in to cover the Sadat visit to Jerusalem in November 1977. In the first seven weeks of the *intifada*, 580 visiting reporters arrived in Israel. The bureaus of the TV networks become "mini-armies." For example, in the 1973 war the U.S. network ABC expanded to some 150 personnel including eight correspondents brought in from abroad.

THE CONFLICT ELEMENT

A substantial part of foreign media reporting from Israel is taken up with the Arab-Israeli conflict and, through it, with the army and defense policy. An analysis by the author of 21 years of reporting by the Israel bureau of the Associated Press news agency found that military news and diplomatic news about the peace process dominated AP's coverage over such other news themes as Israel's foreign relations, internal politics, the economy, crime, culture, science, religion, immigration, sport, and Israeli-Jewish Diaspora news. Given the agenda-setting role which news agencies play in the media as a whole, these findings are important to note. With the exception of 6 of the 21 years examined, military and peace diplomacy reporting accounted for more than 60% of the bureau's reportage. There was a mean average of seven military or peace diplomacy news items per week in a regular period.

In times of war or major crisis media interest increases substantially. During the first week of the major wars of 1967, 1973 and 1982, the AP news agency sent 147, 190, and 113 items respectively from its Israel bureau, and all items concerned the war in its various aspects. Noteworthy is the smaller size of attention which the *intifada* received than did the wars. In the first week of the *intifada* (December 7–13 1987), AP sent from Israel 40 reports on the *intifada* and 16 additional non-*intifada*-related items. While during the major wars there was also very wide coverage by AP bureaus from Arab countries, in the *intifada* nearly all the reporting was done by the bureau in Israel. Yet notwithstanding this, coverage of the *intifada* was very considerable in the beginning months. During its first four months, the *New York Times* printed an average of two stories a day, a total of 242 stories; ABC TV aired 136 stories, NBC 126, and CBS 112.[1] The *Washington Post* published an estimated 300,000 words, including analysis and commentary, in the first five months of the *intifada*, an average of two articles daily — of which nearly a quarter appeared on the front page.[2] A survey of the *International Herald Tribune* from mid-March to mid-May 1988 found that with one exception Israel featured in every issue, with an average of three stories per issue. Of 31 *intifada*-related photographs, 18 were on the front page.[3]

FACTORS EXPLAINING THE NEWS INTEREST

The incidence of war and terrorism is itself not enough to explain foreign media coverage of Israel. There are many conflicts around the world which fail to draw considerable media focus. One factor is the dramatic nature of some of the wars and terrorist incidents involving Israel. Another factor is the fear, right or wrong, that an Arab-Israeli war could spark a third world war or could result in the deployment of nuclear weaponry. Indeed, the dramatic nature of past episodes of the Arab-Israeli conflict ensures media interest in even the potential of an outbreak of fighting such as threats and challenges by one side or the other. Audience identification of a black and white, of a good and bad, contributes to focusing attention on the conflict and the parties involved. Yet another factor for the news interest is the short duration of the 1967, 1973 and 1982 wars. The 1969–1970 Egyptian-Israeli War of Attrition lasted too long, and the level of violence did not dramatically change enough to hold the attention of the foreign media apart from the serious newspapers. Wide media interest in the *intifada* declined early on as the violence failed to result in popular revolution and pose a serious challenge to Israeli rule.

Democratic values, cultural ties and bilateral relations between Israel and Western countries provide the basis to the media interest, as evidenced by the dominance of North America and West Europe in the geographical make-up of the foreign press corps. Israel is seen by audiences in fellow democratic societies as a democracy in a sea of non-democratic states. The strategic and economic significance of the U.S.-Israeli relationship make Israel and the Arab-Israeli conflict particularly relevant to American audiences. The conflict is a major foreign news story in the U.S. media. In 1977–1981 the three U.S. TV networks gave the Middle East 32.4% of foreign newstime compared to West Europe (21.1%), East Europe (10.8%), Asia (9.5%), and Latin America (6.2%).[4] The Middle East and Israel received 9.4% in the U.S. press in 1970.[5]4 A study of foreign coverage by the *New York Times* in the first half of 1979 found that Israel was the most covered country.[6] The oil embargo imposed by Arab oil producing states at the time of the 1973 war made the region of direct relevance to both West European and U.S. audiences but this has since declined in importance in news interest.

Thomas Friedman, the former *New York Times* Israel correspondent, has argued that the cultural legacy of the Jewish and Christian traditions explains the interest in America for Israel. Jewish, Christian, and Muslim holidays, as well as related topics like archaeology are occasional subjects of news reporting, particularly with the visual media. Memories of the Holocaust, and feelings of moral responsibility, make Israel relevant particularly for older audiences. It explains the wide interest which the Eichmann trial generated, and more recently the interest in the trial of John Demjanjuk. But the cultural factor is a latent rather that actual factor. The latent news interest caused by the historico-cultural connection has become actualized through the dramatic wars and terrorism.

Another factor contributing to considerable coverage is the ease of access which foreign correspondents in Israel enjoy to news sources and to zones of combat at times of conflict. It contrasts with relatively limited access in most Arab countries. Reporters benefit from the relative proximity of Israel's border to bureaus in Tel Aviv and Jerusalem. Parallel to the ease of access in Israel are the good communications facilities it offers for transferring information. Israel was hooked up to a communications satellite already before the 1973 war in contrast to most Arab countries which became hooked up only in the latter 1970s. The use of video in the case of TV organizations and facsimile machines and computer word processors for print journalists, not to mention such gadgetry as car phones, makes the lead time between the occurrence of an event and its news transmission often negligible. Media technology and access have, in turn, contributed to greater cultural proximity between Israel and foreign audiences, making the former seemingly more relevant to the latter.

Foreign media interest is not only determined by the intrinsic type of event inside Israel but also by what else is happening around the world. It is particularly true with foreign news that the media appear able to focus on only a couple of international crises at any one time. The longest curfew imposed during the *intifada* — in the first week of June 1989 — failed to be covered in the foreign media due to the turbulent events unraveling in China's Tiananmen Square, Poland, Iran, and the Soviet Union at that time. With the notable exception of the 1991 Gulf War and the period leading up to hostilities, political change throughout Eastern Europe at the end of the 1980s and early 1990s reduced media concentration on the Middle East.

THE IMPACT OF MEDIA COVERAGE

Intensive foreign media coverage of Israel's conflicts raises the question of the impact of this coverage upon Israel's foreign relations. Up to the mid-1970s the U.S. media were inclined to be editorially supportive of Israel. Arab states and the Palestinians were seen as the obstructionist party. The Sadat visit to Israel and the Camp David peace accords turned U.S. media attitudes more in favor of the Arabs and away from Israel. Up to then, with a few exceptions (the *Washington Post, Christian Science Monitor*, and the *St. Louis Post-Despatch*), the U.S. media was broadly supportive of the pro-Israeli policies of successive U.S. administrations.[7] The Sabra and Shatilla killings dropped U.S. public support for Israel to an all-time low of 32% (in May 1982, for example, U.S. public support for Israel had been 51%), and increased support for the Arabs to a high of 28%. U.S. public support for Israel rallied by the mid-1980s. In June 1986, for example, the Roper poll found that 53% of Americans supported Israel more and 8% supported the Arabs more. Yet, in April 1988, the effect of the *intifada* dropped support for Israel to 37%, although support for the Arabs increased only to 13%.[8]

In the 1960s and 1970s there was an inclination for audiences to identify with Israel — the David in the topdog-underdog relationship. But once these roles were reversed there was less inclination to stay with, and understand the motives of, what was perceived as the David-turned-Goliath. The perceived failure of Israel to live up to the higher Western as well as Jewish moral values — in spite of the challenges to its security — created a double standard in reporting and commentary about Israel. It even contributed to anti-Semitism. For example, of 73 terrorist incidents in West Europe against Jewish or Israeli targets in the two-year period September 1980

Foreign correspondents and local journalists at the Jerusalem Hilton Hotel waiting for a press conference to begin in January 1991 prior to the Gulf War (GPO, Jerusalem)

to October 1982, 30 took place during the Lebanon War, between June and October 1982.[9]

There is wide exposure to the foreign media among decisionmakers at times of crisis. Fast channels of newsgathering can prove more efficient as an intelligence source than the ambassador's dispatch. Yet apart from crises, the media's predilection not to cover foreign affairs makes the news media, with the exception of serious quality newspapers and periodicals, of secondary value to the diplomatic or intelligence report which has been crafted specifically from the perspective of the government's interest.

There are occasions when the exposure of policymakers and the public to the news media can produce a change in policy. For example, in the Gulf War the considerable coverage of the first Scud attacks from Israel — broadcast within minutes by TV crews positioned in Tel Aviv — and the damage inflicted on Israeli civilians contributed to the arrival of the Patriot missiles, sent by the U.S. government, within 29 hours from the first attack. The Israeli army's response in dealing with the Arab uprising in the *intifada* as portrayed on American television shocked Bush, according to his aides. A UPI photograph in the Lebanon war showing a baby without arms and which incorrectly claimed to have been caused by an Israeli shell so moved President Reagan that he placed it on his desk in the Oval Room; "it had more impact on him than fifty position papers," remarked a presidential aide.[10]

ISRAELI OFFICIALDOM AND THE FOREIGN MEDIA

Israeli leaders have long given priority to cultivating public support abroad. The Zionist movement in the 1930s and 1940s recognized the importance of propaganda in its political activities. In the final years of the British Mandate, the activities of the Jewish Agency's Political Department included maintaining contact with the foreign press corps, while Jewish Agency representatives in Europe were in touch with editors of the local press. Foreign correspondents in Palestine covering the armed struggle for independence followed the fighting from the Haganah spokesman who issued communiqués, and via the Jewish underground's radio station. Later the Haganah established an office specifically to provide information to the foreign and Hebrew media. With the establishment of the state, an attempt was made to set up a single government information service. However, after its prospective head, Gershon Agron, failed to receive a place in the cabinet, it did not materialize. David Ben-Gurion argued that information matters should be subordinate to political policy, and reserved the informational element within the Prime Minister's Office — even if in practice he had little time to deal with the subject. In its place, an information service in the new Ministry of Interior dealt with information requirements of home government departments, and a similar service in the new Foreign Ministry dealt with information work abroad.

Since then there have been a series of departmental amalgamations and reorganizations in the handling of information matters. Today, a number of government departments deal directly with the foreign media. The Foreign Ministry, through its press and information attachés at Israel's diplomatic missions around the world, maintains contact with local editors and broadcast producers providing them with a stream of information. In Jerusalem, the ministry briefs the foreign press corps several times weekly. The army, Israel Defense Force (IDF), though it holds no regular briefings for foreign correspondents except during major crises, remains an important source of information for correspondents about day-to-day military incidents. The Government Press Office provides technical facilities for permanently based and visiting foreign reporters, and the Prime Minister's Spokesman is a source for information about governmental thinking.

The Israeli Government's ability to manipulate public channels of information is largely limited by those matters which are of interest to the media and the public. Governmental relations with the foreign media in open societies are characterized as being "reaction-orientated" in the main, responding to public reactions and media inquiries on issues which arouse concern and interest. Nevertheless, through engaging in information work and providing reporters with information and with access to sources and events, Israeli officials have had the potential to "balance" the information which reporters gather from other sources, and have ensured that the government's account and interpretation of events are included in the media's reportage.

THE ROLE OF THE ARMY SPOKESMAN

Given that the Arab-Israeli conflict takes up a central part of foreign reporting about Israel, the army is a key component in the government-foreign media relationship. Yet as an organization structured on discipline and tactical surprise, armed forces are least equipped to cope with media interest. Up to the 1967 war a senior officer in the IDF Intelligence Corps doubled as Army Spokesman and as coordinator with the censor and other government ministries. His functions included explaining the country's defense problems to both the Israeli and foreign publics, and developing information programs such as written materials for distribution to these publics. The location of the department within the Intelligence Corps reflected the fact that psychological warfare was part of the department's tools of trade. Over the years the IDF has become more accustomed to the idea of the open society and to meeting the requirements of access for journalists to military information and to areas of combat irrespective of whether or not the event itself serves the country's information cause. Following the 1973 war, when the Army Spokesman's credibility came under question, the unit was taken out of the Intelligence Corps and became part of the General Staff. It was also a recognition of a contradiction between intelligence, which stands for secrecy, and spokesmanship, which implies openness.

Through being the subject of media and public attention, the Israeli army possesses the potential to generate at home public support, such as on the defense budget, and abroad to project the country's deterrent posture. For a long time the structure of the Army Spokesman's media liaison branch was divided into three sub-sections — the Israeli military correspondents, the foreign media, and the Israeli media (apart from the military correspondents). In 1990 the sub-section dealing with the foreign media became a fully fledged branch of the unit reflecting the size and importance of the foreign press corps.

Much of the work of the Army Spokesman's Unit is taken up with escorting reporters to events and bases and, during times of combat, to front lines. Given the small number of commissioned officers, the overwhelming part of escort work is done by reservists, the number of which are estimated to have increased six-fold in the last 15 years. In 1991 the unit was estimated to have about 1,000 reservists.[11] Escort officers require a combination of qualifications including, first, combat experience and knowledge of the military infrastructure — knowing their way around the military, including at times of war, being able to take correspondents close to sometimes rapidly changing front lines. Second, escort officers should possess a solid understanding of a military situation. In the 1982 war, escorts were found to be ignorant of the Israeli-Lebanese military situation even though there had been speculation for more than six months about a possible Israeli operation in southern Lebanon following katyusha attacks by the PLO on Israeli settlements on the northern border. Thirdly, they need an appreciation of the requirements of the media — helping the reporter through the military bureaucracy to meet edition time notwithstanding the obligation to submit the material for censorship clearance. Yet many correspondents perceive the escort officer as a hindrance. According to the report of the State Comptroller in 1990 only some 15% of reservists had the required informational experience.[12]

Army-media relations during the *intifada* were characterized in part by clashes involving soldiers and journalists covering the unrest. In the first five months of the *intifada*, the Army Spokesman reported 31 incidents involving the army and journalists covering the unrest; the Foreign

Press Association, however, reported over 100 incidents in the first six-and-a-half months. The Army Spokesman and the IDF Education Corps recognized a need to educate soldiers about how to respond in low-intensity conflict situations and how to cope with the media's presence. A program of lectures and videos was produced to show regular soldiers and reservists serving in the territories how to act and react in riot control situations, including instructions on opening fire on civilians. For example, an IDF film, *The Camera Sees All*, on dos and don'ts in dealing with non-peaceful behavior, was shown to all troops about to commence a period of service in the administered territories.

MEDIA DIPLOMACY

Israel's Foreign Service has long recognized that information work or *hasbarah* (explanation) is an integral part of the implementation of foreign policy. In addition to the work of press and information attachés abroad, a major part of the work of an ambassador is also in *hasbarah*. Yet the role which diplomats abroad play in the formation of Israel's image in the media requires to be qualified since much of what appears in the media is reported from inside the country itself whether by the news organizations' own correspondents or by news agency correspondents or video news agency teams. Diplomats abroad serve a secondary role through cultivating editiorial commentators and editors, and by maintaining contact with other sections of informed opinion including local politicians, academics, and clergy.[13] Local Jewish groups are encouraged to put pressure upon news organizations.

The Foreign Ministry's Hasbarah Department over the years produced an array of information materials to generate foreign public support. For example, a series of "pink papers" comprising policy positions on a range of foreign policy and defense matters were sent to informed opinion groups. Videos on economic, scientific and cultural themes have been screened at small gatherings as well as distributed to local TV stations. Pre-packaged radio taped programs have been distributed to radio stations. Yet the value of such electronic information materials is limited given the hesitancy of major Western broadcasting organizations to use officially produced material. Smaller stations are willing to use officially-sponsored material. They include dozens of local college, Catholic, Black and other radio and TV stations in the U.S. In the latter 1980s the Foreign Ministry funded a radio producer to supply news clips to dozens of radio stations around the world. But most of these stations were outside the main target regions of Israeli information policy, North America, and West Europe. In 1993 the Hasbarah Department was disbanded and its personnel amalgamated with the Press Department, headed by the ministry spokesman, to form a Media & Public Affairs Division which would focus resources towards the news media. It reflected skepticism about the value of officially sponsored information materials, a recognition of the important role of television in providing live and continuous coverage of events, and the fact that target audiences themselves are informed through the news media.

INFORMATION POLICY

An examination of recent crises shows that informational considerations are not always incorporated into decisionmaking. For example, in the Litani Operation into Lebanon in March 1978 the Army Spokesman was only informed at the General Staff planning stage about the operation a few hours before the actual operation began. This was in spite of the informational element of the operation, namely, the terrorist threat to Israel. As a result, escort officers were not called up or briefed, and written information background materials were not ready at the outset. The need for operational secrecy was further complicated by the fact that reservist escort officers include journalists.[14] Past informational lessons were not applied when the 1982 Lebanon War broke out. A draft plan was drawn up by the Army Spokesman Brigadier General Yaacov Even, which would allow Israeli reporters and foreign journalists to accompany the advancing troops into Lebanon. It would have enabled them to report on the operation as it unfolded, including the care taken by the troops not to inflict wanton damage on the civilian population. The plan was overridden by the defense minister and chief of staff.[15] In the war, journalists were not shown the PLO arms stores which the IDF discovered in southern Lebanon. Another lost opportunity was the local Lebanese civilians who had suffered under the PLO's reign of terror in the south of the country. When the *intifada* broke out, the Army Spokesman's Unit itself was caught by surprise, the spokesman having failed to evaluate the size of the wave of the violence.

Notwithstanding these cases, there is an upward trend over the years towards information planning. In the case of the Army Spokesman, for example, a monitoring group comprising reservists in the unit who possessed expertise in public relations was established following the 1973 Middle

October 5, 1992, press conference in Prime Minister Rabins' office (GPO, Jerusalem)

East War to act as a think tank and provide input into information policy flow. The think tank's outsider-insider perspective meant that an unorthodox perspective entered into informational decisions taken by the military. In the Lebanon War the think tank was responsible for the innovative proposal to open IDF Spokesman's stations in Beirut and Sídon (in addition to those set up at the border points at Gesher Haziv and Metullah) which resulted in journalists on the Lebanese side of the fighting being exposed to the Israeli viewpoint. Errors in information handling in the war resulted in the decision taken after the war for the Army Spokesman, the Defense Minister's media adviser, and the Defense Ministry spokesman to sit in at planning sessions of future military operations. At the tactical level, army commanders today take into account likely reactions abroad to particular decisions. Military information planning also has a macro sense. Yet even if there is greater awareness among the military echelon in Israel about the importance to brief the media, the long-term implications of options of foreign media coverage are not a factor in planning military strategy and tactics. In order to give greater weight at the cabinet level to the PR aspects of military actions some have advocated over the years the appointment of a minister or deputy minister of information.

Another element of information policy is the need for fast response during periods of high tension like wars. Yet the authorities' ability to respond quickly is conditioned by the need for accuracy in order to maintain credibility. Ten days elapsed until the Israeli authorities responded to wildly exaggerated claims about casualties and refugees at the outset of the Lebanon War. Claims by the Beirut representative of the International Committee of the Red Cross that there were 600,000 Lebanese and Palestinians homeless as a result of Israel's putsch to Beirut, and by the Palestine Red Crescent that 15,000 persons had been killed and 10,000 wounded, achieved wide currency. In the *intifada* there were many cases when the government spent months checking into the facts behind a particular incident. In other types of war situations, where it is known what the tanks, artillery, air force, and other units are doing, fast reaction is more possible.

The Gulf War was characterized by past lessons of information planning having been learnt. It is possible to identify an information element in Israeli decisionmaking in the stages leading up to, and during, the war. In the lead-up to the war, there was a need for the spokesman, Brigadier General Nahman Shai, to issue warnings of the dire consequences if Saddam tried to carry out his threat to "burn half of Israel" without provoking him unduly, on the one hand, and calm a somewhat distraught population at home who were being given gas masks and instructions on sealing their homes in the event of a gas attack, on the other hand. Among the information-related questions in the war handled by the Army Spokesman were the need to explain the arrival of the Patriot missiles; how to explain the arrival of U.S. (i.e., foreign) troops on Israeli soil to man the Patriots; how to reconcile the public's dilemma as to whether the best defense against the Scuds was to use gas masks inside sealed rooms above ground level or to enter air raid shelters since none of the Scud missiles had chemical warheads; how the military should give voice to their intelligence that many Iraqi missile launchers had not been destroyed in spite of U.S. claims to the contrary, and to do so without coming into conflict with Washington; and the level of public exposure of the Army Spokesman in the Israeli media — which in the event of an error could be costly to overall credibility.

Some draw from the IDF's doctrine of minimal force in dealing with a problem which can cost soldiers' lives evidence of a running concern about foreign governmental and public reactions. And some on Israel's political Right have claimed that civil disturbances in the Administered Territories could have been dealt with more efficiently through a more brutal manner, were it not for likely foreign governmental criticism. Underlying this doctrine is a basically humane outlook, dubbed "the purity of arms" (*tohar ha-neshek*), which owes its origins to the fabric of a Jewish country and its army, and to achieving military objectives by limiting damage inflicted among an enemy civilian population and property at the same time as minimizing losses among its own forces. To the extent that public opinion considerations coincide with this doctrine public opinion may be said to have an impact in military planning.

GOVERNMENTAL COORDINATION

A positive image in the media and the public is conditioned in part on the projection of a unified government view. Both the Government Press Office, which acts as a conduit to the foreign press corps in Israel, and the Foreign Ministry, are dependent on the Army Spokesman's Unit for information about events of a military-related nature. Notwithstanding cases of lack of coordination, there is also considerable evidence where interdepartmental coordination succeeded. In the 1991 Gulf War the army and the Foreign Ministry jointly established press centers in Tel Aviv and Jerusalem. Similarly, in the Lebanon war the press center set up in Beirut was organized jointly by the army and the Foreign Ministry. In the early period of the *intifada*, in spite of basic policy differences between the coalition government of Likkud and Labor, senior officials handling information in the Prime Minister's Office, Defense Ministry, Foreign Ministry, and Government Press Office worked in general harmony — notwithstanding the need initially for the Foreign Ministry to press the Army Spokesman for more information on specific incidents.

Ad hoc coordination has rarely extended into more long-term structural linkage. The 1969 Peled Inquiry on the *Hasbarah* Apparatus said that one of the weaknesses of the information apparatus was the large number of agencies involved and recommended a single information authority. Its functions would include ongoing analysis of trends in Israel's image abroad; activating official reaction on a 24-hour, daily basis; the preparation of printed and broadcast information materials; and the making of information policy. However, successive foreign ministers have torpedoed what would amount to a single information ministry. They have argued that information work is an integral part of diplomatic representation. An attempt to put the proposal into effect was made in 1974 with the establishment of an information ministry. Ironically, while coordination with the Defense Ministry worked efficiently, it was both foreign Minister Yigal Allon's opposition to the new ministry which he saw as carrying out functions traditionally done by the Foreign Ministry, and the lack of attention at the Cabinet level to the informational element in policy which led, in March 1975, to the resignation of Information Minister Aharon Yariv and, subsequently, to the dismantling of the ministry. Instead of a fully fledged ministry, a compromise formula proposed at different times has been the appointment of a deputy minister of information who would have a coordinating role between the Foreign Ministry, Army Spokesman's Unit, the Defense Ministry and other relevant agencies, in addition to providing policy input at the Cabinet level has been mooted at different times over the years.

OPTIONS AND DILEMMAS

Israel has only limited control over the fate of its public image. In an open society organs of government are largely dependent for their image on how the media cover them. When the government wants to convey a specific message to the public at home or abroad it must, in giving its side of what is happening, break into the market forces of news values; in so doing the government becomes dependent on whether the particular subject is defined as newsworthy or not by journalists. The age when a single political personality could heavily control the public image at a time of crisis has given way in the so-called global village to the instant transfer of information across national boundaries. The important role which television plays in covering conflict was revolutionized again in the Gulf War with live 24-hour coverage by Cable News Network of unfolding events at the various war zones. By contrast, closed societies, which include a large number of Arab states, are characterized by authoritarian governments enjoying wide-ranging powers limiting what their own population knows, as well as being able to control to a great extent what the world outside knows about the country.

The wider interpretation of Israel's image problem in terms of news interest is sometimes lost on those who express criticism of the foreign media for imbalanced, biased, or inaccurate reporting. There have been instances of intentional invention of facts by individual journalists. Yet the frequency of cases of the intentional invention of facts when compared with the total flow of 25 years of foreign reporting of the conflict should not be exaggerated given that reporters and editors are anxious to maintain credibility in the eyes of both their audiences and their professional superiors. A different type of distortion is incomplete knowledge among reporters at the newsgathering stage. Working often with fast deadlines, reporters have to unearth facts to a particular situation and obtain reactions which are often slow in coming from the parties concerned, sometimes intentionally slow. The permanent foreign press corps in Israel is able to draw on wide experience and knowledge of Israel, as well as wide contacts, which limit distortion caused by incomplete knowledge to the maximum possible. This is less true in the case of the many visiting reporters at times of crisis.

A different form of media distortion than intentional invention of facts is the selection of facts, or the influence of tone, in the preparation of a news report or feature article or program. The traditional separation in journalism between news and comment has become blurred owing to a trend towards contextualized journalism. Incorporation of analysis and background — a feature of news magazine journalism — also marks broadcast journalism. And as newspapers lose their role to the broadcasting media of being the providers of breaking news, some in print journalism have redefined their function as being more in the provision of background to the news. In spite of a trend among news media towards contextualized journalism, much reporting remains spasmodic, concentrating on the "bang-bang" of an event and little else. The innovation of live television coverage of events has a structural bias against interpretation and towards unedited footage of the action. Yet, there is little solution to the absence of context and background. The journalist, as distinct from the historian, cannot be expected to rehash to foreign audiences the background and history of the Arab-Israeli conflict for the umpteenth time after each incident.

The major form of media bias is the bias of omission not by the individual journalist but resulting from the news production process itself and the market forces of news values. The lobbying by Jewish organizations of the media regarding specific cases of alleged inaccurate or biased reporting has limited impact on the overall image of Israel. Some complaints have as their basis a complaint that Israel is "too newsworthy" — a language which is meaningless to those working in the media. Notwithstanding this, the ongoing watchdog efforts of these organizations, in addition to winning corrections in specific cases of distorted or inaccurate reporting, are a constant reminder to editors and producers of the requirement for objective and accurate reporting.

There is wide news interest in military matters and in foreign policy regarding the Arab-Israeli peace process. Yet many aspects of Israeli foreign and defense policies are of importance to only certain informed sections of the public. Israel has over the years sought to foster the image of a Western-style democratic society, absorbing immigrants from different social backgrounds, an economy undergoing transformation, and a cultural tradition drawing on the historical past. However, there is little news interest in other news from Israel such as domestic politics, the economy, culture, and science. An irony of 25 years of fairly continuous media interest is that the focus of interest remains the Israeli-Arab conflict rather than Israel proper. Interest in Israel proper has still not come centerfold in the way, for example, foreign reporting from West European countries focuses on the society itself. To be true, some of the interest in the conflict has spilled over to these other stories. Yet, to the extent that they are covered, it is often done within one context or another of the conflict.

The Israel Government has been able to draw on certain existing powers to limit coverage. The military censor is empowered to prohibit the publication of classified information, and the Army Spokesman influences the access to IDF information and to zones of conflict for reporters. These controls are limited to protecting military information. Yet there have been instances in the past when information casting a negative image about an event or the IDF itself was banned, if the information fell within the parameters of military-sensitive information.

Successive Israel governments have been discriminatory at times in providing access when an event is likely to be portrayed in a positive light, and not to provide it for events which are more negative. One school of thought, however, can be identified in recent years among Israeli officialdom arguing that in an open society the information will come out from one source or another and that the government, given its interest to get its views on record, should adopt a less discriminatory and more realistic approach, and provide this access.

In curtailing access to the media, the authorities have had resort to certain legal powers. The Israeli withdrawal from Yammit, Sinai, in 1982 — in which the IDF was faced with settlers refusing to leave their homes voluntarily and threatening to forcibly resist any attempts by the army

— is illustrative. The IDF decided that no reporters, Israeli or foreign, would be present. Subsequently, after protests from news organizations and journalists' associations, the IDF agreed to a pool of 16 Israeli and 16 foreign reporters. The Israeli courts subsequently backed the IDF in the decision and said that the evacuation from Yammit was an unprecedented event of special complexity and importance. Noteworthy is that the court added in its judgment that in normal circumstances the journalists had a right to free access, implying that the foreign journalists had a right of access equal to that of the Israeli journalists. This view could be challenged by the argument that the Israel government, like any other democratic government, is only obligated to keep its own media and its own public informed; it has no obligation of accountability to foreign audiences as distinct to a policy interest to explain its position. This view was succinctly stated by Brig.- Gen. Even who said in a 1983 interview that "the access to the theater of hostilities which the IDF provides to journalists is given because of the public's right to know what is happening. This privilege does not extend to the same degree to foreign newsmen, because my responsibility is to the Israelis."

During the *intifada* the Administered Territories were closed off to the media for three days in March 1988, as well as at prayer times on Fridays, for reasons of "national security." The presence of journalists was likely to encourage demonstrations. But the fact that local army commanders were given powers to close off areas at short notice — and did so sometimes only once they saw a journalist approaching at a distance — together with the lack of differentiation between TV crews, who can be identified as such by local Arabs, and ordinary print journalists, who cannot, confirmed to some people the belief that these measures were taken for political rather than security reasons.

Limits on access can only be effective where the media cannot get the information from alternative sources. Some Israeli officials in the case of *intifada*, including then Defense Minister Yitzḥak Rabin, questioned whether it was possible practically to close off the territories since there were alternative means to get information. There were side roads to reach the Administered Territories. Journalists could enter in Arab taxis. Journalists had contacts among the Arab population, and foreign news organizations had local Arab journalists in the territories who acted as tipsters. One network trained local Arab residents in the use of minicam cameras. Local Palestinian translation agencies sprouted up in major towns providing a range of services to journalists including translation of the Arab media, escorting journalists, and providing information about breaking events. Yet, other officials, including Prime Minister Shamir's spokesman, argued that the strongest army in the region was capable of a limited policing operation. Any explicit limit on access, however, needs to be weighed against the questionable ethics of censorship of the press, as well as a flow of embarrassing articles about press censorship itself which initially follow the introduction of such measures. Further, the importance of the American-Israeli relationship would argue that wideranging closure of media access should only be contemplated in a rare circumstance.

Israeli policymakers, in addition to themselves taking into account the informational element in choosing which tactics to use to achieve their political, diplomatic and military objectives, can draw certain comfort from the dynamics of news interest themselves. Media coverage of a specific event is determined by whether the event's news interest is maintained over a long period or, as in so many situations, the event lacks importance or changes dramatically. And even if an event is lengthy in duration, there exists an inverse relationship between coverage and the length of an event. The longer an event continues the less will be the audience interest in it except if the event itself changes in a dramatic manner, such as a rise in a level of violence. The news story also competes heavily with other stories going on abroad at the same time. The occurrence of news events elsewhere in the world of equal or greater news significance reduces further this news interest.

As reflected by the level of sympathy for Israel in Western countries, Israel's image has largely survived the cost of the society's openness. The overall impact of the foreign media and foreign opinion on Israel's foreign relations is generally small. Were the conflict to be resolved, the level of foreign media interest would decline significantly. Yet Israel could remain a base from which to report the Middle East as a whole given the country's openness, ease of media communications, and travel connections to neighboring states.

Notes

1. Center for Media & Public Affairs (Washington, D.C.), *Middle East Monitor*, 2:4 (May 1988).
2. *Washington Post*, May 23, 1988.
3. E. Tal, *Israel in Media Land* (1989).
4. J. B. Weaver, J. Porter, and E. Evans, "Patterns in Foreign News Coverage on U.S. Network TV: A Ten Year Analysis," in: *Journalism Quarterly* (Summer 1984).
5. G. Gerbner and Marvanyi, "The Many Worlds of the World's Press," in: *Journal of Communication* (Winter 1977).

6. G. W. Hopple, "International News Coverage in Two Elite Newspapers,", in: *Journal of Communication* (Winter 1977).
7. For a study on U.S. editorial attitudes in the 1970s, see R. H. Trice, "The American Elite Press and the Arab-Israeli Conflict," in: *Middle East Journal* (Summer 1979) 310–25.
8. D. Singer and R. Cohen, *Israel and the Intifada: Findings of the April 1989 Roper Poll* (1989), Appendix: Table 1.
9. ADL European Foundation, Paris.
10. *Time*, Aug. 16, 1982.
11. *Maariv*, June 16, 1991.
12. *State Comptroller's Report* (1990), 383.
13. For an insider's view of the Israel Foreign Ministry's information program see M. Yegar, *The Growth of Israel's Foreign Information Machinery*, [Hebrew] (1986). (A veteran diplomat, Yegar was assistant director-general for information.)
14. Z. Schiff, "Military Hasbara in the Stocks," in: *Israel Journalists' Yearbook* (1979).
15. G. Avner, "The Renewed Hasbara Debate in Israel," Report of the Israel Office of the American Jewish Committee (August 25, 1982).

Intermarriage in the United States

Mervin F. Verbit

Intermarriage has always been a danger to the Jewish People. Any group that lives as a minority has the potential of being absorbed by its host society. Some contact among the groups within a society is inevitable, but that contact can take many forms as relations among groups are played out — not always in consistent patterns — along several dimensions: cultural, institutional, residential, social, and familial. Because these dimensions can be independent of one another, acculturation, for example, need not lead to residential integration, nor does residential integration necessarily bring about socializing across group lines. Almost all kinds of acculturation and integration are compatible with continued group identity, at least theoretically. Integration at the familial level, on the other hand, is a sufficient condition for total assimilation by a sub-group into the larger society and its eventual disappearance as an identifiable group. Although most social identities are transmitted through families, Jewishness, going much further, explicitly defines itself in familial terms. Intermarriage thus is seen as the very antithesis of Jewish continuity. From the time that Abraham sent his servant to choose a wife for Isaac from among his own people through Ezra's expulsion of the non-Jewish wives of the Jews who returned to establish the Second Commonwealth to the recent practice of severing all ties with and sitting *shivah* for intermarried children, exogamy was one of the most energetically discouraged and forcefully condemned acts that a Jew could perform.

Most of the research on intermarriage has been done on American Jewry, which serves as the focus of this article, but much of the analysis can *mutatis mutandis* be extended to other Diaspora communities. In the last three decades or so, intermarriage has changed dramatically in the United States — not only in quantity, but also in its meaning and in the reactions it engenders. Although a number of books and articles on intermarriage written before the 1960s viewed it with alarm as "an epidemic," intermarriage was not then generally seen as a serious communal threat, and the data on which those works rested pale in the perspective of the 1990s. Widespread communal concern with intermarriage followed the publication of Erich Rosenthal's "Studies of Jewish Intermarriage in the United States" in the 1963 *American Jewish Year Book* and a cover story on "The Vanishing American Jew" in *Look* magazine. These two articles left the Jews of the time shaken and less assured about the future of the American Jewish community. They had come to believe that, while the Jewishness of their children would not be the same as that of earlier generations, the changes that they had made in order to "modernize" Judaism would guarantee that future generations would maintain their Jewishness even as they acquired full economic, political, civic, and cultural equality as American citizens. They knew that some would intermarry and be lost, but not enough, they were convinced, seriously to weaken American Jewish life. Most Jews entering the 1960s felt themselves part of what had become the world's premier Jewish community, at least in the Diaspora, and, for all of its problems, they felt secure in its future.

In the late 1960s and early 1970s many committees, commissions, and task forces were established by Jewish organizations to propose ways of reducing what was viewed as a dangerously high intermarriage rate. Despite those efforts, in the intervening years the rate increased.

The latest national study, undertaken by the Council of Jewish Federations in 1990, reports that 52% of the Jews who married between 1985 and 1990 married non-Jews (and another 5% married converts to Judaism). The exogamy rate climbed dramatically from decade to decade from the comparatively low and stable level characteristic of the period before the 1960s. Another recent study, by the Center for Modern Jewish Studies at Brandeis University, also reports recent intermarriage rates for successive decades, in eight communities in various parts of the country. Although the figures are somewhat lower than in the CJF study, the increase over time is equally steep. (The overall lower rates may be due to a combination of factors: the communities chosen, the decade break points, and the way Jews became eligible for the sample.) Whatever the precise

The rising tide in intermarriage is a topic engaging the interest of American Jews, an example being the February 1991 cover of *Moment Magazine* (Reprinted courtesy of *Moment Magazine*, Washington, D.C.)

figures may be, it is clear that at this point exogamy is as common as endogamy among American Jews.

Which Jews are most likely to intermarry? Until recently, men were twice as likely as women to marry non-Jews. In recent years, however, the gap has narrowed considerably. It also used to be the case that intermarriage was most frequent among Jews with the highest educational and income levels, but recent studies call this pattern into question. Now, when such variables as age are controlled, Jews at the top of the socioeconomic scale turn out to be less likely to intermarry than those toward the middle, but the differences are small. It is also found that the older Jews are at the time of their first marriage, the more likely they are to be exogamous. This is probably due to the fact that older people are more independent, have a wider network of professional and business contacts including non-Jews, and face a shrinking pool of potential partners. Second marriages after divorce are also much more likely than first marriages to involve a non-Jewish partner. The higher tendency to exogamy among the divorced may be strengthened by their desire for a second spouse "different" from the first and by their greater independence from ties to family and community. Geographic variations are important. Generally, areas of high Jewish concentration have less intermarriage, but some cities with large Jewish populations have very high intermarriage rates (San Francisco, Denver, and Washington, D.C., are examples). The less traditional the religious "movement"with which a Jew identifies, the more likely that Jew is to intermarry, with the highest rates of intermarriage among those who identify with no religious movement at all and claim to be "just Jewish."

During most of the 1980s it was generally believed that in about one-third of the marriages between Jews and partners born non-Jews, the originally non-Jewish partner converted to Judaism according to the norms and practices of one or another of American Judaism's religious movements, either before or after the marriage. (That phenomenon led to the adoption of a more elaborate terminology in which "intermarriage" is often used to refer to any marriage between a Jew and someone born not Jewish, "conversionary marriage" refers to a marriage between a Jew and a non-Jew who converts to Judaism, and "mixed marriage" is the term reserved for marriages in which one partner is Jewish and the other is not.) The most recent studies show that a much smaller proportion of intermarriages is conversionary than had previously been thought to be the case.

Another terminological development is use of the phrase "Jews-by-choice" instead of "convert." Many feel that the former term is more positive. It is also seen as a way at least partly to get around some of the problems that arise from different definitions of conversion held by various segments of the Jewish community. The latest statistical projection estimates that there are now approximately 185,000 "Jews-by-choice" in North America.

Trying to assess the demographic impact of intermarriage, optimistic analysts used to point out that if half of the children of intermarried couples are Jewish there should be no net loss in the size of the Jewish community. Recent studies show, however, that far fewer than half of the children of intermarriage identify as Jews, even by the most liberal criteria. Moreover, those who do consider themselves Jews have weaker Jewish identity on the whole than do born Jews, and they are themselves far more likely to intermarry in turn. The 1990 CJF study projects that there are about 415,000 adults in North America who are descended from Jews but were raised from birth in another religion and another 700,000 children under eighteen years of age who are not identified as Jews but have a Jewish parent or grandparent.

The organized Jewish community in North America is now expressing renewed alarm over intermarriage. Not only has the rate risen dramatically over the last couple of decades, but the demographic impact is seen as more threatening than had been hoped. Many federations and other Jewish organizations have begun to address what they articulate as the problem in "Jewish continuity." Several inquiries have been undertaken into what can be done to bolster Jewish identity, Jewish organizations and agencies have been encouraged in a number of communities to strengthen those aspects of their programs that are seen as contributing to Jewish identity, and some funds are being allocated for activities designed to enhance Jewish continuity.

In order to understand intermarriage in the contemporary Jewish community, it is essential to recognize that its very meaning has changed. In earlier periods intermarriage was often a rebellion against Jewishness or a quiet renunciation of Jewish identity — if not for oneself, then for one's children. There were several variations on that theme. Intermarriage could be a way of breaking free from what were felt as the constraints of Jewish life and the discrimination to which Jews were subjected. It could be an extreme means to declare independence from, perhaps even to punish, parents. For the upwardly mobile, it could provide entry into desired social circles. Whatever the motives, however, intermarriage was understood as sufficiently incompatible with Jewish identity to constitute a decisive break with Jewishness. It was in that context that Jewish parents and, reflecting their sentiments, Jewish organizations reacted so forcefully when the intermarriage statistics of the 1960s were published.

Jewish identity had been re-shaped in America in the 20th century, but most Jews were not assimilationists. The dominant belief in American Jewry in the first two-thirds of the 20th century was that while Jewishness should undergo some acculturation in order to fit comfortably into modern Western culture, it should survive as a separate identity. Indeed, most Jews believed that acculturation was precisely what would guarantee Jewish continuity. If Jewishness were not adjusted according to the norms of the larger society, they were convinced, it would be too culturally deviant for coming generations, which would consequently reject it altogether. Most American Jews understood, however, that intermarriage was the ultimate vehicle of assimilation. They could accept, if with some regret, whatever other changes their children made in Jewish self-expression. Exogamy, by contrast, was the decisive indicator of a failure to perpetuate Jewishness. Ironically, the changes in Jewish identity that were made in order to preserve Jewishness can now be seen as having engendered the kind of Jewish identity which is not inconsistent with intermarriage. It is for that reason that many young Jews came to view intermarriage as compatible with continued Jewish identity and as an essentially unremarkable act.

The Jewish identity of 20th century American Jewry can best be understood as an outgrowth of "Emancipation." The fundamental change in the Jews' status that is denoted by the term "Emancipation" occurred in central and western Europe at the turn of the 19th century. The French Revolution was, of course, the threshold event which offered Jews citizenship as individuals. For the preceding two millenia Jews had had corporate status as part of the Jewish community. The shift to individual political status, generally and for the Jews, made its way across Europe, unevenly, during the 19th and early 20th centuries.

To appreciate the cultural dynamics of Jews in contemporary America, however, it is necessary to remember that about nine-tenths of American Jewry is descended from the major wave of Jewish immigration to the United States from Eastern Europe between 1881 and 1924. In other words, most American Jews are only two or three generations removed from the kind of intensive and enclosed Jewish life that prevailed in the Pale of Settlement and other Jewish areas of eastern Europe. For the Jews who came to America in the 40 years around the turn of the 20th century, the trip was not a journey for political freedom and economic opportunity alone. It was, rather, a fundamental transition to a "new world" in every sense. For them, their voyage was the "Emancipation".

The marginal generation, those who carved out a new American identity (specifically, the children of older immigrants and the younger immigrants themselves), made two basic changes in Jewish identity. One concerned its scope; the other, its content. The marginal generation, welcoming America's offer of equal status, sought to specify the part of behavior that should appropriately be molded by Jewishness, leaving the rest to other elements in each person's overall identity. The most frequent position was that Jewishness was religion, defined narrowly as including some theological assertions, ethical injunctions, and ritual observances, none of which was thought (by most American Jews) to interfere with the larger society's normative expectations regarding occupational, political, recreational, social, or even familial patterns of behavior. For other Jews, Jewishness was manifested in a special enjoyment of Hebrew and/or Yiddish literature. Still others expressed Jewishness through philanthropic activity, giving their largest financial contributions to Jewish causes and devoting significant portions of their volunteer time to service in those causes. In another alternative, the focus of Jewish activity was participation in efforts to enhance intergroup amity and to diminish prejudice and discrimination. Finally, there were Jews whose Jewishness found expression in their choice of other Jews as friends, but whose activities with those friends had no particular Jewish content.

These five general approaches to the limitation of the scope of Jewishness were reflected in the organizations of American Jewry. Most Jewish organizations in the earlier part of the 20th century had closely defined purposes, and activity outside of an organization's prescribed scope was usually discouraged. Moreover, while Jews could, and did, belong to organizations in more than one category of Jewish self-expression, most Jews tended to express themselves primarily in one or another mode.

The second fundamental change which the marginal generation made in Jewish identity concerned the extent to which Jewishness is distinctive. During virtually all of Jewish history, Jews were different from their non-Jewish neighbors in ideologically important and personally profoud ways. American Jews in the early 20th century tried to convey the idea that being Jewish did not make them different from non-Jews in any significant way. There were several reasons for their effort. They wanted to reassure other Americans that the offer of equal status for the Jews was appropriate. More generally, the underlying ideology of intergroup relations activities during that period was that emphasis on the commonness of all humanity would encourage tolerance. It was believed that if people could accept that all human beings are fundamentally the same, then mutual respect and amity would grow. The basis of the approach was the combination of individualism and universalism that reached its apex at that time and which also found expression in a downplaying of other dimensions of identity such as race, ethnicity, and even family. (Now the emphasis is on cultural differences and the need to recognize and respect them, but that approach began to gain strength only in the 1960s.)

In the context of the early 20th century, then, it is not surprising that American Jews tended to articulate a Jewishness whose differentiating impact was restricted to detail. Most Jews preferred to emphasize what they had in common with non-Jews and to insist that what they had in common mattered much more than what set them apart. It is hard to assess the extent to which they believed their own claim, but the fact that they made it had its impact.

The children of the marginal generation were effectively the first "post-Emancipation" generation, and their Jewish identity differed in a number of far-reaching ways from that of previous generations of Jews. First, while all identities have both individual, and collective aspects, the relationship between those two aspects varies. Before Emancipation, a person's Jewishness was derived from his/her being part of the Jewish people. "Jewish" was understood primarily as the designation of a group, and a "Jew" was someone who belonged to that group. For American Jews

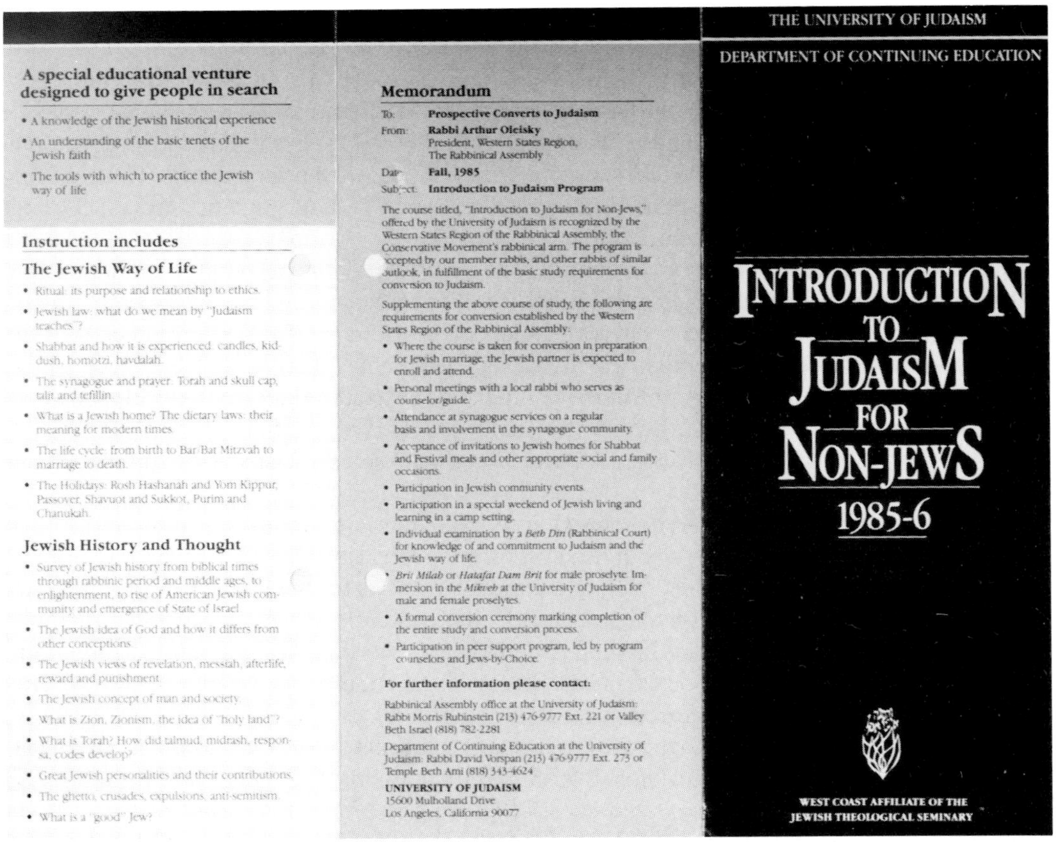

A special educational venture designed to give people in search

- A knowledge of the Jewish historical experience
- An understanding of the basic tenets of the Jewish faith
- The tools with which to practice the Jewish way of life

Instruction includes

The Jewish Way of Life

- Ritual: its purpose and relationship to ethics.
- Jewish law: what do we mean by "Judaism teaches"?
- Shabbat and how it is experienced: candles, kiddush, homotzi, havdalah.
- The synagogue and prayer: Torah and skull cap, talit and tefillin.
- What is a Jewish home? The dietary laws: their meaning for modern times.
- The life cycle: from birth to Bar/Bat Mitzvah to marriage to death.
- The Holidays: Rosh Hashanah and Yom Kippur, Passover, Shavuot and Sukkot, Purim and Chanukah.

Jewish History and Thought

- Survey of Jewish history from biblical times through rabbinic period and middle ages, to enlightenment, to rise of American Jewish community and emergence of State of Israel.
- The Jewish idea of God and how it differs from other conceptions.
- The Jewish views of revelation, messiah, afterlife, reward and punishment.
- The Jewish concept of man and society.
- What is Zion, Zionism, the idea of "holy land"?
- What is Torah? How did talmud, midrash, responsa, codes develop?
- Great Jewish personalities and their contributions.
- The ghetto, crusades, expulsions, anti-semitism.
- What is a "good" Jew?

Memorandum

To: **Prospective Converts to Judaism**
From: **Rabbi Arthur Oleisky**
President, Western States Region,
The Rabbinical Assembly
Date: **Fall, 1985**
Subject: **Introduction to Judaism Program**

The course titled, "Introduction to Judaism for Non-Jews," offered by the University of Judaism is recognized by the Western States Region of the Rabbinical Assembly, the Conservative Movement's rabbinical arm. The program is accepted by our member rabbis, and other rabbis of similar outlook, in fulfillment of the basic study requirements for conversion to Judaism.

Supplementing the above course of study, the following are requirements for conversion established by the Western States Region of the Rabbinical Assembly:

- Where the course is taken for conversion in preparation for Jewish marriage, the Jewish partner is expected to enroll and attend.
- Personal meetings with a local rabbi who serves as counselor/guide.
- Attendance at synagogue services on a regular basis and involvement in the synagogue community.
- Acceptance of invitations to Jewish homes for Shabbat and Festival meals and other appropriate social and family occasions.
- Participation in Jewish community events.
- Participation in a special weekend of Jewish living and learning in a camp setting.
- Individual examination by a *Beth Din* (Rabbinical Court) for knowledge of and commitment to Judaism and the Jewish way of life.
- *Brit Milah* or *Hatafat Dam Brit* for male proselyte. Immersion in the *Mikveh* at the University of Judaism for male and female proselytes.
- A formal conversion ceremony marking completion of the entire study and conversion process.
- Participation in peer support program, led by program counselors and Jews-by-Choice.

For further information please contact:

Rabbinical Assembly office at the University of Judaism: Rabbi Morris Rubinstein (213) 476-9777 Ext. 221 or Valley Beth Israel (818) 782-2281

Department of Continuing Education at the University of Judaism: Rabbi David Vorspan (213) 476-9777 Ext. 273 or Temple Beth Ami (818) 343-4624

UNIVERSITY OF JUDAISM
15600 Mulholland Drive
Los Angeles, California 90077

THE UNIVERSITY OF JUDAISM

DEPARTMENT OF CONTINUING EDUCATION

INTRODUCTION TO JUDAISM FOR NON-JEWS

1985-6

WEST COAST AFFILIATE OF THE JEWISH THEOLOGICAL SEMINARY

The University of Judaism in Los Angeles offers an introductory course in Judaism for non-Jews; if the course is taken for conversion towards Jewish marriage, the Jewish partner is expected to enroll and attend.

of the mid-20th century, "Jewish" described an individual first. Its application to organizations and communities was derived from the Jewishness of their members. In America's political ideology Jewishness was the private business of individuals and of no official public relevance. Jewish organizations were understood as nothing more than voluntary associations of Jews who made them and could use them for whatever ends they wished. During this time, the phrase "Jewish people" was almost always used as the plural of Jewish person rather than to denote an entity with its own inherent meaning.

Jewishness in mid-20th century America was most often conceptualized as one role among the many roles that every person plays. A typical man would see himself in many roles — husband, father, son, brother, neighbor, friend, lawyer, golfer, Democrat, Jew, Chicagoan, tenant, investor, contributor, and so forth. Each role had its own institutionalized set of relationships, its own mandated behaviors, and, consequently, its own well-delineated sphere of relevance. Pre-Emancipation Jews also had multiple roles, of course, even though they were less likely to say it that way. The difference is that Jewishness cannot properly be viewed as one of their roles. It would be more correct to see it as the substance with which all role behaviors were specified and evaluated. Another way of saying the same thing is that, for most Jews, Jewishness was transformed from a diffuse characteristic into a very specific one.

Something can be of specific relevance, yet still be very important. However, most post-Emancipation American Jews not only restricted the scope of Jewishness; they also greatly diminished its power. For the typical pre-Emancipation Jew, the fact that s/he was Jewish took priority over virtually every competing claim to time, energy, or normative prescription. By contrast, most American Jews in the mid-20th century made Jewish self-expression fit into the time, energy, and options left by almost the entire range of other claims — occupational, educational, recreational, civic, social.

The Jews growing up as a post-Emancipation generation heard from their parents that Jewishness did not make a Jew different in any major way. Young Jews learned that Judaism was one of the world's great monotheistic religions, and if there was pride to be found in the fact that it was the first, that, after all, was a matter of history and of little contemporary consequence. In Will Herberg's well-known formulation, a person could be a good American in any one of three ways, by being a Protestant, a Catholic, or a Jew. All were seen as acceptable variations on a common theme, and what mattered was the basic set of values and styles that constituted the American way of life, not the specific literature and symbolism with which the three religions were supposed to convey that way of life. In earlier periods, of course, Jewishness had made Jews different in many far-reaching and fundamental ways, as was fully recognized by both Jews and non-Jews.

Because Jewishness was so narrowly restricted and made subordinate to external contexts of interpretation, most post-Emancipation Jews lost the kind of familiarity with Jewish behavior that people have with their own culture. It is probably a fair rule of thumb that the more internalized an item of culture is, the fewer directions a person needs when performing it. Thus, the inability of most post-Emancipation Jews to carry out Jewish acts without guidance says much about their level of estrangement from the content of Jewishness.

This description does not apply to all Jews in the mid-1900s. Some purposely assimilated altogether; others maintained Jewish identities that were far more comprehensive, primary, distinguishing, internalized, and rooted in Jewish peoplehood past and present. The vast middle group, however, molded a Jewish identity which, though generally positive, was not compelling. Although the Holocaust and the establishment of the State of Israel certainly affected Jewish identity, they did not alter its basic structure of place in the lives of most American Jews.

The key point is that the kind of Jewish identity described here is not a barrier to intermarriage, nor is intermarriage incompatible with that kind of Jewish identity. America is an open society, and the American ethos places overwhelming importance on individual choice in most things. While some group-based hurdles to individual choice remain, marriage across religious and ethnic lines is not discouraged. Rather, even in a period which has for the last two or three decades seen increasing emphasis placed on religion and on ethnic identity, interreligious and interethnic marriages are likely to be viewed as helping to demonstrate the compatibility of disparate traditions and the possibility of amity, even of love, across lines. Other factors encouraging intermarriage are improvement in the socioeconomic standing of Jews and increased acceptance of Jews as friends and as potential marriage partners. As a result, most Jews have circles of colleagues, classmates, and friends that include non-Jewish peers. Inevitably, these relationships often lead to romance.

When subjective feelings of romance begin to grow between two people, they make judgments about whether their differences are numerous enough, large enough, or profound enough to be a barrier to marriage. If not, then the differences become the issues over which the compromises that are part of any marriage are worked out. Otherwise, one party or the other will end the relationship.

If Jewishness is seen to consist of some rather vague ideas about God's existence and providence, a number of almost universally endorsed ethical principles, two or three holiday dinners a year, a Ḥanukkah lamp in the house in December, brief attendance at synagogue services once or twice a year, the obligation to give some emphasis to Jewish causes among one's charitable donations, a somewhat higher and more consistent level of political support for Israel than other pro-Israel Americans offer, a political stance generally in the "liberal" camp, and pride in the Jewish achievements of the past, then Jewishness is compatible with intermarriage. No loving non-Jewish spouse is likely to find these behaviors and attitudes objectionable, and none of them requires the kind of joint participation by a spouse that a non-Jew cannot easily and readily provide. If we add some Jewish art and artifacts to the decorations of the home, a few hours of Jewish education for one's children for a few years, and some ceremonial recognition that those children are (at least "partly") Jewish, which is how ritual circumcision and Bar or Bat Mitzvah are sometimes conceptualized, exogamy still need not be an impediment to continued Jewishness. It is possible for a Jew to be proud of his/her Jewishness, enjoy it, and consider it "important" and yet give it a form which is not pervasive enough and a content which is not distinguishing enough to interfere with a satisfying intermarriage. By contrast, when Jewishness orders one's priorities, locates a person in history and society, provides basic goals and norms, furnishes the cultural materials for the expression of "self," and marks out life's rhythm, then marriage to a non-Jewish spouse is inconceivable without either a total transformation of self or a severe narrowing of the normal marital relationship.

The intermarriage rate has risen as it has, not because Jews want to escape their Jewishness, but because they see intermarriage as quite compatible with their Jewishness. As Marshall Sklare explained, young Jews who marry non-Jews are likely to see themselves not as intermarrying, but merely as marrying.

In another sense, however, intermarriage is not that simple. Resistance is likely to arise from several quarters. Parents and other relatives, synagogues and rabbis, and Jewish communal institutions can all be expected to express some level of opposition to intermarriage. The desire to include Jewish elements in the wedding ceremony or to raise children as Jews can elicit concern from the non-Jewish partner and/or his/her family. The many compromises that need to be made can be harder to work out than was anticipated. Normally suppressed stereotypes and resentments can emerge. Perhaps most indicative of the current mood regarding exogamy is the appearance in the last decade of several books of advice on how to carry out a successful intermarriage.

These books usually deal with reactions of parents and other relatives, planning the wedding ceremony, the raising of children, and ways of handling Jewish and Christian institutions. While some set forth the advantages of religious homogeneity and clarity in the home, others offer guidance on how to maintain active links to both traditions.

The responses of the organized Jewish community to intermarriage fall into two broad categories — opposition and outreach. As the 1990 CJF study shows, many Jews do not oppose intermarriage at all. Only 22% of the respondents who were born Jews and list Judaism as their religion said that they would oppose the marriage of their child to a non-Jew. The corresponding statistic for secular Jews is 4%. Among those Jews who do oppose intermarriage, either in general or in specific cases when they arise, there are several positions about what form opposition should take. Some Jews, though decreasing in number, still break all relationships with relatives and friends who marry non-Jews. Others reduce their relationships with people in mixed marriages, but do not sever them altogether. Yet others express opposition to intermarriage and try, with varying degrees of determination, to urge the Jewish partner to withdraw from the planned marriage or to bring about the conversion of the non-Jewish partner, but accept the marriage once it is a *fait accompli.*

Advertisement by a synagogue conducting only marriages in which both partners are Jewish.

Most Jewish institutions take the position that intermarriage should be discouraged but the intermarried should not be rejected. While that position has a tone that seems resonant with both Jewish principle and the ideology of individual choice and universal human concern, it is hard to specify what coherent attitudes or concrete behaviors it implies.

Just as opposition takes many forms, so does outreach, and the two modes of response are usually in interplay with each other. Sometimes the effort to bring the non-Jewish partner to convert is explicit. Sometimes it is offered as one option. A frequently expressed view is that, where conversion does not seem immediately likely, it is important to maintain linkage to and positive feelings about the Jewish community in the hope that conversion may eventually ensue and that, even if it does not, there will be more readiness to transmit some Jewish identity to the children and a positive feeling toward the Jewish community by the children. In general, the more liberal the religious movement, the greater its emphasis on outreach relative to opposition as the proper response to intermarriage.

The religious movements deal with intermarriage and its consequences at four specific points. First, rabbis are often asked to officiate or co-officiate at intermarriages. The Orthodox and Conservative rabbinates refuse to participate in intermarriages. The Reform movement officially leaves the decision about participating in intermarriages to its individual rabbis, who are divided on this issue. Many liberal rabbis who will not take part in intermarriages themselves will, nevertheless, counsel interreligious couples or refer them to colleagues willing to be available.

The second issue that arises concerns the status of the children of intermarriage and of converts. Orthodoxy, following *halakhah*, defines Jewishness as acquired by being born to a Jewish mother or through a conversion that meets the standards of traditional Jewish law. Since the Reform movement does not adhere to traditional Jewish law in conversions and Conservative rabbis are not uniformly careful in applying Jewish law, Orthodoxy generally does not accept conversions under non-Orthodox auspices. those Conservative rabbis who do adhere to traditional law have similar problems with Reform conversions, but the Conservative movement's emphasis on pluralism makes it harder for them to be publicly explicit on this matter. The Reform movement's formal adoption of the principle of patrilineal descent, which it had practiced quietly for decades before declaring it officially, complicated the issue. By defining Jews differently from traditional Jewish law, it created a category of people who are Jewish by the standards of some Jews and not Jewish by the standards of others. Although there have long been such people, their number is growing and the resolution on patrilineality made the controversy over their status and the potential difficulty of their situation more severe. The Reform rabbinate decided that its action was justified, nonetheless, as a way to compensate for demographic decline by broadening the definition of Jewry and by extending a welcome and a sense of legitimacy to people who, it felt, would otherwise most likely be lost to the Jewish community. The traditional view is that, since those people are not Jews, they are lost in any case.

The third specific issue with which synagogues must deal is the participation of non-Jewish spouses in synagogue activities. Membership in synagogues is normally a family matter, and members can, of course, hold positions of leadership and play a number of roles in the ritual. Many intermarried Jews wish to join synagogues, and many synagogues, for outreach and other reasons, are willing, even eager, to welcome interreligious families. The consequence is that synagogues, especially but not only the more liberal ones, must make decisions about which roles can be played in leadership and in ritual by intermarried members and by their non-Jewish spouses.

Admission of children of intermarried couples to religious school, especially when those children are not Jewish, also poses difficulties. Their parents may want to enroll them in order to make Jewishness an option or simply to give them some information about part of their family

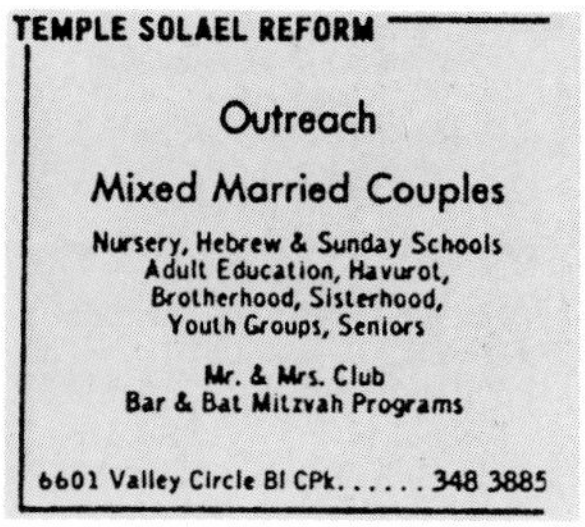

A response to intermarriage — welcoming of mixed couples.

background. However, the curricular challenges of simultaneously teaching children from Jewish homes and from mixed homes are formidable.

Other organizations in the Jewish community must also delineate which roles, as participants and as leaders, can appropriately be played by intermarried Jews and, what is more difficult, by their non-Jewish spouses. Jewish organizations which cut across "movement" lines also have the problem that their members do not agree on which other members are Jewish.

Beyond the concerns about the status and roles of individual members, there is the problem of program. It cannot be entirely comfortable for a Jewish organization to deliberate about and then adopt a program whose goal is to discourage intermarriage when a not insubstantial proportion of its members and leaders are themselves intermarried or have accepted intermarriage among their children.

There is currently controversy over the proper balance between opposition and outreach as responses to intermarriage. Advocates of opposition argue that efforts must be made to strengthen a more comprehensive, distinctive, and rewarding Jewish identity in Jews and that, in the meantime, Jewish institutions and organizations should unambiguously convey Judaism's position that only that kind of identity, in individuals and embodied in family life, is authentic and viable. Their acceptance of outreach is limited to attempts to bring non-Jewish spouses and prospective spouses to conversion. Advocates of outreach, by contrast, usually despair of changing the overall character of Jewish identity in America and predict that the intermarriage rate will not decline significantly as a result of any Jewish policy or program. Their approach to assuring Jewish continuity, therefore, rests on encouraging intermarried families to maintain positive links to the Jewish community and on increasing the number of people who are considered Jews by expanding the lines of Jewish descent and broadening the criteria and methods by which people can be treated as Jews-by-choice. What balance between these two modes of response will ultimately be struck, and with what consequences, remains to be seen.

A Fading Heritage: The Fate of Central and Southern European Synagogues

Rivka and Ben-Zion Dorfman

The original objective of our first field trip to Italy in 1987 was to look for Jewish sites during a vacation, in the custom of Jewish tourists. In Parma we met a young Israeli medical student who told us of the many undisturbed, unfamiliar synagogues in Piedmont, and we unhesitatingly changed our itinerary in that direction. Arriving in the regional capital, Turin, on the eve of Israel's Independence Day, when the Jewish community assembled to celebrate in noisy Israeli style, we met people who enabled us to visit many synagogues of the province where there were no resident Jews.

The architecture and decorations of these buildings were such a revelation to us that we felt challenged to record them in depth before time and urban renewal might take their toll. From that time on we have compulsively been engaged in synagogue art documentation.

We returned to Italy for a longer period in the following summer and made an intensive synagogue circuit from Turin to Trieste, revisiting important locations, and adding new synagogues to our list. A year later we discovered the rich Jewish heritage in Hungary and Czechoslovakia. With two additional journeys of more than four months each, we were able to work at almost all of the important surviving synagogues in these countries, and to visit many of the Jewish sites of Greece, Austria, and Yugoslavia as well.

In all, we have documented about 350 synagogues in almost as many localities. Often, we also photographed the Jewish quarter, school, rabbi's house, cemetery, or other aspect of the former Jewish presence. Our archive presently contains about 20,000 photographs, over 120 hours of taped interviews, 25 hours of video record, and many relevant documents from local and regional archives and museums.

It was not emotionally easy to wander from place to place in search of Jewish communal relics in regions of formerly dense Jewish settlement. Not much is left of the once ubiquitous Jewish presence in central Europe, but small Jewish populations carry on in the capitals where they are only partially organized and are touched by assimilationist tendencies. In our concern to keep alive the detailed memory of the many European Jewish communities that no longer exist, the art and architecture of the synagogues become relevant to an appreciation of the prewar milieu in which the Jews once thrived and were an influential factor. Paradoxically, we met researchers in a number of places, mostly non-Jews, who were dedicated to studying Jewish customs, religion, history, and physical remnants of former Jewish presence, as well as others who worked to preserve synagogues or cemeteries.

Wherever the synagogue building still stands it may now be the sole reminder, other than an overgrown cemetery, of a historic Jewish settlement. Real property of the Jewish communities destroyed in the Holocaust was left ownerless, at the mercy of local populations. Houses and personal property were promptly seized by aggressive neighbors. Factories and workshops were reorganized under ad hoc non-Jewish management that devolved into ownership. Community buildings, such as rabbis' residences, or village synagogues that were easily convertible to dwellings, were adapted with alacrity for living quarters.

The post-Emancipation synagogues presented problems of a different scale. These were ordinarily large public buildings with high ceilings, even in the small towns, and they usually contained a women's gallery on an upper level, open to the prayer hall below. Their exploitation for business or public use when the Jews were gone may have been determined by commercial or political authorities whose perspectives were seldom consistent with preservation of the buildings. The process of synagogue destruction, viciously begun by the Nazis, continued as mindless attrition under the communist postwar regimes of eastern Europe. At Bratislava and Hlohevec in western Slovakia, historic synagogues were demolished over tumultuous objection to make way for road bridges. In the east Slovakian cities, Humenne and Michalovce, relatively modern synagogue buildings were bulldozed as unfit neighbors when Communist Party headquarters were erected in their central-city vicinities. The grand Neolog synagogue at Mako, Hungary, was likewise destroyed under a communist regime.

Many synagogues that escaped destruction over the decades were adapted for use as churches, storerooms, workshops, and less often, as museums and archives. Others were converted to bakeries, gymnasiums, fire stations, a hairdressing salon, flower shop, police station, driving school and so forth — or else they stand empty and deteriorating, if not actually in ruin.

Ironically, the situation may worsen as the eastern European countries embrace democracy, if, indeed, that is how they will go. The dynamics of political change are accompanied by social unrest and outbursts of local patriotism, xenophobia and blatant anti-Semitism. The physical state of towns and cities is undergoing rapid alterations that will speed up as revisions in the economic order take hold. Most synagogues are literally in the middle of the urban turmoil because they occupy choice locations in or near the old centers of the cities. Previously only moderately secure in the stagnant communist reign, they are now in danger of accelerated vandalism or demolition under the new dynamism.

The few decimated Jewish communities that were revived outside of the capital cities after the war were not always able to keep possession of their former synagogue buildings. Existing communities are still too small to use more than the *bet ha-midrash* (study room) section for religious services or for social events, and they seldom have a source of money with which to maintain the large, prestigious synagogues. A positive example, however is to be seen in Pecs and in Szeged, Hungary, where the synagogues are maintained by the Jews as public museums, while their own assembly needs are provided for in smaller places nearby. Another example is from Subotica, Serbia, where the Jewish community retained the privilege of Jewish use of its illustrious Art Nouveau synagogue while ceding it to the city. The municipality, in turn, was committed to renovate the building in adherence to its original design and to maintain it for cultural enjoyment by the general public.

Disposition of synagogues where there are no Jews varies widely among the countries and the localities. Hungary was among the first to take advantage of the possible social benefit of the ownerless synagogue buildings. A number of them were renovated to house concert halls, libraries, art galleries, television house in Obuda, or, as at Kecskemet, a congress hall. A memorial tablet acknowledging the Jewish origin of the building and the destruction of the local Jewish community was typical.

Czechoslovakia was slower to appreciate the potential public value of the synagogues, but many of the buildings, storerooms until recently, are now under the protection of laws for the preservation of historic sites. With an eye to the growing tourist traffic, municipal officials increasingly plan to restore synagogues for cultural use, and authenticity is now perceived as an asset. Moreover, Czechoslovakia was prompt to adopt a policy of property restitution soon after the "velvet revolution" of 1989. Some synagogues and other real estate have already been restored under this provision to the Jewish community, as represented in the capitals, Prague, Brno, and Bratislava, and additional claims are pending.

At Eisenstadt, Austria, where there are no Jews, a synagogue in a former home is part of an elaborate Jewish museum. In other parts of Burgenland synagogues have been modified beyond recognition to fire stations or municipal offices, whereas an institute for research on the Jewish presence in Austria occupies a well-restored synagogue building in St. Polten. There are two major synagogues in Jewish use in Vienna and a few smaller, informal ones.

Synagogues in Italian localities without Jews have often remained the property of Jewish individuals who now reside in the large cities. The Jews of Greece have also demonstrated an amazing tenacity. Their communities are functioning despite small numbers, and they retain ownership, if not always use, of their old, traditional synagogues.

Photos by Rivka and Ben-Zion Dorfman unless noted otherwise.

Jewish property

Makó, Hungary (1870, neo-Moresque). Orthodox synagogue, in poor condition, still in occasional use by visiting Jews. The elegant Neolog synagogue, built in 1904 by Lipot Baumhorn nearby on the same street, was destroyed during communist rule in the 1960s.

Szeged, Hungary (1903, Late Eclectic, Lipót Baumhorn, architect). Synagogue exterior. One of the finest synagogues of Europe, it is operated by the Jewish community as a public museum since it was renovated, about 1988.

Szeged (1903). Synagogue interior, resplendent in lavish architectural embellishment with elaborate frescoed inscriptions and naturalistic motifs.

Jánoshalma, Hungary (1850). Synagogue interior, to the women's gallery. The synagogue is still in Jewish ownership, but is not used, except for annual memorial services in June. Dusty leaves of dried up *lulav* still decorate the reader's stand.

Bardejov, Slovakia (1927, neo-Gothic). Ark of the relatively recent synagogue, Klaus Bikur Cholim. It is still attended and maintained by one of only two Jews in Bardejov, Max Spira.

Pilsen, Bohemia (1892, neo-Moresque). View to the ark and poetically inscribed reader's platform in the Neolog synagogue, one of three that survive in Pilsen. Situated on a major street, the synagogue is the second largest in Eastern Europe, and quite exceptionally retains its original furniture. It is owned by the small Jewish community, which lacks the funds to renovate the synagogue to Jewish museum status.

Massimo del Sette, synagogue caretaker in Biella, Italy, reading an old document kept in the synagogue which gives an accounting of expenses incurred in celebrating the emancipation of the Jews in 1848 by King Carlo Alberto of Piedmont. The sum of L71.40 included wine, candles, salami, printing and invitations, flags and lights.

Dubrovnik, Croatia (1532, Medieval, Baroque restoration). View of the reader's platform and arched support partition. The synagogue is kept by the Jewish community as a public museum. The Jewish quarter nestles in the heart of ancient Dubrovnik, in the steep alleys that slope down to the picturesque port. This area suffered heavy naval shelling in 1991.

Subotica, Serbia (1901, Art Nouveau, Marczel Komor and Dezso Jakab, architects). Over the portal: "This is the gateway to the Lord, the righteous shall enter therein" (Psalms 118:20). The synagogue was turned into a theater but is due to be restored by the city.

Deserted

Kőszeg, Hungary (1858, neo-Classical-Romantic). View of the synagogue from above. The building is round, with three apses and an entrance flanked by square towers.

Kőszeg, Hungary. Women's gallery and part of the dome.

Mateszalka, Hungary (1857, neo-Classical). Ceiling decoration. The synagogue is owned by a Jewish community too small to use it and without the means to repair it.

Pápa, Hungary (1845, neo-Romanesque). Interior, main hall and galleries. The synagogue dominates a large former Jewish quarter of several streets, towering over the old one-story residences in an area undergoing active urban renewal, and now stands empty.

Above: Vercelli, Italy (1878, neo-Moresque, Giuseppi Locarno, architect). View to the ark through a missing pane in the stained glass window. Unused since World War II, the Jewish-owned synagogue is in structurally poor condition.

Above left: Lučenec, Slovakia (1925, neo-Moresque, Lipót Baumhorn, architect). The north facade. The building has been owned by the municipality for many years, yet, despite recognition as one of the architecturally outstanding buildings in Lučenec, it remained unprotected and has been heavily vandalized. The small Jewish congregation of Lučenec uses a small prayer room elsewhere.

Left: Lučenec, Slovakia. View of the interior, with open floor of the women's gallery at the left.

Veria, Greece (16th c.). Facade and portal in the old Jewish quarter. The synagogue is unused but is carefully kept by the small Jewish community.

Veria, Greece. Interior, toward the ark, set into a niche behind a rise of several steps. The tiny schoolroom consisted of one row of chairs under the women's gallery off to the right.

Březnice, Bohemia. Interior to the ark. The vaulted ceiling under a hip roof is typical of the period. Above the ark, the inscription: "Thou shalt love thy neighbor as thyself" (Leviticus 19:18).

Březnice, Bohemia (1725, rural Baroque). The portal, with its inscription (Psalm 118:19). The synagogue stands in the middle of a large open square, surrounded by what was once the Jewish ghetto on all sides. Plans for renovation are held in abeyance for lack of funds.

Ruined or demolished

Szentes, Hungary (1870, neo-Romanesque). View of the synagogue. Roof and internal floors have been removed, the debris cleaned out, and the bare walls stand waiting. Restoration might be attempted if money for the purpose were available.

České Budějovice, Bohemia. (1888, neo-Gothic, Max Fleischer, architect). An old postcard shows the synagogue, which was the architectural pride of the city. It was designed in faithful adherence to the Gothic style, including the flying buttresses.

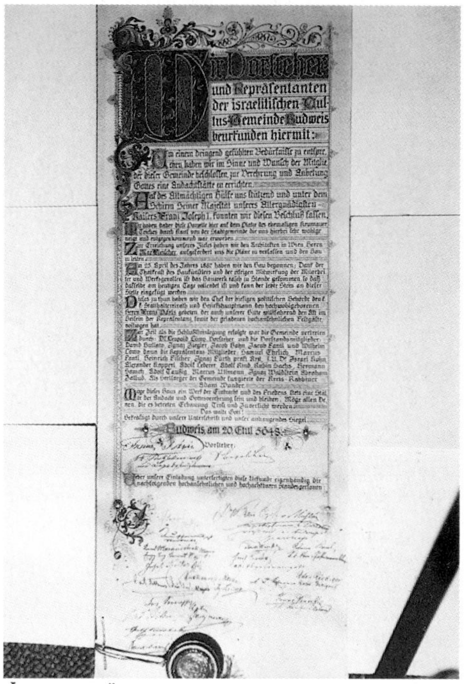
Die Vorsteher
und Repräsentanten
der israelitischen Cul-
tus-Gemeinde Budweis
beurkunden hiermit:

Um einem dringend gefühlten Bedürfnisse zu entsprechen, haben wir im Sinne und Wunsch der Mitglieder dieser Gemeinde beschlossen, zur Verehrung und Anbetung Gottes eine Andachtsstätte zu errichten.

Auf des Allmächtigen Hülfe uns stützend und unter dem Schirm Seiner Majestät unseres Allergnädigsten Kaisers Franz Joseph I. konnten wir diesen Beschluß fassen.

Das walte Gott!

Budweis, am 20. Elul 5648.

České Budějovice. The original deed, signed by Emperor Franz Josef on June 8, 1888, granting permission to the Jewish community to build a synagogue in České Budějovice. The deed is now in the municipal museum.

České Budějovice. Facing the ark, in the interior of the synagogue. The Nazis destroyed the building on June 5, 1942, refusing all appeals to preserve it for use as a municipal museum. Photo: Municipal Archive, České Budějovice.

Trnava, Slovakia (1891, neo-Moresque). The huge niche of the ark in the "Status-quo" synagogue. Restoration of this synagogue, initially begun about 20 years ago, was stopped for lack of money, and the building now stands open, brutally vandalized.

Trnava, Slovakia. Moshe Glück, of nearby Hlohevec, at the entrance to the ruined synagogue.

České Budějovice. The region where the ark stood, soon after the synagogue was dynamited. Photo: Municipal Archive, České Budějovice.

Klagenfurt, Austria. A marble monument on the site of the local synagogue, destroyed on *Kristallnacht,* November 9, 1938. It also memorializes the Jewish community of Klagenfort, deported and murdered by the Nazis.

Berettyóujfalu, Hungary (late 19th c.). Walls and ark niche of former synagogue, now a metal workshop.

Hartmanice, Bohemia (c.1850). Interior view of the building. The originally arched windows were modified at some time to rectangular shape, presumably to negate their synagogue origin when secular use was commenced. Nevertheless, it has been abandoned even as a carpentry shop. There is renewed interest in its restoration as a Jewish museum.

In commercial use

Halič, Slovakia (mid 19th c.). Facade. Built in the old technique of mixed brick and stone under the plaster, it is still an imposing structure in this tiny village and is now used to store building materials (photo to the right).

Strážnice, Moravia (rebuilt from much older beginnings after 1869, neo-Romanesque, and renewed again in 1906). Part of the ceiling and the makeshift floor, built at mid-height of the prayer hall to increase furniture storage capacity.

Bonyhád, Hungary (1795, Lvov four-pillared style). The four-pillared reader's platform. The main hall is used for storage of paper products, a shoe factory utilizes the women's gallery, and the space underneath serves an agricultural supply house for storage of fertilizer and other bulk commodities.

Bardejov, Slovakia (1830, neo-Classical). The women's gallery in the older of two synagogues in Bardejov. This one is part of a large former Jewish compound that includes several buildings, all devoted to building construction materials. The synagogue, which has been formally protected as an historic site since June 1991, is used to store plumbing supplies and appliances.

Úštěk, Bohemia (1794, probably rebuilt since, ca. 1900, neo Classical). Interior of the synagogue, now used as a pen for a ferocious dog, with appropriate sign "Pozor pes" "Beware the dog."

Jičín, Bohemia (earlier than 1840, neo-Classical-Baroque). City cultural director helps storeroom personnel to clear sacks of tea and of orange peels from the vicinity of the reader's platform and the ark so that the Dorfmans could photograph them. The city would like to restore the synagogue-- if the money were found.

Divišov, Bohemia. Interior of the synagogue, much modified.

Divišov, Bohemia (mid-19th c., Empire). Facade. The building has been in use as a beauty salon, "Kadernictví," since the late 1950s.

As Churches

Humpolec, Bohemia (mid-18th c., Baroque, renovated 1870). Clean line of the ark wall, supporting the Hussite cross.

Kutná Hora, Bohemia (1902, neo-Classical). Facade of the synagogue, as a Hussite church. The stone "tablets of the law," now resting quietly on the platform of the back entrance, have been replaced by the Hussite church symbol - the chalice and the cross.

Osijek, Serbia. The ark, retained and renovated by the Pentecostalist church. In the battles at Osijek, 1991, the synagogue was damaged and was temporarily abandoned for safety by the church and school.

Milevsko, Bohemia (1919, neo-Classical-Cubist, Strilek, architect). The synagogue exterior, with the chalice and cross of the Hussite church added to the unique Cubist tympanum.

Milevsko, Bohemia. The marble ark, preserved behind a screen-wall erected by the church on the outer edge of the reader's platform.

Humpolec, Bohemia. Vignette of a prayer inscription, typical of the period, in the northeast corner. It is one of several that were preserved in adapting this synagogue to church use. The rabbi's house, part of the same building, houses church personnel.

Prostějov, Moravia (1904, was Art Nouveau). The cross that replaces the ark in the south wall of the Neolog synagogue. The four pillar style still divides the ceiling into nine arched bays, but the pillars are far from the center and no longer serve to define the reader's platform area. The facade was radically modified.

Slovenské Nové Masto, Slovakia (early 19th c., Romantic). Facade. Now Catholic, it is the only synagogue of Slovakia converted to a church.

Secular, Cultural Use

Volyně, Bohemia (1849, neo-Classical). Facade. The stucco decorations in the tympanum, lions guarding a heraldic shield containing a clock and an unusual poetic dedication, were preserved when the building became a cinema (photo to the right).

Subotica, Serbia (1901, Art Nouveau, Marczel Komor and Dezső Jacob, architects). Interior, toward the ark. The congregation of Subotica accepted the plans for this temple from that of Szeged. With minor adaptation for a stage, this synagogue served for a long time as a theater. In 1990 the Jewish community ceded its ownership to the city in exchange for renovation to cultural use and availability for Jewish functions.

Baja, Hungary (1846, neo-Classical). Interior toward the women's gallery. Reverently adapted as a library, the restoration was done with careful regard to preservation of the original. The painted baldacchino around the ark was often used as a decorative element, but the birds gripping its folds are distinctive to Baja.

Zalaegerszeg, Hungary (1903, neo-Moresque). Twin-towered facade. In the conversion of the synagogue to a concert hall, the decorative exterior red accents and the dressing-room annex at the rear were added.

Zalaegerszeg, Hungary. The interior as a concert hall. The women's gallery above serves as an art gallery.

Trenčín, Slovakia (1913, proto-Modern, Oriental, R. Schneiber, architect). Facade. Although this property was formally restituted to the Jewish community, an agreement extends its use as an art gallery for another ten years. The small Jewish community of Trencin uses the *bet ha-midrash* on the side.

Trenčín, Slovakia. Interior of the art gallery. The chandelier and dome decor retain the original design.

Hradec Králové, Bohemia (1905, Art Nouveau, V. Weinzettel, architect). The impressive synagogue structure dominating a major intersection in the heart of the city. The interior was completely modified to serve as a science library, but on the outside oriental decorative elements, the sculpted palmettes and the two-tiered roof pagoda still adorn the facade.

Apostag, Hungary (1842, neo-Classical-Lvov four-pillared style). Interior, with reader's platform and ark. Well restored by the voluntary effort of the residents in this miniscule town, it was awarded the Europa Nostra prize for authentic restoration. With 48 comfortable seats, the prayer hall serves as wedding salon and concert chamber, and the gallery is an elegant library. Near the ark two museum cabinets display Jewish artifacts and memorabilia of local Jews, while the lobby boasts an array of pictures of World War II Hungarian heroes. It has become an attraction for visiting tourist groups and schoolchildren.

Mikulov, Moravia (1550, Renaissance, renovated 1723). The newly restored marble columns, ceiling, and stucco decorations.

Mikulov, Moravia. A flute and piano concert. After eleven years of restoration activity, the first concert in the hall, with repertoire, Israeli and Theresientadt-composed music was presented in by Israeli artists, Wendy Eisler-Kashy, flute, and pianist Alan Sternfeld. Photo: Dobromila Brichtova, curator of the municipal museum, Mikulov.

In restoration

Right: Liptovský Mikuláš, Slovakia (1842, neo-Classical, restored by Lipot Baumhorn after a fire, in 1906). Facade. The synagogue was long used as a storeroom, but money is being raised for its elaborate restoration to cultural use - concert and theater.

Right middle: Kunszentmárton, Hungary (1912, Secessionist, Jozsef Doborszky, architect). Facade. Adapted for use as a storeroom for a carpentry shop, but emptied now in the hope of eventual restoration. Some roof repairs have been made.

Right bottom: Liptovský Mikuláš, Slovakia. Interior, toward the ark. The cloth that descends from above the ark was part of the decor for a recent benefit concert. On it are written in memoriam the names of some of the Jews deported from Liptovský Mikuláš and murdered in the Holocaust. The balustrade of the reader's platform was demolished by vandalism in recent years.

Bottom: Hódmezővásárhely, Hungary (1856, Romantic, renovated in 1906 by Muller Gyula). Facade, partly restored, in 1990. The only entry is from the steps in the back, literally through the back of the *aron*. Restoration has been going on for several years, with closer attention to authenticity of the exterior than of the interior.

Above: Vrbové, Slovakia. Interior, the impressively detailed ceiling.

Right above: Győr, Hungary (1866, neo-Moresque, Benko Károly, architect). Facade. Like many others, this synagogue was a storeroom during most of the period of communist rule in Hungary. Restoration was begun at one of the two school/office wings, which was made into a music school. More recently, restoration of the second wing for expansion of the music school was completed, and restoration of the synagogue itself was begun.

Right middle: Vrbové, Slovakia (1882, neo-Moresque). Facade. Restoration of the exterior was almost complete in 1991, but work on the interior had not yet begun. A few Jewish families still live in Vrbove.

Right: Boskovice, Moravia (1698, Baroque, renovated 1836, Neo-Gothic, and again during the 1930s). The ark, shorn of its ornaments. Real restoration of this synagogue by the municipality had to wait until after the "velvet revolution" of November 1989. One of the difficulties in restoring it is that much of the walls and arches were covered with plaster painted prayer inscriptions that are particularly difficult and expensive to restore.

Novi Sad, Serbia (1906, Eclectic, Lipót Baumhorn, architect). Interior of the dome. The Jewish architect, Lipót Baumhorn, designed 24 synagogues that were built. In his later work, as here at Novi Sad, he regularly used the symbol of the tablets within the capitals of columns.

Novi Sad, Serbia. Interior, from the women's gallery. By the summer of 1991, work on the synagogue, sponsored by the municipality, was approaching completion. Its brown and white facade was freshly cleaned and painted, and the interior was in the last stages of restoration.

Cemeteries

Mikulov, Moravia. Moses, son of Joseph Austerlitz, 1770. Poetic inscription describes his many devotional qualities.

Kobersdorf, Austria. David Tzevi Reininger, of the house of Levi, 1889, "who knocked on the doors of the synagogue twice daily...and worshiped his Creator without remiss...," dying in venerable old age.

Left: Sarajevo, Bosnia, Monument to 900 Jewish victims of the Nazis, whose remains were buried here in a common grave. Serbian forces shelled the city massively from this hill during the Yugoslav civil war 1992-1993.

Left bottom: Sarajevo, Bosnia. Old section of Jewish cemetery, with typical tent shaped gravestones, reminiscent of small sarcophagi.

Bottom: Heřmanův Meštec, Moravia. General view of the cemetery, with unusual inclined shape of gravestones.

Pečovska Nová Vés, Slovakia. Rabbi Naphtali Sofer and his wife traveled from Brooklyn, N.Y., to visit the grave of his uncle in the hilltop cemetery of this tiny village.

Tokaj, Hungary. Zissel Moshkowitz, 1885, "...an important yet humble woman." A sculpted urn on the stone face is filled with drooping foliage - an iconographic symbol of death. The cemetery is cleaned and maintained by Lőwy Lajos, one of the few remaining Jews in the town.

Genoa, Italy. General view of the Jewish section of the Staglieno cemetery.

Genoa, Italy. The Jewish section of the Staglieno cemetery. Ornate marble sarcophagus decorated with symbolic jugs overflowing with water, and a *menorah.*

Last (or nearly last) Jew

Jirí Mahler of Světlá nad Sázavou, Bohemia, is proud of his relation to the composer, Gustav Mahler.

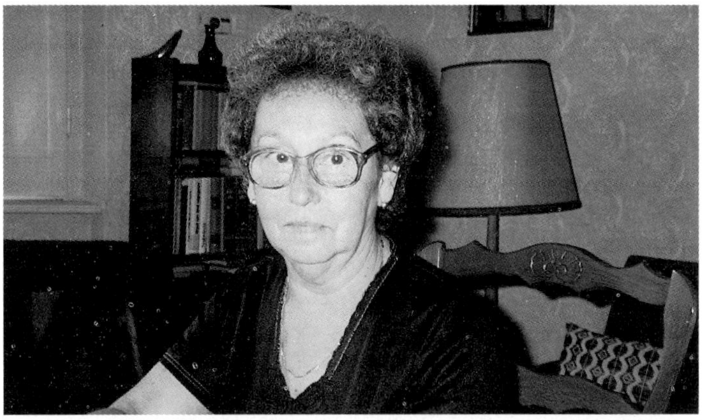

Dr. Agnes Nádas, Kunszentmárton, Hungary was a member of Ha-Shomer Ḥa-Ẓa'ir in her youth. She left *hakhsharah* for medical school and completed a full career as a gynecologist. Today, "I meet my Jews only in the cemetery."

Imre Samosné is the widow of a former head of the congregation of Jánoshalma, Hungary. She retains access to the synagogue and shows it to visitors, welcoming contributions.

Helena Vankatová, Ivancicé, Moravia.

Mrs. Rosenberg and son, in Karcag, Hungary, were preparing for a bar mitzvah ceremony. They complained bitterly that the synagogue windows were repeatedly broken by stone-throwers, and that the cost of a rabbi from Budapest for the bar-mitzvah was prohibitive.

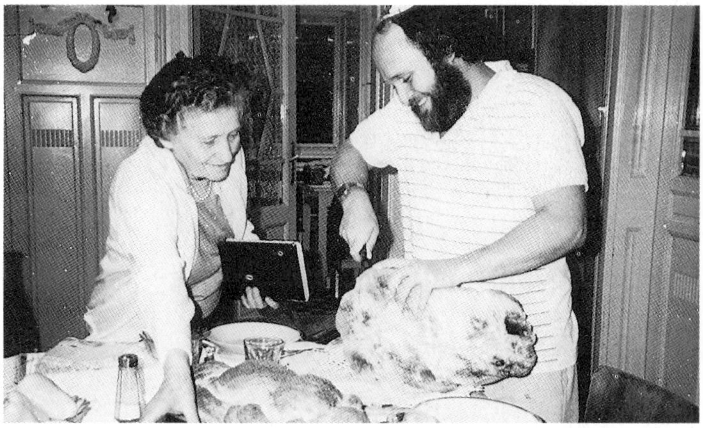

Peter Feldmaijer and his mother, in Nagykőrös, Hungary. They represent a rare instance of almost isolated Jews who maintain a full Jewish family life of three generations in three branches. Peter, a lawyer, devoted several years, together with his sister, Dr. Livia Feldmaijer Albane, also a lawyer, to assembling information about Jewish victims of the Holocaust in Hungary. He has become the head of the Hungarian Jewish community.

Budai Gyulané, Makó, Hungary. Supported largely by former Makó Jews who come to visit the cemetery and the synagogue, she explains her biding in Makó as loyalty to the visitors.

Josef Roth of Golčův-Jeníkov, Bohemia, had not met a Jew in many years until the visit of the Dorfmans.

Árpád Stern, and his wife, Trnava, Slovakia.

Moise Eliasaf with the key to the ancient synagogue in Ioannina, Greece.

Dr. Marco Levi, Mondoví, Italy. Long retired, Dr. Levi, alone, maintains the synagogue and a home that is distinctly Jewish. He has "planted" a grove of trees in Israel in memory of the Jews of Mondoví.

Above: Lucia Sulam is the synagogue caretaker in Rhodes, Greece.

Left, above: Max Spira of Bardejov, Slovakia supports himself as a cantor and *shoḥet* for the few Jews of eastern Slovakia. In Bardejov, he conducts complete Sabbath services at the synagogue, all alone.

Left, middie: Aharon Armando in Corfu, Greece, supports his family with income from his small retail clothing store.

Left, bottom: Zdenko Kohn of Osijek, Serbia, is an occupational psychologist who went on *aliyah* to Israel with his family in the summer of 1991 to escape the civil war that raged in northern Yugoslavia at the time.

Miriam Ferrera, in office of the ancient synagogue, in Dubrovnik, Croatia.

Eva Justová teaches English in Vrbové, Slovakia, where the synagogue is under restoration for cultural use.

Ladislav Mareš was not deported with other Jews from Heřmanův Městec because only his mother was Jewish. After the war he went to Theresienstadt to bring her home. He retired only recently from his career with the municipality and devotes himself to the care of the old Jewish cemetery and to raising funds for restoration of the synagogue and the Jewish quarter.

Roberto Segré came from Turin to Cherasco, Italy, especially to open the synagogue, owned by his family who formerly lived in the small apartment below, for the Dorfmans to document. It is a charming example of rural Baroque.

Pepice Misic of Split, Croatia, a former professional tour guide, speaks volubly and interestingly about the many sights of Split. In the old Jewish quarter, she points to a doorpost on which a *mezuzah* had formerly been mounted.

The An-Sky Collections: Jewish Collections of the State Ethnographic Museum in St. Petersburg

Judith C. E. Belinfante and Ludmilla Uritskaya

For many years the existence of the legendary An-Sky collections was doubted outside the Soviet Union, even maybe outside the walls of the State Ethnographic Museum. All that was known about them was the description of the ethnographical expeditions of 1910–1916, headed by the well-known dramatist S. Z. Rapoport (*An-Ski), written by one of its members, Abraham Rechtman. He gave a list of their finds: 700 ceremonial objects, 2,000 photographs, music recorded on 500 wax cylinders, and many folktales, articles of everyday life, and documents. Due to the consequences of the Russian Revolution, two world wars, and official Soviet anti-Semitism, only a fraction of these items survived in the Russian collection. In 1992, 90% of these remnants, approximately 330 objects, were shown for the first time outside Russia, in Amsterdam, in the Jewish Historical Museum.

The State Ethnographic Museum and the Jewish Historical Museum joined forces to register, describe, photograph, and publish these traces of the once important center of Jewish culture and history; the Pale of Settlement in Tsarist Russia.

The history of the Jewish collections in the State Ethnographic Museum in St. Petersburg began early in the century. The scale of collection and completing material related to the Jewish culture and way of life has varied greatly at different times — after all, it had to deal with no fewer than six million people who lived within the Pale of Settlement.

The first entries related to the subject date from 1904 to 1912, when the cultural heritage of the peoples inhabiting the vast territories of the Russian Empire attracted special interest. It was a time when there were thorough studies of the way of life among national minorities, when ethnographical expeditions were undertaken, and folklore collected. The enlightened section of the Russian intelligentsia appreciated that rapid urbanization was taking place throughout the country and feared the consequent destruction of traditional forms of folk life, including that of the Russian Jews. Among this group were F. K. Volkov, an expert in Ukrainian ethnography, A. K. Serzhputovsky, a researcher in Byelorussian ethnography, and A. A. Miller, a specialist in

Purimshpil

Klezmer

Jew with phylacteries

40-year-old Jewish man, Ukraine, c. 1900

the people of the Caucasus, the one who made the first contribution to the Jewish collections.

The second fruitful period for the Jewish collections was during the 1930s when the Jewish section of the St. Petersburg (Leningrad) Museum was headed by I. M. Pulner. His aim was not only to expand the collection but also to form a comprehensive exhibition entitled "The Jews in Tsarist Russia and the U.S.S.R." This exhibition opened in 1939 and turned out to have a rather propagandistic character, which only seemed natural in those years.

After World War II the purposeful collection of ethnographical data relating to Russian Jews was virtually finished. The Pale of Settlement was now past history, while the years of brutal fascist occupation of the Ukraine, Belorussia, and Lithuania destroyed vast quantities of cultural material.

There was also strongly anti-religious propaganda, which became the policy of the Soviet Union and destroyed the last vestiges of spiritual life — that is, the Jewish religious communities.

During the postwar years the collections were mostly augmented with gifts from other museums as well as rare purchases and private donations. A large collection from the former Moscow Museum of the Peoples of the U.S.S.R., which was passed on to the St. Petersburg Museum in 1948, should be mentioned in this respect.

The S. A. Rapoport (An-Sky) Collection is held to be the heart of the Ashkenazi collection. An-Sky headed a number of ethnographical expeditions during 1911–12, working in the provinces of Podolia, Volhynia, and Kiev. The items collected were intended for exhibition in the Jewish Museum formed as a section of the St. Petersburg Society of History and Ethnography. The *Evreyskaya Starina* ("Jewish Antiquity") magazine, the published organ of the society, printed articles on the collecting activities of the museum. In 1914–1916 An-Sky was known to be working in the front lines of Galicia, helping to evacuate historical valuables. This mission was formed by the State Duma (the Russian Parliament), and the data he collected while there were delivered to St. Petersburg. In 1917–18 *Evreyskaya Starina* reported on "Robbery and Pogroms that have been taking place since autumn 1917, which force us to close the museum and pack the exhibits into boxes to be kept in a safe place." From the published An-Sky will it is known that "5 boxes and suitcases with exhibits were given to be kept in the Alexander III Museum," now the State Ethnographic Museum.

As we now have no precise documents or lists it is quite difficult to identify whether certain An-Sky exhibits date back to 1911–12 or to the times of his expeditions of 1914–16. Unfortunately, the documents relating to these expeditions are lost and it proves impossible to identify the geographical source of objects. Indirect indications helping to date the items can be found when deciphering the inscriptions and also in the writings of A. Rechtman. We can, however, only make guesses as to the routes An-Sky followed and the places where he found his exhibits.

The Jewish Ashkenazi collections of the State Ethnographic Museum present a historical and cultural heritage, covering the period from the late 18th to the early 20th century. In terms of geography it embraces most of the area where the Pale of Settlement was introduced after 1795 (the third partition of Poland).

The Judaica occupy a central place in the museum's collection, together with household objects and personal belongings.

The Tsarist policy towards the Jews was ambivalent. It forced the Jews to live in the Pale of Settlement, where they formed 5% of the population. On the other hand, they tried to assimilate the Jews in their culture. Hundreds of measures were taken to achieve these goals, but without success. The Jews, speaking their own language, keeping their own religion and its traditions, resisted this policy.

But, as in all other communities, their material culture was heavily influenced by the Russian surroundings. The most exciting examples are the so-called Lubok paintings, Russian folk art used for decoration at home, but also as amulets to keep evil out of the house. In Judaica, often made by Jewish craftsmen, Russian folk elements like deer, birds, lions, and flowers decorated the Ḥanukkah lamps, spice boxes, and *rimmonim.* The Tsarist crown can be seen on covers for synagogue arks.

Another important part of the collection is clothing: the specific "brustichel" for women, and the headgear for men, both decorated with the so-called "spanjerwerk," gold embroidery. There are also the simple home-made wooden chess set, Ḥanukkah cards, and the models of cookies, specific for the Jewish kitchen like the bridal cake in a Star of David form.

The remnants of the An-Sky Collection, modest as they are in number, should be treasured for the wealth of background they give of a poor man's deeply felt Jewish culture of bygone days. And we hope that through the exhibitions and through the publications of the material (see the catalogue *Tracing An-Sky: Jewish Collections from the State Ethnographbic Museum in St. Petersburg* with excerpts from A. Rechtman and articles by Igor Krupnik and by Ludmilla Uritskaya, 1992), new generations can benefit from its resurgence.

New Facts, New Entries

New Facts, New Entries

ABELLA, Canadian family. IRVING ABELLA (1940), academic and Jewish leader. He is known for his historical research on the Canadian labor movement and in particular for his pathbreaking study with Harold Troper, *None Is Too Many: Canada and the Jews of Europe, 1933–1948*, which won the National Jewish Book Award in the United States. The book shows how Canadian officials kept Canada closed to Jewish refugees from Nazism during the critical period before the outbreak of the war and during the war itself. The findings had a profound effect on how Canadian Jews viewed their own past and their country.

Rosalie Silberman Abella (Photo Paul J. Lawrence, Toronto)

Abella was educated at the University of Toronto, from which he received his Ph.D. in 1969. His academic appointments have been at Glendon College of York University in Toronto, where he is professor of history. Among his books are *Nationalism, Communism and Canadian Labour, The Canadian Labour Movement, 1902–1906, The Canadian Worker in the Twentieth Century*, and several on Canadian history.

In 1992 he was elected president of the Canadian Jewish Congress, the culmination of a distinguished career of community leadership. Abella has also served as chair of the CJC Archives, the Canadian Professors for Peace in the Middle East, and the Canadian Seminar on Zionist Thought.

His wife, ROSALIE SILBERMAN ABELLA (1946–), lawyer and judge, was born in Stuttgart, Germany, but was taken as a child to Toronto, where she studied at the University of Toronto. Following admission to the Bar and four years in private practice, she was appointed as a judge of the Ontario Family Court in 1976, a post that she held until 1987.

Judge Abella has held a number of public positions in Ontario, including membership on the Public Service Labor Relations Tribunal and the Human Rights Commission and co-chairmanship of the University of Toronto Academic Discipline Tribunal. She also served as a member of the Premier's Advisory Committee on Confederation and as chairman of the Study of the Access to Legal Services by the Disabled. Since 1984 she has been the chair of the Ontario Labor Relations Board and is now chair of the Ontario Law Reform Commission. She is particularly noted for service as a one-person Royal Commission on Equality in Employment for the federal government in 1983–84. Her report was considered a landmark development in the struggle to eliminate discrimination in the employment field.

She has co-edited *Justice Beyond Orwell* with M. L. Rothman and *Family Law: Dimensions of Justice* with Claire L'Heureux-Dube and has written widely in legal journals on topics such as administrative law, equality, judicial role, and family law. [H.M.W.].

ALASKA (see **2**:513). The Jewish community of Alaska has grown and changed with the growth of the oil industry. Once primarily a military community, current estimates are that there are between 2,000 and 2,500 Jews in the state with less than 100 in the military. Anchorage has the largest Jewish population in the State of Alaska with approximately 1,200 people.

The past years have seen the Jewish community become more organized. A Reform congregation, Beth Sholom of Anchorage, is the largest Jewish group in Alaska, and in 1988 it built the second synagogue in its 30-year history. Shomrei Ohr, a small Orthodox congregation, also makes its home in Anchorage. Juneau and Fairbanks each have small formal congregations, and there are small groups meeting in the towns of Kenai, Valdez, Ketchikan, and Petersburg. In addition, Jews can be found in most of the major rural towns and villages.

For most of its history, only military rabbis served Alaska's Jews. In 1978, the first civilian rabbi, Lester Polonsky, was called to serve Beth Sholom in Anchorage. The last military rabbi left the state in 1983 and in the late 1980s the only ordained rabbi in Alaska was Harry Rosenfeld of Beth Sholom.

The first Jews came to Alaska with the Russian explorer Vitus Bering. Under Russian rule, the Jews of Alaska were trappers and traders. With the American purchase of Alaska, and the discovery of gold, Jews continued to go to Alaska to trade.

Jacob Gottstein came to Anchorage at its founding in 1915. He established a trading and warehouse business, the J. B. Gottstein company. Still a family owned business, it combined with Carrs Grocery chain to form Carr-Goldstein, Inc., the largest private employer in Alaska.

Jews have long been politically active in Alaska. The first mayor of Anchorage was David Leopold; several years later Zachary Loussac served in the same capacity. Ernest *Gruening held the office of Territorial Governor and then U.S. Senator.

Jews currently make up 5% of the State Legislature and the Anchoral Municipal Assembly as well as holding other elected positions in the State. [HA. RO.]

ALBAHARI, DAVID (1948–), Yugoslav translator. Born in Pec, Albahari graduated from Teachers College in

Belgrade and settled in Zemun as a free-lance writer of short stories and novels. His prose interweaves abstraction and reality, the lyric and the fantastic. He has edited literary magazines and translated literature from English, and is a member of the PEN club, the writers' union of Serbia, and the association of literary translators of Serbia. As a Jewish communal worker he has served as deputy president of the Federation of Jewish Communities of Yugoslavia. His books include the collected short stories *Family Time* (1973), *Ordinary Tales* (1978), *Description of Death* (1982), and *Simplicity* (1988); the novels *The Judge Dimitrievich* (1982), *Shock in the Shed* (1984), and *Zinc*; and the anthology *Contemporary World Short Stories* (1982), in two volumes. Some of his stories and novels have been translated into Hebrew, English, Hungarian, and other languages. [E.WE]

ALTER, ROBERT B. (1936–), U.S. literary critic. Born in the Bronx, New York, Alter taught at Columbia University from 1962 to 1966. In 1967, he joined the faculty of the University of California at Berkeley reading Hebrew and Comparative Literature.

Alter has published works on English, French and American literature. A specialist in modern Jewish literature and culture, he has written numerous articles for the *New York Times Book Review*, the *Times Literary Supplement*, and *Commentary*.

In *After the Tradition: Essays on Modern Jewish Writing* (1969), Alter explored the meaning of tradition in post-Holocaust Jewish literature, examining the works of such writers as Elie Wiesel, Saul Bellow, S. Y. Agnon, and Bernard Malamud. In *Defenses of the Imagination: Jewish Writers and Modern Historical Crisis* (1977), he saw Jewish writing as emerging from the problems of the 20th century and concentrated on Jewish writers such as Gershom Scholem and Osip Mandelshtam. He has also explored the profound influence of 20th-century wars on such writers as Norman Mailer and Joseph Heller, and the influence of historical forces on such writers as Saul Bellow.

Alter has also been deeply concerned with biblical narrative, showing how literary scholarship may be utilized in Bible study so as to enhance appreciation of the Bible as both a literary and religious document. [SU. STR.]

ALTMAN, SIDNEY (1939–), research biologist and educator. Altman, born in Montreal, Canada, received his doctorate in biophysics from the University of Colorado in 1967. He joined the department of biology at Yale University in 1971, becoming a professor in 1980 and serving as chairman of the department 1983–85. He was the dean of Yale College in 1985. In 1989 he shared the Nobel Prize in chemistry with Thomas Cech of the University of Colorado for similar discoveries they made in the 1970s and early 1980s while working independently. They found out that in contrast to the idea that RNA (ribonucleic acid) was only a passive bearer of genetic information between DNA (dioxyribonucleic acid) molecules, it could process genetic information and actively aid chemical reactions.

AMERICAN SEPHARDI FEDERATION (ASF). The American Sephardi Federation was reconstituted in 1973 in order to make a cohesive effort, by the Sephardim of the U.S.A., to promote their distinguished heritage as well as Jewish identity and Zionism. A member of the World Sephardi Federation, the American Sephardi Federation has branches in Miami Beach and Seattle, with its main office in New York City.

Since the Federation's membership is drawn from Balkan and Middle Eastern countries and represents some of the oldest Jewish communities in the world, the ASF maintains intercommunications among its varied ethnic strains through religious, educational, and cultural social events.

The Sephardim were the first Jews to settle in the Western hemisphere, and the ASF seeks to educate the broader American Jewish and non-Jewish communities about the unique history and values it perpetuates, while revitalizing a sense of affiliation and commitment among the younger Sephardi generations. In cooperation with universities, it has sponsored Jewish study programs and symposia on Sephardi subject matter. From its very inception, the ASF was youth oriented, intiating numerous functions for young adults.

ANTI-SEMITISM (see **3**:87). **1983–1992.** In the Western world, the decade 1982–92 began with a wave of anti-Semitism sparked off by the Lebanon war. There followed a decline in public expressions of it until the late 1980s when economic recession took hold, far-right parties made significant advances, and newer forms of anti-Semitic expression gained ground. The resurgence of grassroots anti-Semitism in Eastern Europe, following the collapse of Communism, gave encouragement to anti-Semitic groups in the West, and by 1992 it was clear that a wave of resurgent anti-Semitism was under way.

The West: New Forms of Anti-Semitic Expression. In the United States and Germany, anti-Jewish sentiment, as measured by opinion polls, declined steadily, and in other countries no marked increases in anti-Semitic sentiment were recorded. However, even in countries where polls indicated decreasing levels of anti-Semitism, the number of anti-Semitic incidents appeared to rise steadily and become more violent and abusive. A particularly gruesome example was the desecration in May 1990 of the Jewish cemetery in Carpentras, France, where a corpse was dug up. This shocked many and a huge demonstration led by President Mitterrand, took to the streets of Paris.

In the U.S., skinhead groups were thought to be responsible for the rise in anti-Semitic incidents in the mid-1980s which continued until 1992 when there was a reported decrease in such incidents for the first time in six years. Skinhead groups were also a source of concern in the United Kingdom, Italy, France, Germany, and Canada, where they were thought to be behind the increase in anti-Semitic attacks over the decade.

Many neo-Nazi groups were formed during the 1980s. Most remained electorally marginal, although some were thought to be responsible for the more violent attacks. There was increased international co-operation between extremist groups in terms of the publication and distribution of propaganda and the organization of conferences and speaking tours.

By the mid-1980s, disillusionment with established political parties, rising nationalism, ethnic conflicts, and an influx of immigrants and asylum-seekers from Eastern Europe led to increased electoral gains for far-right parties in Western Europe. These parties were principally anti-immigrant but their leaders used anti-Semitic innuendo to make it clear to supporters that anti-Semitism was part of the fundamental ideological outlook. Anti-Semitism was far more open at local party level. Racial violence was directed mostly at blacks, Asians, Turks — anyone seen as a "foreigner" — and not at Jews. Yet anti-Semitic slogans and rhetoric often seemed to be employed by those perpetrating such violence.

In France, the Front National consistently achieved between 9 and 15 percent of the vote. By the late 1980s far-right parties such as the German Republikaner Partei, the Belgian Vlaams Blok, and the Austrian Freiheits Partei also won seats at local and national levels. In 1984, for the first time, the far-right parties had sufficient numbers in the Euro-

ANTISEM
by
Goygoy

The Conciliatory Society is proud to present to the Unchosen this choice selection of healing verse by Goygoy.

9. MORE FRANK
Where is the genuine Anne Frank
beneath all the hanky and pank -
with a crooked papa -
one fake diary too
and a Yiddish brainwash think tank.

13. PLUS^3
Why not six million and one?
surely *one* more is not overdone?
A little more gas...
One more squeezed in that mass...
One more Jew gets a place in the sun.

Anti-Semitic doggerel ridiculing the Holocaust (Courtesy G. Wigoder, Jerusalem)

pean Parliament to form the Group of the European Right, entitling them to EC funding.

In the U.S., David Duke, the former Ku Klux Klan leader, and Pat Buchanan, known for anti-Jewish comments, were candidates for the 1992 Republican Party's presidential nomination. Although both failed, there was considerable unease at the willingness of the American body politic to embrace these candidates.

Black anti-Semitism was a serious concern through the 1980s in the U.S. Two of its principal sources were Louis Farrakhan, leader of the Nation of Islam Movement, and the Reverend Jesse Jackson, the black contender for the 1988 Democratic party presidential nomination. Further tension was caused when, in 1991, a black child was run over by a Ḥasidic driver in the Crown Heights district of New York and a seminary student was murdered in riots which followed.

The "Pollard affair," in which Jonathan Pollard, a U.S. citizen was convicted of spying for Israel, caused anxiety in the Jewish community. However, fears that the affair would result in the traditional anti-Semitic accusation of dual loyalties were allayed by opinion polls which indicated that it had little negative effect.

Anti-Semitism in Latin America was marginal during the period, except in the case of Argentina. Under the Argentine military junta, anti-Semitism had been a factor in the violent campaign waged against perceived political enemies. When democracy was restored after the Falklands/Malvinas war, expressions of anti-Semitism in publications increased markedly. However, by the end of the decade, even in Argentina, anti-Semitism appeared to be decreasing in significance.

In South Africa, Australia, New Zealand, and other countries in the Asia-Pacific region, anti-Semitism remained essentially marginal, although overtly anti-Semitic groups existed and their activities were occasionally cause for concern.

Church anti-Semitism decreased in significance during the period, although it increased markedly after the start of the *intifada*. Interfaith dialogue played an important role in countering anti-Semitism in the churches, particularly among the clergy, but did not appear to have sufficient impact on the grassroots.

The Post-Communist Societies of East-Central Europe — From Institutionalized to Grassroots Anti-Semitism. The early 1980s were for the Soviet Union a transitional phase between the bureaucratic stagnation of the Brezhnev era and the reformism of the Andropov-Gorbachev regimes. Beginning around the years 1982–83, there was a shift away from the state-sponsored ideological and political media campaign against Zionism and Israel which had begun in the late 1960s in response mainly to the emigration movement of Soviet Jewry. The campaign had been expressed in Marxist-Leninist terms but elements of it had been marked by transparent anti-Jewish imagery, in particular the invocation of an alleged "Zionist"-Masonic world conspiracy against Moscow and the Soviet Bloc.

As the political wind changed, some writers, propagandists and activists who had specialized in this form of propaganda paid lip service to *perestroika*, others joined the burgeoning chauvinistic and anti-Semitic groups which had sprung up in Russia, yet others disappeared from view.

With the failure of reform, the economic, political, and social fabric of the Soviet Union deteriorated. This was accompanied by ethnic strife in a number of republics. In December 1992 the Soviet Union finally collapsed and was replaced in part by the shaky Commonwealth of Independent States; the three Baltic states had earlier successfuly sued for independence from Moscow.

By the beginning of the 1990s, the situation with regard to anti-Semitic expression in Central and Eastern Europe had changed radically. In not a single country was anti-Semitism tolerated as a state policy. On the contrary, Jewish culture was undergoing an unimpeded renaissance, emigration was virtually unrestricted, and the leaders of the new states were concerned both with combating xenophobia, racism, and anti-Semitism by political and legal means and with maintaining good relations with Israel.

At the same time, the collapse of the Communist system was accompanied in several of the countries by the rise of grassroots anti-Jewish movements of varying degrees of importance. One particular source of danger was tactical alliances between "unreconstructed" Communists and extreme nationalists. Another source of concern, in particular in the Baltic countries, was the rehabilitation of accomplices of the Nazis in implementing the "Final Solution."

At the turn of the decade, the principal danger spots in post-Communist Central and Eastern Europe appeared to be Russia, where the far right embraced both the would-be respectable National Salvation Front and numerous Pamyat-style neo-Nazi and neo-fascist groups; Hungary, where the far-right parliamentarian and writer Istvan Csurka had been expelled from the governing party and had started up a party of his own; and Romania, where the governing coalition depended on the support of a number of xenophobic parties. While there appeared to be relatively little popular prejudice against Jews in any of the post-Communist countries — there was no shortage of ethnic scapegoats — the economic, political, and social dislocation which followed the collapse of Communism remained serious cause for alarm. The bitter warfare in the former Yugoslavia, with its abhorrent practice of "ethnic cleansing," served as a solemn reminder of the depths to which ethnic strife could descend.

Anti-Zionism and Anti-Semitism. Much expression of anti-Semitism at the beginning of the 1980s was disguised as anti-Zionism. Although by no means all anti-Zionists were anti-Semites, many groups across the political spectrum, but particularly on the extreme left, couched their anti-Semitism in anti-Zionist rhetoric. For some Communist countries too, anti-Zionism was a convenient tool for concealing state-sponsored anti-Semitism. UN General Assembly resolution 3379, which equated Zionism with racism, was a principal tool of the anti-Semitic anti-Zionist campaign.

The Israeli invasion of Lebanon in 1982 sparked off a wave of anti-Semitism which was closely related to negative images of Israel. In the following few years, criticism of Israel provided effective cover for expressions of anti-Semitism, generating considerable debate as to the relationship between anti-Zionism and anti-Semitism. Some believed that since anti-Zionism denied the rights of Jews on a collective level, it was the equivalent of denying the Jew individual rights — a classic element of anti-Semitism.

As the 1980s wore on, however, anti-Zionism began to diminish. The Third Worldist forums in which anti-Zionist rhetoric was constantly featured declined in importance as many of the participants saw that it brought them no benefit. The collapse of the Soviet empire led to an end to Communist state-sponsored anti-Zionism. Far-right groups which utilized anti-Zionism continued to do so but, as anti-Zionism became less of an acceptable notion on the international political stage, it became less useful to those seeking a "respectable" front for their anti-Semitism. In addition, as socialism appeared to be discredited, far-left anti-Semitic anti-Zionism declined markedly.

In many Arab countries anti-Semitism was used in the continuous fight against Zionism and the state of Israel. Much of this anti-Semitism was imposed from above since practically all Arab governments exercised strict control of the media. However, in some countries, Egypt in particular, there was clear evidence of anti-Semitism becoming increasingly a grassroots phenomenon, linked to the rise of Islamic fundamentalism.

Anti-Semitism from Islamic fundamentalist sources became a cause of increasing concern during the period, with extremist groups in certain Western countries propagating violent anti-Jewish rhetoric and using traditional far-right anti-Semitic themes. Much of this activity was encouraged by Iran and although it resulted in little actual violence against Jews outside of the Middle East, the potential for violence was certainly increasing at the end of the period under review.

Holocaust Denial. During the 1980s, Holocaust-deniers sought to depict denial as a scholarly endeavor, issuing "research" purporting to prove that the Holocaust was a hoax. Their main focus was on the gas chambers, particularly at Auschwitz.

Fred Leuchter, who invented the lethal injection system used for executions in some American states, was commissioned to analyze the gas chambers "scientifically." Leuchter's work, which claimed to prove the gas chambers a physical impossibility, was disseminated widely by Holocaust-deniers, although it was found to contain fundamental scientific errors and historical inaccuracies. In Britain, the so-called *Leuchter Report* was published by the far-right historian David Irving.

Other Holocaust-deniers who have provided the "conceptual" framework for the deniers' arguments include Robert Faurisson, a former professor of comparative literature in France, and Arthur Butz, a professor of electrical engineering in the United States.

Young people have been targeted by deniers in an attempt to spread doubt about the Holocaust and the veracity of such works as the *Diary of Anne Frank*. They placed advertisements denying the Holocaust in American campus newspapers. A significant number of papers accepted the ads, contending that they presented "ideas" and "points of view" which, however odious, deserved to be heard. In addition, the deniers established ties with European extremist groups.

Sample of anti-Semitic propaganda distributed in England in 1992 (Courtesy G. Wigoder, Jerusalem)

Certain countries tried to use the courts as a means of controlling Holocaust-denial activities. However, such legal measures are often difficult to sustain. In 1992, the Canadian Supreme Court overturned the conviction of prominent Holocaust-denier Ernst Zundel, ruling that the prohibition against spreading false news likely to cause injury to a public interest was too vague and possibly restricted legitimate forms of speech.

Conclusion. By 1992, it was clear that new patterns of anti-Semitic expression had emerged. Older forms — discrimination in employment and education, parties with anti-Jewish platforms, Jews as the primary target of ideological racism, state-sponsored anti-Semitism in Eastern Europe — had largely disappeared. Distance from the Holocaust appeared to encourage a greater tolerance of anti-Semitic sentiment. Holocaust denial was common to practically all groups expressing either overt or covert anti-Semitism. "Antisemitism without Jews" — in countries like Poland, Romania, Japan — was a significant feature of this period. And after the collapse of Communism, grassroots anti-Semitism and anti-Semitism in mainstream politics were important factors in former Communist states.

The countering of anti-Semitism developed considerably during the decade. Much was done in the framework of international human rights bodies like the Conference on Security and Co-operation in Europe (the "Helsinki Process"). Many states adopted legislation outlawing incitement to race hatred, although rarely singling out anti-Semitism by name, and a few countries implemented legislation against denial of the Holocaust. Education remained a significant means of countering anti-Semitism, and significant initiatives were taken in the U.S.A., the UK, Germany, and other countries, both privately and through state education systems, to raise awareness of the dangers of anti-Semitism.

[H.AH./AN.LE./JU.SCH./HO.SP.]

ARCHAEOLOGY (see **3**:303; **Dc./17**:155). **Chalcolithic Period** (4000–3100 B.C.E.). The investigation of Chalcolithic sites in the Golan was continued and excavations carried out at Rasm el-Kabash and on a site near the south Daliyyot waterfall. In both, the settlement is situated on two sides of perennial streams and most of the houses — consisting of parallel chains of buildings — concentrate on one bank, while isolated dwellings or small groups of one or two houses are scattered on the periphery.

A further group of subterranean dwellings belonging to the

Beersheba Chalcolithic culture was excavated at Neveh Noy, on the southwestern outskirts of Beersheba. The dwellings had a central courtyard from which entrances to subterranean rooms and tunnels were cut. The population hunted, raised livestock, and produced dairy products. Copper-working was quite common. Another site of Beersheba culture was investigated at Shikmim in the northwestern Negev. The remains belong to a large village with four phases of mud-brick rectangular buildings.

Early Canaanite Period (3100–2100 B.C.E.). At Yiftahel in Lower Galilee, the remains of a village from the late fourth-early third millennium B.C.E. have been excavated. The abundant and well-preserved architectural remains point to probable links with roughly contemporaneous sites in Phoenicia (e.g., Sidon-Dakerman and Byblos). In the City of David in Jerusalem remains were found of a rectangular domestic structure built on bedrock, dating from ca. 3000 B.C.E.

At Tel Arad northeast of Beersheba the excavators explored the remains of a water reservoir which served the city during the early Canaanite period. Its importance is manifested by the impressive girdle of buildings surrounding it, each of which seems to have had a special function in the water administration of the city authorities including a building of five parallel long and narrow halls, identified as a "water citadel."

Middle Canaanite I (2100–1950 B.C.E.). Tombs dating from the Middle Canaanite period have been discovered in different parts of the country, e.g., at Tel Amal and kibbutz Ha-Zorea in the Valley of Jezreel and Jebel Ta'amur 12 km (7 miles) northeast of Jerusalem. A small excavation was carried out at Naḥal Nissana in the western Negev, close to the Israel-Egypt frontier. The settlement on the site is the largest in the Negev from that period. Similar settlements were also explored at Mashabbei Sadeh and Ein Zik in the central Negev.

A large area was excavated along Naḥal Rephaim, southwest of Jerusalem. A large Canaanite settlement was found with two main strata. The lower stratum included houses built of mudbrick on fieldstone foundation, dating to the Middle Canaanite (Bronze Age) I period. An upper stratum of houses dated to the Middle Canaanite (Bronze) IIb period. The site is identified with biblical Manahat (Septuagint) Josh. 15:59.

Several rooms and a large hall belonging to a palace from the Middle Bronze II period have been excavated in Kabri, in western Galilee. A hall of considerable size has been uncovered, with its floor painted with floral motifs in a very naturalistlic style.

Middle Canaanite II (1950–1550 B.C.E.). Excavations have established that the reemergence of sedentary life along the coastal plain, whether in the form of rural communities

View of the remains of houses found at the Naḥal Rephaim site (Courtesy of the Israel Antiquities Authority)

Triple-arched gate of Laish–Dan of the Middle Canaanite Period. (Courtesy The Nelson Glueck School of Biblical Archaeology, Jerusalem; photo Zev Radovan)

or important fortified cities, started in early Middle Canaanite IIA and probably preceded the reappearance of urban centers in the hilly interior of the country by about a century. At Tel Aphek, on the springs of the Yarkon River, the excavators reached the earliest of six second-millenium B.C.E. palaces. The palace from the 18th–17th centuries B.C.E. proved to be by far larger and more impressive than anticipated. Fortifications from the same period have been examined on the mound of ancient Acre.

The excavation of the gate of Laish (Dan) at the head of the river Jordan has been completed. The triple-gate was built of sun-dried mud bricks. It was found in an excellent state of preservation and its three arches are still standing intact. The gate stands to a height of 7 m (22.7 ft). Twenty steps led from a small stone-paved piazza down into the city to a street made of pebbles. Pottery fragments from the gate show that it was constructed and filled in sometime between ca. 1775–1725 B.C.E.

In the City of David in Jerusalem the excavators cleared parts of the 18th-century B.C.E. city walls. Fortifications dating from a late stage in Middle Canaanite II were dug at Shiloh. The city wall and a retaining wall as well as a glacis facilitating the defense of the area close to the city were examined.

Late Canaanite (1550–1200 B.C.E.). A large residence from the 13th century B.C.E., perhaps the palace of the local ruler, was partly excavated at Tel Yenoam in the Jabneel Valley (eastern Galilee). Of special interest is a well-made iron bowl and a workshop, possibly of an ironsmith. This seems to be the earliest evidence of this kind from Israel, dating from a period in which iron working was still very rare and in its initial stages.

In the City of David in Jerusalem, the excavators investigated a massive stone podium at the northeastern end of the hill of the City of David on which was built a substantial structure, possibly the Canaanite citadel of the 14th–13th centuries B.C.E. It is likely that the citadel of David's and Solomon's times reused these massive remains of the Canaanite podium.

Israelite Period I (1200–1000 B.C.E.). The last excavation of the late Prof. Y. Yadin was devoted to a reexamination of the levels from the Early Israelite period at Beth Shean. It revealed a stratum with a series of buildings dating from the reign of Ramses III. This came to an end with a devastating fire and was followed by an occupation by people who dug numerous storage pits and built poorly constructed thin mud and rubble walls. This seems to indicate that the destruction of Beth Shean in the time of Ramses III (first half of the 12th century B.C.E.) was followed, for a while, by a settlement of

Pottery assemblage from a burial cave of Ketef Hinnom, Jerusalem, First Temple period. (Courtesy Israel Antiquities Authority; photo Israel Museum, Jerusalem)

a type usually associated with that of the Israelite tribes.

Important work has been done at Shiloh, the site of the Tabernacle. The excavators cleared further buildings dating from the mid-twelfth to mid-eleventh centuries B.C.E. Shiloh was destroyed by fire, apparently by the Philistines, after the defeat of the Israelites at Eben-Ezer. This destruction is evident on the site. Debris, which may have come from the Tabernacle or a building connected to it, contained pottery fragments of a cult stand, and vessels decorated in relief with figures of a lioness, a horse, and a leopard attacking a ram. Numerous objects from the Middle and Late Canaanite periods may indicate that a sanctuary existed on the site long before the Israelite Tabernacle was brought there.

An intriguing discovery was made on the northeastern side of Mt. Ebal. At a height of 940 m (3,055 ft) above sea level and about 150 m (488 ft) below the peak, an early Israelite cult site dating from the 12th century B.C.E. was discovered, with a rectangular structure constructed of large unhewn stones. The structure was deliberately filled with stones, soil, and ashes containing sheep bones upon which was built a stone pavement. A narrow ramp seems to lead up to the top of the structure which may have been an altar. In the surrounding area refuse pits with pottery fragements and bones were found. While there is no proof that the site is directly connected with Joshua and the traditions related in Deut. 27 and Josh. 8, it seems to be an early Israelite worship place.

Israelite Period II (1000-586 B.C.E.). In the City of David in Jerusalem excavations yielded new evidence on the fortifications and buildings from the 10th century to the destruction of Jerusalem by the Babylonians in 586 B.C.E. Above a plaster floor were found a group of pottery vessels, some of unique forms, bronze and iron arrowheads, and 50 clay bullae which had been baked by the fire of the destruction in 586 B.C.E., most of them with readable names, for example, "(belonging) to Benayahu son of Hoshayahu" and "Gemaryahu son of Shaphan," perhaps the scribe of King Jehoiakim (Jer. 36:9-12).

On the border between the Kingdom of Israel and Phoenicia, the site of ancient Cabul (Josh. 19:27) was identified on a hill 15 km (9.3 miles) east-south-east from Acre. It was first settled in the early days of Israelite Period I and fortified during the 10th century B.C.E. The city was given by King Solomon to Hiram, king of Tyre (I Kings 9:13), and was destroyed in the 10th century B.C.E.

On a low hill south of Arad, an Edomite shrine was excavated. A large amount of cult objects point to the function of the site, which date from around 600 B.C.E. Outstanding is a figurine of a goddess with a three-horned miter which served as her divine crown. A large amount of pottery known as "Edomite" led to the conclusion that larger areas in the south of Judea fell into the hands of Edomites who entered from Transjordan than had been supposed.

In Tel Mikne, several strata dated to Iron Age II, were exposed in all digging areas. Of outstanding importance are several stone altars with horns on all four corners, dated to the 7th century B.C.E. The finds point to the destruction of the site by Nebuchadnezzar, in his 603 B.C.E. campaign.

In 1986 publicity was given to the finds from an excavation carried out in Jerusalem during 1979–80 on the hill below the Scottish Church of St. Andrew's above the valley of Ben Hinnom. Revealed were several rock-cut tombs — one of which was found intact — bearing architectural characteristics typical of the First Temple Period (7th–6th cent. B.C.E.). Most of the caves have one chamber with benches along three walls, upon which the dead were placed. The small finds included two silver plaques, both rolled into scroll-like objects. These could be worn on the body with the help of a threaded string. Upon the thin leaves, delicately engraved inscriptions could be deciphered. The main text of each plaque contains the Priestly Benediction, slightly different from the biblical version in Numbers 6:24–26. This is the earliest known biblical text, predating by ca. 500 years the previously known oldest extant text. It is also the only biblical text originating in the First Temple Period.

In Tel Dan the expedition excavated around the site where the *bamah* (high place) identified with the activities of King *Jeroboam had been previously uncovered. Two shovels made of iron were most probably used on the altar, to take off or manipulate the ashes on it.

A massive stone-built fort was excavated at Ḥorvat Rosh Zayit, at the western edge of Lower Galilee, east of Akko (Acre). It is a square fort in which a series of rooms surrounds a central hall. The basement of the fort was used for storage as attested by more than 300 storage jars. The fort was in use in the tenth and ninth centuries B.C.E. The site probably served as an administrative center in the "Land of Cabul" (I Kings 9:13).

The Persian Period (538–333 B.C.E.). Interesting remains from the Persian period came to light at Dor, on the coast south of Haifa. Here a two-chambered city gate, with access through a stone-paved square was unearthed. The gate and city wall went out of use sometime during the fourth century B.C.E., before the conquest by Alexander the Great. In a cave on the cliffs to the west and above Jericho, traces of occupation were found below remains of the Byzantine period. The most important find is a written document on papyrus in Aramaic. It consists of names of Jewish origin with different numerals and the letter *sh*, abbreviation of *shekel*. It seems to be a list of loans. The dating of the document has been

Small silver plaque containing the Priestly Blessing found in Jerusalem, excavated by Dr. Gabriel Barkai. (Courtesy Israel Antiquities Authority; photo Israel Museum, Jerusalem)

ascribed to the middle of the fourth century B.C.E.

The Hellenistic Period (333–37 B.C.E.). Impressive fortifications dating from the Hellenistic period have also been excavated at Dor. A stone wall 2 m (6.5 ft) thick was built along the eastern slope of the mound during the third century B.C.E.. The residential quarter of the Hellenistic period followed the same orthogonal plan adopted in the Persian period.

In the sea off the coast of Athlit south of Haifa, in a depth of 3 m (9.7 ft) a unique bronze ram of a warship was discovered, evidently from a galley dating from the Hellenistic period. The ram, a masterpiece of ancient metal casting, is decorated on its sides with a trident, Poseidon's symbols, head of an eagle (of Zeus?), and a helmet of the Dioscuri.

At Jericho further work has been done on the site of the Hasmonean palaces from the late second-early first century B.C.E.

An outstanding find was the discovery of a wooden boat, found in the mud on the shore of the Sea of Galilee near kibbutz Ginossar. The boat is *ca.* 8 m (26 ft) long. Since in the close vicinity fragments of other boats were found, it seems that the site served as a yard for building or storing boats. The boat was used for fishing on the lake or for maritime transport. A cooking pot and oil lamp found nearby, as well as radiocarbon dating, point to a date in the late Hellenistic period.

On the top of Mount Gerizim several houses, some preserved to the second floor, have been excavated. In the debris of a walled enclosure a large amount of animal bones was discovered. These are related to the sacrifices brought to the Hellenistic Samaritan Temple which stood there. Among the fallen stones and those reused in later periods are an abundance of inscriptions in Hebrew, Aramaic, and Greek. The inscriptions mainly mention offerings given to the Temple. Traces of destruction by fire as well as an abundance of coins minted by John Hyrcanus I provide evidence of the destruction of the Samaritan Temple as attested by Josephus.

Early Roman Period (37 B.C.E.–96 C.E.). The exploration and excavation of King Herod's palaces at Jericho was continued. Herod built three palaces on both sides of Wadi Qelt in the oasis of Jericho. Recent work revealed further structures and swimming pools. Further excavations were carried out at another site founded by Herod — Herodium, southeast of Bethlehem. The large pool in Lower Herodium was cleared and a large bath from the period of Herod unearthed. It was built according to the Roman style and techniques and is similar to Herod's baths on other sites. A magnificent building constructed by Herod was excavated at Sartaba/Alexandrium. This structure, decorated with frescos and stucco, is similar to the panoramic peristyle structure of the northern palace at Masada.

The synagogue at Gamla in the Golan is, perhaps, the earliest known example of a synagogue. Objects recovered from the debris below its floor demonstrate, however, that it does not antedate the later part of Herod's reign and was in use until the conquest of Gamla by the Romans in 68 C.E.

The base of the two towers of the entrance to the ancient harbor of Caesarea, mentioned by Josephus, were identified during underwater explorations. Various submerged quays and breakwaters of the harbor built by Herod were also explored and mapped.

A major project of excavations was undertaken at Banias (Casearea Philippi) at the sources of the river Jordan. Part of the temple dedicated to the Greek deity Pan has been found attached to the famous cave whence the source springs. A monumental building incorporating a series of 12 gigantic vaults, completely preserved, is under excavation.

Middle and Late Roman Period (96–396 C.E.). In numerous areas along the Shephelah, the hilly countryside of western Judah, as well as southeast of Bethlehem, further examples of complex subterranean tunnels and hiding places dating from the period of the Bar Kokhba war (132–135 C.E.) were discovered. The rebels seem to have concentrated most of their military forces in such subterranean hide-outs from which they attacked the Romans in surprise sorties.

A Roman theater was excavated at Neapolis (Shechem), on the slopes of Mt. Gerizim. It was built in the 2nd century C.E., and had some 6,000–7,000 seats. In Byzantine times, the orchestra was turned into a pool used for water performances. A hippodrome and amphitheater from the 2nd and 3rd centuries C.E. were also excavated. A small theater or odeum was excavated at Antipatris (Aphek) by the spring of the Yarkon river. The construction of the theater was never completed and it was destroyed, together with the rest of the city, in the earthquake of 361 C.E. Remains of a Roman amphitheater have been uncovered at Eleutheropolis (Beth Guvrin). Further excavation at the Roman temple at Kedesh Naphtali, on the Israel-Lebanon frontier, established that it dates from the 2nd–3rd centuries C.E.

The synagogue of Hammath Gader, southeast of Tiberias, was first excavated in 1932. New explorations below the 6th-century C.E. mosaic pavement established that the synagogue had two earlier phases. In the 4th cent. C.E. it was

Caldarium in the thermae, Bet Shean (Courtesy of the Israel Antiquities Authority)

paved with a patterned grey stone pavement and even earlier is a simple white mosaic pavement which may belong to a 3rd century C.E. synagogue. A synagogue from the 3rd–4th centuries C.E. has been partly excavated at Kh. Shua, east of Rosh Pinnah. A similar basilical synagogue has been excavated at Yesud ha-Ma'alah, north of Tiberias.

Near the gate of the Roman fort near Yotvatah (in the southern Arabah) a monumental Latin inscription was accidentally found. Nine lines mention eternal peace and the names of emperors, Diocletian, Maximianus, and Constantius. The inscription commemorates the building of the fort's gate in the late 3rd century C.E.

In a survey carried out in a subterranean shelter in Ḥorvat Alim (near Mạreshah in the Shephelah) a unique lead weight was found. It bears a Hebrew inscription in square script: *Sm'on bn ksba nsi' isr'l wprnsw prs* meaning: Shim'on ben Kosba prince of Israel and his parnas, pras. Ben Kosba is the authentic name of *Bar Kokhba, the famous leader of the second revolt against the Romans. *Parnas* was probably the title of the official responsible for the authenticity and accuracy of the weights, and *pras*, the measure of the weight.

Excavations at Sepphoris have yielded many finds including a large mansion, located just to the south of the Roman theater. In the center of the building a large *triclinium* (dining room and guest room) was exposed, paved with a magnificent mosaic pavement, one of the richest in decoration and most delicate in workmanship ever found in Israel. The central "carpet" depicts scenes from the life cycle of Dionysos, the Greek god of wine, and his cult. The villa was built in the 3rd century C.E. and was probably destroyed by the earthquake of 363 C.E.

At Shuni, northwest of Caesarea, the remains of a Roman theater are under excavation.

The Byzantine Period (396–636). A basilical church was excavated at Dor. It was built in the 4th century B.C.E. on the site of a pagan temple and rebuilt after a fire in the late 4th or early 5th century C.E. During the excavation in the ruins of the healing baths of Hammath Gader, an inscribed marble slab was discovered bearing a 17-line poem in Greek by Empress Eudocia, wife of Theodosius II, who died in Jerusalem in 460 C.E. The poem praises Clibanus,the hot-water spring of the baths.

In the Jewish Quarter of the Old City in Jerusalem a further section of the Byzantine *cardo maximus* (main thoroughfare) was cleared, bringing the total length to about 80 m. It had two colonnades and on its western side are preserved small chambers, which probably served as shops. The *cardo* has been reconstructed and opened for visits by the public. Also in the Jewish Quarter the southern lateral apse of the magnificent Nea Church built by Justinian (527–565 C.E.) was excavated.

A rescue excavation within the premises of kibbutz Sedot Yam revealed a section of a solid city wall and gate, part of the outmost fortification of *Caesarea Maritima. The gate was blocked with discarded columns, capitals, and four late Roman statues.

In Khirbet Beit Loya, southeast of Beth Guvrin, a large monastic complex was excavated, including a church paved with magnificent mosaics which made use of figurative and animal patterns. However the central parts of the figures were obliterated in antiquity. It seems that the Christians themselves defaced their mosaic floors in accordance with the decree of the Caliph Yazid II, c. 721 C.E.

Since 1986, a large-scale project of excavations and reconstruction has been undertaken in Beth Shean (Scythopolis) which has already been developed into a major tourist attraction. It has concentrated on the Roman and Byzantine periods, exposing public monuments and urban layout. Among the main elements are the amphitheater, which accommodated 5–7,000 spectators; the Thermae which cover 1.5 acres; the Odeon (a small auditorium); and the Theater, seating 6,000, which is the best-preserved in the country. A long colonnaded street leads to the façade of a temple and other monuments. There is also a Roman colonnade and a Byzantine street.

In the Mamillah area close to the Jaffa Gate in Jerusalem, a small chapel and adjacent crypt were excavated. The simple mosaic pavement included a Greek inscription asking for salvation for those people whose names are known only to the Lord. It seems that in the crypt a large number of victims of the Persian invasion of 614 C.E. were buried, as mentioned in the writings of the Church Fathers.

From the Arab Conquest to the Fall of the Crusader Kingdom (636–1291 C.E.). In the baths at Hammath Gader a Greek inscription was discovered, dating from December 5, 662. It is dedicated to the rebuilding of the baths by the Arab governor. A hoard of 282 Umayyad gold coins was discovered at Capernaum buried under the floor of a house from the Umayyad period. It seems that this level was destroyed by earthquake in 746. Numerous coin hoards were discovered buried in the ruins of the Umayyad palace south of the Temple Mount in Jerusalem.

General Information. In August 1989 the Knesset passed a bill by which the Israel Department of Antiquities, which was a department within the Ministry of Education and Culture, was turned into an independent body: the Israel Antiquities Authority (IAA). [D.Ba./Ro.R/Ed.]

ARENS, MOSHE (1925–), Israeli politician and professor of aeronautical engineering. Arens was born in Kovno, Lithuania and immigrated to the United States in 1939 with his family. After serving in the United States army (1944–46), he studied mechanical engineering at the Massachusetts Institute of Technology. He was active in American Betar and during the Israel War of Independence fought as a member of the *Irgun. After the war he continued to reside in Israel and worked in agriculture at Mevo'ot Betar, until he went back to the United States to further his education at the California Institute of Technology from which he received a master's degree in aeronautical engineering in 1953. Arens returned to Israel in 1957 and became a professor of engineering at the Technion in Haifa. From 1962 to 1971 he was deputy director of engineering at the Israel Aircraft Industry working on development projects which culminated in aircraft such as the Aravah and the Kfir. In 1971 he received the Israel Security award.

He was elected to the Ninth Knesset in 1974 as a representative of Herut and reelected in 1977 for the Likkud. His consistently hawkish approach on security matters in combination with a quiet, businesslike style brought him to the fore. Arens opposed the Camp David Agreements and the Peace Treaty with Egypt. In the 10th Knesset he served as chairman of the Foreign Affairs and Security Committee. He was appointed Israel's ambassador to the United States in 1982. When Ariel Sharon resigned upon the publication of the recommendations of the Kahan Commission, Arens was appointed minister of defense. After the Knesset elections of 1984 he became minister without portfolio in the National Unity government led by Shimon Peres. In Dec. 1988 he was appointed foreign minister in the second National Unity Government. From June 1990 until July 1992 he served again as defense minister. He retired from politics in July 1992 following the Likkud's defeat in the Knesset elections. [ED.]

ARGENTINA (see **3**:408; **Dc./17**:162). **Demography.** The most recent demographic studies confirmed the real size of the Argentinian Jewish community, estimated in 1970 at 500,000 and alleged by some anti-Semitic groups to be in the region of one or two millions! Since 1980, religion has not been specified in Argentinian censuses, and these can therefore no longer serve as a source for official data. The work of the U. O. Schmelz and S. DellaPergola (1985) estimates fairly precisely the number of Jews in Argentina at 233,000 in 1982 (out of a total population of 33,000,000), with a tendency to decrease for various reasons: low fertility, assimilation, small but persistent *aliyah* to Israel, a high percentage of outmarriage, and cessation of immigration from other countries.

Another study carried out by AMIA (the Buenos Aires Jewish community organization) and its education center, and directed by Yaakov Robel (1986), counted 11,700 families with children in the Jewish education network of Buenos Aires and the rest of the country (involving approximately 50,000 Jews). This count covers 90 percent of the families with children studying in Jewish schools; the study revealed that 94 percent of the respondents were born in Argentina, and the majority of the community is concentrated in urban areas. It also showed the rapid rise of educational achievements through a comparison of different age groups: the proportion of those with secondary or university education (whether completed or not) rose from 2.2 percent among Jews aged over 65 to 21.1 percent in the age group 15–19 years old.

In the professional field, the same study showed a strong overrepresentation of the "owners, partners and managers" category in relation to the general population, to the detriment of the "salaried workers" category. Professional statistics — for instance, through a comparison of censuses of different decades — showed that the Jewish population has gravitated towards the tertiary branches of the economy and is concentrated in the "middle class." It is thus (together with members of the middle class in general) in an anomalous position: it has relative economic security, but at the same time it has no real political influence.

Memorial service at Buenos Aires' Jewish cemetery for soldiers killed in wars of Israel; trees stand in the name of fallen Argentinian IDF soldiers. (Courtesy AMIA, Buenos Aires)

In the last two decades the sociological structure of Argentinian Jewry has been subjected to a series of slow but profound changes, that have not yet been quantified. A polarization has been observed similar in nature to that detected in the overall Argentinian population: a small percentage of Jewish families have risen to the upper class, including entry into agricultural–stock farming (land-owning) or large-scale contracting-commercial activities, and participation in the financial and services sector. On the other hand, thousands of impoverished Jews, often from the decaying middle class, have joined the marginal population sectors (employees, professionals, and small merchants who suffer severely from the economic reorientation).

As a reflection of this development, the identification models of the members of the community have been modified. Some integrate more easily into community work, guided less by their adherence to religious practice and more by identification with the State of Israel, which replaces the traditional (religious and cultural) sources. Others add cosmopolitan imports to this "liberal" Argentinian Jewish identity, even adopting models of the North American or French Jewish community. The hybrid models of the majority — with the exception of religious-Orthodox or ideological-Zionist remnants in separate groups — produce a confused identity in large sectors of the community, in which an important role is played by guilt feelings (guilt at not being a good Jew, at not having emigrated to Israel for Zionists, at not respecting traditional religious precepts, at having suddenly grown rich and at realizing their Jewish ignorance).

Argentinian Politics and the Jewish Community. The Falklands (Malvinas) War against Great Britain (April–May 1982) and the consequences of Argentina's military defeat marked the beginning of the end for the regime installed by the military junta in 1976. During the hostilities in the south of Argentina, rabbis traveled to the war zone to serve as chaplains for the Jewish soldiers. In the following year, sectors of the community publicly supported the protests concerning the victims who had been arrested and disappeared during the repression practiced by the military junta. "Never Again," the report prepared by CONADEP (National Commission for the Missing Persons) published in 1985, revealed a special degree of atrocity in the treatment and torture of many Jewish citizens figuring in the dreadful lists: of the 30,000 "missing persons," about 1,500 were Jews. Some of the survivors testified to the pictures of Hitler and the anti-Semitic watchwords that formed the "habitual decor" of many torture rooms.

The establishment of a democratic regime represented a relief for most Argentinians, including the Jews, many of whom became active participants in the Union Civica Radical (UCR), a party traditionally aligned with the middle classes. The Sociedad Hebraica Argentina's Israeli dance troupe, "Darkeinu," celebrated the arrival of democracy at the Obelisk, together with the people.

Raúl Alfonsin, a progressive and charismatic president, surrounded himself with many figures prominent in other spheres of life: Rabbi Marshall Meyer and Professor Gregorio Klimovsky joined CONADEP (chaired by writer Ernesto Sabato); Bernardo Grinspun became minister of the economy and Mario Brodersohn district secretary; Adolfo Gass obtained a seat in the Senate, Marcelo Stubrin and Cesar Jaroslavsky (the latter, head of the district bank) entered the Chamber of Deputies and Jacobo Fiterman — ex-president of the Argentinian Zionist Organization — became secretary of public works in the Buenos Aires municipality.

In the field of education and culture, traditionally a Catholic enclave, Marcos Aguinis became minister of national culture, Manuel Sadosky was minister of science and technology, and Oscar Shuberoff was appointed rector of Buenos Aires University. The Jewish Human Rights Movement was established, and the San Martin General Cultural Center, seat of a hitherto unknown pluralism, inaugurated a Jewish Culture Sphere. It may well have been this Jewish participation in public life that led Monsignor Antonio Plaza spokesman of the most rightwing sectors of the Argentinian bishopric, to declare in March 1987 that "the government is full of Jews." A fresh anti-Semitic campaign throughout the initial democratic years of this regime, spoke of the "radical synagogue," a reference to the Jewish community's alleged influence.

The trial of the leaders of the military junta, at the initiative of Alfonsin and many Argentinians, petered out as support for the government began to wane and economic problems worsened. The decline of the "Austral Plan" presented by the new minister for the economy, Juan Sourrille, and the return of inflation, were accompanied by the opposition of the Peronist central trade-union, which organized 14 general strikes during the Alfonsin regime.

The first counterattack by the army's "hardliners," led by the "carapintadas" (Aldo Rico and Mohamed Ali Seineldin, who had fought in the Falklands War), took place in April (Holy Week) 1987 and assumed the character of a military coup, that the civilian president had great difficulty in putting down. Successive concessions to the military disregarded the danger of institutional failure and put an end to trials of soldiers for human rights violations. The renewed insurgency of the "carapintadas" groups in 1988, although failing to obtain their objective, extended their base of support with sectors of the extreme right such as Alejandro Biondini's Nazi group, that claimed to be part of the National Justice Movement. The precarious situation was further destabilized by the confused events of January 1989, when several score soldiers of the Todos por la Patria Movement — a heterogeneous national-Marxist group, influenced by surviving sectors of the guerrilla movement of the previous decade — tried to take by assault a military barracks at La Tablada (a province of Buenos Aires) and were wiped out after many hours of combat.

These episodes indirectly affected the Jewish community, since the "carapintada" sector leader, Colonel Mohamed Ali Seineldin was a fanatic Catholic and an avowed anti-Semite ("I know no green horses or decent Jews" is the best-known phrase with which he harangued his troops).

November 1985 saw the arrest of the Nazi war criminal Walter Kutschmann, but the extradition demand was delayed by legal appeals and Kutschmann died in prison in August 1986 without having been sent to Europe. In March 1986, a group of participants in a public meeting of the General Confederation of Labor (CGT) made anti-Semitic remarks that were later repudiated in a document issued by the Labor Central's governing board. DAIA successfully negotiated modification in a regulation, so that henceforth Jewish relatives could honor their deceased with identification of their faith (through the Star of David) in the obituary columns of the Argentinian press. The year 1987 saw continued anti-Jewish attacks, this time on the Sephardi Congregation and the AISA cemetery in Ciudadela. The Jewish community organized a mass demonstration at the central Houssay Square in Buenos Aires (November 1987), with the participation of Argentinian political, trade union, and religious leaders, to demand the speedy ratification of an anti-discrimination law to penalize any expression of anti-Semitism (this was achieved in the following year).

The social problems continued to increase. In early 1989 President Alfonsin fell victim to an "economic coup" engineered by the financial sectors, which unleashed a hyperinflation that culminated in pillaging of the supermarkets, general disturbances, and the early surrender of power (in July 1989) to the president-elect, Carlos E. Menem. The new president, who came from a Syrian Muslim family (although a convert to Catholicism), was very aware of the prejudices regarding his personal history (closely linked with the Argentinian Arab community), and to the prejudices of sectors of his "Justicialist" movement, which in the past had combined a degree of populism with a certain authoritarian tendency. His public acts soon allayed anxieties in these respects: he personally participated in the event organized by the Jewish community at the Calle Libertad synagogue to denounce the desecration of the Jewish cemetery of Carpentras in France, expressing his "profound indignation" at an act of sacrilege and "absolute solidarity with the Jewish community." Nazi war criminal Joseph Schwamberger, commandant of a concentration camp in Poland (arrested in Cordoba in 1987), was extradited in 1989 to stand trial in Germany. In 1992 Menem announced the decision to "open the Nazi archives" to the investigators, a political measure of great significance (since Eichmann, Mengele, and dozens of other Nazi leaders resided in Argentina or had entered the country in the post-war period, under Peron's benevolent acquiescence) but with few practical results: the files now revealed, carefully expurgated, contain newspaper clippings, with almost no documental value. The Argentinian Chancellery was pressured by the press and political figures to hand over the documents that certainly exist on the immigration of the Nazi criminals from Europe to Argentina.

The centenary of Jewish Settlement in Argentina (1889–1989) was celebrated by various events in the capital and in the rest of the country, with the participation of political authorities. The culmination was in Moisesville, the colony founded by Baron Maurice Hirsch's Jewish Colonization Association (ICA). In 1991, various celebrations marked the first centennial of the arrival of Jewish immigrants to Colonia Mauricio (Carlos Casares).

In general politics, Menem executed a dramatic volte-face when he pardoned the soldiers condemned for human rights violations and allied himself with representatives of business and financial sectors in order to commence privatization of state enterprises and introduced stringent economic regulations. Denouncing the failure by members of the Menem government to fulfill commitments, Colonel Seineldin headed a bloody "carapintada" uprising in December 1990, that ended with the defeat of this nationalist and anti-Semitic sector. While a ministerial reshuffle transferred science and education posts from Jewish to Catholic personalities participating in the new power alliance, no signs of particular discrimination were revealed and important posts went to personalities such as Moises Ikonicoff (minister of planning), Enrique Kaplan (director of protocol), Nestor Perl (governor of Chubut) and Carlos Corach (presidential adviser). Argentinian citizens of Jewish origin now participate together with their compatriots in various administrative and political posts, with some tacit restrictions in the military diplomacy, and the higher levels of the judiciary.

Jewish cemeteries were once more desecrated in 1992, in the province of Buenos Aires. A bus taking Jewish schoolchildren on a holiday trip came under fire in the province of Cordoba. In certain football clubs, groups of fans set fire to flags bearing swastikas and chanted anti-Jewish slogans. The fluctuations in anti-Semitism would seem to reflect an inherent tension between xenophobia and prejudice with the cosmopolitanism and culture expressions of Argentina's liberal urban society. Sociological studies carried out in Argentina have shown, for decades, the presence of a strong element of latent anti-Jewish prejudice, the magnitude and intensity of which grow in relation to the deterioration of the economic situation. In recent years, Chinese and Korean immigrants, particularly in Buenos Aires, have in some cases replaced the Jews as the traditional scapegoat for Argentinian xenophobia.

Argentina–Israel Relations. In the first democratic government after the military dictatorship (1983–1989) Chancellor Caputo's foreign policy attempted to achieve an alliance both with Third World and developed countries at one and the same time. To these ends special attention had to be paid to the demands of the Arab bloc, while a barely correct profile was maintained in relations with Israel. This in no way influenced the ideology of the ruling party (UCR), that was traditionally democratic and opposed to the fascistic groups. In 1992 then ex-president Alfonsin visited Israel, as did the possible radical candidate in the next presidential election, Fernando de la Rua.

Relations between Argentina and Israel, despite the initial prejudices, have been concretely upgraded since Menem came to power in 1989. The association between Argentina, Egypt, and Iraq for the construction of the Condor II missile was frozen and then disbanded. The missile was finally destroyed as a result of U.S. government pressure. Official visits at the highest level have increased: in late 1989 Israeli president Chaim Herzog visited Argentina, where he addressed the National Congress; in 1991 Menem became the first Argentine president to visit Israel. Before and after these visits, parliamentary and ministerial missions were exchanged between both countries for discussion of issues of mutual interest.

During the 1990 Persian Gulf crisis, the Argentinian government opposed the Iraqi invasion of Kuwait and sent two frigates to join the United Nations force that attacked the aggressor. This active position was a source of controversy in Argentinian political sectors and, manifestly, in the president's own family (ex-first lady Zulema Yoma, deputy Alberto Samid, and other members of the presidential "entourage" publicly sided with Saddam Hussein, while other members of the family, connected with the Syrian Ba'ath party, aligned themselves with Menem).

In other aspects connected with the Middle East, the Alfonsin and Menem governments resisted PLO efforts to open an office in the country in order to obtain diplomatic recognition. In 1985 leaders of the Jewish community appealed to representatives of all the political streams to condemn UN General Assembly Resolution 3378 equation "Zionism" with "racism"; in the following years, the resolution was condemned by the Argentinian parliament (1990). In 1988, Buenos Aires and Tel Aviv became "twinned" cities.

In March 1992, the Israeli embassy in Buenos Aires was destroyed in a brutal attack that left 20 dead and hundreds of wounded, including passers-by and neighbors as well as embassy personnel The dimensions of the explosion represented a new stage in the political situation (never before had Buenos Aires suffered an attack on civilians of such magnitude). The press compared the attack with Beirut or Medellin. Speculations regards motive ranged from the vengeance of Islamic groups for the military situation in Lebanon (death of the pro-Iran Hamas leader) to "messages" to the Argentinian government regarding the opening of the Nazi archives (a month previously) or its participation in the anti-Iraq coalition during the Gulf War. Tens of thousands of Argentinian citizens filed past the ruins of the embassy building in an expression of solidarity with the victims and condemnation of the barbaric act. President Menem and his ministers, ex-president Alfonsin, and representatives across almost the entire political, trade-union, and intellectual spectrum participated in this show of solidarity.

Internal Development of the Jewish Community. The community models and the institutions founded in the first decades of the century have passed through a "structural crisis" in recent years. There is a strong trend towards professionalization in social, educational, and cultural work. This has a technical advantage, in that the workers are trained in the complexities of modern life; but an ideological disadvantage for the voluntary activists, who fear that the original Jewish feeling of solidarity and a common mission will be lost in the process of transforming the institutions into pragmatic, efficient bodies, managed by capable directors but empty of content.

This debate, which commenced in the 1990s, coincides with the decline of the central institutions and the sudden flowering of an intensive cultural activity. In 1986 the first encounter of intellectuals was held, dealing with the subject of "Pluralism and Identity: Jewish Content in Latin American Literature," under the auspices of AMIA and the Cultural Secretary of the Buenos Aires Municipality. The reports of this international meeting constitute the first title of the Mila Publishing House, founded by the Jewish Community of Buenos Aires at the end of the same year. In its first six years of work, this publishing house published a hundred books (about 500,000 copies), including the RAICES-Biblioteca de Cultura Judia collection, copies of which were sold for 50 consecutive weeks in all the kiosks of the country. In 1988 the Fifth Congress of LAJSA (Latinoamerican Jewish Studies Association) was held. In 1990 the Nissim Elnecave School of Journalism was inaugurated, to train young journalists for the Jewish media; 1991 saw the appearance of the review "Raices Judaismo Contemporaneo," a quarterly publication of a high intellectual level, edited by AMIA, in collaboration with a private publishing house. Coinciding with the events to mark the 500 years of the Spanish Expulsion, the Sefarad 92 Congress was held in Buenos Aires.

In the last few years there have also been signs of a growing return to religion in sectors of the Jewish community, especially around the Conservative movement, that has successfully increased its congregational activities. Through its Latin American Rabbinical Seminary, it provides local spiritual leaders, teachers, and a publication program. The ultra-Orthodox Agudat Israel and Ḥabad Lubavicher movement have extended their influence to some Jewish groups in Buenos Aires and the provinces, especially in Sephardi sectors. Ḥabad activities have a high profile in the streets of Argentina, with the lighting of an enormous Ḥanukkah lamps at Ḥanukkah time in the central parks and with the militant presentation of their message on university campuses and in populous neighborhoods. The Argentinian Association for a Secular and Humanistic Judaism was also created and is chaired by scientist Gregorio Klimovsky, who published the review *Judaismo Laico*.

Publications that have appeared include *Megamot* (Jewish review of Social Sciences, AMIA), *Coloquio* (Latin American Jewish Congress), *Indice* (published by DAIA's Centre of Social Studies), and *Controversia* that reflects the meetings of the ideological circle of intellectuals backed by the World Zionist Organization. A decline has been observed in Yiddish journalism and culture. (*Di Presse* survives with great difficulty and few readers) and various Jewish newspapers continue to appear in Spanish: *Mundo Israelita* (weekly), *Comunidades* and *Nueva Sion* (every three weeks), *La Luz*

Jewish Gaucho, wearing a *tallit*, drinking mate (1984) (Beth Hatefutsoth — "Jewish Heritage in the Eye of the Camera," 1984; photo Gustavo A. Cohen, Argentina)

(Sephardi monthly), *La Voz Judia* (monthly of the Orthodox that also supports the Yehuda Publishing House), and *Semanario Israelita* (bilingual monthly of German Jews). *Jueva Presencia*, which was a widely distributed weekly prominent in the struggle for human rights between 1977 and 1987, changed its orientation several times and by the 1990s has become almost non-existent and with no clear policy. Other smaller publications come and go sporadically. Two or three radio broadcasts are maintained with relative stability, and are transmitted once a week. They contain Jewish and Israeli music and community news.

In this period, following the debate on the forms to be taken by the institutions, the Fundacion Tzedaka was established (1992) in response to the new socioeconomic composition of the community. The Fundacion Tzedaka's Chagall Cultural Center involves in its cultural activities thousands of Jews who have never before participated actively in community affairs. The activities are held at Ayacucho 832, the main Jewish education building, serving secondary and tertiary institutions which, as a result of the economic crisis were deregulated and privatized through agreements with other Jewish bodies. School registration continues to be high — about 20,000 pupils — and the ORT technical schools are enjoying expansion and high prestige. There is, however, an open controversy on the profile that the community should assume: a central community that includes every type of Jew and activity (cultural, social, burial, religious affairs, youth, groups from throughout Argentina); or, decentralized and smaller more self-sufficient institutions, in the North American style. What should be done with the marginal sectors of the community that cannot afford a private Jewish education for their children? These questions will stand high on the agenda in the coming years. [RI. FEI.]

ATTALI, JACQUES (1943–), French economist and special adviser to President Mitterrand. Attali was born in Algiers and was educated there and in France. In 1981 he was appointed special adviser to President Mitterrand and in that capacity was influential on both internal and foreign issues and was sent on several highly confidential missions. In addition to being an economist he is a philosopher and has written a number of works which include *Analyse économique de la vie politique* (1973), *Modèles politiques* (1973), *L'Anti-économique* (1974), *La parole et l'Outil* (1975), *La Nouvelle economie française* (1978), and *Les Trois Mondes* (1981). Before taking office in the Socialist government, Attali was very active in Jewish affairs and held the post of vice-president of the Fonds Social Juif.

In 1990 Attali was appointed to a four-year term as president of the European Bank for Reconstruction and Development (BERD) with headquarters in London. [GI.KO./ED.]

AUERBACH, CARL A. (1915–). U.S. law professor. Born in New York, Auerbach graduated from Long Island University in 1935 and from Harvard Law School, in 1938. He then took a position in the Department of Labor, followed by positions in the National Defense Commission and the Office of Price Administration. In the latter agency he served as assistant general counsel. For two of the war years he served in the army, and then reentered federal government service, where he held important legal positions, including that of general counsel of the Office of Price Administration (O.P.A.). From 1947 to 1961 he was a professor at the University of Wisconsin Law School and then served for 25 years as a professor at the University of Minnesota Law School. As a law teacher and legal scholar, his chief subjects were administrative law, constitutional law, civil rights, legal education, and law and the social sciences. In 1972 Auerbach was appointed acting dean at Minnesota, and was dean from 1973 to 1979.

Auerbach is the author or coauthor of several books on the regulation of transportation and on the legal process. He identified himself with the mainstream of American liberal thought, with the reform-liberal program and policies of Hubert Humphrey; he was one of the founders of Americans for Democratic Action. He believed that the best critical legal thought should have a bearing on important social and political issues and policies. His writings contributed to the planning that resulted in the civil rights legislation of Congress; and while he questioned the wisdom of the Communist Control Act of 1954, he defended its constitutionality. [M.R.K.]

AUSCHWITZ CONVENT. In 1984 Cardinal Macharski, archbishop of Cracow, announced the establishment of a Carmelite convent in Auschwitz in a building on the camp periphery which had orginally been a theater but was used during World War II to store the poison gas used in the Auschwitz crematoria. When a Catholic organization called Aid to the Church in Distress issued an appeal to mark the pope's visit to the Benelux countries in 1985 under the slogan "Your gift to the Pope — a convent in Auschwitz," the Jewish community — initially in Belgium — reacted with outrage. They were joined in their protest by leading Catholic dignitaries in Western Europe. Jews stressed that although others had suffered there, Auschwitz had become a symbol of Jewish martyrdom and while not objecting to a convent devoted to commemoration of Catholic suffering in Auschwitz, it should not be sited within the boundaries of the camp.

The building which housed the controversial convent at Auschwitz (Photo Ruth E. Gruber, Rome)

Although similar Christian institutions existed in other camp sites, Auschwitz, it was felt, was different. The presence of the convent would contribute to the minimization of the Jewish aspect, already scarcely mentioned in the official descriptions on the site as prepared by the Polish government. One reaction in Polish circles was to emphasize the theme of the fate of Poles for whom Auschwitz was also "a synonym of martyrdom and extermination." The issue exercised the Jewish world and became the major subject in Jewish-Catholic discussions, overshadowing all other aspects of the ongoing dialogue.

Two top level meetings in Geneva in 1986 and 1987 (attended on the Catholic side by four cardinals and on the Jewish side by West European leaders) led to the undertaking by the Catholics to create a new "center of information, education, meeting, and prayer outside the area of the Auschwitz-Birkenau camps" with the Carmelite convent transferred to this new area. Cardinal Macharski, who was one of the participants, undertook that the nuns would be moved to the new site within two years.

The issue then dropped to the background and only came again to the fore as the two-year deadline approached and there was still no sign of progress and indications that the Catholics were not fulfilling the Geneva promises. Macharski claimed that the problems encountered with the Polish authorities over the new site made postponement inevitable. Moreover the nuns in the convent and some elements in the Polish Catholic Church were opposed to the move. Tensions rose as the Catholics announced a delay, and the Jews complained that no indication was being given for the fulfillment of the agreement. Jews were further incensed by reports of a large cross having been erected in the grounds of the convent. Protests and demonstrations were now held in various countries. A French-Belgian delegation brought a petition signed by 800 Belgian Catholics requesting the removal of the convent but were not received by the nuns. On the other side, over a thousand inhabitants of the town of Oswiecim (Auschwitz) protested "the illegal demands of the Jews to ruthlessly carry out an unwarranted eviction of the nuns," while other anti-Jewish reactions were reported from elsewhere in Poland.

As the new deadline of July 22, 1989, approached, tensions rose still higher. One indication was the call of the Board of Deputies of British Jews for prayers to be recited in all synagogues in Britain calling for the removal of the convent. The Catholics restated that they intended to keep the agreement but that an educational program had first to be implemented in Poland. The situation reached flashpoint when an American rabbi, Abraham Weiss, and six colleagues dressed in concentration camp garb scaled the walls of the convent and were dragged away, screaming "Nazi anti-Semites." Reactions were divided in the Jewish world to the demonstration, but Polish sources saw it as an attempted attack on the nuns. The deadline passed with a march around the convent by 300 European Jewish students, to the sound of the *shofar*. In August Cardinal Macharski announced that in reaction to the Jewish campaign, the agreement was to be canceled and the nuns would remain where they were.

At this time the archbishop of Warsaw, Cardinal Glemp, delivered a sermon in Czestochowa to a congregation of 100,000 including the Polish premier, which was seen as anti-Semitic when he called on the Jews "not to talk to us from the position of a superior nation and do not dictate terms that cannot be fulfilled...Your strength is in the mass media, at your disposal in many countries. Do not use it to spread anti-Polonism." Glemp's remarks were condemned not only by Jews but also in Polish quarters, with Lech Walesa calling them "a shame and a disgrace." Glemp's attacks on the Geneva agreement were also seen as revealing a rift with his fellow Cardinal Macharski and indicating a division in the Polish Catholic hierarchy. The three western cardinals who had signed the agreement — Cardinal Decourtray of Lyons, Cardinal Lustiger of Paris, and Cardinal Daneels of Brussels — also publicly opposed Glemp.

In September the Vatican spoke out for the first time supporting the relocation of the convent in order to restore good relations with the Jews and even expressed its willingness to contribute financially to the project. Cardinal Glemp, who was then visiting England, executed a volte-face and two days after a speech calling the agreement "a form of wishful thinking," he wrote a letter (the Vatican statement had appeared in the meanwhile) stating that the convent should be moved as soon as possible. With this the crisis was defused.

Although the original deadline for the new complex, set in 1990, proved over-optimistic, work progressed on the interfaith center and the convent which was ready in 1993. Nevertheless the nuns continued to be reluctant to leave the old building, and this was only accomplished in the summer of 1993 following a letter from the pope and pressure from the Polish Bishops' Conference. Seven of the 14 nuns agreed to move to the new convent, the others going elsewhere. Jewish-Catholic relations returned to normal and the dialogue was resumed. In particular Jews were encouraged by the understanding that had been evinced towards Jewish sensibilities by many Catholic quarters.

Jewish sensitivity to Auschwitz was also recognized by the new Polish regime, which succeeded the communists, and a special commission was set up, with the participation of Jewish scholars, to prepare completely new texts for the information and inscriptions presented in Auschwitz-Birkenau and the literature available at the site, in which due prominence would be given to the Jewish aspects and to the fact that of the 1,600,000 victims at Auschwitz, 1,350,000 were Jews (the others being approximately 83,000 Poles, 20,000 Gypsies, and 12,000 Russians). [G.W.]

AUSTRALIA (see **3**:877; **Dc./17**:165). During the decade 1983–1992 Australia enjoyed a period of growing prosperity followed, after 1990, by a severe recession and increased unemployment. Its traditional links with Britain declined in this period and most Australian leaders saw its future as linked with the East Asia–Pacific region.

The Jewish community in Australia is by far the largest and best organized in the region and a community of growing importance and visibility in the Diaspora with a wide range of institutions. Anti-Semitism has always been low and Jews have risen to high places. Links between Australia and Israel have always been strong, although in the past decade they have been troubled by repeatedly critical comments voiced by the government about Israel's West Bank policies, similar to those made by other Western governments. In general, however, the decade under review witnessed a period of growth and maturation for Australian Jewry.

Demography. Australian censuses are held every five years, most recently in April 1991. An optional religious question is asked, from which it is possible to establish a lower limit of the number of Jews. About 25 percent of the Australian population give "no religion" or "religion not stated" in response to this question, while it is known that many Jews decline to answer this question, either out of fear of possible anti-Semitism, because they regard it as an invasion of privacy, or because of self-identity as Jews in a non-religious sense. The 1986 figures, the most recent available, are by state: New South Wales, 28,236; Victoria, 32,387; Western Australia, 3,919; Queensland, 2,632; South Australia, 1,144; Tasmania, 161; Australian Capital Territory (ACT), 502; Northern Territory, 110. The total number of persons declaring themselves to be Jewish by religion in the 1986 census was 69,091. Most demographers believe this figure is a serious understatement of the true picture, with the total number of Jews in the range of 90,000–100,000. Some new statistical basis for this higher figure was available from two new sources. The 1986 census uniquely asked for respondents to identify their "ethnic" origin, and by adding those respondents denoting a "Jewish" ethnic origin, to the Jewish religious figure, Dr. Charles Price of the Australian National University arrived at a total of "about 90,000 Jews" in Australia (*Journal of the Australian Jewish Historical Society* II (1991), pt. 3, p. 530). Secondly, the Jewish Welfare Society in Melbourne released some details of the master list it maintains of Jewish persons in Victoria (whose capital is Melbourne) for the first time. According to its list there were in November 1988 a total of 41,276 Jews known to it and the Welfare Society believed its list to be 95 percent complete, which would raise the Victorian total to 43,448 in November 1988, suggesting a national total of 92,800. In November 1992 the number of Jews known to it in Victoria had risen to 45,590 in 17,121 households (an average of 2.66 persons per household) suggesting that very significant Jewish population growth — an increase of about 10 percent in only four years — was continuing.

The results of the April 1991 census were delayed by computer problems, and complete census figures for Jews were not available by the end of 1992, except for the small communities of Tasmania and the Australian Capital Territory (Canberra). In Tasmania, there were 194 Jews, compared with 160 in 1986, a rise of 21.3 percent; in the A.C.T. there were 512, an increase of 2.2 percent over the 1991 figure of 501.

During the decade, immigration continued from a number of sources, especially the Soviet Union/Russia, the source of about 3,500 Jewish migrants to Australia in this period. Immigration from South Africa, particularly during the early 1980s, was also significant. In general the integration of South Africans into the Australian community was smooth, with the two communities enjoying a similar institutional structure and language. The integration of Russian/Soviet Jewry was, however, more difficult, with Soviet Jews often reluctant to associate with existing institutions and often experiencing economic and social difficulties. A number of organizations, like the Association of Jews from the Commonwealth of Independent States (formerly "Shalom") in Melbourne existed to assist Russian Jewish integration.

Melbourne remained the largest Jewish community in Australia, with a Jewish population of 40–50,000. Sydney was the second largest community with about 35,000. Perth, in Western Australia, with about 5,000 Jews, grew strongly, sparked by many South African arrivals.

Intermarriage in Australia is low by most Diaspora standards. In Victoria in 1986, according to the census, only 7.9 percent of Jewish wives had non-Jewish husbands, with 9.4 percent of Jewish husbands having non-Jewish wives, a marginal rise (less than 1 percent) from 1981. Figures from the other states were not available, but were believed to be higher in New South Wales (Sydney) and higher still in the other states with smaller Jewish communities. Some commentators on Australian Jewish affairs would place the Australian intermarriage rate higher still, in the 20–30 percent range, but without factual evidence. This relatively fortunate state of affairs, compared with, say, the United States, may be ascribed to a number of factors, including the greater strength of Orthodoxy in Australia, the geographically contiguous nature of most Jewish communities, the fact that most Australian university students live at home and associate in Jewish circles, and, most of all, the existence of a particularly well-developed Jewish day school network.

Mr. I. J. Leibler (right), president of the Executive Council of Australian Jewry, meets with Malcolm Fraser, Australian prime minister, 1982. (Courtesy of Rabbi Israel Porush, Australia)

In socio-economic terms, Jews clearly belonged to the upper middle classes, with most Jews employed in managerial or professional fields. "Rich lists" of Australia's 200 wealthiest persons and families during the 1980s invariably showed that about 25 percent of such persons were Jewish, a vast over-representation of the Jewish proportion in the overall population of 0.6 percent. Australia experienced a boom of wealthy self-made men during the 1980s; only a few of the most visible of these were Jewish, possibly accounting for the relative lack of discernable anti-Semitism these figures engendered. Among the best-known Australian Jewish entrepreneurs were the Smorgon family (meat retailing and manufacturing), Richard Pratt (packaging), Sir Peter Abeles (transport). John Gandel (clothing), Isidore Magid (property development), Marc Besen (clothing), and Isi Leibler (travel agency). Many of these were Holocaust survivors or their relatives and together with self-made men of other backgrounds, were sometimes seen as comprising a "new boy network" (the title of a well-publicized study of these men by Ruth Ostrow), challenging the traditional Anglo-Saxon "Establishment" of old money. Many, too were closely associated with the Jewish community and its causes. Leibler, the founder of Jetset, Australia's largest travel agency, was co-chairman of the World Jewish Congress and internationally known in the Jewish world.

On the other hand, many Australian Jews were certainly far from rich. Apart from chronic poverty among the elderly and newly arrived immigrants, the recession which began in the later 1980s struck particularly hard at the Jewish community, especially in Melbourne, with the facilities of the Jewish Welfare Society and similar bodies stretched to the limits. The Jewish Welfare Society in Melbourne reported that cases brought to its attention rose from about 1,500 per year in the late 1980s to 2,250 cases in the financial year 1991–92 (of which 424 were recent Soviet migrants and 660 calls for information or referral). Australian Jewry also differs from other Diaspora communities in containing relatively few academics and intellectuals, and Jews were seldom seen as important participants in national debates.

Education. Several full-time Jewish day schools were founded over the past decade. In Sydney, Emanuel School in the suburb of Woolhara was established in 1983. It is associated with the Progressive movement's Temple Emanuel, and takes both primary and secondary students. In Melbourne, the North-Eastern Jewish Day School was established in 1989 to serve the community of Doncaster, somewhat removed from the center of Jewish life. Although associated with the Ḥabad movement, it drew students from other backgrounds and currently serves the primary grades only.

View of the Nathan and Miriam Solomon Center with the Adelaide Hebrew Congregation to the left and the school, Massada College, to the right (Courtesy A. Bensimon,. Adelaide Hebrew Congregation)

Queensland was long the only mainland state capital in Australia without a Jewish day school. In 1990 Sinai College, in the suburb of Burbank, catering for primary students, was established. The foundation of these three schools brought the total number of full-time Jewish day schools in Australia to eighteen: nine in Melbourne, six in Sydney, and one each in Perth, Adelaide, and Brisbane. These represent the various streams in Australian Jewish life, with three schools in Melbourne, for instance, representing strict Orthodoxy, and the other schools associated with the Mizrachi movement, mainstream Orthodoxy, and with the Progressive movements, with secular Yiddish culture, and with secular Zionism.

Enrollments continued to climb at these schools during the past decade. In Melbourne, they rose from 4,840 at all schools in 1982 to 5,492 in 1989, and about 6,000 in 1992. In Sydney, the rise was even more spectacular, from 1,594 in 1982 to 3,041 in 1988. Carmel College in Perth (Western Australia) had 968 students in 1992. During the severe recession of the early 1990s, doubts were widely expressed about the continued viability of several Jewish schools, all of which are fee-paying although they each receive some state government assistance. It seems probable that enrollments will level off for the time being, and some schools, like Masada College in Sydney, did see declining numbers in 1991–92. Nevertheless enrollments at Jewish day schools in Australia probably represented a higher percentage of the local Jewish community than in any other significant Diaspora community, with over 50 percent of Jewish school-age children attending one or another school.

Australia's oldest and largest Jewish day school, Mount Scopus College, with 2,700 students, chose a new head master in 1991, Dr. Bill Altshul, an American-born educator, to replace Dr. Stephen Lorch, who moved to Israel. In 1992 Carmel College in Perth admitted adherents of the Progressive movement, including students not regarded as Jewish according to Orthodox *halakhah*, for the first time.

Advances were made in this period in tertiary Jewish education, long an area of neglect, especially in comparison with the well-developed day school movement. By 1992, the University of Sydney and three universities in Victoria — Melbourne, Monash, and Deakin — were offering or actively planning Jewish studies programs, a notable advance on the situation a decade before. Lecturers in Modern Jewish History were appointed at Melbourne and Monash Universities in, respectively, 1988 and 1992. An Australian Association for Jewish Studies was established in 1987 and has held annual conferences since then; nearly 200 scholarly papers, representing all facets of Jewish studies, have been presented in the first five years. Several Orthodox *kollels* also exist.

Congregational. There were approximately 71 synagogues and Jewish religious congregations in Australia in 1992, of which 31 were in Victoria, 24 in New South Wales, four in Western Australia, five in Queensland, two in South Australia, four in Tasmania, and one in the Australian Capital Territory. (This figure includes Habad houses but excludes a number of unofficial religious groups which meet regularly.) Most streams in contemporary Jewry are represented among these congregations, from strict Orthodoxy to the Progressive movement, with the exception of the Conservative movement, which has no representation in Australia. Of these synagogues and congregations, about 12 are strictly Orthodox (Lubavitcher or Adass), three Sephardi, 12 Progressive, and the other mainstream Orthodox, stemming either from Anglo-Orthodox or East-European origins and traditions. Most synagogues are in a healthy state and most reported outstanding attendances throughout this period, especially on High Holy Days. About 80 percent of Australian Jews were regarded as Orthodox and 20 percent Progressive; perhaps 15 percent were adherents of a strictly Orthodox synagogue.

In 1989 the Hobart Synagogue, founded as an Orthodox synagogue in 1845 but in steady decline in this century, joined the Progressive movement after a vote of its members. A major new Adelaide complex, containing an Orthodox synagogue, day school, and communal center, the Nathan and Miriam Solomon Center, was dedicated in July 1990 by Australia's Governor-General, Bill Hayden. New congregations in Perth and in East Gosford, NSW were established in the period of 1989–92, as well as a number of Ḥabad houses in Melbourne, Sydney, and in Tasmania. The Orthodox Bankstown and District Synagogue in western Sydney, founded in 1912, closed down in 1991 after a fire.

The Melbourne Hebrew Congregation, Melbourne's oldest synagogue, celebrated its 150th anniversary in 1992 with the publication of a major history by Yossi Aron and Judy Arndt, *The Enduring Remnant: The First 150 years of the Melbourne Hebrew Congregation* (1992).

Rabbi Dr. Israel Porush, rabbi of the Great Synagogue in Sydney from 1940 to 1972 and the author of much of the material on Australia in the *Encyclopaedia Judaica* and its supplements, died in 1991 at the age of 84. He was regarded as the doyen of the Orthodox rabbinate in Australia. Rabbi Ronald Lubofsky, of the historic St. Kilda Hebrew Congregation in Melbourne, retired in 1984 and was replaced by Rabbi Philip Heilbrunn. Rabbi Jonathan Sacks, the new chief rabbi of the United Hebrew Congregations of Great Britain, visited Australia in mid-1991.

Relations between Orthodox and Progressive synagogues in Australia have always been less than outstanding and were particularly bad in the period 1983–92, with many acrimonious exchanges, especially in Melbourne, among the Orthodox and Progressive rabbinate. These probably peaked around 1986 on the occasion of a visit to Australia of Israel's President Chaim Herzog, whose itinerary was a matter of dispute by both streams. Recently efforts have been made by Melbourne leaders to hold discussions aimed at improving relations.

Israel and Zionism. In general, relations between Australia and Israel were very good in the period 1983–92. A clear pattern emerged, however, of criticism of Israeli policy vis-à-vis the West Bank being voiced by the Australian government at the UN or other international bodies, leading to a spirited response by the Australian Jewish community, generally in the form of a meeting between the prime minister and foreign minister and senior leader of the Excecutive Council of Australian Jewry and the Zionist Federation of Australia. These meetings were generally productive from the Jewish community's viewpoint. This pattern continued in the period 1989–92. A meeting held between Prime Minister Bob Hawke, Foreign Minister Gareth Evans, and 24 Jewish leaders in May 1989 occurred after the upgrading of contacts with the PLO and some unfortunate remarks by Australia's UN officials. In January 1991 Australia sent three naval frigates so support the UN action against Iraq, and there was general public support for the Gulf War.

In December 1991 Prime Minister Bob Hawke was replaced by Paul Keating, formerly federal treasurer. Whereas Hawke had a long-standing commitment to Israel (which diminished considerably during the Likkud years of rule), Keating's views on the Middle East were unknown. Keating came from a faction of the Australian Labor party, the "New South Wales right," which was generally very friendly to Israel, but in his constituency were many Muslims and he was not known to be close to Jewish advisers or supporters. Asked for his views soon after, he stated that he "was a supporter of Israel but not one-eyed [one-sided]," In general, during the first year of Keating's rule Australia took a lower profile on the Arab-Israeli dispute, probably because of the start of Arab-Israeli peace negotiations and Australia's pressing domestic concerns. The only untoward incident arose out of a trip to the Middle East by Australian Foreign Minister Gareth Evans, who was reported as making a number of anti-Israel remarks and was photographed, amid much publicity, playing soccer with Palestinians on the West Bank. Talks on his return with Jewish leaders, especially Australian Zionist Federation President Mark Leibler, produced a more conciliatory statement.

Yehuda Avner, an experienced diplomat, was appointed Israeli ambassador to Australia at the end of 1992, replacing Zvi Kedar.

Communal. The "roof body" of the Jewish community in Australia, the Executive Council of Australian Jewry (ECAJ) rotates its headquarters between Sydney and Melbourne every few years. Presidents in recent years have included Isi Leibler (1982–85, 1987–89, 1992–) of Melbourne and Leslie Caplan (1985–87, 1989–92) of Sydney. The representative body of the Jewish community in New South Wales, the N.S.W. Jewish Board of Deputies, has been headed by Dr. Graham de Vahl Davis (1985–89), Gerry Levy (1989–92), and Michael Marx (1992–). Its equivalent in Victoria, the Victorian Jewish Board of Deputies, changed its name to the Jewish Community Council of Victoria in 1988. Its presidents in recent years have been Robert Zablud (1980–86), Shmuel Rosenkranz (1987–90), and Joe Gersh (1990–). The important Zionist Federation of Australia has been headed by Melbourne lawyer Mark Leibler since 1984. His brother Isi Leibler is head of the Australian Institute of Jewish Affairs and in 1990 was awarded an honorary degree by Deakin University in Victoria for his efforts on behalf of Soviet Jewry.

Anti-Semitism and Anti-Zionism. Australia has experienced comparatively little anti-Semitism. Most anti-Semitism emanates from a few predictable sources, especially the Australian League of Rights, an extreme right-wing body which distributes anti-Semitic and "Holocaust revisionist" materials. A faction of the anti-Semitic La Rouche movement came to light in Australia in 1991. Several neo-Nazi "skinhead" groups have surfaced in Australia in recent years, generally attacking Asian rather than Jewish targets. A powerful, controversial Australian film about neo-Nazi skinheads, *Romber Stomper*, was released in 1992.

Attacks against Jewish persons or properties are rare in Australia. Distrubing exceptions to this trend occurred in 1990 and 1991 when over 150 anti-Semitic incidents were reported to the Jewish community in each year, peaking around Hitler's birthday in April. These included over a dozen arson attacks on synagogues in Sydney and Melbourne. Attacks were also reported during the Gulf War period in 1990, but declined significantly after mid-1991.

A government committee taking evidence on racist violence in Australia in 1991 found that of 225 such acts reported to it, 115 were directed against Aboriginals, 53 against Asians, but only 17 against Jews. Laws making racial incitement or vilification illegal were passed in several Australian states including New South Wales. In 1992 the federal government announced its intention to pass national legislation making racial vilification illegal and to forbid the visit to Australia of racist activists from abroad.

Hostility to Israel, often bordering on anti-Semitism, emerged strongly from extreme left sources in Australia in the 1970s but has, generally, declined since the end of the Lebanon War of 1982–84. Concern has often been voiced in the Jewish community at reportage on the Arab-Israeli conflict on the ABC, Australia's national television network, and on SBS, an "ethnic" television network, both of which are allegedly controlled by leftists with an anti-Israel agenda. Complaints peaked during the Gulf War, when the ABC's coverage was widely seen by Jews as anti-American. There are also other sources of Australian anti-Zionism. Leftist-dominated church groups, especially the Australian Council of Churches and "social responsibility" groups in the Uniting (i.e., Methodist/Presbyterian) churches, have issued one-sided attacks on Israel regarded as virtually anti-Semitic. Extremist Muslim sources have also given rise to considerable concern, especially the blatantly anti-Semitic Sydney Arab-language newspaper *An Nahar*, and an anti-Semitic Sydney imam, Sheikh Taj al-Hilaly.

The murder of Australian Yeshivah student Yankel Rosenbaum by anti-Semitic blacks in Crown Heights, Brooklyn, New York in August 1991 was greeted with particular outrage in Melbourne, where he lived and was well known in the *Lubavitcher* community. His murder and the subsequent acquittal of his alleged murderer received considerable publicity in the Australian media.

War Crimes. In 1988 Australia passed a War Crimes Act, making possible the prosecution in Australia of East European immigrants accused of complicity in the Holocaust. Two such prosecutions have been brought — against former Ukrainians resident in Adelaide, Ivan Polyukovich, and, separately, Heinrich Wagner.

The Australian War Crimes Act aroused considerable controversy, especially from conservative sources, when it was passed. The federal government spent over $15 million on identifying suspected war criminals in Australia, but the apparently meager results — only two viable prosecutions out of 820 suspected persons in four years — caused the federal Government, in July 1992, to cease funding the Special Investigations Unit created to proceed against alleged war criminals in Australia.

Culture. Australia has a growing number of significant Jewish cultural figures and institutions. Notable Australian Jewish writers who have made an impact in recent years include Dr. Serge Liberman, a gifted short story writer, controversial playwright Ron Elisha, and poets Fay Zwicky, Lily Brett, and Mal Morgan. A rich Yiddish culture survives, especially in Melbourne, in the form of the Sholem Aleichem School, a weekly newspaper, several hours of broadcast time on two "ethnic" radio stations, and a Yiddish-English quarterly, *The Melbourne Chronicle.* Melbourne writer Arnold Zable's *Jewels and Ashes* (1991), an autobiographical account of his trip to his parents' *shtetl* in Poland, won several awards. A Jewish Festival of the Arts was held in Melbourne in 1991 and 1993, while a Jewish Film Festival, held annually since 1990, is now the second largest in the world. Australian theatrical impresario Elijah Moshinsky is internationally known. The revamped *Australian Jewish News*, the Jewish community's weekly newspaper, is now, under the editorship of Sam Lipski and Susan Bures, of high quality, while several other Jewish periodicals, including *Generation* (a quarterly on Jewish topics) and *Without Prejudice* (on racism) have been founded in recent years.

The period since 1982 has seen a great increase in writings on Australian Jewish history, with histories of the Australian Jewish community by Suzanne Rutland *Edge of the Diaspora*, 1987) and Hilary L. and W.D. Rubinstein (*The Jews in Australia: A Thematic History*, 2 vol., 1991), and a history of Western Australian Jewry by David Mossenson and Louise Hoffman, *Hebrew, Israelite, Jew* (1990). Important works on Australian attitudes during the Holocaust period have been written by Michael Blakeney, Paul R. Bartrop, Colin Golvan, and others, as well as studies of Australian Zionism by Rodney Gouttman. *The Journal of the Australian Jewish Historical Society*, founded in 1939, has emerged in recent years as an important venue of serious Australian Jewish historiography, while a scholarly quarterly on Jewish subjects, *The Australian Journal of Jewish Studies* (formerly *Menorah*) was founded by the Australian Association for Jewish Studies in 1988, under the editorship of Dr. Evan Zuesse and Dr. Rachel Kohn. Jacques Adler's *The Jews of Paris and the Final Solution*, by a former member of the French Resistance now in Melbourne, is internationally known.

A Jewish Museum of Australia was founded in Melbourne in 1982, with a smaller one in Sydney opening the same year, while Holocaust Museums have been established in Melbourne (1984) and Sydney (1992). A novel of rescue during the Holocaust by non-Jewish Australian novelist Thomas Keneally, *Schindler's Ark* (1982) became an international best-seller. [W.D.R.]

AUSTRIA (see **3**:887; **Dc./17**:167). In 1985 the first conference of the World Jewish Congress in Vienna was overshadowed by the populist Freedom party's defense minister fetching at the same time in his official helicopter the Nazi war criminal Walter Reder when he was released from an Italian prison. (He had slaughtered 1,500 Italian civilians.)

The year 1986 was dominated by the election of President Kurt Waldheim — the most important event of the 1980s for the Austrian state and the Jewish community, causing a most serious crisis for both. The World Jewish Congress charged Waldheim with wartime involvement in Nazi activities in the Balkans as a staff member of General Löhr who was executed as a war criminal by the Yugoslavs in 1947. During Waldheim's election campaign strong anti-Semitic feelings were openly expressed by parts of the population, and also by several politicians and the media, especially by the two dailies, *Die Presse* and *Neue Kronen Zeitung*. The latter, which has a circulation of 1.5 million in a country of 7 million, had already in 1974 published a notorious series about the Jews by Viktor Reimann which was strongly attacked as anti-Semitic and discontinued. Waldheim's election was opposed by many intellectuals and artists, who formed a new club called "New Austria" and organized demonstrations, symposia, vigils, press conferences, and publications in order to recall Austria's responsibility for the Nazi crimes. Many Jews considered emigrating and felt homeless again. Although Israel recalled its ambassador and replaced him by a chargé d'affaires, many joint projects between the two countries were realized. The coolness between the two countries lasted until Waldheim left the presidency in 1992.

Because of the Waldheim affair the so-called "Bedenkjahr" (year of commemoration), which in 1988 marked the 50th anniversary of the "Anschluss" of Austria to Nazi Germany was taken very seriously. At the state ceremony and the festive event in Parliament on March 11 the leading role was played by the socialist Austrian chancellor Franz Vranitzky. Whole series of symposia, exhibitions, lectures, discussion groups, etc., were organized, especially at universities and schools (including many top events fostering the Christian-Jewish dialogue). This was a new experience for Austria, confronting it at last with the historic truth. In June 1988 the heads of the Austrian Jewish community, Chief Rabbi Paul Chaim Eisenberg and President Paul Grosz, were received by Pope John Paul II during his visit to Vienna. In July Helmut Zilk, the mayor of Vienna, commissioned from the sculptor Alfred Hrdlicka a monument to commemorate "the victims of war and fascism" in the center of Vienna. It shows a kneeling Jew being forced by the Nazis to clean the streets in 1938. This caused great controversy among the Jewish community because of the Jew's humiliating posture. In June 1991 Vranitzky made a speech in Parliament, in which he fully acknowledged Austria's moral guilt and responsibility for the Nazi crimes — the first such speech by the head of an Austrian government. Despite all efforts and several legal improvements, many questions concerning reparations remained open and remain to be negotiated. When Simon Wiesenthal in 1987 wanted to found an institute for research on anti-Semitism in Vienna he found no financial support in official Austria.

Anti-Semitism. In June 1987 the deputy mayor of Linz wrote an open letter to Edgar Bronfman, head of the World Jewish Congress, comparing his attitude to Waldheim with the "show trial of the Jews about Jesus." In November of that year Michael Graff, the general secretary of the People's party, resigned because he had said: "as long as there is no proof that Waldheim strangled six Jews with his own hands, there will be no problem"; however, he remained active in politics. When in October 1991 the Jewish cemetery of Vienna was desecrated, 10,000 people took part in a silent march against anti-Semitism in Vienna. It was supported by the People's party and the socialists, but not by the mayor

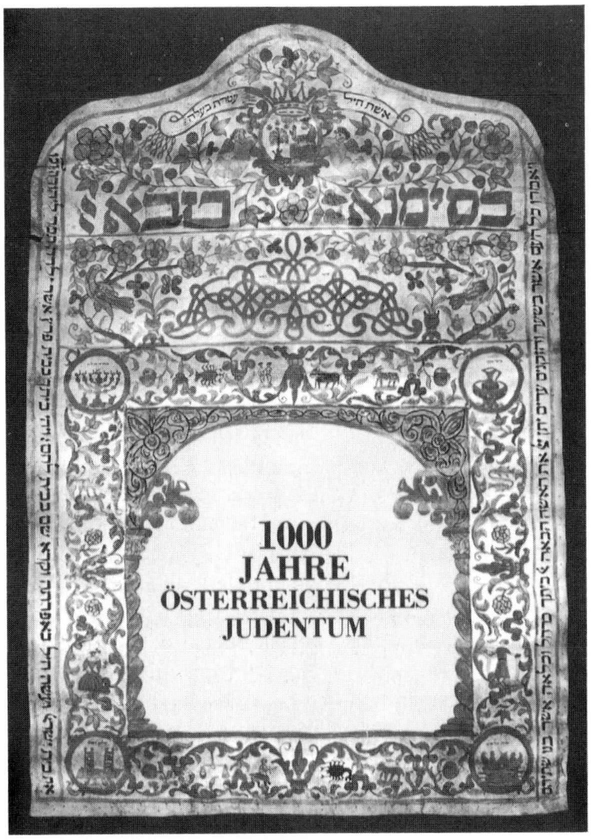

Cover of exhibition catalogue for "1000 Years of Austrian Jewry," the first exhibit at the Austrian Jewish Museum in Eisenstadt

of Vienna. In October 1992, the Jewish cemetery of Eisenstadt, (the location of the Austrian Jewish museum), was desecrated and Chancellor Vranitzky and Paul Grosz attended a commemorative ceremony.

In spring 1991 Jörg Haider, the populist leader of the Freedom party, praised the "decent and proper employment-policies" in Nazi Germany, for which he was voted out of his office as governor of Carinthia. A year later a committee of prominent artists and publicists organized a "concert for Austria" on the Heldenplatz in Vienna against rightist tendencies in Austrian politics. Elie Wiesel was invited to speak from the huge balcony — the first person since Hitler who spoke from there. Even more people — about 250,000 — took part in a "sea of lights" in January 1993 opposing a petition of Haider's Freedom party against the immigration of foreigners, which was signed by 417,000 people, far fewer than expected. Opinion polls throughout these years show that the score of anti-Semites in the Austrian population can be estimated as 20%. After the law against neo-Nazism was amended one of the most vicious Austrian neo-Nazis was sentenced to 18 months imprisonment and more Nazi trials are expected.

Communal. In 1986 the Jewish community had 6,000 members which was a historic low. Today it has 7,400 members, of whom about 800 had lived in Vienna before 1938, 1,500 are Soviet immigrants, and the rest originate mainly from Poland, Hungary, and other Eastern European countries. It is estimated that there are several thousand Jews, many of them Russians, outside the community.

In 1984 the historic Chajesgymnasium, which was founded by Ẓevi Perez *Chajes in 1919, was reopened as the only Jewish high school in a German-speaking country today. Together with the schools of the ultra-Orthodox community there are today 900 pupils who receive a Jewish education in Vienna. In 1984 the Art Nouveau Synagogue in St. Pölten was renovated and in its building was established a new Institute for the History of the Jews of Austria under the directorship of Dr. Klaus Lohrmann, who is also the vice-president of the "action against anti-Semitism in Austria" (the president of which is the actress Elisabeth Orth). In 1988 the historic Stadttempel, the main synagogue of Vienna, was reopened after its renovation in the presence of Chancellor Vranitzky, who in 1989 received the gold medal of the Austrian B'nai B'rith. In 1989 the Jewish Institute of Adult Education was founded, and offers many excellent courses and symposia. For the Russian Sephardim the Jewish community built a new "Sephardi Center" with two beautiful synagogues (officially opened in 1992 by President Thomas Klestil.) But in fall 1991 a well-prepared international conference on anti-Semitism under the auspices of the American Jewish Committee in collaboration with the city of Vienna was postponed by the mayor because of forthcoming local elections and was never held. Since 1990 a Reform Jewish community, Or Chadasch, has existed in Vienna. It has about 100 members and engaged Rabbi Michael König from 1993 with the support of the World Union of Progressive Judaism, but it is not recognized by the Jewish community (Kultusgemeinde).

In October 1992, the Vienna-born Jerusalem mayor Teddy Kollek officially visited Vienna and came again in January 1993, to inaugurate the Austrian branch of the Jerusalem Foundation. The visit of Israel foreign minister Shimon Peres in November 1992 and his official invitation to President Klestil and Chancellor Vranitzky to Israel, together with the inauguration of several Austrian-Israeli projects, marked a new era in the relationship of the two countries.

In 1984 "Versunkene Welt" on the lost culture of Eastern Jewry (with a photographic exhibition, a highly qualified symposium, a film festival, a TV-discussion and an excellent book), was organized by Leon Zelman's Jewish Welcome Service. In March 1990 the Vienna Jewish museum, which was founded through the initiative of Mayor Helmut Zilk, was provisionally opened in the historic building of the Jewish community in the Seitenstettengasse and will be permanently housed in the Palais Eskeles. The city of Vienna bought the famous Judaica collection of Max Berger for the museum, which has already held several exhibitions, some of them in collaboration with the Diaspora Museum in Tel Aviv.

In spring 1992 a week of Jewish culture was for the first time part of the Vienna "Festwochen" and will be continued, as will the Jewish cultural weeks in fall. They were organized in collaboration with the city of Vienna, including a Jewish film festival, and attracted over 10,000 people. [E.AD.]

AVINERI, SHLOMO (1933–), Israeli political scientist and educator. Born in Bielsko, Poland, Avineri arrived in Palestine in 1939 with his family who settled in Herzliyya. Avineri studied political science and history at the Hebrew University of Jerusalem, and received his doctorate for a thesis "The Concept of Revolution."

Avineri has served on the academic faculty of the Hebrew University since 1959. His research work was initially an extension of his doctoral thesis, dealing with the social and political thought of Karl Marx. It was connected to the discovery and publication of the philosophical manuscripts of the young Karl Marx. His research addressed the relationship between the philosophical humanistic, and anthropological writings of the young Marx and his economically orientated later writings. He claimed there was a degree of continuity in Marx's thought and that the mature Marx cannot be understood without the presuppositions of earlier thought.

This research led Avineri to consider the philosophy of Hegel and its relationship with modern totalitarianism (of the left and the right). His research showed that the view presented by Karl Popper of Hegelian philosophy as a form of modern totalitarianism did not present an adequate picture of the Hegelian philosophy and its heritage.

In 1970 Avineri published an article in *Commentary* calling for a dialogue with the Palestinians. In the following year he edited a book *Israel and the Palestinians*, which explored the possibility of negotiations with the PLO. When he was appointed director-general of the Foreign Ministry by Foreign Minister Yigal Allon, the Likkud opposition took exception to Avineri's statements calling for the establishment of a Palestinian state in the West Bank and tried unsuccessfully to block his appointment by a parliamentary motion.

After his year in the Foreign Ministry, Avineri devoted himself to researching the intellecutal origins of Zionism. He tried to place Zionism in the context of 19th-century socialism and nationalistic movements. He has taken a deep interest in recent developments in East Europe where he was one of the first Israeli academics to be invited to give talks in seminars in the Soviet Academy of Sciences in the U.S.S.R., Poland, Hungary, and the former German Democratic Republic. He was an observer to the 1989 elections in Hungary and Czechoslovakia.

His books include several works on Marx and Marxism as well as *The Making of Modern Zionism* (1982), *Moses Hess: Prophet of Communism and Zionism* (1985), and *Arlosoroff: An Intellectual Biography* (1989). [E.HO.]

AZERBAIJAN, one of the independent states of the CIS, gaining its independence with the breakup of the U.S.S.R. In 1979 the republic had 35,500 Jews and in 1989 — 30,800 (of whom 22,700 Ashkenazi Jews lived in Baku).

In the wake of the continuing warfare between Azerbaijan

and Armenia over Nagorny-Karabakh in 1989, 1,981 Jews (97.5% or 1,933 of them, from Baku) emigrated. In 1990, 7,673 Jews immigrated to Israel from Azerbaijan and in 1991 — 5,968 (with 5,513 of them coming from Baku).

Baku has a Jewish culture club, "Alef." In 1992 Azerbaijani Jews began issuing the newspaper *Aziz* (an abbreviation of "Azerbaijan-Israel"). In deference to local nationalism, the newspaper has published anti-Armenian articles. The government and the Popular Front of Azerbaijan have publicly condemned anti-Semitism on more than one occasion. The Jewish Agency is allowed to operate openly in Baku. [MI.BE.]

B

BADINTER, ROBERT (1928–), French lawyer and minister of justice. Born in Paris, Badinter studied law there and at Columbia University. A lawyer and a professor of law, Badinter is a well-known opponent of the death penalty and fighter for civil rights. After taking office as minister of justice under President Mitterrand in 1981 he promoted and

Robert Badinter (Courtesy Embassy of France, Tel Aviv; photo Bourcier/Sipa Press)

had passed — sometimes in the face of considerable opposition — legislation towards the abrogation of the death penalty, abrogation of the special tribunal for security offenses ("cour de sécurité de l'Etat"), and curtailment of the powers of the police. His militant stand on these and related issues made him the target of virulent attacks, sometimes of an anti-Semitic nature. However, he enjoyed the support of President Mitterrand. Badinter published *L'Execution* (1973) and *Liberté*, (1976). Prior to his joining the government he had been active in Jewish organizations.

Before the change of regime in 1986, Badinter was appointed President of the Constitutional Council, which is the highest authority in France for interpreting the constitution. [GI.KO.]

BAKSHI-DORON, ELIAHU (1941–), rabbi, Sephardi chief rabbi of Israel. Bakshi-Doron was born in Jerusalem, where he studied at Hebron yeshivah and in the *kollelim* of Mosad Ha-Rav Kook and Kol Ya'akov.

He served as a neighborhood rabbi in Bat Yam, becoming the city's chief rabbi in 1972. In 1975 he was appointed chief Sephardi rabbi of Haifa, serving in that capacity until elected Sephardi chief rabbi of Israel in 1993.

Bakshi-Doron has published dozens of articles reflecting his Torah learning, studies dealing with halakhic solutions to medical, economic, legal, and social problems as well as facets of political science. His work *Binyan Av* (vol. 1, 1982; vol. 2, 1989) deals with many facets of *halakhah* and also gives rabbinic responses to current issues. A third volume recently appeared following the order of the weekly Torah readings to which Rabbi Bakshi-Doron brings new light to *aggadah* and Jewish thought. The book also contains speeches given by the rabbi.

Eliahu Bakshi-Doron, Sephardi chief rabbi of Israel (GPO, Jerusalem)

Throughout his career, Rabbi Bakshi-Doron has worked for Torah education, establishing, among others, a *kolel* in Tel Aviv, an advanced *bet midrash* in Bat Yam, and a Torah learning center in Haifa. [ED.]

BARAK, EHUD (1942–), 14th chief of staff of the Israel Defense Forces (from 1991). Born in Mishmar ha-Sharon, he served in one of the IDF's select reconnaissance squads and commanded it. During the Yom Kippur War he led an armored batallion; in 1982–83 he was head of the Planning Branch General Headquarter; 1983–86, commanding officer of the Central Command; and 1987–91, assistant chief of staff and head of Operations Branch at GHQ. He holds a bachelor's degree in physics and mathematics from the Hebrew University of Jerusalem and received his master's degree in systems analysis from Stanford University. [ED.]

BARBIE, NIKOLAUS ("KLAUS"), TRIAL OF, trial in Lyons, France of SS Hauptsturmfuehrer (captain) Klaus Barbie (b. 1913). Known as "the Butcher of Lyons" for his wartime activities in France, Barbie joined the Nazi Party in 1932 and in 1935 became the personal adjutant to the head of the local Nazi party office in Trier. In late September 1935 he also joined the SS, working in the SD (Security Service) main office and then as a specialist in the Duesseldorf region. On April 20, 1940, he was made an SS second lieutenant (Untersturmfuehrer). On May 29, 1940, shortly after the fall of the Netherlands. Barbie was assigned to the "culture" section of the SD in Amsterdam. His job was to monitor anti-Nazi tendencies in the fields of science, education, religion, sport, entertainment, and propaganda. In November of that year he was promoted to SS first lieutenant (Obersturmfuehrer); exactly two years later he would reach the rank of Hauptsturmfuehrer. During the disturbances in Amsterdam in February 1941, Barbie had acid thrown into his face by the Jewish owners of the "Koko" ice cream parlor. In reprisal over four hundred young Jewish men were arrested and sent to Mauthausen, where most of them perished.

Barbie was made the head of the Gestapo (KdS) in Lyons in November 1942 and remained in that post for nearly two years. To foil the Resistance, Barbie ordered that raids be conducted against arbitrary targets as well as places suspected of underground activity. His work was characterized by a combination of guile and cruelty. He was apparently responsible for the arrest of René Hardy, a resistance leader. Twice tried after the war, Hardy was found innocent of charges that he had divulged the names of French underground leaders to Barbie. Nevertheless, shortly after Hardy was interrogated, Barbie arrested Jean Moulin, Charles de Gaulle's representative in southern France. Moulin had unified the major undergrounds and resistance movements under the National Resistance Council, which was founded on May 27, 1943. During the course of Barbie's interrogation, Moulin was brutally tortured, but apparently gave away nothing before he died. Barbie was involved in the deportation of at least 842 other people from Lyons and its environs. Half of them belonged to the Resistance, and half of them were Jews. He also personally shot a number of persons and was responsible for the death of others from the villages of St. Rambert-en-Bugey, Evosges, Nivollet-Montgriffen, the Montluc prison in Lyons, and other places.

Perhaps his most ignominious act was the seizure and deportation of 41 children and five women who were found hiding in Izieu, a village about 44 miles (70 km.) east of Lyons on April 6, 1944. They were sent to Auschwitz on August 11, 1944. Barbie also was responsible for the deportation of 85 Jews taken in a raid on the headquarters of the Union Générale des Israélites de France (UGIF), on February 9, 1943, in Lyons.

In the spring of 1947, Barbie began working for the Counter Intelligence Corps of the U.S. army in Germany. He became such a valuable informant that his superiors protected him from French attempts to extradite him and helped him escape to Bolivia. Arriving in Bolivia in 1951, he assumed the alias Klaus Altmann, eventually becoming an important advisor to several Bolivian governments. Barbie was tried in abstentia in France in 1952 and in 1954. In the first trial he was charged with atrocities committed in the Jura region against the civilian population and the underground. In the second trial he was charged with committing a massacre at St. Genis-Laval and numerous shootings at the Montluc prison in Lyons. Both trials led to his conviction and sentences of death. In 1971 Barbie was found in La Paz, Bolivia, by Beate and Serge Klarsfeld, French hunters of Nazis. It was not until 1983, however, following repeated appeals by the French, that he was expelled from Bolivia and brought to France for trial.

Barbie was charged with the raid on the UGIF office and the deportation of the Jews from Izieu, two acts for which he had not been previously tried. Coming under the rubric of Crimes Against Humanity, these acts were not subject to the statute of limitation in France. The main proceedings against Barbie took place between May 11 and July 4, 1987. The trial aroused a great deal of interest in France and the rest of the world. Many Frenchmen had mixed feelings about the trial or opposed it. Some Jews thought it might arouse anti-Semitism or become a forum for the denial of the Holocaust. Extreme right wingers actually advanced the claim that Barbie's behavior was no worse than that of the Allies, who had bombed German cities and caused the death of civilians. Some feared it would raise the question again of events surrounding the death of Jean Moulin and of French collaboration with the Nazis.

Barbie himself, after making an early appearance in the courtroom, refused to be present for most of the trial. He was found guilty on July 4, 1987, and given the maximum penalty under French law, life imprisonment. He died Sept. 25, 1991.

Bibliography: T. Bower, *Klaus Barbie Butcher of Lyon* (1984); A.J. Ryan, Jr. (ed.), *Klaus Barbie and the United States Government* (1984). [RO.ROZ.]

BAUER, YEHUDA (1926–), historian and educator. Bauer was born in Prague, Czechoslovakia. He immigrated to Palestine in 1939, joined the Palmaḥ, and participated in the Israeli War of Independence. He earned his B.A. and M.A. at the University of Cardiff, Wales, and his Ph.D, at the Hebrew University of Jerusalem. He has been a member of kibbutz Shuval since 1952. From 1962, he taught at the Institute of Contemporary Jewry at the Hebrew University of Jerusalem, where he became professor of Holocaust Studies in 1973. Since 1983 he has also served as the academic chairman of the International Center for the Study of Antisemitism, at the Hebrew University. In 1986 Bauer became the editor-in-chief of the journal *Holocaust and Genocide Studies.* He is a member of the Scientific Committee of Yad Vashem. He also served on the editorial boards of *Yad Vashem Studies* and *Yalkut Moreshet*, on the curatorium of Bet Loḥamei ha-Getta'ot museum, and on the Holocaust Commission of the Memorial Foundation for Jewish Culture.

Bauer initially wrote about modern Jewish history, especially in the period immediately before, during, and after World War II. His first major studies were about the Joint Distribution Committee from 1919 to 1945 (*My Brother's Keeper* [1974] and *American Jewry and the Holocaust* [1981]): the *Beriḥah (*Flight and Rescue: Brichah* [1970]); and the Yishuv during the Holocaust (*From Diplomacy to Resistance* [1963]). After the untimely death of Shaul Esh who had taught the Holocaust at the Hebrew University, Bauer succeeded him, turning his attention almost entirely to the study and teaching of the Holocaust, on which he was recognized as one of the outstanding authorities in the world. In his writings on the subject (among them *The Holocaust in Historical Perspective* [1978] and *The Jewish Emergence from Powerlessness* [1979]), Bauer has explored broader topics such as the relationship between information about the Holocaust and rescue, and negotiation as a form of rescue. Perhaps more than any other historian of his generation, he has articulated the major issues in Holocaust research and education. In 1982 he published a text book entitled *A History of the Holocaust.*

Bauer also heads the Israel movement for a humanistic Judaism. [RO.ROZ.]

BECKER, GARY STANLEY (1930–), American economist, Nobel prize winner. Becker was educated at Princeton and the University of Chicago. He was the Arthur Lehman Professor of Economics at the University of Chicago and, from 1985, a columnist for *Business Week* magazine.

Early in his career he decided that racial and ethnic bias could be maintained only if markets were not completely competitive. In his 1964 book, *Human Capital*, he raised the idea of considering education as an economic decision.

Becker is a free-market philosopher and has applied his thinking to a wide variety of subjects. He examined the family unit, considering the household as a small business the behavior of which could be analyzed by applying economic principles. In 1992 he was awarded the Nobel Memorial Prize in Economic Science "for having extended the domain of economic theory to aspects of human behavior which had previously been dealt with — if at all — by other social science disciplines such as sociology, demography, and criminology." [ED.]

BEINART, HAIM (1917–), Jewish historian specializing in Spanish Jewry in the Middle Ages. Born in Pskow, Russia, Beinart received a traditional Jewish and general education at the Hebrew High School in Riga. He arrived in Palestine in 1937 as a student and commenced his academic studies at the Hebrew University in Jerusalem.

Concentrating on the history of the Jews in Spain, Beinart spent a research year in the Archivo Historico Nacional in Madrid and in the Archiva General de la Corona de Aragon in Barcelona. He received his Ph.D. in 1955 for his thesis on

"The Trials of the Inquisition against the Judaizers in Toledo in the period of the Expulsion of the Jews from Spain."

Beinart taught in the department of Jewish history at the Hebrew University from 1952, becoming a full professor in 1972.

From 1965 to 1969 he served as academic adviser for the Faculty of Humanities and Social Sciences at what was to become the Ben-Gurion University of the Negev, and was dean of the faculty from 1969 to 1973.

Beinart's research work has dealt extensively with the history of Spanish Jewry in the Middle Ages, based on original sources he has uncovered through his meticulous searches in various libraries throughout the world. His research has concentrated on the century before the expulsion of the Jews from Spain in 1492, although he has researched numerous other areas including studies on the Jews expelled from Spain and their search for refuge in other countries. This includes archival material about Marranos who formed the nucleus for the revival of Jewish communities outside of Spain.

Beinart has published hundreds of scholarly articles in various journals in Spanish, Hebrew and English. His four-volume *Records of the Trials of the Spanish Inquisition in Ciudad Real*, which includes the reports of the trials against the Marranos during the Spanish Inquisition, and his *Conversos on Trial* have made a major contribution to the study of the era.

Beinart founded and edited the *Hispania Judaica Series* (1978–) which publishes historical monographs on the Jewish community in Spain. He is a member of the editorial board of the quarterly *Zion*, of *The Shorter Jewish Encyclopaedia in Russian*, and was editor of the history of the Jews in Spain for the *Encyclopaedia Judaica*. [E.HO.]

BELARUS (formerly **Belorussia**; see **4**:443), independent republic of the CIS. In 1979 Belorussia's Jewish population amounted to 135,400 and in 1989 to 112,000 (with 39,100 in Minsk, 31,800 in Gomel province, and 18,400 in Mogilev province). In 1988–89 the birthrate of Belorussian Jews was 8.2 per 1,000 and their mortality rate — 17.9 per 1,000.

During 1989–91 a total of 49,008 Jews emigrated (the data for 1990–91 reflects only emigration to Israel). The breakdown for these years was: 17,289 from Minsk, 13,370 from Gomel, and 5,575 from Bobruisk. In 1991 15,049 Jews immigrated to Israel, including 5,130 from Minsk.

One Jew was elected to the republic's Supreme Soviet in 1990. Anti-Semitism within the Belorussian national movement militated against its receiving support from Jewish organizations. Anti-Semitic propaganda was rife in such publications as *Politicheskii sobesednik*, *Slavianskie vedomosti*, and *Sem' dnei*. The year 1991 saw the desecration of the Jewish cemetery in Borisov.

The monthly Jewish newspaper *Aviv* began to appear in 1992. Like the local press as a whole, the Jewish paper devotes considerable attention to the topic of World War II. In 1992 Rabbi Yitzhak Volpin came from New York to occupy the long vacant pulpit in the Minsk synagogue.

In the spring of the same year Belarus established diplomatic relations with Israel. [MI.BE.]

BELGIUM (see **4**:416; **Dc./17**:176). Since 1980 the country has undergone deep structural modifications. Belgium is almost a federal country composed of Brussels, Flanders, and Wallonia.

The estimated Jewish population is about 30,000 people equally distributed between the French-speaking community and the Flemish community.

Politics and Terrorism. After the municipal (October 1988) and European elections (June 1989), the general elections (October 1991), confirmed the success of the right-wing parties by electing politicians openly against immigration as well as against Jews (in Antwerp 20 percent of the population voted for them). This is not a specifically Belgian phenomenon but an international one, as was stressed at the conference of the World Jewish Congress held in Brussels in July 1992, called "My Brother's Keeper."

Also, giving rise for concern was the killing in 1989 of Professor Joseph Wybran, president of the political body of Belgian Jewry (it is still not known who was responsible); the release (July 1990) of a Palestinian terrorist (see **Dc./17**:177) in exchange for the freedom of four Belgian hostages held by the Abu Nidal group; and anti-Semitic slogans painted on walls. All these events brought protests from Jewish bodies to the government which reacted positively.

Religious Life. About 14,000 people attend the 48 synagogues and places of worship (28 in Antwerp, 13 in Brussels and one each in Arlon, Charleroi, Ghent, Knokke, Liège, Mons (NATO), and Ostend) during the High Holidays. A Jewish chapel opened (1986) at the Brussels international airport, following the request of Orthodox travelers. Fifteen recognized religious communities (seven in Brussels, three in Antwerp, and one each in Arlon, Charleroi, Ghent, Liège, and Ostend) are represented at the Consistoire Central Israélite of Belgium (CCIB), the only national Jewish body officially recognized by the State, which employs 27 rabbis and religious functionaries.

Religious life continues to be much more intense in Antwerp than in Brussels. Over the past few years, however, Brussels has witnessed a strengthening of its more traditionalist religious life — the creation of two new Orthodox communities, the suppression of the organ, and the mixed choir at the principal synagogue, the opening of a *kasher* restaurant and of a yeshivah. The Israelite Community of Waterloo and of Southern Brabant, which belonged also to this current, was recognized (1992) by the Cult Administration only four years after its creation. The new congregation is the result of changes in the urbanization of the Brussels area; its membership consists largely of English-speaking expatriates. The Liberal congregation has grown steadily and in 1984 founded its own burial society with its own cemetery. Like the Ḥasidim (Belz and Satmar), it wishes to be recognized by the state but is not able, for the moment, to get past the first obstacle which is the agreement of the CCIB where there is opposition.

Education. Jewish education has benefited from the liberal Belgian system. A two-hour per week course is given by 61 teachers appointed by the Consistoire and paid for by the State to 1,300 students attending 247 schools — primary, secondary, and technical — scattered throughout the country, and to the six private Jewish day schools (three in Brussels for more than 1,200 pupils and three in Antwerp for

General Assembly of Belgian Consistory, Pres. George Schnek speaking, at Machzike Hadass, Feb. 1989 (Courtesy Belgian Consistory, Brussels)

about 2,100 children), the latter substantially subsidized by the State. In Antwerp, there are also pupils in other Jewish day schools not recognized by the State.

The constant growth in the number of pupils attending Jewish schools has led to the need to enlarge premises. In Brussels, "Beth Aviv" bought an adjacent house and "Maïmonide" completely rebuilt its premises; in Antwerp, "Yessode Hatorah" is renovating some of its class rooms.

Altogether, more than 6,500 students are receiving a Jewish education. The Ministry of Education also largely supports a free faculty of Jewish studies called "Institut Universitaire d'Etudes du Judaïsme" founded in 1972. Since the academic year 1986–1987, a special degree in Jewish history, thought, and civilization has been recognized by the Free University of Brussels. In the Flemish section (created in 1983 at the Vrije Universiteit te Brussel and in 1988 at the Universitaire Faculteiten St Ignatius Antwerpen) evening classes and courses are taught by professors from Belgium and abroad.

Other forms of education are to be found in Talmud Torahs, in Zionist youth movements, in summer camps, and in community centers where courses are taught on Judaism, Zionism, modern Hebrew, and Yiddish. In Brussels, since Oct. 1984, a "Tzugrapschule" has been open every Sunday morning, and since 1985, three public daily nurseries operate there. With the help of the Antwerp Jewish social welfare institutions, a school called "Tikvatenoe" caters to learning-disabled and problematic children, most of them from Ḥasidic families.

Remembering the Holocaust. During the period under review, Holocaust consciousness was heightened among Belgian Jewry. The case of the Carmelite convent in Auschwitz (see p. 108) was first taken up in Belgium. Actions around this affair froze the official interfaith relations, although in 1993 a "Committee of Consultations between Jews and Christians in Belgium" was set up. After the publication of Professor M. Steinberg's thesis on "The History of Jews in Belgium between 1940 and 1944," an international colloquium on "The Holocaust Period in Belgium" was organized in Bar Ilan University in Israel (1989). Belgium television (French and Dutch channel) produced and broadcast several documentaries on this subject followed by discussions.

As approximately 20,000 Jews were hidden by Christians during the last period of the Holocaust, several memorials were opened in remote places by different associations, one of which, the Belgian Hidden Children Association, helped organize the first congress in New York on this subject.

The fiftieth anniversaries of several historical events were commemorated by impressive ceremonies attended by thousands of Jews and non-Jews. For the 45th celebration of VE-day, King Baudouin attended a gathering in the Jewish National Memorial; it was the first time in the history of Belgium that the ruling king came to a Jewish monument.

Culture. As in the past, cultural and communal life in Belgium is very intensive and is reflected in the Jewish press. Newspapers in Yiddish and in Judeo-Spanish are published regularly as well as old-established journals in French and Dutch. Radio Judaica is still flourishing along with several other institutions. The commemoration of the 500th anniversary of the Spanish Expulsion was celebrated in different ways. The Jewish Museum of Belgium was opened in temporary premises in 1990.

Relations with Israel. In March 1992, elections were held to the Zionist Congress: 3,140 voted (25 percent more than in 1987). The results showed a shift to the right, possibly because the leader of the left was involved in organizing a meeting with Palestinians. The anti-Israel feelings prevailing in the media since the Lebanon War are still felt among the population and the flow of tourists going to Israel has dropped. One consequence was the closing of the Israel Tourist Office in Brussels.

Since 1992, Israel has had two ambassadors in Brussels, one for the EEC, the other for Belgium. [DA.DR.]

BEN-DAVID, JOSEPH (1920–1986), Israeli sociologist. Ben-David was born in Gyor, Hungary, and immigrated to Israel in 1941. He studied at the London School of Economics from 1947–1949. He received his M.A. in history and sociology in 1950 and Ph.D. in sociology in 1955, both from the Hebrew University.

In 1951 he was appointed George Wise Professor of Sociology at the Hebrew University, in 1968 research associate and visiting professor of sociology at the University of Chicago, and in 1979 the Stella M. Rowley Professor of Education and professor of sociology at the University of Chicago.

Ben-David's sociological research and publications reflect his interest in the interaction between macrolevel historical events and microlevel sociological processes in the areas of the development of science, higher education, and the professions and social stratification.

His publications included: *Fundamental Research and the Universities: Some Comments on International Differences* (1968), *The Scientist's Role in Society: A Comparative Study* (1971); *American Higher Education: Directions Old and New* (1972), and *Centers of Learning: Britain, France, Germany and the United States* (1971). [BE.M.]

BENKOW, JO (Josef Elias; 1924–), Norwegian politician. Born in Trondheim, he was a photographer by profession like his father and grandfather. Towards the end of the 1920s the family settled in Bærum, a municipality near Oslo. In World War II he and other male members of his family (his father, brother, and uncle) succeeded in fleeing to Sweden. The female members of his family were deported to Auschwitz. In March 1944 he left Sweden for service in the Norwegian Air Force in England and Canada.

In the 1950s his political interests brought him posts in the liberal conservative party Høyre, the second-largest political party. He was elected as a member of the Bærum local council in 1959, a deputy member of the Storting (the Norwegian parliament) in 1961, becoming the first Jewish-born member of the Storting in 1965. He was the chairman of Høyre in 1981–85, and was then elected president of the Storting. His Jewish connection has been expressed through his interest for Israel (e.g., as a speaker) and his involvement in the cause of Soviet Jewry. Through his objectivity, command of language, and calm and dignified behavior, Benkow has won widespread respect and recognition.

In 1985 Benkow published his autobiography *Fra synagogen til Lovebakken* ("From the Synagogue to Lion Hill," a popular name for the Storting), which was a great success, more than 160,000 copies being sold. In it, he describes his childhood and youth, his Jewish family and Jewish connections, his opinions concerning religious faith and absence of faith and tells about his political life. He also writes about general prejudices and touches on Jewish history (the history of his own family), Jewish customs, discrimination against Jews in the Soviet Union, and tells about his relations with Israel ("a turning point in Jewish self-understanding," as he says). [O.M..]

BERKOFF, STEVEN (1937–), English actor, director, and writer. Born in Stepney, London, he studied drama at the Webber-Douglas School in London and mime at the Ecole Jacque le Coq in Paris.

He has established himself as one of the most innovative theater personalities in the last quarter of the 20th century. As a writer he has adapted many works for the stage including Kafka's *The Trial* and "Metamorphosis" and Poe's "The Fall of the House of Usher." His first professional production was an adaptation of Kafka's "In the Penal Colony."

His personal acting style is original and highly physically controlled — the expression both hypnotic and threatening; although controlled, his stage rages are full of hurt and foreboding leaving an audience little solace. Each performance is unique.

Steven Berkoff (Courtesy Rosica Colin Ltd., London)

He is a prolific playwright whose original works include *Decadence, Greek, West,* and *East.* Much of his work is based on the vernacular of the present day — *West* with the social language and mores of the "West End"; *East* with the "East End" of London, for example. *Kvetch* is, at the same time, amusing and discomfiting; it received the London drama critics' award as the best comedy of 1991. The language of his works is acerbic, clear, intelligent, and unpretentious. Many of his chosen characters as writer or actor are either disturbed or social misfits. He is also a master in the transposition of mythology on to modern life.

He has appeared in a number of films and TV productions, such as *Octopussy, Beverly Hills Cop, Rambo,* and *The Krays,* playing "baddies" (film villains) with relish and undisguised glee.

Berkoff has toured and acted in his own productions of *Hamlet, Macbeth, Salome,* and *Coriolanus* throughout Europe, Israel, and Australia. In his book on the theater *Coriolanus in Deutschland* he describes his unease as a Jew in Munich. Other publications include *I Am Hamlet* and *A Prisoner in Rio.*

In 1983 Steven Berkoff received the Los Angeles Drama Critics Award for directing. [SA.WH.]

BETA ISRAEL (Falashas; see **6:**1143; **Dc./17:**245). In a decade of dramatic changes for World Jewry, the Beta Israel (formerly known as the Falashas regarded by them as a term of contempt) stand out as the Jewish community that has undergone the most dramatic transformation. At the end of 1982 the number of Ethiopian immigrants in Israel stood at about 2,300 and the vast majority of community members were still in Ethiopia. Ten years later the Beta Israel as a diaspora community had ceased to exist. By the end of 1992 over 45,000 Ethiopian immigrants had settled in Israel. When those born in Israel are included and those who have died subtracted, the total number of Ethiopian Jews in Israel exceeds 50,000.

Despite the relatively short period within which the Beta Israel were brought to Israel, each period in their immigration had different characteristics. Most of those who came prior to 1984 were from the Tigre and Walqayit regions of northern Ethiopia. They arrived in small numbers through the Sudan and were gradually settled throughout Israel. In 1984 over ten thousand Jews from the Gondar region of Ethiopia flooded into Sudanese refugee camps. Initially they

Meeting between brothers at the Ashkelon transit center, 1984 (Courtesy Beth Hatefutsoth, Tel Aviv; photo Doron Bacher)

Table 1. Ethiopian Jews in Israel

Year	Ethiopian Immigrants
1972–1979	268
1979–1984	14,037
1984–1990	7,323
1991	19,879
1992 (est.)	3,500
	Israel-born
1977–1990	5,422
1991–92 (est.)	1,000
Total	51,429

were brought out a few hundred at a time, but deteriorating conditions necessitated a more dramatic approach. During a period of less than two months starting in mid-November 1984, more than 6,500 Beta Israel were airlifted to Israel in what became known as "Operation Moses." Premature publicity brought the operation to a halt, but in March 1985 a further 650 Jews were rescued in "Operation Joshua." During the period from March 1985 to October 1989 only a relatively small number of Jews managed to leave Ethiopia. The renewal of diplomatic relations between Israel and Ethiopia, however, paved the way for legal emigration on the basis of family reunification. By the summer of 1990 over twenty thousand Ethiopian Jews had migrated to Addis Ababa in the hope of being taken to Israel. During 36 hours between May 24 and 25 as rebel troops threatened to conquer the capital, over 14,000 Beta Israel were airlifted to Israel in "Operation Solomon." In the succeeding year and a half, several thousand more Beta Israel were brought to Israel. By the end of 1992 only a handful of Beta Israel remained in Ethiopia. A large number (estimates vary between 30–250,000) of *falas moura* (Christians of Beta Israel descent) remained in Ethiopia.

Although all the Beta Israel have left Ethiopia, their resettlement in Israel is far from complete. Virtually every aspect of their absorption process remains fraught with difficulties, and a clear danger exists that Ethiopian Jews in Israel will find themselves marginalized geographically, socially, and religiously.

Despite clearly stated criteria for dispersing Ethiopian immigrants around the country, settling them in permanent apartments has always proven difficult. Housing in the designated sites has not always been available, while local authorities and residents have not necessarily welcomed the influx of a dependent population. For their part the Ethiopians have been reluctant to abandon the protection of immigrant housing and have often refused to do so unless provided with housing that meets all of their criteria regarding cost, proximity to relatives, climate, and employment opportunities. Only after immigrants have been settled in permanent apartments can issues such as children's education and long-term employment be seriously confronted.

As of September 1992 almost half the Ethiopian immigrants in the country were still in temporary housing: 2,500 were in hotels, 7,600 were in regular absorption centers, and 15,000 were living in mobile homes. Each of these groups presents officials with a different set of difficulties, but the last is probably the most problematic. Mobile homes for Ethiopian immigrants (as well as a relatively small number of Russians and veteran Israelis) are situated in 22 sites around the country. Most are located in isolated areas far removed from other Israelis, schools, and employment opportunities. At present it is anticipated that many immigrants will continue to live in such quarters for at least 3 or 4 years.

So long as the Ethiopians remain in temporary quarters, it will be extremely difficult to complete their educational, social, and occupational absorption. Although official statistics were never released, it was generally estimated that prior to 1991, 80% of Ethiopian immigrants eligible for work had found jobs. Those who have arrived in the past two years have had a much harder time finding employment both because of their geographic isolation and difficult conditions in the Israeli economy.

Although more than two decades have passed since Rabbi Ovadiah Yosef (at the time Sephardi chief rabbi) ruled that the Falasha were Jews, many details of their religious status remain unresolved. Despite recurrent demonstrations and court appeals, most Israeli marriage registrars continue to follow the Chief Rabbinate's guidelines and require Ethiopian immigrants wishing to marry to undergo ritual immersion. Rabbi David Chelouche of Netanya and other rabbis designated by him require no such ceremony and continue to perform weddings for Ethiopian Jews throughout the country. Some Ethiopian activists have demanded that *qessotch* (priests), the community's religious leaders, be allowed to conduct weddings and perform divorces as in Ethiopia. The Chief Rabbinate has firmly rejected this demand. Instead it has agreed to allow the *qessotch* to serve on religious councils in areas with large Ethiopian populations and has suggested that they study to become marriage registrars.

The ongoing controversy concerning marriages and the status of the *qessotch* is not merely a halakhic-legal issue. It is also symptomatic of the vast changes that have shaken the Ethiopian family in the past decade. Couples have divorced and remarried, children have asserted an unprecedented degree of independence, and women have redefined their roles. Changes have, moreover, not been limited to the restructuring of relations within the family. The family's relationship to the surrounding society has also been radically changed. In Ethiopia families and households were the foundation of rural communal life and served as schools, workshops, clinics, reformatories, and credit organizations. In Israel most of these functions have become the primary responsibility of other institutions. Thus, the past decade has witnessed not only a dramatic and irreversible change of location (in a geographic sense) for the Ethiopian family. It has also produced a no less revolutionary transformation of its place (in a social-economic sense) and its relationship to its surroundings. [ST.K.]

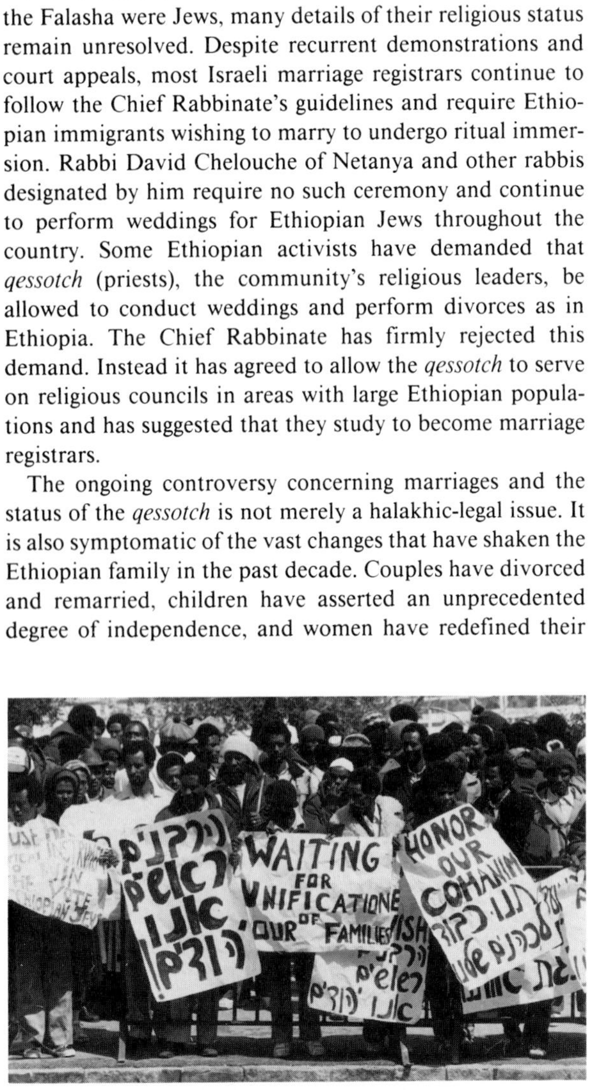

Ethiopian immigrants demonstrate outside the Knesset against attitudes of the Chief Rabbinate, the Jewish Agency, and the absorption authorities, March 24, 1986 (GPO, Jerusalem)

BIRAN (Bergman), AVRAHAM (1909–), archaeologist and diplomat. Born in Petaḥ Tikvah, of a third generation Ereẓ Israel family, Biran received his education at the Reali Secondary School in Haifa and at the David Yellin College in Bet ha-Kerem, Jerusalem. He obtained his M.A. and Ph.D. from Johns Hopkins University in Baltimore, where he studied with William Foxwell *Albright.

From 1935 to 1937 he participated in various archaeological excavations with the University of Pennsylvania in Iraq and with the American Schools of Oriental Research near Irbid in Jordan. He also accompanied Nelson *Glueck on his discoveries along the Gulf of Elath, and in Palestine directed the excavations of the birthplace of the prophet Jeremiah in Anathoth (1935).

In 1937, Biran was appointed District Officer of the Palestine Mandatory Government for the area of the Jezreel Valley. During this period he carried out an archaeological survey of the area. Transferring to Jerusalem in 1945, he became District Officer of the Mandatory Government for Jerusalem. He served as liaison between the United Nations representatives and the Jewish military authorities during the fighting before the 1948 Declaration of Independence.

Biran held a variety of positions with the government of Israel, initially as administrative assistant to Dov *Joseph, the military governor of Jerusalem, becoming governor of Jerusalem for several months. From 1949 to 1958 he was Israel Consul-General in Los Angeles and in 1958 was the director of the Armistice Affairs in the Foreign Ministry.

Returning to archaeology, Biran took up the position of director of Antiquities and Museums of Israel and in 1974 became director of the Nelson Glueck School of Biblical Archaeology of the Hebrew Union College–Jewish Institute of Religion in Jerusalem. In this capacity he directed the excavation of the Israelite sites of Ira and Aroer in the Negev; the ancient synagogue of Yesud ha-Ma'alah; and the longest ongoing excavations in Israel, at Tel Dan. These last excavations revealed a city founded in the 6th millennium B.C.E.; massive fortifications of the 2nd millennium, including a unique triple-arched gate of the 18th century B.C.E. still standing as originally built; a 14th-century B.C.E. tomb with Mycenean imports; evidence for the first settlement of the tribe of Dan, their installations for metal work; the Israelite sanctuary where *Jeroboam had set the golden calf, the religious center of northern Israel with its high place, chambers, altars; a royal scepter; and a dedicatory inscription in Greek and Aramaic — "To the God who is in Dan."

Biran is chairman of the Israel Exploration Society, the Government Names Committee, and president of the International Committee of Museums and Sites (Israel) of UNESCO. [E.HO.]

BLAU, PETER (1918–), U.S. sociologist. Peter Blau was born in Austria and immigrated to America where he was educated at Elmhurst College and Columbia University. He also studied at Cambridge University. Blau was an instructor in sociology at Wayne State University and Cornell University, and a professor at University of Chicago, Columbia University, and the University of Cambridge. He has been a fellow at the Center for Advanced Studies in Behavioral Sciences and the recipient of several National Science Fellowship grants. He was a member of the American Sociological Association and served as its president from 1973 to 1974.

On the basis of his research subject matter and methodology, Blau is associated with the American School of Sociology. His work has centered in two main areas: organizations and social stratification. His book *Formal Organizations* (1963), written with W. Richard Scott, has become a standard textbook on the nature and functioning of formally constituted organization in society. He developed a useful system of typologizing organizations according to the identity of their prime beneficiary. His book *The Dynamics of Bureaucracy* (1955) is a pioneer study in the analysis of the interrelations between formal arrangements and informal relations in organizations. With respect to his interest in stratification, in *Exchange and Power in Social Life* (1964), Blau revealed how normative processes came to govern the exchange between individuals in society. That study was also an ambitious attempt to derive macrolevel sociological institutions from microlevel social processes.

His other publications include: *Bureaucracy in Modern Society* (1956), *The American Occupational Structure* with Otis Dudley Duncan (1967), *The Organization of Academic Work* (1973), and *Inequality and Heterogeneity: A Primitive Theory of Social Structure* (1977). [BE.M.]

BLEUSTEIN-BLANCHET, MARCEL (1906–), French advertising executive and radio pioneer. Born in Enghien, France, Bleustein-Blanchet founded a number of businesses over the years through which he became the foremost individual in advertising in France, a field which he virtually established by introducing advertising into French film, radio, and television. Among his companies were "Publicis" (est. 1927), the largest privately owned advertising agency in France; Radio Cité (1935); Regie Press of which he is chairman (founded 1938); and Cinéma et Publicité (1938). In the early 1920s Bleustein-Blanchet established a private company, "Radio Paris," making him a pioneer of French radio broadcasting. He is sole or part owner of other types of businesses as well, such as the Drugstore restaurants in Paris, and he is the owner of the sixth television network of France, specializing in music.

During World War II he was an active member of the Resistance. He served as Conseilleur of French Foreign Commerce from 1973 to 1975. Bleustein-Blanchet was active in the support of social welfare of the French Jewish community and was president of the Montmartre Israelite Center from 1965. He has received France's highest award, Grand Officer of the Legion of Honor.

He wrote *La rage de convaincre* (1970), *La nostalgie du futur* (1978), and *Les ondes de la liberté* (1984). [GI.KO.]

BOGALE, YONA (1908–1987), Ethiopian Jewish (Beta Israel) personality. Bogale was born in 1908 (some sources say 1910 or 1911) in the village of Wolleqa northeast of the important Ethiopian city of Gondar. His father was a weaver, who also worked as a tenant farmer for a local Christian nobleman. In 1921 Jacques *Faitlovitch visited Ethiopia for the fourth time and spent several months in Walleqa. At the end of his stay he took Yona Bogale with him to study in Europe. Bogale studied two years at the Mizrachi Tahkemoni School in Jerusalem before continuing his education in Frankfort, Switzerland, and France. By the time he returned to Ethiopia he had learned to speak over half a dozen languages. Until the Italian conquest of Ethiopia in 1935/6 Bogale worked as a teacher in the "*Falasha" school which had been established by Faitlovitch and Taamrat Emmanuel in Addis Ababa in 1923. Following the end of the Fascist occupation in 1941 Yona worked for the Ethiopian Ministry of Education. He resigned in 1953 to devote himself to the Beta Israel community, and played a crucial role in the establishment and operation of the Jewish Agency's schools in Ethiopia. Following the closure of these schools Yona continued to work among his people and served as the major mediator for contact between Ethiopian and World Jewry. Perhaps the clearest reflection of his attempts to create a bridge between the two communities were his writings, *A "Falasha" Book of Jewish Festivals*, an Amharic translation of portions of *Pirke Avot*, and a Hebrew-Amharic dictionary. Although generally treated by outsiders as "the leader" of the Beta Israel, within the community his position was ambiguous and he often came into conflict with other important community members. In 1979, Yona immigrated to Israel where he continued his activities on behalf of the Beta Israel. [ST.K.]

BOGORAD, LAWRENCE (1921–), U.S. biologist. Bogorad was born in Tashkent, Russia, but was taken to the United States as an infant. He became a naturalized U.S. citizen in 1935. Bogorad studied at the University of Chicago, where he received a B.S. in botany (1942) and a Ph.D. in plant physiology (1949). From 1951 to 1953 he was a fellow at the Rockefeller Institute working in the laboratory of Prof. Sam Granick. In 1953 he returned to the University of Chicago, joining the faculty of the Department of Botany and became a professor of botany in 1961. Bogorad became professor of biology at Harvard University in 1967, and was chairman of the Department of Biological Sciences (1974–1976), and director of the Maria Moors Cabot Foundation in 1976. He was named the Maria Moors Cabot Professor of Biology in 1980. Bogorad is a fellow of the American Academy of Arts and Sciences, a member of the National Academy of Sciences, and a foreign member of the Royal Danish Academy of Sciences and Letters. He has been president of the Society for Developmental Biology and of the American Society of Plant Physiologists. Bogorad has been on a number of editorial boards and served on national committees as well as having served on the Council and Executive Committee of the American Society of Cell Biology. In 1985 he was elected president of the American Association for the Advancement of Science, which has close to 300 national and regional scientific societies and academies as formal affiliates and 130,000 individual members.

Bogorad's research has concentrated on chlorophyll synthesis, particularly the investigation of the effects of light in the induction of the complex greening process through which pale, etiolated leaves of plants grown in the dark become green and active in photosynthesis. Early work on the enzymes involved in chlorophyll synthesis with algae furthered our understanding of the biosynthesis of hemes and bile pigment. Bogorad's work from the mid-1960s on has dealt with the biogenesis of chloroplasts, the nature of the organelle of DNA, and its function in the synthesis of chloroplast proteins as well as other phytomolecular biological processes.

Bibliography: H. Swift, in: *Science* 229 (1985), 353–54 [ED.]

BOYCOTT, ARAB (see **4**:1282). The Arab boycott of Israel began even before the establishment of the State of Israel but in 1951 the Arab League formally organized a systematic effort designed to thwart the economic development of the fledgling state. The boycott, however, went far beyond the customary boycott of one nation against another, the so-called primary boycott. The Arab League, a loose federation of 20 Arab countries, issued a complex system of regulations designed to create a "blacklist" of companies with which it was improper to trade. This has been described as a secondary boycott. The League went even further and declared a tertiary boycott against any companies dealing with a blacklisted company. The League then established a "Central Office for the Boycott of Israel" in Damascus and a boycott bureaucracy was soon appointed to administer the boycott. The blacklistings and the removals from the blacklist are announced at the semi-annual meetings of the Central Office attended by the boycott commissioners from the various Arab states. In addition, individuals or organizations not involved in any commercial venture but who are Zionists or support Israeli causes are frequently blacklisted for appearing in films decreed by the boycott apparatus to be friendly to Israel. The findings of the Damascus office are, however, merely recommendations which the League members are free to accept, reject, or modify.

Some Arab states, notably Bahrein, Iraq, Jordan, Kuwait, Lebanon, Libya, Oman, Qatar, Saudi Arabia, Syria, United Arab Emirates, and Yemen, participate in the secondary boycott but the remaining eight do not. Among these are Algeria, Morocco, and Tunisia.

While primary boycotts on one nation against another are not uncommon, e.g., India and Pakistan, U.S.A. and Cuba, Taiwan and China (they are recognized as legitimate in international law), secondary boycotts against commercial firms are unprecedented and are deemed impermissible by international law experts.

The 12 Arab countries engaging in the secondary boycott require foreign firms seeking contracts or commercial deals to submit certificates attesting to their lack of economic ties to Israel. The Arab League Boycott Office has issued a model questionnaire to be answered by foreign companies. The questions asked are whether the firm now or in the past:

1. Has a company, factory or assembly plant in Israel.
2. Maintains general agencies or offices in Israel.
3. Has granted the right to use its name, trademarks or copyrights to Israel or Israeli corporations.
4. Has participated in Israel corporations or enterprises.
5. Has provided consultative services or technical assistance to any Israeli enterprise.
6. Represents any Israeli firm inside or outside Israel.

There is no question about the export and sale of goods to Israel or about the import and purchase of Israeli goods. Apparently boycott officials believe that merely selling goods to Israel or buying from it does not strengthen the Israeli economy. What the boycott seeks to do is to deter investments from abroad in Israel.

What is puzzling about the boycott is the failure of the Arab League to publish the so-called blacklist of foreign firms violating boycott rules. Boycott experts believe that the Arab League refrains from such publication so that its members may have the maximum freedom to make exceptions to these rules or disregard them whenever it suits them. Thus, in practice, the entire blacklisting process seems capricious and suspicions of corrupt deals are frequent.

The Unites States mammoth conglomerate, General Electric, manufactures jet engines for Israeli fighter planes. Yet GE has never been placed on an Arab blacklist nor has any other U.S. military contractor.

Arab boycott threats are often mere bluster. When the Chase National Bank in the U.S. became the fiscal agent for Israeli bonds, it was threatened with a boycott if it persisted. It paid no attention to this threat and nothing happened.

Similarly, when Arabs threatened cruise ships stopping in Israel and hotel chains building hotels in Israel, these threats were disregarded. Not only did nothing happen, but the boycott regulations were amended to exclude such cruise ships and such hotels. In 1992 the Arab League threatened to boycott any airline that transported Jewish immigrants from Russia to Israel. The carriers paid no attention to the threat and again nothing happened.

Nevertheless, for some companies, being blacklisted results in their being cut out of the Arab market and such companies go to great lengths and great expense to get their names off the blacklist. In the U.S. the Baxter Corporation, probably the largest health care company in the world, is now under criminal investigation in the U.S. because of its efforts to get off the blacklist.

Until recently, the trading companies of the world, with the sole exception of the U.S.A. and the Netherlands, made no effort to resist the blacklist and allowed their enterprises to comply with various boycott rules. In the U.S., however, because of the organized pressure of the Jewish community during the Carter administration, the U.S. added anti-boycott provisions to the Export Administration Act. A year earlier the Internal Revenue Code was amended to deny foreign tax credits to American companies participating in the Arab boycott.

The Export Administration Act requires any American firm receiving a boycott-related request from abroad to file a copy of that request with the Commerce Department and to state whether or not it will comply with such request. These reports are public documents. The EAA provisions are enforced by a tiny unit in the Commerce Department called the Office of Antiboycott Compliance, with a yearly budget of about one million dollars. Nevertheless, the OAC has over the years imposed penalties amounting to millions of dollars on giant firms in the U.S.

The Dutch law of 1984 follows the U.S. model except that the reports submitted to the ministries are not made public and the ministries themselves do not seem to prosecute anyone. Weaker laws also have been enacted in the Canadian provinces of Ontario and Manitoba. The French law enacted in 1976 was not enforced for many years. Today it has been interpreted by the government export insurance agency, COFAGE, to refuse to insure on contracts containing boycott clauses.

There has been much speculation about the economic effects of the boycott upon Israel's economy. One answer came in 1992 when the economists of the Israeli chambers of commerce estimated that in terms of lost foreign investments and reduced exports abroad, Israel in the last 40 years had lost $49 billion dollars.

The first crack in the western indifference to the boycott came in 1991 at the London meeting of the so-called G7. The seven chief industrial powers of the world, Canada, France, Germany, Italy, Japan, the U.K., and the U.S., issued a declaration calling upon the Arab states to suspend their boycott of Israel (not specifying if primary or secondary) and calling upon Israel to suspend settlement activity. The appeal fell on deaf ears.

The situation changed dramatically after the Rabin government took power in July 1992 and the Israeli prime minister promised to curb "political settlements." In rapid succession thereafter, Prime Minister Major, President Mitterrand, Chancellor Kohl, and Foreign Minister Watanabe issued public declarations calling for an end to the secondary boycott with no linkage to any other goal. In the U.S. the anti-boycott forces redoubled their efforts and obtained pledges from both major parties.

As the Clinton administration took over, it found three new anti-boycott laws to enforce, involving the Defense Department, the State Department, and the U.S. Trade Representative.

Meanwhile, as Kuwait slowly recovered from the Iraq

invasion, it sought to stave off mounting U.S. pressure by informally notifying U.S. authorities that it would not enforce boycott regulations on American exporters. A similar policy was adopted by Saudi Arabia, again without public announcement. The other four members of the Gulf Cooperation Council are following a similar rule.

Bibliography: A. J. Sarna, *Boycott and Blacklist, A History of Arab Economic Warfare Against Israel* (1980); K. L. Teslik, *Congress, the Executive Branch and Special Interests, the American Response to the Arab Boycott of Israel* (1982); W. H. Nelson and T. Pritties, *The Economic War Against the Jews* (1977); W. Maslow (ed.), *Boycott Report*, a monthly newsletter published by the American Jewish Congress; H. B. Fenton III, "United States Antiboycott Laws: An Assessment of their Impact Ten Years After Adoption," in: *The Hastings International and Comparative Law Review* (1987); *Palestinian Yearbook of International Law*, 1986 and 1987, contains English text of official boycott regulations. [W.M.]

BRAZIL (see **4**:1322; **Dc./17**:196). The decade 1983–1992 began and ended with dramatic political turmoil that affected the Jewish community, along with the rest of the population. The years 1983–1984 marked the end of more than 22 years of military rule, and the preparations for the election of the first president of a newly democratic government. However, the president elected in 1985 died before assuming office, and his vice-president, José Sarney, became president of Brazil until 1990. By the end of 1992, the president who took office in 1990, Fernando Collor de Mello, was impeached and resigned in disgrace.

While the first two years of the Sarney government were a time of optimism and hope for economic development in Brazil, the 1980s have generally been considered the "lost decade" for Brazil, as well as the rest of Latin America. There has been virtually no economic growth, rampant inflation, and no solution for a staggering external debt. Brazil is very much a dual society, with the vast majority of its population of 150 million people living in poverty, with no prospects for improving their condition. With some exceptions, the Jewish community, which is only 0.1 percent of the population, is in the upper stratum of the society.

There has never been a census by Brazil's Jewish community, and the only one done by the São Paulo community was in 1968, therefore, current reliable demographic data are not available. Religious data from a 1990–91 government census have not yet been released, but Jewish communal leaders doubt they will be accurate. Educated estimates put the number of Jews in Brazil at about 150,000–170,000, with more than half of them living in São Paulo. The second largest population, is in Rio de Janeiro, and the third, with perhaps 10,000–12,000 people, is in Porto Alegre. The rest of the population is spread out in small communities throughout Brazil, especially in the capital cities such as Belo Horizonte, Curitiba, Recife, Belém, Brasilia, Salvador, and Manaus.

The Jewish community's cultural life is relatively rich for its size. Periodicals include the *Shalom Notícia* weekly newsletter, *Shalom Magazine* (quarterly), and several other magazines of Jewish interest, and *Resenha Judaica*, a semi-monthly community newspaper. A weekly Jewish television program, *Mosaico*, airs every Sunday on a commercial network. There have been a number of important fiction and non-fiction books published in the original Portuguese, as well as Portuguese translations of some of the best Hebrew and English books. Authentically Brazilian-Jewish fiction by Moacyr Scliar has also been published in English translations abroad. There have been major museum exhibits on Jewish immigration to Brazil, the Warsaw Ghetto, and modern and ancient art from Israel. Belated, disparate, and incomplete efforts to preserve and commemorate the history of Brazil's Jewish community are underway in a number of locations.

The Center for Jewish Studies of University of São Paulo (USP), the Federal University in Rio de Janeiro, the Marc Chagall Institute in Porto Alegre, and other institutions have sponsored such activities as lecture series, conferences, and courses on academic subjects of Jewish interest. During 1989 a Master's degree in Jewish Studies was initiated at the University of São Paulo. There were two major international conferences on the theme of the Inquisition, in 1987 and 1992. There have also been Jewish theatrical productions and Jewish and Israeli film festivals in São Paulo and Rio de Janeiro. Special commemorative and cultural events are held in conjunction with Holocaust Memorial Day and Israel Independence Day. There are large Jewish social clubs in both São Paulo and Rio de Janeiro.

Regarding religious observance, São Paulo offers a wide range of choices: Congregação Israelita Paulista was founded in the 1930s in the German Liberal tradition and is the largest congregation in Latin America, with a membership of 2,000 families. At the other end of the spectrum are several tiny Orthodox *shtiebls*. In between are a number of large and small Sephardi and Ashkenazi congregations. In Rio de Janeiro, which also has a variety of synagogues, Congregação Judaica do Brasil, a new synagogue generally in the Conservative egalitarian tradition, was founded during the past decade. The Ḥabad-Lubavich movement has grown remarkably in the past decade, and has synagogues and schools in most major cities in Brazil. Their presence is one reason that the availability of *kosher* meat, imported and local products, and restaurants has increased significantly in the last few years.

An important Catholic-Jewish dialogue exists, under the sponsorship of the National Conference of Brazilian Bishops. Rabbi Henry Sobel is responsible for the Jewish side of the dialogue. As Brazil is the largest Catholic country in the world and the Jewish community is so small, most members of the non-Orthodox Jewish community support this effort. A delegation of Jewish leaders met with Pope John Paul II when he was in Brazil in 1991, and Madame Sadat spoke at a major interfaith event in 1989, sponsored by the Bishops' Conference and Latin American Jewish Congress. The Latin American Jewish Conference also sponsored former U.S.S.R. leader Mikhail Gorbachev's appearance at a Jewish communal event in 1992.

On the political scene, members of the Jewish community have played an important role. In 1992, Dr. Eva Alterman Blay, a professor heading the University of São Paulo's sociology department, became the first Jewish woman to serve in the Senate of Brazil. Dr. Celso Lafer and Dr. José Goldemberg, two other University of São Paulo professors and members of the community, were, respectively the foreign minister and education minister. A leader in the Green Movement in Brazil, Federal Deputy Fabio Feldmann,

Dedication of Maimonides Square, São Paulo, Brazil, 1987; from left to right, José Knoplich, president of the Jewish Federation of the State of São Paulo, Zvi Caspi, consul general of Israel, and Mayor M. Covas. (Courtesy Israel Consulate, São Paulo)

Mikhail Gorbachev (left) in São Paulo, Brazil, with Rabbi Henry Sobel, Dec. 1992.

played a key role in the Eco-92 international ecological conference held in Rio de Janeiro in June 1992. In the 1991 United Nations vote that reversed the infamous "Zionism is racism" resolution, Brazil (which originally voted for the resolution) voted for the reversal.

While the world Jewish community showed little interest in Eco-92, members of the local Jewish community took an active part. In addition to Feldmann, Goldemberg and Lafer's participation as government officials, Rabbi Nilton Bonder of Congregação Judaica do Brazil led Jewish efforts among the Non-Governmental Organizations at the Global Forum. He organized a Jewish prayer tent for a nightlong interfaith prayer vigil where the worshipers included the Dalai Lama.

In September 1992, a group of twelve "Skinhead" or "White Power" members in a city in greater São Paulo beat up two Jewish young men wearing *kippot* (head coverings). The incident occurred near their school, which is connected with the Lubavich-Ḥabad movement. Some Jewish institutes throughout Brazil have also received threatening mail from the skinheads, and Jewish buildings and cemeteries have been desecrated in Rio de Janeiro and the state of Rio Grande do Sul during 1992. While there is no tradition of anti-Semitism in Brazil, the combination of resurgent nationalism and the current rampant inflation and unemployment create a situation that bears careful watching.

After incidents such as the above, and others against poor migrants from the northeast of Brazil, the Jewish Federation of São Paulo and more than 100 human rights organizations formally created the Democratic Movement Against Nazism and All Forms of Discrimination. Such a coalition is unprecedented in Brazil.

The São Paulo Jewish Federation, like Jewish Federations in the other major cities in Brazil, is part of the Jewish Confederation of Brazil. The Confederation, in turn, is part of the Latin American Jewish Congress, which in 1992 had its first Brazilian president, Benno Milnitzky. There is also a wide range of Zionist activities, with adult organizations, youth groups, *sheliḥim* (emissaries from Israel), and Seminars on Zionist Thought. [RO.SA.]

BRODSKI, YOSIF (see **4**:1395; **Dc./17**:197). Brodski received the Nobel Prize in literature for 1987. In May 1991 Brodski was named the fifth U.S. poet laureate.

BRONFMAN, EDGAR MILES (1929–), industrialist and Jewish leader. Bronfman was born in Montreal to Saidye and Samuel *Bronfman. In 1953 he joined Distillers Corp.–Seagram Ltd. (now the Seagram Company Ltd.) in Canada. In 1955 Bronfman moved to New York where he became a naturalized citizen of the U.S. In 1957 he became president of the U.S. subsidiary of Seagram and undertook the con-

Edgar Miles Bronfman

struction of a new corporate headquarters, the Seagram Building, a New York City landmark skyscraper. After his father's death in 1971 Bronfman assumed complete control of the firm, becoming chairman and chief executive officer of the Seagram Company Ltd., the Canadian parent firm, and of Joseph E. Seagram & Sons, Inc., the U.S. subsidiary, in 1975. Under his leadership the Seagram empire has grown and diversified, from natural gas and oil holdings in Asia and Europe to a significant interest in the international chemical firm E.I. du Pont de Nemours & Company.

Bronfman has had a notable career as a Jewish communal leader and philanthropist. Foremost among his positions is that of president (from 1981) of the *World Jewish Congress, an association of Jewish representative organizations in over 80 countries. Bronfman has taken that organization through a period of consolidation and has taken an active role on behalf of Jewish communities and causes in many parts of the world. He also holds significant positions with many other Jewish and non-Jewish organizations, such as the American Jewish Committee, the American Jewish Congress, the ADL, and the National Urban League. [M.FRI]

BROOKNER, ANITA (1938–), writer and art historian. Brookner was born in London, England, into a family of Polish origin. She was educated at the University of London and at the Courtauld Institute in London. In her professional life, her achievements have been in the areas both of art history and English literature. She was a visiting lecturer at the University of Reading from 1958 to 1964 and shortly thereafter became a lecturer in art history at the Courtauld Institute. From 1967 to 1968 she was Slade Professor at Cambridge University, the first woman to hold that position. She is considered an international authority on 18th- and 19th-century painting. Her academic works include *The Genius of the Future: — Studies in French Art Criticism* (1971) and *Greuze: The Rise and Fall of an Eighteenth-Century Phenomenon* (1972).

In the field of literature, Anita Brookner has written literary reviews for the *Times Literary Supplement, Observer, London Review of Books*, and the *Times* (London). However, she is best known for her novels. She wrote *A Start in Life* (1981; U.S. title *The Debut*), *Providence* (1982), *Look at Me*

(1983), *Hotel du Lac* (1984) for which she was awarded the Booker Prize of 1984, *Family and Friends* (1985), and *Fraud* (1992).

Brookner's literary style very much reflects her background in art. She writes in an elegantly formal, highly structured prose reminiscent of the staid, carefully composed, character studies found in 18th- and 19th-century portraits of individuals. With the exception of *Family and Friends* her novels are, in fact, verbal portraits of a single main character.

Brookner's novels concern the relationships between men and women in modern society. She depicts men as the activists and catalysts in the world, while women, though competent and accomplished, are presented as meek, lonely objects waiting for men to confer love upon them in order to deliver them from their prudent, patient, long-suffering lives.

Bibliography: H. May (ed.), *Contemporary Authors*, 114, 77–78; S. Hall (ed.), *Contemporary Literary Criticism, Yearbook* 34, (1984), 136. [BE.M.]

BROWN, MICHAEL STUART (1941–), U.S. medical geneticist and Nobel Prize winner. Brown was born in New York. After attending the University of Pennsylvania from which he obtained a B.A. (1962) and a doctorate from the School of Medicine (1966), he interned at Massachusetts General Hospital in Boston where he met his scientific collaborator, Joseph Goldstein, with whom he shared the 1985 Nobel Prize for medicine. Upon completion of his internship he worked at the institute of the National Institutes of Health in Bethesda, Maryland; the National Institute of Arthritis and Metabolic Diseases; and then in the biochemistry laboratory of the National Heart Institute. He and Dr. Goldstein devoted attention to cholesterol metabolism disorders.

In 1971 Dr. Brown moved to Texas when he joined the faculty of the Southwestern Medical School of the University of Texas at Dallas. He became the Paul J. Thomas Professor of Genetics in 1977 as well as the director of the Center for Genetic Diseases of the Health Science Center of the university.

Brown and Goldstein took up joint research in Texas in 1972 and in 1985 were awarded the Nobel Prize in recognition of the significant advances in knowledge about how the body absorbs cholesterol and towards an understanding of familial hypercholestrolemia as a genetic defect in which cells are not able to absorb low-density lipoprotein. [ED.]

°BRUNNER, ALOIS (1912–), Nazi deportation expert. Brunner was born in Rohrbrunn, Austria.

"He was an extremely unscrupulous individual, one of the best tools of *Eichmann. He never had an opinion of his own, and as Eichmann himself described him, he was 'one of my best men.'" Adolf Eichmann's reliance on Alois Brunner confirms this Nuremberg testimony of Dieter Wisliceny, Brunner's coworker in the SS program to deport Europe's Jews to Poland.

Adolf Eichmann turned over the Central Office of Jewish Emigration in Vienna to Brunner, who organized the first European experiments in deportation of the Jews as early as October 1939. As director of the Central Office in 1941 and 1942, Brunner coopted Jewish leadership by threats and promises; after decimating the Austrian Jewish community, he was promoted to SS Hauptsturmfuehrer in 1942. In the fall of 1942 Brunner applied the methods he had used in Vienna in Berlin. Then, in February 1943 Eichmann posted Brunner to command technical aspects of deportation in Salonika, Greece, the center of Sephardi Judaism in Europe. There Brunner perfected his methods of pressure and deception, destroying in six weeks a community that had flourished for five centuries.

In order to accelerate the deportation program in France, Eichmann sent Brunner to France's main transit camp, Drancy, where he was commandant from June 1943 to August 1944. Brunner radically altered Drancy, and with it the condition of the Jews in France: he denied French officials access to the camp, provisioned it with funds taken from Jews, deceived and tortured the inmates, and deported even those with *de facto* exemptions — Jews from neutral or friendly states, welfare workers, orphans, and French-Jewish nationals. When Germany occupied the Italian zone of southern France in September 1943, Brunner took charge of one of the most brutal roundups in Western Europe, sending off transports even as the Germans retreated from France. He then took up his last post, commandant of Camp Sered, the deportation center of Slovakia.

In Slovakia, from September 1944 to April 1945, Brunner dismantled the Jewish community, and punished both Jews and Nazis who had negotiated to ransom Jewish lives. In 1945, as Russian troops approached, Brunner disappeared. According to his own account, Brunner was arrested by Czechs, Americans, and British, but released under a false name. He obtained false papers and left Europe in 1954 for Egypt and then Damascus, Syria, where he lived under the name Georg Fischer. Brunner claimed to have planned to bomb a World Jewish Congress meeting in Vienna, with Syrian help, and also to abduct Eichmann from Israel. Warrants for his arrest are on the books in Germany and Austria; France sentenced him to death *in absentia*; West Germany requested his extradition in 1984, but the Syrian government refused to respond.

Brunner deported at least 129,000 people to ghettos and death camps in Poland — 47,000 from Vienna, 44,000 from Salonika, 24,000 from France, and 14,000 from Slovakia.

Bibliography: M. Felstiner, "Alois Brunner, Eichmann's Best Tool," in: *Simon Wiesenthal Center Annual* (1986); D. Wisliceny testimonies, in: *The Holocaust: Selected Documents*, J. Mendelsohn (ed.), vol. 8, and in *Trial of the Major War Criminals before the International Military Tribunal*, vol. 4; Brunner interview, *Bunte* 45, 46 (Oct. 30, Nov. 7, 1985). [M.FEL.]

C

CAHN, SAMMY (1913–1993), U.S. songwriter. Born in New York to parents of Galician origin, he learned the violin when a boy. He earned a living in various dance bands and his first musical successes were in Tin Pan Alley in cooperation with Saul Chaplin. Early successes included "Rhythm is our Business," which became the theme tune for the Jimmie Lunceford Band, "Shoe Shine" recorded by Louis Armstrong, and the adapted Yiddish melody "Bei Mir Bist Du Schön" which sold over a million copies in the Andrews Sisters recording. Later Cahn linked up with Jules Styne and in the 1940s wrote a series of hits for Frank Sinatra, with whom Cahn was long associated. These included "I Fall in Love Too Easily" and "Saturday Night is the Loneliest Night of the Week." He also wrote "It's Magic" for Doris Day. In the 1950s he teamed up with Jimmy Van Heusen. Among Cahn's many further hits were "Three Coins in the Fountain," "All the Way," and "High Hopes" adapted as John F. Kennedy's campaign theme in 1960. Cahn was a noted raconteur and had a great success in the 1970s with a one-man stage show presenting his tunes and an autobiography, *I Should Care* (1974). [ED.]

CANADA (see **5**:102; **Dc./17**:201). Canadian Jews were concerned primarily with political developments in their own country and with matters concerning Israel. Given that a substantial portion of the community lived in Quebec, a

Memorial service in Montreal for Jews massacred in Istanbul, Sept. 1986; left to right; Morton Bessner, chairman CJC Quebec Region, Rabbi Howard Joseph, Spanish and Portuguese Cong., Montreal; Dorothy Reitman, president, CJC (Courtesy CJC, Montreal)

province where latent separatist tendencies reappeared, Jews were particularly sensitive about questions of national unity. The new constitution, adopted in 1982, failed to resolve the issue because it was passed without Quebec's agreement. As a consequence, when Brian Mulroney became prime minister in 1984, he made the resolution of the constitutional problem one of his highest priorities.

The negotiations that he initiated led to two major apparent agreements, both of which ultimately failed. The Meech Lake Accord of 1987 was not ratified by enough provincial legislatures within the three-year time limit, while the Charlottetown Accord of 1992 was defeated in a national referendum. Both agreements, which had the backing of the Quebec government, would have recognized that province as a distinct society and weakened federal power somewhat. Jews generally supported both initiatives because of their desire to see the country hold together. The inability of the country to resolve its constitutional dilemma left Montreal's Jews in a quandary regarding their future, especially in light of the revival of nationalist sentiment in Quebec produced by the debate over Meech Lake. The possibility that Quebec might become independent during the 1990s was most unsettling for the approximately 30 percent of Canadian Jews who live in Montreal. As a result, the intensity of Jewish community support, especially from the established organizations, was a notable aspect of the struggle to pass the Charlottetown Accord.

Israel. Israel's well being was a prominent concern of Canadian Jewry. The 1982 Lebanon War and its aftermath proved to be very trying. Although the general instinct of the community is to close ranks with Israel in time of crisis, the controversial nature of the war led to more open expressions of dissent than had been witnessed in the past. Intense discussions within all sectors of the community produced a variety of public declarations, including demonstrations. Generally, official community organizations defended the rationale of the war while the dissent came from ad hoc groupings. The refugee camp massacres injected a further note of divisiveness.

This trend continued during the Palestinian uprising that began in 1987. The *intifada* caused further public relations problems for Israel in Canada and made relationships between the Jewish community and the Canadian government more difficult. The effects of the *intifada* were to undermine public support for Israel and to exacerbate tensions within the community. Individual Jews, as well as groups like Canadian Friends of Peace Now, were increasingly likely to take issue publicly with Israeli policies, thereby making it difficult for the main Jewish organizations to maintain their traditional unified stance on matters involving Israel. Israel's positions regarding the *intifada* and other foreign policy issues were articulated forcefully in June 1990 by President Chaim Herzog during a state visit.

During the 1991 Gulf War, when Israel was under attack by Iraqi missiles, both public and elite opinion shifted toward Israel and there were numerous expressions of solidarity. On the other hand, in the aftermath of that war, as attention turned toward a renewed emphasis on the Arab-Israeli peace process, External Affairs Minister Joe Clark and Prime Minister Mulroney had sharp differences of opinion regarding their expectations of Israel, especially with respect to the role of the PLO. Clark, who had insisted for years that he did not favor the creation of an independent Palestinian state, nevertheless took steps that enhanced the status of the PLO. In 1992 Ottawa hosted sessions of the multilateral peace talks regarding refugees, but Israel refused to participate due to objections to the nature of the Palestinian representation.

Anti-Semitism and Holocaust Denial. The decade was one in which this issue was very high on the Jewish agenda. Lengthy legal proceedings tested the utility of criminal laws that proscribed the fomenting of hatred or the dissemination of "false news." James Keegstra, a high school social studies teacher and mayor of a small town in Alberta, was charged under the anti-hate law because he had been teaching anti-Semitic ideas for years. He also lost his job and was defeated for re-election. Among his teachings were Holocaust denial and international conspiracy theories regarding Jews. Keegstra was convicted in 1985, but eventually had the conviction overturned on appeal in 1991, even though the constitutionality of the law had been upheld by the Supreme Court of Canada in 1990. He was convicted again at a second trial in 1992 and fined $3,000. Keegstra intended to appeal that conviction as well.

Another celebrated case was that of Ernst Zundel, a German immigrant in the printing business in Toronto who was accused of distributing anti-Semitic hate literature in Canada and abroad, especially material denying the historical authenticity of the Holocaust. He was charged under an obscure provision of the Criminal Code for publishing false statements that were likely to cause injury to the public interest. After a lengthy trial that included extensive testimony of Holocaust deniers, Zundel was convicted in 1985 and sentenced to 15 months in prison and three years probation. He also faced deportation. His conviction was overturned by the Ontario Court of Appeal in 1987, but he was retried in 1988, convicted, and sentenced to nine months in prison. After years of appeal, the Supreme Court in 1992 struck down the law as unconstitutional, thereby reversing his conviction.

The third major case of anti-Semitism involved Malcolm Ross, a New Brunswick teacher. Ross had published anti-Semitic views, but, unlike Keegstra, was not accused of dis-

Israel Pres. Herzog addressing Canadian Parliament during his June 1989 state visit. Canadian Prime Minister Mulroney, in front, far left (GPO, Jerusalem)

seminating them in the classroom. Nevertheless, members of the Jewish community questioned his fitness to teach. After many delays due to a variety of investigations and hearings, Ross was eventually removed from the classroom in 1991.

In the three cases of Keegstra, Zundel, and Ross, Jewish community organizations, especially Canadian Jewish Congress and B'nai B'rith, maintained steady pressure on governments to act and saw to it that the issues remained on the public agenda. They reflected a strong consensus in the community that public displays of anti-Semitism had to be dealt with severely, using the power of the law when available.

In a related matter, a British historian who is a Holocaust denier, David Irving, has tried to mount speaking tours in Canada on several occasions, but has encountered strong opposition from Jewish groups. Finally in 1992 he was denied entry by the government because of a 1991 hate law conviction in Germany. Nevertheless he entered Canada using deception and managed to give a speech in British Columbia. After his arrest and the issuance of a departure order, he managed to give another talk in Toronto, prior to being deported.

Nazi War Criminals. One of the key issues of the decade was the question of what to do with alleged Nazi war criminals living in Canada, especially given a government reluctance to deal with the situation. An early case involved Albert Helmut Rauca, who was wanted by the Federal Republic of Germany for the murder of numerous Jews in Lithuania during World War II. After much prodding from Jewish groups, the government moved in 1983 to extradite him. Despite the time required by the novel legal issues involved, he was sent back to Germany, where he died in custody while awaiting trial.

As further information regarding other war criminals and the ways in which they entered Canada became public, there was increasing clamor for government action. In an effort to shift attention from the political sphere, the government appointed Justice Jules Deschenes in 1986 as a one-man commission to investigate the situation and make recommendations. The result was the publication in 1987 of a report that was a shocking and biting criticism of morally bankrupt government policies and practices that continued virtually until the establishment of the Commission. Deschenes showed how Canada had permitted people with dubious pasts to immigrate, often waiving regulations that might have resulted in their exclusion. After following up leads about some 1,700 individuals, he finally recommended investigation of about 250, of whom about 20 warranted immediate action by the government. His suggestion that the government permit trials in Canada for war crimes was enacted into law.

The record of the resultant legal proceedings was disappointing for the Jewish community. Imre Finta, accused of aiding the Nazis in their efforts to deport Hungarian Jews to concentration camps, was acquitted by a jury in 1990 after a lengthy trial that had included extensive testimony concerning his role in loading Jews into freight cars. Michael Pawlawski was charged in 1989 with participating in the killing of nearly 500 Jews and Poles in 1942 in Belorussia. However, the Crown dropped the case in 1992 before trial on the grounds that judicial rulings about gathering evidence from abroad made it impossible to prosecute. The Justice Department's War Crimes Unit was criticized by Jewish organizations both for that decision and for dropping the charges in 1991 against Stephen Reistetter, who had been charged with kidnapping and placing Jews on trains headed for concentration camps. On the other hand, Jacob Luitjens, who had collaborated with the Nazis in his native Holland, was stripped of his Canadian citizenship and deported in 1992. The government was planning an appeal in the Finta case.

Demographic and Social Trends. The 1981 census showed a total Jewish population, measured by religion, of 296,425, of whom 148,255 lived in Ontario (123,730 in the Toronto area), 102,355 in Quebec, 15,670 in Manitoba, 10,655 in Alberta, and 14,680 in British Columbia. The Jewish population increased by about eight percent from 1971 to 1981 and constituted about 1.2 percent of the total population of Canada. The mid-decade census in 1986 provided more ambiguous data because it only asked about ethnic origin, not religion. The result was that 245,855 people listed only Jewish ethnicity, while an additional 97,655 listed Jewish as one of two or more ethnic origins. Thus there were some 343,510

Canadian Jewish Congress rally in 1987 in support of Anatoly Sharansky, held on his birthday prior to his release (Courtesy CJC, Montreal)

people who might have been considered Jewish in some way. A reasonable estimate that errs on the side of inclusion would be that the number of Jews who identify as such would be between 315,000 and 330,000.

There were a number of demographic trends evident. In terms of population distribution, there has been a definite movement toward Ontario and particularly to greater Toronto at the expense of Montreal and a number of small communities. About half of Canada's Jews live in Ontario, with Toronto clearly eclipsing Montreal as the main Jewish city. In the Toronto area, the more distant suburbs are growing rapidly with new facilities springing up in areas that have not had much of a Jewish presence. Sephardim are growing in numbers and influence, both in Montreal and Toronto and now claim to constitute about one-sixth of the community nationally. Intermarriage is increasing towards levels comparable to those in the United States. Only the ultra-Orthodox and Sephardim are producing enough children to create population growth. Other Jewish groups exhibit low fertility and tend to have a high marriage age. Finally, studies that showed about 20 percent of the community to be living below the poverty line prompted greater attention to the problem on the part of the local federations.

Organizational Life. There was considerable focus on the formal structure of major community organizations. Changes in the community and its relationship to the external world necessitated a re-examination of some key assumptions about the various bodies representing Canadian Jewry. Serious financial problems, resulting from a prolonged period of hard economic times around the end of the decade, had several effects, including lower budgets for the Canadian Jewish Congress and other countrywide organizations, an enhanced role for the National Budgeting Conference, and austerity programs in the local federations. The two largest federations changed their names in 1991 and 1992 to the Jewish Federation of Greater Toronto and Federation CJA in Montreal.

The collapse of the Reichmann real estate empire in 1992 had very deleterious effects on a number of ultra-Orthodox institutions that the family had been supporting in Toronto and Israel.

Community Relations. There were several major developments in this area. The knotty problem of divorce where the husband refuses to issue a *get* was ameliorated somewhat when Ontario and later the federal government passed laws designed to deter those who would use the withholding of a *get* to extort a better civil divorce settlement.

Jewish day schools in Quebec, British Columbia, and Alberta enjoyed government financial support, but in Ontario, the seemingly endless campaign to obtain government funding remained unsuccessful. Various legal cases claiming inequality of treatment compared to the Catholic schools, for example, as well as direct political approaches failed to produce the desired result, putting the schools and parents under increasing financial pressure. In contrast, in both Ontario and Quebec, long struggles finally succeeded in legalizing Sunday shopping, although of course that issue was not completely a Jewish one.

Culture. Several books with Canadian authors won the U.S. National Jewish Book Award during the decade: *None Is Too Many* by Irving Abella and Harold Troper, *Vichy France and the Jews* by Michael Marrus and Robert Paxton, *Art of the Holocaust* by Janet Blatter and Sybil Milton, and *Maintaining Consensus: The Canadian Jewish Polity in the Postwar World* by Daniel J. Elazar and Harold M. Waller. Other major publications included *Canada and the Birth of Israel* by David J. Bercuson, *The New Jewish Identity in America* by Rabbi Stuart Rosenberg, *The Coming Cataclysm* by Rabbi Reuven Bulka, *Mr. Sam: The Life and Times of Samuel Bronfman* by Marrus, and *A Little Love in Big Manhattan: Two Yiddish Poets* by Ruth Wisse. The decade also saw the exhibition *Coat of Many Colors*, a depiction of the history of the Canadian Jewish community, tour the country and the presentation of the Jacob Lowy Collection of Incunabula, Hebraica, and Judaica to the National Library of Canada.

Personalities. A number of Jews played prominent roles in public life: Robert Kaplan, Herbert Gray, Senator Jack Austin, and Gerald Weiner all served in the federal cabinet. Norman Spector served as chief of staff to the prime minister and later was appointed ambassador to Israel. Stanley Hartt and Hugh Segal also served as chiefs of staff. Bora Laskin was chief justice of the Supreme Court of Canada, Allan Gottlieb served as ambassador to the U.S., and Stephen Lewis was ambassador to the UN. Larry Grossman led the Ontario Progressive Conservative Party. Victor Goldbloom became commissioner of official languages. Charles Dubin became chief justice of Ontario while Rosalie Abella and Morris Fish were appointed to the Ontario and Quebec Courts of Appeal respectively and Alan Gold served for several years as chief justice of the Superior Court of Quebec. Within the community, Irwin Cotler, Dorothy Reitman, Les Scheininger, and Irving Abella held the post of president of Canadian Jewish Congress. Dorothy Heppner became the first woman president of the Montreal federation and Jack Silverstone was selected as national executive director of CJC.

Among the deaths recorded by the community were Chief Justice Bora Laskin, aged 71 in 1983; Zionist federation executive Leon Kronitz, aged 68 in 1985; educator Shloime Wiseman, aged 86 in 1985; noted lawyer and senator Lazarus Phillips, aged 91 in 1987; leading demographer and civil servant Louis Rosenberg, aged 94 in 1987; novelist Margaret Laurence, aged 60 in 1987; Bible scholar and historian Frank Talmage, aged 50 in 1988; theatrical director John Hirsch, aged 59 in 1989; businessman and community leader Ray Wolfe, aged 72 in 1990; prolific writer Rabbi Stuart Rosenberg, aged 67 in 1990; comedian Johnny Wayne, aged 72 in 1990; trailblazing politician Sen. David Croll, aged 91 in 1991; United Israel Appeal executive Walter Hess, aged 53 in 1991; leading philanthropist Joseph Tanenbaum, aged 87 in 1992; noted television journalist Barbara Frum, aged 54, in 1992; and renowned Talmudic scholar Rabbi Gedalia Felder, aged 70 in 1992. [H.M.W.]

CARIBBEAN JEWISH COMMUNITIES (see **16**:473). The decline of active Jewish life in the Caribbean area that began in the middle of the 19th century has continued in recent years. This is linked to the diminishing numbers of Jews living in the area. The Caribbean area — once the scene of flourishing Jewish communities in the 17th and 18th centuries, when in some places, as in Surinam, Curaçao, and St. Eustatius, the Jews constituted the majority of the free population — now has very few Jewish communities, who are trying their best to preserve Jewish life.

The Caribbeans ceded their central place in the economic life of the Americas to more flourishing centers in North and South America. The cultivation and export of tropical products to Europe declined sharply, especially when European countries began to grow and refine their own sugar, and Africa became a cheaper and just as reliable competitor in the export of coffee, cocoa, vanilla, and coconuts. The liberation of the Spanish colonies in Central and South America in the 19th century brought a wave of emigration of Caribbean Jews to the newly formed republics. Jewish communities were formed in Barranquilla, Colombia; Coro, Barcelona, and Tucacas in Venezuela; Colón and Panama City in Panama; Cartago and San José in Costa Rica; and in Santo Domingo in the Dominican Republic. There the Jews

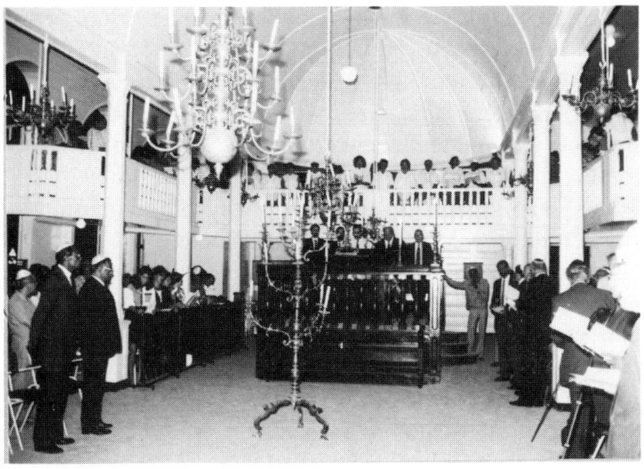

Special commemorative prayer in Zedek ve Shalom synagogue in Paramaribo in Surinam, in memory of Jews expelled from Spain and 500 years since Columbus's discovery of America, August 1992. (Courtesy the Mordechai Arbell Collection)

re-encountered the language and customs of their Iberian forefathers which made their life easier and new opportunities opened, although in some places they also encountered the pressures of the Catholic Church. Most of these communities have disappeared today, except in Panama City where there is an active Spanish-Portuguese Jewish community, Kol Shearit Israel. One of its members, Eric Delvalle, president of Panama in 1988–89, is the nephew of Max Shalom *Delvalle, president of Panama in 1969. In the other cities there are only individuals remembering their Jewish past. Intermarriage is the main cause of the disappearance of Jewish life there.

The opening of the Panama Canal after World War I brought another wave of Jewish emigration from the Caribbeans to Latin America. The majority of the Jews from St. Thomas in the Virgin Islands, and many Jewish families from Jamaica and Curaçao settled in Panama.

From the mid-1980s until peace was restored in summer 1992, Surinam was the scene of a series of revolutions and civil wars which devastated parts of the country and brought economic life close to a standstill. Jews emigrated, mostly to Holland and some to Israel. Today a group of 20–30 families, under the leadership of Rene Fernandes, is trying to restore Jewish life in Surinam. The two wooden synagogues with sand-covered floors in Paramaribo — Zedek ve Shalom (1716) and Neve Shalom (1735) — have been restored to their former glory. In those synagogues the community held an impressive ceremony commemorating 500 years of the expulsion of Jews from Spain and the subsequent settlement of Jews in America. Surinam issued a special postage stamp for the occasion. The civil war has left the old Jewish cemetery in Casioperra inaccessible from jungle growth, and the cemetery of the "Jewish Savanna" (Joden Savane) in a sorry state with its poetic Hebrew inscriptions almost completely obliterated and the ruins of the old synagogue "Beraha ve Shalom" (1685) still standing, untouched by the civil war. The ruins of the old Jewish plantations with their biblical names — Dothan, Mahanaim, Beersheba — could still be seen ten years ago, but have now disappeared under the encroaching jungle.

The 400-strong Jewish community in Curaçao is active; its numbers have remained relatively stable over the past ten years. The synagogue Mikveh Israel (1732) is the center of Jewish life, whereas Temple Emanuel, the other synagogue, has been converted into a movie-house. The old Jewish cemetery near the refinery has suffered damage from its fumes. Some of the historical tombstones, however, are now located in the synagogue yard.

The instability in Jamaica has hurt Jewish life there, and the Jewish population has declined. Once home to a number of Jewish communities, Jamaica in the early 1990s had about 400 Jews. Community services continue to function and the synagogue Shaarei Shamaim is active under the guidance of Ernst de Souza. There is an Israeli embassy in the capital, Kingston.

Barbados, considered by many as the site of the earliest Jewish settlement on the American continent (1628), has no descendant from the first Jewish settlers. Some 20–30 Jewish families, mostly from Eastern Europe, now live there. This group established under Paul Altman "The Synagogue Restoration Project" which acquired the old synagogue, Nidhei Israel (1654) and rededicated it in 1987. A series of four stamps were issued on the occasion.

In Charlotte Amalie, capital of St. Thomas, one of the Virgin Islands, there is only a handful of descendants of the original Jewish settlers. A new Jewish community has been formed, consisting mostly of people from the United States, and has some 400 members. Active Jewish life is maintained in the old synagogue Beraha ve Shalom ve Gemilut Hassadim (1796) and the community also preserves a big

First day cover of a 1987 Barbados series of stamps to commemorate the re-opening of the synagogue; the façade and interior of the synagogue, the Ten Commandments, and a marble laver for ritual washing of the hands (Courtesy the Mordechai Arbell Collection)

Jewish cemetery. The old Jewish cemetery, dating from the time of the Danish West Indies, is abandoned.

On other Caribbean islands, once the home of settlements of Spanish-Portuguese Jews, there are only ruins and cemeteries — mute witnesses of Jewish life that existed there. On the island of St. Eustatius (Netherlands Dutch Indies) — the ruins of the synagogue Honen Dalim (1738) and an old cemetery, kept up by the local government, still exist. In the island of Nevis an enterprising couple from the United States, Florence and Robert Abrahams, restored the Jewish cemetery; in Coro, Venezuela, the old Jewish cemetery has been declared a national monument; and in Barranquilla, Colombia, the cemetery of the Spanish-Portuguese Jewish settlers is intact, witness to the old Jewish history of the city. In the island of Tobago a sign notes the place where the Jews settled in 1660 when the site was under the Dutch. In the island of St. Maarte in the Netherlands Antilles, a restaurant discotheque is built on the foundation of the old synagogue, and in Belize there is an abandoned Jewish cemetery in the marshes near Belize City.

On several of the Caribbean islands, new Jewish communities have appeared. In Haiti there was a limited Jewish settlement of Spanish-Portuguese Jews who have long since left. A small Jewish cemetery has been uncovered in Cape Haitien. In the beginning of the 20th century a number of Jews, mostly of Syrian origin, settled in Haiti. During the instability after the fall of the Duvalier family most of them left.

Trinidad, which had only a handful of Spanish-Portuguese Jewish families in the 19th century, mostly from Curaçao and Venezuela, saw an influx of about 300 Jews during World War II. Those who came from Germany were detained as enemy aliens in internment camps. Most of them left after the war, and their cemetery tells the story. Today Trinidad has no more than three or four Jewish families.

In the Dominican Republic, a prosperous settlement of German Jewish refugees from Nazi persecution in Sosúa on the Atlantic Coast has been decimated by intermarriage and emigration. In the capital, Santo Domingo, there are less than a hundred Jews.

After the exodus of Jews from Cuba with the advent of Fidel Castro, there remain some 100 to 150 Jewish families out of the 12,000 Jews who were there in 1948. They still maintain three synagogues and a Jewish center.

In Martinique where a limited number of Jews lived in the 17th and 18th centuries, a few Jewish families from North Africa have recently formed a congregation.

In the island of Aruba there is a small, active Jewish community of about fifty people who try to maintain Jewish life around the Beth Israel Congregation.

The Jewish population of Puerto Rico numbers about 2,000 and is made up of people who arrived from the United States after World War II and from Cuba in 1959.

[M.ARB.]

CELAN (Antschel), PAUL (1920–1970), Romanian-born German poet. Celan grew up in Czernowitz, Bukovina, the only child of middle-class, partly assimilated Jewish parents. He learned Romanian at school, studied Hebrew until his bar mitzvah, and after a year in France, began studying Romance philology in 1939. During the Nazis' June 1942 deportations from Czernowitz, Celan fled but his parents were sent to Transnistria and soon were killed. He spent 18 months at forced labor and returned home in 1944, shortly before the Soviets annexed northern Bukovina. In 1945 Celan left his homeland for Bucharest, fled in 1947 to Vienna where he published his early poems, *Der Sand aus den Urnen* ("The Sand from the Urns," 1948), and in 1949, he settled in Paris. He married the artist Gisèle de Lestrange in 1952, had a son, taught German at the École Normale Supérieure, and continued writing poetry.

The bitter "Todesfuge" ("Deathfugue"), in his first major collection *Mohn und Gedächtnis* ("Poppy and Remembrance," 1952), made a great impact in Germany. He won the Bremen Prize in 1958, the Büchner Prize in 1960, and others, publishing eight books of poetry and many translations from French, Russian, and English. In 1960 a groundless plagiarism charge against Celan, publicized in Germany and exacerbated by his vulnerability to German neo-Nazism and anti-Semitism, acutely afflicted the poet. At the same time he succored his friend Nelly *Sachs, also undergoing a nervous crisis. Celan's most pervasively Jewish writings emerged from this period, in *Die Niemandsrose* ("The No-One's-Rose," 1963). He visited Israel in 1969, appeared intensely affected by it, and considered settling there. But in late April 1970, aged 49, he drowned himself in the Seine.

"Todesfuge" (1944–45) remained Celan's best-known work (particularly in German school books). "Black milk of daybreak we drink it at dusk," a voice begins, "we shovel a grave in the sky." A commandant orders Jews to "strike up for the dance," then writes home to his beloved Margarete. The poem ends by counterpointing her "golden hair" with "your ashen hair Shulamith."

Celan's writing never dismissed the Jewish dead, personified in his mother, or neutralized the shock of the Holocaust on articulate existence — even when he explored wholly different regions: geology, geography, botany, physiology. What critics called obscurity in his later verse, Celan insisted was exemplary clarity. "The Meridian" (1960), his major speech on poetry, says "Go with art into your very selfmost straits. And set yourself free."

Celan's last poems, issued posthumously as *Zeitgehöft* ("Homestead of Time," 1976), aim at a final yet originative point of rest. The collection includes 20 lyrics inspired by Celan's visit to Israel, expressing a fitful hope "that Jerusalem *is*," that "we're finally there." The last poem he wrote, ten days before his death, speaks of vinegrowers digging up "the darkhoured clock," and ends with a stone — usually a sign of muteness, blindness, and death for Celan — now resting not upon but "behind the eyes — it knows you, come the Sabbath."

Celan's literary translations reached the height of that art. He made ingenious versions from Rimbaud, Valéry, and other French poets, did the German script for Resnais' *Night and Fog* (1956), and translated Yevtushenko's "Babi Yar." Having learned Russian during the war, Celan in 1957 began translating Aleksandr Blok, Sergei Esenin, and Osip Mandelshtam. In Mandelshtam he recognized a brother, affecting him in ways that tested and deepened his own poetic identity. Celan also responded to the taut, tragic vision of Emily Dickinson, and to Shakespeare's sonnets on beauty and death in German visions that often intensify their original.

While Celan's affinities with Hölderlin, Rilke, Heidegger, and others ally him to German tradition, the strain of Jewishness marks his writing in the mother tongue: "Circumcise the word," pleads a poem on Kafka and the *golem*. His prose "Conversation in the Mountains" (1959) voices in quasi-Yiddish cadences a Jew's search for himself and lost kin, for "the love of those not loved." Throughout Celan's work Jewish terms persist, including Hebrew and Yiddish, amid many other references. Gershom Scholem's Kabbalah studies heightened Celan's mystical, messianic sense of language, and the addressable "Thou" his poems sought reflects his reading of Buber. He felt a lifelong kindredness with Kafka, leaning toward East European Judaism yet at odds with Orthodox spirituality: "Apostate only am I faithful."

Bibliography: *Text u. Kritik* 53/54, (1984^2) and *Studies in Twenti-*

eth Century Literature 8,1 (1983) include bibliographies; D. Meinecke (ed.), *Über Paul Celan* (1970); P. Szondi, *Celan-Studien* (1972); J. Glenn, *Paul Celan* (1973); B. Böschenstein, *Leuchttürme; von Hölderlin zu Celan* (1977); I. Chalfen, *Paul Celan: Eine Biographie seiner Jugend* (1979); L. Olschner, *Der feste Buchstab: Erläuterungen zu Paul Celans Gedichtübertragungen* (1985); J. Derrida, *Schibboleth: Pour Paul Celan* (1986) [J.FE.]

CHARPAK, GEORGES (1924–), French physicist and Nobel Prize winner. Born in Dabrovica, Poland, Charpak came to France as a child with his parents. He was in Dachau in 1943–45, after having been captured by the Germans as a member of the French resistance in World War II.

He studied at the Ecole des Mines de Paris and was a professor at the Ecole Superieure de Physiques et Chemie in Paris. Charpak is a researcher at the European Laboratory for Particle Physics (CERN) in Geneva, where he has been working since 1959. He was awarded the 1992 Nobel Prize in physics for his invention of particle detectors in high-energy physics so that, as stated in the Swedish Academy of Sciences citation, "largely due to his work, particle physicists have been able to focus their interest on very rare particle interactions, which often reveal the secrets of the inner parts of matter." His invention of the multiwire proportional chamber, enabling the collection of data a thousand times faster than with the old photographic methods was particularly noted.

In 1985 he was elected a member of the French Academy of Sciences [ED.]

CLAL — The National Jewish Center for Learning and Leadership. CLAL was founded in 1974 by Rabbi Irving *Greenberg, Elie *Wiesel, and Rabbi Steven Shaw. In 1983 the Institute for Jewish Experience founded by Rabbi Shlomo Riskin merged with CLAL.

The name CLAL, taken from the term Clal Israel referring to the entire, indivisible Jewish community, alludes to the various aims of the center. One major goal is that of Jewish-Jewish dialogue, intercommunication with respect between the trends in contemporary Judaism, Orthodox, Conservative, Reform, and Reconstructionist, all to be conducted in a spirit of pluralism.

From the *CLAL Perspectives* publications. N.Y.

CLAL conducts programs geared to the training of knowledgeable Jewish leaders through the teaching of Jewish history and source materials, to the strengthening of Jewish unity, to achieving a meaningful appreciation of Jewish culture and religion, and to the preparation of well-equipped, informed individuals — especially with leadership potential — who can meet the challenges of the modern era with authentic Jewish responses. Increased commitment to the Jewish people and community is consciously striven for, particularly among those of little Jewish background or experience.

Programs directed by CLAL are: (1) Shamor, for leadership education. It involves learning and pluralistic religious experiences as well as the development of community leadership. The programs are generally conducted in coordination with local Jewish federations or agencies. There are some 30 ongoing classes in five cities in the United States. Weekends and seminars have been held in over 50 Jewish communities in the United States and Canada.

(2) Chevra, a program for rabbis and academicians, rabbis from the four trends meet to learn and to examine diverse issues facing the Jewish community.

(3) Zachor, the Holocaust Research Center, whose aim is to commemorate and examine the basic challenges inherent within the Holocaust. It was involved in the establishment of the United States Holocaust Memorial Council.

CLAL, whose headquarters are in New York, publishes monographs on topics such as charity, pluralism, and ethic. A retreat center, Bet Clal, in Goshen, N.Y., was purchased in 1986. [ED.]

COALITION FOR THE ADVANCEMENT OF JEWISH EDUCATION (CAJE; formerly Coalition for Alternatives in Jewish Education). The Coalition for Alternatives in Jewish Education (CAJE) was conceived in Boston, in 1975, by a group of graduate students from the North American Jewish Students' Network, whose primary goal was to make a contribution to the improvement of the quality of Jewish education. These students sought to present alternatives to Jewish educational organizations, which they said served administrators and were divided, counterproductively, into Orthodox, Conservative, and Reform denominations. CAJE's first task was the organization of a conference to serve as a forum for "teaching, learning, and sharing."

The first CAJE conference, held in 1976 at Brown University, Providence, Rhode Island, attracted 500 participants. Since that time, conferences have been held yearly in sites throughout the United States and have grown steadily in both size and content. Conferences now include workshops, lectures, movies, seminars and displays of educational materials.

Membership in CAJE and participation in its conferences is open to anyone concerned with the transmission of Jewish custom, culture, and belief. No standards or prerequisites exist, and members are composed of various age and ideological, professional and geographical backgrounds. Orthodox, Conservative, Reform, Reconstructionist and secular Jews come together with the common goal of improving Jewish education. The coalition's constituents come primarily from North America, but also from Europe, Israel, Morocco, and Australia.

Aside from its annual conference, CAJE concentrates on creating networks for those in the field of Jewish education. The CAJE network operates through "Mekasher," a computerized listing of members according to their areas of expertise. "Mekasher" printouts also list the teachers' addresses, phone numbers and teaching age levels. Task forces, composed of small groups of people interested in specific projects or subjects, are also run through CAJE. Task force issues have included: research in Jewish education; women in Jewish education; special education; and computer applications to Jewish education.

CAJE, which is based in New York City, is developing a curriculum bank, career clearinghouse, continuing education for members, and a journal. [RO.REB]

COHEN, ARTHUR A. (1928–1987), U.S. novelist, publisher, art historian, and theologian. Born in New York, Cohen received his B.A. (1946) and M.A. (1949) from the University of Chicago and then continued with studies in medieval Jewish philosophy at the Jewish Theological Seminary. He founded, with Cecil Hemley, Noonday Press in 1951; in 1956 he began Meridian Books. From 1960 to 1974, when he founded Ex Libris Publishing Company, he worked as an editor. He wrote essays, works of non-fiction on Jewish subjects, and novels.

Arthur Cohen (photo Pepe Diniz)

His *The Natural and the Supernatural Jew* (1962) sets the most insistent theme of his theological writings. Since Enlightenment, he avers, Jewish thought and imagination have with ever-increasing measure focused on the "natural" Jew enmeshed in immediate social and political concerns. Cohen fears that this understandable attention to the interests of the natural Jew, abetted by secular attitudes and biases of the modern period, has led to the neglect of the "supernatural" Jew, the Jew of the covenant conscious of his transcendent responsibilities. Accordingly, the urgent task of contemporary Jewish religious thought is to develop a strategy to reintegrate the natural and the supernatural Jew, otherwise the prospect looms that although the supernatural Jew may survive, Judaism will perish. Because of the experience of the modern, secular world, however, the supernatural vocation of the Jew could no longer be naively affirmed. To be spiritually and intellectually engaging, Cohen holds, the presuppositions of classical Jewish belief must be first "theologically reconstructed." Cohen's conception of this endeavor is inspired largely by the German Jewish thinker Franz *Rosenzweig whose uncompromising affirmation of theistic belief — grounded in the experiential categories of creation, revelation, and redemption — was supplemented by an equally unyielding adherence to rigorous philosophical reflection and honesty. For Cohen, the task of theological reconstruction is rendered all the more urgent by the Holocaust which in disclosing "the *tremendum* of evil" has so radically challenged the presuppositions of Jewish belief that to avoid this task is to relegate Judaism to blind faith and atavistic sentiment. Clearly, as Cohen argues in *The Tremendum. A Theological Interpretation of the Holocaust* (1981), the retreat to an unthinking, platitudinous posture endangers the recovery of Judaism as a supernatural vocation. These themes are echoed in Cohen's novels, among them *The Carpenter Years* (1967), *In the Days of Simon Stern* (1973), *A Hero in His Time* (1976), *Acts of Theft* (1980), and *An Admirable Woman* (1983). He coedited, with Paul Mendes-Flohr, *Contemporary Jewish Religious Thought* (1987). [P.M.-F.]

COHEN, STANLEY (1922–), U.S. biochemist. Cohen was born in Brooklyn, New York. After studying at Brooklyn College (B.A., 1943) and Oberlin College (M.A., 1945), he received his Ph.D. in biochemistry from the University of Michigan in 1948. From then until 1952 he worked at the University of Colorado. Cohen then proceeded to Washington University in St. Louis in 1953 where he was an American Cancer Society Fellow. There he worked with Dr. Rita Levi-Montalcini (q.v.) and they isolated the protein which is recognized as the nerve growth factor. Cohen's later individual research led him to the discovery of the epidermal growth factor which oversees cell development in the skin. The two researchers were the corecipients of the 1986 Nobel Prize for physiology or medicine for having "opened new fields of widespread importance to basic science" with these discoveries.

Cohen remained at Washington University until 1967 when he became a professor of biochemistry at Vanderbilt University. He was an American Cancer Society research professor in 1976 and is a member of the National Academy of Science. He and Dr. Levi-Montalcini were also the corecipients of the 1986 Lasker Award. [ED.]

CONSERVATIVE JUDAISM (see **5**:901). **1970–1990. Demography.** Although the roots of Conservatism can be traced to Germany in the early and middle 1900s, in the 20th century it has flourished most in the United States. According to *The American Jewish Yearbook 1989*, from the end of World War II to the present a plurality of American Jewish adults have identified themselves as Conservative Jews. After the decimation of European Jewry in the Holocaust, American Jews have constituted the world's largest Jewish population with the most financial resources, the predominance of Conservative Judaism in America then being especially significant.

A major shift, however, has occurred in American Jewry in the last two decades. While 33% of American Jews still consider themselves Conservative (in comparison to 9% Orthodox, 2% Reconstructionist, and 30% Reform), a full 26% no longer identify with any of the religious movements. Jews now feel totally at home in America, and their understanding of America is quite secular — more secular, in fact, than most American Christians take it to be. Even those Jews who do see themselves in religious terms do not necessarily join synagogues. Nationwide, in fact, only about half of American Jews are currently synagogue members, with the weakest affiliation rates in some of the largest Jewish communities. This, represents a major decrease in membership and impact for all three of the major religious movements in American Judaism. Their primary challenge is not the competition engendered by each other, but the secularism.

The Search for Definition. These demographic factors were one important stimulus for the drive within the Conservative Movement during the 1970s and 1980s to formulate a clearer definition of the meaning of Conservative Judaism. No longer would adult Jews join synagogues almost automatically as a result of social pressure; now they must be convinced to take on a religious form of Judaism in the first place, and a Conservative form in particular. To accomplish this, the movement could no longer satisfy itself with a vague understanding of its principles on the part of its leaders and constituents; it would have to articulate its principles and programs clearly in order to mount a campaign to convince unaffiliated Jews to join.

In addition to these demographic pressures, two events

Derrida's sophisticatedly written philosophy resists systematic presentation. Rather, it itself is a critical reflection upon the spirit of system, upon the closedness of the Western philosophical tradition. This tradition establishes, in effect, a metaphysics of presence and origin, an ontology of plenitude. It is based on a phonocentric conception of language, which attributes a "natural" power of transparence and immediacy to the "living" word, relating it to the Logos; writing in comparison is commonly relegated to a marginal "technical" aspect of signification. The horizon of knowledge is thus seen, due to an ideological illusion, as artificially divided between "interior" and "exterior," between "intelligible" and "sensory"; such a dualism disregards the essentially metaphorical and subversive nature of language. One can go beyond this binary logic, the exposition of rhetorical ambiguities: Derrida, in the spirit of Nietzsche or Heidegger, undertakes the task of rupturing the logocentric system. Writing differs from speech not so much in medium (graphic vs. vocal) as by a certain mediatedness. As the sign of a sign, the written word is by definition estranged from its origin, and as such becomes emblematic of a culture based on the "arbitrariness of sign" (Saussure).

Founded on a network of oppositions, language posits the "instituted trace" as its very principle. The literary work as a totality gives way to Text: the site of an endless play of recurrent signifiers, and of the dissemination of meaning.

Derridian criticism is thus a practice of reading dedicated to the "deconstruction" of semiotic poor faith and of a "will to power" that are commensurate with the political and philosophical history of the Western world. It demonstrates the "indecidability" which necessarily causes any text, whether literary or philosophic, to exceed the bounds of its affirmed meaning by way of innumerable fissures. Thus the classics of philosophy from Plato to Hegel are rigorously sifted through, and most contemporary texts (from Levi-Strauss to Lacan) as well.

Derrida's rewriting, which extends to art and poetry, opens itself in its turn to a free proliferation of signs, constructed in a series of ambiguous terms ("différance," "supplément," "passe-partout") and word plays, dizzying play which ends by "disconcerting all opposition" between text and conceivable "paratext."

His works include: *L'Ecriture et la différence* (1967), *La Voix et le phénomène* (1967), *De la Grammatologie* (1967) *La Dissémination* (1972); *Marge — de la philosophie* (1972) *Glas* (1974), and *Schibboleth* (1986). [BE.R.]

DERSHOWITZ, ALAN M. (1938–), U.S. law professor and civil liberties lawyer. Dershowitz was born in Brooklyn, New York, graduated from Yeshiva University high school and Brooklyn College. He received his law degree from Yale Law School, where he was editor-in-chief of the *Yale Law Journal*. He was law clerk to Chief Judge David Bazelon, U.S. Court of Appeals, and Justice Arthur Goldberg of the U.S. Supreme Court. In 1967 he was appointed professor at Harvard Law School, where his special subjects have been criminal law, psychiatry and law, and constitutional litigation. He has served as consultant to the government of China on the revision of its criminal code, as a member of the President's Commission on Marijuana and Drug Abuse, the President's Commission on Causes and Prevention of Violence, and the President's Commission on Civil Disorders, and he has been director of the National Institute of Mental Health.

Dershowitz has been chairman of the civil rights commission for New England of the Anti-Defamation League of B'nai B'rith, and has been a prominent member of the board of directors of the American Civil Liberties Union.

He has lectured widely and written extensively (in books, in magazines, and newspaper articles) on civil liberties and public affairs. He has been identified as counsel in many important legal cases involving civil liberties, and became a public figure especially through his participation in television programs and interviews.

Dershowitz has played a leading role in influencing Congress in projecting the theory of "presumptive sentencing," which is intended to obviate discrepancy in criminal sentencing for the same crimes.

Between 1967 and 1986 Dershowitz represented clients in eleven cases in the U.S. Supreme Court. Some of his cases have attracted national attention, including those in which he represented Patricia Hearst, Claus von Bülow the trial lawyer, F. Lee Bailey, and Kenneth Tyson. Although stridently loyal to Jewish causes, he defended the constitutional right of the American Nazi party in 1977 to march in Skokie, Illinois, for he maintains that as a civil libertarian it was his duty to uphold the constitutional right of free speech, which includes the right to demonstrate peacefully. Dershowitz thinks of himself as a liberal in the tradition of John F. Kennedy and Hubert Humphrey. Although opposed to the philosophy and actions of the Jewish Defense League, he in 1972 successfully defended Sheldon Siegel, a member of the J.D.L., on a murder charge arising out of the blowing up of the offices of Sol Hurok to protest Hurok's sponsorship of Russian performers. Dershowitz succeeded at the trial of Siegel to expose the case as a police frameup. *Time* magazine has called him, "the top lawyer of last resort in the country." *Newsweek* has described Dershowitz as "the nation's most peripatetic civil liberties lawyer and one of its most distinguished defenders of individual rights."

Dershowitz is author of several books, including *The Best Defense* (1982); *Reversal of Fortune: Inside the von Bülow Case* (1982), which was made into a successful film; his autobiography *Chutzpah* (1991); and *Contrary to Public Opinion* (1992). [M.R.K.]

DOCTOROW, EDGAR LAWRENCE (1931–), U.S. novelist and editor. Born in the Bronx, New York, Doctorow began his career as a reader of fiction for TV and film studios. This led him into editorial work, first at New American Library (1959–1964) and then as editor-in-chief for Dial Press in the 1960s. His reading of mediocre filmscripts for western movies helped inspire his first novel. *Welcome to Hard Times* (1960), a black comedy of the Wild West. His second novel, *Big as Life* (1966), a semi-science fiction tale, described two huge, naked figures being introduced to New York. Several critics saw these figures as an allegory of the atom bomb.

In 1971, Doctorow published *The Book of Daniel*, a fictionalized account of the celebrated Rosenberg trial and its radical legacy. The novel is a portrait of the defendants' son "Daniel" who was profoundly affected by the death of his parents at the hands of a ruthless and indifferent society. The novel's style anticipates many of the innovative literary techniques employed in his later novels — juxtaposition of historical fact and fantasy and cinematic switches of tense, scene and voice. The novel was made into a film.

Ragtime (1975) weaves a story around a host of early 20th century figures in the United States, among them Houdini, Freud, Jung, Emma Goldman, Theodore Roosevelt, Henry Ford, Woodrow Wilson and Albert Einstein, together with ironic comment on their achievements and later effects. *Ragtime* was awarded the National Book Critics Circle Award in 1975. The film version was directed by Milos Forman. His *Loon Lake* (1980) dealt with life during the Depression; *World's Fair* (1985) culminates in a boy's visit to the New York World's Fair in 1939; and *Billy Bathgate* was made into a movie. Doctorow's fiction utilizes the past to explore parallel tendencies in the present and the inability of the present to learn from the past and escape its errors.

Doctorow has also written a play, *Drinks Before Dinner* (1979), which was first produced at the New York Shakespeare Festival's Public Theater.

Doctorow was a writer-in-residence at the University of California at Irvine and taught at Sarah Lawrence College in Bronxville, New York. [SU. STR.]

DONSKOY, MARK SEMENOVICH (1901-1981), Soviet film director. Born in Odessa, he began working in films in 1926. Most of his films were made from his own scenarios. He became famous with *Pesnya o schast'e* ("Song of Happiness," 1934). His trilogy based on Maxim Gorky's autobiographical accounts: *Detstvo Gor'kogo (Gorky's Childhood," 1938), V lyudjakh* ("Among People," 1939) and *Moi universitety* ("My Universities," 1940) are distinguished by the vividness and precision of the depiction of Russian provincial life at the end of the 19th century and by the psychological acuteness of his presentation of character. The direct and candid depiction of suffering in the partisan movement in the Ukraine as seen in *Raduga* ("Rainbow," 1944) and *Nepokorennye* ("The Undefeated," 1945; according to B. Goratov's novella) made a strong impression and influenced the masters of the Italian neo-realistic cinema. In the second of these two films there is a particularly striking episode depicting the mass execution of Jews in a Nazi-occupied city. *Sel'skaya uchitel'nitsa* ("The Village School Mistress," 1947) enjoyed considerable popularity. Later films included one about Lenin's mother and screen versions of Gorky's novels *Mat'* ("The Mother," 1956) and *Foma Gordeev* ("Foma Gordeev," 1959).

Donskoy was awarded three Stalin Prizes, and one State Prize and the honorary titles of Peoples' Artist of the U.S.S.R. (1956) and Hero of Socialist Labor (1971). [S.J.E.R.]

DOTHAN, MOSHE (1919-), Israeli archaeologist. After graduating from high school in his native Cracow, Dothan received an entry permit to study in Palestine at the Hebrew University of Jerusalem. He arrived in 1938 but his studies were soon interrupted by the outbreak of World War II. He spent two years in kibbutz Naḥshonim (today kibbutz Ma'apil) and then joined the British Army in 1942. His service took him to Malta, North Africa, and Italy. When in Italy, he first felt an interest in archaeology.

In 1946 he returned to Palestine and completed a master's degree in archaeology and Jewish history and while working from 1950 in the Department of Antiquities in Jerusalem was able to conclude his doctorate. His thesis (1959) was on the late Chalcolithic period (4000-3000 B.C.E.) and much of his research was based on his findings at Tel Asor (near Naḥal Iron), a site where a mass grave from that period was discovered.

He headed numerous excavations including Tel Afula (1951); Mezer in Naḥal Iron; the 1956 survey of Kadesh-Barnea in northern Sinai of the Israelite town of the 10th century B.C.E.; Tel Mor, the ancient port dating from 1600 B.C.E. where Ashdod port stands today; the excavations of the important Philistine town of Ashdod (1960-1977); Ḥammath Tiberias (1962) where the excavations revealed an early synagogue dated approximately 250 C.E. under other synagogues which had been constructed on top of it; and Tel Acre (1972-1989) where he headed excavations whose finds went back to the 10th century B.C.E..

From 1972 to 1988 Dothan was a professor at Haifa University where he founded the department of maritime civilization and in 1976 the department of archaeology.

He published over 150 articles, primarily in English. He is married to Trude Dothan (see below). [E.HO.]

DOTHAN, TRUDE (1923-), Israeli archaeologist. Dothan was born in Vienna, daughter of the artists Greta and Leopold *Krakauer. The family arrived in Palestine in 1925. Trude Dothan studied at the Hebrew University of Jerusalem and continued her post-graduate studies at the Oriental Institute of the University of Chicago, and the Institute of Archaeology at the University of London. Returning to Israel, she received her Ph.D. in archaeology for her thesis on "Philistine and Egyptian Material Culture in the Twelfth and Eleventh Century B.C.E." She joined the academic staff at the Hebrew University in 1963 and became a full professor in 1981.

She has worked on numerous archaeological excavations under the auspices of the Institute of Archaeology of the Hebrew University paying special attention to the interconnections between the Aegean and the Orient. She participated in the Tel Qasile excavations of the Philistine city and was a member of the archaeological team of the Hazor excavations from 1952 where her main emphasis was on Canaanite cult and culture.

From 1961 to 1962 she co-directed the Ein Gedi excavation and in the 1971-72 seasons was co-director at the Athienou excavations in Cyprus where the first and only archaeological excavation outside of Israel was carried out by the Hebrew University. In Cyprus the excavation was of the sanctuary of the cult and industry (metal work) of the Cypriot Mycenean culture and its interconnections with other cultures.

Dothan was the director of the Deir el-Balaḥ excavations in the Gaza Strip which was an Egyptian outpost on the road from Egypt to Canaan. During these excavations the anthropoid coffins of an Egyptian-style settlement and a cemetery from the 18th-19th dynasty were found. She has been serving as co-director of the Tel Mikne-Ekron excavations and publications project which examines the rise and decline of one of the five Philistine cities from its initial settlement in the 12th century. The excavations have uncovered a fortified city with its palaces and cult relating to the Aegean background, a flourishing city in the eighth and seventh centuries B.C.E. which was destroyed and left desolate in 603 B.C.E., and what was one of the largest centers for the production of olive oil in the ancient world.

Dothan has published numerous articles. Her books published in English include *The Philistine Material Culture* (1982).

She is married to the archaeologist Moshe Dothan (see above). [E.HO.]

DREIFUSS, RUTH (1940-), first Jew elected to the Bundesrat, the seven-member federal government of Switzerland. Born in St. Gall to a family which had its roots in the

Ruth Dreifuss

old "Judendorf" of Endingen, Dreifuss grew up in Berne and Geneva and joined the socialist party. She worked at the Swiss Ministry of Foreign Affairs and from 1981 was secretary–general of the Swiss Federation of Labor. When, in the summer of 1992, it was first suggested that she may become a member of the Bundesrat, the idea was immediately dismissed as unrealistic, on the grounds that Switzerland would not yet be ready to elect a Jew to such a high position. But in March 1993, Dreifuss was elected by the Bundesversammlung, combining both houses of parliament, to the Bundesrat after a political crisis which threatened the "magic formula" of Swiss politics. This unwritten agreement as well as popular pressure demanded that the new member of the Bundesrat should be a socialist, female, and French-speaking, while the constitution excluded anybody from one of the cantons already represented in the Bundesrat. After her election, she took over the Department of Internal Affairs.

While no longer a member of any Jewish congregation, Dreifuss has always maintained contacts with the Jewish community and steadfastly insisted on her Jewish origins. Under the rules of the Swiss system, she can be expected to become (the first female and the first Jewish) president of the Swiss confederacy by or before the end of the century. [MA. MAR.]

DWORKIN, RONALD (1931–), U.S. legal philosopher. Dworkin received a B.A. degree from Harvard in 1953 and another B.A. degree in 1955 from Oxford. Two years later he received his law degree from Harvard. After admission to the New York bar, he joined the law firm Sullivan and Cromwell as an associate. In 1962 he joined the faculty of Yale Law School, where he was named Hohfeld Professor in 1968. In 1969 he was appointed professor of jurisprudence and Fellow at University College, Oxford; in 1977 he became professor of law at New York University without resigning his position at Oxford.

Dworkin is recognized as a leading philosopher of law. His best-known works are *Taking Rights Seriously* (1977), *A Matter of Principle* (1985), and *Law's Empire* (1986). In his work Dworkin has contended against the philosophy of legal positivism, identified with Jeremy Bentham, John Austin and more recently H.L.A. Hart. Legal decisions, he maintains, should be based on principles and pre–existing rights, rather than on discretion or policy. While rights may be controversial, Dworkin holds that nonetheless there is always only one right answer in hard cases. Rights, he holds, are inherent in the Constitution and in the precedents that interpret it. Judges make moral judgments as they apply precedents to factual situations — precedents on which principles are based and which are the bases of decisions.

In *Ronald Dworkin and Contemporary Jurisprudence* (1984), the editor — Professor Marshall Cohen — states, "In the opinion of the editor, the jurisprudential writings of Ronald Dworkin constitute the finest contribution yet made by an American writer to the philosophy of law."

Despite Dworkin's close association, as student and as teacher, with Oxford, he is basically an American thinker. Much more than would be true of a British jurist, Dworkin has been influenced by American constitutional law and constitutional jurisprudence. His emphasis on principle is a reflection of this influence. [M.R.K.]

E

ELAZAR, DANIEL J. (1934–), political scientist. He was born in Minneapolis and received his Ph.D. from the University of Chicago. He was appointed professor of political science at Temple University in Philadelphia, where he directs the Center for the Study of Federalism. A leading authority on the subject, he is a founding president of the International Association for Federal Studies.

Elazar divides his time between the U.S. and Israel where he is professor of intergovernmental relations at Bar-Ilan University and president of the Jerusalem Center for Public Affairs, which he founded. In 1986 he was appointed by Pres. Reagan to be a member of the U.S. Advisory Commission on Intergovernmental Relations and was reappointed by Pres. Bush in 1991. He has served as a consultant to many governments in various parts of the world.

Daniel J. Elazar (Photo Debbi Cooper, Jerusalem)

Elazar has written or edited over 50 books and many other publications, including *Community and Polity*, an in-depth study of the American Jewish community and its institutions, *People and Polity, The Organization Dynamics of World Jewry*, a study of the communities and institutions of World Jewry, *Understanding the Jewish Agency*, and *Israel: Building a New Society*. Some of his books have sought a solution to the Israel-Palestinian problem based on federal principles. He edits *Publius*, the journal of Federalism, and *The Jewish Political Studies Review*. Together with his brother, David H. Elazar, he published *A Classification System for Libraries of Judaica*.

Elazar is active in the World Sephardi Federation and was president of the American Sephardi Federation. [YI.K.]

ELIAHU, MORDECHAI (1929–), chief rabbi of Israel. Born in the Old City of Jerusalem, Eliahu studied at the Porat Yosef yeshivah, the oldest and largest Sephardi yeshivah in Jerusalem. He was appointed *dayyan* when he was 30 and served in Beersheba and Jerusalem until his appointment to the High Rabbinical Court in 1973. He was elected Sephardi chief rabbi of Israel in March 1983 and invested soon thereafter as the *rishon-le-ẓion*.

Mordechai Eliahu

ELION, GERTRUDE BELL (1918–), research scientist and pharmacology educator, Nobel Prize laureate. Miss Elion was born in New York City and educated at Hunter

College and NYU from which she received a M.S. degree in 1941. After working as a research assistant in organic synthesis at Johnson & Johnson in New Brunswick, New Jersey (1943–44), she began her long-term association with Wellcome Research Laboratory, first in New York and then with Burroughs Wellcome in North Carolina. From 1944 to 1950 she was a biochemist for Wellcome, becoming a senior

Gertrude Bell Elion

research chemist in the latter year. Her other positions with the laboratory were assistant to the associate research director (1955–62), assistant to the research director (1963–66), and head of experimental therapy from 1966 to 1983 when she became scientist emeritus.

Miss Elion was adjunct professor of pharmacology at Duke University from 1970 and research professor in 1983. Among her other activities she was a consultant for the United States Public Health Service (1960–64) and chairman of the Gordon Conference on Coenzymes and Metabolic Pathways in 1966. She was a member of the board of scientific counselors to the National Cancer Institute from 1980 to 1984 and of the American Cancer Society (1983–86).

She was the recipient in 1983 of the Judd award of the Sloan-Kettering Cancer Center, and in 1984 of the Cain award of the American Association for Cancer Research of which she was president 1983–84.

In 1988 she was awarded, along with her colleague George Hitchings, the Nobel Prize in medicine for 40 years of research into cell metabolism and work leading to the production of the first chemotherapy drugs and antiviral drugs. (Sir James Black of Britain also shared in the 1988 Nobel Prize in medicine for his work.) In 1957 they developed azathioprine which helps in the control of rejection in organ transplants; this was followed by the introduction of acyclovir used in treating herpes and the development of AZT, the only drug — as of 1988 — approved by the U.S. government for use in cases of AIDS. [ED.]

ELKIN, STANLEY (1930–), U.S. novelist and short story writer. From 1955 to 1957, he served in the U.S. Army. From 1960, he taught and wrote at Washington University in St. Louis, Missouri, where he was appointed professor of English in 1968.

Elkin has been described as a black humorist. His fiction, which dramatizes the conflicts and vulgarity of contemporary popular culture in the U.S.A. has become increasingly popular since the 1960s. His first novel *Boswell: a Modern Comedy* (1964) chronicles the post-World War II era as seen through the eyes of a cynical outside observer. His 1976 novel *The Franchiser* describes the life of Ben Flesh who collects franchises, lives out of his Cadillac, eats fast food and sleeps in motels. Only serious illness forces Ben to confront the sterility of his life.

Elkin's fiction is peopled by fantastically comic characters. In his third novel, *The Dick Gibson Show* (1971), Elkin utilizes a radio talk show format to recreate a set of eccentric comic personalities. His novella *The Living End* (1979) traces the lives of hold-up victims in Minneapolis-St. Paul, the cast of characters including Jesus, Mary and Joseph and others both living and dead.

Elkin often uses the Jew and his exile as analogy for man's striving for freedom. In his first collection of short stories, *Cries and Kibitzers, Kibitzers and Criers* (1966), Elkin evokes the atmosphere of growing up Jewish in the late 1930s.

Elkin's other works have included the novel *A Bad Man* (1967) and the volume of short stories *Searches and Seizure (1973), George Mills* (1982), for which he won the 1983 National Book Critics Circle Award, and *Magic Kingdom* (1985). [SU.STR.]

ENGLAND (**6**:747; **Dc./17**:234). **Demography and Social Structure.** Calculations have indicated the Jewish population falling from 336,000 (plus or minus 10%) in 1983, to 330,000 in 1986, to below 300,000 in 1990. However, these are approximate figures since it is difficult to compute the number of non-affiliated Jews. There are also few statistics on the number of Israelis in Britain which may be between 30,000 and 50,000.

The percentage of Jews who were members of synagogues in the central Orthodox stream fell from 70.5% in 1983 to 64% in 1990. The percentage of those affiliated to the right-wing Orthodox community increased from 4.4% in 1983 to 10% in 1984, falling to 6.9% in 1990. Only the Progressive movements showed signs of consistent growth. In 1983, 22.4% of Jews affiliated to synagogues belonged to Reform and Liberal congregations. According to 1990 figures, the Reform Synagogues of Great Britain accounted for 17%, the Union of Liberal and Progressive Synagogues claimed 7%, with the Masorti movement taking a small, but growing share. The Sephardi community held steady at just under 3% of the total.

Cover of souvenir brochure produced for "The Jewish East End: A Celebration"

The geographical and social distribution of British Jews has barely altered. Two-thirds continue to inhabit the capital. The only growth areas are the "sun-belt" towns on the South Coast such as Brighton, the largest with 10,000. Manchester Jewry maintains its numbers at around 30,000, but Leeds has seen a fall from around 14,000 to about 11,000. A similar drop is estimated for Glasgow. Within each metropolitan center, Jews remain concentrated in a small number of prosperous, suburban, middle-class districts: Bury in Manchester, Moortown in Leeds, north-west London and Redbridge, an eastern suburb of the capital. The first centers of settlement are now almost bereft of Jewish residents or institutions.

The Jews in British Politics and Society. The last decade has seen a shift of political allegiances among British Jews from the left to the right. Affluence and self-interest have underpinned the trend, but it has been abetted by the perceived anti-Zionism of the Labor Party and the appeal of Mrs. Thatcher, prime minister for most of the period, who was seen as "strong" on Jewish issues. Yet the same period saw manifestations of a stubborn prejudice against Jews within Conservative political circles.

In the June 1983 General Election, 28 Jewish M.P.s were elected of whom 17 were Conservative and 11 Labor. Three Jews were appointed to serve in the new cabinet, rising to four in 1984 and briefly five in 1986. The General Election of June 1987 saw 63 Jewish candidates. Of these, 16 Conservative and 7 Labor candidates were elected. This marked the second highest ever number of Jewish Tory M.P.s and a big fall in the number of Jewish Laborites. In the June 1992 General Election out of 43 Jewish Parliamentary candidates, 11 Tory, 8 Labor and 1 Liberal Democrat were successful. The unsuccessful candidates included 4 Jewish Greens, a new phenomenon. Three Jewish Conservative M.P.s retired and two others were defeated. Among the appointments to the new cabinet made by the prime minister, John Major, were two Jews: Michael Howard, secretary of state for the environment (home secretary in 1993) and Malcolm Rifkind, secretary of state for defense.

Unlike the rest of Europe, the far-right has been conspicuously unsuccessful in British electoral politics at either a local or national level. In April 1992, the British National Party obtained a mere 7,000 votes for the 13 candidates it fielded. The National Front did even worse, winning under 5,000 votes in 13 constituencies. A visit to Britain by M. Le Pen in December 1991 was met by Jewish protests and antifascist demonstrations.

The government's stand on immigration and asylum issues throughout the decade has aroused disquiet among sections of the Jewish population. In February 1992, a delegation from the Jewish Council for Community Relations saw the then home secretary, Kenneth Baker, to protest against the Asylum Bill. The Board of Deputies also expressed its concern. The Jewish historical experience was alluded to several times by Jewish speakers in the debates accompanying the Asylum Bill's passage through Parliament during 1991–93.

Another long-running Parliamentary issue of Jewish concern was the punishment of alleged Nazi war criminals and collaborators domiciled in the United Kingdom. An All-Party Parliamentary War Crimes Group was formed in November 1986 to press first for a government investigation and, subsequently, for action against suspected was criminals. Intense lobbying and media revelations caused the government to announce an inquiry in February 1988. Its report in July 1989 called for legislation to enable the trial in Britain of men suspected of committing war crimes in Nazi-occupied Europe at a time when they were not of British nationality. Legislation was introduced into Parliament in November 1989, but opposition by a minority of M.P.s and a majority of Peers delayed its passage into law until May 1991. The debates about the bill exposed the persistence of many negative stereotypes about the Jews. By April 1992, around £10 million had been spent on the investigations being conducted by the Metropolitan War Crimes Unit and its Scottish counterpart. Over 90 cases were being looked into, but there was still no indication of any case coming to trial.

In July 1992, Antony Gecas, a former member of the 11th Lithuanian Police Battalion who had lived in Scotland since 1946, lost his libel case against Scottish TV for a program which had accused him of being a war criminal. The hearing lasted four months and cost £650,000. In his ruling, the presiding judge, Lord Milligan, concluded that Gecas had "participated in many operations involving the killing of innocent Soviet citizens including Jews in particular." Despite this, Gecas has not been charged with war crimes under the 1991 Act.

Anti-Jewish prejudice surfaced in politics and society, Leon Brittan, the trade and industry secretary who resigned from the cabinet over the "Westland Affair" in 1986, Lord Young, secretary of state for trade and industry who Mrs. Thatcher wanted to take over the chairmanship of the Conservative Party, and Edwina Currie (née Cohen), a junior health minister who resigned in December 1988 over her pronouncements on salmonella in eggs, were all thought to have been victims of a "whispering campaign" among Tory backbenchers.

A series of criminal cases involving Jews attracted much attention and discussion during the late 1980s. The Jewishness of those involved was mentioned sometimes directly, sometimes obliquely, and efforts were made to find a link between this and the malfeasance in question. Such commentary could be open and well-intentioned, but at other times it was insidious and malevolent.

In August 1990, the first trial in the Guinness fraud case, which had lasted 113 days, resulted in the conviction of Gerald Ronson, Sir Jack Lyons, Anthony Parnes, and Ernest Saunders. Parnes, Ronson, and Lyons were Jews, the last two being notable donors to Jewish causes. Saunders was Viennese-born of Jewish parents, but raised as a Christian. In the two subsequent trials connected with the Guinness affair, none of the defendants was Jewish and none was convicted. This fostered the sense that the defendants in the first case had been at best "fall-guys" or, at worst, victimized.

The sensational death of Robert Maxwell in November 1991 was followed rapidly by the collapse of his business empire and the revelation that he had stolen hundreds of millions of pounds from his employees' pension fund in order to prop up the share value of his companies. His sons were subsequently arrested for abetting this fraud and await trial. Although Maxwell's ostentatious burial on the Mount of Olives could not help but draw attention to his Jewish roots, media commentary was relatively restrained. However, it was widely considered that Maxwell and the Jewish entrepreneurs in the Guinness case were outsiders in the City. This denied them protection by the "old boys" network when their schemes, in no way unique, ran foul of the law.

British Jews were, on the whole, spared violent forms of anti-Semitism. The exception was 1990 when, over a twelve-month period there were 29 cases of vandalism against Jewish cemeteries, synagogues, and Holocaust Memorials in the London area alone and 7 reported cases of physical assault on Jewish persons. This violence is miniscule compared to the assault on non-white minorities, but the attacks provoked media comment and provoked reassuring statements from the prime minister in May 1990.

The most prevalent form of anti-Jewish action in Britain

has been the distribution of anti-Semitic literature. In November 1990, Greville Janner, M.P., sponsored an early day motion in the House of Commons which attracted the names of 100 M.P.s in support of suppressing the circulation of Holocaust Denial material. In March 1991, Dowager Lady Birdwood was charged under the Public Order Act (1986) for distributing the ritual murder accusation against the Jews. She was subsequently found guilty and given a two-year unconditional discharge. In December 1992, glossily produced pseudo-Hanukkah cards containing doggerel that embraced anti-Semitic libels were sent to hundreds of Jewish organizations and prominent individuals. Police investigations failed to identify the source of this "hate mail" and the Government has consistently rebuffed pleas by the Board of Deputies, most recently in October 1992, for a community libel law.

The announcement that a gathering of Holocaust Denial practitioners would be held in London in November 1991 led to demands that the home secretary ban the entry of Robert Faurrison and Fred Leuchter. Leuchter actually entered the country illegally and was deported after showing up at a "conference" that was heavily-picketed by anti-fascist groups. David Irving, sometime British historian and now a propagandist well known for addressing neo-Nazi rallies in Germany, has become a linchpin in this shadowy global network.

Jews and the Holocaust figured in several historical controversies. In 1987 Jim Allen's anti-Zionist play *Perdition* deployed the canard that Zionists collaborated with the Nazis. Production was canceled after expressions of outrage from the Jewish community and intense media scrutiny, but this only inflamed the debate. The War Crimes Bill occasioned many reflections on the Holocaust, often yoked disturbingly to Jewish terrorism in Palestine in 1946–47. In January 1992, when Irving claimed to have discovered new Eichmann papers the press treated him as a right-wing historian whose views merited serious reportage. In July 1992, the *Sunday Times* caused a storm of controversy by employing him to transcribe and comment on newly revealed portions of Goebbels' diary.

Alan Clark, junior defense minister, was widely condemned in December 1991 for attending a party to launch the revised version of Irving's book *Hitler's War* in which Irving states that Hitler was innocent of the Final Solution and denies the existence of gas chambers for killing Jews. Clark later endorsed a political biography of Churchill by John Charmley, which appeared in January 1993, that suggested Britain should have made peace with Hitler in 1940 or 1941. Clark and Charmley agreed that there was little to choose between Stalinism and Nazism, and that the plight of the Jews under Nazism was a marginal issue. The exposure in the *Guardian* newspaper in May and December 1992 of war crimes in the Nazi-occupied Channel Islands, and the concurrence of the local authorities in the deportation of Jews, shed a different light on the matter.

Controversy also surrounded efforts to set up an *eruv* in the London borough of Barnet. The project was launched by the United Synagogue "*Eruv* Committee" in 1987. In June 1992 it was passed by the Public Works Committee of Barnet Council. It was then considered by the Hampstead Garden Suburb Trust, which manages this architecturally unique suburban area. At a stormy meeting in September 1992, the Trust's chairman, Lord MacGregor, was censured for approving a letter to Barnet Council advising it to reject the plan and calling the *eruv* "a very unpleasant exhibition of fundamentalism." He subsequently resigned. This fracas made the *eruv* into a heated issue locally and in the national newspapers. On February 24, 1993, the council's planning committee defeated the *eruv* proposal by 11 to 7 votes. Jewish councillors were split and it generated fierce opposition from both Orthodox and "assimilationist" Jews. It was also attacked by non-Jews unable to accept the public expression of Jewish difference.

Britain and Israel. From 1983 to 1989, British foreign policy was conducted by Sir Geoffrey Howe. Britain urged the PLO to recognize Israel and renounce terrorism, while calling on Israel to halt settlements in the occupied territories as a *quid pro quo.* Between 1984 and 1987 there were several friendly high-level exchange visits, but British unease about conditions in the Gaza Strip were forcefully expressed by junior Foreign Office Minister David Mellor during a visit in January 1988. After Yassir Arafat announced acceptance of UN resolutions 242 and 338 and renounced the armed struggle, William Waldegrave, Mellor's successor, met with Abu Bassam Sharrif of the PLO.

The outbreak of the *intifada* in 1989 led to the revival of the propaganda war in the media and in student politics. British Government officials repeatedly expressed concern at Israeli handling of the disturbances. In March 1990, the new foreign secretary, Douglas Hurd, met with Abu Bassam Sharrif, although the Palestinian terrorist attack on Israel in May 1990 led to demands to sever links with the PLO. Hurd issued a call to the Palestinians to curb terrorism, but contacts with the PLO continued. The situation was transformed by Iraq's invasion of Kuwait in August 1990. The British Government deplored PLO support for Saddam Hussein and rejected any "linkage" between Iraq's invasion and the Palestinian problem, although in October 1990 it said that Israeli policy towards the Palestinians could not go unchanged. In November 1991, Britain resumed diplomatic ties with Syria, severed after the 1988 Lockerbie disaster, which was now a member of the anti-Iraq coalition.

When the war started, hundreds of British Jews, including the chief rabbi, went to Israel on solidarity missions. Prime Minister John Major, congratulated Israel on its "admirable restraint" following Iraqi missile attacks. Popular attitudes towards Israel and the Palestinians changed radically, although British official policy soon reverted to type. In January 1992 Mr. Major addressed a letter to the Zionist Federation of Great Britain calling on Anglo-Jewish leaders to intervene with the Israel Government against the deportation of 12 Palestinian activists. On July 30, 1992, Mr. Major addressed the annual dinner of the Conservative Friends of Israel. He called the settlements "a major impediment to the peace process," denounced the Arab boycott as "iniquitous" and said it should be ended in return for freezing the settlements.

Prime Minister Margaret Thatcher with Israel Prime Minister Peres at a reception in her honor at Claridge's Hotel London, Jan. 23, 1986 (GPO, Jerusalem)

Politics, Society and Culture of Anglo-Jewry. The Board of Deputies acquired a new chief executive in February 1991 when Neville Nagler, a senior civil servant, succeeded Hayyim Pinner, holder of the position for 14 years. In June 1991, Judge Israel Finestein, Q.C., won the election for the presidency of the Board of Deputies and succeeded the outgoing Dr. Lionel Kopelowitz who had held office since 1985. Rosalind Preston was elected the first woman vice-president of the Board. Finestein announced that he intended to increase democracy in Anglo-Jewry and secure greater participation in communal governance by the young, women, regional communities, and academics.

Chief Rabbi Dr. Immanuel Jakobovits was elevated to the House of Lords in January 1988 and in March 1991 was awarded the prestigious Templeton Prize for progress in religion. In May 1991 he was criticized by figures in the Joint Israel Appeal because of an interview in the *Evening Standard* newspaper in which he expressed reservations concerning Israeli conduct in the Administered Territories. He was succeeded in September 1991 by Rabbi Dr. Jonathan Sacks. As principal of Jews' College, in 1989 Sacks organized two important conferences on "traditional alternatives" in Judaism, one on general and another on specifically women's issues.

In February 1992, the new chief rabbi unveiled his review of women's role in Jewish life and named Rosalind Preston as its head. This followed a bitter struggle over women's services in Stanmore Synagogue. Although in April 1991 he resigned from a Jewish education "think tank" because it included a Reform rabbi, in April 1992 Chief Rabbi Dr. Sacks led a delegation that embraced Reform and Liberal rabbis (including a woman) to a major interfaith conference.

In September 1992 a report on the United Synagogue, conducted under the guidance of Stanley Kalms, found "mistakes, miscalculations, poor management, and financial errors" and revealed a debt of £9 million. The report also noted that a majority of members felt alienated by the rightward trend of the rabbinate and recommended an "inclusivist" position. It precipitated the resignation of Sidney Frosh, the president. In December 1992, the United Synagogue announced £0.8 million of cuts and a freeze on rabbis' salaries. It wound up its three-year old *sheḥitah* operation, established as a result of the bitter "*sheḥitah* wars" in the 1980s, with a loss of £0.7 million.

The search for economies underlay the amalgamation of the Jewish Blind Society and the Jewish Welfare Board to form Jewish Care in December 1988. In the recession of the early 1980s and again in the slump of 1990–92, Jewish welfare organizations had to cater for Jewish unemployed persons, too, despite a shrinking income base. The second recession saw many of the fortunes built up by Jewish entrepreneurs in the 1980s crumble. Grodzinski, the *kasher* baker, went into receivership in February 1991 after trading for 102 years. The famous *kasher* caterer Schaverin suffered a similar fate in November 1991. In June 1992, the Glasgow *Jewish Echo* closed down after 64 years of publication.

Nor was Anglo-Jewry immune to the social problems afflicting the rest of society. In July 1991 David Rubin, son of an eminent rabbi, absconded after allegedly defrauding fellow-Jews of millions of pounds. A few weeks later, a child-abuse case in the Orthodox community of Stamford Hill led to violent demonstrations by members of the community against the family that had taken the matter to the police.

Jewish education and culture recovered from a lean period in the early 1980s. In 1984, Jews' College moved to new accomodations and the Manor House Sternberg Center for Reform Judaism was set up. Jewish museums were founded in London and Manchester. In 1990–92 there were several conferences and publications on the preservation of the documents, artefacts, and buildings that constitute the Jewish heritage in Britain. Sadly, Bevis Marks synagogue suffered collateral damage from an IRA bomb attack in London in August 1992. In 1991, Immanuel College was opened and the Jewish Chronicle Chair in Modern Jewish History was established at University College London to mark the paper's 150th anniversary and a chair in Modern Jewish Studies was dedicated at the University of Manchester. During 1992–93, lectureships in Modern Jewish History were established at Warwick and Leicester Universities. In 1992, Dr. David Paterson was succeeded by Professor Phillip Alexander as head of the Oxford Center for Postgraduate Hebrew Studies, having secured its future. Jewish schools topped the national league for the award of "A" Levels in August 1992. Less happy publicity was created by the decision of state-aided Jewish schools in Liverpool and Manchester in September 1991 not to admit Jewish children from a Reform Jewish background.

Yarnton Manor, home of the Kressel Collection and the Oxford Centre for Postgraduate Hebrew Studies (Courtesy Oxford Centre of Postgraduate Hebrew Studies, the Kressel Collection, Oxford)

Jewish culture found diverse expression in the courses of the Spiro Institute throughout the decade. There were festivals of Yiddish culture on the South Bank in 1986 and 1992, an annual Jewish Film Festival and Jewish music festival. In December 1991, *Leon the Pig Farmer*, an independent film funded largely by Jews and on a Jewish subject, won awards at the Edinburgh and Venice Film Festivals. In 1988, the conference "Remembering for the Future" inquired into the Holocaust. The anniversary of the massacre at Clifford's Tower in York in 1090 occasioned several solemn events. The fiftieth anniversary of the 1942 Wannsee Conference was the subject of an international conference in London organized principally by the Wiener Library. During 1992 there were many celebrations of the Sephardi experience to mark the anniversary of the expulsion from Spain.

[D.CE.]

ENGLISH LITERATURE (see **6**:773; **Dc./17**:237). In the last decade Anglo-Jewish literature has undergone something of a transformation. Instead of specifically English concerns and forms of expression, many recent Anglo-Jewish novelists are influenced by the American Jewish novel and incorporate European Jewish history and the contemporary State of Israel into their fiction. This marked lack of parochialism is reflected in novels, often first novels, published in the 1980s by Elaine Feinstein (q.v.), Howard Jacobson (q.v.), Emanuel *Litvinoff, Simon Louvish, Bernice Rubens (q.v.), and Clive Sinclair.

In 1985, the London *Times Literary Supplement* indicated a serious general interest in Anglo-Jewish literature by organizing a symposium for English and American Jewish writers of the role of Hebrew and Yiddish culture in the writer's life and work. In general, national British radio, television, and press have devoted a significant amount of time to Anglo-Jewish literature which, in recent years, has included many individual profiles of Jewish novelists in England. Clive Sinclair and Howard Jacobson, in particular, have achieved national prominence with Sinclair, in 1983, designated one of the twenty "Best of Young British Novelists" and Jacobson's *Peeping Tom* (1984), his second novel, winning a special *Guardian* fiction prize. Since 1984, the Institute of Jewish Affairs, the London-based research arm of the World Jewish Congress, has organized a regular Jewish writers' circle which has brought together many Anglo-Jewish writers for the first time. This group has grown out of a colloquium in 1984 on Literature and the Contemporary Jewish Experience which included the participation of the Israeli writer Aharon *Appelfeld and the literary critic George *Steiner.

In contrast to Anglo-Jewish literature which includes explicitly Jewish concerns, many Jewish writers in England continue to abstain from overt expression of their Jewishness in a fictional context. Prominent examples, in these terms, include Anita Brookner's (q.v.) *Hotel du Lac* (1984), which won the Booker McConnel Prize for Fiction in 1984, Gabriel Josopovici's (q.v.) *Conversations in Another Room* (1984), and Russell Hoban's *Pilgermann* (1983). Against this trend, however, Anita Brookner's *Family and Friends* (1985), for the first time in her fiction, obliquely refers to the author's European Jewish background and her *The Latecomers* (1988) makes explicit her grief for a lost European past as well as her Central European Jewish antecedents. Gabriel Josopovici's literary criticism reveals a profound interest and knowledge of Jewish literature. Two of Josipovici's novels, *The Big Glass* (1991) and *In a Hotel Garden* (1993), are concerned, respectively, with a Hebraic understanding of art and the continued European dialogue with Jewish history. Josipovici has also published his much acclaimed *The Book of God: A Response to the Bible* (1988) which has had a considerable impact on his fiction. Josopovici has also written the introduction to the English translation of Aharon Appelfeld's *The Retreat* (1985).

A young Anglo-Jewish playwright, who has emerged in the last decade, is Stephen Poliakoff, whose plays have been regularly produced in both London and New York. Older playwrights, Bernard *Kops and Arnold *Wesker, continue to produce drama of interest, especially Bernard Kops' *Ezra* (1980) and Arnold Wesker's *The Merchant* (1977). Between 1977 and 1981 Harold *Pinter's collected *Plays* were published to much acclaim and Peter *Shaffer, the author of *Amadeus* (1980), staged *Yonadab* (1985), a play based on Dan *Jacobson's *The Rape of Tamar* (1970), which played in a West End London theater. Jacobson, who was born in South Africa and has lived in England for nearly three decades, continues to produce fiction of high quality as demonstrated by his autobiographical set of short stories, *Time and Time Again* (1985) and his novel *The God-Fearer*. The poet Dannie *Abse has published *A Strong Dose of Myself* (1983), the third volume of his autobiography, and his *Collected Poems: 1945–1976* appeared in 1977.

Much Anglo-Jewish literature continues to situate Jewish characters in a specifically English context. In a comic tour de force, Howard Jacobson contrasts Englishness and Jewishness in his popular campus novel, *Coming From Behind* (1983). Jacobson's *Peeping Tom* (1984), is a brilliant and lasting comic treatment of the same theme. His *The Very Model of a Man* (1992) and *Roots Shmoots: Journeys among Jews* (1993) are explorations of his Jewishness.

Frederic *Raphael's *Heaven and Earth* (1985) examines Anglo-Jewishness in the political context of an amoral English conservatism. A more conventional account of middle class Jewish life in England — and its relationship to the State of Israel — is provided by Rosemary Friedman's trilogy, *Proofs of Affection* (1982), *Rose of Jericho* (1984), and *To Live in Peace* (1986). Friedman's fiction demonstrates that the family saga continues to be a popular form of Anglo-Jewish self-expression. Chaim *Bermant's *The Patriarch: A Jewish Family Saga* (1981) is another example of this genre, as is Maisie Mosco's bestselling *Almonds and Raisins* trilogy (1979–1981). Judith Summers' first novel, *Dear Sister* (1985), is a woman-centered Jewish family saga.

While much Anglo-Jewish literature continues to be set in an English milieu, many Jewish novelists have begun to reveal a fruitful interest in European Jewish history and the contemporary State of Israel. Emanuel Litvinoff's *Falls The Shadow* (1983), using the form of a detective novel, examines the Jewishness of modern-day Israel and the relationship of the Jewish State to the Holocaust. A more controversial account of these themes is found in George Steiner's *The Portage to San Cristobal of A.H.* (1981). The 1982 West End stage version of this novella excited a prolonged exchange of articles and letters in the London *Times* and *The Jewish Chronicle*. Steiner also published an interesting work of fiction, *Proofs and Three Fables* (1992). Other works of fiction by Jewish critics include Al Alvarez's *Day of Atonement* (1991) and Harold Pinter's autobiographical novel *The Dwarfs* (1990 but mainly written in the 1950s). Pinter, like Steven Berkoff (q.v.) in his challenging plays, was deeply influenced by his poor London East End Jewish background. Provocative fictional accounts of contemporary Israel are found in Simon Louvish's novels, *The Therapy of Avram Blok* (1985), *The Death of Moishe-Ganel* (1986), *City of Blok* (1988), *The Last Trump of Avram Blok* (1990), and *The Silencer* (1991). Louvish, who lives London, was raised in Jerusalem and served in the Six-Day War. His fiction is an iconoclastic, deliberately grotesque, portrait of the State of Israel. Clive Sinclair's *Blood Libels* (1985), his second novel, also utilizes Israeli history, especially the Lebanon War, and combines such history with a haunting imagination. In fact, Sinclair epitomizes the explicitly Jewish self-assertion and maturity of a new generation of Anglo-Jewish writers that has emerged in the 1980s. He describes himself as a Jewish writer "in a national sense" and so situates his fiction in Eastern Europe, America, and Israel. In this way, he eschews the usual self-referring, parochial concerns of the Anglo-Jewish novel. This is especially true in his collection of short stories, *Hearts of Gold* (1979) — which won the Somerset Maugham Award in 1981 — and *Bedbugs* (1982). His later works are *Cosmetic Effects* (1989), *Augustus Rex* (1992), and *Diaspora Blues: A View of Israel* (1987).

Elaine Feinstein is another Anglo-Jewish writer who, over the last decade, has consistently produced fiction of the highest literary excellence and has demonstrated a profound engagement with European history. Her fiction, especially *Children of the Rose* (1975), *The Ecstasy of Dr. Miriam Gardner* (1976), *The Shadow Master* (1978), *The Survivors* (1982), and *The Border* (1984) all demonstrate the persistence of the past in her characters' lives. Apart from *The Survivors*, all of these novels have a continental European setting. That is, Feinstein's fiction has successfully drawn on European Jewish history in a bid to understand her own sense of Jewishness. In recent years this has been clearly focused in her autobiographical *The Survivors*, set in England, and her less overtly autobiographical *The Border* which is set in Central Europe in 1938. *The Border* received high critical acclaim. The novel, using the form of a collection of letters and diaries, enacts the irrevocable march of history leading up to the outbreak of World War II. In juxtaposition to this historical backdrop, Feinstein's rare lucidity evokes her characters' passionately differing sense of reality. Bernice Rubens' *Brothers* (1983) utilizes modern Jewish history in more expansive terms than Feinstein, but perhaps, because of this, with less success.

The growing strength of British-Jewish writing is further indicated by a younger generation of Jewish novelists which is now emerging. Work by them includes Jenny Diski's *Like Mother* (1988), Will Self's *Cock and Bull* (1992), and Jonathan Wilson's *Schoom* (1993). When this writing is coupled with the plays of a number of young Jewish dramatists such as Diane Samuels, Julia Pascall, and Gavin Kostick, then the future of British-Jewish literature looks particularly healthy.

The last decade has demonstrated that there is a coincidence of interests between English literature in general and the concerns of the Anglo-Jewish novel. In recent years, much of the best English fiction looks to Asia, the Americas, and continental Europe for its subject matter and sense of history. It is not uncommon, therefore, for non-Jewish writers to incorporate Jewish history into their novels. With regard to the Holocaust, two of the most prominent examples of this phenomena are Thomas Keneally's Booker Prize winning *Schindler's Ark* (1982) — based on the life of the righteous gentile Oskar *Schindler — and D.M. Thomas' controversial *The White Hotel* (1981). [B.C.]

ESTONIA (see 6:916). The republic declared its independence from the U.S.S.R. in August 1991. In 1979 it had 5,000 Jews and in 1989 — 4,600. In 1989 169 Jews emigrated while 501 immigrated to Israel in 1990. In 1991 211 Jews immigrated to Israel from Tallinn alone. This community is highly assimilated: in 1987 42.7% of the children born to Jewish mothers had non-Jewish fathers.

The monthly Jewish newspaper *Khashakhar*, the first legal and independent Jewish newspaper in the Soviet Union during *perestroika*, began to appear in December 1988. The Jewish community of Estonia receives substantial material support from the Scandinavian Jewish communities, including Finland. Until the secession of Estonia, the half-Jew Evgenii Kogan headed the International Front, which was oriented towards preserving the U.S.S.R.

In November 1991 a meeting of fighters for the freedom of Estonia included members of the 20th Estonian SS Division, which had fought on the side of the Nazis. This participation was protested by the Jewish Culture Association and the Jewish religious community. The Estonian president responded that those who participated in the mass murder of Jews during World War II would not be rehabilitated.

On November 29, 1991, the Jewish cemetery in Tartu was desecrated; swastikas were painted on tombstones and others were damaged. [MI.BE.]

EVANS, ELI (1936–), U.S. administrator and Jewish historian. Evans was born in Durham, North Carolina, where his father served as mayor from 1950 to 1962. His grandmother founded the first southern chapter of the Hadassah Organization in the pre-World War I period.

After graduating from the University of North Carolina in 1958, he took a law degree at Yale University in 1963. He worked in various branches of government, state and national, as a speech writer and as a White House assistant.

In 1973, he published *The Provincials: A Personal History of Jews in the South*. The book provided an insight into the Jewry of the southern United States which had never been studied in depth previously. One of Evans' most revealing statistics was that over 45 Jews held mayorships and other leading government positions in southern communities. The book generated a new field of study of southern Jewry.

In 1977 Evans became the president of the Revson Foundation, which he guided in four specific areas: urban affairs, with special emphasis on New York City; education; biomedical research policy; and Jewish philanthropy and education.

In the Jewish field the foundation has made a number of significant gifts. The first major grant helped to underwrite the ten-part television series "Civilization and the Jews" narrated by Abba Eban. A second gift made possible the production of "Sesame Street" in Hebrew by Israel Education Television. A further large gift was allocated to the Jewish Museum, New York, for its remodeling and expansion which will provide an electronics education center on all aspects of Judaism.

In 1988 Evans published a biography of the Civil War personality, *Judah P. Benjamin: The Jewish Confederate*. Evans mined previously untapped sources and demonstrated aspects of Benjamin's personality which reflected the continuing strain of his Judaism even though this famous southerner did not practice his faith. [M.D.G.]

EZRA, DEREK, LORD (1919–), British industrial administrator. Ezra was educated at Magdalene College, Cambridge, and served in the British army during World War II, being appointed a member of the Order of the British Empire and awarded the United States Bronze Star. In 1947 he joined the newly nationalized coal industry. After holding posts in sales and marketing on the National Coal Board, he became a member of the board in 1965 and deputy chairman in 1967, and was chairman, the highest position in the industry, from 1971 to 1982. His period of office included the 1974 miners' strike, but he was generally characterized by a conciliatory attitude in industrial relations. Ezra was knighted in 1974 and created a life peer in 1983. After retirement from the coal board, he joined the Social Democratic Party in the House of Lords and held numerous British and European directorships and advisory posts in industry and commerce. He was appointed a Grand Officer of the Italian Order of Merit and held French and Luxembourg decorations. [V.D.L.]

F

FABIUS, LAURENT (1946–), French politician — the youngest premier in the history of the Republic. Fabius was born in France to a Jewish family which converted to Catholicism during World War II. After completing his studies in political science and humanities, he became active in the Socialist party. In 1978 he was elected deputé to the French Assembly. When François Mitterrand was elected president of the Republic in 1981, Fabius joined the government, first as minister in charge of the budget (1981–83) and then as minister for industry and research (1983–84). In 1984, with the collapse of the alliance between the Socialists

Laurent Fabius (Courtesy Embassy of France, Tel Aviv; photo Bourcier-Sipa)

and the Communists and the generally poor showing of the government in the public opinion polls, Mitterrand called in Fabius, as a representative of the new technocratic trend in the Socialist party, to lead the new government. With the appointment of the young, articulate politician, polls took an upswing. "Modernization and unity — these will be the priorities of my government," stated Fabius when taking office.

In 1986, the Socialists were ousted by a right-wing government and Fabius ceased to be prime minister. When the Socialists returned to power in 1988, Fabius was elected president of the National Assembly, a position he held until he became first secretary of the Socialist party in 1992. He had the difficult task of pulling the party out of a slump but support for the Socialists continued to plummet. At the end of 1992, the party agreed to send him and two former health ministers to trial for their ministerial responsibility for a 1985 scandal when HIV-contaminated blood had been knowingly distributed by high officials; over 1,000 people had acquired the HIV virus and 200 have died. The National Assembly and the Senate endorsed the decision to send the three for trial. Fabius asked to be brought to trial saying to the Senate "Innocent and recognized as such, I come before you to ask you to charge me with errors I did not commit." [GI.KO.]

FEIFFER, JULES (1929–), U.S. cartoonist and writer. Born in the Bronx, New York, Feiffer drew a Sunday cartoon page feature called "Clifford," from 1949 to 1951. He served in the U.S. Army from 1951 to 1953, working with a cartoon animation unit. Upon leaving the army, Feiffer worked in a number of jobs until in 1956, the New York weekly magazine *The Village Voice* began to publish his cartoons which were an immediate success. His cartoons have since appeared regularly in *The Village Voice* and are also internationally syndicated. His satirical cartoons make moral and political statements on a wide range of contemporary issues, both political and personal — from nuclear holocaust, the arms race and presidential politics to male-female relationships and human fears and neuroses. His cartoons are characterized by the revelation of private thoughts of his characters to the reader.

Although known primarily for his cartoons, Feiffer has also achieved success as a playwright, screenwriter, and novelist. His plays of the late 1960s, *Little Murders* (1967), *God Bless* (1968), and *The White House Murder Case* (1969), were all highly political. *Little Murders*, which depicted the horrors of urban life, was later made into a film. In 1963, he came out against the Vietnam War, subsequently speaking at peace demonstrations in Washington.

His screenplay for the 1971 movie *Carnal Knowledge* and his play *Knock Knock* (1976) dealt with more personal issues, the former with middle-age crisis and the latter with social values. His play *Grownups* (1981) focused on interfamily relationships and conflicts. [SU. STR.]

Topical issues of the day as seen through the eyes of Jules Feiffer (From *Jules Feiffer's America*, published by Alfred A. Knopf, New York)

FEINSTEIN, ELAINE (1930–), English novelist, poet, and translator. Born in Bootle, Feinstein was educated at Cambridge University. She has worked as an editor for the Cambridge University Press and lectured in English at Bishop's Stortford Training College and the University of Essex until 1970. She is now a full-time writer. Feinstein published her first novel, *The Circle*, in 1970. She also translated *The Selected Poems of Marina Tsvetayeva* (1971) and *Three Russian Poets: Margarita Aliger, Yunna Moritz, Bella Akhmadulina*, (1978). As an editor she has chosen the *Selected Poems of John Clare* (1968) and, with Fay Weldon, *New Stories 4* (1979). She has also published volumes of short stories and plays, *Breath* (1975) and *Echoes* (1980). The Holocaust is central to *Children of the Rose* (1975) and *The Border* (1984). She also wrote a book on the blues singer Bessie Smith (1985).

Her prodigious literary output includes volumes of poetry such as *The Magic Apple Tree* (1971), *At The Edge* (1972) and *The Celebrants and Other Poems* (1973). Feinstein is regarded as an important English novelist. She has described her early fiction as an "extension" of her poetry as her novels combine the poetic with a larger historical canvas. Her fiction, therefore, has ranged through European history and, at the same time, has retained a poetic use of language and myth. With remarkable economy, several of Feinstein's novels, *Children of the Rose* (1975), *The Ecstasy of Dr. Miriam Garner* (1976), *The Shadow Master* (1978), and *The Border* (1984), incorporate the violence, fanaticism, and pseudo-apocalyptic character of modern history. The ever-present themes of exile and betrayal in Feinstein's novels are given a wider historical dimension which shapes the lives of her cosmopolitan characters. *The Survivors* (1982), an autobiographical novel, has an exclusively English setting and uses the compressed form of a conventional family saga.

Feinstein consciously writes in a Central European literary tradition. She is the first post-war English-Jewish novelist to successfully eschew the parochial concerns and forms of expression of the Anglo-Jewish novel and has located her sence of Jewishness in a wider European context. *The Border* is a representative example of Feinstein's ability to express in an exciting love story a multifarious vision of the world made up of history and autobiography, poetry and myth, literature and science. In this way, Feinstein has managed to broaden the concerns of the Anglo-Jewish novel and develop a lasting poetic voice in a distinct and imaginative manner.

Bibliography: J. Vinson (ed.), *Contemporary Novelists* (1982) 211–12. [B.C.]

FINKIELKRAUT, ALAIN (1949–), French author and thinker. After a short academic career in which he taught in France and the United States, Finkielkraut devoted himself to writing books, articles, and radio programs, all of which deal with issues of contemporary Jewry. His books delineated the problems of the Jew in the Diaspora from the cultural and social aspects as well as the problem of his link to Jewish history and to Israel as a central issue. He has dealt with anti-Semitism, the revisionist historians who have distorted the history of World War II, and incitement against the State of Israel, using a system close to that of the "New Philosophers" of France. His thought was also influenced by that of the Jewish philosopher Emanuel *Levinas. In 1986 he became the youngest recipient to be awarded the prestigious prize of French Jewry, the Prix de la Foundation du Judaisme Français. He is considered the most significant of young French thinkers who deal with current issues of Jewish existence.

He has written *Le Juif imaginaire* (1980), *L'avenir d'une negation* (1982), *La reprobation d'Israel* (1983), and *La sagesse de l'amour* (1984). [GI.KO/ED.]

FINNISTON, SIR HAROLD MONTAGUE (Monty; 1912–1991), British metallurgist and industrial administrator. Finniston was born in Glasgow (whose accent he retained), educated at Glasgow University, and became a lecturer at the Royal College of Science and Technology, Glasgow. He then became a metallurgist in industry and served in the Royal Naval Scientific Service during World War II. He was chief metallurgist at the United Kingdom Atomic Energy Authority, Harwell, from 1948 to 1958, and managing director of the International Research and Development Company from 1959 to 1967. He joined the board of the recently renationalized steel industry (British Steel Corporation) as deputy chairman (technical) in 1967, becoming chief executive in 1971 and chairman from 1973 to 1976. From 1976 he was active as chairman or director of industrial companies and from 1980 as a business consultant. Finniston was involved in many fields of research and in the Jewish community. He was chairman of the independent "think tank" of the Policies Institute from 1975 to 1984, chancellor of Stirling University, and pro-chancellor of the University of Surrey. He was knighted in 1975, had 15 honorary doctorates conferred upon him, and in 1969 was elected a Fellow of the Royal Society, of which he was later a vice-president. [V.D.L.]

FITERMAN, CHARLES (1933–), French politician. Born in Saint Etienne, France, Fiterman, a qualified electrician by trade, made his way to the number two position in the French Communist party, the second largest communist party in the Western world. In the first Mitterrand administration (1981–1984) he was one of the four communist ministers and was in charge of transport. Fiterman is a cool, moderate politician who follows traditional party lines.

His unsuccessful challenge to the leadership of the Communist party by Georges Marchais led to his exclusion from central positions in the party and he became one of the leaders of the "reformers" wing demanding reform and modernization of the remaining traditional communist parties in the world. [GI.KO.]

FRANCE (see **7**:7; **Dc./17**:248). **Demography.** The Jewish population of France, estimated at 530,000 at the beginning of the 1980s, is considered stable. Following the decolonization of the former French possessions in North Africa, the Jewish population of France doubled between 1955 and 1965. Afterwards immigration was numerically insignificant. However, French Jewry changed from having an Ashkenazi majority to a Sephardi one.

In the early 1990s the second as well as the third generation is French-born and educated. They are, of course, French, but maintain a conscious Jewish identity. As elsewhere in the Diaspora, the community is aging and there is an increase in mixed marriages.

Some 50%–55% of French Jews live in Paris and its suburbs. Among the provincial communities the largest are those of Marseilles, Nice, Toulouse, and Montpellier in the south, Lyons and Grenoble in the southeast, and Strasbourg in Alsace. Jews also live scattered throughout the country, while having a tendency to congregate in middle-sized cities owing to the attraction of a better organized community life.

Economic and political situation. The French economy went through great changes during the decade under review. It has become information oriented and automated, with a considerable increase in its production capacity. The battle against inflation succeeded and the currency has been stabilized. The economy played an important and influential role in the creation of the European Economic Community whose borders opened on January 1, 1993, to free movement of goods among the 12 member-countries. European political union is more difficult to put into effect: in France, the September 20, 1992, referendum on the treaty of the European Union, called the Maastricht treaty, barely received a majority (51%); voting in favor was supported by several Jewish personalities.

This modernization of the economy has a corollary in increased unemployment. At the end of 1992, the threshold of three million unemployed was reached. Jews, too, have been affected by this calamity, and social cases and problems reappeared. Poverty is also found among the Jews; in December 1992, Jewish social services launched an appeal called Tsedaka to collect funds to bring relief to 25,000 needy Jews.

During the decade 1982–1992, France's president was François Mitterrand and its various governments had a socialist majority (except for the period of "cohabitation" from 1986 to 1988 during which the right-wing government was led by Jacques Chirac). Elected for the first time as president of the Republic in May 1981, Mitterrand was re-elected with 54% of the votes in 1988 for another seven-year period. During the Gulf War in which France participated with the allies in Operation Desert Storm, presidential and government action was supported by a certain consensus between the democratic left and right. However, the situation has subsequently deteriorated. Since the end of the 1980s, some of the elected Socialists and also some of the politicians of the right have been implicated in a series of scandals involving the collection and use of funds intended for financing the parties and their electoral campaigns. More serious was the "drama of the blood." AIDS has spread in France as elsewhere. In October 1985 stored blood, contaminated with the disease, was used for transfusions. Hundreds of patients became serum positive: some of them have died. During summer 1992 the main people administratively responsible for this situation were tried and found guilty. Public opinion also called for trying the ministers responsible for public health as well as Laurent Fabius (q.v.), who had been prime minister at that time. According to the terms of the French Constitution, only a special court, the High Court of Justice is enabled to judge charges of offenses committed by a minister in fulfillment of his functions. Following violent debates, the creation of such a High Court of Justice was decided upon in December 1992, by the deputies and senators. The passions aroused by the contaminated blood affair gave rise to a deep political and moral malaise in French society.

In any event, the role of politicians, has had a bad press in France. New parties have emerged: among them, the ecologists who earned 15% of the votes in the regional elections of March 1992.

In this context of crisis, the danger to democracy is most clearly posed by the National Front (F.N.) whose platform is openly xenophobic and racist. The F.N. had its first national electoral success (11% of the votes) in 1984 in the elections for the European Parliament. Since then it has garnered nationally 14%–15% of the vote, while in certain regions, most particularly in the south of France, the F.N. is securely embedded and attracts greater numbers of votes. In France the main victims of racism are first- and second-generation immigrant Arab workers. The F.N and its publications, however, are also anti-Semitic.

Elections at different levels of political life are held frequently in France, and Jewish voters are regularly solicited by the political parties. Following an old tradition, the main Jewish organizations do not give any directions on how to vote. Nevertheless, some of them warn against voting for the F.N. Jews constitute about 1% of the French electorate. Their votes can only play an important role in specific localities such as Paris and Marseilles. On the basis of analyses of voting behavior, it is known that the Jewish vote is spread

Pres. Mitterrand (left) meeting with Chief Rabbi Sirat, 1987 (Courtesy Service Photographique, Presidence de la Republique Française)

among all parties, while within the machinery of every party Jews are active.

Community. From 1982 to 1992 organized community life was characterized by the rise of ever-increasing numbers of Sephardi Jews to positions of leadership and by a certain return to religion in strong opposition to humanistic and secular initiatives. The organization of the Jewish community of France reflects the ideological heterogeneity of its members.

The consistoires, created by Napoleon I in 1808, are the oldest French Jewish institution. The Central Consistory stands over the local and regional consistories. The main task of the consistories is the organization of Jewish religious worship and observances, but they tend to extend their spheres of activities.

Since 1981 the chief rabbis of France have been Sephardi: Rene Samuel Sirat (q.v), born in Bone, Algeria, held the title from 1981 to 1988; Joseph Sitruk (q.v.), born in Tunis, succeeded him for a seven-year term which may be extended. Jean-Paul Elkann was president of the Central Consistory in the 1980s. In June 1992, Jean-Pierre Bansard was elected to this position. Born in 1940 in Oran, Algeria, and president of a financial company, Bansard represents a new Jewish leadership.

The most important changes, however, have taken place since 1989 in the Conseil d'Administration de l'Association Culturelle de Paris (ACIP) which is the most important regional consistory in France. A new team of a stricter Orthodoxy than its predecessor, headed by Benny Cohen, was elected, calling vigorously for a return to religious practice. This new tendency is strongly opposed by some of their coreligionists who affirm their Jewish identity only in a cultural mode. There are also more Orthodox Jews: in Paris, as in other cities, ultra-Orthodox groups and notably the Lubavich Ḥasidim took root during the 1980s. They have established their neighborhoods and made their Judaism "visible" through billboard campaigns at Jewish holiday times and through lighting Ḥanukkah candles in large public places in Paris.

At the end of 1992, the new team of the ACIP changed some of the rules governing their association. As voted on December 20, 1992, the ACIP which became the "consistory of Paris and the Ile de France" sought to reinforce its position as the heart of the central consistory organization and increase its powers with an eye on stricter observance of the *halakhah.*

This transformation met with lively opposition on the part of representatives of more liberal tendencies within the consistory spheres themselves.

Two other institutions strive to activate and above all federate the many French Jewish organizations. The Conseil Representatif des Institutions Juives de France (CRIF) encompasses some 50 institutions, among them the most important in the country. Created at the end of World War II, CRIF is officially charged with relations with the public authorities. Its presidents have been Theo Klein (q.v.) (1983–89) and Jean Kahn (q.v.) (from 1989). From 1982 to 1992, CRIF not only fought against anti-Semitism but also expanded its activities in the sphere of defense of human rights. Moreover, since 1986, first Theo Klein and then Jean Kahn were president of the European Jewish Congress (CJE) created at the initiative of the World Jewish Congress. Since 1989 CJE has developed activities involving French Jewry, directly or indirectly, in behalf of Jewish communities in the ex-communist bloc. In 1992, Jean Kahn, within the framework of his functions, took part in humanitarian actions in the territory of former Yugoslavia.

The Fonds Social Juif Unifie (F.S.J.U.) celebrated in 1991 its fortieth anniversary. This is the most important organization supporting and coordinating French Jewry's social, educational, and cultural activities. Since 1982 David de Rothschild has been its president.

Among the large Jewish organizations in France the Alliance Israélite Universelle (A.I.U.), founded in 1860, plays an important role in the cultural domain. Prof. Ady Steg has been its leader since 1985. In September 1989 the A.I.U. inaugurated a new library which is now the largest Jewish library in Europe. It also has a College of Jewish Studies focusing its activities, under the direction of Shmuel Trigano, on in-depth study of Jewish thought in its various expressions.

This overview of the large organizations gives only a partial picture of actual Jewish life in France. There are several hundred Jewish organizations in France, some with thousands of members, others with only a few dozen. Moreover, despite the impressive number of organizations, only 30% to 40% of the Jews have relations with the so-called organized community. For some ten years now there has been widespread discussion of the "return to Judaism." This return in not only an intensive return to Orthodoxy. It expresses itself in a number of ways, such as in the search for the affirmation of Jewish identity, not solely religious but also cultural.

Since the end of the 1980s on, some Jewish secular and humanist movements have been organized, at least among the Ashkenazi Jews, and more recently, also among Sephardim.

It may be asked if one may speak of "a Jewish community" in the case of France. Heterogeneous in origins and orientations, embedded in a social, cultural, and political environment which offer aspirations different from those presented

Leading French educators and representatives of Jewish organizatons on the panel of the 1988 Bible contest for Jewish youth, Paris (Courtesy Dept. of Torah Education in the Diaspora, Jewish Agency, Paris)

Cover of catalogue for "Juifs & Citoyens" exhibit, 1989, organized by the Alliance Israélite Universelle, the Paris Consistoire, and the Musée d'Art et d'Histoire du Judaïsme (Courtesy Musée d'Art et d'Histoire du Judaïsme, Paris)

by Judaism, the French Diaspora does not constitute, a comunity, in the strict sense. To be sure, at the local level or as voluntary societies based on origin or ideological sector, communities can come into being; they provide a firm foundation on which to affirm one's quest for Jewish identity. But this search exhibits different facets, even though, in France today, Jewish life is essentially crystallized around three poles: religion; culture; and the attitude to the State of Israel.

Education and Culture. Jewish education has developed considerably in comparison to the 1970s. In 1976 the F.S.J.U. and the Jewish Agency created Fonds d'Investissement Pour l'Education (F.I.P.E.), which, with the support and participation of a number of religious organizations, led to a significant expansion of the network of Jewish day schools.

According to a study made by Erik Cohen in 1986/88 (see bibliography), the number of full-time Jewish educational institutions—from nursery school to high schools—has doubled, increasing from 44 in 1976 to 88 in 1986/87, at which time, 16,000 children and teenagers attended full-time Jewish schools. This trend has continued: in 1992, 20% to 25% of school-age Jews attend full-time Jewish schools. If one adds the Talmud Torahs (preparatory courses for Bar Mitzvah and Bat Mitzvah), the youth movements, and other Jewish recreational organizations, 75% of Jewish youth have some more or less long term formal Jewish education.

Non-practicing Jewish families had, in the 1980s, a more favorable attitude than in the past to full-time Jewish education, but, more than the others, the religious circles have the maximum commitment to Jewish education. According to Cohen's study, in 1986/87, about one-third of the Jewish day schools were affiliated with organizations such as Lubavich, Otzar Ha-Torah, or Or Yossef. This work is far from complete and stress is now on teacher training.

In the public school system, Hebrew is taught at a number of high schools as a foreign language which fulfills the matriculation requirement. In the universities, the study of Hebrew, Jewish languages, and Jewish civilization is now well represented.

In Paris as elsewhere, the years 1982–92 were marked by a large number of cultural events — conferences, colloquia, exhibitions — organized either by Jewish institutions or by some of the universities of the National Center for Scientific Research (CNRS). Among these events, history played an important role. In 1989 Jewish intellectuals and artists participated actively in celebrating the bicentennial of the

March in commemoration of the 40th anniversary of French Jews' deportation to the death camps in WWII, Paris, April 17, 1983 (Photo Daniel Franck, Paris)

emancipation of the Jews of France. In 1992 several colloquia were devoted to the history of Spanish Jews and the commemoration of 500 years since their expulsion. University scholars and representatives of French Jewry took part as well in the commemorative events held in Spain.

The year 1992 was also for the Jews of France the 50th anniversary of the beginning of the mass deportations: the Holocaust is at the heart of Jewish memory. During this decade, there was a significant increase in research studies into the responsibility of the Vichy government for the persecution of the Jews. President Mitterrand has been called upon to admit officially France's responsibility for this persecution.

The intellectual and cultural vitality of French Jewry is attested by artistic, literary, and scientific output. Each year, 200 to 300 works on Jewish themes are published in France. They cover the gamut of the field of Jewish studies, from the translation and interpretation of traditional texts of Jewish thought to the study of contemporary Jewish issues. At the same time, novels with Jewish themes are published and plays, movies, and works in the plastic arts are produced. The interest in Judaism and its culture is shared by the Jewish and non-Jewish public.

Terrorism, Racism, and Anti-Semitism. French Jewry has been called on to meet the challenge of the rise in xenophobia, racism, and anti-Semitism.

Against the background of social and economic crises during the decade under review, offical reports and opinion surveys have alerted the public authorities to these dangers. In 1990, the Gayssot law reinforced the anti-racist legislation. It limits the questioning of the existence of crimes against humanity and the publication and distribution of racist anti-Semitic and revisionist writings. Some revisionist university workers have been found guilty of questioning the Holocaust, but the suppression of anti-Semitic writings is insufficient.

Terrorism and anti-Semitic incidents marked the years 1982 to 1992. At the beginning of the 1980s, a wave of terrorism raged with the bloodiest attack against Jews carried out in August 1982 against the Jo Goldenberg restaurant. At the end of the 1980s and in the early 1990s, desecrations of synagogues and, above all, cemeteries were prevalent. The most serious incident took place in Carpentras in 1990. At the end of 1992, the desecrations increased, particularly in Alsace where German Neo-Nazism and the French extreme-right cooperate. Only rarely have those guilty of these attacks been apprehended.

Other incidents were connected to the Holocaust past. In 1987 the trial against Klaus Barbie had widespread publicity. Sentenced to life imprisonment, Barbie died in prison on September 25, 1991. (See Barbie Trial.)

Barbie was German, but the case of French Paul Touvier is more complicated. Touvier, head of the Lyon militia and Gestapo collaborator, was arrested in May 1989. On July 11, 1991, the Paris court (Chambre d'accusation) decided to release him. On April 13, 1992, this same court gave Touvier a general acquittal. This decision was accompanied by an interpretation of the Vichy role in the persecution of the Jews, considering it as totally subordinate to German authority. This decision unleashed fierce emotion in France and was repealed, at least in part, on November 27, 1992, by the Paris High Court of Appeal. The trial against Touvier, for the murder of seven Jews in June 1944, will be examined as a charge concerning crimes against humanity. The other dossiers against him were dismissed.

In November 1991 the media announced that the card file of the census of the Jews made in 1940 by the Vichy police had been found by the lawyer Serge Klarsfeld in the Ministry of Veteran Affairs. For 50 years historians have searched for

Pres. Mitterrand addressing the Israel Knesset, 1982 (Courtesy Service Photographique, Presidence de la Republique Française)

this card file which had been said to have been destroyed. The file was transferred to the National Archives where it was studied by a commission of historians. On December 31, 1992, the Ministry of Culture made public the results of its study: this card file deals only with those Jews arrested and/or deported. The census made under the Vichy government seems to have been in fact destroyed in 1948 or 1949. A new polemic has already arisen: the memory of the somber years of France under Vichy continues to haunt the French Republic.

Relations between France and Israel. On the whole, French Jewry and its main leaders have been pro-Israel. In spite of a difference of opinion over the role to be played by the PLO in the peace negotiation process, relations between the French and Israeli governments are cordial. President Mitterrand paid official visits to Israel in March 1982 and November 1992 and there were frequent exchanges at the ministerial level

In November 1992, President Mitterrand and President Herzog inaugurated the Maison France-Israel located in the heart of Paris. This new institution, conceived and realized by Lionel Stoleru, former minister and president of the France-Israel Chamber of Commerce, has as its goal the development of economic relations and their expansion to all Europe. It will be a new meeting point for Frenchmen and Israelis.

Bibliiography: D. Bensimon, *Les Juifs de France et leurs relations avec Israël: 1945-1988* (1989); B. Berg, *Histoire du rabbinat français: XVie-XXe siècle* (1992); P. Birnbaum, *Histoire politique des Juifs de France* (1990); E. Cohen, *L'étude et l'éducation juive en France* (1991); R. Remond, *Paul Touvier et l'Eglise* (1992); S. Trigano, *La société juive a travers l'histoire* (4 vol.; 1992/93). [D.BS.]

FRANCO, AVRAHAM (1894–1993), Sephardi leader. Franco was born and raised in Hebron where his father was a religious leader. He had a traditional religious education and succeeded his father as *shoḥet* of the Sephardi community. In Hebron he taught Arabic at the New Talmud Torah but went on to study pharmacy, becoming the pharmacist of the Hebron municipality.

In World War I he served in the Turkish army, and after the war was a pharmacist at the Rothschild Hospital (which became the Hadassah Hospital) in Jerusalem. He then entered government service as a translator and became secretary of the Jerusalem municipality. As secretary of the Sephardi Federation, he introduced organizational changes in Jerusalem's Sephardi Public Council.

After the 1929 Hebron riots, he was active on behalf of the Hebron refugees, in aid of whom he went to London where he raised money, enabling some of the families to return to Hebron.

Avraham Franco, 1932

In 1947, Franco, as a Jewish employee of the Jerusalem municipality, was a target for assassination by Arabs. Sometime after escaping a bombing attempt aimed against the Jewish employees, two Arabs saved him from being stabbed by a potential assassin who entered the municipality specifically to kill him.

As secretary of the municipal council, he served as a bridge between Jews and Arabs. His experiences growing up in Hebron and living with Arabs helped him considerably in making friendships and initiating Jewish-Arab cooperation. [Yi.K.]

FRIEDAN, BETTY (1921–), U.S. writer and feminist. Born Naomi Goldstein in Peoria, Illinois, she received her B.A. in Psychology from Smith College in 1942. She then held a research fellowship in psychology at the University of California at Berkeley, assisted in early group dynamics at the University of Iowa, and worked as a clinical psychologist and in applied social research. She also turned to free-lance writing, contributing to various magazines.

After her marriage in 1947, her main efforts were devoted to raising her three children. In 1963 she published *The Feminine Mystique* which focused on the plight of women and their lack of equality with men. This represented the start of the women's movement in the United States.

Friedan was the founder of the National Organization of Women (NOW) and served as its president from 1966 to 1970. The organization aimed at bringing women into full equal participation in American society, exercising all privileges and responsibilities. In 1970, she organized a march of 50,000 women through New York City.

In 1978 she chaired the Emergency Project for Equal Rights and the following year the National Assembly on the Future of the Family. Her second book, *The Second Stage* (1981), outlined new directions for the women's movement based on shared female experience.

Friedan was seen in the 1980s as one of America's senior statespersons in the struggle for equal rights and was outspoken over what was perceived as backsliding on the issue of women's rights under the Reagan administration. During the span of her career she became more closely identified with Jewish issues and served on the board of *Present Tense — the Magazine of World Jewish Affairs*. She also denounced anti-Semitism and anti-Zionism at the UN. [Su. Str.]

FRIEDMAN, JEROME ISAAC (1930–), physicist. Friedman studied at the University of Chicago from which he received his A.B. (1950), his M.A. (1953), and his Ph.D. (1956) in physics. After working as a research associate there and at Stanford University, he joined the faculty of MIT in 1960, becoming a professor in 1967. At MIT he was also the director of the laboratory for nuclear science (1980–83) and head of the physics department (1983–88). He was co-recipient of the 1990 Nobel Prize in physics with Richard Taylor and Henry Kendal for work they had done at the Stanford Linear Acceleration Center 1967–73, which showed that protons and neutrons were quarks rather than fundamental particles. In doing so they also proved the existence of quarks which had been regarded until then as theoretical. [Ed.]

FRIENDLY, HENRY JACOB (1903–1986), U.S. judge. Considered by lawyers, judges, and legal scholars as one of the ablest lawyers of his generation and the preeminent federal appellate judge of his time, Friendly made a legendary record as a student at Harvard Law School. He became law clerk to Justice Louis D. Brandeis. He turned down an offer to teach at Harvard Law School and joined the prestigious Stanford Linear Acceleration Center 1967–73, which showed that protons and neutrons were quarks rather than fundamental particles. In doing so they also proved the existence of quarks which had been regarded until then as theoretical. [Ed.]

The Honorable Henry J. Friendly (Courtesy U.S. Court of Appeals, Second District, N.Y.)

public activities. In 1959 he was appointed judge of the United States Court of Appeals for the Second Circuit, in which he served until his death in March 1986. In the estimation of the legal profession, Friendly deserved to be coupled with Learned Hand for judicial competence and eminence. Felix Frankfurter in 1963 considered him the best judge writing judicial opinions. Professor Paul Freund wrote that Friendly "combined massive documentation and sharply critical, often astringent, analysis with invariably constructive, or reconstructive, proposals." He was especially expert in administrative law, federal jurisdiction, criminal procedure, trademark, railroad, and commercial law. He was chief judge of his court for two years, and from 1974 to the time of his death he was also presiding judge of the special court set up by an act of Congress on railroad reorganization.

Judge Friendly served on the Council of the American Law Institute, on the board of overseers of Harvard University, and was the author of several books, including *Benchmarks* (1967) and *Federal Jurisdiction: a General View* (1973). In 1977 he was awarded the Presidential Medal of Freedom, and in the following year the Thomas Jefferson Memorial Award in Law.

Bibliography: *Harvard Law Rev* 99 (1986); K. Johnson, *N.Y. Times* (June 10, 1986). [M.R.K.]

GAMUS GALLEGOS, PAULINA (b. Caracas), Venezuelan lawyer and politician. Paulina Gamus Gallegos was born in Venezuela and attended the Moral y Luces Herzl–Bialik High School there. She obtained her law degree from the Universidad Central de Venezuela in 1959. After working as a lawyer for two years, she served in various capacities in public administration. In 1974 she became adjunct legal adviser to the president of the country and executive secretary of the Women's Advisory Commission of the president. She served as director of information of the Ministry of Education from 1975 to 1977 and in the latter year was vice minister of information and tourism.

Paulina Gamas Gallegos

In 1977 she was also chosen by presidential candidate Luis Pinerua Ordaz as his campaign public relations director. Gamus Gallegos was elected councillor representing the Democratic Action Party for the Federal District in 1977, becoming head of that faction in 1981. She chaired the Committee on Environment and was a member of the Permanent Committee for Culture and Town Planning. In December 1983 she was elected principal delegate of the Democratic Action Party in the Federal District and in January 1984 became the co–director of the parliamentary faction. She belonged to the Legislative Commission, to the bicameral commission for a new Employment law, to the bicameral commission for the reform of municipal government, and was chairman of a number of special committees. In January 1986 she was appointed a minister in the government, Ministra de Estado–Presidenta del Consejo Nacional de la Cultura (CONAC).

Gamus Gallegos was a journalist from 1969 with a column in the daily newspaper *El Nacional* and from 1981 with a column in the daily newspaper of Caracas. She has also contributed to the magazines *Resumen* and *De Frente*. In addition, she has represented Venezuela at numerous international meetings. [ED.]

GANS, MOZES ("Max") H. (1917–1987), author, jeweler, and communal worker. Gans grew up while living in the Amsterdam Jewish Quarter in the building of the "Joodse Invalide," the institute for poor Jewish invalids, of which his father, Isaac Gans, was the director.

In 1943 he managed to escape to Switzerland where he was as active as possible on behalf of the Jews under Nazi occupation in Holland. Upon his return to Amsterdam he took over the jeweler's shop of his father–in–law (who had been deported to his death), Premsela & Hamburger, which specialized in silverware, and later wrote a work on antique silver, which became standard.

At the same time he was active in Jewish affairs, becoming the head of the Central Committee for Jewish Education of the Netherlands Ashkenazi Congregation (NIK) and in 1950 assistant editor and then, from 1956 to 1966, the editor of the Dutch Jewish Weekly *Nieuw Israelitisch Weekblad (NIW)*.

A private collector of Judaica, he published in 1971 his monumental *Memorbook*, A Pictorial History of Dutch Jewry from the Renaissance to 1940, with some 1,100 illustrations, which in 1987 went into its sixth printing, and of which an English translation was published in 1977. In addition, he published three smaller albums on the Amsterdam Jewish quarter, on how it was prior to 1940 and its current condition, all of which were also translated into English. In 1973, on the 150th anniversary of the Premsela & Hamburger firm, he published a history of the business.

In 1976–77 he held the appointment of professor extraordinary in Dutch Jewish History at the University of Leyden. [H.BO.]

GEKHT, SEMEN GRIGOREVICH (1903–1963), Russian writer. Gekht was born in Odessa and from the mid–1920s lived in Moscow where he worked on the newspaper *Gudok*. With his first prose work, the novella *Chelovek, kotoryj zabyl svoya zhizn'* ("The Person Who Forgot His Life," 1927) Gekht appeared as a representative of Russian–Jewish literature. The basic theme of his books (including the novel *Pouchitel' naya istoriya* ("An Instructive Story," 1939); stories for children; *Syn sapozhnika* ("Son of the Cobbler," 1931); *Efim Kalyuzhny iz Smidovichey* ("Efim Kalyuzhny from Smidovichi," 1931), etc., is the transformation of Jewish life in the post–revolutionary period and the participation of Jewish youth from the shtetl in the struggle for the industrialization of the country. In his major novel *Parokhod idet v Yaffu i obratno* ("The Steamship Goes to Jaffa and Back," 1936), set in Palestine of the first third of the 20th century. Gekht describes positively the daily life of the *ḥalutzim*, accurately depicts the bloody attacks of the Arabs in Jerusalem and Jaffa, and reproduces at length passionate speeches of Zionists about assimilation and anti–Semitism. Some Soviet critics accused the novel of manifesting "camouflaged Zionism."

During World War II Gekht was military correspondent for the newspaper *Gudok*. At the end of the 1940s his works were suppressed but he was rehabilitated in 1956.

Gekht maintained his Jewish themes throughout his career (cf. *Budka solov'ya* ("Nightingale Booth," 1957), or *Dolgi serdtsa* ("Debts of the Heart," 1963)). His heroes are Jews whose lives are ruined by the war. Even his works in which the characters are non–Jews, contain tragic motifs concerning the destruction of Ukrainian Jewry, with references to Babi Yar, the tractor factory in Kharkov (the site of another massacre of Ukrainian Jews), and so on. In 1960 Gekht wrote memoirs about E. Bagritsky, I. *Ilf, and others. He translated from Yiddish works by Sholem *Asch, *Shalom Aleichem, and M. *Daniel. [MA. KI./S.J.E.R.]

GELFOND (Gelfand), ALEXANDER LAZAREVICH (Israel; main pseud. **Parvus**; 1869–1924), active member of both the Russian and German revolutionary movements. Born in Berezino, Minsk province, he graduated from high school in Odessa in 1885 and in 1891, from the University of Basle in Switzerland. From the late 1890s he lived in Germany. Gelfond joined the left wing of the German social–democratic movement and edited the newspaper *Sachseche Arbeiterzeitung* (1897–98), which opposed the policies of Eduard *Bernstein. In 1898 he published in Munich the weekly *Aus der Weltpolitik*. By the end of the 1890s he had gained the reputation of a major Marxist expert on world economy and politics. From the early 1900s he participated in the work of the Russian social–democratic movement. He organized the publication of the newspaper *Iskra* in Leipzig and published articles in it and in the journal *Zarya* under the pseudonym Molotov. In 1903 he joined the Mensheviks. For his revolutionary activities he was exiled from several German states. In 1905 he returned to Russia where he became a member of the executive committee and one of the leaders of the St. Petersburg soviet of workers' deputies. Together with Rosa *Luxemburg he supported the theory of "permanent revolution" which was later elaborated on by Leon *Trotsky. In December 1905 Gelfond was arrested and sentenced to three years of Siberian exile. He escaped from the convoy on the way and fled to Germany. From 1910 to 1915 he lived in Turkey and in the Balkans where he became wealthy through commerce. During World War I he was a supplier to the German army and in Berlin he published the journal *Die Glocke* in which he supported German victory. He proposed a plan to the German Ministry of Foreign Affairs and General Staff to get Russia to withdraw from the war by supporting the Russian revolutionary movement. Under cover of commercial operations he sent money received from the German government to various Russian revolutionary parties. After the February Revolution of 1917 the bulk of these funds went to the Bolsheviks. After the October Revolution of 1917 he wanted to return to Russia, but Lenin, fearing to compromise the Party and himself by the arrival of Gelfond, whose ties with the German government had become widely known, refused Gelfond permission to return. After the German Revolution of November 1918 Gelfond attempted to settle in Switzerland, but was deported. He returned to Germany, abandoned political activity and worked in an institute he founded for studying World War I. He died in Germany in 1924.

Both during his lifetime and posthumously Gelfond was accused of moral turpitude (by Maxim Gorky in his *V.I. Lenin*), and of chauvinism (by A. Solzhenitsyn in his *Lenin in Zurich*, 1975, although the depiction of Gelfond in the latter work does not correspond to his role in the history of the Russian and European revolutionary movements).

Gelfond's son, EVGENIY ALEKSANDROVICH GNEDIN-GELFAND (1898–1983) was until 1939 a high official in the Russia Peoples' Commisariat of Foreign Affairs. From 1939 to 1955 he was in Soviet forced labor camps and exile. He actively participated in samizdats in the 1960s and 1970s. In 1977 his memoirs *Kataztrofa i vtoroe rozhdenie* ("Catastrophe and Second Birth") were published in Amsterdam.

[MA. KI./S.J.E.R.]

GENIZAH (see **7**:404; **Dc./17**:259). Research of the *Genizah* continues in various spheres of Jewish studies.

Biblical Commentary. The following are worthy of note.

(1) The commentary on the Pentateuch by Judah ben Shemariah, published from a *Genizah* MS in Cambridge. The pages printed contain interpretations of several weekly portions in Exodus and Leviticus. The author explains the text through interpretative sources using **peshat*, **derash*, *kabbalah (mysticism) and philosophical proofs. Composition of the MS dates from the fourteenth century. There is reason to presume that R. Judah ben Shemariah lived at approximately that time in Germany and Italy and was the disciple of R. Meir of Rothenburg.

(2) New sections of *The Commentary of Saadiah Gaon on Isaiah*. From 1896 (the year of Joseph Derenburg's publication of Saadiah Gaon's translation of Isaiah) through 1983 about 49 fragments of Saadiah Gaon's commentary on Isaiah were printed; in Fragment 7, published from Cambridge MS collection and the Bodleian Library, Oxford, Saadiah mentions *Ḥiwi al-Balkhi, and a reasonable assumption emerges that Saadiah composed his commentary on Isaiah after having crystallized his response to Ḥiwi al-Balkhi.

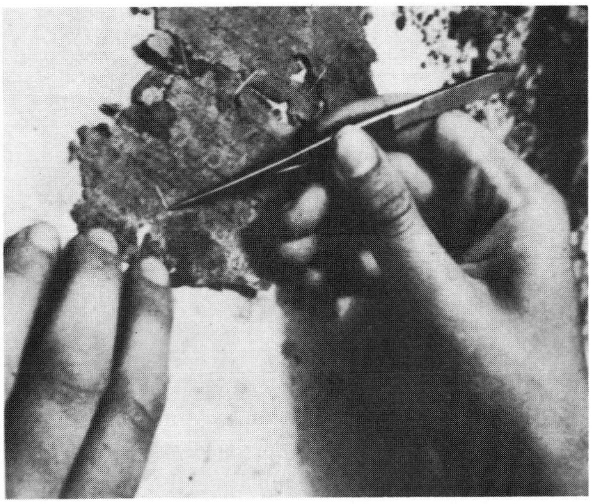

Repairing a paper manuscript from the *Genizah* in Cambridge, 1975 (Courtesy Taylor–Schechter Genizah Research Unit, University of Cambridge)

Commentaries on the Talmud. Fragments which are in the course of publication cover 16 pages of the Cairo *Genizah* in Cambridge, including the commentary of Hananel b. Ḥushiel's commentaries on *Bava Kamma* 114b–116a and the Cairo *Genizah* contains fragments of Hananel b. Ḥushiel's commentaries on various tractates of the Talmud.

Midrash. *The Genizah Fragments of Bereshit Rabbah*, published by M. Sokoloff, have been assembled through searches in the microfilm collection of the Institute of Hebrew MS Photographs in the Jewish National and University Library, by investigation of the few available catalogues of *Genizah* collections, and from announcements concerning *Genizah* fragments in scholarly literature. The new aspect of the material published here is that the *Genizah* fragments published thus far have been from hitherto unknown Midrashim. M. Margalioth has added *Genizah* fragments of *Leviticus Rabbah* to his edition of *Midrash Va-Yikra Rabbah* in the form of an appendix. Editions of *Genesis Rabbah* have thus far contained but a few *Genizah* fragments. Theodor–Albeck used a number of photographs or copies from the Bodleian Library in their edition of *Genesis Rabbah*, and this prompted Sokoloff to collect *Genesis Rabbah* fragments and to publish them along with a linguistic analysis of them in order to advance research into the language of Mishnaic Hebrew and Galilean Aramaic as well as research of the midrash. Of the 12 MSS to have been published, there is special importance to MSS 2 and 10 — a Christian Palestinian Aramaic and a Greek palimpsest — which display the original Palestinian orthography of the Amoraic period.

Maimonides. Five orders of Maimonides' *Commentary on the Mishnah* have been found in almost complete form, in Maimonides' own handwriting. An outline version of the introduction to the order *Tohorot* has been published by J. Blau and A. Scheiber (Jerusalem, 1981). Two fragments from the Cairo *Genizah* have been identified:

(a) the Adler–New York collection: one page of the opening of the introduction, which contains two continuous folios;

(b) the Antonin collection (Leningrad): two pages of fragments of the continuation of the introduction, which were identified by A. Scheiber (1978).

Piyyut and Poetry. The following have been published:

(1) The *piyyutim* of the German *paytan* R. Simeon bar Isaac. With the help of the variant readings included in this printing, it is now possible to complete the well known *piyyut Amiẓ ha-Menusseh* and various individual letters lacking in other sources.

(2) Fragments of the *kerovah Aḥat Sha'alti* from Oxford and Cambridge MSS, a special *Kiddush* for *Shabbat Parah* by Eleazar *Kallir. These fragments testify to rather wide circulation of the *kerovah* in the Orient.
(3) *The "Azharot" of Solomon Ibn Gabirol*, based on rare MSS and a volume printed by David Bitton (1980). The *Azharot* are part of the liturgical poetry of Ibn Gabirol.
(4) *Kerovat Yannai* for the chapter *Emor el ha-Kohanim* (Leviticus 21:1) — completed with *Genizah* material.
(5) New poems of Judah Halevi from the Cairo Genizah in Leningrad. Editor Arye Wilsker (Leningrad) wrote in the journal *Sovetish Heymland* of the existence of new poems by Judah Halevi from an unknown diwan from the Cairo *Genizah* material in Leningrad. N. Allony notes in surveying this publication that six new points which emerge from the writings of the Russian researcher. Among them is the very existence of the diwan, in which a list of the openings of the poems of Judah Halevi is found as well. Wilsker's book cites 22 openings of hitherto unknown poems by Judah Halevi. The discovery of a love poem by Judah Halevi, based on five MSS — four in Russia and one in the Cambridge Cairo *Genizah* collection — is especially worthy of note.
(6) Another study on the poetry of Rabbi Hai Gaon has been produced.
(7) An elegy on the death of the wife of the Gaon Nethanel Halevi — head of the Cairo academy in 1160–70 — from the Kaufmann *Genizah* collection. A song of praise in his honor has been found in the Cambridge *Genizah* collection.
(8) A few fragments of poems attributed to Abraham Ibn Ezra have been found in the Cambridge *Genizah* material.

History

(1) A letter sent from the city of Shamtoniya in Iraq (located on the Euphrates River between Nehardea and the Tomb of Ezekiel) in the early eleventh century to Goma-Mazod (a town close to Baghdad) has been published. Its writer — a physician named Jacob from Goma-Mazod — comments that upon arriving in Baghdad he refrained from joining either the academy of Sura or that of Pumbedita, lest this not be to the liking of the rejected academy. The editor of this letter — S.D. Goitein — infers therefrom that the synagogue in the traveler's town was not subject to the permanent influence of either of the two aforementioned academies. Goitein also raises the possibility of a further conclusion: that central spiritual authority had slackened at the time. There is some question as to how this letter — sent to a destination east of Baghdad — reached the *Genizah* of Egypt.
(2) M. Gil reviews the state of historical research on the Cairo *Genizah* documents and describes the state of research on Palestine: history, settlement, community, and leadership.
(3) Two *Genizah* fragments were published dealing with commercial transactions between Crete and Egypt.

Genizah manuscript fragment, a section of the *piyyut Kiddush Yeraḥim* by R. Pinḥas ben R. Jacob Hacohen of Kafra, 11th century (Cambridge University Library, T-S NS 275:184)

Language and Linguistics.

(1) A Cambridge *Genizah* fragment containing a translation of commentary upon portions of *Pirkei Avot* in Old Yiddish, attributed to the fifteenth century, has now been printed. Variant readings and parallels from four similar Yiddish compositions are added. Special importance accrues to Yiddish texts from the *Genizah* because, despite their modest number and scope, they have contributed much to our understanding of the earliest stages of the development of Yiddish literature and the Ashkenazic language at the end of the medieval period.
(2) Three fragments from the Cairo *Genizah* which contains *Karka'ot ha-Dikduk* by Joshua ben Abraham in Judeo-Persian are now in print. The Hebrew words therein are vocalized according to the Tiberian system. The fragment is written in Judeo-Persian; its composition apparently dates from the 12th century. This work deals with the letters and their functions, and adds to our knowledge of the Hebrew language textbooks used in the Jewish communities scattered throughout central Asia.
(3) Ashkenazic fragments in the *Genizah* material have been printed which contained ancient Ashkenazic *piyyutim*, literary texts in Judeo-Ashkenazic, and a number of letters which are dated 1567. The *piyyutim* constitute a complement of sorts to fragmentary *piyyutim* for which no such complement has been found in any other source. They inform us that the Jews of Ashkenaz (Franco-Germany) were no more detached spiritually then in other respects from their gentile surrounding, and knew the vernacular of those in whose midst they had settled. The oldest MS in Judeo-Ashkenazic bears a specific date: קמ"ג (1382–83).

Collected Papers. A. Scheiber's *Genizah Studies* appeared in 1981. The collection includes 65 papers published by Scheiber beginning in 1947, with many findings relating to *Genizah* texts, especially from the collection of David Kaufmann in Budapest and from other *Genizah* collections.

In a critical essay (KS 58 (1983), 159–62), M. Gil classifies the papers into nine groups according to subject matter. Of these, special mention should be made of the following: (1) liturgy and poetry; (2) Rabbi Saadiah Gaon; (3) the problem of "the old questions" (i.e., Land of Israel liturgy); (4) Land of Israel affairs; (5) Egypt; (6) proselytes.

The book is an important contribution to the field of Genizah studies.

Bibliography: BIBLE: L. N. Goldfeld, in: *Kovez al-Yad*, n.s. 10(20), (1982, 123–60; Y. Ratzaby, in: *Sinai*, 89 (1980–1981), 193–216; *ibid.*, 90(1981–1982), 193–231; *ibid.*, 93 (1982–1983), 1–16. TALMUD: A. L. Rosenthal, *Sefer Zikkaron la-Rav Shneor Kolter* (1982–1983), 8–18. MIDRASH: M. Sokoloff, *The Genizah Fragments of Bereshit Rabbah* (1982). MAIMONIDES: N Allony, in: *Sinai*, 92 (1982–1983), 189–91. PIYYUT AND POETRY: A. M. Habermann, *K'vusei Yaḥad* (1980), 15–19; S. Elitzur, in: *Kovez al-Yad*, n.s. 10(20), 1982, 13–55; D. Bitton, (ed.), *Azharoth of Ibn Gabirol* (1980); Z. M. Rabinowitz, in: *Iyyunim be-Sifrut Ḥazal ba-Mikra u-ve-Toledot Yisrael*, dedicated to A. Z. Melamed (1981–1982), 363–75; N. Allony, in: *Sinai*, 93 (1982–1983), 17–24; E. Fleischer, in: *Habermann Memorial Volume* (1983), 109–29; A. Scheiber, in: *Habermann Memorial Volume* (1983), 153–58; A. Saenz-Badillos, in: *Habermann Memorial Volume* (1983), 103–107. HISTORY: S. D. Goitein, *Studies in the History of Iraqi Jewry I* (1981), 12–18; M. Gil, in: *Newsletter of World Union of Jewish Studies* (1983), 17–29; M. Benayahu, in: *Habermann Memorial Volume* (1983), 255–65. LANGUAGE AND LINGUISTICS: S. Hopkins, in: *Tarbiz*, 52 (1983), 459–67; N. Alonny, *Iyunnim be-Sifrut Ḥazal li-Khevod A. Z. Melamed* (1981–1982), 291–311; A. M. Habermann, *K'vusei Yaḥad* (1980), 15–19.

[YO.H.]

GEONIC LITERATURE. This entry includes the basic books of geonic literature, which were compiled during the geonic period — from the year 600 to 1040, approximately. Geonic literature includes several types of works:

(1) Commentaries on the Bible
(2) Commentaries on the Mishnah and Talmud
(3) Books of *Halakhah*, Judgments, and Regulations *(takkanot)*
(4) Responsa
(5) Documents and Letters
(6) Jewish Thought and Ethics
(7) Prayers (prayer-books) and Liturgical Poetry
(8) Language and Grammar

Title page of *Sefer Mishpetei Shevu'ot* (Book of Laws of Oaths) by Hai Gaon, printed by Daniel Zanetti, Venice, 1602 (JNUL, Jerusalem)

Commentaries on the Bible. COMMENTARIES ON THE PENTATEUCH (TORAH). *Saadiah Gaon. Torah with Arabic translation (Constantinople, 1546); *Tafsir al-Torah bi-al-Arabiya* (Paris, 1893); *Keter Torah*, known as *Tag'* (Jerusalem, 1894–1901); Commentary on the Torah — Kafaḥ edition (1963); Torah Commentary on Genesis (Zucker edition 1984).

**Samuel ben Hophni Gaon*. Commentary on the book of Genesis, A. Greenbaum (ed.), 1978. Selections of his commentary on other parts of the Torah have also been published.

COMMENTARIES ON THE PROPHETS AND THE HAGIOGRAPHA. From Saadiah's translation of biblical books, *Tafsir*, there remain those of the Pentateuch, Isaiah, Proverbs, Job, the Five Scrolls, and Psalms, all with commentary. They were published from 1546 to 1970, with new sections of his commentaries on Isaiah, Lamentations, and the Book of Esther appearing more recently.

Saadiah's introduction to his *Pitron Shivim Millim* was printed in N. Allony's *Studies in Medieval Philosophy and Literature I: Saadiah Works* (1986). Various geonic commentaries on the Bible are scattered throughout the geonic responsa and referred to in geonic essays; they were collected in various anthologies.

Commentaries on the Mishnah and Talmud. COMMENTARIES ON THE MISHNAH (1) The only geonic commentary on the Mishnah extant in its entirety is on the order *Tohorot* (J. N. Epstein edition, edited by E. Z. Melammed, 1982); it is attributed to *Hai Gaon and may be an adaptation of Saadiah's commentary. (2) Geonic commentaries on the Mishnah collected from various sources appear in *Ozar ha-Geonim* ("The Treasure of the Geonim"; 13 vols., 1928–62) by Benjamin M. *Lewin. (3) Saadiah's *Millot ha-Mishnah* ("Words of the Mishnah") appeared in various journals.

COMMENTARIES ON THE TALMUD. (1) Talmud commentaries of the early *geonim* were incorporated into the Talmud. For a long time the geonic commentaries were found among those of the French and Spanish commentators. Some of these were thought irretrievably lost, with fragments being rediscovered only during the past 100 years. They were published in various articles, anthologies, and in Lewin's *Ozar ha-Geonim*. (2) Talmud commentaries by Paltoi Gaon, Sherira Gaon, and Hai Gaon, mentioned in various sources, have not reached us in their entirety. (3) The Talmudic dictionary of the *gaon* Samuel ben Hophni was published by S. Abramson in *A. Even Shoshan* (1985), 13–65.

INTRODUCTORY BOOKS TO THE TALMUD. These works include material dealing with methodology as well as with history.

(1) *Seder Tannaim ve-Amoraim*, compiled c. 884–886, was first published in Leghorn in 1796; an edition by Kalman Kahana appeared in 1935. The author's name is unknown. It contains a summary of the chain of tradition of the oral Law up to the Saboraim, including regulations for passing halakhic judgments. (2) Saadiah Gaon's Introduction to the Talmud, which has been lost. (3) Samuel ben Hophni's "Introduction to the Talmud." Selected chapters of this work with the Arabic source and Hebrew translation, accompanied by an introduction and notes, were published by S. Abramson (1990). This volume is the second part of the work Samuel b. Hophni called *Mevo li-Yedi'at ha-Mishnah ve-ha-Talmud*. Extant from the first part are most of the book's index and several sections from the text (see S. Abramson, in: *Sinai* 88 (1980), 193). (4) *Iggeret Rav Sherira Gaon* (see **14**:1381) was published by B. M. Lewin (1921) in both known versions, the so-called *"nosaḥ Sefarad"* and *"nosaḥ Ẓarefat,"* i.e., a "version from Spain" and a "version from France" (in which there is a difference of opinion as to whether the Mishnah was already written down in the time of Rabbi Judah ha-Nasi or

merely remembered orally), on the basis of manuscripts and Genizah fragments.

Books of Halakhah. (1) *She'iltot* (Venice, 1566), by *Aḥa of Shabḥa (680–752), *gaon* of Pumbedita. Robert Brody's *The Textual History of the She'iltot* (1991) is a study aimed at reconstructing as closely as possible the original text of *Sefer ha-She'iltot*. This work prepares the way for a new edition of the *She'iltot* which will contain additional textual vestiges, particularly from the Cairo *Genizah*.

(2) The book *Ve-Hizhir* (see **2**:450), an imitation of *She'iltot*.

(3) Legal decisions by *Yehudai Gaon (head of Sura academy, 757–761), to whom the book *Halakhot Pesukot* is attributed. He is the first *gaon* whose responsa have been preserved.

(4) *Halakhot de-Rab Abba*, a student of Yehudai Gaon, excerpts of which were published by J. N. Epstein in *Madda'ei he-Yahadut* (1927).

(5) **Halakhot Gedolot*. In addition to the 1548 and 1885 editions, a new edition according to a manuscript in the Ambrosiana Library, Milan, was edited by A. Hildesheimer (grandson of the 1885-edition editor): (a) *Seder Mo'ed* (1972); (b) *Seder Nashim* (first three tractates, 1980), part 3, edited by E. Hildesheimer, introduction, 11–26, and *Hakdamat Halakhot Gedolot*, edited by N. Z. Hildesheimer (1987), 9–52. (For the relationship between *Halakhot Gedolot* and *Halakhot Pesukot*, see **Dc./17**:285).

(6) **Halakhot Pesukot* or *Hilkhot Re'u*, attributed to the disciples of Yehudai Gaon, published in 1886 and in the Sasson Edition (1951).

(7) **Halakhot Kezuvot*, published by M. Margaliot in 1942.

(8) Books of *Halakhah* by Saadiah Gaon (see **14**:547–48). Saadiah wrote monographs on various halakhic subjects, but only a small part has reached us in its entirety. A study on Saadiah's *Sefer ha-Edut ve-ha-Shetarot* by M. Ben-Sasson appeared in the *Annual of Jewish Law* (1984–86), 135–278. A new edition of *Sefer ha-Mizvot*, with commentary by Y. Y. F. Perla, pts. 1–3 appeared 1989.

(9) Sherira Gaon who is famous for his *Iggeret* mentioned above. Approximately half of the geonic responsa in our possession were written by Sherira and his son Hai Gaon. Parts of Sherira's commentaries on certain Talmudic tractates have also been preserved.

(10) Hai Gaon (see 7:1131) did not compile any book of *halakhah* on all the Talmudic laws, but devoted a separate composition to each subject, as did Saadiah and Samuel ben Hophni. Five additional chapters of *Sefer ha-Mekkaḥ ve-ha-Mimkar* ("Treatise on Commercial Transactions") were published by S. Abramson in the *Joseph Dov Soloveitchik Festschrift*, vol. 2 (1984), 1312–1379. There is also mention of a Book of Oaths in verse. Chapters of monetary laws of commerce and chapters of oaths in verse have appeared in part in various collections.

(11) Samuel ben Hophni. Of his many works, only a few have reached us. In recent years excerpts have been published of his books from the *Genizah*. He wrote monographs on *halakhah* which are still being published. Mention should be made of the following: Chapters on Blessings (in *Ozar ha-Geonim*, tractate *Berakhot*, commentaries, pp. 65–77), the Book of Gifts, divorce laws, obligations of religious judges and the Book of Pledge, etc.

Other halakhic essays from the period of the Geonim include: (a) *Sefer Metivot*: a book of laws arranged according to the order of tractates of the Talmud. B. M. Levin collected all the citations from the book which were mentioned in earlier books and arranged them in the Talmudic order in this book *Metivot* (1934). (b) *Sefer Ḥefez*: There are many speculations concerning the authorship and place of origin of this book. Many of the early authorities discussing halakhic matters use *Sefer Ḥefez* as their source. Levin is of the opinion that *Metivot* served as an example for *Sefer Ḥefez*. (c) *The Book of Mitzvot of Ḥefetz ben Yatzliaḥ*: (B. Halper edition 1915). This book includes all the laws of the Torah, and it is "a treasury of halakhah, philology and philosophy as they were in the time of the author".

HALAKHIC LITERATURE IN EREẒ ISRAEL IN THE PERIOD OF THE GEONIM. In recent years, there were discovered in the *Genizah, Hilkhot Tereifot shel Erez Israel* — in the style of *Halakhot Pesukot*. An important find was remnants of *Sefer ha-Ma'asim li-Venei Erez Yisrael*, and parts of this book were published by Levin, Epstein, Mann, and Aptowitzer, between the years 1930–1974. It is assumed that *Sefer ha-Ma'asim* served as a source for the compiler of *Halakhot Gedolot*, and possibly also for *Sefer ha-She'iltot*. There is a theory that *Sefer ha-Ma'asim* is another title for *Sefer ha-She'iltot*. During the Geonic period, the following important literary activities were undertaken in Ereẓ Israel: the translation of works from Aramaic to Hebrew: Rav Yehudai's *Halakhot Pesukot* was translated into Hebrew under the title *Hilkhot Re'u*, taken from the opening words of the book "*Re'u ki Adonai natan lakhem et yom ha-Shabbat....*"

RULES, REGULATIONS AND CUSTOMS. The Geonim set down various legal decisions and customs. At the beginning of the Geonic period, an essay was written by a sage in Ereẓ Israel, under the title: "Controversies between Easterners and those who dwell in Ereẓ Israel" (pub. M. Margaliot, 1938). It includes a list of 55 customs upon which Jews in Babylonia disagreed with Jews in Ereẓ Israel, and this book formed the foundations for all subsequent books of customs. "The Book of Change of Customs" (Müller, 1878) and the "Treasury of Differences of Custom between Babylonian and Palestinian Jewries" (ed. Levin, 1942) are also available.

GEONIC EDICTS (TAKKANOT). Geonim sought to issue decrees based on Talmudic conclusions, and to establish regulations to cover all aspects of Jewish life. In the course of time, it became necessary to supplement Talmudic regulations and to introduce new laws according to the reguirements of the period. These laws encompass various areas, and in particular deal with laws of personal status, money matters, oaths, and evidence. The sources for these ordinances are the geonic literature and they are collected in H. Tykocinski's *The Gaonic Ordinances*, translation and notes by H. Ḥavazelet (1959). I. Schipansky's, *The Takkanot*

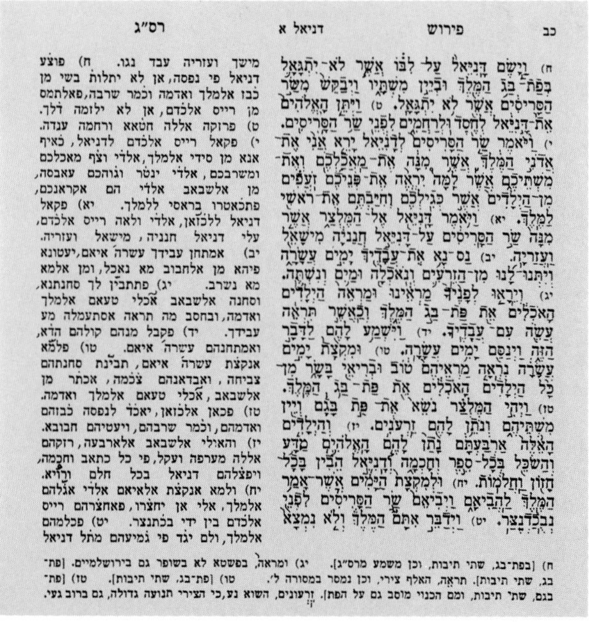

Book of Daniel; with Arabic translation and commentary by Saadiah Gaon (Dror Publishing House, 1981)

of Israel — v. 3, *Geonic Enactments* (1992) contains *takkanot* by sages from Israel and geonim of Babylonian yeshivot from the close of the Talmud to the period of the Rishonim presented in three sections: introduction to geonic *takkanot* by famous *geonim* of Sura and Pumbedita, and other *takkanot* from the same period.

Jewish Thought and Ethics. In this sphere mention must be made of Saadiah Gaon's *Emunot ve-De'ot*, translated from Arabic by Judah Ibn Tibbon (Constantinople, 1562) under the title *Sefer ha-Nivḥar ve-Emunot ve-De'ot* (J. Kappaḥ edition, 1970). Other works are *Rhymes on Moral Instruction attributed to R. Hai Gaon* (ed. H. Gollancz, 1922); Saadiah's "Epistle on Ethics to the Jewish Communities of Spain" (in Saadiah's *Bible Commentary* — Pt. 2, 1960), and *Ethics of the Dayyanim* by Hai Gaon. Other works by Saadiah Gaon: *Esa Meshali*, a rhymed polemic devoted against the teaching of Anan b. David, in: *Devir*, 1(1923), 180ff; and a polemic against Ḥiwi al-Balkhi, published by Y. Davidson, in the introduction to his edition of this work (1915), 11–37. (See **8**:792–93.)

PRAYERS AND LITURGICAL POETRY. Of note are two prayerbooks; the *Siddur* of *Amram Gaon, of which a scientific edition by D. Goldschmidt appeared in 1972, and the *Siddur* of Saadiah Gaon, published 1941.

Geonic Responsa. Scores of collections of geonic responsa exist, comprising thousands of answers sent by the *geonim* to queries received from correspondents throughout the geonic period. A large number of responsa were discovered in the *Genizah* and several excerpts have been published. The first collection of geonic responsa appeared in 1516 in Constantinople. G. Harpnas's *Teshuvot ha-Geonim she-Heishivu Ge'onei Sura u-Pumbedita* ("Responsa of Geonim of Sura and Pumbedita," 1992) has the responsa arranged topically and provides cross references.

Documents and Letters. Many documents and letters of the Geonim have reached us. These were written in answer to specific questions which were addressed to them, or which the Geonim wished to make known among Jewish communities outside Ereẓ Israel — especially as regards specific subjects related to religious fundamentals to taking a stand on current matters. In this connection the *Iggeret* ("Epistle") of *Pirkoi ben Baboi (turn of the ninth century) should be mentioned as it is one of the earliest literary writings from the geonic period and is also the first known instance in the literature advocating the dissemination of the Babylonian Talmud. In this connection, see also the *Iggeret* of Sherira Gaon mentioned above.

Among the many sources of geonic letters are: J. Mann, *Texts and Studies I* (1931); L. Ginzberg, *Genizah Studies II* (1929), which contains a collection of all the letters of the Babylonian *geonim*; S. Abramson, *Be-Merkazim u-va-Tefuẓot* (1965).

Throughout the Geonic period, the Geonim occupied themselves with prayerbooks, establishing the versions of prayers, and dealing with the obligation and value of prayer. *Natronai bar Hilai (mid-ninth century) compiled a prayer book, *Me'ah Berakhot* ("Prayer Book of the Hundred Benedictions"), and *Israel ben Samuel bar Hophni (gaon of Sura from about 1017 to 1033) deals with the "obligation to pray."

Many liturgical hymns have reached us from the time of the Geonim. Saadiah's *Siddur* contains *bakkashot* (petitions) and *azharot; "Otiyyot Rav Saadiah"* contains rhymes on the letters of the alphabet with annotations by Elijah (Baḥur) *Levita at the end of his book *Masoret ha-Masoret* (1538). Many liturgical hymns of the Geonim were discovered in the *Genizah* and have appeared in various publications and anthologies.

Language and Grammar. The *geonim* also engaged in the study of Hebrew language and grammar. Saadiah wrote *Ha-Egron* (edition N. Allony, 1969), containing a Hebrew dictionary, with Hebrew grammar rules, and also a summary of the basis of Hebrew poetry. Additional information on Geonic Hebrew is in *Zaḥut ha-Lashon ha-Ivrit* in: *Allony Studies*, (1986), 205–31.

Bibliography: L. Ginzberg, *Geonica II. The Halakhic Literature of the Geonim* (1909), 72–200; I. H. Weiss, *Dor Dor ve-Doreshav*, 4 (1911), 1–41, 99–184; I. Halevy, *Dorot ha-Rishonim*, 3 (1923), 147–305; M. Waxman, *History of Jewish Literature*, 1 (1936), 182–86, 253–55, 310–312; H. Graetz, *History of the Jews*, 3 (1939), 86–126, 177–179; on Saadiah, 187–250; on Sherira, 231–33; on Hai, 233–253; V. Aptowitzer, *Meḥkarim be-Sifrut ha-Geonim* (1941); M. Margolis and A. Marx, *History of the Jewish People* (1945), 264–76; H. Tchernowitz (Rav Ẓa'ir), *Toledot ha-Posekim*, 1 (1946), 18–130; S. Assaf, *Tekufat ha-Geonim ve-Sifrutah* (1955); S. W. Baron, *A Social and Religious History of the Jews*, vols. 5–7 (1957/58); see Baron, Index, Geonim and also under individual *geonim*; B. Dinur, *Yisrael ba-Golah*, 1, Bk. 2 (1961), chp. 9, 78–151; chp. 13 (Saadiah), 380–469; *Sefer ha-Mekorot shel ha-Milon ha-Histori le-Lashon ha-Ivrit*, 1 (1963), *Sifrut ha-Geonim*, 76–90; Z. Jawitz, *Toledot Yisrael*, 9 (1963), 82–115; 1–174; M. Elon, *Jewish Law*, 2 (1973), 528–46; 3, 949–64; S. Abramson, *Inyanut be-Sifrut ha-Geonim* (1974); M. Kasher and J. Mandelbaum (eds.) *Sarei ha-Elef* (2 pts.; 1978); A. Kimmelman, "A Guide to commentaries in the Geonic Period," in: *Annual of the Institute for Research in Jewish Law*, vol. 11–12 (1984–86), 463–587.

COMMENTARIES ON THE PENTATEUCH (TORAH). *Saadiah:* I. Ta-Shema, in: KS, 44 (1969), 442, Y. Ratzaby, in: *Sinai*, 91 (1982), 196–222; idem in *Sinai*, 94 (1984), 4–27; idem in *Sinai*, 95 (1984), 1–26; idem in *Sinai*, 96 (1985), 1–17; idem, in: *Sinai*, 107 (1991), 97–126; A. Kimmelman, in: *Guide*, 475–507. *Samuel b. Hophni*: A. Greenbaum, in the Yechiel Jacob Weinberg Memorial Book (1970), 257–83; idem in: *Areshet*, 5 (1972), 7–33; idem, in: *Ha-Darom*, 3 (1980), 139–41; idem, in: *Introduction to the Commentary on Genesis* (1978), 11–115; idem, in: *Sinai Jubilee Volume*, 100 (1987), 273–90; M. Sokolof, in: *Alei Sefer*, 8 (1980), 137–39; N. Allony, in: *Beth Mikra*, *25 (1980), 85–90*; G. Vajda, in: *REJ*, *139 (1980), 143–47*; N. Allony, in: *Immanuel*, 12 (1981), 96–101.

COMMENTARIES ON PROPHETS AND HAGIOGRAPHA: *Saadiah:* H. Avenari, in: HUCA, 39 (1968), 145–62; I. Tobi, in: KS, 50 (1975), 654–62; B. Z. Kedar, in *Jerusalem in the Middle Ages* (1979), 107–2; L. E. Gordon, in: *Studies in Jewish Philosophy*, 3 (1982); N. Allony, in: *Studies in Medieval Philology*, I. *Saadia Works* (1986), 9–23; Y. Ratzaby, in: *Sinai*, 89 (1981), 193–216; idem, in: *Sinai*, 90 (1982) 193–231; idem, in: *Sinai*, 93 (1983), 1–116, idem, in: *Sinai*, 105 (1990), 193–211; idem, in *Bar-Ilan*, 20–21 (1983), 349–81; idem, in: *J. B. Soloveitchik Jubilee Volume*, II (1984), 1153–78, *Saadiah:* Hapax Legomena: S. Buber, in: *Ozar ha-Sifrut*, I (1887), 33–52; B. Klar, in: *Saadiah Volume* (1943), 275–90; N. Allony, in: *Sinai* 37 (1955), 245–60: H. Mutins, in *Biblische Notizen — Beiträge zur exegitischen Diskussion (BNBD)*, 8 (1979), 18–21; N. Allony, in *Studies* (1986), 95–117, *Various Geonic commentaries on the Bible:* M. B. Lerner, in: *Koveẓ al Yad*, 8 (1976), 141–64; N. Allony, in: *Alei Sefer*, 9 (1981), 56–62.

COMMENTARIES ON THE MISHNAH: I. N. Epstein, Introduction to commentary on *Seder Tohorot* (1982), 10–146; S. Assaf, *Tekufat ha-Geonim ve-Sifruta* (1955), 137–46; 294–322. *Millot ha-Mishnah — Saadiah:* N. Allony, in: *Leshonenu*, 18 (1953), 176–78, 22 (1958), 147–72; S. Abramson, *Leshonenu*, 19 (1954), 49–50; Y. Ratzaby, *Leshonenu*, 20 (1956), 41–44; 23 (1959) 125–26, *Milon ha-Mishnah — Saadiah:* N. Allony, in: *Studies* (1986), 137–50; A. Kimmelmann, *Guide to Commentaries in the Geonic Period — Annual Jewish Law*, XI–XII (1984–86), 509–87. COMMENTARIES ON THE TALMUD: *Commentary of Saadia to tractate Berakhot*, ed. Wertheimer (1908); I. L. Sachs, in: *Sinai* 13 (1943), 49–54; S. D. Goitein, in: KS, 31 (1956), 368–70; B. M. Lewin, *Marei Makom avur Ozar ha-Geonim le-Massekhet Bava Batra u-Hullin*, in: *Jewish Law Annual*, A. Kimelmann (ed.), 543–56; 565–77.

INTRODUCTORY BOOKS TO TALMUD:

(1) *Seder Tanaim ve-Amoraim:* S. Assaf, *Tekufat ha-Geonim*, 147–48; Waxmann, I 315–16; *Sarei ha-Elef*, M. Kasher, J. Mandelbaum (eds.), I (1978), 163; II (79), 582; S. Abramson, in: *E. Z. Melammed Jubilee Volume* (1982), 215–47. (2) *Saadiah: Introduction to the Talmud:* Assaf 148–49, in: KS. 52 (1977), 381–82.

(3) *Samuel b. Hophni: Introduction:* Assaf, 149; J. N. Epstein, in: *Kovez al Yad,* 13 (1940), 3–8; S. Abramson, in: *Tarbiz,* 26 (1957), 421–23. (4) *Iggeret Rav Sherira:* B. M. Lewin, *Introduction to Iggeret;* Assaf, 149–53; Waxman, I, 427–29; J. N. Epstein, *Mevo'ot le-Sifrut ha-Amoraim* (1963), 610–15; M. Ber, in: *Bar-Ilan,* 4–5 (1967), 181–96; I. Blidstein, in: *Daat,* 4 (1980), 5–16.

BOOKS OF HALAKHAH: (1) *Sheiltot:* Aḥa of Shabḥa, *Sarei ha-Elef,* 96–97; II, 573; A. Kaminka, in: *A. Schwarz Jubilee Volume* (1917), 437–53; idem, in: *Sinai,* 6 (1940), 179–92; A. Aptowitzer, in: MGWJ (1932), 558–75; J. N. Epstein, in: *Tarbiz,* 6 (1935), 460–97; 7 (1936), 1–30; 8 (1937), 5–54; A. Weiss, in: *Sefer S. Assaf* (1953), 293–301; S. K. Mirski, in: *Proceedings of World Congress of Jewish Studies* (1967). 127–29; Baron, History, VI 37; Sh. Morell, in: HUCA, 43 (1972), 253–68; M. Elon, Jew. Law III, 949–52. (2) *Ve-Hizhir:* Rav Ẓair (H. Tschernowitz), *Toledot ha-Posekim* I, 127–30; Assaf, 161–63, 178; Baron, VI 40, 339; *Sarei ha-Elef* I, 68 NO. 27; (3) *Decisions of Yehudai Gaon:* see **16:**731–32; M. Herschler, in: *Sinai,* 70 (1972), 121–25. (4) *Halakhot de Rav Abba:* J.N. Epstein, in; *Maddaei ha-Yahadut, II* (1927), 149–61. (5) *Halakhot Gedolot:* see 7:1167–1170; **Dc./17:**285–86; Rav Ẓair, I 70–84; Assaf, 165–71; Baron, IV 195; VI 23, 81, 98, 121, 364ff; E. Hildesheimer, in: *Moria* 12, 144-46; I. Ta-Shema, in: KS, 55 (1986), 197–201; M. Elon, Law III, 954. (6) *Halakhot Pesukot — Hilkhot Re'u:* see **7:**1171–1172 *Hal. Pesukot:* Elon III, 952–53; S. Morag, in: *Leshonenu* 32 (1968), 67–88; M. Ben Asher, in: *Leshonenu.* 34 (1970), 278–86; idem, in: *Leshonenu,* 35 (1971), 20–35; E. Hildesheimer. in: *Weinberg Memorial Book* (1970), 303–12; idem, in: *D. Ochs Memorial Book* (1978), 153–71; S. Morel, in: HUCA, 43 (1972), 253–68; HUCA, 46 (1975), 510–32; HUCA, 50 (1980), 11–32; J. Yalon, in: *Leshonenu,* 37 (1973), 161–64; Y. Ez-Haijm, in: *Alei Sefer,* 11 (1984), 9–36; idem, in: *Sidra,* 2 (1986), 77–124. (7) *Halakhot Kezuvot.* see **7:**1170; Rav *Ẓair I, 112–16; Baron VI, 108, 356, 366; E. Hildesheimer, in: Sinai,* 13 (1943), 271–87; idem, in: *Sinai,* 14 (1944), 21–32. 82–94. (8) *Books on Halakhah by Saadiah:* Rav Ẓair I, 85–94; S. Assaf, 185–93. idem, in: *Saadiah Volume* (1943), 65–97, 674–76; Elon III, 957–59; S. Abramson, in: KS, 23 (1947), 231–32; A. Scheiber — I. Han in *Tarbiz,* 25 (1956), 323–30; *Tarbiz,* 28 (1959), 48–53; D. Z. Baneth, in: *Saadia Book* (1943), 365–81; "Book of Commandments," in: *Tarbiz,* 41 (1972), 170–82. (10) *Hai Gaon:* Rav Ẓair I, 95–105; Assaf, 198–202; Baron VI, 70ff, 395ff; Elon III, 962–63; S. Abramson, in: *Epstein Jubilee Book* (1950), 296–315; M. Havazelet, in: *Tarbiz* 35 (1966), 39–47; *Sarei ha-Elef* II, 390, 650. (11) *Samuel b. Hophni:* Assaf, 194; Elon III, 960–62; I. Friedlander, in: *Hoffman Jubilee Volume* (1914), 83–97; B. M. Lewin, in: *Sinai,* 6 (1940), 390–97; S. Assaf — S. Abramson, in: *Tarbiz,* 18 (1947), 28–33, 34–46; S. Assaf, in: *Sinai,* 17 (1945), 113–55; A. Greenbaum, in: KS, 46 (1971), 154–69; idem, in: *Sinai* ,72 (1973), 205–21; *Sinai,* 73 (1973), 97–117; idem in: *Sinai,* 77 (1975), 97–115; S. Emanuel, in: KS, 59 (1984), 962–66; N. Z. Hildesheimer, in: *Moria,* 15 (1987), 17–31. G. Libson, in: *Annual of Jewish Law,* 11–12 (1984–86), 337–92. (12) *General.* D. Groner, "*Mi-Sifrei Halakhah shel ha-Ge'onim,*" in: *Alei Sefer,* 15 (1988/89), 31–35.

Sefer Metivot: Assaf, 203–204; D. S. Loewinger, in: *Ginzei* Kaufmann (1949), 42–58. *Sefer Hefez:* Rav Ẓair I, 123–27; Assaf, 204–206; V. Aptowitzer, in: *Tarbiz,* 4 (1933), 127–52. *Sefer Hamizvot of Hefez b. Yazli'ah:* Rav Ẓair I, 117–23; Assaf, 206–207; Baron VI, 59, 93ff; B. Halper, in: JQR, 4 (1913/14), 519–75; ibid., 5 (1914/15), 29–90, 345–441; 6 (1915/16), 97–156; M. Zucker, in: *Proceedings,* 29 (1961), 1–68. *Sefer ha-Mikzo'ot:* Assaf 207–209ff.; *Hilkhot Tereifot Shel Erez Israel:* Assaf, 175; M. Margaliot, *Hilkhot Erez Israel me-ha-Genizah* (1973), 95–117; *Sefer ha-Ma'asim li-Venei Erez Israel:* Rav Zair I. 106–108; Assaf, 175–178; Baron II, 283, 422,; III, IIIf.; VI, 64f.; 355; *Sarei ha-Elef* II, 386–87; J. N. Epstein, in: *Tarbiz,* 2 (1936), 33–42; I. Mann, in: *Tarbiz,* 3 (1930), 1–14; and remarks of Epstein, 143–53; Z. M. Rabinowitz, in: *Tarbiz,* 41 (1972), 275–305; M. D. Herr, in: *Tarbiz,* 49 (1980), 62–80; I. Ta-Shema, in: KS, 60 (1985), 306.

RULES REGULATIONS: *Controversies...* M. Margalioth. in: *Mavo* to the book, Assaf, 179; S. H. Kook, *Iyyunim ve-Meḥkarim,* I (1959), 286. TAKKANOT: I. H. Weiss, *Dor Dor we-Dorshav,* IV, 177–84; Assaf, 62–64; I. Shzipanski, in: *Ha-Darom,* 24 (1967), 135–97; 26 (1968), 203–10; M. Elon, *Jewish Law,* 2 (1973), 531–46; Y. Brody, in: *Annual of Jewish Law,* 11–12 (1984–86), 279–315; A. Shochetman, in: Annual, 655–86.

PRAYERS AND LITURGICAL POETRY: *Siddur of Amram Gaon:* D. Goldschmidt, Introduction to his edition of this *siddur,* G. Orman, in: KS, 47 (1972), 376–81; Assaf, 180–184; H. J. Zimmels, in: *Sinai,* 18 (1946), 362–73; *Sarei ha-Elef* 2, 394–95.

Prayer Book of Saadiah Gaon: Introduction to the ed. of Siddur (1941) — S. Bernstein, in: *Bizaron* (1942), 845–57; Review of D. Goldschmidt, B. Klar, in: KS, 18 (1942), 336–48; L. Ginzberg, in: JQR, 33 (1942/3), 315–63; H. J. Zimmels — H. Yalon, in: *Saadia Volume* (1943), 537–66; S. Krauss, in: *Sinai,* 15 (1945), 302–11; M. Zulai, in: *Tarbiz,* 16 (1945), 57–70; N. Wieder, in: *Assaf— Volume* (1953), 237–60; B. Klar, *Mehkarim ve-Iyyunim* (1954), 136–45; A. Scheiber, in: *Sinai,* 11 (1957), 59–60; *Sarei ha-Elef,* 2 (1979), 393–94; Sh. Tal, in: *Sinai,* 90 (1982), 95–96; idem, in: *Sinai,* 95 (1984), 249.

LITURGICAL POETRY: *Otiyyot R. Saadiah: Sarei ha-Elef* II, 420, 659; Baron Index 53, 119; VII, 63ff, 78, 103, 111f, 132f, 274f. H. Brody, *Yedi'ot ha-Makhon le-Ḥeker ha-Shirah ha-Ivrit,* III 1937, 5ff.; idem, in: *Sinai,* 2 (1938), 516ff; Y. Rafael, in: *Sinai,* 12 (1938), 592–676; Habermann, in: *Tarbiz* 13 (1942), 52–59; M. Zulai, *Ha-Eskolah ha-Paytanit shel R. Saadiah Gaon (Rasag)* (1964); idem, in: *Tarbiz,* 23 (1952), 112–19; I. Tobi, in: *Tarbiz,* 53 (1984), 221–53.

RESPONSA: See **14:**84–85; Geonic Period; Assaf, 211–20; Baron V: 52; VI: 29, 115, 339, 385, VIII: 229; Z. Groner, in: *Sinai,* 79 (1976), 42–229; idem, in: *Alei Sefer,* 8 (1980), 5–22; idem, in: *Alei Sefer,* 13 (1986), contains a list of Hai Gaon's Responsa: M. A Friedmann, in: *Meḥkarim be-Sifrut ha-Talmud* (1983), 71f; J. Lipschitz, in: *Moria,* 7 (1978), 4–5; A. Eisenbach, *Tzefunot,* 1–3 (1989), 4–7; M. A. Friedman, in: *Sinai,* 109 (1992), 125–44.

DOCUMENTS AND LETTERS: Pirkoi B. Baboi, see **13:**560–561 and Bibliography; Rav Ẓair I, 109–12; Baron V: 32; VI: 29, 109–116, 339, 381–85.

LANGUAGE AND GRAMMAR: *Saadiah's Grammatical Work.* S. Abramson, in: *Tarbiz,* 19 (1948), 104; S. L. Skoss, in: JQR, 23 (1932/33), 329–36; JQR, 33 (1942/3), 171–212; JQR, 42 (1952), 283–317; JQR 42 (1951/2), 283–89; idem, in: *Proceedings,* 21 (1952), 75–100; 22 (1953), 65–90; 23 (1954), 59–73; idem, *Saadia Gaon, the Earliest Hebrew Grammarian* (1955); Review in N. Allony, *Studies,* 381–84; N. Allony, *Introduction to ha-Egron* (1969); D. Tene, in: KS, 47 (1972), 545–53; A. Goldenberg, in: *Leshonenu,* 37 (1973), 117–36, 275–90; 38 (1974), 78–90; Y. Eldor, in: *Leshonenu, 45 (1981), 105–32; N. Allony, Studies* (1986), 205–31; 233–281; 325–34; Baron VII: 15, 26, 32, 39; S. Abramson, *"Sefer ha-Me'assef le-Rav Hai Gaon,"* in: *Leshonenu,* 41 (1977), 108–16.

RESEARCH ON GEONIC LITERATURE. Ḥayyim Loven, in: *The Young Israel Rabbinical Council in Israel Annual,* 2 (1988), 87–123; Y. Blumberg in: *Hebrew Law Annual,* 14–15 (1988/89), 61–87; D. Groner, *Pe'amim,* 38 (1989), 49–57; Y. Horowitz, *Meḥkarei Ḥag,* 1 (1988), 49–56; idem, 3 (1992), 6–14.

RESEARCH ON SAADIAH GAON AND HAI GAON. Saadiah Gaon, A. Schlossberg, in: *Shema'tin* (1988), 18–23; idem, in: *Meḥkarei Ḥag,* 4 (1992), 74–82; H. Ben Shammai, *Sefer ha-Yovel li-Shelomo Pines,* 1 (1988), 127–46; Y. Horowitz, in: *Meḥkarei Ḥag,* 2 (1990), 54–62; idem, *Meḥkarei Ḥag,* 4 (1992), 83–87; A. Lasker and D. Lasker, in: *Tarbiz,* 61 (1991), 119–28; Y. Ratzaby, in: *Sinai,* 109 (1992), 97–117; E. Fleischer, in: *Sefer Zikkaron Pagis* 1988), 661–681; Z. Rothstein, in: *Esh Tamid* (1989), 21–30; Y. Gertner, in: *Sinai,* 107 (1991), 202–12. [Y. HO.]

GEORGIA (see **7:**423). A CIS republic, Georgia declared its independence in 1991. Since then it has been the arena of uninterrupted military conflict, first between President Zviad Gamsakhurdiia and the opposition and then, after the former was driven out in January 1992, between the government of Eduard Shevardnadze and separatists in Southern Osetia and Abkhazia.

Soviet censuses reported 28,300 Jews in 1979 and 24,800 in 1989; 14,300 of the latter were Georgian Jews who have preserved their ethnic and religious distinctiveness despite speaking the same language as their host nationality. At the end of 1991, there were 21,700 Jews in Georgia.

In 1989, 488 Jews emigrated. In 1990, 1,603 (including 911 from Tbilisi) immigrated to Israel. The corresponding figure for 1991 were 1,502 and 822. Economically and socially the Georgian Jews are well integrated in the larger community. They generally have been less interested in emigration than the Jews in other republics.

A 1992 statement by local Jewish organizations stated that

anti-Semitism has been and continues to be alien to Georgia. The approximately 20 Jewish organizations in Tbilisi mostly consist of Ashkenazi Jews. One of Gamsakhurdiia's advisors was Isai Goldshtien, a former refusenik who became an anti-Zionist. Most Georgian Jews, however, have been reluctant to become involved in the recent struggles for power.

[MI BE.]

GERMANY (see **7**:457; **Dc./17**:261). The history of post-war German Jewry follows several distinct phases. In the West, the first period, from 1945 to 1950, is that of the *She'erit ha-Peletah* (the Holocaust survivors), during which time over 200,000 Jews, most of them in Displaced Persons' camps, lived in Germany, trying to make their way to Palestine or waiting for passage to the United States and other countries. For a few years, this camp life produced a flourishing, mostly Yiddish, culture in which Zionism emerged as the dominant theme. To this day, this period has been largely neglected by historical research. This first period is characterized by a group of mostly German Jews with personal charisma who has come into close contact with Eastern European Jews in the concentration camps, who were thus able to mediate between the two groups, and who had to negotiate with German and allied authorities as well as with international Jewish organizations. The most important of these leaders was Norbert Wollheim who was the liaison to Jewish organizations in Britain and was instrumental in founding the Central Council of Jews in Germany, designed originally to deal with claims to Bonn for restitution and to coordinate the activities of Jewish communities throughout Germany. Other important figures in this early period include Philipp Auerbach in Munich, Rabbi Wilhelm Weinberg in Frankfurt, Hans-Erich Fabian in Berlin, and Josef Rosensaft and Hadassah (Bimko) Rosensaft in Belsen; by 1952, these and a number of other leaders had left Germany or had died.

The second postwar period, from about 1951 to 1969, is that of bureaucratic consolidation, under the leadership of Karl Marx — who in the 1940s had founded the *Allgemeine Wochenzeitung der Juden in Deutschland* — and Hendrik George van Dam, the first general secretary of the Zentralrat and an outstanding lawyer who — while excluded from negotiations leading to the treaty of The Hague — helped bring about a wide net of legislation that was to compensate Jews living in Germany for their material losses. Jewry during this period developed a mentality of heightened vigilance and of "living on packed suitcases" while their leadership, despised as traitors and isolated by world Jewry for living in Germany, tended toward a tacit accommodation with the German political class and a definition of Jewish existence in Germany.

The third period, which might be called one of representationism, dates from Werner Nachmann's election to the chair of the Central Council in 1969 to the death of his successor, Heinz Galinski, in August 1992. In this period, the sentiment at least of the leadership, moved from the earlier "vigilance" to a desire for normalizing relations with Germany; public pronouncements stress German-Jewish understanding and define the Jewish role as the guardian of memory and advocacy of minorities in general. This leadership portrayed itself as martyr-founders of the new German Jewry and although it slowly lost political significance sought a strong public and political presence in Germany, resulting in what one critic called the "memorial site and state Jewry" (Gedenkstätten- und Staatsjudentum). With the election of Ignatz Bubis of Frankfurt to the chair of the Central Council in 1992, the Jewish community has moved in a new direction.

Encyclopaedia Judaica Decennial Book 1973–82 painted, correctly for that time, a dim and stagnant picture of German Jewry and concluded that "religious and communal life is at a low level." In this regard there have recently been significant changes.

Demography. As of January 1983, Jewish communities in West Germany had 28,202 registered members, virtually unchanged for many years. In January 1993, the demographic flux, due to the Russian immigration, was so great that the Jewish Central Welfare Agency (Zentralwohlfahrtsstelle) for the second year in a row was unable to provide official figures. In February 1993, however Ignaz Bubis spoke of 11,000 new members over the past years. Using this figure, there would be approximately 40,000 Jews in Germany in 1993. Following the American demographer Sidney Goldstein's distinction of core and periphery groups, this group might be called the Jewish core group which includes converts to Judaism estimated in the many hundreds; it excludes, however, secular-minded Jews who chose not to register with the Jewish communities, one reason being to avoid paying state church tax. The core group figures also exclude considerable numbers of people of Jewish ancestry who may not necessarily identify as Jews. Around 1990, for example, there were about 500 Jews registered with the Jewish communities in East Germany; but from the over 3,500 pensions paid to "racially persecuted" victims of Fascism (Opfer des Faschismus), it can be concluded that well over 4,000 individuals of at least partial Jewish ancestry live in East Germany. Moreover, in light of a high intermarriage rate of at least 65% and up to 50% halakhically non-Jewish partners among recent Russian emigres and other non-Jewish spouses there may well be a Jewish periphery of over 55,000 persons, bringing the Jewish core and the Jewish periphery groups to a combined total of close to 100,000 individuals.

As far as religious and Jewish communal life are concerned, the Russian influx is of extraordinary significance especially for mid-sized communities. In Hamburg, for example, membership has increased by 28% in three years, from 1,344 to 1,724 members, whereas in Stuttgart, membership has almost doubled, from about 650 to 1,200 members. The Russian influx is of very great importance also for Berlin, the largest Jewish community, where membership has increased from about 6,000 to 9,000, and where, with the addition of the previous Soviet-Israeli "dropouts" who came to Berlin from the late 1970s onwards, Jews from former Soviet lands now constitute two-thirds of the entire community. The important question is whether and how the newcomers will be integrated into the communities and how they might develop their Jewish identity in Germany, especially vis-à-vis Israel and Germany. In light of their frequent intermarriage and estrangement from the religious culture, it will be important to see how they will be accommodated by a largely Orthodox rabbinate and a mostly conservative leadership not prone to experiments and new departures.

The classicist Rothschild Palais in Frankfort, home of the Jewish Museum (Courtesy Jüdisches Museum Frankfurt am Main)

Community Life. The other significant development is the appearance of organized Jewish life from the grassroots and outside the official Jewish community. This development dates back to 1982 when a younger generation of Jews, many of them involved in the 1968 student movement, spoke out against the Israeli invasion of Lebanon and found themselves severely censored by the official Jewish leadership. This evolved into small but vocal dissident groups, Jüdische Gruppen, active especially in Frankfurt and Berlin. Two significant periodicals have come out of this milieu, the scholarly *Babylon* and the popular, muckracking *Semit–Times*. Besides these groups, originally non–religious, some others, as in Hamburg, Cologne, and the Jüdischer Kulturverein in East Berlin, have developed distinct religious orientations. In Berlin as well Adass Jisroel, the famous neo–Orthodox Austrittsgemeinde, was reestablished in the late 1980s with the assistance of the East German authorities, especially Lothar de Maiziere, later the last prime minister of the GDR. Adass Jisroel was subjected to intensive obstruction by the large Gemeinde, especially under the late Heinz Galinski. Galinski objected in particular to Adass Jisroel receiving status as a Körperschaft des öffentlichen Rechts (public corporation), which undermined the Gemeinde's claim to be the sole representative of Berlin Jewry. The new Adass community has laid claim to, and partly occupies, its historic building in the expensive old center of Berlin; it has opened a restaurant and a *kasher* store. The large Berlin community followed suit with its second cafe in nearby Oranienburgerstrasse where the former Neue Synagoge, Berlin's largest, is currently being reconstructed as the Centrum Judaicum, a cultural center and museum.

Jewish leadership is undergoing profound changes, too. The old authoritarian and sometimes corrupt leadership, as in the conduct of Werner Nachmann, an unresolved case which allegedly involves funneling Holocaust victims' money to political parties, has virtually come to an end with the death of such leaders as Günter Singer of Hamburg and Heinz Galinski in Berlin. Ignatz Bubis, the new chair of the Central Council, is distinctly liberal and pluralist, and moreover has attained extraordinary moral stature in Germany. The position of German Jewry vis–à–vis world Jewry is nevertheless precarious. In 1990, for example, the first meeting of the World Jewish Congress in Germany in 40 years — the last one was in Frankfurt in 1950 — was boycotted by a number of delegates, and in the controversy over the Jewish cemetery in Hamburg–Ottensen in 1991–93, where construction was planned on the site of a cemetery desecrated by the Nazis and then sold by the Jewish community, an agreement was arrived at over the heads of the local community between rabbinical authorities in Israel, the company involved, and the city of Hamburg.

German–Jewish Relations. Since the early 1980s, there has been an ever stronger evolution of two countervailing trends in West Germany, and as is now apparent, in East Germany as well. The first one consists of pro–Jewish and sometimes pro–Israeli currents with often strongly idealizing and romanticizing elements; the other, in the wake of growing racism, of more virulent forms of anti–Semitism. In the past, surveys have shown that the right–wing potential — expressed, for example, in sympathy for the moderate right–wing Republikaner party (roughly equivalent to France's Front National) or by core anti–Semitic attitudes — has been at about 15%. In recent years, however, the Right has experienced clear gains. This has to do with the traumatic experience of unification for many East Germans, and Germany experiencing the highest growth in foreign population of any state in the European community and far larger absolute numbers of immigrants than Britain or France, former colonial powers. In 1992 alone, willingness to vote for a right–

Announcement for Jüdische Lebenswelten ("Patterns of Jewish Life in the World") Exhibition, Berlin, Jan.–April 1992

wing party jumped from 12% to 19% in the West, from 8% to 12% in the East; Gerhard Frey's Deutsche Volksunion (DVU), the right of the Republikaner, grew from 22,000 to 24,000 members.

Moreover, blatantly neo–Nazi groups, such as the Deutsche Alternative (AD) of the late Michael Kuhnen, grew from a few dozen members in the 1980s to over 1,000 in 1992, with a substantial growth in particular localities in the East. Neo–Nazi, skinhead–type activists increased concurrently from 1,000 to about 6,000 in early 1993, while the total right–wing extremist membership must be estimated at well over 40,000 members. With this growth and the crystallization of right–wing movements into ever more stable parties and other institutions, anti–Semitism, previously often underground, is now out in the open and acceptable again in some quarters. This goes hand in hand with desecrations of cemeteries, synagogues, monuments, and plaques commemorating the Holocaust (including, for example, the burning of a barracks at Sachsenhausen), with occasional attacks against individual Jews. These sentiments are often located in the lower and lower–middle class, as well as among some noteworthy neo–conservative and right–wing intellectuals. In order to contain the Right within its ranks, the governing CDU has largely downplayed the seriousness of these developments. While they represent a serious threat, as shown in the pogrom–like acts in Moellin, Rostock, or Hoyerswerda, the recent massive resistance against the Right is at least as noteworthy, especially the anniversary of Kristallnacht which is turning increasingly into a central day of anti–racist action, with hundreds of thousands in the large cities demonstrating against racism and the asylum policies of the government. Some in the Jewish community, notably Central Council Chair Ignatz Bubis, have been important voices in this regard.

Within this middle–class milieu, there has also been unprecedented interest in the Jewish world and its traditions. *Jüdische Lebenswelten*, the largest, most expensive exhibit of

Judaica ever, opened in January 1992 in Berlin and ran until April; during that time it attracted over 350,000 visitors. This Gropius–Bau Exhibit had to schedule additional hours to accommodate the unexpectedly high number of visitors. Its opening coincided with the dedication of a Holocaust commemorative center, the Wannsee Villa, where in January 1942 Nazi officials decided on the "final solution." A second, major exhibit on the Jüdische Kulturbund in Nazi Germany ran concurrently elsewhere in Berlin, and other important exhibits have been organized especially at the Jewish museum in Frankfurt which opened in this period. Several papers, particularly *Die Tageszeitung* in Berlin, write in great detail and knowledgeably about Jewish affairs, usually far out of proportion to other minorities in German society. The interest in Jewish Studies among Germans is very high, as seen in enrollments in the Judaica departments in German universities, and a large majority of students at the College for Jewish Studies in Heidelberg, now under the direction of Julius Carlebach, are also non–Jewish.

German–Israel Relations. Germany and Israel are locked into a continuing raucous, yet close, relationship full of disappointments about the other partner; and yet, neither partner could do without the other. In 1990, Germany gave Israel DM 63.6 million development aid in the form of loans and other contributions; while in 1981, imports into Israel amounted to DM 1724.4 million, by 1991 they had risen to DM 3036.4 million; Israeli exports to Germany grew, from DM 1,077.1 to DM 1,464.4 million. During the Gulf War, the debate between the "pacifists and bellicists" cut across all parties in Germany, and the Israeli public and politicians were angered about the neutral and sometimes anti–Israel stance taken by German politicians and the media, especially in light of the military hardware and poison gas installations given to Iraq by German firms. Partly because of the uproar caused by this, Germany promised Israel $670 million in aid; it supported the war effort with $5.5 billion and sent military goods and gas masks valued at $60 million. These monetary moves vis–à–vis Israel were complemented by a flurry of visits, including that of Foreign Minister Genscher, to Israel and meetings by Chancellor Kohl and others with major international Jewish organizations.

Apart from the Gulf War and despite all historical obstacles, contacts have been intensifying all along. Even before unification, for example, the speakers of both the West and East German parliaments, Rita Süssmuth and Sabine Bergmann–Pohl, in a demonstrative act both for international and domestic consumption, undertook to visit *Yad Vashem in Jerusalem, and the number of mutual political visits in general is steadily growing. Over the past ten years, both presidents, Chaim Herzog and Richard von Weizsäcker, have paid a major visit to each other's country, and there are

Israel Pres. Herzog reciting *kaddish* in Bergen–Belsen, 1987 (GPO, Jerusalem)

Reception in East Berlin for Jewish–Christian colloquium, from left to right: translator, East German Minister of Religions Klaus Gyzy, Rabbi Isaac Newman, Victor Goldbloom, and Coos Schoneveld (of the Int. Council of Christians and Jews), 1987 (Courtesy G. Wigoder, Jerusalem)

virtually annual visits by the foreign ministers as well as occasional visits by the prime minister of Israel to Germany and by the German chancellor to Israel.

Exchanges are also intensifying at the cultural and scientific levels. After the death of Herbert van Karajan (whose activities in World War II were regarded with suspicion) in 1989, the Berlin Philharmonic Orchestra could finally visit Israel the following year, and even Gottfried Wagner, great–grandson of Richard Wagner, was invited in 1990 to participate in lectures and discussions. Israeli academics receive study grants to Germany. Israeli artists, likewise, receive considerable attention in Germany; most noteworthy was the 1990 meeting of Israel and German authors in Mainz, with Aharon Meged, Yoram Kaniuk, Ruth Almog, and David Grossman. In 1991 Amos Oz received the prestigious award of the Frankfurt Book Fair.

Today, in an ironic twist and despite all ambivalences, bitterness, and mutual misunderstandings, the presence of Israel is greater in Germany then in any other European country, and Germany has become the major advocate of Israeli interests and concerns in Europe.

East Germany–German Democratic Republic. DEMOGRAPHY. In 1945, the eight Jewish communities in the Soviet–occupied zone numbered 3,100 members. Many of these emigrated shortly thereafter, but others, mostly German–Jewish communists or "anti–Fascists," returned from exile and, especially after the *Kielce pogroms in 1947, some Polish Jews made their way to what was to become the GDR.

Of the 2,600 Jews in the time of the Stalinist anti–Jewish campaigns in 1952–3, over 500 fled from East Germany ,and there has been a continuous, slow exodus ever since; according to the first offical statistics released in 1989 by the East German Federation of Jewish Communities, 370 Jews were members of these communities, including about 200 in East Berlin. Most of the remainder lived in Dresden, Leipzig, Erfurt, and Magdeburg. This count, however, ignores several thousand individuals of Jewish ancestry who chose not to register with the communities. With the influx of Russian Jews since 1989, membership has increased significantly, doubling or even tripling some of the communities and raising the total to well over 500; but here as in the West, there are no reliable figures at present.

HISTORY. From the late 1940s onwards, there were two separate Jewish milieux in the East: a more religious, partly Eastern Jewish, element that found its place in the communities, and a secular, German Jewish, highly assimilated element that identified strongly with a German state supposedly cleansed of Nazism. The years until 1952 were most favorable

Oranienburgerstrasse synagogue (Courtesy Geoffrey Wigoder, Jerusalem)

to religious, communist and "anti-fascist" Jews alike. This changed briefly and abruptly with the anti-Semitic campaign of 1952–3, less severe in the GDR than elsewhere in Eastern Europe, despite the temporary shutdown of all Jewish institutions and the sudden flight of the leaders of all communities. Subsequently, the personally favorable conditions of many Jews notwithstanding, the Jewish communities were kept on a tight leash and Jewish life, without rabbis and Jewish infrastructure, remained relatively stagnant. This changed slowly by the mid-1980s when the regime decided that in order to strengthen its acceptability and its ties to the West, especially to the United States, and at the same time reasserting its anti-fascist character, Jews in the GDR should attain greater visibility. With this new policy, a significant number of individuals, often children or grandchildren of Jewish communists, discovered their Jewish roots, and in East Berlin, some of these joined "We for Ourselves," a group of mostly marginally Jewish individuals who stood in an ambivalent relationship to the community; several of its members have since been accepted into the Jewish community. With the Honecker government's new attention to the Jews, a number of important initiatives became possible. East Berlin was able to appoint an American rabbi, Isaak Neuman, who was in office there for a short period from 1987 to 1988. At around the same time, the Weissensee Jewish cemetery, Europe's largest, was rehabilitated, and a descendant of one of the families that belonged to the former neo-Orthodox community Adass Jisroel, Mario Offenberg, negotiated with the GDR in order to reestablish this community in East Berlin. Moreover, the Neue Synagoge in Berlin, ruined in wartime, was now turned into a cultural center and archive, Centrum Judaicum, financed mostly through small private donations from East German individuals. The community in East Berlin reached the height of activity in 1988 and 1989, the two final years of its full independence: 1988 saw the first large observances of Kristallnacht, in a meeting of younger Jews from East and West Germany in East Berlin; an exhibit *Und lehret sie Gedächtnis* was shown there in the reconstructed Ephraim Palais, the residence of King Frederick II's Jewish financier; on May 10, 1989, for the first time, *Ha-Tikvah* was sung and a community membership meeting referred to Israel Independence Day. After the collapse of the Wall, numerous, especially Israel-oriented activities, intensified; on November 11, 1989, for the first time, a large Israeli flag was diplayed in West Berlin and a GDR-Israel Friendship society began to be formed. These independent Eastern initiatives came to a halt very soon, however. Very much in step with the rapid unification of East and West Germany, the Western Central Council of Jews and the West Berlin Jewish community took control of their Eastern counterparts, and on January 1, 1991, the East Berlin Jewish community ceased to exist.

Bibliography: R. Ostow, *Jews in Contemporary East Germany. The Children of Moses in the Land of Marx* (1989). [Y.M.B.]

GERY, a small group of ethnic Russians who adhere to Judaism. As a separate religious group the Gery emerged in the early 19th century from the sect of the Subbotniki (Sabbatarians) and in the late 19th–early 20th centuries adopted Orthodox Judaism. The Gery strive to observe all the commandments of the Jewish religion and to merge totally with Jews of Jewish ethnic origin, including by marriage. Many Gery sent their children to **yeshivot*. They lived scattered through many provinces of Russia (Astrakhan, Saratov, Tambov, Voronezh) on the Don, in the Kuban, in Northern Caucasus and Transcaucasus, and in Siberia where they were sent as exiles. They were persecuted by the Tsarist government and the Russian Orthodox Church which considered "Judaizing" sects especially dangerous. Cases are known of Jews serving the Gery as rabbis, ritual slaughterers, and teachers. Important roles in their religious education were played by an anonymous Jewish distiller from Tambov province who lived among the Gery from 1805 and in the 1880s by a Lithuanian Jew, David Teitelbaum. Many Gery families settled in the land of Israel in the 19th century, particulary in Galilee (Yesud ha-Ma'alah, Bet-Gan, etc.) and within two–three generations were completely assimilated into the surrounding Jewish populations. After the Russian proclamation of the freedom of religion in 1905, the Gery, now known as "sabbatarians of the Jewish faith," gained the right to legal recognition of their communities and the right to build synagogues (e.g., at Stantsiya Zima in Irkutsk province, Tiflis). Although the number of Gery has significantly declined, they still continue to exist (in Voronezh province, on the Don, in Northern Caucasus, and elsewhere).

In Israel the Gery are recognized as Jews both from the point of view of **Halakhah* and by the laws of the state. Many Gery in the Soviet Union are actively fighting for emigration to Israel and a number of Gery families left for Israel between 1971 and 1980. Twenty families from the village of Il'inka, Talov region, Voronezh province who moved to Israel in 1973–76 evidently came from a Gery background.

[S.J.E.R.]

GILBERT, MARTIN (1936–), British historian. Born in London, the son of a jeweler, Gilbert was educated at Highgate School and Magdalen College, Oxford. His earliest work concerned British foreign policy in the 1930s which in 1962 brought him into contact with Randolph Churchill. Between 1962 and 1968 he worked as research assistant to Randolph Churchill on the official biography of Sir Winston Churchill. From 1968, Martin Gilbert was the sole author of what became the most voluminous biography ever written, totalling over nine million words and running to six volumes plus an as yet unfinished set of companion volumes containing documents. Appointed a fellow of Merton College, Oxford, in 1962, Gilbert has been on an extended sabbatical since he engaged in the biography during which time he has also produced a series of major studies on the creation of the State of Israel, the Holocaust, and World War II. A tireless worker on behalf of Soviet Jewry, he was at one time writing over a dozen letters a day to refuseniks and became personally known to many Russian Jews during his frequent visits to the U.S.S.R. He has written on the situation of Soviet Jewry and authored a biography of Anatoly Shcharansky. In 1987 he was a non-governmental representative on the UN Commission on Human Rights (43rd session) in Geneva. Gilbert has undertaken a history of the 20th century to be completed in time for the new millennium. He is a highly popular author although some historians have criticized his preference for pure narrative history. He defends his choice to abstain from judgments and has said that "By what you select you make plain your views." Volume 6 of the Churchill biography, *Finest Hour, 1939–41*, won the 1983 Wolfson Award. In 1988 he was awarded the Ka-Zetnik Prize for Literature by Yad Vashem and the Holocaust Memorial Foundation. Since 1978, Gilbert has been a governor of the Hebrew University of Jerusalem. He has homes in London and Jerusalem.

In addition to the Churchill biography, completed in 1988, Martin Gilbert's publications include: *The Appeasers* [with Richard Gott] (1963); *The European Powers 1900–45* (1965); *The Roots of Appeasement* (1966); *Exile and Return: a study of the emergence of Jewish Statehood* (1978); *Churchill: a photographic portrait* (1974); *Churchill's Political Philosophy* (1981); *Auschwitz and the Allies* (1981); *The Jews of Hope: the plight of Soviet Jewry today* (1984); *Jerusalem, rebirth of a city* (1985); *Shcharansky: hero of our time* (1986); *The Holocaust; the Jewish tragedy* (1986); *Second World War* (1989); three edited collections of documents, 12 historical atlases including *Atlas of Jewish History* and *Atlas of the Holocaust.* [D.CE.]

GOLD, PHILIP (1936–), Canadian medical researcher. Gold was born in Montreal and studied at McGill University from which he holds both an M.D. degreee and a Ph.D. From 1973 he was professor of medicine at McGill with a joint appointment in the Department of Physiology from 1974. Among the other major academic and research appointments that he has held are: director of the McGill Cancer Center, director of the McGill Clinic and physician-in-chief of the Montreal General Hospital, and chairman of McGill's Department of Medicine.

Gold is widely known for his development of an important diagnostic test for cancer; his work won him international renown and brought him numerous awards. He is a Companion of the Order of Canada and a Fellow of the Royal Society of Canada.

In his professional work Gold has written innumerable scientific papers and is co-editor of *Clinical Immunology.* He served as president of the Canadian Society of Immunology from 1975 to 1977. [H.M.W.]

GOLDSTEIN, JOSEPH LEONARD (1940–), U.S. medical geneticist and Nobel Prize laureate. Born in Sumter, South Carolina, Goldstein received his medical degree from Southwestern Medical School of the University of Texas at Dallas in 1966. He then did his internship and residency at Massachusetts General Hospital in Boston where he became acquainted with his collaborator and corecipient of the Nobel Prize, Michael Brown. From Massachusetts General he proceeded to the National Heart Institute of the National Institutes of Health at Bethesda, Maryland, where he was a clinical associate in the biochemical genetics laboratory. In 1972 he became a faculty member at the University of Texas in Dallas where he could work with Dr. Brown who had moved there the precious year.

Dr. Michael S. Brown (left) and Dr. Joseph L. Goldstein, corecipients of the 1985 Nobel Prize in medicine (Courtesy University of Texas Health Center, Dallas)

Goldstein and Brown were awarded the 1985 Nobel Prize for medicine or physiology for their research into the body's mechanisms for aborbing cholestrol and for making a significant contribution towards understanding of a genetic defect which blocks the absorption of cholestrol from the bloodstream, familial hypercholestrolemia. [ED.]

GORDIMER, NADINE (see **7**:786). Gordimer was the recipient of the Nobel Prize for literature in 1991.

GORNICK, VIVIAN (1935–), U.S. author, a product of New York city's vibrant, multi-ethnic, and often socialist urban environment, Gornick attended City College and received her Master's Degree from New York University. A veteran journalist, she has written for the *Village Voice*, the *Atlantic Monthly*, the *Washington Post, The Nation, Ms* magazine, and the *New York Times Book Review* and *Sunday Magazine.* She has also taught at University of Colorado and Pennsylvania State University.

Gornick rose to prominence in the early 1970s as one of the most articulate of the feminist writers. Her essay "Woman as Outsider" in *Women in Sexist Society: Studies in Power and Powerlessness* (1971), which she edited, paints an unflattering portrait of women's role "in the fierce unjoyousness of Hebraism." Later books explored a variety of subjects, including *In Search of Ali Mahmoud: An American Woman in Egypt* (1973); *The Romance of American Communism* (1977); *Essays in Feminism* (1978). *Women in Science: Recovering the Life Within* (1983), and the novel/memoir *Fierce Attachments* (1987). [S.B.F.]

GOULD, MILTON S. (1909–), U.S. lawyer. Born in New York City, Gould graduated from Cornell University with a B.A. degree in 1930 and a law degree in 1933. From 1935 to 1937 he served under Federal Judge Samuel H. Kaufman as special attorney and special assistant in the U.S. Department of Justice. He was in private practice for years with the firm Kaufman, Weitzner & Celler; then in 1964 he formed the firm Shea & Gould, in which he is a senior partner. In the 1930s he was legislative adviser to the Commissioner of Immigration and Naturalization and to the Assistant Attorney General in charge of the criminal division. In his private practice he specialized in corporate litigation arising under the Securities Exchange Act of 1934, the Investment Company Act of 1940, and the Public Utilities Holding Company Act. He has also been active in litigation for utility companies. Gould has also participated in the prosecution and defense of criminal cases in the Federal courts. He especially attracted public notice internationally for his representation of Gen. Ariel Sharon who sued Time, Inc., for libel, arising out of the Israeli action in Lebanon in the early 1980s, and in which the jury's finding was that Sharon had in fact been libeled, although no money damages were awarded.

Gould served as an adjunct professor at Cornell Law School and at New York Law School, and lectured at the law school of the Hebrew University. He was active for the United Jewish Appeal. He was the author of two books: *The Witness Who Spoke With God* (1979) and *A Cast of Hawks* (1985). [M.R.K.]

Herman Graebe receiving Righteous Gentile award from Dr. Kubovy (standing) at a ceremony in Yad Vashem (Courtesy Yad Vashem, Jerusalem)

***GRAEBE, HERMANN FRIEDRICH** (1900–1986), non-Jew who saved Jews during the Holocaust. A native of Solingen, Germany, Graebe worked for the construction company, Jung. At one point he joined the Nazi party, but after speaking out against them, he was sentenced to a short term in prison. The Jung company sent Graebe to Zdolbunov, Volhynia, in October 1941. There he was to be responsible for their undertakings for the German civil administration.

The Jung company employed thousands of Jews and Graebe did his best to ensure they were treated reasonably. In November 1941 and again in July 1942, he safeguarded his Jewish workers from being sent to their death, through contacts with the SD in Rovno. Sensing that the Jews who worked in the Jung head office in Zdolbunov were in danger, Graebe provided them with papers which represented them as Aryans and transferred them to Poltava. Ostensibly they were to work for Jung there, but in fact Graebe had moved them without the company's knowledge and supported them himself. In the fall, Graebe went to Dubno, where he saved the lives of several dozen Jews during the final *Aktion*. He described this incident at the Nuremberg Trial. After the trial, he emigrated to the United States. In 1966 he was officially recognized by *Yad Vashem for his courageous deeds.

[RO.ROZ.]

GREECE (see **7**:687; **Dc./17**:279). The time period under review can be characterized by a diplomatic rapprochement between Greece and Israel, and the beginning of an active historical commemoration of the Judeo-Greek and the Sephardi heritages in Greece. Greek Jewry has aged, but a new generation of youth is being educated. Assimilation has taken a great toll and the legalization of civil marriages by the Papandreou government at the beginning of the 1980s greatly accelerated the process. Since then, most marriages are mixed and conducted outside of the synagogue, and unlike the past, there is no compelling need for the female to convert to Judaism. Jewish communities have dwindled due to deaths in places such as Corfu, and Ioanina, while elsewhere — as in Didamotiko, Zakynthos, and Cavalla — deaths of influential leaders and the elderly have brought Jewish commmunal life to an end. During the Lebanon War, Greek society was very critical of Israel and hostile to Israeli tourists and athletes. The press and the media vociferously condemned Israel for its invasion into Lebanon, the course of the war, the bombing of civilian targets, and its treatment of Palestinian refugees in Lebanon. Greek Jewry was very uncomfortable during this period. Since then, sporadic unrelated anti-Semitic incidents have periodically continued to occur.

The main event of the 1980s was the culmination of the process lasting throughout most of the decade in preparing the terms and the establishment of full *de jure* diplomatic relations between Greece and Israel, which was technically achieved on May 21, 1990. With the election of the Socialist Pasok Party in 1982 under the leadership of Andreas Papandreou, gradual preparations were made for eventual full diplomatic relations between Greece and Israel. Most of the process was conducted by the Socialist Papandreou government and the Likkud government (except for a two-year Israeli Labor rule in the mid-1980s, and a Greek centrist Nea Demokratia political turnover at the end of the process). Early official contact between the two nations resulted from visits of opposition parliamentarian Shulamit Aloni and Foreign Minister Yiẓhak Shamir to Greece and the Jerusalem visit of Greek Foreign Minister Karolas Papoulias, who was noted for his intervention in attempting to release Israeli prisoners of war from Lebanon and occupied Syrian areas. In Athens, the Israeli consul, Moshe Gilboa, succeeded in bridging the technical problems, and when the moderate Nea Demokratia Party came into power in 1989 and agreed to institute full diplomatic relations with Israel, he was elevated to the position of Israel's first ambassador to Greece. In turn, Greece sent Ambassador Constantinos Tsokos to Tel Aviv, as their first ambassador to Israel. In November 1991, Greek Prime Minister Constantinos Mitsotakis paid an official State visit to Israel.

Moshe Gilboa also prepared the way for the exit of more than 300 Albanian Jews, most of whom are of Greek Ioaniote origin, to immigrate to Israel.

Until 1985, *Yad Vashem had only recognized 42 Greeks as Righteous Gentiles during the Holocaust. By 1993, some 120 were recognized and another 300 were in the process of being recommended. Noteworthy are the Salonikan lawyer Dimitri Spiliakos, who saved more than 30 Jews by taking them out of the Salonikan ghetto and bringing them to Italian

Nikos Stavroulakis, director of the Jewish Museum, at work on conservation of a 19th-century "Aleph" birth amulet, from Ioannina (Courtesy the Jewish Museum of Greece; photo Timothy DeVinney)

diplomats, who sent them on Italian military trains to the less dangerous Italian zone of southern Greece in Athens; Alexandros Kallodopoulos, who recruited dozens of Salonikan youth and accompanied them to the leftist E.L.A.S.-E.A.M. partisan movement in the mountains; Sotiris Papastratis, who coordinated illegal immigration activities for the latter movement and assisted some 800 Greek Jews in their escape from Athens to the Evia Peninsula, where they eventually found transport to Turkey in fishing boats arranged by the Mosad le-Aliyah Bet (the Palestinian Jews organization to provide "illegal" immigration); and Salahattin Ulkumen, who as a 29-year-old Turkish consul in Rhodes, risked his life by saving some 46 local Jews, most of whom were not Turkish subjects. In October 1992, at the dedication of Yad Vashem's Valley of the Communities, Greek Jewry was represented with stones for the Jewish communities of Salonika and Rhodes, and one general stone with the names of the other communities from which Greek Jews were annihilated by the Germans in the Holocaust. Yad Vashem is establishing a room in their archive in memory of the Jewish community of Rhodes, which was annihilated in the Holocaust. In the past several years at Yad Vashem, Bracha Rivlin has been editing *Pinkas Kehillot Yavan*, a memorial volume on the history of the Jewish communities of Greece before their members were executed in the Nazi extermination camps in World War II, with the assistance of the historians Yitzchak Kerem and Leah Bornstein-Makovetsky. The Holocaust Museum of Kibbutz Loḥamei ha-Gettaot is planning a permanent exhibition on Salonikan Jewry, the largest Jewish community of Greece annihilated in the Holocaust.

The gem of Greek Jewry has been the Jewish Museum founded in 1979 by the art historian Nikos Stavroulakis. He, together with the assistance of assistant Ida Mordoh, the photographer Timothy DeVinney, a devoted staff of volunteers, and the United States-based Friends of the Jewish Museum of Greece, have produced an official established museum. After being housed on Amalias Street in Athens for several years, a new building purchased on Nikis Street is being renovated as the permanent site of the museum. The museum has benefited from inheriting artifacts of Thracian Jewry confiscated in World War II, which were returned by the Bulgarian government in the late 1980s, and the Salonikan German deportation registration lists of the local Jewish population during the Holocaust. Under the auspices of the museum, Stavrolakis has published numerous books and pamphlets, including works on Jewish Ottoman dress, a cookbook, historical essays, and a guide to Greek Jewish sites. Stavrolakis is also currently planning to restore the remaining neglected synagogue of Chania, Crete, and turn it into a Jewish museum.

Greek Jewry, in particular in Athens, has in recent years lost many of its elderly dynamic leaders: including Joseph Lovinger, president of the Board of Jewish Communities in Greece (KIS); the lawyer Daniel Alhanati, the founder of KIS and former local Jewish National Fund representative; former Athenian Jewish community leader Marco Osmos; and from Ioannina, the Jewish scholar Yosef Matsas. Other deaths connected to the Greek-Jewish community were; the Salonikan Alberto Lavi of Tel Aviv, who played a heroic role in the Warsaw Ghetto in the Holocaust: the Salonikan-raised Auschwitz women's orchestra member, Lili Asael, of New York, whose renown included teaching the piano to the concert pianist Murray Perahia; Rae Dalven, researcher into Judeo-Greek literature (and editor of that department in the *Encyclopaedia Judaica*); and scholars: Miriam Movitch (Kibbutz Loḥamei Hagettaot), Enrique Saporta y Beja (Paris), Georgos Zogratakis (Salonika), Yaakov Tzur (Jerusalem), author Georgos Ioannou (Athens), and Shlomo

Taking out the Torah at Greek Jewish summer camp, 1987 (Rabbi Tzvi Marx and Yitzḥak Kerem)

Reuvain — Ladino poet, Salonikan Betar leader in the 1930s, and founding Tel Aviv president of the Israeli-Greek Friendship League. The doctors Albert Menasche and Marco Nahon, who wrote valuable memoirs of their Auschwitz-Birkenau experiences, passed away in U.S.A. in 1991–2.

In Athens a new middle-aged Jewish leadership under the party list of Solon Ben-Ardot, local travel agent and Maccabi organizer, has been elected to be a coalition partner in the Athenian Jewish communal leadership. Due to transportation problems in the vast Athenian metropolis and outer socio-geographic Jewish mobility, enrollment in the Jewish elementary school has decreased greatly. The Jewish summer camp in Loutraki, financed and run by the Salonikan Jewish community, serving all the Jewish youth of Greece, increased its enrollment significantly in the latter half of the 1980s.

Some changes were made among the religious leaders of Greek Jewry. In the absence of a rabbi in Salonika for several years, after Veria-born Rabbi Shabetai Azaria passed away, the retired scrapyard owner and pre-World War II Salonikan ordained rabbi, Moshe Halegua, became a functioning rabbi in the late 1980s. Recently a Moroccan Israeli rabbi has been hired in the community. In Trikala, native-born Rabbi Elie Shabetai left his position in Athens as clerk at KIS and returned to function as communal rabbi. The Trikala Jewish community has also been strengthened by a young cantor from Istanbul. In Corfu, the few remaining youth have benefited from a resident Hebrew teacher at the beginning of the 1990s.

Several anti-Semitic events have passed in the 1980s with little publicity and repercussions. During the Lebanon War, the doors of the Corfiote synagogue were damaged. The local Athenian and KIS Jewish leadership hesitated to react to the existence of Jimmy's Coin and Stamp Store on Stadiou Street, which sold numerous Nazi emblems and knives and enjoyed 24-hour police protection, and to some 13 stores distributing neo-Nazi propaganda, denying the existence of the Holocaust. In the 1989 Greek election campaign, the campaign staff of Prime Minister Papandreou maliciously produced a false picture of opposition leader Mitsotakis arm in arm with two Nazi soldiers, when the latter was an officer in Crete in the resistance forces to the Germans, and the event was interpreted negatively at the time by the Israeli newspaper *Haaretz*. In Larissa, the Holocaust martyrs' memorial has been defaced several times with anti-Semitic graffiti. In 1992, a Princeton University computer technician detected the use of Neo-Nazi anti-Semitic propaganda through electronic mail at Aristotle University in Salonika.

On an emotional level, in the 1980s Greek society shared identification with Jewish suffering in the Holocaust. Much attention has been given in the press, in publications, and in public lectures in Greece to the role of Greek Jewish soldiers fighting against the invading Italian army from Albania in 1940 and the heroic role of Colonel Mordechai Frizis who died in battle. Other signs of official Greek recognition of the suffering of Greek Jews in the Holocaust, was the laying of a wreath by Prime Minister Andreas Papandreou for Greek Jewry at Auschwitz in November 1984, and the publicity of the ceremony for the deceased controversial Salonikan Rabbi Zvi Koretz, who died of typhus shortly following the liberation after suffering as a prisoner in Bergen-Belsen, at his grave in Trebitz (in former East Germany).

In the 1980s, 40 years after the Holocaust, the primarily Sephardi survivors of Greece — like other Jewish survivors — have begun to speak of their World War II experiences. By the beginning of the 1990s several books of Greek Jewish survivor testimonies were published: the Salonikans Yaakov Handeli and Moshe Aelion (Israel), Beri Nahmias (b. Castoria) of Athens, and the Rhodian Rebecca Levy (Los Angeles). Currently the Salonikan Auschwitz violinist Jacques Strumza (Jerusalem), Ioaniote Solomon Cohen (Haifa), and Daniel Haguel (Seattle) are preparing their testimonies for publication. In 1985, "Dor Hemshech," the second generation of Greek Jewish Holocaust survivors in Tel Aviv, was founded by the student of Sephardi literature Shmuel Raphael, the Judeo-Spanish poet Margalit Mattiyahu, and other Israeli-born descendants of Greek-Jewish concentration camp survivors. It publishes a pamphlet of essays on Greek Jewry and the Holocaust each year on Holocaust Remembrance Day.

The Salonikan Jewish community has been active in preserving its rich history. Local Jewish community historian Albertos Nar established a study center of Salonikan Jewry in 1985. Local historian Rena Molho and other young Salonikan Jews founded the Society for the Study of the Jews of Greece, and organized an academic conference in fall 1991. A year later the local Jewish community, the Center for Balkan Studies, and the Modern Greek History Department of Aristotle University, sponsored a six-day international interdisciplinary academic conference of over 50 scholars on the theme "The Jewish Communities of Southeastern Europe, from the Fifteenth Century to the End of World War II," focusing on Greek Jewry, but also bringing from abroad scholars on Albanian and Yugoslavian Jewry. While the Soviet Union was crumbling at the beginning of the 1990s, Soviet-captured German archives from World War II, which contained Jewish communal documents confiscated by the Germans in Salonika, were located in Moscow and lengthy negotiations are still being conducted in order to duplicate the material and bring it to Israel. Research on Cairo *Genizah* documents housed at the library of Cambridge University in England has also recently uncovered rare material connected to Greek-speaking Jews, Greek Jewry, and post-Spanish expulsion Sephardi Jewry. Historian Yitzchak Kerem uncovered a rare photo collection of the Bulgarian deportation of Jews of Serbian Macedonia and Greek Thrace in World War II to Treblinka.

In England, at Cambridge Univeristy, Prof. Nicholas de Lange and Judith Humphrey established the *Bulletin of Judeo-Greek Studies* to coordinate international research into subjects related to the study of Greek Jewry. In Israel, David Recanati finished editing the second volume of the monumental *Zikhron Saloniki* ("Salonika Memoir"), published in 1986. Also in Israel, Yitzchak Kerem and academic Jewish computer network and expert Avrum Goodblatt have established the Sephardic Electronic Archive, a computer network for the international academic and lay community connected to Sephardi studies and affairs, which is computerizing the numerous archival collections of Sephardi Jewry to provide a Sephardi data bank and genealogical Sephardi tracing service, create an ongoing bibliography on Sephardi Jewry, sponsor a computerized academic Sephardi journal and publish a monthly bulletin of Sephardi events and studies throughout the globe.

Greek Jewry has received growing exposure through the arts. Films on Greek Jewish themes in the 1980s and early 1990s include *Auschwitz-Saloniki* (Gidon Grief and Israeli Educational TV), *Ioannina, Athens, Jerusalem* (Yitzchak Kerem, Israeli Television, & Nehora Film Society), *Because of that War* (Yehuda Polikar, Gilad, and directed by Orna Niv), *Salonique Ville Du Souvenir, Ville De L'Oubli* (Alain Penso), and *Ottoman Salonica* (Robert Bedford, Dr. Joe Halio, and Stuart Fishelman). The following photo exhibitions were produced: "Scattered Lights, The Dying Jewish Communities of Rural Greece" (Joshua Plaut), "Historical Photographs of Greek Jewry" (Yitzchak Kerem), and "Faces and Facets: The Jews of Greece" (Morris Camhi). As part of the Sepharad '92 quincentennial activities in Salonika, Israeli Ottoman historian Ilan Carmi and the Salonikan Jewish community organized an exhibition on Salonikan and Cavallan Jewry, and an international Judeo-Spanish song concert was organized bringing guest artists from Turkey, Germany, Israel, Bulgaria, Austria, Italy, and Athens.

Numerous public scandals connected to Greek Jewry have broken out in the past years. During the 1985–86 Austrian presidential election campaign, former UN secretary Kurt Waldheim was accused of covering up his World War II Wehrmacht activities in Yugoslavia and Greece, which included his service as an intelligence officer based at Arsakli, outside of Salonika, and allegations were raised accusing him of connections to the deportations of the Jews of Ioannina, Crete, Corfu, and Rhodes. Greek and Israeli historians participated in an international committee of scholars formed by the Austrian government to review charges against Waldheim, and the British historian of Greece in World War II, Mark Mazower, organized a filmed staged public trial of Waldheim under the auspices of the BBC. The Salonikan Buna (Auschwitz III) champion boxer Jacko Razon is still battling a 1990 27-million-dollar lawsuit in Los Angeles courts against his former best friend and boxing apprentice Salomon Arouch, producer Arnold Koppelson, and Epic and Nova film companies for allegedly stealing his identity in the film *Triumph of the Spirit*. The problem of a group of 700 Israeli Greek Holocaust survivors, who never received reparations from Germany, was aired on Israeli TV. The Israel government began to grant some of the survivors indemnities, but the Claims Conference, despite promises in writing in 1980 by its president Nahum Goldmann, has still not recognized this large group of Holocaust survivors as eligible for German reparations. Rhodian Jews living in the U.S.A. who lost their Italian citizenship or Yugoslavian Jews residing in Israel who were deported from Greece have also never been recognized by their governments as eligible for reparations. Rhodian Jewish survivors, dispersed throughout the Americas, Africa, Europe, and Israel, who retained Italian citizenship, only received reparations by way of the Italian government in 1975.

Prominent Greek Jews include filmmaker and author Nestoros Matsas, radio interviewer Maria Rezan, radio music commentator and entertainer Jak Menachem, play director Albert Ashkenazi, Post Office Director-General Moisis Kostantini, former Energy Ministry Director-General Raphael Moissis, retired brigadier-general Marcos Moustakis, and retired military colonels Edgar Allalouf and Doctor Errikos Levi.

Salonikan Jewish community president Leon Benmaior represented the community in fall 1991 when Spanish Prince Felipe awarded the annual prestigious Principe de Asturia a la Concordia prize to Yugoslavian-born Haham Solomon

Gaon in the name of the Sephardi communities of the world.

The Jews of Rhodes in the Americas, Belgium, and Ashdod, Israel, under the inspiration of Hillel Franco of New York founded the Jewish Community of Rhodes Heritage Foundation, Inc., which raised money to preserve the synagogue and the deteriorating Jewish cemetery in Rhodes, and organized a reunion of Rhodian Jewry, throughout the world, in Rhodes and Israel in the latter part of July 1991.

[YI.K.]

GREEK LITERATURE, MODERN (7:898). Frequent references are to be found in modern Greek literature to the Jewish people in general and more specifically to Greek Jews and the Holocaust. A number of the authors concerned emanate from or had close connections with Thessaloniki (Salonika) or Ioannina with their famed Jewish communities. The works are often inspired by personal experiences based on relations with Jewish friends annihilated in the Holocaust. Many of these appeared in the 1960s with the stimulation of public interest through the trial of the Nazi Dr. Merten in Greece and the *Eichmann trial in Israel.

Traditional Greek language and literature created a mass of negative stereotypes of the Jew, as found in proverbs, folksongs, and the shadow-theater. The figure of the Jew in this pre-modern literature has often no relation to reality. This has often passed into modern works. In the words of the outstanding writer Yiorgos Ioannou in 1979, "The still unstable modern Greek society does not even have the time and strength to collect its energy to combat the poisonous luxury of anti-Semitism and racial discrimination."

However, other voices were heard also in the past. The national poet of Greece, Dionysios Solomos (1798–1857), published in 1822 a series of sonnets inspired by the Bible. In one of these he compared the revolutionary Greek nation to Zion reborn. The poet K. P. Kavafi (1863–1933) wrote two poems about the Jews of the Hellenistic period. In the poem "About the Jew — 50 BCE," his protagonist is the imaginary Ianthis Antoniou who desires that "there always will be Jews, holy Jews." The second poem relates to Alexander Yannai and his wife, Hellenizing rulers of the Jewish state at the end of the Hasmonean era. Kostas Palamas (1852–1943) extravagantly praised the Zionist movement and was deeply impressed by Max Nordau. Alexander Papadiamantis (1851–1911) started from negative positions but revised his views, notably in his article "The Repercussion of Sense" where he reacted to the 1891 pogrom of the Jews in Corfu.

Of all the later writers, pride of place goes to Nikos Kazantakis (1883–1957) who relates in his autobiography *Relation to Greco* that he persuaded his father to permit him to study Hebrew with the rabbi of Irakleon but was prevented due to the prejudices of the rest of his family. He also presents impressions of travelers from Jerusalem and Sinai who expound on the virtues of the Jewish people. In the memoirs of his mature age, he speaks of his bond with the German Jew, Rachel Lipstein, which is also indirectly reflected in his novels *Christ Recrucified* and *Captain Michael*.

Of later works, mention should be made of the fictional biography by M. Karagatsi (1908–1960) *King Laskos*, whose hero is in charge of a boatload of Jewish immigrants trying to beat the British blockade of Palestine, and the novel *Sergio and Bacchante* which pays tribute to the role of Jews in modern civilization. Ilia Venezi (1904–1973) wrote travel impressions from modern Israel as well as stories against the background of the 1948 Arab-Israel War. Yianni Berati (1904–1968) in his book *The Wide River* writes of the heroism of the Greek Jewish soldiers in the Greco-Italian War of 1940. Dimitri Yatha (1907–1979), the leading theatrical author, writer, and humorist, describes his recollections of a Jewish family of bankers in his *The Land of the Sea*. Strati Mirivili (1892–1963) also refers to Jewish soldiers in the anti-war chronicle *Life in a Grave*. Kosma Politi (1893–1974) preserved aspects of the Jewish community of Izmir in his book *To a Western European Pilgrim*. Dimitri Hatzi (1914–1981) described the Jewish community of Ionina in his story "Shabetai Kabilli" in his book *The End of our Small City*, and Toli Kazantzi in his narrations sketches the coexistence of Greeks and Jews in pre-War Salonika.

A body of poetic work has been inspired by the Holocaust. Among the poets mention should be made of Manoli Anagnostaki (b. 1925), Taki Barvitsioti (b. 1916), Nino Kokkalidou-Nahmia (b. 1922), I. A. Nikolaidi (b. 1936), Marino Charalambous (b. 1937), Dino Christianopoulo (b. 1931), Yiorgos Ioannou (1927–1985), G. Th. Vafopoulou (b. 1903), the surrealistic Niko Engonopoulo (1910–1986), George Kaftantzi (b. 1920), and Prodromo Markoglou (b. 1935), and Kimona Tzalla (1917–1988). Outstanding is the poem of Zoe Karelli (b. 1901) "Israel," which harks back to the sufferings of the Jews in biblical times and links them with the tragic fate of the Jews of Salonika. She seeks the causes of anti-Semitism and of the Holocaust, showing the common element throughout history, and also shows how Jews always maintained a discreet strength in their resistance to persecutions.

Among prose writers who have been affected by the Holocaust are G. Th. Vafopoulouy in his *Pages of Autobiographies*; Ilia Venezi (1904–1973) in the fictionalized biography *Archbishop Damaskinos*; the diary of Iakavou Kampanelli (b. 1922) *Mauthausen*; the tender novel *Tziokonta* of Nikou Kokantzi (b. 1927); Nikou Bakala (b. 1927) in his novel *The Big Square* and works by Vasili Vasilikou (b. 1934), Georgou Theotoka (1905–1966), Yianni Lambrinou (1909–1949), Nestoria Matsa (b. 1932), Kostoulas Mitropoulou (b. 1940), I. M. Papagiotopoulou (1901–1981), Yianni Starki (1919–1987), and Friksou Tzioba (b. 1919).

The major author who wrote of the Holocaust of Salonika Jewry is Yiorgos Ioannou. In his poems "Iliotropia" (1954) and "The Thousand Trees" (1963), he describes the last night of a Jewish family who lived in a nearby apartment and of his grief over their unbelievable disappearance. His book *For the Honor* (1964) describes the leveling of the old Jewish cemetery of Salonika. In *The Sarcophagus* (1971), *Our Own Blood* (1978) and *The Capital of the Refugees* (1984), he wonders at the persecution of the Jews in his neighborhood which culminated in the pillage of their homes and the testimony of his own father, a railroad worker, who experienced at first hand the songs sung on the journeys to the death camps from inside the sealed animal wagons.

All these works face the Jews with reverence and treat their suffering with the utmost respect and sympathy, emanating from the recognition of a longtime harmonious symbiosis.

[AL.NAR]

GREENBERG, MOSHE (1928–), biblical scholar. Greenberg was born in Philadelphia, where he obtained his Ph.D. in Oriental Studies from the University of Pennsylvania in 1956. He received his rabbinical training at the Jewish Theological Seminary of America from which he also has a master's degree in Hebrew Literature.

He held various academic appointments at the University of Pennsylvania from 1954 to 1970, from assistant professor of Hebrew and Semitic languages and literature.

He became professor of Bible at the Hebrew University of Jerusalem in 1970. From 1971 to 1981 he served as academic advisor for Bible curriculum at the Israel Ministry of Education and Culture where he endeavored to place the study of Bible in the school system into a Jewish context.

Greenberg's grammar of Biblical Hebrew is widely used.

In *The Religion of Israel* (1971) he made the work of Bible scholar Yehezkel *Kaufmann accessible to the international community in his one-volume abridgment and English translation of Kaufmann's monumental work. His biblical commentaries, notably on Exodus (*Understanding Exodus*, 1969) and Ezekiel (Anchor Bible, 1983) have emphasized a holistic approach to the text, and represent a unique contribution to understanding the Bible within the context of critical biblical context. He has sought to understand the value system underlying biblical literature and its relationship both to the Ancient Near East and Jewish thought.

Greenberg served as the divisional editor (law and society in the Bible) for the *Encyclopaedia Judaica*, 1968–71, and was a member of the Bible translation committee for the Jewish Publication Society of America (1966–82).

From 1982 he was a member of the academic council of the Open University of Israel and from 1985 served as editor for a commentary series entitled *Bible for Israel.*

His other writings include *The Hab/piru* (1955) and *On the Bible and Judaism: A Collection of Writings* (Hebrew; 1985).

[E.HO.]

GREENFIELD, JONAS CARL (1926–), Bible scholar, specializing in the languages and culture of the Ancient Near East. Born in New York, he received his early education from both public school and *yeshivot.* Greenfield showed early interest in Semitic Near Eastern Languages, learning both Arabic and Aramaic in his youth. He received his bachelor's degree from CCNY in English literature in 1949. In that

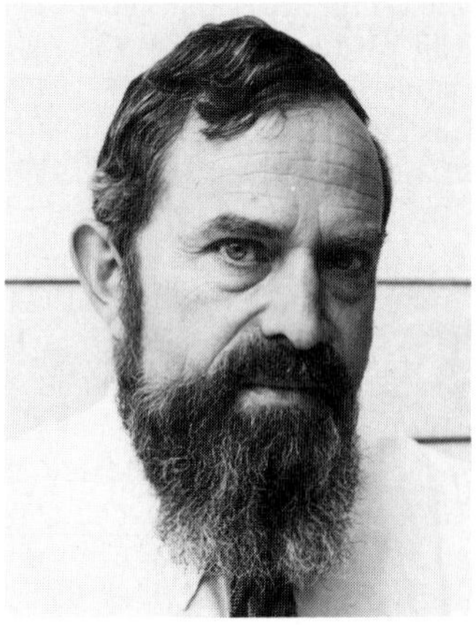

Jonas Carl Greenfield (Courtesy Hebrew University of Jerusalem, Dept. of Information and Public Affairs)

same year he was ordained rabbi at Metivta Torah Vadaath. He received his doctorate from Yale University (1956) for his thesis "The Lexical Status of Mishnaic Hebrew."

Starting his teaching career in 1954 as instructor in Semitics at Brandeis University, he became assistant and later associate professor of Semitics at the University of California at Los Angeles (1956–65) and then professor of Semitics at the University of California at Berkeley (1965–71).

In 1971 Greenfield moved to Jerusalem where he is professor of Ancient Semitic languages at the Hebrew University. He also taught during the 1970s and early 1980s at Bar-Ilan University.

His interests within the field of Ancient Semitic languages are diverse. He is a known authority on comparative Semitic philology, Aramaic dialectology and lexicography, Ugaritic language and literature, Northwest Semitic epigraphy, and Canaanite and Aramaic religion, and he is also interested in the social history of the period, legal matters, and Iranian studies.

He is a member of the publication supervisory committee for the Dead Sea Scrolls and is engaged in the publication of the papyri from Naḥal Ḥever and Naḥal Ẓe'elim.

Since 1967 Greenfield has been editor of the *Israel Exploration Journal*, associate editor of the *bulletin of the American School of Oriental Research.* He is a former member of the editorial committee of the Jewish Publication society of America and was on the committee for the new JPS translation of the Hagiographia.

His works include *Jews of Elephantine and Arameans of Syene* (with B. Porter, 1974); and *The Bisiton Inscription* (with B. Porter, 1982/3). [E.HO.]

GRINSPUN, BERNARDO (1926–), Argentinian economist and statesman, specializing in international economic and foreign debt. He belongs to the outstanding Argentinian circle of economists of our time (Aldo Ferrer, Guido Di Tella, etc.) and was linked with the group that controlled economic affairs during the former Radical party's government of President Illia (1963–66) on whose staff Grinspun held the post of secretary of commerce. He is also connected with the enterprise group which led the Federation Economica de Buenos Aires and specially the medium-size entrepreneurs. When democratic rule was restored to Argentina in 1983, Grinspun was appointed minister of finance in the cabinet of President Raul Alfonsin, in which capacity he sought to extract the country from the serious economic plight in which it had been left by the military junta.

[JO.NA./N.H.-D.NA.]

GROSSMAN, DAVID (1954–), Israeli writer. Born in Jerusalem Grossman studied philosophy and theater at the Hebrew University, receiving his B.A. in 1979. From a young age, he worked for the Israel radio becoming a news editor and broadcaster until his left-wing political views led to a severance of his employment.

Grossman achieved international fame as one of the leading Israeli writers of his generation. His novel *Smile of the Lamb* (1983) already shows his preoccupation with the Israel-Palestinian problem, with the conquered psychologically overcoming the conqueror. His second novel, *See Under: Love* (1986; translated into several languages) is set during and immediately after the period of the Holocaust and centers on the struggle of the individual against meaninglessness. It includes the internal monologue of an anguished child Holocaust survivor, the encapsulation of the life of a dead child in the form of an encyclopedia, and a section about the Polish-Jewish author Bruno Schulz. His *The Yellow Wind* (1987; translated into 12 languages and serialized in the *New Yorker*) collects his impressions from the West Bank, written before the *intifada*, predicts the dehumanization which could only deteriorate. In 1991 he published a book based on the Gulf War.

Grossman has also written a series of popular children's books based on a character Ittamar (the name of his son).

[ED.]

GUREVICH, MIKHAIL IOSIFOVICH (1893–1976), Soviet aviation constructor. Gurevich was born in 1893 in the village of Rubanshchina which is in today's Kursk province. He graduated from the airplane construction faculty of the Kharkov Technological Institute in 1925. In 1929 he began working in the aviation industry and from 1938 to 1957 held the rank of deputy chief constructor and from 1957–1964 of chief constructor. He received the degree doctor of technological sciences in 1964. Together with Ar. I. Mikoyan in 1940 he planned and built the high-speed fighter plane the MiG-I (the name being an abbreviation of Mikoyan and Gurevich). After being upgraded, as the MiG-3, this plane was widely employed during World War II. After the war, the same duo designed the first Soviet supersonic jet fighters (also part of the MiG series). Gurevich was awarded the orders of the U.S.S.R., the Stalin Prize (in 1941, 1947, 1948, and 1953), and the Lenin Prize (in 1962). He was designated a Hero of Socialist Labor in 1957. [S.J.E.R.]

GUSH EMUNIM ("Block of the Faithful"; see **Dc./17**:281). Gush Emunim has played a significant role in Israeli political life since 1977. Although the declared ideology of the movement continues to emphasize Zionist renewal in all spheres of life, in practice the Gush is concerned with the implementation of policies which will make impossible the return of any of the West Bank (Judea and Samaria) as a result of future peace treaties or negotiations. The retention of Israeli (Jewish) control over this region is viewed as being divinely ordained, and thus not to be negated by human or democratic decision, even if it is the elected government of the State of Israel. This element of fundamentalist belief underlies all of Gush Emunim's activities. However the activities themselves — the creation of irreversible settlements facts — are implemented through the most pragmatic of means.

Following the coming to power of the Likkud Government in 1977, the Gush presented a short-term "emergency" settlement plan to the new government, the objective of which was the establishment of 12 new settlements throughout the West Bank at locations previously rejected by the Labor government. The majority of these locations were indeed settled during the subsequent eighteen months. In October 1978, Gush Emunim presented a more comprehensive blueprint for settlement in the region. This plan focused on the establishment of a widespread network of both rural and urban settlements as a means through which Israeli sovereignty over the region could be emphasized. This plan was similar in nature to parallel blueprints proposed by the joint head of

Map showing settlements of Amana settlement movement of Gush Emunim (gray) and others (black) in Judea, Samaria, and Gaza Strip. All are beyond the pre-1967 border of Israel. (Courtesy Amana)

the Settlement Department of the Jewish Agency, Herut appointee Matityahu Drobles, and the minister of agriculture, Ariel Sharon. Despite the lack of any formal government or cabinet decision in favor of these plans, public resources were nevertheless made available for their gradual implementation.

The implementation of Gush Emunim settlement policy is carried out by its operational arm, the Amanah settlement movement. Formal government recognition of this movement, enabling it to become the recipient of government aid and funds, together with the legalization of the two existing Gush settlements at Ofrah and Camp Kaddum afforded legitimization to the Gush Emunim settlement objectives. Amanah now includes well over 50 settlements, of which nearly all are located in the West Bank. The majority of these settlements are of the *yishuv kehillati* (community settlement) type, these being largely dormitory settlements, wherein the settlers commute to the Israeli metropolitan centers for their employment. Despite their lack of domestic economic base, these settlements maintain a closed social unit and new or potential candidates must be approved by general vote. They range in size from around 15 to 20 families in the smaller newer settlements to over 500 families in the larger, more veteran units such as Kedumim, Bet Aryeh, and Elkanah.

Gush Emunim as such does not have any formal membership and it is therefore difficult to estimate its size or actual support. While the settlers themselves constitute the grass roots of power of the movement, the Gush has also succeeded in obtaining support from a variety of Knesset members in the right-of-center political parties. Although the Gush has not transformed itself into a political party as such, many of its members and activists have become leading figures in other parties. Knesset members of the Teḥiyyah Party from 1981 and of the Matzad faction (a break away from the National Religious Party) between 1984–1986 were Gush Emunim activists. Such personalities include Gush Emunim founder Ḥanan Porat of Kefar Eẓyon, Rabbi Chaim Druckman — a leading figure in the Benei Akiva national religious youth movement — and Rabbi Eliezer Waldman, a head of the Kiryat Arba yeshivah.

Other leading activists have become the administrators of the regional councils set up to provide municipal services to the new settlements. These regional councils receive their budgets through Ministry of Interior grants as well as by means of local taxes. Thus the administrators have become, de facto, public service workers, in a position to advance their political objectives through the control and allocation of municipal funds. Additional organizations, such as the Council of Settlements in Judea, Samaria and Gaza (Mo'eẓet Yesha) and the Sheva finance company, established to promote Jewish settlement activity in the West Bank, are largely manned by Gush Emunim personalities. This gradual process of institutionalization has not included the charismatic figure of Rabbi Moshe Levinger, who had continued to propound the mystical fundamental tenets of the Gush Emunim ideology. His position as the unofficial leader of Gush Emunim received a setback in 1984, following the appointment of an official general secretary for the movement, Daniella Weiss — a resident of Kedumim.

The Gush attempts to promote a populist image by means of an annual Independence Day Rally and hike through the West Bank as well as through organizing occasional demonstrations. The most significant rallying of ranks took place in the wake of the Camp David Accords and the subsequent withdrawal from Sinai. Gush Emunim and its leaders provided a focus for the Movement to Stop the Withdrawal from Sinai. Gush Emunim viewed the withdrawal from Sinai in general, and the destruction of Jewish settlements in particular, as a dangerous precedent for the West Bank. Many of their supporters remained in Yamit as a final protest before being forcibly removed by the Israeli army. (See **YB 83–85**:431.)

The discovery of a Jewish underground in the West Bank and its terrorist activities in 1984, and the subsequent arrest, trial, and imprisonment of 20 Jewish settlers, three of them for life terms, caused an ideological crisis amongst the Gush Emunim ranks. Their supporters were split into two, with one camp openly denouncing the underground activity as being outside the legitimate field of play, the other camp supporting the actions as being legitimate in the face of what they saw as non-action on the part of the Israeli government to safeguard their interests. The former viewpoint was put forward by many of the Gush Emunim founders and focused around the personality of Yoel Bin-Nun from the Ofrah settlement. In time, these two camps became largely reconciled around the question of clemency for the Jewish prisoners.

Opposition to Gush Emunim and their ideology remains intense, in both secular and religious sectors of the population.The Peace Now Movement (see **Dc./17**:502) continues to protest against the establishment of settlements in the West Bank, which it views as obstacles in the achievement of any peace agreement between Israel and Palestinians. Religious opposition groups, Oz VeShalom and Netivot Shalom, which stress religious values of peace and the need for interethnic mutual respect, rather than the territorialism and nationalism preached by the Gush, have remained small and without influence, owing to the general identification of the religious population with the Gush Emunim viewpoint. The Gush derides the opposition movements as "speakers" only and points to their "doing" as proof of their commitment to their cause. Opponents tend to be labeled as *"yefei nefesh"* ("genteel souls") and as traitors to the cause of "Greater Israel."

The Gush Emunim ideology is expounded in the monthly magazine *Nekudah* (and its occasional English version, *Counterpoint*), published by Mo'eẓet Yesha. Recent years have witnessed a surprising amount of academic research into Gush Emunim, focusing on the group's origins, ideological viewpoints, and the functioning of the settlement network.

The change in government in 1992 had a major impact on the West Bank settler population. On the one hand, much of the Gush Emunim political lobby was lost when the Teḥiyyah party failed to gain any seats in the new Knesset. The Teḥiyyah failure was attributed, by many, to the decision of Rabbi Levinger and Daniela Weiss to run as a separate party list. This resulted in a split in the traditional Gush Emunim vote, with neither party obtaining any seats.

With the intensification of the peace talks under the Rabin government, new groups were established among the West Bank settlers to replace the now defunct Gush Emunim. These included the "Emunim" movement, supposed to represent the next generation of ideologically inspired settlers, but free of the traditional Gush leadership. In addition, national-religious rabbis of the West Bank settlements formed their own organization, aimed at providing "halakhically" inspired answers to the new political dilemmas facing the settlers. Their basic message was uncompromising, returning to the traditional national-religious argument that the Divine Right to the Land of Israel cannot be voted away by government. They provided religious backing for opposition to the Rabin government peace initiatives.

By 1992, the West Bank settler population (excluding East Jerusalem) had increased to beyond 100,000. Most of these continued to live in the communities and townships of Western Samaria, close to the metropolitan center of Israel. Particular emphasis was placed along the new west-east highway connecting Tel Aviv to the Jordan Valley. Along this route lies the expanding town of Ariel, as well as the ultra-Orthodox township of Emanuel. The Gush Etzion region, to the south of Jerusalem, also underwent internal growth, centered around the township of Efrat. The West Bank settlement network itself was greatly affected by the change in government. The new planning priorities redirected resources out of the Administered Territories and back into Israel itself — especially into the Negev and Galilee. Settlers who had previously been beneficiaries of tax concessions, easy-term mortgages, low-priced land, by virtue of their living beyond the green line, now found themselves facing conditions equal to any other region in the country.

Bibliography: M. Aronoff, in: *Political Anthropology*, 3 (1985), E. Don-Yihya, in *Middle Eastern Studies*, 24 (1988), 215–234; G. Goldberg and E. Ben-Zadok, in: *Middle Eastern Studies*, 22 (1986), 52–73; D. Newman, "The Role of Gush Emunim and the Yishuv Kehillati in the West Bank," Ph.D. diss., University of Durham (1981); idem, in: *Jerusalem Quarterly*, 39 (1986); D. Newman (ed.), *The Impact of Gush Emunim* (1985); idem, in: *Middle Eastern Studies*, 28 (1992), 509–530; Tzvi Ra'anan; *Gush Emunim* (Hebrew; 1980); E. Sprinzak, in: *Jerusalem Quarterly*, 21 (1981), 28–47; L. Weissbrod, in: *Middle Eastern Studies*, 18 (1982), 265–275. [D.NE.]

GUTMAN, ISRAEL (1923–), historian and educator. Born in Warsaw, Poland, Gutman took part in the Warsaw Ghetto Uprising and in its aftermath was imprisoned in Auschwitz. He immigrated to Palestine in 1947. Gutman studied at the Hebrew University of Jerusalem and received his Ph.D. in 1975. From 1971 he served as the director of research and publications at Yad Vashem, where he headed the Scientific Committee from 1974. He also taught at the Institute of Contemporary Jewry, at the Hebrew University of Jerusalem, which he headed (1985–88). He is an advisor to the United States Holocaust Memorial Commission and has served on the editorial committees of *Yad Vashem Studies, Studies in Contemporary Jewry, Yalkut Moreshet, Polin,* and *Zion.* He was also the editor-in-chief of *The Encyclopedia of the Holocaust* (1960). Gutman's book *The Jews of Warsaw 1939–1943* (1982; Hebrew edition, 1976) is considered the definite work on that subject. He was awarded the Shlonsky Award for Literature (1976), the Yiẓhak Sadeh Award for Military Research (1978), and the Polish Jewry Research Award (1979). Among Gutman's other publications are *Unequal Victims: Poles and Jews during World War Two* (co-author Shmuel Krakowski, 1986); and *Fighters Among the Ruins* (Hebrew, 1988). [RO.ROZ.]

H

HAMMER, ARMAND (1898–1990), U.S. industrialist and art collector. When studying at Columbia Medical School in his native New York in 1918, he joined his father's business, a chain of drug stores which was about to go bankrupt. Hammer demonstrated his business acumen when he bought quantities of medicine cheaply at the end of World War I and sold them as the price rose quickly, making $1 million.

After graduating medical school in 1921, he took off six months before beginning his internship and went to the U.S.S.R. His father was a member of the Communist party of America and a strong supporter of the Russian Revolution. Hammer went to help set up medical clinics in Moscow and other Russian cities. In the aftermath of the Revolution, the health-care system no longer existed and he made a significant contribution.

A businessman by nature, Hammer began arranging busi-

A 1984 meeting in Jerusalem between Armand Hammer (right) and Israel prime minister Shimon Peres (GPO, Jerusalem)

ness deals for the Soviet Union. The first major one was an American wheat purchase in exchange for Russian furs and caviar. When Lenin saw Hammer's capabilities, the Russian leader gave the young man mining rights in Siberia. To show his appreciation, Hammer engineered deals involving Ford, U.S. Rubber, and other large companies with the Soviet Union.

Remaining in Russia for nine years until 1930, he and his brother, who had joined him, bought up Russian art treasures which were available for needed cash. He made another $1 million when Lenin granted him the exclusive rights to manufacture wooden pencils in the Soviet Union.

On his return to the U.S.A. with an enormous horde of art treasures, many from the royal Romanov family, he had trouble selling the works because of the Depression. To be innovative, he merchandized the paintings and other art objects through major department stores such as Macy's and Gimbels. His first book dealt with his adventures collecting art in Russia and was entitled *The Quest for the Romanoff Treasure.* During the next 25 years, he earned a major fortune buying and selling distilleries. He retired in California in 1956, but within a short time he bought the controlling interest in Occidental Petroleum Company, a company about to fail. He struck oil with several new leases, soon registering major profits amounting to $300 million a year. This company, under his leadership, became the largest oil company in the world under private ownership.

In the early 1970s his close relationship with the Soviet government resulted in his negotiating a major fertilizer purchase by the Russians from an American company worth $8 billion. His ties with Russia helped to reawaken his Jewish roots. Although secret at the time, it is now clear that Hammer intervened to seek to persuade Russian leaders to permit Soviet Jews to leave the U.S.S.R. in the 1970s — ultimately almost 200,000 then emigrated.

Although publicly non-committal about Israel and his Judaism until the 1980s, he visited the country secretly and also tried to help develop certain business ties for Israel with various countries, which had no relations with her. From the mid-1980s, he was active in getting refuseniks released and he flew Ida Nudel to Israel in his own plane when she was finally freed. He also invested in oil explorations in Israel and in offshore sites nearby, none of which produced any marketable finds. He died in his sleep only a few days before he was to have had a belated bar mitzvah. [M.D.G.]

HARAN (Dyman), MENAHEM (1925–), Israeli scholar in Bible and Jewish studies. Born into a Zionist family in Moscow, as a child Haran received a traditional Jewish education. In 1933 his family moved to Palestine where he attended schools in Tel Aviv. He received his doctorate in Bible studies in 1956 from the Hebrew University of Jerusalem. His thesis was concerned with the importance of the symbolism of worshiping idols in the biblical period.

In 1950 Haran served as deputy editor for the bi-weekly journal *Be-Terem*, which dealt with social and political issues, and in 1954 began his career as lecturer in Bible studies at the Hebrew University. He founded and organized the departments for Bible studies at the universities of Tel Aviv and Haifa in the 1960s and served as one of the deputy editors of the *Enziklopediyyah Mikrait* and consulting editor of the *Encyclopaedia Judaica.*

Haran has not restricted himself to one aspect in his biblical studies but has dealt with such diverse areas as literacy and historical analysis of biblical texts, religious and social history of the biblical period; patterns in biblical style; canonization of the Bible; Bible exegesis; and biblical research and criticism. This has led him to the study of Jewish Thought and he has also published papers on Samaritan liturgy.

His work on the Priestly source in the Pentateuch led him to the conclusion that the full description of the Priestly cult of ancient Israel belongs to the pre-exilic and not post-exilic period as is usually perceived in modern scholarship.

Haran has also worked on the style of writing and literary activity of the scribe in the biblical period where he has been concerned with the developing format of the Hebrew Bible.

He has published over 200 papers, mainly in Hebrew and English. His books include: *Between Former Prophecies and New Prophecies* (1963); *Ages and Institutions in the Bible* (1973); and *Temples and Temple Service in Ancient Israel* (1979; 1985). [E.Ho.]

HARTMAN, DAVID (1931–), rabbi, educator, and philosopher. Born in the Brownsville section of Brooklyn, New York, David Hartman attended Yeshiva Chaim Berlin and the Lubavich *yeshivah.* He received his rabbinical ordination at Yeshiva University's Rabbi Isaac Elhanan Theological Seminary from Rabbi Joseph B. *Soloveitchik. He continued to study with Rabbi Soloveitchik until 1960 fostering his belief that halakhic Judaism can be integrated with a love for knowledge regardless of its source. Simultaneously, he continued his graduate studies towards his M.A. in philosophy under Robert C. Pollock of Fordham University.

After serving as the rabbi of the Anshei Emet congregation in the Bronx, New York (1955–1960), he moved to Montreal to take on the position of rabbi of the Tiferet Beit David Jerusalem congregation, while also studying and teaching at McGill University, where he received his Ph.D. in philosophy.

Emigrating with his family to Jerusalem, Israel, in 1971, he joined the department of Jewish philosophy at the Hebrew University. In 1976 he founded the Shalom Hartman Institute in Jerusalem, named after his late father who was born in the Old City of Jerusalem. He has directed the institution since its inauguration, leading a team of young research scholars who combine the study of traditional Judaic sources exploring new ways to understand and interpret and apply talmudic law and Jewish ethics and political thought with concerned involvement with contemporary issues of Israeli and Jewish life.

Rabbi Hartman has twice been the recipient of the National Jewish Book Award, for a scholarly study of Maimonides and for his book *A Living Covenant* (1985), the culmination of his thoughts on Orthodox Judaism in modern society.

His work emphasizes the centrality of the rebirth of the State of Israel and the challenge and opportunities it offers Judaism. Among his concerns is the difficulty of bringing

Jews from diverse ideological backgrounds together to form a viable nation. His teachings, drawing upon the writing of the Talmud, Maimonides, and Rabbi Soloveitchik, emphasize the importance of community and the dignity of the individual, freedom of conscience and human rights. His major theological concern is to offer a way of affirming new possibilities for love of God and Torah under conditions of religious freedom and religious tolerance.

His publications include: *Maimonides: Torah and Philosophic Quest* (1976); *Joy and Responsibility: Israel, Modernity and the Renewal of Judaism* (1978); *The Breakdown of Tradition and the Quest for Renewal: Reflections on Three Jewish Responses to Modernity* (1980); *Crisis and Leadership:* and *Three Epistles of Maimonides* (1985). [E.Ho.]

ḤAVURAH. As Bernard Reisman stated in his *The Chavurah: A Contemporary Jewish Experience* (1977), "the chavurah is a relatively recent movement in the intellectual life of American Jewry. The term, best translated as 'fellowship,' has been used to describe a wide range of approaches in which relatively small groups of Jews come together regularly for programs which include Jewish study, celebration, and personal association. Although current folklore attributes [the origin] of the chavurah movement to the establishment in 1968 of Chavurat Shalom in Somerville, Massachusetts, the chavurah concept itself is more than 2,000 years old. Moreover, the idea of fellowship — of which the chavurah is but one manifestation — is a tradition with a long and distinguished place in Jewish history."

The ḥavurah movement has developed in the United States as part of the search for Jewish community. Although intellectual and educational values are primary in the ḥavurah, it is distinguished from ordinary synagogue-related activities by its emphasis on the social component. While the traditional Jewish sense of responsibility for the larger Jewish community has been retained, and in some instances, amplified, some ḥavurot were established because of their young members' need to exercise greater influence over their destiny, and to protect the rights of individual members to be free from external control.

Ḥavurah members create the structure of their group. They decide when, where, and how often they are to meet, how their meetings will be conducted, and what they will do together. Some ḥavurot are composed solely of adults, while others include entire families. Itself a surrogate extended family, the ḥavurah broadens the network of people available to provide support to its members, and affords husbands, wives, and children a sense of belonging. Both during periods of crisis and at times of celebration, families can turn to one another for support.

According to a survey conducted at the start of the movement, during the early 1970s, members tend to be young, with young children. Most of them are native-born Americans and highly educated professionals. The average level of Jewish education is significant but not necessarily impressive. While they are more observant than other representative groups of Jews, they are not specifically committed to the synagogue as the only means of Jewish expression.

Because of the innovative and autonomous leadership of the ḥavurah, the motivation for most participants to maintain a steady level of involvement is high. The average rate of attendance in sample groups was 85%, indicating that members were serious in their commitment to the group.

In contrast with study groups conducted by a rabbi, ḥavurah members assume responsibility for defining the content of their group meetings and presenting the material to be learned. Issues and experiences are discussed from many points of view.

Jewish programs make the ḥavurah a specifically Jewish experience. Studying and socializing are combined. In a typical ḥavurah, the members construct their own *sukkah*, instead of merely visiting the synagogue's *sukkah*. In lieu of attending a lecture on Sabbath, they make *ḥallah* and participate in their own Sabbath ceremonies at home.

The major reason offered by the members for joining the ḥavurot is to fulfill Jewish objectives and obtain individual and family Jewish enrichment. The importance of the Jewish motivation of the participants is borne out in what they do in their group meetings. Jewish holiday celebration and Jewish study are the predominant activities of ḥavurot.

There are various kinds of ḥavurot. For example, the New York Ḥavurah, initially organized in 1969, included weekly Sabbath services, study sessions, and monthly retreats during which the group would spend a weekend together in the country. As individuals, members participated in various secular and Jewish concerns, including projects on behalf of Soviet Jewry and Israel.

The Washington-based Fabrengen added unstructured activities to its educational program, in an attempt to meet the needs of young Jews in the downtown area. Among the services provided were a Thursday drop-in center with the aid of a young social worker from the Jewish Social Service Agency, personal and psychological counseling, and a Saturday night "coffee house" — with musical entertainment, improvisational theater, movies, and original films.

Some ḥavurah-style groups function as *ẓedakah* (charity) collectives, with members pooling their resources to give to projects of their choice. Other groups, such as Project Ezra and Dorot, are modeled on *bikkur ḥolim* (visiting the sick) principles, with participants planning holiday celebrations and spending time visiting the Jewish elderly and poor in New York's lower East Side and upper West Side.

The ḥavurah movement grew rapidly in the 1970s. According to a spokesperson from the National Ḥavurah Committee, there are ḥavurot throughout the United States, and groups have also been organized in England, Australia, and Israel.

The Committee, begun several years ago to organize summer institutes for ḥavurah members, has expanded its programming and publishes a magazine, *New Traditions*, a newsletter, and study guides for prospective members on how to organize a ḥavurah.

While the individual orientation of ḥavurot makes the total membership difficult to estimate, more and more synagogue-affiliated ḥavurot are being formed, as both rabbis and members discover that the groups are a positive force for Jewish renewal and the rediscovery of Judaism as an organic part of life.

Bibliography: I. M. Goldman, *Lifelong Learning Among Jews* (1975); R. Kanter, *Commitment and Community* (1972); J. Neusner, *The Havurah Idea* (1967); idem, *Judaism in the Secular Age: Essays on Fellowship, Community, and Freedom* (1970); idem, *Contemporary Judaic Fellowship in Theory and in Practice* (1973); idem, *Understanding American Judaism* (2 vols.; 1975); B. Reisman, *The Chavurah: A Contemporary Jewish Experience* (1977). [Ju. Ba.]

ḤAZZAN (1983–1992) (see **7**:1542; **Dc./17**:289). **Israel.** *Ḥazzanut* is gradually disappearing from synagogues in Israel, with only a few synagogues employing professional cantors. The only synagogue in the country with a permanent choir for Sabbaths and holidays is the Great Synagogue in Jerusalem led by Eli Jaffe. Concert *ḥazzanut* is replacing synagogue *ḥazzanut* as the number of well-attended cantorial concerts continues to grow. In 1986 Dr. Mordecai Sobol established the Yuval Ensemble composed of cantors, singers, and instrumentalists. The ensemble appears in liturgical music concerts throughout Israel; it also took part in the Israel Festival in 1991. Cantorial training schools were founded in Tel Aviv, Bat Yam, Petaḥ Tikvah, and Jerusalem. The Renanot Institute, directed by Ezra Barnea during the period under review, continued the dissemination of the melodies of the various Jewish communities. Tape recordings were produced for the High Holy Day, Festival, and Sabbath prayers and for the Passover *Seder* in the style of the different Jewish communities. The series of books edited by Yehuda Kadari, *Ve-Shinantem le-Vanekha*, for the study of Torah cantillation in the tradition of the various Jewish communities, was completed. Renanot published *Mi-Zimrat Kedem*, edited by Edwin Seroussi, on the life of the Turkish cantor and rabbi Isaac Algazi, one of the greatest Sephardi cantors.

The Tel Aviv Beth Hatefutsoth Museum's Center for Jewish Music, under the direction of Dr. Avner Bahat, began operations in 1982 and among other things has produced tapes of prayers in the traditions of the Jewish communities of Koenigsberg and Danzig sung by Cantor Naftaly Herstik as well as of works by the composer Alberto Hamzi. Tel Aviv University's music department marked the eightieth birthday of Prof. Ḥanoch Avenary, an outstanding contemporary scholar of Jewish music and *ḥazzanut*, with a special edition of its journal, *Orbis Musica.* Two books by Akiva Zimmerman appeared in Tel Aviv, *Be-Ron Yaḥad* (1988), on the world of liturgical and Jewish music, and *Sha'arei Ron* (1992), on *ḥazzanut* in responsa literature and Jewish law. In 1992, upon the fiftieth anniversary of the death of the singer and cantor Joseph Schmidt, there was established in Tel Aviv, a public committee to perpetuate his memory. Thus far there has appeared a memorial tape with selections of prayers and songs from Joseph Schmidt's repertoire sung by Cantor Moshe Stern. This tape was produced by the curator of the Jewish museum in Augsburg, Ayala-Helga Deutsch.

Prof. Isaac Bacon of Beersheba and Bar-Ilan universities published a book in 1991 containing the tunes of his father, Cantor Hirsch Leib Bacon. This is the first time the melodies of this cantor, who was extremely well known in Galicia, have appeared in print. Worthy of note is the book of melodies published by Dr. Zvi Talmon, *Pa'amei ha-Heikhal* (1992), which offers tunes for Sabbath and Festival prayers and is a continuation of his first book, *Rinat ha-Heikhal* which appeared in 1965.

Europe. The memorial day in honor of Solomon *Sulzer in commemoration of 100 years since his death was marked in his city of birth, Hohenems, with the naming of a street after him. In 1990, the Austrian government produced a special postage stamp in his honor. In 1985 Prof. Ḥanoch Avenary published a book devoted to Sulzer and his times. An important work for the field of *ḥazzanut, Hebrew Notated Manuscript Sources up to circa 1840*, written by Prof. Israel Adler, head of Jerusalem's Center for Jewish Music, appeared in 1985.

Three works treating liturgical traditions of Amsterdam Jewish communities appeared; *Shirei Ḥazzanei Amsterdam*, edited by Cantor Hans Blumenthal, is devoted to the prayer services of the Amsterdam Ashkenazi congregation, while *Tenu Shevah ve-Shirah* and *Mi-Yagon le-Simḥah.* edited by Cantor Abraham Lopes Cardozo, addresses itself to the tunes of Amsterdam's Portuguese community.

In England the status of *ḥazzanut* declined and the London synagogues were forced to reduce cantor's salaries. In 1988 a concert including cantorial music was given in commemoration of the fiftieth anniversary of Crystal Night.

Soon after the collapse of the Communist regime in Eastern Europe, concerts of cantorial music were held in Poland, Hungary, Romania, and the area of the former U.S.S.R. with the participation of cantors from Israel and the United States. An academy for Jewish music and *ḥazzanut* was established in Moscow with the support of the Joint Distribution Committee and Cantor Joseph Malovany its director.

Upon his retirement in 1992 Cantor Avraham Adler (left) of Vienna received a medal and scroll of appreciation from the president of the Jewish community, Paul Gross (right), with Chief Rabbi P. Eisenberg looking on. (From the Akiva Zimmerman Collection, Tel Aviv)

The chief cantor of the Vienna Jewish community, Abraham Adler, who retired in 1992 after holding the position for 17 years, published two volumes of his works as *Zeluta de-Avraham.*

The final stamp minted by East Germany prior to its reunification with West Germany in 1991 featured the composer Louis Lewandowski, who had been the choir conductor at the Oranienburgerstrasse synagogue in Berlin, a synagogue destroyed on Crystal Night and now being restored.

In 1985 a Joseph Schmidt Archive was established in Rueti near Zurich. The collection contains recordings, documents, announcements, and much other material on the life history of the singer and cantor Joseph Schmidt. The initiator of the archive and its director is Alfred Fassbind, who in commemoration of the fiftieth anniversary of Schmidt's death, published a biography on him. The book, *"Ein Lied geht um die Welt" — Spuren einer Legende, Eine Biographie — Joseph Schmidt* (1992), includes the first discography of Schmidt's recordings.

United States. The largest center in the world for cantorial music is the United States where great changes took place in the field of *ḥazzanut* in the period under review. Orthodox synagogues hardly employ any professional cantors at all, and in Conservative and Reform synagogues the main function of the cantor is that of musical director. The Reform cantors' association is headed by a woman, and from 1990 the Cantors Assembly of the Conservative movement, the largest cantors' organization in the world, also granted women full membership. The acceptance of women into the Cantors Assembly involved a long struggle, and although most of the members voted against accepting women, the executive board decided to take them in on the basis of a paragraph in the group's regulations.

In 1991 women were voted on to the Cantors Assembly board and the number of U.S. synagogues employing female cantors is increasing. A small minority of the Cantors Assembly broke away and attempted to form a new organization, Traditional Cantors, which held a convention in Toronto, Canada, in October 1991.

Most of the Orthodox cantors belong to the Cantorial Council of America which holds a convention yearly and publishes an annual volume.

The Cantors Assembly held two conventions in Israel, one in 1987, marking 20 years of a united Jerusalem, and the second in 1992, noting 25 years of a united city. In addition, in 1991, during the Gulf War, a delegation of its members went to Israel and made concerts as a sign of identification with

Photo of the first woman trained as a cantor at the Jewish Theological Seminary of America (Photo Debbi Cooper, Jerusalem)

the State of Israel. A special committee, led by Cantor Sol Mendelson, was set up to maintain links with Israel.

Among cantorial activities of note in the U.S. were Special Sabbaths organized by Park Synagogue in New York City devoted to the works of cantors and composers of earlier generation as well as to contemporary ones. In charge of music activities in Park Synagogue are the cantor David Lefkowitz and the conductor Abraham Kaplan.

In commemoration of 100 years since the death of Solomon Sulzer a symposium was held in his memory sponsored by the Hebrew Union College, the Jewish Theological Seminary of America, the Leo Baeck Institute, and the Austrian Cultural Institute. Selections of prayers set to his music were aired and a special exhibit was mounted in his memory. The director of the event was Dr. Neil Levin.

Among U.S. cantors who died in the past decade were some of the most famous of this generation, and they include Shlomo Katz (1982), David Koussevitzky (1985), Samuel Malovsky (1985), and Zvi Aharoni (1990). In honor of Aharoni the University of Florida at Boca Raton established a memorial room which houses the important books in the fields of cantorial and Jewish music.

Books of notes in the sphere of cantorial music which appeared in the U.S. include *Chosen Voices* (1989) by Mark Slobin, surveying the history of *ḥazzanut* in the U.S.; *Synagogue Song in America* (1989) by Joseph A. Levin; and *The Golden Age of Cantors* (1992), edited by Velvel Pasternak and Noah Schall, which contains works by cantors of the "Golden Age" in America, biographies, an introduction by Irene Heskes, and tape cassetes with the cantors performing their works.

Compact discs containing cantorial music have begun to appear, some feature contemporary cantors, others are re-recordings of music which previously appeared on phonograph records. There are also now video tapes of cantors. Of particular interest is a video made in 1990 by the National Center for Jewish Film of Brandeis University and produced by Sharon Puker Rivo and Cantor Murray E. Simon. It is of a film originally made in 1931 with the cantors Yossele Rosenblatt, Mordechai Herschman, Adolf Katchko, David Roitman, and Joseph Shlisky. Added to the film now are explanatory comments by the cantor, Prof. Max Wohlberg.

[AK.Z.]

HEBREW LITERATURE, MODERN (see **8**:175; **Dc./17**:295). **Prose.** Intense activity in the sphere of prose characterizes the period 1983–1992 in Hebrew literature. To a great extent it overshadowed the other branches of literary creativity. In the field of prose, members of a number of literary generations were writing at the same time: from the "Palmaḥ generation," which recently marked 50 years since its appearance on the literary scene, to writers who were born in the 1960s and published their first works in the 1980s. The prose of this period was extremely varied as to themes, attitudes, and means of expression, yet a number of leading processes and common characteristics may be indicated.

Ideologically this prose for the most part continues the established tradition of modern Hebrew literature which has always served as a means for examining and grappling with the basic questions of Jewish-Israeli existence by exposing the collective tensions in individual characters and fates. Among the basic questions repeatedly treated were the nature of Israeli identity, the Israeli's confrontation with his Jewish roots, scrutiny of the validity and destiny of the Zionist vision, the changes of values within Israeli society, the relations between Israel and the Diaspora, the Israeli's confrontation with the memory of the Holocaust, the problems of absorption in Israel faced by immigrants from a variety of countries. In order to grapple with these issues writers selected the appropriate genres, such as the historical novel, the family saga, or realistic allegories. Some authors (such as Aharon Meged, Moshe Shamir, A.B. Yehoshua, Amos Oz, David Grossman, Shulamith Hareven) went beyond imaginative fiction and published collections of essays on social and political topics. Toward the end of the decade, however, there were signs of "fatigue" with the grand historical themes among the new generation of writers who now aimed to focus on constricted private worlds, distanced from the relentlessness of time.

This strong awareness of the social, ideological dimension is prominent, indeed, mainly among the senior authors, of the Palmaḥ generation, such as Moshe Shamir and Aharon Meged. In 1992 Shamir completed his historical trilogy *Raḥok mi-Peninim*, the first part of which appeared in 1974 and the second in 1985. This wide-sweeping work follows the life of a woman who is the model type of idealistic Jewish pioneer who represents through a century of the struggles and achievements of Zionism. Great interest was sparked by Aharon Meged's novel *Fogelman* (1987), which examines the tensions between Hebrew and Yiddish culture, on the one hand, and Israel and the Diaspora, on the other, by means of the story of the complex attitude of an Israeli historian to an old, embittered Yiddish poet. Benjamin Tammuz's final work *Ha-Zikkit ve-ha-Zamir* ("Chameleon and Nightingale," 1989), which appeared shortly before his death, presents the history of one Jewish family over a period of more than 1,300 years using a special literary technique combining passages from diaries, letters, and wills, collected and translated, as it were from the family archive. The fate of this family's members is interwoven with the collective, tragic, and heroic fate of the Jewish people in its dispersal and in the Land of Israel. These three examples are representative of dozens of literary works by this generation of authors (among whom are Ḥanoch Bartov, Shlomo Nitzan, Nathan Shaḥam, Mati Meged, Aharon Amir, Amos Kenan, David Shaḥar, and Yonat and Alexander Sened) which appeared during the period under review whose plots involve in various ways the "Jewish situation" and the "Israeli situation." The Israeli reading audience received a jolting surprise with the appearance of the novel *Mikdamot* (1992) by S. Yizhar, the most revered storyteller of his generation, after an almost 30-year stretch in which he refrained from publishing prose. This is a lyrical, nostalgic novel reconstructing the author's early childhood in Palestine in the 1920s, and the texture of his language equals his finest achievements of the 1940s and 1950s.

Thematically these years saw a great expansion in the range of topics. The historical span depicted in this literature runs from the biblical period — as in the novel *Uzzai* (1983) by Ricky Keller and the biblical novellas by Shulamith

Hareven *Sonei ha-Nissim* ("The Miracle Hater," 1983) and *Navi* ("Prophet," 1989) — to the *intifada* — as in *Ta'atu'on* (1989) by Yitzḥak Ben-Ner and *The Third Condition* (1991) by Amos Oz. The geographical range was also enriched with the increasing tendency of Israel authors to present their protagonists as immigrants or tourists in foreign countries (Jacob Shabtai, Mati Meged, Ḥanoch Bartov, Nathan Shaḥam, and many others). Most prominent in this period was the rich variety of social groups given expression through literature by new authors who grew up among them. For example, the world of the dismal, overcrowded neighborhoods of North African immigrants on the outer fringes of Jerusalem received powerful expression in *Akud* ("The Bound," 1990) by Albert Souissa. The veteran Jerusalem neighborhoods of Oriental Jews were shown in a fantastic-grotesque light in the books of Dan Benaya-Seri, *Zipporei Ẓel* ("Birds of Shade," 1987) and *Mishael* (1992). The alienated world of the "Yekkes," German Jewish immigrants to Palestine who never fully integrated into it, is depicted in the innovative work of Yoel Hoffman (*Sefer Yosef* ["The Book of Joseph"], 1988); *Bernhard* (1908); *Kristos shel Dagim* ["The Christ of Fish"], 1991), and broken, deformed figures from Jerusalem's religious society appear in the stories (*Likro la-Atalefim* ["To Call the Bats"], 1990) — by Ḥanna Bat-Shaḥar, an ultra-Orthodox Jew writing under a pseudonym.

As to the "division of labor" among the literary generations, the literature of these years seems to divide itself into two groups. On the one hand there is wide-ranging activity on the part of the writers of the "generation of the State," each of whom published more than one novel in the past ten years, and among them are A. B. Yehoshua, Amos Oz, Amalia Kahana-Carmon, Joshua Kenaz, Aharon Appelfeld, Yoram Kaniuk, Ruth Almog, Yitzḥak Ben-Ner, Yitzḥak Orpaz, Shulamith Hareven, David Schutz, and Ḥaim Be'er. One must add Yehudit Hendel and Yeshayahu Koren, who were discovered anew as it were after years of silence and who reappeared in a newer, maturer form, and also Jacob Shabtai (1934–1981), whose excellent final work, *Sof Davar* ("Past Perfect"), was edited after his death and appeared in 1984. This group of writers was focal for the reading audience and for critics, and two of them deserve special mention: A. B. Yehoshua and Joshua Kenaz, whose last two novels each are masterpieces.

Cover of Aharon Appelfeld's novel *Mesillat Barzel* ("Railway," 1992) which appeared in the Ẓad Ha-Tefer literature series edited by Yigael Schwartz.

In 1987 A. B. Yehoshua published his novel *Five Seasons (Molcho)*, which is concerned with a description of the attempt by the hero, Molcho, to free himself from the memory of his dead wife. With rare powers of psychological insight and with sensitive design of the texture of the text, Yehoshua builds up the mental process through which the hero is going, one of cycles of conflict and identification with the dead woman. The novel is designed as a perfect network of details and minutiae that build up a ramified system of motifs, parallels, and contrasts. With Yehoshua's style one can identify, under the realistic surface, layers of ideas and allegories from areas of Jewish history, Zionist ideology, and the history of Hebrew literature. Besides its other qualities the novel excels in humor, at times macabre. In 1990 Yehoshua published the novel *Mr. Mani*, another many layered work in which the familial-genetic-psychological element is closely bound with a wide historiosophical system. The novel, which spans a period of 150 years, is a saga of a Sephardi family whose history for five generations is linked to the focal events in Jewish, Zionist, and Israeli history. Its distinctive innovation is its sophisticated structure, which is based on five mono-dialogues (conversations in which only one speaker is heard), in each of which a member of the Mani family is covered but through the words of an external observer. Tracing the Mani family through these generations reveals a multifaceted system of repeated strange, deviant modes of behavior, which are generally connected to some sexual transgression and to odd socio-political positions. At the same time the history of this family forms a continuous "alternative history" whereby Yehoshua expresses his opinion on a series of missed historical opportunities, which had they been seized would have been able to change the course of Jewish history. Beyond his rich network of analogies, each chapter stands as a virtuoso performance, moving from realism to the grotesque, of the reconstruction of a period with its various types and its special language.

Joshua Kenaz published, in 1986, *Hitganevut Yeḥidim* ("Heart Murmur"), a realistic novel that describes the adventures of a group of recruits in the Israeli army of the mid-1950s. It presents a reliable sample of the mosaic of contradictory tensions and forces from which Israeli society has been built. But on a more significant level this is a story of the maturation and education of an artist, in which basic human contrasts are portrayed and examined: between the individual and society, between inside and outside, between beauty and ugliness, and between ethics and aesthetics. In 1991 Kenaz published his novel *Ba-Derekh el ha-Ḥatulim* ("The Way to the Cats"), which constructs with careful precision the world of an old woman in a geriatric hospital. The distinctiveness of this novel is in its realistic, exacting, patient depiction which contains no false or harsh note. Kenaz is a past master at empathy-laden, slow-motion scrutiny paying attention to the tiniest details which comprise a human portrait, social behavior, monotonous daily routine, a landscape, or a string of speech in broken Hebrew. On the realistic level the world depicted is hard and cruel, depressing and hopeless, but what turns this into a purifying reading experience is the manner in which the protagonist's image is sculpted, which awakens empathy and respect on the part of the reader for her struggle with aging as well as for her reconciliation with her approaching end.

Kenaz, Yehoshua, and other members of their generation are representative of one central group in contemporary Hebrew literature, which first appeared in the 1960s, yet parallel to them and following in their wake there came in the past decade a large group of new writers, most of them young, who attracted ever-increasing attention. In a general, schematic division two contrasting poetic trends in the writing of these authors can be discerned. One clings firmly to the realistic modes of expression and traditional conventions of depiction which these authors inherited from their predecessors, developing them in their own way. An example is the first collection of stories by Judith Katzir, *Sogerim et ha-Yam* ("Fellini's Shoes," 1990). Reviewers stressed the sensitive, mature narrative ability of this young author, her success in constructing vibrant, richly detailed worlds, and her facility in fashioning romantic figures who are the prisoners of false perceptions which they are destined to destroy. Another instance is Yitzḥak Bar-Yosef, who in two short-story anthologies and the novella he published during this period conveyed the sensuous, violent aspects of Israeli life. Others from this group include: Israel Hameiri, Ḥanna Bat-Shaḥar, Ofra Offer, Savyon Liebrecht, Lily Perry-Amitai, Miri Varon, Nava Semel, Ronit Matalon, Lea Aini, Zipora Dolan, and Gabriela Avigur-Rotem. It is no accident that most of them are women, for one of the characteristics of this past decade is the appearance of a growing number of women writers, an unprecedented blossoming of the feminine voice in prose.

In contrast to this "conservative" group stands another group whose common denominator is a tendency towards experimentalism, often in a post-Modernist spirit, which has left its traces in all of the Israeli arts in recent years. Noticeable in their works is the desire to break down in various ways the traditional formalistic consensus on the novel and the structure of reality fashioned in it in order to draw attention to the linguistic medium. One of the outstanding writers in this group is Orly Castel-Bloom, who has published since 1987 two collections of stories and two novels (*Lo Raḥok mi-Merkaz ha-Ir* ("Not Far from the City Center"); *Sevivah Oyenet* ("Hostile Surroundings"); *Heikhan Ani Nimzet* ("Where Am I"); *Doli Siti* ("Dolly City")) whose outstanding features were "spare," economic language, fragmentation of the text and the world, parody of cliches of language and thought, a deviant, alienated reality, and an atmosphere of nihilism, estrangement, and despair. The first novel by Yuval Shimoni, *Ma'of ha-Yonah* ("The Flight of the Dove," 1990), was widely praised. Set in Paris, it comprises three parallel plots: the dull lives of an aging American tourist couple; the suicide of a young French woman; a previous love affair of the narrator. The uniqueness of this book is in the "non-Israeliness" of its subject matter and in the complex web of connection woven among the various plots which lead them to a joint conclusion concerning the vapidity of human existence. Extremely bold experiments are exemplified by the novels by Yoel Hoffman, *Bernhard* and *Kristos shel Dagim*, which are made up of short, carefully designed sections with associative links. Wild connections and an insane reality are in the novel *Aggadat ha-Agammim ha-Azuvim* ("The Legend of the Sad Lakes") by Itamar Levi which is an attempt by a young Israeli author to confront the subject of the Holocaust in a fantastic, surrealistic manner, to the point of blurring the border between murderer and victim. Fantastic-grotesque elements and meta-fictitious games characterize the two novels by Meir Shalev, *Roman Rusi* ("A Russian Novel," 1988) and *Esav* ("Esau," 1991). Other new authors who applied various experimental techniques during this period were Chaim Nagid, Avner Shalev, Amnon Navot, Israel Berama, and Jonathan Ben Nahoom. This reflexive trend, which indulges itself with literary forms and tensions between the different levels of reality and imagination and which mix reality and fantasy, were not the exclusive domain of the young. During the past decade novels innovative in their structure and techniques were published by Amos Oz (*Kufsah Sheḥorah* ["Black Box"], 1987), Yitzḥak Orpaz (*Ha-Kallah ha-Nizḥit* ["The Eternal Bride], 1987), David Schutz (*Shoshan Lavan, Shoshan Adom* "White Rose, Red Rose", 1988), and Moshe Shamir (*Ad ha-Sof* ["To the End"], 1991).

These two contrasting trends, the "conservative" and "the experimental," meld in the writing of the most outstanding young author to emerge in the 1980s, David Grossman (b. 1954). His wide-ranging works, appearing from 1983 on, comprise thus far a collection of stories and three novels in addition to two non-fiction works dealing with the Israel-Arab conflict, plays, and children's books. Grossman's poetic innovativeness is most pronounced in the novel in which he grapples with the Holocaust, *Ayyen Erekh Ahavah* ("See Entry: 'Love'," 1986). This is a novel complex in structure and plot, each of whose four parts is written according to a different literary code. More than attempting to deal with the Holocaust itself, it is a metapoetic novel that tries to examine whether the topic can be portrayed at all in a literary manner. From this the novel creates a complex interweaving of viewpoints, planes of reality and fiction that are mixed and conflict with one another, a jumble of literary genres (with a strong tendency toward wild fantasy) and changing techniques of narration. In contrast, Grossman's next novel, *Sefer ha-Dikduk ha-Penimi* ("The Book of Internal Grammar," 1991) appears to be very conservative in topic (the adolescent travails of a young man growing up in a Jerusalem neighborhood in the 1960s) and in the crafting of its structure and language. Yet one can find in it Grossman's pronounced penchant for grotesque forms in the design of the situations and the language, without his shattering the realistic appearance of the fictional world.

At the initiative of publishers and editors, valuable books of earlier generations were republished. Prominent activities in this sphere included: the collection of David Vogel's prose works, the novel *Ḥayyei Nisu'im* ("Married Life") and the anthology of novellae *Taḥanot Kavot* ("Stories: Diary"); the publication of the trilogy *Ad Yerushalayim* ("Even to Jerusalem") by A. Reuveni; Jacob Ḥurgin's short-story anthology *Professor Leonardo*; and Dov Kimḥi's novel *Beit Ḥafez*. Dvir Publishing Company initiated a special series entitled "*Kolot*," which published novels and anthologies of stories by the classic Hebrew authors, such as *Mendele Mokher Seforim, M. J. *Berdyczewski, David *Frischmann, Y. Ḥ. *Brenner, L. A. Arieli-Orloff, and Avigdor *Hameiri, accompanied by introductions and annotations. Renewed interest in and appreciation of the fiction of the "Palmaḥ Generation" led to reprintings of some of the outstanding writers of that generation, such as S. *Yizhar, Ḥanoch Bartov, Igal Mossinsohn, Shlomo Nitzan, and Benjamin Tammuz.

Poetry. The most striking phenomenon in Hebrew poetry in the early 1980s was the outpouring of a wave of protest poems prompted by the Lebanon War of 1982–1983. These poems were collected in two anthologies which appeared in 1983, *Ḥazayat Gevul* ("Border Crossing") and *Ve-Ein Tikhlah li-Keravot u-le-Hereg* ("Fighting and Killing without

End"). Along with poets belonging to the literary establishment, such as Natan Zach, Dalia Rabikovitch, Yehuda Amichai, Dan Pagis, Ya'ir Hurvitz, Meir Wieseltier, Moshe Dor, and Aryeh Sivan there appeared younger poets, in these anthologies such as Maya Bejerano, Yosef Sharon, and Yitzhac Laor. Towards the end of the decade several poets responded in similar protest to the events of the *intifada.* Their poems express fear and frustration in light of the continuation and shame of the Israel-Palestine conflict. Prominent among them were Moshe Dor in the poems collected in *Overim et ha-Nahar* ("Passing the River"); Aryeh Sivan (*Kaf ha-Kela* ["Hollow of the Sling"]); Yizhac Laor (*Shirim be-Emek ha-Barzel* ["Poems in the Iron Valley"]); and Dalia Rabikovitch (*Ima im Yeled* ["Mother with Child"]). The impact of the early 1991 Gulf War was echoed almost immediately in Hebrew poetry, as in the anthologies published by David Avidan and Ilan Sheinfeld. Poetry books also appeared expressing through their topics and their linguistic design a yearning for the European refinement and alienated, pure aesthetics, such as poetry anthologies by Mordechai Geldman, Lea Snir, Tuvia Ruebner, and Asher Reich. The tendency of contemporary Hebrew poets to reflect upon the essence of the medium of language was broadly represented in two anthologies edited by Ruth Kartun-Blum: *Shirah bi-Re'i Aẓmah* ("Poetry as Its Own Mirror," 1982) and *Yad Kotevet Yad* ("Self-Reflexive Hebrew Poetry — Forty Years," 1989).

The main thrust of Hebrew poetry in the period under review continued to revolve around the world of the individual, with prominent personal-universal motifs in it. Many poets have shown a tendency toward thoughtful elegiac writing, toward personal statements and soul-searching, on a background of experiences of growing old, being ill, and taking leave of parents and other close friends who have died. Others have written about love, landscapes, city life, the craft of writing, travels abroad, and other components from the broad range of human experiences. The most widespread form of expression is the lyric poem that is limited in its topic, and constitutes a direct or nearly direct autobiographical expression, and that generally abstains from pathetic rhetoric or metaphor, but rather achieves its color by the combination of concrete details taken from reality. It is hard to point to distinct groups, streams, or schools of Hebrew poetry in the 1980s, which seems to have blurred the boundaries between the "generational" categories defined in precious decades, and now stands for heterogeneity and individualism.

One reason for this is that during this period at least five different generations of poets were simultaneously active on the literary scene. During the 1980s several poets born in the early part of this century were still active and continue to produce excellent poetry. Among those who died in the past decade are: Simon *Halkin (1898–1987), Avoth Yeshurun (1902–1992), Shin Shalom (1904–1990), Zerubavel Gilead (1912–1988), David Rokeaḥ (1912–1985), Zelda Shneurson-Mishkovsky (1914–1984), Amir Gilboa (1914–1984), Gabriel Talpir (1901–1990), and Yehoshua Tan-Pai (1914–1987). Other members of this generation are Yehoshua Rabinov, K.A. Bertini, and Gabriel Preil. Much interest was stimulated by Avoth Yeshurun's next-to-last book *Adon Menuḥah* ("Master of Rest," 1990), which expressed the poet's yearnings for his town in Poland and for the members of his family who perished in the Holocaust, while at the same time there is a brave, sensitive confrontation with the ever-growing presence of approaching death. A number of poets belonging to younger generations also passed away while at the height of their poetic powers — Abba Kovner (1918–1987), Hillel Omer (1926–1990), Dan Pagis (1930–1986), Aryeh Sachs (1932–1992), Ya'ir Hurvitz (1941–1988), Yona Wallach (1944–1985) — all of whom published important collections of poems in the 1980s, and Yitzḥak Shalev (1919–1992), whose main contributions to Hebrew poetry were made many years ago.

Artistic maturity and personal depth characterized the writing of the veteran poets of the "Palmaḥ Generation" and of the "generation of the State" which appeared in the 1940s and 1950s. In 1987 Ḥaim Gouri published *Ḥeshbon Over* ("Selected Poems"), which represents 42 years of creativity and incorporates intimate-personal life experience with collective national memories. Yehuda Amichai published during this decade three collections of poems which, as is customary for him, determined the existence and happiness of the individual as the highest value, according to which all other values are measured. In the books of other poets belonging to that generation, such as Natan Zach, Pinḥas Sadeh, Dalia Rabikovitch, Moshe Dor, and Yaakov Besser, a tone of maturity and sobriety dominates, and there is a tendency to concentrate on what is happening here and now, to avoid universal abstractions and romantic voyages to other times and places, to increase autobiographical elements on the one hand and involvement in current political events, on the other. All of this is expressed in poetic language whose rhythmic structures and connotative depths are disguised under an ostensibly simple, spoken-language style surface.

A striking phenomenon of the 1980s is the enhanced interest in the works of poets of the 1940s–1950s generation which had been initially overshadowed by their dominant contemporaries. In the 1980s, new conditions arose allowing for their distinctive voices to be heard, both as a result of changes in literary norms and the recognition of the freshness in their poetry. An outstanding example is the poetry of Avner Treinin, with its balance between a dry, quasi-scientific description of laws and cyclic processes in nature and intimate childhood memories. Another example is Aharon Shabtai's poetry which passed through a few developmental stages from its beginning in the 1960s, and which, at the close of the 1980s, with the publication of *Ziva,* was the object of much attention because of its daring, bold eroticism, probably the first of its kind to be written in Hebrew. Much attention was paid to Dan Pagis's final poetry collections, *Millim Nirdafot* ("Double Exposure," 1982) and *Shirim Aḥaronim* ("Last Poems," 1987), whose intellectual and ironic complexity earn for him a central position in this generation's poetry. The poetry of Aryeh Sivan, Ori Bernshtein, and Israel Pincas also aroused fresh interest and appreciation.

Among the poets born in the 1940s prominent in the 1980s were Meir Wieseltier, whose book *Mikhtavim ve-Shirim Aḥerim* ("Letters & Other Poems," 1986) gives bold, classical expression to intimate experiences and childhood memories as well as current events; Yitzhac Laor, whose early work was prominently marked by biting political protest, and now writes more refined poetry, and in his 1992 book, *Laila be-Malon Zar* ("A Night in a Foreign Hotel") gives delicate, complex expression to experience of loss, love, and wandering; Maya Bejerano, who made extensive semantic experiments in expanding the boundaries of poetic language, as in her *Livyatan* ("Leviathan," 1990;) Roni Somek, who in his poems constructs a very "with-it" world, founded upon refreshing observations about trivial objects; and Pereẓ-Dror Banai, from whose poetry, combining East and West, emanates human warmth. Among the younger poets, born in the 1950s and 1960s, there is a multiplicity of voices and aims with no distinctive poetic center. Their poetry treats every topic freely, and does not recoil from explicit presentation of subjects considered taboo for Hebrew literature in the past, such as coarse erotic descriptions or experiences of male and of female homosexual relations. The most prominent names

Gershon Shaked's *Ha-Sipporet ha-Ivrit 1880–1980* ("Hebrew Narrative Fiction 1880–1980") is a multi-volume historiographic work on Modern Hebrew Literature.

in this group are: Ilan Sheinfeld, Amir Or, Admiel Kosman, Yosef Sharon, Zruyah Shalev, Ẓvi Atzmon, Leah Ayalon, Nitsa Kann, and Ḥezi Leskli.

In contrast to fiction, which aroused great public and media attention, the influence of poetry did not extend beyond the small circles of literary devotees. Critics argued among themselves whether this was due to a weakening of poetry itself or from sociocultural changes of wider scope. Some took this to be part of a regular cycle of various genres which has characterized Hebrew literature since the 19th century, and defined the present generation in Hebrew literature as "the prose era." A practical reflection is the very limited distribution of books of poetry, the reluctance of major publishing houses to put out works of poetry, and the increasing financial difficulties encountered by poets when they tried to publish their poems. However, this decade saw the establishment of special journals paying special attention to Hebrew poetry, such as *Hadarim* and *Helicon*, along with the continued appearance of poetry in the established journals such as *Moznayim, Iton 77, Siman Kri'a*, and *Akhshav*. An important contribution to the dissemination of Hebrew poetry (and narrative) outside of Israel was made by the periodicals *Tel-Aviv Review* and *Modern Hebrew Literature*, since they included English translations of poems and stories as well as critical essays on Hebrew literature.

In addition to the continuous appearance of new books of poetry, the works of leading poets of previous generations were collected on a large scale. The two main projects in this sphere, both under the direction of Dan Miron, were the scholarly edition of Ḥayyim Naḥman Bialik's poetry in two volumes (1983; 1990), and the comprehensive publication of the writings of Uri Ẓevi Greenberg, the first four volumes of which have been published. Other poets whose works were collected after their deaths were Yitzḥak Katzenelson, Avraham Ben-Yitzḥak, Yehuda Karni, Esther Raab, Avraham Ḥalfi, Amir Gilboa, Dan Pagis, and Ya'ir Hurvitz. A previously unknown volume of the poetry of David Fogel, *Le'ever Hadmama*, appeared in 1983, almost forty years after the author's death. Formerly uncollected units of Nathan Alterman's works continued to appear in the past decade in the series *Maḥberot Alterman*. Other poets issued their own comprehensive anthologies representing decades of creative activity. Among them were K. A. Bertini, Aharon Amir, Tuvia Ruebner, Yaakov Besser, Moshe Dor, and Itamar Yaoz-Kest.

Criticism. The achievements in the study of modern Hebrew literature in 1983–1992 may be found in four main areas: historiography, monographs, the study of genres, and historical poetics.

HISTORIOGRAPHY. In the field of historiography three outstanding works of research have surveyed and mapped extensive aspects of Hebrew literature in recent generations. Gershon Shaked published the second (1983) and third (1988) volume of his study *Ha-Sipporet ha-Ivrit 1880–1980* ("Hebrew Narrative Fiction 1880–1980"). The second volume treats the realistic literature written in Palestine by prose writers of the First, Second, and Third Aliyah while also examining S. Y. Agnon's writing, presenting them as the conduit into which flow all the norms and the principal changes in Hebrew literature which preceded him. The third volume also has two foci. The first part describes modernistic Hebrew literature written between the two world wars, and the second section is an introduction to the literary works of authors living in Israel from the 1940s on.

Hillel Barzel published three volumes of his historiographical project in which he plans to cover the history of Hebrew poetry over the past 100 years. The first volume (1987) surveys "The Ḥibbat Zion Poetry" at the end of the 19th century. The second volume (1990) is devoted to the works of Ḥayyim Naḥman Bialik, and the third (1993) to the writings of Saul Tchernichowsky. Uriel Ofek (1926–1987), the most important scholar in the field of Hebrew literature for children, completed two monumental works a short time before his death: *Leksikon Ofek le-Sifrut Yeladim* ("The Who's Who of Children's Literature"), which contains 2,000 detailed entries from all areas of Hebrew and world children's literature; and *Sifrut ha-Yeladim ha-Ivrit 1900–1948* (1988), which is centered on a description of the development of a natural and ramified children's literature in Ereẓ Israel, on a wide social and cultural background. Also of note is the appearance of *Leksikon ha-Itonut ha-Ivrit ba-Me'ot ha-18 ve-ha-19* ("Hebrew periodicals in the 18th and 19th centuries," 1992) by Menucha Gilboa, which for the first time documents hundreds of Hebrew periodicals and newspapers running the entire ideological and literary gamut.

MONOGRAPHS. In the field of monographs three trends were prevalent. One trend concentrated on the poetics and thematics of the works themselves, such as in the books on Amir Gilboa (by Hillel Barzel); Saul Tchernichowsky (by Avraham Shaanan); Uri Ẓevi Greenberg (by Shalom Lindenbaum); Amalia Kahana-Carmon (by Lily Rattok); L. A. Arieli-Orloff (by Gila Ramras-Rauch); Jacob Horowitz (by Rachel Frenkel); Shin Shalom (by Avidov Lipsker); Rachel [Blubstein] (by Reuven Kritz); Amos Oz (by Avraham Balaban); Yehuda Amichai (by Boaz Arpali); M.J. Berdyczewski (by Ẓipora Kagan and Isaac Ben-Mordechai); Nathan Yonathan, Yaakov Fichman, and Ozer Rabin (by Zvi Luz). The second trend interwove literary discussion with the biographical and historical contexts, while inquiring into the portrait of the artist as a person seen against the background of his time. This is the case in the books by Nurit

THE AN-SKY COLLECTIONS
(see page 91)

Costumes

Klezmer

Mordecai *Purim-shpil* costume sketch by Yudovin

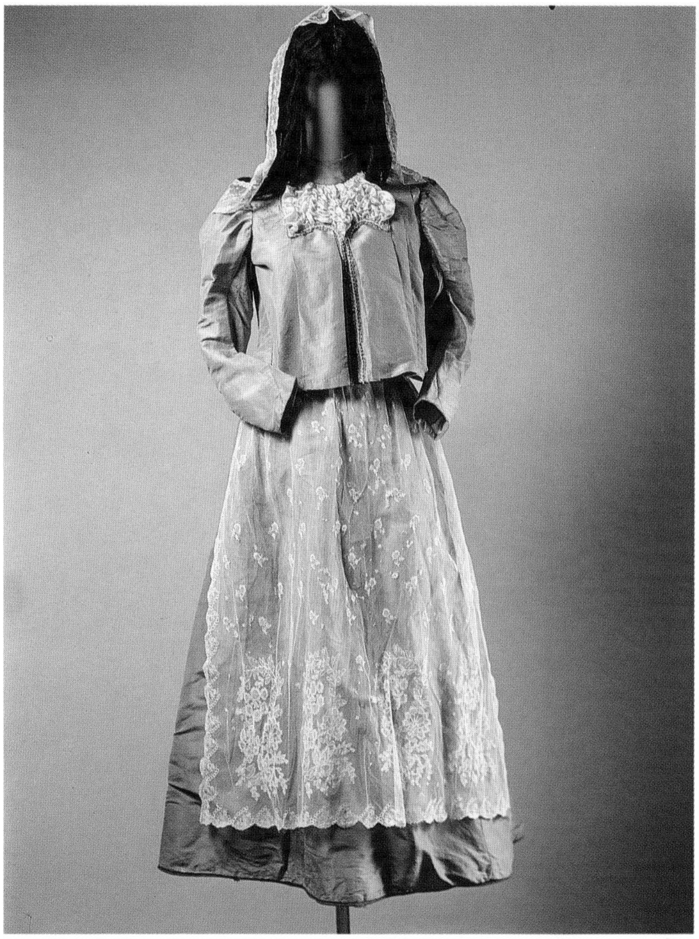

Complete woman's costume with skirt, blouse, kerchief, apron, and wig

Ahasuerus *Purim-shpil* costume sketch by Yudovin

Haman *Purim-shpil* costume sketch by Yudovin

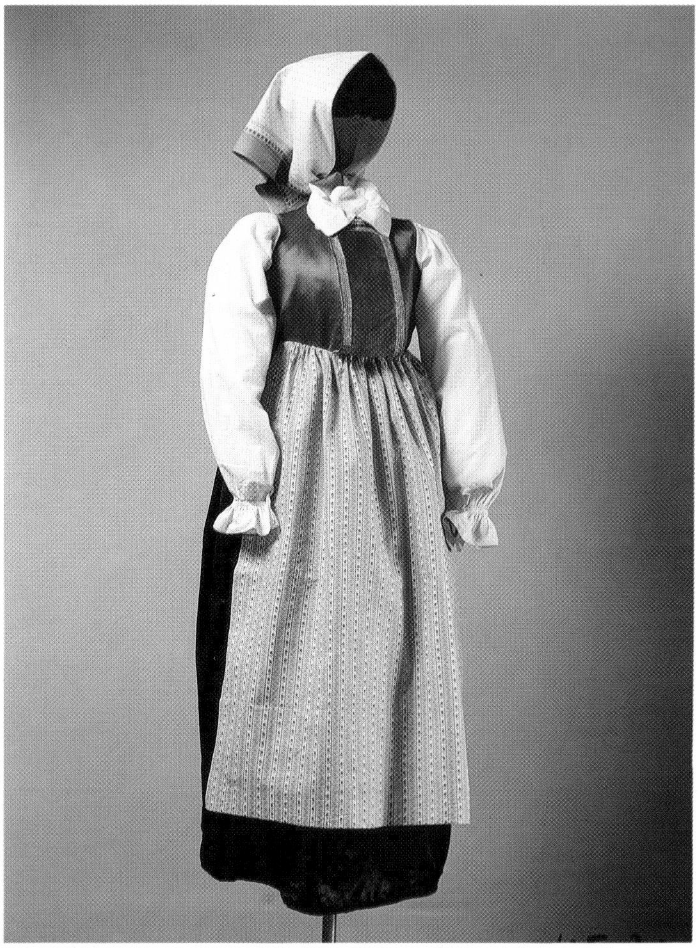

Complete woman's costume with necklace, blouse, brustichel, wig, skirt, and apron

Medzibezh

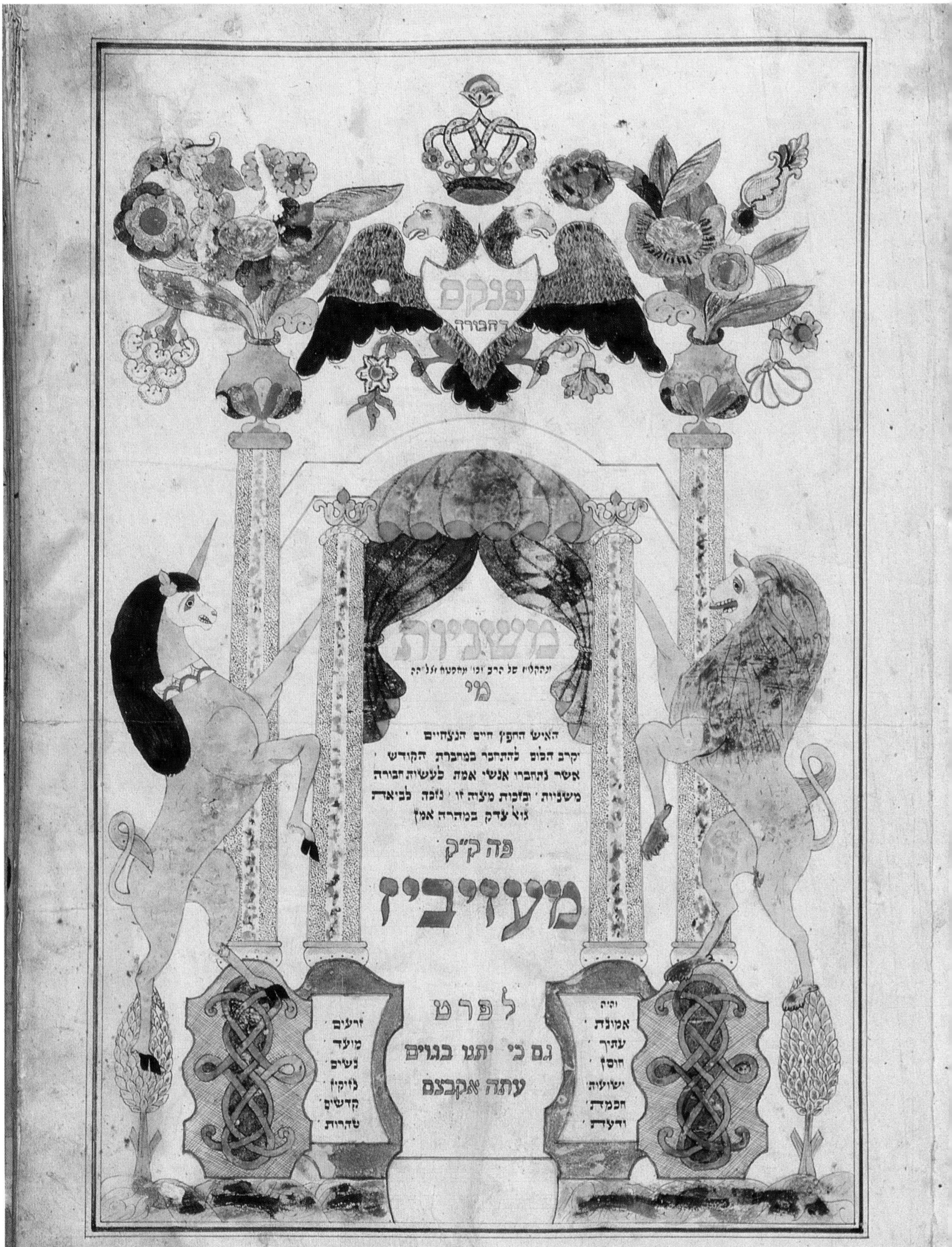

Front page of a *pinkas* (communal register) from Medzibezh

Illuminated page from *pinkas* Medzibezh

Folk Prints

Western Ukraine, 1880-1915

The Story of Lot

Seder Meal

Rebecca and Eliezer

Balaam and the Ass

Jacob's Funeral

David and Goliath

Games

Set of wooden chess men

Set of Ḥanukkah playing cards

Amulets and Pottery

Folk print of David and Bathsheba which also served as an amulet

China Ḥanukkah lamp from the pottery factory in Grodnitsa (late 19th century)

Amulets to protect women in childbirth

SYNAGOGUES IN CENTRAL AND SOUTHERN EUROPE (see page 65)

Jewish property

Above, left: Ancona, Italy (c.1550, Baroque). The Scuola Levantina synagogue's ornate Baroque ark on an elevated platform. The synagogue is meticulously cared for by the small, devoted Jewish community.

Above, right: Rhodes, Greece (12th c., rebuilt 16th c.). Interior of the synagogue toward the entrance court, showing the reader's platform and the arched construction. Renovated in recent years, the synagogue is Jewish owned, but there are only a handful of Jews in Rhodes, and no prayer quorum. The crystal chandeliers are typical of Greek synagogues.

Right: Biella, Italy (c.1750, Baroque). Fine Italian wood craftsmanship is evident in the ark of this intimate synagogue in a town where the Jews number less than a prayer quorum.

Churches

Osijek, Serbia (1867, Romantic). Facade of the synagogue, now a Pentecostalist church. A cross has been added over the portal and above the original tablets, still in place. The church maintains a divinity school located in the building that was once the rabbi's house, behind the synagogue.

Secular, Cultural Use

Apostag, Hungary (1842, neo-Classical-Lvov four-pillared style). Interior, with reader's platform and ark. Exceptionally well restored by the voluntary effort of the residents in this miniscule town, it was awarded the Europa Nostra prize for authentic restoration. With 48 comfortable seats, the prayer hall serves as wedding salon and concert chamber and the gallery is an elegant library. Near the ark two museum cabinets display Jewish artifacts and memorabilia of local Jews.

Kecskemet, Hungary (1871, Neo-Moresque, Janos Zitterbarth, architect). Facade. A town landmark with its single domed tower and gleaming white exterior, the synagogue building serves many purposes. The prayer hall and gallery have been converted into two assembly halls for conventions; the ground floor includes a clubroom and a used-clothing bazaar, the top floor lobby houses a collection of replicas of sculptures by Michelangelo.

In restoration

Vrbové, Slovakia. Interior, the impressively detailed ceiling.

Kunszentmárton, Hungary. Stylized star-of-David in a stained glass window at an upper level, affording a view of the town and the church steeple.

Govrin on Gershon Shofman and Devorah Baron; Jacob Kabakoff's book on Naphtali Herz Imber; Ḥagit Halperin on Alexander Penn; Avner Holtzman on Avigdor Hameiri; Yosef Halevi on Mordechai Tabib; Yael Feldman (in English) on Gabriel Preil; and Michael Stanislawski (in English) on Judah Leib Gordon. The third trend was biographies on Hebrew writers written by historians who are not literary scholars and whose research methods do not enable them to give deep literary analysis. The two most prominent examples are Yehoshua Porath's book on Yonathan Ratosh and Joseph Goldstein's book on Aḥad Ha-Am. In addition, there appeared comprehensive bibliographies of the works of M.J. Berdyczewski, Y. Ḥ. Brenner, Ḥayyim Hazaz, G. Kressel, Dov Sadan, and Amos Oz, and collections of articles on U.N. Gnessin, Yehuda Amichai, Abba Kovner, Asher Barash, David Frischman, Aharon Reuveni, and Yonathan Ratosh.

Four authors, who are the mainstays of Hebrew literature in 20th-century prose and poetry, were the object of particularly intense interest by literary critics: Y. Ḥ. Brenner, S. Y. Agnon, Ḥ. N. Bialik, and N. Alterman. Each of them was, over the past decade, the subject of at least ten books and scores of scholarly articles, some of which have been anthologized. Broad sections of Brenner's biography were highlighted in books by Nurit Govrin and Yitzḥak Bakon, which analyze his relations with his literary colleague, the various spheres of his activity, and the way in which his writing was nourished by events in his life. Ideational and poetic aspects in Brenner's works were explicated by Ada Zemach, Menaḥem Brinker, and Boaz Arpali. The life and works of Agnon, too, were studied from different angles. Over the decade volumes of stories and letters from his estate continued to appear, expanding knowledge of his life and writings. A concise biography of Agnon accompanied by documents was published by Avinoam Barshai, who edited a series of volumes of collections of scholarly articles and literary criticism on his works. Agnon's connections to Brenner and Bialik were described in a comprehensive and documented biographical study written by Ḥaim Be'er, and Yitzḥak Bakon discussed Agnon's early years as a writer. Research works into the poetics in Agnon's writings were published by Gershon Shaked (in Hebrew and English), Dan Laor, Esther Fuchs, Shmuel Katz, Hillel Weiss, Gedalya Nigheal, Judith Halevi Zwick, Aliza Shenhar, Dov Landau, and Yair Mazor as well as by Amos Oz, the author, who devoted a special book to a close reading from a personal perspective of three stories by Agnon.

The swirl of activity around Bialik's works yielded a number of books on a variety of aspects of his life and writings: the first decade of his poetry (Dan Miron), his prose works (Samuel Werses, Ruth Shenfeld), the prosody of his poetry (Uzi Shavit), his poetic concepts (Ẓvi Luz, Ziva Shamir), his origins in Russian poetry (Esther Nathan), his affinity for folk literature (Ziva Shamir), his writings for children (Uriel Ofek, Ziva Shamir), his Yiddish works (Yitzḥak Bakon), the structure of language in his writings (Dov Sadan). Separate books were devoted to interpretations of individual works (Reuven Kritz, Ziva Shamir). Shlomo Shva and David Aberbach wrote general biographies of Bialik. Nathan Alterman, too, was the object of detailed biographical research (by Menachem Dorman) and notable among the studies on his lyrical and political poetry are the works by Dan Miron, Dan Laor, Ruth Kartun-Blum, Boaz Arpali, and Ziva Shamir as well as Moshe Shamir's book on Alterman's political activity in his last years.

GENRE STUDIES. The decade 1983–1992 saw the appearance of the first studies on some of the outstanding genres in Hebrew literature, in poetry and in fiction. Regarding poetry the outstanding work was Shlomo Yaniv's book on the history of the Hebrew ballad from its beginning until the present, in light of its links to the tradition of the European ballad. Studies by Uzi Shavit and Yehudit Bar-El contributed to the understanding of the roots and crystallization of the Hebrew long poem. Ḥaim Shoham on the idylls, Reuven Tsur wrote about the hypnotic poem, Ziva Ben-Porat studied the pop song, and Ruth Kartun-Blum investigated the self-reflexive poem. Among those in the realm of prose, noteworthy were the books by Ortsion Bartana on fantasy, Ruth Shenfeld on the Hebrew historical novel in the 20th century, Malka Shaked on the family saga, Lea Hadomi on utopias, Lily Rattok on the lyrical story, Hamutal Bar-Yosef on narrative notes, and Hannah Naveh on the prose of confession. Ben-Ami Feingold wrote on the subject of the Holocaust in Hebrew drama.

HISTORICAL POETICS. The field of historical poetics evinced great interest in the period between the closing years of the 19th century and early part of the 20th. A systematic, useful introduction in English to this period is found in Nurit Govrin's *Alienation and Regeneration*, which presents the classic authors of Hebrew prose in the Diaspora and Israel from Berdyczewski to Agnon. Two books by Dan Miron dealt with changes that occurred in Hebrew literature during the transition from the 19th to the modernism of the 20th century, and with the biographical and collective poetical portraits of the creators of Hebrew literature in the early 20th century. Simon Halkin, Samuel Werses, Alan Mintz, and Ortsion Bartana also devoted scholarly works to this dramatic period, which set the foundations of modern Hebrew literature.

The growth of the Hebrew literary center in Palestine from the time of the First Aliyah up to World War II was described in scholarly books by Nurit Govrin, Zohar Shavit, Nurith Gertz, and Nili Sadan-Loebenstein. Hebrew literature's reaction to the War of Independence was described by Dan Miron (in the field of poetry) and Mishka Ben-David (in the field of prose), and the changeover of generations in Israeli prose from the "Palmaḥ Generation" to the writers of the 1960s was covered in studies by Nurith Gertz.

Advances in research were made also in other fields, such as: the poetics of Haskalah literature, prosody of Hebrew poetry, literary journals, literary-psychoanalytical analysis, Holocaust literature, and the bilingual (Hebrew and Yiddish) literary system. Initial studies were made in the field of Hebrew women's literature, under the influence of the premises of feminist criticism. New periodicals were founded for the study of Hebrew literature: *Meḥkarei Yerushalayim be-Sifrut Ivrit* ("Jerusalem Studies in Hebrew Literature"), *Dappim le-Meḥkar ha-Sifrut* ("Dappim — Research in Literature"), and the English-language *Prooftexts*. [AV.HOLZ.]

HERZOG, CHAIM (1918–), sixth president of Israel. [This entry replaces the one in **8**:424.] Herzog was born in

Chaim Herzog

Belfast, Northern Ireland, to R. Isaac and Sarah *Herzog and lived in Dublin from 1919. He immigrated to Palestine in

1935, studying at Hebron Yeshivah and the Government of Palestine Law School. He served in the Haganah during the Arab revolt, 1936–38, and in the British army in World War II. He crossed to Normandy and was stationed in northwest Germany, participating in the liberation of some of the concentration camps. Herzog graduated at the Royal Military College and returned to Palestine where he fought in the War of Independence and served as director of Military Intelligence, 1948–50 and 1959–62. From 1950 to 1954 he was defense attaché at the Israel embassy in Washington. After holding various field commands, he retired from regular service in 1962 with the rank of *aluf* (major-general) and went into business, heading an industrial development group and founding a law firm in Tel Aviv. In the period of the Six-Day War, he became Israel's best known military commentator and after the war he was the first military governor of the West Bank. From 1975 to 1978 he was Israel's ambassador to the United Nations where he led the struggle against the 1975 Zionism=Racism resolution and at the conclusion of his speech tore up the document containing the resolution. He was president of the World ORT Union and was awarded an honorary British knighthood in 1970. From 1981 to 1983, he was a Labor member of the Knesset.

In 1983 Herzog was elected president of Israel, serving for ten years. In that period he paid official visits to some 30 countries and addressed 15 Parliaments, including both houses of the U.S. Congress, both houses of the Canadian Parliament, the Argentine Congress, and the Polish Sejm as well as the Bulgarian parliament, being the first foreigner in history to do so.

He also wrote prolifically in the press in Israel and abroad. His books include *Israel's Finest Hour* (1967), *Days of Awe* (1967), *The War of Atonement* (1975), and *The Arab–Israeli Wars* (1982).

His wife, AURA, established the Council for a Beautiful Israel. [ED.]

HILBERG, RAUL (1926–), political scientist and authority on the Holocaust. Hilberg was born in Vienna, Austria, and went to the United States in 1939. He received his undergraduate degree from Brooklyn College and his doctorate in public law and government from Columbia University. In 1951–52, he served as a research specialist in the War Documentation Project in Alexandria, Virginia. From 1956 he taught at the University of Vermont at Burlington. He has served on both the United States President's Commission on the Holocaust and the United States Holocaust Memorial Council.

Hilberg's major work, *The Destruction of the European Jews* (1961, revised ed. 1985), is one of the most important contributions to date to Holocaust historiography. It was one of the first attempts to write a comprehensive history of the Holocaust based on German documentation and it discusses, country by country, how the Nazis and their collaborators attempted to carry out the annihilation of the Jews in their domain. Its great importance notwithstanding, Hilberg's book has also been the subject of controversy among historians. His negative portrayal of Jewish response during the period has been attacked as unbalanced, since it is based primarily on German documentation and related little to Jewish sources. His other works include *Documents of Destruction* (1971), *The Warsaw Diary of Adam Czerniakow* (1979), and *Special Trains to Auschwitz* (1981). [RO.RO.]

HIRSCHMANN, IRA ARTHUR (1901–1989), U.S. business executive. He held key positions in several large New York department stores, eventually becoming vice-president of Saks Fifth Avenue, 1931–1938, and vice-president, Bloomingdale Brothers, 1938–1946. In 1935 he served as the chairman of the board of the University-in-Exile which employed many refugees from Nazi Germany. That year he also joined the New York City Department of Education. In July 1938 he was an observer at the *Evian Conference on refugees, which led him to more intensified action on behalf of those who sought to flee from Hitler. A supporter of President Franklin D. Roosevelt, Hirschmann was named special assistant to William H. Davis of the National War Labor Board in 1942. The Emergency Committee to Save the Jewish People in Europe (the Bergson Group) asked him to investigate rescue possibilities in mid-1943.

In February 1944 he arrived in Turkey as the Special Representative of the War Refugee Board. Working with the United States ambassador, Laurence Steinhardt, Hirschmann helped convince the Turkish authorities to allow refugees to pass through Turkey on their way to Palestine. He made a great effort to find a suitable sea-route to Turkey from the Balkans and procure shipping for the refugees. Hirschmann also played a key role in the Transnistria scheme. Through the International Red Cross, he met the Romanian ambassador in Turkey, Alexander Cretzianu, and induced him to press his government to permit the return to the traditional areas of Romania of the remaining Jews, who had been deported to Transnistria. Hirschmann also assisted Hungarian Jewry. After interviewing Joel *Brand, he recommended that the Western Allies enter into negotiations with the Nazis, with the hope that the process would earn valuable time and thereby save their lives. With the help of Monsignor Angelo Roncalli (later Pope *John XXIII), Hirschmann obtained baptismal certificates for Hungarian Jews. He also successfully prevailed upon the Romanians to allow Hungarian refugees into Romania in the summer of 1944. Through the Bulgarian minister in Turkey, Nicholas Balabanoff, he persuaded the Bulgarians to revoke their anti-Jewish legislation.

In 1946 Hirschmann went to work for the United Nations Relief and Rehabilitation Administration (UNRRA) as a special inspector-general. In that capacity he toured displaced person's camps in Germany and contributed to the improvement of conditions in them. In addition to his other interests, Hirschmann was a talented pianist and musicologist. He established and assumed the presidency of the New Friends of Music in 1946. That same year he became the president of the Metropolitan Broadcasting and Television Inc. Hirschmann published two memoirs, *Lifeline to a Promised Land* (1946) and *Caution to the Winds* (1962).

Bibliography: H. L. Feingold, *The Politics of Rescue: The Roosevelt Administration and the Holocaust, 1938–1945* (1980); D. Morse, *While Six Million Died; A Chronicle of American Apathy* (1968); D. A. Wyman, *The Abandonment of the Jews: America and the Holocaust, 1941–1945* (1984). [RO.ROZ.]

HOROVITZ, ISRAEL (1939–), U.S. playwright. Born in Wakefield, Mass., Horovitz in 1965 became the first American playwright-in-residence for England's prestigious Royal Shakespeare Company. He burst on the New York scene in 1967 with four one-act plays and received acclaim the following year for *The Indian Wants the Bronx* which introduced Al Pacino to broadway and won several awards. A prolific writer, Horovitz followed this success with a number of plays including *Rats, Morning, Morning Noon and Night* (1968); *Trees* (1969); *Acrobats* (1970); *Line* (1971); *Leader* (1972); *The Honest-to-God Schnozzola* (1969); *Shooting Gallery* (1973); *The Primary English Class* (1976), which starred Diane Keaton; and *The Reason We Eat* (1977). In 1970 his screenplay for the film, *The Strawberry Statement*, won the Prix de Jury at the Cannes Film Festival.

His later work has been more experimental in form and style, with deep character introspection and incidents of mental disorientation. In general he has written ensemble pieces rather than star vehicles, and his work has exhibited a profound social commitment. [ED.]

HUNGARY (see **8**:1078; **Dc./17**:317). Over the past decade a revolution of sorts occurred within the Jewish community in Hungary, with repercussions on its existence and development. This change can be defined as mainly one of quality but also one of quantity: there are now many more Hungarian Jews than there were a decade or two ago, that is, many more people of Jewish origin are now willing to identify themselves as Jews and no longer feel or see a need to hide their Jewishness.

The freedom which returned to Hungary with the fall of communism in Eastern Europe also gave back to its Jews, who had suffered greatly, a sense of being free to be Jews, to maintain a natural link to the State of Israel, and to try to give Jewish education to their children. At the same time, anti-Semitism reappeared, and the Jews now faced the same choices as their brethren in the West: identification with Zionism and possible *aliyah*; or accelerated assimilation; or carefully walking the tightrope between the two.

Assimilation, Zionism, Aliyah. Assimilation continued apace among the Jews of Hungary. The recent controversy over the problem of intermarriage showed that almost every Jewish family in Hungary has been affected by it.

As soon as it was legally possible, a Zionist Federation was founded in Hungary, led by psychologist Dr. Tibor (Samuel) Englander, but it has little influence and only a tiny fraction of Hungarian Jews are active in it. In 1992 no more than 100 Jews emigrated to Israel.

An impartial observer receives the impression that he is seeing vibrant Jewish life. Dozens of organizations — B'nai B'rith, WIZO, Na'amat, the Jewish Culture Organization, Zionist youth movements from Benei Akiva to Ha-Shomer ha-Ẓa'ir, Ḥabad, and so on — carry on feverish activity which touches only a small part of the Jewish population. The Jewish Agency has an office in Budapest, but there is no emissary for educational affairs and after the Russian immigrants to Israel stopped using the transit center in Hungary, the Agency's role and importance diminished. The World Jewish Congress, one of the first organizations to set up a representation in Hungary after the change of regime in 1990, was about to close its office and transfer it to Moscow.

Anti-Semitism. Paradoxically, Jews seem to have been goaded into "Jewish life" by the anti-Semitism which reasserted itself under the new rule. Although it is still illegal, the police in a liberal regime are unable — and the government apparently does not care — to enforce this law. The result has been a great spurt in anti-Semitic journalism and hateful anti-Semitic remarks by a few of the elected representatives of the Democratic Forum (M.D.F.), the ruling party. The most prominent of the anti-Semitic papers are the *Magyar Forum*, under the editorship of the author Istvan Csurka, and *Szent Korona* ("The Holy Crown"), edited by Laszlo Romhany. Romhany has been convicted of incitement to murder. In 1992 and early 1993 there were many incidents of attacks on foreign students as well as against gypsies and Jews by young persons called "nationalists," who identify themselves with the skinheads, and in the Hungarian Parliament they have a patron in the person of Isabella B. Kiraly (M.D.F.). At a large demonstration in front of the Parliament in October 1992, groups of young people showed up in Nazi uniforms and the writer Csurka accused the president of Hungary, the liberal Arpad Gönz of having "the agents who pull the strings in New York, Paris, and Tel Aviv, guide his path in Hungarian politics," which according to Csurka are still ruled by the Jews as are the communications media.

In Satoraljaujhely, Hungary, Holocaust survivor Rosika Roth, 73, maintains a Jewish life and *kasher* home despite being one of only seven Jews in the town, Oct. 1992. (Photo Ruth E. Gruber)

In 1983 the then chief rabbi of Hungary, Joel Shoner (far left), greeted the German chancellor, Helmut Schmidt, upon his visit to Budapest. (Courtesy Naftali Kraus)

In spring 1993 anti-Semitic feelings were aroused by an interview given by the head of the Jewish community, Gusztav Zoltai, and the chief rabbi of Budapest, Georg Landesman, to a Catholic weekly. The rabbi made a few lame statements which were seen as contemptuous of Hungarian culture. The rabbi apologized, but his opponents in the community used the ensuing storm of public opinion to call for his resignation. The Hungarian prime minister, Jozef Antal, addressed himself — in an unprecedented step — not to the board of the Jewish community, but to the Israel ambassador in Budapest, David Kraus, and demanded the dismissal of the rabbi, whose remarks were, as stated in Antal's letter, "false, shocking, detrimental to the Hungarian people, and likely to cause an outbreak of anti-Semitism." The ambassador rejected the letter's contents, but the Hungarian minister of the interior ordered that an investigation be opened to see whether there is any basis for accusing the rabbi of "causing hatred of Jews." After Rabbi Landesman apologized, but refused to resign, the community board canceled the position of chief rabbi and its duties were divided among the other rabbis. Landesman did stay on as the rabbi of the Great Synagogue on Dohany Street.

Jewish Education. At the close of 1992 three Jewish schools were in operation with a total of 1,000 pupils, less than one percent of the Hungarian Jewish population, estimated at 100,000. There was also a kindergarten, founded in 1992, from which, according to the plan, another elementary school will develop and which will be operated by the Jewish community.

At present the schools are: Moreshet Avot, founded by the Canadian Reichmann family. It has 12 grades (some with two classes) and some 500 pupils. A special rabbi brought from Israel, Rabbi Jacob Zinger of Givat Shemuel, is respon-

Gusztav Zoltai, head of the Hungarian Jewish community (Courtesy Naftali Kraus)

sible for seeing that only Jewish pupils are accepted by the school. The school has 55 teachers, 10 from Israel, who are changed yearly. The salary of the principal, Avi Teitelbaum, is paid for by the Jewish Agency. The school maintains a moderate religious atmosphere and promises the pupils "international" matriculation in English.

Yavneh School (founded by the Lauder Foundation) defines itself as a "secular Jewish school," and is open, by declaration, to non-Jews (indeed over half of its pupils are not Jewish). The school is overcrowded and only one of every three applicants is accepted. In spirit Yavneh is akin to the Jewish Culture Organization, and in its three years of existence has had four principals.

The Anne Frank Gymnasium is the oldest of today's three Hungarian Jewish schools. It was the only Jewish school not closed by the Communist regime, although it was severely limited by it, so much so that by the end of the 1970s only 15 pupils were enrolled in its four classes. Currently there are 200 pupils (only Jews are accepted); the principal, Rozsa T. Berendt, and most of the teachers are Jewish. Organizationally the school belongs to the Jewish community. Hebrew instruction is given by a teacher from Israel.

Study groups are conducted by the Lubavich movement and its emissary, Rabbi Baruch Oberlander, as well as by the Jewish Culture Organization, which also published a bi-monthly journal, *Szombat* ("Sabbath"). The famous Budapest Rabbinical Seminary, founded nearly 120 years ago, recently ceased functioning in that capacity — from lack of interest and pupils — and is now a teachers' training college preparing a group of young people for teaching in the Jewish schools. In 1986, a centennial volume on the seminary, edited by Moshe Carmilly-Weinberger, was published in New York.

Organizational Structure. At the head of organized Hungarian Jewry stands Mazsihisz, the federation of Jewish communities, which unites the organized Jewish communities, the largest and most important of which is the capital Budapest, with the greatest concentration of Jews; others exist in Debrecen, Miskolc, Szeged, and elsewhere. The majority of Jews in Hungary do not belong to any organized community or to any Jewish organization. The leaders of the federation are its president, the lawyer Peter Feldmayer, and the acting chairman, Gustav Zoltai. After a 50-year break, during which the Jewish leaders were appointed by the Communist regime, elections were held in 1990 and since then an elected directorate has been in operation. Among all Jewish organizations listed above, the largest and strongest is the culture organization, Mazsike, and even its membership does not exceed a few hundred. The community publishes a biweekly called *Uj Elet* ("New Life").

Rabbis and Spiritual Leadership. There are some 12 rabbis today in Hungary, all belonging to the Neolog (akin to Reform) stream. For the few dozen Orthodox Jews, the rabbi is Rabbi Jacob Zinger of the Reichmann school. The elected chief rabbi is Georg (Joshua) Landesman and the director of the former rabbinical seminary is Rabbi Josef Schweitzer. In the different regions of Budapest, congregational rabbis are: Rabbi Tamas Lővy; Rabbi Tamas Raj (also a member of Parliament for the Free Democrats party); Rabbi Judah (Robert) Deutsch, director of the Budapest rabbinate office; Rabbi Dr. Oedon Zinger, rabbi of Buda; Rabbi Istvan Doman; Rabbi Peter Kardos, editor of the community biweekly; Rabbi Istevan Berger, rabbi of the city of Pecs; Rabbi Arpad Vèrtes, rabbi of Gyor; and Rabbi Baruch Oberlander, the Lubavich emissary, who has his own synagogue in Budapest and who publishes his own organ, *Egyseg* ("Unity"). A ritual bath operates in Budapest and the rabbinical council recently published an open letter stressing the importance of observing the laws of family purity.

Hungary-Israel Relations. These relations, established and developed by Shlomo Marom, the first Israel ambassador to Hungary after the resumption of diplomatic relations, are satisfactory and have continued to improve during the term of the current ambassador, David Kraus. On Hungary's part, from 1990 through 1992, visitors to Israel have included President Arpad Gőnz, Prime Minister Jozef Antall, and Foreign Minister Geza Jeszensky. Israel President Herzog visited Budapest (amid rumors that Arabs tried to assassinate him while there). Hungary was of great assistance to Israel in the transit of immigrants from the Soviet Union to Israel when they passed through the Budapest transit center. In 1992 terrorists attacked a busload of Soviet Jewish immigrants; although they were not hurt, two Hungarian policemen were injured. Mutual tourism is growing as are relations between cities and increased cooperation at international forums — all of which are characteristic of the relations between the two countries since the resumption of diplomatic relations. [N.KR.]

I

IBIZA and FORMENTERA, third and fourth largest of the Balearic Islands. Situated south to south-east of Majorca, equidistant to North Africa and mainland Spain, the islands provided a strong commercial attraction to Jewish traders from the periods of Phoenician and Roman occupation, particularly for their bountiful saltpans and the dyeing industries.

Hitherto, historians have concluded that the Jews in the smaller Balearics suffered similar oppression to their coreligionists some 100 miles away in Palma, capital city of controlling Majorca. This misconception was enhanced because the name "Majorca" was given to the whole Balearic area.

The inhabitants of Ibiza and Formentera (Ibicencos) to this day bitterly resent the 700 years of Majorcan domination and greatly prize personal freedom. Local piracy, smuggling, and the proximity and affinity to Islamic Barbary all contributed to a hatred of prying eyes and the facility to hide Jews from the Inquisition.

Sixth-century church documents mention the considerable size of the Jewish population and, contrary to other Iberian centers of that period, their lack of interest in conversion to Christianity. The Jewish population increased with the annexation by James I, the "Conquistor," in 1235. In 1254, the king arranged their property assessments as part of the Aljama of Majorca. In 1329, the Jews of Ibiza requested separation from the Majorcan community which was refused.

In the terrible year for the Jews of Spain, 1391, there is no mention of outrages in Ibiza or Formentera, or of an exodus in the fateful year of 1492. All documents relating to visits by the officers of the Inquisition from 1423 onwards state that nobody was found practicing the Laws of Moses, yet research indicates that Jews continued to reside in the Islands and assisted many from elsewhere to escape the clutches of the Inquisition.

The Juderiá (ghetto) in Ibiza was in use as such until the 19th century and efforts are now being made for its restoration. Part of the nearby Convent of San Christobel (built in 1600) was used as a synagogue.

In 1867 a clearly defined Jewish community was described by Prinz Luis Salvador of Hamburg in German in his first book on the Balearic Islands but was deleted in all subsequent editions until 1979.

The survival of Jewish customs was described by visitors to the Islands as late as the 1930s. The Spanish Civil War (1936–39) and the influence of the German SS in Majorca brought fear and conversions to Catholicism. Yet the islanders protected Jewish arrivals fleeing the Nazis.

A small number of Jews of various origins now reside there and have formed a group to support the many interested in their Jewish roots and desirous of strengthening these affiliations.

Bibliography: B. Braunstein, *Chuetas of Majorca* (1952), 117; I. Macabich, *Costumbre* (1966), 19; G. Mound in *Papers 4th and 5th British Judeo-Spanish Seminars*, Glasgow, 1984 (1986); I. Cohen, *Travels in Jewry* (1952); JC (Sept. 4, 1936); Jerusalem Post (March 17, 1983); *Die Balearen in Wort und Bild* (1867); Prinz Luis Salvador, *Los Antiguas Pitiusas* (fascimile, 1979), 137. GL.M.]

INDIA (see **8:**1349; **Dc./17:**319). There has been no dramatic change in the number of Jews in India over the past decade. The community has faced no crisis and there has been no immigration. However there has been a trickle of emigration to Israel, averaging about 200 a year. It is estimated that the community (now consisting mainly of *Bene Israel) has dwindled from about 7,000 to about 5,000. No precise figures are available as no community-wide census or survey has been organized. At its height, in the 1940s, Indian Jewry numbered over 30,000, the largest community in the Far East, with a full range of social, cultural, Zionist, charitable, and sports activities.

There has been no evidence of anti-Semitism although damage has been done to a synagogue in Poona by vandals. Relations between the government at central and state levels continue to be cordial. The community was encouraged by the establishment of diplomatic relations between India and Israel in 1992 which resulted in a tremendous upsurge of interest in Israel and its international stance, especially as India shares many problems with Israel. There has been considerable progress in the spheres of trade, defense, and scientific and cultural exchanges.

In religious life, an American rabbi, Rabbi Gradstein, was financed by the Joint Distribution Committee to serve in Bombay in 1992–3. Difficulties have been experienced in organizing services in Baghdadian and Cochin synagogues due to lack of numbers, but the Bene Israel synagogues and prayer halls, including the Reform, have been functioning normally.

Special Zionist activity over the decade has consisted mainly in organizing celebrations to mark Israel's Independence Day by the local Zionist associations, in Bombay in cooperation with the Israel consulate. The consulate was established in 1952 but kept a low profile as it was accredited not to India but to the State of Maharashta, in order to placate pro-Arab sentiment in ruling circles. This has now changed dramatically and in May 1992 there was a great celebration to mark the 25th anniversary of the reunification of Jerusalem held at the Magen David Synagogue in Byculla, Bombay which was established in 1861.

Passover Haggadah, 1875, India. From the exhibition *Jews of India*, Jewish Museum, N.Y., 1985–86. Collection of the Jewish Theological Seminary, N.Y.

Indian representatives attended meetings of the Commonwealth Jewish council of which Calcutta-born Lieutenant-General Jack Jacob, the only Jewish general in the Indian army, became vice-president.

An outstanding event in 1985 was the centenary celebration of the Keneset Eliahu Synagogue in Fort Bombay, the largest center of Indian Jewry. The events were inaugurated by the president of India, Gyani Zail Singh. Prime Minister Rajiv Gandhi sent a message praising the major contributions of India's small Jewish community. The main address in the synagogue was given by Percy S. Gourgey. Another centenary celebration was held that year for the Magen David Synagogue in Calcutta. Also in 1985 the Jewish Museum in New York presented an exhibition on India's three Jewish communities — the Bene Israel, the Baghdadian (Babylonian), and the Cochin Jews. In 1987, the Jewish Religious Youth Union launched a history project about Jewish landmarks in Bombay, and 1988 saw the building of a memorial pillar at the Bene Israel cemetery at Navgaon, near Bombay, where according to their tradition the ancestors of the Bene Israel landed 2,000 years ago. Three books on Indian Jewry were published in 1990: *Jews in British India: Identity in a Colonial Era* by Joan Roland; *India's Bene Israel* by Shirley Isenberg; and *Indian Jews and the Indian Freedom Struggle* by Percy S. Gourgey. In 1992 an Indo-Israel Friendship League was formed in Bombay. [P.S.G.]

INSTITUTE OF JEWISH AFFAIRS (IJA), international research body based in London, which deals with contemporary issues affecting Jews and Jewish communities worldwide. The institute monitors and analyzes trends and developments in international relations, politics, human rights, sociology, economy, and culture. It acts as a forum for discussion and presentation of policy options on matters of Jewish concern. The IJA is a leading research and documentation center on international anti-Semitism and publishes *Antisemitism World Report*, an annual survey of anti-Semitism and right-wing extremism in the world. The IJA's publications include *Patterns of Prejudice*, an academic journal devoted to the study of racial and religious prejudice with a special reference to anti-Semitism; *East European Jewish Affairs*, a journal dealing with Jewish problems in Eastern and Central Europe and the countries of the former Soviet Union; *Research Reports*, a series of background surveys on international affairs; *IJA Analysis*, papers commenting on current events and developments affecting Jews; *IJA Intelligence Reports*, concise assessments of the Jewish significance of developments in current affairs worldwide. Its journal *Christian-Jewish Relations* ceased to appear in 1990. Long-term research projects are published in book-form. The IJA's public activities range from academic conferences, symposia, and seminars to lecture series.

History. The Institute was founded in 1941 in New York by the World Jewish Congress to study problems facing Jewry after World War II. In the post-war period the IJA played a vital role in preparing blueprints for compensation to victims of Nazism, assisting in war-crimes trials and contributing to international legislation on human rights and related issues. It was headed successively by Jacob Robinson, Nehemia Robinson, and, after its transfer to London in 1966, by Stephen J. Roth. Its present director is Antony Lerman.

IRAN (see **8**:1439; **Dc./17**:231). In 1978, an estimated 80,000 Jews were living in Iran, of whom 60,000 were in Teheran, 8,000 in Shiraz, 3,000 in Isfahan, and 1,500 in Kermanshah with 2,000 in the Khuzistan townships. Their cultural, economic, and professional importance far exceeded their proportion in the population. Some 10% were very wealthy, a similar number very poor, while the economic status of the others was satisfactory. Some 6% of the country's 10,000 doctors were Jews, and 4% of the students and 2% of academicians. In the course of a single generation Iranian Jews had made impressive advances, participating in the economic boom which followed the "White Revolution" of 1963.

From early 1978, parallel to the turbulence in Iranian society, the Jewish community underwent difficult internal conflicts, reflected in the bitter struggle between the Organization of Radical Intellectual Jews in Iran and the Teheran community council. The former identified with the Khomeini revolution of January 1979 and published a manifesto expressing the "solidarity" of Iranian Jewry with the aims of the "Islamic Revolution," praising the PLO, and attacking Zionism and the Israel government.

On coming to power Khomeini issued conflicting proclamations concerning the regime's attitude to Iranian Jews. In its early years a number of Jews, most of them wealthy industrialists, were executed but the motivation seems to have been economic and not anti-Jewish. Khomeini promised a delegation of Iranian Jews in 1979 that he would maintain the welfare and security of the "Jewish Iranians as long as they remained far removed from Zionism and the state of Israel," but on other occasions made humiliating statements concerning the Jews which caused apprehension in the community. In its early years the revolutionary regime confiscated much Jewish property, on a much more systematic basis than confiscations from Muslims. It was estimated that the value of Jewish property expropriated exceeded a billion dollars.

Many Iranian Jews saw the revolution as a danger signal and emigrated. From the early 1980s a considerable number arrived in the United States, especially California, while others went to Great Britain, Italy, and France. According to the Iranian constitution, Jews continued to have the right to elect one representative to the Majlis (the Iranian parliament). The Jewish representative has followed the regime's line with respect to foreign and domestic policy, which features rabid anti-Zionist propaganda. Young Jews serve in the Iranian army where they are permitted to observe Jewish holidays and several Jews fell in the Iraqi-Iranian War.

During that war, much was written in the Western world about the sale of military equipment from Israel to Iran. There is no doubt that Israel favored Iran, feeling that an Iraqi victory would make Saddam Hussein an even more dangerous figure in the Middle East. Israeli figures were involved in the "Irangate" affair in which Israel acted in behalf of the United States in conveying weapons to Iran in the hope of receiving in return the release of western hostages held in Lebanon. In Sept. 1985, Prime Minister Shimon Peres announced that Israel would not sell weapons to Iran.

After the 1982 Lebanon War, Iran became deeply involved in developments there through its support of the extremist Shi'ite organizations, notably the Hizbollah and later Hamas, through money (estimated at $100 million a year), armaments, and training. The Hizbollah became outstanding for its desperate actions and its adamant stance for an all-out war of destruction against Israel.

Iran has remained steadfast in its extreme anti-Israel attitudes in the United Nations and in international forums. The phrase "Israel must be destroyed" was uttered by its representative in the UN, and it annually advocated the expulsion of Israel from the world body. During the war against Iraq, Saddam Hussein was denounced as a "Zionist"(!) and several of the Iranian military operations were dedicated to the "liberation of Jerusalem." An Iranian stamp depicted the mosques on the Temple Mount with the inscription "Let us liberate Jerusalem." The last day of Ramadan each year was established as "Jerusalem Day," when anti-Israel slogans are disseminated. In 1982–3, the religious and lay heads of the Jewish community published an announcement requesting the Jews of Iran to contribute to the war effort and to protest "the cruel Zionist invasion of Lebanon, the repression of the Palestinians, and for the liberation of Jerusalem."

During 1986–87, the rate of emigration of Jews from Iran increased, mainly following Iraq's aerial bombing of the large towns, in which the Jews were concentrated. One consequence of the exodus of many young men was that it became increasingly difficult for girls to find Jewish husbands and there was an increase in intermarriage between Jewish girls and Muslim men (permitted in Islamic law, unlike marriages between Muslim girls and Jewish men). Most of the 23 Jewish schools in Teheran were taken over by Muslims while in the others, Muslim pupils constituted a majority. Education in general is Islamic and Jewish pupils are exposed to constant Islamic propaganda.

After the death of Khomeini and the end of the war with Iraq, a slight improvement in government attitudes to Iranian Jews was discerned. The economic position of many Jews improved, a sizable number even became rich, and some Jewish leaders became friendly with high members of the ruling circle. The Jews continued to publicly stress their enmity to Zionism and the state of Israel, and their sympathy for the Islamic revolution. However the beneficial changes were few. Some Jews whose property had been confiscated and who had been imprisoned or whose freedom of movement had been restricted had part of their property returned and were allowed to leave the country.

The active participation of Iranian Jews in the war against Iraq, both as soldiers at the front and through material aid and care for the wounded in the Teheran Jewish hospital enhanced the image of the Jews as loyal citizens. Moreover their continuing denunciations of the "Zionist state" have been appreciated not only by the authorities but also by the general public.

The Jews now number about 25,000 and are mainly concentrated in Teheran. The provincial cities have been largely emptied of their Jews who have moved to the capital. Although the Jews are not numerically significant, the authorities attribute importance to them at the economic level and for international propaganda purposes. The intellectual sector of the Jewish population is relatively large and the government sees them as having links to Jews in Europe and the U.S. with political and economic influence.

In 1992 there was an increase in the number of Iranian Jewish expatriates in the U.S. who returned to Iran to run their businesses and even to resettle there. There are no precise statistics on this "return movement." At the same time, hundreds of wealthy Jews and those considered close to Israel and to the royal family are still blacklisted with their names published from time to time in the local press.

Iran's hostility to Israel continues to be expressed on every possible occasion by word and deed. The local press is filled with vilification of Israel, in the basest terms, reminiscent of the worst Nazi propaganda. The papers declare that *aliyah* endangers the world, that the Palestine problem is what matters rather than the Gulf situation, and that Hizbollah in Lebanon must be made stronger so that it can destroy Israel. It is claimed that Israel is helping the Serbs to annihilate the Muslims in Bosnia. No day passes without the press mentioning the *intifada*, and Israel's "genocide and killing of Muslim children." In many scenes, Israel is depicted as the devil, conniving to take over the world. Frequently this hatred of Zionism and Israel is hard to distinguish from anti-Judaism. Iran is the only country in the world whose leaders openly declare that the state of Israel must be destroyed, a slogan that continues to appear on walls of houses, stores, schools, and buses.

Apart from its support of Hizbollah and Hamas in Lebanon, Iran is involved in terror at the international level, both directly as in the bombing of the Israel embassy in Buenos Aires, and indirectly as in the bombing of the World Trade Center in New York. The regime has increased its support for fanatical groups in the U.S. which wish to expand the building of mosques in the big cities and to distribute newspapers and other publications.

Since the breakup of the Soviet Union, the regime in Iran has been expending great efforts and investing huge sums in the Muslim republics of Asia, especially those adjoining Iran. Every effort is made to export the ideas of an Islamic state to these republics. The influence of Iranian propaganda in Arab countries is also strong. Evidence of this is the impact on extremist Muslims of Egypt, Jordan, and Algeria. Iran is the only country strongly opposed to the Israel-Arab peace talks, thereby encouraging extremist groups in the Arab world.

Since the Gulf War, the Western powers have begun to understand the threat posed by Iran to Western interests. In particular there is concern over the development of the country's nuclear potential. Iran is cooperating on nuclear research with Far Eastern countries and has acquired large quantities of weapons, apparently from Kazakhstan. It is scrambling to obtain weapons of mass destruction from every place, the world over, and is developing its long-range missile capacity. [AM.N.]

IRELAND (see **8**:1464; **Dc./17**:322). One of the most remarkable features of Irish Jewish fortunes in the decade under review is the continuing decline in numbers. The 1971 Government Census put the Jewish population at 2,633; in 1981 it was 2,127; and current estimates are 1,400. At the same time, there has been a rise in Jewish participation in the top sectors of public life. Throughout various general elections, three Jewish TDs (members of the Dail, the Irish parliament) have retained their seats — one for each of the main parties. Ben Briscoe who represented Fianna Fail was also lord mayor of Dublin in the city's millennium year (1988), following in the footsteps of his father, Robert *Briscoe. Alan Shatter of Fine Gael was also appointed his party's environment spokesman. Mervyn Taylor of the Labor Party in 1993 became Ireland's first Jewish cabinet minister.

Israel president Chaim Herzog (see p. 181), who was born in Belfast and educated in Dublin, paid a State visit to Ireland in 1985. On this occasion he opened the Irish Jewish Museum in the former Walworth Road Synagogue. Diplomatic relations between Ireland and Israel remain at the level of non-resident ambassadors, Israel being represented by its ambassador in London (Yehuda Avner, 1984; Yoav Biran, 1989). A pro-PLO Palestine Information Office was established in Dublin in 1986. In 1992 Ireland appointed an honorary consul in Israel.

Rabbi David Rosen served as chief rabbi of Ireland until 1984 when he settled in Israel. He was succeeded by Rabbi Ephraim Mirvis who went to England in 1992. There are now two major Orthodox synagogues in Dublin: Adelaide Road (which celebrated its centenary in 1992) and Terenure, and two minor congregations: Machzikei Hadass (formerly St. Kevin's Parade, which celebrated its centenary in 1983) and the Abraham Gittleson synagogue in the Jewish Home for the Aged, opened in 1991. The Dublin Jewish Progressive congregation marked its 40th anniversary in 1986. The Greenville Hall synagogue was sold in 1986 but the developers have retained the original perimeter walls, windows and

Herzog Family Exhibit in the Irish Jewish Museum, Dublin (Courtesy Asher Benson, Dublin)

Presidential visit to Terenure Synagogue, Dublin, June 1991: (left to right) Mrs. Mirvis, Rabbi Mirvis, Pres. Mary Robinson, Judge Hubert Wine, Mr. Nick Robinson, Mr. Maurice Abrahamson (Courtesy Asher Benson, Dublin)

cupola, and welcome visitors. The *mikveh* was restored in 1984. A major community survey made in 1986 recommended the rationalization of communal resources, including a single Dublin congregation, but little had been done by the end of the decade.

The main educational facility, Stratford College, was rebuilt after an arson attack in 1983, and its three-tier educational complex remains in full operation. It was awarded the Jerusalem Prize for Jewish education in 1989. The Edmonstown Golf Club built a new 6,000-square-foot clubhouse, opened in 1990. The old Jewish cemetery at Ballybough, which was in use from 1718 to 1890, was reopened to the public in 1990. An extension to the Jewish Home for the Aged was opened by the Irish president, Mary Robinson, in 1992. The old headquarters of the Board of Guardians and former Talmud Torah premises in Bloomfield Avenue were sold in 1983.

A number of new organizations have been founded: the Irish Council of Christians and Jews in 1983; the Ireland-Israel Economic and Business Association in 1992; while the Irish-Israel Friendship Association was revived in 1989.

Among the anniversaries celebrated during this period were the 50th anniversary of Dublin Ziona (WIZO) in 1987; the 60th anniversary of the 16th Dublin Jewish Scouts in 1987; and the centenary of the Board of Guardians in 1986.

A number of international conferences of Jewish interest were held in Dublin. These included the International Council of Jewish Women (1985); the International Council of Christians and Jews (1985); the International James Joyce Symposium in 1991, which held a session at the Irish Jewish Museum; while the first Irish Genealogical Congress in 1991 held a workshop on Irish Jewry.

Relationships with the authorities continued to be cordial. The president of Ireland, the lord mayor of Dublin, and many dignitaries were guests of honor at Jewish occasions and delegations from the Jewish Representative Council of Ireland reciprocated with courtesy visits. The chief rabbis continued to make TV appearances on major Jewish festivals.

Anti-Semitism was very low-key, although occasionally exacerbated by casualties suffered by Irish troops serving in UN troops in Lebanon. The tiny Nationalist Socialist Irish Workers' party, which exported anti-Jewish pamphlets to the United Kingdom in 1984, has not surfaced for years. A survey by St. Patrick's College, Maynooth, found only 40% of the respondents would marry or welcome Jews into their family (which should be seen partly against religious backgrounds) while 13% did not welcome them as Irish citizens.

Apart from Dublin, the only other community that still exists in the Republic of Ireland is in Cork, which has a burial ground and synagogue. However services take place only during the High Holy-days when the requisite number for the *minyan* is made up to strength by volunteers from Dublin. Park Shalom was dedicated by Cork Corporation and the Irish Gas Board, 1989, in fond memory of the city's Jewish community, and is appropriately situated in the area where they lived.

The disused Limerick Jewish cemetery (early 20th century) was restored 1990, by the Limerick Civic Trust. The ceremony was attended by many church and civic leaders.

The troubles that have beset Northern Ireland have led to a dwindling of the Belfast Jewish community, now estimated at about 200 families, which maintain an active communal life. [ASH.B.]

ISAACS, JEREMY (1932–), English producer and arts executive. Isaacs was educated at Oxford, where he was president of the Union in 1955. In television, his main interests were in documentaries and current affairs, and he was responsible for celebrated series and programs both for BBC (Panorama) and Independent Television as producer, controller, editor, and sometimes journalist. The 26-part series *The World at War* about World War II, which received worldwide praise, was initiated and produced by Isaacs in 1974. As an independent he produced "A Sense of Freedom" for Scottish TV and a series for BBC, *Ireland — a Television History*.

He became founding chief executive of Channel 4 in 1981, creating a much-envied model for cultural television. He was a major influence in the arts by attaching a high priority to opera and ballet as well as literature and the visual arts.

In 1988 Isaacs was appointed general director of the Royal Opera House, Convent Garden, where he had served as a member of the board since 1985. Despite great financial difficulties in the arts and much media criticism of the Royal Opera House, Isaacs brought Covent Garden back to internationally acclaimed artistic levels.

A private and somewhat reserved personality, he is also a distinguished TV interviewer of singular discretion allowing recognition for the personality being addressed (he rarely appears on the screen himself). He suffered a personal tragedy when his brother was killed by a terrorist bomb in Jerusalem in 1975.

Isaacs has been the recipient of many honors and awards and has been a governor of the British film Institute since 1979. France made him a Commandeur de l'Ordre des Arts et de Lettres in 1988. [SA.WH.]

ISAACSON, JOSÉ (1924–), Argentinian writer, essayist, and lyric poet. Many of his works have received awards, including *Amor y Amar, Elogio de la Poesía*, and *El poeta en la sociedad de masas*, the last an audacious literary anthology which won the National Prize for Linguistic Sciences. Other noteworthy works were *Kafka, la imposibilidad como proyecto* (1974) and "Cauderno Spinoza," (1977) a philosophical poem conceived as an incarnation of the apogee of 18th-century reason before the advent of the crisis of contemporary thought and the alienation of 20th-century man.

In 1980 he received the Latin American Prize for intellectual Jewish merit, conferred by the Latin American branch of the World Jewish Congress. From the Jewish perspective José Isaacson writes about the post-emancipation period and from the perspective of Argentine history, his literary production belongs to the most pluralistic and humanist tradition generated by Liberalism. Thus he appealed both to Jewish intellectuals and to the non-Jewish cultural world which appreciated his human, universal and abstract values. He was president of the Argentine branch of the International Pen Club. From 1953 to 1970 he was board secretary of the Jewish-Argentine quarterly *Comentario.*

[J.L.NA/N.H.DN.]

ISRAEL STATE OF GENERAL SURVEY (see **9**:404; **Dc.17**:326).

1982–1991. In a broad perspective of Israeli history, the decade of the 1980s was a period of internal strife, growing dissent over major issues such as the war in Lebanon, an era of economic reverses, serious decline in immigration but ending with a major influx, especially from the Soviet Union, and finally — the *intifada*, which brought Israel to face a renewed outburst of Palestinian nationalism.

The Lebanese War, which started on June 6, 1982, was long in the planning and was expected by many Israelis, who felt that the northern border area could not be left exposed to terrorist attacks emanating from the mini-PLO state which had emerged in southern Lebanon. Initially, there was little public debate on the wisdom of the invasion. It was assumed that it would amount to a brief operation lasting less than a week, with few casualties, and covering a limited area, not dissimilar to other operations taken in the past. The Israel Defense Forces (IDF) planners, and above all the key figure pushing for war, Defense Minister Ariel Sharon, based their plans on a number of assumptions. They assumed that a brief operation would not be opposed by the United States, and that the Soviet Union would not get involved. They assumed correctly that apart from Syria, no other Arab state would intervene. They thought that Israel would need some five to seven days to complete the destruction of the mini-PLO state. They assumed that the Lebanese Christian forces would participate alongside Israel and that once the aims would be achieved, a central and effective government would be installed in Beirut which would sign a peace treaty with Israel. Sharon thought that the destruction of the PLO bases in Lebanon would allow him to deal more effectively with the Palestinians in the West Bank and Gaza. He also thought that in the future Israel and Syria would have to collaborate on deciding the future of Lebanon. Most of these assumptions proved to have been correct.

There were also a number of dissenting voices. The defense minister was warned by both the Mossad and Army Intelligence *(Aman)* that the Christian forces were an unreliable element, more of an armed militia than a trained and disciplined fighting army. Israeli planners did not understand the nature of Lebanon and its society, being more of a tribal and communal nation than a unified one. Above all, the planners failed to gauge reaction inside Israel to a prolonged war which would demand a high number of casualties, and would give the IDF a new role — that of police force in a neighboring country. The official aims, contained in the government's announcement of June 6, 1982, were the removal of the Northern Galilee settlements out of PLO artillery and katyusha range, the removal from Lebanon of external forces, and the restoration to that country of a centralized authority which would sign a peace treaty with Israel. It called on Syria not to participate in the war and promised not to attack its troops in Lebanon.

Major Haddad with Lebanese and Israeli troops greeted by Lebanese village women, June 8, 1982 (GPO, Jerusalem)

Within five days, most of the military aims were achieved. The IDF expelled the PLO units from southern Lebanon and destroyed the mini-state it had created there. But this was done with a higher casualty rate than anticipated, and with Syrian involvement. Superior Israeli military technology resulted in the destruction of over 100 Syrian jet fighters and a vast number of Syrian missile batteries on Lebanese territory. By the fifth day Israeli military units reached the edge of Beirut. It was then that the United States ordered Israel to cease fire, claiming that it had far exceeded its limited territorial war aims by moving farther north than the 40 kilometers it spoke of initially. Israel Premier Menahem Begin had to accept a cease-fire, which actually never came into being as Palestinian troops continued to fight, as did the Syrian army, now threatened in its positions along the strategic Beirut-Damascus highway. By the end of the first week, public opinion in Israel was aroused. Questions were being asked about the true agenda of the government, the real war aims, the growing number of casualties, and above all how long the IDF intended to stay in Lebanon and in what role. During June, July, and August 1982, while diplomats tried to hammer out an agreement which would remove the PLO from Lebanon and bring about a new order in that country, Israeli troops continued to shell Muslim West Beirut, cutting off water, power, and food. The aerial and artillery bombardment of West Beirut aroused growing international criticism and created hostile world public opinion. In Western media Israel was portrayed as an aggressor fighting helpless civilians, creating a new refugee problem, this time in Lebanon. Feeble Israeli efforts to explain the true causes of the war and the need to remove the PLO threat to Israel fell on deaf ears. Growing dissent inside Israel was also reflected in the Western media. It became clear that Israel was becoming mired in the Lebanese bog with few considering how to extricate the IDF from that country. Prime Minister Begin argued that the achievements in Lebanon erased the shame of the Yom Kippur War, but that did not convince many Israelis of the need to remain in that country for any length of time.

Protracted negotiations led to the removal of both the Syrian army and the PLO from Lebanon. Israel was instrumental in getting Christian forces leader Basheer Gemayel elected as president of Lebanon. But on September 1, 1982, Israel suffered two major setbacks. The first was the announcement of Gemayel, in a meeting with Prime Minister Begin, that he did not intend to sign a peace treaty with Israel, because he was first and foremost an Arab. The second was the proclamation of the "Reagan Plan" for a Palestinian settlement, which called on Israel to withdraw from most of the territories it held, and return them to Jordan in the context of a peace treaty. There was to be no Palestinian state, but Jordan would grant special status to the West Bank and Gaza. The situation of Jerusalem would have to be negotiated in the future. Begin, who had no prior notice of the plan, rejected it outright, saying it was not even a basis for negotiations. It looked as though the war in Lebanon had yielded little apart from securing northern Galilee and destroying the PLO as a military force and an important element in the Arab world.

The Kahan Commission findings had their opponents as well, February 1983. (GPO, Jerusalem)

The assassination of Basheer Gemayel shortly before his inauguration (September 14, 1982) was the signal for a vicious reprisal by his Christian forces on Palestinians living in two refugee camps in Beirut — Sabra and Shatilla. With the IDF standing by not far from the camps, and unaware of the magnitude of the massacre which lasted three days (September 17–19, 1982), some 400 Palestinians, men, women, and children, were massacred before the IDF put an end to the killing. A clamor went up in Israel to establish a commission of inquiry to investigate the events in the camps. The demand, backed by a demonstration organized in Tel Aviv by left wing parties and groups in Israel, reputedly attracted some 400,000 people, the largest ever held in Israel. When Begin still resisted, he was confronted with a threat by President Navon to resign his office. Finally, the prime minister relented and a commission was constituted headed by Supreme Court President Justice Kahan. While it began its work, tempers cooled and the country awaited two decisions — the verdict of the commission and a political decision on how long and within which borders the IDF would remain in Lebanon.

The government decided to order the IDF to remain in Beirut until an agreement could be worked out with the new Lebanese government headed by Amin Gemayel, the brother of the late Basheer Gemayel. As time went on, the IDF became involved in local communal strife in Lebanon. The Kahan commission issued its report in February 1983. It found the IDF indirectly responsible for the massacre, calling for the resignation of the defense minister and senior army officers. Ariel Sharon had to leave his post but remained in the government as minister without portfolio. Senior officers also had to leave, among them the director of military intelligence. Others, including the chief of staff, did not have their term of duty extended.

On May 17, 1983, after long and difficult negotiations with the participation of U.S. Secretary of State George Shultz, Israel and Lebanon signed an agreement which fell short of a peace treaty. It ended the state of war, recognized Israel's need to have a security zone in southern Lebanon under its control, called for Israeli diplomatic presence in Beirut, and demanded the withdrawal of all foreign troops from Lebanon, which meant in effect Syrian troops. The agreement was hinged on this withdrawal. When Syria announced that it would not withdraw its troops, the agreement became a dead letter. Nine months later the Lebanese parliament failed to ratify it and the agreement in effect lapsed. For the next two years, the IDF sought ways to extricate itself from Lebanon, finally withdrawing under orders from the National Unity Government which came into being in 1984. By the summer of 1985, the Lebanese episode ended, leaving Israel in a security zone in southern Lebanon, the PLO re-established in Tunisia, the Syrian army in Lebanon, and Israeli public opinion highly uncertain whether the toll of three years in Lebanon — 659 dead and thousands wounded — had been worthwhile.

In 1983 Israel faced an unprecedented economic threat, caused by the over-valuation of bank shares, inflated by the banks themselves. When the public began to unload these bank shares, there was a danger that the Israeli financial institutions would collapse and that overseas investors and depositors would remove billions of dollars leaving the Israeli economy in the lurch. In October 1983 the Tel Aviv stock market was closed for 17 days and the government decided to buy the bank shares at a cost to the Israeli taxpayer of some 7 billion dollars. By late 1983 inflation in Israel reached the figure of 200% annually and by 1984 it had amounted to 448%. Inflation was destructive for the country's economic growth, morale, overseas investments, and labor relations. Even the resignation of Finance Minister Yoram Aridor, whose policies brought Israel to the brink of economic disaster, did not alleviate the situation. It took the Government of National Unity's rescue plan (July 1985), which froze prices and wages and put in a mechanism of retrenchment to save the situation. Within a year, the rate of inflation was down to 20%. The plan was made possible by the cooperation of the government, the Histadrut (Trade Union Federation), and the Manufacturers' Association. The three factors realized that with no serious action, Israel's economy would literally collapse. The rescue operation was engineered by Prime Minister Peres, with the help of Finance Minister Yitzhak Modai and the Histadrut leadership. The Israeli public, asked to make sacrifices in lowering its standard of living, agreed once it saw a coherent economic policy.

The Government of National Unity (see Israel: Political Life and Parties) brought about three major achievements — it extricated Israel from Lebanon, it rescued its economy, and restored public confidence in the economy and the leadership. It failed to attract a mass wave of immigration, and the decade of the 1980s up to 1989 saw an average of some 12,000 immigrants a year, while the number of emigrants leaving Israel reached similar figures. The gates of the Soviet Union were closed and immigration from the free world dwindled. The outstanding exception was the airlift of 17,000 Ethiopian Jews to Israel in 1984. The Jewish Agency decided to transfer to the government much responsibility in the area of immigrant absorption, previously under its domain. The peace process was virtually at a standstill because of the vast chasm between the views of the Likkud and those of Labor (see Israel: Foreign Relations).

The absence of meaningful progress towards peace, the growth of a generation of young Palestinians who knew nothing else but Israeli occupation, an economic recession in the oil-producing Arab states which drastically reduced flow of funds to the areas held by Israel causing serious economic hardship, and above all resentment of the prolonged Israeli presence on the one hand and the impotence of the PLO and the Arab governments to change the situation, all this erupted in late 1987 in an uprising called the *intifada* ("shaking off"). A series of demonstrations in the Gaza Strip on December 9, 1987, signaled the beginning of the *intifada*, led by young men in their early twenties, asserting themselves against both Israel and their elders. Starting with demonstrations, throwing stones, burning tires, the aims of the *intifada* were to call attention to the plight of the Palestinians, to the prolonged occupation in all its ramifications, to

The stock market crash: shocked customers line up in front of a bank (Courtesy *Koteret Rashit*, photo courtesy Chibi Shichman)

Rioting in the *casbah* of Nablus, the *intifada* in action, 1988 (GPO, Jerusalem)

focus on the Palestinization of the conflict, to force the Arab states to take notice, to move the rest of the world to take action, and to make the Israel public and government take decisions on future policies. The major achievement of the *intifada* in its first four years were mainly in the area of public relations. Israel's image in the Western media plunged dramatically. The *intifada* leaders forced the PLO to follow its lead. It hurt the Israeli economy by calling on Arabs in the areas to boycott Israeli goods. It helped to precipitate the decision of the U.S. government to recognize the PLO in December 1988, after the latter announced the creation of a Palestine State in the 1947 partition borders, the acceptance of Israel, and what appeared to be a renunciation of terror. The U.S then embarked on a dialogue with the PLO. The *intifada* created major problems for Israel, whose army now had to deal with civil unrest, the mass demonstrations manned by women and young children. This time, unlike the years that followed the 1967 war, the bulk of the Palestinian Arab population seemed to support the uprising, as did a growing number of Israeli Arabs.

Faced with a new type of war, the IDF had to consider the ethical and moral issues involved in fighting against civilians. It was initially thought that if the *intifada* leaders would be caught and deported or imprisoned, the wave of attacks would die down, but this was not the case. As the *intifada* spread from Gaza to the West Bank, it began to claim Israeli lives, both civilian and military. By early 1993, some 160 Israelis had lost their lives. In that period over 1,600 Palestinian Arabs were killed, the majority at the hands of other Arabs accusing their victims of collaborating with Israel. The IDF found itself having to fight what was essentially an unpleasant, at times "dirty," war. On the whole it succeeded, but there were cases of torture, unnecessary shooting and killing and a number of Israeli officers and soldiers were court-martialed for using illegal force. These were highly publicized in Israel and abroad, where the issue of human rights was prominent in the headlines and Israel was often the object of criticism.

The impact of the *intifada* on Israelis was at first marginal, but as time went on it became central. There was a feeling of loss of personal safety, and as more acts of terror were committed in Israeli cities, Israelis realized that they were facing a new breed of Palestinians, some of whom were even prepared to engage in suicide attacks. The Gulf War and the resultant peace process put the *intifada* on the back burner for a time, but it remained a major problem for all Israeli governments who feared that if not dealt with properly, the allegiance of the Palestinians would move from the PLO to the Hamas (Islamic fundamentalists) who opposed the peace process, negotiations with Israel, and called for the elimination of the Jewish state. By 1991 the areas held by Israel were the arena for a fight for the hearts, minds, and souls of the Palestinians between the PLO and the Hamas movement. There was also a growing demand in Israel for unilateral withdrawal from the Gaza Strip and gradual disengagement from the West Bank as well. The reliance on some 120,000 laborers from these areas meant that Israeli agriculture, housing construction, and many services were now manned by Palestinians, whose absence could cause havoc. Measures were undertaken to replace Palestinians by Israelis, but there was need to find employment for Palestinians, as long as they remained an Israeli responsibility. Massive unemployment in the areas could result in an explosion, it was argued.

By the end of the 1980s, the continued *intifada*, the wave of immigration from the Soviet Union, and the end of the Cold War brought about the need for Israel to reconsider many of its social, political, and economic institutions. Many of them served the country well in its formative years, but no longer provided answers to the complex issues of the final decade of the twentieth century. It was widely agreed that reforms were sorely needed in the Histadrut, government corporations, political parties, the electoral system, and government control of many aspects of the life of its citizens; there was need to reconsider the relations between the secular majority and the Orthodox minority. Questions dealing with the nature of Israeli politics and the ties between big business and government had to be considered.The 1991 Gulf War also resulted in serious questioning of Israel's military and strategic doctrines and the realization that future wars would not differentiate between civilians and soldiers.

Some changes were made in the political system. There was greater internal democratization in the political parties, where candidates for office were elected in a primary system. From 1996 Israel will elect its prime minister on a personal basis, as it does its mayors. There was progress towards codifying a constitution. However, the arrival of some half a million new immigrants between 1989 and 1993 meant that Israel was once again thrown into a turmoil involving the postponement of many crucial decisions on essential reforms. [M.ME.]

CENTRAL GOVERNMENT

The main feature of the central government between 1984 and 1990 was the existence of the Government of National Unity based on the two major political blocs. It was a unique Israeli creation and an unprecedented political arrangement. In view of the failure of both Labor and Likkud to win an absolute majority in the 1984 elections to the 10th Knesset, and in order not to rely on radical left-wing or right-wing parties or an ultra-Orthodox non-Zionist parties, and in view of the economic crisis and the presence of the Israel army in Lebanon, the Likkud and Labor entered into an agreement on the following arrangement (September 13, 1984). The prime minister for the first two years of the Knesset term would be Shimon Peres (Labor), while Yiẓhak Shamir, Likkud's leader, would be vice-premier and minister for foreign affairs. At the end of two years they would rotate their respective positions. The key body dealing with foreign affairs and defense was to be an "Inner Cabinet" consisting of five ministers from the two major parties. This body was also empowered to deal with settlement and had the same authority as the previous Ministerial Committee for Defense and Foreign Affairs. The defense minister (Yitzḥak Rabin, Labor) would serve for the entire four-year term, so would the finance minister (Yitzḥak Modai, Likkud). Each of these two was to have a deputy minister from the other party.

This arrangement worked well during the term of the 10th Knesset. Peres relinquished the premiership to Shamir in 1986 and assumed the post of foreign minister. The results of the elections for the 12th Knesset were such that the arrangement was continued, but it was decided that Shamir would be premier for the entire four years, Peres would be vice premier and finance minister while Rabin would continue as defense minister. The National Unity Government finally broke up in March 1990 over serious disagreements concerning the peace process. While in office, the government was able to extricate Israel from Lebanon, initiate a new economic policy which virtually saved Israel's economy from imminent collapse, and improve Israel's international standing.

Another feature relevant to this era was the rise in influence of the state comptroller. Former Supreme Court Justice Miriam Ben-Porat, appointed state comptroller in 1983,

Miriam Ben-Porat (GPO, Jerusalem)

began to issue scathing reports detailing serious flaws in the government's operations and management. Some of her findings led to criminal charges against ministers and deputy ministers. She did not spare any institution under review and while not all her findings were corrected, she did create an atmosphere of greater adherence to the laws and regulations directing the work of the government.

This era also witnessed a growing politization of the civil service which did not contribute to the maintenance of an apolitical civil service. Both major parties appointed to various offices party stalwarts, who in many cases lacked any competence in the field in which they found themselves. Most glaring were the appointments of party loyalists to positions of directors over the 140 government corporations. Many lacked any experience and training and were chosen to enhance the "camp" of the respective minister who appointed them. Similarly, there was a growth in the number of deputy ministers and the re-establishment of ministries that were once abolished (Ministry of Police recreated in 1984). Efficiency and saving of public funds were not priorities for the politicians. This situation was also a perennial feature in the annual report of the state comptroller.

There was a vast growth in appeals to the Supreme Court to rule on many issues that were once the domain of the Knesset and the government. There was also a growing number of officials, Knesset members, deputy ministers, and even cabinet members against whom police investigations were commenced on charges of mishandling public funds, diverting funds to their parties or special institutions, and evading various regulations governing disbursal of public funds. Special inquiries were held to determine how funds were used during election campaigns.

This situation meant that there was increasing public disillusionment with politicians and with the institution of the Knesset, while two institutions rose in public esteem — the Supreme Court and the state comptroller. Israeli democracy remained intact, protected as it were by the latter bodies, as well as by a free and very vociferous and investigative media. [M.ME.]

POLITICAL LIFE AND PARTIES

(see **9**:656; **Dc./17**:334)

Israeli political life in the 1980s revolved around the elections for the 11th and 12th Knessets (1984 and 1988). The Knesset is the central arena for Israeli politics and much of the inter- and intra-party infighting was over the control of the party leadership, seats in the Knesset, and cabinet posts. The decade witnessed a continued struggle within the Likkud Party for the eventual succession to Yizḥak Shamir, and in the Labor Party the ongoing leadership struggle between the two veteran leaders, Shimon *Peres and Yizḥak *Rabin. There was growing demand on the part of the rank and file in both large parties for greater democratization and mass participation in the selection of the candidates for the Knesset and the premiership.

Yizḥak Shamir (GPO, Jerusalem)

There was a noticeable decline in party ideology and considerable crossing over from one party to another for the sake of personal gain and promotion. Some of these maneuvers added to public cynicism and disenchantment with the political system, and there were loud calls for the reform of the electoral system in order to make the Knesset members responsible to the voters and not solely to their party's central committee. Many attempts to write and legislate a constitution for Israel failed, mainly because of opposition stemming from the Orthodox parties who feared secular influence and a parallel decline in the authority and jurisdiction of the religious institutions. Since both Labor and Likkud sought the support of the Orthodox parties in order to govern the country, they were content to leave the matter of a constitution in abeyance.

Yizḥak Rabin (GPO, Jerusalem)

The resignation of Menaḥem Begin as prime minister in August 1983 did not usher in a period of struggle for his succession. Yizḥak Shamir was seen by all party factions as the heir-apparent because of his seniority and also in order to avoid a vicious fight between many contenders while Israel was still involved in Lebanon and in the midst of a severe economic crisis. Shamir favored a passive type of leadership, not imposing his will nor demonstrating charismatic traits. Not an orator, he preferred to pursue a very careful and cautious domestic and foreign policy, leaving decisions to the last minute, playing his cards very close to his chest, and above all unwilling to experiment both at home and abroad. He did groom, however, a number of younger leaders who were seen as the core of his camp. Among them were Moshe *Arens, his protegé Binyamin Netanyahu, Ehud Olmert, Dan Meridor, and later Binyamin Ze'ev Begin (son of Menaḥem Begin). In the 1980s they were included in the inner group that advised Shamir on major issues. Shamir followed the Likkud's line of no Palestinian state, no talks with the PLO, no territorial concessions, no alienation of territory held by Israel, no change in the sovereignty and status of Jerusalem, continued large-scale settlement in the Administered Areas. At home, the party called for greater liberalization of the economy, sale of public corporations, massive investments to create jobs, reduction of taxes and limitations on the powers of the Histadrut. Likkud also favored a national health service. On issues of the relations between the secular majority and the Orthodox minority, Likkud was prepared to give in to Orthodox demands in order to maintain their coalition, especially in areas of special funding of religious schools, no change in the jurisdiction of the religious courts and rabbinate, and the preservation of the status quo on religious matters.

In the 1984 elections the Likkud obtained 41 seats (2 less than in the May 1977 landslide that brought the Likkud to power), but Labor received 44 seats (12 more than in 1977) and became the largest party bloc in the Knesset. Likkud had to settle for a Government of National Unity in which the offices of prime minister and foreign minister were rotated

Shimon Peres (GPO, Jerusalem)

between Peres and Shamir after an interval of two years. During this time, there was an intensification of the inner struggle within the party and growing dissatisfaction with Shamir's leadership. The two main challengers were Ariel (Arik) *Sharon and David Levy (q.v.). Both began to form their camps in the hope of winning votes in the 2,100-strong Ḥerut Central Committee. This infighting continued well into the early 1990s and was one of the major reasons for the defeat of the Likkud in the June 1992 elections for the 13th Knesset. None of the contenders challenged the ideology of the leader, stressing mainly their electoral appeal and marketability to younger voters. Levy leaned heavily on Jews originating from Muslim lands, especially Morocco, stressing his "ethnic" background. Sharon campaigned on the basis of his military record and his tough stand on the Palestinian issue and the need to eradicate terrorism. None of the contenders was above gaining supporters in various, sometimes dubious, means, which did not enhance their integrity. Shamir's protegés managed to gain much experience in government and emerged in the public eye as much engaging and trustworthy leaders whose future was still ahead of them. Meridor's term as minister of justice and Olmert's stewardship in the ministry of health were successful. Netanyahu had a meteroic rise from the post of ambassador

Television ads have become part of Israel's election campaigns; above, Labor Party election team analyzes another party's ad, June 1992. (GPO, Jerusalem)

to the United Nations, to Knesset member (1988) and deputy foreign minister and emerged as one of Israel's best-known international spokesmen. All this did not help the Likkud which lost a seat in the 1988 elections, gaining only 40 seats. However, Labor dropped to 39 and the National Unity Government was continued until it broke up over the peace process issue in March 1990. In its final years in power, Likkud was accused of mass appointments of party loyalists to various posts and boards of directors for which they were ill-suited. The party's finances also came under the State Comptroller's scrutiny and police inquiries were started. Secret deals with various politicians were revealed. Finally, the relations between the old time Ḥerut and their Liberal partners were never happy and the coalition between these two blocs collapsed in 1992.

Labor did not fare much better than the Likkud in the 1980s. Its politics were dominated by the seemingly unending struggle between Peres and Rabin for the position of party chairman and its candidate for the office of the prime minister. Both were of the same age, and while Rabin boasted of an impeccable record as chief of staff, ambassador to the United States, and prime minister (1974–1977), Peres ran on his record as the moving spirit behind Israel's nuclear and aviation industry program and the defense industries as a whole, his close association with David *Ben-Gurion, and his achievements as defense minister between 1974 and 1977. There were no ideological differences between these two leaders. The key issue was who could lead Labor to a victory in the next elections. Peres tried and failed in 1981, 1984, and 1988; Rabin tried and succeeded in 1992. In its foreign policy, Labor supported a "Jordanian option," negotiating with Jordan a Palestinian settlement. It was prepared to cede land for peace, it accepted the 1978 Camp David Accords as the basis for peace, it saw in certain Palestinian leaders in the areas possible interlocutors, and sought better ties with Europe, both on government level and through the Socialist International of which Peres was vice-chaiman. It insisted that Jerusalem must be united under Israeli sovereignty and remain the capital of Israel. With the Likkud it shared the view that the Jordan River must be Israel's security border in the east and that Israel should remain on the Golan Heights. It objected to removal of Jewish settlements in the West Bank and Gaza in case of withdrawal. It rejected the Likkud concept that "the entire world is against us," and called for a more open-minded approach to the world and said that Israel must come to terms with the new world of science and technology, where borders were being erased and new horizons were being created. It wanted a change in school curriculum which would not only stress the sufferings of the Jews but also the new opportunities and challenges ahead in an industrially-technologically oriented society. Labor was tied to the Histadrut in its domestic platform, unsure how to proceed on the matter of National Health Service bound to undermine the Histadrut's sick-fund (Kupat Ḥolim). It wanted to preserve the special privileges of the kibbutzim and moshavim, but noted the need to modernize the country, to reform its institutions, and was the first party to institute primary elections which determined in 1992 both its candidate for prime minister (Rabin) and its Knesset candidates' list. The primary system was later adopted by Likkud when it elected Netanyahu to succeed Shamir as Likkud chairman in March 1993. The Rabin-Peres leadership struggle so dominated labor politics that it delayed the emergence of younger men to positions of influence and leadership. Similar to Likkud, Labor was not beneath stooping to questionable tactics when it came to attempting to form a government, wooing certain politicians from Likkud with promises of Knesset seats and respectable jobs. These shady tactics did not endear the party to potential voters who sought other parties, seen as more "clean" and honest. In 1992 many such voters cast their ballots for the Ẓomet party (8 seats) and Mereẓ (12 seats).

In the 1980s there was a temporary resurgence among the parties on the right, which included Teḥiyyah, Moledet, and Kakh. The radical right wing parties were united in their opposition to territorial concessions to Arabs and caving in to American pressure. They called for massive settlement of the areas, and the institution of Israeli law and administration in the West Bank and Gaza. They demanded the death penalty for terrorists, greater use of the explusion measure and in the case of Moledet, "voluntary" resettlement ("transfer") of Arabs from the Areas in the neighboring countries. Kakh advocated a blend of radical Judaism and nationalism, calling for expelling the Arabs both from Israel and the Areas and the final institution of a halakhic state in Israel. Teḥiyyah won five seats in 1984, three seats in 1988, and in 1992 failed to win even one seat. Moledet won two seats in 1988 and three in 1992. Ẓomet appeared on the scene in 1988 as the "clean" party, won two seats. It quadrupled them in 1992, becoming the fourth largest party in Israel. Kakh won one seat in 1981 and was later barred from the elections by the Supreme Court which ruled that the party's platform included racial slurs.

On the extreme left there were two Arab parties which called for a unilateral Israeli withdrawal from the areas and the creation of a Palestinian state. They won two seats in 1988, similar to their strength in 1984. The Communist party, now called Democratic Front for Peace and Equality, was able to maintain its four members in the Knesset in the 1980s. Taking its line, funding, and orders from Moscow, it called on Israel to withdraw from the areas, create a Palestinian state, and pursue a non-aligned foreign policy. Naturally, they demanded nationalization of all means of production

Raphael ("Raful") Eitan, with back to camera, greets Rabbi Pinḥasi of Shas, 1992 (GPO, Jerusalem)

and a struggle against capitalism. The Communists gained much of their support from the Israeli Arab population, which cast a protest vote in this manner. They were never considered coalition partners by Labor and remained in the opposition. Another long-time opposition party was Citizens' Rights and Peace Movement, composed mainly of Ashkenazi Jews of some affluence and considerable education, who wanted to reform Israel's antiquated political system as well as bring about a separation of the state from religion and who called for the protection of the rights of the secular majority, and opposed Orthodox domination. It also stressed the need for politics of peace, based on conciliation, end of the occupation, readiness to make concessions in return for peace. They were not prepared to compromise on matters of national security although they called for closer supervision of Israel's security services. They won three seats in 1984, rose to five in 1988, and after uniting with Shinui, won 12 seats in the 1992 elections, joining Rabin's government. While Mapam was formally part of the Labor Alignment in the 1980s, it did maintain its own separate political framework, basing its power on its kibbutzim. When it ran separately in 1988, it won a mere three seats.

The religious bloc was noted for the emergence of a new, ultra-Orthodox Sephardi-based party called Shas (Sephardi Torah Guardians). They seceded from the Ashkenazi-dominated Agudat Israel, claiming that they were being discriminated against in school funding, positions, and influence. The spiritual leader of Shas was Rabbi Ovadiah Yosef, former Sephardi chief rabbi of Israel. The party sought to enhance the cause of its followers — relatively poor, less educated, urban-slum dwellers, Sephardi Jews with large families. Promising immediate material support in the shape of a long school day, warm meals in schools, special benefits to large families, and funding of various educational and social institutions, Shas was able to win four seats in 1984, rose to six in 1988, and held this number in 1992. They joined the government coalitions, even though their leadership proclaimed that they were not bound by the secular Knesset law but by a higher, Torah law, as interpreted by their sages. They viewed the state as a necessary evil and agreed to participate in the political game as long as it served their special interest. Almost from the start, the party was accused of highly irregular financial deals, channeling in an illegal manner vast amounts of money to their own institutions. Their leaders were investigated and one former member of the Knesset was sentenced to five years in jail in 1993. Their leader, Arieh Deri, was under police investigation from 1989, refusing to answer police questions until early 1993. In its foreign policy, Shas was moderate, supporting territorial concessions since peace means saving of life. They admitted that their main concern was preservation of religious gains and the furtherance of religious legislation which will make Israel a halakhic-Jewish state. For their support of the National Unity Government and later the Likkud government, they were awarded the Ministry of the Interior and between 1990 and 1992 the Ministry of Immigrant Absorption.

The National Religious Party (NRP) witnessed a vast decline in its fortunes in the 1980s. While in 1977 it was able to win 12 seats, it shrank to 4 in 1984 and 5 in 1988, and 6 in 1992. The reasons were the tilt of the party towards the radical nationalist settlers' movement called Gush Emunim, their total support for the Likkud from 1977, and the rise of competing Orthodox parties which took away Sephardi voters. There were also leadership squabbles, mainly after the departure from politics of party leader Dr. Joseph Burg. The NRP continued, however, to support the notion of co-existence with the secular parties and remained a Zionist party stressing that the laws of the Knesset were binding. They did not have a Council of Torah Sages or Elders to determine their policies and brought about greater democratization in the inner working of the party, including the selection of leaders and Knesset members.

Political life in Israel was very intense. In cases of disputes, there was often recourse to the legal system. Leaks to the press, libel, and vilification of opponents were common. Politicians began to employ public relations and media advisers, who counseled them how to appear on television, how to sell themselves to their party leaders and to the rank and file. Speech writers were employed and foreign experts hired (by Labor in 1984 and 1988). Election campaigns became very costly and donations were sought both in Israel and overseas. The State Comptroller investigated in depth the parties' election expenses in 1988 and fined some of them heavily for various transgressions of the Elections Law. As in the past, the two main parties continued to look to the Israel Defense Forces as a reservoir for future politicians, seen by the public as "clean" figures with integrity and honor. This practice often created difficulties, because generals were approached while they were still in uniform, in contradiction to the strict separation of the army from politics applied by Ben-Gurion in the early years of statehood. The practice of parachuting generals into the Knesset also clashed with the ambitions of budding politicians who came through the political ladder starting with the local branch, rising to regional and later national prominence.

In spite of many faults and flaws, the Israeli democracy continued to flourish, defended by a free press, the Supreme Court, the State Comptroller, the subservience of the army to civilian rule and public alertness. Apart from some irregularities, elections were clean and honest, transfer of power orderly and normal (and that included the 1986 rotation between Peres and Shamir). When it came to core issues, there was unanimity among all Zionist parties. All favored unlimited immigration, the need to keep Israel a Jewish State, rescue of Jews, the struggle against worldwide anti-Semitism, the pursuit of peace with security, the need to improve the country's social and educational and health services, the need to reform the system and to modernize Israel in order to make it more attractive to immigrants, tourists, and investors from the West. Israeli democracy flourished even in the face of mass immigration from 1989. New immigrants soon found themselves involved in the politics of their new country. The vote of many new immigrants from Russia, who were not satisfied with their integration in Israel, was instrumental in the defeat of the Likkud, the party in power when they arrived. The role of the Israeli media also helped to protect the country's democracy.

Many decried the loss of ideology and the trend towards voting for "names" rather than for a program. In the 1980s there was no radical change similar to that which occurred in 1977. Both the Likkud and Labor maintained some 40 seats in the Knesset and none was able to obtain an absolute majority. Coalitions were required and although these helped to protect democracy, they were not conducive to efficiency and savings, rather the opposite. Even the June 1992 elections which returned Labor to power after 15 years were not really a major upset. The camp of the national right continued to have some 50 Knesset seats, the center-left a similar number, with the rest divided among small parties with a rigid following which does not float during elections. On the basis of the Israeli democratic system, Begin was able to obtain a large majority for the Camp David and the Israel–Egypt Peace Treaty which called for the withdrawal from Sinai and the dismantling of settlements in that peninsula. One meaningful constitutional change occurred in 1992 when the Knesset decided that the prime minister will be elected on a personal basis. [M.ME.]

DEFENSE FORCES (see **9**:681; **Dc./17**:337)

The period under review was marked by four major events. The first was the war in Lebanon (1982–1985); the second was the slow withdrawal from Lebanon (1985); the third was the outbreak of the *intifada* (1987); and the fourth, Israel's experience during the 1991 Gulf War.

The decision to go to war in Lebanon was the result of many factors, among them the desire to put an end to the emerging PLO mini-state, in Southern Lebanon and the destruction of the PLO forces, headquarters and supply depots strewn throughout Southern Lebanon. There was a feeling that once the PLO would disappear from the Middle Eastern scene, Israel would find it easier to negotiate with Palestinian leaders in the territories under its control who would be free to deal directly with Israel. There was hope that war in Lebanon would bring about Israel–Syria negotiations over the future of that country. Above all, there was the desire to free Galilee from the constant threat of shelling and attacks by PLO elements. There was also the aspiration to bring about the creation of a central government in Lebanon, that would be able to demand the withdrawal of Syrian forces from Lebanon and eventually sign a peace treaty with Israel.

The shooting of the Israel ambassador, Shelomoh Argov, in London by members of the Abu Nidal terrorist group on June 2, 1982, served as the reason for Israel to enter Lebanon on June 6, 1982. Announcing the military action and the codename "Peace in Galilee," Israel said it was aimed at clearing a zone of 40 miles from its borders from the PLO. It stated that if Syrian forces would remain neutral, Israel would not attack them. Within one week, Israeli forces occupied most of Southern Lebanon, reaching the outskirts of Beirut. Hopes that the Lebanese Christian forces under the command of Basheer Gemayel, with whom prior coordination existed, would join the war did not materialize. The IDF did engage Syrian troops in various parts of Lebanon, culminating in the destruction of Syrian anti-aircraft missiles and the shooting down of close to 100 Syrian jet fighters and bombers. When a cease-fire was proclaimed on June 11, the Israel Defense Forces (IDF) deployed along the Beirut–Damascus road and inside Beirut. It had captured vast quantities of PLO equipment, including tanks and artillery. To induce Yasser Arafat, trapped in West Beirut to leave the city, the IDF began to besiege West Beirut. During June, July, and August sporadic fighting continued in Lebanon while Israeli and American diplomats sought a diplomatic solution that would enable the PLO to depart from Lebanon. An arrangement was reached in late August and the PLO withdrew on September 1, moving its headquarters to Tunis. Technically the war aims were achieved.

However, already in mid-June, there was growing dissent in Israel over the continued war in Lebanon and over its final aims. For the first time during the war, Israelis were questioning its aims and the real intent of the political leadership. The public was shocked when elements of the Lebanese Christian forces carried out a massacre of hundreds of Palestinians in two refugee camps Sabra and Shatilla in Beirut on September 16–18. A demonstration in Tel Aviv, with an estimated 400,000 protesters, forced the government to appoint a commission of inquiry. The final report of the Kahan Commission did not blame the IDF for the massacre, but found it indirectly responsible for not anticipating the consequences of the Christian forces entry into West Beirut. It recommended the removal of the defense minister and other senior officers from their posts. By then, there had been over 200 Israeli casualties in Lebanon. The impact of the war on the morale of the IDF was highly negative. A new chief of staff, General Moshe Levy, replaced General Rafael Eitan in April 1983 and began to plan a slow disengagement in Leba-

Israel Air Force Phantom jet flying over Beirut, August 1982 (GPO, Jerusalem)

Tel Aviv, 1990 — a view from west to east shows a sprawling, modern metropolis (GPO, Jerusalem)

population of the whole conurbation of Tel Aviv is added a total is reached of 1.5 to 1.8 million, depending on how the boundaries of the metropolitan area are defined. The population of the Haifa conurbation is 447,000.

Within the rural area, the population of the moshavim and the kibbutzim grew at a slower rate than did the total Jewish population, so that the percent of the population residing in moshavim declined within a decade from 4.5% to 4.0% and that of the kibbutzim from 3.5% to 3.0%.

Human Resources. In 1992 the labor force of Israel (i.e., those employed and those unemployed seeking work) numbered 1,850,000. In the decade from 1982 to 1992, the labor force grew by some 480,000 (i.e., by more than a third or 3.0% per annum). Parallel to the population change, the labor force grew at a slow pace in the period 1982 to 1989 (by 2.3% yearly), and at a much higher rate in the period of the mass immigration (by 4.9% per year).

This decade marked a high increase in unemployment compared to that of the employed. While in 1982 the rate of unemployment (unemployed as a percent of the labor force) was 5% it increased to 6.4% in 1988 and increased sharply up to 11% in 1992. This was caused partly by the entry into the labor force of a large number of new immigrants who were still looking for a job in the first stages of their stay in the country.

The main trends regarding labor force participation found in the 1970s continued through the 1980s and the beginning of the 1990s. The major development is the continuous increase in the participation of women in the labor force; from 36% of the women aged 15 and over in the labor force in 1982 to 42.5% in 1992, with women constituting 42% of all the labor force. Another continuous trend was the decrease in the labor force participation of men, mostly in the retirement and pre-retirement ages. The participation of men aged 55–64 in the labor force declined from more than 80% in 1982 to 70% in 1992, and of those aged 65 and over from 28% to 18%. Smaller declines are also found in age 35 and over. Thus, the labor force has become more feminine and of a younger age. The continuous increase in the proportion of those aged 35–44 in the labor force was related to the changes in the age structure and to the decline in participation in other ages.

The labor force is of a higher level of education. Thus persons who had 13 years and over of schooling constituted 28% of the labor force in 1982 and 36% in 1992 (17% had 16 years and over of schooling). The high level of education of the mass immigration which arrived from 1990 contributed to this trend.

Table 8. Employed Persons by Economic Branch

	1991/92		1982
	'000's	percent	percent
All Employed	1,583*	100.0	100.0
Agriculture	56	3.4	5.7
Industry	340	21.4	22.9
Electricity & Water	17	1.1	1.1
Construction	96	6.6	6.2
Commerce & Restaurants	224	14.0	12.1
Transport & Communication	97	6.3	6.8
Financing & Business Service	161	10.0	9.0
Public & Community Services	468	29.6	30.1
Personal & Other Services	115	7.5	6.1

* Includes "unknown branch"

The average number of hours worked by the employed population was 36.0 per week. No important trend changes were noticed in the decade 1982–1992.

The large increase of the employed population between 1982 and 1992 was absorbed in the various branches of the economy in similar proportions. Some differences were noticed; a continued decrease in the proportion of those employed in agriculture and industry; the proportion working in construction increased as activity in this branch grew in 1990–91 owing to the large-scale building for immigrants. In addition to the Israelis employed in the construction industry, some 70,000 workers from Judea and Samaria and the Gaza Region were employed in this branch in Israel. The proportion of those working in commerce, business, and personal services continued its growth.

The occupational distribution of the employed population did undergo some changes: the percent of those in scientific, academic, professional, managerial, and technical occupations increased from 27% to 31%, the percent of those in sales and service workers increased, while the proportions of employed in other occupational groups decreased.

Some 81% of all employed persons in 1992 were wage and salary earners, 14% were employers, self-employed persons and members of cooperatives, 4% were kibbutz members, and 1% were unpaid family workers.

Table 9. Employed persons by Occupation

	1991		1982
	'000's	percent	percent
All Employed	1,583*	100.0	100.0
Scientific & Academic	140	8.9	8.4
Professional & Technical	263	16.8	14.6
Administrators	79	5.1	4.2
Clerical	258	16.5	18.5
Sales	136	8.7	7.5
Service Workers	208	13.2	12.0
Agricultural	54	3.4	5.2
Skilled	371	23.7	25.1
Other & Unskilled	60	3.8	4.3

* Includes unknown occupations

The Israeli Household. The average Israeli household (i.e., the group of people living regularly in the same apartment and sharing common meals, including households of one person) consisted in 1991 of 3.7 persons (3.4 persons in the Jewish household and 5.5 persons in the Arab household).

There were in Israel in 1991, 1.3 million households (1.14 million Jewish and 150 thousand Arab). The typical household (75% of all households) consisted of a couple with or without children, and in some of them also additional members; 15% were households of one person (i.e., widows living alone, young persons living on their own outside their family, etc.), 4% were one-parent households with children. Other households consisted of various other structures.

The long-term trend of a slow decrease in the size of the average Israeli household was not found in the 1990s. This trend was reversed in the Jewish population, and a small increase was registered in the Jewish population. This resulted from the entrance of immigrants in 1990–92 in larger households. Though immigrants from Russia came in small nuclear families, some proportion of the families lived together in the same household (i.e., a couple with a parent or parents of the husband or wife).

Table 10. Average Size of Household

	1981	1989	1991
Total	3.66	3.62	3.68
Jews	3.42	3.34	3.43
Arabs	5.35	5.78	5.53

The proportion of single-member households, which increased continuously up to 1989 (15% of Jewish households in 1981 and 17% in 1989) decreased somewhat (16.2% in 1992), while larger households of 5 members and over did increase (from 27.2% in 1989 to 28.4% in 1991). Large differences in the size of households were found between households of various communities. The average household of those born in Africa in 1991 was 3.94, in Asia 3.52, and in Europe and America 2.83. The household of those born in Israel was 3.76, resulting from the young age structure of this group.

HOUSEHOLD FORMATION AND DISSOLUTION. The number of marriages and their frequency continued decreasing in the 1980s, as formal marriage was postponed, by some one year for grooms and brides who married for the first time. This occurred as cohabitation of younger men and women continued increasing. The decrease in the marriage rate was found in all age groups but especially in the younger age groups.

The dissolution of families by divorce increased to a small extent. One of every eight marriages contracted in Israel was broken by divorce. The divorced couple was married on the average for 11.5 years and had 1.8 children on divorcing.

[M.SIC.]

THE ARAB POPULATION (9:1021; Dc./17:342)

Israel. In the early 1990s the Arab population of Israel was close to 730,000 (compared to 150,000 when the state was established, and excluding the East Jerusalem Arabs who are not citizens of Israel, estimated in 1993 to number 170,000).

During the 1980s the social and political consciousness of the Israeli Arabs crystallized, having been deeply influenced by pivotal political events in the region; the Lebanon War (1982–1983), the *intifada* in the Administered Territories (1987 ff.), and the Gulf crisis and war (1990–1991). Despite the high tension these events created in the relations between Jews and Arabs in general, the Israeli Arabs became more integrated and more involved in the life of the state. They were seriously opposed to the war against the PLO in Lebanon, expressed in various ways solidarity with the *intifada* in the Administered Territories, and demonstrated sympathy for Saddam Hussein, but all of this did not lead to deep rifts between them and the Israeli-Jewish establishment. In many ways the opposite is true. Israeli Arabs conducted their political struggle through legitimate channels while emphasizing their being Israeli citizens. Their fight took the form of opposition to government policy and stressing their separate national identity while desirous of striving for principles of equality within the Israeli democratic frameworks.

A school building in Umm el-Faḥm (GPO, Jerusalem)

The nature of the Israeli Arabs' struggles is best exemplified by the *intifada* which engulfed the entire area of Judea, Samaria, East Jerusalem, and the Gaza Region, but in which Israeli Arabs did not take part. The manifestations of civil disobedience in the Administered Territories did not appear at all among the Israeli Arabs. Although there were occasional instances of rock throwing or the waving of the Palestinian flag in Arab settlements in Israel, it can still be said that the Israeli Arabs did not participate in the *intifada.*

The separate identity of Arab citizens of Israel (from that of the Administered Territories' Arabs) was given expression in the establishment of new public bodies and in the founding of political parties and social movements. In 1982, in the wake of the Lebanon War, a "Supreme Watch Committee" was set up which in the 1980s turned into a quasi-representative body for the entire Arab population of Israel. This grew out of the committee of Arab mayors and gradually took on high political and social standing. Its members are the heads of the Arab locales, Arab Knesset members from all parties, the Arab representatives in the Histadrut, and leaders of various political movements. The committee has no recognized legal standing and reaches its decisions most often by general agreement, but it has great prestige and influence. It made the decisions to give assistance of a humanitarian nature to Administered Territory residents and to express identification with their struggle, took decisions on the behavior of the Arab populace on memorial days and on the annual Land Day, and also discussed the issues of readying the Arab public for elections to the Knesset, the Histadrut, and the city and village councils.

While in previous years the Israeli authorities did everything possible to prevent the establishment of separate Arab bodies for fear of the consolidation of Arab nationalism hostile to the state, from the early 1980s on the Israeli regime was tolerant on this issue. The members of the Israeli Arabs' Supreme Watch Committee acted in concert (not officially) with factors within the overall Israeli social and political system.

In contrast to the first decades of the state in which the Israeli Arabs were divided generally into supporters of the Communist party or suppporters of Zionist parties, in the 1980s a different party-political structure took shape. The

Communist party declined, with the decline of the Communist regimes. Its position was claimed by two movements of an Arab-National nature, namely, "The Progressive List for Peace" (initially an Jewish-Arab party) and the "Democratic List" (led by Abd al-Wahab Darousheh who left the Labor party). A more important change came with the rise of a new powerful factor — the Islamic Movement. This movement did not compete in Knesset elections; its strength was seen in the election campaigns for the local authorities. The Islamic Movement won, among others, the mayoralty of Umm al-Faḥm as well as the chairmanship of other councils mainly in the central district bordering Samaria. In Galilee, with its high concentration of Christians, the Islamic Movement had only modest success. The movement rose against the background of the flourishing of similar movements throughout the Arab east. The ideological stances of the Islamic Movement in Israel are more moderate than those of its sister movements in the Administered Territories, the Hamas and the Islamic Jihad, which call for violent struggle against the state.

The 1980s were a time of significant development in the local rule in Israeli Arab villages. Seventeen new authorities (about one-quarter of all Arab authorities in the country) were established. In some places the locality's status was changed and large settlements were recognized as cities. Although the average socio-economic standing of the Arab public is still lower than that of the Jews, there was accelerated development of various public services.

Administered Territories. At the start of the 1980s a gap, which became even wider, opened between the Israeli administration and Palestinians' leaders and their institutions in Judea, Samaria, and the Gaza Region. Talks about instituting autonomy in the Administered Territories according to the Camp David Accords ceased when no real progress was made. Israel proposed personal autonomy, for the residents only, with no territorial ramifications, while the Egyptian proposals spoke of Palestinian administration which would in effect lead to total Israeli withdrawal from the territories. When Ariel Sharon was defense minister (in the second Likkud government elected in 1981), there were many settlement campaigns.

The most prominent change in the Territories in 1981–1984 was the emergence of village leagues. The Israeli administration which nurtured them saw these leagues as representing the silent majority of the inhabitants of the villages in Judea and Samaria who ostensibly opposed the preeminence of the PLO-supporting radical city dwellers. The government gave the heads of the leagues and their activists wide authority and budgets, and residents were directed to the leagues in order to obtain permits and recommendations for various petitions to the administration.

The village leagues attracted marginal members of the Palestinian population. Many people saw them as a collection of doubtful individuals collaborating with the Israeli regime. In order to protect the league people, the Israeli administration allowed their leaders to start militias which were given weapons for self-defense by the Israel Defense Forces (IDF). In March 1982 Jordan published an official report according to which membership in village leagues would be considered an act of treason punishable by death.This led to the collapse of the leagues, some of whose major activists had previously been considered traditionally loyal to the rule in Amman. After 1984 the Israel administration gradually ceased supporting the leagues. In the mid-1980s the leagues' activities were greatly reduced, and they are remembered as the only episode in which the Israeli administration tried to encourage a political group in the territories.

The Lebanon War that began in June 1982 with the aim of damaging the PLO organizational infrastructure succeeded in effecting the removal of its headquarters and offices from Lebanon.

The events in Lebanon led to closer relations between the PLO and Jordan as well as to an improvement in the relations between the Administered Territories' residents and the Jordanian government. In Amman the work of the Jordan-PLO committee became regularized, and large sums of money were poured into the territories. The Jordanian Parliament convened in Jan. 1984 for the first time in nine years, with representatives from the West Bank.

In the Administered Territories the Lebanon War gave rise to a gradual increase in disturbances and acts of terror against Israel. Elements in the Israel military tendered the explanation that the retreat from Lebanon under terrorist pressure and attrition had reinforced the feeling among young Arabs that it was possible to fight against Israel using those means. Immediately after two Jews were killed, an underground group of Jewish settlers attacked the Muslim college in Hebron, killing three Arab students and wounding several. The police and security services captured members of a "Jewish underground" who confessed to a number of acts against Arabs, including mayors of cities, and to planning to blow up the Dome of the Rock.

In early 1985 an agreement was signed by which the Popular Front for the Liberation of Palestine–The General Command, led by Aḥmad Jibril, released the few Israeli prisoners of war from the Lebanon War and Israel freed from Israeli prisons 1,150 prisoners convicted of membership in terrorist organizations and of carrying out terrorist acts. Most of the Arabs returned to their homes in the Administered Territories and within Israel and were not deported. The Palestinian public saw this as a great victory.

After the breakdown of an agreement between King Hussein and Arafat in Feb. 1986, the Jordanians increased efforts to acquire influence in the Administered Territories. The Jordan government published a five-year plan for the territories' development while at the same time announcing the closure of the PLO office in Amman.

On Dec. 9, 1987, the popular rebellion, the *intifada* ("shaking off"), broke out in the Administered Territories. On that day an Israeli truck ran over four Arab workers from the Gaza Region as they returned from work in Israel. Three days earlier an Israeli merchant had been stabbed to death in Gaza, and a rumor ran among the Arab populace that the traffic accident was really an Israeli act of revenge. During the funerals wild disturbances broke out during which another three Gaza residents were killed.

Besides the broad economic, social, and political circumstances which led to the uprising, there were other contributory developments. During summer and fall 1987 the U.S. government did not succeed in promoting any ideas towards a settlement in the region. In November an Arab summit meeting took place in Amman which disappointed the Palestinians, since it refrained from discussing their issues. At the end of November a young Palestinian coming from Lebanon managed to infiltrate an Israeli army camp near Kiryat Shemonah by use of a glider. He shot and killed six Israeli soldiers before being killed. The Administered Territories populace was thrilled by the success of this suicide mission as well as by the deaths of Israeli soldiers and the escape from prison of a number of security prisoners connected to the Islamic extremists from Gaza.

The first weeks of the *intifada* were characterized by spontaneous large-scale outbursts of demonstrations along with commercial and school strikes throughout the territories and in East Jerusalem. No organization or guiding hand was behind this. Handbills were printed daily, slogans were painted on walls, and calls were heard to fight against Israeli rule. Almost daily reports were received of Arabs injured in

Bir Zeit University students carrying the Palestinian flag at a demonstration during the first month of the *intifada*, Jan. 5, 1988 (GPO, Jerusalem)

clashes with Israeli soldiers. World media showed increasing interest.

Even during the first month Israel security forces arrested hundreds of Arabs suspected of instigating strikes and demonstrations, and on Jan. 3, 1988, expulsion orders against nine Administered Territories activists were issued. The Israeli measures did not lead to any calming down of the situation and the foment in the Administered Territories reached new heights.

During Feb.–March 1988 there were indications of the intent to turn the uprising into organized civil disobedience against Israeli rule. Handbills signed by a body called "The United Intifada Command" began to appear with instructions to the people. Representatives of the different PLO faction and activists from the Islamic movements took part in the Command. Announcements were broadcast on a number of PLO radio stations, and the youths who heard them printed transcripts, photocopied them, and distributed them in cities, villages, and refugee camps.

The civil disobedience which coalesced at the start of the *intifada* was organized by activists sympathetic to the PLO with the aim of creating the widest breach possible between the Arab–Palestinian population and the institutions of the Israeli administration. Most of the Administered Territories' educational institutes, including the universities and colleges, were closed by military orders in the middle of the 1988 school year since they were hotbeds for demonstrations, and in effect the educational system was shut down. Heavy pressure was applied on other Arabs employed by the Israeli administration to leave their jobs. Particularly targeted were those who came into contact with the broad public. Workers of the Department of Motor Vehicles, those who check and test drivers and vehicles, were asked to quit. The same was true for workers in taxation departments, in civil courts, and offices in the Israeli administration civil service system. Those who did not quit received threats; stones and Molotov cocktails were thrown at their homes.

One of the areas of civil disobedience intended to lead to a break between the residents and the Israeli regime was the declaration of a boycott on all Israel-made goods. The tradesmen were requested to rid themselves of all products bought or made in Israel for which a local substitute could be found. In addition, the residents were asked to try to avoid turning to the Israeli authorities on any issue whatsoever, to shun the civil courts operating within the framework of the Israel Civil Administration, and to refrain as much as possible from working in Israel and from trading with Israelis.

Unified Intifada Command instructed the residents to institute an austerity regime. It was forbidden to hold weddings with many guests or have other parties. The purchase of luxury items, including new cars, was interdicted. The inhabitants were requested to avoid going out for recreation, to refrain from seeking entertainment, not to eat in restaurants and not to visit the seashore or vacation spots in Israel. In many places Arabs who had private gardens were made to uproot shrubs and flowers and tear out grass in order to make room to plant vegetables for home use to replace the Israel produce.

Storekeepers were ordered to keep their stores closed almost completely and to open them only as directed in the handbills. Gradually an arrangement took shape whereby it was permitted to open businesses for three hours in the morning and only on those days on which there was no general strike. In the afternoons and on the frequent strike days all public institutions, such as municipalities and public transportation, were shut down. Even owners of private cars were told not to drive on the roads.

All of these moves were prompted by "Popular Committees" formed in villages, refugee camps, and urban neighborhoods. Many of the committees were based on youth organization clubs found practically everywhere in the Administered Territories: the (PLO) "Shabiba" and other groups identified with the left-wing Palestinians organizations.

Popular education committees were set up to arrange for school-like frameworks in private houses in place of the closed schools. Hundreds of adjudication committees were set up to which the residents were to turn in place of the courts to settle disputes. The local committees tried to create the impression of creating the structure of an independent Palestinian regime. They set up roadblocks at entrances to villages which they declared "liberated territory."

The *intifada*'s political effects became more noticeable in summer 1988. At the end of May, U.S. Assistant Secretary of State Richard Murphy, responsible for dealing with the region's affairs, announced that the U.S. would consider opening a dialogue with the PLO on the condition that the organization accept UN resolutions 232 and 338 and condemn the use of terror. At the end of July, King Hussein announced that his country had no claims on the West Bank and was in effect breaking relations with the Administered Territories. Residents of Judea, Samaria, and East Jerusalem, most of whom were still Jordanian citizens, feared that this decision would prove detrimental to them but in actuality it did them relatively little harm. Pension payments to Jordanian civil servants in the territories continued as usual as did export (mainly agricultural produce) from the territories to the eastern side of the Jordan. Administered Territory residents could continue to use their Jordanian passports.

This break was a political victory for the Palestinian national leadership in the Administered Territories and for the PLO command in Tunis, for this was an unequivocal declaration that the PLO institutions were the only and sole representations for territory residents, with no challenge to this from Jordan.

The Jordanian statement and the continued *intifada* paved the way for the dramatic decisions by the Palestinian National Council (PNC), meeting in Algiers. *Intifada* activists applied great pressure to the PLO leaders to transform the successes of civil disobedience into political achievements. On Nov. 15 the PNC declared the "establishment of an independent state" and its acceptance of UN resolution 242. The latter made it possible for Arafat to appear before the UN assembly meeting in Geneva in Dec. 1988. At a press meeting held there he declared that the meaning of the PNC decision was recognition of the State of Israel and demurring from acts of terror. Arafat's statement had been coordinated with the U.S. which announced that the U.S. was opening a dialogue with the PLO. This development was the zenith of the *intifada*'s political achievements.

In the Administered Territories the Palestinian declaration of independence was accepted enthusiastically and general support given to the Palestinian leadership's new political line. On Dec. 9, with the first anniversary of the *intifada*, sources in the Administered Territories claimed that over the course of the year more than 300 Arabs had been killed and some 20,000 injured. Israel gave similar figures. The number of Arabs arrested or detained in Israeli prisons was close to 12,000.

During the *intifada*'s second year (1989) cracks and internal dissension began to show. One of the most salient was the phenomenon of intra-Arab murders of people suspected of collaborating with the Israeli rule. The ongoing *intifada* pattern yielded great suffering for the Administered Territories residents. The suspension of the education system, lengthy strikes, and severe Israeli punitive measures all led to a lowering of the standard of living across the board. In some places there were residents who refused to comply with the demands of the United Command leaflets and who tried to oppose the young activists' directives.

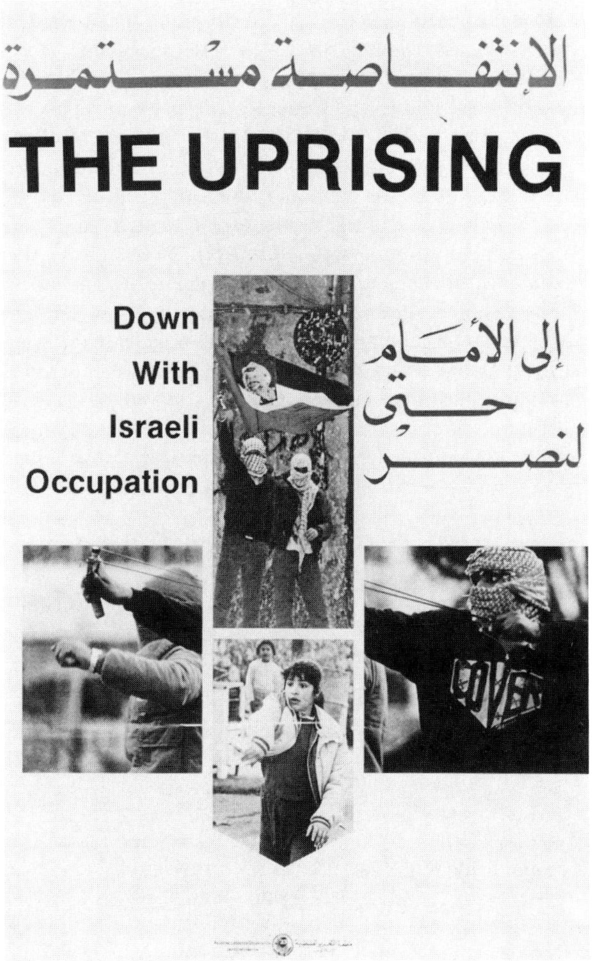

Touting the *intifada* — a PLO poster printed in Tunis

While in 1988 some 20 suspected collaborators were murdered, in 1989 the victims numbered over 150. In 1990 and 1991, the number of Palestinians killed by security forces declined, while there was a steep increase in those killed by other Arabs as suspected collaborators. By the start of 1992 the number of Arabs killed during the *intifada* was 2,000 — 600 of whom had been murdered as suspected collaborators.

The severe hardships suffered by the people led, as early as the second year of the *intifada*, to calls for its cessation in return for the start of political negotiations. In early 1989 exploratory moves were made towards creating an Israeli political program which would bring calm to Judea, Samaria, and Gaza. A number of prominent Palestinians in the Administered Territories were informed of the details of the plan fashioned by Defense Minister Yiẓḥak Rabin. It included a proposal to hold general elections in the territories as an initial step towards designating a representation accepted by the Arab presidents. After a series of contacts and recommendations raised by representatives of the U.S. and Egyptian president Husni Mubarak, sharp differences of opinion broke out within the Israeli government (regarding East Jerusalem residents' participation in the elections in the territories) leading eventually to the dissolution of the National Unity Government.

The atmosphere in the Administered Territories changed from the end of 1989 as the result of the upheavals taking place in Eastern Europe. For nearly 40 years the Communist bloc countries had served as strong political support for sizeable parts of the Arab world, including the Palestinians, besides providing aid in the form of money, weapons, military training, and grants to students. As those countries began to collapse, a feeling of dismay and confusion arose among the Palestinians as the Eastern European countries established diplomatic relations with the State of Israel and a large wave of emigration of Jews from the former Soviet Union was set into motion.

In 1990 calls were heard in the Administered Territories for a return to the "armed struggle" against Israel, that is, acts of terror and the use of firearms. On June 1 terrorist cells belonging to the pro-Iraqi organizations linked to the PLO tried to attack Israeli bathers on the southern shores of the country. In the wake of this (abortive) attempt, the American administration suspended its dialogue with the PLO whose leadership refused to oust from its ranks Abu al-Abbas, the head of the organization taking responsibility for this act.

The *intifada* began to lose the public enthusiasm which had characterized its beginning. Mass demonstration ceased. Public opinion and the world media paid attention to happenings in Eastern Europe and largely stopped covering the Middle East. Gradually schooling was resumed on a regular basis, and in the large cities *intifada* activists allowed the storekeepers to keep their stores open for longer hours. To a significant degree life returned to what it had been prior to the outbreak of the popular uprising.

On Aug. 2, 1990, a dramatic change occurred with Iraq's conquest of Kuwait. The Palestinian population and its leadership took a stance in favor of Iraq and its ruler Saddam Hussein who, from the outset of the crisis, linked the solution of the problem he had created in the Gulf with a solution to the Palestinian problem. The Kingdom of Jordan with its large Palestinian population also joined the supporters of Iraq.

During the continuing tension in the Gulf, a serious incident occurred in the Old City of Jerusalem. On the broad plaza of the Temple Mount mosques there erupted a demonstration of Muslim worshipers who began to throw rocks on

Masked Palestinians out in support of Saddam Hussein and Yasser Arafat in Sa'ir, near Hebron, during the waiting period prior to the start of the Gulf War, Jan. 13, 1991 (GPO, Jerusalem)

Jewish worshipers at the Western Wall. Israeli soldiers and policemen who broke into the plaza shot 18 Arabs to death and wounded dozens of others. The incident was prompted by rumors concerning the activity of a group of Israelis called the "Temple Mount Faithful" which has demanded over the years removing the control of the mosques to Israeli authorities.

The incident sparked new foment in the Administered Territories. Orthodox Muslim groups, which had organized themselves into the "Islamic Resistance Movement" (whose Arabic initials form "Hamas"), had been prominent. They even published a manifest claiming that all of the country's land was Muslim *hekdesh* (consecrated property) meaning that the very existence of the State of Israel contradicted Islamic teachings. Stabbing attacks on Israelis by Muslim extremists became evermore frequent. In most cases the Administered Territories attackers acted alone, unprompted by any organization and ready to die as a martyr. Attempting to thwart these strikes, Israeli security authorities limited the right of free passage of Administered Territories Arabs into pre-1967 Israel.

The number of Administered Territories inhabitants working in the Israeli economy dropped from 130,000 to 50,000 in the period following, with the average number in the early 1990s being about 80,000. The Israeli public became more fearful of employing Arabs from the Administered Territories as knifing attacks by young Administered Territories Arabs occurred from time to time.

The Administered Territories' economic situation was severely affected by the Gulf War events. Besides limitations on working in Israel, there was an almost complete halt of the transfer of money to the Administered Territories by relatives working in the Gulf oil-producing countries. After the war, there began mass expulsions of Palestinians who had worked in Kuwait. Some 20,000 who had Israeli Military Administration identity cards rejoined their families in the Administered Territories. The great need in Israel for construction workers to erect housing for new immigrants somewhat alleviated the Administered Territories economic distress.

Following the outcome of the Gulf War, political activity in the region aimed at convening a peace conference stepped up. The Palestinian stances in the new world order, after the Soviet Union's collapse and Iraq's defeat, became more flexible and allowed for a compromise with Israeli demands. With American mediation a Palestinian delegation was composed with members from the Administered Territories and quasi-official East Jerusalem advisers.

At the end of Oct. 1991 the Palestinian delegation from the Administered Territories, without PLO representatives, took part in the Madrid peace conference in which delegations and observers from most Arab countries participated. Additional meetings were held throughout 1992 in Washington, Moscow, and other world capitals. The discussions encountered many stumbling blocks. The main demand of the Administered Territories delegates was the cessation of the widespread settlement activity in the Administered Territories sponsored by the Israel government. Opposition to the peace process, rooted in Muslim extremist circles, also developed in the Administered Territories. [DA.RU.]

FOREIGN RELATIONS AND INTERNATIONAL AFFAIRS

(see **9**:421; **Dc./17**:331)

The decade of the 1980s began with Israel's international standing and image seriously tarnished by the war in Lebanon, and ended, in 1991 and 1992 in a major breakthrough on the international arena, the beginning of a peace process, and the acceptance of Israel by major powers who had traditionally shunned it, among them China and India. Israel also resumed diplomatic ties with nations who broke them in 1967 (Eastern European nations) and in 1973 (most of the African nations). In spite of repeated periods of strain, Israel–American relations remained very friendly and a close strategic cooperation marked the ties in many spheres. There was also a noted improvement in Israel's economic performance. Two rescue operations which brought to Israel over 30,000 Ethiopian Jews, and the beginning of massive immigration from the Soviet Union, restored Israel to its proclaimed role as a haven for oppressed Jews.

The peace process which began in 1977 following Egyptian President Anwar Sadat's visit to Jerusalem, the Camp David Accords (1978), and the Israel–Egypt Peace Treaty (1979), was halted when Egypt suspended the talks on the implementation of the Camp David interim autonomy regime for the West Bank and Gaza (1981). Shortly after that President Sadat was assassinated in Cairo. His successor, Hosni Mubarak, was busy building his own regime and waiting for the last Israeli soldier and settler to evacuate Sinai. This was done on April 26, 1982. Two months later, the Israel Defense Forces (IDF) entered Lebanon to destroy the PLO power base there, to seek the creation of a unified central government in Lebanon, and sign a peace treaty with it. Above all, Israel wanted to protect Galilee from PLO attacks that stemmed from Lebanon in spite of a cease fire agreement which was brokered by the United States in July 1981. The war in Lebanon generated much ill-will for Israel in the international media. Exaggerated reports on the number of Lebanese and Palestinian civilian casualties as well as physical destruction of cities and refugee camps placed Israel on the defensive. Domestic Israeli opposition to the war also helped Israel's detractors to portray that country as an aggressor.

An aerial view of Yammit in April 1979 (GPO, Jerusalem)

The Yammit area ready to be returned to Egypt, April 23, 1982 (GPO, Jerusalem)

The siege of West Beirut and the massacre in the Sabra and Shatilla camps carried out by the Phalange (Christian Lebanese Forces) resulted in an outcry against Israel. Egypt withdrew its ambassador from Tel Aviv, and the Security Council adopted a number of condemnatory resolutions. When the dust settled down, it was American diplomacy which once again was instrumental in arranging for an agreement to end the state of war between Israel and Lebanon and create a security zone for Israel in southern Lebanon. It even called for the establishment of diplomatic ties between Jerusalem and Beirut. When a peace treaty was actualized, although it fell short of the one Prime Minister Begin wanted, it was an important milestone. It was based on the assumption that all foreign forces, among them the Syrian forces, would leave Lebanon. When this did not happen, it was clear that the agreement was invalid. Nine months after it was signed (Jan. 13, 1984), the Lebanese parliament failed to approve it and it lapsed.

For the next two years, 1983 and 1984, Israel sought ways to maintain a military presence in Lebanon, while keeping the number of its casualties to the minimum and attempting to refrain from becoming involved in ethnic strife. The government of Yiẓhak Shamir, which took office in September 1983 following the resignation of Prime Minister Begin a month earlier, sought ways and means to extricate the IDF from Lebanon, but felt that it could not do so unless peace was insured for Galilee. Meanwhile there was no progress on the negotiations for autonomy for the Palestinians. Relations with various European and Latin American nations soured as a result of Israel's Lebanese involvement. The Government of National Unity, which came into being in September 1984 under Shimon Peres, placed as its central foreign policy objectives the continuation of the peace process, consolidation of the peace with Egypt, and withdrawal of the IDF from Lebanon, while insuring the security of the northern settlements. The government would also strive to restore links with the Soviet Union and African and Latin American states that had suspended such ties. At the top of the agenda was the fostering and deepening of the relations of friendship and understanding with the U.S.

The first priority was the withdrawal of the IDF from Lebanon. This was achieved in three stages in the course of 1985, leaving a security zone in southern Lebanon manned by pro-Israeli Southern Lebanese Army units. Parallel to this track, efforts were made to settle outstanding issues with Egypt. The issue of Taba, a small border area which was a thorn in the ties between the two nations, was resolved in 1988 after years of protracted negotiations and international arbitration when Israel agreed to turn Taba over to Egypt, which reappointed its ambassador to Tel Aviv. However, efforts to inject some warmth into Israel–Egyptian relations were, on the whole, unsuccessful. Egypt preferred to maintain a cold peace between the two governments and objected to attempts to create people-to-people ties. The military arrangements of the peace treaty were usually adhered to by both parties.

The major difficulty was over the Palestinian issue. Prime Minister Peres sought to break the stand-off, but was unable to convince his Likkud partners over the modalities and procedures required to achieve progress. While Labor and Likkud agreed that in the future, under any circumstances, the Jordan River must be Israel's security border in the East, Jerusalem must never be divided or placed under foreign rule and would remain Israel's capital, there would be no Palestinian state between the Mediterranean Sea and the desert, there would be no negotiations with the PLO, and the Israeli settlements in the territories would remain under Israeli jurisdiction, there were disagreements on how to proceed. Peres hoped that Israel would be able to negotiate with local Palestinian leadership who would be part of the Jordanian–Palestinian delegation but would not include Arabs from East Jerusalem and the Palestinian diaspora. He was not averse to an international "event" or "happening" to mark the opening of the negotiations, before moving on to face-to-face talks with the Arab states and the Palestinians. The aim of the talks would be to implement the autonomy regime for a five-year transition period. Various contacts between Israeli leaders and King Hussein of Jordan convinced Peres that Jordan would accept such an arrangement, which was finally agreed upon in a secret meeting in London between Peres and Rabin and King Hussein (April 11, 1987).

The agreement, however, was not accepted by the Likkud which vetoed it in the inner cabinet. The Likkud's position consisted of vehement opposition to an international event of any sort, to the participation of the European Economic Community and the United Nations, to Soviet involvement, and even to American mediation. The Likkud objected to the concept of "Land for Peace" which Labor was prepared to follow, and championed the concept of "Peace for Peace." An important event took place in July 1986 when Premier Peres paid an official visit to Morocco as guest of King Hassan II. While no concrete results were achieved, here was another Arab state that was prepared to deal openly with Israel. A major role was played by the United States in efforts to resume the stalled peace process. The Reagan Administration, mainly in the person of Secretary of State George Shultz, devised many formulae to close the gap between the Israeli and the Arab positions. But it was evident that King Hussein could not make an independent move without the approval of Syria and the PLO. Syria, still heavily dependent on the Soviet Union for military, economic, and political support, adhered to the Soviet line that called for the resolu-

During second stage of withdrawal, IDF convoy on way to redeploying in security zone in south Lebanon after leaving Tyre, April 29, 1985 (GPO, Jerusalem)

Israeli policeman surveying ruins of house in southern Tel Aviv after Iraqi Scud missile attack, Jan, 18, 1991 (GPO, Jerusalem)

tion of the Arab–Israel conflict on the basis of various United Nations resolutions through an international conference chaired by both the Soviet Union and the United States. In the second half of the 1980s there was little pressure on Israel to make concessions to the Arabs. The Middle East was wracked by the Iraq–Iran war, the military situation along the Israel–Lebanon border was quiet, the peace treaty with Egypt was working, and the Palestinians in the areas were relatively quiet. In 1988 both Israel and the United States held elections, and the issue of the peace process was shelved for the duration of the election campaigns. The onset of the *intifada* (Palestinian uprising) in December 1987 and the decision of the Reagan Administration to enter into a dialogue with the PLO in December 1988, placed Israel in a difficult position forcing its government to come up with a new peace plan. This initiative, announced on May 14, 1989, called for negotiations with Palestinians for an interim agreement based on the Camp David autonomy plan. At the end of a five-year transition period, discussions would be held for the final resolution of the issues. The U.S. welcomed the plan as a very useful step but both the PLO and King Hussein rejected it. In an effort to move the process forward, U.S. Secretary of State James Baker devised a five-point plan in October 1989 calling for Israeli–Palestinian dialogue in Cairo. The next problem was how to put together a list of Palestinian delegates acceptable to all. Shamir objected to East Jerusalem and "Palestinian Diaspora" delegates while Peres was prepared to be more conciliatory on the issue. The problem brought down the government of National Unity in March 1990. There was little movement while Shamir constituted his new government, and when the parties were ready to state their positions, the Iraqi dictator Saddam Hussein had invaded Kuwait (August 2, 1990) plunging the Middle East into a major crisis which dwarfed the Arab–Israel conflict.

As the United States began to build its anti-Iraqi coalition, which included Syria, Egypt, Saudi Arabia, and the Gulf States, Israel feared that Washington would link the resolution of the Iraqi crisis to that of the Arab–Israel conflict and would make concessions at Israel's expense to maintain its war coalition. In a number of high level meetings in Washington between Prime Minister Shamir, Defense Minister Arens, and senior members of the Bush administation, agreement on military and strategic cooperation was reached and greater coordination arranged. Israel was assured that no deals would be made at its expense. Meanwhile, the PLO lost much credibility in the West when it openly supported Iraq's invasion of Kuwait. The PLO was joined by Yemen, Libya and Algeria. Palestinians in the territories, then in the third year of the *intifada*, also hoped for an Iraqi victory. King Hussein quietly supported Iraq, although he was warned by Israel that entry of Iraqi forces into Jordan would be seen by Israel as a *casus belli*. Israel began to realize that war was imminent and took measures to prepare its civilian population for such an eventuality.

The allied victory over Iraq ushered in a new era for the Middle East. Futhermore, the collapse of the Soviet Union deprived Syria and other Arab states of their military, political, and economic backer, leaving the United States as the sole super power in the region. New thinking was the order of the day. For the Arabs, it was evident that the main threats to their stability and political regimes were Iran, Iraq, and Islamic fundamentalism, leaving Israel as their fourth perceived danger. It was also clear to them that another Middle Eastern war would be fought with non-conventional weapons, unleashing mutual destruction. The Middle East had entered into the era of a regional balance of terror. The United States sought to reorganize the defense of the Middle East and of its own economic and strategic interests, insuring an uninterrupted supply of oil and helping its allies thwart the dangers of Islamic fundamentalism. Israel emerged from the war bruised, sustaining 39 Scud missile attacks from Iraq which caused few casualties but much damage in the greater Tel Aviv and Haifa regions, and paralyzed the country for some three weeks. Israel's economic vulnerability and dependence on the U.S. were exposed. For the first time in its history it did not engage in preventive war or pre-emptive strike or retaliatory action, acceding to the request of the

United States not to become militarily involved in the war. It allowed the stationing on its territory of American, Dutch, and German soldiers who were manning Patriot anti-missile missiles. The Palestinians emerged from the war badly hurt. Some 350,000 Palestinians were expelled from Kuwait in the wake of the war; the PLO was totally discredited in the West; Palestinians in the areas who supported Iraq were in despair. The Soviet Union, preoccupied with its own internal affairs, was content to let the United States manage the restructuring of the Middle East peace process as long as it was kept in the picture formally as an equal partner.

Between March and October 1991, Secretary of State James Baker visited the Middle East eight times in order to prepare the ground for the resumption of the peace process. The breakthrough came when in July, Syria agreed to attend a peace conference and negotiate directly with Israel. It was agreed that a Palestinian delegation would formally be part of the Jordanian delegation. The U.S. and the Soviet Union would be co-chairmen of the peace conference which was to commence in a ceremonial event and continue in a series of bilateral and multilateral talks. The latter would deal with issues of water, refugees, disarmament, economic development, and environment. The bilateral talks were to focus on borders (withdrawal), the nature of peace, security arrangements, and economic issues. The letter of invitation to the Madrid Peace Conference (October 30, 1991) spelled out the terms of reference under which the Palestinian issue would be discussed; at its core was the creation of a five-year autonomy regime. A final settlement and the issue of Jerusalem were not to be discussed at this stage. Eight rounds of talks took place in Washington in the course of 1991 and 1992, which defined the issues but did not achieve any concrete results. The peace process, however, had become a reality in the Middle East.

Parallel to this development, there was a major improvement of Israel's international standing. Already in the 1980s relations were resumed with a number of African nations starting with Zaire and the Ivory Coast. As Eastern Europe freed itself from Soviet domination in the late 1980s, Israel resumed diplomatic relations with Poland, Hungary, Bulgaria, Czechoslovakia, and on the eve of the Madrid Conference with the Soviet Union. Israel conditioned UN participation in the peace process on the revocation of the infamous General Assembly Resolution 3379 (Zionism = Racism) and this was done on December 16, 1991. On the Asian continent, full diplomatic ties were established with China and India, an embassy was opened in South Korea, and there was a major improvement in Israel–Japan relations, with more Japanese companies defying the Arab economic boycott and selling directly to Israel. Contacts with Vietnam were entered into while the Israeli ambassador was

Soon after resumption of relations the president of Zaire, Mobutu Sese Seka, visited Israel; above, greeted upon arrival in Israel, to his left Pres. and Mrs. Herzog. (GPO, Jerusalem)

also named ambassador to Outer Mongolia. The breakup of the Soviet Union into the 16 republics of the Commonwealth of Independent States resulted in the establishment of Israeli diplomatic representations in the Ukraine, Belarus, and the Baltic States, Kazakhstan, and Kirghizia in addition to the Russian Republic.

Relations with the United States were on the whole close and friendly. Israel and the United States agreed on certain principles, among them: The peace process will be based on Resolutions 242 and 338; the PLO would not take part; there would be no Palestinian State; Jerusalem will not be divided again; Israel would only be asked to withdraw from the areas in the context of a peace treaty; close military and strategic cooperation would continue; and Israel would be entitled to economic and military aid and the regional balance of power would be maintained in such a manner to insure Israel's qualitative edge. There were also agreements on freedom of navigation and Israel's water rights. But there were also a series of disagreements, among them: Israel's eastern borders, the future of the Golan Heights, and the resolution of the Palestinian issue (the favored American position was the return of the West Bank and Gaza to Jordan and the granting by Jordan of a special status to these areas). There was constant disagreement over the future of Jerusalem with the U.S. opposed to Israeli sovereignty over Jerusalem. There were arguments over American arms sales to Arab states and Israeli arms sales to various nations, over Israel's nuclear development, over Israel's presence in Lebanon, over whether Israel or Egypt should play a greater role in the American planning in the Middle East. The main disagreement was over the key issue of the meaning and nature of Israel's security and who will determine its needs. On a number of occasions there was much strain in the personal relations between President Bush and Prime Minister Shamir, considered by the United States as an "ideological" leader, meaning inflexible and rigid. A major problem occurred in December 1988 when the U.S. decided to recognize the PLO and enter into a dialogue with this terrorist organization. This dialogue, however, was suspended in June 1990 when the PLO refused to denounce a terrorist attack on Israel which had been foiled by the IDF. There were also disagreements on the interpretation of the Camp David Accords, the meaning of the balance of power, and the nature of the autonomy plan.

While Israel became an associate member of the European Economic Community, and maintained growing economic ties with the nations of Western Europe, there were serious disagreements on the peace process. The EEC's traditional position called for an international peace conference, the creation of a Palestinian state in the areas, and the re-division of Jerusalem. There were constant arguments over the role played by certain European countries in the arming of Iraq and the building of its war machine. The EEC never failed to condemn Israel for its behavior in the areas and the criticism grew stronger as the *intifada* broke out and Israel took stern measures.

The traditional friendly ties between Israel and the Latin American continent continued, with Israel extending much technical assistance to various states and training a growing number of students from that continent. Similar close relations were maintained with Australia and New Zealand, even while disagreeing on the resolution of the Arab–Israel conflict. President Herzog of Israel traveled extensively during his two terms of office to the U.S., Canada, Britain, France, Holland, Belgium, Poland, Czechoslovakia, Romania, South American nations, Spain, Australia and New Zealand, Singapore and Sri Lanka.

Jewish communities worldwide continued to be Israel's most loyal and trusted allies. They were thrilled when Israel

King Taufa'ahau Tupou IV of Tonga conversing with Israeli president Herzog at the king's summer palace, Nov. 14, 1986. (GPO, Jerusalem)

airlifted Ethiopian Jews in two daring operations (Moses in 1984 and Solomon in 1991), airlifted the Jewish community of Albania (1992), and began the herculean task of absorbing the hundreds of thousands of Jews who began to stream to its shores from the Soviet Union, once the gates were opened in October 1989. Between that date and April 1993, some 425,000 Jews arrived in Israel from the former U.S.S.R. Israel was instrumental in getting the Syrian government to allow the emigration of hundreds of the previously besieged members of the Syrian Jewish community and to start the process whereby the remnant of the Jews of Yemen were reunited with families overseas. Yet there were also ongoing debates on the centrality of Israel in Jewish life and on organizational frameworks in which to achieve common goals. The Jewish Agency for Israel continued to be the most effective body for the implementation of the immigration and absorption process, combining in it the Zionist (mainly Israeli) element with the New Zionists (mainly fund raisers) from the diaspora. [M.ME.]

ALIYAH AND ABSORPTION (see **9**:515; **Dc./17**:345)

The decade 1982–1992 witnessed both the lowest annual immigration figures and the highest recorded since the first years of statehood. The decade also marked the reopening of the gates of the Soviet Union, a cherished dream, and the completion of the evacuation of Jews from certain countries of stress. Some 573,000 new immigrants arrived in this decade and in many respects revolutionized Israeli society. Between 1989 and 1992 some 476,000 immigrants came, the majority from the former Soviet Union, compared with a yearly average of 12,000 during previous years.

For decades, Israeli governmental and non-governmental bodies had worked for the eventual emigration of Soviet Jews. Massive pressures were exerted by Israel and world Jewry through a variety of organizations and institutions to bring about a change in Soviet emigration policy, and eventually these bore fruit. The Soviet Government, in return for winning a most-favored nation status in its trade relations with the United States, began to ease emigration restrictions. In the two decades, 1969–1989, some 190,000 Soviet Jews arrived in Israel, of whom 170,000 remained. However, this period was also marked by a growing number of Soviet Jews opting to drop out on the way to Israel and travel to settle in the United States and to other countries. The percentage of these dropouts reached 90% in the mid-1970s. Since these Jews were leaving the Soviet Union on the basis of a scheme for family reunion in Israel, this trend endangered the operation. Israel found itself confronting a growing number of American Jewish organizations who favored the freedom of choice of Soviet Jewish emigrants to decide their destination. Israel claimed that there was no point in moving Russian Jews from one diaspora to another. The issue was resolved in 1989 in an agreement between Israel, the Soviet Union, and the United States, whereby from October 1, 1989, Russian Jews who wished to travel to the United States (or elsewhere) would have to obtain an entry visa in the embassies of their country of destination in Moscow. The United States established a quota of 40,000 emigrants a year. Those traveling to Israel would get their entry visa in the Israeli consulate in Moscow, which had been reopened in 1988.

The end of the 1980s also marked a massive change in Soviet–American relations with the realization of the Soviet president Mikhail Gorbachev, that his country's economic development would require massive Western, especially American, aid. This meant that he had to reduce elements of friction with the United States, one of them being the issue of human rights in general and Jewish emigration in particu-

Soviet Jews deplane in Israel after direct flight from Moscow, Sept. 1990. (GPO, Jerusalem)

Settlement advertisement from the 1980s stressing quality of life in settlements over the Green Line. (Courtesy David Newman)

lar. The end of the Cold War in 1989 brought about radical changes in Soviet emigration policies, which allowed most Jews who so wished to leave for Israel, although restricting the movements of a few hundred whom the Soviet government claimed were in possession of state secrets because of previous employment.

The massive wave began in late 1989 and soon swelled into a human tide. The Jewish Agency, which was responsible for the movement of immigrants to Israel, established transit stations for Soviet Jews on their way to Israel in Budapest, Warsaw, and Bucharest. A few traveled through Prague and Helsinki. These stations played a major role in the transit of Jews who came from the Soviet Union by bus, train, and plane, sometimes in private cars, to Israel. The reestablishment of consular, and later full diplomatic, relations between Israel and the Soviet Union also facilitated the transit of Jews. After 1989 the Jewish Agency was permitted to set up Hebrew classes in various parts of the Soviet Union and send emissaries and teachers to prepare Jews for *aliyah* and to teach them Hebrew, Judaism, and Jewish history.

The Soviet Government estimated in late 1988 that there were some 1.8 million Jews in the country, the Israelis put the figure at 2.8 million. By early 1993, some 420,000 Soviet Jews had gone to Israel, another 150,000 to North America, and some 20,000 to Germany. In April 1993 there were still some 1.7 million Jews in the CIS (Commonwealth of Independent States), a million of whom were holding Israeli documents as a first step towards their immigration. It was assumed that at the current rate of emigration (70,000 a year), some 500,000 Jews would remain in the CIS at the end of the century.

Jewish emigration was a result of both a push and a pull. The push came in 1989 when Jews feared that there might not be much time before the Iron Curtain would slam down again and left en masse. There was genuine fear that the collapse of the Soviet empire would be accompanied by a civil war in which the Jews would be the main victims. They thought that in a period of vast social, economic, and political instability, anti-Semitism, long ingrained in Russia, would reappear. Moreover the greater democratization allowed in Russia meant that anti-Semitic propaganda and organizations were also permitted. Chief among these groups was Pamyat, a virulently anti-Jewish nationalist, organization. Jews felt that life in the former Soviet Union was becoming intolerable for them. There were limited economic and occupational possibilities. Promotion in the army and government was very limited and there were quotas on the number of Jewish students at universities. Academic and professional promotion was also very slow. Many wanted to reunite with families already in Israel. The majority of the immigrants were not permeated by Zionist or even Jewish sentiments. The majority were secular, some third having married non-Jews. But as the Iron Curtain lifted, more people discovered their Jewishness and wanted to leave, most of them for economic reasons. There were some drawbacks. A number feared that the Jewish state was a theocracy. Being secular, and cut off from Judaism for seventy years, this could have problems, mainly for those with non-Jewish spouses. There was concern over military service, *intifada*, and above all fear that the professionals among them would not be able to find suitable jobs. The last concern proved to be true. A number of Jews chose to remain behind to participate in the building of a new society in the CIS, but many of these became disappointed, especially those who found themselves in the midst of civil war in Moldova, Abkhazia, and Tadjikistan.

From a figure of some 200,000 in 1990, 176,000 in 1991, the numbers dropped to 76,000 in 1992. The task of moving Russian Jews to Israel and settling them there was shared by the *Jewish Agency, representing world Jewry, and the government of Israel. The Agency launched a fundraising campaign called "Exodus" which resulted in over $500 million being raised in three years to help cover the costs of flying the Jews to Israel, bringing their luggage and helping in their initial absorption. The government of Israel provided housing, education, health care, and welfare.

Unlike previous years, when immigrants were directed to absorption centers where they would learn the language before being let out into the Israeli economy and society, the majority of Soviet Jews were absorbed in what was termed "direct absorption track," in which they were given a yearly allowance to cover costs of housing and subsistence, were told to look for work, put their children into school, and become absorbed almost overnight. This, on the whole, proved successful. By 1993 some 35,000 Soviet Jews had found work in industry, others in professions and trades. A major problem was posed by the large number (over 16%) of immigrants over 65 years old who were no longer productive and became the responsibility of the local and national governments. Another difficulty arose with those immigrants who had to be certified again by Israel before they could practice, among them physicians and engineers. They had to be maintained while studying for their qualifying examinations. Many had to be re-trained as the number of physicians, for example, who came between 1989 and 1993 was 12,000 as against the 16,000 doctors already practicing in Israel. Scientists and academics also found difficulties obtaining suitable jobs. But only 2.8% of the immigrants who arrived since 1989 left Israel. Immigrants continued to arrive even during the Gulf War when Israel was attacked by Iraqi Scuds.

The addition of some 420,000 high quality immigrants from the CIS had vast strategic implications for Israel. The Jewish population increased by 12% in three years. The quality of the immigrants was remarkable. They raised the cultural level of Israel, in music, arts, literature, and drama. Three new orchestras were created for immigrants. They began slowly to replace some Arabs from the Administered Territories who were working in Israel. Their numbers meant that once again there was a Jewish majority in Galilee. Strenuous Arab efforts to stop this immigration demonstrated that the Arab states realized the magnitude of this immigration and its potential for Israel in the scientific, technological, and

Ethiopian Jews calling in Sept. 1992 for re-unification with their *falas moura* relatives left behind: Hebrew signs read, "Complete Operation Solomon," "Our Jewish brethren! Like us, like you..." (GPO, Jerusalem)

military areas. The immigration also had an impact on the peace process. Israel with over 4.4 million Jews was a different country from previously. The new reality was slowly grasped by Arab governments, especially after their efforts to block the *aliyah* failed. Sheer numbers enabled the Israel army to consider reducing the length of military service. Israel's economy received a tremendous boost by the arrival of almost half a million new consumers. In 1992 the country recorded a 6.4% growth in its Gross Domestic Product and a rise in exports.

The major problems accompanying this immigration were in the social sphere. Israeli society welcomed immigrants with open arms. They were absorbed mainly by voluntary organizations, previous Russian immigrants, and local authorities. But there were strains, some of them due to a different mentality. Since most of the immigrants were not motivated by Jewish or Zionist ideology, they had to be re-educated in many ways about the meaning and nature of life in a Jewish State. There was some grumbling among Jews of Asian and African origin who feared that well-educated Russian Jews would get the better positions. The ultra-Orthodox and the Orthodox were dismayed over the prospect of the Russian immigrants voting mainly for secular parties, and affecting their political clout. Inevitably, there was considerable disappointment and disillusionment among many of the newcomers. For all the efforts to help a quick absorption, the country could not cope with many of the problems while the immigrants found themselves in unaccustomed surroundings and faced with a new language which some could not master. It was the economic problems that were uppermost. While the immigrants received grants for their initial period, this ran out and they had to face the challenge of finding work, with the possibilities especially limited in the professions and arts. Many found themselves unemployed and others took menial jobs in order to survive. Some of them organized demonstrations to draw attention to their plight. Reports of these difficulties reaching Russia dampened the enthusiasm of many potential immigrants and were a major factor in the drop in immigration figures from 1990 to 1991 and from 1991 to 1992. But on the whole, the Russian immigrants absorbed themselves well into Israeli society and many were beginning to make meaningful contributions to its economy, science, and technology.

The decade also witnessed the end of a number of diasporas. In two dramatic air lifts, the government of Israel and the Jewish Agency brought to Israel over 22,000 Ethiopian Jews. Some 7,500 were airlifted at the end of 1984 from Sudan in an operation called "Moses." To escape famine Ethiopian Jews walked hundreds of miles to Sudan and from there, were taken to Israel with the help of the United States government and air force. Between 1985 and 1991, Israeli emissaries brought thousands of Ethiopian Jews to Addis Ababa to prepare them for immigration. Two days before the final collapse of the Mengistu government, in May 1991, and with the active help of the United States, Israel secured use of the Addis Ababa airport for thirty-six hours. During this time 41 flights brought to Israel 14,440 Jews in "Operation Solomon." Subsequently the rest of Ethiopian Jewry was brought to Israel and effectively, apart from *Falas Moura*, converts to Christianity, the Jewish community of Ethiopia ceased to exist.

By the end of 1992, Israel airlifted the entire Jewish community of Albania (350 souls) while over a 1,000 Jews were rescued from the civil war which engulfed Yugoslavia. Eventually, the numbers of Jews in distressed countries diminished significantly during the decade under review. In 1948 there were over 800,000 Jews in Arab countries, by 1993 there remained some 60,000 Jews in those countries, the three largest communities being Iran, Turkey, and Morocco with c. 20,000 Jews in each.

Immigration from Western countries continued to arrive in a trickle. Some 2,500 Jews came annually from North America, hundreds from South Africa, Australia, France, and Britain.

Table 1. Aliyah by Country of Origin, 1948–1992 (%)

Country	Percent
CIS	27.0
Morocco, Tunisia, & Algeria	15.0
Romania	12.0
Poland	7.5
Iraq	5.7
Iran	3.3
U.S.	2.9
Turkey	2.7
Yemen/Aden	2.2
Argentina	1.9
Bulgaria	1.9
Other	17.7

Table 2. Age Structure of Immigrants from the Former Soviet Union, 1989–1992 (%)

Ages	%
0–14	19.3
15–24	15.7
25–34	15.9
35–44	14.8
45–54	10.7
55–64	9.6
65–74	8.8
75+	5.2

Table 3. Immigration to Israel, 1982–1992

Year	Number of Immigrants
1982	13,723
1983	16,906
1984	19,981
1985	10,642
1986	9,505
1987	12,965
1988	13,034
1989	24,050
1990	199,516
1991	176,110
1992	76,554

[M.ME.]

NEW SETTLEMENT (see **9**:546; **Dc./17**:349)
Between 1983 and 1992, the size of settlement and its regional distribution depended largely on the influence of the main political parties and their approach to Israel's current situation. The Likkud and Gush Emunim (whose settlement association is named Amana) persevered in putting the emphasis on Judea-Samaria (the West Bank) and the Gaza Strip. The Ma'arakh Labor Bloc, on the other hand, insisted on restricting new settlement beyond the pre-1967 areas to the Allon Plan (see **Dc./17**:349) areas that had been envisaged for development after the Six-Day War. It explained that the peace process had to be kept going without the impediment of settlement in areas closely inhabited by Arabs. When the National Unity government was established in 1985, the Likkud partners had to be content with a compromise that permitted the establishment of only a few new settlements in the Administered Areas.

Foreign powers showed increased interest in the settlements. The U.S. kept repeating its wish that Israel refrain from further settlement in the territories and, especially, from directing new immigrants to them. The U.S.S.R. made full renewal of diplomatic relations conditional upon Israel's readiness for compromise concerning the territories although the relations were eventually restored without any concessions. The Arabs made cessation of settlement part of their conditions in peace negotiations.

Community village Kedumim in Samaria, founded 1975, as it appeared in spring 1982; low buildings in the front are original settler housing in stucco block, behind them private homes in stages of construction. (Courtesy World Zionist Press Service, Jerusalem)

Israel's right wing endeavored to make up for the decrease in new foundings by "thickening" the territories' Jewish population through speedy enlargement of existing places, aspiring to obtain appropriate budgets for land purchase, road construction, and other investments. Their success was considerable. In Judea-Samaria, the number of Jews rose from 22,800 in mid-1983 to 63,000 at the end of 1988, and in the Gaza Strip from 900 to 2,700. In 1989, growth was even quicker. However, Teḥiyyah and other right-wing parties opposing the National Unity government complained that far from enough was being done for expansion.

Within the pre-1967 boundaries, Galilee and the Negev were the locales for few new settlements. In the Golan Heights no change was made.

Between 1983 and 1988, 83 places were founded: 34 in Judea-Samaria; 5 in the Gaza Strip; 3 in the Golan; 41 within pre-1967 Israel. Of the 83, 48 were established in 1986, 18 in 1984, and only 17 during the following four years. In fact, however, the total of additions in the period was smaller, because the survey indicates as founding date the year when it recognizes a settlement's existence, which is frequently later than the foundations are laid.

A trend discernible in the 1980s is the preference given to the novel forms of "community village" or "private village." Permitting settlers much greater freedom in their occupational and private sphere than do the veteran kibbutz or moshav, the community village not only attracted nuclei of new settlers but also groups which had originally intended to choose one of the traditional forms. Even a number of existing settlements decided, or were considering, to turn themselves into community villages. The designers of the new forms had predicted that they would each contain 200 or more families. While most community villages remained below this size, a few had grown beyond it and become, or were on the way to becoming, urban localities.

Of the sites available for new settlement both within pre-1967 Israel and in the Administered Areas, very few have at their disposal a minimum of cultivable soil. Therefore only a very small number of the new settlements included farming in their economic projection. This was encouraged by the fact that the size of cultivable acreage is no longer seen as decisive for Israel's farming capacity and profitability. Instead, most new places endeavor to promote industry, tourism, and other productive services or are content that most of their members commute to their work places in the country's major agglomerations. Among the settlement sites, those which are easily accessible for commuters have an advantage. Construction of good and easy roads has thus become an integral part of regional development. [E.O.]

Aerial view of the *mizpim*, observation outpost communities, in the Segev region in Galilee. (Photo Richard Nowitz, Jerusalem)

REGIONAL AND SETTLEMENT PLANNING
(9:546; **Dc./17:**349)

Regional planning in Israel has always been a highly centralized activity, formulated through a series of statutory national, district, and local guidelines. The National Council for Planning and Construction prepared occasional outline plans at the country-wide level, and these provide the framework for more detailed district and local plans. The National Council is chaired by the chief planner of the Ministry of Interior and is composed of members representing other government ministries (such as Housing and Construction; Education; Economic Planning) and other major interests (the Committee for Land Preservation; environmental groups and so on).

In 1985, the National Council for Planning completed the Outline Plan (No. 16) for the Geographical Distribution of Seven Million Inhabitants, expected to occur during the 1990s. This plan replaced the existing Outline Plan (No. 6) for Five Million inhabitants which had been completed in 1975. The expected distribution of population was divided among the six major administrative districts of the country (see Table 1).

Table 1. Expected Distribution of Population (for seven million inhabitants)

DISTRICT	POPULATION	% OF TOTAL
Jerusalem District	900,000	13% (incl. East Jer.).
Northern District	1,513,000	22%
Haifa District	1,006,000	14%
Central District	1,230,000	17%
Tel Aviv District	1,252,000	18%
Southern District	1,006,000	14%
Administered Territories	125,000	2% (Jewish pop. only; excl. East Jerusalem).
TOTAL	7,032,000	

The demographic assumptions behind the plan assumed continued natural growth coupled with significant immigration. While at first these assumptions did not appear realistic, the sudden influx of Russian immigrants between 1989 and 1991 transformed the Seven Million Plan into a realistic indicator of demographic growth for the 1990s.

The urban landscape continued to grow, with some 20 percent of Israel's population residing in the four major towns of Tel Aviv, Haifa, Jerusalem, and Beersheba, by the year 1992. Within the Dan Bloc metropolitan region, encompassing Tel Aviv and the surrounding towns from Kefar Sava and Netanyah in the north, to Ashdod in the south and Petaḥ Tikvah to the east, over half of the country's population resided on only 25 percent of the country's land surface, with 40 percent of the population within the metropolitan center alone. This was in direct contrast to the peripheral regions, especially the Negev, wherein less than 10 percent of the population lived in 60% of the country's land area. Despite government attempts to promote population dispersal, through the granting of tax cuts, cheap mortgages and other benefits, the population showed its preference for the center of the country.

A major change to have taken place within Israel's settlement landscape during the 1980s was the continued transformation of the rural landscape. What had previously been a largely homogeneous settlement pattern, composed of cooperative agricultural communities, such as the kibbutz and the moshav ovedim, now gave way to a more varied pattern. On the one hand, many of the existing agricultural communities underwent functional transformation, as many of the residents ceased working in agriculture, taking up alternative employment in nearby towns. This was particularly true of the moshav sector, not least because of the severe economic problems which afflicted these communities in the wake of the high inflation of the early part of the decade.

Of greater significance was the founding of over 100 dormitory communities, similar in nature to the exurban commuting villages to be found throughout the Western world. Approximately two-thirds of these new communities were established in the West Bank, many of them by Gush Emunim adherents, this region lying within the natural commuting hinterland of both the Tel Aviv and Jerusalem metropolitan regions. A large number of these exurban communities were also founded in Galilee, mostly in the western Galilee region of Segev. These communities were distinct from the traditional agricultural cooperatives in many respects. In the first place, little — if any — employment takes place within the village itself. Nearly all the working residents commute to the nearby towns for their employment. Moreover, these communities are based on a vision of "Western high quality-of-life" living standards characterized by the private construction of large detached houses, giving further evidence of the clear emergence of a growing Israeli middle-class. While the majority of these communities were founded with substantial governmental assistance, private investment was responsible for a minority of cases (approximately 20 communities). The private communities were, on the whole, extremely large from the outset, with some of them (such as Metar in the northern Negev, or Koḥav Ya'ir in the center of the country) reaching 1,000 households (5–6,000 people) by the early 1990s.

The sudden arrival of the mass Russian immigration in 1990 and 1991, resulted in short-term, dramatic changes in both planning and construction. At the national level, the National Council for Planning prepared an Outline Plan for the distribution of population, as expected to take place by 1995 — reaching a total of 6.1 million inhabitants. This plan followed the general trend already noted in the Plan for Seven Million Inhabitants, although it proposed some variations on the detailed patterns of distribution (see Table 2).

The lack of sufficient housing for all of the immigrants led to the granting of emergency powers, designed to shortcut the normal bureaucratic delays encountered in the housing process, to the respective ministries, and in particular to the Ministry of Housing and Construction. Large-scale construction programs were put into effect throughout the country. The varied building programs included the construction of both high and low density neighborhoods, some of which consisted of imported housing units. Some of

Table 2. Expected Distribution of Population by 1995

DISTRICT	POPULATION 1989	% of TOTAL	EXPECTED INCREASE 1989–1995	POPULATION 1995	% of TOTAL
Northern Planning Region	654,200	14.3%	225,800	880,000	14.4%
Haifa Planning Region	532,300	11.7%	167,700	700,000	11.4%
Ḥaderah Planning Region	188,700	4.1%	66,300	255,000	4.1%
Central Planning Region	969,800	21.3%	335,200	1,305,000	21.3%
Tel Aviv Planning Region	1,043,500	22.9%	166,500	1,210,000	19.7%
Jerusalem Planning Region	556,000	12.2%	169,000	725,000	11.8%
Ashkelon Planning Region	224,300	4.9%	140,700	365,000	6.0%
Southern & Eilat P.R.	317,600	7.0%	232,400	550,000	9.0%
Judea & Samaria	73,000	1.6%	67,000	140,000	2.3%
TOTAL	7,032,000	100%	1,570,600	6,130,000	100%

the smaller development towns underwent substantial population increase — as much as 25–30% — in the space of only one or two years. However, this has resulted in significant municipal and functional problems for the local authorities in their attempt to continue to supply a reasonable level of municipal services.

In addition to the major programs of housing construction, thousands of mobile caravan units were imported in order to provide short-term housing solutions until the solid housing would be completed. The government was conscious of the fact that the large caravan estates which sprang up throughout the country could lead to the development of social and economic conditions similar to those which occurred in the immigrant camps of the 1950s. As a result, the new government of June 1992, declared its intention of evacuating all of these camps within as short a time period as possible and encouraging their residents to move into the permanent housing.

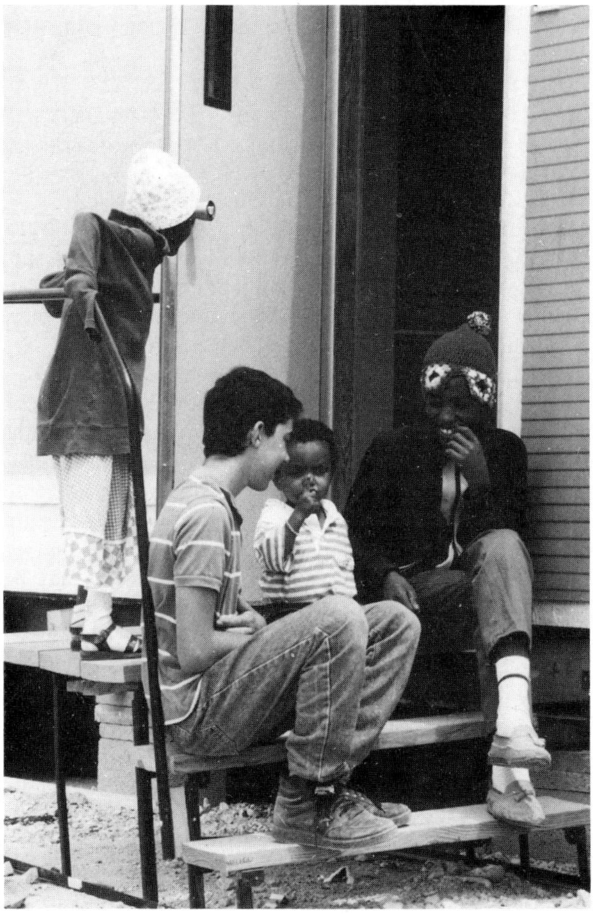

Israeli boy (left) from Kefar Tavor visits Ethiopian Jewish immigrant children in their nearby caravan neighborhood. (GPO, Jerusalem)

Bibliography: L. Applebaum, L. D. Newman, *Between Village and Suburb: New Settlement Forms in Israel* (in Hebrew; 1989); Y. Golani, S. Elidor, and M. Garon (eds.), *Planning and Housing in Israel in the Wake of Rapid Changes* (1992). [DA.NE.]

LEGAL AND JUDICIAL SYSTEM

(see **9**:626; **Dc./17**:361)

The following is a summary of some of the important laws passed by the Knesset during the period under review:

THE CRIMINAL REGISTER AND LENIENCY TO THE REPENTANT LAW — 1983. This law requires the police to keep a criminal register which is to be restricted, and the information contained therein is revealed under limited circumstances.

THE RESTRICTION ON ADVERTISING TOBACCO PRODUCTS FOR SMOKING LAW — 1983 prohibits such advertising, including any "tobacco product" — except on an authorized signboard, where a warning is to be added stating: "The Minister of Health has determined that smoking is harmful to health."

This was followed by the RESTRICTON ON SMOKING IN PUBLIC PLACES LAW — 1983 which imposed restrictions on smoking in places such as cinemas, theaters, concert halls, a hospital clinic, a library, a place of learning, an elevator, taxi, or bus.

THE DECEPTION IN KASHRUT LAW — 1983 was designed to prevent false representation as to *kashrut* of food and drink including meat and meat products.

THE PREVENTION OF SEA POLLUTION (DUMPING OF WASTE) LAW — 1984. This takes upon itself international obligations and adherence to the Protocol for Prevention of Pollution in the Mediterranean annexed to the Barcelona Convention of 1976.

THE USE OF HYPNOSIS LAW — 1984 limits the use of hypnosis to legitimate objectives and provides for the registration of persons qualified to engage in this practice.

THE DISCHARGED SOLDIERS LAW — 1984 provides for the preferment of discharged soldiers to facilitate their re-integration into civilian life, enduring for three years after the discharge. It includes reductions in tuition fees, and acceptance to courses and dormitory accommodation, and applies also to women who have done at least two years national service in lieu of army service.

THE FREE TRADE ZONE IN ELATH LAW — 1985. This law provides tax exemption for Elath's residents and introduces exemptions from some tax dues relating to international flights.

THE BASIC LAW, THE KNESSET (AMENDMENT No. 9) — 1985. This law came to remedy the situation in which two political parties, banned by the Central Elections Committee on the ground of incitement to racism and danger to state security, respectively, were allowed by the Supreme Court to participate since there was no legislation on the subject. This law enabled the committee to disqualify any list that rejects the existence of the State of Israel, rejects the democratic nature of the state, or incites to racism.

THE ADMINISTRATIVE OFFENSES LAW — 1985. This law provides for the administrative imposition of fines for technical offenses (i.e., other than felonies) in the fields of labor conditions, marketing, health, tourism, the practice of medicine, dentistry and pharmacy, and fiscal offenses.

THE PREVENTION OF TERRORISM (AMENDMENT No. 2) — 1986, and THE PENAL LAW (AMENDMENT No. 20) — 1986. These laws relate to racism: The first makes it an offense for an Israeli citizen or resident to have contact, knowingly and without legal authority, in Israel or elsewhere, with any person connected with a body declared by the government as a terrorist organization. This does not apply if such contact is for family reasons or at academic or scientific conferences provided there is no contact on a political subject.

The anti-racism element of the second law was to combat public expression of degradation based on race or nationality and the publication of incitement to racism.

PASSOVER: PROHIBITION OF "ḤAMEẒ" [LEAVENED FOOD] LAW — 1986. Under this law it became an offense for the owner of a business publicly to exhibit, for sale or use during the Passover festival, bread, rolls, or any other leavened flour product. It did not apply to local government areas where the majority of inhabitants were not Jewish.

THE WOMEN'S LABOR LAW (AMENDMENT No. 7) — 1986. This law abrogated the general prohibition, enacted in 1984, of the employment of women at night except in certain recognized categories such as hospitals and restaurants, and enabled the minister of labor to make regulations for the night employment of women.

THE DEBIT CARD LAW — 1986 recognized modern trends in commerce for the use of credit cards instead of cash and laid down express conditions relating to the use of the cards and the obligations of bodies issuing such cards.

THE PROHIBITION OF DENYING THE HOLOCAUST — 1986. The law, reacting to propaganda denying the Holocaust, rendered liable to five years' imprisonment anyone publicly denying the crimes perpetrated during the Nazi era, including crimes against the Jewish people or against humanity, or belittling their magnitude.

BEZEK (ISRAEL COMMUNICATIONS COMPANY LTD.) AMENDMENT LAW — 1986. The increased use of cable television was the basis for this law, providing for the establishment of a council consisting of government and public representation to determine policy regarding telecasts and dealing with the granting of concession for television and tenders, and television by satellite.

MINIMUM WAGE LAW — 1987. This law provided for the laying down and computation of a minimum wage for workers, including workers under collective labor agreements.

PENAL LAW OF 1977 (AMENDMENT No. 21) — 1987. This amendment empowers the court to order a convicted person, in certain circumstances, to serve a term of public service in a government or public institutions. Provisions are made for the payment of wages and expenses. The law also applies to persons convicted in Courts Martial.

MEDICAL PRACTITIONERS ORDINANCE (CONSOLIDATED VERSION) of 1970 (AMENDMENT) — 1987. This amendment empowers the minister of health to reserve certain aspects of medical practice for specialists only. It also deals with medical practice by foreigners and the practice of acupuncture, and contains revised disciplinary provision for unprofessional conduct.

THE BASIC LAW: THE STATE COMPTROLLER — 1988. Like other Basic Laws this is intended to be part of the constitution of the State of Israel. Its purpose is to ensure the independence of the comptroller who is to be elected by the Knesset in a secret ballot by a two-thirds majority of those voting.

THE GALILEE LAW — 1988. In order to encourage the development of Galilee, this law provides for the establishment of a Galilee Council including representatives of the government, the Nature Reserve Authority, the World Zionist Organization, the Histadrut, a recognized industrial federation, and in addition, five public members.

THE AUTHORITY FOR COMBATING DRUGS LAW — 1988. This law provides for the appointment of a Council to frame a policy for governmental action to prevent the use of drugs and for the punishment and rehabilitation of drug offenders.

THE EQUAL OPPORTUNITY IN LABOR LAW — 1988. This law protects the right of women to equal opportunity in employment, and forbids discrimination except where the nature of the employment so demands. It also proscribes sex discrimination in employment advertisements, and provides for the punishment of sexual harassment by employers.

THE SPORTS LAW — 1988. This law empowers the ministers of education and culture to supervise sports activities. It provides that coaches and trainers must be properly qualified, and includes directives for insurance, safety measures, and drug control. It demands equal opportunity for women and requires local authorities to establish sports facilities.

THE LAW FOR THE SUSPENSION OF THE PUBLIC PERFORMANCE (CENSORSHIP) ORDINANCE — 1989. This law suspended, for two years, the censorship of plays and films introduced during the British Mandate in 1927 in preparation for a more sophisticated law on the subject.

PENAL LAW OF 1977 (AMENDMENT No. 26) — 1989. This amendment deals with the protection of minors and neglected children, aged and sick persons and others needing protection. It imposes upon doctors, nurses, and the general public the duty of reporting offenses and includes rules to facilitate testimony by minors, as well as by children against parents.

THE STATE SERVICE (RESTRICTON ON PARTY POLITICAL ACTIVITY AND FUND-RAISING) LAW OF 1959 (AMENDMENT No. 2) — 1989. This amendment restricts the political activity of civil servants, and officials of local authorities, the World Zionist Organization, and the Jewish Agency.

THE TOWN PLANNING AND BUILDING PROCEDURES (INTERIM PROVISIONS) LAW — 1990. This law contains special provisions for the confirmation of building plans in an attempt to find urgent solutions to the problems of new immigrants, young couples, and homeless persons.

THE LAW GOVERNING THE PRACTICE OF OPTOMETRY — 1991. This law re-defines the qualifications of candidates who seek to be granted licenses by the Ministry of Health.

THE LAW GOVERNING VETERINARY SURGEONS — 1991. This law sets out the requirements for obtaining a license from the relevant departments of the Ministry of Health. Provision is made for an advisory council whom the director should consult — appeals against their decisions may be made to the District Court.

THE MORTGAGE LAW — 1992. In an endeavor to assist discharged soldiers, young couples, and new immigrants to acquire their own homes, the law empowers the minister of finance, with the approval of the Finance Committee of the Knesset, to grant loans of between 70,000 and 160,000 shekels for 25–30 years, bearing a 4% rate of interest linked to the cost-of-living index.

THE LAW FOR A SECOND AUTHORITY IN TELEVISION AND RADIO (AMENDMENT No. 2) — 1992. This law introduces important amendments designed to promote private investment in broadcast and to exercise control.

Supreme Court Decisions. The following judgments of the

Supreme Court of Israel during the period under review are among those of special interest.

The High Court of Justice (H.C. 243/82 — judgment handed down March 24, 1983) laid down the principles which should govern the Directors of the Broadcasting Authority regarding publicity to be given to the PLO and its spokesmen. The Board contended that it was not obliged to provide a platform for enemy propaganda as evident in the "Palestine National Convention" of 1968. While the public had the right to receive full and balanced information that was to be measured by what is said and also by the personality of the person making the statement.

A matter of principle regarding adoption was the basis of an appeal (C. A. 518/83 — March 1, 1984). Under the Adoption Law, a court may declare a child adopted if the parent has abandoned the child for six consecutive months or shown by his conduct that he is incapable of caring for the child properly. In the case under consideration the child was brought to the hospital, aged four months, with clear signs of having been a battered child. The court upheld a decision of the District Court that the ill-treatment had resulted from the social conditions under which the family had lived. The ill-treatment itself did not justify taking the child away — it was a passing phase. The integrity of the family unit should be preserved.

The right of the public to demonstrate was defined in detail in the case of two petitioners against the police (H. C. 153/83 — May 13, 1984). Following the Peace Now demonstration held opposite the Prime Minister's Office in Jerusalem in February 1983, in the course of which a demonstrator, Emil Grunzweig, was killed, the "Committee against the War in Lebanon" applied to the police for a permit to conduct a procession at the same site on the thirtieth day after Grunzweig's death. The police refused. The Court laid down that freedom of expression was vital to "those who cannot avail themselves of governmental and commercial media." This right is not absolute but limited by the need to preserve public order and security — and a balance had to be found between the two. The Court expressed its displeasure at the refusal of the police to allow the procession along other routes, and they were ordered to grant the requisite permit.

The conflict between the concepts of marriage under Rabbinical Law and Civil Law were outlined in a appeal before the Court of Civil Appeals (C. A. 593/83 — September 1983, 1984). Two Israel citizens, a man who was a *Kohen* (member of the priestly sect) and a divorced woman were married in Italy. The Rabbinical Court in Israel had held that since the marriage was forbidden by Jewish law, the parties must be divorced. The Supreme Court dealt with the issue of maintenance which, it was claimed, was due on the grounds of the marriage abroad. The Court held that the wife was obliged to accept a divorce since it was a forbidden marriage, without any right to maintenance as long as the man did not delay the divorce proceedings.

Deportations have been brought before the court on various occasions. An example is H. C. 159/84 — February 17, 1985. The petitioner asked the Court to cancel an expulsion order issued by the Gaza army commander. He had infiltrated from Gaza into Israel after the Six-Day War, was caught and sentenced to a term of prison. While he was in prison a deportation order was issued against him. This was subsequently canceled by the army but issued anew. The court held that a reassessment of the position was not only permissible but obligatory, and the application to revoke the second deportation was dismissed.

The status of *dayyanim* (religious court judges) was ventilated in a petition to the Supreme Court (H. C. 732/84 — July 10, 1986) by a member of the Knesset against the Ministry of Religious Affairs and a rabbi who was both a *dayyan* and a member of the body of Torah Sages. He acted as an advisor to political parties and even decided whether a particular party should join the government coalition. The Court held that a *dayyan* — like any judge — could only express his opinion via the ballot box and the petition was granted.

The exact relationship between halakhic (Jewish religious) law and the civil law was reviewed in a hearing against the Ministry of Interior (H. C. 230/86 — December 2, 1986). The petitioner converted to Judaism within the Reform movement in the United States. She entered Israel as an immigrant under the Law of Return, but when she applied to the ministry for an identity card, the official refused to register her as Jewish but only as "Jewish converted." The petition requested that the reference to conversion be omitted. Quoting the judgment of a former chief justice the court stressed that the establishment of the State of Israel was not intended to drive a wedge between Jews and Israelis, and ordered the petitioner to be registered simply as a Jew.

Restrictions on the right of the Film and Theater Censorship Board to ban a controversial play was laid down in a case (H. C. 141/86 — February 5, 1987). The board had refused to license a performance of a play on the grounds that it purported to show the Israel army as a degrading subhuman and predatory body with clear comparisons to the Nazi regime. The court held that the purpose of the law was to prohibit performances offending against the existence of the state, and public peace, order and morality. This was not the case here, however, revolting the play might be. The board's ban was accordingly canceled.

The nature of journalists' rights not to disclose their sources of information was the basic theme of actions before the Supreme Court (298/56, 368/86 — April 7, 1987). Two applicants, journalists, made allegations about two advocates before a disciplinary court of the Bar but claimed privilege not to disclose their sources. The Court rejected their claim and imposed a fine. The Supreme Court reversed the verdict and the fines, holding that the privilege should have been recognized.

The right of a prisoner to home leave in order to exercise his conjugal relations with his wife was the subject of an application by a long-term prisoner seeking an order against the prison governor (H. C. 114/86 — August 9, 1987). The regulations permit ordinary leave once in three months (after one-quarter of the sentence has been served) and certain special leave once in one or two months. The Court held that the application for leave once a month for the stated purpose involved a change of the regulations which was the prerogative of the legislature and the prison authorities; the Court would not intervene.

The right of a common-law wife to inherit her deceased partner's property on intestacy — to the exclusion of a daughter, the only remaining child of an earlier marriage — was upheld in a judgment (CA/107 — April 27, 1989). The couple had lived together for six years until the man's death, sharing accommodation, social life, and a bank account. The daughter resented the relationship and had ceased visiting her father. The District Court had rejected the daughter's claims holding that the Succession Law of 1965 gave the female full rights to inherit as a wife, and the Supreme Court upheld the lower court's decision.

The eligibility of Reform rabbis to perform marriages in Israel was considered in detail before five judges in H. C. 471/82. The judgment was delivered on July 24, 1989, after a protracted delay due to an unsuccessful attempt to find a solution. Two petitioners applied to the Ministry for Religious Affairs to recognize two Reform rabbis as "registering authorities" for performing marriage under the law. All five judges held that granting the application would be contrary to existing law — which the Court was obliged to uphold.

The Attorney-General's prerogative to decide not to prosecute in certain circumstances was challenged in a petition to set aside his decision not to prosecute those allegedly responsible for manipulating bank shares, resulting in the stock exchange crisis of October 1983 (H. C. 935 — May 19, 1990). The Court held that the decision that there was "no public interest" in instituting the prosecution should be set aside as being "inherently unreasonable."

The nature of the crime of treason was examined in the celebrated Vanunu case. Vanunu had worked as a technician at a nuclear research institution, had left the country, converted to Christianity while abroad, and deliberately sought out a journalist of a prominent London newspaper and revealed full details, together with sketches, of his work at the institute — information which received worldwide publicity. He was tried before a District Court and found guilty of aiding an enemy in war, and divulging secret information with intent to impair state security. Vanunu's appeal (C. A. 172/88) was dismissed. Judgment was given on May 27, 1990, and released for publication after certain passages had been deleted, on Aug. 29, 1990.

The issue of working women and discrimination came before the Supreme Court in the petition of a woman sociologist employed by the Jewish Agency and who was required, in terms of a collective work agreement, to retire on her 60th birthday whereas the age for retirement for men was 65 (H. C. 104/87 — October 22, 1990). The Court noted that Knesset legislation in March 1987, while giving women the option of early retirement, had laid down an equal compulsory retiring age for men and women. Although technically the law was enacted after the appeal was lodged, the new law made it clear that the previously existing discrimination had been unlawful. The petitioner was accordingly granted the right to negotiate for her rights.

The right to end one's own life in certain circumstances was recognized by the District Court in Tel Aviv. (O. S. 1141/90 — October 25, 1990). The plaintiff suffered from a terminal disease which brought about progressive paralysis — a course which was irreversible and which would lead to his life becoming "a hell on earth." The plaintiff accordingly applied to the Court to order the hospital, in due course, to comply with his desire not to be attached to a life-support system. The application was granted.

The paramount right of natural parents to the custody of their children was reaffirmed when a Brazilian mother claimed her young daughter from an Israel couple (H. C. 248/88 — March 28, 1991). The latter couple tried in vain to adopt a child in Israel and eventually traveled to Brazil. There they contacted a local advocate and transacted a complicated arrangement through him. Ultimately they were handed a child together with what purported to be her birth certificate and an adoption certificate in their favor. These documents turned out to be forged, and it emerged that the girl had been abducted from her home — without the would-be parents being aware of any wrong doing. After weighing all the facts the Court ordered the child to be restored to her parents.

Principles concerning the liability of dog owners for injury or harm caused to a person were enunciated in two appeals which were heard together (C/A 3934 and 385/89 — October 22, 1991). In the first case the complainant was thrown to the ground by the appellant's Great Dane; in the second, the appellant's German wolfhound threw to the ground and bit a child. According to the penal code a person negligently omitting to take precautions against possible danger from an animal in his possession is liable to imprisonment, but as this was a criminal, and not a civil case, the degree of negligence to be proved was higher. This degree had not been established by the prosecution and both appeals were accordingly dismissed. [A.F.L./S.Lev.]

ECONOMIC AFFAIRS

(see **9**:697; **Dc./17**:364)

Even for the Israeli economy, which has never been characterized by excess stability, the 1980s were marked by severe shifts. For the first five years, through mid-1985, galloping inflation was rampant, almost reaching the dimensions of hyperinflation, and there was a severe decline in growth and an overriding deficit in the balance of payments accompanied by a dangerous drop in the country's foreign currency reserves. Inflation and deficits in international payments are not unusual in the Israeli economy but their dimensions were more threatening in 1980–1985. Moreover, at that time an additional factor was the war being waged in Lebanon without a national consensus whose economic repercussions made the evident negative processes even more severe. The Tel Aviv Stock Exchange, which at the opening of the decade had been surging to new highs, collapsed. The stock market was hit especially hard by the downfall of the bank stocks which until then had been considered reliable and returning real earnings over the rate of inflation of the period. In order to prevent very serious damage to the investing public, trading in those stocks was halted, and for a number of years a floor was fixed for their price guaranteed by the government, turning them in effect into dollar-linked bonds. When the government redeemed them, it became in effect the owner of the Israeli banks. The cost of this government intervention in liabilities to the public

In Nov. 1984 Prime Minister Peres in an Ashkelon supermarket sees how the price freeze affected shoppers. (GPO, Jerusalem)

was estimated by the State Comptroller at $9 billion dollars at 1992 prices. Many experts are convinced that even under optimal conditions the government will not be able to realize even half this sum by selling the banks.

A critical factor in these happenings was a policy of deficit budgets which reached 15 percent of the Gross Domestic Product. This deficit fanned inflation and goaded the general public into searching for alternative ways to stabilize the discretionary resources it had available and to daily linkage to foreign currency for the determination of the financial-economic values needed for ongoing activity. Even though the politicians then in power (the Likkud at the time) had explanations and theories for the trends that emerged, it was obvious that the Ministry of Finance and Bank of Israel had lost control. Indeed, the finance minister was replaced at the height of the difficulties, but even that was not enough. Various partial attempts at stabilization did not succeed because of the public's lack of faith in them.

In summer 1985, when the regime, after elections, became a National Unity Government based on a large majority of the Knesset members, a comprehensive, energetic plan for stabilization was put into effect and applied with determination earning the public's trust. Measures included drastic reduction of the budget deficit, inroads into the cost-of-living adjustments of workers' salaries which seriously dampened the public's buying power, a one-time adjustment of the exchange rate by anchoring it (in contrast to the daily change prior to the reform), and a draconic interest rate which not only turned all financial monetary speculation into losses but also scared off any investment activity. Moreover, all inflationary investments in the recent past became unremunerative under the new normal conditions and were a burden on their holders. This led to serious difficulties in broad sectors of the economy, particularly in agriculture where careless investments were now unproductive.

Yet, there is no doubt that the stabilization plan's designers were highly successful. Inflation declined to an annual rate of some 20 percent in contrast to an average annual rate of about 400 percent before the reform (and an annual marginal rate on the basis of the last month prior to the stabilization of 1,600 percent). Within a short time there were real signs of an improvement in the balance of payments. Foreign currency reserves began to increase (also owing to aid from America which looked favorably upon the stabilization of the Israeli economy). A feeling that the Israeli economy was on the right track prevailed. Growth rejuvenated to a certain extent but it is difficult to pinpoint any impressive result. Over the decade the government expended great effort to maintain the gains of the reform, to a large extent through allowing only a slow, slight change in the exchange rate of the shekel to the dollar. Obviously this policy and the interest policy made production and export more difficult. Under such circumstances it is not surprising that unemployment cropped up and worsened as the decade drew to a close.

From 1989 on a significant external factor was added which dramatically changed the situation of the economy. Large-scale immigration began to arrive, mainly from the former Soviet Union and from Ethiopia. Within three years some half million immigrants entered the country. Over most of the decade immigration averaged 15,000 people a year, then in 1989–1992 the rate was about 150,000 each year, and even in 1992, when the flow diminished, some 80,000 people arrived. Historical experience has shown that large-scale immigration is followed by heightened economic activity. The reasons for that are simple. The absorption system requires the influx of additional means to the economy for the absorption of immigrants — housing, education, and occupational retraining, further investments in infrastructure, in systems of production, and so on; all of these accelerate activity. Indeed, the growth rates which were characterized by a low average rate across the decade (about 3 percent a year), doubled, and since the mass immigration began this growth has been about 6 percent a year.

The economic policy met the challenge admirably. Budget deficit limits were not breached and inflation even continued to decline in the early 1990s to an annual rate of about 10%. This policy was backed by the high foreign currency reserves and the American government's decision to guarantee ten billion dollars of international loans for Israel over a period of five years. This guarantee in the annual sum of two billion dollars enabled Israel to obtain cheap loans and signaled the creditworthiness of the Israel economy to the international financial community. Indeed, the new government which came to power after the summer 1992 elections, a government of a more center left, laborite nature, set itself the aim of carrying out an ambitious program for the expansion of the infrastructure, a change in its order of priorities, both economic (such as forgoing investments in the Administered Territories) as well as social (such as education), and was determined to stress realistic attempts for achieving peace. The government's hope is that this reorganization and its efforts at privatizing an important part of the public sector will attract investments to Israel.

All the above shows that the practical aim of the economic policy is to absorb the large-scale immigration at the cost of an intentional worsening of the balance of payments, so as to maintain internal stability until the investments materialize which it is hoped will stabilize the balance of payments, absorb the surplus manpower created as a result of the consistent policy of restraint in effect since the 1985 reform as well as the addition to the labor force (unskilled from the point of view of the economy) from the immigration.

The most pressing problem — both politically and economically the legacy of the 1980s and the mass immigration which developed at its close — is the widespread, deep unemployment. At the end of 1992 it had reached 11 percent of the civilian labor force (that is, without taking into account the not inconsiderable number of those "employed" by the army which is relatively greater than the norm in Western countries). Although the average rate of unemployment is as stated above, there are certain regions of the country where the employment structure is of very limited range (one or two enterprises) and among the uneducated, unskilled population the rate of unemployment was over 15 percent near the end of 1992 creating pockets of socioeconomic distress worrisome to the government bodies whose efforts at easing the situation were thwarted by lack of resources. The fact that among the immigrants the unemployment rate was almost double the national average, 20 percent, was taken by the public as a "natural" phenomenon but causes great suffering to the immigrants and their families as well as negative feedback to potential immigrants in their countries of origin.

Over the years the argument has been heard that true unemployment is lower since relatively generous unemployment benefits are preferred by some of the unemployed over simple jobs. Government efforts in the period under review did not lead to the employment of this group nor to any solution of the problem of pseudo-unemployment. Yet, it is doubtful that this is a serious problem. Apparently in Israel as in all Western countries the solution is in productive investment which over time will absorb the excess labor force. But in a country absorbing *aliyah* this is not enough. At the end of the period covered here the government tended increasingly to initiate public works projects of scant economic value in order to employ the excess labor force.

It may be that an important non-economic event, namely the *intifada*, will contribute in the long run to increased employment of Israelis. Whereas the Palestinians provided

Table 1. Distinctive Indications of Economic Development 1980–1992 (Changes in average annual % [rounded])

	1980–88	1986–89	1990–92
Gross Domestic Product (GDP)	3.0	3.5	6.0
Business Sector Product	3.5	4.5	6.5
Current Deficit in Balance of Payment (changes in billion $)	0.5	−0.5	0.5
Unemployment	5.5	7.0	10.5
Foreign Debt as % of the GDP	66.5	48.5	27.5
Increase in Immigrants (in 1000's)	15.0	15.0	150.5

Sources: Israel Central Bureau of Statistics and Bank of Israel

Table 2. Population, Labor Force, and Employment (changes in % each Year as compared to the previous year)

	1987	1988	1989	1990	1991	1992
Population (Average)	1.6	1.7	1.7	3.1	6.1	3.5
Civilian Labor Force	1.5	3.9	3.2	2.9	7.3	4.7
Employed Persons	2.6	3.5	0.5	2.1	6.1	4.1
Work Hours of Employed Persons	2.3	3.4	1.9	1.5	5.9	7.3
Employees	2.4	4.0	1.1	2.3	8.0	4.8
Work Hours of Employees	2.2	3.9	2.5	1.9	7.8	7.8

Source: Israel Central Bureau of Statistics

some 5–6 percent of the labor force in the Israeli economy, their violent behavior both in the Administered Territories and in Israel resulted in a lessening of dependence upon them. The government decided to create an additional decline in the number of Arab workers from the territories by increasing control over the number of workers as well as seeking employment for Palestinians in their own locales. If peace agreements will be reached, this topic will have to be faced squarely since without work in Israel, unemployment in the territories, particularly in the Gaza region, reaches as high as 50 percent. This process of change cannot take place without an economic price to the employers and the Israeli economy, since at issue are the replacement of cheap labor and jobs of low social status. Most salient are the fields of construction, agriculture, and certain services which many Israelis and immigrants shun. A two-pronged solution would require more investments in the affected economic branches and a higher wage to Israelis and immigrants who will replace the Arabs.

As an overview of the 12 years covered here, three periods can be discerned: (1) until 1985 an economy in a dangerous spiral according to all relevant indicators; (2) determined stabilization until 1989 which yielded not only positive results as presented at the time but also distress through lack of growth in production and ever-increasing unemployment; (3) from 1989 on, massive immigration into Israel mainly from the former Soviet Union which caused a flurry of activity but also led to an additional expansion in unemployment. [Y.J.T.]

Energy Resources (see 9:790). SUPPLY, USE, AND DEVELOPMENT. During the period 1982–1992 the Israeli energy economy went through a transition phase and achieved a higher degree of sophistication as compared to the previous years. Although the basic problems related to energy, mainly that of the almost total dependence upon imported energy have not been resolved, the understanding of the present international energy market and the relaxation of the stresses on that market eased the energy situation in Israel. Changes in the energy scene occurred mainly as a result of the structural changes in the international energy producers' arena and also due to changes in technologies used, e.g., the use of coal and gas-fired plants instead of oil. Those changes considerably eased the pressures upon the Israeli energy economy as compared to the years following the two oil price shocks in 1973 and 1979. Consumption of primary energy in million ton per year increased from a value of 6.57 in 1974 to a quantity of 8.60 in 1984, an average increase of approximately 2.7% per annum. Total consumption of energy in 1991 was 11.2 million ton oil equivalent per annum. The average rate of increase of energy utilization between the years 1984 and 1991 is about 3.9% per annum. Concurrently the annual electricity consumption increased at a higher pace. Between 1980 and 1991 the electricity consumption increased from 11,057 million kilowatthours (kwh) consumed per year to 19,265 million kwh, an average yearly increase of 5.2% per annum.

THE ELECTRICITY SECTOR. It is evident that the yearly electricity growth rate is higher than the total energy growth rate. The dollar value of energy imported to Israel, in current values, went down from 1.8 billion dollars in 1980 for imported oil, to a 1 billion dollar "price tag" in 1991. The value of coal imports went up from a sum of 22 million dollars in 1981 to 191 million in 1991.

In 1991, the energy necessary to supply electricity to the grid accounted for approximately 43% of all the primary energy used in Israel.

The electric power system is now comprised of three main types of power plants; coal-fired, heavy fuel oil-fired, and gas turbines fired with light fuel oil.

In 1991, 52.1% of the electricity was produced from coal: 43.3% from heavy fuel oil and 4.6% from light fuel oil.

The installed capacity of the various power plants as divided into the previous categories, are as follows; Coal-fired plants having a common capacity of 2,525 electric megawatts, heavy fuel oil-fired plants of 2,150 electric megawatts capacity, and gas turbines having a capacity of 1,155 electric megawatts using light fuel oil.

The first coal-fired power station at Ḥaderah started operation in 1982, and since then all the base load power stations are coal-fired. The latest two coal-fired plants were started in 1991 at the Rutenberg site near Ashkelon. Conforming to the government resolution, those plants are dual-fuel plants and may also use heavy fuel oil as alternate fuel. During the last few years additional gas turbines were installed to cope with unexpected growth in the electricity demand. The peak electricity demand in December 1992 was 5,010 megawatts, as compared to a peak of 4,050 megawatts a year earlier.

The increase in electricity demand also brought the construction of a 400 kilovolt electricity supply trunk that will serve as the main electricity carrier during the next century. As a result of the increase in the use of electricity by the many households, deriving from the increase in the population and of the standard of living during the last decade, the electric grid was found to be inadequate to cope with the demand for electricity. To alleviate this situation the Israel Electric Corporation (IEC) embarked on an accelerated program of improving the low voltage distribution system including connections of electricity lines to dwellings in old houses. This program will continue for a few years to come until the issue is resolved.

The Oil Supply Sector. The quantities of oil imported to Israel between 1980 to 1991 did not vary much. In 1980 Israel imported 7.4 million tons of oil compared to 8.1 million ton in 1991, an increase of about 9.5% in 11 years. Most of the increase in energy consumption was due to the increase in coal imports to Israel in that period. The maximum yearly quantity ever to be imported was 8.3 million ton per annum in 1982 and the minimum was 6.3 million ton oil in 1985. This difference does not show the fluctuation in demand but rather emphasizes the flexibility of the Israeli oil purchasing agents in utilizing world oil prices and Israeli oil stocks to achieve an optimum mix of oil purchases. Following government decisions, oil is now purchased in two ways; (a) Contractual purchases to the order of 4 million tons from oil producing countries such as Mexico, Norway, and Egypt; (b) Oil spot market purchases — the entire oil purchasing operation, is carried out by commercial bodies and not by a government entity. The division of the overall quantity purchased by the oil importing companies is determined by the oil companies and is approved by the government.

The present distillation capacity of Israel's oil refineries is ca. 10.5 million ton oil per annum. This means that Israel now possesses about 1.5–2 million ton per annum of excess capacity in the refinery business. This excess capacity is available for the refining of crude oil for export, under special contractual arrangements. Israel oil refineries are owned by the Israeli government (74%) and by private investors (26%) and are operated as a commercial company.

The Coal Supply Sector. Coal is used in Israel as the main fuel for the new coal-fired power plants. The coal is imported to Israel by the National Coal Supply Company, a government company jointly owned by the government (74%) and the Israel Electric Corporation (26%). The coal company now operates two ships for coal shipments; *Ḥaderah* with a capacity of 166 thousands, and *Leon* with a capacity of 129 thousand tons. Coal is purchased from Australia, Colombia, South Africa, and the U.S.A. It is brought into two importation ports, the coal unloading jetty port at Ḥaderah, and the coal pier at Ashdod. The main coal stockpile is located close to the Ashdod port. This stockpile, operated by the National Coal Supply Company, can stock about 700 thousand tons. Israeli industry uses only small amounts of coal — about 200 thousands tons per annum, but this is expected to increase to about half a million ton per year by the year 2000.

HARNESSING OF LOCAL ENERGY. Oil shales are the most abundant fossil energy resource discovered up until now in Israel. The estimated quantities are about 12 billion ton of oil shales. Analysis has shown that those oil shales contain about 12%–14% of kerogen oil that can be used as replacement for crude oil.

The PAMA energy company, established about 10 years ago by the Israel Chemicals Corporation, the three Israeli oil companies Paz, Delek, and Sonol, and the Israeli Refineries, dealt with developing exploitation methods to use the oil shale resource in two ways; (1) Direct combustion in oil shale-fired power plants; and (2) Oil extraction through retorting of the shales.

After a few years of operation, the oil companies sold their share in the PAMA company to the Israel Electric Corporation. Following this restructuring, the Israel Electric Corporation now holds 50% of the shares and each of the other companies 25%. Investment in the PAMA company up to now is 50 million dollars in current value, about half by the Ministry of Energy and Infrastructure.

A pilot plant for the production of electricity and steam by direct combustion of oil shales was built by PAMA in the Negev, south of Arad. The plant, which started operation in 1989, produces 5 megawatt of electricity and 50 ton of steam per hour. Electricity is fed to the grid and steam is utilized by the Rotem company fertilizers plant located near the power plant. Lessons learned from the operation of this power plant demonstrate that the building of a large oil shale-fired power plant, using Israeli low calorific value oil shales, is indeed feasible.

Israel Electric Corporation (IEC) is now considering the building of additional oil shale-fired power plants in modules of 100–150 electric megawatts. A total of 1,000 electric megawatts of oil shale-fired power plants is envisaged. Many foreign companies have shown interest in building these oil shale plants.

Wind Energy. Israel did not develop indigenous wind energy machines. The policy of the Ministry of Energy and Infrastructure is to install wind turbines of a well-proven design, so as to assure the highest performance possible. Five wind demonstration units were installed in Israel, in different locations spread all over the country. The demonstration units are located at Katif in the Golan Heights, Yodfat in Galilee, Maaleh Gilboa in the Gilboa range, Eilon Moreh in Samaria, and in Beit Yatir west of Arad. In addition to these demonstration units, a private company installed, in the Golan Heights, a wind farm of 5 electric megawatts., The best sites for the installation of additional wind farms are located in the Golan Heights, where wind velocities of more than 8 m/sec. were recorded. The Golan Heights can provide sites for the installation of about 300 megawatts of wind power.

The Israel Electric Corporation is also reviewing the possibility of installing a wind farm of 70 megawatts at a Golan Heights site. The Ministry of Energy and Infrastructure is planning to have about 50–75 megawatt of wind power installed by the year 2000.

Solar energy. Levels of solar insolation in Israel are very high. The insolation levels in the Negev are about 2 mwh/year for every square meter. In theory, all the present power requirements of Israel could be supplied using solar irradiation from an area of only 12 square kilometers. Even assuming an area utilization factor of 1/3, the total area to supply all the present power needs of Israel would be only a square of 6 × 6 km. The Ministry of Energy and Infrastructure has thus far invested about 56 million dollars in research into means of extracting solar energy. A similar amount was invested by other government funds under the auspices of the Ministry of Trade and Industry and the Ministry of Science and Technology. Private companies among them Luz, the most successful from the technical point of view, spent even higher sums for solar energy research out of their own resources. The total amount spent until now on solar energy research in Israel is about 200 million dollars. The solar energy now used in Israel accounts for 3% of the overall amount of energy used. More than two-thirds of the households in Israel are using solar heaters for water heating.

Solar energy research in Israel is carried out mainly in the Weizmann Institute in Rehovot and the solar experimentation center at Sedeh-Boker, a branch of the Ben-Gurion University of the Negev. Four large solar experiments are being conducted at the Weizmann Institute using the solar tower, which has an array of 64 heliostats that concentrate sunlight into focal points on the central tower. In the first experiment, solar heat was collected in a central collector to heat air to a temperature of 1200° centigrade and the heated air expanded in a gas turbine to produce electricity. This experiment was sponsored by the Israel Electric Corporation and by private bodies. The second experiment is related to chemical heat collection of solar energy. In this experiment, solar energy is collected through the conversion of two inert gases into two other inert gases that can be catalyzed to form the initial components, yielding solar energy that is stored during the conversion process. Storage of solar energy, as well as conveying the energy in pipes until recombination of the solar gases takes place, is thus possible. In the third experiment, steam was generated by directly heating a ceramic steam boiler, through focusing sun rays into it. This experiment has now been terminated, mainly since most relevant data had been collected on all the main issues. The fourth, most advanced, experiment, is the solar pumped laser exper-

Solar energy at Sedeh Boker where work is also being done on Direct Steam Generation. (Courtesy Ben-Gurion University of the Negev)

iment, in which a coherent laser light beam is created by directing concentrated sun light on a crystal that emits coherent light. All these experiments are being supported by the Ministry of Energy and Infrastructure.

The second center where solar experiments are being performed is the Solar Experimentation Center in Sedeh Boker, which tests different solar technologies. Among the technologies tested are "LUZ type" parabolic trough collectors, deep trough collectors "CPC type" and various photovoltaic cell collectors; stationary, single axis tracking and double axis tracking.

The role of Luz corporation in the development of solar energy the world over must be mentioned. Luz, a Jerusalem-based company, developed, designed and constructed solar energy power plants on a large scale. It built 9 solar power plants in Barstow, Kramer Junction, and Harper Lake in the Mojave Desert in California. The total power installed in those stations is 350 electric megawatts. The stations are operating as of now and supply electricity to the Southern California Edison Electricity Company under standard electricity supply contracts. Luz corporation went bankrupt in 1991 because of financing problems before the start of the construction of power station no. 10 to be erected at Harper Lake in the Mojave Desert.

In the Luz system, electrical energy is produced by steam generated via solar heating. Solar energy, collected by linear parabolic troughs, heats collecting elements located in the foci of those troughs. Mineral oil flowing through the heat collecting elements is heated to a temperature of about 390°C. The mineral oil is then pumped to heat exchangers and steam generators in which steam is produced. The steam is then expanded in steam turbines as in any other conventional steam power plant. Following condensation of the steam to water, the water is pumped back to the steam generator. Gas steam boilers were supplied with the plant to provide back up during cloudy and overcast days.

Before its collapse, Luz corporation intended to develop a solar power plant system based upon direct steam generation in the heat-collecting element located in the foci of the parabolic troughs of the solar collectors, instead of heating oil in them. This system (DSG, i.e., Direct Steam Generation) was to be tested at the Sedeh Boker test facility. The Ministry of Energy and Infrastructure contributed to the installation of all the infrastructure for that experiment.

Following the demise of Luz all the technology it had developed was acquired by the Belgian company, Belgian Instruments International (BII). BII continues to market the previous Luz technology, and is active in developing the new DSG technology in the Sedeh Boker site.

The Paz-Pimat company developed solar heating systems operating at low-range temperatures (70°–140°C). This system is used to heat water and produce low pressure steam for industrial facilities and hospitals.

Another company, Paz-Gal, developed an absorption chiller using the heat collected by the trough solar collectors designed by Paz-Pimat. The absorption chiller fluids are a mixture of an organic oil and an "environmentally friendly" gas to be used with new chillers and air conditioners replacing the commonly previously used Freon-derived gases.

Oil and Gas Exploration and Production. Oil exploration in Israel started in 1953, since when 395 boreholes have been sunk. Successful strikes were scarce and the yield of local oil fields is no more than 700 barrels of oil per day. Present exploration efforts concentrate on the continental shelf of the Mediterranean, the Dead Sea, the Jordan Valley, and eastern and western regions of the Negev. Since 1975, 365 million dollars were invested in oil and gas exploration of which 135 million were invested by the state. The Ministry of Energy and Infrastructure policy is to encourage private sector investments in explorations and production, providing infrastructure services through government-owned companies. The services include geophysical surveys by the Institute of Petroleum Research and Geophysics and also drilling and other well services by different government companies.

The area designated for oil exploration totals about 36,000 square kilometers, of which 29,000 are on land and the rest offshore.

Exploration and production of oil requires licencing as defined by the Israel Petroleum Law.

Energy Conservation and Miscellaneous Projects. Energy conservation measures include improving the efficiency of energy systems, utilizing waste energy, and the efficient energy use by the energy consumer. The Ministry of Energy and Infrastructure provides grants of up to 15% of the investments for energy conservation activities.

Among the projects sponsored by the MOEI is a cold storage facility at the Metullah sports center. Its unique feature is the use of the ice layer of the skating rink as the main cold storing facility, in addition to utilizing the waste heat from the ice generation system for sanitary and pool heating.

Another project utilizes soluble organic waste effluents from a yeast plant to produce methane gas using controlled anaerobic fermentation of the waste effluents. The methane gas is used to produce steam for the fermentation process.

Because of the large desert area of Israel, an effort is being made to investigate the possibility of changing the microclimate within the buildings in the desert areas, in order to provide temperate climate for its inhabitants. The ministry supports research in that field, which was summarized in guidelines published as a handbook *Energy Aspects of Design in Arid Zones.* Low energy-consuming houses, using desert architecture design principles, were built at the Sedeh Boker campus of the Ben-Gurion University of the Negev.

A small hydroelectric power station was built on the northern section of the Jordan River. The 2.6 megawatt plant came into operation in December 1991. The plant and ancillary ponds and pipelines were designed to conform to environmental requirements for the preservation of indigenous flora and fauna.

In summary. The Israel government energy policy as carried out in the past ten years by the Ministry of Energy and Infrastructure, demonstrated the ability of the Israeli administration to cope with many crisis situations in the energy supply areas. The numerous energy projects, developed by Israeli scientists, show the ability of the technical community in Israel to provide economically viable solutions to many problems in the energy field. [AM.E.]

RELIGIOUS LIFE

Jews (see **9**:887; **Dc./17**:390). Jewish religious institutions continued to be linked to political developments, with a drop in the influence of the modern Orthodox and a parallel rise in the ultra-Orthodox (*haredi*) community. Politically, the National Religious Party, which spoke for modern Orthodoxy, declined sharply from the 1960s, when it had 11 or 12 representatives in the Knesset. In the 1984 elections, this party won four seats, in 1988, five, and in 1992, six. In contrast, the parties to the religious right of the NRP, which had had six seats in the 1960s, won eight seats in 1984, 13 seats in 1988, and ten in 1992.

The modern Orthodox camp, and in particular, the National Religious Party, had become identified with Gush Emunim, the movement favoring Jewish settlement of the entire Land of Israel, and in particular, the Administered Territories. The religious obligation to retain all of the Land of Israel was associated with a belief in the potential arrival of the Messiah. The most extreme form of this messianism found expression in movements aimed at restoring a Jewish presence on the Temple Mount, either in addition to, or in place of, the Muslim shrines occupying the site. One small group of extremists was arrested while planning to destroy the mosques there. A group known as the Faithful of the Temple Mount, which had previously attempted unsuccessfully to conduct public Jewish prayer on the Temple Mount, organized a "cornerstone-laying" ceremony with a bloc of stone weighing several tons, but was barred from the area by the police. Another organization, the Jerusalem Temple Institute, occupied itself with creating ritual objects and garments to be used in the Temple upon its restoration.

A relatively small number of Orthodox leaders tried to dissociate themselves from this trend, by organizing, in 1982, Netivot Shalom, a religious group loosely identified with the Israeli peace movement, and founding Meimad, a moderate religious party, in 1988. Although Meimad won considerable sympathy in left-wing non-Orthodox circles, it failed to garner even the minimum of votes needed for one seat in the Knesset.

Political developments in the ultra-Orthodox camp were highlighted by the fragmentation of Agudat Israel, which had formerly been its sole political representative. Shas, a Sephardi ultra-Orthodox movement, combined religious fervor with bitterness over the discrimination and wrongs of the past. The party participated in the 1983 Jerusalem municipal election and then went on nationally to become the dominant ultra-Orthodox voice. Seeking votes outside the traditional ultra-Orthodox strongholds, Shas brought a new flavor to the local political scene, especially in the 1988 elections when the secular public was bemused to see a television election advertisement in which a group of black-clad rabbis pronounced a formula releasing voters from promises to vote for other parties.

Degel ha-Torah, organized in 1988, was an Ashkenazi split-off from Agudat Israel. Despite the desertions, Agudat Israel enjoyed considerable success in this election, thanks to the support of the Ḥabad Ḥasidim, who had previously refrained from supporting any party. The change was a result

Rabbi Eliezer Shach. (GPO, Jerusalem)

of the bitter attacks by Degel ha-Torah's leader, Rabbi Eliezer Schach, head of the anti-hasidic camp, on Ḥabad's Rabbi Menachem Mendel Schneerson, the Lubavicher

Jerusalem demonstration by secular Jews in favor of opening of movie theaters on the Sabbath, August 1987. (GPO, Jerusalem)

Rebbe, a fellow nonagenarian. Rabbi Schach, who enjoyed an adulation from his followers not unlike that bestowed on ḥasidic rebbes, became the object of harsh criticism in the wake of the 1988 elections, when he ruled out any coalition with Labor because of the lack of religious observance in kibbutzim, whose very Jewishness he questioned.

An apparent victory for the NRP was the election, in 1983, for a ten-year term, of Ashkenazi Chief Rabbi Avraham Shapiro and Sephardi Chief Rabbi Mordechai Eliahu, both identified with the nationalist-religious ideology of the NRP. Rabbi Shapiro, in particular, was the principal of the Merkaz ha-Rav yeshivah, the ideological cradle of Gush Emunim. However, the chief rabbinate became more alienated from the secular Jewish majority, while in Orthodox circles, an increasing public looked to the ultra-Orthodox *ḥaredi* rabbis for spiritual leadership.

The challenge to the chief rabbis was especially effective from Rabbi Ovadiah Yosef, Eliahu's predecessor, who continued to be regarded by many as the rightful leader of Sephardi Jewry. Yosef, the spiritual mentor of Shas, challenged a halakhic ruling by Shapiro and Eliahu that it was impermissible to give up any part of the Land of Israel, even for the sake of peace. Yosef ruled that territorial concessions were permissible to prevent bloodshed.

Another challenge to the chief rabbis regarded the observance of the sabbatical year, during which it is forbidden to work the land of Israel. Prior to the sabbatical year which began in October 1986, the chief rabbis, following a precedent set by their predecessors, ruled that in order to promote Jewish settlement, it was permitted, and even desirable, for Jewish farmers to nominally "sell" their land to a non-Jew and continue to work it. The *ḥaredi* rabbis ruled that one could not eat produce grown as a result of such a ruling and succeeded in convincing the Ministry of Commerce and Industry to import grain so bakeries would not use that grown locally. This incident highlighted a tendency by food producers to seek kashrut certification from *ḥaredi* institutions, although legally, only the official rabbinates were empowered to issue such certification.

In the schools, a growing number of parents preferred the *ḥaredi* schools over the modern Orthodox State Religious system. Even within the State Religious system there was a tendency for extremism, with the establishment of new schools to cater to a more religiously strict public and many existing schools opting for separate classes for boys and girls. Part of the success of the *ḥaredi* schools networks could be attributed to the increasing funds allocated to them as the price for government coalitions. Especially remarkable was the flourishing of *ḥaredi yeshivot*, where a growing number of adults studied religious subjects full-time. It was estimated that there were more yeshivah students than ever before in Jewish history.

The growth of the *yeshivot* became a source of contention with the secular majority, many of whom were unhappy at the government subsidies which went to such institutions. Both the secular and many modern Orthodox objected to the fact that in a country in which universal military service was the rule, the yeshivah students received automatic deferment, often until an age at which they were no longer fit for military service. At one point it was estimated that some 20,000 young men were enjoying such deferment.

The question of public Sabbath observance continued to be an issue, with a tendency for some public desecration of the Sabbath, despite repeated protests and demonstrations. In particular in Jerusalem, for the first time, several cinemas began to have Friday night showings and a large number of pubs, discotheques, and cafes opened their doors on the Sabbath.

There were acrimonious disputes in Jerusalem over the issue of the exhumation of the bones of Jews. According to the ultra-Orthodox interpretation, land even suspected of containing Jewish remains should remain untouched, so as to facilitate resurrection of the dead. This interpretation led to considerable conflict between Atra Kadisha, an organization devoted to preserving Jewish burial sites, and archeologists and civil engineers. In 1982 and 1983, Atra Kadisha led public protests against the archeological excavations at the City of David. According to Atra Kadisha, the site contained a medieval Jewish cemetery. The archeologists, who denied this, succeeded in completing the excavations. In 1992, a number of tombs from the Second Temple period were uncovered during construction of a major highway interchange in French Hill and a large burial area which archeologists insisted was Christian, because of the presence of Christian symbols, was uncovered during construction of the Mamilla project. Archeologists removed and then, following violent protests, returned for burial, the bones and sarcophagi of one tomb from French Hill. At Mamilla, the builders removed the bones and bulldozed the burial area in the dead of night. The young demonstrators who reacted introduced a new level of violence into religious-secular disputes, violently confronting the police, stoning cars, and burning garbage dumpsters.

The immigration of Jews, both from Ethiopia and from the former Soviet Union, presented a challenge to the religious establishment. The Ethiopian Jews (see BETA ISRAEL) were intensely observant, but their practice differed considerably from normative Judaism. When large numbers began to arrive as a result of Operation Moses in 1984, the chief rabbis ruled that they would have to undergo a symbolic conversion ceremony before they could be married. In protest over what they saw as a questioning of their Jewishness, the Ethiopian

Ethiopians in front of a spiritual absorption center in Netanyah, 1992. (Courtesy Netanyah Municipality)

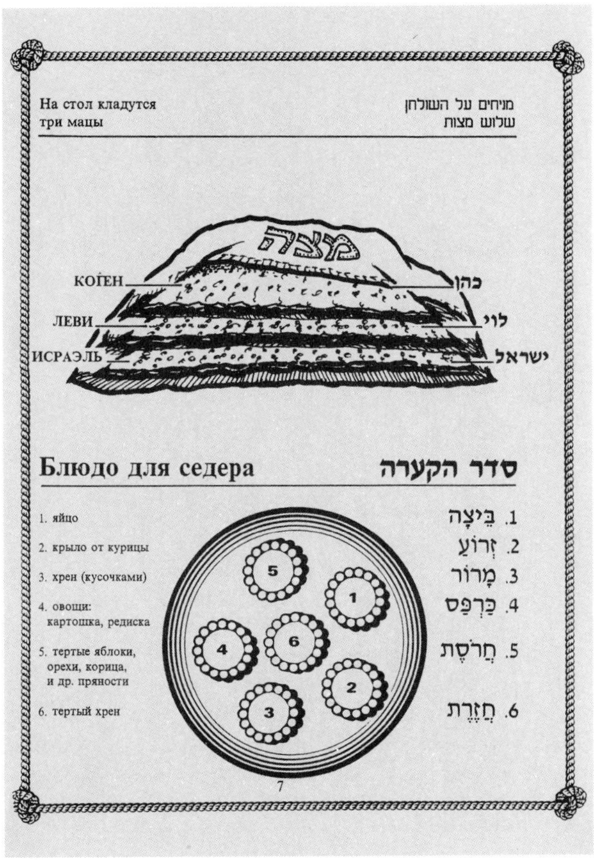

A Russian-Hebrew Passover *Haggadah* published in 1991 by the Ministry of Absorption's Department of Social Absorption. (Courtesy Ministry of Absorption, Jerusalem)

Jews objected to the ruling and held a sit-in strike for a month, across from the offices of the chief rabbis. Although the Ethiopian Jews garnered considerable public sympathy and support, they were unable to win over the chief rabbis, who eventually circumvented the issue by allowing a rabbi sympathetic to their cause to register their marriages. In 1992, the Ethiopian Jewish community was again unsuccessful in a confrontation with the chief rabbinate, this time in a bid for the community's traditional religious leaders, the *qessim* (Amharic: *qessotch*), to be allowed to perform marriages and carry out divorces in Israel.

Yet another religious dilemma faced the Ethiopian Jewish community after Operation Solomon, the mass airlift in which the bulk of Ethiopian Jewry was brought to Israel in May 1991. Remaining in Ethiopia were thousands of *Falash-Mura (falas moura)*, Jews who had become estranged from the Jewish community and in many cases had converted to Christianity. Although the *qessim*, for the most part, regarded these people as renegades, to be abandoned, most members of the community in Israel agitated for them to be returned to Judaism and brought to Israel. The government eventually decided that close relatives of those living in Israel could be brought in as a humanitarian gesture.

A different type of problem resulted from the mass immigration from the former Soviet Union. Although some of the immigrants from the Baltic states and Central Asia had some basic knowledge of Judaism, many of the others were almost totally ignorant of even the most basic elements of Jewish history, religion, and culture. A considerable number of these immigrants were either the offspring of mixed marriages or brought with them non-Jewish spouses. It was not clear how many were actually Jewish according to *halakhah*. During the years that Rabbi Yitzḥak Peretz of Shas was the Absorption Minister, the ministry embarked on a campaign of "spiritual absorption," introducing the immigrants to the practices of ultra-Orthodoxy, with questionable success. The immigrants studied some essentials about Judaism at the ulpanim in which they learned Hebrew and a wide variety of public institutions and organizations offered courses in Judaism. Perhaps the most promising indication of the immigrants' desire to return to Judaism was the frequency with which they asked to be circumcised.

Demonstration by Shoshana Miller (center) against decision by Ministry of Interior to write "convert" on her Israel identity card. (Courtesy *Koteret Rashit*; photo Chibi Shichman)

Non-Orthodox movements continued to make limited progress. Their main success was in barring a change in the Law of Return, which would have, in effect, excluded those converted to Judaism by Conservative and Reform rabbis abroad from recognition as Jews eligible for Israeli citizenship. Although the number of such converts immigrating to Israel was minimal, many Jews abroad, particularly in the U.S., saw this as a crucial issue, in view of the high rate of mixed marriages and the fact that a growing part of the American Jewish community included converts or their children. The failure of the religious parties to gain support on this issue from the other parties was a result of massive pressure by American Jewish organizations.

A related issue was the decision of the Interior Ministry not to register such converts as Jews in their identity cards and in the population registry. After Shoshana Miller, a Reform convert from the U.S., successfully petitioned the High Court of Justice to be registered as a Jew, the ministry continued to try to circumvent the decision. It proposed registering all converts as such in the identity cards, a move that aroused opposition not only from the non-Orthodox, but from the chief rabbis and many other Orthodox rabbis, who pointed out that Jewish law forbade reminding a convert of his or her non-Jewish origins.

In 1992, the first woman rabbi, Naama Kelman-Ezrachi, was ordained by Israel's Reform rabbinical school and in the same year, the rabbinical school of the local Conservative (Masorti) movement decided to admit women as students in its rabbinical program. In 1986, Leah Shakdiel, an Orthodox schoolteacher, was elected to the religious council of Yeruḥam, the first woman to be elected to such a body, but she did not take her seat until the High Court of Justice ordered the Religious Affairs Minister to validate her election two years later. In 1988, women won the right to serve on the body electing the Tel Aviv chief rabbi.

However, the High Court rejected the petition of another women's group, the Women of the Wall, which included women of all religious streams who aroused the fury of ultra-Orthodox worshipers when they attempted to read from a Torah scroll at the Western Wall. The Court upheld a Religious Affairs Ministry ruling which forbade them to wear prayer shawls, read from a Torah scroll, or even sing aloud at the Western Wall. [HA.SH.]

Christians (see **9**:910; **Dc./17**:393). According to the Central Bureau of Statistics, the estimated Christian population of the State of Israel at the end of 1991 was 128,000, compared with 94,170 Christian inhabitants counted in the 1983 decennial census. Estimates vary greatly regarding the extent to which this number has been augmented by Russian and Ethiopian Christians who arrived in Israel with the most recent waves of immigration from those countries. On the other hand, Christian sources note that in the face of continuing political tension and an uncertain future in the Middle East, a growing number of Christian families in Jerusalem and the Territories have now chosen emigration to the West.

The various strands — Christian, Israeli, Arab, Palestinian — intertwined in the identities of Christians in the land, have been colored by political conflicts in the area during the past decade. The civil and religious strife in Lebanon and renewed contact with fellow-Christians there in the wake of the 1982 War in Lebanon, stirred, especially among Christians in Galilee, stronger feelings of identity with their particular Christian community. The protracted *intifada*, on the other hand, has induced many Christians living in Jerusalem and the Territories to accentuate their Palestinian identity and advocate solidarity with their Muslim neighbors, despite, or perhaps because of, rising Islamic fundamentalism. In the latter circumstance, some Christians have begun

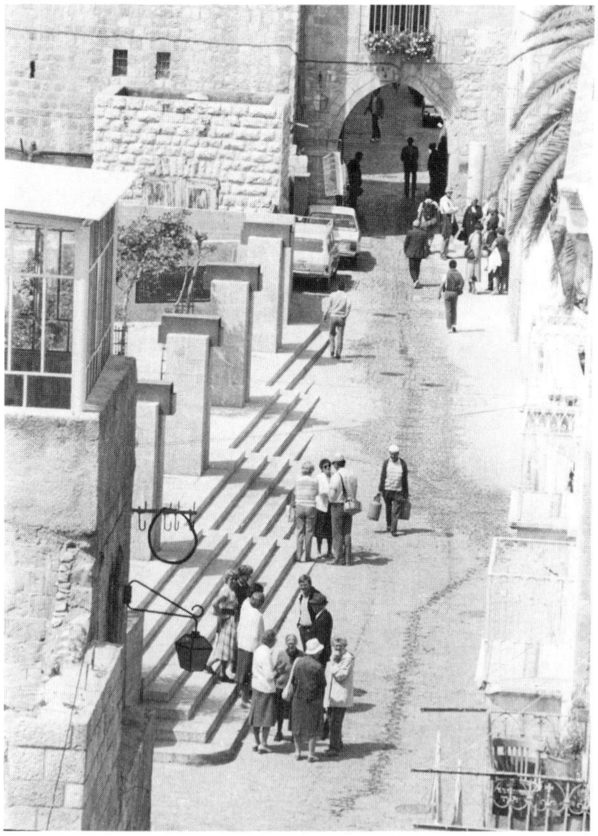

Renovated Via Dolorosa as seen from the rampart above the Lion's Gate with pilgrim way station to the left. (Photo Isaiah Karlinsky, Jerusalem)

to formulate a Palestinian Christian "theology of liberation," designed to strengthen local Christians in their Palestinian context and identity. Church leaders in Jerusalem on their part have issued with increasing frequency joint public statements and pastoral letters expressing their deep dismay over the suffering of their faithful. Israel government officials in turn have accused Church leaders of being one-sided in their political positions, and fault them for their failure to speak out on Palestinian violence and their refusal to publicly acknowledge recurrent instances of Muslim extremism directed against their members and institutions.

The sensitive situation of the Christian communities in the present political climate was brought to the fore in 1990 by the St. John's Hospice Affair. Over the past decade, Muslims have continued without opposition to purchase, lease, or rent many properties in the Christian Quarter of Jerusalem's Old City. However, when a group of Orthodox Jews managed with assistance from the Ministry of Housing to sub-lease and subsequently take up residence in a building in the vicinity of the Holy Sepulcher owned by the Greek Orthodox Patriarchate, Christians felt obliged to protest loudly in order to avert Muslim accusations of collusion with Zionist designs. The initial support for the Christian side which was forthcoming from many Jewish circles weakened significantly when the Greek Orthodox Patriarch of Jerusalem Diodoros I, traveled to Rome to enlist the support of the pope, and to Damascus where President Asad readily offered his help to defend the Christians of the Holy Land.

In line with a process of indigenization in evidence throughout the Catholic world, for the first time in the history of the Latin Patriarchate a local Arab Christian, Monsignor Michel Asad Sabbaḥ, took office as Latin Patriarch in Jerusalem in January 1988. During the past decade his Church and the various Uniate Catholic communities have dedicated a significant number of new houses of worship and refurbished many of their older churches and convents throughout the country. The spiritual life of the local Catholic Church has been strengthened by the arrival of 11 additional religious orders and congregations, and by the publication of a new missal and lectionnaire in Arabic in accord with the liturgical reforms recommended by the Second Vatican Council.

Through official visits to the leaders of Orthodox Churches abroad and by hosting them in Jerusalem, the Greek Orthodox patriarch of Jerusalem has attempted to reassert the centrality of Jerusalem as the "Mother" Church of the Christian oecumene. For the first time in several centuries, representatives of Orthodox Churches from throughout the world gathered in Jerusalem in October 1986 at his initiative to discuss issues of world peace. The patriarch has also labored to more effectively capitalize on the extensive real estate holdings of his Church in order to generate the funds required for an ambitious project of renovation of the Patriarchate's historic shrines and convents throughout the country. The Palestinian laity of his community, both in Israel and in Jordan, have lobbied ever more forcefully for a greater say in the affairs of the Patriarchate and for the redirecting of its resources to educational and welfare projects for their benefit.

In February 1990, Yegishe Derderian, passed away after 30 years of service as Armenian Patriarch, during which the Jerusalem Patriarchate played a central role in the religious and cultural life of the Armenian diaspora. Under the leadership of his successor, Archbishop Torkom Manoogian, renewed access to the Armenian homeland has brought benefit to the community, but also the burden of the tragedies and tribulations of their fellow-Armenians living there.

The religio-political divide within the Protestant communities in the country has widened during the last decade. Among those who deeply identify with Jews, whether as an affirmation of the Jewish roots of their faith or with an aim to pave a path for missionary inroads, western evangelical circles close to the International Christian Embassy have been ever more vocal in their political support for the State of Israel, at times in ways which have irritated the indigenous Churches. On the other hand, most Arab Protestants and many of the expatriate Christians who work among and emphathize with them, have adopted a much more critical posture vis-à-vis the State of Israel and endeavor to distance themselves from any religious or political links, past or present, with Israel.

Holy Places. Significant progress has been made in the restoration of major Christian shrines throughout the country. Renovations in the Church of the Holy Sepulcher have continued, although in parts of the basilica progress is still impeded by age-old disputes concerning the Status Quo. The three principal communities — Greek Orthodox, Armenian, and Latin — have completed most of the works of restoration and beautification in the sections of the shrine held respectively by them and have finally jointly agreed concerning the embellishment of the ceiling of the dome of the Rotunda, darkened for decades by the ugly scaffolding left in place pending the outcome of their deliberations. The Civil Administration in Judea and Samaria has repeatedly patched the roof of the Basilica of the Nativity in Bethlehem but has not been able to achieve agreement among the Churches concerning the major repairs called for since the days of the British Mandate. The annual general cleaning of that shrine has become in recent years the scene of altercations between the three main communities. Both the Egyptian and Ethiopian governments have continued to actively press for a resolution of the long-standing Coptic-Ethiopian dispute over Deir al-Sultan, the monastery on the roof of the Holy Sepulcher, which would favor their respective countrymen.

General Secretary of the International Council of Christians and Jews, Rev. Dr. Jacobus Schoneveld (left) with Teddy Kollek, mayor of Jerusalem, 1990. (Courtesy ICCJ, Heppenheim)

Among other holy places which have been reconstructed or undergone repairs are the Church of the Multiplication of the Loaves and Fishes at Tabgha, the traditional house of St. Peter in Capernaum, over which a controversial octagonal "memorial" structure has been erected, and the Tomb of the Virgin near the Garden of Gethsemane. The Cenacle on Mount Zion, traditional site of the Last Supper, has been refurbished by the present caretaker, the Ministry for Religious Affairs, and the East Jerusalem Development Corporation has esthetically renovated the Via Dolorosa. The traditional place of the baptism of Jesus at Qasr al Yahud, located in a closed security zone along the Jordan River southeast of Jericho, remains inaccessible to the general public, but in recent years the Civil Administration in the Administered Territories has made arrangements for an annual Catholic pilgrimage to the site, and for the Orthodox celebration of the Feast of Epiphany there. The Government Tourist Corporation has developed baptismal facilities for the convenience of pilgrim groups along the Jordan river just south of the Sea of Galilee.

Education, Social, and Cultural. Nearly all the Christian schools in the State of Israel, with the exception of those in East Jerusalem, have in the course of the last decade received official recognition from the Ministry of Education and Culture and now benefit from extensive funding from the state budget, which has made it possible for them to expand and improve their programs. Christian schools in the Territories have been severely affected by the civil unrest and repeated closures during the *intifada*. However, there too Christian educational activities have continued to expand, for example through additional facilities inaugurated at Bethlehem University and at the Salesian Technical School in Bethlehem, as well as through a new theological seminary opened in the village of Beit Sahour by the Greek (Melkite) Catholic Church.

The dozens of study frameworks available to Christians from abroad have been augmented by the Vatican-sponsored Centre Chrétien des Etudes Juives opened in Jerusalem in 1987 at the Monastery of Saint Pierre de Sion (Ratisbonne). The new graduate institute is run under the academic direction of the Institut Catholique de Paris, and like many other Christian study programs in Israel, benefits from close collaboration with the Hebrew University. Among Jewish educational institutions in the capital which have developed special study programs for Christians are the Shalom Hartman Institute for Advanced Jewish Studies and the Melitz Centers for Jewish-Zionist Education.

A protracted controversy surrounding the construction of

a new Mormon Church-affiliated Brigham Young University study center on Mount Scopus was defused by a written undertaking of officials of the Church that the center's staff and students will scrupulously refrain from any missionary activity in the country.

The local Churches, with the financial support of Western coreligionists, have devoted increasing attention to the social and cultural needs of their communities. The Greek, Armenian, and Coptic Orthodox, as well as the Latin, Syrian, Greek, and Maronite Catholics, have all established additional community and retreat centers or expanded existing facilities.

Several Churches have initiated much-needed housing projects for Christian residents. Christian medical services have been expanded and improved, *inter alia*, at the Caritas Baby Hospital and the Holy Family Maternity Hospital in Bethlehem and at the Scottish Hospital in Nazareth. Historical museums have been opened to the public in Jerusalem by the Latins, Armenians, Greek Orthodox, and Greek Catholics. During the past decade many of the Christian hospices have been renovated and modernized to meet the needs of today's pilgrim.

The Jerusalem Municipality has honored several Christian personalities with the title "Distinguished Citizen of Jerusalem" and, in January 1987, the Knesset paid special tribute to "Righteous Gentiles" living in Israel.

Ecumenical and Interfaith. Ecumenical and interfaith activities in Israel have continued to attract primarily persons of Western background. Attempts to involve representatives of the dominantly eastern or Arab Christian population have met with little success. Ecumenical contacts among local Christians have focused mainly on discussion of political rather than theological issues. Steps have been taken to establish an Arab Christian–Muslim dialogue, but significant progress has been impeded by difficulties, magnified by present political realities, in coming to grips with the less than happy history of Muslim–Christian relations in the region.

The opening of formal talks between representatives of the Vatican and the Government of Israel in 1992 has been received with mixed emotions by many Christians in the country. There is, on the one hand, deep apprehension that official Vatican recognition of the State of Israel might imperil their fragile relations with their Muslim neighbors, and on the other, the cautious hope that formal agreements between the State and the Vatican will clarify and even enhance their position in local society. Both the Government and the Vatican have stressed that the outcome of the talks will in no way prejudice the existing Status Quo in the Holy Places and that any rights and privileges which might be secured by the Catholic Churches and institutions would be extended to other Christian communities in the country as well. [D.Ros.]

Muslims (see **9**:919; **Dc./17**:395). Since the establishment of the State of Israel, the Muslim religious institutions have changed considerably. Due to the growing number of the Muslim population (over 14% of the total population), many needs and problems have emerged. Some of these problems have been solved while others still await solutions.

Muslim Institutions. *Courts.* The Muslim courts are called Shari'a courts after the name of the Muslim law, and are located in areas which are heavily inhabited by Muslims. There are seven regional courts covering all the areas in Israel which are inhabited by Muslims: Acre, Haifa, Nazareth, Jaffa, Taibeh, Jerusalem, and Beersheba.

In spite of the fact that seven Shari'a courts exist, there are, for the time being, only five judges (kadis), after the death of the kadi of Acre, serving in these courts. Ever since the establishment of the Beersheba court (about 10 years ago), no kadi has ever been appointed for that court. The kadi of Jaffa, therefore, visits that court on a weekly basis. For each regional court one kadi is appointed to deal with the cases of his region.

Aerial view of Ramadan prayers by the Muslim faithful on the Temple Mount in Jerusalem. (GPO, Jerusalem)

There is also the Shari'a Court of Appeal, which according to the law is located in Jerusalem. The number of kadis who should serve in this court is three; yet there is only one permanent kadi functioning — the head of the Court of Appeal. The other two members are recruited by this kadi from among the regional kadis to fill the vacant places, a situation which has its disadvantages especially as regional kadis deal with cases of their fellow kadis of similar rank. According to the law, every kadi is automatically considered a member of the Court of Appeal; however, it is possible to hold the sessions of the Court of Appeal with only two members present.

In the Shari'a courts the Muslim religious law *(Shari'a)* is the dominant law.

Mosques. The increase in number of the Muslim population and the growth of religious movements among Muslim youths have led to a noticeable increase in building houses of worship for religious services. There are 180 mosques registered in the Ministry of Religious Affairs. New mosques have been constructed and old ones have been renovated or expanded. The budget needed for such enterprises comes, mainly, from contributions of local Muslim organizations and individuals in addition to a sum of money donated by the Ministry of Religious Affairs. The annual budget allocated by the ministry ranges from NIS 5,000 to NIS 10,000. Another source of support is the revenues of the Muslim Waqf (religious trust).

The Waqf. In several towns (such as Jaffa, Ramleh, Lydda, Haifa and Acre) the government has appointed special committees in order to administer the Waqf's properties in these places, to collect the rentals, and to spend them on religious projects, mainly maintenance of mosques. The most famous project, with which the Waqf committee of Jaffa has been involved, is the reconstruction of Hassan Bey Mosque. Efforts are being made to renovate Seedna Ali Mosque which was damaged by sand fall. For that object a special Muslim association from the "triangle" region has been established.

Religious Officials and Functionaries. Hundreds of Muslim functionaries are working in the religious sphere of life in addition to the kadis and the clerks of the Shari'a courts.

This group includes: Imams — conductors of religious services; Muezzins — those who call for prayers; and Ma'zuns — writers of marriage contracts. The first two groups (about 270 persons) were not considered as government officials and were deprived of all kinds of social benefits such as pensions, widows' allowances, clothing, recreation, etc. After a lengthy struggle 214 functionaries achieved the status of State employees with all the mentioned benefits in 1981. The rest (56 persons) are still awaiting recognition as State employees. The third group, composed of writers of marriage contracts, are appointed by the kadis each in his own region and have no rights whatsoever. The income of this group is gained by collecting fixed fees upon writing of the marriage contract from the partners concerned.

Spiritual and Cultural Activities. Until 1978, Muslims in Israel were denied the right to fulfill the fifth religious pillar of Islam — the Hajj, i.e., the pilgrimage to the holy places of Mecca and Medina in Saudi Arabia. In 1978 an unwritten agreement between Israel, Jordan, and Saudi Arabia made possible the carrying out of the Hajj for thousands of Muslims in Israel.

The mass media in both Israel and the neighboring Arab countries broadcast special programs on various religious occasions such as Ramadan — the month of fasting, *'id al-Fitr*, the feast which marks the end of Ramadan; *'id ad-Adha* the feast of sacrifice; the Prophet Muhammad's Birthday; the Hijra New Year and other occasions. The Friday prayers are usually broadcast live by these stations.

The Shari'a Law and the Israeli Law. Shari'a courts implement the Shari'a law and have the sole authority to deal with matters of personal status according to articles 51 and 52 of the Palestine Order in Council of 1922.

These matters include marriage, divorce, custody, maintenance, and other personal issues. Israeli law has narrowed the courts' authorities in specific issues such as inheritance, where the law gives parallel authority to the Civil District Court. The Shari'a Court is not allowed to deal with cases of inheritance unless all beneficiaries sign an agreement for that matter.

The Israeli law prohibits Muslim men to divorce their wives without their consent. Moreover, it prohibits bigamy and the marriage of under-age girls (those under the age of 17 years). Should such violations take place, although they are permitted by the Shari'a law, it is the kadi's responsibility to notify the authorities. These laws, in addition to the Law of Equal Rights for Men and Women of 1951, have caused dramatic positive changes in the status of Muslim women.

[AW.HAB.]

EDUCATION (see **9**:928; **Dc./17**:389)

Since the birth of the State, education has been given a high priority in Israel. The great value that the Jewish people have traditionally accorded to education has been enhanced by the challenge of consolidating a modern state and a democratic society composed of disparate elements. Faced with the tasks of integrating a highly diverse immigrant population, diminishing the economic, social, and cultural barriers which divide the Oriental and Ashkenazi, as well as the Arab, communities and cultivating the human resources necessary for prosperity and independence, the government has demonstrated a constant concern with the maintenance of high standards of education.

1981–85. The education momentum of the 1970s was halted during the 1980s as, under the stress of a faltering economy, the ministry was forced to cut back on initiatives and slow down many of the programs introduced during the previous decade. In contrast to the 1970s, the 1980s were a time of containment and consolidation. During the period 1981–86, soaring costs and a restrictive budget compelled the ministry to forgo the idea of making major innovations and to direct its energy and resources to the task of finding a way simply to keep things going.

The proportion of the national budget allocated to education dropped and the funds within the budget available for programming declined sharply. Rising costs, especially in the areas of teachers' salaries and maintenance, absorbed funds that were previously used for educational programs. The substantial rise in teachers' salaries stems from the recommendations of the Etzioni committee.

In 1978 the minister of education ended a teacher's strike by having the government appoint a committee headed by Dr. Moshe Etzioni, a former Supreme Court justice, to examine the status of teachers. In 1979, the committee presented its findings which included a number of recommendations directed to improving the professional status of teachers. Among other things, they recommended that teachers' salaries be raised and that teaching hours be cut. The government's commitment to abide by the recommendations of the Etzioni committee was made just before the onset of the economic crisis, and the changed economic situation made it difficult for the government to honor its commitment. However, the government found itself facing strong teachers' organizations. The teachers' unions — of which there are two: the Irgun Morim and the Histadrut Morim — came into their own during the 1980s. Teachers' strikes were once rare in Israel, but between 1981 and 1985 there was a strike or the threat of a strike virtually every year. The power of the teachers' unions derives in part from the fact that working mothers represent a significant percentage of the labor force, so that a strike which keeps working mothers home has a broad and substantial impact on the general economy. Rejecting the government's position that it was unable to honor the recommendations of the Etzioni committee, the teachers' unions succeeded in forcing the government to stand by its original commitment to carry out many of the recommendations, particularly as regards raising salaries. Teachers' salaries moved from 68% of the Ministry of Education budget in 1979 to 73% of the budget in 1985. This process has seriously decreased the funds available for programming.

The economic difficulties which faced the ministry during the years 1981–1985 severely curtailed but did not totally suppress all initiative and innovation. Four notable innovations were introduced: (1) As a result of studies which showed that the reading ability of students was below standard, a remedial reading program was introduced into the schools. (2) The ministry implemented new policies designed to improve the evaluation of student achievement. (3) Computer education courses were established in schools. (4) The requirements for admission and the academic standards of teacher training institutions were raised, thus enhancing the quality of new teachers entering the school system.

The 1980s witnessed one structural change which is potentially of great significance. The 1970s had been a period of increased centralization culminating in the establishment of a curriculum institute which standardized curricula throughout the country. By the end of the decade the Ministry of Education had become so highly bureaucratic that its heavy organizational apparatus actually diminished its ability to respond quickly and sensitively to the everchanging needs of the dynamic Israeli society. The ministry initiated a process of decentralization. It divided the school system into six districts and allocated substantial responsibilities to the local district authorities, including the authority to distribute supplementary hours for educational initiatives and to allocate certain budgets. School supervisors were made responsible to district heads rather than to the central office of the Ministry of Education. Although the movement toward greater local autonomy was initiated as a corrective to overbureaucratization, it acquired a new momentum in the 1980s. Throughout the Western world there has been a trend toward decentralization in education, and the 1980s witnessed changes and developments in Israeli society which created a demand for greater local autonomy.

(1) The 1980s brought with it a more critical attitude toward the central authority of the government. Israelis are simply less willing to relinquish their responsibility for their children's education to a central government agency. (2) The Sephardi community has progressed to the point of possessing the human resources for taking a leadership role in a modern educational system. In the 1950s and 1960s the principals and teachers of schools in development towns were nearly always Ashkenazi outsiders appointed by the central authority of the Ministry of Education. Today, most of the principals in development towns are local people. In Beth Shean, for example, almost every principal in both elementary and high schools comes from the local community. (3) As the Sephardi community emerged from the shock of its sudden displacement into a modern Western society, it renewed its pride in its traditions and demanded independence from the western intellectual establishment which still largely controls the ministry.

The decentralization of the ministry is reflected in the structure of both the elementary schools and the high schools. In the 1970s, elementary schools were strictly supervised by the central office of the ministry which exercised extensive power over the functioning of local schools. The principal, for example, could not hire a teacher without his supervisor's approval. Today the ministry is far more flexible. The curriculum of elementary schools reflects this new flexibility as it is now divided into three categories: (1) obligatory courses, (2) elective courses of which a certain number must be chosen, and (3) courses which are completely elective. Thus, the principal, in consultation with teachers and parents, can now design a curriculum which is sensitive to the needs and preferences of the community served by his school.

The same trend is evident in high schools. Whereas, in the 1970s, the curriculum of the high schools was rigidly prescribed by the ministry, today's curriculum is largely determined by the students themselves. The move from the track system to the elective system has established a situation in which there is no standard curriculum in high schools. Students choose their own curriculum and come up with every imaginable combination of courses. The high schools have also become more heterogeneous as the law of compulsory education has drawn students into the high schools from socioeconomic classes previously not represented in the high school student population.

Other changes in the ministry during the 1980s reflect the change in policies instituted by education minister Itzhak Navon. Zevulun Hammer, the former minister, initiated Jewish identity programs in the schools and chose themes for emphasis during the school year that pertained to matters of traditional Jewish concern, such as the unity of the Jewish people and the love which Jews should feel for one another. Navon continued the Jewish identity programs, but chose different central themes reflecting new developments in Israeli society and the dominant concerns of the political party he represents: Jewish–Arab coexistence and the value of democracy. He also initiated a program of encounters and discussions between Jewish and Arab students to promote mutual understanding. Navon's choice of themes suggests his concern with the increased polarization in Israeli society.

Integration remains a major concern of the ministry that has acquired, in the context of growing polarization of Israeli society, a new urgency. Both the religious and the secular school systems reflect that polarization. In the religious school system it can be seen in the establishment of schools which provided deeper Torah studies than those provided by the standard curriculum of the government religious schools. The No'am schools, which largely serve the Ashkenazi religious community, represent, in the eyes of the ministry, a threat to the goal of integration because, offering a more thorough Torah studies program, they tend to drain off the better students from the school system and isolate them in a school of their own. Sephardi *talmud torahs* have been established, which, very much like No'am, have attracted the best students and separated them from the rest of the student community. In the secular schools, polarization is expressed in growing political rightism (which is found among the religious as well) and disturbing signs of ignorance and increasing hostility toward religion. The Ministry of Education, continuing its long-established policy, remains nevertheless committed to the goal of using the school system to promote mutual understanding, tolerance, and social integration.

Yeshivot. Although the educational system under the jurisdiction of the Ministry of Education includes a system of religious schools, religious education in Israel, particularly higher education, is largely the province of yeshivot established and maintained by the religious communities they serve. Although most yeshivot receive financial assistance from the government, they are independent institutions which offer a curriculum of study that reflects the practice and traditions of their communities. The yeshivot are not associated with any central governing authority. They are, nevertheless, bound together to form a coherent system of institutions by their own common ideology and the mutual dependence and concern of the various religious communities. The yeshivot represent an entire educational system which includes nursery schools, primary schools *(heder)*, secondary schools *(yeshivah tikhonit)*, *yeshivah ketannah*, and institutions of higher learning *(yeshivah gedolah* and *kolel)*. The yeshivot have flourished in Israel and many young people from Orthodox communities in the Diaspora attend yeshivot in Israel. The number of foreign students in yeshivot exceeds the number of foreign students attending the universities.

Yeshivah students are exempt from military service so long as they are engaged in full-time study. They do their service in the Israel Defense Forces after leaving the yeshivah. Some yeshivot have made an arrangement with the government whereby students in the yeshivah divide their study years between military service and yeshivah study. Yeshivot which have accepted this arrangement are commonly referred to as *yeshivot hesder*.

Teachers' Training. The process of academization of the teachers' seminaries that began in the late 1970s continued throughout the 1980s. Smaller seminars were closed down in order to concentrate and enhance the resources available for training teachers in larger, better equipped institutions. Both admission requirements and the requirements for receiving teaching certification have been raised, resulting in a student body that represents a higher standard of academic achievement. Students are no longer admitted to teacher training programs unless they have completed all their matriculation exams, which in the past they were allowed to complete during their first year of training. The curriculum in the teachers' seminaries has been extended from two to three years, and since 1980s several seminaries have been accredited to award B.A. degrees.

Jewish Identity Education. Jewish identity education was a focus of a major educational initiative during the 1980s. A new curriculum in the oral tradition was drawn up for the elementary schools, an original curriculum stressing value education, *Benei Mitzvah*, was introduced into the seventh and eighth grades, and a new curriculum was introduced for teaching Bible in the general school system. An experimental project in teaching the prayer book was introduced. These programs are reactions to a general feeling that the students

One of the new assets during this time was the building and establishment in 1989 of the Suzanne Dellal Center for Theater and Dance in Tel Aviv in an area that had been dilapidated and is now a focus of cultural activity, with the Batsheva and the Inbal companies based there. In 1988, the first annual dance festival was held in Karmiel in Galilee. It is primarily a folk dance event with thousands of folk dancers from Israel and abroad coming together.

The events in Karmiel always include performances by Israeli professional dance companies and one foreign company. Among the latter the London Contemporary Dance Theater, the Poznan Ballet (Poland), and the Bolshoi Ballet (Moscow) have appeared.

At the Suzanne Dellal Center a major event was an International Modern Dance Competition in which a core of contestants from abroad took part. The center is directed by Israeli Yair Vardi who danced for several years with the Ballet Rambert in Britain and directed a company there before returning to Israel.

The Bat-Dor Dance Company founded in 1968 by Batsheva de Rothschild, (who had founded the Batsheva Company in 1964) went through a serious crisis in 1992 when the Rothschild support was cut by half. Artistic director Jeannette Ordman continued with a reduced company until the influx of dancers from Eastern Europe replaced a number of dancers who had left. The company was given assistance with the task of absorbing the immigrants and is now thriving again, giving weekly performances at its own little theater in Tel Aviv. Ordman has served three times on the jury of the Jackson Mississippi International Ballet Competition (1982, 1986, 1990) and is the first Israeli to serve on the jury of the Contemporary Dance section of the Paris International Competition (1992).

The Kibbutz Contemporary Dance Company during the past decade has increased its tours abroad, visiting Britain, Czechoslovakia (where its founder-director Yehudit Arnon was born), Holland, and Germany.

In the past ten years, the Israel Ballet (classical) founded by its directors, husband and wife Hillel Markman and Berta Yampolsky 26 years ago, has grown more conspicuous on the dance scene. Yampolsky has developed into a noted choreographer.

The Inbal Dance Theater has a new artistic director, Rina Sharett, who replaced founder-choreographer-director Sara Levi-Tanai, who became Inbal President. The company continues to train dancers in the ethnic tradition that Levi-Tanai established. It still stages some of her works as well as those of others, including Sharett.

Not everything in the past ten years moved forward. One company, the Tamar Dance Company, was started in Ramle but closed down after two years because of a lack of funds. It was reformed in Jerusalem in 1987, but the subsidy from the Jerusalem Foundation was withdrawn in 1992 and it folded.

Several companies visited Israel in recent years. Among them were two from Spain, the Hoyas Flamenco and the Antalogia de la Zarzuela, and the Basel Ballet of Switzerland, the Alvin Ailey Dance Theater (U.S.A.), the Pina Bausch Company from Wupperthal (Germany), the Maurice Bejart Ballet (Lausanne), the Kirov Maly Ballet (Moscow), and Daniel Ezralow's ISO (U.S.A.).

Celebrated teachers have included Nina Timofeyeva (former Bolshoi prima ballerina) for the Rubin Academy Dance Department in Jerusalem; Jane Dudley (former Martha Graham dancer) from the London Contemporary Dance School; Ivan Kramer from the Netherlands Dance Theater, for the Bat-Dor company; Ivan Marko (formerly of the Gyorgy Ballet, Hungary), Brenda Bufalino (U.S.A.) for the Jazz-Tap

Batsheva Dance Company performing *Rituals*, choreography by Robert North. (Photo Eldad Maestro)

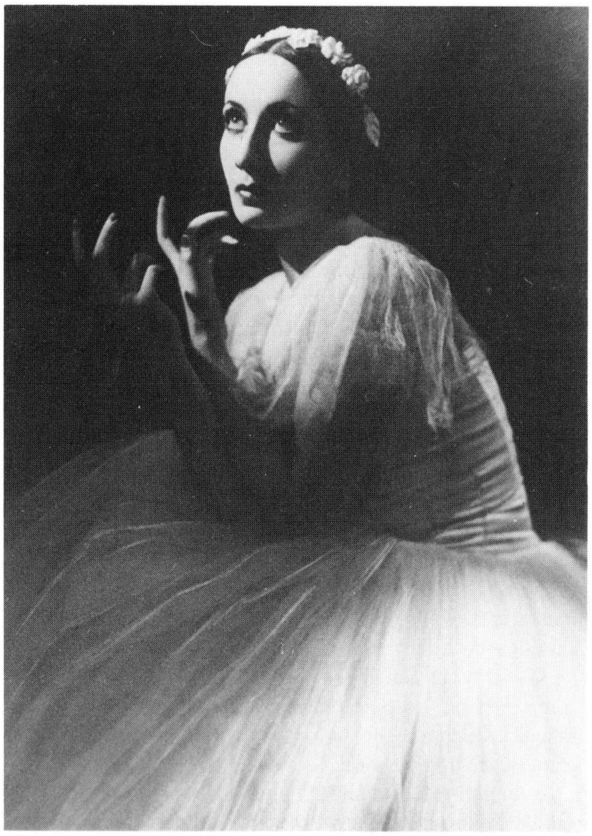

Mia Arbatova in *The Sylphides*. (Courtesy the Mia Arbatova Competition Foundation and Zohara Simkins-Manor, T.A.)

Festivals organized by Avi Miller, Tel Aviv; William Louther and Galina Panova (now prima ballerina in Bonn) for Tamara Mielnik's dance school in Jerusalem.

The deaths of Mia Arbatova, veteran classical dance teacher (a ballerina from Riga), and of Shalom Hermon, pioneer creator of folk dance and supervisor of dance as a subject in school curricula were serious losses. A Ballet Competition in memory of Arbatova has been founded in Tel Aviv. [D.L.S.]

Art (see **9**:1009; **Dc./17**:402). Israeli art in the decade 1983–1992 can be characterized by its increasing pluralism and by the expansion of its significant dialogue with major urban centers of international art. Although minimalism and conceptualism were clearly hallmarks of the 1970s, the art scene has grown more complex largely due to the increasing number of artists. One can, however, cautiously generalize art of the early 1980s as more emotional and expressionistic in character, while in the late 1980s and early 1990s, a more intellectual, understated, and intentional approach is discernible.

The undaunted art lover can see in Israel's museums, galleries, and beyond (in out- and indoor monuments, parks, or nature reserves, etc.) a dizzying number of exhibitions. The Gabriel Sherover Information Center for Israeli Art at the Israel Museum records approximately 2,000 per year. Older or established artists are often seen in solo retrospectives, and the younger generation is exposed in group or thematic shows.

Important internal art stimuli during the past decade have included biannual exhibitions for sculpture (since 1988), and photography (since 1986). There were four Tel Ḥai events for outdoor environmental sculpture (since 1980). There are also prizes awarded by the Tel Aviv Museum of Art, the Israel Museum, Jerusalem, the America–Israel Cultural Foundation, and the Minister of Education to encourage the young artist. The opening of the Museum of Israeli Art, Ramat Gan, in 1987 added another exhibition space for emerging talent. Smaller museums in Arad, Bat-Yam, Herẓliyyah, Petaḥ-Tikvah, and Tefen also contribute to the dynamism.

Not all art in Israel is in the museums. In the field of sculpture, man-made efforts are united with nature's aesthetic in reserves or parks, such as the Desert Sculpture Park on the Edge of the Ramon Crater (curated by Ezra Orion). A project which began in the early 1960s but was only realized in the mid-1980s, its object was to add contemporary sculpture along the rim of the cliff which was sculpted by nature itself into geometrical rock formations. Israeli sculptors who worked there in dolomite stone from 1986 to 1988 were Ezra Orion, Dalia Meiri, Noam Rabinovich, Itzu Rimmer, Hava Mahutan, Dov Heller, Sa'ul Salo, Berny Fink, and David Fein. Israel Hadany, whose work can be found in many sculpture gardens and urban spaces, also sculpted a stone monument for the Albert Promenade to counterbalance the natural beauty of Miẓpeh Rimon (1992).

In an effort to bring art to the streets of Tel Aviv, its municipality sponsored a project which brought 15 sculptures to the Tel Aviv–Jaffa area from 1989 to 1992. Participants in the project were Ilan Averbuch, Zadok Ben-David, Gideon Gechtman, Isaac Golombeck, Yaacov Dorchin, Yaacov Hefetz, Dina Kahana-Gueler, Motti Mizrachi, Lawrence McNabb, Sigal Primor, Gabi Klasmer, Zvika Kantor, Yuval Rimon, and Yehiel Shemi.

Dani Karavan's "White Square" environmental sculpture of stone, water, and landscaping was completed in 1988 in the Wolfson Park, Tel Aviv. A homage to the pioneers of the "White City" — Tel Aviv — it was one of four works chosen to represent Israel in the architectural biennale in Venice (1991). [The others were the Sherover Promenade in Jerusalem by Shlomo Aharonson, Zvi Hecker's spiral house in Ramat Gan, and Moshe Safdie's design of the extension of the Hebrew Union College in Jerusalem.]

The international Tel Ḥai Contemporary Art Meeting, a project of the Upper Galilee Regional Council, began in 1980 with the aim of promoting sculpture in nature, installations in interior spaces, and of creating an alternative space to the sociocultural concept of museums. It provided artists with a place of historical meaning and sentimental identity. Three additional Tel Ḥai events (1983, 1987, and 1990) attracted scores of local and some international participants as well.

In the final analysis, however, the museums carry the greatest weight concerning artistic quality. In the past decade there were homage to solo figures considered to be singularly important and influential artists. Following are short descriptions regarding a limited number of them, chosen because they signify unique trends and/or are of seminal importance throughout the period under discussion.

Micha Ullman, "Container (Day)," 1988, iron plates, sand, Israel Museum Collection, Gift of Dr. and Mrs. Raymond Sackler, N.Y. (Israel Museum; photo Avraham Hay)

Ilan Averbuch: "Fata Morgana," from the exhibition *80 Years of Sculpture in Israel*, at the Israel Museum, May 1984. (Israel Museum, Jerusalem)

Homage was paid to Moshe Kupferman (b. 1926) in an exhibition at the Israel Museum and Tel Aviv Museum of Art in 1984–85 (curator: Yona Fischer) which surveyed this prominent non-representational artist's work in paint and on paper from 1963 to 1984. Employing purposely limited color palette and formal vocabulary, Kupferman constructs his unique oeuvre by a process combining subtle layering, erasing and recombining color, and adding and subtracting planes and lines. The resulting abstract black-white-violet grid and scaffold compositions formed by decisive strokes of the brush are laden with emotion and expressionism relating to the artist's own outlook on life.

Abstraction in contemporary art has another strong protagonist in Lea Nikel (b. 1918) whose solo exhibition at the Israel Museum in 1985 (curator: Yigal Zalmona) was devoted to her thunderously bright, multicolored canvases. Nikel's paintings are afire with painterly instinct and values, which she has never deserted for any kind of propaganda content in her work.

Philosophical and poetic qualities can be found in the work of the minimalistic sculptor Micha Ullman (b. 1940), who was chosen to participate in the last two Documentas (8 and 9). Ullman's "Containers" were the subject of an exhibition at the Israel Museum (curator: Yigal Zalmona) in 1988. To his simple formal vocabulary of forms (often chairs and pits made of clay, mud, soil), Ullman added massive steel house-like elements ("Day," "Night," and "Havdalah") to express the nuances of concepts like borders, shelter/grave, reincarnation. In his latest work he dealt with negative and positive areas in red sand within a steel and glass vitrine, another variation on the theme of the relationship between the container and the contained.

The versatility of Menashe Kadishman (b. 1932) spans three decades and three major areas: painting, sculpture, and prints. In the past decade he has dealt with humanistic and universal themes: the sacrifice of man, as portrayed by the Abraham–Isaac/lamb–God story (an example stands in the plaza before the Tel Aviv Museum of Art in corten steel); births: the subject of an exhibition of that title in the Israel Museum in 1990 (curator Yigal Zalmona); nature, focusing on trees — as cotton sheets in the 1970s, and later on in prints and in steel. Examples of the latter are the blue metal tree silhouettes before the Wolfson Towers and near the Knesset in Jerusalem.

Oswaldo Romberg (b. 1938) is an architect-artist-teacher concerned with the language of art. "Building Footprints," a mixed-media installation at the Israel Museum in 1991 (curator: Yigal Zalmona), was another step in his continuing research of prominent art historical paintings and monuments. By isolating their formal and/or color components, Romberg helps the viewer analyze the details of the powerful whole.

Yigal Tumarkin (b. 1933) has been on the map of Israeli art since the late 1950s as a painter, sculptor, and printmaker. A retrospective on his sculpture covered the decades 1957–1992 at the Tel Aviv Museum of Art (curator: Ellen Ginton). It surveyed his artistic growth from his earlier tortured and maimed Grunewaldesque bronze figures, his anti-war mixed media paintings to his most recent period with more abstract/less explicit metal sculptures.

As an artist and teacher at the Bezalel Academy of Art and Design, Jerusalem, Pinchas Cohen Gan (b. 1942) has played an influential role on the younger generation of artists. Active in different media (painting, printmaking, photography), Cohen Gan works with conceptual and socio-political content while he varies stylistically from expressionistic to minimalistic. The Tel Aviv Museum of Art (curator: Talia Rappaport) devoted a retrospective "Works on Paper 1969–1992" to him. A stick-like human figure, often running, and a big human head are recurring motifs in his work and hint at the trials of an Everyman in constant search of answers.

In the 1980s, there were a series of historical exhibitions which were critical attempts to understand the roots of earlier Israeli art. These exhibitions may have actually raised questions relating to national identity before they were asked in other fields. The conflict between localism and internationalism, between provincialism and urban centers, between group vs. individual values were relevant to the art arena as well as reflecting the duality of Israeli society's values.

At the President's House, Jerusalem, an exhibition in 1983 entitled "The Archetype of the Pioneer in Israeli Art" (curator Dr. Gideon Ofrat) traced the subject from the early 20th century until the 1980s in two- and three-dimensional works. Artists working in the 1980s and concerned with this vein of ideological expression included the late Abraham Ofek, Naftali Bezem, Yossl Bergner, Yair Garbuz, Oded Lerer, Motti Mizrahi, and Menashe Kadishman.

Another manifestation of the historical/heroic approach was seen in the graphic work of David Tartakover, who often nostalgically bases his images on idealistic graphics of the Mandate Period. Tartakover also created a series of famous "Tel Avivians," paying homage to local heroes of the first Jewish city in 2,000 years. The name of the exhibition "Produce of Israel" (curator: Izzika Gaon) at the Israel Museum and Tel Aviv Museum of Art, 1983–84, was devoted to many positive aspects of Israeli cultural life.

A few years later, in 1987, "To Live With the Dream" at the Tel Aviv Museum of Art (curator: Batia Donner) presented an analysis of the idealism and the following disillusionments using documentation from graphic, painting, and sculpture media from the Mandate to post-statehood decades. Stereotypes, cultural heroes, places, cultural symbols, borders, and territory were the sub-topics of the show. (In 1980 an important exhibition entitled "Borders" [curator: Stephanie Rachum] also investigated how artists define this concept.)

After the Gulf War in 1991 an exhibition called "Real Time" at the Tel Aviv Museum of Art (curator: Batia Donner) reviewed the patriotic expressions, largely in the graphics medium, seen on billboards, in newspaper advertisements, posters, etc., during the war itself. Many of them used the blue-white motif of the flag as a rallying point. However, this type of expression was as short-lived as the war, and Israeli society quickly returned to normalcy and its ideological problems.

At the Israel Museum in 1991, 24 artists participated in

"Routes of Wandering: Nomadism, Voyages and Transitions in Contemporary Israeli Art" (curator: Sarit Shapira). The show dealt with questions relating to the most contemporary version of the pioneer/place/land ideology. Art and philosophy seem to have gone full circle. Deterritorialization has replaced the concept of "place," with borders being burst both conceptually and actually. The show dealt with images relating to means of transportation in Israeli art; maps; and most importantly, the concepts represented by travel and moving around. Some examples of the work on exhibit were Moshe Gershuni's "There"; Benni Efrat's 1989 sculpture, "Quests for Air Spring 2037," a bed-shaped cell with a suitcase in it; and Moshe Ninio's "Exit," blurred text on a photograph. The few human figures were generalized and transitory, like Pinchas Cohen Gan's arrangement of a "Cardboard Box Figure," an image of an anywhere man fleeing.

As mentioned above, the types of art available reflect the pluralistic approach dominant in Israel's museums and galleries. If one is looking for specific information or documentation of contemporary life, there are few painters working in a realistic style. Outstanding among them are Israel Hershberg, who paints fastidiously hyper-realistic still lifes and interiors; Pamela Levy, who bases her paintings on photographs of leisure time and situations (such as swimming) which she reworks into allegorical and tense situations; David Reeb, also inspired by televised or photographic images of actualia, such as soldiers in action, converts them into compelling paintings freezing significant and formerly fleeting images; and Ivan Schwebel depicts biblical stories by placing his characters in contemporary cityscapes, such as Jerusalem's Ben-Yehudah Street, to give the viewer a feeling that the ancient conflicts are still relevant to our own times.

There is a significant group of artists whose work reacts to the political climate from symbolic, emotional angles. An exhibition in New York's Jewish Museum (curator: Susan Goodman) entitled "In the Shadow of Conflict: Israeli Art, 1980–1989" summarized a decade of work along this line with a wide variety of artistic reactions to war, the neither-nor situation, and the dream of peace. Artists included in the show were Arnon Ben-David, Pinchas Cohen Gan, Yair Garbuz, Moshe Gershuni, Tsibi Geva, Michael Gitlin, Menashe Kadishman, Gabi Glasmer, Moshe Kupferman, Dudu Mezah, Motti Mizrachi, Avner Moriah, Moshe Muller, Joshua Neustein, David Reeb, Igael Tumarkin, Micha Ullman, and the late Aviva Uri.

Although much is heard of orientalizing music, levantization in the visual arts is rare. The closest to it are the paintings of Tsibi Geva, with their Islamic-inspired style or content: allover patterns with overtones of meanings such as the 'kefiya' paintings or patterns of terrazzo floor tiles; or a series of works which combine names of Arabic words and towns written in Hebrew with illustrations ostensibly drawn by Arab children.

Since 1981 there have been a series of group exhibitions by Jewish and Palestinian artists whose aims were to promote both political and artistic peaceful co-existence by constructing bridges of understanding. Several exhibitions were held at the Artists House and at the "El-Quwaiti" theater in Jerusalem during this period. There were group exhibitions of Palestinian artists in 1988 and 1990 at the Artists House, Jerusalem. In 1992 the group of 12 Palestinian and Israeli Artists (curator: Ariella Azoulai) joined forces again in a show which coincided with the peace negotiations and renewed their commitment to the process. Participating were Moshe Gershuni, Tamar Getter, Pamela Levy, Assad Azi, Arnon Ben-David, David Reeb, Sliman Mansour, Nabil Anani, Taisin Barkat, Kamal Butalah, Khalil Rabel, and Taleb Dweik. Sliman Manzur and Israel Rabinovitz were invited by the Swedish Socialist Party in Stockholm for a joint exhibition, "Out of the Same Earth," which contained a work they created together.

On the international scene, and in Israel as well, compelling work has been based on the written word as the central image. An exhibition at the Janco-Dada Museum, Ein Hod, entitled "Imagewriting" (curator: Sara Hakkerts, 1992) investigated how 24 Israeli artists use letters, words, and sentences in their work, and in this way illustrate their points of view about local events. There were very few political statements (with the exception of works by Yair Garbuz, Arnon Ben-David, and Tsibi Geva). Other participants included Nurit Isaac-Polachek, Shaul Bauman, Jenifer Bar-Lev, Eli Gur Arie, Tamar Getter, Michael Grubman, Moshe Gershuni, Elisha Dagan, Svetlana Dubrovsky, Alexander Rudakov, Nurit David, Rachel Heller, Boris Yuchvitz, Pinchas Cohen Gan, Raffi Lavie, Chaim Maor, Bashir Makhoul, Michal Na-aman, Moshe Amar, and Michal Shamir.

Poetic texts written by Oded Yedaya in white or black ink on black and white photographs were the subject of an exhibition curated by Nissan Peretz at the Israel Museum in 1988. Yedaya's compositions combine figurative elements (images and words) with a strong abstract substructure.

In a solo exhibition at the Tel Aviv Museum of Art 1992 (curator: Ellen Ginton) dreams were Jenifer Bar-Lev's subject. She interspersed original stream-of-consciousness poems in English with Hebrew biblical texts with a patchwork of painted shapes and/or other materials, like blue jeans or kitsch paintings.

Nurit David and Yocheved Weinfeld are two other artists whose multimedia creations intersperse textual elements with imagery. Zvi Goldstein is another multimedia artist whose texts are integral to his work. His verbal manifestos are of a didactic rather than a personal nature, and he combines them with objects that look as if they belong to a highly technologically advanced culture. These installations deal with the position and options of a third world country.

Recently there have been very personal, humoristic works which contain underlying, serious meanings created by a few mavericks in the art world. Philip Rantzer converts found objects into adult, kinetic toys which provide the museum viewers with a piquant black humor. In his exhibition "Sometimes I Get a Hankering for My Wife" at the Israel Museum in 1992 (curator: Yigal Zalmona), he created a house with his ready-mades and collectibles, running water, and delectable, sundry items such as a breadbox with a small video screen and songs by the Andrews Sisters.

Zvika Kantor uses banal, domestic objects but constructs them out of absurd kitschy materials. An example is his "Duet of Happiness" piano made not for music lovers but for those with a sweet tooth, as it is made only of sugar cubes and chocolate. Dudu Gerstein also makes light colorful and amusing sculpure cutouts, such as a flowering plant, by painting aluminum with duco paint. Elisha Dagan paints wood with industrial paint and makes three-dimensional word sculptures, such as "Oh Baby Wolffff" and "Motherrrr" which can be read by looking down at the generally waist-high structures.

Dr. Gideon Ofrat's choice for Israel's representative to the Biennale was Avital Geva, a conceptual anti-art establishment artist who has chosen not to be exhibited since the early 1970s, when he executed some bold conceptual projects (like the yellow line beginning on the road near his kibbutz, Ein Shemer, and ending at the Israel Museum). Geva has spent the past years experimenting with knowledge in the form of growing tomatoes and fish, and thus studying the artistic process.

Photography clearly influences a number of contemporary

artists, who rework it in other media. However, it is also the chosen sole media for certain artists. There were many exhibitions devoted to young and established photographers concentrating on this art form alone. Notable among them were exhibitions showing the work of Pesi Girsch, Bareket Ben Yaakov, Judy Orgel Lester, and nostalgic shows by the young Gabi Salzberger called "Rusted Pioneers" and homage to the late Alfred Bernheim, all curated by Nissan Peretz at the Israel Museum. At the Museum of Israeli Art in Ramat-Gan there was another homage to the late Alfonse Himmelreich, "Dance Photographs: Mood and Movement," curated by Vivienne Silver in 1987. Moshe Ninio's exhibition entitled "Cycle of Days" in 1991 at the Israel Museum (curator: Yigal Zalmona) incorporated mixed media with photography. His blurred, enlarged photographic details printed on metal plates were clearly detached from their original contexts and the sparse, iconic images resulting were intended to supply new meanings, above and beyond the former content.

Zvi Tolkovsky, a versatile painter and printmaker, organized a quasi-documentary exhibition in 1991 containing photographs and found objects which had been left at the deserted refugee camp of Nueima, at the Israel Museum (curator: Rika Gonen). Displayed like archeological remnants from a forgotten people, the show brought out the poignancy of this relatively recent "tel."

In 1992 Sigal Primor's "The Antarctic Challenge," (curator: Yigal Zalmona) at the Israel Museum moved from Alfred Hitchcock's *Psycho* to the South Pole, and the indefatigable sculptor Ezra Orion celebrated the space year by transmitting a laser beam column to infinity from Israel and international locations. [EL.VA.]

Motion Pictures (see **12**:460). The period 1983–1992 has seen a further maturing in Israeli cinema, and even if the process has not been a consistent one, nor as radical as some would like to have seen, the undeniable increase in activity in the local film world is in itself a promising sign.

The year 1982 had been an eventful one: the high taxes on movie tickets were abolished, the war in Lebanon provided a military conflict that would spawn, after a few years, a rash of filmic reactions, and directors Daniel Wachsman and Itzhak "Zeppel" Yeshurun produced their most highly regarded works, respectively, *Hamsin* and *Noa at 17.*

Amos Gutman made a bold feature film debut in 1983 with *Drifting*, which sought to deal with the homosexual scene in Tel Aviv. Towards the end of that year, Haifa, which had been the venue for film festivals in the 1950s, resumed the custom and Jerusalem, not to be outdone, followed suit in mid-1984 with a burst of visiting starpower that included Lillian Gish, Jeanne Moreau, and Warren Beatty. Both these festivals are now well-established annual events, as is Tel Aviv's international festival of student films.

Beyond the Walls, by Uri Barabash, proved that there was a viable alternative to the production of innocuous low-budget, naive comedies (which continue to be blithely churned out in spite of all critical derision). This 1984 film united Arab and Jew against authority in a prison environment, also casting against type by having swarthy Arnon Tzadok play the Jew while his counterpart was fair-skinned Mukhammed Bakri. Winning the Critics' Prize at the Venice Film Festival as well as being nominated for an American Academy Award, it put Israel back on the map and helped bring about increased investment in the industry.

Two years later, another surprise success, made on a shoestring budget, also did much to change the perception of what local talent could achieve: *Avanti Populo.* The humanity and humor with which first-time feature director Rafi Bukaee treated his heroes — two Egyptian soldiers trying to retreat to the Suez Canal at the end of the Six-Day War — won over audiences and critics alike.

Major changes, the effects of which are still unfolding, began to be felt in the late 1980s. The rapid spread of video (cable TV was introduced in 1990) has caused cinema owners to undramatically but steadily reduce the number of seats in theaters while increasing the number of screens (241 nationwide in 1992). These factors, while adversely affecting

Scene from *Beyond the Walls*, with Mukhammed Bakri (center left) and Arnon Tzadok (center right). (Courtesy *Koteret Rashit*)

the cinematheques, have had a net result of greatly increasing the choice of viewing open to audiences and generally stimulating interest in motion pictures.

Film students protesting the meager resources allocated to their department at the Beit Zvi school in late 1988 and early 1989 paved the way for the department's closure and the opening of Israel's first independent academy for filmmaking, The Jerusalem National Film and Television School. Under the directorship of Renen Schorr, best known for his 1987 feature *Late Summer Blues*, the first 21 students graduated at the end of 1992, amid extensive media attention and speculation regarding the possible change in direction this new avenue into the industry could herald.

Meanwhile, the films of the past five years have contained an increasing percentage of serious works demanding attention, many by newcomers. Apart from Eli Cohen's *Ricochets* in 1987, it was only at the very end of the decade that filmmakers began to tackle Israel's controversial military involvement in Lebanon head-on. Yossi Sommer's *Burning Memory* concentrated on battle-shock and its treatment as a means of addressing the responsibility of those who send men to war. Surreal imagery and some overdone symbolism characterized Chaim Buzaglo's *Time for Cherries*, in which an American TV journalist covers the last days of a reserve soldier fated to become a casualty. The most successful of this batch of films was *Cup Final*, by Eran Riklis. In it, a common love of football leads to mutual respect between an Israeli soldier in Lebanon and his Palestinian captors.

Cup Final's star, on whom much of the film rested, was Moshe Ibgi. Having just starred in Shabi Gavison's offbeat Tel Aviv social comedy, the hit *Shuru*, Ibgi became a top male actor.

Shuru was only one of several major films that strayed from the often tiring preoccupation with the Arab–Israeli conflict. Two highly acclaimed motion pictures dealt with the lingering memory of the Holocaust. *The Summer of Aviya* was based on the childhood of its star, Gila Almagor. Eli Cohen was the director who brought to the screen the poignant tale of the young girl who witnesses the mental disintegration of her mother, a Holocaust survivor. The feature-length documentary *Because of That War*, by Orna Ben-Dor Niv, looked at popular rock musician Yehuda Poliker, his partner Ya'acov Gilad, and the way the experiences of their Holocaust survivor parents have found musical expression.

Other quality productions of the early 1990s included *Laura Adler*, by respected writer-director Avraham Heffner, a melancholy eulogy to Yiddish theater, and Daniel Wachsman's *The Appointed*, which was set in contemporary Galilee and dealt with fraudulent and genuine religious mysticism.

A large boost was given to foreign and co-produced filmmaking in Israel with the opening of the new G. G. studio complex at Neveh Ilan, on the outskirts of Jerusalem. Boasting three large soundstages and the full range of auxiliary facilities, it has so far managed to maintain the impressive schedule announced for it, including films featuring well-known actors, such a Tony Curtis and Chuck Norris.

The Fund for the Promotion of Israeli Quality Films, in operation since 1979, has grown to the point where it is now a partner in most prominent Israeli features, as well as helping to develop dozens of projects annually. The most recent of these include *Over the Ocean, Tel-Aviv Stories, Black Box, Amazing Grace*, and *Life According to Agfa*. The last, directed and scripted by Assi Dayan, was an apocalyptic vision of Israel in a hypothetical "year from today," and it swept the board at the 1992 awards of the Israel Film Academy, founded the previous year. Gidi Dar's somewhat surreal debut feature, *Eddie King*, was also a strong contender in the awards stakes. Both films starred Shuli Rand, one of a roster of new on-screen talent that includes Sharon Alexander, Irit Frank, Bruria Albek, and Limor Goldstein. Goldstein starred in Shmuel Imberman's *Overdose* in 1993, a tale of teenage drug addiction that saw the return to the screen of Amos Lavie after winning his own battle with drugs.

Film director Amos Gutman died of AIDS early in 1993 at the age of 38. Gutman's fourth feature film, *Amazing Grace*, was an extremely personal work that itself focused on a homosexual protagonist under a similar sentence. The film won the Jerusalem Film Festival's Wolgin award before being released in 1992.

The hopes held for increased official assistance for filmmaking that were nurtured by many after 1992's change of government did not seem unjustified after the Education and Culture Ministry doubled its participation in the Fund for the Promotion of Israeli Quality Films, enabling the Fund to invest $3.5m in Israeli cinema during 1993.

[H.TRY.]

ISRAEL PRIZE (see **Dc./7:**410). **1982.**

AMICHAI, YEHUDA (see **2:**838), for Hebrew poetry.

AMIRAN, RUTH (see **2:**849), for archaeology.

Ruth Amiran. (Dept. of Public Relations, Israel Museum, Jerusalem)

BACCHI, ROBERTO (see **4:**53), for economics and demography.

BENVENISTI, DAVID (see **Dc./17:**183), for teaching towards an appreciation of the Land of Israel and its lore. He died in 1993.

GILBOA, AMIR (see **7:**569), for Hebrew poetry.

GVATI, CHAIM (1901–1990), for his contribution to the development of the state as a *ḥalutz* ("pioneer") and for his role in the establishment and development of agricultural settlements. Chaim Gvati was born in Poland and emigrated to Eretz Israel in 1924. One of the founders of kibbutz Gevat in 1926, he later helped found kibbutz Yifat where he remained. Gvati was minister of agriculture from 1964 to 1974 in Labor governments.

VILNAY, ZEV (see **16:**151), for *yedi'at ha-aretz* ("knowledge of Israel").

YASKI, AVRAHAM (1927–), for architecture. Born in Kishinev, he was brought to Palestine in 1935. A prize-winning architect, he designed the social sciences wing of the Givat Ram campus of the Hebrew University, the IBM building in Tel Aviv, the Ben-Gurion University of the Negev campus, and the Gilo neighborhood in Jerusalem.

YURTNER, YEHOSHUA (1933–), for chemistry. Born in Tarnow, Poland, he has been a professor of chemistry at Tel Aviv University since 1966 and was chief scientist in the Ministry of Communications (1970–72).

1983. APPELFELD, AHARON (see **3:**222), for Hebrew literature.

FRIEDLANDER, SAUL (see **7:**182), for history.

ḤEFER, ḤAYIM (see **8:**241), for Israeli song.

SALTMAN, AVROM (1925–), for history. Born in

England, Saltman emigrated to Israel in 1957 and is professor of history at Bar-Ilan University.

SHEMER, NAOMI (see **12**:707), for Israeli song.

WARHAFTIG, ZERAḤ (see **16**:30), for special contribution to law and society.

WILENSKY, MOSHE (see **Dc./17**:476), for Israeli song.

1984. BONDI, ARON (see **5**:380), for agriculture.

DEVELOPMENT TOWNS' PROJECT, for special contribution to society and the State.

JAMMER, MOSHE, (1915–), for the history of science. Born in Berlin, he emigrated to Palestine in 1935 and studied at the Hebrew University of Jerusalem. After lecturing at American universities (1949–55), he became physics professor at Bar-Ilan University of which he was later rector and president.

NAḤAL (see **12**:768), for special contribution to society and the State.

RABICOVITCH, SHELOMOH, for agriculture.

RODENSKY, SHEMUEL (1902–1989), for theater arts. Born in Poland, Rodensky was an actor with Habimah and played a variety of roles, often Jewish folk types. After playing Tevya in *Fiddler on the Roof* in Israel, he did the same in West Germany to high praises.

TCHERNOWITZ-AVIDAR, YEMIMAH (see **15**:885), for children's literature.

1985. BLAU, JOSHUA (see **4**:1075), for Hebrew language and linguistics.

ISRAEL TELEVISION ARABIC, for its special contribution to society and the State.

MAKHON BEN-ZVI (The Ben-Zvi Institute for the Study of Jewish Communities of the East), for research into the Eastern Oriental Jewish communities.

NEUFELD, HENRY (1923–), for medicine. Neufeld was born in Lvov, Poland. He emigrated to Israel in 1951 and in 1962 became director of the institute of cardiology at Tel ha-Shomer, introducing cardiac intensive care into Israel for the first time. Neufeld became professor of medicine at the Hebrew University of Jerusalem in 1965. He served for eight years as the senior scientist of the Ministry of Health and developed the department of cardiology at Tel Aviv University. He was elected president of the International Cardiological Federation in 1978.

PADEH, BARUCH (1908–), for public health services. Padeh was born in Russia. He completed his medical studies in Prague in 1934 and immigrated to Palestine. He was one of the founders of medical services to the armed forces in the War of Independence, which became the Medical Corps, and was appointed senior medical officer of the IDF in 1956. He was director-general of the Ministry of Health 1971–1974.

SUTZKEVER, ABRAHAM (see **15**:538), for Yiddish literature.

1986. AVRECH, YESHAYAHU (1916–), for his essays. Avrech was born in Kiev and settled in Palestine in 1935. In 1949 he became the first general secretary of the Ministry of Education. A member of the Histadrut executive from 1965, he founded the department of higher education, Tel Aviv University labor studies, and the Golda Meir Institute. He published hundreds of articles and essays in *Davar.*

DEMALACH, YOEL (1924–), for his investigation and teaching of arid region agriculture. Demalach was born in Italy and settled in Palestine in 1939. He joined kibbutz Revivim where he devoted himself to Negev agricultural development and invented irrigation methods for arid zone agriculture.

EVENARI, MICHAEL (see **6**:983), for his research into ancient and current agricultural systems in the Negev region. He died in 1989.

HATOKAI, ALDIN (1944–), for managing a work crew of Jews, Muslims, Druze, and Circassians in an exemplary manner and setting an outstanding example as an employee of the American–Israeli Paper Mills in Ḥaderah.

KATZNELSON, SHULAMIT, for her pioneering work in adult education and in the teaching of spoken Hebrew and Arabic. In 1951 she founded one of the first three *ulpanim* (Hebrew language intensive courses) in Israel. As founder and director of Ulpan Akiva in Netanyah, she was cited as an outstanding example of Hebrew humanism in adult education.

LISHANSKY, BATYA (see **3**:605), for sculpture. She died in 1992.

ROSENFELD, SHALOM (1914–), for political journalism and essays. Rosenfeld was born in Poland and settled in Palestine in 1934. Deputy editor (1960–1974) and editor-in-chief (1974–1979) of *Maariv*, he then headed the Journalism Studies Program at Tel Aviv University.

SA'ID, YONA, for being an outstanding example in her job at the Israel Aircraft Industries.

SHEMI, YEHIEL (see **14**:137), for sculpture.

ZAK, GERSHON, for education. Zak was founder of the Beit Ḥinnukh and Ha-Kefar ha-Yarok schools.

1987. BEIN, ALEXANDER (see **4**:401), for his contribution to Zionist historiography. He died in 1988.

HARARI, OVADIAH (1943–), for technology and engineering. Harari was born in Cairo and came with his family to Israel in 1957. He studied aeronautical engineering at the Technion in Haifa and served in the Israel Air Force in his profession and then worked on development projects. He was the recipient of the Israel Security Prize for 1975. In 1978 he was appointed head of the Lavi fighter airplane project which employed about 1,800 people, half of whom were engineers.

KHOURI, MAKRAM (1945–), for theater, cinema, and television arts. Khouri, an Israeli Arab, was born in Jerusalem and raised in Acre. He performed with the Cameri Theater and then with the Haifa Municipal Theater. He appeared frequently on Arabic and Hebrew general Israeli television as well as on educational television and played in films.

KONIG, LEA for theater, cinema, and television arts. Born in Poland, she moved to Romania after World War II. She studied acting at the Romanian Academy of Art in Bucharest and from the age of 17 appeared with the National Jewish Theater. After immigrating to Israel in 1961 she studied Hebrew and continued her acting career. She has appeared in more than 50 roles ranging from the classical repertoire to the modern and has always maintained her connection to Yiddish theater.

MELAMED, EZRA ZION (see **11**:1275), for Torah literature and commentary on the sources.

YAARI, MENAḤEM (1935–), for economics. Yaari was born in Jerusalem and studied at the Hebrew University and Stanford University in California. Professor of mathematical economics at the Hebrew University, Yaari has been since 1985 director of its Institute for Advanced Studies. He has published papers on subjects such as consumerism under conditions of uncertainty, the allotment of resources over time, and insurance and economic justice.

ZOHAR, MIRIAM, for theater, cinema, and television arts. Born in Czernowitz, Romania, Miriam Zohar was in a concentration camp in the Ukraine during World War II. In 1948 she was among the illegal immigrants to Palestine on the *Pan York* all of whose passengers were sent to Cyprus. There she began to perform in an amateur theater. After arriving in Israel she worked in a Yiddish theater. From 1951, she appeared in Habimah theater.

1988. ARGOV, ALEXANDER (Sascha; 1914–), for Hebrew song. Argov was born in Moscow and came to Palestine in 1934. He wrote over 1,000 songs, from those for pioneering settlers to the Israel army entertainment troupes and on to musical theater.

DAMARI, SHOSHANA (see **12**:687), for Hebrew song.

ELIAV, ARIE (Lova; 1921–), for exemplary lifelong service to society and the State. Eliav was born in Moscow and was brought to Palestine in 1924. From 1936 to 1940 he was in the Haganah, from 1945 he assisted with the "illegal"

Arie Eliav. (Photohouse Prior, Tel Aviv)

immigration to Palestine, and in the Israel War of Independence achieved the rank of lieutenant colonel. In the 1950s and 1960s he worked with new immigrants and "established" the Lachish region as well as planning and establishing the Arad district. In 1956 he was in charge of the project for saving the Jews of Port Said during the Sinai Campaign.

In 1958–60, he was first secretary in the Israel embassy in Moscow; 1966–73, the Israel Representative to the European Council in Strasbourg; 1970–72, general secretary of the Israel Labor Party; a member of the sixth through ninth Knessets and of the twelfth; deputy minister of commerce and industry as well as absorption and chairman of the "Sheli" movement. He was instrumental in negotiations for the release of Israeli prisoners in Lebanon.

GOLDBLUM, NATAN (1920–), for life sciences. Born in Poland, Goldblum immigrated in 1938 to Palestine where he studied at the Hebrew University where he later became professor of virology. He was vice-president of the university, 1974–77. His early work was on malaria and efforts to eliminate it in the Huleh valley. He studied the preparation of polio vaccine with Prof. Jonas Salk in the United States and upon his return to Israel applied this knowledge to produce the vaccine with which some 60,000 Israeli children were inoculated. For over 30 years he continued research on polio. Among his other research subjects were Israel snake venom, molecular identification of viruses transmitted by insects, and hoof-and-mouth disease.

GOSHEN-GOTTSTEIN, MOSHE (1925–1991), in Jewish studies. Born in Berlin, Goshen-Gottstein emigrated to Palestine in 1939. He studied at the Hebrew University of Jerusalem and taught there from 1950 on, becoming professor of Semitic linguistics and biblical philology in 1967. He was also director of the lexicographical institute and biblical research institute of Bar-Ilan University.

His three areas of research were biblical studies, Hebrew linguistics, and Semitic linguistics. His numerous articles and books included *Medieval Hebrew Syntax and Vocabulary as Influenced by Arabic*, *Introduction to the Lexicography of Modern Hebrew*, and *The Aleppo Codex*. He worked on a number of dictionaries, among them the *Millon ha-Ivrit ha-Ḥadashah* ("Dictionary of Modern Hebrew"), the first synchronic dictionary of Hebrew.

GOURI, HAIM (see **7**:832), for poetry.

HECHT, REUBEN (see **Dc./17**:301), for exemplary lifelong service to society and State. Hecht died in 1993.

KOLLEK, THEODORE (Teddy; see **10**:1163), for exemplary lifelong service to society and the State.

SHAMIR, MOSHE (see **14**:1289), for fiction.

STEINSALTZ, ADIN (see p. 354).

1989. AHARONOV, YAKIR (1932–), for exact sciences. Born in Haifa, Aharonov studied at Haifa Technion and at Bristol University in England where he discovered in 1959, working under Prof. Boehm, the Aharonov-Boehm Effect, essential to quantum theory and of far-reaching effect on modern physics. He is professor of theoretical physics at Tel Aviv University and served as chairman department of the high energy physics department.

FROMAN, IAN (1937–), for sport and physical culture. Born in Johannesburg, South Africa, Froman received his degree in dentistry in 1961. In 1964 he immigrated to Israel. A tennis player from his youth, he was captain of the Israeli Davis Cup team and trainer of the national tennis team. From 1974 he devoted himself full time to advancing tennis centers for Israeli youth.

HARARI, ḤAYYIM (1940–), for exact sciences. Born in Jerusalem, Harari completed his doctorate at the Hebrew University in 1965. Since 1970 he has held the Chair in High Energy Physics at the Weizmann Institute in Reḥovot of which he became president in 1988. He has published over 100 articles on particle physics.

ḤAZAN, YA'AKOV (see **7**:1523), for exemplary lifelong service to society and the State. He died in 1992.

ISRAEL EXPLORATION SOCIETY (see **9**:1060), for special contribution in national and social fields.

KATZ, ELIHU (1926–), for social sciences. Born in New York, Katz received his doctorate from Columbia University. In 1963 he immigrated to Israel and joined the Guttman Institute for Applied Social Research. He founded the Communications Institute at the Hebrew University in 1966, heading it until 1980. He was concurrently a professor of sociology and communications at the Hebrew University and at the University of Southern California. He has published extensively.

ROTHSCHILD, BATHSHEVA DE (Bethsabée; see **14**:340), for special contribution in national and social fields. In addition to the Bathsheva Dance Company, Bathsheva de Rothschild founded the Bat-Dor Dance Company, which combines classical ballet and modern dance. Among her other endeavors are the project to translate ancient literature into Hebrew and a music library in Tel Aviv.

WERSES, SAMUEL (1915–), for research in Hebrew literature. Born in Vilna, Poland, Werses immigrated to Palestine in 1936 where he studied Hebrew literature. From 1953 he was a member of the Hebrew Literature department of the Hebrew University. His research focused on Haskalah and modern Hebrew literature, with an emphasis on studying literary genre as they developed and their links to world literature.

WINGATE INSTITUTE FOR PHYSICAL EDUCATION AND SPORT (see **9**:1020), for education and physical culture.

YEIVIN, ISRAEL (1923–), for research in Hebrew language. The son of Yehoshua Heschel *Yeivin, he was born in Berlin and in 1925 came to Palestine. In addition to supervising the ancient literature section in the Academy of the Hebrew Language's Historical Hebrew Language Dictionary project, he does research on ancient biblical manuscripts as part of the Hebrew University Bible project. He is a professor in the Hebrew University Hebrew Language department.

1990. ALTBAUER, MOSHE (see **1**:27), for the humanities.

LEVITZKI, ALEXANDER (1940–), for life sciences. Born in Jerusalem, in 1975 Levitzki joined the faculty of the Hebrew University and was chairman of the biological chemistry department. From 1989 he was director of the life sciences institute there. He is one of the pioneers in the study of receptors in the cells which serve to transmit biochemical signals through the cell membranes.

POLLACK, ISRAEL (1910–1992), for special contribution in national and social fields. Pollack was born in Transylvania and raised in Bukovina where he opened his first textile factory in 1935. In 1947 he moved to Chile. In the early 1960s he established the Polgat textile works in Kiryat Gat, which grew to over a dozen locations in Israel and hundreds of workers.

PRYWES, MOSHE (see **Dc./17**:514), for life sciences.

SPIEGEL, NATHAN (1905–), for Jewish studies. Spiegel grew up in Galicia, Moravia, and the Ukraine. After World War II he was a high school teacher in Poland and from 1952 the rector of a Warsaw institute of education. He immigrated to Israel in 1957. In 1965 he began to teach at Ben-Gurion University and served as head of the department of general studies. Among his works are books on leading figures of the Greek and Hellenic world.

STREICHMANN, YEḤEZKIEL (see **3**:611), for the plastic arts.

TARIF, AMIN (c. 1900–1993), for special contribution in national and social fields. Tarif was the spiritual leader of the Druze community in Israel and the president of the Druze High Court.

WEISS, MEIR (1902–), for Jewish studies. Born in Budapest, in 1933 he became a rabbi and received a doctorate from the Royal Sciences University of Hungary. He emigrated to Israel in 1945 and from 1957 lectured in Bible at Bar-Ilan University and from 1960 at the Hebrew University where he became a professor in 1972. The uniqueness of his approach to Bible study was in his holistic appreciation of each book for its own sake.

WEITZ, RA'ANAN (see **Dc./17**:616), for exemplary lifelong service to society and the State.

WILCHEK, MEIR (1935–), for life sciences. Born in Warsaw, he came to Israel in 1949. He received his doctorate from the Weizmann Institute and teaches there in the department of biophysics. He was awarded the Israel Prize for his discovery and development of technology of chromotographic linkage.

YAVETS, ZVI (1925–), for the humanities. Yavets was born in Czernowitz, Romania, and came to Palestine in 1944. From 1958 he has been chairman of the Department of History at Tel Aviv University, holding the chair in Roman History since 1976. His book *Princeps and Plebs* (1969) was of seminal importance to the field of Roman history.

1991. AGMON, SHMUEL (1922–), for exact sciences. Born in Tel Aviv, the distinguished mathematician Agmon received his doctorate from the University of Paris in 1949. His work focused on the theory of partial differential elliptical equations and problems of linear language as well as the spectral theory of Schrodinger operations.

BEINART, HAIM (see **1**:28), in Jewish History.

BEN-PORAT, MIRIAM (1918–), for special contribution to society and the State. Born in Vitebsk, Russia, she grew up in Lithuania and emigrated to Palestine in 1931. From 1950 to 1958 she served as Deputy State Attorney at the Ministry of Justice, from 1958 to 1975 as judge of the District Court of Jerusalem, and appointed its president in Dec. 1975. In Nov. 1976 she was appointed acting judge of the Supreme Court and a permanent justice in 1977; from 1983 to 1988 she was vice-president of the court. In 1988 she retired from the court and was chosen as State Comptroller.

BERTONOFF, DEBORAH (see **4**:699), for Dance.

FEINBRUN-DOTHAN, NAOMI (1900–), for knowledge of the Land of Israel. Born in Moscow and raised in Kishinev, she immigrated to Palestine in 1924. Working with Alexander *Eig, she helped gather the plants which formed the basis for the Hebrew University's herbarium. She was part of the Hebrew University for its establishment, becoming a full professor in botany 1966. She was instrumental in preparation and publishing of *Flora Palaestina.*

FRIEDMAN, DANIEL (1936–), for social sciences. Born in Israel, he studied law at the Hebrew University of Jerusalem prior to his army service. He is a professor of law at Tel Aviv University, where he was also dean of the Law Faculty, 1974–1978. He has published numerous books on various spheres of law: insurance, contract, damages, and other topics.

FROMAN, DOV (1939–), for engineering and technology. Born in Amsterdam, Froman reached Israel with Youth Aliyah, his parents have been murdered in the Holocaust. He studied at the Haifa Technion and at the University of California, Berkeley, from which he received his Ph.D. in 1969. Much of his work has been devoted to the development of semi-conductor memories, and he developed the first EPROM products. Joining the staff of the Hebrew University in 1974, he headed the School for Applied Science and Technology there, 1975–1980, during which time he established a laboratory for the development of semi-conductor devices as a basis for applied research on memory devices. In 1981 he began to direct Intel activity in Israel, eventually becoming its general manager in Israel.

HELFMAN, ELḤANAN (1946–), for social sciences. Born in the U.S.S.R., he lived in Poland until 11, when his family moved to Israel. He studied economics and statistics at Tel Aviv University. He received his doctorate from Harvard in 1974. He is a professor at Tel Aviv University and holds the chair in International Economic Relations. In 1988 he was elected a member of the Israel Academy of Science.

LANDAU, MOSHE (1912–), for social sciences. Born in Danzig, he studied in London and went to Palestine in 1933, engaging in private law in practice until 1940. From 1940–48 he was a judge in the Haifa Magistrates Court, and after the establishment of the State became a district court judge. In 1953 he was appointed to the Supreme Court. He was the presiding judge at the *Eichmann trial. From 1980 to 1982 he was president of the Supreme Court after having been permanent substitute for the president since 1976.

WERTHEIMER, STEF (1926–), for special contribution to society and the State. Born in Germany, he came to Palestine with his family in 1937. After service during Israel's War of Independence he continued with the development of armaments. In 1951 he founded the ISCAR (Israel Carbides) company. In 1981, after four years in the Knesset, he devoted his efforts to developing the Galilee, with a residential project, Kefar Veradim, and the Tefen industrial park. He initiated the establishment of several other Galilee industrial parks.

YADIN, YOSEF (see **16**:696), for screen and theater arts.

YESHIVOT HESDER, for special contribution to society and the State. The Hesder program combines Israel army service with intensive yeshivah studies. In 1991 there were 3,300 students in the program. The Israel Prize was given to it in recognition of its students excelling in the study halls and in the IDF's elite combat units.

1992. ERLIK, DAVID (1909–), in life sciences. Born in Russia, he came to Palestine in 1924. He completed his medical studies in Strasbourg. In 1948 he was asked by Israel's Ministry of Health to assemble the surgical department at the abandoned Mandatory (now Rambam) Hospital in Haifa. He made the surgical department the central one for the north of Israel and headed it for several years. He is a pioneer and innovator of surgical procedures involving the blood vessels in the abdomen and the kidneys.

FEUERSTEIN, REUVEN (see **13**:1346), in social sciences. Two of the items he developed are particularly well known: the Learning Potential Assessment Devices, for evaluating learning potential, and the Instrumental Enrichment Program, for improving an individual's way of thinking and functioning.

HABIBI, EMIL (1922–), for literature and poetry. A Christian Arab born in Haifa, after 1948 he was a founder of the Israel Communist Party and Knesset member on its behalf. He left the Knesset in 1972, to allow for his being the editor of *Al-Ittihad* and for his literary work. In 1991 he withdrew from active political endeavors. He has written several novels as well as shorter items, much of which has been translated from the Arabic.

ISRAELI, SHAUL (1910–), in Jewish studies. A rabbi and Torah scholar, Israel was born in Slutzk. He came to Palestine during the Mandate period and studied at Mercaz Harav yeshivah. He was the first rabbi of Ha-Po'el ha-Mizrachi settlements, a founder of Yeshivot Benei Akiva high schools, and a member of the Chief Rabbinate. He published *Ereẓ Ḥemdah* on religious laws relating to the Land of Israel.

KIEL, YEHUDA (1917–), in Jewish studies. Born in Petrograd, as a child he lived in Lithuania and Latvia. Arriving in Palestine in 1935, he helped develop the state religious education system and was its national supervisor of elementary and secondary education. He received the Israel Prize in recognition of his commentary on books of the Bible, particularly his wideranging ones on First and Second Chronicles.

LISSAK, MOSHE (1928–), in social sciences. Born in Tel Aviv, he received his doctorate in sociology from the Hebrew University, where he became a professor of sociology in 1978. He has done research and written on topics such as social and political history of the Yishuv, society–army relations in Israel and in South East Asia, and on ethnic group relations in Israel.

NAVON, DAVID (1943–), for social sciences. Born in Tel Aviv, he studied at the Hebrew University of Jerusalem and received his doctorate in psychology from San Diego University in California. He teaches at Haifa University where he became a professor in 1984 and was dean of the Faculty of Psychology. He is a leading researcher in cognitive psychology.

SPERBER, DANIEL (1940–), for Jewish studies. Born in Wales in 1940, he moved to Israel after high school and studied at Kol Torah and Hebron yeshivot. In the 1960s he studied the history of art at England's Courtauld Institute. In 1978 he became a full professor of Talmud at Bar Ilan University. He has written on economic history, as in *Roman Palestine, 200–400: Money and Prices* and in *Roman Palestine, 200–400: The Land* and on Jewish art and history, among other topics. From 1985 he was a member of the Academy of the Hebrew Language.

WAHL, ISAAK (1915–), in life sciences. Born in 1915 in Kherson, Russia, he immigrated to Palestine at 18 and studied at the Hebrew University, majoring in botany. He is recognized as one of the founders of phytopathology in Israel.

YESHURUN, AVOT (see **16**:773), for literature and poetry. He died in 1992.

ITALY (see **9**:1115; **Dc./17**:411). **Demography.** Totaling 32,000 in 1983 and 31,000 in 1992/93, the population of Jews officially registered in Italian communities remained largely stable, with an estimated additional 10–15,000 unaffiliated. Mixed marriages fell from 50% to 40% in ten years. The Rome community numbers c. 15,000 with 10,000

Fifth graders in the Milan Jewish day school, Milan. (Courtesy Scuole della Comunia Israelita, Milan)

in Milan and the rest dispersed in 19 smaller communities such as Turin, Venice, Genoa, Padua, Trieste, Bologna, Ferrara, Mantua, Ancona, Naples, and tiny Tuscan communities in Lucca, Siena, Pisa, Viareggio, etc. In this period some small communities died out. Rome Jewry is the most homogeneous, made up mostly of families — most of them store owners — who survived the War and a dynamic post-1967 Libyan Jewish community by now well-integrated although they have their own synagogue. The Milan community is of international origin with groups of Syrian, Iranian, Lebanese Jews and others, each with their own synagogues. Lubavich families have settled in various cities, attracting some of the youth. Friction arose initially because the Lubavich rabbis accused the Italian rabbis of laxity in maintaining halakhic standards, challenging Italian Jewry's elastic traditions of accommodating all forms of religiosity under an umbrella definition of Orthodoxy. A *modus vivendi* was found, resulting in greater cooperation. No Conservative or Reformed congregations exist in Italy because they are traditionally regarded as a threat to Jewish unity and a step towards assimilation.

Community Life. The Union of Italian Jewish Communities held national congresses in 1982, 1986, and 1990. Tullia Zevi, a journalist from Rome, was elected as the UIJC's first woman president in 1982, a position she still held in 1992. The 1982 keynote address on the importance of historical memory was written by Primo Levi, the distinguished novelist and Auschwitz survivor. The Italian Jewish biologist, Rita Levi Montalcini, co-winner of the 1986 Nobel Prize in medicine, addressed that year's UIJC Congress which was also attended by the president of the Italian Republic, Francesco Cossiga.

In 1984, the Italian Constitutional Court repealed a 1930 law requiring compulsory membership and taxation of Jews by local communities. This law was successfully contested by a Libyan Jewish immigrant. In 1987, a new *intesa* (agreement) between the UIJC and the Italian government was signed, becoming effective in March 1989 and containing allowances for Sabbath requirements, legalizing rabbinic marriages, and making rabbinic ordination equivalent to university degrees.

Similar *intese* were stipulated with other religious minorities in Italy and in 1992 negotiations began between the government and the c. 100,000-strong community of Muslim immigrants.

Italy became a state of religious pluralism on February 18, 1984, when a revised Concordat between the Holy See and the Italian Republic abolished Catholicism's privilege of being the "state religion," for the first time in 16 centuries.

In December 1992 the UIJC decided to call a special

national congress on the possibility of financing the Jewish communities by opting for voluntary contributions from tax payers of "8 per 1000 lire" of their income taxes — a system already adopted by the Catholic Church, Protestants, Seventh Day Adventists, and Mormons.

Culture. JEWISH HERITAGE. Major efforts were made to preserve Italy's vast and precious but rapidly deteriorating Jewish heritage. Private foundations and government sponsorship could only partially cover the enormous costs required for maintenance and restoration.

The National Jewish Bibliographic Center was established in Rome in 1984 and in 1990 a wing was inaugurated. In 1986 a grant from the Olivetti group permitted work to begin on the collection and preservation of about 25,000 volumes of archival and bibliographical materials from extinct and small communities all over Italy. Other contributions included a donation by Nobel Prize winner Rita Levi-Montalcini. Israeli experts came to help in the framework of Italy–Israel cultural agreements, and regular expertise was given by Father Pierfrancesco Fumagalli, secretary of the Vatican's Commission for Religious Relations with Jews, himself a specialist in illuminated Hebrew manuscripts. In April 1992 a three-year agreement was made with the musicological departments of the University of Cremona and Hebrew University for collecting, recording, and transcribing liturgical and other music by Italian Jewish composers for a special section of the Library.

The Vatican transferred the custody of the Roman Jewish catacombs to the Italian state in 1985; but for lack of funds for guardians and upkeep, the Villa Torlonia catacombs are not yet open to the public.

The Venice and Rome synagogues were refurbished and the restoration of ancient synagogues and cemeteries in small communities were under way. Excavations in Calabria unearthed a 4th-century synagogue.

In 1990, the Italian government announced plans for renovating the Roman ghetto.

CONGRESSES. Among initiatives made possible by renewed Italy–Israel cultural and scientific agreements were five international "Italia Judaica" conferences including in Genoa, 1984, on "Italian Jewry in the Renaissance and Baroque Periods"; in Tel Aviv, 1986, on "Jews in Italy from Ghetto Times to the First Emancipation"; in Siena, 1989, on "The Jews in United Italy 1870–1945"; and in Palermo, 1992, on "Jews in Sicily up to the Expulsion in 1492."

Throughout 1992 Italy commemorated the 500th anniversary of the arrival in Italy of Jews expelled from Spain. A major international congress was held in Genoa. In Ancona, a monument was unveiled to the memory of a group of Marranos burned at the stake in 1556.

EXHIBITIONS. In 1989 a "Gardens and Ghettos" exhibition on Italian Jewish art was shown in New York and Ferrara, and 1992 saw an important exhibition in Rome of all Judaica literature published in Italy 1955–1990.

HOLOCAUST STUDIES. A special commemorative edition of Italy's 1939 racial laws was published in 1989 by Italian authorities in Rome. In Florence, Israeli architect David Cassuto was awarded a silver medal in honor of his father, Rabbi Nathan Cassuto, for moral courage in wartime Italy.

In 1986, RAI-TV produced a series of programs on Nicola Caracciolo's book on Italians and Jews in World War II; in 1987 Susan Zuccotti's *The Italians and the Holocaust* was translated into Italian; in 1991 Liliana Picciotto Fargian's *Libro della Memoria* containing the individual stories of every deportee from 1943 to 1945, published by the Milan Jewish Documentation Center (C.D.E.C.), was presented in a solemn public ceremony in Rome.

EDUCATION AGAINST ANTI-SEMITISM AND ANTI-ZIONISM. In 1992, C.D.E.C., with government sponsorship, inaugurated a "Videotheque of Jewish Memory," offering 700 selected videocassettes for free loans to individuals and groups. On November 10, 1992, the Italian Ministry of Education made an agreement with the Union of Italian Jewish Communities on the use in schools of audiovisual programs on Jewish history. A course on Israel for high school teachers was held in Bergamo, organized by the Federation of Italy–Israel Friendship Associations.

Politics. ITALY–ISRAEL RELATIONS. A Palestinian terrorist attack on the Rome synagogue on October 9, 1982, resulted in the death of a 2-year-old boy and 40 Jews were wounded. In October 1985, the Italian cruiser *Achille Lauro* was hijacked and an invalid Jewish passenger, Leon Klinghoffer shot and thrown overboard. On December 27, 1985, terrorists struck at the El Al counter of Rome's Airport, leaving many dead and wounded. In June 1986, the Italian government signed an agreement with the U.S. for cooperation against terrorism.

The Lebanese war in 1982 and the *intifada* in 1987 set off media campaigns against Israel, often tinged with anti-Semitism. Newborn Italian "Progressive Judaism" movements proposing a two-state solution for Israelis and Palestinians began a constructive dialogue with the traditionally critical Italian Left. An Israeli–Palestinian meeting was held in 1989 by the Milan Center for Peace in the Middle East. Jewish and Italian groups joined Shalom Akhshav in a Jerusalem "Time for Peace" march in 1989.

During the Gulf War, the Italy–Israel Friendship Association staged a 1,000-person Solidarity for Israel demonstration outside Israel's Rome Embassy.

On May 25, 1992, Oscar Luigi Scalfaro was elected president of the Italian Republic only 2 months after having been nominated the first president of a newly formed Italy–Israel Parliamentary Friendship Association. On March 20, he had defended Israel as "a land for which we Europeans have still not been able to assure the basic requisites of security."

Two Italian Jews were elected to parliament: Bruno Zevi on the Radical ticket in 1987 and Enrico Modigliani, a Republican, in 1992. With Italian support, the European Economic Community lifted the freeze on scientific cooperation with Israel in 1991.

In 1991–2 economic instability and political scandals shook coalition alliance parties and strengthened the newly emerged Northern Lombard League favoring regional autonomy, a stop to immigration, and the expulsion of southern Italian migrants. Italy's extreme-right fringe became more audacious, permitting fascist salutes and racist slogans. There were anti-Semitic outbursts in sports stadiums (rival teams being referred to as "Jews"), desecrations of Jewish cemeteries, and violence against foreign immigrants. In June 1992 an international revisionist congress was held in Rome but Italian authorities blocked further meetings.

A massive Kristallnacht anniversary demonstration against anti-Semitism in Italy's major cities on November 9, 1992, concluded a week of chain reactions to a misleadingly alarmistic report on anti-Semitism in the weekly *Espresso.* Following the issue, 30 Jewish stores in Rome were plastered with yellow stars with the message "Zionists Out of Italy" and other graffiti proclaimed "Jews — Back to Africa". About 100 Jewish youths then stormed the headquarters of the fascist "Movimento Politico Occidentale."

At the end of 1992 parliament was debating a bill updating and reinforcing existing laws against anti-Semitism, neo-Fascism and racism in all its forms.

TOURISM TO ISRAEL. A record total of Italian tourists, mostly pilgrims, went to Israel in 1992. El-Al increased flights and extended coverage to Venice, Verona, and Bergamo. From 1992 all organized pilgrimages included visits to Yad Vashem. In February 1991, Milan's Cardinal Martini led 1,250 pilgrims, traveling in four planes from Milan and two from Rome. The Italian Touring Club published its first "Green Guide" to Israel in 1993.

Catholic–Jewish Relations 1983–1992. A special document on Ecumenism by the Diocese of Rome in 1983 called for the Church to insure that sermons did not contain "any form or vestige of anti-Semitism," and called for "a rediscovery of our Jewish roots."

After the revision in 1984 of the Concordat between Italy and the Holy See, Catholicism was no longer a "state religion" and attendance at Catholic religious courses in schools became voluntary.

In 1985 the Vatican's Commission for Religious Relations with Jews promulgated *Notes on the Correct Way to Present Jews and Judaism in Preaching and Catechesis.* These were discussed in the Vatican by a Jewish delegation which was received by Pope John Paul II to mark the 20th anniversary of the *Nostra Aetate* declaration.

On April 13, 1986, John Paul II visited Rome's main synagogue, the first such visit by a pope in history, and addressed Jews as "our cherished older brothers."

In October 1986 the pope invited leaders of the world's main religions to prayer at Assisi. Judaism was represented by ADL Representative Dr. Joseph Lichten and Rome's Chief Rabbi Elio Toaff who led a study session in front of an ancient synagogue.

In 1987 the pope received Austrian President Kurt Waldheim in private audience, arousing worldwide Jewish protest.

The 1988 the Vatican Document *The Church and Racism* contained the statement "Anti-Zionism serves at times as a screen for anti-Semitism, feeding on it and leading to it."

On January 17, 1990, the Italian Episcopal Conference celebrated its first annual national day of dialogue with Judaism in parish churches throughout Italy — so far the only national Episcopal Conference to have taken this initiative.

That same year the cult of "Saint Domenichino" (an alleged Jewish ritual murder victim) in Massa Carrara was abolished by the Catholic Church, declared illegitimate, and without any historical foundation.

In November, 1990 the Pope declared that "Anti-Semitism is a sin against God and man," endorsing a statement made by the International Catholic–Jewish Liaison Committee in Prague, in September 1990.

On July 29, 1992, a bilateral permanent working commission was established between "the Holy See and the State of Israel in order to study and define together issues of reciprocal interest and in view of normalizing relations," according to a joint communiqué. This was described as a first step towards diplomatic recognition.

Pope John Paul II, accompanied by Rabbi Toaff, chief rabbi of Italy, during his visit to the Synagogue of Rome, April 13, 1986. (Courtesy Beth Hatefutsoth, Tel Aviv, and Emmanuele Pacifici, Rome)

Prime Minister Ciriaco de Mita (right) greeting Israel President Herzog while on visit to Jerusalem, with Italy's foreign minister Andreotti looking on, April 1989 (GPO, Jerusalem)

Soviet Transmigrants in Italy. The last groups of Soviet transmigrants left Italy in 1990 after 100,000 had passed through Rome, Ostia, and Ladispoli during the previous two decades. Changed U.S. immigration laws in 1989 and direct processing of visas for Israel in Moscow, ended the flux that had been coordinated by HIAS, the Joint Distribution Committee, the Jewish Agency, and Italian authorities who set up schools and social centers, with religious help from the Lubavich movement.

Necrology. Losses of Italian Jewry between 1983 and 1992 include:

1983 — Julius Dresner (b. Podvoloschiska), American Joint representative during and after the war, *Davar, Aufbau,* JTA corrspondent in Rome for 25 years;

1986 — Augusto Segre (79), rabbi, writer, professor at Rome's Rabbinical College and Pontifical Lateran University, UIJC Secretary, editor of *La Rassegna Mensile d'Israel*; Sergio Tagliacozzo (52), president of Rome Jewish community;

1987 — Dr. Joseph Lichten, Rome and Vatican Anti-Defamation League Representative for 25 years; Arnaldo Momigliano, outstanding scholar and authority on ancient history; Edoardo Vitta (74), professor of International Law at several Italian universities, author, former president of Florence community, senior ranking official at Israeli Justice Ministry, and member of Israel's Commission for the Preparation of a Constitution; Primo Levi, author, chemist, and Auschwitz survivor

1988 — Paolo Milano (84), distinguished literary critic;

1989 — Cesare Musatti (82), leading psychoanalyst; Fausto Sabatello (84), founder and for 50 years director of the Italian branch of the Jewish National Fund; Emilio Segre (84), co-winner of 1959 Nobel Prize for Physics;

1991 — Leonardo Israelovici, for many years president of Italian B'nai B'rith, benefactor;

1992 — Fritz Becker (b. Vienna), World Jewish Congress representative in Rome and Vatican for 45 years; Emanuele Artom, former chief rabbi of Venice and Turin, scholar, author of Hebrew–Italian dictionary, liturgical and pedagogical texts, emissary of Jewish Agency, died in Jerusalem; Dr. Boldo Viterbo, legal coroner for Italian state, benefactor, Venice.

In 1992 Italian Jewry also mourned Beniamino Carucci, distinguished publisher of Jewish texts, and Giorgio Perlasca, a Yad Vashem "righteous gentile" who saved 5,000 Jews when he was stranded in Budapest during the war, risking his life by posing as the Spanish consul, issuing false identity papers and organizing a block of protected housing for refugees. He became famous only in his later years, after he had been sought out by the people he saved. He died in his native Padua. [L.P.-B.]

JACOBSON, HOWARD (1942–), English novelist and broadcaster. Born in Manchester, Jacobson was educated at Cambridge University where he was strongly influenced by F. R. Leavis, the English literary critic. He then lectured in English literature at Sydney University, Australia, and, on his return to England, supervised students at Cambridge University. After a variety of jobs in publishing, teaching, and retailing, he was appointed a Lecturer in English at Wolverhampton Polytechnic. This experience was to provide the material for his first novel, *Coming from Behind*, published in 1983. Jacobson, with Wilbur Sanders, has also jointly published a critical study entitled *Shakespeare's Magnanimity* (1978).

Jacobson is widely regarded as one of the most original and brilliant comic voices to have emerged in post-war England. *Coming From Behind*, a campus novel, was widely reviewed in England and quickly established Jacobson as a comic writer. According to Jacobson, the novel was meant to be "the last word in academic novels," but, instead, he found himself "writing about gentileness; about what a foreign place England is to a Jew."

Peeping Tom (1984), Jacobson's second and far more substantial novel, examines the consequences of being a culturally dispossessed Jew in a "foreign" country. In this novel, Jacobsons's Jewish persona is contrasted with "peeping" Thomas Hardy and the English literary rural tradition. Jacobson, with a considerable ironic punch, then goes on to transform his persona into Hardy's reincarnation. Hardy, that is, provides the "negative" Jew with his identity.

Jacobson's distances himself from what he calls the "super-Anglicization" of many Anglo-Jewish writers in the 1980s who, with a welcome self-assurance, examine and take risks with their Jewish identity in a literary context. Jacobson, for this reason, has been compared to American-Jewish comic writers Woody Allen and Philip Roth. He has also expanded his comic talent in a series of radio broadcasts.

Bibliography: *The Jewish Quarterly*, 32 (1985), 117; *Times Literary Supplement*, (May 3, 1985). [B.C.]

JAPAN (see **9**:1280; **Dc./17**:416). **Community.** In 1992 approximately 1,000 Jews resided in Japan, most of them in the greater Tokyo area. The permanent Jewish population, however, is less than 200. About 60% come from the U.S., 25% from Israel, and the rest from all over the Jewish world. Within the community are only a handful of Japanese converts. Most Jews residing in Japan are expatriates representing major businesses, banks, and financial institutions. There are also journalists and students. The Jewish Community Center of Japan, located in Tokyo, houses the city's only synagogue, a religious school, a Judaica and general library, a *mikveh*, *ḥevra kaddisha*, social area, and administrative offices. Religious services are held every Sabbath and on holidays. *Kasher* food products are imported from abroad and other religious needs and requirements are met. There are also youth programs, adult education courses, and cultural and social activities. The community is a member of the World Jewish Congress, the Asia Pacific Jewish Association, and the B'nai B'rith and also contributes to the United Israel Appeal.

The only other organized Jewish community is located in Kobe which consists of about 35 Jewish families in Kobe itself and about 35 families in other parts of the Kansai region (Kyoto and Osaka).

Jews in the American military stationed in Japan are usually serviced by two Jewish chaplains. One is stationed in Yokosuka Naval Base outside of Tokyo and the other in Okinawa. There are about 100–200 Jews stationed in Japan.

The Jewish Community Center continues to serve as the home for the Japan-Israel Women's Welfare Organization (JIWWO) and the Japan-Israel Friendship Association (JIFA).

Especially since 1986, numerous books about Jews and Judaism have been published in Japan. Several of them have been anti-Semitic but have not led to any significant acts of anti-Semitism. The Japanese government's response has been vague and non-committal.

Jewish subjects are taught from time to time in Japanese

Tashlikh over the bridge in Arisugawa Park, Tokyo, Japan, 1984 (Courtesy Jewish Community of Japan, Tokyo)

universities. There is a Jewish Studies Section of the Institute of Social Sciences at the prestigious Waseda University. It was founded in 1976, has 16 academic members, and meets several times a year. There is also the *Studies on Jewish Life and Culture*, a journal by the Japan Society for Jewish Studies, which has published several issues since 1961.

The Makuya and the Christian Friends of Israel, two new religious Japanese sects, continue in their strong support of the State of Israel and in their warm ties to the Jewish community.

However, the average Japanese still has very little knowledge or understanding of Jews. The information about Jews and Judaism available in Japanese is limited and often skewed or misleading. This has led to the current situation in which the little that the Japanese do know about Jews is often based on the typical Western stereotypes. Lacking the proper context to put such misinformation into perspective, many Japanese find any statement about Jews believable. The Jewish community of Japan is working at giving better access to accurate information about Jews.

Relations with Israel. Japan's main exports to Israel are transportation machinery and processing machinery. Its main imports from Israel are processed diamonds and chemical products.

Israel was one of the very few nations in the world to run a trade surplus with Japan, primarily because of booming diamond imports by the Japanese.

Although there have been some tentative movements toward increasing trade relations with Israel by small and medium-sized Japanese firms, most major Japanese companies continue to adhere to the Arab economic boycott of Israel. However, in 1992 the Japanese Foreign Ministry advised Japanese companies to cease cooperating with the boycott and Japan called on Arab countries to stop the boycott.

In 1987 an economic mission from Israel, led by representatives of the Israeli Manufacturers Association, visited Japan. A return delegation of businessmen from Japan, led by representatives of the Federation of Economic Organizations of Japan (Keidanren), followed to Israel. In 1988, a conference on the Japanese economy was held in Israel and an Israeli Economy Seminar was held in Tokyo.

Politics. On the political scene, since before the Yom Kippur War, Japan has maintained a pro-Arab stance due to immense Arab pressure and Japan's heavy dependence on oil. However, as Japan is now emerging as a world power and is being pressured by the West to be more active in international affairs, Japan may find it necessary to maintain a more neutral stand concerning Mid-East problems.

This is evidenced by increased political contacts as exemplified by the first visit to Israel by a Japanese cabinet member, Foreign Minister Sousuke Uno in June 1988, and by a visit by Israel Foreign Minister Shimon Peres to Japan in 1992. [M.J.SH.]

JERUSALEM (see **9**:1378; **Dc./17**:417). Jerusalem continued to be a city of tensions, primarily between Arabs and Jews. The initial post-1967 goal of an integrated population foundered, largely as a result of a long series of attacks (often stabbings) carried out by Arabs, sometimes evoking reprisals by Jews. In 1990, in an incident on the Temple Mount 21 Arabs were killed and over 100 injured by Israeli forces. Tensions were also exacerbated, especially during the Shamir regime, when Jews moved in to Muslim neighborhoods, including the Muslim Quarter of the Old City and the village of Silwan. In many respects the city was divided almost as much as before 1967 with little social intercourse between Jews and Arabs.

The Palestinian *intifada* brought many instances of stone-throwing by Arabs at Jewish buses and cars in East Jerusalem. There was a prolonged protest shutdown of Arab stores and a sharp fall-off in the number of Jews visiting the Arab parts of the city, including the formerly crowded marketplaces of the Old City. The Palestinians reiterated that in some form Jerusalem, or part of it, must be included in any Palestinian entity. The issue was not squarely faced in the first rounds of the peace process, but Israel refused to have Jerusalemites included in the Palestinian delegation.

The population of Jerusalem at the end of 1992 was 558,000 of whom 401,000 were Jews and 157,000 Arabs (whose percentage in the total population had risen from 25 to 28 since 1967). The growth in the Jewish population was largely due to the Russian immigration, and the new suburbs of Gilo, Neveh Ya'akov, Har Nof, Pisgat Ze'ev, and Ramot mushroomed. There was also, however, an outflow of the Jewish population as many were attracted by the favorable terms offered by settlements in the West Bank within easy commuting distance of Jerusalem.

The ultra-Orthodox (*ḥaredi*) population continued to thrive and hundreds of new yeshivot and synagogues have been built in the city since 1967. There were not infrequent tensions with the ultra-Orthodox who often held protest demonstrations to protest Sabbath desecrations and alleged desecrations of graves by archeologists or construction workers. Their projections in the population grew constantly due to immigration and a very high fertility rate, and they now constitute over 20% of the Jewish population. Jerusalem's Sabbath character took a surprising turn in the late 1980s when for the first time pubs, discotheques, and some cinemas began to open on Friday nights. In the past, ultra-Orthodox protests had managed to snuff out attempts to open entertainment facilities on Sabbath eve and young Jerusalemites who sought such outlets had to travel to Tel Aviv. In time, the Friday night life in Jerusalem became so lively that it even occasionally drew Tel Aviv youth.

A quarter-century after its unification in the 1967 Six-Day War, Jerusalem continued its dynamic transformation into a modern urban center. With the completion of most of the new housing developments launched in the wake of the 1967 war, efforts focused on providing facilities to serve the vastly increased population. In the south of the city, a 15,000-seat soccer stadium was opened in 1991, providing Jerusalem with its first major sports facility. At the insistence of its foreign donor, it was named Teddy stadium, honoring Mayor Teddy Kollek. Nearby, a 100,000-square-meter enclosed shopping mall, said to be the largest in the Middle East, was opened in 1993. Opposite Jaffa Gate, development of the new Mamilla quarter as a commercial-residential link between the Old City and West Jerusalem finally began with the construction of luxury housing, more than a decade after the previous inhabitants of the area had been evacuated. An

Mayor Teddy Kollek (left) receiving award from neighborhood resident at the opening of Teddy Stadium, 1991 (GPO, Jerusalem)

Israel's new Supreme Court Building in Jerusalem, 1992 (GPO, Jerusalem)

ambitious new City Hall complex was dedicated alongside the building that had filled that role for half a century.

A major new road, Road Number One, was built to bring traffic from north Jerusalem to the city center, via Damascus Gate. The road's three kilometer alignment followed the line that had served as no-man's-land between Israeli and Jordanian Jerusalem before the Six-Day War. A new museum complex began to take shape alongside the Israel Museum with the dedication of the Bible Lands Museum and a science museum. The Israel Supreme Court moved in 1992 from its old quarters in the center of the city to a much acclaimed new building in the Government Center. The biblical zoo also shifted to more elaborate new quarters in the south of the city. A major expansion of the Binyanei Ha'ooma Convention Center was launched to help meet the growing demand of international congresses seeking to hold their meetings in Jerusalem. In northern Jerusalem, the last and largest of the massive post-Six-Day War housing developments, Pisgat Ze'ev, with 12,000 units, was nearing completion.

On the Temple Mount in the Old City, the gold-colored annodized aluminum dome covering the Islamic shrine, the Dome of the Rock, was replaced by a dome gilded with real gold.

Teddy Kollek, first elected mayor in 1965, served in that capacity until replaced in the 1993 elections by Ehud Olmert. [A.RA.]

JEWISH AGENCY (see **10**:26). Since the mid-1980s, the Jewish Agency (JA) and World Zionist Organization (WZO) have sought ways to redefine many of their traditional programs and modes of operation as well as to effect a new division between them. This process emerged in response to changes in Israel-Diaspora relations, but it was also shaped by ongoing tensions and differences in the relative strength of the constituent groups of these bodies. As a result, major transformations occurred.

Far-reaching programmatic and operational modifications have been made in an effort to streamline bureaucracy and bring about cost efficiency. In 1988 alone, 559 budgeted personnel positions were terminated in the JA. By 1990, one-third of all JA employees had been made redundant. Traditional Agency departments: Aliyah, Youth Aliyah, Rural Settlement, and Project Renewal were restructured. Another three departments, Torah Education & Culture, General Education & Culture, and Youth & He-Ḥalutz, formerly solely in the domain of the WZO, have come under the budgetary and programmatic aegis of a newly created JA/WZO Authority for Jewish Zionist Education. Initially it was envisaged that the budget of the Authority would be about $50 million a year approximating the aggregate of the separate departments, but the 1993 budget allocated only $33.9 million.

In 1993, the departments of Rural Settlement and Renewal & Development were merged into a combined Department for Rural and Urban Development. This culminated a process which began at the June 1991 Assembly. The new department was mandated to operate on a time and resource limited project base.

Budgetary constraints also forced a gradual reduction in the total number of youngsters in the care of the Youth Aliyah Department from 19,000 in the fiscal year 1986/87 to 14,000 in 1992/93. This cutback was made despite the massive inflow of immigrants and the deteriorating economic state of broad sections of Israeli society. Here, as in the case of rural settlement and urban renewal, the economies of scale followed on studies conducted by consultants appointed by the JA Board of Governors.

Several catalysts together generated the changes. Among these were an extended world business slump, demands that funds raised in the Diaspora be used domestically, and the unforeseen enormous costs of financing *aliyah* from the former Soviet Union and Ethiopia. The personalities of the leaders of the WZO and the JA, and the divergent political, public, and business cultures from which they hailed also contributed to the shifts. Overriding all these components was the difficult structural and philosophic interface between two systems — the political WZO and the philanthropic/communal JA.

Almost all the leadership elites of the JA reside overseas and are appointed to their positions, whereas the majority of WZO officials live in Israel and are elected through political parties.

Jewish communal life in the Diaspora revolves around the maintenance of educational systems, welfare institutions, synagogues and other functions, all of which require funding; this calls for a highly complex fundraising capacity. Lacking the means to levy taxes, the compelling issue facing those structures is the mobilization of funds. Since fundraising is not a democratic activity, cost efficiency is arguably at the top of campaigns considerations. The role of major

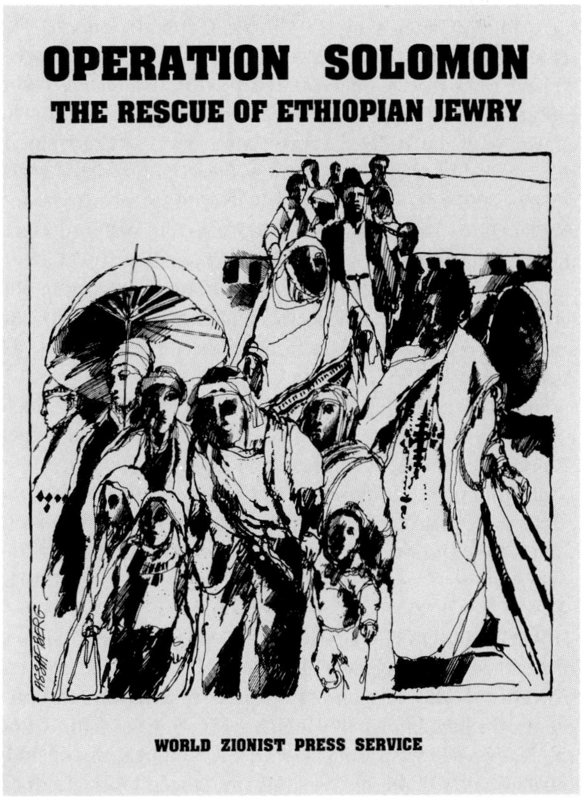

Cover of World Zionist Press Service information folder on Operation Solomon, 1991 (Courtesy WZO, Jerusalem)

contributors is thus perpetuated, which in turn coalesces into an oligarchy.

In the WZO, leadership is by demonstrated electability. While Zionists are critical of what they term dominance by people of wealth, community leaders in the Diaspora are equally critical about what they term the exaggerated politicizing of Israeli-Zionist leadership and the attendant political coloration of policy.

In 1971, the Reconstituted Jewish Agency was composed of representatives of institutional Jewish life in the Diaspora, e.g., the communal federation system and the fund-raising community, who joined the existing structure — which had been made up exclusively of Zionists — in a fifty-fifty partnership. Subsequently, the creation of JA governing bodies — an Executive, a Board of Governors, and an Assembly — separated the JA from the WZO's governing bodies — an Executive, the Zionist General Council, and Zionist Congress. (By statute, however, certain positions, particularly those of the chairman and the treasurer of the Executive, remained common to both.) The result was that the JA became an autonomous organization in which the leadership of Diaspora communities initially acquired equal responsibility, and later supremacy in determining policy and budget.

Until February 1988, the Jewish Agency Executive like that of the WZO, worked both ideologically and operationally as a collective. This meant that the chairman functioned as the "first among equals," with decisions taken as a group. In response to the demand by Diaspora members of the Board of Governors, particularly the Americans, to institute a corporate managerial style, each head of department within the JA has tacitly agreed in 1992 that the chairman of the Executive may operate, when necessary, with decision-making authority. In addition, prior to February 1988, the director-general of the JA merely had a coordinating role. Subsequently, all department directors-general, and the secretary-general of the JA, are professionally responsible to the director-general.

Certain checks-and-balances were incorporated into the JA system. Fifty percent of the representatives in the 398-member Assembly of the JA (convened annually) are elected for a four-year term by the Zionist General Council. The remaining members are appointed by the United Jewish Appeal (30%) for a one-year term, while Keren ha-Yesod (20%) appoints representatives for a four-year period. The chairman of the WZO Executive also serves as chairman of the Assembly which determines basic policy and goals, reviews and acts upon budgets, determines priorities and directions of future budgets, adopts resolutions and elects the Board of Governors. The 75-member Board of Governors, which meets in between Assemblies to determine policy, manage, supervise, control, and direct operations and activities, is composed according to the same key as the JA Assembly.

The challenges met during the last decade by the JA have been its greatest since the early days of the State of Israel. The twin chapters of immigration from the former Soviet Union and from Ethiopia appear to have had an exhilarating effect on Jews around the world, effecting a great increase in fundraising and wrenching it out of the doldrums of eroding incomes. [AM.H.]

JEWISH BOOK COUNCIL, U.S. organization that promotes the publishing and reading of books of Jewish interest. Toward this end, it sponsors a variety of activities and programs, the best-known of which are Jewish Book Month and the National Jewish Book Awards. Its publications include the *Jewish Book Annual*, various specialized bibliographies, and *Jewish Book World*, a quarterly newsletter.

The Council's origins date back to 1925, when Fanny

1991 Jewish Book Month poster by Neil Waldman (Courtesy Jewish Book Council, sponsored by the JCC Association, New York)

Goldstein, the librarian of the West End Branch of the Boston Public Library, prepared a Judaica book exhibit and called it Jewish Book Week. In 1940, a National Committee for Jewish Book Week was founded, with Miss Goldstein as its chairman. The committee included representatives of major American Jewish organizations, as well as figures from Jewish educational and literary life. Mordecai Soltes became the chairman the following year. The Histadruth Ivrith of America and Yiddishist organizations such as YIVO and the Central Yiddish Cultural Organization (CYCO) influenced the Council to give the role of Yiddish and Hebrew literature a prominent place in its programs.

Since 1942, the National Committee has published the trilingual *Jewish Book Week Annual*. Initially edited by Solomon *Grayzel, the *Annual* included bibliographies in English, Hebrew, and Yiddish, and several articles on Jewish literary activity. This basic format has been maintained since the first volume.

In 1943 the week-long Jewish Book observance was extended to a month. That same year the Jewish Book Council of America became the successor organization to the National Committee for Jewish Book Week. In 1944, the National Jewish Welfare Board (now known as JWB), entered into an agreement with the Council to become its official sponsoring and coordinating organization. JWB provided financial support to the Council, as well as organizational expertise and professional guidance.

To carry out its objectives, the Council has developed a range of programs. These include: Jewish Book Month, which is observed annually in the United States and Canada during the month before Ḥanukkah. Among the Book Month activities are exhibits in libraries and schools and lectures. The Council distributes educational and promotional materials such as posters, bookmarks, and book lists aimed at the building of home Jewish libraries. Also part of Book Month activities are the more than 50 community-wide Book Fairs held at Jewish Community Centers across the U.S. many smaller book fairs and exhibits are also held.

The National Jewish Book Awards, conferred annually

since 1943, are intended to recognize outstanding writers and to encourage the reading of worthwhile books. Panels of judges examine new works in biography, children's literature, scholarship, and other fields. With the exception of the Israel category, winning authors must be United States citizens or residents.

Starting in 1948, the Council began granting citations of merit to libraries of Jewish Community Centers, Jewish schools, synagogues, and other Jewish agencies. These Library Citations are given to libraries that meet minimum requirements as to size of collection, staffing, and acquisition budget. The criteria developed by the Council are widely used as a guide in the development of libraries.

A major part of the Council's program has been the preparation of specialized publications. Since 1942 the Council has been the principal distributor of bibliographies of Jewish interest, covering children's literature, Hebrew literature in translation, Israel, the Holocaust, Sephardi Jewry, and other subjects. The *Jewish Book Annual* continues to appear. Other publications include *Jewish Book World*, a quarterly with brief descriptions of new books of Jewish interest, articles, reviews, and news of Jewish book publishing, and *Jewish Books in Review*, a syndicated service that provides book reviews to newspapers and magazines in the U.S. and Canada. The JBC has also sponsored conferences meant to bring together writers, publishers, and others involved with Jewish book publishing. [WI.W.]

JEWISH-CHRISTIAN RELATIONS (see **Dc./17**:421; **YB 83–85**:375). Throughout the years since World War II, and under the impact of the revelation of the facts of the Holocaust and the establishment of the State of Israel, Christians individually and collectively have felt themselves impelled to reassess their relationships with Jews and Judaism, and at the very least to repudiate traditional anti-Semitism and the "teaching of contempt." This movement has been expressed in Church documents, in theological writings, and in dialogue with Jews. By 1985 the main lines had been drawn, and the last years of the 1980s were essentially a period of consolidation, and of educational initiatives to ensure that the guidelines of Churches would be absorbed into teaching and preaching. At the same time, however, a number of "sticking points" in the dialogue emerged clearly, and a series of incidents created tensions.

The Church of Rome. High level dialogue between the Roman Catholic Church and the Jewish people is undertaken by the International Catholic-Jewish Liaison Committee (ILC). On the Catholic side, this consists of representatives of the Holy See's Commission on Religious Relations with the Jews, an office within the secretariat for Promoting Christian Unity. On the Jewish side, the representative body is the International Jewish Committee on Interreligious Consultations (IJCIC), composed of the World Jewish Congress, the Synagogue Council of America, the American Jewish Committee, B'nai B'rith International — Anti-Defamation League, and the Israel Jewish Council for Interreligious Relations.

The 1985 meeting of the ILC took place on October 28–30 in Rome, and was a major commemoration and reassessment of the publication 20 years previously of *Nostra Aetate* no. 4, part of the "Declaration on the Relationship of the Church to non-Christian Religions," the Second Vatican Council document which paved the way for the subsequent development of Catholic attitudes to Jews and Judaism. The progress which had taken place in the intervening years was evaluated, a program for the future outlined, and the importance attached by the Church to the proceedings emphasized by an audience with Pope John Paul II. An added touch to all of the foregoing activity was the recognition, by a special lecture, of the 850th anniversary of the death of Maimonides.

The most substantial discussions at the Rome meeting, however, were in connection with the newly prepared Vatican document, "Notes on the correct way to present the Jews and Judaism in preaching and catechesis in the Roman Catholic Church." This "internal" Church document, intended to develop the teaching of *Nostra Aetate* and to help integrate it into the everyday life of the Church, met with a mixed response from the Jewish delegation. On the positive side, the State of Israel was for the first time mentioned in a Vatican document, Jewish suffering in the Holocaust recognized, the "ongoing spiritual vitality of Judaism" to modern times

May 1989 WIZO protest demonstration, "Get the Carmelite Convent Out of Auschwitz," in front of the Carmelite convent at Auschwitz; president of World WIZO, Raya Jaglom, in center between two Israeli flags (Courtesy WIZO, T.A.; photo Rachel Hirsch, T.A.)

appreciated, and guidance given on how to interpret New Testament texts without deriving anti-Semitism from them. On the other hand, Jews were upset that they had not been fully consulted in preparing the document, felt that treatment of the Holocaust failed to acknowledge any Christian guilt, were dissatisfied with the lack of a positive theological evaluation of Israel, and detected inconsistencies in the theological sections, including remnants of typology and "replacement theology."

On Sunday April 13, 1986, Pope John Paul II made a historic visit across the Tiber to the synagogue in Rome, where he was welcomed by Chief Rabbi Elio Toaff. The president of the Jewish community, Professor Giacomo Saban, reminded the pope of the illustrious history of the Roman Jewish community, extending back to pre-Christian times. Generally, the visit was welcomed by Catholic and Jewish leaders as a signal of the pope's personal commitment to carrying forward the initiative of *Nostra Aetate*; indeed, the pope has lost no opportunity to address Jewish communities in the numerous cities he has visited around the world, has frequently welcomed visiting Jewish dignitaries at the Vatican, and has used these occasions repeatedly to denounce anti-Semitism and to recognize Jewish sufferings in the "Shoah," as he consistently calls the Holocaust.

It was at about this time that the Auschwitz Convent (q.v.) controversy erupted (the Cracow Church's approval for the project had been given on September 30, 1984, without attracting attention), and plans for a major Consultation of the ILC on the subject of the Holocaust were postponed indefinitely. Relations were further exacerbated when the World Jewish Congress, in the form of a letter from its president, Edgar Bronfman, dated December 4, 1986, while declaring that its commitment to improving relations with the Catholic Church had never been stronger, launched a "global campaign" to force the Holy See to "recognize" Israel. Although the steering committee of the ILC continued to meet, no full Consultation took place until that in Prague in September 1990. One of the effects of this postponement was delay in producing a comprehensive Vatican statement on the Holocaust, which is still awaited. Archbishop Edward (later Cardinal) Cassidy, who led the Catholic delegation at Prague in his capacity as president of the Commission on Religious Relations with the Jews in succession to Cardinal Willebrands, declared in his opening remarks "that anti-Semitism has found a place in Christian thought and practice calls for an act of *Teshuvah* (repentance) and of reconciliation on our part as we gather here in this city which is a testimony to our failure to be authentic witnesses to our faith at times in the past." The Statement issued from the Prague meeting cited these words and is the first document with Vatican authority to acknowledge, if somewhat obliquely, Catholic guilt in relation to the Holocaust. The Statement also stressed the educational task in Jewish-Christian relations, and the opportunities for common social work and spiritual witness. The statement was endorsed by John Paul II when he received the ILC on the occasion of the 25th anniversary of Nostra Aetate in December 1990.

Relations moved further ahead as a result of a Conference of the ILC in Baltimore in 1992 when the Vatican participants proposed the establishment of Joint Catholic-Jewish delegations to appear before international bodies on matters of mutual concern. They also undertook to extend to other countries the initiative of the Italian bishops who had declared that one day a year in their dioceses would be devoted to the study of Judaism and the Jewish people. In the summer of 1992, the Vatican announced the opening of discussions with Israel for the normalization of relations between the two countries towards the establishment of diplomatic ties which was finally achieved at the end of 1993. (See article VATICAN, Relations With Israel, page 385.)

The World Council of Churches and Protestant Churches. The World Council of Churches (WCC), while unrelenting in its opposition to anti-Semitism, has progressed only slowly in dialogue in the period under review. This is thought to be partly because of political pressure from the Middle East Council of Churches, and partly because of the reluctance of some member Churches to abandon an actively evangelical approach towards non-Christians including Jews. Moreover, whereas the Catholic Church has several times stated that relations with Jews and Judaism are at the center of Christian concern, the World Council tends to place the matter lower on its scale of priorities. The World Council is an amorphous federation rather than a hierarchical structure like the Roman Church; it cannot determine standards from the top down, but must work on the basis of consensus.

Some progress was made at the "Consultation on the Church and the Jewish People" in Arnoldshain, West Germany, February 10–14, 1986, but the most significant advance was the document formulated at the November 1988 meeting at Sigtuna, Sweden, of the WCC's Committee on the Church and the Jewish People. This document recognizes the lack of consensus among its members on mission and on the significance of the Land of Israel, but claimed wide agreement for the following:

1. The covenant of God with the Jewish people remains valid.
2. Anti-Semitism and all forms of the teaching of contempt for Judaism are to be repudiated.
3. The living tradition of Judaism is a gift of God.
4. Coercive proselytism directed towards Jews is incompatible with Christian faith.
5. Jews and Christians bear a common responsibility as witnesses to God's righteousness and peace in the world.

In addition, it agreed nine affirmations, which recognized Israel's call, acknowledged the spiritual treasures shared by Jews and Christians, made clear that Jews should not be blamed for Jesus' passion, and expressed sorrow at the Christian share of responsibility for Jewish suffering, culminating in the Holocaust.

Like the Vatican, the WCC engages in dialogue at the highest level with IJCIC. One of their most notable joint ventures was an African Christian-Jewish Consultation which took place in Nairobi, Kenya, from November 10–13, 1986; the emphasis here was on the shared concern of Jews and African Christians with tradition and its relationship with Scripture. As was aptly remarked, "Scripture is not a European creation."

Since the WCC can work only by consensus the Statements of its individual constituent Churches are of significance.

The Anglican Communion held its own Consultation with IJCIC at Shallowford House, Stafford (England), in 1986, focusing on two issues of common concern to Jews and Anglicans, AIDS and inner city deprivation, though few who were present would deny that the high point of that Consultation was Dr. Gerhart Riegner's spontaneous and moving narration of the events of 1942 when, from his Geneva office, he had battled against immense resistance to inform the unbelieving world of the implementation of the "Final Solution."

This Consultation undoubtedly fed into the 1988 Lambeth Conference, the 10-yearly gathering of Anglican Bishops from around the world. For the first time in their history they devoted attention to Christian-Jewish relations, and produced and unanimously commended a document "Jews, Christians and Muslims: the Way of Dialogue." This, far from assimilating the relationship with Judaism to that with all monotheists, clearly spelled out its special nature and obligations, Christian guilt for the "teaching of contempt" which provided the soil in which Nazism could thrive, and the nature of Judaism as a living religion not to be confused with a literal reading of the Old Testament.

The Lutheran Churches in Germany and elsewhere were among the first and most copious in the production of documents. The Lutheran European Commission "Church and the Jewish People," in its May 8, 1990, "Statement on the Encounter between Lutheran Christians and Jews" (Driebergen, Netherlands) recognizes that a prerequisite to a new, more tolerant relationship with the Jewish faith is "a partial renunciation of the requirement for evangelization of Jews, as well as the call for a self-critical analysis of the Lutherans' own theology."

Excellent statements and guidelines have emanated from other church groups within the WCC, such as Methodists and Presbyterians — and even from those outside the WCC, such as the Unification Church.

Special mention should be made of the June 12, 1990, "Statement by the Synod of the Reformed Church in Hungary on its Relations with the Jews," perhaps the first document of this nature to emanate from a non-Catholic Church in Central Europe since the imposition of communism, yet able to confess repentance in the words of a 1946 statement of its Reformed Free Council: "Under the responsibility resting upon us because of sins committed against the Jews, however late, we now ask the Hungarian Jews before God to forgive us."

The International Council of Christians and Jews and National CCJ's. Much of the dialogue at "grass-roots" level is undertaken through local branches of the national Councils of Christians and Jews (CCJ's). The national councils are members of the International Council of Christians and Jews (ICCJ). With the admission in 1990 of CCJ's in Poland, Czechoslovakia, Hungary, and New Zealand, there are now 23 national groups.

Members of the national CCJ's are able to meet at the ICCJ's International Colloquium, held each year in a different country. In the period under consideration they have met in Dublin (1985), Salamanca (1986), Fribourg (1978), Montreal (1988), Lille (1989), and Prague (1990). The Salamanca meeting was notable for its strong Muslim participation, and some element of this has been maintained. At the Prague meeting delegates from Central and East European countries outlined their local situations and problems. Each colloquium is combined with a women's symposium and a young leadership conference, though in 1990 the young leadership conference took place separately, in Israel.

ICCJ had sponsored other major meetings and initiatives, including "Identity and Commitment in the Religious Encounter," Jerusalem, December 1986. It had a first conference in Eastern Europe with its 1985 meeting in Budapest (see below). This was followed, in September 1987, with a second "Seminar of Jews and Christians from the East and the West" in Buckow, then East Germany—an occasion remarkable for the presence of 12 Israeli scholars. Together with the Konrad Adenauer Stiftung it held a Symposium of Jews, Christians and Muslims from May 29–June 2, 1988 in Sankt Augustin, near Bonn, where there was much discussion of the stereotypes which hinder mutual understanding.

The largest popular gathering in Christian-Jewish relations is the National Workshop of the NCCJ in the United States. Such workshops (Baltimore, 1986; Minneapolis, 1987; Charleston, 1989) attract well in excess of a thousand participants.

Opening up the East. THE DIALOGUE. Long before the demise of communism in Central Europe in 1989 contact had been established with the Churches and with the small remaining Jewish communities and the foundations laid for a positive development in Jewish-Christian relations. At that time the Churches themselves were struggling to exist in the face of a hostile regime. This gave them a sense of solidarity with the Jewish minority, but as against this was the lack of familiarity with Western developments in Christian theology, lack of knowledge of Judaism, and lack of local Jews with knowledge of their own faith.

In November 1985 the International Council of Christians and Jews, together with the Interchurch Peace Council in Hungary, sponsored a four-day conference on "Jewish-Christian Dialogue and its Contribution to Peace." Hungary has not only a substantial Jewish community but also several native Jewish scholars. Mention has already been made of the September 1987 "Seminar of Jews and Christians from the East and the West" which took place in East Germany.

In Poland there had been, through much of the communist era, a fascination with Jewish culture, as manifested for instance in the continuation of the Yiddish theater, but only in the 1980s did a serious attempt at critical reassessment of the past commence. The pope, in his 1979 visit to Auschwitz, had perhaps initiated the process by referring there to "the great sufferings of the Jewish people." A highly significant series of articles appeared in the Catholic journals *ZNAK* and *Tygodnik Powszechny*, commencing in 1983; Jan Blonski's challenging 1987 article "The Poor Poles Look at the Ghetto" deserves special mention. In May 1986 the Polish Bishops' Conference set up a sub-commission (later upgraded to a full commission) to examine, in a Polish context, relationships with Jews and Judaism, and under its chairman, Bishop Henrik Muszynski of Wloclawek, this group has led the Polish church to take seriously the new attitudes to Jews and Judaism emanating from Rome, and in 1990 published a book of recent Catholic documentation on Judaism and the Jews. Since the beginning of the decade there have been large international scholarly gatherings on the history and culture of Polish Jews; the Jagellonian University at Cracow has a special department for these subjects. International conferences on Jewish-Christian relations have also taken place, including one arranged by the Bishops' Commission together with the Anti-Defamation League of B'nai B'rith (Tyniec, 1987), and another at Cracow in November 1989, at which the Catholic sponsors were the KIK (Catholic Intellectuals' Club) of Cracow, which has all along taken a leading part in these matters. Educational work has proceeded apace; 22 Polish seminary professors spent seven weeks in Chicago in 1989 studying together with rabbis and other Jewish scholars, and in April 1990 a British scholar, Rabbi Norman Solomon, lectured at the Academy of Catholic Theology in Warsaw.

THE CHURCHES AND THE RESURGENCE OF ANTI-SEMITISM. On the downside of the 1989 Central European rejection of communism has been a resurgence of anti-Semitism, coinciding with similar phenomena in Western Europe. It is difficult to know how much of this arises from Church influence, and how much from nationalist sentiment, but it has been interesting to observe the reactions of the Churches which, far from encouraging such attitudes, have been strongly condemnatory. In his letter of August 8, 1990, Dr. Emilio Castro, the general secretary of the World Council of Churches, reaffirmed the council's 1948 pronouncement that "anti-Semitism is a sin against God and man" reminded Christians of their special responsibility for anti-Semitism, and called upon them not to fail in resolute action against it. Responses from the Vatican and from the Lutheran World Federation were equally strong, and have been followed by declarations from numerous church bodies and leaders worldwide. The real interest focused on the Orthodox Churches which, though members of the World Council, have not previously evinced much interest in dialogue, they are dominant in many of the countries in which incidents have occurred; it was therefore reassuring that Archbishop Kirill, of the Russian Orthodox Church, unambiguously condemned, with the authority of January 30–31, 1990, meeting of his episcopal synod, "any teaching of hatred, violence or national exclusivity," though it remains to be seen to what extent this condemnation will influence the behavior of Russian Christians.

The problem is that though the Churches do indeed condemn anti-Semitism they will continue to foster it unintentionally unless they can achieve the reinterpretation of basic Christian teachings in the light of the new theology, thus abandoning "replacement theology" and the "teaching of contempt." One should not underestimate the magnitude of such a task especially in countries where clergy training is minimal and old habits of thought persistent.

Latin America and the Theology of Liberation. Whereas for Europeans and North Americans the Holocaust casts its shadow over contemporary theology, the burning issue in South American and much third world theology has been liberation from the centuries of bondage and oppression, even genocide, imposed by European Christian colonists, and from the grinding poverty and deprivation suffered by the masses still today. The biblical Exodus is the great paradigm for the theology of liberation, though too few liberation theologians have perceived its relevance to the story of the modern Jewish liberation from the bondage of European oppression and Nazism to the freedom of independent statehood in Israel. Still, the return through Exodus to the "Jewish Old Testament," and the emphasis of the new theology on "praxis" rather than theory, have combined with some influx of the new Catholic outlook on Jews and Judaism to enable serious Jewish-Christian dialogue to get under way.

The first Pan-American Conference on Catholic-Jewish Relations, jointly arranged by the American Jewish committee and the National Conference of Brazilian Bishops, São Paulo, Brazil, took place on November 3–5, 1985. The most recent major gathering was the November 1990 25th anniversary commemoration of *Nostra Aetate*, attended by Archbishop Cassidy, who agreed to transmit back to Rome a number of resolutions of the Brazilian National Commission on Catholic-Jewish Religious Dialogue, including a protest against the proposed canonization of Queen Isabella, and a denunciation of anti-Zionism as a current form of anti-Semitism.

Obstacles and Irritants. Incidents apart, there are two themes which constantly give rise to friction within the dialogue.

The first of these is the Christian commitment to evangelization. While the Roman Catholic Church and many other major Churches no longer target Jews, only a few Christians, whether because of the Holocaust or for more fundamental theological reasons, would demand the positive exclusion of Jews from evangelization. All nowadays reject coercive or deceitful evangelization, though definitions differ. However, a recent feature of Christian life has been the rise of small, independent evangelical sects who are beyond the control of the major Churches; some such groups do target Jews. Moreover, the 1990s have been declared a "decade of evangelism," and a fine balance will have to be struck between mission and dialogue. The 1980s saw a strong growth of Jewish anti-missionary groups, and it is difficult for mainstream Jews and Christians engaged in serious dialogue to remain indifferent to the snapping at their heels on both sides.

The second major topic of friction is Israel, and this has both a political and a theological dimension. On the political level, both Jews and many Catholics found it hard during the period under review to accept the failure of the Holy See to establish normal diplomatic relations with the State of Israel. Of course, only the Roman church had this problem, as other churches do not claim to be sovereign territories. What is often overlooked is the extent to which documents from the non-Roman Churches affirm the existence of Israel. For instance, the World Council of Churches, in the Statement on the Middle East it adopted at its Sixth Assembly in Vancouver in 1983 and upheld subsequently, unambiguously affirmed "the right of all states, including Israel and Arab states, to live in peace with secure and recognized boundaries," reflecting the terminology of United Nations Security Council Resolution 242. The Lambeth Conference Resolutions of 1988 were similarly forthright, though few churches have gone as far as the Hungarian Reformed Church which declared, in the document cited above, "We express our joy over the fact that our country established diplomatic relations with Israel."

Theological views differ. Conservative Evangelicals are often the strongest supporters of Israel, because they see the state as the fulfillment of prophecy, heralding the second coming of Jesus—and the conversion of any remaining Jews! The Roman Catholic Church made clear in the 1985 Notes that, while it understands the Jewish religious attachment to the Land, the Church itself related to the State of Israel solely on the basis of international law; Church spokesmen strongly denied that there was any theological impediment to full diplomatic relations. Others steer a middle course, seeing the restoration of the Jews to Israel as a significant divine act, but without commitment to literal interpretation of prophecy.

There are several irritants which one hopes will prove temporary rather than permanent sources of friction within the dialogue. The Auschwitz convent has been one of them, and the beatifications of Edith Stein and Maximilian Kolbe another. Requests for the beatification of Queen Isabella in 1992 have been formulated in certain Spanish Catholic circles. Several actions of the pope—his reception of Yasser Arafat and of Kurt Waldheim, some unfortunate Easter sermons—have been irksome. In the non-Catholic world Passion Plays, such as that at Oberammergau (greatly improved in 1990), have strained the Jewish-Christian relationship.

Conclusion. The 1980s saw a proliferation of writing in Jewish-Christian relations. Scholarly and deeply sensitive works appeared by Protestant scholars such as Hans-Joachim Krauss, Roy Eckardt, and Paul van Buren, and Catholics such as Franz Mussner, John Pawlikowski, and Eberhard Bethge. Churches of many denominations and in many countries produced statements and guidelines. Serious consideration has been given to the reinterpretation of fundamental Christian beliefs in the light of the new understanding of Jews and Judaism.

The Jewish-Christian dialogue reached a stage of maturity. It is not without problems and is not yet firmly rooted in either of the religious communities involved. The main task, however, remains that of education, of ensuring that the new insights of the Churches and their theologians actually become part of normal Christian teaching and preaching, not only in the better educated West, but amongst Christians in all lands.

Bibliography: *Christian-Jewish Relations*, a quarterly published by the Institute of Jewish Affairs, London, in conjunction with the World Jewish Congress, published not only academic articles on the important themes, but the major documents and reports on events, including those in Israel. It ceased to appear in 1993. *Immanuel*, published by the Ecumenical Research Fraternity in Jerusalem, carries high caliber theological and historical articles, many of them translations of Hebrew articles. Other journals carrying documentary and original material are the SIDIC newsletter published in Rome by the Sisters of Sion and *El Olivo*, published in Madrid by the Centro de Estudios Judeo-Cristianos.

The last years of the 1980s saw a proliferation of books summing up the dialogue so far. In 1988 the International Catholic-Jewish Liaison Committee published its account of "Fifteen Years of Catholic-Jewish Dialogue 1970–1985" through the official Vatican publishers. In the same year the World Council of Churches published its documents and those of member churches, with an illuminating commentary by Allan Brockway and others, and an authoritative Jewish account of the dialogue, *Jewish-Christian Relations since the Second World War*, by Geoffrey Wigoder also appeared in 1988. David Novak's *Jewish-Christian Dialogue: a Jewish Justification* was published in 1989. One of the most sensitive and balanced Christian accounts is Marcus Braybrooke's *Time to Meet: Towards a Deeper Relationship between Jews and Christians* (1990).

Of the documentary collections the most comprehensive (though there are lacunae) is Rolf Rendtorff and Hans Hermann Henrix's *Die Kirchen und das Judentum: Dokumente von 1945–1985*. For English readers, the two volumes of *Stepping Stones* edited by Helga Croner (1977 and 1985) are the most useful. [NO.SO.]

JEWISH DAILY FORWARD (Forverts) (see **10**:49). Since 1990, it has published the weekly *Forward* in English as well as the Yiddish-English *Forverts*.

JONG, ERICA (1942–), U.S. novelist and poet. Born Erica Mann in New York, where she was educated and began to write poetry, she lived in Heidelberg, Germany, from 1966 to 1969, where her husband (from whom she was later divorced) was serving in the U.S. Army. Her experiences there were featured in the autobiographical novel *Fear of Flying* (1973). In Germany she continued to write poetry which

Erica Jong (Bar-David, T.A.)

began to evolve a feminist outlook. In 1971, she published her first collection of poetry, *Fruits and Vegetables*, much of which explored the position of women as artists. Her second volume of poetry, *Half-Lives* (1973), continued to explore feminist and psychological issues.

The publication of *Fear of Flying* established her popularity as a novelist. The novel, which describes the search for self-identity and analyses the upbringing, neuroses, and sexuality of its heroine, Isadora Wing, mirrored much of Jong's own intellectual background and Jewish upbringing. It includes a chapter describing her life in Germany and its effect on her Jewish consciousness. The novel's sexual frankness sparked much controversy.

In 1977, she published her second novel, *How to Save Your Own Life*, a sequel to *Fear of Flying* which explored Isadora Wing's experiences with fame, divorce, and new relationships. This was followed in 1980 by *Fanny: Being the True History of the Adventures of Fanny Hackabout-Jones*, a contemporary "18th-century novel" describing the adventures of a female Tom Jones.

Jong has also published volumes of poetry, *Loveroot* (1975) and *At the Edges of the Body* (1979). [SU.STR.]

JOSIPOVICI, GABRIEL (1940–), English novelist, playwright, and literary critic. Born in Nice, France, Josipovici was educated at Victoria College, Cairo, and at Oxford University. From 1963 he taught at the University of Sussex where he became a professor of English Literature. In 1981 he was made the Northcliffe Lecturer at University College, London. His first novel, *The Inventory*, was published in 1968 and his outstanding work of literary criticism, *The World and the Book: A Study of Modern Fiction*, appeared in 1971. He also wrote *The Lessons of Modernism and Other Essays* (1977) and edited *The Modern English Novel: The Reader, The Writer, and the Work* (1976). As well as his acclaimed literary criticism, Josipovici published *Four Stories* (1977), a collection of short stories, and ten stage and radio plays. *Mobius the Stripper: Stories and Short Plays* (1974) contains an important selection of this work.

Josipovici is a consciously postmodernist writer who has rejected the tradition of 19th-century realism. Instead, his literary tradition is made up of Marcel *Proust, Franz *Kafka, Rainer Maria Rilke, T. S. Eliot and, more recently, Samuel Beckett, Alaine Robbe-Grillet, Jorge Luis *Borges and George Perec (q.v.). All of these writers transcend a too easy identification with a national culture. Their "rootlessly self-contained" art, in the words of one critic, corresponds to Josipovici's own abstract, vulnerable, inconclusive short novels. Much of his fiction, such as *The Inventory*, *Words* (1971), and *Conversations in Another Room* (1984), juxtaposes the lightness and musicality of the author's dialogue with a series of haunting, unanswered questions. *Migrations*, on the other hand, lacks a narrative thread as it moves between nameless, displaced individuals who are related only by the author's recurring images.

Josipovici's disdain for fiction which is based on large historical questions means that his novels do not deal explicitly with Jewish themes. The Jewish writers which interest him the most are, therefore, those that write outside of a defined Jewish tradition—such as Saul *Bellow, Bernard *Malamud, and, of course, Kafka and Proust — and not such "insiders," in Josipovici's terms, as Isaac Bashevis *Singer and S. Y. *Agnon. It was only after the Six-Day War that Josipovici began to explore his Jewishness with considerable interest. He has written the introduction to the English edition of Aharon *Appelfeld's *The Retreat* (1985) and he is a regular contributor to *European Judaism* and *The Jewish Quarterly*.

Bibliography: J. Vinson (ed.), *Contemporary Novelists*, (1982) 356–357; *The Jewish Quarterly*, 32 (1985). [B.C.]

K

KAHLER, ERICH (1885–1970), historian and philosopher. Born in Prague, raised in Vienna, educated at the universities of Berlin, Munich, Heidelberg and Vienna, he settled in Munich after obtaining his doctorate in Vienna (1908) with his dissertation *Recht und Moral* (published 1911). His study, *Das Geschlecht Hapsburg* (1919) was followed by *Der Beruf der Wissenschaft* (1920), a polemic directed against Max Weber's *Wissenschaft als Beruf*. A publisher to whom he submitted the manuscript of his major work, *Der deutsche Charakter in der Geschichte Europas*, denounced him to the Nazis in 1933, but he had already escaped to Vienna, afterwards to Czechoslovakia, and then to Switzerland, where the book appeared in 1937 and aroused much attention. In 1938 he found a permanent refuge in Princeton. His public lectures and seminars at American universities, primarily at Cornell from 1947 to 1955, resulted in seven scholarly volumes. A book of tributes to him by John Berryman, G.A. Borgese, Hermann Broch, Albert Einstein, Rudolf Kassner, Thomas Mann, Wolfgang Pauli, and others appeared in 1951.

Kahler's approach to history was characterized by Hermann Broch as moral anthropology. This approach was apparent in his study of the Hapsburgs which considered the royal family as an historical organism with common psychological traits throughout six centuries. In his sociological and historical study *Israel unter den Völkern* (1936) he found a common Jewish type persisting down the millennia from its tribal origin until the twentieth century. In *Der deutsche Charakter in der Geschichte Europas*, he presented the Germans as a specific historic organism, its evolution and its impact upon Europe. Its ideas continued to occupy Kahler's thinking and formed the basis for *The Germans* published in 1974. In it, the material was presented not topically, as in the earlier volume, but rather chronologically, from the confrontation of the German tribes with the Roman Empire until the Nazi assumption of power and the catastrophe of World War II.

Kahler's most important work, *Man the Measure* (1943), was subtitled *A New Approach to History*. It studied the human species as an organism whose historical changes were grafted on to an enduring psychic structure. It emphasized the evolution and transformation of human consciousness.

The Tower and the Abyss (1957) may be regarded as a sequel to *Man the Measure*. As an inquiry into the transformation of the individual, it stressed the evolutionary forces which converged to bring about the disruption, disintegration, and fragmentation of the contemporary individual personality from without and from within. Kahler sees the present as a state of transition from an individual form of existence to a supra-individual form, whose character is still obscure. He concludes with his own vision of a possible Utopia, which will permit the reintegration of fragmented Man in free communities.

Kahler's essays were collected in the German volume *Die Verantwortung des Geistes* (1952) and in the English volumes *Out of the Labyrinth* (1947), *The Disintegration of Form in the Arts* (1968), and *The Inward Turn of the Narrative* (1973).

Bibliography: S. Liptzin, *Germany's Stepchildren* (1944), 275–81.

[S.L.]

KAHN, JEAN (1929–), French Jewish leader. Kahn was born in Strasbourg where he attended school and the university law school. He received his doctorate in law for a thesis on "Marriage in Jewish and Roman Law." Kahn qualified as a lawyer in 1953 but gave up his practice to enter the family textile business. He was early involved in communal affairs

Jean Kahn (Courtesy CRIF, Paris)

and from 1969 to 1990 was president of the Strasbourg Jewish Community. Active in the World Jewish Congress from 1979, he became president of its European Commission in 1979 and president of the European Jewish Congress in 1991. In 1983, Kahn was elected vice-president of CRIF (the French Jewish Representative Council) and in 1989, by a 75% vote, he became its president. He has been involved in various major problems facing the European Jewish community, especially in view of the recrudescence of anti-Semitism. He was active in the efforts to transfer the Carmelite convent from Auschwitz, in the protests against the desecration of Jewish graves in the Carpentras cemetery, and in the struggle against France's National Front Party, including a crucial intervention in having the parliamentary immunity of its leader, Jean-Marie le Pen, lifted so he could face charges before the European Parliament. In 1991 he became president of the Bas-Rhin Consistoire. He has been awarded the Legion of Honor and other honors. [G.KO.]

KAMPELMAN, MAX M. (1920–), U.S. lawyer and diplomat. Born in New York, Kampelman received his undergraduate and legal education at New York University, and his M.A. and Ph.D. in political science at the University of Minnesota. He taught political science at the University of Minnesota (1946–48), and at Bennington College (1948–50).

Max Kampelman

He came under the influence of Senator Hubert H. Humphrey and served as his legislative counsel (1949–1955). He then joined the law firm of Fried, Frank, Harris, Shriver and Kampelman, in Washington, D.C. He served as director and as chairman of the executive committee of the District of Columbia National Bank (1962–66). For three years (1967–70), he was moderator of the popular television program, "Washington Week in Review."

Kampelman has had an active career as a major American diplomat, serving in several very important and delicate negotiations. He has served as senior adviser to the U.S. delegation to the United Nations. From 1980 to 1983, by appointment of President Carter and then of President Reagan, he was ambassador and head of the U.S. delegation to the Conference on Security and Cooperation in Europe (under the Final Act signed in Helsinki in 1975). Then he was appointed by President Ronald Reagan as ambassador and head of the Delegation on Negotiations on Nuclear and Space Arms.

Kampelman has a long and distinguished record of public and philanthropic service. By appointment of the president of the United States, he was chairman of the board of trustees of the Woodrow Wilson International Center for Scholars (1979–81), and continued as a member of the board of trustees. He was chairman of Freedom House (1983–85). He has served on the board of directors of Georgetown University, on the board of advisers of the Kennedy Institute of Ethics, on the board of trustees of the Law Center Foundation of New York University, on the board of trustees of the U.S. Council for International Business, as vice-president of the Helen Dwight Reid Educational Foundation, vice-chairman of the Coalition for a Democratic Majority, a member of the executive committee of the Committee on the Present Danger, a member of the board of directors of the Atlantic Council of the United States, and other organizations and institutions.

Kampelman has been actively identified with many Jewish and Israeli interests. He has served as honorary vice-chairman of the B'nai B'rith Anti-Defamation League; as a member of the board of governors of Tel Aviv University and of Haifa University; as chairman of the National Advisory Committee of the American Jewish Committee; as a member of the board of directors of HIAS; as vice-president of the Jewish Publication Society, on the board of trustees of the America-Israel Cultural Foundation and of the American Friends of the Israel Conservatory of Music, and on the board of trustees of the American Histadrut Cultural Exchange Institute.

Kampelman is the author of many articles and pamphlets on public affairs, American foreign policy, and on Jewish subjects. [M.R.K.]

KANETI, SELIM (1934–1992), Turkish lawyer and communal leader. Kaneti graduated from Istanbul University Law Faculty in 1956 and was appointed an assistant professor, becoming a full professor of civil law in 1972. From 1984 he was chairman of the University's Department of Public Finance and Economic Law. He was also vice-president of the university's Comparative Law Institute. From 1957 he was a member of the Istanbul Bar and wrote many works on civil law and tax law.

An active member of the Jewish community, he served on the council of the Turkish chief rabbinate from 1972, and as its chairman in 1991–92. [ED.]

KANIEVSKY, JACOB ISRAEL ("the Steipler"; 1899–1985), rabbi. Kanievsky was born in Hornistopol from which his appelation, "the Steipler," was derived. From an early age he studied at the yeshivah of Gomel, which was directed by the "elder of Novogrudok," Joseph Yozel Hurwitz. Kanievsky soon became known as the *illui* ("genius") from Stopol. At the end of his teens he was pressed into service in the Russian army.

In 1925 his first book, *Sha'arei Tevunah*, was published. After the Ḥazon Ish, Rabbi Avraham Yeshayahu *Karelitz, read the work, he offered his sister Miriam in marriage to Rabbi Kanievsky and the two were married. Immigrating to Palestine in 1934 — about a year and a half after his brother-in-law had settled in Bene-Berak — Rabbi Kanievsky was appointed the head of Bet Yosef-Novohardok yeshivah in Bene-Berak. Rabbi Karelitz was once asked was there any man in his generation for whom one could recite the blessing "blessed is He for having shared His wisdom with His reverers," and the reply of the Ḥazon Ish was, "the Steipler."

Kanievsky was the author of nearly 30 books and devoted much time to writing, teaching, and dealing with the vast public which constantly streamed to his home seeking spiritual guidance. Religious and non-religious alike sought his counsel, and Jews from many communities looked to him for guidance. Some 200,000 people from all over Israel attended his funeral. [ED.]

KANOVICH, GRIGORY (pseudonym of **Yakov Semenovich**; 1929–), Soviet prose writer, poet, and dramatist. Kanovich, who writes in Russian and Lithuanian, was born in the town of Ionava near Kaunas or, according to another source, in Kaunas itself, into the family of an observant Jewish tailor. In 1953 he graduated from Vilnius University. His first writings were published in 1949. He has written collections of poetry in Russian: *Debroye utro* ("Good Morning," 1955) and *Vesenniy grom* ("Spring Thunder," 1960); of literary epigrams and parodies in Lithuanian ("*With a Joyful Eye*," 1964; *Naked Ones on Olympus*, 1981), 30 plays and film scenarios (some co-authored) on contemporary themes, and has translated literary prose from Lithuanian into Russian.

Kanovich's Russian prose works are almost all devoted to the life of Lithuanian Jewry. The theme of the moral quest of a Jewish boy from a Lithuanian shtetl in his long stories "Ya smotryu na zvezdy" ("I Gaze at the Stars," 1959) and "Lichnaya zhizn'" ("Private Life," 1967) is developed in his trilogy *Svechi na vetru* ("Candles in the Wind") consisting of the novels: *Ptitsy nad kladbishchem* ("Birds over the Cemetery," 1974), *Blagoslovi i list'ya i ogon'* ("Bless Both the Leaves and the Fire," 1977), *Kolybel'naya snezhnoy babe* ("Lullaby for a Snowman," 1979, translated into Hebrew in 1983). The trilogy, the action of which takes place between 1937 and 1943, recreates the traditional world and spirituality of East European Jewry. The events, even those on the most massive scale such as the Holocaust, are presented through the eyes of a youth and, as he develops, of a young man; in its structure the novel in places resembles a lyrical diary. An epic, philosophic element predominates in Kanovich's cycle of novels devoted to Jewish shtetl life of the end of the 19th and early 20th centuries — *Slëzy i molitvy durakov* ("Tears and Prayers of Fools," 1983); *I net rabam raya* ("There's No Heaven for Slaves," 1985), *Kozlenok za dva grosha* ("A Kid for Two Pennies"). The ethnic character of the novels (the heroes' way of thinking, reminiscent of Talmudic dialectics, and their way of speaking) and the problems they raise (the aspiration of the Jewish masses for national self-preservation, the feeling of responsibility for the ethical and ethnic essence of the people, the tendency of part of the Jewish intelligentsia to reject its identity for the sake of career, and assimilation) brought these works popularity among Soviet Jews. Kanovich visited Israel in 1980 and settled there in 1993. [S.J.E.R.]

KARAITES (see **10**:762). CONTEMPORARY KARAITE LIFE. From the 1970s, the Karaite community in Israel has grown in numbers and has seen the consolidation of its institutions. The major force behind this Karaite strengthening has been Chief Rabbi Haim Hallevi of Ashdod. For many years, Hallevi was acting chief rabbi of the Israeli Karaites, becoming chief rabbi in title, as well as in fact, with the death of the previous chief rabbi, David ben Moses Yerushalmi, in 1987. (Yerushalmi became chief rabbi in 1976, having succeeded the late Shelomo ben Shabbetai Nono.) Hallevi has overseen the Karaite institutions in Israel, including the national religious council, the Karaite religious court, and eleven synagogues (two in Ramleh, and one each in Acre, Ashdod, Bat Yam, Beersheba, Jerusalem, Kiryat Gat, Maẓli'aḥ, Ofakim, and Rannen). In addition to the chief rabbi, Israel's Karaites are served by 14 other rabbis and a larger number of *ḥazzanim*. Some of the rabbis function also as ritual slaughterers and circumcisers. According to Karaite sources, there are now approximately 20,000–25,000 Karaites living in Israel.

Israeli Karaites, the majority of whom are of Egyptian origin, have had difficulty maintaining their religious customs and their independent identity since immigrating to Israel, mostly in the 1950s. There are two basic problems. On the one hand, they have encountered many of the same phenomena of secularization as have confronted other traditional Jewish groups from Islamic countries. On the other hand, there are strong forces of assimilation into the general Rabbanite Jewish community. For instance, since the Karaite holidays do not always coincide with those of most Israeli Jews, demands of work, army, and school make it difficult for many Karaites to continue their own customs. While Ḥanukkah is not considered a religious holiday by Karaites, it is often observed anyway as an Israeli national

Interior view of the only intact Karaite synagogue in Turkey, Hasköy (Istanbul) (Photo Eli Cittone, Istanbul)

holiday. Though Karaism has its own laws of ritual slaughter, many Karaites are satisfied with the meat produced under Rabbanite supervision which is more easily available. Some Karaites try to avoid any possibility of stigmatization by severing their ties with the Karaite community completely.

The Karaite leadership in Israel has tried to maintain the loyalty of their faithful by promoting various religious, cultural, and educational activities. Children participate in after school classes (there are no independent Karaite public schools) and summer camps. It is still too early to determine how successful these measures will be. Some of the questions of Karaite assimilation and acculturation have bee investigated by Emanuela Trevisan Semi, especially in her *Gli ebrei caraiti tra etnia e religione*, 1984 (which also deals with non-Israeli Karaites), and by Sumi E. Colligan in her dissertation, *Religion, Nationalism, and Ethnicity in Israel: The Case of the Karaite Jews*, 1980.

Intermarriage between Karaites and Rabbanites, frowned upon by both groups, is generally allowed by the official (Rabbanite) rabbinate if the Karaite member of the couple is willing formally to accept Rabbanism. Not all Rabbanite rabbis, however, are prepared to accept such intermarriages because of the problems of *mamzerut* (see **mamzer*). Karaites maintain de facto, but not de jure, authority over intra-Karaite marriage and uncontested divorce. These issues are discussed by Michael Corinaldi in his *The Personal Status of the Karaites in Israel*, 1984.

In 1983, the Karaite Jews of America was incorporated as a religious organization. Karaites claim that there are at least 1,200 and perhaps as many as 10,000 Karaite Jews of Egyptian origin in the United States, most of whom live in the San Francisco Bay Area of California. The Karaites in that region conduct services, either in private homes or monthly at a Conservative synagogue in Foster City. Other small concentrations of American Karaites are found in the New York and Chicago areas. There appears to be strong evidence of Americanization of this community.

The Karaites of Turkey are grouped particularly in Istanbul, but their deep religious attachment has led many to Israel in order to find Karaite mates to marry. Those who marry non-Karaite Jews or partners from other communities are automatically segregated from the community and constitute a loss for the Istanbul community which numbers 50–60 families.

In recent years, many young Karaites have studied medicine, while others have tended towards craftsmanship such as jewelry. In some cases the jewelry artisanship is handed down from father to son and practiced in the Covered Bazaar in Istanbul. One Covered Bazaar street is called "The Street of the Karaites." Similarly, an important business center of Istanbul has retained its name — "Karaköy."

Following the destruction by fire of the great Karaite Synagogue, the Karaites are using the Hasköy Karaite Synagogue. This is the last available and usable Karaite sanctuary. Because their dwellings (Moda, Şişli, Nişantaşl, Gayrettepe, etc.) are far away from the synagogue, Karaites are not able to attend as frequently as previously. The synagogue, led by Yusuf Sadik, never witnesses three generations attending together. Only during rare religious holidays do a few Karaites, usually elderly, come to pray. Nevertheless, the Karaites continue to survive and strive to maintain their numbers.

There are still Karaite communities in Cairo (a handful of mostly older people who are looking after the Karaite synagogue and precious manuscripts), Poland (perhaps 200 individuals), and Russia. The last group, which for centuries made up the bulk of the world's Karaites, has dwindled in numbers and does not maintain contact with the Karaites in Israel. In 1970, 4,571 Karaites were reported to be in Russia.

The Israeli Karaite community has been active in editing previously unpublished Karaite works or reissuing unavailable classics. These works include Aaron ben Elijah's *Keter Torah* and *Gan Eden* (both reissued, 1972), Isaac Troki's *Ḥizzuk Emunah* (1975), Caleb Afendopolo's *Patshegen Ketav ha-Dat* (1977), Simḥah Isaac Luẓki's *Ṭurei Zahav im Nekudat ha-Kesef* (1978), and Shelomo Afida Ha-Kohen's *Yeri'ot Shelomo* (1986). While not produced critically, these editions are useful for research into Karaism.

A major Karaite project is the multi-volume work on Karaite history and life by Rabbi Yosef Algamil. The first two volumes discuss in general the history of Karaism and Karaites, and the third volume is devoted to the Karaite community of Egypt. While characterized by a partisan Karaite interpretation of Karaite origins and history, these books contain much material about Karaism unavailable elsewhere. The personal accounts of Karaite communities and the many illustrations are especially important. Another recent one-sided exposition of Karaism is by the Paris-based Polish Karaite Simon Szyszman, *Le Karaisme*, 1980. Szyszman has also begun a journal entitled *Bulletin d'Études Karaïtes*.

Scholarship on Karaism and the Karaites. Leon *Nemoy continued to be the doyen of Karaite scholarship, still publishing on the subject almost 60 years after his first article on Kirkisani. His many publications of the last 20 years, ranging from early Karaism (and Kirkisani studies) to contemporary Karaism, have contributed greatly to Karaite studies. In honor of Nemoy's eightieth birthday, two *Festschriften* were published (*Studies in Judaica, Karaitica, and Islamica*, 1983, and *Jewish Quarterly Review* 73:2, October 1982), both with articles about many aspects of Karaism.

Karaite studies were greatly impoverished by the passing of Georges *Vajda in 1981. In addition to his many publications in all fields of Jewish and Islamic thought, Vajda took special interest in early Karaite philosophy, law, and exegesis. Two of his books are mentioned below.

The one question of Karaite studies which continues to intrigue scholars more than any other is the issue of Karaite origins and the possible relation between medieval sectarianism and Jewish groups of the Second Temple period. The issue, simply put, is whether Karaism was founded in the eighth century by *Anan ben David, or whether Anan merely reorganized and consolidated non-Rabbinic groups which had existed for hundreds of years. The discovery 40 years ago of the *Dead Sea Scrolls, with certain obvious parallels to Karaite literature, occasioned a flurry of research comparing the ancient scrolls with medieval writings. While more and more parallels have been adduced between apocryphal and Qumranian literature, on the one hand, and Karaism, on the other hand, there is yet not decisive proof that an organic connection can be shown between Second Temple groups and Karaites. While new theories of Karaites origins continue to be propounded, and old theories are revived, there have, unfortunately, been no more new discoveries which could decide this difficult question. Most scholars, however, no longer accept the simplistic Rabbanite view of Karaism as a schismatic heresy begun by a single disgruntled individual, Anan. Some of the scholars who have addressed themselves recently to these issues are Haggai Ben-Shammai, Martin A. Cohen, Yoram Erder, and Moshe Gil (who has also published *The Tustaris, Family and Sect*, 1981, about a sub-group of Karaites).

Research in Karaite exegesis has revolved mainly around the works of *Salmon ben Jeroham and *Japheth ben Ali Ha-Levi. Georges Vajda wrote extensively about these commentators, especially in his *Deux commentaires karaïtes sur l'Ecclésiaste*, 1971. Uriel Simon, *Four Approaches to the Book of Psalms*, 1982, bases his discussion of the Karaite approach upon the opinions of Salmon and Japheth. Haggai Ben-Shammai presents Japheth's (and Kirkisani's) philosophy in his dissertation, *The Doctrines of Religious Thought of Abû Yûsuf Yaʿqûb al-Qirqisânî and Yefet ben ʿElī*, 1977. Moshe Sokolow's dissertation, *The Commentary of Yefet ben Ali on Deuteronomy XXXII*, 1974, provides an Arabic edition and Hebrew translation of part of Japheth's Torah commentary, and subsequent articles have dealt with other aspects of Karaite biblical exegesis in Arabic.

The most significant recent contribution to the study of Karaite philosophy has been the posthumous appearance of Georges Vajda's edition of Joseph al-*Baṣīr's *Kitāb al-Muḥtawī* (edited by David R. Blumenthal). The book includes an edition of the original Arabic text and French translations or paraphrases, accompanied by extensive commentaries showing al-Baṣīr's dependence on contemporary Muslim Kalām, especially the works of ʿAbd al-Jabbār. Haggai ben-Shammai's publications concerning early Karaite authors and their philosophies (*Daniel ben Moses al-Qūmisī, Kirkisani, Japheth ben Ali, *Jeshua ben Judah) have also shown the Kalamic milieu of these Karaite thinkers. Daniel J. Lasker's studies of late Karaite philosophy (Judah *Hadassi, *Aaron ben Elijah, Elijah *Bashyazi) have challenged the widely held assumption that Karaites invariably remained loyal to the early Karaite Kalamic thought. In fact, Aaron ben Elijah was greatly influenced by Aristotelianism, and Bashyazi was a follower of Maimonides. Mention should also be made of Sarah Stroumsa's dissertation edition of David *Al-Mukammis' *ʿIshrūn Maqāla*, 1983, though it is unclear if the latter was indeed a Karaite.

Studies in Karaite philology and linguistics were pursued by the late Nehemia Allony, who concentrated on Arabic writings, and by Paul Wexler, Wolf Moskovich, and Boris Tukan who have examined the Tataric language of Eastern European Karaites.

Karaite ethnomusicology has been investigated extensively by Jehoash Hirshberg, who has compared the changes that have taken place in Egyptian Karaite musical traditions in Israel and in the United States. Rachel Kollender has specialized in Karaite liturgical music. Both authors have noted the role music has played in preserving Karaite identity.

The fate of Karaites during the Holocaust has been discussed recently by Warren P. Green and by Shmuel Spector. All evidence seems to point to the conclusion that while individual groups of Karaites were murdered, generally the Nazis regarded European Karaites as a Tataric group similar to other Crimeans.

Other significant works are Bruno Chiesa and Wilfrid Lockwood's *Yaʿqub al-Qirqisani on Jewish Sects and Christianity*; Baruch Ehrlich's dissertation, "Laws of Sabbath in Yehudah Hadassi's *Eshkol Hak-Kofer*," 1974; and Philip E. Miller's dissertation "At the Twilight of Byzantine Karaism: The Anachronism of Judah Gibbor," 1984.

Other scholars who have been engaged in Karaite research include the late Alexander Scheiber, and Naphtali Wieder, Giuliano Tamami, William Brinner, and Jonathan Shunari.

Future Karaite studies will probably turn toward a greater appreciation of the multifaceted nature of Karaite cultural achievements, overturning the generally held notion that after its initial founding and the Golden Age of the tenth and eleventh centuries, Karaism became a conservative and static phenomenon. No doubt much research will center around the Firkovitch collection of manuscripts found in Leningrad. These works are now slowly becoming available to Western scholars for the first time in many years. A major desideratum of Karaite studies is the scientific edition of Karaite texts, many of which remain either in manuscript or in inferior printed editions. [D.J.L./EL.C.]

KASPAROV GARY (1963–). Soviet chess master. Kasparov, whose father was Jewish and whose mother was an Armenian, was born in Baku. He was taught the basic rules of chess by his father, Kim, an engineer who was killed in an accident when Kasparov was seven years of age. As his career in chess developed, he adopted his mother's maiden name — apparently at the behest of the Soviet authorities. After his exceptionally great talent for chess was discovered he was taught intensively by the former world champion Mikhail *Botvinnik who clearly understood the great potential which Kasparov had in the field of chess. His career was meteoric: in 1980 he earned the title of grand master and won the World Junior Chess Championship; in 1981 he became chess champion of the Soviet Union. His path to the world championship was paved by his victory in the Moscow interdistrict competition. He then won matches against the grandmasters Alexander Blaiavsky and Viktor Korchnoi as well as defeating former world champion Vasili Smislov. The height of his achievement came after three dramatic duels against his immediate predecessor as holder of the world title, the Russian Anatoly Karpov. The first duel was called to a halt at the end of 1984 after 48 games because of the physical and mental fatigue of Karpov. Kasparov did not refrain from accusing FIDE (the World Chess Federation) and the Russian chess establishment of trying to aid his opponent. In the second battle, which was limited to 24 games and which ended in November 1985, Kasparov was the victor, the result being 13:11. He thus became the youngest person ever to hold the title of world champion. In the rematch which took place in London and Leningrad in 1986 Kasparov retained the title of world champion by a score of 12.5:11.5. As world champion he also played against — and defeated — some of the greatest players in the West, including among them Olaf Anderson of Sweden, Jan Timmam of the Netherlands, and Anthony Miles of Great Britain.

Kasparov's style of playing is deep, original, and devious. He tends to make bold moves and take chances in order to assume the offensive role. Kasparov puts great weight on the psychological aspects of the game and particularly on the ability to rebound after losses. He applied this in the 1986 match with Karpov after suffering three losses in a row. In 1990 he defeated Karpov again in the final meeting of a 24-game contest. He won 4, lost 3, and drew 17. In 1993 he retained his title, defeating Nigel Short of Britain.

Kasparov has written a number of books which deal with the theory of openings of games and an analysis of a selection of his games. [YI.SH.]

KAUFMAN, AVRAHAM YOSIFOVICH (1885–1971), Jewish public figure, head of Jewish communities in the Far East. He was born in Mglin, Chernigov province, into a family of Ḥasidim and, on his mother's side, he was great grandson of the founder of this movement, *Shneur Zalman of Lyady. In 1903 Kaufman graduated from high school in Perm where he became an enthusiastic Zionist. From 1904 to 1908, he studied medicine at Berne University in Switzerland where he was vice-chairman of the Union of Jewish Students. In 1908 Kaufman returned to Russia where, at the initiative of Jehiel *Tschlenow, he visited the cities of the Volga and Ural regions to disseminate Zionism. He was a delegate to three Zionist Congresses.

In 1912 Kaufman moved to *Harbin in Manchuria where he became involved in communal and Zionist activity. In late 1918 he was chosen vice-chairman of the National Council of Jews of Siberia and the Urals (the chairman was Moshe *Novomeysky). From 1919 to 1931 and 1933 to 1945 Kaufman was chairman of the Harbin Jewish community. During that period he was representative in China of the *Jewish National Fund and *Keren Hayesod, and official representative of the *World Zionist Organization and the *Jewish Agency, chairman of the Zionist Organization of China and head of almost all the cultural and social institutions of the Jews of Harbin. From 1921 to 1943 he was editor of the Russian language weekly *Yevreyskaya zhizn'* ("Jewish Life"). At the same time he worked as chief physician at the Jewish hospital in Harbin which he had founded. From 1937 he was chairman of the National Council of Jews of East Asia (i.e., the Far East).

Kaufman was a brilliant orator and publicist and was very knowledgeable about Judaism. He devoted considerable efforts to Jewish education. Recognized as the spiritual leader of Chinese Jewry, he staunchly opposed anti-Semitic tendencies among the Russian emigrés in Harbin which became particularly strong after the Japanese occupation of Manchuria in 1931. Due to his indefatigable energy and personal charm, he was able to establish direct contact with the Japanese authorities in Tokyo and succeeded in having countermanded the orders issued at Hitler's urging for concentrating the Jews of China under Japanese occupation into camps specially established for that purpose.

When the Soviet Army occupied Harbin in August 1945, Kaufman was among the many arrested and taken to the Soviet Union. He was accused of spying and Zionist activities and sentenced to 25 years imprisonment. He spent 11 years in confinement (three years in a solitary cell in Moscow and eight years in prison camp). He was released in 1956 with his criminal record erased and sent to Karaganda in Kazakhstan. During his five-year stay there he endeavored to reach Israel and succeeded in 1961. For the rest of his life he worked as a physician in an ambulatory care clinic in Ramat Gan. He also wrote his memoirs as well as a history of the Jewish communities in the Far East. He vividly described his life in the Soviet Union in his book *Lagerniy vrach* ("Camp Physician," Hebrew, 1971; Russian, Tel Aviv, 1973). [S.J.E.R.]

KAZAKHSTAN, independent republic of the CIS. In 1979 its Jewish population totaled 23,500 and in 1989, 19,900. In 1989, 220 Jews emigrated (118 from the capital Alma Ata), and in 1990, 2,109 Jews (1,254 from Alma Ata) immigrated to Israel. In 1991 the figures were 1,925 and 1,062).

The Jewish community is very assimilated. In 1987 47.2% of children born to Jewish mothers had non-Jewish fathers.

No Jews were elected to the Supreme Soviet of the Republic in 1990. Islamic fundamentalism is not widespread. Recent years have seen the appearance of a number of very successful Jewish businessmen. The Jewish Agency is now operating in Alma Ata. [MI.BE.]

KIRSZENSTEIN-SZEWINSKA, IRENA (1946–), Polish Olympic champion. Born in Leningrad, U.S.S.R., where her parents took refuge during World War II, Kirszenstein returned with her family to Poland, where she began her athletic career as a Warsaw schoolgirl. She became a world-ranked sprinter and long-jumper at the age of 17 and an Olympic champion a year later, in the 1964 Olympic Games held in Tokyo, Japan, when she won a gold medal as a member of Poland's 400-meter relay team, and silver medals in the 200-meter run and the long jump.

In 1968, in the Olympic Games at Mexico City, she won another gold medal in the 200-meter run and a bronze medal in the 100-meter dash. Her 200-meter time set a new world record.

In the Munich Olympics in 1972 she added another bronze medal in the 200-meter run; she won a gold medal in the 400-meter run in the 1976 Olympics in Montreal. The latter also set a new world record. In 1974 she became the first woman to run 400 meters in under 50 seconds and was proclaimed Woman Athlete of the Year.

In addition to her world records and Olympic successes Kirszenstein-Szewinska has won 10 medals in the European Track and Field championships. [J.H.S.]

KIS, DANILO (Daniel; 1935–1989), Yugoslav author and translator. Born in Subotica, Kis survived the Holocaust and after the war completed high school in Cetinje, Montenegro. He received his B.A. from the Faculty of Philosophy at the University of Belgrade. He was a free-lance writer, dramaturge in Belgrade Atelier 212 Theater, and lector for Serbo-Croat at various French universities. Kis wrote short stories, novels, essays, dramas, and television screenplays, translated poetry from French and Hungarian. He published *The Mansard, Psalm* 44 (1962), but made his name with the meditative novel *Garden, Ashes* (1965) in which the fascinating image of his Jewish father who was killed in Auschwitz in 1944 appears for the first time. He went on to publish *Early Griefs* (1969) and *Hourglass* (1969) for which he was awarded the 1972 Belgrade NIN magazine prize for the best novel in Yugoslavia.

A master of style, modern in expression, and an outstanding talent, Kis was attacked after his anti-Stalinist book *A Tomb for Boris Davidovich* (1976) by a group of Belgrade writers and journalists. His reply was the polemic treatise *The Anatomy Lesson* (1978). He lived in isolation in Paris, away from public life, but surrounded by friends. In Paris he wrote *The Encyclopedia of the Dead* (1983). In 1984 he was awarded the Ivo Andric Prize in Belgrade and in 1989 received the Bruno Schulz Prize in New York. He was a member of the Serbian Academy of Sciences and Arts and a Chevalier des arts et lettres (Paris, 1986). His works have been translated into English, French, German, Russian, Hungarian, Hebrew, and other languages. [E.WE.]

Beate and Serge Klarsfeld accepting the prize of Arts, Letters, and Science of French Jewry, for their action against Nazi War Criminals, by the Foundation of French Jewry, May 28, 1984 (Bar-David, Tel Aviv)

°**KLARSFELD, BEATE AUGUSTE** (née **Kunzel**; 1939–), anti-Nazi, pro-Israel activist. Beate Klarsfeld was born in Berlin to a Protestant family and began her working career as a secretary. In 1960 she went to Paris where in 1963 she married a Jewish lawyer, Serge Klarsfeld (q.v.), a Holocaust survivor.

Beate Klarsfeld began to take a deep interest in the Holocaust and into the efforts necessary to locate Nazi war criminals and bring them to justice. In 1967 the Klarsfelds authored a series of articles in the newspaper *Combat* in which they attacked Chancellor Kurt Kiesinger of Germany for his Nazi past. For this series Beate was dismissed by the French-German Youth Office.

In November 1968, at a Christian Democrat party rally, she went to the podium and slapped the chancellor, calling him, "Nazi criminal." For this act Mrs. Klarsfeld was sentenced to one year in prison. She successfully fought against the appointment of a former Nazi diplomat, Ernst Aschenbach, to the Commission of the European Economic Community as representative of the German Federal Republic and led a four-year campaign in which she succeeded in having the Bundestag ratify the Franco-German judicial convention of 1971, authorizing the trial in Germany of directors of the Nazi police system who had been active in France. Beate Klarsfeld devoted other efforts towards the bringing to justice of Kurt Lischka, one of the persons responsible for the deportation of the Jews of France; he was convicted in 1980 and sentenced to a long prison term.

Beate Klarsfeld carried her endeavors to South America where she worked undauntedly even in the face of dictatorships: in 1972 in Bolivia where she located Klaus Barbie, in 1977 in Argentina and Uruguay where she protested repressive measures and the use of torture, and in 1984 in Chile and 1985 in Paraguay. In 1986 she campaigned vociferously against Kurt Waldheim's candidacy for president of Austria because of his Nazi past. She was arrested in Warsaw in 1970 and in Prague in 1971 for protesting against anti-Semitism and repression.

Mrs. Klarsfeld has also held personal protests in Middle Eastern countries. She went to Damascus after the Six-Day War to obtain a list of the Israeli prisoners held by the Syrians and to protest the conditions of the Syrian Jews, and in 1974 was arrested in Rabat at the October summit meeting of the Arab countries for distributing tracts calling for peace between Israel and the Arab states. In early 1986 she spent a month in west Beirut, offering to substitute herself for the Lebanese Jewish hostages held by terrorists.

She and her husband have been the recipients of numerous prestigious awards in recognition of the importance of their activities. [ED.]

KLARSFELD, SERGE (1932–), lawyer, historian, and Nazi-hunter. Klarsfeld was born in Bucharest and moved with his family to France as a child. While he, his mother and sister remained in hiding in Nice, his father was arrested there in 1943 and deported to Auschwitz where he perished. Serge Klarsfeld has a varied academic background with a degree in history from the Sorbonne, a law degree from the Paris Faculty of Law, and a diploma from the Institute of Political Science in Paris. While a student he met his wife Beate (q.v.).

Klarsfeld has devoted himself to seeking out Nazi criminals who were successful in evading punishment and seeing that they be brought to justice. Working as a team, he and his wife have focused on Kurt Lischka, Klaus Barbie, and several others. He located Alois Brunner (q.v.) in Syria and traveled there to seek Brunner's extradition; in this instance, he was not successful.

The Klarsfelds were instrumental in locating Klaus Barbie in Bolivia in 1972 and continued their struggle to have him brought to trial in France for over ten years. At the 1987 trial, Serge was the first of many private prosecution lawyers testifying against Barbie who was ultimately sentenced to life imprisonment.

Serge Klarsfeld has published a number of works, including *Vichy–Auschwitz — The role of Vichy in the Final Solution to the Jewish Question in France* (1983); *Memorial to the Jews Deported from France, 1942–1944* (1978), which includes the names and vital statistics of the 75,721 Jews deported from France to extermination camps in Eastern Europe; and *The Holocaust and the Neo-Nazi Mythomania* (1978).

He protested the execution of Jewish community leaders in Teheran in 1979 by going there to intercede on behalf of those members of the community still in prison, and in February 1986 he went to Beirut to show his condemnation of the execution of Lebanese Jews who had been taken hostage.

Serge Klarsfeld was president of the Association of Sons and Daughters of the Jews Deported from France. [ED.]

KLEIN, THEODORE (Theo; 1920–), French lawyer and Jewish communal leader. Klein was born in Paris and completed his studies in law and political science there. A successful lawyer who has worked both in France and in Israel (a member of the Israel Lawyers' Association since 1970), he has also been extremely active in Jewish communal affairs.

Theo Klein
(Courtesy CRIF, Paris)

He was president of CRIF, the representative body of French Jewry, 1983–9 and president of the European Jewish Congress 1986–91. His term as leader of the French Jewish community coincided with an increase in the influence of that community during the tenure of President Mitterrand who is a personal friend of Klein. Klein is also close to the leaders of the French Socialist Party and the Israeli Labor Party. He took a leading role in the negotiations to remove the Carmelite convent from Auschwitz. He wrote *La guerre des civils* (1974). [GI.KO.]

KLUG, AARON (1926–), British chemist and Nobel laureate. Born in Lithuania, Klug was taken by his parents to South Africa at the age of three. As a youngster he was a member of the Habonim Zionist youth movement. In 1949, after attending the University of Witwatersrand and the University of Cape Town, he moved to Cambridge, England, where he obtained his doctorate from Trinity College of Cambridge University. He pursued his academic career at Birkbeck College of the University of London studying viruses, especially the tobacco mosaic virus, and in 1958 he became director of the Virus Structure Research Group there. In 1962 he returned to Cambridge to become a staff member of the Medical Research Council; he was appointed joint head of the division of structural studies in 1978.

Klug was awarded the Nobel Prize in Chemistry in 1982 for his contribution towards the advancement of science through his study of the three-dimensional structure of the combinations of nucleic acids and proteins. He developed techniques which benefited the study of crystalline material and led to crystallographic electron microscopy with which he has demonstrated that a combination of a series of electron micrographs taken at different angles can provide a three-dimensional image of particles, a method which is of use in studying proteins and viruses. [ED.]

KNUT, DOVID (pseudonym of **David Mironovich Fichman** 1900–1955). Russian poet, Knut was born in Kishinev into a merchant family and made his literary debut in the Kishinev press: in 1918 he edited the journal *Molodaya mysl'* ("Young Thought"). In 1920 he emigrated to Paris where he participated in circles of Russian-language poets, and organized the group of poets "Palata poetov" ("Palace of Poets"). He published in emigré journals and edited *Noviy dom* (1925–27), the Russian-language Jewish newspaper **Razsvet*, and other publications. In 1925 he published *Moikh tysyacheletiy* ("My Millennia") which included many poems infused with biblical motifs and allusions, and with consideration of the historical fate of the Jewish people. In subsequent collections, *Vtoraya kniga stikhov* ("Second Book of Verses," 1928); *Parizhskie nochi* ("Parisian Nights," 1932); *Nasushchnaya lyubov'* ("True Love," 1938) the predominant themes are love, loneliness, death, rejection of the city, the oppression of life, and unrealizability of hopes. Knut dedicated a cycle of poems to his visit to Palestine in the mid-1930s; this was called "Prarodina" ("Original Homeland," published in periodicals from 1938 to 1948 and partially included in *Izbrannye stikhi* ("Selected Poetry", 1949)). Initially Knut's poetry was close to that of the Acmeists. His outstanding talents as a publicist were demonstrated in his essays (*Al'bom puteshestvennika*; in *Zh. Russkiye Zapiski*, 1938).

In August 1940 Knut joined the Jewish resistance movement (L'Armée juive) in France whose activity he described in "Contribution to the History of the Jewish Resistance in France, 1940–1944" (in French, 1947). In 1949 he moved to Israel and settled in Tel Aviv, where he continued his literary activity and began to write poems in Hebrew.

Knut's wife ARIADNA (Sarah after her conversion to Judaism; 1905–44), daughter of the composer Scriabin, was a Russian poet. Her book *Stikhi* ("Poems", 1924) contains a poem on the biblical Joshua. While an active participant in the Jewish Combat Organization she transported a group of Jewish refugees to Switzerland. Killed in July 1944 in Toulouse in a clash with policemen collaborating with the Nazis, she was posthumously awarded the first French "military cross" and "medal of resistance." [MA.KI./S.J.E.R.]

KODER, SHABDAI SAMUEL (1907–), Jewish communal leader in Cochin. He was educated in Cochin and at Madras University, after which he entered the family business. For 12 years he represented the Jews of Cochin in the Cochin Legislative Assembly. He was honorary consul for the Netherlands and on his retirement received a knighthood of the Order of Nassau. Koder held high office in Rotary International and the Freemasons. In 1968 he presided at the 400th anniversary of Cochin's famous Paradeis synagogue, which was attended by Indian Prime Minister, Indira Gandhi. Koder is the author of a number of articles on the history of Cochin Jewry. [P.S.G.]

KOLODIN, IRVING (1908–1988), U.S. music critic. Born in New York City, Kolodin was raised in Newark, New Jersey, where he began to study music at an early age. From 1927 to 1931 he attended the Institute of Musical Art in New York. Beginning his career as assistant music critic to W.J. Henderson at the New York *Sun*, he eventually became the newspaper's chief critic, leaving there in 1950. He was also a critic of recordings and published a number of books of record reviews: *A Guide to Recorded Music* (1941), *Mozart on Records* (1942), *The Saturday Review Home Book of Recorded Music and Sound Reproduction* (1952; revised 1956), and *Orchestral Music* (1955). In 1970 he chose the classical music which was included in the first official White House music library. He taught criticism at the Juilliard School from 1968 to 1986.

Kolodin was well known as a historian of the New York Metropolitan Opera, publishing *The Metropolitan Opera: 1883–1935* (1936); a second edition, *The Story of the Metropolitan Opera, 1883–1950*, appeared in 1953 and was again updated in 1966.

Among his other works are *The Interior Beethoven* (1975), *The Opera Omnibus* (1976), and *In Quest of Music* (1980). [ED.]

KOL'TSOV, MIKHAIL (pseudonym of **Mikhail Yefimovich Fridland**; 1898–1940), Soviet publicist and social activist. Kol'tsov was born in Kiev and in 1915 he entered the Petrograd Psychoneurological Institute. He took part in the February and October Revolutions in Petrograd (1917) and in the Civil War, the subject of a series of sketches in his books *Petlyurovshcina* ("The Petlyura Terror," 1922), *Sotvrorenie mia* ("Creation of the World," 1928), and others. In 1920 he began working in Moscow in the press department of the People's Commissariat of Foreign Affairs. From 1922 he worked for *Pravda*, publishing almost daily a topical feuilleton on domestic and foreign policy. His keen observation, inexhaustible humor, and biting sarcasm, as well as the ability to manipulate facts, together with a keen political sensitivity allowed Kol'tsov to follow every fluctuation of Soviet policy, thanks to which he became one of the most authoritative and popular Soviet journalists of the 1920s and 1930s. Enjoying the confidence and support of the "authorities," he was editor of the journal *Ogonëk* which he founded in 1923, editor of the satirical journals *Chudak* (1928–30) and *Krokodil* (1934–38), co-editor (with Maxim Gorky) of the journal *Za rubezhom* (1932–38); member of the editorial

Ashkenazi Jews and did not retain a separate identity.

Although already in the 13th century some of the Crimean Jews spoke Turkish, and the final crystallization of the Krimchaks into a separate ethnic and linguistic group occurred in the 14th–16th centuries, a number of historians — Simon *Dubnow included — thought that the Krimchak community descended from the ancient Jewry of the Crimea.

History. THE BOSPHORUS PERIOD. The appearance of the Jews in the Crimea was connected with the Greek colonization of the shores of the Black Sea in the 2nd–1st centuries B.C.E. The Jews seem to have arrived in the Crimea from Asia Minor, although it is possible that they had reached the Crimea from the Caucasus through Taman peninsula already at the time of the Assyrian and Babylonian invasions (7th–6th centuries B.C.E.).

The first mention of the Crimean Jews is from the 1st century C.E. They are found in documents concerning the liberation of the slaves by their Jewish owners and epitaphs discovered mainly in the south-eastern part of the Crimea and on the Taman peninsula.

The documents concerning the slaves refer to the obligations imposed on them to visit regularly the synagogue under the supervision of the Jewish community. Thus, the Hellenized Jewish communities of the Bosphorus Kingdom, never having suffered from persecutions or limitations of any kind, grew — thanks to the conversion of the liberated slaves to Judaism. Moreover, the so-called *Sebomenoi*, non-Jews partially observing Jewish law, also tended to join the Jewish communities. A fourth-century inscription has been found on the construction of the synagogue in Panthikapei, now Kerch.

Little is known about the occupations of the Crimean Jews of the period. They must have dealt mostly in trades and crafts. The Jews also occupied state positions and served in the army, as evidenced by a 1st-century tombstone found in Taman. The tombstones of the 3rd and 4th centuries preserve, besides Greek inscriptions, a Hebrew inscription, as well as Hebrew names and symbols.

In the 2nd and 3rd centuries, the Jews moved along the southern coast of the Crimea. In 300, the Jews are mentioned in Kherson, in south-western Crimea, in connection with the rebellion of the local population protesting the introduction of Christianity.

In the late 4th century, *Jerome wrote about Jews in the Bosphorus Kingdom. Traditionally they included descendants of families who had been exiled by the Assyrians and the Babylonians, as well as of imprisoned warriors of Bar Kokhba.

The invasion of Huns in the 370s destroyed the Bosphorus Kingdom, and another state arose on its ruins — the Alan-Hun, which ceased to exist in the early 6th century. Those events contributed to the further dehellenization of the Crimean Jews, evidenced by the tombstones of the period, usually without inscriptions of names but with Jewish symbols such as the seven-branches candelabrum.

At the beginning of the 6th century the territory was invaded by the Byzantine Empire, and Byzantine chroniclers mention Jews in the area. In the Taman region, Jewish tombstones of the 6th–8th centuries have been excavated.

THE KHAZAR PERIOD. In the middle of the 7th century *Khazars occupied most of the Crimean territory.

The Jewish population might have played a decisive role in the process of establishing Judaism among the Khazars, who adopted Judaism as their religion in the late 8th–early 9th century.

The Jewish population also grew as a result of the influx of Jewish refugees coming mostly from the Byzantine Empire where Jews were periodically persecuted (843, 873–874, and 943). Judaism in the Crimea was greatly influenced by the Jewish refugees from the Byzantine Empire and by constant contacts with Byzantine Jewry. Under this influence the so-called "Crimean Rite" was elaborated. The most ancient of all known synagogues on Russian territory was built in 909 in Kaffa (Feodosiya). Several sources mention authors of religious hymns (*piyyutim) in the region, such as Abraham ben Simḥah ha-Sefaradi (died 1027). Silk-processing, fabric-dyeing, and trade were the main occupations of the Jews.

From the mid-9th century the power of the Khazars in the Crimea weakened as a result of invasions and also because of renewed wars with the Byzantine Empire. In 940–941 the Kiev princedom at the instigation of the Byzantines, waged war against the Khazar state, resulting in the victory of the Khazars who recaptured the southern and south-western parts of the Crimea up to Kherson. Attempts by the Byzantine Church to convert the Crimean Jews to Chrstianity failed.

The Khazar ruler Joseph wrote to *Ḥisdai ibn Shaprut, approximately in 960, stating that he ruled over many other areas besides the twelve settlements in the Crimea and in Taman. The most numerous Jewish communities existing at the time were in the towns of Samkush or Samkersh (Tmutarakan), Mangup (Doros), and Sudak. Large Jewish communities were known in the towns of Solkhat (presently Stariy Kryn), Kaffa (presently Feodosiya), and Kherson, where already in 861 Cyril, a preacher of Christianity, found a Jewish community of long standing including Khazars converted to Judaism. The decline of the Khazar kingdom began after Prince Svyatoslav defeated the Khazars in 965.

In 1096 the Byzantine emperor Alexei I ordered that all Jews should be driven from Kherson and their property confiscated. The exiles from Kherson must have settled in those regions of the Crimea where the Byzantines did not reach. However 60–70 years later the Jews were still living in the Byzantine part too as *Benjamin of Tudela in the 1160s reported on the existence of a community of Rabbanite Jews in the town of Sogdia (presently Sudak), which was a significant Crimean port. At that time the Jews of the Crimea comprised a provincial part of the Romaniot community, whose members spoke Greek.

Khazars observing Judaism must have assimilated among the Jewish population of the Crimea. Some of the immigrant Jews were Karaites. In approximately 1175, the traveler Pethahiah of Regensburg confirmed the existence of Jewish groups in the region of the Azov Sea, whose customs were identical with those of the Karaites. The Jews of the Crimea continued to maintain contact with the Jews of the Byzantine Empire and of Islamic countries.

THE TATAR PERIOD. In 1239 the steppe area of the Crimea was occupied by the Tatars and Mongols. Along the southern coast, the colonies of Genoa entrenched themselves. Thanks to the Genoese colonies the Crimea became an important trading center attracting numerous Jewish emigrants from the eastern countries (Persia, Asia Minor, Egypt) as well as from the West (Italy, and later, Spain).

The economic flourishing of the Jewish communities contributed to their cultural development. *Sefat Emet* ("Language of Truth"), a rationalistic commentary on the Pentateuch by Avraham Kirimi (i.e., of Crimea), written in 1315, is the first known original work by a Crimean Jew. Several sources point to the town of Solkhat (where Kirimi was born and lived), as an important center of Jewish rationalism at the time.

From the 14th century on, the Karaite communities were centered in Chufut-Kale and in Mangup. Most Rabbanite Jews settled in Solkhat, and later in Karasu-Bazar. However Kaffa was the largest Jewish community in the Crimea with both Rabbanite and Karaite Jews.

Bazaar in Simferopol, Jewish merchant is mounted on horse; drawing by Leipzig engraver Greissler in series of a *Journey through Old Russia by the Privy Councillor of the Palatinate* in 1794–1802 (JNUL Photo Archives, Jerusalem)

The Genoese authorities endeavored to calm the tensions between various ethnic and religious groups in their colonies related, in particular, to the forced conversations of the Jews to Christianity and the plunder of property. In 1449 they issued a decree for the Black Sea colonies, which included a confirmation of the rights of all peoples and groups including the Jews to observe their own religion. Later decrees from the Genoese ordered that the Jews be free from interference in their affairs, so that the Jews enjoyed freedom until the conquest of Kaffa by the Turkish troops in 1475.

Already prior to 1475, some Jews living in Kaffa had established contacts with the court of the Crimean Khans in Solkhat. One of these Jews, Khozya Kokos, a merchant, mediated in 1472–86 the negotiations between the Grand Duke of Moscow, Ivan III, and the Crimean Khan, Mengly-Girei, a part of the correspondence being written in Hebrew.

Centuries of Tatar rule resulted in a considerable orientalization of the Crimean Jews: to a great extent they adopted the language, customs, and mores of the Moslem Tatars. Already in the 13th century some of the Crimean Jews spoke Turkish. The Bible was translated into Krimchak. The decline of trade led to the increased share of crafts and agriculture in the occupations of the Crimean Jews. Many Jews in Mangup and Chufut-Kale engaged in leather tanning, mountain vegetable gardening, and viticulture. The Jewish merchants obtained credentials from the ruler to protect themselves and their property from the encroachment of local feudal lords.

Throughout their history the Krimchaks absorbed Jews coming from other communities: the Byzantine Empire, Babylonia and the Khazar kingdom, Italy, and the Caucasus, as well as Ashkenazi Jews brought to the Crimea as prisoners of the Tatars, or those who fled from pogroms and later moved to the Crimea for economic reasons.

Prior to the conquest of the Crimea by Russia, all Rabbanite Jews in the Crimea merged with the Krimchak community, and it was only in the 19th-early 20th century that a separate Ashkenazi community emerged. The merger of the various communities resulted in a special prayer rite incorporating elements of different communities *(minhag Kaffa).* Various trends of Jewish mysticism made their impact on Krimchak tradition: *Ḥasidei Ashkenaz, the Kabbalah of the Zohar, Isaac *Luria, and especially, practical kabbalah. Rabbi Moses ben Jacob, who went to the Crimea from Kiev, reconciled the different traditions and elaborated the single rite compiling the prayer book *Maḥzor Minhag Kaffa*; he also established rules for guiding community life.

The Russian Period. The successful struggle of Karaites to be exempted from the anti-Jewish laws of the Russian Empire and their move from the dilapidated town-fortresses to other regions of the Crimea for economic reasons led to a complete break in relations between the Karaites and the Krimchaks.

From 1866 to 1899 Ḥayyim Hezekiah *Medini (born in Jerusalem in 1832, and died in 1904) was chief rabbi of Karasu-Bazar. He raised the spiritual and cultural level of the Krimchaks, increasing the Sephardi infuence. He introduced changes in the community's customs, and founded several schools, and a yeshivah.

In his monumental multi-volume *Sedei Ḥemed* Medini described at length Krimchak traditions and elaborated his own regulations (**takkanot*). In 1899 Medini returned to Ereẓ Israel to publish religious literature with translations into Krimchak.

Polygamy among the Krimchaks disappeared early in the 19th century. Girls married at an early age, and marriages between close relatives, such as an uncle and his niece, were permitted. Widows could never remarry because a husband and wife were considered inseparable also after death.

The everyday life of the Krimchaks was influenced by that of the Crimean Tatars. The patriarchal nature of the family was preserved up to the end of the 19th century. The practice of good deeds was regarded as of great significance. They carried out charity extensively, cared for widows and orphans, no beggars were found in their midst, and the poor received firewood, flour, and candles at the community's expense.

In the 19th century the Krimchaks lived in small poor communities almost untouched by the European enlightenment. Most of them were craftsmen, and the minority were engaged in agriculture, gardening, and vine-growing, with only a few in trade.

In 1840 the Krimchaks founded an agricultural settlement, Rogatlikoy, with 140 members. However, in 1859 the Krimchak peasants received the status of middle-class citizens of the town of Karasu-Bazar, and their lands were transferred to Russian Christian settlers. Count A. Stroganov, governor-general of Novorossijsk, interceded for the Jews who wanted to acquire property in the Crimea and as a result the transfer decree failed to be ratified by the Czarist government in 1861. The attitude of the Russian authorities to the "Talmudic Jews" in the Crimea was relatively favorable: the community enjoyed several privileges in the fields of taxation and conscription.

The Krimchaks created a rich folklore: collections of legends, songs, riddles, and proverbs, written by hand in Hebrew letters and passed from one generation to another. Samples of their folklore were published in the original with translations into Russian, Yiddish, and Hebrew. Literature in Krimchak consisted, apart from folklore, mainly in translations of religious texts.

Drawn into Russian culture from the beginning of the 20th century, some of the Krimchaks participated in revolutionary movements and a considerable part of them joined Zionist organizations.

After the Revolution of 1917, the Krimchaks were subject to the same social and demographic processes as all the other Jewish ethnic and linguistic groups. The considerable increase in their educational level led to a decline in everyday traditional life. Many Krimchaks who had received professional education as physicians, engineers, and teachers severed contacts with their native community.

In October 1941 German troops occupied the Crimea, and only an insignificant number of Krimchaks managed to leave the area. The occupying authorities, not sure whether the Krimchaks belonged to "the Jewish race," turned to Berlin for guidance. The answer was that the Krimchak community should be destroyed with the rest of the Jewish population.

There were 6,000 Krimchaks among the 40,000 Crimean Jews killed by the Nazis. According to the reports of the Nazi murder squads, the *Einsatzgruppen*, 2,504 of Krimchaks perished in the anti-Jewish actions of November 15 to December 16, 1941, in eastern Crimea. Krimchaks from Simferopol were executed on December 11 near the village of Mazanka. The Krimchaks of Feodosiya met their death on December 15, on the same date as the Krimchaks of Kerch, and on January 18, 1942, 2,000 Krimchaks of Karasu-Bazar met their death in gas chambers.

Krimchaks fought in the Soviet army and in partisan detachments. Many perished, including the poet Ya. I. Chapichev (1909–1945) who received the posthumous title of Hero of the Soviet Union.

At present, the remnants of the Krimchaks are being rapidly assimilated, and their culture inadequately preserved. In the post-war period, they were officially defined in the Soviet Union as a special nationality of mixed ethnic origin, mostly non-Jewish. [MI.Z./D.KH./S.J.E.R.]

קונטרס הכללים
ספר
שדי חמד
חלק ראשון
כולל אות א. ב. ג. ד. ה.
יבואו בו כללי הש״ס וכללי הפוסקים דברים ברורים. ליקוטאי נינהו מספרן של צדיקים המה הגבורים. אשר דברו בקדשם אחת הנה ואחת הנה במקומות מפוזרים. ואסיפת דינים, אמרי פנינים. מפי סופרים ומפי ספרים. בדבר הנהוגים נפשי איותה ללקט אמרים. בעזרת האל יתברך בורא רוח ויוצר הרים. למדנו חיפוש מחיפוש חופש כל חדרי חדרים. תיקנתים אף עשיתים ע״ס א״ב מאל״ף ועד ת״ו מסודרים. להועיל לקטנים כמוני מילדי העברים. את כל אלה ידי עשתה אנכי הדל צעיר שבצעירים. מבני ציון עיר קדשנו ירושלים משוש תפארתנו במהרה בימינו תבנה ותכונן בראש ההרים, גר אנכי לעתות כאל באתת מעיירות קירים. קראסוב בזאר עיר קטנה ואנשי קדש בתוכה טובים ויקרים.
הצ״יר חיים חזקיהו מדיני המכונה חח״ם ה״יו בלא״א הרב החסיד ועניו מוהר״ר רפאל אליה מדיני זלה״ה תנצב״ה נהנה מזיו השכינה באספקלריא המאירה אור לישרים.
הובא לבית הדפוס ע״י בית מסחר הספרים של הר״ר שמשון ובנו הר״ר יצחק סובאלסקי נ״י. בווארשא רחוב דזיקא 40
ווארשא
אם אתן שנת אמרתי הנה באתי במגלת ספר כתוב.
בדפוס לוין-עפשטין, סניה 88.
בית הספרים הלאומי והאוניברסיטאי ירושלים

Title page of part one of *Sedei Ḥemed* by Rabbi Ḥayyim Hezekiah Medini (JNUL, Jerusalem)

KUN, BÉLA (see **10**:1290). The Soviet Communist Party informed the Hungarian Communist Party that Béla Kun was executed on August 29, 1938, and not in 1939 as it had previously claimed (and as published in the *Encyclopaedia Judaica*). It announced that he was tried during the Stalinist purges on charges of being "a Trotskyite conspirator, plotting to undermine the Communist International," and executed several hours after being sentenced to death. He was rehabilitated in 1955.

KUNIN, MADELEINE (1933–), U.S. politician, Kunin was born in Zurich, Switzerland, and was brought to the United States by her parents in 1940. She became a naturalized citizen in 1947. Her political career was initiated in 1972 with her election to the Vermont House of Representatives where she spent a total of three terms. During her second term she was chosen Democratic whip. For two terms she was on the House Appropriations Committee, eventually becoming chairman of that committee — the first Democrat and first woman to do so. For two terms, from 1978 to 1982, she was lieutenant governor of Vermont; in this capacity she gave substance to what was a mainly ceremonial office by prompting studies on day care, highway safety, and energy conservation. She was defeated in a 1982 bid for the position of governor, but was elected in the 1984 gubernatorial contest, becoming the first Jewish woman governor elected in the United States, and the third Democratic governor of Vermont in 130 years. She served until 1991. [ED.]

KUSHNER, ALEKSANDER SEMENOVICH (1936–), Russian poet and translator. Kushner was born in Leningrad. In 1959 he graduated from the philological faculty of Leningrad's Herzen Pedagogical Institute and until 1970 worked as an evening school teacher. He began publishing poetry in 1957. His first collections of verse *Pervoe vpechatlenie* ("First Impression," 1962) and *Nochnoy dozor* ("Night Watch," 1966) reflect to some degree the influence of V. *Khodasevich. Starting from the collection *Primety* ("Omens," 1969). Kushner can be linked with the tradition of the Acmeists (particularly with O. Mandelshtam [see **Dc./17**:459]). However, his verse is distinguished by considerable semantic simplicity and restraint in the choice of metaphor, which imparts an electric tension to his poetry. Kushner's poetry is written in classical meter, in strophes with a precise, somewhat subdued, rhythm. Basic motifs in his poetry are: the inevitability of death, suffering, and persecution as necessary conditions for happiness, external lack of freedom as the source of internal freedom, solitude, and the metaphysical exile of the individual. His philosophical lyrics are based on rejection of the perceptible reality of daily life, of the urban scene, on precise and concrete observation, and filled with associations, reminiscences, and veiled allusions to the cultural symbols of all times and peoples (excluding, however, allusions to the Hebrew Bible). From the late 1960s, both Kushner and his poetry were criticized, and after an attack by the secretary of the Leningrad Party provincial committee of the Communist Party, he was not published for a while.

He became well known with the publication of his collections *Pis'mo* ("Letter," 1974) and *Pryamaya rech'* ("Direct Speech," 1975). The appearance of his collection *Golos* ("Voice," 1978) coincided with a raging argument, encompassing the Soviet *samizdat* (underground press) and emigré press, about the place and significance of his poetry which some considered the most outstanding in contemporary Russian literature. His book of selected poems *Kanva* ("Canvas," 1981) was succeeded by the collections *Tavricheskiy sad* ("Tauride Garden," 1984) and *Dnevnie sny* ("Day Dreams", 1986). Aleksander Kushner also published books of poems for children: *Zavetnoe zhelanie* ("Secret Wish," 1973), *Gorod v podarok* ("City as Gift," 1976) and *Velosiped* ("Bicycle," 1979).

In Kushner's poetry Jewish motifs appear only in references or allusions. An exception is the poem "Kogda tot pol' skiy pedadog..." ("When That Polish Pedadogue") about the educator and writer Janusz *Korczak. Upholding the principle of not leaving the Soviet Union and of not expressing an attitude about the Soviet regime, Kushner reacted to the mass emigration of other Jews from the Soviet Union with poems such as "The next time too I want to live in Russia." [YU.KU./S.J.E.R.]

KYRGYZSTAN (formerly Kirghizia), one of the independent states of the Commonwealth of Independent States, bordered on the north and northwest by Kazakhstan, to the southwest by Uzbekstan, and on the south by Tadzhikistan, with a population of some 4,500,000 people. In 1979 Kirghizia had a Jewish population of 6,900 (with 5,700 living in the capital Frunze, which in 1991 was renamed Bishkek). In 1989 the Jewish population of the republic was 6,000 (with 5,200 in the capital); 178 Jews emigrated in 1989. In 1990, 1,170 Jews of Krygyzstan immigrated to Israel, 1,111 of them from Frunze. In 1991, the year the republic gained independence, the corresponding figures were 696 and 629.

One Jew was elected to the Supreme Soviet of the republic in 1990. The government of the republic has expressed its opposition to Islamic fundamentalism. In 1992 Kyrgyzstan passed a law making knowledge of the Kirghiz language a prerequisite for high government positions. This latter condition effectively bars most Jews from holding high government offices. [MI.BE.]

L

LANG, JACK (1939–), French public figure and minister of culture. Lang studied law and politics before turning to theater and theater management. He directed the Festival Mondial du Théatre Universitaire (1963–1972) and also the Chaillot Theater (the former T.N.P.) in Paris (1972–1974). In 1978 Lang was appointed special adviser to the first secretary of the Socialist party and in 1979 he became director of the cultural activities of the party. In 1981 he was appointed minister of culture in the Socialist government under President Mitterrand. In this position, Lang sought to implement the cultural platform of the Socialist party, to encourage popular theater and culture and government support for films. At one time violently opposed to "American cultural imperialism," Lang subsequently toned down his criticism while making an all out effort to promote French culture on the international scene. He devoted much attention to promoting youth activities, including rock performances. He ceased to be minister with the defeat of the Socialists in 1993. [GI.KO.]

LANZMANN, CLAUDE (1925–), French cinema director and essayist. Lanzmann was born in Paris and during World War II was active in the Resistance. After completing his studies in philosophy in France, he lectured at the University of Berlin in 1948–49. In 1952 he became acquainted with Jean Paul Sartre and Simone de Beauvoir, becoming their personal friend and a partner in their philosophical and public endeavors. He was adviser and close personal friend of Simone de Beauvoir in her later years. Sartre, de Beauvoir, and Lanzmann founded the journal *Les temps modernes* (1946) of which Lanzmann was an editor.

In 1970 Lanzmann left journalism for film and spent three years preparing *Pourquoi Israel?* which received warm reviews when it was screened in 1973, and was even called "the best movie ever made about Israel." Lanzmann's talents especially came to the fore in his monumental film *Shoah* on which he worked for over ten years. The film premiered in France in 1985 and President Mitterrand of France attended its opening. The film was subsequently shown in London, New York, Israel, and elsewhere, including on Polish television despite an initial protest on the part of the Polish government which objected to the portrait of Polish people as collaborators with the Nazis in the destruction of the Jews.

Shoah is a nine-hour film, which consists of continuous interviews with Jews, Nazis, and Poles. The film uses no documentary footage and constructs a spiral of tension and shock using trains to link the interviews. The very power of the film emerges from the description of the terrifying events by the interviewees. For this project, Lanzmann was awarded the most prestigious prize of French Jewry, the Prix de la Fondation du judaisme français (1985). [GI.KO.]

LATVIA (see **10**:1462). Latvia regained its independence in 1991. The Jewish population of Latvia declined from 28,300 in 1979 to 22,900 in 1989, when 18,800 of its Jews lived in the capital Riga. In 1988–89 the Jewish birth rate was 7.0 per 1,000 and the Jewish mortality rate — 18.3 per 1,000. The rate of intermarriage is high. In 1987, 39.7% of children born of Jewish mothers had non-Jewish fathers. A large percentage of the Jewish population in Latvia is composed of postwar immigrants from other republics of the U.S.S.R. According to legislation passed by the newly independent country, these new Latvian Jews do not have an automatic right of citizenship as do ethnic Latvians.

In 1989, 1,588 Jews emigrated from Latvia (1,536 of them from Riga). In 1990, 3,388 Jews immigrated to Israel (2,837 of them from Riga). The number of immigrants to Israel from Riga in 1991 was 1,087.

While striving toward independence the Latvian national

movement sought to make common cause with the Jews in the republic. July 4 was established in Latvia as a memorial day for the victims of the Holocaust.

Many Jewish organizations are operating in the country. The elite of the Jewish intelligentsia is not involved in Jewish communal life. In 1992 there was a perceptible increase in anti-Semitism. [MI.BE.]

LAU, ISRAEL MEIR (1937–), Ashkenazi chief rabbi of Israel. Born in Piotrkow, Poland, Lau is a member of a rabbinic family, descendants of Meir ben Isaac *Katzenellenbogen, the Maharam of Padua. His father, Rabbi Moshe Ḥayyim Lau, who perished in Treblinka, was the last rabbi of Piotrkow.

Israel Meir Lau (GPO, Jerusalem)

As a young child Israel Lau experienced the Holocaust in the Piotrkow ghetto, the Czestochowa work camp, and the Buchenwald concentration camp from which he was liberated at the end of the war with his brother Naftali. He was brought to Palestine by Youth Aliyah on a ship of child Holocaust survivors.

He lived with his uncle, the rabbi of Kiryat Motzkin, near Haifa, until the age of 13 and then spent many years studying in yeshivot in Jerusalem, Bene Berak, and elsewhere in Israel. He was ordained as a rabbi in 1960 and served as a congregational rabbi in Tel Aviv for 11 years, after which he was appointed regional Tel Aviv rabbi. In 1979 he became chief rabbi of Netanyah where, among other communal and educational activities, he founded the Ohel Mosheh yeshivah in his father's memory.

From 1983 he served on the council of the Chief Rabbinate, and in 1988 he was chosen chief rabbi of Tel Aviv. In March 1993 he was elected chief Ashkenazi rabbi of Israel.

In 1978 he published *Yahadut Halakhah le-Ma'aseh* ("Judaism in Practice"). [ED.]

LEDERMAN, LEON MAX (1922–), physicist, educator, Nobel Prize winner. Lederman was born in New York City and attended the College of the City of New York from which

Leon M. Lederman (Courtesy Fermilab Visual Media Services, Illinois)

he received his B.S. in 1943. He earned his M.A. (1948) and Ph.D. (1951) from Columbia University. Working at Columbia in the physics department from 1951, he was assistant professor (1952–54), associate professor (1954–58), and professor from 1958. In 1973 he was appointed the Eugene Higgins Professor of Physics there. From 1979 he was director of the Fermi National Accelerator Laboratory in Batavia, Illinois. He was a consultant to the European Organization for Nuclear Research (CERN) in Geneva, Switzerland from 1970.

The author of numerous scientific articles, he was the recipient among other awards of the National Medal of Science in 1965, the Elliot Cresson Medal of the Franklin Institute in 1976, and the Wolf Prize in 1983. Lederman is a member of the National Academy of Science.

In 1988 he was awarded the Nobel Prize in physics along with Melvin Schwartz (q.v.) and Jack Steinberger (q.v.), who had been his colleagues at Columbia University in the 1960s, for their research which contributed to a greater understanding of particle physics. [ED.]

LEVI-MONTALCINI, RITA (1911–), developmental biologist; Nobel Prize winner. Levi-Montalcini was born in Italy and grew up in Turin. She earned her degree in medicine at the University of Turin where she was employed until 1939 when she was barred by the Fascists from practicing medicine and from working in the university. Undaunted she continued her cell research by conducting experiments in an improvised laboratory in her bedroom with embryos from eggs which she had begged for to feed "needy children." Since she was a member of the "Jewish race," the results of the experiments could not be published in fascist Italy, but they did appear in Belgium, establishing her scientific reputation.

The family fled to Belgium, but with Hitler's invasion of the country in 1940 returned to Italy. They hid in Florence under the name "Lovisato," claiming to be southern Italians — with a northern accent.

In 1947 Levi-Montalcini accepted a teaching and research position at Washington University in St. Louis, Missouri, with Professor Viktor Hamburger. There in June 1951 she made the discovery for which she and Dr. Stanley Cohen (q.v.), who worked with her at that time, were awarded the 1986 Nobel Prize for medicine, the isolation of the nerve growth factor (NGF), a protein which stimulates the growth of sensory and sympathetic nerves in animals and in cultures.

Levi-Montalcini, who holds both United States and Italian citizenship, returned to Italy in 1977 to head a research laboratory of the National Council of Scientific Research in Rome. She was the first woman elected to the Pontifical Academy of Science and the sixth woman to be accepted into the American Academy of Science (1968).

In addition to the Nobel Prize, Levi-Montalcini received the Medicineltrinelli in 1969, the St. Vincent prize in 1980, and the Albert Lasker Basic Medical Research Award for 1986. [ED.]

LEVIN, A. LEO (1919–), U.S. law professor and administrator. Born in New York City, Levin, son of an Orthodox rabbi and Mizrachi leader, was graduated with a B.A. degree from Yeshiva University and a law degree from the University of Pennsylvania Law School. He began to teach law at the University of Pennsylvania in 1949 and became a full professor in 1953. From 1963 to 1968 he was vice-provost at the university, and then for a year (1969–1970) he served as vice-president for academic affairs at Yeshiva University. He returned to teaching law at the University of Pennsylvania in 1970.

In addition to teaching law, Levin has been prominently involved in judicial administration. In 1977 he was appointed director of the Federal Judicial Center in Washington, D.C., an agency created by an act of Congress in 1967, to conduct research on the operation of federal courts, to conduct training programs for judges and court personnel, and to engage in related activities designed to make the federal court system efficient.

A. Leo Levin (Courtesy Yeshiva University, N.Y.)

Other positions that Levin has held have been as executive director of the Commission on Revision of the Federal Courts Appellate System (1973–75); chairman of the Pennsylvania State Legislative Reapportionment Commission (1971–73); founding director of the National Institute for Trial Advocacy; member of the Standing Committee on Practice and Procedure, Judicial Conference of the United States (1977–78); conference coordinator, National Conference on Causes of Dissatisfaction with the Administration of Justice (the so-called Pound Conference, 1976–77); and he has been a member of the National Institute of Corrections since 1977.

Levin is a Fellow of the American Academy of Arts and Sciences and an honorary trustee of Bar-Ilan University. He was formerly president of the Jewish Publication Society, and is a member of the Board of Directors of the American Judicature Society.

Among his publications are a study of judicial administration in Pennsylvania, a case book on civil procedure, and a book on trial advocacy, as well as numerous law review articles. [M.R.K.].

LEVY, DAVID (1937–), Israel politician. Levy was born in Rabat, Morocco, where his father, a carpenter, ensured that his children received a traditional Jewish upbringing and education. Arriving in Israel in 1957, the Levy family

David Levy (GPO, Jerusalem)

settled in the northern town of Beth Shean. Initially Levy was employed by neighboring kibbutzim as a hired agricultural laborer and then worked on various building sites where he proved himself to be an outstanding scaffolding erector. However, like many new immigrants in the 1950s, Levy could not always find employment.

In 1966, he was elected to the municipal council of Beth Shean and acted as deputy mayor. In this period he was also elected to the executive committee of the General Federation of Labor where he became chairman of the Likkud faction which, during his period of leadership, grew in strength and numbers, contributing to the success of the Likkud party in the 1977 general elections.

Levy himself was elected to the Seventh Knesset and in 1977, was appointed minister for immigrant absorption. In addition, in 1979, he became minister for construction and housing, a position he held for 11 years, during which time 300,000 new apartments were built, 220 settlements (both communal and agricultural) were established as were 13 new towns, in Galilee and the Negev as well as in Judea, Samaria, and the Gaza strip. He was also the minister responsible for Project Renewal, an extensive neighborhood project carried out in 100 towns and settlements which helped to raise the standard of housing and the self-image of the population.

From 1981, David Levy functioned as deputy prime minister of Israel, and from 1990 to 1992 as minister of foreign affairs. [E.Ho.]

LITHUANIA (see **11**:361). Lithuania seceded from the U.S.S.R., in August 1991. In 1979 the republic's Jewish population was recorded at 14,700 and in 1989 as 12,400. In 1988–89 the Jewish birthrate was 7.5 per 1,000 and mortality rate was 17.8 per 1,000.

In 1989, 780 Jews (743 of them from the capital Vilnius [Vilna]) emigrated. Immigration to Israel amounted to 2,962 (2,355 from Vilnius) in 1990 and to 1,103 in 1991.

There is no state anti-Semitism in Lithuania. In 1990 Emanuel Zingeris, an activist of the Lithuanian national front Sajudis and now co-chairman of the Jewish culture Association of Lithuania, was elected as a deputy to the Supreme Soviet of Lithuania. The other co-chairman was Lithuanian-Jewish writer Grigorii Kanovich (who writes in Russian, but whose basic theme is Jewish life, particularly of the past, in his region). A Jewish museum has been opened in Vilnius and a monthly newspaper, *Litovskii Ierusalim* ("Jerusalem of Lithuania"), appears in Yiddish, Russian, Lithuanian, and English. September 23, the day the Vilna ghetto was destroyed, has been set aside to commemorate the mass murder of the Jews of Lithuania. A memorial complex, where annual public meetings are held, has been built at the site of mass executions at Ponary. A Jewish guide to Vilnius has been published. In November 1991 a Council of Jewish Communities of Lithuania was established. Due to the small number of Jews remaining in the country the majority of the numerous Jewish organizations registered in Lithuania have no more than a few members and scarcely function, and according to one local activist, "There are no Jews, there are just Jewish representatives."

On June 1, 1992, an air route was opened between Vilnius and Israel. [Mi.Be.]

LOS ANGELES (see **11**:497). **1970–1990. Introduction.** Jewish life in Los Angeles was profoundly affected by swift currents of change that swept over the Jewish community during the 1970s and 80s. In summary they were: (1) The drastically reshaped demographics of a city which at a mindboggling pace underwent an immigrant-driven transformation into America's first Third World city. This ethnic revolution had powerful Jewish consequences including the need for reexamination of Jewish self-identity; (2) Profound internal religious changes, marked by significant movement toward increased adherence to historical traditions, alongside equally striking departures from traditional views and practices; (3) The assumption by the Los Angeles Jewish Federation of responsibilities and objectives commensurate with newly perceived qualitative needs of the world's second largest Jewish community (after New York).

The Demographic Revolution in Los Angeles. California in the 1980s grew by six million people, the biggest human surge in any state in U.S. history, with estimates of an additional million immigrants by the end of the century. One third of the new arrivals settled in the Los Angeles Area, increasing its population to 14.5 million. Greater Los Angeles had abruptly become the largest metropolitan center in the country.

It also had ceased to be a European outpost and was now a multi-racial world nation. Some 75% of the immigrants were Hispanic, Asian, and black. By the end of the 1980s 51% of Los Angeles residents were Hispanic or nonwhite. This was true of 75% of the students in the public school system who spoke in 83 mother tongues.

The Asian community, largely Chinese and Japanese, who in the 19th century were viewed as ignorant, laboring class "coolies," now immigrated to the West Coast as colonizers of the Pacific rim. Many were "Yuppies," well educated with massive investments in corporations and real estate. Others from Korea, Philippines, Vietnam and dozens of other countries seemingly overnight established and built retail businesses, bought homes, and transformed neighborhoods.

As examples, Monterey Park, a former Jewish enclave, became the Western world's first Chinese suburban city. Elite San Marino, which once staunchly restricted Jews, became 46% Asian. Congregation Judea in the midst of the Jewish Fairfax area was transformed in 1975 into a robust Korean Presbyterian church, the center piece of a new and thriving Korean commercial district.

California State University, Los Angeles, in 1989 had the following student profile: of 20,000 students, 30% were Latino, 11.5% Asian, 11.5% black, and 30% white. The vice-president for academic affairs of the state college system announced that "Cal State-LA is probably close in its student body representation to what any university campus in California, public or private, is going to look like in the early 21st century." These demographic estimates were inescapably destined to be among the powerful determinants of the character of Jewish life in the coming century.

The Jewish Population of Los Angeles. By 1989, Los Angeles Jewry was estimated to have grown to 650,000 Jews from 500,000 in 1972 and 350,000 at the end of World War II. Another 90,000 Jews had settled in neighboring Orange County. The Greater Los Angeles Jewish community was now numerically larger than the Jewish population of any country other than the United States, Israel, and the Soviet Union.

Some of the population increase represented the sunbelt-driven migration from the East and Middle West to Florida and the West Coast. A substantial portion of the new immigrants came from Israel (probably 50,000, although estimates ranged as high as 150,000). The Soviet Jews were estimated at between 25,000–40,000 and the Iranian community at 20,000–30,000. In addition there were sizeable contingents from South Africa, South America, Australia, and Mexico. These immigrants provided a challenge to the Los Angeles Jewish community in terms of their integration and acculturation.

A major implication for the Jewish community was that with Los Angeles now a multi-racial nation with ethnic ties to every race and region in the world, the Jewish community had thrust upon it a double identity. It had the obligation to assert itself and protect its rights. But in a situation without precedent the Jewish community was now additionally the principal representative of the white establishment. This is illustrated by the following:

They were the prominent residents in the finest sections of the city: Beverly Hills, Bel Air, Westwood, San Fernando Valley, Santa Monica, Pacific Palisades.

They played a major role in the political life of the community: the City Council, Board of Supervisors, State Legislature, the House of Congress. In addition the Jewish community could count on the non-Jewish congressmen and senators to vote with friendly sensitivity on matters of Jewish interest.

They were conspicuous in the cultural, philanthropic, and economic life of the city.

They were the most cohesive, best organized white body in the city with ties to the instruments of civic power.

These new realities contrasted sharply with the years from 1900 to 1960 when no Jew was elected to the City Council or the Board of Supervisors or to represent California in Sacramento or Washington. Nor were Jews considered worthy to be mentioned in the society pages of the *Los Angeles Times* or in the published social register.

This new status now meant that the organized Jewish community was, as a minority, enjoined to protect and advance its own interest but equally responsible, as a principal member of the white establishment, to seek the peace of the city, recognizing, to paraphrase Jeremiah, that only in its welfare, would they be at peace. This double identity was bound to create ambivalence and tension in the Jewish community in the years ahead.

The Religious Community. Judaism in Los Angeles was decisively shaped by a number of rabbis of varying denominations who were drawn to the city by personal visions of what they might accomplish in a city which was responsible

The AIDS Committee of the Pacific Southwest Council, UAHC
welcomes you to:

A Service of Remembrance,
Healing and Hope
In support of
People with AIDS
and
Their Loved Ones

Leo Baeck Temple
March 12, 1989

Title page of a special service held at Los Angeles's Leo Baeck Temple in support of people with AIDS and their friends and families, March 1989 (Courtesy Andrea London, Jerusalem)

to religious enterprise as it was to other forms of individual endeavor. These rabbis, in a community capable of providing considerable human and physical resources if properly motivated, were given an opportunity to concentrate their energies as religious leaders for purposes compatible with their personal interests and concerns. They became what might be termed rabbi-institution builders, rabbi-communal leaders, rabbi-social activists, rabbi-educators.

The following is a sampling of the impact on Judaism in Los Angeles by a few of the over 200 Los Angeles area rabbis.

RABBI-INSTITUTION BUILDERS. The Orthodox leaders in Los Angeles before World War II had such little faith in their own future that their leading synagogue was called "the modern synagogue," and their significant events were given enhanced status by the participation of a local Reform Rabbi or his president.

The resurgence of Orthodoxy in post-war Los Angeles was fueled by some determined rabbis, who were confident that American Jews however acculturated, would be receptive to a return to authentic tradition if it were attractively clothed in American values, if it secured serious media attention, and if it could be identified as the natural heir to the Jewish heart.

Rabbi Baruch Shlomo Kunin introduced the Ḥabad movement to Los Angeles in the 1950s. In subsequent years, he became a major religious force in the state with an operating budget of 15 million dollars from 50,000 contributors and was supported by a rabbinic staff of 106 impassioned young graduates of their yeshivah in Brooklyn. He established and controlled an imposing and growing array of synagogues, day schools, adult Torah study centers, and social projects such as a shelter for the homeless, a counseling center for battered women, and two drug treatment centers financed substantially by federal grants. Woven into the program were public relations sorties, featuring Judaism in the streets such as *Mitzvah* mobiles, and Ḥanukkah lighting celebrations in shopping malls and city halls. The annual climax was a hyperkinetic telethon in which movie and television personalities vied for the *mitzvah* of raising millions of dollars for Ḥasidic Judaism — Western style.

Rabbi Marvin Hier moved into Los Angeles from Vancouver in 1977, intending to establish a yeshivah, but instead founded the Simon Wiesenthal Center which became the Los Angeles community's first national and international Jewish organization. Rabbi Hier succeeded in implanting Holocaust Judaism into a Jewish people seeking a way to sacrilize the Holocaust. Rabbi Hier propelled the Holocaust Center to stake out an independent claim as an activist leader in the fight against anti-Semitism.

Rabbi Nahum Braverman came to Los Angeles in the mid-1980s to establish a western outpost of Aish Hatorah. In a few short years he created an outreach program of one-to-one Torah learning. He established a chain of study sessions in private offices and conference rooms and began the process of organizing Aish Hatorah synagogues. The students were prominent business and community leaders. The program created a network of intellectual *Ba'alei teshuvah* (newly Orthodox), sympathetic to "authentic" Judaism and often prepared to support it, even though not necessarily embodying it in their lifestyles.

Rabbi Daniel Lapin arrived from South Africa in 1977. Although only a young man he was already an engineer, physicist, airplane pilot, sailor, and Orthodox rabbi. Together with Michael Medved, best-selling writer and movie critic on public TV, they took over a minuscule store front synagogue on the Venice beach, operated by and for a few remaining elderly Jews, and established the Pacific Jewish Center. It was an unusual strictly Orthodox synagogue in which financial participation was voluntary, participation in Torah study compulsory, and outdoors adventuring a *mitzvah*. At first the members were overwhelmingly single; in time they married, moved into the neighborhood to be within walking distance of the synagogue, and so created a living and learning community, which former and disaffected members described as "cultlike."

The official Jewish establishment, acutely conscious of the strategic necessity of maintaining the historic separation of church and state, was likewise periodically constrained to remain mute and resigned while the Ḥabad aggressively broke down barriers between religion and the state in its public square religious practices; and while the Wiesenthal Center was prevailing on the California Legislature and the United State Congress each to contribute five million dollars to the Center's projected Museum of Tolerance, which opened in 1992.

These rabbinical leaders of the *Ba'al teshuvah* movements represented a new American meld; totally Orthodox, totally American, technologically advanced and with their work largely financed by non-Orthodox supporters.

During the 1970s reform rabbi Isaiah Zeldin, who had come to Los Angeles to represent The Union of American Hebrew Congregations and subsequently became rabbi of Temple Emanuel in Beverly Hills, left his congregation and founded Stephen S. Wise Temple in the sparsely settled Mulholland Drive area of western Los Angeles.

In the course of 15 years, the congregation grew in numbers and in program to become one of America's largest, with a membership of 3,000 families, with an annual budget in excess of 11 million dollars, and a physical plant of monumental proportions. Its campus on 10 acres of land was *sui generis*: a total of 1,200 students in its school system, ranging from pre-school to an elementary day school through grade six, an all-day junior high school, and most recently an all-day high school; its parenting center; its faculty with four rabbis at the helm assisted by a staff of 250 permanent personnel; imposing facilities that included an immense special parking structure, Olympic swimming facilities, and a variety of specially designed and constructed recreational area.

Rabbi Harold Schulweis moved to the Encino area of the San Fernando Valley from Oakland. With a rare combination of philosophical profundity and Jewish social engineering genius, he established a series of programs which stamped his congregation as a creative center of Jewish life:

A ḥavurah program in which the bulk of the members participated, a para-professional counselling center whose first lay counsellors were volunteers from the board of directors who studied and trained for several years for this opportunity to serve: a para-rabbinic training program in which the synagogue leadership similarly learned to become rabbinic aides qualified to meet with members and teach them how to be Jews at home as well as in the synagogue; an outreach program which accepted the inevitability of an increasing proportion of interfaith marriages in our open society and chose to deal with it on the basis of inclusivity rather than a posture of exclusivity; and an assistant rabbi, engaged by the congregation after her ordination in 1990 who was herself a Jew by choice. Most of these and other innovative experiments were emulated nationwide.

RABBI-COMMUNITY BUILDERS. Some of the rabbis transcended their responsibilities to their synagogue by sharing their energies with the larger Jewish community. Rabbi Jacob Pressman arrived in Los Angeles in 1946 to assist Rabbi Jacob Kohn at Sinai Temple. A few years later he left to join a small congregation which grew to become Temple Beth Am one of the large and influential Los Angeles synagogues. Simultaneously he became a central figure in the building of Jewish institutions in the city.

He was a key figure in the organization of the University

of Judaism in 1947 and served as its volunteer founding registrar. He was one of the founders of Camp Ramah and the Los Angeles Hebrew High School. He established Herzl Academy, one of the first day schools in the Los Angeles Conservative community. He established the synagogue Israel Bond Appeal program and headed the synagogue division of Los Angeles Bonds. He was chairman of the Los Angeles Board of Rabbis as well as of the Western States region of the Rabbinical Assembly. Ten of his students went on to become rabbis.

The most significant centrist Orthodox synagogues, the Beth Jacob Congregation in Beverly Hills, had been originally established by Rabbi Simon Dolgin in the 1950s. He moved to Israel in 1971 and was replaced by Rabbi Maurice Lamm. Upon his retirement Rabbi Abner Weiss, from South Africa, became spiritual leader of the congregation. He was also the representative of moderate Orthodoxy in Los Angeles communal, religious and educational circles. His congregants who once rode to the synagogue, now walked if possible.

Rabbi Weiss also took pride in the "upstairs *minyan*" in which younger members were given an opportunity to take charge of their own Sabbath service as a popular alternative to the more staid and formal sanctuary service.

Rabbi Harvey Fields is the chief rabbi of the venerable Wilshire Temple, the first and still arguably the largest Jewish congregation in Los Angeles. He became chairman of the Middle East commission of the Jewish Federation Council. A congregation which historically had rejected many traditions, now settled into a life style which was comfortable with Hebrew instruction, bar mitzvah, bat mitzvah, and a *shofar.*

RABBI-SOCIAL ACTIVISTS. A number of rabbis, mostly in the Reform movement, became leaders in movements dealing with peace, poverty, racial harmony, and AIDS.

Rabbi Leonard Beerman established a congregation in the spirit and name of Leo Baeck, which over the years fostered an environment which made involvement in human concerns a normal congregational function.

As one example among many, Rabbi Beerman led his congregation to join forces with the All Saints Episcopal Church in Pasadena to establish a professionally run "Interfaith Center to Reverse the Arms Race." For years they supported and maintained a peace movement which gave serious attention to the world's ultimate long-term threat. When world events signaled a suspension of the arms race, both congregations shifted their energies to establishing a shelter for the homeless in downtown Los Angeles.

At the same time Rabbi Alfred Wolf, a long time associate of Rabbi Magnin at Wilshire Temple, set himself to bridge the gulf between the faiths. In 1975 he knit together the Roman Catholic Archdiocese of Los Angeles, with the Southern California Board of Rabbis and the American Jewish Committee. Together they established the Los Angeles Roman Catholic/Jewish Respect Life Committee which annually issued pastoral statements on subjects like "reflections on abortion and related issues," "caring for the dying person," "the single parent family," "nuclear reality," and "a covenant of care." He was one of the architects of the Southern California Interreligious Council for rabbis, ministers, and priests which met regularly with Muslim, Buddhist, Sikh, and Bahai leaders. He also presided over the County Commission on Human Relations. When the pope came to Los Angeles on a formal visit in 1989, Rabbi Wolf was chosen on behalf of the rabbinate to speak to him and he said, "we urge you, as we urge all our friends, to assist us in the continuing struggle against anti-Semitism — and in securing peace in Israel — including full diplomatic relations with the Vatican."

Rabbi Wolf upon retirement after 36 years of active service, became director of the newly established Skirball Institute on American Values.

Rabbi Allen Freehling of University Synagogue was deeply immersed in social action issues. He was much honored, receiving the Los Angeles social responsibility award from the Los Angeles Urban League, and the National Council of Christians and Jews honored him with the Humanitarian Responsibility Award. He was on the Los Angeles Commission to draft an ethics code for Los Angeles city government. He received the National Friendship Award by the parents and friends of lesbians and gays in 1989.

When the AIDS epidemic began to spread, Rabbi Freehling became Los Angeles' heroic voice on behalf of Jewish religious action for AIDS victims. He was the city wide chairman of the Committee for AIDS, the founding chairperson of the County Commission on AIDS, and the founding chair of the AIDS Interfaith Council of Southern California.

RABBI-EDUCATORS. In immediate post-World War II Los Angeles there was no learning beyond bar mitzvah and no employed Jewish scholars other than Dr. Samuel Dinin, head of the Bureau of Jewish Education and Rabbi Jacob Kohn at Sinai Temple. Forty years later, the University of Judaism was esconced on 25 acres of land on Mulholland Drive, the Hebrew Union College was in the process of building a major cultural center in neighborly proximity, and Yeshiva University was building a multi-story building on its site on Pico Boulevard. Additionally UCLA and the state universities had developed serious programs of advanced Jewish studies as an integral part of their academic offerings, and a substantial community of Jewishly committed academics was helping to transform a Jewish desert into a possible oasis of Judaism.

This came about largely through the efforts of rabbi-educators who put their lifetime learning and teaching experience to the task of building Jewish educational institutions.

The Union of American Hebrew Congregations (UAHC) in 1947, established in Los Angeles a college of Jewish studies to engage in teacher training and adult education. Five years later the Cincinnati-based Hebrew Union College formed a degree-granting California school. Eventually the school absorbed the UAHC College of Jewish Studies into a School of Education and Jewish Studies. In 1957, freshly ordained Rabbi Alfred Gottschalk, was appointed dean of the school. He enrolled at the University of Southern California Graduate School of Religion to get a doctorate in Bible.

Dr. Uri Herscher (right), executive v.p. of HUC-JIR, views model of HUC/Skirball Cultural Center, a project now under way, with visitors from the Times-Mirror Co. in Los Angeles (Courtesy HUC, L.A.; photo Allen Dean Walker, Santa Monica, Calif.)

University of Judaism Sunny and Isadore Familian Campus, Los Angeles, 1986, with academic wing and sculpture garden in the foreground, residence halls in the rear (Courtesy University of Judaism, Los Angeles)

While there he became good friends with the dean of the School of Religion. Their joint dream of the future bore fruit when in time an academic reciprocity agreement was negotiated whereby HUC would move to a major urban renewal site near USC, and the HUC students would get a dual USC-HUC degree in selected graduate programs. HUC in turn would serve as the Jewish studies provider for the university. The campus was built and dedicated in 1971.

The Rabbinical School was the centerpiece of the program. Joining it was the School of Jewish Communal service. The Rhea School of Education graduated educational administrators and teachers.

The Skirball Museum and the American Jewish Archives were transferred from Cincinnati to Los Angeles expanding considerably the educational and cultural horizons of the school. It now increasingly regarded itself, except for its rabbinical department, as an institution for the entire Jewish community.

When Gottschalk moved to Cincinnati to become fifth president of HUC, Uri D. Herscher became executive vice-president of the Hebrew Union College JIR world-wide and dean of the local school. He took the lead in conceptualizing and implementing a plan to build an imposing HUC Skirball cultural center. The academic department, integrated with USC would remain on its existing site. The rest of the college would move to the new campus. By 1990 the concept, the new campus, and the funds were securely in hand. The renowned Israeli architect, Moshe Safdie, was commissioned to design a cultural center on an acquired choice Mulholland area site.

The University of Judaism was founded in 1947 by the Jewish Theological Seminary in response to a visionary concept by Mordecai M. Kaplan. He proposed to establish a Jewish institution with the academic rigor of a general university but devoted to specialized research, training, and education for a Judaism defined as a civilization. At the same time the Los Angeles Bureau of Jewish Education was prodding the seminary to provide them with a school that could qualify prospective teachers who would be needed for the growing Jewish school system. Additionally the university planners saw the mission of the university as providing adult education, stimulating Jewish artistic expression, and offering continuing education to the young rabbis now flocking westward. Simon Greenberg volunteered to act as founding director, and Samuel Dinin as founding dean.

David Lieber came to the University of Judaism in 1956, as dean of students and in 1962, became president. Early on he formulated educational and management principles which guided him through the decades of university growth: uncompromising academic excellence; partnership with scholars and laity in the running of the school; unswerving attachment to the principle of pluralism in recognizing the legitimate diversities in Judaism and in the faculty; the ultimate establishment of a liberal arts college which would integrate both Jewish and Western cultures in one school and in one curriculum.

The university was radically reconstituted. A new campus was built in western Los Angeles which included residence halls for individuals and families which in time transformed the university from a commuting to a residential campus, from a local and Western institution to a national and international center. The school embarked upon a major program of expansion and diversification. The Hebrew teachers college was replaced by a master's program in Jewish education which qualified teachers to serve as administrators and educators; the courses for rabbis were replaced by a graduate school in Judaica for prospective rabbis who studied for two years at the UJ then spent a year in Israel and completed their training at the seminary in New York. A masters of business administration program was established under the direction of Dr. Leslie Koltai whose purpose was to train future executives for Jewish and for not-for-profit secular institutions. In 1989 there were approximately 25 students in each of three graduate programs.

In 1982 a four-year liberal arts college (Lee College) was established at the university. Students were grounded in both the Jewish and Western civilizations, with majors in a wide array of disciplines and qualified for graduate work in universities of their choice. In 1990 the student body was 75 full-time students. The continuing education program of the university grew to become the largest of its kind in the United States. Its annual catalogue of more than 50 pages described dozens of courses, an annual lecture series of six lectures held in five communities attracted a yearly audience of 25,000–40,000 persons; its elder hostel program was considered to be the most popular in the country.

A vigorous arts program attested to the continuing concentration on the arts as being integral to Jewish education.

Two new policy institutes were established in the late 1980s. The Wilstein Institute, was an activist think tank which researched and recommended public policy on vital Jewish issues. In its first two years of existence conferences on public policy were held in subjects relating to Jewish identity, crime and punishment, Soviet Jews in their homeland, Jews and other ethnics in America. The Whizin Institute, researched and experimented with new directions for the Jewish family, the synagogue, and the Jewish community.

By the 1990s, both the University of Judaism and the Hebrew Union College were thriving institutions with differing but also overlapping types of leadership and goals, who were beginning to establish modes of cooperation.

The Jewish Federation Council. The Federation of Jewish Welfare Organizations was established in 1912 to serve as the disbursement, coordinating, and lobbying body for the 12 Jewish recipient agencies of the Los Angeles Community Chest. In addition the federation took responsibility for raising modest sums for supplementary assistance. Under this arrangement only local Jewish needs were served.

In 1929, responding to appeals from European and Palestine Jewry, and to local needs not supported by the federation a separate funding mechanism was established, the United Jewish Welfare fund. Its first campaign year produced $93,000. By 1933, it became increasingly evident that there was need for a representative body that would be empowered to unite the Jewish community, including newer arrivals, around local concerns not addressed by the Federation or the Welfare Fund, such as Jewish education, youth organization, *kashrut* supervision, newly formed synagogues. In response an umbrella body called the United Jewish Community was founded which in 1936 comprised 92 constituent organizations, congregations, and societies.

In 1937, the United Jewish Community and the United Jewish Welfare Fund merged into a new body called the Jewish Community Council which a few years later was given the authority to allocate the monies raised by the United Jewish Welfare Fund. There were a Federation and a Council. The Council became increasingly preeminent as it attracted the new leadership in the growing Jewish community, while the Federation remained the bastion of the traditional and largely German leadership; 156 of the 350 eligible Jewish organizations joined the council. The new Jewish immigrants now arriving from the East Coast in increasing numbers tended to be politically liberal, equal-rights oriented, and devoted to Zionism and overseas needs.

This contrasted strongly with the Federation of Jewish Welfare Organizations which was conservative, local-needs oriented, lukewarm to Zionism. The spectacular increase in fundraising from $2,750,000 in 1945 to $10 million in 1948, and from 33 to 58 thousand contributors convinced the Federation leadership that their future was dismal, especially since Community Chest support, their major source of Jewish institutional income, was increasingly inadequate and increased public Jewish support was essential.

The Federation and the Council negotiated for three years; the result was the Jewish Federation Council (JFC). In the decades ahead the Federation-Council moved to become not only the spokesman but the driving force behind Jewish community growth and development. It continued to expand its sense of community responsibility. Its goals originally were quantitative and defensive: raising more money from each contributor and from more contributors; dealing with emergencies that upset Jewish unity and harmony and so affect fund raising; helping to maintain good relations in the community at large.

In the wake of the Yom Kippur War, the Federation leadership began to consider the responsibilities of the Federation as potentially transcending practical needs. The Federation was already deeply involved in Jewish education. Its bureau of Jewish Education guided, supported, subvented and served as chief advocate for Jewish schools. Since its organization in 1937, it had striven to establish and raise standards, attract and increase financial support, help to create a teaching profession. Under the initiative of Emil Jacoby, its director since 1983, a number of programs were established which sought to raise the level and standards and effectiveness of Jewish education.

However some thought more could be done to establish federation responsibility for the welfare of Judaism as well as of Jews. Sensitive to the danger of crossing the line between religious autonomy and Federation responsibility, they suggested that the Los Angeles Federation formally accept responsibility for a community stake in what they termed "the quality of Jewish life." This was to be a revolutionary departure. Until now Jewish communities were divided into "organized" and "religious." Jewish organizational life mandated mutual independence between "church" and "state."

Three major undertakings were established by the Federation-Council which blurred the line of demarcation between religious and secular.

(1) The absorption by the Federation of the Board of Rabbis. The previously independent Board of Rabbis was taken over as a Federation responsibility. The advantage to the rabbis was that they finally had the financial security and staffing that enabled them to function more vigorously and effectively. The disadvantage was implicit control over policies and resolutions that might be unacceptable to the board or to the professional staff. Wise leadership on both sides kept resentments to a minimum and allowed this arrangement to become permanent.

(2) The establishment of the "council on Jewish life." In 1973 a Committee on Jewish Life was established by the JFC with the avowed goals of reducing tensions and adding to the potential cooperation between the communal and the congregational sectors of Jewish life.

A year later the committee made its report and recommendations; as a result, in the fall of 1974, the Council of Jewish Life was established to implement the report. Its mandate at the time was to improve relationships between synagogues and JFC; develop an outreach program to the unaffiliated including promotion of synagogue affiliation; and support of existing adult education programs.

In succeeding years the Council on Jewish Life expanded its program which aimed at "raising the quality of Jewish life." It established a number of commissions which undertook projects with cultural, educational, and religious goals. It established a commission on synagogue affairs which organized synagogue councils in outlying areas, developed a task force on synagogue finance and administration and circulated widely a letter written by the president of the JFC to welfare fund contributors describing the synagogue as "an indispensable link for the preservation and transmission of an authentic Jewish way of life" and urging affiliation with a synagogue. Nine hundred responses were received in response to this unprecedented appeal by a Jewish community organization which openly committed itself to the synagogue as essential to the creative survival of Jewish life in America.

Over the years the council established commissions which operated in areas considered significant. In 1988, they were adult Jewish education, the arts in Jewish life, the disabled, the Israelis, outreach to intermarried, outreach to singles, spirituality, synagogue funding. The council appropriated approximately $100,000 a year for support of synagogue proposals which were innovative. The grants were awarded by the committee on synagogue funding on a three-year basis. Grant requests by the end of the 1980s increasingly dealt with outreach concerns such as reaching the unaffiliated, the singles, the intermarried, the disaffected.

(3) Commission on the Jewish Future. In 1988, the Jewish Federation Council established a potentially far reaching commission to study anticipated needs of the Jewish community in the last decade of this century. A number of social scientists were commissioned to study and recommend policies. They concluded that the first community responsibility must be to meet the Jewish needs of those who will constitute the coming generation and then set out to determine the first priorities in meeting these needs. They included the supplying of day care in a community in which 50% of the mothers with children under six hold full time jobs; raising 20 million dollars in 10 years to be divided between scholarships; raising teacher salaries and benefits to meet a disastrous shortage; and reaching Jewish youth through alternative experiences such as trips to Israel or camping.

The committee determined that its overarching goal was to find a meaningful Jewish identity for an emerging generation whose chief Jewish disability was likely to be rootlessness. They agreed too that this was only the beginning of a comprehensive plan to help structure a Jewish future for the Jews of Los Angeles and that the organized Jewish community must take full responsibility for its ultimate implementation. [M.V.]

LOTMAN, YURI MIKHAILOVICH (1922–), literary scholar and cultural anthropologist. Lotman was born in Petrograd into an assimilated Jewish family, and studied in the philological faculty of Leningrad University from 1939 to 1950, except for the years 1940–46 when he was in the Red Army, mainly at the front. From 1950 to 1954 Lotman worked at Tartu Teachers' Institute in Estonia, and from 1954 was at Tartu University where from 1960 to 1977 he was head of the Chair of Russian Literature. His main works are concerned with the history of Russian literature and social thought from the end of the 18th to the early 19th century, the theory of literature, cultural history, and semiotics. Basing himself on the work of the "formalist school," Lotman developed a methodology of analyzing the internal structure of poetic texts, applying quantitative methods of research to the semantics of verbal art. He developed ways of studying the links between the author, the structure, and addressees of artistic works, thus emerging as one of the first theoreticians of structuralism in literary study. His major works *Lektsii po struktural'nou poetike* ("Lectures on Structural Poetics," 1964); *Struktura khudozhestvennogo teksta* ("The Structure of the Artistic Text," 1970); *Analiz poeticheskogo teksta* ("Analysis of the Poetic Text," 1972); *Semiotika jino i problemy kinoestetiki* ("Semiotics of Cinema and Problems of Cinema Aesthetics," 1973, etc.) established principles of structural-semiotic research in the fields of literature and art. Many scholars, including Roman *Jakobson, took part in the Summer School for Modeling Systems which he organized in Tartu in 1964, 1966, 1968, and 1970. In 1964, Lotman inaugurated the publication of the series *Trudy po znakovym sistemam* ("Works on Signal Systems").

His sister, LIDIYA MIKHAYLOVNA LOTMAN (1917–) is also a literary scholar, who has written on general problems of Russian literature of the 19th century. Her monograph *Realizm russkoy literatury 60–x godov 19 v.* ("Realism of Russian Literature of the 60s of the 19th Century," 1974) is characterized by a complex elaboration of literary-historical and theoretical issues. [MA.KI./S.J.E.R.]

°**LUTZ, CARL** (Charles; 1895–1975), Swiss diplomat who was responsible for saving Jewish lives in World War II. Lutz was made responsible for the interests of a number of countries who had severed relations with Hungary. He arrived in Budapest on January 2, 1942. As the representative of British interests, he came into contact with Moshe (Miklos) Krausz, the Jewish Agency immigration representative in Budapest. They developed a good relationship, working to maintain the modest flow of immigrants from Hungary to Palestine until the German occupation in March 1944.

Following the German occupation, Lutz gave Krausz and his team diplomatic protection in a Swiss office building. During the concentration and ensuing deportation of Hungarian Jewry, Krausz continued to try to foster emigration to Palestine and implored the Swiss and the Jewish Agency to influence the British to declare the holders of Palestine visas potential British citizens. At the height of the deportations, in late June 1944, the British agreed to Krausz's proposal. On July 7, the Hungarian regent, Miklos Horthy, declared that the deportations must cease. Soon after he also declared his willingness to allow 7,500 Jews to immigrate to Palestine, along with their families. This became known as the Horthy Offer, and it rendered Palestine visas even more valuable.

Working with Lutz, Krausz assembled a team which was comprised mostly of Zionist youth movement members. From the Glass House on Vadasz Utca, a Swiss holding, they distributed Palestine visas along with *Schutzbriefe*, letters of protection in the name of Switzerland. Some 50,000 *Schutzbriefe* were disseminated. After October 15, 1944, when the fascist Arrow Cross leader Ferenc Szalasi was brought to power by the Nazis, Lutz and other neutral diplomats redoubled their efforts to protect Jews from deportation. In addition to safeguarding those Jews who held legitimate *Schutzbriefe*, they also tried to help the thousands who held counterfeit documents. They intervened with the Hungarian authorities, trying to stop the deportations altogether, and — until that was possible — to mitigate their effect.

In November, the Hungarian authorities declared that a ghetto must be established for those Jews without *Schutzbriefe*, while Jews holding legitimate papers would be housed under the auspices of their foreign protectors. Lutz and the other neutral diplomats did what they could to prevent the founding of the ghetto. Although they managed to have its establishment postponed, they could not avert its ultimate creation. Once it was set up, they did their best to care for the Jews' day to day needs, working with the Zionist youth underground. Lutz, along with other neutral diplomats, also procured homes for the Jews under his protection. Jews, bearing false *Schutzbriefe*, found their way in to these homes and Lutz did his best to protect them as well. Nonetheless, both he and Raoul *Wallenberg, a Swedish attaché, were forced to delineate between Jews with real documents and Jews with forged papers at the concentration point in Obuda. Lutz also tried to save the deportees, who were being marched from Obuda to the Austrian border by foot. He filled out unused Salvadorean visas in their names and managed to pluck Jews from the lines of the Death March. With the conquest of Pest by the Soviets in mid-January 1945, Lutz moved to Buda. There he protected Jews in a Swiss building until that side of the city was also taken in mid-February. Lutz's work in saving Jews was officially recognized by *Yad Va-Shem in 1965.

Bibliography: A. Grossman, *Nur das Gewissen: Carl Lutz und seine Budapester Aktion; Geschichte und Portrait* (1986). [RO.ROZ.]

M

MALAMAT, ABRAHAM (1922–). Israel Bible scholar. Born in Vienna, Malamat settled in Palestine in 1935 and received his doctorate from the Hebrew University of Jerusalem in 1951 for a thesis on the history of the Arameans.

Many of his writings are concerned with the relationship between the history of ancient Mesopotamia to Ancient Egypt and the Bible. He has made a major contribution through his discoveries of the relation of the ancient *Mari inscriptions to the study of the Bible. His record and study of Mari in the 3rd and 2nd millennium of the Bible period contributed to our understanding of the historical background of the patriarchal period.

In 1954 he was appointed lecturer in Biblical and Ancient Jewish History at the Hebrew University of Jerusalem and professor in 1964. He has served as editor of the Hebrew bulletin of the Israel Exploration Society and is a member of the board and scientific council of the Israel Society for Military History, the international editorial board of the *Zeitschrift fuer die alttestamentlische Wissenschaft*, and the *Journal for the Study of the Old Testament*.

Malamat has published over 150 papers in Hebrew, English, and German. His Hebrew works include: *Israel in Bible Times — Historical Essays* (1983–1984); *Jeremiah, Chap. One — The Prophetic Call* (1954), and *The Arameans in Aram Naharayim* (1952). [E.HO.]

MARCUS, RUDOLPH ARTHUR (1923–), chemist and Nobel Prize winner. Marcus was born in Montreal, Canada,

Rudolph Marcus (Courtesy California Institute of Technology, Pasadena; photo Bob Paz/Caltech)

and educated there at McGill University. He taught at the Polytechnical Institute of Brooklyn, N.Y., 1951–64, at the University of Illinois, 1964–1968, and at the California Institute of Technology, where he became the Arthur Amos Noyes Professor of Chemistry in 1978.

Marcus was awarded the Nobel Prize in Chemistry in 1992 for his mathematical analysis of the cause and effect of electrons jumping from one molecule to another, ideas which he developed from 1956 to 1965. When electrons in molecules in a solution jump from one molecule to another, the structure of both molecules changes. The occurrence of this change temporarily increases the energy of the molecular system, resulting in a "driving force" for electron transfer. It was only in the 1980s that Marcus's theories were finally confirmed by experiments. His work has been useful in understanding many complicated chemical reactions, among them photosynthesis.

MARKOWITZ, HARRY M. (1927–), economist and Nobel Prize winner. Born in Chicago, he received his higher education, B.A. through Ph.D. (1954), at the University of Chicago. He was on the research staff of the Rand Corporation and technical director of Consolidated Analysis Centers, both in Santa Monica, California. After serving as a professor in UCLA, 1968–69, he moved to New York where he was president of the Arbitrage Management Company (1969–72), worked as a private consultant (1972–74), and was a member of the research staff of T. J. Watson Research Center of IBM (1974–83). Since 1982 he has been the Speiser Professor of Finance at Baruch College of CUNY. From 1990 he was research director at Diawa Securities Trust. In 1990 he shared the Nobel Prize in economics with William Sharpe of Stanford University and Merton Miller of the University of Chicago. The Nobel award was in honor of Markowitz's theory, first defined in the 1950s, of "portfolio choice," which showed that investors would do best if they built up a diversified investment portfolio. [ED.]

MATSAS, JOSEPH (1918–1986), Greek merchant, partisan, and researcher, the foremost Jewish intellectual in Greece after World War II. Matsas lived most of his life in Ioannina and devoted himself to his city, to his Jewish community, and to the research of the Jews in Ioannina and Greece.

Joseph Matsas (Courtesy Allegra Matsa, Ioannina)

Coming from a line of merchants, he owned a glass product store in the heart of the Ioannina bazaar, where Ionnaiote Jewish merchants had worked and thrived for generations. By the beginning of World War II, he had finished his studies in philosophy at Aristotle University in Thessalonika (Salonika) and was teaching high school in a village near Kilkis. When the ghettoization process started in Salonika in late January–early February 1943, the youth of the Jewish community started to flee in small numbers to the mountains in order to join the partisans. The Jews were welcomed by the military arm ELAS, which belonged to the leftist resistance movement EAM (The National Liberation Front), and Matsas was one of the first to leave to join.

After facing great difficulties in escaping from Salonika,

crossing rivers and avoiding German-controlled bridges, he reached the partisans. Since he had been a fighting soldier in the Greek army in the Albanian campaign, he was integrated into ELAS as fighting combattant, together with nine other Jews in a unit of 40 men. At the end of 1943, he went with his unit to Western Macedonia where the allies dropped equipment to them by parachute. In general, his unit lived under difficult circumstances in the mountains of Pieras, Vermious, and Pindou.

After the war Joseph Matsas established himself in Ioannina. In 1945 he was president of the Ioannina Jewish Council and in 1947 Matsas became the secretary of the Jewish community.

Matsas's main scholarly contribution lay in his research on the language, culture, and ancient traditions of the Romaniot Jews of Ioannina. His research into Judeo-Greek was a pioneering and valuable scholarly effort. In Ioannina in 1953 he published *Yianniotika Evraika Tragoudia* ("Greek Jewish Songs"), which consisted of 16 hymns taken from two manuscripts written between 1853 and 1870, translated into modern Greek. In 1955 he also published *Ta Onomata Ton Evraion Sta Ioannina* ("The Names of the Jews of Ioannina").

In the field of poetry he researched Judeo-Greek *kinot* (elegies) from Corfu from as early as the 13th century. He uncovered valuable collections of centuries-old Judeo-Greek *piyyutim* from Ioannina and contributed research and documentation to Jerusalem's Ben-Zvi Institute on Judeo-Greek poetry and language. He published several articles on the unique festivities of the Sicilian Purim celebrated in Ioannina.

Bibliography. R. Dalven, *The Jews of Ioannina* (1990); Y. Kerem, *The History of the Jews in Greece, 1821–1940. Part I* (1985); idem, "*Darkhei Hazalah shel Yehudim be-Yavan be-Milhemet ha-Olam ha-Sheniyyah*," in: *Pe'amim*, No. 27 (1986), 77–105. [YI.K.]

MAXWELL, ROBERT (1923–1991), British publisher. Maxwell was born Jan Ludvik Hoch, son of a poor Jewish farm laborer, in Solotvino in the Carpathians, then part of Czechoslovakia. Although his family were Orthodox Jews, he appears to have abandoned Judaism at about the time he left his native village and traveled to Budapest. Maxwell later stated that "I ceased to be a practicing Jew just before the war... I certainly do consider myself a Jew. I was born Jewish and I shall die Jewish." After the German occupation of Czechoslovakia in March 1939, Maxwell made his way to Hungary where he was arrested at the end of the year. He escaped and made his way to southern France where he joined members of the free Czech forces with whom he was transported to Britain in 1940. After a spell in the Czech Legion and the British Pioneer Corps, he joined the North Staffordshire Regiment in 1943 and served with distinction during the campaign in Northern Europe. He was decorated with the Military Cross in 1945 and had risen from the rank of corporal to captain by the end of the war. He served with the Allied Control Commission in the British Zone of Occupation in Germany in the department of Public Relations and Information Services Control. At this time he also engaged in commercial activities and following his demobilization in 1947 he entered business, specializing in import and export between Britain and Eastern Europe where he established extensive connections. He first entered publishing by way of an agreement to distribute German scientific periodicals in 1947. Two years later he acquired Pergamon Press, although he lost control of the company for a time in the early 1970s when his business activities were subjected to a critical report by the Department of Trade and Industry. In 1981 he bought the British Printing and Communication Corporation, of which he was chairman, and in 1984 acquired Mirror Group Newspapers (MGN). As chairman of MGN he became the publisher of several mass-circulation titles. Pergamon Press is today the world's largest distributor of scientific periodicals. Maxwell had extensive interest in the U.S. including the Macmillan Publishing Co. He also invested heavily in Central and Eastern Europe. Between 1964 and 1970, Robert Maxwell was Labor Member of Parliament for Buckinghamshire. He was active in various philanthropic causes and was chairman of the National AIDS Trust. In 1986 he was involved in the financing of the Commonwealth Games in Edinburgh and had an interest in several football clubs, notably Oxford United and Derby County. Most of his own family perished in the Holocaust and in 1988, he provided £1 million to fund the major international conference on the Holocaust, "Remembering for the Future," which took place in London and Oxford. Maxwell had business interests in Israel — Pergamon Media purchased a 45% stake in Modi'in Publishing House which owned the Israeli daily newspaper *Ma'ariv* — and invested in: Scitex, Keter Publishing House, and Teva Pharmaceutical Industries Ltd.

Maxwell was drowned at sea on falling from his yacht and was buried in Jerusalem on the Mount of Olives. After his death it was discovered he faced massive debts and had used the pension fund of MGN to meet the growing demands of his creditors. The possibility was mooted that his death was suicide, and two of his sons faced fraud charges in connection with the operations and collapse of what was known as the "Maxwell Empire." [D.CE.]

MEMORIAL FOUNDATION FOR JEWISH CULTURE, a worldwide funding body which seeks to stimulate Jewish scholarship and Jewish education, encourage the documentation and commemoration of the Holocaust, and offer succor to communities struggling to maintain their Jewish identity. It is based in New York. Established in 1964 as a living memorial to the victims of the Holocaust, the foundation aims to help assure a creative Jewish future throughout the world. The foundation's grants to institutions are for: (a) projects in Jewish scholarship; (b) Jewish education; (c) research and publication on the Holocaust; and (d) support for religious and educational programs in Jewishly deprived communities. The foundation's grants to individuals are for: (a) community service scholarships, to enable persons to get professional training in Jewish education, Jewish social service, the rabbinate, *shehitah*, and *milah* so that they can help communities where such professional personnel are urgently needed; (b) doctoral scholarships, to help train people for careers in Jewish scholarship and for leadership positions in the Jewish community; (c) postrabbinic scholarships, to help newly ordained rabbis get advanced training for careers as judges on rabbinical courts *(dayyanim)*, heads of institutions of higher Jewish learning, or other advanced leadership positions; and (d) fellowships, to help individuals do independent work of a significant nature in Jewish scholarship, literature, or art. [JE. HO.]

MILSTEIN, CESAR (1927–), immunologist and Nobel Prize laureate in medicine. Milstein was born in Bahia Blanca, Argentina. He studied at the University of Buenos Aires and received his doctorate from Cambridge University in 1960. From 1961 to 1963, when he emigrated from Argentina to England, he was affiliated with the National Institute of Microbiology in Buenos Aires. From 1963 he was with Cambridge University and headed its division of protein and nucleic chemistry. In 1980 he was the recipient of the Wolf Prize in medicine. In 1984 he was a co-recipient of the Nobel prize in medicine with George Koehler and Niels Jerne for their research into the body's immunological system and their development of a revolutionary method for producing antibodies, a technique which gave rise to new fields of endeavor for theoretical and applied biomedical research. [ED.]

MNOUCHKINE, ALEXANDRE (1908–1993), French film producer. Mnouchkine was born in Petrograd, Russia. One of the most influential producers in France, his endeavors left their mark on French cinema from the 1930s through the 1980s. He produced films with most of the great artists of his time and a number of his films are among the greatest box-office successes of France. He founded Majestic Films which operated from 1935 to 1940, and from 1945 he was chairman of Ariane Films.

Among the films he produced were: *Les parents terribles* (1948), *Fanfan la Tulipe* (1951), *Babette s'en va-t-en guerre* (1959), *Cartouche* (1961), *L'Homme de Rio* (1965), *Le Train* (1964), *Stavisky* (1974), *Garde a vue* (1981), and *La Balance* (1983).

His daughter ARIANE (1939–) is the founder and main director of the world-famous theater, Theatre du Soleil (established 1964). Mnouchkine and the actors in her company — most of whom come from academic backgrounds — live together in a kind of commune. Their creative activities take place in a former ammunition warehouse in a Paris suburb which was put at their disposal in 1972. They renovated the building and turned it into a theater setting, La Cartouche de Vincennes.

In 1960 Mnouchkine had established the A.T.E.P., the Paris University Theater. She studied the forms of Oriental theater in Cambodia and Japan in 1962. The Theatre du Soleil had its initial success with its presentation of *The Kitchen* by Arnold Wesker which was given in a Circus Medrano tent. The world-wide reputation of the theater was gained by its performance of *1789* in Milan in 1970 and of *1793* in Paris in 1972. The Mnouchkine formula for total theater includes physical expression and body language, the use of elements taken from the circus world, and audience participation. The performances also demonstrated a politically left-wing outlook on life.

A movie made by the Theatre du Soleil on the life of Molière was also a great success. In 1984 Mnouchkine participated very successfully in the Los Angeles international theater festival where the troupe presented three plays by Shakespeare, *Richard II, Henry IV*, and *Twelfth Night* in a Japanese-Oriental adaptation. In 1992 she presented her production of *Les Atrides* in England. [GI.KO.]

MOATI, SERGE (1946–), French television director. Moati was born in Tunis. From 1982 to 1986 he was the head of the state-owned channel 3 of French television (FR3), where he had been director of programming in 1981–1982. In addition to his work in television, he has directed a number of feature films and is a film critic. He has been awarded several prizes for his television programs, among them a prize for a documentary film (Prague, 1970), a prize for the best French-language film (1970), television critics award (1973), and the International Critics Award at the Monte Carlo festival in 1980. [GI.KO.]

MODIANO, PATRICK (1945–), French writer. Modiano was born in a suburb of Paris. His first book, *La Place de l'Étoile* (1968), gained him immediate fame and recognition. It is the story of a young French Jew caught in the turmoil of the war years in occupied Paris. Though Modiano was born after World War II, that period appears to fascinate him, and he goes back to it time and again in search of inspiration. Anti-Semitism and collaboration, black market and resistance, spies and doubtful heroes; these are the theme of his work. In *Lacombe Lucien* (1974), made into a successful film by Louis Malle, Modiano caused a furore by delving into the murky relationship between a young French Nazi and a Jewish girl. His other works include: *La Ronde de nuit* (1969), *Les Boulevards de ceinture* (1972), *Ville triste* (1975), *Livret de famille* (1977), *Rue des boutiques obscure*, winner of the 1978 Goncourt Prize. [GI.KO.]

MODIGLIANI, FRANCO (1918–), economist and Nobel Prize laureate. Modigliani was born in Rome. After earning a law degree at the University of Rome, he escaped the Fascist regime in Italy and moved to the United States in 1939. In New York he studied at the New School for Social Research, obtaining his Ph.D. in social sciences in 1944. He

Franco Modigliani (Courtesy of MIT, Cambridge, Massachusetts)

has been on the faculty of the Massachusetts Institute of Technology since 1962. Modigliani's research work focused on the analysis of household savings, wherein he determined that people save towards retirement rather than to amass money to be left as inheritance for the next generation, and on the different types of national pension programs and their effects. He also was highly influential in the area of corporate finance by directing attention to the fact that future earnings of a company serve to determine stock market values. The Nobel Prize in economic science for 1985 was awarded to him for "his pioneering analyses of saving and financial markets," for work which he published in the second half of the 1950s. [ED.]

MOLDOVA (formerly **Moldavia**), independent state of the CIS, which proclaimed its independence in May 1990. In 1979 it had 80,100 Jews and in 1989 — 65,800 (of whom 35,700 lived in Kishinev). The estimated Jewish population at the end of 1991 was 28,500. In 1988 the Jewish birth rate was 9.3 per 1,000 and mortality rate — 17.1 per 1,000.

Emigration in 1989 was 4,304 (3,702 from Kishinev). Immigration to Israel in 1990 amounted to 12,080 (7,578 from Kishinev); the corresponding figures the following year were 17,305 and 9,487.

The Jewish organizations in Moldova include the Moldova-Israel Friendship Association (established in November 1991), the Moldova-Israel Foreign Trade Association, and the Jewish Museum. The monthly Jewish newspaper *Nash golos* began appearing in March 1990. In June of that year the paper printed an interview with Prime Minister Mircea Druk, who stated that he had never concealed his revulsion for anti-Semitism and stressed the need to normalize relations between Moldovans and Jews. The prime minister also came out in favor of education in Hebrew for Jews in the republic.

Moldovan Jews appear to be worried about their future. Not a single Jew was elected to the Supreme Soviet in 1990. A law was passed making knowledge of the Moldovian language mandatory; this created difficulties for the basically Russian-speaking Moldovan Jews. Intensive Jewish emigration was renewed in mid-1992 in the wake of fighting in Trans-Dnistria.

Both the Joint Distribution Committee and the Jewish Agency have begun operating in Kishinev. Direct flights from Moldova to Israel started in January 1992. [MI.BE.]

MOSHINSKY, ELIJAH (1946–), opera and theater producer-director. He was educated at Melbourne University (B.A.) and St. Anthony's College, Oxford.

He was appointed associate producer at the Royal Opera House in 1979 where he is now principal producer. His most successful productions for Covent Garden have included *Peter Grimes, Othello, Samson and Delilah*, and *Simon Boccanegra*. West End productions have included the prize-winning *Shadowlands* and *Cyrano de Bergerac*. He has also produced five plays in the BBC Shakespeare cycle.

Moshinsky's preferences incline towards the classics which include Chekhov and Ibsen, and he is considered a leading Verdi expert. However, the 20th-century Ligeti's *Le Grand Macabre*, Berg's *Wozzeck*, and Sir Michael Tippett's *A Midsummer Marriage* are among his operatic productions.

Moshinsky has described his favored method of working; he is first and foremost a respecter of the creative forces of composer and writer and is therefore not a believer in the current vogue of innovation for its own sake.

Moshinsky has also mounted operas for the New York Metropolitan, Australian Opera, Welsh National Opera, the Chicago Lyric Opera, and for the houses of Paris, Geneva, Amsterdam, and the Maggio Musicale in Florence.

[SA.WH.]

MOTION PICTURES (see **12**:463) and **TELEVISION** (see **15**:927). The following capsule biographies supplement the list which appeared in volume 12. Since many of the individuals noted appear in both media the list is a combined one.

ASNER, EDWARD (1929–), actor. Born in Kansas City, Mo., Asner first gained attention as the gruff, but gentle television station manager, Lou Grant on the long running "The Mary Tyler Moore Show." A spin-off from this successful production provided Asner with his own star vehicle, "Lou Grant." Over a six year period, Asner received six Emmy Awards and four Golden Globe Awards for his show, a highly successful series critically and commercially. In 1981, Asner was elected president of the Screen Actors Guild and had a starring role in the film *Fort Apache, The Bronx*.

BACALL, LAUREN (Betty Joan Perske; 1924–), U.S. actress. Born in New York, Bacall studied at the American Academy of Dramatic Arts and then turned to modeling. She was featured on the cover of Harper's Bazaar and within one month had a Hollywood contract. Bacall co-starred in her first film with Humphrey Bogart whom she married one year later (1945). Her most outstanding films were made with Bogart — *To Have And Have Not, The Big Sleep, Dark Passage*, and *Key Largo*. In 1970 she won the Tony Award for her performance in the Broadway musical *Applause*.

BOONE, RICHARD (1916–), U.S. actor. Born in Los Angeles, Boone prepared for his career at New York's Actors Studio and debuted on Broadway in Judith Anderson's *Medea*. He made his motion picture debut in 1951 in *The Halls of Montezuma* and since then has appeared in over 30 films, including *The Robe, The Alamo, Hombre, Madron*, and *The Shootist*. Boone's name became a household word in the U.S. because of his starring roles on television in such series as "Medic," "Have Gun Will Travel" and "The Richard Boone Show."

BROOKS, MEL (Melvin Kaminsky; 1926–), U.S. comedian, actor, director. Born in New York, Brooks started as a gag writer for Sid Caesar's "Your Show Of Shows" and then created Don Adams' star comedy vehicle "Get Smart." He also teamed with fellow writer Carl Reiner on a number of big selling comedy albums based on Brooks' character, "The 2,000 Year Old Man." He broke into films by writing and directing the critical success (and commercial failure) *The Producers*. Brooks' second film, *The Twelve Chairs* met a similar fate, but his third effort, *Blazing Saddles*, was a box-office hit, and has been followed by many others including *Silent Movie* (1976), *High Anxiety* (1977), *History of the World, Part I* (1981), and a remake of the wartime comedy *To Be or Not To Be* in which Brooks costarred with his wife Anne Bancroft.

CRYSTAL, BILLY (1947–), U.S. actor. Born in New York, Crystal first achieved national recognition through regular appearances on the "Saturday Night Live" television comedy show. Crystal eventually graduated to feature film work and built up a steady following with roles in *This Is Spinal Tap* (1984), *Running Scared* (1986), *The Princess Bride* (1987), *Throw Mamma from the Train* (1987), and *Memories of Me* (1988), which Crystal co-scripted and co-produced with Alan King. Crystal then catapulted to star status in the hugely popular *When Harry Met Sally* (1989) and he followed this with the equally successful *City Slickers* (1990). His next film was *Mr. Saturday Night* (1992) which he also directed. Crystal was the host of the annual Academy Award presentations in Hollywood from 1990 to 1993.

FALK, PETER (1927–), U.S. actor. Born in New York, Falk worked for the Budget Bureau of the state of Connecticut as an efficiency expert after receiving his M.B.A. in public administration. Bored with his job, he turned first to theater and television and then to film, eventually receiving Oscar nominations for his performances in *Murder Inc.* and *Pocketful of Miracles*. In the 1970s Falk made a convincing impression in the films *Husbands* and *A Woman Under the Influence* and starred in his own popular television detective series "Columbo," new episodes of which were filmed after more than a 20-year break. In 1972 Falk won the Tony Award for his performance on Broadway in *The Prisoner of Second Avenue*.

FRIEDKIN, WILLIAM (1939–), U.S. director. Born in Chicago, Illinois, Friedkin began his career directing live broadcasts on a local television station. He then moved up to network television, but only after ten years did Friedkin have the opportunity to direct a feature film, *Good Times* (1967), with Sonny and Cher. He swiftly advanced to major motion pictures with *The Night They Raided Minsky's* (1968), and then directed a number of successful, critically acclaimed films, including *The Boys in the Band* (1970), *The French Connection* (1971), winner of Academy Award as best picture, and *The Exorcist* (1973).

GORDON, MICHAEL (1909–1993), U.S. director. Born in Baltimore, Gordon began directing feature films in 1942 and was highly successful critically and commercially with *Another Part of the Forest*, and his adaptation of Rostand's *Cyrano de Bergerac*. Gordon was blacklisted because of the House Un-American Activities Committee hearings. Away from Hollywood for a decade, he returned with an unrecognizable but successful style, directing slick, glossy hits such as *Pillow Talk, For Love Or Money*, and *Move Over Darling*.

HAMLISCH, MARVIN (1944–), U.S. composer and arranger. Born in New York City, Hamlisch was the youngest student (at age seven) ever admitted to the Juilliard School of Music (which he attended until 1964). He is the composer and/or arranger of music scores for such films as *The Swimmer* (1968), *Take The Money and Run* (1969), *Bananas* (1971), *Save The Tiger* (1973) and *Kotch* (1971). In 1974, Hamlisch became the first individual to receive three Academy Awards in one night — one for best scoring of *The Sting*, one for best original dramatic score for *The Way We Were*, and one for best original song (also, "The Way We Were"). He also received Four Grammy's for his work on *The Sting*. Hamlich also won a Pulitzer prize and Tony Award for composing the score of the Broadway musical *Chorus Line* (1976).

HARRIS, BARBARA (Sandra Markowitz; 1937–), U.S. actress. Born in Evanston, Ill., Harris attended the Goodman Theater School and the University of Chicago. She began her career with the famous Second City improvisation troupe and moved from there to Broadway where she won a Tony Award (1967) for her performance in *The Apple Tree*. Harris made her film debut in the bittersweet comedy *A Thousand Clowns* and went on to star in such films as *Plaza Suite, Who is Harry Kellerman and Why Is He Saying Those Terrible Things About Me?, The War Between Men and Women, Nashville, Movie Movie*, and *The Senator*.

HENRY, BUCK (Buck Henry Zuckerman; 1930–), U.S. screenwriter and actor. Born in New York, Henry began his career at age 16 in the cast of the long-running Broadway production *Life With Father*. Henry saw military service with the army during the Korean

War and afterwards found work writing jokes for the Steve Allen and Garry Moore television shows. His first big success was as co-writer of the hit comedy series "Get Smart." Henry became a member of a screenwriter's elite when he shared credit for the script of the feature film *The Graduate*, and since then has written the screenplay for such films as *Catch-22, What's Up Doc?, The Day of the Dolphin*, and *Heaven Can Wait*.

HERSHEY, BARBARA (Barbara Herzstein; 1948–), U.S. actress. Born in Hollywood, Calif., Hershey starred as a teenager on the television show "The Monroes," and from the late 1960s on acted in such feature films as *Last Summer, The Liberation of L. B. Jones, The Baby Maker, Dealing, Boxcar Bertha, The Stunt Man, A Man Called Intrepid, The Right Stuff, The Natural, Hannah and Her Sisters, Tin Men, Shy People* (Cannes Film Festival award for Best actress, 1987), *A World Apart* (Cannes Film Festival award for Best Actress, 1988), *The Last Temptation*, and *Public Eye*.

LASSER, LOUISE (1941–), U.S. actress. Born in New York, in 1964 she joined the cast of Elaine May's improvisation troupe *The Third Ear* and later appeared in several Broadway and off-Broadway productions. Lasser was married to Woody Allen for several years and acted in four of his early films, *What's New Pussycat?, What's Up Tiger Lily?, Bananas* and *Everything You Always Wanted To Know About Sex But Were Afraid To Ask*. In 1976, Lasser attained national stardom as a result of her title role in the television series "Mary Hartman, Mary Hartman."

LEAR, NORMAN (1922–), U.S. writer, producer, director of TV and films. Born in New Haven, Connecticut in 1922, Lear served in the U.S. Army Air Force during World War II (1941–45). At the war's end Lear was decorated with the Air Medal with four oak leaf clusters. Lear began his career in films, producing and writing such motion pictures as *Come Blow Your Horn* (1963), *Divorce, American Style* (1967) and *The Night They Raided Minsky's* (1968). He then turned to developing and creating television shows, beginning with "All In the Family" in 1971 and including "Maude" (1972). "Sanford & Son" (1972), "Good Times" (1974), "The Jeffersons" (1975), "Mary Hartman, Mary Hartman" (1976), and "One Day At A Time" (1976). Lear has been president of the American Civil Liberties Foundation from 1973 and founded People for the American Way in 1980. He was also a member of the advisory board to the National Women's Political Caucus. In 1973, Lear was named Man of the Year by the Hollywood chapter of the National Academy of Television Arts and Sciences. Lear also received three Emmy Awards for "All In the Family" (1970–73) and a Peabody Award (1978).

LEVINSON, BARRY (1942–), U.S. director and writer. Born in Baltimore, Levinson began his show business career writing for and performing on television's "Carol Burnett Show." Levinson moved up to feature film work by helping write two of Mel Brooks' screenplays, *Silent Movie* and *High Anxiety*. He then made his directorial debut with his semi-autobiographical *Diner* (1982), the first of three Levinson films to be set in his home town of Baltimore. Levinson followed with *The Natural* (1984), based on Bernard Malamud's novel, *Young Sherlock Holmes* (1985), *Tin Men* (1987), and the box-office smash hit *Good Morning, Vietnam* (1987). Levinson's next movie was *Rain Man* (1988), which won that year's Academy Award for Best Picture plus an Oscar for Levinson as Best Director. Levinson's three subsequent directorial efforts were *Avalon* (1990), *Bugsy* (1991), and *Toys* (1992).

MATTHAU, WALTER (1920–), U.S. actor. Born in New York, Matthau served as a gunner on an Army Air Force bomber during WWII. Afterwards he attended acting classes and performed on Broadway. Matthau made his film debut in *The Kentuckian* in 1955 and since then has acted in over 40 films, including *Lonely Are the Brave, Charade, Fail Safe, Mirage, The Odd Couple, Hello Dolly!, Cactus Flower, Plaza Suite, Charley Varrick*, and *Hopscotch*. In 1966 Matthau won an Oscar as best supporting actor for his role as "Whiplash Willie" Gingrich in *The Fortune Cookie*, co-starring with Jack Lemmon with whom he appeared in a number of films, and was nominated twice for best actor, for his roles in *Kotch* (1971) and *The Sunshine Boys* (1975).

MAZURSKY, PAUL (1930–), U.S. director, producer, screenwriter and actor. Born in Brooklyn, New York, Mazursky began work in films as an actor, playing small parts in *Fear and Desire* (1953) and *The Blackboard Jungle* (1955). He then turned to writing for television ("The Danny Kaye Show") in collaboration with Larry Tucker. In 1968, Mazursky and Tucker wrote the screenplay for *I Love You, Alice B. Toklas*. In 1969, Mazursky directed his first film, *Bob & Carol & Ted & Alice*. He followed it by directing such motion pictures as *Alex In Wonderland* (1970), *Blume In Love* (1973), *Harry and Tonto* (1974), *Next Stop Greenwich Village* (1976), *An Unmarried Woman* (1978), *Tempest* (1983), *Moscow on the Hudson*, and *Down and Out in Beverly Hills* (1986).

NEWLEY, ANTHONY (1931–), English actor and singer. Born in London, Newley found stardom as a teenager in David Lean's film of Dickens' *Oliver Twist* (1948) and continued in lead roles in such films as *The Cockleshell Heroes, The Good Companions, How To Marry A Rich Uncle, Fire Down Below, Killers of Kilimanjaro* and *Doctor Dolittle*. Newley co-authored and co-composed (with Leslie Bricusse) the hit Broadway musical *Stop the World — I Want To Get Off* and wrote the music for the Gene Wilder film, *Willy Wonka and the Chocolate Factory*.

REINER, ROB (1945–), U.S. director and actor. Born in New York, the son of actor/writer/director Carl Reiner, Rob Reiner began as a sketch writer for television's "Smothers Brothers Comedy Hour." Reiner's breakthrough as an actor came in 1971 when he was chosen for the part of Mike Stivic ("Meathead") on the popular TV comedy series "All in the Family." Finding only limited movement in his acting career, Reiner turned to directing and his feature film the mock-documentary *This Is Spinal Tap* (1984) was a surprise hit. Reiner followed this success with five straight money-makers, *Stand by Me* (1986), *The Princess Bride* (1987), *When Harry Met Sally* (1989), *Misery* (1990), and *A Few Good Men* (1992), which earned an Academy Award nomination for Best Picture of the Year.

RYDER, WINONA (Winona Horowitz, 1970–), U.S. film actress. Born in Winona, Minnesota, she appeared in such popular films as *Beetlejuice, Night on Earth*, and *Edward Scissorhands*. At age 22, Ryder achieved the status of one of Hollywood's most sought after actresses with starring roles in Coppola's *Dracula* and Scorsese's *Age of Innocence*.

SEGAL, GEORGE (1934–), U.S. actor. Born in New York, Segal began his career on the off-Broadway stage. He moved on to television and Broadway, then made his film debut in 1961 in *The Young Doctors*. Segal's stardom was assured with two performances in successive films, *King Rat* (1965) and *Who's Afraid of Virginia Woolf?* (1966), the latter winning him an Oscar nomination for best supporting actor. Segal has starred in over two dozen motion pictures including, *The Quiller Memorandum, Bye Bye Braverman, No Way To Treat A Lady, Where's Poppa?, The Hot Rock, A Touch of Class, Blume In Love*, and *California Split*.

SPIELBERG, STEVEN (1947–), director. Born in Cincinnati, Ohio, Spielberg began his career early in his youth, directing home movies. At age 13 he entered and won his first contest with a 40-minute war film. While attending California State College he directed five films and made his professional debut with a 24-minute short, *Amblin*, which was shown at the 1969 Atlanta Film Festival.

Steven Spielberg (Bar-David, Tel Aviv)

Its success led to a contract with Universal Studios that soon found Spielberg directing movies for television such as *Duel* and *Something Evil*. His debut as a feature film director was *Sugarland Express* (1974). Spielberg followed this with a series of some of the most successful motion pictures in cinema history. They included *Jaws* (1975), *Close Encounters of the Third Kind* (1977), *Raiders of the Lost Ark* (1981), *E.T.* (1982), *Indiana Jones and the Temple of Doom* (1984), *The Color Purple* (1985), *Empire of the Sun* (1987), *Indiana Jones and the Last Crusade* (1989), and *Schindler's List* (1993). In 1990 the Academy of the Motion Pictures, Arts and Sciences presented Spielberg with the Irving Thalberg Memorial Award for his ongoing contribution to the Excellence of Cinema.

STONE, OLIVER (1946–), U.S. film director. Born in New

Gene Wilder (center) and Richard Pryor (right) in the Columbia Pictures film *Stir Crazy* (*Jerusalem Post* Archive, Jerusalem)

York, Stone spent two years in Vietnam (1967–68) as a U.S. Infantry Specialist 4th class and received both the Purple Heart and a Bronze Star with Oak Leaf Cluster honors. Stone began his feature film career at the highest level, writing the screenplay of Alan Parker's *Midnight Express* (1978), for which he received an Oscar. Stone then wrote the script for *Scarface* (1983) and then directed his first feature, *Salvador* (1986), which he also co-scripted and co-produced. Stone's next directorial effort was the hugely successful *Platoon* (1986), which received the Academy Award for Best Picture of the year and an Oscar for Stone for Best Director. Stone then directed *Wall Street* (1987) and *Talk Radio* (1988), both of which he also co-scripted. His next film, *Born on the Fourth of July* (1989) won him his second Academy Award for Best Director. Stone then directed *The Doors* (1990) and the highly controversial *J.F.K.* (1991).

WILDER, GENE (Jerry Silberman; 1935–), U.S. actor. Born in Milwaukee, Wisc., Wilder taught fencing before making his off-Broadway debut in 1961 and made his film debut as the undertaker in *Bonnie and Clyde* (1967). Wilder was nominated for an Academy Award for his next film, *The Producers* (1968), and since then has starred in a variety of comedy vehicles including *Start the Revolution Without Me, Blazing Saddles, Young Frankenstein, Silver Streak*, and *The Cisco Kid.* [JO.LI.]

MOUNTAIN JEWS (see **12**:478). The following article is based on supplementary material that has become known in recent years as a result of the arrival of Russian Jewish scholars in Israel.

A Jewish ethnic and linguistic group living mainly in Soviet Azerbaijan and Daghestan, the name "Mountain Jews" emerged in the first half of the 19th century when the Russian Empire annexed those territories. The Mountain Jews call themselves *Juhur*. According to estimates based on the Soviet censuses of 1959 and 1970 they numbered between 50,000 and 70,000 in 1970. Of these, 17,109 registered as Tats in the 1970 census so as to escape being registered as Jews and discriminated against by the authorities. About 22,000 did so in the 1979 census.

They speak several dialects (similar to each other) of the Tat language (see *Judeo-Tat), which belongs to the western branch of the Iranian languages group.

Their main centers of settlement are: in Azerbaijan, *Baku, capital of the republic, and the town of Kuba where the majority of Mountain Jews live in the suburb of Krasnaya Sloboda which has an all-Jewish population; in Daghestan, *Derbent, Makhachkalah, capital of the republic (which was called Petrovsk Port until 1922), and Buynaksk (Temir-Khan Shurah prior to 1922). Outside Azerbaijan and Daghestan considerable numbers of Mountain Jews live in Nalchik, in the suburb of Yevreyskaya Kolonka, and also in the town of Grozny.

Linguistic and indirect historical evidence indicates that the community of Mountain Jews was formed as a result of constant immigration of Jews from northern Persia — and perhaps also from nearby regions of the Byzantine Empire — to the Transcaucasian Azerbaijan where they settled in its eastern and north-eastern regions among a population speaking the Tat language which they also adopted in time.

The immigration of the Jews evidently began when the Muslims invaded those regions in 639–643, and it continued for the whole period from the Arab to the 13th-century Mongol invasion. Apparently the main waves of migration ceased in the early 11th century under the impact of the mass invasion of a Turkic nomadic tribe. This intrusion might also have forced many of the Tat-speaking Jewish inhabitants of Transcaucasian Azerbaijan to move further north to Daghestan.

There they contacted remnants of the *Khazars who had adopted Judaism in the 8th century. Already in 1254 the monk Wilhelm Rubruquis, a Flemish traveler, noted the existence of "a great number of Jews" throughout eastern Caucasus, in both Daghestan and Azerbaijan.

The Mountain Jews had contacts with the Jewish communities of the Mediterranean region. Tagriberdi (1409–1470), the Muslim historiographer from Egypt, wrote of Jewish merchants from "Circassia" (i.e., from Caucasus) visiting Cairo. Through such contacts printed books reached the Mountain Jews. In the town of Kuba books were preserved until the beginning of the 20th century that had been printed in Venice in the late 16th and early 17th centuries.

From the 14th to the 16th centuries European travelers did not reach those regions but rumors spread in Europe in the 16th and 17th centuries about "nine and a half Jewish tribes" driven by "Alexander the Great" behind the Caspian Mountains, i.e., into Daghestan. Those rumors might have originated with Jewish merchants from the eastern Caucasus appearing at the time in Italy. N. Vitsen, a Dutch traveler, who visited Daghestan in 1690 found many Jews there, especially in the village of Buynak, not far from the present Buynaksk, as well as in the Khanate of Qaraqaitagh where, according to him 15,000 Jews lived. The 17th and early 18th centuries can perhaps be considered for the Jews a period of relative peace and prosperity. A solid area of Jewish settlement existed in the north of present-day Azerbaidjan and in southern Daghestan, in the region between the towns of Kuba and Derbent. A valley near Derbent, called by the Muslim Juhud-Kata (Jewish Valley), was inhabited evidently, mainly by Jews. Its largest settlement named Aba-Sava served as the spiritual center of the community. Several *piyyutim* (liturgical poems) written in Hebrew by Elishah ben Samuel who lived in the region have been preserved. Also in Aba-Sava there lived a scholar called Gershon Lalah ben Moses Naqdi who wrote a commentary on Maimonides' *Mishneh Torah.* Mattathias ben Samuel ha-Kohen from Shemakha to the south of Kuba wrote between 1806 and 1828 a kabbalistic work, *Kol Mevasser*, which is the last evidence of religious creativity in Hebrew in the community.

From the second half of the 18th century, the situation of the Mountain Jews severely deteriorated as the result of the struggle to conquer their region involving Russia, Persia, Turkey, and a number of local rulers. The Persian commander Nadir, who later became the Shah of Persia (1736–47), managed in the early 1730s to drive Turkey out of Azerbaijan and successfully to withstand Russian efforts to possess Daghestan. Several settlements of Mountain Jews were almost entirely destroyed by his troops, a number of others were partially demolished and plundered. The Jews saved from destruction settled in the town of Kuba under the protection of its ruler Khan Hussein. In 1797 or 1799 Surkhan-Khan (the Muslim ruler of *qazimuqs* or *laks*) attacked Aba-Sava and, after a severe battle in which 157 defenders of the settlements perished, killed all the male prisoners, took the women and children prisoners, and destroyed the settlement. Thus the settlements of the Jewish valley came to an end. Those Jews who were so fortunate as to remain alive found refuge in Derbent under the protection of the local ruler, Fatkh-Ali-Khan, whose lands stretched to the town of Kuba.

In 1806 Russia annexed Derbent and the surrounding areas. In 1813 Transcaucasian Azerbaijan was annexed, the formal right to possession being finalized in 1828. Thus the majority of Mountain Jews who lived in these regions found themselves under Russian rule.

In 1830 a rebellion against Russia broke out in Daghestan, except for the coastal region including Derbent. The rebellion, headed by Shamil, continued with interruptions up to 1859. Its slogan was *Jihad* — holy war against non-believers, i.e., non-Muslims. Grave assaults on Mountain Jews occurred: the inhabitants of a number of *auls* (villages) were forced to convert to Islam, and in time they merged completely with the surrounding population. However, for several generations, the memory of their Jewish origin lingered. In 1840 the community heads of Mountain Jews in Derbent appealed to Czar Nicholas I in a petition (in Hebrew) beseeching the Russians to "gather the Jews dispersed in the mountains, the forests, and little villages, suffering under Tatars" (meaning the rebellious Muslims) "and settle them in towns and settlements" (meaning in areas controlled by the Russians).

The turning of the Mountain Jews to Russia for protection did not lead to immediate changes in their situation, occupations, or community structure.

Such changes emerged slowly only toward the end of the 19th century. In 1835 of 7,649 Mountain Jews under Russian rule 58.3% were involved in agriculture and 41.7% were urban dwellers. The town population, however, also engaged to a considerable extent in agriculture, mainly in viticulture and winemaking, especially in Kuba and Derbent; they also grew rubia, a plant from the roots of which red paint was extracted.

The rich families among the Mountain Jews were wine producers: the Ḥanukaevs, owners of a company for producing and selling wine, and the Dadashevs, who besides wine production founded the largest fishing company in Daghestan.

The raising of rubia was almost entirely dropped by the early 20th century due to the development of aniline dye production; most Mountain Jews who had been involved in the business lost their property and became casual workers. This became their job mainly in Baku, where the number of Mountain Jews increased only toward the end of the 19th century, and to some extent also in Derbent, where the bankrupt Jews turned mostly to door to door trading or became seasonal fishing workers.

Almost all the Mountain Jews engaged in viticulture worked also in gardening. In some settlements of Azerbaijan they grew tobacco, and in Qaitagh and Tabasaran (Daghestan) they were engaged in land cultivation, an occupation which was also common in several villages of Azerbaijan.

In some of the villages their main employment was leather processing. This branch came to a standstill in the early 20th century when the Russian authorities forbade Mountain Jews to enter Central Asia where they used to buy the raw skins. A significant part of the leather processors became town laborers.

The number of Mountain Jews in petty trade, including peddling, was relatively small in the initial period of Russian power, but grew significantly from the late 19th century. The few affluent Jewish merchants lived mainly in Kuba and Derbent, and from the end of the 19th century they also began to settle in the towns of in Baku and Temir-Khan-Shura where they most notably dealt in textiles and carpet selling.

The main social framework of the Mountain Jews up to the end of the 1920s was a large family unit encompassing three or four generations and reaching 70 or more people in number. As a rule, the extended family lived around a large single "yard" where each nuclear family, consisting of a father and mother with their children, occupied a separate house. The Mountain Jews practiced polygamy and two or three wives at a time were common up to the Soviet period.

If a nuclear family consisted of a husband and two or three wives, then each wife with her children occupied a separate house. The father was head of the family, and after his death was succeeded by his eldest son. The head of family took care of the property shared by all members of the family. He also fixed the work schedule for all the men in the family and his authority was beyond question.

The mother of the family, or in the polygamous families the first wife of the father, conducted the household and watched over the housework: cooking the food for all the family, cleaning the yard and the house, and so on.

Several large families originating from the same ancestor formed the broader and loosely connected community, *tukhum* (literally "seed"). Family links were of special importance in vendettas; if the murderer appeared Jewish and the relatives did not manage to avenge the blood of the victim within three days after the murder, then the families of the murderer and the victim reconciled, and considered themselves tied by the bonds of blood kinship.

The population of the Jewish village consisted as a rule of three to five large families. The head of the rural community originated from the most respected or most numerous family of the settlement.

In the towns the Jews lived in special suburbs as in Kuba, or in a separate Jewish quarter as in Derbent. From the 1860s

Title of a Judeo-Tat language textbook by Levi Natranova, 1927 (JNUL Photo Collection, Jerusalem)

Mountain Jews began to live in towns where they had never lived before (Baku, Temir-Khan-Shura), and in towns founded by the Russians: Petrovsk Port, Nalchik, and Grozny. Such moves often resulted in the disintegration of the structure of the large family, for only part of it — one or two nuclear families — moved to a new settlement. Even in the towns where Mountain Jews had lived for a long time, such as Kuba and Derbent (but not in the villages), the process of the disintegration of large families began toward the end of the 19th century.

Precise data on the administrative structure of urbanized Mountain Jews is available only for Derbent, where the community was headed by three elected members. One of these took the post of head and the two others served as his deputies. They were responsible both for the relations with the authorities and for the internal affairs of the community.

The rabbinical hierarchy had two levels: "rabbi" and *"dayyan."* The rabbi served as *ḥazzan* and preacher in the *namaz* (synagogue) of his village or his quarter of the town, and also as a teacher in *talmid-khuna (ḥeder)* and as religious slaughterer *(shoḥet).* The *dayyan* was the chief rabbi of the town: he was elected by the leaders of the community, and was the highest religious authority not only for his town, but also for the neighboring settlements; he chaired the religious court (**bet din*). He was also the *ḥazzan* and preacher in the main synagogue of the town and headed the yeshivah.

The level of halakhic knowledge among the yeshivah graduates was about that of a ritual slaughterer elsewhere, but they were reverently called "rabbi." From the middle of the 19th century a number of Mountain Jews studied in Ashkenazi yeshivot in Russia, mostly in Lithuania; there they were granted only the title of *shoḥet* but on returning to the Caucasus they served as rabbis. Very few of these Jews who studied in the yeshivot of Russia received the title of rabbi. From the mid-19th century, the Czarist authorities acknowledged the *dayyan* of Temir-Khan-Shra as the chief rabbi of northern Daghestan and northern Caucasus, and the *dayyan* of Derbent as chief rabbi of southern Daghestan and Azerbaijan. Besides their traditional duties, they acted as **kazyonny ravvin* (official rabbis in behalf of the authorities).

In the pre-Russian period, relations between the Mountain Jews and Muslims was determined by the so-called Covenant of *Omar, the special set of Islamic directives regarding **dhimmis* (non-Muslim protected citizens). However, the application of those laws in these regions was accompanied by special humiliation since the Mountain Jews depended to a great extent on the local ruler. According to the description of the German traveler I. Gerber, published in 1728, they had to pay a special ransom to the Muslim rulers for protection. Moreover, they had "to perform all kinds of difficult, dirty jobs which could not be enforced on a Muslim." The Jews had to give the ruler some of their yields free of charge: tobacco, rubia, tanned skins, and so on; they worked on his fields in harvest time, built and repaired his house, did gardening jobs, and were engaged in his vineyard. They also gave the ruler their horses on special occasions. Muslim soldiers who were feasting in the house of a Jew could demand money from their host "for causing them toothache."

Up to the end of the 1860s the Jews of certain mountain regions in Daghestan continued to pay ransom to the previous Muslim rulers of those regions, or to their descendants to whom the Czarist government has given rights equal to Russian noblemen, leaving the estates in their possession.

*Blood libels occurred in these regions only after they came under Russian rule. In 1814 disturbances occurred as the result of a blood libel in Baku; the Jews affected, mostly originating from Iran, fled to Kuba for protection. In 1878 on a similar allegation, dozens of Kuba Jews were arrested, and in 1911 the Jews of the settlement of Tarki suffered after being accused of kidnapping a Muslim girl.

The first contacts between the Mountain Jews and Ashkenazi Jews were established in the 1820s or 1830s. These links were reinforced and became more frequent only after regulations appeared which allowed those Russian Jews permitted to live outside the Pale of Settlement to move to areas where Mountain Jews were living.

In the 1870s the chief rabbi of Derbent. R. Jacob Itzhakovich-Yiẓhaki (1848–1917) contacted a number of Jewish scholars living in St. Petersburg. In 1884 R. Sharbat Nissim-Oghly, the chief rabbi of Temir-Khan-Shura, sent his son Elijah to the Higher Technical School in Moscow, and he became the first Mountain Jew to receive higher secular education. In the early 20th century Russian-language schools, where both religious and secular subjects were taught, were opened for Mountain Jews in Baku, Derbent, and Kuba.

Already in the 1840s or 1850s the yearning for the Holy Land led some Mountain Jews to Ereẓ Israel. In the 1870s and 1880s Jerusalem emissaries regularly visited Daghestan to collect **ḥalukkah* money. In the second half of the 1880s a Kolel Daghestan (Daghestan congregation) already existed in Jerusalem. R. Sharbat Nissim-Oghly settled in Jerusalem at the end of the 1880s or in the early 1890s. In 1894 he issued there a brochure, *Kadmoniyyot Yehudei he-Harim* ("The Ancient Traditions of the Mountain Jews"). In 1898 representatives of the Mountain Jews participated in the Second Zionist Congress in Basle. In 1907 R. Jacob Itzhakovich-Yiẓhaki moved to Ereẓ Israel and headed a group of 56 founders — mostly Mountain Jews — of the settlement Be'er Ya'akov near Ramleh, which is named for him.

Another group tried without success to settle in Maḥanaim in Upper Galilee in 1909–1911. Ezekiel Nisanov who went to the country in 1908 became a pioneer of the *Ha-Shomer organization and was killed by the Arabs in 1911. His brothers Judah and Ẓevi also joined Ha-Shomer. Before World War I, the number of Mountain Jews in Ereẓ Israel reached several hundred, most of them living in the Beth Israel quarter of Jerusalem.

Asaf Pinhasov became an active advocate of Zionism among the Mountain Jews at the beginning of the 20th century. In Vilna he published in 1908 his Judeo-Tat translation from the Russian of Joseph Sapir's book *Zionism*, the first book published in the language of the Mountain Jews.

The varied Zionist activities in Baku during World War I attracted Mountain Jews. After the 1917 February Revolution, these activities gained some momentum. Four representatives of the Mountain Jews, one of them a woman, participated in the Conference of Caucasian Zionists, in August 1917.

In November 1917, the Bolsheviks seized power in Baku, but in September 1918 the independent Azerbaijan Republic was proclaimed. These changes left Zionist activity undisturbed up to the second Sovietization of Azerbaijan in 1921. The national Jewish Council of Azerbaijan headed by Zionists established the Jewish People's University in 1919 and Mountain Jews were among the students. In the same year the Regional Caucasian Zionist Committee started to issue in Baku a Judeo-Tat newspaper called *Tobushi sabaḥi* ("Twilight"). Among the Zionists, Gershon Muradoy and Asaf Pinhasov were outstanding.

The Mountain Jews in Daghestan viewed the struggle between Soviets and the local separatists as the continuation of the traditional fight between Russians and Muslims, and they therefore mostly sympathized with the Russians, i.e., with the Soviet rule. Seventy percent of the Red Guards of Daghestan were of the Mountain Jews. The Daghestan separatists and their Turkish supporters, for their part, destroyed

Jewish settlements and massacred their population. Consequently the majority of Jews living in the mountains had to move to towns situated along the coast of the Caspian Sea, mainly to Derbent, Makhachkalah, and Buynaksk.

After Soviet power established itself in Daghestan, anti-Semitism did not disappear. In 1926 and 1929 the Jews faced blood libels, that of 1926 being accompanied by pogroms.

In the early 1920s, about 300 families of Mountain Jews from Azerbaijan and Daghestan managed to leave for Palestine. The majority of them settled in Tel Aviv where they established a Caucasian quarter. (One of the outstanding leaders of this immigration was Yehuda Adamovich, father of Yekutiel Adam, deputy chief of staff of the Israel Defense Forces who was killed in the 1982 Lebanon War.)

In 1921–22 organized Zionist activities among the Mountain Jews were disrupted; immigration to Ereẓ Israel also subsided. In the period between the end of the Civil War in Russia and World War II, the main goal of the Soviet authorities for the Mountain Jews was their productivization and eradication of religious feeling. With the former objective, Jewish collective farms were established. Two Jewish collective farms were founded in the settlements of Bagdanovka and Ganshtakovka where about 320 families worked in 1929. The settlements were situated in the North-Caucasian Territory, presently Krasnodar Territory. In 1931 about 970 Mountain Jewish families were drawn into collective farms in Daghestan. In Azerbaijan collective farms were established in Jewish villages and in the Jewish suburb of the town of Kuba. In 1927 members of 250 Mountain Jewish families became collective farmers in the Republic.

However, toward the end of the 1930s the Mountain Jews began to abandon collective farming, although many Jewish collective farms were still in existence after World War II: in the beginning of the 1970s about 10 percent of the community members remained in collective farms.

As far as religion was concerned, the authorities preferred not to destroy it immediately, in accordance with their general policy in the eastern provinces of the U.S.S.R., but to undermine religious tradition gradually by secularizing the community. For this purpose a wide network of schools was established, and special attention given to indoctrinating youth and adults in the framework of clubs.

In 1922 the first Soviet newspaper in Judeo-Tat appeared in Baku called *Karsokh* ("Worker"). It was sponsored by the Caucasian Regional Committee of the Jewish Communist Party and its Youth Section. The Poalei Zion newspaper did not find support among the authorities and soon ceased to exist. In 1928 another Mountain Jewish newspaper appeared called *Zaḥmatkash* ("The Laborers") and it was issued in Derbent. From 1929 to 1930 Judeo-Tat was given in the Latin script instead of Hebrew, and from 1938 the Russian (Cyrillic) alphabet has been used. In 1934 the Tat Literary Circle was established in Derbent, and in 1936 a Tat Section was created in the Union of Soviet Writers of Daghestan.

Works by Mountain Jewish writers of the period evince strong Communist indoctrination, especially in drama which was considered by the authorities as the most effective propaganda weapon. As a result, amateur theatrical groups proliferated and later, in 1935, the professional Mountain Jewish theater opened in Derbent.

During World War II the Germans for a short time occupied the regions of the northern Caucasus populated by Mountain Jews. In those areas with mixed Ashkenazi and Mountain Jewish population — in Kislovodsk, Pyatigorsk, and so on — all the Jews were killed. The same fate struck the Mountain Jewish collective farms in Krasnodar Territory, and also the Crimean settlements of Mountain Jews founded in the 1920s. In the regions encompassing the towns of Nalchik and Grozny the Germans were awaiting instructions on how to deal with "the Jewish problem" but these did not arrive before they had to retreat from these areas.

After World War II the anti-religious campaign gained momentum. In the period 1948–53 teaching in Judeo-Tat ended, and all the Mountain Jews' schools were conducted in Russian. *Zakhmatash* no longer appeared and all literary activities in Judeo-Tat were ended.

In the latter part of the 1970s, the Mountain Jews became victims of assault in several towns, in particular Nalchik, because of their struggle to leave for Israel. Cultural and literary activities in Judeo-Tat, revived after Stalin's death remained rudimentary in nature. From the end of 1953 up to 1986, two books a year were published on the average.

The main — and at times the sole — language of the youth was now Russian. Even the middle generation used the language of their community only at home in the family circle: to discuss more sophisticated topics they had to turn to Russian. This development was most noticeable among the small urban population of Mountain Jews, as for example, in Baku, and also among persons of higher education.

Religious tradition suffered, but was still partly retained, especially in comparison with the Ashkenazi community of the Soviet Union. The majority of the Mountain Jews continued to observe customs connected with the Jewish life cycle. The dietary laws are observed in many homes. However, Sabbath observance has been mostly abandoned, and the same is true of the Jewish festivals, except Rosh ha-Shanah and Yom Kippur, the Passover *seder* and the eating of *mazzot*. The knowledge of reading prayers and prayer rituals has been also largely lost.

Despite all this, the level of Jewish consciousness among the Mountain Jews has remained high and their Jewish identity is being preserved, even by those who formally register themselves as Tats. The mass emigration to Israel was resumed rather later than among other groups of Soviet Jewry; they began to leave not in 1971 but at the end of 1973 and early 1974 after the Yom Kippur War. About 12,000 Mountain Jews had arrived in Israel by the mid-1980s, and from 1989 through 1992 about another 5,000 reached Israel.

[MI.Z./S.J.E.R.]

MUSEUMS (see **12**:538). **In the United States.** THE JEWISH MUSEUM. The first documented, formal collection of Judaica established at an American Jewish institution was the donation in 1904 by Judge Mayer *Sulzberger of 26 objects "used in various rites and ceremonies" of Jewish life, to the library of the Jewish Theological Seminary (JTS) in New York City. With this donation, the Jewish Museum was established. Subsequent acquisitions of several major collections of Jewish ceremonial art, as well as continuing donations of Judaica, have made it one of the largest and most comprehensive collections of Judaica in the world.

Until 1944, the growing collection was housed in the Seminary's library. In that year, Frieda Schiff Warburg, widow of Felix *Warburg, presented the family home at the corner of 92nd Street and Fifth Avenue, a landmark building, to the Seminary for use as a museum. A sculpture court was installed in 1959, and the Vera and Albert A. List Building was added in 1963 to provide additional exhibition and program space. In 1993, the rebuilt Museum was opened with a doubling of gallery space and additional educational and public use areas.

The Jewish Museum's collections and exhibitions address the entire Jewish experience from biblical times to the present. Numbering over 16,000 objects, the collections are divided among the areas of Judaica (75%), fine arts, and broadcast materials. Included are paintings, prints and drawings, photographs, sculpture, decorative arts, ceremonial objects, textiles, antiquities, wood and metal work, manuscripts, coins and medals. Collection strengths include one of the finest collections of Ḥanukkah lamps in the world and a comprehensive collection of treasures of the city of Danzig which were entrusted to the JTS by communal elders on the eve of the Nazi invasion of Poland in 1939.

Some 6,000 objects in the Jewish Museum's collections, encompassing ceremonial art, fine arts, and archaeological material, were donated by businessman and philanthropist Harry G. Friedman between 1941 and 1965. A collection of 3,000 coins and medals assembled by the late Samuel Friedenberg and his son Daniel was donated between 1935 and 1948.

Archaeological artifacts constitute a significant aspect of the permanent collection, and the Jewish Museum's holdings in Israeli art rank as the most important publicly held representation in the United States. The National Jewish Archive of Broadcasting, established in 1981, maintains over 2,100 television and radio programs of Jewish interest, documenting in eyewitness interviews, performances, educational programs, and other expressions in audio and video recordings, the twentieth-century Jewish experience as well as the extraordinary contribution of Jewish writers, producers, actors, and comedians to American radio and television.

An Education Department was established in 1976 to coordinate tours and to implement a full range of family, school, and adult interpretive programs.

HEBREW UNION COLLEGE SKIRBALL MUSEUM. Comparable in size, scope, and quality to the collections of the Jewish Museum in New York, are the holdings of the Hebrew Union College Skirball Museum in Los Angeles, originally housed at the Hebrew Union College campus in Cincinnati. The Los Angeles location adjacent to the University of Southern California was opened to the public in 1972.

The programmatic emphases of the HUC Skirball Museum have encompassed exhibitions, cataloguing, and conservation of collections, innovative educational programming, and collection development. Building upon collection strengths in ceremonial art and Near Eastern antiquities, a major environmental installation devoted to biblical archaeology and ritual art, *A Walk Through the Past*, opened in 1974. In 1981, the permanent exhibition was renovated and expanded with the installation of *The Realm of Torah.*

Documented in exhibition catalogues and a 20,000-item slide library, the HUC Skirball Museum collections, also numbering nearly 20,000 objects, span 4,000 years of Jewish history. Collection strengths include the Nelson Glueck Memorial collection of archaeological artifacts, 1,300 rare Judaic textiles (including 600 Bavarian *wimpels*, illustrated or embroidered Torah binders), over 350 Italian *ketubbot* (illuminated marriage contracts), and major works of European silver Judaica. The Hebrew Union College Skirball Museum has undertaken a major national survey and collecting campaign called "Project Americana," designed to collect American Judaica.

One of the primary emphases of the HUC Skirball Museum, interpretive programming, includes docent-led tours, intergenerational programs, lectures and film series, and a pioneering endeavor initiated in 1976 entitled "M.U.S.E." ("Museum Utilization for Student Education"), which provides collection-based curricula on Jewish subjects for use in the multicultural classrooms of Los Angeles public schools as well as in Jewish educational settings.

B'NAI B'RITH KLUTZNICK MUSEUM. The third Jewish museum to be established in the United States was the B'nai B'rith Kluznick Museum, founded in 1957. Located at the headquarters of B'nai B'rith in Washington, D.C., the Klutznick Museum maintains a permanent collection of more than 600 Jewish ceremonial and folk art objects, prints and drawings, paintings and sculpture. An additional 12,000 B'nai B'rith documents and 3,000-volume library are housed and maintained by the Museum. It maintains a collection of ancient coins as well as the historic correspondence between President George Washington and Moses Seixas, sexton of the Hebrew Congregation at Newport, Rhode Island, dated 1790.

JUDAH L. MAGNES MEMORIAL MUSEUM. The first Jewish museum established in the Western United States, the Judah L. Magnes Memorial Museum, opened in Oakland, California, in 1962, and moved to its present Berkeley location in the historic Burke mansion in 1966. It holds the distinction of being the first American Jewish museum to be formally accredited by the American Association of Museums (1974).

The museum maintains a permanent collection of Jewish art from around the world, including ceremonial and fine art, textiles and costumes from North Africa and Europe, one of the largest Torah binder collections, documents and artifacts from the Jews of India, a Holocaust collection, and coins, medals, and amulets. In the museum's early years, missions were sent to vanishing Jewish communities such as those in Morocco, Tunisia, Egypt, India, Czechoslovakia, and Yugoslavia, to recover ceremonial art and books.

The Magnes Museum houses two significant archival and library resources. The Western Jewish History Center, founded in 1967, is an archival research library documenting the influence of the Jewish population on the development, character and culture of the Far West, from the Gold Rush to the present, and the Harry and Dorothy Blumenthal Rare Book and Manuscript Library which contains over 10,000 books and periodicals in English, Hebrew, Yiddish, and Ladino, as well as the Frydman Listening Center for Jewish music. Among the highlights of the library's holdings are a 5,000-item manuscript collection.

SPERTUS MUSEUM OF JUDAICA. Chicago's Spertus Museum of Judaica was opened to the public in 1968. It maintains a collection of approximately 3,000 objects with particular strengths in the area of ceremonial art, including textiles and costumes, and in Holocaust artifacts. The collections include a number of archaeological artifacts, paintings, sculpture, and graphics, 19th-century Yemenite manuscripts, as well as several examples of North African ritual art.

Most of the Spertus Museum collection does not predate the 18th century, and some of its more impressive artifacts reflect the aesthetics and art movements of the early 20th century.

In recent years, the major thrust of the Spertus Museum has been the development of educational applications in the museum setting. Materials are developed in conjunction with most exhibition offerings to augment appreciation of exhibits by younger viewers, to provide supplementary learning modules for teachers' use in the classroom, and to correlate exhibition designs and museum programs with educators' needs and curricular emphases.

YESHIVA UNIVERSITY MUSEUM. The Yeshiva University Museum was established in 1973. Occupying the main floor of a campus building in New York City's Washington Heights section, the museum opened with an exhibition of architectural models of ten historic synagogues, presented alongside a cybernetic map of Jewish history and three audiovisual programs on the history of the synagogues. In 1975 the Yeshiva University Museum began an ambitious program of exhibition development.

Its collections comprise ceremonial objects, textiles, and costumes of the 18th and 19th centuries, paintings, graphics, sculpture, rare books and manuscripts, and slides and photographs, and also include important examples of Americana and a collection of paintings, sculptures, and woodcuts by

Torah ark, mixed materials, Jerusalem, 1912–1913, by the Bezalel Art School, in the Spertus Museum of Judaica, Chicago. (Courtesy Spertus Museum of Judaica, Chicago)

artists of the early Zionist period and the beginning of the State of Israel.

NATIONAL MUSEUM OF AMERICAN JEWISH HISTORY. During the year of America's Bicentennial celebration, 1976, the nation's seventh Jewish museum was founded by Philadelphia's historic Congregation Mikveh Israel. The museum is intended both to celebrate the Jewish settlement in America and to provide an understanding of the universal struggles and triumphs of all ethnic groups in America's history.

Its collections today number nearly 3,000 artifacts. Comprising Jewish ceremonial art, fine arts, and decorative art relating to American Jewish history from colonial times to the present, the collections of the museum are augmented by the historical artifacts and archives maintained by Congregation Mikveh Israel.

Interpretive programs are regularly offered as a complement to its exhibitions. Lectures, concerts, theatrical performances, and family crafts workshops are sponsored in addition to docent-guided tours, and an annual film series has been developed drawing upon the resources of the museum's Ralph Lopatin Memorial Film Library.

COUNCIL OF AMERICAN JEWISH MUSEUMS. Recognizing their mutual concerns, and anticipating that the sharing of information between professionals would be likely to yield creative solutions, these museums formed the Council of American Jewish Museum (CAJM) in 1977. Its objectives and purposes are "to encourage, support and further the development of the Jewish museums in collecting, preserving, and interpreting Jewish art and artifacts for public education and the advancement of scholarship; to foster cooperative efforts among institutions maintaining Judaica collections; to advance understanding and support by the Jewish, general, and museum communities; and to facilitate the optimum utilization of collections embracing the significant Jewish aspects of the arts, humanities, and social sciences."

The National Foundation for Jewish Culture (NFJC) serves as the sponsoring agency for the Council, providing staff, office support, travel subsidies, seed money for particular projects, advocacy with the Council of Jewish Federations, and coordinates biannual conferences.

By 1988, 26 museums were affiliated. In recent years, an increasing number of smaller Jewish museums, historical societies, and other exhibiting organizations wished to become affiliated and the CAJM "Associates Program" was established to "nurture the development of the work of smaller Jewish museums and historical societies in the field of Jewish art and culture."

Among the museums newly affiliated is the Plotkin Judaica Museum of Greater Phoenix, Arizona, which has a collection of holiday and life cycle objects, including the Steven Orlikoff Tunisian collection comprising ceremonials, books, documents, typical clothing of the later 19th and early 20th centuries, and artifacts from the closed Koskas synagogue of Tunis.

Other CAJM affiliates include the Museum of Congregation Emanu-el of the City of New York; the Temple Museum of Religious Art, Cleveland, Ohio, founded in 1950 and notable for its Abba Hillel Silver archives; the Philadelphia Museum of Judaica of Congregation Rodeph Shalom, founded in 1975, which maintains on permanent display the Leon and Julia Obermayer Collection of Jewish Ceremonial Art; the Fenster Museum of Jewish Art, Tulsa, Oklahoma; the Mixel Museum of Judaica, Denver, Colorado, founded in 1982; and the Starr Gallery of the Jewish Community Center, Newton Center, Massachusetts.

Additional CAJM members are the American Jewish Historical Society, Waltham, Massachusetts; Central Synagogue, New York City; Benjamin and Dr. Edgar R. Cofeld Judaic Museum of Temple Beth Zion, Buffalo, New York; Congregation Beth Ahabah Museum and Archives Trust, Richmond, Virginia; Jewish War Veterans, USA, National Memorial, Washington, D.C.; Hebrew Home for the Aged at Riverdale's Judaica Museum; the Jewish Historical Society of Maryland; May Museum of Temple Israel, Lawrence, New York; Park Avenue Synagogue, New York City; the Fred Wolf, Jr. Gallery of the Klein Branch Jewish Community Center, Philadelphia, and the two satellite galleries affiliated with Hebrew Union College–Jewish Institute of Religion.

Many notable Jewish museums are not yet formally affiliated, including the Jane L. and Robert H. Weiner Judaic Museum located in the Goldman Fine Arts Gallery of the Jewish Community Center of Greater Washington and the Jewish Community Museum of San Francisco, opened in 1983.

HOLOCAUST MUSEUMS AND MEMORIALS. The U.S. has witnessed a proliferation of Holocaust memorials and museums since the late 1970s. In addition to such regional entities as the Dallas Memorial Center for Holocaust Studies and the Holocaust Memorial Center in West Bloomfield, Michigan, three institutions are sponsoring the development of museums that will reach out to a national audience. In Los Angeles, the Simon Wiesenthal Center has opened a "Museum of Tolerance," as part of its overall educational program to study the Holocaust, its contemporary implications, and related human rights issues.

The United States Holocaust Memorial Council, established by Congress in 1980, planned and built the U.S. Holocaust Memorial Museum in Washington, D.C., on property adjacent to the National Mall. This national museum opened in 1993, and contains a memorial Hall of Remembrance, a permanent exhibition on the history of the Holocaust, the national Holocaust library and archives, two auditoriums, and education center, two changing exhibition galleries and a Scholars' Center.

Finally, "A Living Memorial to the Holocaust — Museum of Jewish Heritage" is being planned by the New York Holocaust Memorial Commission to be New York City's principal public memorial to the six million Jews murdered during the Holocaust. Situated in Battery Park City in view of the Statue of Liberty and Ellis Island, the museum will honor the memory of Holocaust victims by documenting "the world before" (European Jewish culture and civilization prior to the Nazi assault), the Holocaust itself, the aftermath of the Holocaust (refugees and displaced persons, establishment of the State of Israel, pursuit of Nazi war criminals), and renewal in America.

Bibliography: N. Frazier, Jewish Museums of North America: A Guide to Collections, Artifacts and Memorabilia (1993).

In Europe. THE NETHERLANDS. The Jewish Historical Museum in Amsterdam was housed from 1932 on the top floor of the medieval weigh-house. By 1975 the collection had become so large that it occupied almost the entire building. The Amsterdam City Council decided that the abandoned Ashkenazi Synagogue complex, consisting of four historic 17th- and 18th-century synagogues, should become the new home of the Jewish Historical Museum. After careful art-historical and archival research, they were restored to their early 19th-century state, and to unite the four separate buildings, a new wing and a glass-roofed alleyway were added.

The museum displays objects of an artistic and historic nature, which combine to provide a picture of the rich cultural heritage of Dutch Jewry. The synagogues themselves provide a highly appropriate background for the collection. The permanent displays emphasizes the many-sidedness of Judaism; in the introductory section it focuses on five aspects which characterize contemporary Jewish identity in the Diaspora: religion, the bond with Israel; persecution and the will to survive; personal history; and the interaction with the majority culture. In the section presenting Jewish religion, the differences between Orthodox, Reform, and Conservative are shown. The collection of ceremonial objects illustrates both the dignified richness of the affluent Jews of Portuguese descent in Amsterdam and The Hague, as well as the charming simplicity of provincial Ashkenazi communities. The third section focuses on the social history of Dutch Jews presented through the development of ideas connected with *zedakah* (charity). The remaining space is used for temporary exhibitions, two large (art) historical exhibitions and four smaller ones annually. With its computerized documentation, the museum attracts students and scholars from far and wide. Since its opening in May 1987 this museum, the largest of its kind in Western Europe, has had over 120,000 visitors annually.

Elsewhere in the Netherlands, some 15 synagogues have been restored in recent years and now serve a cultural function. The most prominent is the Groningen Synagogue, an oriental-style building dating from 1906, in which regular Jewish worship is held concurrently with exhibitions on Jewish themes. The main building of the Amsterdam Lekstraat Synagogue, dating from 1937, has since 1984 become the home of the Amsterdam Museum of the Dutch Resistance.

GERMANY. In various parts of Germany interest is shown in Jewish ceremonial art and local Jewish history. An example is the Museum of Jewish Culture in the synagogue of Augsburg in southern Germany. Dedicated in 1917 and badly damaged in 1938, the former synagogue has served since 1985 as a Jewish museum. The Fränkische Schweiz Museum in the Bavarian village of Tüchersfeld is located in a beautiful 18th-century synagogue. The museum, opened in 1985, shows some fine Judaica. The Rashi House is the former wedding hall of the Jewish quarter of Worms. In 1982 the house was turned into a Jewish Museum and City Archive. The permanent exhibition is dedicated to the history of the Jewish community of Worms from the Middle Ages until the present. History and culture of North German Jewry are shown in the Jewish department of the Landesmuseum in Brunswick, which opened in 1987. The museum possesses a remarkable collection of Torah binders, the oldest dating from the 17th century. Inspired by the exhibition Monumenta Judaica in 1963–64, the Cologne Historical Museum started its own Judaic collection. The history of the Jews in Schleswig–Holstein, the region north of Hamburg, can be seen in the former synagogue of Rendsburg. There the sanctuary, religious school, and ritual bath have been used since 1987 as exhibition space.

In 1988, a new Jewish Museum was opened in Frankfurt on Main. Located in the Rothschild mansion, it forms part of Frankfurt's prestigious museums on the river bank *(Museumufer)*. The museum, the largest of its kind in German, focuses on the history and culture of its once flourishing Jewish community. The museum is educationally oriented. It shows the history of the community from its ghetto origins up to the deportation and beyond. Such aspects as the Jewish contribution to German society and Jewish religious life are given equal treatment. Museum publications also stress this approach.

Equally ambitious are plans to expand the Jewish department of the Berlin Museum. A semi-permanent display of history, culture, and religion of Berlin Jews can now be seen on the second floor of the Martin Gropius building. When the plans to expand this museum are realized in the 1990s, the Jewish department will form a separate but integrated part of the Berlin Museum. The infamous past is shown in a most impressive presentation in the ruins of the former Nazi Gestapo headquarters, "Topography of Terror." The Berlin Wannsee villa, the place where the "final solution" was discussed in 1942, has also been turned into a documentation center.

The famous synagogue at Oranienburger Strasse, of which only the façade still stood after bombings at the end of the war, is being reconstructed and will house a memorial, a synagogue, and a museum.

OTHER MUSEUMS IN WESTERN EUROPE. *Austria.* The Austrian Jewish museum in Eisenstadt was founded in 1982. It documents the contribution of Austrian Jews from the Middle Ages to the present. The museum is housed in the mansion of the Court Jew Samson Wertheimer (1658–1724), whose private synagogue is preserved. The Institute of Jewish Studies of Vienna University is responsible for its exhibitions. There are also plans to start a Jewish Museum in Vienna.

In former Yugoslavia, the Jewish Historical Museum of Belgrade and the Jewish Museum of Sarajevo were the major exhibitions.

Greece. The Jewish Museum of Greece in Athens was founded in 1977. It collects documents, and exhibits the material evidence of 2,400 years of Jewish presence in this country. The museum collection includes ceremonial art, costumes, and historical photographs.

Italy. In Italy, the Jewish Museum in the Scuola Tedesca in Venice's Ghetto Nuovo, opened in 1952, was fully renovated in 1986. It contains an exquisite collection of ceremonial silver and textiles, dating from the 16th century onward, and wedding contracts from several Italian cities. The Jewish Museum in Florence, founded in 1982 and located in the community center, focuses on the equally superb treasures of this city. The Jewish Museum of Soragna near Parma, also established in 1982, marks a change in the previous policy to dismantle and virtually rebuild synagogue interiors in Israel. Through local effort, the neoclassical synagogue (1855) was preserved and turned into a museum and cultural center. In Rome, the Jewish Museum, which opened in 1977, is near the Great Synagogue.

Spain and Portugal. Political changes in the Iberian Peninsula have led to new interest in the Sephardi heritage. Thus, the Museo Lusu-Hebraico Abraham Zacuto, in the 15th-century synagogue of Tomar in Portugal, though already founded in 1939, recently became known to a wider public. In this charming building, the oldest synagogue in the country, some ancient Jewish tombstones are exhibited, next to a more general presentation of Jewish ceremonial art. In 1985 the original *mikveh* was discovered and excavated. The Sephardi Museum of Toledo, Spain, set up in 1964 by the Spanish government is housed in the 14th-century "El Transito" synagogue. The emphasis here is on the sparse remains of pre-expulsion Jewish culture and on the Spanish Diaspora.

England. In England, the London Jewish Museum in Woburn House exhibits its famous collection of Judaica. Recently, two new Jewish museums have been set up in England, both developing a more active policy of collecting and exhibiting. The London Museum of Jewish Life, founded in 1983 and located in the Sternberg Center in the northern part of the City, focuses on the social life of London Jews. Its collection includes a large number of memorabilia from the turn of the century, the accent lying on the frequently neglected everyday life. The Czech Memorial Scrolls Center on the third floor of Kent House, London, was opened to the public in 1988. Its collection of binders is one of the largest in the world, and many are on display at the center. The Manchester Jewish Museum, in the Cheetham Hill Road Sephardi Synagogue, opened in 1984, documents two centuries of local Jewish history.

Elijah's chair, Germany or Austria, 1791, in the collection of the Jewish Museum of Switzerland, Basle. (Courtesy of the Jewish Museum of Switzerland, Basle; photo D. Widmer, Basle)

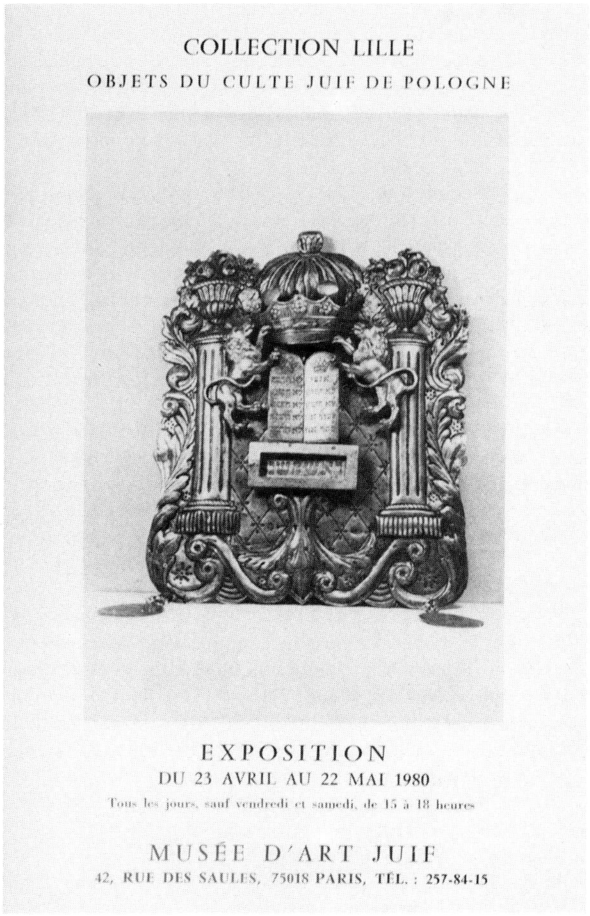

Cover of catalogue for the exhibition of the Lille Collection of Jewish religious objects from Poland at the Museum of Jewish Art, Paris, April–May 1980 (Courtesy Musée d'Art Juif, Paris)

Ireland. The Irish Jewish Museum opened in 1985 in the former Walworth Road Synagogue in Dublin. The building was completely restored: the sanctuary, women's gallery, and attached rooms have been turned into exhibition areas. The history of Irish Jewry over the past centuries receives ample attention.

Scandinavia. In Scandinavia two new Jewish Museums were recently founded. The Danish Jewish Museum in Copenhagen opened its doors in 1985 to show an impressive collection of ceremonial art, including some 250 Torah binders from various Jewish communities in Denmark. The impressive way in which Danish Jewry was saved during the Holocaust and the immigration of Polish Jews in 1970s also receives attention. In 1988 it was decided to turn the former synagogue, once a railroad station, and community building of Trondheim, Norway, into a Jewish Museum.

Switzerland. The Jewish Museum of Switzerland opened in Basle in 1966, beginning with a Judaica collection from the Folklore Museum of Switzerland in Basle, containing mainly objects from Switzerland and its neighboring countries. The museum's main objective is to remind Jews of their past and tradition and to introduce non-Jews to the Jewish way of life and holidays. The now much enlarged collection is displayed under three headings, the Law, the Jewish Year, and Everyday-life. The collection contains, among other items, silver objects from big cities and simple artifacts of brass, tin, wood, and pewter from rural areas, richly embroidered textiles, and amulets. There are Hebrew books printed in Basle from the 16th century on. A series of local Jewish tombstones from the 13th century through 1348 and documents of medieval Jewish communities in Basle are of special importance. A small collection of jars and coins from biblical times and a survey of Zionist documents — the first

Zionist Congress was held in Basle in 1897 — link the museum with Israel.

France and Belgium. In France, ambitious plans have been made to move the Paris Museum of Jewish Art, to the Hotel de Saint-Aignan, in the Marais quarter. The museum has an active exhibition schedule that supplements the display of the permanent collection of ceremonial and contemporary art. The important Strauss–Rothschild Collection of Judaica has since 1890 been part of the Cluny Museum. In Belgium, a Jewish Museum opened in Brussels in 1990.

EASTERN EUROPE. *Poland.* Within Poland, a permanent exhibition devoted to the history and culture of Cracow Jews was installed in 1980 in Cracow's 16th-century Old Synagogue. Attempts are being made to recover and preserve the rich Polish Jewish heritage.

Czechoslovakia. Over the past decade the State Jewish Museum in Prague, housed in the ancient synagogue of the ghetto, has successfully updated many of its displays. The restoration of the Pinkas Synagogue, with the names of the deported Czech Jews, is still in progress.

Hungary. The Jewish Museum of Budapest, founded in 1895 and since 1932 located in a separate building next to Dohany Synagogue, completely changed its display in 1984. The museum, which belongs to the Jewish community, received government support for this project. The permanent show documents the rich history and culture of Hungarian Jewry from the third century onwards. There is a section on the Nazi period and one on contemporary Jewish life. Elsewhere in Hungary some old synagogues have been restored; the modest exhibitions inside indicate the new sensitivity to the past. Two 14th-century synagogues in Sopron, for example, are now open to the public. The remains of 13th- and 15th-century synagogues at the castle of Budapest, destroyed at the time of the Turkish occupation, also attract visitors. [AL.GR./E.V.V.]

Note: This entry is an abridged addition of the entry on Jewish Museums which appeared in the Encyclopaedia Judaica Year Book 1988–89.

MUSIC, POPULAR. The following entries are on individuals who have had careers of note in the various fields within popular music.

ALPERT, HERB (1935–), U.S. musician and producer. Born in Los Angeles, Alpert first achieved success in the music industry by writing and recording the instrumental hit "The Lonely Bull" (1962) with his backup group the Tijuana Brass. Alpert used his royalty money to purchase the old Charlie Chaplin studio and form A&M Records in partnership with Jerry Moss. Under Alpert's guidance, A&M signed many famous pop performers such as the Police, Cat Stevens, Joan Baez and the Carpenters. In addition, Alpert himself recorded the number one hit single "This Guy's in Love" (1972).

BALIN, MARTY (Martyn Buchwald; 1942–), U.S. singer and songwriter. Born in Cincinnati, Balin founded the seminal Bay Area rock group Jefferson Airplane (1965–71). In 1975, Balin re-formed the band under the new name of Jefferson Starship and immediately had a top-of-the-chart album, *Red Octobus.* Balin is the president of the Great Pyramid Ltd. and owner of Diamondback Music Co. His hit songs include "It's No Secret" (1966), "Plastic Fantastic Lover" (1967), "Young Girls" (1968), "Sunday Blues" (1969), "Volunteers" (1970), and "Miracles" (1979).

DIAMOND, NEIL (1941–), U.S. singer and songwriter. Born in New York, Diamond began his music career as a staff songwriter for Bang Records. He wrote hit songs for the Monkees, "I'm A Believer" (1965), and "A Little Bit Me, A Little Bit You" (1967), and then recorded his own smash single "Cherry Cherry." Diamond followed this up with a long series of Top Ten songs, including "Kentucky Woman," "Sweet Caroline," "I Am I Said" and "Solitary Man." He then scored the soundtrack for the movie, *Jonathan Livingston Seagull* (1971) and wrote the number one single "You Don't Send Me Flowers Anymore" (1979) which he recorded as a duet with Barbra Streisand.

FOGELBERG, DAN (1951–), U.S. composer and recording artist. Born in Peoria, Ill., Fogelberg's first album, *Home-free* (1972), attracted little attention. His second album, *Souvenirs* (1974), however, proved to be one of the finest collection of songs written in the 1970s. Fogelberg was chosen as pop music's Newcomer of the year and since then has recorded a number of best-selling albums including *Captured Angel* (1975), *Twin Sons of Different Mothers* (1979) with Tim Weisberg, *Phoenix* (1980), and *The Innocent Age* (1981).

GARFUNKLE, ART (1941–), U.S. singer and actor. Born in Forest Hills, New York, Garfunkle met singer/songwriter Paul Simon while they were both in their early teens. They formed the duo Simon & Garfunkle and began recording Simon's songs together in 1960 ("Hey, Schoolgirl"). In 1964, Simon and Garfunkle signed a one-album contract with Columbia Records and released *Wednesday Morning, 3 a.m.* It failed to generate interest and Garfunkle left the music business to teach mathematics. The sudden and unexpected success of a single song culled from the album ("The Sounds of Silence") brought Garfunkle back with Simon and together they recorded a long string of hit songs that include "Homeward Bound," "I Am A Rock," "A Hazy Shade of Winter," "The Dangling Conversation," "The 59th St. Bridge Song," "Mrs. Robinson," "The Boxer," "Fakin' It," and "Bridge Over Troubled Water." In 1973, Garfunkle began a solo career and recorded such albums as *Angel Clare* (1973), *Breakaway* (1975), *Watermark* (1978), *Fate For Breakfast (Double For Dessert)* (1979), *Art Garfunkle* (1979), and *Scissors Cut* (1981). Garfunkle is the recipient of Grammy Awards for "Mrs. Robinson" (1969) and "Bridge Over Troubled Water" (1970). As an actor, Garfunkle has appeared in such films as *Catch-22* (1970), *Carnal Knowledge* (1971), and *Bad Timing* (1980).

GEFFEN, DAVID (1944–), U.S. record producer. Born in New York, Geffen began his career in the mailroom of the William Morris Agency, moved up the ladder to a position as agent and then founded his own agency with Elliot Roberts in 1968. Taking such stars as Joni Mitchell and Neil Young under his managerial wing, Geffen founded the now major recording label Asylum Records (1970). He picked up recording artists such as Jackson Browne and built his company up to the point where it merged with long-established Electra Records, with Geffen installed as president (1973–76). In 1975 he was made vice-chairman of Warner Brothers Pictures and in 1977 became executive assistant to the chairman of Warner Communications. In 1980, Geffen founded a new record label under his own name and signed John Lennon and Yoko Ono. The Lennon-Ono *Double Fantasy* (1980) album was the first released on Geffen Records. Geffen has also been a member of Yale University's music faculty since 1978.

IAN, JANIS (Janis Fink; 1951–), U.S. singer and songwriter. Born in New York, Ian was discovered at the age of 14 by Leonard Bernstein, who played her song, "Society's Child" (1967), on his televised Concerts for Youth series. The song became a nationwide hit, but Ian had trouble repeating her success and was eventually released by her record label, Columbia. She managed to revive her career in Australia, then triumphantly reentered the American music scene at 26 with her deeply etched portrait of adolescent pain "At Seventeen" (1975).

JOEL, BILLY (1949–), U.S. singer and songwriter. Born in New York, the son of a Holocaust survivor who came to New York by way of Cuba, Billy Joel first climbed the music charts with his self-confessed autobiographical sketch "The Piano Man" (1976). This was followed by a series of eclectic hit singles such as "Just the Way You Are" (1977), "She's Only a Woman to Me" (1978), "It's Still Rock and Roll to Me" (1979), and "Allentown" (1981).

KING, CAROLE (Carole Klein; 1942–), U.S. singer and songwriter. Born in Brooklyn, King entered into a songwriting partnership with her husband Gerry Goffin (from whom she was divorced in 1968), and became part of one of the most successful songwriting teams of pop music of the early 1960s. They wrote such hits as "Will You Still Love Me Tomorrow?" (1960) for the Shirelles, "He's a Rebel" (1960) for the Chiffons, "The Locomotion" (1961) for Little Eva, "Go Away Little Girl" (1962) for Steve Lawrence, "Up on the Roof" (1962) for the Drifters, "Take Good Care of My Baby" (1963) for Bobby Vee, "I'm into Something Good" (1964) for Herman's Hermits, and "Natural Woman" (1965) for Aretha Franklin. Soon after her divorce King started a solo career as a recording artist. Her album *Tapestry* (1970), was one of the biggest-selling albums in pop music annals with a recorded worldwide sales of 20,000,000. King won four Grammy Awards for this album. She went on to write and record such hit songs as "It's Too Late" (1971) and "You've Got a Friend" (1972).

KNOPFLER, MARK (1949–), U.K. singer, songwriter, and producer. After working as a journalist, Knopfler formed the rock group Dire Straits, which established itself as a serious force to be reckoned within the late 1970s. "Sultans of Swing" (1978) was critically lionized and shot out of nowhere to the top of the album charts. Knopfler followed this smash debut with three more hit Dire Straits albums, "Communique" (1979), "Making Movies" (1980), and "Love over Gold" (1982) which included the no. 2 single, "Private Investigations." During this time Knopfler also became recognized as an outstanding guitarist. In 1985, Knopfler released Dire Straits' "Brothers in Arms," which dwarfed every other record in its wake and became one of the biggest selling albums in the history of the music industry. The album included the U.S. #1 single, "Money for Nothing." Knopfler was then acknowledged (with Paul McCartney and David Bowie) as one of the three richest recording artists in the U.K. Knopfler waited six years before issuing a sixth Dire Straits album, "On Every Street" (1991), which became an instant #1 on the album charts, but only briefly. Knopfler also wrote the film score for the movie *Local Hero* (1983) and produced high quality albums for Bob Dylan ("Infidels," 1983) and Randy Newman ("Land of Dreams," 1988).

MANILOW, BARRY (1946–), U.S. singer, producer, and songwriter. Born in New York, Manilow entered the music business writing commercial jingles. He became rich with his famous "You Deserve A Break Today" (1973) commercial for the MacDonald's hamburger empire. Soon after, Manilow became Bette Midler's record producer and then turned performer himself. His first record, *Mandy* (1974), went straight to first place on the charts. Manilow then adapted a Chopin sonata and turned it into the hit song "Magic" (1975). He has since recorded a long succession of Top Ten singles, such as "I Write the Songs" (1976), "Copacabana" (1978) and "What a Friend You Turned Out to Be" (1983).

MIDLER, BETTE (1945–), U.S. singer, entertainer, and actress. Born in Honolulu, Midler entered show business as a member of the *Fiddler on the Roof* cast for four years (1966–69). She gained notoriety as a popular performer in the Baths cabaret, a meeting place for homosexuals, and then scored a hit single with the frequently recorded "Do You Wanna Dance?" (1974). She followed this success with her top-selling album *The Divine Miss M.* and a popular film of her live act called *Divine Madness* (1979). Midler turned actress in a movie loosely based on the life of Janis Joplin, *The Rose* (1981), and divides her time equally between live shows, albums and non-musical films.

Bette Midler (Bar-David, Tel Aviv)

NEWMAN, RANDI (1943–), U.S. singer, songwriter, composer, and arranger. Born in Los Angeles, Newman received his first opportunity when Judy Collins recorded his plaintive song "I Think It's Going to Rain Today" in 1966. This initial success brought him to the attention of the Los Angeles music community and soon recording artists such as Peggy Lee, Three Dog Night, Harry Nillson, Neil Diamond, Art Garfunkle, Barbra Streisand, the Everly Brothers and Ringo Starr were recording Newman's material. He had difficulty achieving commercial success with his own albums until the release of *Little Criminals* in 1977, which included Neuman's controversial number one hit single "Short People." He was nominated for an Academy Award in 1981 for his score for the movie *Ragtime.*

SIMON PAUL (1943–), U.S. singer and songwriter. Born in New York, Simon formed a musical partnership with his childhood friend Art Garfunkle and entered the musical scene with his song "The Sounds of Silence" (1964). This best-selling single was followed in rapid succession by a number of his songs including "Homeward Bound" (1965), "I Am a Rock" (1965), "The Dangling Conversation" (1966), and "A Hazy Shade of Winter" (1967). Simon and Garfunkle's popularity soared when Simon's music was chosen to accompany the highly successful film *The Graduate* in 1967. Their 1970 album *Bridge Over Troubled Water* received six Grammy awards including best song and best album. Simon began a career as a solo performer in 1971. His song "An American Tune" was voted Song of the Year in 1975 by *Rolling Stone Magazine.* Simon and Garfunkle have come briefly together for a number of mass-audience appearances, including one in Tel Aviv. [JO.LI.]

MUSICIANS (see **12**:679; **Dc.17**:472).

ABILEAH, ARIE (1885–1985), Israel pianist. Born in Russia, Abileah gave his first concert at the age of six. Studied at the Conservatory of Petersburg under Marie Benoit, Liadov, and Glazounov. He completed his artistic training in Geneva with Stavenhagen and appeared as accompanist of Joseph *Szigeti, Josef *Achron, and Maurice Maréchal. In 1914 he was appointed chairman of the piano department at the Music Academy in Geneva, a position he held until 1922. He was active in 1922–1926 as piano teacher in Tel Aviv. During 1926–1932 Abileah performed in concerts in Paris and New York. In 1932 he settled in Jerusalem where he was appointed professor at the Music Academy and, as chairman of the Musicians' Association, organized chamber music concert series. He made recordings for the Israel Broadcasting Authority.

Arie Abileah (Courtesy of Mrs. Miriam Bendor, Bloomingburg, N.Y.)

BERGEL, BERND (1909–1966), Israel composer. Bergel was born in Hohensalza, Germany, the nephew of Sammy *Gronemann, one of the principal leaders of the Zionist movement in pre-World War II Germany. He studied at the Berlin Music Academy where he was a student of Arnold *Schoenberg. He settled in Tel Aviv in 1938. Bergel was invited by the Music of the Twentieth Century Festival 1954 in Rome to compose his *Prayer of a Man in the Year 2100* for solo voice and 11 instruments. His works include *Divertimento* for small orchestra; *Variations* for orchestra (Israel Philharmonic Orchestra Prize); and the opera *Jacob's Dream* (1961) based on text by Richard Beer-Hoffmann.

BOEHM, YOHANAN (1914–1986), Israel composer, hornplayer, and music critic. Born in Breslau, Germany, Boehm immigrated to Palestine in 1936. He taught at the Jerusalem Music Academy and was music program editor and tone master at the Israel Broadcasting Service and the World Zionist Organization Broadcasting Service for the Diaspora *(Kol Ẓiyyon la-Golah).* He composed songs, chamber music, and symphonies in a late romantic style, wrote articles on music, was a contributor to the *Encyclopaedia Judaica,* and served as the music critic for the *Jerusalem Post.* Boehm founded the Jerusalem Youth Orchestra in 1959 and directed it for 20 years. He was music advisor to the Jerusalem municipality and was a jury member of the International Harp Contest in Israel.

EVEN-OR, MARY (1939–1989), Israel composer. Even-Or studied at the Music Teachers' Seminary in Tel Aviv in 1959, the Oranim Seminary in 1960–62, and with Yehezkel Braun. She studied law at Tel Aviv University and music in 1976–80 at the Rubin Academy of Music in Tel Aviv and Tel Aviv University. Even-Or was a member of the Israel Composers' League from 1980; from 1981 she was a member of ACUM and of the International Association of Women Composers. Her works include *Dances* for flute, clarinet, violin, bass and percussion (1961); *Dreams* for flute, clarinet and guitar (1977); *Music for Strings* (1979); *Espressioni Musicali* for choir a cappella (1981); *Cardioyada* for brass quintet (1981); *Musikinesis* for symphony orchestra (1983). [U.E.]

NARKISS, BEZALEL (1926–), Jewish art historian. Narkiss was born in Jerusalem, son of Mordechai *Narkiss, director of the Bezalel Art Museum. He studied at the Hebrew University of Jerusalem and then taught history for five years at a secondary school in Haifa. It was only after his father's death, whilst examining and arranging his papers, that Narkiss found his vocation; to establish Jewish art as a specialized academic discipline. Consequently, he retrained, studying at the Courtauld and Warburg Institutions at the University of London.

Specializing in the history of medieval art, where his interests are divided between iconographic and stylistic studies, he was particularly influenced in his approach to art by Hugo Buchthal and Francis Wormald, his supervisors in London, and Yitzḥak Baer, professor of medieval Jewish history in Jerusalem. After his return to Israel in 1963, Narkiss taught in the department of art history at the Hebrew University.

Through Narkiss's work, the study of Jewish art has been transformed into a specialized academic discipline. He has stressed the relationship of the style to that of the general art of the region, while pointing to specific Jewish elements and iconography. As a result of his methodology, a school of students and researchers has evolved.

As director of the Index of Jewish Art since 1974, he has undertaken the task of indexing all works of Jewish art and has computerized this index in his capacity as director of the Center for Jewish Art at the Hebrew University.

He has served in various editorial capacities, as art editor of Masada Press (1963–73), and foreign editor of *Gesta* International Center of Medieval Art (1973–1980). He was from 1974 the editor-in-chief of the *Journal of Jewish Art* and director of the Catalogue of Hebrew Illustrated Manuscripts of the British Isles. He was also the art adviser to the Diaspora Museum (Beth Hatefutsoth). Narkiss has published numerous articles and introductions to art books [E.HO]

NATIONAL JEWISH WELFARE BOARD (JWB) (**12**:872). In 1990, the JWB, after 73 years of existence, changed its name to Jewish Community Centers Association of North America. It had 275 YM/YWHAs and camps in North America and served the community in the areas of informal education and Jewish culture through the Jewish Book Council, the Jewish Music Council, its Lecture Bureau, and a variety of Israel-related projects. It retained the name Jewish Welfare Board for its work on behalf of soldiers.

NEHAMA, JOSEPH (1880–1971), Greek educator and historian. In his capacity as teacher and school principal of the local Alliance Israélite Universelle, Nehama devoted his life to educating several generations of Salonikan youth.

For a number of periods, Nehama was a member of the Committee of the Jewish Community of Salonika representing the non-Zionist general stream of the Jewish community. As a historian he made a major pioneering effort in tracing the Salonikan Jewish community's roots in his seven-volume work, *Histoire des Israélites de Salonique*. Another noteworthy work was *La Ville Convaitée*.

As a writer Nehama's literary ability was demonstrated in the dozens of essays he contributed to such French literary publications as *Mercure de France*. He wrote numerous studies and articles in Judeo-Spanish on Jewish history, health codes, and commerce which appeared in the press of Salonika and Paris. Nehama made a great contribution to the propagation and research of the Judeo-Spanish language by writing a comprehensive Judeo-Spanish — French dictionary. The work, entitled *Dictionnaire du Judeo-Espagnol*, was published in 1977 several years after his death.

Nehama was a prominent banker in his capacity as president of the Banque Union. During the Holocaust, Nehama managed to escape the Germans in Salonika by fleeing to Athens. However he was caught by the Nazis and deported on March 25, 1944, to Auschwitz. He was liberated by the American Army in the last days of the war.

The Holocaust not only was a personal tragedy for Nehama, but a changing point in his attitude toward Zionism. Previously he had little belief in the potential of political Zionism and its ability to create a viable and prosperous homeland for the Jews. He had been one of the key community leaders in the 1930s who encouraged Jews to stay in Salonika and not immigrate to Palestine. After the Holocaust Nehama was greatly saddened that the prosperous Diaspora center of Salonika had come to an end and regretted his earlier stand against emigration. He was joint author (with Michael Molho) of *The Destruction of Greek Jewry 1941–1944* (Hebrew, 1965). [YI.K.]

NETHERLANDS, THE (see **12**:793; **Dc./17**:488). **Demography.** The Jewish population of the Netherlands at the end of 1992 was estimated at some 25,000, out of a total population of 15,250,000. No reliable figures exist about the Jewish presence in the Netherlands. The last demographic survey was published in 1971, with data obtained in 1966. In 1983 the Board of the Jewish Social Welfare Foundation (Joods Maatschappelijk Werk, or J.M.W.) initiated a proposal for a new demographic survey, but due to strong opposition from several quarters, the plan was soon shelved and never revived. The reasons for the opposition were, on the one hand, that the board of J.M.W. wanted to broaden the definition of who is Jewish and wanted to include not only those who are halakhically Jewish and/or are members of a Jewish congregation, but also those who have a Jewish "attachment" only, whatever this may mean. There was also opposition from those fearing that registration of Jews might have the same dire results as during the German occupation, even though J.M.W. promised that the published results would contain no names.

Religious Life. The large majority of persons of Jewish origin in the Netherlands were no longer members of any Jewish congregation. In its Annual Survey for the year 1991 the secretary of the Netherlands Ashkenazi Congregation or Nederlands Israelitisch Kerkgenootschap (N.I.K.), Joseph Sanders, analyzed the phenomenon of most persons of Jewish origin no longer belonging to a Jewish congregation and found various reasons. One was widespread secularization; assistance to the poor is no longer the responsibility of religious institutions but of the government; the existence of Jewish social activities outside synagogues and the fact that synagogue membership is no longer required for membership in organizations such as B'nai B'rith or J.M.W.; the high synagogue membership fees; and the growing number of mixed marriages. Previously many remained members of a congregation in order to be buried in a Jewish cemetery, but with the steep increase in cremation this motive too lost its force.

The N.I.K., still the largest Jewish congregation in the Netherlands, from 1992 used a different method of counting its members. Hitherto it had considered as members all those who were virtually known as Jewish and were not members of either the Sephardi or the Liberal Jewish congregations. Now it counted only those who paid their membership fees or were exempt. Thus, whereas in 1983 the number of members of the N.I.K. was still given as 11,600, including 8,100 in Amsterdam, this figure was reduced by 1992 to 5,600, of whom over 3,000 were in Amsterdam. The Hague and Rotterdam showed no significant changes at 400 and 375, respectively. The number of congregations of the N.I.K.

Conversation at the 350th anniversary of the Ashkenazi Congregation of Amsterdam, held on Sept. 1, 1985, in the Sephardi Esnoga, between Prince Claus (left), Queen Beatrix of the Netherlands, and Dr. Henri Markens, chairman of the Ashkenazi Congregation and an attendee (Photo Han Singels, Amsterdam)

dropped from 39 in 1982 to 30 in 1992. The Central Council of the N.I.K. in 1988 adopted amendments in its Regulations by which congregations with fewer than 25 souls could be ordered in principle to enter into a cooperative association with a larger nearby congregation or be dissolved. The four congregations in the province of Limburg — Maastricht, Venlo, Roermond, and Heerlen — combined to form the congregation of Limburg, with its seat in Maastricht.

The attempts to establish a single Ashkenazi Chief Rabbinate for the Netherlands, instead of the four existing nominally, failed, owing to problems of competence, and was indefinitely shelved, although only two chief rabbis remained—Rabbi Meir Just of Amsterdam and Rabbi Eliezer Berlinger of Utrecht, for the rest of the Netherlands. After the death of the latter in 1985, the seat of the Chief Rabbinate for the provinces, with the exception of Amsterdam, The Hague, and Rotterdam, partly from Utrecht to Amersfoort. S. Jacobs and S. Evers, and American-born Rabbi A. L. Heintz represents it at Utrecht. A long-standing conflict with Chief Rabbi Just was solved through the mediation of the Ashkenazi chief rabbi of Israel, Avraham Shapiro, in 1986. Chief Rabbi Just was allowed to carry the title of chairman of the Chief Rabbinate of the Netherlands for another three years and to continue supervising *kashrut* for export, to grant divorces, and accept conversions.

The General Council of the N.I.K. as long ago as 1982 voted in favor of the vote for women in congregational councils. The proposal, however, was vetoed by the Chief Rabbinate.

The Sephardi Congregation had some 500 members, including some recent immigrants from Morocco and from Middle East countries. Much of its attention centered on the repair of its famous 17th-century synagogue. About half the sum needed was given by the government and the Amsterdam municipality. A fundraising committee, consisting partly of non-Jews, was established to raise funds for the other half, both in the Netherlands and abroad, mainly in the United States.

The Liberal Jewish Congregation remained with a membership of some 2,250, of whom several were halakhically not Jewish or partners in mixed marriages. It continued to have six congregations, of which only two—Amsterdam and The Hague—had regular services every Sabbath. The other four were in Brobart, Twenthe, Rotterdam, and Arnhem. The Leo Baeck Liberal Jewish elementary school, established in Amsterdam in 1982 had to close in 1991 as it had only 20 pupils.

The strictly Orthodox Jewish school, Cheider, in Amsterdam, established in 1974 with only five pupils at the behest of the Lubavicher Rebbe in New York, in 1992 had nearly 300 pupils in its kindergarten and elementary and secondary school. The Cheider attracts children of parents who think that the two long-established Jewish day schools— the elementary school and kindergarten Rosh Pinah and the Maimonides Lyceum—do not provide sufficient Jewish knowledge.

In Rotterdam, the Jewish elementary school Etgar, which was established in 1988 at private Jewish initiative had to close down in 1992 for lack of pupils.

Of the some 100 synagogue buildings that existed in 1940, 30 were still in use as such, although regular services were still held only in a minority.

Some synagogues that were still in use had to reduce the size of their main hall, as it had become too big for the number of worshipers. In Amsterdam, the Lekstreet synagogue, which was inaugurated in 1938 was declared a protected monument, as a fine example of the New Business School of Architecture. The main hall was leased permanently to the newly established Dutch Resistance Museum, which was dedicated in 1987, and a much smaller synagogue was opened in part of the building.

In The Hague in 1980 the monumental central Ashkenazi synagogue was sold to the Hague Municipality, which placed it at the disposal of a Turkish Muslim congregation, and turned it into the Al-Aqsa mosque. The Hague Ashkenazi congregation in its turn bought a former Protestant church in the Bezuidenhout district and turned it into its synagouge and communal center. However, its maintenance proved too costly, and it was decided to demolish it and to construct an apartment building on the site, the ground floor of which was to serve as the synagogue and communal center.

The ancient Jewish burial ground at Scheveningseweg in The Hague — where the first Jewish burials took place around 1700 — which was in a neglected condition, was restored.

Maimonides Jewish Lyceum, Amsterdam (Courtesy Geoffrey Wigoder, Jerusalem)

The restoration of the oldest part of the famous old Sephardi burial ground at Ouderkerk-on-the-Amstel, southeast of Amsterdam, the Beth Chaim, was carried out by volunteers and by persons employed by the Municipalities of Amsterdam and Ouderamstel. The work temporarily stopped in 1992, as neither the Amsterdam Municipality nor the Sephardi congregation had more funds available.

Community Life. Beth Shalom, the Home for the Jewish Elderly in Amsterdam, formerly far from the centers of Jewish residence, was reopened by the Queen Mother Juliana in 1991 in new premises in the southern suburb of Buitenveldert, where many Jews now live. The residents of the Rabbi de Vries Home in Haarlem were also transferred to the new building. Its ground floor contains the *kasher* restaurant, Hatikvah, formerly elsewhere in Amsterdam.

The sole Jewish Children's Home in Amsterdam, Bethenu, was closed in 1983 with the five remaining children being placed with private families.

The Jewish Social Welfare Board (J.M.W.), which previously dealt mainly with the processing of applications under the Law for Payments to War Victims, now devoted itself to problems of the post-war generation, organizing seminars on such issues as Jewish identity.

The Netherlands Society for Jewish Genealogy was established in 1987 and by 1992 had more than 400 members, many of whom were non-Jews with one or more Jewish ancestors, and about an additional 50 members abroad, mainly in the U.S. and Israel.

Shalhomo is a society of Jewish Gays and Lesbians in Holland established in 1979; it publishes its own paper, *Shalhomo*. In 1989 it was host to the Tenth International Conference of Jewish Homosexuals, which was opened by the mayor of Amsterdam.

Amsterdam was also the venue in 1991 of an International Yiddish Festival. Yiddish groups from various countries gave performances and several groups performed Klezmer music. A small theatrical company for Yiddish plays, the Anthony Theater, was established by a non-Jew and existed for some time.

The Jewish Historical Museum which had existed in modest premises from 1934 was transferred to much larger premises and offically opened there in 1987 (see entry Museums). In May 1989 its director, Judith Belinfante, received the European Museum of the Year Award of the Council of Europe.

Zionism. Attempts to expand the Netherlands Zionist Organization (N.Z.B.) and to increase its importance and influence both in general society and in the Jewish community were not successful. Its membership was officially given as about 1,200.

One reason for its failure to attract new members was that its tasks had largely been taken over by the Israel Embassy and by the C.I.D.I., the Center for Information and Documentation on Israel, established in 1974 jointly by several Jewish organizations, with a professional salaried staff to give information about Israel.

To expand the influence of Zionism, the Annual Conference of the N.Z.B. in 1991 decided to convert the N.Z.B. into a Federation of Netherlands Zionists (F.N.Z.) that would incorporate the various Zionist political parties and Arza as well as a group of Zionists not affiliated to any particular party.

A number of small but vocal groups, were engaged in criticizing the policy of the Israel government with regard to the Palestinians and the Administered Areas. A Dutch branch of Peace Now was established in 1982. "Blanes" was a small group which sometimes demonstrated in front of the Israel embassy. They also showed a great interest in Yiddish. "Women in Black," from 1990 onwards, demonstrated twice a month for an hour in the center of Amsterdam to protest against Israeli occupation of the Administered Areas. The Netherlands Palestine Committee, established in 1989, published a monthly periodical, later called *Soemoed* which emphasized the violations of Palestinians' human rights by Israel.

The P.L.O. office in The Hague, which was opened as an information office, was not accorded diplomatic status by the Dutch government.

The plan to establish a Holland Village of caravans in the southern outskirts of Jerusalem, near Beit Safafa, for the temporary absorption of Ethiopian Jews, which was partly financed by the "Christians for Israel" Society, aroused some opposition as its site was partly on land beyond the Green Line. The project, however, went ahead and was inaugurated in 1992.

Issues Related to the Holocaust. THE TWO OF BREDA. An issue which had aroused strong emotions for many years — the possible release from prison of the "Two of Breda" (called after the prison in Breda, where they were held for some 40 years)—the last two war criminals, both Germans, remaining in prison in Holland (Ferdinand H. Aus der Funten and Franz Fischer)—came to a conclusion in 1989 when they were handed over to the West German authorities. Originally there had been four such prisoners, all of them Germans. One, Willy Dages, was returned to West Germany in the mid–1960s, as he was believed to be mortally ill; he died there several years later. The other, Joseph Kotalla, died in prison, after a long illness, in 1988. Lages, Aus der Funten, and Fischer had occupied key positions in the mass deportation of Jews from Amsterdam and The Hague, respectively, in 1942–44.

The release of the two was sparked off by a letter to the minister of justice early in 1989, by 19 prominent Dutchmen, many of them lawyers and/or men who had been active in Dutch wartime resistance, among them two Jews. It stated that the continued imprisonment of the Two, then respectively 79 and 87, was inhuman and did not serve any purpose. In a parliamentary debate on the issue, it was decided by a vote of 83 to 55 to expel them. A few hours later the two men were handed to the West German police. Both Aus der Funten and Fischer died that same year.

In 1990, the Special Public Prosecutor for War Crimes announced that no more trials of war criminals could be expected.

AID TO WAR VICTIMS. The Ministry of Welfare and Culture from 1989 granted the sum of F. 750,000 annually for three years to enable institutions engaged in non-material aid to war victims to increase their staff in order to help war victims with problems resulting from the release of the Two.

The Institute for the Study of Psychotrauma in Utrecht, in a report published in 1990, concluded that one quarter of all the "Second Generation Jews" born between 1945 and 1970 were in need of psychotherapeutic treatment as a result of the war traumata of their parents.

The problems of children who had been hidden with non-Jews during the Nazi occupation of Holland received increasing attention. Some 4,000 Jewish children survived in this way, half of whom were reunited with at least one surviving parent after the war. About 1,000 were returned to Jewish relatives or the Jewish community after the war, and about 1,000 remained with their non-Jewish foster-parents. A number of these Hidden Children participated in the first Hidden Children Conference held in New York in 1991. A Hidden Children Conference for those who had lived in hiding in Holland, and were now living in many different countries, was held in Amsterdam in 1992 with 500 participants.

WESTERBORK. The former Westerbork transit and concentration camp in northeast Netherlands, from where some 100,000 Jews were deported to their deaths between July 1942 and September 1944, was turned into a sober memorial in 1983, due largely to non-Jewish initiative and was officially dedicated by Queen Beatrix. The main feature was a monument, by the Jewish artist Ralph Prins (who as a child had himself been at Westerbork) consisting of two broken railway tracks symbolizing the trains by which the Jews had been deported to their deaths.

On the 40th anniversary of the liberation of Westerbork on April 18, 1945, a ceremony was held there, in the presence of former Queen Juliana and some 600 former inmates and their relatives.

In 1992 the commemoration center which had been entirely renovated was officially reopened, this time by Princess Margriet. To the monument by Ralph Prins has been added a field of 102,000 bricks in the shape of a map of The Netherlands, and on each brick is a small *magen David.*

COMMEMORATIONS. The year 1985, the 40th anniversary of the liberation of The Netherlands from Nazi occupation, sparked off a series of commemorations and commemorative publications, with special attention to the suffering of the Jews, which had hitherto been largely ignored. This flow has continued ever since.

Monuments or memorial tablets were unveiled in 1985 in Bught, Zwolle, Coevorden, Cuyk, Doesburg, Elburg, Raalte, Weesp, and Zaandam, sometimes accompanied by a memorial exhibition. In the following years further memorials were set up in the town hall of Dordrecht, at Gornichem and Denekamp at the sites of demolished synagogues, in Leyden at the site of the former Jewish orphanage, several in Amsterdam including one at the site of the Jewish Ashkenazi Boys' Orphanage, from where nearly 100 pupils were deported in March 1943. In 1986, a monument, the work of the Dutch-Jewish sculptor Appie Drielsma, was unveiled at Mauthausen concentration camp in Austria where 1,700 Dutchmen, primarily Jews, died.

Other memorial tablets or monuments for local Jews who perished were unveiled: in Leeuwarden, in Beek, near Maastricht, in Oud-Beyerland, near Dordtrecht, and Barneveld. At Loosdrecht, near Hilversum, a monument with the names of 23 Youth Aliyah wards who lost their lives was dedicated.

The Netherlands and Israel. Netherlands governments in various coalitions continued to adhere to the Declaration of Venice of 1980. On several occasions The Netherlands succeeded in having a UN anti-Israel draft resolution toned down.

In the UN General Assembly Dec. 4, 1985, it was one of 16 countries voting against a resolution demanding unconditional withdrawal by Israel from all Palestinian and other Arab territories occupied since 1967. It was also among the 22 countries voting against a resolution calling the Israel decision of Dec. 1981 to introduce Israel laws and jurisdiction and Israeli administration into the Golan Heights an act of aggression and demanding a military, economic, diplomatic, and cultural boycott of Israel. On the other hand, it voted in favor of a resolution calling the incorporation by Israel of Jerusalem unlawful. The Dutch government criticized Israel for its bombardment of PLO headquarters in Tunisia.

The Netherlands withheld diplomatic recognition of the PLO and continued to limit the status of the Palestinian office in the Hague, which was opened in July 1983, to that of an Information Office.

In July 1983 the government, with the full approval of Parliament, decided to withdraw the Dutch Unifil battalion from South Lebanon as from October 19, 1983, as it could no longer play a useful role there.

1989 Passover Guide of The Hague Jewish community

The Netherlands continued to represent Israel's interests in Moscow and to mediate in the applications for visas to Israel by Soviet Jews until Israel was able to open its own consulate in Moscow.

In the Gulf War the Netherlands fully supported the American stand against Iraq and participated in the Allied forces, be it in a modest way.

At the end of January 1991 the entire Second Chamber of Parliament, with the exception of a few members of the Green Left party, approved the government decision to lend eight Patriot systems to Israel, with 70 instructors and maintenance personnel. By the time they arrived in Israel the Iraqi Scud attacks had ceased, so that they never went into action. At the same time the government, in addition to the F. 3,000,000 it had donated already for food for the Palestinians in the Administered Areas, gave another F. 2,000,000 for this purpose, plus 10,000 gas masks. The newsmedia had repeatedly pointed to the absence of gas masks for the Palestinians.

The *intifada,* from its start, received very great attention in the Dutch news media. The emphasis was often on the "cruelty" of the Israeli soldiers firing at young children who merely threw stones. Among the organizations showing great sympathy for the Palestinians was the Netherlands Council of Churches (mainly Protestant) and the Dutch branch of the Roman Catholic "Pax Christi."

Two small extreme left-wing parties, the P.R.P. (Political Radical Party) and the P.S.P. (Pacifist Socialist Party), often publicly criticized Israel. In 1987, together with the small Communist Party (CPN), they merged into the Green Left which often criticized Israel, as did some members of the Labor left wing.

On the second anniversary of the outbreak of the *intifada* the PLO representative in The Hague, Afif Safieh, organized a large-scale meeting, to which he invited representatives of all the major parties as speakers, but all declined. Nor was any official representative of the Foreign Ministry present.

The meeting was addressed by the chairman of the Netherlands Council of Churches, Prof. Dirk C. Mulder.

The Israel-Palestine peace talks in Madrid had orginially been scheduled to take place in The Hague, but Syria had objected for a number of reasons. The Hague was thus dropped, much to the relief of the Dutch authorities, in view of the vast organizational and security problems it would have caused.

No Palestinian terrorist attacks against Jewish persons or property took place throughout the decade under review.

On January 19–21, 1986, Israel's prime minister, Shimon Peres, paid an official visit to Holland, where he also met Spanish premier, Felipe Gonzalez. Lubbers.

The I.C.N. or Israel Committee Netherlands, which consists of orthodox Protestants, is fully pro-Israel and every year from 1980 sent tens of thousand of flower bulbs to Israel to adorn its public gardens.

The Collective Israel Actie (United Israel Appeal) in 1992 raised some F. 9,240,000, of which F. 6,260,000 came from the campaign itself and some F. 3,000,000 from bequests. This was a reduction of F. 2,500,000 against 1991, but F. 2,500,000 more than in 1989. In contrast to the situation in the 1950s and 1960s, many Israeli institutions now freely solicit funds in Holland.

The disaster of the El Al Boeing 747 cargo aircraft which crashed into two tall apartment buildings in the Bijlmer district of southeastern Amsterdam on Oct. 4, 1992, made a deep impression. In addition to the three Israeli crew members and one Israeli woman passenger, 43 local residents were killed and four seriously wounded, nearly all of them recent immigrants from Third World countries. In all, 80 apartments were destroyed and 160 others were no longer safe for habitation. The ultimate blame for the disaster was eventually placed upon the Boeing company.

Interreligious Relations. The OJEC (Consultative Council of Jews and Christians) was established in 1981 at the initiative of the Dutch-born Protestant theologian Dr. Jacob J. Schoneveld, director of the International Council of Jews and Christians. In 1992 the Protestant Rev. Simon Schoon, who had been its chairman since its establishment, retired. In his farewell address he regretted the general lack of interest in the Council, among both Christians and Jews.

The Dutch Reformed Council for the Church and the Jews decided in Dec. 1992 to liquidate its permanent representation in Jerusalem, which had been occupied for some ten years by Rev. Dr. G. H. Cohen Stuart, and to replace him by a visiting clergyman. Cohen Stuart had often been believed to be closer to the Israeli Jews than to the Palestinians, including the Christians among them.

Attempts to establish a consultative council of Jews and Muslims proved unsuccessful.

Soviet Jewry. The Dutch Solidarity Committee with Soviet Jewry remained very active as long as this was required. Its chairman, Liberal Rabbi Avraham Soetendorp, spent some months in Moscow after the liberalization of Russian policy towards the Jews, to acquaint Jews there with Judaism. The Netherlands Ashkenazi Congregation subsidized a number of Jewish educational projects in Moscow and in Kiev.

In 1991–1992 a few hundred Russians arrived in Holland from Israel to demand political asylum, claiming they had been discriminated against in Israel because they, or one of their partners in a mixed marriage, were not considered Jewish. Their request was rejected and they had to leave Holland. However, a number succeeded to go into hiding. They received no financial or moral support from the Jewish Welfare Board or the rabbinate. Support, however, was given to some 400 Russian Jews who went to Holland directly from the Soviet Union and requested political asylum. This was granted them collectively by the Dutch government at the end of 1992, the first time in the postwar period that this was done for such a large group.

Culture. The main cultural event during the period under review was the opening of the Jewish Historical Museum in Amsterdam on May 3, 1987, in its new premises (see above).

In the Amsterdam Historical Museum an exhibition, "Exodo: Portuguese Jews in Amsterdam, 1600–1680," was held from Dec. 1987 to Feb. 1988, within the framework of the Dutch-Portuguese cultural agreement.

Dr. Rena Fuks, at the University of Amsterdam, was appointed professor in Jewish history, and Dr. Ido Abram, professor in Holocaust education. Channah Safrai replaced Yehuda Ashkenazi in 1991 as teacher of Talmudics at the Roman Catholic Theological Academies of Amsterdam and of Utrecht.

The Symposia on Dutch-Jewish History which have been held every couple of years alternately in Holland and in Israel since 1980, continued. They were organized by the Institute for Dutch-Jewish History in Jerusalem and by related institutions in Holland.

Maurits Kopuit, chief editor of the N.I.W., *Nieuw Israelisch Weekblad*, the only Jewish weekly in Holland, died and was succeeded by Tamarah Benima. Its editorial staff now consists of women only.

Deaths. HARTOG BEEM (1898–1987), author of numerous publications on the prewar Jewish countryside in the Netherlands and on the Dutch variant of Yiddish; Rabbi ELIEZER BERLINGER (1905–1980), who was first a rabbi in Sweden and Finland before coming to Holland in 1955 where he was chief rabbi of the Utrecht District; NICO BOEKEN (1920–1992), past director of the Jewish Social Welfare Foundation and for many years on the executive of the Liberal Jewish Congregation in Amsterdam; GODFRIED ("FREEDY") BOLLE (1914-1984), a lifelong Zionist who in a volunteer capacity headed the Jewish National Fund in the Netherlands for 25 years; SIEGFRIED TEN BRINK (1926–1991), vice-chairman of the Netherlands Zionist Federation and chief editor of its periodical, *De Joodse Wachter*; HANS EVERS (1925–1992), from 1980 to 1985 chairman of the Amsterdam Ashkenazi Congregation Council and also very active in the Netherlands Zionist Federation and the Consultative Council of Jews and Christians; M. H. GANS (1917–1987), a jeweler by profession, he was the author of the *Memorbook* on the History of Dutch Jewry and of several other works on Dutch-Jewish history and 1955–60 editor of the Dutch-Jewish weekly *Nieuw Israelietisch Weekblad*; J. GLAZER (1916–1989), past director of the Jewish Social Welfare Foundation; MURITS GOUDEKET (1912–1988), chairman of the Jewish Social Welfare Foundation and for very many years chairman of the Netherlands Liberal Jewish Congregation and of its Amsterdam branch; R. GOUDSMIT (1924–1991), chairman of the board of the Home for the Jewish Elderly Beth Shalom, of the Foundation for Jewish Daytime Schools (J.B.O.), and of other Jewish organizations; EVA HALERSTADT (1915–1990), one of the founding members of the Netherlands Auschwitz Committee, of which she was chairman for many years; ABEL J. HERZBERG (1893–1988), lawyer and 1935–1939 chairman of the Netherlands Zionist Federation and after 1945 the author of many books on Jewish subjects; ABRAHAM HORODISCH (1890–1987), who came to Amsterdam from Berlin in 1933 and opened the antiquarian bookshop Erasmus, specializing in bibliophile editions, and author of many publications on booklore; MRS. H. KOHNSTAMM (1908–1988), for many years chair of WIZO Netherlands; MAURITS KOPUIT (1930-1992), from 1973 chief editor of the Dutch-Jewish weekly *Nieuw Israëlietisch Weekblad*; HERMAN MUSAPH (1915–1992), professor of sexual psychiatry in Utrecht and past chairman of Netherlands Liberal Congregation; LOUIS ALVAREZ VEGA (1905–1984), for many years secretary of the Sephardi Jewish Congregation of Amsterdam and keeper of the Sephardi Burial Ground at Ouderkerk near Amsterdam, on which he published a book. [H.BO.]

NEWMAN, PETER C. (1929–), Canadian journalist, editor, and author. Newman was born in Vienna and went to Canada at the age of 11; he was educated in Toronto. He has written 12 books.

His journalistic career has been spent mainly in Toronto and Ottawa. He served 15 years as Ottawa editor of *Maclean's* and then the *Toronto Star*. While with the latter newspaper, he became a nationally syndicated columnist with a wide following. Subsequently he became editor-in-chief of the *Star*, but soon afterwards was appointed to the same post at *Maclean's*, Canada's only domestic weekly newsmagazine. In his 11 years as editor-in-chief of *Maclean's* he played a key role in the development of the magazine. After retiring from that position, he continued his association with *Maclean's* as senior contributing editor and also appeared regularly on television.

After leaving his editorial career Newman concentrated on writing books. Some of his outstanding books, many of which became bestsellers, are: *Renegade in Power, The Diefenbaker Years, The Distemper of Our Time, The Canadian Establishment* (2 vols.), *The Bronfman Dynasty*, and *The Company of Adventures*. His books have focused on Canadian business and politics and the personalities in those fields. As an offshoot of his writing he has also been involved in preparing television productions, especially an award-winning, seven-part series on "The Canadian Establishment." [H.M.W.]

NEW ZEALAND (see **12:**1127; **Dc./17:**165). New Zealand is an English-speaking democracy and member of the British Commonwealth, where Jews have lived since the earliest days of white settlement in the 1840s. Most New Zealand Jews were and are of British descent; New Zealand admitted only about 900 refugees from Nazi Germany and few post-war survivors. In recent years, however, significant numbers of Jews have settled in New Zealand from the former U.S.S.R. and especially from South Africa.

The number of Jews by religion reported in the 1991 New Zealand Census was 3,126. Most observers regard the actual number as significantly higher, in the range of 4,500–5,000.

There are at present six synagogues in New Zealand. Three (the Auckland Hebrew Congregation, Wellington Hebrew Congregation, and Canterbury Hebrew Congregations) are affiliated with the United Hebrew Congregations of the Commonwealth and traditionally reflect a moderate Anglo-Orthodox outlook. Three (Beth Shalom, in Auckland; Wellington Liberal Jewish Congregation; and Dunedin Jewish Congregation) are affiliated to the Australian and New Zealand Union for Progressive Judaism. The Dunedin Congregation changed its affiliation from Orthodox to Progressive in 1989. There are also a number of Ḥabad groups. The three Orthodox synagogues currently have rabbis but the only progressive rabbi (in Auckland) left at the end of 1992.

Two Jewish day schools exist in New Zealand — Kadimah College in Auckland, opened in the late 1970s, and Moriah College in Wellington, opened in 1987.

The representative body of the Jewish community in New Zealand is the New Zealand Jewish Council, now located in Auckland. Its current president is Mrs. Wendy Ross.

Relations between the Jewish community and the New Zealand government soured considerably under the Labor government led by David Lange (1984–90), which constantly criticized Israeli policy on the West Bank and opened a dialogue with the PLO. Left-wing unions in New Zealand, powerful under the Labor government, tended to be dominated by hard anti-American elements who are also anti-Zionist. Relations improved following the return of the more conservative, pro-American Nationalist party government in 1990.

In 1989 the Anglican Church in New Zealand changed its Prayer Book to omit any references to "Zion," substituting phrases like "God's Holy City." According to Jewish sources, this was made in part through anti-Zionist pressures, although this has been officially denied by the Anglican Church. On the other hand, in recent years, Councils of Christians and Jews have been established in Auckland and Wellington.

There is a small but often noisy extreme right-wing movement in New Zealand associated with the Australian League of Rights, as well as anti-Semitic Christian fundamentalist groups, but levels of anti-Semitism are regarded as low, with few reports of anti-Jewish vandalism or violence. In 1990, there was a serious knife attack on school children at Kadimah College by a deranged non-Jewish woman who was placed under psychiatric care.

A number of books have appeared over the last few years on New Zealand Jewish life, including Ann Beaglehole's *A Small Price to Pay* (1988), on the very restrictive government policy toward Nazi-era refugees; Odeda Rosenthal's *Not Strictly Kosher: Pioneer Jews in New Zealand* (1988); and Ann Gluckman (ed.), *Identity and Involvement: Auckland Jewry Past and Present* (1990). A history of Wellington Jewry, *A Standard For the People* by Dr. Stephen Levine, was written for 1993 to mark the community's 150th anniversary. [W.D.R.]

NOBEL PRIZE (see **12:**1201; **Dc./17:**493). The following individuals are to be added to the list of Jewish Nobel Prize winners

1982 Aaron Klug, in chemistry (see separate entry).
1984 Cesare Milstein, in medicine (see separate entry).
1985 Michael Stuart Brown, in medicine (see separate entry).
Joseph Leonard Goldstein, in medicine (see separate entry).
Modigliani, Franco, in economics (see sep. entry).
1986 Stanley Cohen, in medicine (see separate entry).
Rita Levi-Montalcini, in medicine (see separate entry).
Elie Wiesel (see **16:**507; **Dc./17:**618), for peace.
1987 Joseph Brodsky (see **4:**1395), in literature.
Robert M. Solow, in economics (see separate entry).
1988 Gertrude B. Elion, in medicine (see separate entry).
Leon Lederman, in physics (see separate entry).
Melvin Schwartz, in physics (see separate entry).
Jack Steinberger, in physics (see separate entry).
1989 Sidney Altman, in chemistry, (see separate entry).
Harold Eliot Varmus, in medicine (see separate entry).
1990 Jerome Isaac Friedman, in physics (see sep. entry).
Harry M. Markowitz, in economics (see sep. entry).
1991 Nadine Gordimer, (see **12:**786), in literature,
1992 Gary S. Becker, in economics (see separate entry).
George Charpak, in physics (see separate entry).
Rudolph Arthur Marcus, in chemistry (see separate entry).

NORWAY (see **12:**122; **Dc./17:**494). **Population.** In 1992 the number of Jews in Norway was about 1,300–1,400, of which 200–300 are Israelis. More than 1,000 people (including children) are members of the Jewish congregations in the two

Children in Oslo Jewish kindergarten learn about Sabbath candle blessing from Rabbi Michael Melchior, 1982 (Photo Debbi Cooper, Jerusalem)

Jewish communities in Norway: about 900 in Oslo and 135 in Trondheim. During the period under review 10–15 Christians converted to Judaism, 4 of them men. The Jewish population of Norway today is only three-quarters of that before the German occupation in 1940. A high percentage of community members are older than 65, which explains the relatively high rate of death in proportion to births.

The Jewish Communities. The frequency of people participating in the Sabbath morning-service in Oslo has increased. On other festivals, except Rosh ha-Shanah and Yom Kippur, services are not as well attended. In Trondheim the membership is too small to arrange morning services on Saturday. Services are usually held on Friday afternoons, on Rosh ha-Shanah, Yom Kippur, and some of the other festivals. The service is conducted by the chairman and superintendent Jacob Kommisar. In Oslo, since 1988 the leadership has been divided between the head of the board (administration, from 1991 Robert Katz) and the superintendent of religious affairs (Kai Feinberg). Rabbi Michael Melchior, who settled in Israel in 1986, is still the religious leader of the community, spending about four months a year in Oslo. The cantor is an Israeli and services are also conducted by a young Danish Jew who has settled in Oslo.

The cantor together with some local people teach in the religious afternoon-school (assisted in 1992–93 by two Israeli girls). The number of pupils in Oslo is about 70, in the age group 7–16. In addition to the ordinary lessons, weekend gatherings (also for the children in the kindergarten) are arranged once or twice a year in the community vacation home 12 miles (20 km) from Oslo. Once a year children and their parents spend a weekend in a hotel some 50 miles (80 km) from Oslo. Children from Trondheim have participated in these events and in the summer camps they were joined by children from other places in Norway as well. A young person from Oslo visits Trondheim every two or three weeks to teach and the community leader also teaches. A kindergarten was established in recent years in Trondheim.

The Jewish kindergarten in Oslo, with about 18 children, receives some economic support from the city. Twenty apartments for the elderly, partly subsidized by the city of Oslo, were built alongside of the synagogue and inaugurated in 1988.

The *Jodisk Menighetsblad*, the Jewish community journal, edited by Oskar Mendelsohn, 1976–1991, was succeeded in 1992 by a new, shorter publication, *Hatikwa.*

Since 1991 *kasher* meat has been imported from the U.S. and other *kasher* food from Denmark and Israel.

Community Centenary. In June 1992 the Oslo Jewish community marked its centenary with various celebrations, seminars, and public lectures, while the religious school arranged a walk to and over the Swedish border along one of the routes of escape of fall 1942. There was also an exhibition showing the religious holidays and surveying important events over the course of 100 years, which attracted more than 5,000 schoolchildren, and for which a special catalogue was printed. Pupils from the *ḥeder* together with pupils from another Jewish school published a paper about Jews in Norway which was distributed to schools. The community published a 230-page jubilee book.

The jubilee, held on June 14, started with a ceremony in the Jewish cemetery at the memorial for Jewish victims of World War II. This was followed by a festive service in the synagogue in the presence of Norwegian authorities and representatives of the other Scandinavian Jewish communities. Rabbi Michael Melchior spoke and the cantor, the synagogue choir, and Cantor Joseph Malovany of New York conducted the service, which was transmitted over Norwegian television. Rabbi Melchior was honored in 1993 with the Bridgebuilder Prize of the common council of the Norwegian Church academies for his significant efforts toward creating a dialogue and building bridges between people belonging to different groups and backgrounds to counteract the influence of hatemongers.

Culture. Over the decade books by Norwegian Jews as well as on Norwegian Jewry appeared, only a selection of which are mentioned here. Professor Leo Eitinger edited *Human among Humans: A book of anti-Semitism and hatred against strangers* (1985), the lectures from the Nansen Committee hearing on anti-Semitism. Autobiographies were published by the pianist Robert Levin and by Jo Benkow (q.v.); biographies on Leo Eitinger and Jo Benkow appeared. The Norwegian-Jewish author Eva Scheer published books on

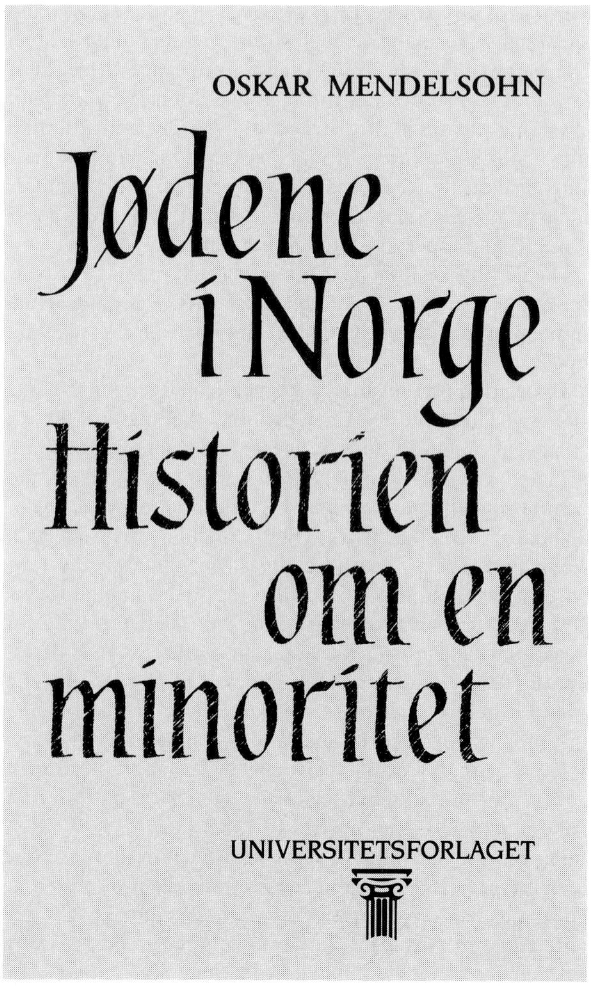

Cover of Oskar Mendelsohn's concise history of the Jews in Norway

19th-century Jewish life in Lithuania and some of her stories were translated into German.

The author of the two-volume *History of the Jews in Norway during 300 Years* (vol. 1, 1969; vol. 2, 1986; second edition, 1987), Oskar Mendelsohn, was made Knight, 1st class, of the Royal Saint Olavs Order in 1989 for his work on the history of the Norwegian Jews and in 1993 received the gold medal of the Royal Norwegian Society of Sciences and Arts, the oldest Norwegian society of science (founded 1760), for his "comprehensive scientific work in the investigation of the history of the Jewish minority in Norway." In 1992 a concise popular edition of Mendelsohn's work was published. Mendelsohn died in 1993.

The Holocaust was the subject of many Norwegian books and of several books translated into Norwegian in the past ten years, since the topic is of interest to the Norwegian reader. Many books of Jewish interest were translated into Norwegian, among them works by Elie Wiesel, Primo Levi, A. B. Yehoshua, Chaim Potok, Saul Bellow, and Simon Wiesenthal. [O.M.]

NOY, DOV (1920–), scholar in Jewish folklore. Born in Kolomyja, Poland, he graduated from a Polish secondary school, and then immigrated to Palestine where he began his academic studies at the Hebrew University of Jerusalem. He interrupted his studies to volunteer for military service in the British Army Royal Engineers during World War II, returning to the Hebrew University to complete his master's degree in Talmud, Jewish History, and Bible studies in 1946. He directed educational and cultural activities in the Cyprus Detention camps of Jewish refugees and worked there until the camps' liberation in 1948. For the next three years he served as editor of the leading Israeli children's weekly *Davar le-Yeladim.*

Returning to his studies, he received his post-graduate education in folklore, comparative literature, and anthropology at Yale University and at Indiana University, from which he obtained his doctorate in 1954, studying under Stith Thompson.

In 1955 he began his teaching career at the Hebrew University of Jerusalem where he taught *aggadah*, folk literature, general folklore, and Yiddish. He became professor and incumbent of the Chair of Folklore and Hebrew Literature. Noy's contribution to Jewish folklore has been pioneering. He founded and directed the Haifa Ethnological Museum and Folklore Archives (1956–1982) and edited the Israel Folktale Archives Publications series until 1981. He founded the Israel Folklore Archives, the largest treasure of Jewish folktales recorded in Israel. He was director of the Hebrew University Folklore Research Center from 1968 and edited *Studies*, its journal. He also trained a generation of researchers and students to tape and collect folk stories from all the various Jewish ethnic groups. He started the folklore section at Haifa University within the department of Hebrew Literature. From 1985, he served as professor of Yiddish Folklore at Bar-Ilan University.

His books cover a wide range of Jewish folklore: European, North African, Yemenite, and others. [E.HO.]

NUDEL, IDA (1931–), Russian Jewish activist and Refusenik. Born in the Crimea, she was trained in Moscow as an economist. Under the impact of the 1967 Six-Day War and the 1970 Leningrad Trial, she and her sister — her sole relative — decided to leave for Israel in 1971. Her sister and her family were permitted to emigrate but Nudel was refused permission on the ground that she was privy to state secrets (she had been working as an accountant in a planning institution which was totally non-secret). Dismissed from her job, she became extremely active in the Jewish Emigration movement and was known as the "guardian angel," caring for Jewish prisoners and their families. Through demonstrations, correspondence, and meetings with foreigners visiting Moscow, she brought the plight of the prisoners to public attention. She was arrested on many occasions, placed under house arrest, harassed frequently and physically abused.

Ida Nudel, upon arrival in Israel (GPO, Jerusalem)

In 1978 she hung a banner on the balcony of her apartment reading "KGB — GIVE ME MY EXIT VISA," as a result of which she was sentenced to four years exile in Siberia on charges of malicious hooliganism. There she suffered great hardships and after her release in 1982 was refused the right to live in a major city and moved from one place to another. In the Western world she became the best-known woman refusenik, winning the active support of many public figures such as Jane Fonda (who visited her in her exile) and Liv Ulmann (who portrayed her in a movie). Finally in 1987 she was permitted to leave for Israel where she settled near her sister in Reḥovot. [ED.]

O

OLSEN, TILLIE (1913–), U.S. author. Born Tillie Lerner in Omaha, Nebraska, the daughter of Russian immigrants, her stature rose steadily over the years and she became regarded as one of America's leading writers. Self-taught, with little formal education, she writes about the world which she is most intimately familiar — the struggles of working people, particularly women.

She was raised in a socialist background and developed her passion for writing as a young girl. In the 1930s she became involved in a variety of political and trade union movements. After dropping out of high school, she was briefly jailed in Kansas City for trying to organize packing-house workers. She then worked full time in various trade unions while writing for left-wing journals.

Married in 1945, she thereafter devoted herself to raising her four daughters, while employed in various menial jobs. A novel began in the 1930s was finished only 40 years later, and her first book *Tell Me a Riddle* (1962), a collection of four stories exploring human relationships, was published when she was nearly 50. The title story, published separately in 1961, received the O. Henry Award. It deals with the last months of a terminally ill elderly woman and her attempts to resolve deep-rooted marital conflicts. Another much-anthologized story in the collection, "I Stand Here Ironing," explores the relationship of mothers and daughters and the repression of women.

As a result of her publication, Olsen began receiving writing fellowships, including grants from the National Endowment of the Arts, and served as a visiting professor at several universities. In 1974, her novel, *Yonnondio: From the Thirties* was finally published to widespread acclaim. The novel deals with the struggles of a midwestern family during the Depression.

Olsen has also written a biographical and literary commentary of the writer Rebecca Harding Davies who was an early influence on her writing, and a collection of essays, *Silences* (1978). In her 1981 play *I Stand Here Mourning* — a monologue — a mother mourns the blighting of her 19-year-old daughter's life. [SU.STR.]

OLYMPIC GAMES (see **12**:1375; **Dc./17**:498). The following names are to be omitted from the list of Jewish Olympic medal winners in **12**:1375–1377: 1908, 1912, 1920, 1924, Paul Anspach; 1912, Henry Anspach; 1912, 1924, Zoltan Schenker; 1912, Margarete Adler; 1912, Klara Milch; 1928, 1932, Istvan Barta; 1932, 1936, Karoly Karpati; 1936, 1948, 1952, Ilona Elek; 1936, Ibolya Csak; 1948, 1952, 1956, 1960, 1964, Dezso Gyarmati; 1972, Nikolai Avilov; 1976, David Rigert; 1976, Nancy Lieberman; and 1980, Shamil Sabyrov

The following Jewish Olympic winners are to be added:

1900 — Edouard Alphonse de Rothschild, France, polo, Bronze (1)
1928, 1936 — Helene Mayer, Germany, fencing, gold (1), silver (1)
1932, 1936 — Miklos Sarkany, Hungary, water polo, gold (2)
1936 — Irving Meretsky, Canada, basketball, silver (1)
1952 — Maria Gorokhovskaya, USSR, gymnastics, gold (2), silver (5)
1968 — Victor Zinger, USSR, ice hockey, gold (1)
1972 — Ildiko Sagine-Rejto, Hungary, fencing, silver (1)
1972 — Mark Rakita, USSR, fencing, silver (1)
1972 — Eduoard Vinokurov, USSR, fencing, silver (1)
1972 — Grigory Kriss, USSR, fencing, bronze (1)
1980 — Johan Harmenberg, Sweden, fencing, fold (1)

Oren Smadga, bronze medalist for judo, 1992

Olympic Games 1984. Jewish medal winners were:

GOLD
Mitch Gaylord, USA, gymnastics (1)
Carina Benninga, Netherlands, field hockey (1)
Dara Torres, USA, swimming (1)

SILVER
Robert Berland, USA, judo (1)
Mitch Gaylord, USA, gymnastics (1)
Bernard Rajzman, Brazil, volleyball (1)

BRONZE
Mitch Gaylord, USA, gymnastics (2)
Mark Berger, Canada, judo (1)

Olympic Games 1988. Jewish medal winners were:

BRONZE
Dara Torres, USA, swimming (1)
Brad Gilbert, USA, tennis (1)
Carina Benninga, Netherlands, field hockey (1)
Seth Bauer, USA, rowing (1)

Olympic Games 1992. Jewish medal winners were:

GOLD
Joseph Jacobi, USA, canoeing (1)
Dara Torres, USA, swimming (1)
Valeri Belenki, Unified Team, gymnastics (1)

SILVER
Yael Arad, Israel, judo (1)
Arbital Selinger, Netherlands, volleyball (1)

BRONZE
Shay Oren Smadga, Israel, judo (1)
Valeri Belenki, Unified Team, gymnastics (1)
Dan Greenbaum, USA, volleyball (1)

[J.H.S.]

ORDMAN, JEANNETTE, Israel ballet dancer and teacher; director of the Bat-Dor Dance Company and school. Born in Germiston, South Africa, her family moved to Johannesburg where she studied dance with Reina Berman and later with Marjorie Sturman, founder of the Johannesburg Festival Ballet (which became the Pact Ballet). She was still in her teens when Anton Dolin who had come to advise on dance selected her to dance the title role in *Giselle.*

Jeannette Ordman

Moving to London, she danced with the Sadler's Wells Opera Ballet and on television. In 1965 she went to Israel as principal dancer of a touring company. When the tour ended abruptly, she opened a studio. Her dancing had already made an impression and pupils flocked to her. At that time Batsheva de Rothschild, who had settled in Israel in 1958 and founded the Batsheva Dance Company in 1964, was looking for a suitable director to open a dance school. With her friend Martha Graham, then visiting Israel, she saw

Ordman's classes. The result was the opening of the Bat-Dor Dance School in 1967 and of the Bat-Dor Dance Company in 1968, with Ordman as director and principal dancer.

From then on, the studio grew in importance and the company is one of the major dance companies in Israel and has toured widely. It was the first professional Israeli company to go to Poland (1987) and to Russia (1989).

After her great success in the Polish tour, Ordman developed hip trouble. After two operations, she made a successful comeback (1989) in Rodney Griffin's *Piaf Vaudeville.* She has three times been invited to serve on the jury of the International Ballet Competition at Jackson, Mississippi (held every fourth year) — the latest in 1990. [D.L.S.]

ORTHODOXY. Modern (see **12**:1491). Orthodox Judaism is by no means monolithic; the diversity in faith and practice is legion; it has no ultimate authority or hierarchy of authorities; and it has never been able to mobilize even one national or international organization in which all of its groups would speak as one. The diversity in halakhic rulings is typical of most legal systems. It stems principally from reliance on different sources all of which are deemed authoritative, or from methods of reasoning, applied to the sources, which are also deemed normative by all halakhists. Philosophy or teleology play little part in the decision-making process except for a few among the Modern Orthodox.

The Modern Orthodox constitute neither sect nor movement. They convene no seminars and no colloquiums. They have no organized group and no publication of their own. There is no list of rabbis or laymen who call themselves "Modern Orthodox." They are at best represented by a group of rabbis who see each other from time to time and share the same commitment, namely that the Torah does not have to be afraid of modernity since there is no challenge that the Torah cannot cope with. Some prefer the word "centrist" because the word "modern" is too often associated with permissiveness. Others reject the term "centrist" because it suggests being in the center on all issues. But the Modern Orthodox are extremists on the positive side of many issues such as the centrality of ethics in religious behavior and the need for improving the status of women in *halakhah.*

The diversity among all Orthodox Jews that evokes the most acrimony revolves around three issues: the nature and scope of Revelation; attitudes toward secular education and modern culture; and the propriety of cooperation with non-Orthodox rabbis. To systematic theology very little attention is given. The writings of the medieval Jewish philosophers are studied and expounded but they appear to stimulate no new approaches. Orthodox Jews are still rationalists or mystics; naturalists or neo-Hegelians; and, even existentialists, most notably Joseph D. *Soloveitchik. Starting with the premise that all the Torah is God's revealed will, he holds that logically all of it must have theological significance. Therefore, he sees the totality of Torah as the realm of ideas in the Platonic sense, given by God for application to the realm of the real. Just as the mathematician creates an internally logical and coherent fabric of formulas with which he interprets and integrates the appearances of the visible world, so the Jew, the "Man of Halakhah," has the Torah as the divine idea that invests all of human life with direction and sanctity. "The *halakhah* is a multi-dimensional ever-expanding continuum that cuts through all levels of human existence from the most primitive and intimate to the most complex relationships." And though the *halakhah* refers to the ideal, its creativity must be affected by the real. "Man's response to the great halakhic challenge asserts itself not only in blind acceptance of the divine imperative but also in assimilating a transcendental content disclosed to him through an apocalyptic revelation and in fashioning it to his peculiar needs. It is rather the experiencing of life's irreconcilable antitheses — the simultaneous affirmation and abnegation of the self, the simultaneous awareness of the temporal and the eternal, the simultaneous clash of freedom and necessity, the simultaneous love and fear of God, and His simultaneous transcendence and immanence."

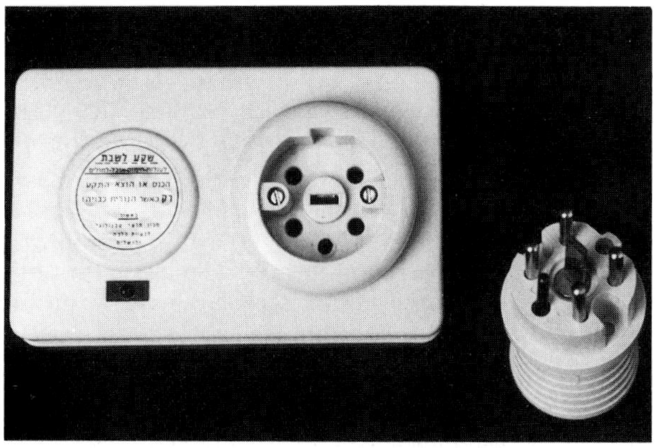

A specially developed, halakhically permissible electrical outlet for use in hospitals on food-warming trolleys on the Sabbath, developed by the Institute for Science and Halakhah, Jerusalem (Courtesy the Institute for Science and Halakhah, Jerusalem)

As for conceptions of the hereafter and resurrection of the dead, Soloveitchik holds with earlier authorities that no man can fathom or visualize precisely what they signify in fact, but the beliefs themselves can be deduced logically from the proposition that God is just and merciful. God's attribute of absolute justice and mercy require that he provide rewards and punishments and that He redeem Himself by being merciful to those most in need of mercy — the dead. Soloveitchik holds with many earlier philosophers that the immortality of the soul after death is to be distinguished from a this-worldly resurrection of the dead in a post-Messianic period; the Messianic period itself will produce only international peace and order.

Essentially the doctrines represent fulfillment of Judaism's commitment to an optimistic philosophy of human existence. In Soloveitchik's intellectual development there was a period when there was a clash, a confrontation between two ways of life and modes of thought; that of Brisk (Brest-Litovsk), where he became the great Talmudist, and that of Berlin, where he later became the great philosopher.

For many of his disciples who call themselves Modern Orthodox there was no such clash. They grew up in both cultures simultaneously and the synthesis they sought and attained was a gradual achievement over a long period, virtually from elementary school days through graduate study. What little they achieved was not born altogether from anguish but more by the slow natural process of intellectual and emotional maturation. That is why they often part with the master in whose thought existentialism plays the major role and they are more likely to embrace a more naturalist theology.

Theology and eschatology generally receive very little attention from Orthodox Jewish thinkers. The case is not so with Revelation, on which, the range in views is enormous. There are those who hold literally that God dictated the Torah to Moses, who wrote each word as dictated, and there are those who maintain that how God communicated with Moses, the Jewish people, the Patriarchs and the Prophets will continue to be a matter of conjecture and interpretation but the crucial point is that He did it in history. As creation is a fact for believers, though they cannot describe how, so Revelation is a fact, though its precise manner is not clear. This less fundamentalist approach would not deny a role to man's subjective response to the encounter with the divine, but all Orthodox Jews would agree that the doctrine of divine Revelation represents direct supernatural communication of content from God to man.

There are those who hold that every event reported in the Torah must be understood literally; some are less rigid in this connection and even regard the Torah as the ultimate source for a Jewish philosophy of history rather than Jewish history itself. This accounts for the fact that presently some authorities insist that Orthodox Jews must hold the age of the earth to be some five thousand years plus, while others have no difficulty in accepting astronomical figures.

The head of the Lubavich movement, Rabbi Menaḥem *Schneerson, insists that the age of the earth is what the tradition holds it to be. The Modern Orthodox are more likely to hold with Rabbi Menaḥem Mendel *Kasher that it is not imperative that one so hold, and he thus advised scientists who sought his definitive opinion on the issue. He made no dogma of the traditional view. There are many Orthodox scientists, researchers, and academicians, who bifurcate their position. They hold to the traditional view as believers and to the scientific views in their professional pursuits — and this schizoid position does not disturb them.

With regard to the legal portions of the Torah, many Orthodox Jews still insist that they are eternal and immutable. Others maintain that the Oral Torah itself affords conclusive proof that there are laws that are neither eternal nor immutable. In the Oral Torah one also finds that some commandments were deemed by one authority or another never to have been mandatory but rather optional. Such were the commandments with regard to the blood-avenger and the appointment of a king. However, exponents of Orthodox Judaism generally affirm eternity and immutability even though they engage in halakhic development without regard to the fiction they verbalize. The Modern Orthodox are more likely not to articulate the fiction as they explore ways to make the eternal law cope with the needs of the period.

With regard to parts of the Bible other than the Pentateuch, some hold that all of them were written because of the Holy Spirit; others are more critical and do not dogmatize with regard to their authorship, accuracy of texts, dates of composition, or literal interpretation. Some extend the doctrine of the inviolability of the Torah to all the sacred writings including the Talmud and the Midrashim and do not permit rejection even of any of the most contradictory legends or maxims. Others are "reductionists" and restrict the notion of inviolability to the Five Books of Moses.

Many of these views were expressed before the modern period. They are found in the writings of Jewish philosophers of the Middle Ages and some are clearly expressed in the Talmud and Midrashim. The so-called Modern Orthodox are more likely to be found among those who hold the more liberal views with regard to these issues. Similarly, on the basis of tradition the Modern Orthodox differ with their colleagues with regard to secular education and modern culture and the cooperation of Orthodox Jews with non-Orthodox Jews.

There were Orthodox rabbis who bemoaned the collapse of the ghetto walls because they fathomed what this would mean to the solidarity of the Jewish community and especially the future of its legal autonomy. *Halakhah*, which had always been applicable to the personal, social, economic, and political existence of Jews, would therafter be relevant to very limited areas in the life of the Jew. These rabbis opposed any form of acculturation with their non-Jewish neighbors. Others advocated acculturation in social and economic matters but retained commitment to a Judaism totally unrelated to, and unaffected by, the ideas and values that dominated the non-Jewish scene. Others advocated the fullest symbiosis, outstanding among them, Rabbis Abraham Isaac Hacohen *Kook and Joseph D. Soloveitchik. Rabbi Kook maintained a very positive attitude to all modern cultural and scientific developments; Rabbi Soloveitchik described the believing Jew as one who is forever in dialectical tension between his being a member of the covenanted community and his obligation to fulfill his socio-ethical responsibilities with and for all humanity in a rapidly changing world. Disciples of theirs even find that their secular education and exposure to modern culture deepen their understanding and appreciation of their own heritage, even as it helps them to evaluate modernity with greater insight and a measure of transcendence.

Because of differences of opinion, one finds contemporary Orthodox Jews holding many different views with respect to their own mode of living, their careers, and the education of their children. Those who want no part of modernity prefer to live in isolation and earn a livelihood by pursuing "safe" careers in business. They want the same for their offspring. Others seek to bifurcate their existence. They are modern in dress, enjoy the culture which surrounds them, but avoid intellectual challenges, and build a protective wall around their religious commitment, forbidding the environment to encroach upon their faith and ancestral practice. Usually they too want for their children what they enjoy and they also encourage their young to pursue "safe" careers at college — courses in business, law, medicine, accounting, but rarely the social sciences or the humanities.

Then there are those who are determined to cope with all the challenges that modernity can offer. Some, like Samuel *Belkin, held to this view but spoke of the "synthesis" between modernity and traditional Judaism as a merging of the two cultures in the personality and outlook of the Orthodox Jew. His predecessor, Bernard *Revel, the first president of Yeshiva University, had a more exciting goal — a genuine synthesis of the best in both worlds. He craved the sanctification of the secular as did Rabbi Kook; the integration of the best that humanity has achieved with the eternal truths of Judaism; the greater appreciation of Judaism because of its differences from other religions and cultures; and the reformulation of the cherished concepts and practices of Judaism and their rationalization in modern terms. This goal has been achieved by only a few, but most of the intelligentsia among the Modern Orthodox share Revel's dream rather than the less difficult goal of Belkin.

U.S. stamp issued in honor of Rabbi Bernard Revel, 1986 (Courtesy U.S. Postal Service)

The attitudes of Orthodox Jews to their non-Orthodox co-religionists also range from one end of the spectrum to the other — from hate presumably based on revered texts to toleration, total acceptance, and even love, similarly based on revered texts. Those indulging in hate are responsible for the physical violence occasionally practiced against any who deviate from the tradition. Theirs is a policy of non-cooperation in any form whatever with any who disagree with them, and they not only pray for the destruction of the State of Israel but even take measures to achieve that end. Others simply desire total separation from those who deviate from their customs and practices even in the matter of dress.

A further group is reconciled to the fact of pluralism in Jewish life but has no affinity whatever for the non-Orthodox. A fourth group loves all Jews irrespective of how they behave but does not accord even a modicum of tolerance to organizations that represent non-Orthodox rabbis and congregations. It is more tolerant of secular groups — no matter how anti-religious. A fifth group is even willing to cooperate with non-Orthodox groups in all matters pertaining to relationships between Jews and non-Jews, at least in the United States. Even they are less open-minded with regard to the situation in Israel. Only a very small group goes all the way with the inescapable implications of the thought of Kook and Soloveitchik and welcomes the challenge of non-Orthodoxy, even as it views secular education and modern culture as positive factors in appreciation of the tradition.

It is also in this last group, Modern Orthodox, that one is likely to find those who will project halakhic decisions that are based on the sources but not necessarily the weight of the authorities. Especially with respect to the inviolability of the persons of all human beings, including Jewish dissenters, they are zealots. Thus they encourage dialogue with all Jews, solutions to the painful problems in Jewish family law, more prohibitions with community sanctions against the unethical behavior of Jews in business, in the exaction of usury, in the evasion of taxes, and in the exploitation of the disadvantaged. They propose the use of more theology and teleology in the process of halakhic decision. Their principal difference with so-called right-wing Conservative rabbis is that they do not wish to "update" the *halakhah* to adjust it to the spirit of the time but rather within the frame and normative procedures of the *halakhah* — its sources and its method of reasoning — to express the implications of the *halakhah* for the modern Jew and his existential situation.

The Modern Orthodox are especially attentive to historical, psychological, sociological, and teleological considerations. A few illustrations may be of interest.

They oppose any form of religious coercion by Jews against Jews and not by resort to the legal fiction that every Jew is now to be considered the equal of one who was taken captive in his early childhood and never raised as a Jew.

The tradition exempts such a person from religious coercion. The Modern Orthodox prefer the approach which says that religious coercion was only permitted when it might truly change the attitude and inner feeling of its victim. However, coercion now only angers the victim more and makes him or her more hostile to Judaism. Therefore, it defeats rather than advances its original purpose.

Similarly, Jewish family law developed to give dignity and sanctity to the status of every member of the family, with every individual enjoying the right freely to serve God and fulfill his or her responsibilities as a member of the family. When Jewish law, however, no longer serves this purpose and becomes an instrument for exploitations of one by another and the literal enslavement of spouses or offspring then there must be legislation and the sooner the better. Therefore, the Modern Orthodox especially favor antenuptial agreements anticipating certain unfortunate events and the reactivation of the annullment of marriages — all of which has ample sources in the halakhic literature.

Last but not least, the Modern Orthodox are more likely than others to give a sympathetic ear to halakhic changes in the face of developments in modern medicine — especially the right to volunteer one's organs for transplanting. This is a field in which very little creative work has been accomplished by rabbis, except to assemble ancient sources with little or no philosophical analysis.

Because of the enormous diversity among Orthodox Jews in both creed and practice, there is a tendency at present to speak of the ultra-Orthodox, the Orthodox, and the Modern Orthodox. Yet in each of these groups there is substantial diversity, and the outlook in a free world and open society is for more, rather than less, of it. [E.RA.]

OURY, GERARD (1919–), dramatic artist, author, film director. Oury was born in Paris. He is one of the leading directors of comedies in the French film industry and has worked with all the great comedians of France. He began his career as an actor in Paris with the Comédie Française in 1939/40, but had to abandon it upon the Nazi conquest. He spent 1943 to 1945 in Geneva, and only returned to the Comédie Française in 1961. Some of his films have featured Jewish characters or elements. Among his many successful films, many featuring Louis de Funès, are: *Le Corniaud* (1964), *La Grande Vadrouille* (1966), *Le Cerveau* (1968), *La Folies des Grandeurs* (1971), *Les Aventures de Rabbi Jacob* (1973), and *L'As des As* (1982). [GI.KO.]

P

PALESTINE LIBERATION ORGANIZATION (PLO). The loss of the PLO's state-within-a-state in Lebanon following the 1982 Israeli invasion forced the PLO into a difficult predicament and generated several processes whose repercussions were still evident by 1992. By shifting its headquarters to Tunis, the PLO lost direct control of all major concentrations of Palestinian population. Deprived of an independent power base, the PLO faced growing dependence on the various Arab states. In view of the dispersion of its forces in Tunisia, Algeria, Yemen, the Sudan, the PLO's strategy of armed struggle to liberate Palestine was proven almost bankrupt. The unveiling in September 1982 of President Reagan's peace plan, which offered the Palestinians an autonomy within Jordan, while explicitly ruling out an independent Palestinian state and any role for the PLO, threatened to leave it out of a settlement of the Arab-Israeli conflict. In order to survive politically, it was essential for the PLO to preserve its independence *vis-à-vis* the various Arab states (the independence of Palestinian decision-making in its terminology), as well as its unity and its status as the sole legitimate representative of the Palestinian people. Consequently, the PLO chairman, Yasser Arafat, and the PLO's mainstream, realized that the political option, though psychologically and ideologically problematic, was the only viable one left for them.

Resentment over negotiations which Arafat had conducted with Jordan since late 1982 and several organizational measures designed to enhance his personal power, provoked in mid-1983 a rebellion among Fataḥ units stationed in the Syrian-controlled Bekaa Valley in Lebanon. Syria, which had always sought to dominate the PLO, and the pro-Syrian organizations militarily supported the dissenters. In December 1983 Arafat and his followers were expelled from Tripoli, their last stronghold in Lebanon.

In order to counterbalance the Syrian pressures, Arafat established an alliance with Egypt, which the PLO had hitherto boycotted, and renewed his contacts with Jordan. Despite Syrian efforts, Arafat managed to reactivate the PLO's institutions and to consolidate his personal leadership over the organization. The pro-Syrian factions established the Palestine National Salvation Front (PNSF), which

Fataḥ poster with theme of conquest of Jerusalem

degenerated into a Syrian tool with insignificant popular backing.

PLO's policy during the years 1984–87 was marked by diplomatic duality, through which the PLO sought to participate in an eventual political settlement, but without making painful ideological concessions. The policy was manifested by signing the Amman Accord with Jordan on Febrary 11, 1985, which asserted the principle of land in exchange for peace in accordance with all UN resolutions, but also the agreement's subsequent abrogation following opposition by the radical organizations. On later occasions, the PLO conditioned its acceptance of Security Council Resolution 242 by adding all relevant UN resolutions, which could be interpreted as implicitly sanctioning the elimination of Israel, while it refused to explicitly recognize Israel. Although preserving the organization's unity, this diplomacy failed to win U.S. recognition of the PLO. It also alienated various Arab governments, each for its own reasons, as manifested in the PLO's low stature during the Amman Arab summit of 1987, which for the first time since 1948 relegated the Palestinian problem to secondary importance.

The PLO did not initiate, and was in fact surprised, by the outbreak in December 1987 of the uprising against Israel in the Territories (the *intifada*). Moreover, to some extent the *intifada* erupted out of frustration over the organization's meager military and political achievements. Yet, the PLO was one of the *intifada*'s major beneficiaries, as the majority of Palestinians rallied behind its banner. The *intifada* tarnished Israel's image abroad while enhancing Western sympathy for the Palestinians. It regenerated the peace process under more favorable terms for the Palestinians. Jordan's legal disengagement from the West Bank removed a major rival for the PLO. The *intifada* also shook Israel's belief that the status quo in the Territories could last indefinitely. Concurrently, the *intifada*'s achievements accelerated the process, which had begun in 1982 of enhancing the inhabitants of the Territories *vis-à-vis* the PLO's establishment in the Palestinian political arena.

Complying with pressures from the Territories to politically capitalize on the *intifada*'s gains, the 19th Palestine National Council (PNC), which convened in Algiers in November 1988, declared the establishment of an independent Palestinian state based on the 1947 UN partition plan. The reference in the declaration to a Jewish state, to the partition plan, and the explicit mentioning of Security Council resolutions 242 and 338 as the basis for convening an international conference brought the PLO closer than ever before to the acceptance of a permanent solution to the conflict based on two states in Palestine. Nevertheless, the PNC resolutions were phrased in a way leaving the door open for the PLO's phased strategy leading to the elimination of Israel. Thus the PLO demanded the implementation of the Palestinian refugees' right of return, designed to achieve Arab demographic superiority within Israel. In addition, it insisted on the Palestinian right of self-determination, which includes the Palestinians residing inside Israel proper. While the Palestinian Covenant, the PLO's constitution, was not mentioned in the resolutions, neither was it abolished nor amended. Even though the radical organizations opposed the resolutions, they did not secede from the PNC, leaving Arafat sufficient latitude to pursue his policies.

Additional statements by Arafat in December 1988 in Geneva of explicitly recognizing Israel, of accepting resolution 242, and of renouncing terrorism prompted the U.S. to initiate an official dialogue with the PLO. The dialogue, however, was suspended in June 1990 when the PLO refused to denounce an attempted terrorist act by the Palestine Liberation Front at the end of May on bathers on Israel's Mediterranean coast. Bowing to popular Palestinian pressure, and resentful at the U.S., the PLO sided with Iraq following its invasion of Kuwait in August 1990. In response, the Gulf states suspended their financial aid to the Organization and expelled more than 300,000 Palestinians who had resided in the region. Considerably weakened internationally, the PLO was forced to accept American terms that a delegation from the Territories would represent the Palestinians in the Madrid Peace Conference of October 1991 and the ensuing negotiations, with the organization playing only an indirect role. In addition, the PLO had to accept an autonomy for the Territories for a transitional period until their final status would be settled.

The *intifada* also engendered the most serious threat to the PLO with the establishment of the Islamic Resistance Movement *(Ḥarakat al-muqawama al-Islamiyya*, Ḥamas), as the military arm of the Muslim Brotherhood in the Territories. Presenting itself as a religious and national alternative to the PLO, Ḥamas castigated the organization for abandoning the goal of liberating all of Palestine and of eliminating Israel, and for seeking to establish a secular Palestinian state rather

PLO flags, swastika, molotov cocktails, and other *intifada* material, Jan. 1990 (GPO, Jerusalem)

than an Islamic one. In contrast to the PLO's establishment, which was tainted with corruption, Ḥamas leadership resided in the Territories, close to its major constituency, and enjoyed a reputation of religious purity. Ḥamas also took advantage of the PLO's financial difficulties and inability to support its institutions in the Territories to expand its organizational and communal services networks. Likewise, it benefited from the growing frustration among the Palestinians over the lack of progress of the peace process, by presenting an attractive ideological alternative. Thus at the end of 1992, while the Palestinians were closer than ever to achieve a peaceful solution to their problem, the PLO faced the danger of losing its dominance in the Palestinian arena. (For further update, see page 33.) [M.LIT.]

PALEY, GRACE (1922–), U.S. author. Born Grace Goodside in the Bronx, New York, the daughter of East European immigrants, Paley's first stories appeared in *Accent* and other small magazines. Among the most important and innovative of contemporary American short story writers, in 1959, she published her first volume of short stories, *The Little Disturbances of Man*, which was widely reviewed and praised. Throughout the 1960s, her stories appeared in such magazines as *Esquire, Atlantic Monthly*, and *New American Review*. In 1974, fifteen of these stories were published in a collection, *Enormous Changes at the Last Minute*, which established her as an original talent in modern fiction. Her collection *Later the Same Day* reintroduces characters from her earlier works; they are older but still outspoken. Paley's writing describes the world with which she is most familiar — contemporary ethnic urban life and social conditions and interpersonal relationships.

Paley is also well known as a peace activist and was a longtime campaigner in the anti-Vietnam War movement. She has been active in numerous campaigns on behalf of peace and civil rights, more recently becoming a leading spokeswoman against nuclear weapons. She was among eleven protesters arrested and found guilty following an anti-nuclear demonstration at the White House in 1978.

From 1966 Paley taught writing at Columbia University, Syracuse University, and Sarah Lawrence College. She was elected to the American Academy and Institute of Arts and Letters in 1980. [SU.STR.]

PAPO, IZIDOR JOSEF (1913–), Yugoslav surgeon. Born in Mostar, Papo received his M.D. from the University of Zagreb in 1937 and specialized in surgery at Sarajevo 1937–1941. During World War II he fought from 1941 in the Yugoslav Liberation Army, advancing to the rank of lieutenant-general. From 1947 he was a professor of surgery

Izidor Josef Papo (Courtesy Eugen Werber, Belgrade)

and in 1948 head of the surgery clinic of the Yugoslav Military Medical Academy and surgeon-in-chief of the Yugoslav Army. He settled in Belgrade. Papo wrote papers in the field of general and cardiovascular surgery and was co-deviser of the method of reconstruction of the esophagus known as Yudin-Papo. He was also responsible for various innovations in cardiovascular surgery. Papo received the Highest Yugoslav and foreign decorations and awards and was made honorary knight commander in the Order of the British Empire and a fellow of the American College of Cardiology as well as of the British Royal College of Surgeons.

[E.WE.]

PEACE MOVEMENTS, RELIGIOUS. Israel. Within Israel, Orthodox Judaism has politically largely become associated with an uncompromising stance concerning issues of territory and the Arab–Israel conflict. This has become an integral part of the ideologies and policies expressed by the *National Religious Party and Gush Emunim (q.v.). Over the years, however, a number of small, religious peace movements have been founded in an attempt to promote an alternative message based, also, on recourse to religious and theological sources.

Oz ve-Shalom ("Strength and Peace") was founded in the 1970s as a religious response to Gush Emunim. Made up of religious intellectuals, this movement failed to have any major impact on its target population, who viewed it as unrepresentative of the religious population. In the wake of the Lebanon War, the Netivot Shalom ("Paths of Peace") Movement was founded by members of the *yeshivat hesder* (yeshivah studies combined with army service) at Har Etzion. The head of the yeshivah, Rabbi Yehudah Amital, favored a more moderate stance on the question of exchanging territory for a peace agreement. During the 1980s, the two movements operated as a single, largely ineffective, organization in their attempt to find a place both among the peace camp of the secular left and the ultra-nationalists of the religious right.

In 1988, a moderate religious political party, Meimad, was founded under the leadership of Rabbi Amital. This party failed to obtain the minimum number of votes necessary for a seat within the Knesset, and this was seen as a clear indication of the limited religious support for a moderate stance on the question of the territories. Meimad was reformed early in 1993, mainly as an ideological and educational organization to lend support to the renewed peace process of the Rabin government. Also in 1992, the Committee of Rabbis for Human Rights was formed and obtained some prominence in their support of Palestinian human rights. Unlike the other religious peace organizations, the Rabbis for Human Rights was composed of rabbis from all the major religious streams — Orthodox, Conservative, and Reform.

Bibliography: T. Hermann of & D. Newman, in: C. Liebman (ed.), *Religious and Secular: Conflict and Accommodation between Jews in Israel* (1992), 151–172; D. Newman, in: *L'eylah*, 31 (1991), 4–10.

[DA.NE.]

PEARLMAN, MOSHE (1911–1986), author and journalist. Pearlman was born in London where he graduated from the London School of Economics. During World War II he served in the British army in North Africa and Greece, attaining the rank of major. Concurrent with his army service and after it, he was involved in the organization of "illegal" immigration, Aliyah Bet. Pearlman was at kibbutz Ein Ḥarod for the year in 1936 and returned to the country as an immigrant in 1948. In the War of Independence he was in charge of the Israel army press liaison unit and served as the army's chief spokesman. He remained head of the Press Unit until 1952 and during the same time period was the organizer and first director of the Government Press Office. From 1952 to 1956 he was the director of the Israel Broadcasting Service, Kol Yisrael. He was sent as an ambassador on a special mission to Zaire (then the Belgian Congo) in 1960 and in 1967 served as special assistant to Defense Minister Moshe Dayan during the period of the Six-Day War. His first book, *Collective Adventure*, described his year on a kibbutz; among his other works are *In the Footsteps of Moses. In the Footsteps of the Prophets*, and *The Capture and Trial of Adolf Eichmann.* He also worked as a collaborator with public figures, for example, with Ben-Gurion on *Ben-Gurion Looks Back*, and with Teddy Kollek on *Jerusalem: A History of 40 Centuries.* [ED.]

PEREC, GEORGES (1936–1982), French author. Grandson of Isaac Leib *Peretz's nephew David, Georges Perec lost his father in the defense of France in 1940 and his mother in the deportation from *Drancy (February 1943). For the major part of the Nazi occupation of France, Perec was hidden in a Catholic boarding school at Villard-de-Lans (Isère) and after the Liberation he was brought up in Paris by his paternal aunt and her husband, a trader in fine pearls. Perec's early orphanage marked him deeply, and lies near the root of his highly defended but engagingly unpretentious literary personality. He was educated in Paris and at Etampes, where his philosophy teacher, Jean Duvignaud, encouraged him in his early decision to become a writer. Perec dropped out of a history degree at the Sorbonne and constructed his own "university" through reading, through friendships (notably with a group of Yugoslav artists and thinkers), and through La Ligne générale (1958–1960), a cultural movement aiming to renew Marxism from within. Perec did two years military service in a parachute regiment (1958–1959), then worked briefly in market research before spending a year at Sfax, in Tunisia. From 1961 until 1978 Perec was employed as a research librarian in a neurophysiological laboratory.

Many of Perec's early writings have been lost. Every one of his published works is an exercise in a different style. *Les Choses. Une histoire des années soixante* (Prix Renaudot 1965; transl. as *Things, A Story of the Sixties*, 1990), is an ironical portrait of a generation bewildered by the arrival of prosperity, written in a deceptively simple language intentionally echoing the style of Flaubert's *Sentimental Education*; it made Perec famous as the "sociologist" of his own generation. Perec's following works were not in the same vein and were less widely read until the 1980s. *Quel Petit Vélo à guidon chromé au fond de la cour?* (1966) is a mock-epic. *Un homme qui dort* (1967; transl. as *A Man Asleep*, 1990) is a second-person narrative of adolescent depression in which the technique of collage is used almost invisibly (a film version was made by Perec and Bernard Queysanne in 1974), and *La Disparition* (1968) is a murder mystery novel written under the constraint of a lipogram on e. Perec became well known in Germany for a series of radio plays: *Die Maschine* (1968, with Eugen Helmle), *L'Augmentation* (1969), *Tagstimmen* (1971, with Eugen Helmle and Philippe Drogoz), etc. He also performed remarkable "alphabetic exercises" as a member of OuLiPo (the "Workshop for Potential Literature" founded by Raymond Queneau) including palindromes, univocalics, and heterogrammatic poetry (*Alphabets*, 1976).

Perec's incessant formal innovations accompany a lifelong concern with autobiography. *La Boutique obscure* (1973) is a record of his dreams; *Espèces d'espaces* (1974) is a personal reflection on his relationship to spatiality; *Je me souviens* (1978, stage adaptation by Sami Frey, 1988) a record of "shared" memories. *W ou le souvenir d'enfance* (1975, incorporating earlier texts, transl. as *W or The Memory of Childhood*, 1988) is Perec's most direct approach to self-description and self-analysis, conducted by unusual means. It consists of two apparently unrelated texts printed in alternating chapters, which converge on a common image, that of the concentration camp. Its deceptive design is to make the reader share some of the inextinguishable anguish and guilt of a childhood survivor of the Holocaust.

La Vie mode d'emploi (Prix Medicis, 1978; transl. as *Life A User's Manual*, 1987) is Perec's masterpiece, "the last great event in the history of the novel" (Italo Calvino). It describes the contents of a block of flats at a frozen moment of time — June 23, 1975, towards eight in the evening — together with the life-histories of the characters and the objects (and even the cats) caught in the novelist-painter's artfully calculated frame. Its success allowed Perec to live thereafter as a full-time writer. He pursued two projects related to the understanding of his own Jewish background: a "genealogical saga" of his family (unfinished), and a television essay on Ellis Island, as a kind of "alternative autobiography" (with Robert Bober, 1979–80). He also produced a film, published a novella about a forged painting representing many other paintings, each of which refer in some way to *Life A User's Manual (Un Cabinet d'Amateur*, 1979), and continued to provide crosswords for the weekly magazine *Le Point.* After 1978, Perec also traveled widely, to Poland, America, Italy, and Australia, where he spent one month as writer in residence at the University of Queensland. He died, leaving many works incomplete. His unfinished "literary thriller" *53 Jours (53 Days)* was published in 1989.

Perec's standing in French and world literature has not ceased to grow since 1982, as the originality and underlying coherence of his extremely diverse output comes into clearer focus.

Bibliography: Benabou, "Georges Perec et la judéité," in: *Cahiers Georges Perec I* (1985); C. Burgelin, *Georges Perec* (1988).

[DA.B.]

PERES, SHIMON (see **13**:278; **Dc./17**:503). From September 13, 1984, to October 13, 1986, Shimon Peres served as the prime minister of Israel, in accordance with the coalition agreement reached following the elections held in July 1984. As of October 1986, Peres became the foreign minister and deputy prime minister, serving until the 1988 elections. In 1992 he became foreign minister in the Labor-led government and conducted the secret negotiations in 1993 with the PLO leading to the Declaration of Principles.

PILCH, JUDAH (1902–1986), United States Jewish educator. Born in the Ukraine, he received a traditional Jewish education in Europe and his ordination as a rabbi in Turkey. He went to the United States in 1928. He received his M.A. degree from Columbia University and his Ph.D. at Dropsie College. He was on the faculty of the College of Jewish Studies at Chicago from 1929 to 1939; for the following five years he was director of the Jewish Education Association in Rochester, N.Y. After serving with the Jewish Education Committee of New York City and the Jewish Education Association of Essex County, N.J., in 1949 Pilch became associated with the American Association for Jewish Education (now the Jewish Educational Services of North America), and from 1952 to 1960 was the executive director. In 1960 he became the founding head of the Association's National Curriculum Research Institute. After his retirement, Pilch moved to Los Angeles, where he was on the faculty of the Institute of Religion at HUC/JIR.

In the early 1950s Pilch organized and led the first Jewish teachers' seminar to Israel. He was president of the National Council for Jewish Education (1945–1950), vice president of the Religious Education Association of the U.S. and Canada in 1953, and president of the National Conference for Jewish Social Service (1954–55). He was vice president of the Histadrut Ivrit (1934–38). Without compromising his devotion to Hebrew, he also was interested in Yiddish literature and served as dean of the Graduate Division of Herzlia-Jewish Teachers' Seminary in New York.

Pilch was a prolific writer in Hebrew, English, and Yiddish. Among his works are *Jewish Life in Our Times* (1943), *Teaching Modern Jewish History* (1948), *Between Two Generations: Selected Essays* (1977), and *The Weak Against The Strong* (1973). He edited the Jewish Education Department of the *Encyclopaedia Judaica*.

Pilch was widely recognized as one of the great leaders of Jewish education in the United States, belonging in the same echelon as Alexander Dushkin, Israel Chipkin, and Samson Benderly. Like them, he combined a European, traditional Jewish education with Western culture, and expertise as a teacher and administrator. He brought to his positions and work an extraordinary single-minded devotion to the furtherance of Jewish education; he sought to pioneer in methodology and stimulated the preparation of newly designed textbooks and the exploration of teaching through technological advances. [M.R.K.]

POETRY, MEDIEVAL HEBREW (see **3**:681; **Dc./17**:510). During the 1980s, a number of noted scholars in the field of Medieval Hebrew Poetry died, namely: A. *Scheiber, J. *Schirmann, N. Allony, A. M. *Habermann, G. *Vajda, H. Schwarzbaum, D. Jarden, D. Goldschmidt, D. Pagis, Y. Heinemann, and A. L. Wilsker. Anthologies of articles from their estates as well as memorial volumes have begun to appear.

In the decade under review editions of poetic texts from all the countries of the Diaspora as well as from Ereẓ Israel were published.

Editions of texts: POETRY. *Ereẓ Israel.* All the *piyyutim* of Yannai (Z. M. Rabinowitz); *piyyutim* of Eleazar Berabbi Kiler (S. Elizur).

Babylonia. Rabbi Hai Gaon (Y. Hasida); Eleazar ben Jacob ha-Bavli (D. Jarden); Rabbi Judah Berabbi Benjamin (S. Elizur).

Byzantium. Simeon bar Megas. (Y. Yahalom).

Spain. Joseph Bensuli (Y. David); A. Ibn Ezra (I. Levin); Y. Ibn Ezra (M. Schmelzer); Joseph Ibn Ẓaddik (Y. David); Samuel ha-Nagid (Ben Mishlei; D. Jarden); Isaac ibn Ghiyyat (Y. David); Judah Halevi (religious poems; D. Jarden); Jehiel ben-Ḥarosh (Y. David); Isaac b. Solomon al-Ahdab (O. Raanan).

Provence. Rabbi Zerahiah ha-Levi Gerondi (I. Meiseles).

North Africa. Fradji Shawat (E. Hazan).

New Editions of Texts. PROSE AND RHYMED PROSE. Isaac Polgar *"Ezer ha-Dat"* (J. S. Levinger); Shem Tov ben Isaac Ardutiel, *"Ma'aseh ha-Rav"* ("The debate between the pen and the scissors"; Y. Nini and M. Fruchtman); Berechiah ha-Nakdan, *Mishle Shu'alim* ("Fox Fables"; H. Schwarzbaum); *Sippurei ben Sira* (E. Yassif).

MONOGRAPHS AND STUDIES. Topics chosen focused on trends and aims in poetry and prose. (1) Poetry. The following poets and topics were studied and annotated: Judah Halevi (A. Doron; E. Hazan); Samuel ha-Nagid (T. Rosen-Moked; A. Zemach); M. Ibn Ezra (J. Dana); Ereẓ Israel *piyyut* (Y. Yahalom); Saadiah Gaon (N. Allony); Eliezer Berabbi Kiler (S. Elizur). (2) Types of Hebrew secular poetry (I. Levin; T. Rosen-Moked; R. Tsur; R. Scheindlin; M. Itzḥaki, Y. Feldman). (3) Types of Hebrew religious poetry and the *piyyut* of Ereẓ Israel (E. Fleischer; D. Goldschmidt; J. J. Petuchowski). (4) Hebrew emblem-riddles in Italy (D. Pagis). (5) The history of Hebrew poetry in Spain, Provence, Italy (J. Schirmann) and Morocco (H. Zafrani).

Edited Texts. (1) V. E. Reichert, *The Taḥkemoni of Judah al-Ḥarizi*, an English translation, vol. I, Introduction and Gates 1–15 (Jer., 1965), 234 pp.; vol. II, Gates 16–50 (Jer., 1973), 443 pp. (2) E. Hazan, *Shirei Fradji Shawat* (Jer., 1976), a critical edition of 91 poems by the most famous Hebrew poet in Tunisia, who apparently lived in the 17th century. He came to Tunisia from Fez, Morocco, and composed a total of 900 poems which were largely religious in nature. The real name of the poet was Raphael Malaḥ, who adopted the equivalent Arabic name Fradji Shawat. (3) Y. Ḥasida, *Rav Hai Gaon, Reshuyyot le-farshiyyot ha-Torah* (Jer., 1977), 63 pp.; the book contains 29 poems for sections of the Torah. (4) R. Bonfils and A. M. Habermann (eds.), *Kalonymus ben Kalonymus, Megillat Setarim al Massekhet Purim* (Jer., 1977), a facsimile of the first edition published in Pesaro in 1513. Along with 24 pages of text there are 34 facsimile pages. The book contains an article by the translator M. D. Cassuto about Kalonymus in Rome and an introduction by Habermann on *Massekhet Purim*, its editions and printings. (5) E. Romero (tr. and ed.), *Selomo ibn Gabirol, Poesia secular* (Madrid, 1978), 532 pp., with an introduction by Dan Pagis. This is a bilingual edition with selected texts, translations, and notes; (6) S. Hopkins, *A Miscellany of literary pieces from the Cambridge Genizah Collection...Old Series, Box A 45* (Cambridge, 1978), 110 pp.; this work has facsimiles and copies along with short introductions and includes *piyyutim* by Kallir and a fragment from *Esa Meshali* by Saadiah Gaon. (7) Y. David, *Piyyutei Yosef Bensuli* ("The Poems of Joseph Bensuli"), critical edition with introduction and commentary (Jer., 1979), 55 pp. Joseph Bensuli was an important Hebrew poet in Toledo, Spain, at the beginning of the 14th century. Fifteen liturgical poems are collected here for the first time from 44 manuscripts and 38 early printed prayer books and liturgical collections found in Spain and elsewhere; (8) H. Schwarzbaum, *The Mishle Shualim* (Fox Fables) *of Rabbi Berechiah Ha-Nakdan; a study in comparative folklore and fable lore* (Kiron, 1979), with introduction and folkloristic commentary on *Mishle Shualim*, 658 pp., bibliography, table of narrative types and table of narrative motifs plus a general index. In this comprehensive work the author presents not only competent translations of all the fables, but examines the various sources which influenced them and offers a comparative folkloristic analysis. (9) Rabbi Shem Tov ben Isaac Ardutiel (or Don Santo de-Carrion), *Ma'ase-Harav (The Debate between the Pen and the Scissors;* Tel Aviv, 1980), 86 pp., edited with introduction, commentary, and notes by Y. Nini and M. Fruchtman; (10) I. Levin, *Shirei ha-Kodesh shel Avraham Ibn Ezra* ("Religious Poems of Abraham Ibn Ezra," 1 (Jer., 1975), 522 pp.; 2 (Jer., 1980), 708 pp. Volume one contains 262 poems and volume two has 247 poems. (11) M. H. Schmelzer, *Yiẓḥak ben Avraham Ibn Ezra, Shirim* ("Isaac ben Abraham Ibn Ezra, Poems"; New York, 1980), 171 pp., edited on the basis of manuscripts, with an introduction and notes; the book contains a letter and 44 annotated poems. (12) L. J. Weinberger, *Sefer ha-Seliḥot ke-Minhag Kehillot ha-Romaniyyotim* ("Romaniote Penitential Poetry"; New York, 1980), 248 pp. (13) A. Saenz-Badillos, *Tešubot de Dunaš ben Labrat*, critical edition and Spanish translation (Granada, 1980), 124 + 164. (14) A. Scheiber, *Geniza Studies* (New York, 1981), 570 pp. (15) Amadis de Gaula (Alilot ha-Abir), Hebrew translation by the physician Jacob di Algaba, first published Constantinople, c. 1541. Critical edition with introduction by Z. Malachi (Tel Aviv, 1981), 240 pp. (16) Varela Moreno Mª Encarnacion, *Tešubot de Yehudi ben Šešet*, edited and translated with commentary (Granada, 1981), 117 pp. (17) Y. David, *The Poems of Joseph Ibn Zaddik* (Jerusalem, 1982). Joseph Ibn Ẓaddik (1075–1149) was well known as a Hebrew poet in Cordoba, Spain, at the beginning of the 12th century. This critical edition of his extant poetry, in which 36 poems are collected for the first time, includes liturgical poems, eulogies, love songs, and four lamentations. (18) D. Jarden, *Divan Shemuel Hanagid*; vol. 2, *Ben Mishlei* ("The

Son of Proverbs"; Jerusalem, 1982), 478 pp. (19) L. J. Weinberger (ed.), *Bulgaria's Synagogue Poets: The Kastoreans*, critical edition with introduction and commentary (Cincinnati, 1983), 175 pp. (20) I. Levin, *Iggeret Hay Ben Mekitz by Abraham Ibn Ezra*, a critical edition supplemented with a Hebrew translation of the Arabic original *Hay Ibn Yaqizan* by Abu Ali Alḥusain Ibn Abdalla Ibn Sina (Tel Aviv, 1983), 99 pp. (21) J. Yahalom, *Piyyutei Shimon bar Megas* (Jerusalem, 1984). The poet Simeon bar Megas lived in Byzantine Palestine in the sixth or seventh century. He is the author of a cycle of over one hundred and fifty *kedushot* based on the triennial cycle then current in Palestine. His writings constitute one of the few resources for information on Palestinian Jewry, its practices and customs, during the crucial period of transition from the Byzantine to the Arabic period. Simeon Bar Megas's 218 poems manifest a special ingenuity in vocabulary and inventiveness, in the use of neologisms, poetic form, and structures. They contribute also to knowledge of Palestinian Hebrew, which according to the editor was still spoken in Simeon Bar Megas's time, at least in the villages. (22) J. S. Levinger, *Isaac Polgar, Ezer ha-Dat* ("A defense of Judaism"), a critical and annotated edition (Tel Aviv, 1984), 197 pp. (23) D. Jarden, *Shirim Ḥadashim le-Rabbi Elazar ben Ya'akov ha-Bavli* ("New Poems of Rabbi Eleazar ha-Bavli"), based on manuscripts and printed editions (Jerusalem, 1984), 60 pp. (24) I. Meiseles, *Shirat ha-Maor. The Poems of Rabbi Zerahia ha-Levy* (Jer., 1984), 186 pp. critical edition with commentary. The complete collection of the liturgical poems of Rabbi Zeraḥiah ha-Levi Gerondi is presented in this volume which contains 51 poems collected from 145 manuscripts located in 32 libraries. (25) L. J. Weinberger, *Jewish Poets in Crete* (Cincinnati, 1985), 211 pp., a critical edition with introduction and commentary. (26) Y. Ratzaby, *A Dictionary of Judeo-Arabic in R. Saadya's Tafsir* (Ramat Gan, 1985), 151 pp. (27) E. Yassif, *Sippurei Ben-Sira bi-Ymei ha-Beinayim* (Jer., 1985), 324 pp. (28) *Ma'aseh Zofar*, an ancient story first printed in Salonika, c. 1600, republished by Z. Malachi (Lod, 1985), 72 pp., a limited edition of 100 copies. (29) Y. David, *The Poems of Yehiel ben-Harosh* (1986), a critical edition with introduction and commentary (Jer., 1986), 65 pp. Rabbi Jehiel ben-Harosh was a theologian, a judge *(dayyan)*, and also a poet of Toledo, Spain, during the 14th century. The poems of Ben-Harosh are offered here in a critical edition of extant works, 15 liturgical poems collected for the first time. The poet was, moreover, a witness of the 1391 massacre in Toledo and his lamentations give a historical perspective of Jewry in the Middle Ages in Spain. (30) D. Jarden, *Shirei ha-Kodesh le-Rabbi Yehuda Halevi* ("The Liturgical Poetry of Judah Halevi," vol. 1: The Winter Festivals (Jer., 1978); vol. 2, The Summer Festivals (Jer., 1980); vol. 3: Other Poems (Jer., 1982); vol. 4, Poems (Jer., 1986)). The four volumes of this edition include 550 poems. In addition to an introduction, a commentary, source references and parallels, and indices are provided. (31) T. Alsina Trias, Olmo Lete, del. G., *El Diwan de Yosef ibn Saddiq*, according to the critical edition by Yonah David. Introduction, text, and notes (Barcelona, 1987), 116 pp. (32) Z. M. Rabinovitz, *The Liturgical Poems of Rabbi Yannai according to the Triennial Cycle of the Pentateuch and the Holidays*, critical edition with introductions and commentary, vol. I: Introduction, Liturgical Poems to Genesis, Exodus, & Leviticus (Jer., 1985), 508 pp.; vol. II: Liturgical Poems to Numbers, Deuteronomy & Holidays and indexes (Jer., 1987); 444 pp. (33) Y. David, *The Poems of Rabbi Isaac Ibn Ghiyyat (Lucena 1038–Cordoba 1089)* (Jer., 1987); the first anthology of 370 poems by this poet. (34) Sh. Elizur, *Rabbi Jehuda Berabbi Binjaminis, Carmina Cuncta.* Ex codicibus edidit, prolegominis et notis instruxit (Jer., 1988), 319 pp. (35) Sh. Elizur, *Kedushah ve-Sir Kedushta'ot le-Shabbatot ha-Nehama le-Rabbi Eleazar Berabi Kiler*, critical edition with commentary and epilogue (Jerusalem 1988), 109 pp. (36) O. Raanan, *The Poems of Ishak ben Shlomo Al-Ahdab based on manuscripts and prints.* Critical edition with commentary (Lod, 1988), 152 pp. The 90 poems in this book represent a great variety of a didactic ethical nature and humorous and satiric elements. The poet was born towards the middle of the 14th century in Castile, Spain, and died after 1429, approximately at the age of 80.

(37) *The Piyyutim of Rabbi Musa Bujnah of Tripoli* (1989), 251 pp., were edited by Ephraim Ḥazan who also wrote the introduction and notes. The book has two parts: the first describes North African Hebrew poetry and discusses the poet and his period, the genre of his poems and their language, while the second offers 109 *piyyutim* by this poet. Appendices provide a table of poetic meters, a list of sources, and an index to the *piyyutim*.

(38) *Pirkei Shirah*, from the treasure-houses of poetry and *piyyut* of Jewish communities, were produced by Yehudit Dishon and Ephraim Ḥazan (1990), 166 pp. The book includes, in addition to the introduction of the editors, chapters by Ya'akov Adler on the explication of a poem by Yosé ben Yosé; Yizḥak Meizlish on a heretofore unknown personal *bakkashah* by Zerahiah ha-Levi; Benjamin bar-Tikvah, on a *kerovah* by Rabbi Berachiah; Judah Razaby, on songs of praise by Joseph ha-Yerushalmi; Hadassah Shai, on a selection from a *maqama* by Joseph ben Tanḥum ha-Yerushalmi: Aaron Mirsky, on poems of Israel Najara from his *She'erit Yisrael*; Ephraim Ḥazan on eight *piyyutim* by Mandil Avi-Zimra; Meir Wallenstein, on the character of Samuel Vitale according to a poetic letter by Moses Judah Abbas.

(39) Ezra Fleischer's *The Proverbs of Sa'id ben Babshad* appeared in 1990 (320 pp.). In this book the author publishes fragments of a major collection of proverbs, written by an unknown medieval Hebrew poet, Said ben Babshad who flourished in Iraq or in Persia at the end of the 10th and beginning of the 11th century. The eleven chapters of the book, in addition to the texts themselves, summarize the progress of this research, the linguistic issues, ideology, and poetics as well as sources of influence upon which the poet drew. The proverbs were culled from 25 manuscripts located in 10 different collections, most prominently from the Cairo *Genizah*.

(40) *Ḥibbat ha-Piyyut* was edited by Eliyahu Gabbai. It is a selection of *piyyutim* representing different Jewish communities. The commentary was provided by Herzl and Balfour Ḥakkak. This is a second edition and it appeared in 1990 (258 pp.). The book has 18 chapters.

(41) Federico Pe'rez Castro published *Poesia secular Hispano-Hebrea* (1989; 399 pp.), which contains translations of 92 Hebrew poems by nine of the most outstanding medieval Hebrew poets, from Menahem ibn Saruq to Judah Halevi. Included are notes and introductions to each poem, edited by H. Schirmann in his *Ha-Shirah ha-Ivrit bi-Sefarad u-ve-Provence.* There are also a general introduction and bibliography.

(42) Carlos del Valle Rodriguez wrote *El Divan Poetico de-Dunash ben Labrat. La introudución de la metrica arabe* (1988), 543 pp. The book has, in addition to an introduction, six chapters: (1) Dunash ben Labrat the man; (2) the poetry of Dunash; (3) language of Dunash; (4) quantitative metrics; (5) a diachronic survey of Hebrew metrics; (6) the terminology of Hebrew poetry. Moreover, all of Dunash poems (including those of doubted attribution) are printed according to N. Allony's edition. The author added two appendices which cite the most significant works which treat Hebrew metrics [text opposite translation] and finally the volume

ends with a bibliography, list of terms, and list of names.

Interpretive Works. (1) C. A. Colahan, *Santob's Debate between the Pen and the Scissors,* Dissertation, University of New Mexico (1977), 360 pp. (2) A. Doron, *Kivvunim u-Megamot be-Heker Shirato shel Yehudah ha-Levi,* Dissertation, Tel Aviv University (1977), 240 pp. (3) N. Ben-Menahem, *Inyanei Ibn-Ezra* (Jerusalem, 1978), 373 pp., an anthology of the author's articles on Abraham Ibn Ezra. (4) E. D. Goldschmidt, *On Jewish Liturgy: essays on prayer and religious poetry* (Jerusalem, 1978), 494 pp. (5) *Mishnato ha-Hagutit shel Rabbi Yehudah ha-Levi,* published by the Ministry of Education and Culture, the Department of Tarbut Toranit (Jerusalem, 1978), 242 pp. The book is divided into four sections: (a) the thought of Judah Halevi, a general discussion, (b) society and state, (c) historical thought, and (d) thought and experience. Eighteen contributors participated in the volume which was dedicated to the 900th anniversary of the birth of Judah Halevi. (6) J. J. Petuchowski, *Theology and Poetry; studies in medieval piyyut* (London, 1978), 153 pp. The book contains ten *piyyutim* in the original language as well as in English translation accompanied by commentary. (7) J. Schirmann, *Le-toledot ha-shirah ve-ha-dramah ha-ivrit* ("Studies in the history of Hebrew poetry and drama; Jerusalem, vol. I, 1979, 438 pp., vol. 2, 1980), 376 pp. A year before his death, Schirmann was able to collect the studies and essays which he had published from 1931 through 1978, and arrange them chronologically according to subject matter. Vol. 1 is devoted to early Palestinian *piyyut* and medieval Spanish and southern French poets. Vol. 2 deals with Hebrew poetry in Italy from its beginnings until approximately 1800, as well as with Hebrew drama during the 16th–18th centuries. The material has been revised and the biography of Judah Halevi rewritten on the basis of the *Genizah* finds of Shlomo Dov Goitein. This is a monumental work distinguished for its erudition, expertise, and meticulous care in dealing with the literary creativity of more than a thousand years. (8) I. Levin, *Me'il Tashbez, The Embroidered Coat: The Genres of Hebrew Secular Poetry in Spain* (Tel Aviv, 1980). The six chapters of the book are divided as follows: (a) the *qasida*; (b) the war poems of Samuel ha-Nagid; (c) songs of praise; (d) poems of glory; (e) poems of complaint; (f) poems of retribution, apology, and abuse. (9) Z. Malachi, *Be-No'am Si'ah, Pleasant Words: Chapters from the History of Hebrew Literature* (Lod, 1983). This volume contains articles dealing with five types of subject matter; (a) studies in *piyyut*; (b) Hebrew poetry in Spain; (c) Medieval Hebrew fiction; (d) the Balbo family of Candia (Crete) in the 15th century; and (e) authors and books of Amsterdam. (10) A. Zemach and T. Rosen-Moked, *Yetsirah mehukhamah: iyyun be-shirei Shemuel ha-Nagid* ("Sophisticated Writing: a study of Samuel ha-Nagid's poems"; Jer., 1983), 158 pp. The authors analyze and explain 17 poems by Samuel ha-Nagid. The book includes three short introductions which treat various biographical, thematic, and methodological aspects of the poet's work. (11) J. Dana, *Ha-Po'etika shel ha-Shirah ha-Ivrit bi Sefarad bi-Ymei ha-Beinayyim al pi Rabbi Moshe ibn Ezra u-Mekoroteha* ("Of Medieval Hebrew Literature, According to Moshe Ibn Ezra"; Tel Aviv, 1983), 337 pp. The book contains, in addition to an introduction, chapters devoted to: (a) content and form, (b) the best poem is that which contains the greatest falsehood, (c) the ornaments in poetry, (d) the qualification and image of the poetic outline, (e) M. Ibn Ezra as poetical theorist and as poet, and (f) influence and originality in the poetics of M. Ibn Ezra. There are also a bibliography and indices. (12) E. Fleischer, *Ha-yozerot be-hithavvutam ve-hitpattehutam* ("The Yotzer, its emergence and development"; Jerusalem, 1984), 795 pp. This is an illuminating and comprehensive scholarly treatment of a thousand years of the development of the *yozer* form, from its beginnings in Byzantine Palestine (c. the 6th century) to its decline in the European Jewish centers. Over two hundred unpublished selections from the Cairo *Genizah* are employed by the author, the first work of its kind in Hebrew. (13) H. Zafrani, *Poesie juive au Maroc,* (ed. by Yosef Tobi; Jer., 1984), 210 pp. (14) A. Doron, *Yehuda Ha-Levi: Repercusion de su obra,* with a biographical sketch of Judah Halevi by Fernando Diaz Estaban (Barcelona, 1985). (15) J. Dishon, *Sefer Sha'ashuim le-Yosef ben Meir ibn Zabara* ("The Book of Delight composed by Joseph ben Meir Zabara"; Jerusalem, 1985), 292 pp. (16) *Studies in the Work of Shlomo Ibn-Gabirol* (Zvi Malachi (ed.), Hanna David (co-ed.); Tel Aviv, 1985). The book contains two collections of articles. The first is dedicated to the philosophical elements in the poetry of Ibn Gabirol, while the second deals with the types of poems by him and the characteristics of his poetry. There were 12 contributors in addition to the editor. (17) J. Yahalom, *Sefer ha-Shir shel ha-Piyyut ha-Erez-yisraeli ha-Kadum* ("Poetic Language in the Early Piyyut"; Jer., 1985), 218 pp. This study deals with the language of the early Erez Israel *piyyutim* which struggled to maintain its independence between the natural needs of expression, rooted in the spoken language, and the archaic literary tradition characteristic of the *piyyutim.* During this confrontation there developed a new independent literary language which bridges the ancient times and the Middle Ages; its distinctive signs are developed and expanded in this work. (18) Y. Silman, *Bein Filosof le-Navi: Hitpattehut Haguto shel R. Yehuda ha-Levi be-Sefer ha-Kuzari* ("Thinker and Seer: The Development of the Thought of R. Yehuda Halevi in the Kuzari"; Ramat Gan, 1985), 325 pp. (19) T. Rosen-Moked, *Le-Ezor Shir* ("The Hebrew Girdle Poem *(Muwashshah)* in the Middle Ages"; Haifa 1985), 245 pp. (20) N. Allony, *Mehkarei Lashon ve-Sifrut: Pirkei Sa'adiah Gaon* (Jer., 1986), 400 pp. (21) E. Hazan, *Torat ha-Shir be-Fiyyut ha-Sefardi le-Or Shirat ha-Kodesh shel R. Yehuda ha-Levi* ("The Poetics of the Sephardi *Piyyut* according to the Liturgical Poetry of Yehuda Halevi"; Jer., 1986), 340 pp.; this work, with introduction, appendices and indices, discusses meter, rhyme, and euphonic word-texture: language, methods of formulation and imagery, and structural methods.

(22) Dan Pagis, *Al Sod Hatum* ("A Secret Sealed," Hebrew Baroque Emblem-Riddles from Italy and Holland; Jerusalem, 1986). This work deals with Hebrew riddles which developed in Italy and Holland in a two-hundred-year period, 1650–1850. The ten chapters of the book cover: the field and its study; the origin of the emblem-riddle and foreign languages; the literary riddle as a social genre; the social role of the emblem-riddle; the "emblem-riddle" and related subjects; tricks of language; Aramaic, Hebrew, and the random interpolation of the key word; the body of the emblem-riddle; the unit of the false "solution"; three emblem-riddles by Rabbi Moses Zacuto. There are also indices, bibliography, and an English summary.

(23) R. P. Scheindlin, *Wine, Women, and Death: Medieval Hebrew Poems on the Good-Life* (Philadelphia, New York, Jerusalem, 1986), 204 pp. The author presents the original Hebrew poem along with his own English translation, followed by commentary which explains its cultural context. Included are 31 poems, grouped into three categories: (a) Wine, description of or meditations on the wine party, a conventional Arabic social gathering; (b) Women, Golden Age poems of love and desire; (c) Death, mellow reflections on the brevity of life. Among the poets whose work is represented in this collection are: Samuel ha-Nagid, Solomon Ibn Gabirol, Moses Ibn Ezra, and Judah Halevi.

(24) M. Itzhaki, *"Ani Hashar": Studies in Secular Poetry in Spain* (Tel Aviv, 1986), 133 pp. This work discusses a num-

ber of poems by Samuel ha-Nagid, Solomon Ibn Gabirol, Moses ibn Ezra, and Judah Halevi in the light of normative poetics of the period. (25) I. Levin, *Ha-Sod ve-ha-Yesod* ("Mystical Trends in the Poetry of Solomon Ibn Gabirol"; Lod, 1986), 174 pp. (26) Y. Feldman, *Bein ha-Kotavim le-Kav ha-Mashveh* ("Semantic Patterns in the Medieval Hebrew Qasida"; Tel Aviv, 1987), 130 pages. The author analyzes through semantic deductions six *qasidot* by Moses Ibn Ezra and thereby demonstrates significant principles of structure which are based on two patterns of organization; opposition or polarization and comparison. (27) M. Itzḥaki, *Ha-Ḥai Gefen ve-ha-Mawet Bozer* ("Man — the Vine; Death — the Reaper: The *Tocheha* Hebrew Admonishment Poetry of Spain"; Tel Aviv, 1987), 82 pp. (28) R. Tsur, *Ha-Shirah ha-Ivrit bi-Ymei ha-Beinayyim be-Perspektivah Kefulah: Ha-Kore ha-Versatili ve-Shirat Sefarad* ("Medieval Hebrew Poetry in a Double Perspective: The Versatile Reader and Hebrew Poetry in Spain." Papers in Cognitive Poetics; Tel Aviv, 1987), 221 pp. The book deals with medieval literature from three perspectives: (a) the analysis and evaluation of the poems as the result of interaction between the ideational generic figurative, and prosodic dimensions as objects of perceived meaning; (b) the skills necessary for a versatile reader to be able to respond to a wide range of literary styles; (c) the contemporary reader's confrontations with the styles of a far-distant literary period. (29) S. Elitzur. *Piyyutei Eleazer berabbi Kiler* (Jer., 1988), 430 pp.

Additional Bibliography. (1) *Todros ha-Levi Abulafia* (1989), 234 pp., was published by Aviva Doron. Todros ha-Levi Abulafia was born in Toledo some hundred years after the transfer of the Jewish cultural centers from Muslim Andalusia to Christian Spain. This book describes the poetry of the Hebrew-Castilian poet against the background of the cultural crossroads in which he lived and worked. The book comprises, in addition to an introduction, a selected bibliography, and three indices (poems treated in the book, subject, and name) eight chapters: (a) the author and his times; (b) Todros ha-Levi, a Hebrew author at the crossroads of literary streams; (c) national and religious expressions in the language of Todros's personal poetry; (d) time in his poetry; (e) the attitude of the poet towards his poetry; (f) love poems; (g) methods of structural and rhetorical design in his poems; (h) comments on a selection of poems from *Gan ha-Meshalim ve-ha-Ḥidot.*

(2) Rina Drory's *The Emergence of Jewish Arabic Literary Contacts at the Beginning of the Tenth Century* appeared in 1988. In addition to an introduction and summary the book has six chapters: (a) the structure of the Jewish literary system at the beginning of the 10th century; (b) the consolidation of Hebrew and Arabic as the written languages for the Jewish literary system; (c) unequivocal literary patterns: Karaite patterns; (d) ambivalent literary patterns: wisdom proverbs; (e) biblical treatment; (f) the role of Saadiah Gaon in contacts with Arabic literature. Indices of names and of works conclude this important contribution to the field.

(3) *Yehuda Halevi*, a selection of critical essays on his poetry, selected with an introduction by Aviva Doron, was published in 1988, 285 pp. It has: (a) studies into the biography of the poet by H. Schirmann, S. D. Goitein, and Yosef Yahalom; (b) articles on his poems — a total of 16 items by Ḥayyim Naḥman Bialik, Franz Rosenzweig, Ben-Zion Dinur, Michael Ish-Shalom, Yitzḥak Heinemann, Aryeh Ludwig Strauss, Yisrael Levin, Moshe Schwartz, Adi Zemaḥ, Aharon Mirsky, Reuven Zur, Dov Sadan, Ezra Fleischer, Ẓevi Malachi, Ephraim Ḥazan, and Aviva Doron; (c) five appendices — Samuel David Luzzatto's *Betulat Bat-Yehudah* (1840); a diwan by Judah Halevi; from Michael Sachs' *Religious Poetry of the Jews* (1845); Heinrich Ḥayyim Brody's *"Rosh Davar"* to a *diwan* by the poet; and from Fritz Yitzḥak Baer's *The History of Jews in Christian Spain* (1945).

(4) *Abraham Ibn Ezra y su tiempo*, the acts of an international symposium held in Madrid, Tudela, and Toledo on February 1–8, 1989, 396 pp., appeared in 1990. This book contains the 45 lectures given by international scholars at the symposium held in honor of the 900th anniversary of the birth of Abraham Ibn Ezra.

Jubilee and Memorial Volmes. (1) *Shai le-Heiman (A. M. Habermann Jubilee Volume)*, edited by Z. Malachi with the assistance of Y. David (Jerusalem, 1977), 385 pp. This volume contains 21 articles, a bibliography of Habermann's works and an index to *piyyutim* he published, prepared by Y. David. (2) J. Blau, S. Pines, M. J. Kister, S. Shaked (eds.), *Ḥakkirei Mizraḥ (Studia Orientalia, Memoriae D. H. Baneth Dedicata)*; Jerusalem 1979, 407 pp. (3) G. Nahon and Ch. Touati, *Hommage à G. Vajda. Etudes d'histoire et de pensée juive éditées par...* (Louvain, 1980), 604 pp. The 40 contributors dealt with Judaica studies. (4) Z. Malachi (ed.), *Yad le-Heiman (The A. M. Habermann Memorial Volume*; Lod, 1983), 434 pp. The five sections of the book deal with Medieval Hebrew literature, the heritage of Eastern Jewry after the Expulsion from Spain, bibliography and study of the Hebrew book, the history of liturgy and customs, and the memory of Prof. Habermann. (5) *Le-Zikhro shel Ḥayyim Schirmann*, published by the Israel National Academy of Science (Jerusalem, 1984). The essays included are "The Position of Prof. Schirmann in the Study of Hebrew Poetry," by S. Abramson; "On Retribution and Redemption in the Religious Poems of Abraham Ibn Ezra," by I. Levin, and "Ups and Downs in Ancient Hebrew Poetry," by A. Mirsky. (6) Z. Malachi (ed), *Be-Oraḥ Mada (Aharon Mirsky Jubilee Volume*, essays on Jewish Culture), Lod 1986, 619 pp. In addition to a selected bibliography of the works of A. Mirsky the book contains essays on Jewish studies, on Hebrew poetry in Spain and North Africa, on poetry and *piyyut* and culture. (7) G. J. Blidstein, Y. Salmon, E. Yassif (eds.), *Eshel Beer-Sheva* ("Essays in Jewish Studies in Memory of Professor Nehemia Allony"; Beersheba, 1986), 371 pp. A bibliography of the works of Nehemiah Allony prepared by R. Attal is included.

Anthologies and Collections. (1) J. Rothenberg, H. Lenowitz, and Ch. Doria, *A Big Jewish Book; poems & other visions of the Jews from tribal times to the present* (New York, 1978), 633 pp. (2) K. Bosley, *The Elek Book of Oriental Verse* (London, 1979). (3) D. Pagis (ed.), *Ke-ḥut ha-shani* ("The Scarlet Thread; Hebrew love poems from Spain, Italy, Turkey and the Yemen; Tel Aviv, 1979), 120 pp. An anthology of 99 poems by 23 poets, dating from the 10th to the 19th centuries. The poems are arranged in 12 sections by subject and motif rather than according to chronological order. (4) *Abraham ibn Ezra Reader* annotated texts with introduction and commentary, by I. Levin, edited by M. Arfa (Tel Aviv, 1985), 438 pp. (5) Angel Saenz-Badillos and Judit Targarona Borras published an anthology, *Poetas Hebreos de-al-Andalus (Siglos X–XII)*, in 1988, 232 pp. This is the first anthology of its type to appear in Spain: it offers selections from 12 of the greatest Hebrew poets of Spain beginning with Menahem ibn Saruq and ending with Abraham Ibn Ezra. The text, in an excellent translation, is accompanied by a selected bibliography.

(6) Aharon Mirsky's 731-page *Ha-Piyyut, The Development of Post-Biblical Poetry in Eretz-Israel and the Diaspora*, appeared in 1990. This large, excellent anthology contains 45 articles representing 40 years of research in the field. There are three sections to the book: (1) 16 articles on the sources of the prayers and the initial steps toward *piyyut* in the Bible; post-biblical poetry; poetry in the talmudic period; delineation of the characteristics of ancient poetry; the schools within ancient Hebrew poetry the *piyyut* tradition in the

Land of Israel, and other items; (2) 15 articles on innovations introduced by early post-biblical poetry, including language and the poetic form; the significance of rhyme in Hebrew poetry; clarification and explication of the language of poetry, and so on; (3) 14 articles on Hebrew poetry in Spain and Germany and the nature of the poetry which began anew in the eastern countries in the 17th and 18th centuries; evaluations of four important poets — Dunash ben Labrat, Rabbenu Gershom Meor ha-Golah, Judah al-Ḥarizi, and Israel Najara. The book ends with indices on subjects, *piyyutim* and *paytanim*.

Liturgy. (1) J. Heinemann and A. Shinan, *Tefillot ha-Keva ve-ha-Ḥovah shel Shabbat ve-Yom Ḥol* (Tel Aviv, 1977), 131 pp., deals with the weekday and Sabbath liturgy and includes explication, history, and discussion of their structure. (2) J. Heinemann, *Prayer in the Talmud* (Berlin, 1977), a revised English edition of the 1964 Hebrew-language version. (3) H. G. Cohen (ed.), *Ha-Tefillah ha-Yehudit* ("Prayer in Judaism: Continuity and Change"; Jerusalem, 1978), 292 pp. (4) J. Heinemann, *Iyyunei Tefillah* ("Studies in Jewish Liturgy"; Jerusalem, 1981), edited by A. Shinan, 205 pp. (5) A. Mirsky, *Yesodei Ẓurot ha-Piyyut* ("The Original Forms of Early Hebrew Poetry"; Jer., 1985), 134 pp., deals with ancient Ereẓ Israel poetry. (6) A. M. Habermann, *Al ha-Tefillah* ("Essays on Prayers"), edited by Z. Malachi (Lod, 1987), 148 pp. This collection is made up of various essays on prayers published during the author's lifetime. (7) The monumental (posthumous) work by D. Goldschmidt, *Meḥkare Tefillah u-Fiyyut*.

Facsimiles and Bibliography. (1) D. S. Loewinger (ed.), *Osef Piyyutei Sepharad* ("Collection of Spanish Piyyutim"; Jerusalem, 1977), 264 pp. Facsimile edition based on Ms. 197 in the David Guenzberg Collection. Lenin Public Library, Moscow. (2) J. Yahalom (ed.), *Kitei ha-genizah shel piyyutei Yannai* ("A Collection of Genizah Fragments of Yannai's Liturgical Poems"; Jerusalem, 1978), 214 pp. (3) E. Koren, *The Alphabetical Index to Israel Najara's Poems* (Tel Aviv, 1978), 44 pp. (4) D. Carpi (ed.), *Italia Judaica bibliography 1964–1973*, comprised by A. Luzzato and M. Moldavi (Rome, 1982). (5) D. Pagis, E. Fleischer (eds.), Y. David (coeditor), *A Bibliography of the Writings of Prof. Jefim (Haim) Schirmann (1904–1981)* (Jer., 1983), 48 pp. (6) "Bibliography of the writing of G. Vajda," in: *Da'at*, 10 (1983), 53–66, 125–126. (7) R. Attal, *Kitvei Professor Nehemya Allony* ("A bibliography of the writings of Prof. N. Allony"; Beersheba, 1984), 33 pp. (8) Y. Ganuz, *Bibliografiyyah shel Kitvei Ḥayyim Schwarzbaum be-Ḥeker ha-Folklore ha-Yehudi ve-ha-Aravi* in: *Yeida-Am* 22 (1984; no. 51–52), 10–19. (9) M. Beit-Arie, *The only dated Medieval Manuscript written in England (1189 C.E.) and the problem of pre-expulsion Anglo-Hebrew manuscripts* (Appendix 1 by M. Banitt; appendix 2 by Z. E. Rokeaḥ), London 1985, 56 pp. (10) Y. David, "A Decade of Research on Medieval Hebrew Literature," in *Jewish Book Annual*, 43 (1985–1986), 107–117; (11) J. Yahalom, *Maḥzor Ereẓ Yisrael, Kodex ha-Genizah* with a paleographic introduction by E. Engel, facsimile edition (1988), 148 pp. (12) *Ḥeqer ha-Shirah ve-ha-Piyyut* ("Research in Poetry and Piyyut") 1948–1978, a cumulative index-bibliography was published by Ben-Gurion University in 1989. There are 451 pages in Hebrew and 31 in other langugages. The editors were Gisella Davidson, Elhanan Adler, Pinḥas Ziv, and Amira Kehat.

The Catalogue of the Jack Mosseri Collection appeared, edited by the Institute of Microfilmed Hebrew Manuscripts, with the collaborations of numerous specialists (1990), 407 pages, with a foreword by Claude Mosseri and a preface by Israel Adler. The catalogue contains, in addition to a concordance of call-numbers and indices of titles, subjects, authors, places, dates, languages, copyists and persons mentioned, and melody indications, a listing on *piyyut* and poetry — genres, subjects, and forms and incipits of the *piyyutim* and the poems. [YO.D.]

POLAND (see **13**:709; **Dc./17**:511). Poland's transition to a democratic system of government and a market economy which began in 1989 after nearly five decades of Communist rule took place against the background of economic crisis and industrial unrest. However, the new freedom experienced by Polish society has had an invigorating effect on the small, mostly elderly, Jewish community which on the eve of the Second World War numbered 3.5 million and is now estimated to number 6,000 people living mainly in Warsaw, Wroclaw (Breslau), Krakow (Cracow), and Lodz with smaller groups in other provincial towns. A significant renewal of Jewish cultural and religious life has taken place, and people previously estranged from Jewish tradition, especially among the younger-age group, have begun to acknowledge their Jewish identity. Communal and cultural activities were strengthened and encouraged by the renewal of ties with Israel and increasing contacts with world Jewry. Two important events exemplify this positive trend: the community acquired its first resident rabbi in over 20 years, and a Co-ordinating Commission of Jewish Organizations, which represents and acts on behalf of the whole community, was established. The new body brought together the Jewish Social and Cultural Association, the Mosaic Religious Association, the Jewish Historical Institute, the Jewish Theater, and the bi-weekly paper *Dos Yiddishe Wort* (formerly *Folks-sztyme*).

A range of educational and cultural activities is provided by the Social and Cultural Association (TSKZ) which has branches in 15 cities. Courses in Jewish history and Yiddish as well as song and dance classes are held. The Jewish Historical Institute conducts research and publishes scholarly papers and books on the history of Jews in Poland. Among

Announcement of a Jewish music concert in Ciesyn, Poland, November 1988

its most recent projects is the provision of teaching materials on the Holocaust. Welfare activities are carried out with the financial support of the American Joint Distribution Committee.

On the positive side of Polish-Jewish relations is the continuing interest in the history and culture of Polish Jews among the Polish intelligentsia. The awareness of the need to preserve the Jewish heritage and recognize the Jewish contribution to Polish culture originated in liberal Catholic, Protestant, and opposition circles in the 1980s.

Among the initiatives taken were annual weeks of Jewish culture, seminars on Jewish subjects, festivals of Jewish films, exhibitions as well as efforts to restore and maintain Jewish cemeteries and monuments. From the mid-1980s, in an attempt to improve their image abroad the Communist authorities encouraged Jewish studies. The Institute for the Study of the History and Culture of the Jews in Poland was created at Krakow's Jagellonian University in 1986. A number of conferences and symposia were held with the support of the state and the participation of Western, including Israeli, scholars. A large number of books on Jewish subjects were published to meet the growing demand. In post-Communist Poland, state authorities have continued to support a range of cultural activities. A foundation called Eternal Memory has been set up by the treasury for the restoration and preservation of Jewish cultural monuments.

The community is, however, experiencing a rising tide of anti-Semitism. The change to a pluralist democracy has opened up opportunities for extremist nationalist groups which have been using anti-Semitism as a tool in the political struggle. Their propaganda identifies Jews with the Communist regime and blames them for all the shortcomings of Polish life. The removal of restraints on freedom of expression has meant that anti-Semitism is now openly voiced in public and every-day life with grass-roots anti-Semitism well attested in public polls.

Government and Solidarity personalities have become targets of anti-Jewish campaigns, which draw attention to their real or alleged Jewish origins. At the time of the 1990 presidential and the 1991 parliamentary elections these tactics were freely used even by the mainstream political groups. Anti-Semitic publications, including reprints of the notorious *Protocols of the Elders of Zion*, have been distributed widely in recent years. Acts of vandalism at Jewish institutions, synagogues, and cemeteries have multiplied as Polish skinheads seek to emulate their Western counterparts. The need to obtain economic assistance from the West, which acted as a brake on political anti-Semitism during the last decade, prompted President Walesa's initiative in 1991 to create a Council on Polish-Jewish Relations. An advisory body attached to the president, its function is to promote better understanding between Poles and Jews by drawing-up educational programs for Polish youth, organizing events and exhibitions, and providing a reaction to anti-Semitic incidents.

Polish Deputy Defense Minister Janusz Onyskiewicz, the former spokesman for Solidarity, addressing a group of visiting American rabbis in Warsaw, Feb. 5, 1990 (Photo Ruth E. Gruber, Rome)

Polish Archbishop Henryk Muszynski and U.S. Rabbi James A. Rudin leading an interfaith memorial service at Birkenau, July 1992 (Photo Ruth E. Gruber, Rome)

The continuing dispute over the Carmelite convent at Auschwitz has been at the center of the crisis in Catholic-Jewish relations for the last decade (see Auschwitz Convent). The controversy was widely debated in the Polish press: a range of views from openly anti-Semitic to liberal was expressed revealing a disquieting level of prejudice and a lack of understanding between Poles and Jews.

While some elements within the Catholic church support right-wing Christian parties with known anti-Semitic tendencies, the Polish bishops, in an effort to improve relations, issued an unprecedented statement taking a clear stand against all manifestations of anti-Semitism. The episcopal letter, read in churches on January 21, 1991, presented Vatican II teachings on the relations between the two faiths and dealt with a number of controversial issues such as Polish responsibility for the Holocaust, alleged Jewish responsibility for Communism, and anti-Semitism past and present. At the same time the Catholic Seminary in Warsaw published a book on Judaism and the Jews for school teachers written in a similar spirit.

Relations with Israel. In 1986 Poland was the first of the Communist bloc countries to re-open low-level diplomatic relations with Israel which had been severed since the Six-Day War. Interest sections dealing with visa regulations and cultural and economic ties were established in Warsaw and Tel Aviv. Full diplomatic relations were restored in 1990. A framework for the promotion of good relations was provided by the establishment of the Polish-Israeli Friendship Society. There has been a steady growth in cultural exchanges and trade expansion. Poland has shown a strong interest in acquiring Israeli technology in the fields of agriculture, telecommunications, health, and hotel industry. There has been an unparalleled growth in tourism, facilitated by direct air links, with Israelis visiting Poland in great numbers. Visits by Israeli and Polish government officials culminated in the visit by President Walesa to Israel in 1991 and President Herzog's visit to Poland in 1992. [L.S.-C.]

POLLARD AFFAIR. Jonathan Jay Pollard, an American Jew, born in 1954 in Galveston, Texas, and educated at Stanford, became an intelligence analyst with the U.S. Naval

Intelligence Service in Suitland, Maryland, in late 1979. He rose in the ranks and had access to sensitive information. In May 1984, he was recruited by Israeli agents and for the next 18 months was "run" by a senior Israeli airforce officer Colonel Aviem Sella, then on study leave in New York. Pollard provided Israel with a vast amount of information pertaining to Israel, the Middle East, and other countries, thus compromising the United States. This information was channeled through an independent intelligence unit called the Scientific Liaison Unit which functioned in the Israeli Defense Ministry from the 1960s and was headed by a veteran Mossad operative, Rafael Eitan. During those 18 months Pollard was paid for his services, traveled to Israel and Europe, and was promised asylum in case of discovery. His recruitment and "running" were never authorized by any Israeli defense minister or the cabinet.

Jonathan Pollard

When FBI agents began to follow Pollard and his wife, they fled to the Israeli embassy in Washington seeking asylum, but were ejected from the embassy's grounds and arrested on November 21, 1985. Their arrest and revelations were leaked to the U.S. media, and the extent of their operation and the Israeli involvement generated an extreme and furious reaction by the American leadership and public opinion. There emerged a serious danger of an open confrontation between Israel and the Reagan Administration and the Congress. The row that erupted required an immediate Israeli effort to stem the tide. By then the Israeli people were appalled over the details of this operation carried out by civil servants which could have created a major crisis with Israel's only major ally, and placed American Jews in a highly delicate situation, accused of dual loyalty.

The U.S. demanded cooperation by Israel in the investigation, and on December 1, 1985, Prime Minister Peres agreed to allow questioning of the involved Israelis by U.S. officials, return all the documents taken by Pollard, disband the Scientific Liaison Unit, and punish the responsible Israelis. The returned documents helped to convict Pollard, who claimed during his trial that being an ardent Zionist he was incensed by the refusal of his government to supply Israel with all intelligence information relating to its security. In June 1986 Pollard pleaded guilty to espionage charges and entered into plea bargaining with the prosecution. But in spite of this he was sentenced in March 1987 to life imprisonment while his wife received a five-year jail term.

A few weeks prior to that, U.S. public opinion was again aroused by the news that Rafael Eitan has been appointed chairman of the board of Israel Chemical Industries, a government corporation, while Aviem Sella was appointed to command a major air base, which meant promotion in rank. Following public outcry in Israel and the U.S., Sella resigned his post. Meanwhile public opinion in Israel demanded the appointment of an inquiry committee to investigate the evolution of the affair and to determine responsibility for this operation. The harshness of the Pollard sentence led the government to appoint a two-man committee (the Tsur-Rotenstreich Committee) on March 12, 1987, while a sub-committee of the Knesset Foreign Affairs and Defense Committee headed by Abba *Eban carried out its own separate and independent investigation. Both committees submitted their reports on May 26, 1987.

The Tsur-Rotenstreich committee felt that the entire cabinet should bear responsibility for the affair. In a secret annex it affixed blame on Prime Ministers Peres and Shamir and Defense Ministers Arens and Rabin for failure to exercise control and supervision over the Scientific Liaison Unit and recommended new procedures in intelligence operations. This body and the Knesset sub-committee felt that the involved civil servants, Eitan and Sella, acted injudiciously and far exceeded their authority, but also blamed the senior political echelon for lack of involvement in such operations and their failure to check the details pertaining to the source of the vast intelligence information flowing to Israel. Both committees severely criticized Israel's leadership for hasty actions and serious errors of judgment, although they justified their cooperation with the United States government.

The affair placed the American Jewish community in an embarrassing situation, their confidence in Israel's leadership seriously shaken, fearing that the affair could be used in the future by anti-Israel and anti-Jewish elements in America. Public opinion both in Israel and the U.S. felt however that the Israeli committees' reports basically amounted to a whitewash and sympathy flowed to Pollard and his wife whose harsh sentence had stunned the public. A fund raising effort on Israeli city streets brought over $150,000 for the Pollard defense fund. Those Israelis who sought to defend their country's actions argued that Israel was still under siege, fighting a battle against terror, and living in a fragile and turbulent Middle East. Israel's strategy rested on early warning with intelligence the key to that strategy. Denying Israel vital information was seen as hurting its vital security interests. In spite of the existing Israel-U.S. Strategic Understanding, some Israelis felt they were not being supplied with all relevant information.

These arguments did not convince many Israelis who felt that a monumental error had been committed and that Israeli leaders were not being required to pay the political price for their lack of judgement and involvement. It was feared that the affair would have long term negative effects on Israel-American relations and the degree of trust and confidence once prevailing in these ties had been seriously compromised. [M.ME.]

PORTER, SIR LESLIE (1920–), British businessman. Porter joined his family's textile business (J. Porter and Company), of which he became managing director in 1955. In 1959 he joined as director the supermarket chain, Tesco, which had been founded by Sir John Edward *Cohen, and after being appointed assistant managing director in 1964 and deputy chairman in 1970, served as chairman from 1973 to 1985. He was president of the Institution of Grocery Distribution from 1977 to 1980. He was active in support for social work as a vice-president of Age Concern, vice-president of the National Playing Fields Association, and chairman of the Sports Aid Foundation. He was deputy chairman of the Board of Governors of Tel Aviv University. He married in 1949, SHIRLEY (1930–), daughter of Sir John Edward* Cohen. In addition to company directorships, including that of Capital Radio, an independent broadcasting company in London, Lady Porter was active in Conservative local politics, serving as a Westminster city councilor from 1974 and as leader of the council from 1983. She was especially concerned about the promotion of the campaign for a cleaner London. [V.D.L.]

PORTUGAL (see **13**:925; **Dc./17**:512). It is estimated that 600 Jews were living in Portugal in 1992 but the figure is conjectural, because there are no reliable updating procedures.

In Lisbon, it is difficult to assemble a *minyan* on Sabbath. Most Portuguese Jews today came from North Africa. There are also a small number of Ashkenazi Jews, some of whom arrived in the country during World War II. Their most serious problems at present are common to other communities, especially the small ones: assimilation and mixed marriages.

In certain mountainous regions far to the north, the remaining crypto-Jews maintain old customs, ways of praying, and special festivities. They were able to survive thanks to the preservation of their tradition and a high rate of endogamic marriages. In 1917, the community of *Belmonte in the Estrella Mountains was discovered. In 1983, a film was produced about those "judeos" of Belmonte, portraying their fidelity to Jewish customs.

During 1982–83 there was a considerable increase in cultural exchange between Portugal and Israel. The Institutos de Relacioes Culturais Portugal-Israel (Institutes for Portuguese-Israel Cultural Relations) was active in Porto and Guarda. In 1983, the Mayor of Lisbon, Nuno Kruz Abecassi, visited Israel to participate in the Fourth Jerusalem Conference of Mayors. [J.L.NA./N.H.DN.]

PRESS. United States (see **13**:1023). In recent decades the Jewish press in the United States has evolved into a serious responsible source of information for the U.S. Jewish com-

THE INTERMOUNTAIN JEWISH NEWS

Vol. 76, No. 40 Elul 29, 5749 September 29, 1989 ©Published every Friday in Denver, CO $1.00

ROSH HASHANAH

L'Chaim — To Life Magazine
"A Week in the Life of Denver Jewry"
"Taking Stock of Our Community"
Community Directory

First-Hand Report from Russia
The Final Installment of IJN Editor and Publisher Miriam Goldberg's Series

Low-Cholesterol New Year
The Sephardic Tradition Has the Key

The Cost of Jewish Living
How Much Does It Cost to be Jewish in Denver?

Retrospective, 5749
Chris Leppek Reviews Events in Denver Jewry, Andrew Carroll in American Jewry

Finance and Business Section
Behind Israel's Recession is Great Strength
Guide to Jewish Life on Campus
How Newspapers Cover 'Jews,' 'Jewish' News

5750

The Sept. 1989 Rosh ha-Shanah edition of *The Intermountain Jewish News*, published in Denver and serving the area from Montana to New Mexico. (Courtesy Mrs. Max Goldberg, *INJW*, Denver)

Death, Lies & Videotape
The Trial of Romania's Ceausescus

INSIDE JEWISH EDUCATION PULL-OUT SECTION

FOUNDED APRIL 22, 1897
Volume LXXXXIV, No. 30,781

FORWARD

Subscriptions 1-800-272-7020
75 cents

New York City August 24, 1990

LETTER FROM MOSCOW
Tsipan's Limbo

Gulf War 'Inevitable' Between Yanks, Iraq
Baghdad Must Lose, Bush Believes

Left Splits Over Saddam

Kremlin Sees Iraqi Envoy

Forward & Back • Jonathan Rosen
Raiders of the Ark

Galinski Cool On Germany

Expanded Iraqi War Coverage, Pages 2-3.

One Special Vacation: Holocaust Education

Pamyat Leader Suffers 'Attack'

Poetic Justice Granted

INSIDE

An issue of *Forward* in its new English-language format (Courtesy *Forward*, N.Y.)

munity. Although the daily Yiddish press of the 1930s and 1940s by and large had high journalistic standards, and sought to alert Diaspora leaders to the growing threat in Nazi Europe, it all too often was brushed aside as too parochial or too alarmist. The English-language Jewish weeklies of a half-century ago by and large did not have the respect of the community that many Jewish newspapers and magazines enjoy today; the Jewish media in America now has clout and influence, but the Yiddish press has lost much ground in terms of circulation and readership.

In the early 1990s, there were three Yiddish weeklies in the United States: the *Forward* (see **Jewish Daily Forward*), once a Bundist socialist medium and now a staunchly Zionist paper, with a steadily declining readership whose average age has been estimated in the seventies and eighties; the *Algemeine Journal*, a lively, Lubavich Ḥasidic-oriented newspaper; and *Der Yid*, the organ of the ultra-Orthodox anti-Zionist Satmar sect. Circulation figures are hard to come by, but it is generally agreed that the combined circulation of all three papers is probably between 40,000–60,000. The *Forward* has readers in all parts of the U.S. while the other two papers circulate primarily in the Greater New York area.

A recent phenomenon is the development of Hebrew-language newspapers in the U.S., directed at the large numbers of former Israelis now residing in America's major cities. *Yisrael Shelanu* is a weekly tabloid produced entirely in New York that seems to enjoy steady sales, particularly in certain areas of New York and Los Angeles where Israeli emigrants are concentrated. In addition, thanks to modern communication satellites, Israelis (and Hebrew-speaking Americans) can now pick up Israel's popular tabloids, *Maariv* and *Yediot Aḥaronot*, a day after they appear in Tel

Aviv. The English-language *The Jerusalem Post* has for years had a loyal readership in the U.S. for its overseas weekly edition, estimated to reach some 25,000 subscribers in America (plus an additional 10,000 in other countries).

It is the English-language press, however, that has made great strides in recent years — in its standards, influence, professionalism, and technological production. The decline of daily newspaper readership in the U.S. brought on partly by the impact of television has reduced the amount of space available to Jewish news, including Israel news, in many metropolitan dailies. American Jews wishing to know what is going on within the American Jewish community, in Israel, and in Jewish communities overseas have begun to depend more and more on local Jewish weeklies and national Jewish periodicals.

A comparison between the English-language Jewish weeklies of today and those of five decades ago demonstrates the

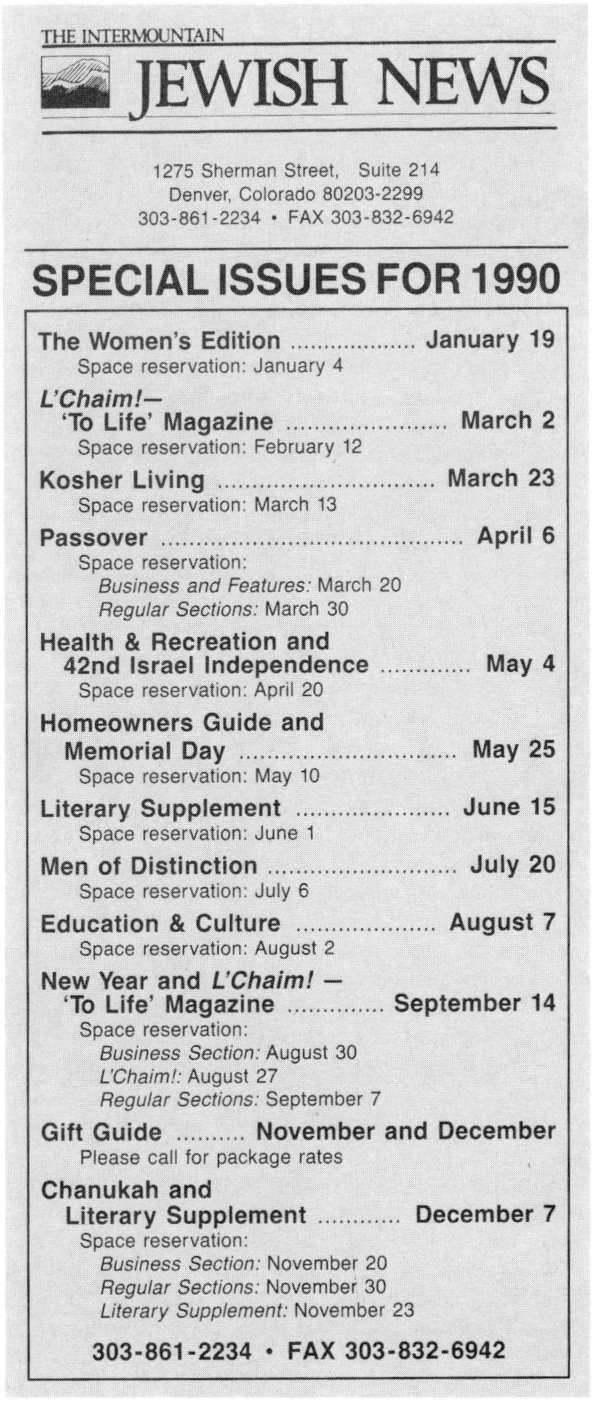

List of 1990 special issues of *The Intermountain Jewish News* shows the active role the paper plays in its community

February 1993 edition of *Moment: The Magazine of Jewish Culture and Opinion*, published in Washington, D.C. (Courtesy *Moment*, Washington, D.C.)

changes that have been taking place in this field. Although local Jewish newspapers still feature reports of weddings, engagements, births, deaths, bar and bat mitzvahs and similar material, a far greater emphasis on full-bodied news about Israel, Soviet Jewry, neo-Nazism worldwide, anti-Semitism in the U.S., assimilation and intermarriage, the paucity of Jewish education, missionaries and cults is now featured in the Jewish media.

Widely divergent views on Jewish life in America may be seen in the national magazines, notably *Commentary* (a conservative monthly published by the American Jewish Committee), *Moment* (published in Washington, D.C.), and *Tikkun* (an independent liberal bi-monthly). Thus, the American Jewish family that belongs to a synagogue and to at least one national Jewish organization and subscribes to the local Jewish weekly receives a steady stream of Jewish reading matter all through the year: the synagogue's weekly bulletin, the weekly Jewish newspaper, and at least one of the national monthlies that come free with membership. In recent years, growing numbers of communities have been purchasing bulk subscriptions to local Jewish weeklies for the benefit of their local campaign donors. Although this phenomenon has led to some charges of unfair local Jewish federation/campaign influence on the Jewish media, it appears that in most cases the papers involved are pleased to have the security of bulk subscribers and have managed to work out effective ways of ensuring their editorial independence.

Some of the English-language Jewish weeklies go back a long time and others are recent — the *American Israelite* in Cincinnati, Ohio, dates from 1854, while the *Palm Beach* (Florida) *Jewish World* was established in 1982. Although Jewish papers are published in virtually every state of the union, New York remains the center of Jewish cultural and press life. Some of the more interesting, unique publications that appear in New York include *Afn Shvel*, a Yiddish quarterly published by the League for Yiddish, Inc.; *Aufbau*, the

German-language bi-weekly read by refugees from central Europe; *Bitzaron*, a Hebrew bi-monthly; *Hadassah Magazine*, which enjoys the world's largest Jewish circulation (some 375,000); *Jewish Braille Review*, for the benefit of its blind members; *Jewish Currents*, a leftist monthly issued by the Association for Promotion of Jewish Secularism; *Jewish Guardian*, a Brooklyn-based irregular (English and Hebrew) publication of Neturei Karta of U.S.A.; *Kosher Directory*, issued by the Union of Orthodox Jewish Congregations of America; *Lilith*, the feminist Jewish quarterly; *Proceedings* of the American Academy of Jewish Research, an annual publication that appears in Hebrew, Arabic, and English; *Shmuessen Mit Kinder Un Yugent*, a Yiddish publication of the Lubavich Ḥasidim aimed at children and teens; *Synagogue Light*, a publication of the Union of Chassidic Rabbis; and *YIVO Annual* of Jewish Social Science.

In recent years local Jewish newspapers have become sources of important information for peripatetic American Jews, including many families moving from the colder northern zones of America to the warmer southern states. Jews have learned that a local Jewish weekly will list synagogues, *kasher* restaurants and butcher shops (if they exist), and will even advertise residences that will appeal to Jews who historically have sought out fellow-Jews among whom to live.

Parents concerned that their children attending out-of-town colleges and universities socialize with other Jews have also discovered the local Jewish weeklies, which feature news of Hillel chapter functions, dances under Jewish auspices, religious services for singles, and similar information.

[D.C.G.]

PUBLISHING. United States (see **13:**1364). The huge changes that continue to engulf the general book publishing field in the United States, and indeed throughout the world, also have made a sharp impact on the specialized area of Jewish publishing. Twenty years ago it was thought that there

Cover of the Los Angeles-area edition of *The Jewish Calendar* provides information on all facets of Jewish living and community events in the region. (The Isaac Nathan Publishing Co.)

were some 600,000 Jewish youngsters attending some kind of Jewish school in the U.S. and Canada, offering a market for textbooks and supplementary reading books that attracted substantial numbers of Jewish publishers. Today, it has been estimated that the number of such students is closer to 300,000, of whom one-third are enrolled in largely Orthodox yeshivot. The results were almost predictable: the innovative Orthodox house, Artscroll, services the Orthodox market; Behrman House continues to be the leader of modern texts for the Conservative area; and the publishing arm of the Reform movement, the Union of American Hebrew Congregations, provides books for the Reform congregations' school needs.

The one area in Jewish school enrollment that has seen a steady rise remains the pre-school nurseries, where children aged three and four are introduced to Judaic concepts through a wide variety of educational material, including video cassettes. It is this slice of the Jewish market that seems to have attracted both general and Jewish publishers in recent years, as the number of full-color illustrated books for very young children continues to mount.

Although an estimated 700 new Jewish books appear every year in the United States, many of these are highly specialized titles meant for limited academic or professional library use. While the number of general Jewish books remains relatively high, and the number of Jewish-theme novels, biographies, general non-fiction, books on Israel, the Holocaust, etc. remains impressive, many publishers are not at all certain how much longer this phenomenon will last, especially as the total number of Jews in the United States is declining for various reasons.

This is not to say that publishers — both general houses and Jewish houses — have given up on Judaica publishing. Jews still buy books in disproportionately large numbers, and every publisher is trying to turn out titles that will capture the community's imagination and become perennial bestsellers. Jewish Book Month, which is sponsored by the Jewish Book Council, an affiliate of the National Jewish Welfare Board, takes place annually in November, with many hundreds of book fairs being held throughout the country.

In New York, a major fair attracted some 15,000 visitors. Some of the authors featured had written general books but since they were themselves well-known Jews, they helped bring in people. A number of authors spoke about such esoteric topics as "The Jewish Detective," "The Jewish Voter" (the fair was held just before the national elections in the U.S.), "How to Care for Your Parents," and "The Jewish Holiday Kitchen." The new books featured at 1988 fairs ranged from a new coffee table volume on Israel published on the state's 40th anniversary, with text by A. B. Yehoshua, to a new volume by Israel's Lova Eliav, titled *New Heart, New Spirit: Biblical Humanism for Modern Israel*, plus a series of new first-person memoirs of the Holocaust, a new series of brief biographies of Rashi, Buber, Bialik and Heine, the autobiography of a former Soviet dissident, fiction by Leon Uris, Amos Keinan, and David Grossman, and scholarly works with such titles as *Jewish Values in Psychotherapy: Essays on Vital Issues of Man's Search for Meaning* by Rabbi Levi Meier.

Although the trend in recent years has been toward smaller numbers of vast publishing empires (Doubleday, once a major general publisher of large numbers of Jewish titles, is now part of the German-owned Bertelsman–Bantam-Doubleday group, while Random House has absorbed Crown, and Macmillan was taken over by Britain's vast Maxwell empire), the number of tiny one or two-man publishing houses has exploded, and now numbers in the thousands. Modern computer technology and desktop publishing have attracted literally thousands of people to set up shop in their homes, basements, and garages, where they issue local, regional or national titles at the rate of two or three a year. This radical new concept has also caught on in the Jewish community.

In addition to the well-known Jewish houses like the Jewish Publication Society, Behrman, Hebrew Publishing, Bloch Publishing, Feldheim, Ktav, Artscroll, and the publishing arms of various religious/educational/rabbinical organizations, one can now find a growing number of small, new Jewish houses: Micah Publications, Alpha Publishing, Bet Shamai Publications, Biblio Press, Bezalel Art, Jewish Historical Society of Oregon, Kar-Ben Copies, Hunter Publishing, Markus Weiner Publishing, Quartet Books, Madison Books, Edwin Mellen Press, Wandering You Press, Mensch Makers Press, Judaica Press, Peartree, Jason Aronson.

The number of Jewish titles appearing on the regular lists of large and small university presses, as well as in the offerings of Christian religious houses, remains high. Abingdon Press, a noted Christian house, issued *A Grammar for Biblical Hebrew* by C. L. Seow in 1988, while Wayne State University Press published a study by Amnon Linder titled *Jews in Roman Imperial Legislation.*

The Jewish Publication Society of America celebrated its 100th anniversary in 1988, noting that it had issued more than 700 titles in that period aggregating more than nine million volumes that it had distributed to its members and the public at large.

A major problem in Jewish publishing in America — distribution — has still not been fully resolved. Books of Jewish interest reviewed in daily or Jewish media, recommended by friends or referred to by a rabbi during a Sabbath sermon, are

The Book of Esther *Artscroll Youth Megillah*, a publication aimed at the young Orthodox reader (Courtesy Artscroll, Jerusalem)

often very hard to come by in general book stores. Although there are some 250 strictly Jewish book shops in all parts of the U.S., and many hundreds of (primarily Conservative and Reform) congregations sell limited numbers of Judaica titles from their volunteer-manned "gift shops," no one has as yet been able to work out an effective method of getting Jewish books into the hands of book buyers on a nationwide scale.

A glance at the catalogs of general houses and Jewish houses will quickly demonstrate that certain broad subjects remain on top of the community's reading agenda: Israel, the Holocaust, anti-Semitism, assimilation, Jewish ethics, culture, and philosophy. In recent years, a number of publishers have begun to issue titles dealing with a subject that is often peripheral in Jewish life — Kabbalah, or Jewish mysticism. Whether this is a reflection of the times or a deep spiritual hunger is hard to say. [D.C.G.]

The Central Conference of American Rabbis published *Shaarei Mitzvah: Gates of Mitzvah* (Courtesy Hebrew Union College, Jerusalem)

R

RABIN, YIZḤAK (see **13**:1471; **Dc./17**: 517). From 1980 to 1984 he was Israel minister of defense. In early 1992 he was chosen head of the Labor party and after the elections in June became prime minister for the second time. He instituted a change of priorities, particularly in cutting back support for the settlements in Judea, Samaria, and Gaza. In August 1993 he announced mutual Israel-PLO recognition and his government began negotiations towards a peace settlement with the Palestinians and with countries bordering Israel.

RAYNE, MAX, LORD (1918–), British businessman and financier. After education at University College London and service in the Royal Air Force during World War II, Rayne was chairman from 1961 of London Merchant Securities, and was also chairman or director of other property and industrial companies. He was active in support for the arts as a governor of the Royal Ballet School, chairman of its London Trust (1967–75) and of the National Theatre Board from 1971 to 1988. His support for medical work included the post of special trustee of St. Thomas's Hospital. He was an honorary vice-president of the (London) Jewish Welfare Board and served on other bodies concerned with social service, including the King Edward VII Hospital Fund for London and St Thomas's Medical School. Rayne was knighted in 1969 and created a life peer in 1976. [V.D.L.]

RAZON, JACKO (1921–), Greek boxer. Born in Salonika, Razon had to terminate his studies when the Germans occupied Salonika in 1941 and was left without a profession. He learned boxing in Maccabi and in 1939 was the middleweight boxing champion of Greece. He was also goalkeeper for the Salonikan soccer team Olympiakos in the Greek National Football League. In 1943, he was deported by the Germans to Auschwitz.

Jacko Razon (Yitzhak Kerem, Jerusalem)

After two months, he was transferred to the Buna labor camp where he organized the boxing at the camp. He had 12 pairs of boxers — Jews and non-Jews, professionals and amateurs, among them Jung Perez, the former Tunisian world lightweight boxing champion. During the day he worked in the kitchen and after working hours he trained the boxers. Razon had to box weekly, often against heavyweights, winning most of his matches. Due to his kitchen connections, he was able to help many prisoners and hundreds owed their lives to him. This ended when Buna was evacuated and the "death march" began.

After a short stay in Gleiwitz, where Jung Perez died, Jacko was moved to Dora. He boxed also there but received little extra food for his talent and managed to feed only a few individuals at most. Transferred to Bergen-Belsen, he found the way to return to kitchen duty and helped Greek Jews in their most dire hour, when the camp was full of living skeletons and food was scarce. He was liberated by the British in May 1945.

After returning to Greece, Razon was a leader of Holocaust survivors who planned to immigrate to Palestine "illegally." They sailed on the *Henrietta Szold*, with 356 passengers, which was met by British warships in Haifa port. Razon led a revolt against the British navy, which was eventually overcome, and he and the other passengers were deported to Cyprus where they were interned for several months.

Eventually he arrived in Palestine and participated in Israel's War of Independence, and was one of the founders of the Organization of Greek Concentation Camp Survivors in Israel.

Bibliography: S. Raphael (ed.), *Binitivei Shaol: Yehudei Yavan Beshoa — Pirkei Aidout* (1988), 454–458. [Yı.K.]

RECANATI (see **13:**1607). ABRAHAM SAMUEL RECANATI (1888–1980). Greek Zionist and journalist. Born and educated in Salonika, Abraham Recanati wrote in the local Jewish Judeo-Spanish press. In the Balkan wars, as a correspondent for the *Jewish Chronicle* and *Die Welt* (Berlin) he brought the suffering of the Jewish community of Salonika to the attention of the Jewish world and to the general European public.

In 1911 he became the head of Maccabi Federation in Salonika, transforming it from a sports organization to a mass youth movement.

Among his writings are *La Poriza dela Familia Judia, Ke es el Tsionismo*, and *Los Judios de Rusia Sofrin Eyos Como Judios*. He also translated *The Jewish State* by Theodor Herzl into French.

Owing to tactical and ideological differences, Abraham Recanati and a group of friends left Maccabi and in 1917 founded the French weekly newspaper *Pro Israel*, which Recanati edited during the ten years in which it appeared. The newspaper had widespread influence on the development of the Zionist movement in Salonika. The connections which developed at that time between Vladimir *Jabotinsky and Recanati brought about the molding of the core group of *Pro Israel* into a branch of the Revisionist Zionists in Salonika.

In 1919, Recanati formed the Histadrut ha-Mizrachi (Mizrachi Organization) in Greece and served as its leader. In 1923 he formed "Ha-Shomer," which was founded to use legal and "illegal" means to work for a Jewish state in Ereẓ Israel.

He was a delegate to various Zionist Congresses and was among the founders of the World Revisionist Organization and a member of its world executive committee.

The Jews always had a small representation in the municipality of Salonika and in 1929 Recanati was appointed assistant mayor of the city.

In 1934 Recanati immigrated to Palestine. He was one of the founders of "Ha-Mizrachi Ha-Mekori," which was a faction in the Tel Aviv branch of the Mizrachi. In 1935 he obtained immigration certificates for Salonikan port-workers, sailors, and fishermen.

In Tel Aviv most of the Salonikan immigrants settled in the Florentin Quarter. Recanati served as vice-chairman of the neighborhood committee under Rabbi Iẓḥak Yedidiah Frenkel and helped in the areas of health, sanitation, education, commerce, and the crafts. During the period of the Holocaust he participated in the formation of the Va'ad ha--Haẓẓalah (Rescue Committee) for Greek Jewry.

As a veteran Revisionist he was elected to the First Knesset in Israel representing the Ḥerut party. He was chairman of the public services committee of the Knesset.

In the last years of his life, he spent much time collecting material and writing for the Salonika memorial book, *Zikhron Salonika* (vol. 1, 1972; vol. 2, 1986).

He was the brother of the banker Yehudah Leib (Leon) Recanati. [Yı.K.]

REFORM JUDAISM (see **14:**23). From the 1930s, Reform Judaism underwent a far-reaching ideological transformation in its perception of Jewish Peoplehood and religious observance. This transformation was embodied in official declarations as well as by internal social changes and by the surge of history. The declarations were responses to the social and political forces, and also served to rally Reform Jews around a new vision. One of the declarations was the Colombus Platform of 1937 in which the Central Conference of American Rabbis (CCAR) acknowledged Jewish Peoplehood, called for the recognition of a Jewish "homeland," the restoration of traditional ritual and ceremonial practices, and the increased usage of Hebrew. This was soon followed by a similar pronouncement by the Union of American Hebrew Congregations (UAHC). In 1943, the

CCAR declared that Zionism and Reform were not incompatible and called for the cessation of anti-Zionist activities by some of its members. By the 1950s, the principles of Reform were becoming reified and institutionalized along expanding fronts.

The Israel-oriented direction of the Reform Movement. Most striking and most symbolic was the establishment of the Hebrew Union College in Jerusalem (1963) under the direction of its president, Nelson Glueck, and in the face of violent anti-Reform opposition, blunted by the decision of the Jerusalem municipality which ceded land to the college for a symbolic annual rental. Beginning as an archaeological center and a place of worship for its local adherents, the college has rapidly become the physical and spiritual focus of Reform in Israel and throughout the world. In 1987, under the leadership of President Alfred Gottschalk, and Board Chairman Richard Scheuer, the college completed an extensive expansion program. It now encompasses the headquarters of the World Union for Progressive Judaism, maintains a hostel for Reform youth from the Diaspora, conducts an intellectual and cultural program for the people of Jerusalem, and provides facilities for a religious action program. At its center, however, is its rabbinic training curriculum which has evolved from its inception. The program requires that candidates for the rabbinate spend the first year of their five-year training in Jerusalem. Later, the college opened a special department for preparing Israelis for the Israeli rabbinate. *Semikhah* (ordination), first granted in 1980, had by 1992 been conferred on 12 graduates of the College in Jerusalem.

Some Reform achievements in Israel preceded the college, establishing a beachhead for a steady advance by the movement. Individual congregations, notably Har-El in Jerusalem (1958), Kedem In Tel Aviv, and Or Chadash in Haifa (1964), persisted in the face of intense opposition. Each now has its own building and is served by a rabbi who has pioneered in behalf of Reform legitimacy in Israel. Today, additional Reform congregations are to be found in Ramat Gan, Ramat ha-Sharon, Ramat Aviv, Kiryat Ono, Netanyah, Nahariyyah, Ḥolon, Rishon le-Zion, Upper Nazareth, Beersheva, and Ra'anannah. They are augmented by a national youth movement, by an assembly of progressive rabbis (Moetzet Rabbanim Mitkadmim), and by a national body representing the Israeli movement, Tnuah l'Yahadut Mitkademet (Telem). The movement has produced a *siddur* (prayer book) and *maḥzor* (festival prayer book).

The Leo Baeck School in Haifa (organized in 1939 as the Hillel Elementary School by Leo Elk) has become the Reform Movement's high school in Israel. Under the direction of Rabbi Robert Samuel, it has developed an expanding program which includes the absorption of American students for semesters of study, the imparting of Jewish values in a progressive idiom, the encouragement of worship in its Ohel Avraham, and more recently the development of a center program for a culturally and socially mixed constituency.

Israeli Reform has, from its inception, been committed to protecting its religious and legal rights. It was long involved in struggles to protect congregations from being evicted from temporary homes or from securing land on which to build. The movement is currently engaged in a legal struggle for the recognition of two of its rabbis, Moshe Zemer and Mordecai Rotem, as official marriage registrars in Israel. It has successfully defended the existing Law of Return from repeated efforts to amend it, and has enlisted the Conservative and other movements in this cause. It has fought in the courts for the legal protection of immigrants who were converted by non-Orthodox Rabbis. True to its Reform mandate, it has intervened in behalf of disadvantaged groups such as immigrants from Ethiopia whose Jewish status was questioned, and it has declared its concern about moral aspects of the Arab uprising. Israeli Reform's halakhic authority, Moshe Zemer, attempts to deal with many of those issues in the con-

HUC rabbinical students presenting Progressive Judaism to an IDF Officers' Course, part of a program with the participation of HUC graduate students (rabbinical, cantorial, Jewish education, and communal service) (Courtesy Hebrew Union College, Jerusalem)

text of Jewish law. The movement has established its Religious Action Center which is committed to confronting social issues affecting Reform and the nation. The Religious Action Center has filed suit in the Supreme Court for approval of a Reform burial society (Menucha Nechona) that will provide burial services under Reform auspices.

Through the Religious Action Center, a social agenda is beginning to be implemented. The center, under the direction of Uri Regev, intends to coordinate a broad spectrum of social issues.

In 1972 and 1973, members of the CCAR in America and in Israel met in Oranim and at the Leo Baeck School with leaders of kibbutz movements to discuss, in Hebrew, the areas of common spiritual and social concern in which each could be helpful to the other. Out of these meetings, lasting several days, emerged a united decision to strive for the creation of a Reform kibbutz.

Consequently, the Reform Movement has created two kibbutzim — Yahel (1977) and Lotan (1983) in the Negev. Both consist of native Israelis and immigrants who, in their economic and social lives and in their religious-cultural experiences, strive to integrate a liberal orientation with an assertive traditionalism. Together with Har he-Ḥalutz, the movement's observation outpost *(mizpeh)* in Galilee (1985), these settlements represent an effort at synthesis of past and present.

Reform in North America. The Pittsburgh Platform of 1885 stressed universalism as paramount in its perception of Judaism. But "A Centenary Perspective" (1976) declared that while "the ethics of universalism implicit in traditional Judaism must be an explicit part of our Jewish duty," yet "the survival of the Jewish People is of highest priority and...in carrying out our Jewish responsibilities we help move humanity toward its messianic fulfillment." While the Reform community continues to respond to the prophetic impulses in Judaism, it appears also to be moving steadily toward ever stronger manifestations of particularity. Both in religious and in ethnic-national terms, Reform is at this period stressing its Jewish uniqueness, if even as an aspect of humanity's "messianic fulfillment." This does not suggest abandonment of Reform's special social consciousness but rather a reordering of priorities in response to the demands of the times. Thus, the Reform stress on Israel, and the spiritual inward turning within Reform, do not invalidate social concern but rather appear to supplement it. Certainly, since 1967, Reform Jews, reacting to the isolation experienced by Jewry prior to the Six-Day War, began to concentrate on the crisis of Jewish existence and to define themselves more as Jews than as Reform Jews. It is no overstatement that Israel has possessed more of the emotional, moral, and religious space of Reform Jews. This is best articulated in the conclusion of a resolution passed by the CCAR during an emergency session in June 21, 1967: "We declare our solidarity with the State and the People of Israel. Their triumphs are our triumphs. Their ordeal is our ordeal. Their fate is our fate." One of the first, if not the first, American Rabbinic conventions was held by the CCAR in Israel on Mt. Scopus, Jerusalem, in June 1970. Others followed in March 1974, June 1981, and March 1988.

On the American scene, the Reform Movement has gone through a period of spiritual creativity unmatched in its previous history. The CCAR has produced a new *siddur, Shaarei Tefillah* (1975), a new *maḥzor, Shaarei Tshuvah* (1978), in expanded traditional yet also new form, with greatly increased use of Hebrew (as well as some Yiddish), with stress on Israel and the Holocaust. It has also published a new manual for rabbis, *Maaglei Zedek* (by David Polish and Gunther Plaut) which reflects many of the changes taking place within Jewish life, such as sexual equality and the spiritual pervasiveness of Israel. The UAHC has produced a modern commentary on the Pentateuch (by Gunther Plaut and Bernard Bamberger), a new *Haggadah* (by Herbert Bronstein and Leonard Baskin), and other works.

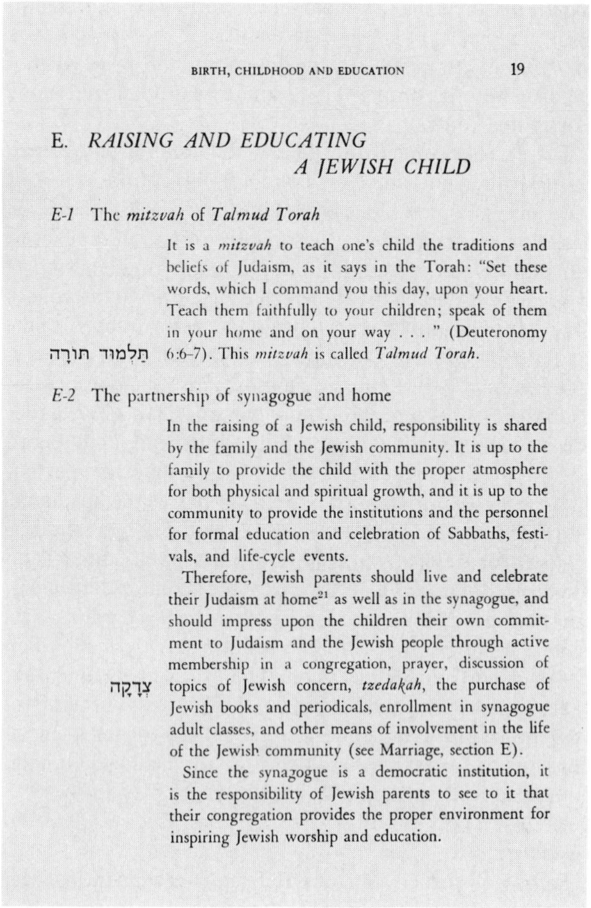
BIRTH, CHILDHOOD AND EDUCATION 19

E. *RAISING AND EDUCATING A JEWISH CHILD*

E-1 The *mitzvah* of *Talmud Torah*

It is a *mitzvah* to teach one's child the traditions and beliefs of Judaism, as it says in the Torah: "Set these words, which I command you this day, upon your heart. Teach them faithfully to your children; speak of them in your home and on your way . . . " (Deuteronomy 6:6–7). This *mitzvah* is called *Talmud Torah*. תַּלְמוּד תּוֹרָה

E-2 The partnership of synagogue and home

In the raising of a Jewish child, responsibility is shared by the family and the Jewish community. It is up to the family to provide the child with the proper atmosphere for both physical and spiritual growth, and it is up to the community to provide the institutions and the personnel for formal education and celebration of Sabbaths, festivals, and life-cycle events.

Therefore, Jewish parents should live and celebrate their Judaism at home[21] as well as in the synagogue, and should impress upon the children their own commitment to Judaism and the Jewish people through active membership in a congregation, prayer, discussion of topics of Jewish concern, *tzedakah*, the purchase of Jewish books and periodicals, enrollment in synagogue adult classes, and other means of involvement in the life of the Jewish community (see Marriage, section E). צְדָקָה

Since the synagogue is a democratic institution, it is the responsibility of Jewish parents to see to it that their congregation provides the proper environment for inspiring Jewish worship and education.

A page on Raising and Educating a Jewish Child from *Gate of Mitzvah*, a guide to the Jewish life cycle (Courtesy Hebrew Union College, Jerusalem)

Preceding these events, the steady alteration of Reform took place from what was primarily a theological, profoundly ideological system, into an extended regimen of doing Jewish deeds, of performing *mitzvot* at home and in the synagogue. This was in keeping with a trend which in part triggered and increasingly responded to the Columbus Platform. In 1957, *A Guide for Reform Jews* (by Doppelt and Polish), stressing the phrase, "it is a mitzvah to," and identifying *mitzvot* with formative moments in Jewish history, was created by individuals for the specific purpose of prompting official Reform responses which came in the form of *Gates of Mitzvah* (1979). The CCAR has also produced *Reform Responsa*, a two-volume collection of hundreds of rabbinic decisions (Walter Jacob, editor, 1983, 1987) and *Gates of the Seasons* (1983). The growing awakening within Reform to what has become a *mitzvah* system, has resulted in widespread observances within congregations where *Seliḥot* services, the second day of Rosh Ha-Shanah, the widespread employment of cantors, the universal practice of Bar and Bat Mitzvah services prevail. In addition, the increased response to the *mitzvah* of *talmud Torah* is resulting in the proliferation of camping programs, Reform day schools, summer pilgrimages to Israel, and extended periods of study in Israel. The Reform Movement is also increasingly stressing the importance of personal and home observance in respect to the Sabbath, festivals, life cycle events, and prayer. Of special significance is a recent effort by the Reform rabbinates of New York and Los Angeles to train corps of *mohalim* and *mohalot* (circumcisers) for Reform communities. The purposes are to encourage the observance of *brit milah* (circumcision) and to counteract the refusal by some Orthodox *mohalim* to officiate for families whose infants may be considered to be halakhically non-Jewish.

All this represents a significant turn toward collective and individual spirituality but it does not necessarily suggest that Reform Judaism is becoming halakhic. As has been noted, the movement has been steadily producing a *mitzvah* system and an accompanying body of literature, and collective consensus. Nevertheless, it would be a fallacy to suggest that this is necessarily leading toward acceptance of *halakhah* as a determinative code for Reform. What can be said is that a substantial, although unmeasured, sector of Reform is taking *halakhah* far more seriously than it may have in the past, although even this must be qualified by many instances of early halakhic discussions over such issues as the circumcision of male converts. Today, however, the number of halakhic inquiries and authoritative responses by Solomon Freehof who published hundreds of responsa, and by his successor, Walter Jacob, who has written and compiled many responsa, attest to the unprecedented interest of Reform Jews in learning what the tradition has to say on a multitude of issues.

At the initiative of Alexander Schindler, president of the UAHC, an intensive program was launched to confront the growing challenge of intermarriage. A special department was established along a national front to reach out to intermarried families and prospectively intermarried couples. This involves classes, conferences, retreats, films and literature, all aimed at stimulating and deepening interest and involvement in Judaism. Also, the CCAR in 1983, passed its Patrilinear resolution, declaring the children of intermarried couples (with either parent Jewish) to be Jewish, subject to the parents' wishes and to the fulfillment of basic *mitzvot* by the children.

As issues broaden and begin to affect the entire Reform community and its own self-definition, the halakhic dilemma becomes far more complex. It is here that we observe sharp divisions between anti-halakhists, non-halakhists, halakhists, and quasi-halakhists. This configuration can best be observed in such issues as medical ethics, intermarriage, women in the rabbinate, and patrilinear descent. Anti-halakhists would argue that a modern, liberal Reform may make its determination without reference to a halakhic system which is not equipped to deal with eventualities unanticipated by the *halakhah*. Halakhists, perhaps the smallest component in the Reform rabbinate, would support halakhic ingenuity in finding solutions for our times. Quasi-halakhists would perceive *halakhah* as an authoritative guide, usually when revealing less restrictive options, but not necessarily determinative. Thus, in 1922, Hebrew Union College Professor Jacob Lauterbach issued a halakhic responsum rejecting the ordination of women, yet the CCAR opposed him, and in 1971 the college ordained the first woman. Despite the clear tendency of the *halakhah* against patrilineality, the CCAR, having searched the *halakhah*, nevertheless took its unequivocal position. In 1973, the CCAR confronted the issue of intermarriage. Following a year of study, a special committee produced and the CCAR adopted a document reaffirming and strengthening an earlier statement of opposition to rabbinic participation at intermarriages, and in that context also reaffirmed the principle of rabbinic autonomy. The latter as applied especially to such an issue is hardly halakhic. The contradiction has been noted. Personal autonomy is unique to the Reform rabbinate. It is perceived by many as a moral force and by others as a stumbling bloc. A definitive Reform view on *halakhah*, if such a view is possible, has not emerged.

An ARZA poster held by Rabbi Charles A. Kroloff, who was ARZA president (Courtesy Association of Reform Zionists of America)

The growth of Reform particularism notwithstanding, the commitment to social activism continues to animate Reform in North America. During the 1960s and 1970s, numbers of Reform rabbis and congregations were involved in the civil rights struggle and in opposition to the Vietnam War. Rabbis and lay people participated in civil rights demonstrations in the North and the South. In a few cases, rabbis' homes and temples in the South were threatened and attacked. Reform activists demonstrated and spoke out against the war, both in their communities and from their pulpits.

Under the auspices of the UAHC, the Religious Action Center in Washington presides over a broad agenda of general and Jewish issues, and for many Reform Jews, social involvement is a primary justification for their Jewish commitment. Under the direction of Rabbi David Saperstein, the center seeks to apply the ethical-social commitments of Judaism to contemporary social and political issues within Jewish, American, and international contexts. Through education, lobbying, activism, involvement of youth and adults on local levels, and collaboration with other Jewish and non-Jewish agencies, it has become a prominent and influential intervening medium on the American and Jewish scenes.

Kelal Israel ("Jewish Community as a Whole"). The creation of the Association of Reform Zionists of America (ARZA, 1977) resulted both in the emergence of a worldwide Reform Zionist body (Artzenu) and for the first time a Zionist organization based on Reform religious Jewish principles. Since its inception, ARZA-Artzenu has been a major factor in the support of the Reform kibbutzim and moshav; it has brought the Religious Action Center in Jerusalem into being; it has had a growing representation in Zionist Congresses since 1978. From 1988 to 1992 it was represented in Zionist councils by Richard Hirsch, as chairman of the Zionist General Council (1987–92), and by Henry Skirball as head of the World Zionist Organization's department of education in the Diaspora (1987–92). With the rest of the movement, it has successfully resisted efforts to amend the Law of Return and at the 1987 Zionist Congress led the successful fight calling for equal treatment for all religious Jewish bodies within Israel (the pluralism resolution). In 1988, it adopted a declaration embodying a comprehensive position on its religious-Zionist philosophy. The Declaration affirms Reform Judaism as committed to the dual traditional stress on piety and justice; it affirms democracy and pluralism in Jewish life which also includes secularism; it affirms the Diaspora and *aliyah* (immigration), and warns the Diaspora to "understand the historical risks entailed by... success." It calls upon the government of Israel to "repudiate religious repression and political violence." It rejects religious extremism, calls for safeguarding the rights of Arabs in the administered territories, and urges a peaceful settlement based on mutual guarantees and concessions.

As a forerunner to ARZA's total involvement in the world Jewish community, the CCAR in 1972 became a member of the World Jewish Congress, and the UAHC joined soon thereafter.

Conclusion. The transformation of Reform Judaism, beginning in the 1930s, advancing in the 1940s, and becoming more extensively institutionalized and internationalized from the 1950s, represents a new phenomenon in Judaism and in Jewish life. It has had its effect not only on its adherents but upon the Jewish world. To be sure, there are contradictions and problematics, but with full consideration of their severity, the tide seems to be moving in a positive and creative direction. The movement which began with hostility towards a Jewish national home is not only securely imbedded in that home but is helping shape its destiny.

[DA.P.]

Attitudes to Homosexuality. On June 25, 1990, at its 101st Convention, the Central Conference of American Rabbis (CCAR) adopted the report of its Ad Hoc Committee on homosexuality and the rabbinate.

This report follows a line of resolutions adopted by the Union of American Hebrew Congregations (UAHC) and the CCAR, dealing mainly with the human and civil rights of homosexuals, and their place in the Jewish community. The present report took this matter one step further and dealt with the highly controversial and sensitive issue of homosexual rabbis.

For Reform Judaism, in dealing with the issue of homosexuality (as with other halakhic issues), the fact that the Torah includes an explicit prohibition against homosexuality, calling it an abomination, is not necessarily the ultimate consideration in forging its contemporary position and attitude. Reform Judaism attempts to investigate the historical circumstances that resulted in a particular biblical or oral law, and confronts it with the present reality, bearing in mind changing scientific, social, and moral circumstances, as well as the dictates of conscience.

In 1969, the leading figure in shaping the American Reform movement's position on *halakhah*, Rabbi Solomon B. Freehof, issued a responsum that followed the traditional position viewing homosexual behavior as sinful, and seeing homosexuality as running "counter to the *sancta* of Jewish life."

The changing position of Reform Judaism on homosexuality is based on the recognition that approximately 10% of the population is homosexual. Equally the growing visibility of homosexuals, and the increasing knowledge about the psychological and etiological foundations of homosexuality have played their part. Even though there is no unanimity in the scientific community as to the sources of homosexuality, it is clear that for many, sexual orientation is not a matter of conscious choice, but is constitutional, and, therefore, not subject to change.

Holding the conviction that all persons are created in the Divine Image and that sexual orientation is irrelevant to one's human worth coupled with the new understanding of homosexuality, Reform Judaism finds it difficult to uphold the traditional view which presupposes choice and therefore sees homosexuality as a deliberate act committed by "heterosexuals" in willful violation of the Divine command.

In 1977, the UAHC and the CCAR passed resolutions calling for equal protection under the law and opposing discrimination against homosexuals in areas of "opportunity, including employment and housing."

The UAHC admitted as members congregations with special outreach to lesbian and gay Jews and in 1987 added a resolution stating that "sexual orientation should not be a criterion for membership of, or participation in, an activity of any synagogue."

In 1989, the UAHC went further, stating that its congregations must be a place where gay and lesbian Jews can know that they are accepted on terms of visibility, not invisibility, and that "no limits are to be placed on their communal or spiritual aspirations."

These resolutions reflect the mood in which the Ad Hoc CCAR committee deliberated on the issue of homosexuality and the rabbinate. The report approved of the new admissions policy to the Hebrew Union College–Jewish Institute of Religion. Until the early 1970s homosexual orientation was perceived as a mental illness or deviance, and anyone who was openly gay was not considered for admission. The new policy considers the sexual orientation of an applicant only within the context of a candidate's overall suitability for the rabbinate, and does not make an *a priori* disqualification on that basis.

The report urged that all rabbis, regardless of sexual orientation, be accorded the opportunity to fulfill the sacred vocation which they have chosen. At the same time the CCAR recognized its limited ability to guarantee the tenure of gay or lesbian rabbis who "come out of the closet." In view of the unique role of the Rabbi and the fact that this is an intensely emotional and potentially divisive issue, the CCAR concluded that the question required further education and dialogue within Reform congregations.

The majority of the committee viewed the issue of choice as crucial and held that heterosexuality is the only appropriate Jewish choice in order to fulfill one's covenantal obligations. It reaffirmed the centrality of heterosexual, monogamous, procreative marriage as the ideal human relationship for the perpetuation of the species, covenantal fulfillment, and the preservation of the Jewish people. Also expressed in the report is a minority viewpoint that accepts homosexuality as a legitimate alternative to heterosexuality. The report met with some criticism from both sides of the debate. There were those who felt that the position expressed is too mild and would like to see a clear validation of homosexual life styles and unions. Others felt that the Reform movement had lost its bearings and standards bowing to the popular and passing mood. The latter group holds to the biblical injuctions and still view homosexuality as an "abnormal and objectionable" lifestyle.

At the same time that the deliberations were taking place in the United States, this matter was being taken up in liberal and progressive Jewish movements throughout the world. In England, for example, the Reform Synagogues of Great Britain published a booklet following a process of study over three years by a group of Reform rabbis and lay leaders. The booklet explained that homosexuality was not a perverse choice and stressed the profound distinction between those who refuse to fulfill their traditional obligations, and those who are unable to do so. The study emphasized the special Jewish obligation towards oppressed minority groups and called for the welcoming of homosexuals in the community.

The Rabbinic Conference of the Union of Liberal & Progressive Synagogues, also in England, has published a position paper on homosexuality, rejecting as morally wrong the harboring of prejudices of discrimination against homosexuals as a group, whether on the basis of an instinctive aversion of biblical teaching. The position paper sees such discrimination as violating Judaism's most fundamental ethical teachings.

Lastly, the Israel Council of Progressive Rabbis has also

formulated its position, rejecting the traditional labeling of homosexuality as an abomination, and expressing its belief in the homosexual's equal rights in society. At the same time the Council views homosexuality as an exceptional phenomenon which cannot be accepted as a norm, equivalent to heterosexuality which represents, in the form of the family unit, the sacred ideal of Jewish tradition. [UR.R.]

RESNICK, JUDITH (1950–1986), U.S. astronaut. Judith Resnick was born in Cleveland, Ohio, and raised in Akron. Her academic training was in electrical engineering and she earned a bachelor's degree from Carnegie-Mellon University and a doctorate from the University of Maryland (1977). Prior to her joining the NASA space flight training program in 1978, she had worked as a design engineer for RCA, as a biomedical engineer in the neurophysiology laboratory of the National Institutes of Health in Bethesda, Maryland (1974–1977), and as a senior systems engineer for the Xerox Corporation. Following her space flight training she worked on projects connected to Orbiter Discovery. She made her first space flight in June 1984 and was the second American woman in space. On that flight she and the five male members of the crew conducted a week-long scientific mission. On January 28, 1986, she was a member of the crew of the space shuttle Challenger which exploded almost immediately after the launch, killing all crew members. [ED.]

RICH, ADRIENNE (1929–), U.S. poet. Rich, who now identifies herself as a lesbian poet and often writes about the shared experiences of females and about historical women, began her career with tightly controlled poetry which brought her early recognition by critics and other poets. Her first book of verse, *A Change of World* (1951), was chosen by W. H. Auden for the Yale Younger Poets Award; a Guggenheim Fellowship followed (1952–53). *The Diamond Cutters and Other Poems* (1955) won the Ridgely Torrence Memorial Award of the Poetry Society of America. She was also awarded the National Institute of Arts and Letters Award for poetry (1960); another Guggenheim Fellowship (1961–62); and a Bollingen Foundation grant for translation of Dutch poetry (1962).

Rich married an economist, had three sons, and served as Phi Betta Kappa poet at William and Mary College, at Swarthmore College, and at Harvard College. After Rich and her family moved to New York City in 1966, she grew active in protests against the war in Vietnam. Rich's poetry became radicalized as well, moving away from the precise blank verse which had been her trademark to freer meters. *Leaflets* (1969) expressed her new conviction that the goal of poetry should be to illuminate the moment, rather than to be worked over for posterity.

In 1970 Rich's husband died and she became increasingly involved in the radical feminist movement. She won the Shelley Memorial Award of the Poetry Society of America in 1971 and served as the Fanny Hurst Visiting Professor of Creative Literature at Brandeis University in 1972–73. When she was awarded a National Book Award for her 1973 book of verse, *Diving into the Wreck*, she refused to accept the award as an individual, and instead accepted it in the name of all women. Her books of poetry include *Poems: Selected and New* (1975) and *A Wild Patience Has Taken Me This Far* (1981). [S.B.F.]

RICHTER, BURTON (1931–), U.S. physicist and Nobel prize winner. Born in New York, Richter received his doctorate from the Massachusetts Institute of Technology in 1956. In the same year he joined the department of Physics of Stanford University as a research associate and remaining with the department became assistant professor (1960), associate professor (1963), and full professor (1967). In 1979 he was appointed the Paul Pigott Professor of Physical Science.

Richter shared the 1976 Nobel Prize in physics with Samuel Ting of MIT for their discovery in 1974 — each working independently — of a new subatomic particle, called "psi" by Richter and "J" by Ting, three times heavier than the proton and with a life-span some 10,000 times longer than anticipated by theory at that time. This significant contribution in the field of elementary particles provided evidence for a fourth quark.

Bibliography: *Science* 194 (1976), 825; *Current Biography* (1977), 359–62. [ED.]

RIEGNER, GERHART (1911–), Jewish public figure. Born in Berlin and trained as a lawyer, from 1936 Riegner was associated with the World Jewish Congress: first as legal officer and then as director of the Geneva office (1939–48), as a member of the World Executive and as director of coordination (1959–64), as secretary-general (1965–83), and as co-chairman of the Governing Board from 1983. He was directly involved in virtually all major Jewish problems from the middle 1930s on.

As international chairman of the World University Service (1949–1955) and as president of the conference of non-governmental organizations in consultative status with the UN (1953–1955) and with Unesco (1956–1958), he established a wide network of international relations among the international leadership and became a leading specialist in this field.

The main features of his activities in the service of the Jewish people include: protection of Jewish rights in the League of Nations under the minorities treaties; decisive information and rescue activities and after World War II, when he was the first to uncover the plan of systematic extermination of the Jews by the Nazi government in August 1942; active involvement in important international conferences, such as the Paris Peace Conference and UN meetings, where he was influential in the shaping of the UN Universal Declaration of Human Rights; a pioneering role in interreligious consultations with the Catholic church (before, during and after Vatican Council II), the World Council of Churches, the Lutheran World Federation, the Orthodox churches, and the Anglican Communion; one of the founders and, from 1982 to 1984, chairman of IJCIC (International Jewish Committee for Interreligious Consultations), which was created in 1969 as a representative platform of the Jewish community in its relations with official church bodies. In 1992, the Vatican conferred on him a papal knighthood of the Order of St. Gregory.

Bibliography: *Christian Jewish Relations*, vol. 24, 1–2 (1991).
[JE.H.]

RIFKIND, MALCOLM (1946–), British Conservative cabinet minister. Rifkind was born in Edinburgh, the son of a credit draper of Lithuanian origin. He was educated locally and graduated with a degree in law from Edinburgh University where he was involved in politics, becoming chairman of the university Conservative Association in 1967. Called to the Bar in 1970 (he was later a Queen's Counsel), in the same year he was elected to Edinburgh Council and unsuccessfully contested the Parliamentary seat of Edinburgh Central. Elected to Parliament for Pentlands in 1974, he was appointed opposition front bench spokesman on Scottish Affairs in 1975. Having served on the Parliamentary committees dealing with foreign affairs, following the Conservative election victory in 1979 he served as minister for home affairs and the environment at the Scottish Office from 1979 to 1982 and Parliamentary undersecretary of state, Foreign and Commonwealth Office, 1983–86. In January 1986 he became the youngest member of the Cabinet and first Jewish secretary of state for Scotland. He held this office until he was appointed secretary of state for transport in 1990. In 1992 he became the first post-war Jewish secretary of state for defense since Emanuel *Shinwell.

Malcolm Rifkind is a participating member of the Edinburgh Jewish community. In public life he has consistently maintained an interest in the affairs of Israel. He opposed the visit of PLO officials to London in 1975 and was honorary secretary of the Parliamentary group of Conservative Friends of Israel 1976–79. [D.CE.]

ROTH, PHILIP (see **14**:330). Roth continues as one of the most brilliant but controversial writers of American Jewish fiction, capturing with wicked accuracy the behavior and foibles of American Jews. For over 10 years, much of Roth's fiction has been devoted to a description of the developing career of novelist Nathan Zuckerman, beginning with *The Ghost Writer* (1979) and continuing with *Zuckerman Unbound* (1981), *Anatomy Lesson* (1983), *Zuckerman Bound* (1985), and culminating in *The Counterlife* (1987).

Nathan Zuckerman is a man of hyperbolic contradictions. He longs for success — but he does not wish to be recognized and hounded by fans once his novels are successful. He behaves as an archetypical good boy to his family, then disobeys his father's orders and publishes fiction which puts his family in a bad light. He craves excitement and he craves quietude; he marries intellectual, stable women and then rejects them because they are intellectual and stable. He pursues sexual adventure but he bitterly resents critical response to his adventures. He writes ribald novels almost exclusively about Jews and cannot understand why the Jewish establishment reacts to him with vocal outrage.

In *The Counterlife*, Roth finally pulls his protagonist out of "the oepidal swamp" of preoccupation with sex and writing. Within the four parts of the novel, Roth plays with the alternative routes which life — and art — can follow. Areas which Roth has left fallow since the stories in *Goodbye Columbus* are picked up in *The Counterlife*, as Roth explores the meaning of contemporary Jewish experience. He articulates an updated argument between various forms of Diaspora and Israeli Judaism, makes them live and breathe and seem like counterlives indeed.

Additional books by Roth include: *Our Gang* (1971); *The Breast* (1972); *My Life As a Man* (1974); *The Great American Novel* (1973); *Reading Myself and Others* (1975); *The Professor of Desire* (1977); and *A Philip Roth Reader* (1981). [S.B.F.]

ROTHSCHILD, NATHANIEL CHARLES JACOB, LORD (1936–), banker and public figure. Born in London, Jacob Rothschild was educated at Eton and Oxford. He

Baron Nathaniel Charles Jacob Rothschild (Courtesy the National Gallery, London)

joined the family bank, N. M. Rothschild in 1964 and by his dynamism revived its fortunes. He left, however, in 1980 after conflict with its head, his cousin Evelyn de Rothschild, over Jacob's conduct of Rothschild Investment Trust. A series of mergers which he subsequently masterminded led to the creation of the influential financial institution Charterhouse J. Rothschild. Since 1971 he has been chairman of St. James's Place Capital (formerly J. Rothschild Holdings plc) and since 1980, chairman of Five Arrows Ltd.

His activity in public life has been focused on culture and the arts. From 1985 to 1991 he was chairman of the board of trustees of the National Gallery and in 1992 was appointed chairman of the new board of trustees of the National Heritage Memorial Fund. In the House of Lords he is independent. In 1992, the year of the opening of the Israeli Supreme Court building, a gift of Yad Hanadiv, the Rothschild family foundation, he was awarded an honorary Ph.D. from the Hebrew University of Jerusalem (1992) and was made an Honorary Fellow of the City of Jerusalem. In the same year he became president of the Institute of Jewish Affairs.

He succeeded his father as Baron Rothschild in 1990. [D.CE.]

ROULEAU, ERIC (Elie Rafoul; 1926–), journalist and diplomat. Rouleau was born in Cairo. From 1953 to 1960 he was an editor for the Middle East service of the Agence France Presse and from 1956 a reporter for *Le Monde*, writing a column on the Near and Middle East from 1960. In the 1970s he spent some time in the United States; in 1974 he was a research associate at the University of California and in 1978–1979 a research associate for the Council of Foreign Affairs in New York and a lecturer at Princeton University. In 1983 he became an adviser to the Television Française 1.

Rouleau is a noted journalist whose recognized expertise is in the areas of the Arab world and Middle Eastern subjects. He has links to excellent sources in Arab countries, particularly in the radical ones. During the course of his career he has interviewed almost all leaders in the Middle East since the 1950s. In 1985 French president Mitterrand appointed him ambassador to Tunisia, but he was forced to resign after a little over a year's service because of opposition to him by the Tunisian government which considered him to be associated with the opposition and the PLO. He was then made a roving ambassador by President Mitterrand.

He has published: *Le Troisième combat* (1967), in collaboration with J. Lacouture and O. F. Held, *Biographie de Kurt Waldheim* (1977), *Entretien avec Abu Iyad* (1979), and *Etude sur les Palestiniens* (1984). [GI.KO.]

RUBENS, BERNICE (1927–), English novelist, film writer, and director. Born in Cardiff, Rubens was educated at University College, South Wales. She taught English and since 1950 has worked as a documentary film writer and director. Her first novel, *Set on Edge*, was published in 1960. She has also published two plays, *Third Party* (1972), and *I Sent a Letter to My Love* (1979) which is based on her novel of the same title.

Rubens first novels, *Set on Edge* (1960), *Madame Sousatzka* (1962), *Mate in Three* (1965), and *The Elected Member* (1969), are all extreme fictional versions of the author's Cardiff Jewish childhood. She has been described as a "chronicler of the frayed edge of middle-class Jewish life." In particular, the question of destructive familial expectations is a central motif in Rubens' early fiction. *Spring Sonata* (1979) addresses this theme from the startling viewpoint of an unborn child and *I Sent a Letter to My Love* (1975) is a Welsh version of this theme.

Rubens' fiction is concerned with marginal characters whose personality is often on the point of breakdown. Representative examples of this preoccupation are *The Elected Member*, her Booker Prize winning novel, *A Five Year Sen-*

tence (1978), *Sunday Best* (1980), a journal of transvestite, and *Mr. Wakefield's Crusade* (1985). For the most part, Rubens avoids a gloomy pessimism — inherent in her subject matter — by dotting her fiction with welcome black humor. In recent years, she has reverted to an exclusively Jewish environment with the publication of *Brothers* (1983), an ambitious Jewish family saga. Above all, Rubens' fiction evoked with considerable power the dark underside of what passes for normal human behavior. In this way, she has challenged the cosy reality of mainstream Anglo-Jewish fiction.

Bibliography: J. Vinson (ed.), *Contemporary Novelists* (1982), 566; *The Jewish Quarterly*, 21, 1–2 (1973). [B.C.]

RUMANIA (ROMANIA: see **14**:386; **Dc./17**:531). **General.** In the decade 1983–1992 the central development in Romanian life and especially in the life of the ever-dwindling Jewish community was the overthrow of the Communist regime and the attempts at introducing democracy into the country along Western lines. The change of rule did not bring in its wake any real changes in the life of the few Jews left in the country.

Over the past decade Jewish life throughout Romania continued to revolve around the synagogues and the *kasher* restaurants, operated by the Federation of Romanian Jewish Communities and funded by the Joint Distribution Committee. The dominating figure in Jewish life has continued to be, Chief Rabbi Moses Rosen, now in his eighties.

Demography and Aliyah. Since the establishment of the State of Israel some 300,000 Romanian Jews have emigrated there. The more the number of Jews in Romania shrinks, the more difficult it is to obtain reliable current Jewish population figures. The Federation of Communities, whose numbers are used by the Joint, estimate that there is a total of 15,000 Jews, 8,000 of whom are in Bucharest, the capital. Timisoara (in Transylvania) and Jassy each has a community of some 900 people; all the others are scattered among a Romanian populace of 22 million people. The official 1992 government yearbook, citing statistical data from a kind of census, states that there are 9,000 Jews. It may be that not all Jews were counted or admitted to being Jewish, particularly those in mixed marriages.

After the death in 1986 of Rabbi I. M. Marilus, the *dayyan* of Bucharest, only two rabbis remained in Romania: Chief Rabbi Dr. Rosen, who is also the president of the Federation of Communities, and Dr. Ernest Neuman of Timisoara. The aging of the leadership as well as the emigration of a few of the leaders to Israel has thinned out their ranks, and Rabbi Rosen had to fill some positions with people who in the past were active in the communist regime and even in the Ministry of Religion, whose function was to oppress religions rather than encourage them.

Sighet, Romania, April 1991: The former home of Elie Wiesel, which the government said would be turned into a museum (Photo Ruth E. Gruber, Rome)

Summer 1992 meeting of Romanian Jewish community leaders: from right to left, Rabbi A. Ehrenfeld of Israel; Rabbi E. Neuman of Timisoara; Chief M. Rabbi Rosen; Mrs. Rosen; Mr. T. Blumenfeld, general director of the Federation of Communities (Courtesy Naftali Kraus, Tel Aviv)

Anti-Semitism and Zionism. In 1992, as part of his effort to reinforce religious leadership, Rabbi Rosen recruited Rabbi Dr. Asher (Georg) Ehrenfeld, a former Israeli army chaplain, to serve as the chief rabbi's deputy and assistant in Bucharest. Ehrenfeld spent about a year in Romania substituting for Rabbi Rosen during his long absences from the country.

The remnants of the Romanian Jewish community welcomed the overthrow of Ceasescu and the community journal published a special issue expressing joy at the change. In the new spirit of freedom Rabbi Rosen was the object of personal attacks by anti-Semitic groups, which accused him of close cooperation with the communist regime. Two anti-Semitic newspapers waged this campaign, which the chief rabbi saw as an attack on the entire community. *Romania Mare* ("Great Romania") and *Europa*, are weeklies publishing virulent anti-Semitic material, aiming their barbs personally at Rabbi Rosen. In 1992 Paul Everac, director of public television, published a book which also contained anti-Semitic material. He claimed, among other things, that the Jews of Romania control everything and that they number more than 30,000 (over double the real figure). Complaints lodged by Rabbi Rosen were rejected on the grounds that they were not of public interest. Rabbi Rosen managed to secure the dismissal of the anti-Semitic attorney general, Cherecheanu.

Some observers have felt that the chief rabbi has exaggerated his cries against anti-Semitism; there have been no physical attacks on Jews, aside from an attempted break-in and robbery at the Ploesti synagogue in June 1992 in which windows were broken and a *parokhet* torn (police in the district claimed that churches in the area had been similarly broken into), and incitement against Jews has not gone beyond the bounds accepted under Ceasescu. They claim that the outcry by Rabbi Rosen has itself fanned the flame of anti-Semitism. Some saw this as the reason for Rabbi Ehrenfeld's leaving his post at the end of a year, while others were convinced that the authorities hinted that he was *non grata* because of his originating in Oradea; he speaks fluent Hungarian and previously served as the rabbi of Debrecen, Hungary. Considering the ethnic tension between Hungary and Romania, this is a likely reason.

There is no Zionism in Romania in the commonly accepted meaning. In the early 1990 attempts were made to organize a branch of the Maccabi sport organization and after the overthrow of Ceasescu, a Romania-Israel Friendship League was established, led by the writer Victor Berlianu. The Jewish Agency emissary in Romania, Tova

Ben-Nun, deals with arrangements for *aliyah*; there are no Zionist youth organizations and Romania is the only country in Eastern Europe — at least in the past few years — which sends no representative to participate in the International Bible Contest for Jewish Youth, held on Independence Day in Jerusalem.

The President in the Great Synagogue. In order to quash the harsh complaints about active anti-Semitism, President Iliescu has invested effort, internally and externally, to placate Chief Rabbi Rosen. In 1993 he took the rabbi with him to the opening of the Holocaust Museum in Washington, D.C., and before that participated in a memorial service for Holocaust victims held in the Bucharest Choral Synagogue, where Iliescu spoke and condemned anti-Semitism.

This seemed to put a stop to the decline in the status of the chief rabbi, who for many over the past 40 years — and to a certain extent correctly — symbolized Romanian Jewry. However, the rabbi's repeated efforts to exploit his international connections in order to insure for Romania a most-favored-nation standing from the U.S. for foreign trade have led nowhere.

The Joint's Rearguard Action. Upon the emigration to Israel of Rabbi Wasserman of Dorhoi, the home for the aged and the *kasher* restaurant there were closed. Otherwise, all the institutions, restaurants, and homes for the aged are still in operation — 10 restaurants and 4 homes (2 in Bucharest, and 2 smaller ones in Arad and Timisoara). Needy Jews receive packages of food and clothing. All this activity is financed by the JDC, fighting a rearguard action to maintain the few remaining Romanian Jews. The situation of the elderly has worsened considerably as their pension's value has eroded to nothing because of inflation, and without the Joint's help they would be starving. The Joint did curtail its budget for Romania with the decline in Jewish population but still finances the ritual slaughterers (three remain), and is prepared to pay the salary for a rabbi if Rabbi Rosen finds a replacement for Rabbi Ehrenfeld. The biweekly paper *Revista*, edited by Chaim Riemer, still appears in four languages. A selection of sermons by Rabbi Rosen has appeared and work is progressing on a book of testimonies which will document the Holocaust of Romanian Jewry.

In an attempt to bring a fresh spirit to the leadership of the communities, Osias Lazar was appointed head of the Bucharest community, while elderly Theodore (Tuvia) Blumenfeld continues to serve as the general secretary of the Federation of Communities. The federation is actually directed by Rabbi Rosen's adviser and confidant, Julian Sorin. Sorin was previously a senior official in the communist Ministry of Religions.

Since Ceasescu's overthrow, a few communities in the provinces — and especially in Transylvania — have tried "to declare independence"; to establish links with other countries and mainly with emigrés from those communities now living in Israel, and even to sell property, without the Federation's approval, an act that was unthinkable during the centralized communist regime. This has created tension between the communities and the chief rabbi, with repercussions even reaching Israel.

Jewish education is almost non-existent. A third of the Jews, whose very number is indeterminate, are involved in mixed marriages, and the majority of the community consists of elderly people whose children and grandchildren live in Israel. Choirs and *talmudei Torah* outside of Bucharest are dwindling along with the Jewish population. Bucharest has been able to maintain its successful choir and a *Talmud Torah* which dozens of children attend on Sundays.

Romania lost its special status regarding relations with Israel, since it is no longer the only Eastern bloc country to have diplomatic relations with the Jewish state. Relations continued to be normal and friendly, with efforts at increasing bilateral trade for which Romania does not have much to offer. Israeli tourism to Romania dropped off. [N.KR.]

RUSSIA (see **14**:433; **Dc./17**:533). **Demography.** In the 1980s the annual decrease in the population among Soviet Jewry reached 2.2%. The Soviet census of January 1989 recorded 1,450,511 people who identified themselves as Jews; this was a decline of 19.9% from the figure of 1,810,876 in 1979. The Jewish population declined sharply in all of the union republics (see Table 1); in Moscow from 223,100 to 175,700. Overall, the percentage of Jews in the Soviet population declined from 0.69% in 1979 to 0.5% in 1989, when 41.5% of Soviet Jewry were residents of Moscow, Leningrad, or the capitals of the union republics.

Soviet Jewry represents an extreme example of an aging, demographically dying, assimilating community. In 1988–89 the birthrate of Jewish mothers was 7.3 per 1,000 Jews (6.3 in the RSFSR). The birthrate in homogenous Jewish families (i.e., where both parents were Jewish) was 4.3 per 1,000 Jews (2.6 in the RSFSR). Fertility of Jewish women in the U.S.S.R. did not exceed 1.6 children per woman. At the same time mortality was high, with 21.3 deaths per 1,000 Jews (the corresponding figure for the RFSFR was 24.4).

The median age of Jews in the U.S.S.R. in 1989 was 49.7 and in Russia it was 52.3. (For comparison, in 1990 the median age of Jews in Israel was 28.4, of Jews in the United States — 37.3, and of the total Soviet population in 1989 — 30.7.) The percentage of aged people (60+) among the Jews of Moscow in 1989 was 39.6%, while that of aged people among the general population in the city was 18.2%. Children up to age 5 made up only 3% of the Jewish population of Moscow while the same age group made up 8% of the general population.

The percentage of mixed marriages among all marriages involving Soviet Jews in 1988 was 58.3% for Jewish men and 47.6% for Jewish women. The same indicators for the RSFSR were 73.2% and 62.8%, respectively. The vast majority of children of mixed marriage who were under 18 were not registered as Jews in the 1979 census. In the U.S.S.R. this involved 90.9% of those children with a Jewish father and a non-Jewish mother; 95.3% of the children with a Jewish mother and a non-Jewish father (for Russia the percentages were 93.9 and 95.5, respectively). The mass emigration of the last few years (see "Emigration and *Aliyah*") has only accelerated the already advanced process of the erosion of Soviet Jewry.

The smaller sub-ethnic Jewish groups largely maintained

Table 1. Distribution of Jewish Population by Union Republic, according to the Censuses of 1979 and 1989, and Estimates for the End of 1991 (in thousands)

Republic	1979 Census	1989 Census	1991 (Estimate for year end)
RSFSR	700.7	551.0	430.0
Ukraine	634.2	487.3	325.0
Belorussia	135.4	112.0	58.0
Uzbekistan	99.9	94.9	55.5
Moldavia	80.1	65.8	28.5
Azerbaijan	35.5	30.8	16.0
Latvia	28.3	22.9	15.8
Georgia	28.3	24.8	20.7
Kazakhstan	23.5	19.9	15.3
Lithuania	14.7	12.4	7.3
Tadzhikistan	14.7	14.8	8.2
Kirghizia	6.9	6.0	3.9
Estonia	5.0	4.6	3.5
Turkmenia	2.8	2.5	2.0
Armenia	1.0	0.7	0.3

Purim party in a Moscow kindergarten in the 1980s (Courtesy the Soviet Jewry Information Center, Jerusalem)

their knowledge of their native languages. The percentage of Ashkenazi Jews with a knowledge of Yiddish may well be even lower than the official 11.1% since the declaration by a Soviet Jew of a Jewish language as his native tongue is often a demonstration of national feelings rather than an indication of a real command of the language.

With the breakup of the U.S.S.R. toward the end of 1991, Soviet Jewry as such disappeared. At the end of that year the number of Jews living in territory of the former Soviet Union was estimated as 990,000, of whom the majority (430,000) lived in Russia. Russian Jewry now no longer constitutes the third largest Jewish community in the world. As of 1992 over half a million Russian-speaking Jews live in Israel.

The Last Years of Stagnation, 1983-1986. OFFICIAL POLICY. A sharp change in Soviet emigration policy in the period 1979–1981 led to the formation of a large group of "refuseniks," i.e., people who were refused permission to emigrate. Reasons given for refusal were often far-fetched pretexts of local OVIR (visa) offices caught between a flood of requests for exit visas and a sharply reduced quota of permits allowed by Moscow. No judicial procedure existed for appealing OVIR decisions. In the early 1980s, the number of refuseniks in the whole country numbered tens of thousand. Besides many had their emigration documents rejected even for consideration by OVIR while others who had an invitation from Israel did not submit their applications due to their conviction that such an attempt would be useless. A whole generation of Soviet Jews grew up "in refusal," including thousands of highly qualified professionals whose careers were irretrievably harmed when they were banned from working in their fields after applying to emigrate. By 1987 refuseniks had become a dominant factor in Soviet Jewish life, a major force for unity among international Jewish organizations, and an important element in Soviet-Western relations.

Table 2. Distribution of Soviet Jews by Sub-Ethnic Groups and Language, according to the Results of the 1989 Census

Sub-ethnic group of Soviet Jews	Population of Group	Consider language of group native tongue (%)
Ashkenazi	1,378,344	11.1
Mountain Jews	18,513	75.8
Georgian Jews	16,054	90.9
Bukharan Jews	36,152	65.1
Krimchaks	1,448	38.9

The Soviet authorities proclaimed that "neither anti-Semitism nor Zionism" would be allowed, suggesting that Soviet Jews forget about emigration and return to "normal" Soviet life. Sometimes refuseniks were even promised that they would be given back their former posts in return for a written statement that they would abandon any idea of emigrating. In fact, anti-Semitism did not decrease; discrimination was manifested against the Jews, as a potentially disloyal part of the population, in regard to acceptance into institutions of higher education, job promotion, and the awarding of prestigious positions, in awarding scientific degrees, etc. In 1980/1981, 3% of Soviet Jews had been studying in institutions of higher education, in 1984/1985 the percentage dropped to 2.6. Between 1982 and 1987 the number of Jews among scientific workers declined from 63,000 to 58,600 and among those with Candidate of Science degrees from 25,800 to 25,200. In the 1980s, in general, there was a relative decline of the status of Jews in Soviet society.

At the same time a campaign gathered momentum against everything connected with Israel, Zionism, Jewish history, Judaism, and Jewish culture. On April 21, 1983, the Soviet Public Anti-Zionist Committee, an ostensibly voluntary organization headed by General David Dragunskii, was established. A group of privileged writers who made a speci-

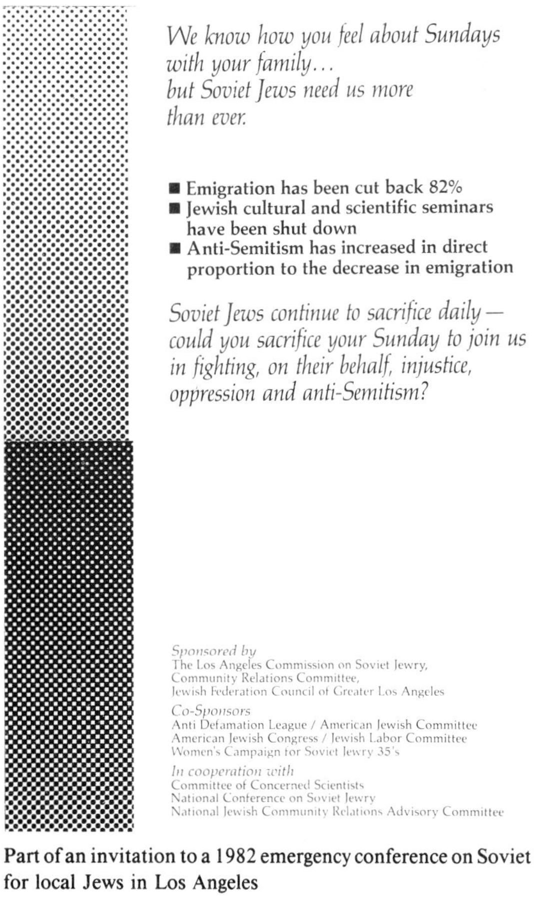
We know how you feel about Sundays with your family...
but Soviet Jews need us more than ever.
■ Emigration has been cut back 82%
■ Jewish cultural and scientific seminars have been shut down
■ Anti-Semitism has increased in direct proportion to the decrease in emigration
Soviet Jews continue to sacrifice daily—could you sacrifice your Sunday to join us in fighting, on their behalf, injustice, oppression and anti-Semitism?
Sponsored by
The Los Angeles Commission on Soviet Jewry,
Community Relations Committee,
Jewish Federation Council of Greater Los Angeles
Co-Sponsors
Anti Defamation League / American Jewish Committee
American Jewish Congress / Jewish Labor Committee
Women's Campaign for Soviet Jewry 35's
In cooperation with
Committee of Concerned Scientists
National Conference on Soviet Jewry
National Jewish Community Relations Advisory Committee

Part of an invitation to a 1982 emergency conference on Soviet Jewry for local Jews in Los Angeles

"Refuseniks" in a Leningrad apartment, from left to right: Daniel Elman, Iosef Radomyselsky, Mikhael Elmlan. (*Jerusalem Post* Archive; photo David Frishman)

ality of "anti-Zionism" emerged at this time; they included: Iurii Ivanov, Lev Korneev, Caesar Solodar, Lionel Dadiani, Evgenii Evseev, and Vladimir Begun. Their works were circulated throughout the country in hundred of thousands of copies. An overtly racist approach characterized the "anti-Zionst" ideology. Soon there was a revival of the notorious myths and libels propagated in the past against the Jews by the Tsarist Black Hundreds and by Nazi propaganda: the myth of the "Judeo-Masonic conspiracy," *The Protocols of the Elders of Zion*, and even the blood libel.

Public criticism of this "anti-Zionism" was not permitted. Thus, the attempt of the Leningrad philologist Ivan Martynov to sue Korneev for libel was turned into judicial persecution of Martynov himself. In the summer of 1986 the book *On the Class Essence of Zionism*, which purported to be a historiographic survey of "anti-Zionist" literature in the previous two decades, was published. Its author, Alexander Romanenko, denied the very existence of the Jewish nation, of any Jewish language (either Hebrew or Yiddish), and of Jewish culture. He justified the pre-revolutionary pogroms as a manifestation of the class struggle against the Jewish bourgeoisie. The Zionists were also blamed for the Holocaust! According to Romanenko, the Zionists were more dangerous than the Nazis since they had succeeded in defeating the latter and then proceeded, by blackmail and threats, in totally bankrupting the Federal Republic of Germany by forcing it to pay reparations to Israel. This fantastic ideology was regularly foisted off on the Soviet population at Party and trade union meetings, on television, and in the press.

The Jews were also being assigned a demonic role in Russian history, for example, in the vulgar historical novels of Valentin Pikul. A special place in this demonology was reserved for Leon Trotsky, who was depicted (for example, in the novel *Petrograd-Brest* [-Liltovsk] by I. Shamiakin) as a symbol of Russia's enemies and described in terms of an anti-Jewish caricature.

One of the aims of the anti-Zionist campaign was to discredit the idea of emigration and to intimidate activists in the growing Jewish national movement in the country. However, despite the jamming of foreign radio stations, a relatively realistic picture of life beyond the "iron curtain" reached Soviet Jews via letters from the thousands of relatives and friends who had already emigrated. This encouraged them to continue the struggle to emigrate.

In an effort to put an end to the refusenik phenomenon, the authorities initially allowed some of the leaders to emigrate. This tactic backfired by increasing the number of activists. Then repression became the order of the day. Special KGB groups were assigned to monitor Jewish activity. They bugged telephone conversations, opened letters, infiltrated informers among the refuseniks, intimidated activists and their families, arranged for some people to be fired from their jobs and for others to be beaten up, and so on. All forms of independent Jewish cultural and public activity were persecuted, including the teaching of Hebrew, the publishing of *samizdat* journals, the organization of kindergartens, the performance of *purimshpils* (often satirical Purim plays) in private apartments, or public meetings to commemorate the Holocaust. There were frequent searches of apartments and jailings of activists on fabricated charges of anti-Soviet activity and propaganda, slander of the Soviet state, and on trumped-up criminal charges, such as possession of narcotics. Sometimes the people arrested were beaten. Occasionally, activists were placed in special psychiatric hospitals. Yet there was a limit to the persecution: mass arrests were not resorted to. The number of Jewish activists imprisoned at one time between 1983 and 1986 amounted to about 15, probably representing the quota decided upon by the central authorities. It appeared that the government wanted to maintain a certain low level of Jewish activity with an eye toward negotiations with the West while the KGB was interested in the continuity of such activity in order to justify the existence of their "anti-Zionist" cadres.

In response to the continued accusations from abroad that they were persecuting Jewish culture in the U.S.S.R., the Soviet authorities did sponsor some Jewish cultural enterprises of their choice. A number of these took place far from the large Jewish population centers, in the so-called Jewish autonomous Oblast (province) of Birobidzhan, the 50th anniversary of which was celebrated in 1984. In 1982 a Yiddish textbook was published there in a miniscule print run and permission was granted for an optional course in Yiddish at one of the schools in the province. At the same time several propaganda booklets were published describing the alleged flourishing of Jewish culture in Birobidzhan. In Lithuania several prose works of Grigorii Kanovich were published on Jewish themes. In 1984 a Russian-Jewish [Yiddish] Dictionary was published in Moscow and an evening celebrating the 125th anniversary of the birth of Sholem Aleichem was held at the Union of Soviet Writers.

In March 1985, General Secretary of the Central Committee of the Communist Party of the Soviet Union Mikhail Gorbachev proclaimed *perestroika*, which originally did not envision any change in official Jewish policy. As late as October 1986 Soviet jails still held 13 Jewish activists, five of whom (Roald Zelichenok, Leonid [Arye] Volvovskii, Evgenii Koifman, Vladimir Lifshits, and Aleksei Magarik) were arrested under Gorbachev. However, to succeed in their intended reforms, the Soviet leadership came to realize that they desperately needed foreign policy successes and economic aid from the West, which increasingly were seen to depend on a liberalization of their policy toward Soviet Jewry.

THE REFUSENIK COMMUNITY. From the early 1980s Soviet Jews found themselves in a hopeless situation. Their social status continued to decline; anti-Semitism prevented them from fully assimilating; almost all expressions of Jewish life were banned; and at the same time permission to emigrate was denied. The response to this situation was the growth of illegal, independent Jewish cultural activity, which was almost completely centered around the refuseniks. The first stirrings of public and cultural activity were felt among the *aliyah* activists in the 1970s. However, only the long period of hiatus in emigration allowed the Jewish movement the opportunity to attain an unprecedented breadth, stability, and continuity of leadership. Often, the veteran refuseniks best known in the West, particularly those who had been imprisoned, ceased playing a leading role but became symbols of the struggle and spokesmen of the movement to the foreign media. New less-known enthusiasts assumed an active role in the organizational, political, and cultural spheres. Veteran leaders, who returned to an active role after being released from prison, could be re-arrested again. Thus, in November 1982, Iosif Begun was imprisoned for the third time.

During their years of "refusal" activists gained experience and knowledge, proved their mettle in confrontations with the authorities, and established contacts with comrades in other communities. They also amassed an unprecedented amount of Jewish cultural materials such as books, textbooks, and religious objects. Interested Jews were able to attend underground classes in Hebrew, Jewish culture, history, and religion, and to enjoy Jewish dramatic productions in private homes. There were activities for children as well. Channels were established for exchanges of information with Israel and the organizations for the rights of Soviet Jewry operating in the West. Thus, any persecution of refuseniks soon became known throughout the world. Those who were arrested (and their families) gained effective legal, medical, and material aid, as well as moral support. Jailed *aliyah* activists, referred to as "prisoners of Zion," knew that they were not abandoned; this often gave them the strength to avoid mental breakdowns and public recantations. Their sense of community helped refuseniks to compensate for the infringement of their rights and their pariah status.

Hebrew teaching occupied a key role in the Jewish movement. Moscow was the center of Hebrew instruction where long-range programs were elaborated, accelerated teacher training organized for teachers from other locations, and teaching materials reproduced and disseminated. Iulii Kosharovskii was one of the main organizers of the teaching network. Teachers of Hebrew, who received special support for their efforts from Israel, became a main target for persecution; they constituted about half the prisoners of Zion. In Moscow alone, the Hebrew teachers Alexander Kholmianskii, Iulii Edelshtein, Leonid Volvovskii, and Aleksei Magarik were arrested between 1984 and 1986.

In Leningrad, starting in late 1979, the center for the Jewish movement was the historical and cultural seminars headed by Grigorii Kanovich (not to be confused with the Lithuanian writer) and Lev Utevskii. In an attempt to halt the seminars, the authorities gave permission for both leaders to emigrate. At the same time a series of round-ups of participants in the seminars took place. Activist Evgenii Lein was arrested in May 1981. After a year-long struggle to maintain the seminars, which had been open to all interested parties, the seminars succumbed. However, a group made up of amateur Jewish historians survived for five more years. Works by members of this group were published in *Leningradskii evreiskii almanakh* (see "The Jewish Press"). An attempt in 1985 to renew popular lectures on Jewish culture in Leningrad ended with the arrest of the organizers, Roald Zelichenok and Vladimir Lifshits.

In contrast to Leningrad, where Jewish history was practically exclusively the domain of refuseniks, Moscow was the site of some permitted Jewish scholarship headed by the professional ethnographers Mikhail Chlenov and Igor Krupnik. In January 1982 there was an announcement of the formation, in conjunction with the journal *Sovetish Heymland*, of a Jewish Historical and Ethnographic Commission. The members of the commission hoped to be able to publish their research without interference. However, the ban on almost everything Jewish often compelled the scholars to restrict themselves to peripheral topics of little social relevance, such as the derivation of Jewish family names and descriptions of small sub-ethnic Jewish groups in the Soviet Union.

The celebration of traditional Jewish holidays and Israel's Independence Day became a widespread expression of national solidarity. In a number of cities Purim was the occasion for the private performance of *purimshpils*, where sharp criticism of the authorities was often presented in disguised form. It is not surprising that the latter activity was particularly subject to government repression.

Demonstration against anti-Semitism in the Leningrad Jewish cemetery, 1987 (Courtesy Beth Hatefutsoth, Tel Aviv; photo Leonid Kelbert)

Another indicator of the growth of national consciousness among Soviet Jews was the public meetings commemorating the mass murder of Jews during World War II. Such meetings were held in Riga at Rumbula forest, in Vilnius at Ponari, in Kiev at Babi Yar, and in Leningrad at the Jewish Preobrazhenskii Cemetery.

The 1980s saw an increased interest in Orthodox Judaism, which had been among the most slandered and persecuted of all the religions in the U.S.S.R. In the course of previous decades, Jewish religious education had suffered particularly. Only a handful of rabbis, *mohalim* (circumcisors), and *shoḥetim* (ritual slaughterers who provided *kasher* meat) were in the whole U.S.S.R. There was no way, either legally or practically, that such knowledgeable Jews could be replaced. Simple Jews who know how to pray were a dying breed. Often Jewish intellectuals who were God-seekers turned to the Russian-Orthodox religion due to their lack of familiarity with their own roots.

In the 1980s in Moscow, Leningrad, and subsequently in other places, informal groups of young people who wanted to study Torah and Jewish tradition were established. Some of the participants became *ḥozrim bi-teshuvah* or "returners to religion." The original impetus for this religious revival was Zionist activity among the refuseniks, which first brought Jews together and provided them with basic knowledge, particularly of Hebrew, without which a mastery of the tradition is hardly possible. The Jewish religious awakening was made possible materially due to the fact that some of the aid from abroad to refuseniks included religious literature, religious objects, and *kasher* food. In the mid-1980s there were up to 2,000 newly observant Orthodox Jews, half of whom resided in Moscow and one-fifth in Leningrad. Despite its relatively small core, the religious community had some impact on a broader range of Jews and even led to the conversion to Judaism of some non-Jews, a unique phenomenon in Soviet history. The religious stream within the total Jewish movement among Soviet Jewry was diminished in 1986-1987 with the emigration of a large segment of the newly religious Jews, including their young leadership.

The religious groups were basically divided into Ḥabad, Agudat Israel, and religious Zionists. In Moscow religious activity originally centered around Vladimir Shakhnovskii, Mikhail Nudler, and Eliahu Essas (Agudat Israel), Mikhail Shnaider and Grigorii Rozenshtein (Ḥabad), and Vladislav Dasheskii, Pinkhas Polonskii, Mikhail Karaevano, and

A typical demonstration on behalf of Soviet Jewry: a 1985 gathering in Montevideo, Uruguay, outside the Soviet embassy (Courtesy the Comite Central Israelita del Uruguay, Montevideo)

Kholmianskii (the religious Zionists). Leningrad with the religious leaders Itzhak Kogan (Ḥabad) and Grigorii Vasserman (Agudat Israel) lacked the religious Zionist orientation.

Although the Jewish movement in the 1980s included in its ranks only several thousand people, in the atmosphere of fear that dominated the Soviet Union at that time, it was virtually the only mass opposition movement in the country. It was not exclusively Zionist. Participation in illegal Jewish activity during their years of refusal, however, increased activists' national consciousness and instilled in many the desire to go straight to Israel as soon as they were free to leave. Many activists after their emigration joined Jewish organizations in Israel and the West (especially in the U.S.), and continued to study and teach Jewish history, Hebrew, and the Jewish religion. A number of books written in refusal have now been published (mostly in Israel). Among them are *Ivrit* ("Hebrew") by Leonid Zeilinger; *Sinagoga-razgromlennaia no nepokorennaia* ("The Synagogue — shattered but unconquered") by Semen Iantovskii (book appeared under the pseudonym of Israel Taiar); *Evrei v Peterburge* (*The Jews of St. Petersburg* [published in Russian and in English]) by Mikhail Beizer; *Delo Dreifusa* ("The Dreyfus Case") by Leonid Praisman; and *Ani Maamin (Ia veriu)* ("I Believe") by Mikhail Shnaider and Grigorii Rozenshtein.

THE STRUGGLE FOR SOVIET JEWRY. The Soviet Jewry movement would never have become an international issue had it not been for support from abroad. The following factors were involved in the struggle in the West: Israel's interest in mass immigration, which reflected both Zionist ideology and Israel's demographic problem; the desire of Western, especially American, Jewish leaders to rally Diaspora Jewry around a goal of importance for the whole Jewish people; the tendency of the American administration to utilize "human rights" and, particularly, the struggle of Soviet Jews for the right to emigrate, as a basic weapon in its ideological confrontation with Communism.

Special organizations were established in the West for the struggle for Soviet Jewry. These included the National Conference on Soviet Jewry, the Student Struggle for Soviet Jewry, the Union of Councils for Soviet Jewry, in the United States, and in Britain the Committee of 35. The organizing center in Israel was the Liaison Bureau for Soviet Jewry of the Foreign Ministry. The Bureau collected information about Soviet Jews, sent them literature and material aid, organized support from the Jewish and international press, and, on occasion, coordinated international protest campaigns in defense of prisoners of Zion and the right of emigration for Soviet Jews. Most aid from the Bureau was given to those refuseniks, especially teachers of Hebrew, who aspired to *aliyah*. Israel regularly provided up-to-date information about emigration statistics, the level of state anti-Semitism, persecution of Hebrew, and the suffering of prisoners of Zion to both Jewish and non-Jewish organizations active in the struggle, as well as to political and social figures. Hundreds of foreign tourists who visited Moscow, Leningrad, and other open cities in the U.S.S.R. were in fact voluntary emissaries of international Jewish organizations or, sometimes, Israeli citizens with dual nationality sent by the Liaison Bureau, to bring in books, *kasher* food, clothing, and other goods, to provide moral support, to give lectures on Jewish history, to share Sabbaths and holidays with their fellow Jews, and to bring back to the West fresh information, texts of protests and appeals, along with various requests for the refuseniks.

The tourists who made contact with Soviet Jewry were often halted by the authorities, searched, subjected to harassment and intimidation, and expelled from the country before the end of their visit; sometimes they were beaten by KGB agents. The Soviet authorities prevented former Israel president Ephraim Katzir, who was visiting the U.S.S.R. as part of a scientific delegation, from meeting with refuseniks. However, even during the most difficult times, the flow of visitors did not cease.

The Public Council for Soviet Jewry (headed by Avraham Harman) supported by the Israel government was founded in 1970. In the 1980s a kind of rival to the council, the Soviet Jewry Education and Information Center (headed by the former refusenik and prisoner of Zion Yosef Mendelevich), was established in affiliation with the American union of Councils. It favored a strategy of public protest while the more moderate national Conference and the Israeli Liaison Bureau pursued a policy of quiet diplomacy.

Due to the efforts of Jewish organizations, the question of the rights of Soviet Jewry gained exposure in parliamentary discussions and in election campaigns in Western democracies. The issue was increasingly raised during intergovernmental contacts with the Soviet government and in the mid-1980s became a focus of demands made on the Soviet Union. In the American congress speeches were often to be heard about refuseniks and prisoners of Zion such as Anatoly Shcharansky, Iosif Begun, and Ida Nudel. When visiting the U.S.S.R., many senators and congressmen met with Jewish activists. U.S. president Reagan and British prime minister Thatcher spoke out in support of the struggle for

Israeli efforts on behalf of refuseniks included Russian immigrants and Israelis, 1986; above, l. to r., Yosef Mendelevich, Vladimir Brodsky, Likkud MK Moshe Arens, Anatoly Shcharansky, and Alignment MK Dedi Zucker. (Courtesy the Soviet Jewry Information Center, Jerusalem)

Soviet Jewry and the issue was also raised in the European Parliament. The International Association of Lawyers encouraged legal experts to provide aid to persecuted and arrested Jews. The situation of individual Soviet Jews was taken up by professional associations in the West, particularly the international scientists' committee which took up the cause of refusenik scientists, including Victor Brailovskii, Alexander Paritskii, and Yurii Tarnopolskii. In New York mass marches and public meetings, which attracted up to 100,000 people, began in 1982.

The well-known British historian Martin Gilbert visited Moscow and Leningrad in 1983 and interviewed a number of leading refuseniks. Although some of the material he collected was confiscated by customs authorities when he was leaving, one year later he published The *Jews of Hope*, which due to his fresh eye-witness point of view and the author's reputation, had considerable influence in mobilizing public support for Soviet Jewry in English-speaking countries and Israel (where the book appeared in Hebrew).

A key event in the struggle was the Third World Conference for Soviet Jewry held in March 1983. The preceding conferences were held in Brussels in 1971 and 1976. The choice of Jerusalem as the location for the third one signified the central role of Israel in the struggle.

Originally the Israel government had preferred to remain in the background so that the issue of Soviet Jewry would be seen not as a parochial problem but as a universal issue of the violation of human rights. Not wishing to complicate the already difficult position of Jewish activists in the U.S.S.R., Israel avoided criticizing the Soviet Union on issues unconnected with Jewish concerns. Tourists sent to the U.S.S.R. by the Liaison Bureau were forbidden to say that they were from Israel and told to travel on second passports. Although following these instructions made the visits less dangerous for the emissaries, this practice gave some Soviet Jewish activists the false impression that they were of more concern to their Western brothers than to the Israelis.

The inclusion of the issue of Soviet Jewry in the agenda of the American-Soviet summit conference in Reykjavik in October 1986 was a considerable achievement. The Soviet delegation there was presented with a list, compiled in Israel, of the names, addresses, and dates of refusal of the many members of the Jewish refusenik community in the U.S.S.R.

The continuing struggle harmed the international reputation of the U.S.S.R., especially after it signed the Helsinki Accords on human rights. On the other hand, the Soviet Union did gain from the international furor. It allowed the Soviets to raise the price on its "merchandise" of Jewish hostages, for example allowing them to exchange individual Jews for Soviet spies caught by the West (as it happened with Anatoly Shcharansky in February 1986) and to use the issue of Soviet Jewry — in terms of a possible concession on the Soviet side in return for American concessions — in its negotiations with the U.S. on limiting strategic and nuclear weapons.

Perestroika and the Breakup of the U.S.S.R. — 1987-1992. Changes in Official Policy and in the Social Status of Soviet Jewry. The primary goal of the policy of *perestroika* was originally to help the Soviet Union emerge from its economic crisis by allowing a degree of democratization, permitting the holding of small private and cooperative property, the weakening of centralization and Party control in the periphery, and the broad encouragement of initiative on the part of the Soviet population. The latter were to be mobilized by granting them a number of civil rights entailing freedom of speech, public organization, and freedom of cultural life *(glasnost)*. Owing to the difficulties of overcoming social inertia and to the opposition of the entrenched bureaucracy, *perestroika* only began to be felt by the public in early 1987. By late 1989 the changes assumed a character unforeseen by the architects of the policy.

Despite the authorities' intentions, *glasnost* was utilized by the peoples of the U.S.S.R. to promote their national aspirations. With the unprecedented burgeoning of national movements that threatened the Soviet Union itself, the issue of the right of Soviet Jews to free emigration and national cultural expression — which had been a major concern of Western public opinion in the 1980s — was no longer so major. At this time of domestic turmoil the Soviet government decided to make concessions on Soviet Jews within the framework of the broadening of civil rights and in exchange for political and economic support from the West.

In January 1987 a new government decree came into effect that regulated entrance into and exit from the U.S.S.R. The decree granted the right to emigrate only for family reunification with close relatives abroad. Still it was an advance, since Soviet emigration procedures were now embodied in law rather than secret government directives. The number of exit visas granted increased each month and in May OVIR began accepting applications to emigrate from people who did not have close relatives abroad. The same year saw applications also accepted for reunification with relatives in countries other than Israel. This change in policy raised the problem of "drop-outs" or those Jewish emigrants who, from the Israeli perspective, denied their tie to the Jewish homeland and chose other destinations.

An indication of a new policy toward emigration was the uncharacteristically mild reaction to the March 1987 demonstration of seven refuseniks in Leningrad. As a result of the demonstration one participant received permission to emigrate while a photograph of the whole group appeared in a local Leningrad newspaper.

Early in the same year several Jewish activists were released from prison before serving their full terms.

The curtailment of the Party's anti-Zionist campaign, a major turnabout, was first signaled by criticism in the journal *Voprosy istorii KPSS* (No. 1, 1987) of Romanenko's *On the Class Essence of Zionism* (see above).

The end came to the ban on importation of Jewish religious literature, Hebrew textbooks, and books on Judaism. The long-standing Soviet domestic policy of proscribing national cultural activity outside the borders of officially designated national regions was rejected in July 1988 when the 19th CPSU Congress passed a resolution granting ethnic groups the right to satisfy their cultural and religious needs throughout the Soviet Union. This change of policy was particularly important for the Jews, almost all of whom live outside their supposed national region, the so-called Jewish Autonomous Oblast in Birobidzhan. One consequence of this new policy was the appearance of many independent Jewish culture associations in all parts of the country. With the simultaneous removal of the ban on discussion in the media of all issues relating to Jews, the number of publications and broadcasts on Jewish topics increased astronomically. The majority of them dealt with domestic concerns rather than the previously common condemnations of Israel. Furthermore, events in the Middle East began to be treated by Soviet journalists in a more objective manner, with Soviet coverage occasionally appearing to be more pro-Israeli than that in the West.

In 1988–1989 almost all remaining veteran refuseniks were given permission to emigrate and the emigration process itself was considerably simplified. The authorities practically ceased persecuting, or even condemning, those who wished to emigrate. Former Soviet citizens living in Israel and the United States, including former Jewish activists, were allowed the possibility of visiting their former homeland without hindrance. Previously miniscule, permitted tourism of Soviet Jews abroad, including to Israel, began to develop. The 1991 law on entrance to and exit from the U.S.S.R. not only guaranteed the right of all Soviet citizens to travel abroad, but also allowed people to emigrate permanently without losing their Soviet passports (as was previously the case with emigrants who "repatriated" to Israel). It also specified timetables and procedures for handling emigration documents so that Soviet emigration legislation finally corresponded with international norms.

Cultural ties between the Soviet Union and Israel began to flourish and, soon thereafter, economic cooperation as well. A series of bilateral diplomatic contacts led in December 1990 to the exchange of consular delegations and one year later to the establishment of full diplomatic relations. The Soviet ambassador to Israel, Alexander Bovin, was the last emissary named by Gorbachev before the formal liquidation of the U.S.S.R. and he remained as the Russian ambassador.

Changes occurred also in the social status and employment profile of Soviet Jewry. Secret restrictions on the acceptance of Jews into institutions of higher education, graduate study, prestigious work, and so on were withdrawn. Jews increasingly appeared among Soviet scientists and cultural figures visiting the West and Israel. Although their numbers hardly increased in the top echelons of Soviet power — the Central Committee of the Communist Party, the government, the army high command, and the diplomatic corps — the number of Jews in secondary positions rose, for example, among government advisers.

There was a perceptible increase in the activity of Jews in social and political life, where a majority of such activists belonged to the liberal-democratic forces. Fifteen Jews were elected to the national congress of People's Deputies of the U.S.S.R. in 1989. The following year 15 Jews passed the first round of elections in the RSFSR, and 9 of them actually became deputies to the Russian Congress of People's Deputies. Some Jews, especially in the Russian hinterland were elected to local city and all-Russian government councils. Jews actively participated in the fights for the general democratization of the Soviet Union, the rights of national minorities, liberalization of the economy, and protection of the environment. There were many Jews among the radically oriented journalists. However, in rare cases, Jews such as the secretary of the board of the Writers' Union of Russia, Anatolii Salutskii, supported Russian nationalist trends.

After the unsuccessful coup in August 1991 and the breakup of the U.S.S.R. at the end of that year, the policy of the Russian government became even more liberal. Direct flights were begun from Moscow and St. Petersburg (the former Leningrad) to Israel. The Russian government even agreed to allow the Jewish Agency to operate in the Soviet Union. In 1992 the vice president of Russia, Alexander Rutskoi, the chairman of the Russian parliament, Ruslan Khasbulatov, and former president of the Soviet Union, Mikhail Gorbachev, all visited Israel.

JEWISH LIFE. During the period of *glasnost* Jewish social and cultural life came to involve many people throughout Russia and the other Soviet republics. This activity was influenced both by the increase of national consciousness among other peoples in the U.S.S.R. and by the growing contacts between Soviet Jews and Israel.

On May 21–22, 1989, a meeting of 120 people representing approximately 50 Jewish social and cultural organizations from 34 Soviet cities took place in Riga. The final document adopted by participants expressed their determination to defend the rights of Soviet Jews to free emigration to Israel and to cultural autonomy within the Soviet Union. The delegates called for the establishment of diplomatic relations between the U.S.S.R. and Israel and the repeal of UN Resolution 3379 which equated Zionism with racism. In the same year 490 delegates took part in a congress of Lithuanian Jews, which elected a Council of Jewish Communities of the republic.

A congress of Jewish community organizations from all over the country took place in Moscow in December 1989. Delegates from approximately 200 bodies and many guests from abroad, including the chairman of the Jewish Agency, Simcha Dinitz, were present. A national umbrella organization — the Council of Jewish Culture Associations of the U.S.S.R. (Vaad) — was established with three co-chairmen, Mikhail Chlenov (Moscow), Yosef Zisels (Chernovtsy), and Samuil Zilberg (Riga). After the dissolution of the U.S.S.R., a Russian Vaad was established at a congress in Nizhni Novgorod in April 1992.

Official, i.e., state-prompted, Jewish figures who, before *perestroika*, had exercised a legal monopoly in representing Soviet Jewry found themselves forced to compete with independent Jewish organizations. One example of this ill-fated effort by these court Jews to sustain their influence took place in early 1989 when a group of people close to the editor of *Sovetish Heymland* founded the short-lived Association of Activists and Friends of Jewish Culture.

Both the leaders of Vaad and the "official" Jewish spokesmen became involved in efforts to resolve the Middle East conflict. With this aim in April 1990 Mikhail Chlenov met with PLO executive committee member, Abu Mazen, while in July former members of the Soviet Public Anti-Zionist Committee announced the establishment of a Peace Today committee (ostensibly on the model of the Israeli Peace Now organization), with its stated goal of facilitating Jewish-Arab dialogue. The second congress of Vaad in January 1991 condemned contacts between the Soviet government and the PLO.

During the August 1991 crisis, Vaad chairman Chlenov did not openly criticize the coup leaders but restricted himself to an expression of concern about the future of Jewish organizations, the possible curtailment of emigration, and the danger of anti-Semitism.

In contrast to Vaad, the opposing wing of Jewish public life is composed of those who consider any Jewish activity in the country either unnecessary or actually harmful unless it is directed toward preparing Soviet Jewry for immigration to Israel. In August 1989 the Hebrew teacher Lev Gorodetskii announced the founding in Moscow of the Zionist Organization in the Soviet Union, which soon opened branches in Leningrad, Riga, Vilnius, Kiev, and Kharkov. Many Zionist youths groups, such as Ha-Shomer ha-Ẓa'ir, Dror, Betar, Maccabi, and Rabim, also began functioning.

A significant feature in Jewish life was the commemoration of the Jewish victims of the Holocaust on the territory of the Soviet Union. This involved groups of Jewish veterans of World War II and concentration camp survivors. In Riga, Vilnius, Leningrad, Minsk, and many other sites, on the anniversaries of mass executions of Jews there, and even in cities which the Nazis did not occupy, increasing numbers of Soviet Jews have been gathering for memorial meetings on Holocaust and Heroism Day (the anniversary of the Warsaw Ghetto uprising). In September 1989 official permission was granted for the first time for such a meeting at *Babi Yar, organized by the Kiev Jewish community. Among the participants were local Party and government officials, leaders of the Ukrainian national movement, and the Church. Finally, after many years, an inscription was placed on the monument indicating, in Russian and in Yiddish, that Jews were the main victims at Babi Yar.

By late 1989 there were almost 200 Jewish associations, clubs, and culture centers in, among other places, Tallinn, Riga, Vilnius, Leningrad, Cheliabinsk, Tashkent, Donetsk,

Former refusenik Iulii Edelshtein (right) with wife and daughter welcomed upon arrival in Israel by Ḥaim Aharon of the Jewish Agency, July 1987. (GPO, Jerusalem)

Baku, Kharkov, Lvov, Chernovtsy, Kiev, Kishinev, Odessa, Minsk, Bobruisk, and Krasnoyarsk. Kiev in late 1989 had 12 different Jewish organizations, including cultural, religious, and even musical groups. In Kishinev the Menora cooperative was established in April 1989; there hundreds of people have studied Hebrew and the fundamentals of Judaism. Tbilisi even granted official recognition to the Aviv association whose goal was to prepare Jews for *aliyah*. Riga Jews have (since July 1988) a culture association, a Yiddish school, and a society for Latvian-Israeli friendship while Vilnius has its own culture association and branches of Betar, B'nai B'rith, and Maccabi.

The greatest number of Jewish culture organizations were concentrated in Moscow. These included: *Iggud morim* (The Association of Teachers of Hebrew, founded 1988), the Association for Friendship and Cultural Ties with Israel (abbreviated ODISKI, summer 1988), the Moscow Jewish Culture and Education Association (MEKPO, September 1987), the Jewish Culture Association, the Gesher youth association, and the Youth Center for Studying and Developing Jewish Culture (abbreviated MTsIRK, 1988). Early 1988 saw the opening of the Solomon Mikhoels Jewish Culture Center and the Shalom Jewish Culture Center.

Efforts have been undertaken to encourage the teaching and study of Jewish studies in the Soviet Union and, after 1991, in its successor, the Commonwealth of Independent States (CIS). Seminars and conferences on Jewish history with the participation of foreign scholars were inaugurated in Moscow and elsewhere.

Jewish religious life ceased to be persecuted. In February 1989, at the initiative of the Israeli rabbi and scholar Adin Steinsaltz, a yeshivah, under the official name of the Center for the Study of Judaism, was established with the Academy of Sciences of the U.S.S.R. Other yeshivot and Torah-study groups sprang up in a number of cities. Among the teachers were a number of Lubavich Ḥasidim from Israel, who had formerly been Soviet citizens.

Due to the lack of trained rabbis, except in Moscow and Leningrad/St. Petersburg, some American rabbis began serving as the spiritual leaders of the main republic synagogues. The national-religious stream in Judaism was represented by Maḥanaim (Hebrew for "two camps"), which had centers in Moscow and Jerusalem. The Bnei Akiva Orthodox Jewish youth movement became active in several localities and, in April 1990, for the first time a progressive (Reform) group, Ineni (Hebrew *Hineni* or "here I am") was registered in Moscow. Camp Ramah, of the Conservative movement, also began to operate. In 1990–1991 Jewish religious holidays were celebrated in public places, including the Palace of Congresses in the Kremlin! Starting in 1992 Russian television began broadcasting programs on basic tenets of Judaism. A number of synagogues confiscated under Stalin were returned to their communities. Nonetheless, it would still be premature to speak of a real religious revival. The majority of newly observant Jews have been emigrating and the Jewish communities do not have the means to either refurbish or maintain their recently regained synagogues.

In connection with the emigration of many nationally oriented Jews, by early 1990 there had been a decline of interest in Jewish culture in the U.S.S.R. A number of Jewish periodicals had ceased appearing and fewer people attended lectures on Jewish history. Interest not only waned in the recently established libraries of the culture centers and synagogues, but those books in demand were increasingly limited to Hebrew study guides and material on *aliyah* and absorption in Israel. The growth in the number of Jewish organizations was accompanied by a decrease in the membership of each of them. At the same time the Jewish elite intelligentsia remained uninvolved in Jewish life.

Israeli and Western Jewish organizations initiated and supported local Jewish institutions and associations. Consequently, the period of amateurs passed — to be replaced by the growth of a significant group of professional Jewish activists directly or indirectly subsidized from abroad. In this environment of support from abroad organizations proliferated, sometimes duplicating existing ones and occasionally being even basically fictitious. In Moscow alone, in 1992 there were several hundred groups. Soviet Jewry, which lacks the experience of autonomous and self-supporting community life, is not able to support its own institutions on the basis of voluntary contributions. This factor lends a somewhat unstable character to the considerable activity that is indeed taking place.

At the same time, some Jewish organizations in Russia and the republics, first of all Vaad, are attempting to chart an independent course while simultaneously trying to gain influence in the international Jewish bodies which provide some of their financing. In May 1991 Vaad became a member of the World Jewish Congress and also has representatives at the Memorial Foundation for Jewish Culture based in New York. In June 1992 at the 32nd World Zionist Congress in Jerusalem, a Vaad delegation and the Zionist Federation of Russia demanded to be represented in all key bodies of the World Zionist Organization which did not agree. There is also a conflict between Vaad and the Jewish Agency since the latter's goal for Soviet Jewry is maximum *aliyah*; Vaad is mainly interested in Jewish revival in Russia and would also like Jews who emigrate to be viewed as part of a Russian-Jewish cultural community rather than have them seen only as part of their new host communities, e.g., Israel and American Jewry.

Yuri Sokol, a Russian Jew, turned his apartment into a Jewish library and reading room. Above, a young Russian Jew and Prof. Dov Levin of Jerusalem in Sokol's apartment (From the Dov Levin Collection, Jerusalem)

A lecture by Cantor Joseph Malovany as part of the Academy for Ḥazzanut and Jewish Music in the Archipova synagogue, Moscow (From the Akiva Zimmerman Collection, Tel Aviv)

The Jewish Press. At the beginning of the 1980s the total legal Jewish press in the U.S.S.R. amounted to two publications in Yiddish: the Moscow Jewish monthly journal *Sovetish Heymland* and the Birobidzhan newspaper *Birobidzhaner Shtern*, plus an annual in the Judeo-Tat language, *Vata Sovetimu*. Issued in languages not understood by the majority of Soviet Jews and consisting largely of propaganda, the existence of these publications was intended to demonstrate that "Jewish culture" was permitted in the Soviet Union.

Attempts in refusenik circles to establish illegal publications were strictly repressed and led to the gradual curtailment of all Jewish *samizdat* publishing. *Evrei v SSSR* ("Jews in the U.S.S.R.," Moscow) ceased publication in 1979, *Nash ivrit* ("Our Hebrew," Moscow) — in 1980, *Din umetsiiut* ("Justice and Reality," Riga) — in 1980, *Evrei sovremennon mire* ("Jews in the Contemporary World," Moscow) — in 1981. The Riga journal *Chaim*, which appeared irregularly starting in 1979, could not fill the vacuum due to its miniscule print-run and its distance from the main Jewish centers. An exception was *Leningradskii evreiskii almanakh* ("Leningrad Jewish Almanac," abbreviated LEA) which first came out in late 1982, at the height of the repressions and succeeded in appearing regularly from 1984 to 1989. The latter publication focused on cultural and historical articles written by Leningrad refuseniks. Due to the size of its print-run (up to 200 — which was large for a *samizdat* publication) and its effective system of distribution, LEA succeeded in reaching distant corners of the country and in demonstrating the need for an independent Jewish press.

Change came with the beginning of the general liberalization in the country. In 1987–1988 several Moscow *samizdat* journals appeared. There were *Evreiskii istoricheskii almankah* ("Jewish Historical Almanac") and *Shalom* with their cultural orientation and several publications dealing with such topics as *aliyah* and absorption in Israel: *Informatsionnyi biulleten po problemam repatriatsii i evreiskoi kultury* ("Information Bulletin of Problems of Repatriation and Jewish Culture"), *Paneninu le-Israel* ("Looking towards Israel"), and *Problemy otkaza v vyezde* iz strany ("Problems of Refusal Regarding Exit from the Country").

There was also a revolution in terms of the technology of publication. While the first illegal publications were typed in multiple copies (occasionally copies were made via photography), the *samizdat* publications of the transitional period were produced on personal computers from abroad and xeroxed so that print-runs were dramatically increased. Several publications were printed in Israel and sent back to the Soviet Union for distribution. In December 1988 the first legally permitted independent Jewish newspaper, *Khashakhar*, was issued in Tallinn by the local Jewish culture association. This publication was typeset and appeared not only in Estonian, but also in Russian, which made it accessible to almost all of Soviet Jewry. Its print-run was over 1,000 and it soon gained a reputation throughout the country.

In Moscow in April 1989 the authorities launched the semi-official *Vestnkik evreiskoi sovetskoi kultury* ("Herald of Soviet Jewish Culture," abbreviated VESK) in an attempt to compete with the independent Jewish press. After a year which saw a change of editor and of name — to *Evreiskaia gazeta* ("Jewish Newspaper") — this publication gained more of an independent status.

In Riga in March 1990 there appeared *Vestnik evreiskoi kultury* ("Herald of Jewish Culture," VEK). In 1990 Jewish newspapers in Russian with real Jewish content began to appear in Kiev (*Vozrozhdenie*, "Revival"), Leningrad (*Narod moi*, "My People"), Kishinev (*Nash golos*, "Our Voice"), Tashkent (*Mizrakh*, "Orient"), Moscow *(Menora)*, Vilnius (*Litovskii Ierusalim*, "Jerusalem of Lithuania"), and elsewhere. These newspapers all gained legal status while those which were issued without permission ceased being persecuted. Thus the distinction between *samizdat* and permitted publications was erased.

Sovetish Heymland softened its hard-line policy and began to publish more cultural and historical materials. In 1990–1991 the former editor of *Birobidzhaner Shtern*, Leonid Shkolnik, began the independent newspaper *Vzgliad* ("View"), which included many items of Jewish interest.

The geographical distribution and sharply increased print-runs, the increased scope of topics treated, and the widely understood Russian language of the majority of publications have made the new Jewish press a significant factor in the formation of Jewish national consciousness and a source of elementary Jewish knowledge for many thousands of people. The press has also become a source of information about emigration and *aliyah*, and both a mirror and monitor of Jewish life in the country. The very fact of the legalization of the Jewish press has made a deep impression on the average Jews who saw that it was no longer necessary to fear public expression of Jewish life.

However, there is also a negative side to the picture. A number of Jewish periodicals ceased publication after their first issues. Few managed to appear more frequently than once a month and the promised periodicity was often not maintained. The professional level of the Jewish press was frequently low. Articles on Jewish culture and history were often reprints or translations from abroad. Factual errors reflecting a lack of basic knowledge of Jewish traditions, Jewish history, and Hebrew among both authors and editors appeared in many articles. These problems stemmed from the lack of publishing experience of those involved, the lack of qualified authors with some Jewish expertise, the difficulties of publication in the Soviet Union, and the considerable turnover of staff as active members of Jewish culture associations often emigrated.

In 1989 the Jewish press consisted of at least 30 publications; more than half of these appeared in Russia, the majority of them in Moscow. Over the following three years, due to the growing role of the Jewish press in the Ukraine, the undisputed dominance of Russia declined while Moscow continued to dominate the scene in Russia. Late 1991 saw the demise of *Sovetish Heymland*. In the same year at least 50 Jewish newspapers and journals appeared, with at least one in practically every republic and some in cities in the hinterland. The Jewish press of the CIS represents a whole range of religious and political orientations, with Israeli and Western organizations sometimes supporting publications which favor their policies. This latter factor suggests some doubts not only about the spontaneity of the Jewish publication boom as well as its actual scope but also about its future.

Anti-Semitism and the Jewish Question. During the years of *perestroika* covert but effective state and bureaucratic anti-Semitism gradually declined while there was a rise in grass roots anti-Jewish trends. The protacted economic crisis and weakening of the central authority produced populist spokesmen who found it easier to cast blame for all the failures of the country, past and present, on various ethnic groups, especially the Jews, than to offer practical solutions for the dire straits of the country. One factor feeding anti-Semitism was envy stemming from the reality that Jews could emigrate while for Russians this way out was basically barred. Further oil to the flame was the fact that Jews could now visit relatives abroad and receive material aid from them.

With *glasnost* Soviet Jewry began encountering overt anti-Semitism in the press and on television, in the pamphlets of political parties, in conversations at work places, on the street and on public transport. Anti-Semitic parties and organizations sprang up like mushrooms. These included: Pamiat (Memory), Rossy (The [Original] Russians), Patriot, Rodina (Homeland), Otechestvo (Fatherland), Nationalno-demokraticheskaia partiia (National Democratic Party), Russkii nationalno-patrioticheskii tsentr (Russian National Patriotic Center), Soius russikh ofitserov (Union of Russian Officers), and Republikanskaia narodnaia partiia Rossii (Republic People's Party of Russia). The year 1989 saw the establishment of the neo-Communist movement Obediennyi front trudiashchikhsia RSFSR (United Front of the Workers of the RSFSR) and in 1991 its spin-off, Rossiiskaia kommunisticheskaia rabochaia partiia (Russian Communist Workers' Party), which espoused anti-Semitism as an organic part of their ideology. About this time Vladimir Zhirinovskii became leader of the rightist populist group which called itself Liberalno-demokraticheskaia partiia Rossii (Liberal Democratic Party of Russia).

The Pamiat Association, originally a conservative movement concerned about the preservation of Russia's past and its environment, became more nationalistic in 1984 when its leadership was taken over by photographer Dmitrii Vasilev. The movement gained notoriety when it blamed Jews for the destruction of Russian churches, and for the serious problem of alcoholism in the country. Originally the authorities did not object to Pamiat's activities and even supported them. In May 1987 Boris Yeltsin, then first secretary of the Moscow city committee of the CPSU, received representatives of Pamiat after a demonstration it staged on Manezh Square. On May 31, 1988, Vasilev announced the transformation of the association into Nationalno-patrioticheskii front "Pamiat" (Pamiat: National Patriotic Front), i.e., a political organization in opposition to the Communist Party. Between 1989 and the early 1990s Pamiat split into several groups, the most extreme of which, Pravoslavnyi nationalno-patrioticheskii front "Pamiat" (Pamiat Orthodox National Patriotic Front) headed by A. Kulakov, espoused restoration of the monarchy while simultaneously expounding the necessity of continuing Stalin's anti-Semitic policy.

Anti-Semitism has not been confined to words. Acts of vandalism have been directed against Jewish targets. In April 1987 the Leningrad Jewish cemetery was desecrated and in the following two years approximately 30 such incidents were recorded in the U.S.S.R. In Moscow attacks were carried out against a Jewish cafe and the editorial offices of *Sovetish Heymland* and arson was committed at the synagogue by the cemetery in Malakhovka. In 1992 a swastika was painted on the Moscow Lubavich Ḥasidic synagogue and a fire-bomb was thrown into the building.

Leningrad, the home of a number of anti-Semitic organizations, became the center of anti-Semitism in 1988–1990. It was a teacher at the Leningrad Technological Institute, Nina Andreeva who, evidently on orders from the central Committee of the CPSU, on March 13, 1988, published a letter, "I Can Not Yield My Principles," calling for the rehabilitation of Stalin and the restoration of the kind of law and order that existed before *perestroika*. In her letter Andreeva attacked the Jews as "cosmopolitans" and a "counter-revolutionary people," who were pushing the Russian people toward a rejection of socialism. In the summer of 1988 Leningrad's Ruminatsev Park was the daily site of Pamiat rallies. The city also regularly heard calls to expel Jews from Russian scientific, cultural, and educational institutions.

In nationalist journals such as *Molodaia gvardiia* ("Young Guard") and *Nash sovremennik* ("Our Contemporary") a group of Moscow writers and journalists, the neo-Slavophiles Valentin Rasputin, Vasillii Belov, Victor Astafev, and Vadim Kozhinov, utilized the traditionally high status of the writer in Russian society to protest ostensibly harmful Jewish influence on Russian culture. For example, they condemned the 1989 publication in the journal *Oktober* of the novella *Vse techet* ("All Is Flowing") by the late writer of Jewish origin Vasili *Grossman, in which the Russian people is allegedly described as having a slave mentality. The January 1990 issue of *Molodaia gvardiia* contained praise of a painting, *The Warning* by Igor Borodin, which the journal claims shows an image of the biblical queen Esther who "after gaining power of the king in his bedroom, and also by clever machinations...urged [King] Artarxerxes to commit the bloody slaughter of 75,000 totally innocent people when there was no threat at all to the Jewish people." The painting (reproduced in the journal) shows Esther on her knees before the tsar while under the throne are visible bloodied heads of famous figures of Russian and world culture and history. In 1992 *Evreiskaia gazaeta* reported the existence of 47 anti-Semitic newspapers and 9 such journals in Russia alone.

Some scientists also denigrated the Jews. Writing appeared denying Jewish contributions to science. A particular target was Albert Einstein, whose discoveries were consistently attributed to others, as in the 1988 monograph of Prof. A. Logunov about Henri Poincaré. The mathematician Igor Shafarevich published a book *Rusofobia* ("Russophobia"), in which a "small people" (for which read "the Jews") was blamed for all the troubles of a "great people," the Russians. In 1992 anti-Semitism among scientists was revealed in elections to the Russian Academy of Sciences. None of the Jews nominated to become members of the academy was elected in contrast to the election of a number of Jews during the pre-Gorbachev "period of stagnation."

A significant indication of anti-Semitic attitudes between 1988 and 1990 was the repeated circulation of rumors about impending pogroms. The first such large-scale pogrom was predicted for June 1988 to coincide with the thousandth anniversary of the baptism of Russia. There were similar rumors in Dnepropetrovsk and other cities in the Ukraine before Easter 1989 and in Leningrad on the eve of elections to local and republic soviets on February 25, 1990. There were rumors of another pogrom set for May 5, 1990, the day of St. George, the patron saint for many nationalists. In that same month a Muslim mob burned and looted dozens of Armenian and Jewish homes in the Uzbek city of Andizhan. Although no exclusively Jewish pogrom took place, the number of reported attacks on individual Jews grew. Soviet Jewry lacked confidence in the ability of the authorities to defend them in the face of failures to prevent or halt interethnic conflict in the republics or to halt the rise in crime in Russia itself.

At the same time that the Jewish population of the country was decreasing due to emigration, the Jewish question increasingly became an issue in the internal Soviet power struggle. In pre-election campaigns the democratic press often indicated its sympathy for the Jews and stressed the anti-Semitism of their political opponents while Russian nationalists often branded as "Jews" anyone who advocated radical reform, the introduction of a market economy, or civil rights. These "Jews" in fact included such non-Jews as Politburo member Alexander Yakovlev; radical opposition leader in the Supreme Soviet of the U.S.S.R., Yurii Afanasev; editor of the *perestroika*-oriented journal *Ogonek*, Vitalii Korotych; and even Boris Yeltsin.

Lithuanian, Ukrainian, and other nationalists saw the Jews in their republics as possible allies in their fight for self-determination against the central authorities and their local Jewish culture movements as forces opposing Russification. On May 28, 1989, a conference of the national movements of Lithuania, Latvia, and Estonia adopted a resolution condemning Soviet anti-Semitism in the past and present and calling for opposition to it. A similar resolution was adopted at its founding meeting in September 1989 by Rukh, the democratic national movement in the Ukraine.

The growing anti-Semitism disturbed the liberal part of the Russian intelligentsia, which saw in it a threat to the overall process of democratization in the country. The "pogrom-like" atmosphere was first protested in an open letter by a group of Moscow intellectuals led by the philologist Sergei Lyosov and the physicist Sergei Tishchenko. Almost simultaneously (on June 7) the Leningrad historian Natalia Iukhneva spoke out in public about increasing anti-Semitism in Russian society. She associated this growth with the unequal position of Jews and Jewish culture in the U.S.S.R. and rejected as false and unjust the attempt to condemn Zionism along with anti-Semitism. Gradually articles against anti-Semitism began to be featured in many *perestroika*-oriented journals and newspapers. Some publications even took a positive rather than defensive approach to Jewish topics. For example, the Moscow journal *Znamia* in 1990–1991 published a whole series of articles on Jewish topics, including a translation of the story "Unto Death" by the Israeli writer Amos Oz. Public opinion also had the opportunity to be influenced by the first objective film on Israel shot *in situ* by Evgenii Kiselev and shown on Soviet television between August and October 1989. Due to the cessation of government funding for "anti-Zionist works," a number of their authors, such as Dadiani, Vladimir Nosenko, Victor Magidson, and Adolf Eidelman, switched camps and became opponents of anti-Semitism, perhaps with the hope of support from Israeli and Western Jewish institutions.

The victory of democratic forces in the elections of local soviets in March 1990 led to the mobilization of law enforcement agencies against anti-Semitic agitation. For the first time in decades the state prosecutor's office prosecuted anti-Semitic actions under article 174 of the Criminal Court of the RFSFR, which deals with the incitement of ethnic strife. The sentencing to a jail term of Pamiat leader Smirnov-Ostashvili (who committed suicide in prison) was viewed as a victory for democracy in the country. Public opinion was favorably influenced toward the Jews in August 1991 when one of the three victims killed defending democracy against the attempted coup turned out to be the young Jew Ilya Krichevskii. The fall 1991 repeal (supported by the Soviet Union) of the UN resolution equating Zionism with racism also was a factor in deflating anti-Semitic propaganda.

In November 1992, almost a year after the dissolution of the Soviet Union, the committee on human rights of the Supreme Soviet of the Russian Federation inaugurated hearings on the problem of anti-Semitism in Russia. The committee concluded that there was a decline in anti-Semitic attitudes in Russian society in 1991–1992 and that anti-Semitic activity was basically restricted to extremist groups and parties. At the same time legislative measures were discussed which, without infringing upon freedom of speech and the press, would stipulate punishment for arousing ethnic hatred. Anti-Semitism is increasingly being treated in Russia as not only a Jewish problem.

Emigration and Aliyah. The number of emigrants fell from 51,300 in 1979 to 1,320 in 1983. Then until 1986 the annual number of exit visas granted hovered around 1,000. Already in the banner year 1979 it was obvious that approximately two-thirds of the emigrants preferred the United States to Israel as their destination. America automatically granted them the status of refugees persecuted on ethnic or religious grounds. The greater part of those who went directly to the U.S. without trying Israel came from the more assimilated regions of the RSFSR and the Ukraine; a small proportion came from the territories annexed by the Soviet Union during World War II and from non-Ashkenazi Jewish communities. Between 1983 and 1986 the proportion of those who went to the U.S. rather than Israel fluctuated between 59 and 78 percent. This situation was viewed with alarm by those Jewish activists within the Soviet Union who had fought for emigration under the banner of "repatriation" to Israel. The refusenik circles in Moscow and Leningrad then succeeded in somewhat lowering the proportion of "drop-outs," as they were called by Israelis and Israel-oriented activists, from these two cities in contrast to other centers of assimilation where pressure to consider *aliyah* was less effective.

In 1987 the number of Soviet Jews emigrating was nine times that of the previous year. In 1988 almost 17,000 Soviet Jews took advantage of the increased opportunity to emigrate directly to the U.S., Canada, Australia, and elsewhere rather than Israel.

Processes that increased under *perestroika*, such as the lack of basic commodities, environmental dangers, and the increase of overt anti-Semitism, encouraged almost everyone to consider emigration. The fact that "the gates" of emigration were open, combined with the fear that they might close again at any time, moved thousands of Jews from all over the country to leave. The number who emigrated between 1988 and 1990 rose dramatically. The vast majority chose to make their new homes elsewhere than in Israel. In this situation Israel demanded that those Jews who were leaving the Soviet Union on Israeli invitations go only to Israel and that the American government cease granting the status of refugees to Jews who were leaving the U.S.S.R. under the status of repatriants to Israel. After long negotiations on this issue, in October 1989 the American govern-

Table 3. Emigration: Immigrants to Israel and "Drop-Outs," 1983-1992

Year	Number of emigrants	Immigrated to Israel	"Drop-outs"	
			Number	%
1983	1,320	399	921	69.8
1984	896	367	529	59.0
1985	1,144	362	782	68.4
1986	914	202	712	77.9
1987	8,147	2,096	6,051	74.3
1988	19,251	2,283	16,968	88.1
1989	71,238	12,932	58,306	81.8
1990	204,700*	185,227	19,500*	9.5
1991	189,800*	147,839	42,000*	22.1
1992	118,600*	65,093	53,500*	45.1

* Minimum estimate: Soviet Jewish emigration to the U.S.: 1988 — 15,000; 1990 — 6,500; 1991 — 34,715; and 1992 — 42,250. Some figures for elsewhere: Germany — not less than 6,000 for the same years; Canada (1992) — 1,500; Australia — 1,000.

Mrs. Medalie (left), the only survivor of a ghetto of 20,000, in front of a memorial to the victims of fascism in Riga. (From the Dov Levin Collection, Jerusalem).

ment introduced a quota on immigrants from the U.S.S.R. and ceased automatically granting refugee status to Israel-invitation holders. One result was the closing of the Italian transit camp at Ladispoli, the way station to the U.S. of a large number of Jews from the U.S.S.R. Another was the fundamental redirection of Soviet Jewish emigration. A more objective picture of Israel in the Soviet media and enthusiastic reports about Israel from Soviet tourists who visited that country also led to a sharp increase in the number of Jews emigrating to Israel. In 1990 over 185,000 Soviet Jewish emigrants went to Israel, establishing an annual record rate for the immigration to Israel from a single country.

In late 1989 the rate of emigration had been limited by the capacity of Soviet OVIR offices, customs, and transportation facilities and by the rate of dispatch of visas from Israel. Bucharest and Budapest served as transit points. By the summer of 1990 the pressure somewhat declined as the process of sending Israeli visas was speeded up and additional routes to Israel were established via Poland, Czechoslovakia, Finland, and other European countries. These emergency measures considerably increased the flow despite attempts by the Palestine Liberation Organization to sabotage the Hungarian and Polish airlines and the refusal of the Soviet Union to allow direct flights to Israel. However, this last obstacle was removed with the normalization of diplomatic relations between Israel and the U.S.S.R. Direct flights were then inaugurated from Moscow, Leningrad, and some republic capitals to Israel.

In 1991–1992 word of the difficulties of absorption into Israeli life and the growing percentage of non-Jews included in the Jewish emigration as parts of mixed families once again turned a not insignificant proportion of the emigration toward the U.S., Germany, and other countries.

Among the immigrants to Israel the median age increased annually while the number of children per family decreased. The percentage of non-Jews also increased. These features reflect demographic processes in the country of emigration. Serious problems in the absorption of these immigrants in Israel stem from two basic problems: the gap between their professional profiles and the needs of the Israel economy; the lack of Jewish traditions and knowledge among most of the immigrants.

Bibliography: Y. Roi, in: *EJ* YB 83-85:405–10; Y. Litvak, in: *EJ* YB 86-87:363–70; R. Vago, in: *EJ* YB 88-89:405–15; M. Beizer, in; *EJ* YB 90-91:388–95; idem, in: *The Shorter Encyclopaedia Judaica in Russian*, Suppl. 1, (1992), 31–41; idem, in: *Jews and Jewish Topics in the Soviet Union and Eastern Europe* (hereafter *Jews and Jewish Topics*), 2:12 (1990), 69–77; idem, in: *Jews and Jewish Topics*, 3:19 (1992) 62-77; T. Friedgut, in: *Soviet Jewry in the 1980s* (1989), 3–25; M. Altshuler, in: *Jews and Jewish Topics*, 2:9 (1989), 5–29; idem, in: *Jews and Jewish Topics*, 3:16 (1991), 224–40; Z. Gitelman, in: *Soviet Jewish Affairs*, 19:2 (1989), 3–4; Y. Florsheim, in: *Jews and Jewish Topics*, 2:15 (1991), 5–14; idem, in: *Jews and Jewish Topics*, 3:19 (1992), 5–15; M. Tolts, in: *Jews and Jewish Topics*, 2:18 (1991), 13–26; idem, in: *East European Jewish Affairs*, 22:2 (1992), 3–19; A. Greenbaum, in: *EJ* YB 90-91:179–83; I. Dymerskaya-Tsigelman, in: *Jews and Jewish Topics*, 3:10 (1989), 49–61; B. Pinkus, in: *Jews and Jewish Topics*, 2:15 (1991), 15–30; M. Gilbert, *The Jews of Hope* (1984); idem, *Ukrainian Diary, September-October, 1991*, manuscript; D. Prital (ed.), *Yehudei Berit ha-Mo'atsot* ("The Jews of the Soviet Union"), vols. 8–15 (1985–1992); "The Second Congress of Vaad," in: *Jews and Jewish Topics*, 3:16 (1991), 224–40; Z. Gitelman, in: *Soviet Jewish Affairs*, 19:2 (1989), 3–4; Y. Florsheim, in: *Jews and Jewish Topics*, 2:15 (1991), 5–14; idem, in: *Jews and Jewish Topics*, 3:19 (1992), 5-15; M. Tolts, in: *Jews and Jewish Topics*, 1:14 (1991), 31–59. [MI.BE.]

S

SACKS, JONATHAN HENRY (1948–), chief rabbi of the British Commonwealth, from 1991. Born in London, Sacks combined brilliant success in secular studies with his Jewish education. He obtained a doctorate in moral philosophy at London University in 1981 and was ordained from both Jews' College and Yeshivat Etz Ḥayyim in London, in 1976. After lecturing in moral philosophy at Middlesex Polytechnic he taught Jewish philosophy and Talmud at Jews' College from 1973 to 1982 and served as the college's principal from 1984 to 1990. Simultaneously he was rabbi of Golders Green Synagogue, 1978–82, and Marble Arch Synagogue, 1983–90. He edited *Tradition and Transition* (1986) and *Traditional Alternatives* (1989) which stemmed from a major conference on contemporary Judaism that he convened in 1989. It was followed in 1990 by a gathering focused on women in Judaism.

A frequent radio broadcaster, Rabbi Dr. Sacks delivered the prestigious Reith Lectures in 1990, subsequently published to wide acclaim as *The Persistence of Faith* (1991). He also published *Tradition in an Untraditional Age* (1991) and *Covenant and Crisis: Jewish Thought after the Holocaust* (1992). His broadcasts and publications established the new chief rabbi as a popular representative of Judaism, although this has not been matched by uniform acceptance among British Jews. He created controversy in 1985 with a pamphlet on Jewish attitudes to wealth and poverty issued by the right-wing Social Affairs Unit.

His scope for initiative in office has been limited by a financial crisis in the United Synagogue and the polarization of Anglo-Jewry. He disappointed Progressive Jews by declining to participate in a radio discussion if a Reform rabbi was included. He inaugurated an unprecedented review of the position of women in the United Synagogue, but his decision to permit women's prayer groups only outside the synagogue, and without use of a Scroll of the Law, was considered a conservative compromise. Popular hostility to the recognition of homosexuals within communal life led him to sanction their exclusion from a fund-raising event, dismaying liberal opinion. These controversies overshadowed his achievements in promoting Jewish learning under the banner "Decade of Renewal." [D.CE.]

SAFIRE, WILLIAM (1929–), columnist. Born in New York, he studied at Syracuse University, but left after only two years in 1949. His first job was as a researcher for Tex McCracy who had a gossip column in the *New York Herald-*

Tribune. After serving as a correspondent in Europe and the Middle East for WNBC radio and TV, he joined the U.S. Army in 1952, working for the Armed Forces Radio Network for the next two years.

On leaving the service, Safire returned to New York where he worked for Tex McCracy's public relations firm and helped to produce McCracy's syndicated radio show. In 1959 Safire opened his own public relations firm and traveled to Moscow that year for the American National Exhibition. While there he met Vice-President Richard Nixon and helped to set up the famous "kitchen debate" between Nixon and Soviet Premier Krushchev in which each leader argued the merits of their particular system of government.

During the 1960 presidential campaign he was in charge of special projects for the Nixon-Lodge candidacy and wrote much of the campaign literature. In 1961 he established Safire Public Relations Inc. which handled the campaigns of a number of New York Republican leaders, including Nelson Rockefeller, Jacob Javits, and John Lindsay. His first two books appeared during this period, *The Relations Explosion* (1963) and *Plunging into Politics* (1964).

From 1965 on Safire was immersed in Richard Nixon's campaign for the presidency. He ghostwrote Nixon's syndicated column and in 1968 authored Nixon's election victory speech. His third book appeared that year entitled *The New Language of Politics*. As a special assistant to President Nixon, Safire wrote major speeches for the president on the Vietnam War and economic policies. On loan to Spiro Agnew in 1972, Safire coined the oftquoted alliterative phrases "nattering nabobs of negativism" and "hopeless hysterical hypochondriacs of history." His articles for the *New York Times* and *Washington Post* during the campaign ultimately led to the invitation for him to write a regular column in the *New York Times*, which he began in 1974.

Safire wrote his White House memoirs in a non-fiction volume entitled *Before the Fall* (1975) and in a political novel, *Full Disclosure* (1977). He combined the talents of columnist and investigative reporter when in 1977 he broke the story on the financial affairs of Bert Lance, President Jimmy Carter's special assistant and key fundraiser. That investigation led to Safire winning a Pulitzer Prize in 1978.

An avowed "hawk" on foreign policy, Safire also strongly supported Israel. He especially championed the government of Menahem Begin and Begin's bombing of the nuclear reactor in Iraq.

His other books have been: *Safire's Political Dictionary* (1978), *On Language* (1980), a collection of his columns in the Times, *Safire's Washington* (1980), and *Lincoln* (1986). Safire's grandfather was the publisher of one of New York's daily Yiddish newspapers. [M.D.G.]

SALOMON, CHARLOTTE (see **14**:694). While a refugee from Nazi Germany, during 1941 and 1942, Charlotte Salomon portrayed her life in an autobiography titled *Leben oder Theater? Ein Singspiel* ("Life or Theater? An Operetta"). It takes the unprecedented form of a musical drama in 1,325 gouaches of astonishing vividness and force. "Life or Theater?" is peopled by characters based on her family and friends, ordered by acts and scenes, narrated by dialogues and commentaries, and accompanied by musical cues.

The autobiography makes one family emblematic of its era. Salomon records the creative milieu of Berlin through the experiences of her stepmother, Paula Salomon-Lindberg, a well-known opera singer, and of her mentor and lover, Alfred Wolfsohn, a philosopher of music. The autobiography also registers the impact of Nazism on an assimilated Jewish family: first Charlotte Salomon's grandparents emigrated from Germany, then her stepmother was restricted to per-

"... Meanwhile, to the tune 'L'amour est un oiseau rebelle,'" Charlotte is sitting on her bed," a page from Charlotte Salomon's *Leben oder Theater?* (Beth Hatefutsoth, Tel Aviv; courtesy Joods Historisch Museum, Amsterdam)

forming for Jewish audiences; her father, Dr. Albert Salomon, was deprived of his professorship at the Berlin University Medical School, then imprisoned in Sachsenhausen. Charlotte Salomon was among the handful of Jewish students admitted to the Berlin Fine Arts Academy, but was expelled in 1938, and left Germany in 1939.

Joining her grandparents in Villefranche on the French Riviera, Salomon witnessed her grandmother's suicide in 1940, and only then learned that her mother's death years earlier was also a suicide. The menace of suicide and the duress of exile forced her to decide, she said, "whether to take her own life or undertake something unheard of and mad" — an autobiography in art. After working more than a year on *Leben oder Theater?*, she gave its paintings and texts to a friend in Villefranche, saying: "Keep this safe. It is my whole life." Marrying another refugee, Alexander Nagler, she lived in relative security until the Germans occupied the Riviera in September 1943. Then the Gestapo conducted one of the most brutal mass roundups in Western Europe. Charlotte Salomon was sent to Drancy, and deported. In October 1943, at age 26, she was killed in Auschwitz.

After the war, her father and stepmother brought "Life or Theater?" to Amsterdam, where it now resides in the Jewish Historical Museum. Exhibitions in Europe, the U.S., and Israel (Beth Hatefutsoth, 1985), as well as published reproductions, a film, and plays, have given "Life or Theater?" international standing as an artwork, autobiography, and historical document.

Bibliography: *Charlotte: Life or Theater? An Autobiographical Play*, intro. by J. Belinfante, G. Schwartz, and J. Herzberg (1981); *Charlotte: A Diary in Pictures*, intro. by E. Straus (1963); "Charlotte" (film) by J. Herzberg and F. Weisz (1981); *Charlotte Salomon — "Leben oder Theater?" Das 'Lebensbild' einr jüdischen Malerin aus Berlin*, ed. C. Fischer-Defoy (for 1986 exhibition, Berlin Fine Arts Academy). [M.FEL.]

SARNA, NAHUM (1923–), Bible scholar. Born in London, Sarna received his training in rabbinics at Jews College, London, and his B.A. and M.A. from the University College London (1946–1949). Settling in the United States in 1951, he studied at Dropsie College, Philadelphia, where he received his Ph.D. in biblical studies and Semitic languages. He taught at Gratz College in Philadelphia from 1951 to 1957 when he was appointed librarian of the Jewish Theological Seminary and member of its faculty. In 1965 he joined the Near Eastern and Judaic Studies Department at Brandeis University.

Nahum Sarna (Courtesy Brandeis University Photography Department)

Sarna was an editor and translator for the new Jewish Publication Society translation of the Bible and is the general editor of its Bible Commentary Project, and, after retiring from Brandeis University, academic consultant for Judaica. He was a departmental editor of the *Encyclopaedia Judaica* and also contributed major articles to the *Encyclopaedia Britannnica*, the *Encyclopaedia Hebraica*, the *Encyclopaedia Biblica Hebraica*, the *Encyclopaedia of Religion*, and the *Oxford Companion to the Bible*.

He has written over 100 scholarly articles. One of the major thrusts of his work has been to make the Bible and biblical scholarship available to the broad Jewish community. For example, his book *Understanding Genesis* (1966) has served as a general introduction to the Bible and was followed by *Exploring Exodus* (1986) and his *Commentary on Genesis* (1989). [E.HO.]

SCHON, FRANK, LORD (1912–), British industrialist. Schon was born in Vienna and educated at the universities of Prague and Vienna, where he studied law. After settling in England, he founded in West Cumberland the chemical manufacturing firm of Marchon Products in 1939 and Solway Chemicals in 1943; he was chairman and managing director of both until 1967. In 1956 Marchon Products became part of Albright and Wilson, of which Schon was a director from 1958 to 1972; he was a director of Blue Circle Industries (formerly Portland Cement) from 1967 to 1982. Schon took a prominent part in the public and cultural life of the north of England, serving on the council and court of Durham University and Newcastle University. He was chairman of the Cumberland Development Council from 1964 to 1968. From 1969 to 1979 he was chairman of the National Research Development Corporation, a public agency concerned with the promotion of inventions in the national interest. He was knighted in 1966 and created a life peer in 1976.

Bibliography: H. Pollins, *Economic History of the Jews in England* (1982), 220–1. [V.D.L.]

SCHORSCH, ISMAR (1925–), Jewish historian and scholar. Born in Germany he went to the United States in his youth. He received his B.A. (1957) from Ursinus College in Pennsylvania and his M.A. (1961) and Ph.D. (1969) from Columbia University. Schorsch was ordained as rabbi from the Jewish Theological Seminary (1962). After serving as a chaplain in the U.S. Army, he joined the faculty of the Seminary in 1964, becoming full professor of history in 1976. From 1975 to 1979 Schorsch was dean of the Seminary's graduate school, and served as provost of the institute from 1980 to 1984. He was elected a fellow in the American Academy of Jewish Research in 1977 and in May 1985 president of the Leo Baeck Institute. In July 1986 he became the chancellor of the Jewish Theological Seminary.

Among his works are the translation of *The Structure of Jewish History and Other Essays* by Heinrich Graetz, which he edited and for which he also wrote the introduction, and *Organized Jewish Reaction to German Anti-Semitism, 1870–1914* (1972). [ED.]

SCHWARTZ, MELVIN (1932–), physicist and businessman, Nobel Prize winner. Born in New York City, Schwartz studied at Columbia University from which he received his Ph.D.) in 1958. He was an associate physicist at Brookhaven National Laboratory from 1956 to 1958 and on the faculty of Columbia University from 1958 to1966, becoming a professor in 1963. From 1966 to 1983 he was a professor at Stanford University. He was chairman of the board of directors of Digital Pathways Inc. in Mountain View, California.

Melvin Schwartz

A member of the American National Academy of Sciences and a fellow of the American Physics Society, he was also on the board of governors of the Weizmann Institute in Israel.

In 1962 he and two colleagues, Jack Steinberger (q.v.) and Leon M. Lederman (q.v.), developed a means for utilizing neutrinos, subatomic particles, to aid in determining the structure of other basic particles. In 1988 they were the recipients of the Nobel Prize in physics in recognition of the greater understanding of elementary particles and forces resulting from their work. [ED.]

SEPHARDIM (see **14:**1164). **1992 — The Quincentennial Year of the Expulsion of the Jews from Spain.** CELEBRATIONS, COMMEMORATION, REMEMBRANCE, AND PUBLIC AWARENESS. The 500th anniversary of the expulsion of the Jews from Spain was commemorated throughout the Sephardi world. In the United States, synagogues put Sephardi themes on their cultural agendas. The community of Indianapolis, for example, produced over 20 relevant events during 1992. Laurence Salzmann's exhibition on Turkish Jewry entitled "Anyos Munchos y Buenos" traveled to dozen of cities in the United States and also in Europe. Other traveling exhibitions included "Mosaic: Jewish Life in Florida"; the Beth Hatefutsoth (Diaspora Museum of Tel Aviv) exhibition "In the Footsteps of Columbus: Jews in America in 1654–1880"; "Turkish Jews: 500 Years of Harmony" — organized by the Quincentennial Foundation of Istanbul (QFI); and the Anti-Defamation League's "Voyages to Freedom: 500 Years of Jewish Life in Latin America and

A reception in Jerusalem by the Sephardi League for the participants of the Fourth Misgav Yerushalayim Sephardi Studies Conference in 1992 — the speaker is Yilmaz Benadrete of Istanbul, vice-president of the World Sephardi Federation. (Yitzhak Kerem and Eti Horn)

the Caribbean." At the Yeshiva University Museum in New York throughout most of the year the exhibition "The Sephardic Journey: 1492–1992" was displayed. The Judeo-Spanish singing groups "Voice of the Turtle" and "Voices of Sepharad" had busy concert schedules in the USA and in Europe.

In addition, in the U.S., various academic conferences were held.

Arizona and Mexico were centers for activities highlighting the recent revelation of numerous crypto-Jews of Spanish-speaking origin among their population. The University of Tucson has taken an active interest in Sephardi studies and promoted Sephardi scholarship and guest lectures.

In England, Rabbi Abraham Levy of the Spanish and Portuguese Lauderdale Road Synagogue produced and sponsored numerous publications, lectures, and other cultural events. The Jewish community of Brussels and its local "Sepharad '92" group were extremely active. In Thessaloniki, Greece, the Society for the Study of Greek Jewry and the local Jewish community organized numerous lectures. Large academic conferences were held in Istanbul and in Thessaloniki. Thessaloniki also hosted an international Judeo-Spanish song festival and an exhibition. France saw a memorial service at the Salonikan-founded Rue de St. Lazare synagogue and an academic conference, part of which was hosted in Geneva, Switzerland.

In Israel, the Shazar Center organized numerous international academic conferences and historical workshops on the Sephardi experience. The Sephardi Public Council of Jerusalem produced several cultural events, and the Committee of Sephardi and Oriental Communities in Jerusalem hosted several concerts. The Center for Spanish Jewish Studies of Lewinsky College in Ramat Aviv presented a lectures program and the Museum of Tel Aviv University put on exhibits on the Jewish experience in Spain. Branches of the Turkish Immigrant Association organized evenings of Judeo-Spanish conversation and song.

Several Sephardi families in Israel organized reunions around the quincentennial year, Castel, Meyuhas, and Abravanel. The Abravanel family sponsored a reunion and conference in New York City, while the Toledanos assembled in Spain.

The Public Council for the 500 Year Festivities was headed by former Israeli president Itzhak Navon who hosted the Israeli Television series "Jerusalem in Spain."

In Spain, the March 31, 1992, ceremony, where King Juan Carlos annulled the expulsion decree, attracted the attention of world Jewry and the media. Spain hosted numerous academic conferences and Spanish presses published hundreds of scholarly books on Spanish and Sephardi Jewry.

The only major foundation created for the 1992 festivities, which produced results, was the Quincentennial Foundation of Istanbul. It organized two major academic conferences and a gala banquet attended by Israeli President Herzog, Turkish President Ozal, and Turkish Prime Minister Demirel, began restoration of the Ochrid Synagogue, sponsored a photo exhibition, a film, concerts; and planned an educational kit.

In Latin America, major conferences were held in Buenos Aires, Argentina, and in Rio de Janeiro and São Paulo, Brazil. The Asociación Internacional de Escritores Judios En Lengua Hispana y Portuguese and *NOAJ, Revista Literaria* sponsored two monumental conferences; one in Jerusalem and another in Miami. In Mexico City, several cultural events were held and Sephardi books were published.

In England, a lengthy film was made on the liturgical music of the Sephardi Diaspora communities. In New York, the film *Ottoman Salonika* was finished and presented at the end of the year. Several of the films about Columbus' discovery of America mentioned the presence of a Jew in his crew, but none went into depth on this point or related to his alleged Jewish background, which in any case was disproved convincingly by two Mexican Jewish historians and the veteran historical biographer of Columbus, Taviani. [YI.K.]

SHAMIR, YIẒḤAK (see **Dc./17:553**). Following the announcement at the end of August 1983 by Prime Minister Begin that he intended to resign, Yiẓḥak Shamir was chosen as the Ḥerut party candidate to succeed him. Shamir received Knesset approval on October 10, 1983 and served as prime minister as well as foreign minister until September 1984. After the elections to the Knesset held in July 1984, Shimon Peres of the alignment became prime minister presiding over the National Unity Government with Shamir as his deputy and foreign minister. Under the coalition agreement, Shamir replaced Peres as prime minister upon completion of 25 months of the term of office, and became prime minister of Israel for a second time when he took over the premiership from Shimon Peres of the Alignment in October 1986 in accordance with the National Unity Government agreement of 1984. After the 1988 elections he remained prime minister, until Likkud lost the 1992 elections.

Israel Prime Minister Shamir (right) with Soviet Foreign Minister Shevardnadze at a press conference in Washington, D.C., Dec. 13, 1990. (GPO, Jerusalem)

SHAPIRO, AVRAHAM (1918–), Ashkenazi chief rabbi of Israel, 1983–93. Born to a family which has lived in Jerusalem for six consecutive generations, Rabbi Shapiro spent the bulk of his career in affiliation with the Merkaz ha-Rav yeshivah founded by Rabbi A. I. *Kook. Following the death of Rabbi Ẓevi Yehudah Kook, son of the founder, Rabbi Shapiro became head of the yeshivah. He also served as a *dayyan* in the High Rabbinical Court in the ten-year period preceding his election as chief rabbi in 1983.

SHAPIRO, BERNARD J. (1935–), Canadian educator and educational administrator. Born in Montreal, Shapiro studied at McGill University. After a stint in the business world, he went to Harvard University for graduate training. His early employment was in the area of educational research, but upon completion of his doctorate he was

Bernard J. Shapiro

appointed to a faculty position in educational statistics and measurement at Boston University, where he remained for nine years in a series of progressively higher administrative posts, ranging from department chairman to associate dean of education. From there he moved to the University of Western Ontario in London for four years, two as dean of education and two as the senior academic officer of the university. He then took over the directorship of Ontario's leading school of education, the Ontario Institute for Studies in Education.

He became minister in the Ministry of Education of Ontario, Canada's largest province. With responsibility for the country's major educational system, he has been in a position to have a significant effect on the direction of Canadian education policy in the future.

Shapiro has published widely on topics ranging from cognitive development to issues involving the future of higher education. He is co-editor of *Contemporary Perspectives in Educational Psychology*. In 1985 he served as a one-man Ontario Royal Commission on policy with regard to private schools. One of the major issues that he had to consider was whether religious day schools should be eligible for public funding, a course of action which he recommended under certain circumstances. Other public service activities include the presidencies of the Social Science Federation of Canada and the Canadian Society for the Study of Education.

[H.M.W.]

SHARANSKY, NATAN (Anatoly Shcharansky; 1948–), Russian Jewish activist. Born in Donetsk, Ukraine, he graduated as a computer scientist from the Moscow Physical Technical Institute. In 1973 he first applied for an emigration visa but was refused. The following year he married Natalya (Avital) who had to leave the U.S.S.R. for Israel a few hours after their marriage as her exit visa was about to expire. Sharansky, who knew English well, became a liaison between the refuseniks (Jews refused an emigration visa) and foreign newspapermen in Moscow, and was the energetic, articulate spokesman for the Aliyah movement. He represented the Jewish Emigration movement in the unofficial Helsinki Monitoring Group, where he successfully fought for its recognition as part of the Human Rights Agenda.

Sharansky medal issued 1983 by the Judah L. Magnes Memorial Museum, designer Alex Shagin (Courtesy Jewish-American Hall of Fame, Magnes Museum, Berkeley, CA; photo Mel Wachs)

In March 1976 the newspaper *Izvestia* accused him of collaborating with the CIA and ten days later he was arrested on charges of treason and espionage. For 18 months he was held in isolation in a Moscow jail, during which time hundreds of Jews were interrogated in an attempt to find evidence against him. Brought to trial, he defended himself with conspicuous courage and made an impressive speech concluding "Next Year in Jerusalem." He was pronounced guilty and sentenced to 13 years imprisonment — three in isolation and ten in a labor camp. This was one of the severest sentences passed on a Jewish activist since the death of Stalin. In fact, he was imprisoned for nine years of which only one- and a half-years were in labor camps and those mostly in punishment cells. In 1981 he was again tried on charges of being a bad influence on other prisoners and sentenced to an additional prison term. In 1982 all basic prison rights were denied him; he was not allowed to meet relatives or send letters. In protest he started a hunger strike which lasted 110 days during which time he was fed forcibly.

Avital Sharansky (Courtesy National Conference on Soviet Jewry, N.Y.)

Outside the U.S.S.R., he was the best-known refusenik as the result of an international campaign in which Avital played a prominent role. His name and plight were increasingly on the international diplomatic agenda, so much so that by 1985 no high-level meeting between Soviet and Western officials took place without a demand being made for his release, even at the level of secretaries of state and foreign ministers. He was released on February 11, 1986, an event that received worldwide publicity. Arriving that night in Israel, he vowed to continue the struggle in behalf of those still in exile and those who remained struggling to emigrate. In the following years he was ceaselessly active on the international scene in this cause and was in time rewarded by seeing the release of the refuseniks. Eventually the Gorbachev government issued a statement exonerating him and after Mikhail Gorbachev was out of office and visited Israel, he held a friendly meeting with Natan Sharansky.

With the renewed large immigration from Russia to Israel from 1989, Sharansky devoted his main attention to problems of the absorption of Russian immigrants in Israel, serving as chairman of the Soviet Jewry Zionist Forum, an umbrella organization of Soviet Jewish activists in Israel. His memoirs *Fear No Evil* appeared in the U.S. in 1988. [ED.]

SHER, ANTHONY (1949–), actor, writer, and artist. Born in Cape Town, Sher was educated at the Webber-Douglas Academy of Dramatic Art, London. He established his reputation on the London stage during the 1980s with a number of virtuoso performances. Unheroic in stature but with an intense, vivid personality, he brings enormous dynamism and panache to every part (rehearsals are always accompanied by body-training).

His extensive repertoire ranged from appearances in *Molière* and *Tartuffe* and the most discussed *Richard III* since Laurence Olivier, to *The Merchant of Venice* and *Singer* for the Royal Shakespeare Company. His roles for the National Theater have included Arturo Ui and Mark Gertler, while his playing of Arnold in *Torch Song Trilogy* was outstanding.

He received the Olivier and Evening Standard Awards for best actor in 1985.

Apart from a consuming acting career Sher is an accomplished artist who has exhibited both at London's Barbican and the National Theater and a highly successful author whose novels *Middlepost* and *The Indoor Boy* both received highly enthusiastic reviews. [SA.WH.]

SHOMRON, DAN (1937–). Israeli soldier, thirteenth chief of staff of the Israel Defense Forces. Shomron was born in kibbutz Ashdot Ya'akov in the Jordan Valley. His military career began in 1956 when he was a paratrooper. During the Six-Day War of 1967 he commanded an armored division in Sinai; and later served as commander of the southern front. After occupying various staff positions, he became deputy chief of staff. In early 1987 he was named chief of staff, taking up the position in April of that year, serving until 1991.

The Entebbe raid (see **Dc./17**:238), later renamed "Operation Yonatan," in which hostages from an air France flight hijacked en route from Tel Aviv to Paris were rescued from Entebbe Airport near Kampala. Uganda, was under the command of Shomron, then a brigadier general, who also planned the operation.

SINCLAIR, CLIVE (1948–), British writer and critic. Sinclair was born in London. In 1973 he published his first novel *Bibliosexuality*. His short stories have been published in two volumes, *Hearts of Gold* (1979) and *Bedbugs* (1982), collections which have established him as a major talent among the younger British writers. A feature of his stories is the strong focus on Jewish and Israeli themes, imagery and idiom. He has written a critical-biographical study of Isaac Bashevis Singer and Israel Joshua Singer, *The Brothers Singer* (1982). Sinclair served as literary editor of the London *Jewish Chronicle*. [SU.STR.]

SITRUK, JOSEPH (1945–), chief rabbi of France. Sitruk was born in Tunisia, but raised from early childhood on in Nice. His brilliant high school record seemed to indicate a career in science, but his extracurricular activities, such as those in the French Jewish scouting movement, led him to choose a career in the rabbinate instead.

After completing his studies at the Seminaire Rabbinique of France, he began in 1970 to serve as the rabbi of Strasbourg. In 1975 Rabbi Jacob Kaplan, chief rabbi of France, put him in charge of the Marseilles community, the second largest in France. Within a few years Sitruk had succeeded in reorganizing this rather disparate community made up of various successive waves of immigration. In ever-increasing numbers Jews began to attend synagogue and return to religious practices.

Rabbi Joseph Sitruk (Courtesy Consistoire Central, Paris)

On June 14, 1987, Joseph Sitruk was elected chief rabbi of France; he assumed office in January 1988. As successor to Chief Rabbi René Sirat, he was the second Sephardi chief rabbi of France. His election confirms the role which Sephardi Jews now play in the leadership of French Jewry following the large immigration of North African Jews to France. [D.BS.]

SOLOW, ROBERT MERTON (1924–), economist, Nobel Prize winner. Born in Brooklyn, Solow was educated at Harvard University from which he received his Ph.D. in 1951. From 1949 he was on the faculty of the Massachusetts Institute of Technology, becoming a professor of economics in 1958 and Institute Professor in 1973.

He was also affiliated with the Council of Economic Advisers, as senior economist (1961–62) and consultant (1962–68), and was a consultant to the RAND corporation (1952–64). He served as a director of the Boston Federal Reserve Bank from 1975 to 1980 and was chairman of the bank in 1979–80.

Among Solow's other activities he has been a member of the President's Commission on Income Maintenance (1968–70), served on the board of directors and as a member of the executive committee of the National Bureau of Economic Research, and served as a trustee of the Institute for Advanced Studies of Princeton University (1972–78).

He is the author of a number of works, including *The Source of Unemployment in the United States* (1964), *Growth Theory* (1970), and *The Behavior of the Price Level* (1970).

A fellow of the American Academy of Arts and Sciences and the recipient of the Seidman award in Political Economics (1983), he was awarded the Nobel Prize in Economic Sciences in 1987 for his significant contributions to the theory of economic growth.

SOUTH AFRICA (see **15**:184; **Dc./17**:588).

Demography. According to the 1991 census there were 59,000 Jews in South Africa, that is approximately half the number enumerated a decade earlier. However, the figure is misleading because, for the first time, the census described the question on religion as optional. As a result one-fifth of all whites did not answer the question. The size of the Jewish population can therefore only be estimated. According to Allie A. Dubb, currently conducting a socio-demographic survey of the South African Jewish population, an estimate based on a range of variables would be between 104,500 and 107,500 — less than 2 percent of the total white population and 0.5 percent of the total population. The size of the community has thus remained fairly constant, despite the emigration of an estimated 40,000 Jews since 1970. (There has been some immigration, including an estimated 6,000 Israelis, and re-immigration.)

The composition and structure of the community has changed significantly because emigration occurred largely among middle-aged couples and their children, with immigrants and returning emigrés having a different profile. Preliminary examination of the age distribution suggests that compared with 1980 the proportion of school-going children and their parents has decreased; those aged 60–70 have decreased and those over 70 have increased. Migration within South Africa has also continued. It is now estimated that Johannesburg has 62,000 Jews (almost 60 percent of all Jews as compared to 54 percent a decade ago) and Cape Town 23,500 (or 22 percent of all Jews). Port Elizabeth's Jewish population is approximately half its 1980 size and Pretoria's population has declined appreciably.

Community. Although funds, skilled personnel, and committed lay leadership are becoming scarce — related to the emigration of young people and the aging of the community — South African Jewry continued to manifest a cohesive communal life. This was exemplified in its two major organizations, the South African Jewish Board of Deputies (SAJBOD) and the South African Zionist Federation (SAZF). The SAJBOD deals essentially with domestic matters and the SAZF with Israel-related activities. However, in view of the changing circumstances in South Africa, it was decided in 1992 to establish a Joint Communal Co-ordinating Committee from the SAJBOD and SAZF to ensure communal unity, loyalty, and discipline. In 1987 the premier fund raising bodies — the United Communal Fund (UCF) and the Israel United Appeal (IUA) — has also merged. The single entity, known as the United Communal Fund (UCF), has unified the community and ensured that the two funds do not compete with each other for contributions. The IUA also enlists the help of the rabbinate and lay leaders of synagogues, with outstanding results. The major beneficiary of the UCF is Israel. Other recipients include the SAJBOD; the Jewish day-school movement; the Union of Orthodox Synagogues; the Union of Progressive Judaism; and the Union of Jewish Women. Congregations and other bodies raise their own funds among their members and with fund-raising drives. Although current demographic trends could eventually force the community to consider rationalizing essential services, the community still operates institutions for the handicapped, aged, and orphaned in all major centers.

According to a study conducted in 1974, 80 percent of South African Jews were affiliated with a religious body, but there is evidence that this number has declined in the interim. About four-fifths belonged to Orthodox congregations and one-fifth to Progressive congregations. There are autonomous bodies, each controlling its own affairs, with religious authority vested in its spiritual leaders. Most of the congregations, however, are affiliated with representative organizations which endeavor to strengthen Jewish religious life.

Helen Suzman at the S.A. Jewish Board of Deputies, Aug. 1989: from left to right: Mr. S. Sacks, Mr. G. Leissner, Mrs. Suzman, Mr. H. Saenger, Mrs. R. Berman (Courtesy the South African Jewish Board of Deputies)

The Union of Orthodox Synagogues (UOS) is the umbrella body for Orthodox congregations throughout South Africa. It consists of 75 synagogues and claims a membership enrollment of approximately 18,500 families. Of the 95 synagogues not more than a handful enjoy the services of a full-time rabbi. The overwhelming majority of rabbis hold down more than one job in order to earn an adequate living. The UOS appoints and maintains the office of the chief rabbi, the Johannesburg Beth Din, and the Cape Beth Din. Since 1987 the office of the chief rabbi has been held by Cyril Harris. He had been a minister of the St. John's Wood Synagogue in London and a fellow of Jews' College, London, before coming to South Africa.

The activities of Jews for Jesus — which has attracted a few hundred Jews to its programs — and other evangelical movements was viewed as a serious problem. A special department was established by the UOS to actively counter this process.

There has been a tremendous growth of the *ba'al teshuvah* movement (newly observant Jews), and 34 small *shtieblach* (synagogues) function mainly in and around Johannesburg. The Lubavich movement has also made inroads in the community, especially in Johannesburg, where it was established in 1972, and Cape Town, from 1976. Although a relatively small proportion of the community is involved in Lubavich activities, programs expanded substantially from the mid-1980s. Adult education, youth clubs, and Shabbatons are particularly popular. Outlying communities are visited periodically by a Mobile Jewish Center — "Mitzvah Tank." This specially designed motor-vehicle houses exhibits, a library, literature, *mezuzot, tefillin*, and so forth. The "tank" periodically visits schools, youth seminars, and predominantly Jewish neighborhoods. In addition, a weekly national radio program, "The Jewish Sound," was initiated and produced by the Lubavich Foundation.

For the Reform sector, the South African Union for Progressive Judaism (affiliated with the World Union of Progressive Judaism) is the co-ordinating body. Estimates of the movement's membership range from 2,500 to 6,500 families, with a total of 12 congregations in the major centers, though only a few are serviced by rabbis. Each temple operates a religious school and there is a separate, independent primary school in Johannesburg under Progressive auspices. In 1992 the Imanu-Shalom Congregations, led by Rabbi Ady Assabi, severed its ties with the South African Union for Progressive Judaism. The new group wishes to distance itself both from the Left and the Right and to find its own solutions to what it means to be Jewish in South Africa.

Education. The South African Board of Jewish Education controls one of the largest Jewish day-school systems in the Diaspora (the King David Schools), though most of its 94 affiliates around the country are afternoon nursery schools. The system maintains its cohesion and strength, even though, apart from Johannesburg and Cape Town, the number of Jewish pupils in day schools has been decreasing over the past few years — a result of demographic shifts within the Jewish population. However, the gradual desegregation of South African education has implications for the Jewish day school. State schools now demand ever-increasing tuition fees and the Jewish day school appears as a bastion of academic excellence. For this reason the relatively few Jewish pupils in the state schools are considering the Jewish day school option.

Jewish day schools provide education from pre-school to the completion of high school for approximately 8,000 pupils — more than 60 percent of all Jewish children in South Africa. They receive a full education following a state syllabus and a Jewish studies program, including religion, history, literature, and Hebrew language. Although all schools have an Orthodox orientation — often described as "national traditional" — some provide a more intensive Orthodox religious education than others. The mainstream Jewish day schools accept children of mixed marriages and Reform converts.

The South African Board of Jewish Education also involves itself with Jewish children who attend state schools and whose main access to Jewish education is through the *Heder* program and by means of religious instruction booklets sent into the schools. It also administers a network of Hebrew nursery schools according to the standards laid down by the Nursery School Association of South Africa. The Cape Council of the South African Jewish Board of Education has its own religious instruction program for Jewish pupils who attend the state schools in the Western Cape Province.

A more intensive Jewish education program is provided for approximately 1,700 pupils by the Yeshivah College; the Torah Academy of the Lubavich Foundation; the Beis Yakov Girls' High School; the Sha'arei Torah Primary School; and the Yeshivat Torat Emet, all in Johannesburg, as well as the Hebrew Academy in Cape Town.

The Progressive movement also maintains a network of supplementary Hebrew and religious classes at its temples. These schools are affiliated with the Union for Progressive Jewish Education. The first multi-racial Progressive Jewish Day School opened in Johannesburg during 1992: the Yael Primary School is the latest addition to the Yael Education Project which operates two nursery and play schools as well as an aftercare center.

At the tertiary level, Hebrew teachers are trained at the Rabbi Zlotnick Hebrew Teachers Training College in Johannesburg. University students are able to take Jewish studies through the Semitics Department of the University of South Africa (UMISA); the Department of Hebrew and Jewish Studies of Natal University; the Department of Hebrew at the University of the Witwatersrand; and the Department of Hebrew and Jewish Studies (including the Isaac and Jessie Kaplan Centre for Jewish Studies and Research) at the University of Cape Town. A Jewish Studies University Program (JSUP) was founded in Johannesburg in 1976 combining traditional Jewish studies with university studies through UMISA. In 1992 JSUP opened a Graduate Law School on its newly renovated campus. A substantial range of Jewish adult education programs is offered in Johannesburg and Cape Town. Some are associated with the university campus while others take place under the auspices of specific movements or groups.

Politics. President P. W. Botha initiated politial reforms to the apartheid systems through the 1980s, amid substantial popular resistance and repression. In 1983 a Tricameral parliament with one chamber each for Whites, Colored, and Indians replaced a whites-only Westminster system. There was a general erosion of "petty" apartheid, including the removal from the statute books of the Immorality Act (which prohibited sexual contact between whites and "non-whites"); and Mixed Marriages Act. Black trade unions were formally accepted; job reservation was modified; pass laws prohibiting the free movement of blacks were repealed; and promises were made to share power with the black majority. Reform gained momentum following the inauguration of F. W. de Klerk as President in 1989. On February 2, 1990, he unbanned all prohibited organizations including the African National Congress (ANC), the South African Communist Party (SACP), and the Pan Africanist Party (PAC). Nelson Mandela was released from prison, political exiles were allowed to return, and the state of emergency was lifted.

Pres. De Klerk of South Africa speaking at a ceremony in his honor in the Rose Garden, Jerusalem, Nov. 10, 1991; Pres. Herzog stands to his right. (GPO, Jerusalem)

South African politics is in a state of transition with political leaders grappling to formulate a new democratic constitution. The process has been characterized by internecine political violence, worker militancy, economic hardship; and social violence. Negotiations broke down temporarily in mid-1992 but towards the end of 1992, bilateral meetings between major political opponents gave some cause for optimism.

The National Party's move away from pure apartheid attracted some Jewish support although the majority of Jews continued to support the liberal opposition Progressive Federal Party, later transformed into the Democratic Party. A substantial number of Jews were engaged in social action and welfare activities. Jews were prominent in various activist organizations including Lawyers for Human Rights, the Legal Resources Center, and the End Conscription Campaign which sought changes to laws regarding compulsory military service for whites. Two specifically Jewish activist organizations were founded in the mid-1980s: Jews for Social Justice in Johannesburg and Jews for Justice in Cape Town. In 1987 Jews for Social Justice participated in the founding of the Five Freedoms Forum, a broad grouping of 25 white organizations opposed to apartheid.

The SAJBOD has fully supported moves away from apartheid. In the early 1980s statements condemned evictions of black leaders and pass-law arrests, detention without trial, a university quota system for blacks, and the treatment of black squatters near Cape Town. At its national conference of 1985, and again in 1987, the Board explicitly rejected apartheid. Changes initiated by President De Klerk have been officially welcomed.

Applauding President De Klerk does not mean unequivocal Jewish confidence in the future. In addition to apprehensions Jews share with many other white South Africans, they also have particular concerns: the freedom to practice a full Jewish life as individuals and as a collectivity, the right to pursue Zionist activities, and the continuation of relations between South Africa and Israel. It was thus not surprising that, shortly after a Jewish cemetery has been desecrated in Pretoria and Mandela had embraced Arafat when the two leaders met in Namibia in 1990, Jews packed meetings in Cape Town and Johannesburg to hear communal leaders, including the chief rabbi, Cyril Harris, assess the Jewish future in South Africa. At each gathering leaders attempted to assuage Jewish fears. They assured their audiences that President De Klerk would not countenance anti-Semitism and that the SAJBOD was monitoring events closely.

The SAJBOD is fully aware that political transformation could generate an anti-Jewish right-wing reaction. However, Jews are not on the agenda of the Conservative Party (CP), the right-wing parliamentary opposition. Nonetheless the brand of nationalism espoused by the CP is Christian-National in content and exclusivist in orientation. The most conspicuous of the ultra-right movements is the Afrikaner-wearstandsbeweging (Afrikaner Resistance Movement), known as the AWB and noted for its swastika-like emblem and brown-shirted cadres. This ostensibly cultural organization made it clear that under an AWB dispensation, Jews (together with other non-Christians) would be deprived of political rights. Anti-Semitic views are also expounded by numerous small white supremacist movements and cells, including the Blanke Bevrydingsbeweging (White Liberation Movement); the World Apartheid Movement; the Israelites; and the Church of the Creator.

Left-wing groups, such as the ANC, the PAC, the Azanian Peoples' Organization (AZAPO), Call of Islam, and Quibla (a Muslim fundamentalist movement), pursue a vigorous anti-Zionist line. Their support builds upon black disappointment at close ties between South Africa and Israel and suspected military co-operation. Anti-Zionist sentiment was already evident at the time of the Lebanon War (1982) and consolidated during the *intifada*. In particular the Muslim population of over 400,000 has pursued a vigorous stance against Israel. This was very evident during the Gulf War. Notwithstanding sympathy for the Palestinian people, black leaders make a clear distinction between anti-Zionism and anti-Semitism. Nonetheless, there are indications of substantial "social distance" between blacks and Jews, including anti-Jewish attitudes among blacks.

Relations with Israel. The SAZF is the representative body co-ordinating Zionist activity and the various Zionist groupings, organizations, and societies are affiliated with it. Its department deal with organization and information, fund raising, youth activities, women's work, and immigration to Israel. A number of Zionist youth movements are affiliated with the SAZF: Habonim, Benei Akiva, Betar, and Maginim. They conduct cultural programs, organize youth activities and run summer camps. In addition university youth have their representative organization — the South African Union of Jewish Students (SAUJS) — affiliated to both the SAJBOD and SAZF.

Political uncertainty generated substantial immigration to Israel and promotion of *aliyah*. South African Zionists succeeded in setting up a co-ordinating committee of the Israeli government's Absorption Ministry, the World Zionist Organization, and their own Israel office.

South Africa consolidated warm relations with Israel through the 1980s. However, as Western pressure against South Africa intensified, Israel was forced into reassessing this relationship. The United States threatened to cut military assistance to countries engaged in military trade with South Africa. In 1987 Israel agreed "to refrain from new undertakings between Israel and South Africa in the realm of defense." In line with its general opposition to sanctions as a policy, the South African Jewish leadership urged Israel not to take that step. Notwithstanding Israeli policy, the South African government continued to accept "approved enterprise to certain categories of investment" in Israel, among them residential housing, subject to certain conditions.

The *intifada* had little impact on South African Jewry and the community continues to demonstrate unquestioning support for Israel. Loyalty was further in evidence during the Gulf War. Solidarity meetings and prayer vigils were held and a "solidarity tour" was undertaken during the war by 70 delegates. President De Klerk sent Prime Minister Shamir a letter of support during the war and later visited Israel to cement ties between South Africa and Israel. In Israel he reaffirmed his appreciation of South African Jewry's contribution to South Africa. [MI.SH.]

SPANISH AND PORTUGUESE LITERATURE. Latin America (see **15**:254; **Dc./17**:559). Latin American Jewish literature developed specifically in the 1970s and 1980s, and can be defined as the treatment of Jewish values in two languages — Spanish and Portuguese, as conceived and spoken in Latin America; and more particularly, as the way in which these languages have left their mark on Latin American Jewry, through those authors who use them as their vehicle.

In other words, the Jewish literature of Latin America exploits the possibilities of expression offered by the Portuguese and Spanish languages to translate, both at the personal and collective level, the way in which basic Jewish values are experienced and interpreted in the framework of living conditions in this part of the world. In the words of literary critic Saul Sonowski, "Jewish literature in Latin America is not built exclusively on the basis of motifs which can easily be identified as Jewish, but as a function of the relationship of these motifs to concrete realities which are in a process of development and transformation: the realities of the Latin American societies in which they must evolve." What he means basically is that the Latin American Jewish writers are an inseparable part of their respective national literatures. Their acknowledgment of their Jewishness resides in their perception of themselves as Uruguayan, Brazilian, Mexican, Venezuelan, Chilean, or Argentine writers whose works and thought integrally include a Jewish thematic variation, which may be more or less frequent, more or less intense, and can be formulated and reelaborated in an infinite variety of ways. The Jewish variation cannot be isolated from the totality which gives its meaning, nor placed in a hierarchy to the detriment of the totality. Nevertheless, Latin American Jewish writers, in order to consolidate their respective identities as Latin American writers, also have to take their positions as Jews. In their work, Jewish and Latin American themes, far from constituting an irreconcilable antithesis, as is often alleged by explicitly anti-Semitic and implicitly discriminatory theses, have become strongly complementary and inseparable.

For many years, in the Latin American cultural arena, the need for an alternative was solicited equally zealously by both the nationalist right and the Marxist-Leninist left: strictly specific characteristics, such as those implicit to the Jewish condition, were to be merged into the national identity (right) or the international proletariat identity (left).

A gathering for Jewish Book Month sponsored by AMIA, August 1988; from left to right: Manuela Fingueret, Saul Sosnowski, Hector Yanover, Arnoldo Liberman, Leonardo Senkman, Gerardo Goldboff, Florinda Goldberg, Eliahu Toker, Daniel Gutman, Alicia Dujovne Ortiz (Courtesy Santiago Kovadloff, Buenos Aires)

Considered "foreign" by the former and "reactionary" by the latter until well into the 1970s, Judaism seemed to have no future as a variation in the composite profile of the Latin American writer. However, the situation began to change in the 1970s. Government terrorism, which raged in every corner of the continent, but with an especially bloody genocide in the southern tip of Latin America, gave rise to a new phenomenon in the region — a diaspora. This bitter experience strongly paralleled Jewish memories.

Discrimination, censorship, persecution, torture, imprisonment, and death were practiced with systematic tenacity by the successive dictatorships, especially against anyone daring to challenge the regime in force; fearing for their lives, many fled their country or even the continent. Jewish writers naturally drew parallels between past and present. At the same time, the seeds of today's Communist crisis were already present. Against this background, the meaning of Judaism, as a constituent element of the personal and historic identity of so many writers, underwent an intense process of redefinition, inspired not only by the suffering but also by its dialectic complement — the spirit of struggle, the capacity to confront adversity. Judaism was beginning to be seen as a determined demand for pluralism, for democratic ideals, for a thirst for dialogue, in open opposition to dogmatism and contempt for differentness. Beyond its possible adherence to theological arguments and religious options of one kind or another, Judaism was conceived, by contemporary Latin American writers, as a moving metaphor of their own experience and was thus ultimately acknowledged as an inalienable part of an individual identity.

"In the countries of Latin America, which have experienced a repression unprecedented in their history, survival — perhaps the basic motif of all Jewish literature — has obviously played a major role" (Saul Sosnowski). And "it is under identical circumstances that some Jewish motifs have become precision instruments in interpreting a reality that centuries of persecution and exile have imprinted in the cultural tradition of the historic Jew" (Saul Sosnowski).

In addition to the decisive theme of survival, other fundamental themes began to appear in poetry, fiction, and drama. Man's dialogue with God with its innumerable variations, the sufferings imposed by prejudice and intolerance, the intensity of nostalgia, exile and its indelible shadow, the meaning of death, the value of memory, mysticism, the warmth of family life, the immigrant origin, the Jewish holidays and history, the unexpected recording of one's own life as an "immigrant," and the presence and ethical and even esthetic weight of tradition all to a great extent shape the repertory of themes which, in numerous forms, run through Latin American Jewish literature. And just as European or North American Jewish literature, for instance, have distinctive traits, specific only to a country or a continent, so Latin American Jewish literature has its own, unique characteristics. Its treatment of proverbially Jewish questions has an unmistakably Latin American emphasis, in that the Jewish models are presented through the subjective, social, and historic experience of the countries of Latin America, with their specific conflicts, resources, and conditions. The Jewish statement is made through the Spanish and Portuguese languages, with their own cultural imprint, and thereby receives a specific bias — accorded by the distinctive intonation of the language in every country and region where it is spoken. This intonation is not only that of the language's rhythm, its euphony, but also that of its semantic weave, which in each locality, and in each consciousness, links the repertoire of resources offered by the language to its users, giving birth to that fertile "hybrid" condition noted by writer Ricardo Feierstein; and to the theme which, among so many other nationalities, both incorporates the Jewish element in and separates it from the Bolivian, Peruvian, Colombian, or Cuban element and elegantly frames a Jewish individuality which, while obviously related to others, is not one of them. This "hybridism" is simply the permanent interweaving of two originally separate traditions — the Jewish and Latin American, which, through the meeting of circumstances, ultimately shaped a new expression. The value and quality of this possibility of expression characterizes Latin American Jewish literature.

In other words, Spanish and Portuguese are not the languages into which the universal nature of Judaism is translated, but the means through which it is constituted and conceived in Latin America. Based in these languages, Jewish poetry, fiction, and drama, as well as essays and critical reviews, are seen as the highest grade of conceptual elaboration which Jewish experience has attained in Latin America. While Latin American Jews do not have to be aware of this in order to be what they are, it is no less true that this knowledge constitutes for them a privileged resource for a greater and better understanding of their identity.

Since the reestablishment of democratic institutions in the 1980s, in particular, Latin American Jewry has encountered a fertile terrain in which to shape itself, demonstrating that a complete manifestation of the universality of Jewish values is possible only when inspired by a concrete historic circumstance. It is in the light of their experience as Latin Americans that the validity of the meaning of Jewishness can be projected in the contemporary world. Every literary work, beyond its value as a comparative model, expresses that moment of luminous encounter between past and present which imbues the experience it describes, the statement it makes, with both an individual, specific, and even regional nuance, and an archetypal, metaphoric, and revealing dimension whose symbolic stature is universal. In this way the yesterday of previous generations who sustained, enjoyed, and suffered the Jewish condition, becomes the today shaped by our circumstances, which are no less worrying or fascinating than those of the past. Through looking at the past one learns to see those who observe from the present; observations of the present brings to the acknowledgment of the validity of this millennia-old message. Latin American Jewish literature proves this eloquently. It is one of the basic indications of Latin American Jewry's intense desire to attain self-understanding. Ideed, to a very great extent literary activity in the 1980s evidenced the resolute initiative and great persistency of this community in examining its condition. Among the events demonstrating this orientation should be noted: two encounters of Latin American Jewish writers held in Buenos Aires in 1986 and in 1988; the proliferation of poetry, fiction and essays, which join together with remarkable elegance the double source of personal identity — Jewish and Latin American; the appearance of *Noaj*, the first Jewish literary review in Spanish and Portuguese edited in Israel; the creation, also in Israel, of a Jewish writers' association in both languages. All these proved decisive acts and showed the extent of Latin American Jewry's eagerness for self-exploration and self-expression. Certainly it is not by chance that all these developments are taking place at a time when the values of political democracy are being progressively restored. Democracy is the most propitious condition for the institution of pluralism; and Judaism, freed from the oppressive yoke placed upon it by totalitarian thinking, finds itself with an auspicious opportunity to say and affirm what it is, and to begin once again to question its own meaning.

[S.KOV.]

SPITZ, MARK (1950–), U.S. Olympic champion. Spitz learned to swim at six and swam in competitions at ten. At 15 he went to Israel for the *Maccabiah games with the

Mark Spitz (left) with Mayor Teddy Kollek at the Philip Lown Community Center in Jerusalem where he gave a swimming demonstration, May 1, 1983 (Photo Keren Benzian, Jerusalem)

United States team. There, in his first international competition, he won four gold medals. Next he set his sites on the 1968 Olympic Games in Mexico City, where much was expected of him. However, a series of unfortunate incidents, including some of an anti-Semitic nature, dealt his Olympic chances a blow. He ended up with only two gold medals in the relays, a silver medal in the 100-meter butterfly and a bronze medal in the 100-meter freestyle — an outstanding feat by most standards but not for someone who many considered the greatest all-round swimmer in history.

Between the 1968 and 1972 Olympic Games Spitz won numerous national and collegiate titles, set many world records, and in 1971 became the first Jewish winner of the AAU's James E. Sullivan Award as his nation's outstanding amateur athlete. He completed his competitive swimming career with an unprecedented seven gold medals in the 1982 Olympic Games in Munich. His victories, all world records, were in the 100- and 200-meter freestyle, the 100- and 200-meter butterfly events and all the relays.

Spitz is a member of the Swimming Hall of Fame and the International Jewish Sports Hall of Fame. [J.H.S.]

SPORTS (see **15**:291; **Dc./17**:563). **1983–1992.**

Association Football (Soccer). Alan Rothenberg, a lawyer, was elected president of the U.S. Soccer Federation in 1990. Rothenberg served as commissioner of soccer in the 1984 Olympic Games. In 1990 Henry Kissinger, former U.S. secretary of state, was named vice chairman of the U.S. World Cup '94 organizing committee.

Yair Allnut was a member of the 1992 U.S. Olympic Games team and a gold medalist in the 1991 Pan American Games. Jeff Agoos represented the U.S. in international competition in 1991 and 1992, and Debbi Belkin performed with the U.S. gold medal team in the inaugural Women's World Championships in China in 1991.

Automobile Racing. Kenny Bernstein won a record-tying four consecutive U.S. National Hot Rod Association Funny Car Championships in 1985–88. He switched to the Top Fuel class in 1990 and the following year had a record six victories in a season. In 1992 Bernstein recorded four wins and became the first drag racer to cover a quarter mile at more than 300 miles per hour.

Baseball. Hank Greenberg, the first Jewish player elected to the Baseball Hall of Fame, died in 1986. His son Steve Greenberg served as the deputy commissioner of baseball in 1989–93. In 1992 Alan (Bud) Selig, owner of the Milwaukee Brewers Baseball Club, was named chairman of baseball's executive council and given the authority to act as commissioner.

Marvin Miller, who had served as the executive director of the Major League Baseball Players Association since 1966, retired in 1983. After seven years Al Rosen, a former all-star third baseman, retired as president and general manager of the San Francisco Giants in 1992. Owner Bob Lurie sold the Giants in 1993.

Al Rosen (Courtesy San Francisco Giants, San Francisco)

Basketball. David Stern became the commissioner of the National Basketball Association in 1983 and in 1992 was named the most powerful person in sports by a national sports publication. *The Sporting News* said of him, "As a direct result of David Stern's progressive leadership, the NBA now has the greatest universal appeal of any professional sport."

Coach Larry Brown, basketball's traveling man, left the NBA New Jersey Nets in 1983 to go to the University of Kansas. In 1988 he went from Kansas to the NBA Antonio Spurs, and in 1992 he moved from San Antonio to the NBA Los Angeles Clippers. Brown's Kansas club won the college (NCAA) championship in 1988, and San Antonio went from a 21–61 record in Brown's first year to 56–26 the following year. The 35-game swing was a one-season NBA record.

Israeli Nadav Henefeld enjoyed an outstanding 1989–90 season at the University of Connecticut. Connecticut won the Big East title and reached the NCAA championship final eight. For his efforts Henefeld was named honorable mention All-America.

Senda Berenson, the "Mother of Women's Basketball" and its first female entrant, and William (Red) Holzman, who

Kenny Bernstein, champion automobile racer (Courtesy, Nat. Hot Rod Association, Glendora, CA)

Memorial plaque in the Los Angeles Coliseum dedicated to the Israeli athletes murdered at the 1972 Munich Olympics (Courtesy Los Angeles Collesium, Sports Arena Complex; photo Andrew D. Bernstein, Pasadena)

coached in the NBA for 18 years, were inducted into the International Basketball Hall of Fame in 1985 and 1986. Holzman's New York Knicks teams won the NBA championships in 1970 and 1973.

Bowling. Bowlers Mark Roth and Marshall Holman, players of the year in 1984 and 1987, were voted into the U.S. Professional Bowlers Association's Hall of Fame in 1987 and 1990. Veteran Barry Asher joined the PBA Hall of Fame in 1988, and the American Bowling Congress' Hall of Fame added Norman Meyers in 1983 and Al Cohn in 1985.

Boxing. French boxers Gilles Elbilia and Fabrice Benichou enjoyed ring successes in the 1980s and 1990s. Elbilia won the French and European welterweight titles in 1982 and 1983 while Benichou won the World and European featherweight championships in 1989 and 1991.

Scotland's Gary (Kid) Jacobs defeated an Australian opponent and won the British Commonwealth welterweight championship in 1988. He lost the title the following year. In 1992 he became the British welterweight champion.

Canoeing. The two-man whitewater team of Joe Jacobi and his partner won a Olympic Games gold medal in 1992. It was only the fifth canoeing or kayaking gold medal won by the U.S. in Olympic Games history.

Equestrian. Margie Goldstein was named the 1989 and 1991 American Grand Prix Rider of the Year. In 1991 she became the first show jumper to win eight Grand Prix events in one season. Serious injuries cost her an Olympic Games opportunity in 1992.

Fencing. American medalists in the Pan American Games were Elaine Cheris, Paul Friedberg, and Jeff Bukantz in 1987 and Nick Bravin, John Friedberg, Chris O'Loughlin, and Joseph Socolof in 1991.

Israel's Udi Carmi placed fourth in the foil competition in the 1987 World Championships.

Field Hockey. A women's Olympic Games gold medalist in 1984, and a bronze medal winner in 1988, Carina Benninga carried the Netherland's flag at the Olympic Games opening ceremony in 1992.

Football (American). Players who performed on Super Bowl teams were Llye Alzado, Los Angeles Raiders, 1984; Ed Newman, Miami Dolphins, 1985 and John Frank and Harris Barton, San Francisco 49ers, 1989 and 1990. Alzado, Frank, and Barton played on winning teams.

Alzado, Newman, Barton, and Brad Edelman of the New Orleans Saints were named to All-Pro teams during this period. With the exception of Barton, all had retired from the game by 1990. Barton, an offensive tackle, was an All-Pro in 1990 and 1992. Alzado died in 1992.

Coach Marv Levy, the Phi Beta Kappa scholar who was hired by the Buffalo Bills in 1986, led the Bills to four consecutive AFC easter division titles (1988–91) and to their first Football Conference championship in 1991.

Coach Sid Gillman and Al Davis were voted into the Professional Football Hall of Fame in 1983 and 1992. In 1989 Gillman was also named to the College Football Hall of Fame. Beginning in 1960 Davis served as a personnel assistant and scout, head coach, general manager, league commissioner, principle team owner, and chief executive officer. Davis was a Gillman assistant in 1960.

Golf. Amy Alcott won 14 tournaments between 1983 and 1992. Her victories included three majors, the Dinah Shore Invitation in 1983, 1988, and 1991. For 12 consecutive years (1975–1986) she registered at least one Ladies Professional Golf Association victory. By the end of 1992 Alcott had 29 wins, just one short of automatic entry into the LPGA Hall of Fame.

After 13 years as a club professional, Bruce Fleischer returned to the tour and won his first Professional Golf Association tournament in 1991. In 1992 Monte Scheinblum won the National Long Drive championship. Entertainer Dinah Shore was the 1985 recipient of the Patty Berg Award for outstanding contributions to women's golf.

Gymnastics. Olympic medalists included Mitch Gaylord of the U.S. and Valeri Balenki of the Unified Team. Gaylord won a gold, a silver, and two bronze medals in 1984 and Balenki a gold and a bronze n 1992.

In 1990 it was learned that Maria Gorckhovskya of the U.S.S.R. was Jewish. Gorckhovskya won two gold and five silver medals in the 1952 Olympic Games.

Americans Lucy Wener and Brian Ginsberg won Pan American Games gold medals in 1983 and 1987.

Horse Racing. Jockeys Walter Blum and Jacob Pincus were enshrined in the U.S. Thoroughbred Racing Hall of Fame in 1987 and 1988. Blum rode 4,382 winners in a 22-year career (1953–1975), and Pincus, a leading 19th-century jockey was also an outstanding trainer. Another Hall of Fame entry in 1990 was owner Sam Rubin's John Henry a two-time American Horse of the Year.

In 1983, with 2,500 victories to his credit, South African jockey Stanley Amos retired, the same year another South African jockey Basil Barcus recorded his 1,000 win.

Ice Skating (Figure and Speed). Dr. Alain Calmat, an Olympic silver medalist in figure skating in 1964 became France's Minister of Youth and Sports in 1984. American Judy Blumberg and her partner won bronze medals in ice dancing in the World Figure Skating Championships in 1983–85. They placed fourth in the 1984 Olympic Games.

In speed skating American Andrew Gabel won seven medals in the Winter World University Games in 1985, 1989, and 1991.

Jai Alai. American Joey Cornblit, a professional for 20 years, won the Tournament of Champions (a meeting of the sport's top players) in 1992 when he also won his ninth Florida singles championship.

Judo. After 40 years Israel won its first Olympic medals in 1992. Yael Arad gained a silver medal in women's competition and Shay Oren Smadga took a bronze in the men's events. Other Olympic medalists were American Robert Berland, silver, and Canadian Mark Berger, bronze, in 1984.

Pan American Games medalists in 1983 and 1987

included Berland, Berger and also American Damon Keeve.

Karate. Between 1986 and 1988 Kathy Jones won two silver and four bronze medals in World Cup and World Championship competition. Danny Hakim of Australia won a silver medal in the 1988 World Championships.

Luge (Toboggan). American Gordy Sheer won gold medals in the North American Championships doubles in 1990 and 1991. Sheer also participated in the 1992 Olympic Games.

Motorboat Racing. Don Aronow, American boat designer and two-time world offshore powerboat champion (1967 and 1969), died in 1987.

Roller Skating. American Scott Cohen, who won the world free skating championships in 1985, 1986, 1989, and 1990, became the first singles skater to win the title four times. Cohen also won a Pan American Games silver medal in 1987.

Rowing. Seth Bauer won an Olympic Games bronze medal in 1988. Other American participants in the 1988 Olympic Games were Sherri Cassuto and Jon Fish. Bauer, Fish, and Cassuto won Pan American Games and World Championships medals between 1985 and 1991.

Pablo Bulgach of Argentina and Betsy Kimmel, U.S., won Pan American Games gold medals in 1987 and 1991.

Shooting. Joelle Fefer of Canada won three Pan American Games medals in 1983 and 1987. Thomas Bernstein, a member of the Norwegian national team, won the U.S. national collegiate (NCAA) rifle championship in 1988.

Skiing. American Hayley Wolff won a grand prix mogul gold medal in 1983 and a silver medal in the first world freestyle championship in 1986.

Surfing. South African Shaun Tomson, who won the world professional championship in 1977, remained among the world's best surfers in 1985. After a decade of competition Tomson had recorded the most victories in the Association of Surfing Professionals world tour.

Swimming and Water Polo. In 1983 Mark Spitz was one of the first 20 Olympians named to the U.S. Olympic Hall of Fame and Museum. Chosen by the National Association of Sportscasters and Sportswriters, Spitz received the second highest number of votes cast; only Track and Field great Jesse Owens received more.

Dara Torres won her second gold and third Olympic medal in 1992. She gained her first gold in 1984 and received a Olympic bronze medal in 1988. Other American medalists in major international competition were John Witchel, 1987, Pan American Games, two golds, and Cheryl Kriegsman, Dan Kutler, and Dan Kanner in the World University Games in 1987 and 1991.

Olympic finalists in 1988 and 1992 were Vadim Alekseev, U.S.S.R., and Tomas Deutsch, Hungary. Alekseev, who is now an Israeli, won a Goodwill Games silver medal in 1990.

In Synchronized Swimming Americans Tracy Long and Ann Miller won Pan American Games gold medals in 1987 and 1991.

Al Schoenfield, publisher and editor of swimming publications, and Dr. Paul Neumann, Austria, 1896 Olympic gold medalist, were named to the International Swimming Hall of Fame in 1985 and 1986.

In Water Polo Australia's Russell Basser and American Charles Harris represented their countries in the 1984 and 1992 Olympic Games. Harris was a silver medalist in the 1991 Pan American Games.

Table Tennis. Ivor Montagu of Great Britain, who became the first chairman of the Table Tennis International Federation and held the post for over 40 years, died in 1984.

Tennis. Two outstanding American players, Brian Gottfried and Harold Solomon, retired from the professional tour in 1984. Other Americans Eloit Telscher, Brad Gilbert, Aaron Krickstein, and Jay Berger and Israel's Amos Mansdorf and Argentina's Martin Jaite joined the world's tennis elite in the 1980s. These players and Shlomo Glickstein, Shahar Perkiss, and Gilad Bloom of Israel and Andrew Sznajder of Canada played in Davis Cup competition. Elise Burgin represented the U.S. in Federation Cup play.

American Jim Grabb was a member of the men's doubles combination that won the U.S. Open championship in 1992, and Brad Gilbert won a men's singles bronze medal in the 1988 Olympic Games.

Joseph Cullman III, who helped launch the women's pro tour, was inducted into the International Tennis Hall of Fame in 1992.

Track & Field. Irena Kiszenstein Szewinska of Poland, who won gold medals in three Olympic Games, was inducted into the International Women's Sports Hall of Fame in 1992. In 1991 another Olympian, America's Abel Kiviat, a 1912 silver medalist, died at the age of 99. Kiviat set a world 1500-meter record in the same Olympic year.

In 1992 Mel Rosen served as the U.S. men's Olympic coach, and Yevgeniy Krasnov of Israel placed eighth in the Olympic pole vault competition.

American Ken Flax won medals in the World University Games in 1989 and 1991 (gold) and was named the ninth ranked hammer thrower in the world in 1991.

Fred Lebow, president of the New York Road Runners Club (the largest American club of its kind) and founder and director of the New York Marathon and the Fifth Avenue Mile, ran in his own marathon in 1992, only two years after he was diagnosed with cancer and given just months to live. It was Lebow's first marathon run in four years.

Volleyball. Doug Beal and Israel's Arie Selinger coached the U.S. Olympic men's and women's teams to gold and silver medals in 1984. They were the first medals ever won by American teams in Olympic competition.

In 1992 Selinger coached the Netherlands men to an Olympic silver medal. Selinger's son Arbital was a member of the Dutch team. Other Olympic Games medalists were Bernard Rajzman, Brazil, silver, 1984, and Dan Greenbaum, U.S, bronze, 1992.

Weightlifting. David Lowenstein of Australia won a Commonwealth Games silver medal in 1986, and Giselle Shepatin and Rachel Silverman won silver medals for the U.S. in the Women's International Weightlifting Tournaments in 1985 and 1987. Allon Kirschner of Israel won a gold medal in the World Powerlifting Championships in 1989.

Wrestling. Pan American Games medalists included Canada's Gary Kallos, sambo wrestling, gold, 1983; Andrew Borodow, free and Greco-Roman wrestling, two silvers, 1991; and also American Andrew Seras, Greco-Roman wrestling, gold, 1991. Seras and Borodow competed in the Olympic Games in 1988 and 1992.

Yachting. American helmsman Larry Klein won four world's championships between 1983 and 1991. He was named U.S. Yachtsman of the Year in 1989. [J.H.S.]

SPORTS IN ISRAEL (see **9**:1019; **Dc./17**:563). **1983–1992.** The decade 1983–1992 was noted in Israel's sports for two major breakthroughs — one in the political domain, the other in the athletic arena.

The political breakthrough began in 1989 when the Soviet Union, under President Gorbachev, relented in its opposition to the acceptance of Israel into the European zone of the various international sport federations. Thus Israel, which had been without a continental affiliation since its expulsion from Asian sports in the mid-1970s, was able to enter the European federations and their regular activities. By 1992 this procedure had been completed for all practical purposes,

Yael Arad (Photo David Ben Dov)

the European Soccer Federation (UEFA) being one of the last federations that had not granted Israel full membership status. At the same time the UEFA from 1987 invited Israel's youth teams to participate in its championships and in 1992 invited the national champion as well as the cup-holder to participate in the annual competitions organized by it.

The major breakthrough in athletics occurred during the Olympic Games in Barcelona in the summer of 1992 when two Judokas succeeded in bringing to Israel for the first time Olympic medals — Yael Arad returning with the silver medal in women's 61 kg. class and Oren Smadja with the bronze medal in the men's 71 kg. class.

Israel had, in fact, been very close to gaining its first Olympic medals already at Seoul in 1988. However, Joel Sela and Eldad Amir had to be satisfied with a fourth place in the Flying Dutchman class of the Olympic yachting competitions, after forfeiting one race because it was held on Yom Kippur. The same couple was placed eighth in the 1984 Olympics at Los Angeles. Similar placings, which were the best during those Olympics, were achieved by the yachtsmen Shimshon Brockman and Eitan Friedlander in the 470 class, as well as by the marksman Yitzchak Yonassi.

In Israel's representation at the Barcelona Olympics, 11 out of the 31 representatives were newcomers to the State of Israel, primarily from the former Soviet Union. The top achievements of those newcomers were the sixth place of weightlifter Andre Danisov in the 100 kg. class and the eighth place of Yevgeni Krasnov in the pole vault.

The significant improvement of the standard of the top athletes can further be seen from a list of achievements in recent years in other sports. In July 1992 Johar Abu-Lashin, a Christian Arab from Nazareth, became the first Israeli professonal athlete to gain a world champion's title, when he became lightweight champion of the World Boxing Federation. The same year windsurfer Amit Inbar was placed second in the world championship (and a disappointing eighth in the Olympics), after having ranked first in the previous year. Another newcomer from the Soviet Union, the wrestler Max Geller, succeeded in winning the silver medal at the European championships in freestyle wrestling in 1991.

On the other hand basketball, which had been the outstanding sport in Israel for its quality for a long time, supplied disappointments in the last decade. Whereas the men's national team was placed second in the European championship in 1979, sixth in 1981, and fifth in 1983, it receded to ninth place in 1985, to eleventh in 1987, and thereafter did not qualify for the final stages of the championship (until 1993). However, in 1986 the team succeeded for the second time in history (after 1954) to qualify for the final stages of the world championship, where it came seventh.

The Maccabi Tel Aviv basketball team also did not succeed in repeating its earlier successes (wins in 1977 and 1981) in the European Champions' Cup games. Although the team reached the finals three years in a row (1987–1989), it was beaten at that stage by teams from Italy and Yugoslavia. After 1989 Maccabi did not manage again to reach the Final Four.

Delegations from the participating countries entering the Ramat Gan Sports Stadium at the opening of the 13th Hapoel Games, May 1987 (GPO, Jerusalem)

The women's national team in basketball succeeded in 1990 to reach the "final eight" in the continental championship, but this turned out to be a one-time achievement.

Israel's tennis managed to be in the limelight from 1986 until 1989, when the men's team held its place among the top 16 nations in the world within the framework of the Davis Cup games. As of 1990 attempts to return to the top have not been successful. The above achievement was mainly due to Israel's no.1 player, Amos Mansdorf, who at the peak of his career (in 1987) ranked no.18 in the world. In the following years Mansdorf had a ranking around no.30.

While soccer remained Israel's most popular sport, the Football Association had very little to show as far as achievements on the international scene were concerned. In 1989 Israel came closest to repeating its appearance in the final stages of the World Cup (the first and only time was in 1970), but drew with Colombia in Ramat Gan, after losing by a single goal in the away game. Israel reached this stage after winning the zone of Oceania, to which it was removed by the FIFA as a result of the Asian boycott and the UEFA's refusal, up to that time, to let Israel participate in the European zone.

In 1988 the Knesset passed the "Sports Law," after tabling it for 13 years. Its major provisions called for manadatory certification of coaches and instructors; mandatory health and loss of income insurance of athletes participating in competitive sports; mandatory periodical medical examinations for participants in competitive sports; and prohibition of the use of any doping materials. The Minister of Education and Culture was given a number of regulatory powers within the frame of the law.

The Knesset also approved, early in 1991, the appointment of a deputy minister in the Ministry of Education and Culture to be in charge of sports. When the Labor Party returned to power in 1992, it too appointed a deputy minister.

The quadrennial Maccabiah and the Hapoel Games continued to be the major sports events in the country. While the participation in the Maccabiah Games expanded — in 1989 athletes from the former Communist bloc participated for the first time — the athletic standard of the Games left much to be desired. The Hapoel Games, on the other hand, developed in scope and in standard up to 1987, but were greatly reduced in 1991 as a result of a serious financial deficit.

[U.S.]

STEG, ADOLPHE (1925–), French surgeon and Jewish community leader. Steg was born in Verecky, Czechoslovakia, and taken to France in 1932. Beginning his activities in the Jewish community at the end of World War II, Steg has held a number of positions of leadership in different Jewish organizations. Initially he was particularly active in student circles and was president of the Union of Jewish Students in Paris (1948) and vice president of the World Union of Jewish Students (1949). He is a leading member of Jewish organizations, the Fonds Social Juif Unifié, the Consistoire, and the Alliance Israélite Universelle. He took part in the creation of the Coordinating Committee of Jewish Institutions in May 1967 on the eve of the Six-Day War. Steg was the founder of the French Association of the Friends of the Hebrew University which he headed from 1965 to 1986. He served as the president of the Conseil Representatif des Juifs de France (C.R.I.F.) from 1969 to 1974 and from 1985 as president of the Alliance Israélite Universelle.

After completing his medical studies, Steg was a surgeon in Paris and became professor of urological surgery at the faculty of Medicine in Paris in 1976. He is a member of the Academy of Surgeons. From 1984 he was secretary general of the European Urological Association and from 1986 president of the French Urology Association.

He is an officer of the Legion of Honor and since 1979 has been a member of the Economic and Social Council of France. [GI.KO.]

STEINBERGER JACK (1921–), physicist, Nobel Prize winner. Steinberger was born in Bad Kissingen, Germany, and emigrated to the United States in 1935. He studied at the University of Chicago from which he received his B.S. in chemistry in 1942 and his Ph.D. in physics in 1948. He was a professor at Columbia University from 1950 to 1971, with the title of Higgins Professor from 1967 to 1971.

He has been affiliated with the European Center for Nuclear Research (CERN) from 1968, serving as its director from 1969 to 1972.

Jack Steinberger (Photo CERN, Geneva)

In the early 1960s Steinberger and two colleagues, Melvin Schwartz (q.v.) and Leon M. Lederman (q.v.) using the power accelerator at Brookhaven National Laboratory in Long Island, developed a method for capturing neutrinos, which are extremely elusive subatomic particles having no mass, no electric charge, one-half unit of spin, and always moving at the speed of light, and using them to help delineate the structure of other basic particles. For their research which led to a better understanding of elementary particles and forces they were awarded the Nobel Prize in physics for 1988.

STEINER, GEORGE (see **6**:790). In 1969 Steiner was made an Extraordinary Fellow of Churchill College, Cambridge, and, from 1974 was the professor of English and Comparative Literature at the University of Geneva. Steiner was appointed president of the English Association in 1975 and is a fellow of the Institute for Advanced Study, Princeton. His distinguished career has been recognized by the universities of East Anglia and Louvain who both awarded him honorary doctorates.

Steiner's publications have included *Extraterritorial: Papers on Literature and the Language Revolution* (1971) and *In Bluebeard's Castle: Some Notes Towards the Re-definition of Culture* (1971), which contains his most comprehensive theory of modern anti-Semitism. *After Babel* was published in 1975 and he has also published *Martin Heidegger* (1980) and a collection of essays, *On Difficulty and Other Essays* (1978). His reputation as one of the world's leading literary critics was confirmed with the publication in 1984 of the anthology, *George Steiner: A Reader.*

Steiner's literary criticism, in recent years, has been complemented by two works of fiction. *The Portage to San Cristobal of A.H.* (1979) and *Antigones* (1984). Both works have received high critical acclaim and the 1982 stage version of *The Portage to San Cristobal of A.H.* excited a prolonged exchange of letters and articles on the meaning of the Holocaust and modern anti-Semitism. Steiner has both an astonishing range as a literary critic and incomparable understanding of Central European Jewish culture. [B.C.]

STEINSALTZ, ADIN (1937–), Israeli rabbi and author. Born in Jerusalem, Steinsaltz acquired a background in Jewish studies as well as chemistry, mathematics, and physics at the Hebrew University of Jerusalem. He was also ordained as a rabbi. After working in education for 13 years in the Negev, he returned to Jerusalem where he taught, did research, and wrote for various periodicals. In 1988 he received the Israel Prize in Jewish Studies.

In 1965 he founded the Israel Institute for Talmudic Publications which undertook the production of a vocalized Babylonian Talmud, accompanied by Hebrew translation and commentary; 25 volumes had appeared by 1993. An English translation of this series has begun; by 1993 eight volumes were available. One volume of the Jerusalem Talmud has been published by the Israel Institute.

Rabbi Steinsaltz founded the "Mekor Ḥayyim" yeshivah in 1984, an institute which has as one of its aims the bridging of the gap between religious and non-religious Jews. In February 1989 he initiated the founding of a yeshivah in Moscow, called the Center for the Study of Judaism.

Each year Rabbi Steinsaltz lectures widely outside of Israel and his books, a number of which have been translated into English, such as *The Essential Talmud, The Thirteen-Petalled Rose*, and *Beggars and Prayers*, reach readers the world over. He has published works on Talmud, bibilical figures, repentance, stories of Rabbi Naḥman of Bratslav, and other topics. [ED.]

STERLING, SIR JEFFREY (MAURICE) (1934–), British businessman and financier. After an education which included studies at the Guildhall School of Music, and activity on the stock exchange from 1957 to 1963, Sterling became successively, finance director of the General Guarantee Corporation (1963–4), managing director of Gula Investments (1964–9), and chairman of the Sterling Guarantee Trust (1969–85), until its merger with Peninsular and Oriental (P. & O.) Steam Navigation Company, a company with wide interests in transportation and commerce, of which he became chairman in 1983. He was a member of the board of British Airways from 1979 to 1982. He gained public recognition for his imaginative work on the celebrations of the Queen's Silver Jubilee (1977), as deputy chairman and honorary treasurer of the London Celebrations Committee, and he also served as special adviser to the Secretary of State for Trade. His interest in the arts found expression as chairman of the Young Vic (theater) Company from 1975 to 1983 and the Royal Ballet School from 1983. From 1986, he was a governor of the Royal Ballet. In social work, he was on the executive board of ORT from 1966, chairman of ORT Technical Services (1974), and vice-president, British ORT, from 1978; and he pioneered new approaches to transport for the disabled as vice-president and chairman of the executive of Motability from 1977. He was knighted in 1985. [V.D.L.]

STERNBERG, SIR SIGMUND (1921–), British businessman and and financier. Sternberg was born in Hungary. After settling in Britain he became prominent as a metal merchant and in property; he was also a Lloyds underwriter (insurer) from 1969. He was a director from 1978 and chairman from 1983 of Commodities Research Unit (Holdings) and chairman of Martin Slowe Estates from 1971. Sternberg was supporter of the Labor Party and founded the research group for the Labor shadow cabinet and served as treasurer of the Labor Finance and Industry Group and on the Economics and Industry Committee of the Fabian Society. He was active in voluntary work for the National Health Service, including the chairmanship of important hospital authorities. He was active also in support for the Hebrew University, of which he was a governor, for the Institute of Jewish Affairs, and for other cultural and educational causes, including the foundation of the Sternberg Centre for Judaism at the Manor House in North West London. He was knighted in 1976, and in 1986 was invested as Knight Commander of the Papal Order of St. Gregory in recognition for his work as chairman of the Executive Committee of the International Council of Christians and Jews. He is also treasurer of the British Council of Christian and Jews. [V.D.L.]

STRAUSS-KAHN, DOMINIQUE (1949–), French economist. Strauss-Kahn graduated in law and then specialized in economics. From 1980 to 1990 she was professor at Paris' Nanterre University. From 1986 she was a deputy in the National Assembly, where she was president of the finance committee before being appointed minister of industry and foreign trade in 1991. She is regarded as one of the leading experts in the Socialist party on economic affairs. Among her many activities as minister were special efforts to strengthen trade relations between France and Israel. [GI.KO.]

SUZMAN, JANET (1939–), actress. Born in Johannesburg, Suzman was educated at the university of Witwatersrand. She first appeared on stage in 1962 in *Billy Liar*, but her modulated voice and diction, elegance and authority led quickly to classical theater, where she specialized in Shakespeare and Classical and 19th-century theater. Her roles with the Royal Shakespeare have included Portia, Rosalind, Ophelia, and Cleopatra. In 1976 she received the *Evening Standard* Award for her portrayal of Masha in Tchekov's *The Three Sisters.* Her many television appearances have included participation in the BBC Shakespeare series along with such varying roles as Charlotte Bronte, Florence Nightingale, Edwina Mountbatten, and Clytemnestra.

Janet Suzman

In films she portrayed Alexandra in *Nicholas and Alexandra*, receiving an Academy Award nomination for best actress for her portrayal of the imperious czarina. In Peter Greenaway's film *The Draughtman's Contract*, her portrayal of the sensual, decadent aristocrat brought great critical acclaim. In recent years she has turned increasingly to character roles and has directed for television *(Othello)* and the theater.

She is a civil rights activist following in the footsteps of her aunt, Helen *Suzman. [SA.WH.]

SWITZERLAND (see **15**:559; **Dc./17**:568). The situation of Swiss Jewry in 1980s and early 1990s has been characterized by two seemingly contradictory developments: a strengthening of its institutions and a weakening of its demographic base. Organized communal life is to be found (in order of descending size of Jewish community) in the towns of Zurich, Basle, Geneva, Lausanne, Berne, Lugano, St. Gall,

Synagogue of Berne, dedicated 1906 (Courtesy Rabbi Marcel Marcus; photo Georges Hill, Berne)

La-Chaux-de-Fonds, Biel, Fribourg, Baden, Winterthur, Vevey, and Kreuzligen.

According to the official census of 1990, 17,577 inhabitants (0.26%) identified themselves as Jews, the lowest level of this century. The age distribution is leveling out: in 1990 26% were over 60, about as many as were under 20. The intermarriage rate (with about 100 marriages a year) has risen to about 60%, although its impact is reduced to about 40% by subsequent conversions.

On the other hand, while in 1960 only about half of Swiss Jewry was organized in one of Switzerland's 25 Jewish congregations, this was true for three-quarters of them in 1980. The 20 communities which form the Swiss Federation of Jewish Communities, the Schweizerischer Israelitischer Gemeindebund (SIG), numbered 5,025 households in 1992, nearly half of them in the Zurich area, with 997 in Basle, and 830 in Geneva. In these cities there are also ultra-Orthodox congregations which are not all members of the SIG, and two Liberal synagogues exist, one each in Zurich and Geneva. The question of granting membership to the Liberal communities, debated for over ten years, gave rise to controversy in 1990/91, with a number of communities threatening to leave the SIG if the Liberals were to be included. A compromise was reached in 1992 which provides for a consulation mechanism without official recognition, especially in questions regarding Israel and anti-Semitism. The large congregations are all modeled on the concept of *Einheitsgemeinde*, while even the *Austrittsgemeinde* is a member of the SIG. Jewish day-schools exist in Zurich, Basle, Geneva, and Lausanne, and a *yeshivah* in Kriens near Lucerne.

The Jewish communities of Basle, Berne, and Fribourg have now gained official status *(öffentliche-rechtliche Anerkennung)* more or less on a par with the established churches. It is hoped that this will become true as well for St. Gall in the near future (it is a matter dealt with by each canton individually). The SIG has established consulting mechanisms with the Federation of Protestant Churches (1987) and with the Roman Catholic Bishops' Conference (1990), while the Council of Christians and Jews, founded in 1949, has seven local branches.

Memorial to Holocaust victims in Berne Jewish cemetery (Courtesy Rabbi Marcel Marcus; photo Georges Hill, Berne)

In his address at the dedication ceremony of a memorial to the victims of the Holocaust in Berne's Jewish cemetery on November 9, 1988, Flavio Cotti, one of the seven members of the Bundesrat, the Swiss federal government, gave what amounted to its first, although guarded, official apology for Switzerland not having saved more Jews during the Holocaust.

There were very few manifestations of anti-Semitism, the majority of the Swiss population feeling more threatened by Muslim and Third World immigrants. Still anti-Semitic graffiti do occur, as do revisionist statements, to which the authorities tend to react quite strongly. A new anti-racialist legislation, passed by parliament in June 1993, makes anti-Semitic propaganda and the denial of the Holocaust a criminal offense. While the election, in March 1993, of Ms. Ruth Dreifuss as the first Jewish member of the Bundesrat came as a surprise to everybody, her Jewish origins were more a matter of curiosity than of political interest.

Bibliography: W. Guggenheim et al, *Juden in der Schweiz* (1982); A. Kamis-Muller et al, *Vie Juive en Suisse* (1992); M. Marcus, in: *European Judaism*, 44 (1990); R. Weill, in: *Judaica*, 1 (1986).

[MA.MAR.]

SYRIA (see **15**:636; **Dc./17**:569). At the end of the decade, the Jewish population of Syria had declined from about 4,000 in 1983 to approximately 1,400. There were some 1,180 left in Damascus, 150 in Aleppo, and 125 in Qamishli.

For virtually the whole of the period, there was no change in the continuing oppressive treatment of the community, denied many basic human rights and civil liberties. Mail, telephone, and telegrams were monitored by the Jewish Division of the Secret Police *(Mukhabarat)*, who kept them under constant surveillance, subjecting them to search and arrest without warrant. Sales of property were prohibited, unless a replacement was being acquired; property belonging to deceased Jews, with no surviving family, was expropriated without compensation. Identity cards continued to bear the word *Mousawi* (Jew), while non-Jews had no religious identification on theirs. The one Jewish school in Damascus (Ben Maimon) and the one in Aleppo (Samuel) were both supervised by Muslims and were allowed to teach only biblical Hebrew, limited to two hours a week.

Contrary to the Universal Declaration of Human Rights, to which Syria was a signatory and unlike the rights granted to other Syrian citizens, the Jews were prohibited from emigrating. Except for six months in 1992 (see below), only a few Jews were permitted to travel abroad for medical or business reasons. In addition to paying bribes, large monetary deposits were required and family members had to be left behind, to guarantee the traveler's return.

The *Mukhabarat* arrested and imprisoned serveral Jews, without charge or trial, for allegedly attempting to leave Syria or for "security offenses." These prisoners were exposed to torture and deprivation of food, clothing, and medicines. Typical of these were the brothers Elie and Selim Swed of Damascus, held for two years without anyone knowing of their arrest. Subsequently, in 1991, a form of "military trial" was held, where no charges were published and their lawyer was prohibited from addressing the "court." They were sentenced to 6½ years in prison, but were released in April 1992.

Earlier, in December 1983, 25-year-old pregnant Lillian Abadi of Aleppo and her young daughter and son were bru-

Demonstration in Italy calling for freedom for Syrian Jewry, 1974

tally murdered and mutilated in their home. Other Jewish families received threats, but no definitive motive for the killings was ever established and nobody was charged.

Nevertheless the Jewish community believed that if the Assad regime was deposed, their treatment by any successor would be even harsher.

The custom of using *Shabbat Zakhor* as the Sabbath for Syrian Jewry, which originated in 1975 in Toronto, Canada, spread to synagogues throughout North America and other countries, highlighting the plight of Syrian Jews, which, over the years, had been substantially ignored by mainline national and interntional Jewish organizations.

Criticism of the Syrians' treatment of its Jewish citizens was latterly raised by several world governments, including Canada, the U.S., and France. The issue was brought before the United Nations Commission on Human Rights. In January 1992, for the first time in responding to the UN body, instead of its traditional posture of merely making denials, the Syrian government issued a detailed "accounting" of the "well-being of its Jews," including a listing of students in educational institutions, places of residence outside the ghettos, and occupations filled by Jews.

During the Assad "re-election" campaign of 1992, the Jewish community was obliged to parade in his support, bearing banners in Hebrew — the first time that language had been permitted to be used in public.

With Syria's participation in the Madrid Peace Conference in 1992, came the announcement — not from the Syrians, but from U.S. Secretary of State James Baker — that Syrian Jews would be permitted to travel abroad. This change, from the prohibition which had been in effect for some 44 years, was not the right to emigrate. The "right to travel" was granted to individuals only under the strict control of the *Mukhabarat*, rather than through the normal channels always available to other Syrians to obtain passports. Permits, when granted, stated that "...the Jew X..." was permitted to travel and the fortunate applicants were obliged to purchase return tickets.

After six months of this seemingly liberalized process, in October 1992, the government, without warning or explanation, discontinued the permits. A large number of applicants were thus unable to leave and many families were caught with some members having permission, while others were refused.

The remnant of a community, which once stood at 40,000, was left with no ritual slaughterers, no *mohalim* (circumcisors), and no undertakers.

A large number of the approximately 2,600 who managed to leave in 1992 joined family in Brooklyn, New York, although some went to other countries.

The U.S. refused to admit them as refugees, but only as "visitors." Thus, they were denied the governmental resettlement facilities available to immigrants, placing a heavy burden on Jewish communal resources, with respect to housing, education, and employment. [J.F.C.]

TADMOR, HAYIM (1923–), Assyriologist and historian of the Ancient Near East. Tadmor was born in Harbin, China, and arrived in Palestine with his family in 1935. He studied at the Hebrew University where he received his doctorate in 1954 for his dissertation on problems in chronology of the Ancient Near East. His postdoctoral studies took him to the Oriental Institute of the University of Chicago where he studied Assyriology under Benno Landsberger.

From 1958 he lectured at the Hebrew University — until 1965 in the Department for Ancient and Near Eastern Studies and then in the Department of Assyriology. In 1971 he was appointed professor of Assyriology and history of the Ancient Near East.

Tadmor is a foremost authority on the history of the first millennium B.C.E. and has made notable contributions to the study of chronology, historiography, and institutions in antiquity as well as to understanding the interrelations between Assyria and the West and the place of Israel in the Ancient Near East.

He applied canons of criticism to inscriptions and historical texts, viewing texts in their broad cultural perspective and emphasizing the value of historiography and literary forms of historical texts. One of his major contributions has been his work on Assyrian and Babylonian royal inscriptions.

He edited, with Moshe Weinfeld, and was a contributor to *History, Historiography and Interpretations — Studies in Biblical and Cuneiform Literature* (1983). He edited *The World History of the Jewish People*, volume 5 (The Restoration, The Persian Period). Tadmor served as a chief editor of the *Enziklopedya Mikra'it* (1971–82) and was a major contributor to *A History of the Jewish People* (edited by H. H. Ben-Sasson, 1969) and the Russian version (edited by S. Ettinger, 1967). He collaborated with M. Katan to produce a *Commentary on Kings* (1988) and is an editor of the ongoing project of the *Shorter Jewish Encyclopedia in Russian* (1976–). [E.Ho.]

TADZHIKISTAN, one of the independent states of the CIS. In 1979 it had 14,700 Jews and in 1989 — 14,800, mainly in the capital Dushanbe. a large proportion of the republic's Jews belong to the Bukharan Jewish community. In 1988–89 the Jewish birthrate was 14.8 per 1,000 and mortality — 8.4 per 1,000.

Emigration totaled 535 in 1989. The following year 2,747 immigrated to Israel (2,473 of these from Dushanbe). In 1991 the corresponding figures were 3,273 and 2,943. The rise of Islamic fundamentalism in the republic, which has led to civil war, has been the major factor in Jewish emigration. [Mi.Be.]

TALMON (Zalmonovitch), SHEMARYAHU (1920–), Bible scholar. Born in Skierniwice, Poland, Talmon received his primary and high school education at the Jüdisches Reform-Real Gymnasium in Breslau, Germany. He immigrated to Palestine in 1939, after being interned for three months in Buchenwald concentration camp.

Talmon obtained his doctorate from the Hebrew University in Jerusalem in 1946, focusing in his doctoral thesis on the text and versions of the Hebrew Bible and in particular on "double meanings" in biblical texts. He refined and supplemented these studies over the years, contributing to many areas of biblical study, applying text-critical procedures to the cultural and literary history of ancient Israel.

His sociological approach to text history advanced the understanding of various aspects of the biblical text, especially with regard to the Qumran scrolls found in the Judean Desert. His interests in the texts found in Qumran and in sociological research were combined in the study of the nature and history of the Qumran monastery.

Talmon was active in the field of biblical education both in Israel and elsewhere. He held the position of director for educational institutions in the "Illegal" Immigration Camps in Cyprus (1947–48). He taught at the major Israeli universities and served as a visiting professor at many institutions throughout the world. He was the dean at Haifa University and of the Faculty of Humanities at the Hebrew University and rector of the Institute of Judaic Studies in Heidelberg.

Talmon is also involved in forging cultural and intellectual links with the World Council of Churches and the Vatican and has been prominent in international Jewish-Christian dialogue.

He has held various editorial positions, published hundreds of articles, and edited numerous books, including *Qumran and the History of the Biblical Text* (1975). His books include *King, Cult, and Calendar* (1986), *Gesellschaft und Literatur in der Hebräischen Bibel* (1988), and *The World of Qumran from Within* (1989). A Festschrift written in his honor, *Sha'arei Talmon*, appeared in 1990. [E.Ho.]

TALMUD, RECENT RESEARCH (see **Dc./17**:571). The items listed in this entry include works on Mishnah, Talmud, and Midrash.

Mishnah. TEXT. (1) *Mishnah Arakhin*, computer-aided critical edition of the Mishnah by M. Krupp (1977) with various readings from manuscripts and early printings. (2) *Avodah Zarah*, critical edition by D. Rosenthal (1980). In an edition prepared by computer, two main textual branches are discerned: the Babylonian Mishnah and the Ereẓ Israel Mishnah. (3) P. J. Haas, *A History of the Mishnaic Law of Agriculture. Tractate Maaser Sheni* (1980), with translation and commentary. (4) A. J. Peck, *The Priestly Gift in the Mishnah. A Study of Tractate Terumot* (1981), with translation of the Mishnah and *Tosefta Terumot.* (5) *Treatise Eruvin* (1986), edited by A. Goldberg, an edition based on Ms. Kaufman and the first printed edition along with variant readings from other early printed manuscripts and *Genizah* fragments.

COMMENTARIES. (1) J. Glikman, *Birkat Emunah* (1985) on Mishnah *Shevi'it.* (2) M. Kesler, *Meor Einayim* (1986). (3) A. Binet, Tractate *Shevi'it* (1986) with explanatory comments from the Babylonian Talmud. (4) J. Ben-Shushan, *Ḥukkat ha-Taharah* on Tract. *Mikva'ot* (1987). (5) Mishnah *Shevi'it* (1985), chap. 1–5, edited by K. Kahana, includes text and commentary. (6) J. Feliks, *Mishnah Shevi'it al pi Ketav Yad Leyden im Shinu'yei Nusḥa'ot* (1987). (7) Two volumes: from Seder *Nezikin*, tract. *Sanhedrin* (v. 5); tractates *Makkot* and *Shavu'ot* (v. 6) in the series *The Mishnah: a new translation with a commentary Yad Avraham anthologized from Talmudic sources and classical commentators* (1987). (8) *Ḥekker ve-Iyyun* in *Mishnah Bikkurim* (1989), ed. by Kalman Kahana. (9) Samuel di Ozida, *Midrash Shemu'el — Oẓar Perushim al Pirkei Avot* (1989); idem, *Midrash Shemu'el — Shitah Mekuẓẓeret al Pirkei Avot* (new edition, 1989). (10) *Shishah Sidrei Mishnah Mefurashim*, with commentaries of Obadiah of Bertinoro and "Mishnah Eliezer" (named after Eliezer Kestenbaum), 3 vol. (1990–1992). (11) N. Eliezer, *Sefer Ḥazon Naḥum* (1986), a work on *mishnayyot*, 2 vols., *Seder Kodashim* and *Seder Tohorot.*

HAGGAHOT. J. D. Bamberger, *Haggahot* on Mishnah, in: *Ha-Ma'yan*, 24 (1984). 55–64, 65–80, 85–96; 25 (1985), 61–79.

DICTIONARY OF MISHNAH. H. Shay, *"Millon le-Lashon ha-Mishnah me-ha-Me'ah 14/15,"* in: *Te'udah*, 3 (1983), 181–213; the author of the dictionary is unknown.

MISHNAH TRANSLATIONS. *English.* Translation with Yad Avraham commentary by A. Y. Rosenberg, *Seder Mo'ed* (1979); R. Cohen, *Mishnah Rosh ha-Shanah* (1981); idem, *Bava Meẓia* (1983); Z. Arom, *Seder Nashim*, tract. *Ketubbot-Nedarim* (1984–85); Ph. Blackman, *Pirkei Avoth* (1985); *Bava Kama* tractate (1988), translated and annotated by Y. (J.) Cohen; *Dutch.* Hebrew-Dutch text, commentary in Dutch, p. 3: *Seder Nashim* (1987), translated and annotated by S. Hamelburg. *French.* Mishnah, translated by the French rabbinate, part 12: *Pea, Demai*, with a French commentary (1982). *German. Seder Tohorot Tractate Tohorot*, by W. Bunte (1981). *Ladino.* O. Schwarzwald, *"Mishnah Pirkei Avot,"* in: *Alei Sefer*, 12 (1986 (95–110). *Spanish* (Madrid, 1981).

MISHNAH RESEARCH BOOKS (1) J. Feliks, *Plants and Animals of the Mishnah* (1983). (2) J. Neusner, *The Memorized Torah; the mnemonic system of the Mishnah* (1985). (3) J. N. Epstein, *Studies in Talmudic Literature and Semitic Languages*, vol. 2, part 1 (1988), 19–99.

BABYLONIAN TALMUD. (1) Babylonian Talmud — extracts, fragments. Fragments of *gemara* chapters and Alfasi (Rif) *halakhot* printed by Spanish and Portuguese Jews before the expulsion from Spain and during the following generation; arranged by H.Z. Dimotrovsky (1979). It is concluded that in less than 50 years five or six editions of Talmud *gemarot* were published by Spanish Jews, with the texts having a specific character even though printed in different times and places. (2) E. Segal, *The Textual Traditions of Tractate Megillah in the Babylonian Talmud* (1981).

TRACTATES WITH COMMENTARIES: (1) B. Noe, *Pesaḥim with Commentary "Gemara Shalem,"* 2 vol. (1960–86), the commentary is up to fol. 15b and includes variant readings and the commentaries of *geonim* and *rishonim.* (2) *Pesaḥim* (2 vol.) with *Halakhah Berurah* by Rabbi A. I. Kook and *"Beirur Halakhah"* by his pupils; the two volumes include chap. 1–10 of the tractate. (3) *Sukkah* (1975; emended ed., 1988) with *Halakhah Berurah* plus *"Berur Halakhah"*; (4) S. Ben-Shemen, tract. *Ta'anit-Moed Katan* with Hebrew translation and commentary (1983). (5) *Yebamoth* (2 vols.), edited by A. Liss for Yad Harav Herzog Institute for the Complete Israel Talmud (1983–86); *Yebamoth*, vol. 3 (1989); (6) *Nedarim*, vol. 2 (1991), edited by M. Herschler for Yad Harav Herzog Institute for the Complete Israel Talmud. (7) Talmud ed. and translated into Hebrew by A. Steinsalz: *Ketubbot* II (1988), *Nedarim* I (1991), II (1992), *Sotah* (1990).

SMALLER TRACTATES OF THE TALMUD. (1) *Tractate Soferim*, Hebrew text with French translation by Obadja ben Isa. The translation is preceded by an introduction dealing with the function and work of the *sofer* (scribe) in Jewish tradition and a discussion of *Tractate Soferim* and the time of its composition. (2) *Masekhet Derekh Ereẓ Zuta*, 2nd edition with commentary by D. Sperber (1982). The commentary deals mainly with different versions, parallels, commentaries and interpretations of words.

COMMENTARIES (without Talmud text): *Oẓar Mefarshei ha-Talmud: Sukkah* I–II (1979–1989); *Bava Kama* — 3 vol. (1981–1991), *Bava Meẓi'a* — 4 vol. (1971–1989), *Makkot* (1975).

DICTIONARY TO TALMUD. M. Meizlish, *Sefer "He-Arukh" al ha-Talmud le-R. Natan ben Yeḥi'el* and *"Musaf he-Arukh" le-R. Binyamin Musafya*, arranged according to the order of pages in the talmudic tractates, with notes, 3 vol. (1992).

INTRODUCTION. (1) H. Strack, *Introduction au Talmud et au Midrash* (1982), a French translation by M. R. Hayoun of the seventh edition of Strack's *Einleitung in Talmud u. Midrash* edited by Sternberger (the book first appeared in 1921). See a review by G. J. Ormann in KS, 63 (1990), ser. 501, 48–49. (2) A. Steinsaltz, *Guide to the Talmud* (1984).

TALMUD TRANSLATIONS. *English. Gittin and Baba Kamma, Selections* (1981), tr. and annotated by B. Elizur-Epstein; *tractate Ḥullin* with notes and glossary by E. Cashdan (1980). Talmud Engl.-American Translation by J. Neusner, 7 vol. (1984); N. Cohen, *Nedarim* (1985); Heb.-Eng. edition of the Bab. Talmud edited by J. Epstein: (1) *Nedarim*, (2) *Nazir-Sotah* (1985). By 1993 eight volumes were available in the English translation of the Babylonian Talmud edited by A. Steinsalz. *French. Tractate Shabbat* by D. Elbeze; *Tractate Megillah* by J. Salper (Paris, 1977–78); French Talmud Selections, ed. L. Berman (1980). Edition by E. Munk, part 2, *Moed* (1981–83); J. Salzer, *Pesaḥim* (1984). *German.* Third edition of L. Goldschmidt translation, 4 vol. (1980); *Nedarim* and *Sukkah* by Ch. Horowitz (1983).

Additional volumes which have appeared in the Talmud edited and translated into Hebrew by A. Steinsaltz are: *Yebamoth*, 2 vols. (1985–86), and *Ketuboth*, pt. 1 (1988).

TALMUD RESEARCH BOOKS. (1) D. Halivni, *Sources and Traditions, A Source Critical Commentary of the Talmud, Seder Moed,* Nashim (2 vols., 1969–1975). (2) A. Oppenheimer, *Babylonian Judaica in the Talmudic Period* (1983); the book contains onomastikon of the Jewish settlements in Babylonia during the Talmudic period based on the Bab. Talmud. (3) Y. Kara, *Babylonian Aramaic in the Yemenite Mss. of the Talmud* (1983). (4) J. Gokavitzki, *Ma'aseh Oreg* (1983), deals with weaving and spinning in the Talmudic period. (5) D. Sperber, *A Dictionary of Greek and Latin Legal Terms in Rabbinic Literature* (1984). (6) M. Catane, *Otzar ha-Laasim*, the French words in Rashi's commentaries on the Talmud, *Recueil des Gloses* (1984). (7) E. Urbach, *Halacha. Its Sources and Development* (1984). (8) M. L. Chernick, *Hermeneutical Studies in Talmudic and Midrashic Literatures* (1984). (9) L. Jacobs, *The Talmudic Argument: A study in talmudic reasoning and methodology* (1984). (10) J. Neusner, *Ancient Judaism* (1984). (11) M. Ayali, A Nomenclature of Workers and Artisans in the Talmudic and Midrashic Literature (1985). (12) A. E. Rivlin, *"Equal to All of Them" — The Pedagogy of the Sages* (1985). (13) J. Z. Feintuch, *Versions and Traditions in the Talmud* (edited by D. Sperber; 1985). (14) G. Harpenas, *The Period of the Talmud*, a historical survey of the Amoraim, Saboraim and Geonim in Palestine and Babylonia (1985). (15) E. Z. Melamed, *Essays in Talmudic Literature* (1986). (16) M. Mielziner, *Hakdamah le-Torat ha-Parshanut be-Talmud* (1986). (17) Z. Safrai (ed.), *The Ancient Synagogue in the Period of the Mishnah and Talmud* (1986); (18) J. N. Epstein, *Studies in Talmudic Literature* II/1–2 (1988). (19) N. Aminoah, *The Redaction of the Tractates Betza, Rosh Hashana and Taanit in the Babylonian Talmud* (1986); idem, *Sukkah, Moed Katan* (1988). (20) M. Ayali, *Po'alim ve-Omanim — Melakhtam u-Ma'amadam be-Sifrut Ḥazal* ("Workers and Artisans — Their Professions and Status in Rabbinic Literature," 1987). (21) E. E. Urbach, *The World of the Sages — Collected Studies* (1988). (22) J. N. Epstein, *Studies in Talmudic Literature and Semitic Languages* I (1983), II/1–2 (1988). (23) I. Schepansky, *The Takkanot of Israel*, part I: talmudic ordinances (1991), a compilation of all statutes and ordinances enacted as legislative supplements of a positive nature to Jewish law and tradition. (24) A. R. Zeini, *Rabbanan Savorei u-Khelalei ha-Ḥalakhah* ("Our Rabbis' Reasons and Rules of Halakhah," 1992). (24) N. M. Weisfish, *Mishnat Kiddushin al Masekhet Kiddushin* ("The Mishnah Kiddush for Tractate Kiddushin," 1992). (25) A study of Rabbi Akiva, P. Lendhardt, *Rabbi Akiva* (1987), a work on the image and thought of R. Akiva in light of texts in Rabbinic literature (explained and translated into German) and various parallels in the New Testament.

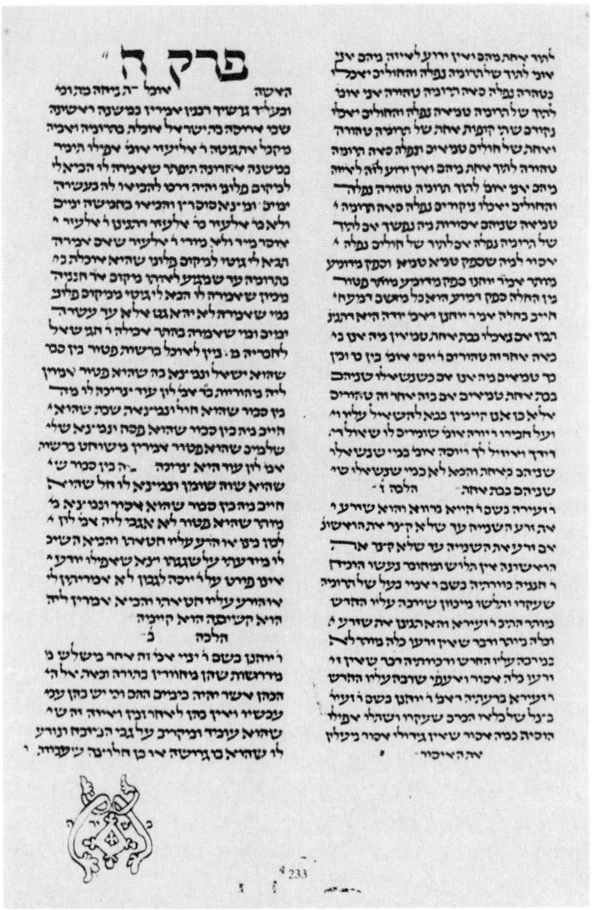

Page from the Jerusalem Talmud, Ms. Vat. Ebr 133, in a Makor facsimile edition, 1971, Jerusalem

TALMUD REALIA. (1) D. Sperber, in: *Sinai*, 93 (1983), 280–83; 94 (1984), 233–36; *ibid*, 96 (1985), 250–59; 98 (1986), 23–38; *Sinai*, 100 (1987), 912–24; 101 (1988), 225–34, (2) idem, in: *Sidra*, 1 (1985), 131–43. (3) Y. Rosenson and Y. Zak, in: *Techumin*, 8 (1987), 417–28. (4) S. Wahrhaftig, in: *Sinai*, 100 (1987), 429–51.

Talmudic Encyclopaedia. Vol. of subject index (1984–85), vol. 18, (1986), v. 19 (1989), v. 20 (1991).

Jerusalem Talmud. TRACTATES, TEXT, AND COMMENTARY. (1) Facsimile edition of Codex Leyden with English and Hebrew Introductions (1982). (2) German translation of tractates *Avodah Zarah* (1980) and *Sanhedrin* (1981). The translation of both tractates is based on the Leyden manuscript, *Genizah* fragments and early printings. (3) *Tractate Shevi'it* with R. Elijah of Vilna's notes and his commentary according to manuscripts and notes as printed in other editions, edited by Kalman Kahana (1980). (4) M. Kasovsky. *Otzar Lashon Talmud Yerushalmi*, Vol. 2 (1982). (5) The order *Nezikin* of Jerusalem Talmud, ed. from the Escorial Ms., Madrid, with an Introduction by E. S. Rosenthal and Introduction and Commentary by P. Liebermann (Israel Academy of Sciences and Humanities, Jerusalem, 1983). The text of the Jerusalem Talmud in all editions is based on the Leyden manuscript. In 1909 L. Ginzberg published *Seridei Yerushalmi* reproducing fragments of the Jerusalem Talmud discovered in the Cairo *Genizah.* The text of the Jerusalem Talmud in Ms. Leyden is corrupt and thus the importance of the discovery of the Spanish Escorial manuscript by Rosenthal which contains the text of *Nezikin: Bava*

Kamma, Bava Mezia and *Bava Batra*. The text in this manuscript preserves very closely the Galilean Aramaic dialect. With the help of the manuscript we can now fill in 23 omissions in the text of Ms. Leyden. The book also contains variae lectiones from Ms. Leyden and four *Genizah* fragments.

(6) Two tractates of the Jerusalem Talmud, *Peah* (1985) and *Terumoth* (1987), have been published by the Mutzal Meesh Institute in New York and include two new commentaries on these tractates *Toledot Yizhak* and *Tevunah* of R. Y. A. Krasilschikov of Poltava. (7) Of Rabbi Issachar Tamar's book *Alei Tamar* (com. and notes), *Seder Nashim* was published (1981). (8) Jer. Talmud *Shevi'it*, text and commentary by Y. Feliks, 2 vols. (1980–87); the text is based on Ms. Leyden, *Genizah* fragments, and the printed Venice edition. (9) J. Sh. Weinfeld, *Tavla'ot Masbirot le-Massekhet Yevamot — Sefer Naḥalat Zevi based on the book of R. Zevi Gutmacher: Naḥalat Zevi* (1986). (10) Jer. Talmud *Ḥallah* (1988) was published by Bet Midrash Gavo'a le-Halakhah be-Hityashvut ha-Ḥakla'it with various commentaries. (11) Jer. Talmud *Peah*, edited by A. Steinsaltz (1988). (12) Jerusalem Talmud with explanation by C. Kanjewski; explanations on tractates from *Seder Zera'im* (1986–1990) and *Shekalim* (1991). (13) Jerusalem Talmud *Ḥallah* (1988) with comments by *Rishonim*, variant readings, and additions (ed. K. Kahana); (14) Tractates *Demai* (1988), *Ma'asarot* and *Ma'aser Sheni* (1991) with the commentary *Toledot Itzḥak* and *Tevunah* by Y. A. Krasilschikov. (15) Y. Tamar, *Alei Tamar*, notes and explanations on the Jerusalem Talmud, *Seder Mo'ed*, v. 1–3 (1992).

JERUSALEM TALMUD RESEARCH. (1) L. Moscovitz, *The Terminology of the Yerushalmi* (1988), a study of ten terms in the Yerushalmi in comparison to the terminology in the Babylonian Talmud. (2) S. Goren, *Ha-Yerushalmi ve-ha-Gra* (1992), a study of the nature and validity of the readings and explications of the Vilna Gaon on the Jerusalem Talmud in comparison to early manuscripts and variant readings and their commentaries; (3) S. Lieberman, *Studies in Palestinian Talmudic Literature* (1991), ed. D. Rosenthal. (4) J. N. Epstein, *Studies*, vol. 2/1 (1988), 249–360. (5) A. van der Hayde, in: *Alei Sefer*, 11 (1984), 153–54. (6 J. Z. Feintuch, in: KS. 59 (1984), 268–70. (7) M. Assis, in: *Teuda*, 3 (1983), 57–70. (8) idem, I. Nissim Mem. Vol., 2 (1985), 49–66, 119–59. (9) idem, *Assufot*, 1 (1987), 29–46. (10) idem, *Tarbiz*, 56 (1987), 147–70. (11) Ch. S. Dimitrovsky, in: *I. Nissim Mem. Vol.*, 2 (1985), 33–47. (12) Y. Feliks, in: *Sinai*, 96 (1985), 18–28. (13) J. Franzos, in: *Sinai*, 101 (1988), 32–43. (14) A. S. Rabinowitz, in: *Moria*, 15 (1987), 39–47. (15) J. Elizur, in: *Sinai*, 101 (1988), 220–24.

Tosefta. (1) *Tosefta Zer'aim* with commentary: *Einayyim la-Mishpat* by Y. Arieli 1980). (2) *Baraita de-Masekhet Middot* with commentary by S. J. C. Kaniewski (1980). (3) *Baraita de-Melekhet ha-Mishkan* with commentary: *Ta'am ve-Da'at* by S. J. C. Kaniewski (1982). (4) H. Natan, *"Mesorato ha-Leshonit shel Ketav Yad Erfurt shel ha-Tosefta,"* [mimeographed] dissertation (1984). (5) idem, *Masorot*, 1 (1984), 121–134; (6) D. Sperber, in *Sidra*, 2 (1986), 145–50 (realia). (7) S. Lieberman, *Tosefta according to Codex Vienna with Variants from Cod. Erfurt Geniza Mss. and Editio princeps* (Venice 1521): Order Nezikin (1988); (8) S. Lieberman, *Tosefta Ki-Pshuta*, v. IX: *Nezikin* (1988); X: *Nezikin* (1988).

CONCORDANCES. (1) M. Kasovsky, *Concordance to the Talmud Yerushalmi*, completion of vol. 3 (1984). (2) M. Kasovsky, *Concordance to Talmud Yerushalmi — Onomasticon — Thesaurus of Proper Names* (1985).

Midrashim. (1) *Midrash Yelammedenu:* German study by Felix Böhe on the formation and editing of the aggadic material of this Midrash according to language patterns, vocabulary and literary-critical analysis of its sources (1977). (2) *Pesikta Rabbati:* German translation with scientific commentary on three portions of the Midrash (34, 36, 37) with an introduction to the literary analysis of the passages and a discussion of the time and place of their composition and parallels from Midrash literature (1978). (3) *Yalkut Shimoni*, Vol. 2 in the Heiman-Shiloni edition on the Book of Exodus (1980). (4) *Midrash Rabbah* on Song of Songs with variant readings, notes and introduction by S. Donsky (1980). (5) Munich *Mekhilta*. J. Goldin edition (1980) with facsimile of Hebrew manuscript and introduction describing the manuscript of the *Mekhilta*. (6) *Midrash Ha-Ḥefez* by Zechariah ben Solomon-Rofe on the five books of the Torah: Genesis edited by M. Ḥavazelet (1981). The edition is based mainly on a British Museum manuscript and includes a Midrashic-philosophic commentary on the Torah; composed in Yemen in the first half of the 15th century and contains selections from different Midrashim and the reflective literature of the Middle Ages. (7) *Ozar de-Vei Eliyahu ha-Shalem* by Y. Bransdorfer (1981). The book contains two parts: Part I — index and all entries for *Tanna de-Vei Eliyahu Rabba* and *Zuta* arranged in alphabetical order; Part II — entries from *Tanna de-Vei Eliyahu* on the Bible. (8) Study on the Midrash "Not by an angel, not by a messenger, but by the Holy One blessed be He Himself" of Pesce Mauro (1979). The author examines the theological view of the direct intervention of the Lord by analyzing sources in the wisdom literature.

Midrash. TEXTS AND COMMENTARIES. (9) Rabbi Simon Hadarshan of Frankfurt, *Yalkut Shimoni*, based on Ms. Oxford, edited by J. Shiloni, 7 vols. (1973–86), Genesis–Numbers. (10) M. Kahana, *Prolegomena to a new edition of the Sifre on Numbers* (1982). (11) M. Sokoloff, *Fragments of Genizah Texts to Midrash Bereshit Rabba* (1982). (12) S. Kolodizki, *Sifri Bamidbar–Devarim with the commentary of R. Hillel b. Elyakim* (1983). (13) M. G. Hirshman, *Kohelet Rabbah*, chap. 1–4 (1983). (14) A. Shinan edited *Shemot Rabbah*, chap. 1–14 (1984). (15) Joseph b. Shalom Ashkenazi, a Kabbalistic commentary to *Bereshit Rabbah* (chap. 1–29), ed. by M. Halamisch (1984). (16) idem, in: *Tishbi Jubilee Volume* (1986), 139–89. (17) Y. Sabar, *Homilies (Midrashim) in the New-Aramaic of the Kurdistani Jews* (1985). The book contains a collection of homilies and commentaries to the Genesis chapter *Va-Yeḥi* and the Exodus chapter *Be-Shalaḥ–Yitro*, written in the Aramaic of Kurdistani Jews. Through this work one can become acquainted with the culture of the Jews of Kurdistan and the new dialects of Aramaic. (18) D. Mandelbaum, an edition of *Pesikta de Rav Kahana* (2 vols., 1987) based on Ms. Oxford and Genizah fragments with commentary. (19) L. Finkelstein, *Sifra on Leviticus according to Vatican Ms. Assemani 66* with variants from the other Ms. *Genizah* fragments, v. 1–5 (1983–1991); (20) A. Shoshana, *Sifra on Leviticus*, according to Vatican Ms. Assemani 66, with medieval commentaries, I (1991), III (1992); (21) *Sifrei*, Midrash Halakhah on *Bemidbar–Devarim* with the commentary of David Pardo, 4 vol. (1990). (22) *Midrash Rabbah ha-Mevo'ar*, assembled and edited by "Makhon ha-Midrash ha-Mevo'ar," 9 parts (1983–1992). (23) *Yalkut Shimoni of R. Simon ha-Darshan* based on Ms. Oxford with variant readings from manuscripts and printed texts, with sources and notes on Deuteronomy, ed. D. Hayman and Y. Shiloni, 2 vol. (1992); (24) *Yalkut Midreshei Teiman: A collection of Yemenite Midrashim on the Pentateuch by an Unknown Medieval Yemenite Scholar*, 2 vol. (1988), ed. A. J. Wertheimer. (25) S. Lieberman, *Yemenite Midrashim*, a lecture on the Yemenite Midrashim, their character, and value (1992^2). (26) *Tibat Marge* (1988), a collection of Samaritan Midrashim, edited, translated and annotated by Ze'ev Ben Ḥayyim.

COLLECTIONS. (1) Y. J. Klapholz, *Yalkut Israel*, 4 vol. (1990); (2) *Midrash Tanḥuma* (English): *Midrash Tanḥuma* translated into English with introduction, indices, and notes by J. T. Townsend (1989), [6. Genesis].

TRANSLATIONS. *English.* (1) J. Nadich, *Jewish Legends of the 2nd Commonwealth* (1983); (2) G. Porton, *Understanding Rabbinic Midrash*, texts and commentary (1985); (3) *Sifra English Selections* (1985), the rabbinic commentary on Leviticus, American translation; (4) *Midrash Rabbah Bereshit* by J. Neusner, 3 vols. (1985). *French.* M. A. Ouaknin–E. Smilevitch, *Pirkei de R. Eliezer* (1983). *German.* H. Bietenhard, *Sifre Deuteronomium* (1984). *Italian.* R. Pacifici, *Midrash Selections* arranged according to subjects in Italian translation (1986).

MIDRASH RESEARCH. (1) Sh. Hofmann, *Music in Midrashim* (1985). (2) J. Neusner, *The Integrity of Leviticus Rabbah* (1985). (3) idem (transl. and ed.), *Genesis and Judaism, the Perspective of Genesis Rabbah* (1985). (4) idem, *Judaism and Scripture, the evidence of Leviticus Rabbah* (1986). (5) J. N. Epstein, *Studies* (1988), vol. 2/pt. 1, 103–233. (6) E. Z. Melamed, *Halachic Midrashim of the Tannaim in the Babylonian Talmud* (1988); (7) Y. Frankel, *Darkhei ha-Aggadah ve-ha-Midrash*, ("Methods of the Aggadah and Midrash," 1991).

Studies. (1) B. M. Bokser, *Post-Mishnaic Judaism in Transition; Samuel on Berachot and the Beginnings of Gemara* (1980). (2) Sh. Albeck, *Battei Ha-Din Bi-Yimei ha-Talmud* (1980), based mainly on legal sources from the days of the Jerusalem Talmud, deals with the theoretical foundations of the activities of the courts of law in the days of the Mishnah and Talmud, the function of the judges and their acts and the part played by the rabbinical courts in determining *halakhot.* (3) D. M. Gordish, *The Exegesis of Mishnah and Baraita of Rab and Samuel* (1980). (4) E. Krupnick, *The Gateway to Learning. A Systematic Introduction to the Study of the Talmud* (1981). (5) D. Pratelli, *Concezioni giuridiche e metodi costruttivi dei giuristi orientali* (1981). Study of the development of Hebrew justice from the beginning of the Return to Zion until the period of the Talmud, relying on sources from the Talmud and Midrash. (6) J. Fraenkel, *Study of the spiritual world of the aggadic tale* (1981). Literary-philosophical analysis of Talmudic *aggadot* with the purpose of understanding the views of Talmud sages on human and spiritual problems and their way of coping with them. (7) H. Strack and G. Stemberger, *Einleitung in Talmud und Midrasch* (1982). Seventh edition of Strack; edited by Stemberger. (8) G. Stemberger, *Der Talmud* (1982). Includes selection from the Talmud. Translated into German with commentary and historical-literary introduction; concludes with a survey of the influence of the Talmud, its rabbinical commentators and Talmud researchers in the last few generations. (9) M. Aberbech, *Jewish Education during the Mishnah and Talmud Period* (1982). The topics dealt with are the development of Jewish education in Ereẓ Israel and Babylon; the teacher's status in society, the relationship between rabbi and pupil in the period of the Talmud, the Hebrew teacher in the period of the Talmud. (10) J. Safran. *Studies in the History of Jewish Education* (1983). Chapters I and II deal with education in the light of Talmud and Midrash sources (pp. 3–51), the conclusion being that for a long time the sages of the Talmud and Midrash devoted themselves to educational work. In Palestine and Babylonia, their chief concern was to make sure the Torah was securely entrenched. The educational planning of the Talmud sages and their educational methods were based on the facts of life and their empirical experience. (11) J. N. Epstein, *Studies in Talmudic Literature and Semitic Languages*, Vol. I (1983). The collection includes 33 studies published in different periodicals in German, English and French in the years 1909–1950; they were translated into Hebrew by Zipporah Epstein, the author's widow, and edited by Ezra Zion Melamed. The collection includes philological-historical selections, Aramaic-Babylonian lexicography and studies in Babylonian Aramaic. (12) Sh. Safrai, *Ereẓ Yisrael ve-Ḥakhameiha bi-Tekufat ha-Mishnah ve-ha-Talmud* (1983).

Biographical Studies and Monographs. (1) Y. D. Gilat, *The Teachings of R. Eliezer b. Hyrcanus* (1968). (2) J. N. Lightstone, *Yose the Galilean, I. Traditions in Mishna-Tosefta* (1979). (3). Sh. Kanter, *Rabban Gamliel II. The Legal Traditions* (1980). (4) A. Cohen, *Mar Bar Rab Ashi and His Literary Contribution* (1980). (5) W. S. Green, *The Traditions of Joshua b. Hananiah. The Early Legal Tradition* (1981). (6) T. R. Ziv, *Shimon ben Lakish — Ha-Ish u-Po'alo* (1981). [Y.HO.]

TAYLOR, SIR PETER MURRAY (1930–), British jurist. Born in Newcastle-on-Tyne, Taylor was educated at Tyne Royal Grammar School and Pembroke College, Cambridge. He served as a captain in the Army Education Corps and captained Northumberland at rugby. Called to the bar in 1954, he was appointed a Queen's Counsel in 1967 and was a prominent prosecutor. He served as recorder of Huddersfield and of Teesside. In 1979–80, he was elected chairman of the Bar. Taylor became a judge of the High Court of Justice in 1980 and was a Lord Justice of Appeal, 1988–92. He achieved national prominence when he conducted the inquiry into the Hillborough (Sheffield) Football Stadium Disaster, and his findings led to the establishment of the Football Licencing Authority. In 1992 he was created Lord Chief Justice of England, the first Jew to hold the post since Rufus Isaacs (Lord *Reading) in 1921. He was a member of the United Hebrew Congregation of Newcastle and was active in the Soviet Jewry campaign in the late 1970s. [D.CE.]

TERKEL, STUDS (Louis; 1912–), U.S. writer and interviewer. Born in New York, the son of immigrant parents, he moved at age eight with his parents to Chicago, a town with which he remained closely associated. His parents opened a boarding-house in an Italian district where he went to school. He attended the University of Chicago and then law school. At the time of the New Deal he got a job on a writers' employment scheme and began to dabble in music, theater, and acting. Gradually he turned to radio and later to television, first as a news commentator and sportscaster, and from the mid-1940s, hosting interview shows. In the early 1990s, his daily hour-long program was still being broadcast throughout the U.S.

Terkel saw the applicability of the tape recorder to social research and utilized oral history as a tool for writing social history. He tracked down ordinary men and women and recorded their story, dramatizing the experience of anonymous Americans who would otherwise have remained anonymous. He made a great impression with *Hard Times; An Oral History of the Great Depression* (1970), following this with other oral histories including *Working* (1974) and *Race* (1992). He also published *Giants of Jazz* (1957). [G.W.]

THEATER (see 15:1077).

HIRSCH, JUDD (1935–), U.S. actor. Born in New York, his first success on Broadway was in a revival of Neil Simon's *Barefoot in the Park* (1966). Hirsch followed this with two off-Broadway hits, *Scuba Duba* (1967) and *Hot L. Baltimore* (1973). He then moved back to Broadway in the play, *Knock Knock* (1975) and won the Drama Desk Award for Best Featured Actor of 1975–76. Hirsch then starred in Neil Simon's *Chapter Two* (1977) and Lanford Wilson's *Talleys' Folly* (1989), for which he won an Obie Award for

Best Actor. Hirsch has also starred in a television series, *Taxi*, and in 1980 he received a nomination for an Oscar as best supporting actor for his work in the film *Ordinary People.*

MAMET, DAVID (1947–), U.S. playwright. Born in Chicago, Illinois, Mamet received a B.A. from Goddard college in 1969 and taught playwriting there for a brief period. He began writing for the stage in 1971 with *The Duck Variations.* In 1973, Mamet founded, along with three friends, his own theater company in Chicago (St. Nicholas) and remained its artistic director through 1975.

Mamet's plays include *Sexual Perversity in Chicago* (1973), *Reunion* (1973), *Squirrels* (1974), *American Buffalo* (1976), *A Life in the Theater* (1976), *The Water Engine* (1976), *The Woods* (1977), *Lone Canoe* (1978), *Prairie du Chien* (1978), *Lakeboat* (1980), *Donny March* (1981), *Edmond* (1982), *The Disappearance of the Jews* (1983), *Glengarry Glen Ross* (1984), and *Speed the Plow* (1990).

Mamet received the New York Drama Critics Circle Award for *American Buffalo* (1977) and *Glengarry Glen Ross* (1984), for which he was also the recipient of the Pulitzer Prize for drama. Mamet has also written screenplays, among them *The Postman Always Rings Twice* (1979), *The Verdict* (1980), *The Untouchables* (1987), *House of Games* (1987, which he also directed), *Things Change* (1988, which he also directed), *Glengarry Glen Ross* (1992, an adaptation of his play), and *Hoffa* (1992).

PAPP, JOSEPH (Joseph Papirofsky; 1921–1991), U.S. theatrical producer. Born in Brooklyn, New York, Papp served in the U.S. Navy during World War II (1942–46). He founded the non-profit Shakespeare Workshop in 1954 and had the name changed to the Shakespeare Festival in 1960 which he directed until 1991.

Papp's off-Broadway productions include *Hair* (1967), *The Basic Training of Pavlo Hummel* (1971), *Short Eyes* (1974), *A Chorus Line* (1975), *For Colored Girls Who Have Considered Suicide/When the Rainbow is Enuf* (1976), and *Streamers* (1976). Papp's on-Broadway productions include, *Two Gentlemen of Verona* (1971), *Sticks and Bones* (1972), *That Championship Season* (1972), *Much Ado About Nothing* (1972), and *The Pirates of Penzance* (1980). Papp also produced *The Haggadah* (1981) for PBS Television.

He taught (as an adjunct professor) at both Yale University and Columbia University and received numerous awards and commendations including Tony Awards in 1957, 1958, 1972, 1973, 1976 and 1981. Papp also received multiple Drama Desk and Drama Critics Circle Awards. In 1979 he received Canada's Commonwealth Award of Distinguished Service and in 1981 the American Academy and Institute of Arts and Letters Gold Medal Award for Distinguished Service to the Arts. He believed in the theater as a social force as well as entertainment.

PRINCE, HAROLD (1928–), U.S. theatrical producer. Born in New York, at age 26 Prince was awarded the first of eight Antoinette Perry Awards for coproducing Broadway's *The Pajama Game* (1954). His other seven awards came for *Damn Yankees* (1955), *Fiorello* (1959, for which he also won the Pulitzer Prize), *A Funny Thing Happened On the Way to the Forum* (1962), *Fiddler on the Roof* (1964), *Cabaret* (1966), *Company* (1970), and *A Little Night Music* (1973).

Prince added directing to his professional activities in 1963, producing and directing *She Loves Me*. Prince directed the successful *Evita* (1978) and *Sweeney Todd, The Demon Barber of Fleet Street* (1979). From 1976 Prince occasionally directed operas.

SCHISGAL, MURRAY (1926–), U.S. playwright. Born in New York, Schisgal's initial intention was to become a lawyer. He received an LL.B. from Brooklyn Law School in 1953. Schisgal's first successful stage hit was the double bill *The Typists* and *The Tiger* (1963) which starred Eli Wallach and Anne Jackson. This was followed by his biggest hit comedy, *Luv* (1964) which was chosen as one of the Best Plays of that season and made into a motion picture with Jack Lemmon and Peter Falk. Schisgal also wrote the play *Jimmy Shine* (1968) which starred Dustin Hoffman.

SONDHEIM, STEPHEN (1930–), U.S. composer, lyricist. Born in New York, his friendship with his neighbor Oscar Hammerstein led him into writing lyrics for stage shows. Sondheim leapt to the forefront of Broadway lyricists while still in his tenties when he coauthored the songs (with Leonard Bernstein) for *West Side Story* (1957). He followed this hugely successful musical with another lyrical triumph, *Gypsy* (1959), and then wrote both the music and lyrics for such hit musicals as *A Funny Thing Happened On the Way to the Forum* (1962), *Company* (1970), *Follies* (1971), *A Little Night Music* (1973), *Pacific Overtures* (1976) and *Sweeney Todd, The Demon Barber of Fleet Street* (1979). Sondheim also wrote the film score for the Alain Resnais film, *Stavisky* (1974) and coauthored the script (with Anthony Perkins) of the motion picture, *The Last of Sheila* (1973). His 1984 *Sunday in the Park with George* was inspired by a painting by the pointilliste artist Seurat.

WASSERMAN, DALE (1917–), U.S. playwright. Born in Rhinelander, Wisconsin, Wasserman came to the fore when he adapted Ken Kesey's novel, *One Flew Over the Cuckoo's Nest* (1963) for the stage. This was followed by *Man of La Mancha* (1965), for which Wasserman received many awards including a Tony Award and a Critics Circle Award. He also wrote screenplays for such feature films as *The Vikings* (1958), *Cleopatra* (1963), and his own *Man of La Mancha* which he also co-produced.

WELLER, MICHAEL (1942–), U.S. playwright. Born in New York, Weller entered the New York theater scene in 1972 with his play, *Moonchildren.* He followed this great success with a number of finely crafted scripts including *Fishing* (1973), *The Greatest Little Show On Earth* (1974), *The Bodybuilders* (1975), *Grant's Movie* (1976), *Dwarfman* (1977) and *Loose Ends* (1978). In 1979 Weller wrote the screenplay for the film version of the musical *Hair.* [Jo.Li.]

TIM (Louis Mitelberg; 1919–), French cartoonist and caricaturist. Born in Kaluszyn, Poland, Tim went to Paris to study at the Ecole des Beaux Arts but fled to England at the beginning of World War II. He returned to Paris at the end of the war and became a regular contributor to some of the world's leading newspapers and news magazines, such as the French *L'Express* and *Le Monde* and the American *Time, Newsweek*, and *The New York Times.*

Known for his incisive, courageous, and sometimes poignant style, Tim first achieved world fame in 1967 with his illustration of the words of General de Gaulle describing the Jewish people as "domineering and sure of itself": a skeleton-thin man in the striped garb of the concentration camp inmates throwing out his chest in a swaggering attitude, with his foot on the barbed wire fence. Tim has illustrated the works of Kafka and Zola and published *Pouvoir civil* (1961) and *Autocaricature* (1974) as well as an album on De Gaulle, *Une Certaine Idée de la France* (1969). In 1984 an exhibition of his works was held at the Musee des Arts Décoratifs de Paris, an almost unprecedented honor for a cartoonist.

[Gi.Ko.]

Cartoon by Tim showing "proud and stiff-necked Jew" (in the words of Charles de Gaulle) wearing a Star of David and behind barbed wire. This cartoon was the first ever to appear in *Le Monde*, 1967.

TRIGANO, SHMOUEL (1948–), French sociologist, writer, and philosopher. Born in Algeria, Shmouel Trigano is a lecturer in sociology at the University of Montpellier and head of the Jewish Studies Center affiliated with the Alliance Israélite Universelle in Paris, He is co-editor, along with Annie Kriegel (q.v.), of the magazine *Pardes.* A leading representative of the new generation of philosophers of French Judaism, his works examine the situation of the Jewish communities and of Zionism today and find a possible solution to their difficulties in a return to the true spirit of Judaism, which he feels is that of Sephardi Judaism. He has written *Le récit de la desparue* (1977), *La nouvelle question juive* (1979), and *La République et les Juifs* (1982). [GI.KO.]

TURKEY (see **15:**1456; **Dc./17:**587). In general, this has been a period of well-being for the Jewish community in Turkey. In spite of increasing Islamic-fundamentalist trends and economic difficulties due to high inflation, the Jews of Turkey have witnessed a demographic growth, an improvement of the relations between the authorities and the community, and a visible awakening of Jewish identity among the members of the community.

The traumatic event of the decade to hit the community, which is usually out of the spotlight, occurred on September 6, 1986, when Arab gunmen attacked worshipers in Istanbul's Neveh Shalom synagogue during Sabbath morning services. Nineteen of the congregation, two of them Israelis, were killed in the massacre as were the two gunmen who apparently blew themselves up. A wave of horror ran through the world and condemnations were heard on all sides, while the subsequent funeral became a protest demonstration. The Turkish prime minister, Turgut Ozal, immediately called an emergency cabinet meeting and sent a message of condemnation and sympathy to the chief rabbi of Turkey, Dr. David Asseo. A subsequent government statement linked the murderers to Iran and pro-Iranian terror organizations. The synagogue was restored and reinaugurated the following year. A monument in memory of the victims was dedicated at the Ulus/Istanbul cemetery in 1989. In another bomb outrage in 1992, an Israel diplomat was killed.

In spite of pressures created by the gradual revival of the Islamic spirit in the country, the Turkish government has shown a closer interest in the problems of the Jewish community and encouraged direct personal contacts to develop between it and the leaders of the community. Unprecedented permission was granted to Jews by allowing members of the community to take part in the assemblies of the World Jewish Congress (WJC). However, this permission marks the only instance, with the exception of Morocco, where a Muslim government has allowed its Jews to participate in a world-wide Jewish activity, is valid solely for the WJC but applies to no other international Jewish organization, and has been granted on condition of the Turkish community not becoming full members but being present only as "observers."

Synagogues, as well as property owned by the community, are considered as "foundations" by Turkish law, and all foundations in Turkey, non-Muslim and Muslim alike, are subject to the control and regulations of the Wakf. Jewish communities have felt the effect of these regulations in their efforts to obtain firm and autonomous possession of their material heritage. By the existing regulations, communities are regarded merely as administrators and not as absolute owners of their immovable property. In the event of Jewish population movement, either within the cities or to the sub-

Mass funeral for the victims of the Neveh Shalom synagogue massacre, Istanbul, September 11, 1986 (*Koteret Rashit*; photo Tom Segev)

Praying at the Ahrida synagogue, built in the 15th century, Balat, Istanbul, 1981 (Courtesy Beth Hatefutsoth, Tel Aviv; photo courtesy Izzet Keribar)

urbs, where Jewish real estate remains in the area where Jews no longer live, it is forfeited by the community to the Wakf administration.

Two main events marked Jewish communal life during the latter part of this period: The reorganization in March 1989 of the Lay Council of the Chief Rabbinate and the positive approach of the Turkish authorities to Jewish communal problems.

Through the reorganization of the Lay Council, communal affairs have been taken over by a younger and more dynamic group which adopted a bolder attitude in solving problems. Both the 80-member General Assembly of the Council and its 15-member Executive Committee include representatives from even the smallest Jewish congregations all over the country. The Chief Rabbinate has thus gained authority and jurisdiction over all the Jews of Turkey while previously its authority was practically limited to Istanbul and was often subject to the whims and goodwill of the communities in other cities.

The new Lay Council also succeeded in establishing closer relations with the authorities which, parallel to the changing international political developments, have been inclined to view the problems of the Jewish community from a more positive angle. As a result of this approach a number of developments beneficial to the community have been achieved: The permission to transfer the Jewish lycée and primary school in Istanbul to an area where Jews had moved during the last 20 years, for which permission had been requested 10 years ago and been left pending, was granted; a law passed six years earlier rendering the teaching of Islamic religion an obligatory part of the curriculum in all primary and secondary schools was abolished; *talmud torah* education in synagogues was officially allowed; a special foundation to commemorate and celebrate the 500th anniversary of the arrival of Jews fleeing the Inquisition on Turkish-Ottoman soil was created jointly by Muslem and Jewish citizens with the support of the government; and a disused synagogue, the Zülfaris, is being turned into a Jewish museum, the only one of its kind in a Muslim country, where Jews constitute less than 5 per 10,000 of the general population; and for the first time ever, Jewish sportsmen were officially authorized to take part in the 1991 Maccabi games in Marseilles under the Turkish flag.

Emigration to Israel has stopped completely, while the number of Jews who had moved to Israel but decided to return to Istanbul in particular has increased considerably. Further, the improved political and social conditions in Turkey have resulted in a sense of security for the Jews and the number of births has risen. The Jewish population grew from 22,000 to 27,000 of whom 2,000 live in Izmir, a few hundred are scattered over western Turkey, and the rest reside in Istanbul. (Censuses do not state the religion of citizens so it is difficult to determine exact figures). Roughly 800–1,000 Turkish Jews are Ashkenazim; the rest Sephardim. The two groups live in complete harmony and all communal welfare institutions are administered jointly by members of both rites. There is only one Ashkenazi synagogue in all Turkey. The religious activities of the two rites are run by the Sephardi chief rabbiate and *beth din* which satisfactorily fulfill Ashkenazi needs.

Economically most of the Turkish Jews continued to be rather well-off, except for some 300 families who were partly or totally supported by the community. However, Jews in general have suffered due to the rampant inflation (a limited number of prominent businessmen constituting an exception).

Members of the community have evinced a marked return to religion and traditions and a keener Jewish consciousness. The number of people who have voluntarily offered to take an active part in communal work and assume their obligations towards the community has grown. The weekly paper *Shalom*, the publication of which had been stopped as a result of its former owner's illness and death, has been taken over by a group of young people who have succeeded in increasing its circulation to 5,000 (thus turning it into a paper read in almost every Jewish household) and giving special emphasis to the revival of Ladino. About one-third of the contents of the paper are in *Ladino and the younger generation has begun to show a greater interest in the language.

A new club was founded to serve the Jewish residents of fashionable quarters on the Asian coast of Istanbul, where almost a fourth of the Jewish population lives, and its new building with sports, recreation, and cultural facilities was inaugurated in 1987. A trend of a more intense search for a Jewish identity has emerged among the younger generation and a greater number of people of all ages are volunteering for communal work.

However, in spite of the socio-cultural revival, the number of intermarriages has increased and has been put at 10%.

The chief rabbi (Hakham Bashi) is the official leader and representative of Turkish Jewry. He is assisted by a religious Council (Beth Din) and the lay Council. In contrast to its glorious past of world-famous rabbis and religious scholars, the community is beginning to feel the shortage of qualified rabbis and other religious functionaries. The only *kasher* restaurant closed when its owner retired.

Jews continue to be politically inactive in the country. As in the past, this is due both to their insignificant numbers as well as to their reluctance to take part in politics. While the majority of Jews voted for the middle-right "Motherland" party in power during the 1986 elections, a religious party advocating antipathy and even hostility towards Israel and the Jews grew much stronger. Occasional incitements by this party have caused the Jewish community anxiety.

The approval by the authorities and their encouragement of the decision to celebrate the 500th anniversary of the settling of the Sephardi Jews on Turkish-Ottoman soil in 1492 was a high point in Jewish communal life. To celebrate the anniversary a series of national and international symposiums, publications, the creation of a Jewish museum and concerts of local Jewish music were prepared for 1990, with the climax in 1992. (See also SEPHARDIM).

No spectacular or sensational changes in the general life of the Jews occurred over this decade. The Jews of Turkey continued to be the only Jewish community to enjoy tranquility and prosperity in a predominantly Muslim country.

[H.Y.]

Poignant meeting in a Odessa synagogue between Jacob Haimovici, comptroller for the Montreal YM-YWHA, and an elderly Jew hungry for contact with Jews from other lands. (Courtesy Allied JCS, Montreal)

UKRAINE (see 15:1513). There were 487,300 Jews living in Ukraine, according to the 1989 census. This figure included 100,600 in Kiev, 69,100 in Odessa province (city and surrounding oblast), 50,100 in Dnepropetrosk province, and 48,900 in Kharkov province. In late 1991 the number of Jews in the Ukraine was estimated at 325,000. The birth rate for Ukrainian Jews in 1988–89 was 6.6 per 1,000 and the mortality rate was 23.4 per 1,000. Ukrainian Jewry is characterized by a high median age (approximately 50), a high proportion of mixed marriages, and a low fertility rate.

The number of Ukrainian Jews emigrating from the late 1980s was: 1988 — 8,770; 1989 (to Israel) — 32,547; 1990 — 60,074, and 1991 (to Israel) — 41,264. The geographical breakdown of emigration for 1989–1991 (from 1990 only to Israel) was: from Kiev — 33,818; Odessa province — 19,741; Kharkov province — 11,945; Dnepropetrosk province — 7,501; and Zhitomir province — 5,005.

Ukraine declared its independence on August 24, 1991, with the majority of the republic's Jews also voting for independence. On a number of occasions the leaders of the Ukrainian national movement "Rukh" expressed a positive attitude toward the Jews of the Ukraine and the desire to cooperate with them. To further that goal, an international conference was held in Kiev in June 1991 on Ukrainian-Jewish relations, with the participation of leading Ukrainian public figures. Ukrainian president Kravchuk spoke at the public meeting commemorating the 50th anniversary of the mass murder of Kiev's Jews at Babi Yar. In his speech the president acknowledged the Ukrainian people's share of guilt for the destruction of the Jews and asked for the Jewish people's forgiveness. He also called for the UN to support the initiative of U.S. president George Bush and rescind the UN resolution equating Zionism with racism. In 1990, before the splitting up of the U.S.S.R., four Jewish deputies were elected to the Supreme Soviet of the Ukrainian republic.

Under Soviet rule, Bogdan *Chmielnicki, the leader responsible for the unprecedented Cossack slaughter of Jews in the mid-17th century, had been considered a Ukrainian national hero. With the growth, however, of Ukrainian separatist feeling, Chmielnicki became less of a hero due to the fact that he had concluded a pact with Moscow which transformed Ukraine into a Russian colony. Today Simon *Petlyura (1879–1926) is considered the pre-eminent national hero since he headed the country during the brief years of its independence after World War I. Petlyura's responsibility for pogroms during the Civil War is denied by Ukrainian nationalists. In Ukraine the Jewish hero Shalom *Schwarzbard, who assassinated Petlyura in Paris for supporting the perpetrators of pogroms, is today viewed as having been a Soviet secret police agent.

Grass roots anti-Semitism has not disappeared in Ukraine. According to the results of a sociological survey conducted in November 1990, 7% of the population firmly believe in the existence of an international "Zionist" conspiracy, while 68% believe that such a conspiracy may exist; 10% believe that the Jews bear considerable responsibility for the suffering of other peoples (e.g., the Ukrainians) in the Soviet Union in the 20th century; and 20% believe that Jews have an unpleasant appearance.

A law on ethnic minorities grants Ukrainian Jews the right of national-cultural autonomy. In 1992 several Jewish publications appeared, including three *(Vozrozhdenie-91, Evreiskie vesti*, and *Khadashot)* in Kiev. Study (often by amateurs) of local Jewish history is being developed in the republics. The Jewish Culture Association of Ukraine is headed by Ilya Levitas; the rival Association of Jewish Public Organizations of Ukraine is headed by the co-chairman of VAAD of the CIS, Iosif Zisels.

In late 1991, 120 Jewish organizations were operating in Ukraine. The Ukrainian Jewish Congress was established in Oct. 1991. The American rabbi Yankel Blau was named chief rabbi of Ukraine. Several synagogues confiscated in the 1920s and 1930s were returned by Ukrainian authorities, among them those of the Jewish communities of Kharkov, Donets, Vinnitsa, Odessa, Lvov, Shepetovka, Kirovograd, and Drahobych. [MI.BE.]

UNITED NATIONS (see **15:**1543). The collapse of the Soviet Union and the end of the Cold War, as well as significant weakening in the Arab position following the Gulf War and the opening of peace talks after the Madrid Conference, led to a significant change in Israel's standing in the United Nations. This manifested itself in the unprecedented repeal on December 15, 1991, of General Assembly Resolution 3379 passed in 1975 which had equated Zionism with racism. The resolution which had been passed by a vote of 72 in favor, 35 against and 32 abstentions, was repealed in 1991 by a vote of 111 in favor, 25 against (including almost all the Arab and Muslim states), and 13 absentions.

Still there remains an anti-Israeli bias at the UN and double standards are applied against it in the General Assembly and other UN forums. However the atmosphere marks an improvement in Israel's position and it has chances to be elected to several UN bodies which were previously closed to it. At the end of 1992 Israel was approached for the first time by the secretary general of the UN, Dr. Butrus-Ghali, about sending professional personnel to participate in UN peacekeeping forces, and agreed.

Resolution 3379 which declared that "Zionism is a form of racism and racial discrimination" marked the climax of the anti-Israel and anti-Semitic campaign in the United Nations. The U.S. ambassador to the UN, Daniel Patrick Moynihan called it a "terrible lie... an infamous act." Israel's then ambassador to the UN, Chaim Herzog, told the General Assembly: "For us, the Jewish people, this resolution based on hatred, falsehood, and arrogance is devoid of any moral or legal value," and then he tore the text of the resolutions in two.

The UN resolution equating Zionism with racism was another Orwellian inversion of language which was common practice at the Soviet-Arab-Third World-dominated General Assembly of the mid-1970s. But unlike other regular generalized attacks on capitalism, democracy, or freedom of the press, here the target was clear and specific: to delegitimize a member state — Israel — and to legitimize anti-Semitism. By equating Zionism, the national liberation movement of the Jewish people, with racism the Jewish state and the Jewish people were formally declared enemies of mankind and were placed beyond the pale of civilized society. The adverse ramifications for Jews and Israelis went far beyond the narrow confines of the United Nations.

Subsequently, the attacks on Israel and Zionism replete with anti-Semitic nuances, spread to all the UN institutions and special agencies, and bore the nature of a campaign to delegitimize the right of the Jewish people to its own independent state. Every year, in every General Assembly, over 30 anti-Israel resolutions were adopted on various aspects of the Arab-Israel conflict. Israel was singled out in General Assembly resolutions for policies of "hegemonism" and "racism" and was accused for being a "non-peace-loving-country" (which, according to the UN Charter, can be expelled from the organization) and a state which is "an affront to humanity" and is "committing war crimes."

The resolutions and papers accepted and distributed within the various organizations of the United Nations were mostly collections of condemnations and abuses, twisted truths, and retouched histories that disregarded and even challenged the right of Israel to exist as a state. At the General Assembly, resolutions called for economic, diplomatic, and military sanctions against Israel which, had they been accepted, would have left Israel helpless against military attacks as well as political and economic ones. UN verbatim records contain many anti-Semitic outbursts, delegitimization attacks, obscene accusations, and diatribes against Israel. A review of the UN assembly papers and examination of the diplomatic effort and the media coverage involved in passing these resolutions creates the feeling that the annual and special UN conferences sometimes became anti-Israel "festivals." The UN played a major role in enhancing the prestige and international standing of the Palestine Liberation Organization (PLO) after the appearance of its leader Yasser Arafat in the General Assembly in November 1974.

In the early 1980s the anti-Israeli campaign shifted to an effort to have the credentials of the Israeli delegation to the General Assembly disqualified, with the goal of having Israel suspended from the deliberations. As a result of the determined American position, accompanied by U.S. threats that it would withdraw if Israel were to be suspended, no deliberation on the disqualification of Israel's credentials has taken place. The decline in the power of the Arab oil-producing countries has also dimished their influence in the UN and has been accompanied by a parallel process of erosion in the status of the PLO in the organization.

The revelations in 1986–7 on the Nazi past of Dr. Kurt Waldheim, the former Secretary General of the UN, dealt another blow to the prestige of the UN. Waldheim's file in the UN War crimes commission was not known to the public when he was elected and serving 10 years in this post.

In the field of UN peacekeeping forces, the Middle East and the Arab-Israeli conflict continued to be an active laboratory for various operations. In addition to the UN Disengagement Observer Force (UNDOF) in the Golan Heights since 1974, the UN Interim Force in Lebanon (UNIFIL) has been stationed in southern Lebanon since 1978. The hostility of the UN General Assembly toward the Camp David Accords and the peace agreements between Israel and Egypt and the opposition of Soviet Union in the Security Council led to the creation of a new framework outside the UN, the Multinational Force, led by the United States, which was stationed in Sinai after Israel's final withdrawal to the international border in April 1982. This Multinational Force replaced the UN forces in Sinai.

There are still about 300 UN personnel in the UN Truce Supervision Organization (UNTSO) which was established in 1948 to supervise the cease-fires and later the armistice agreements between Israel and its neighbors. The UN Relief and Work Agency (UNRWA) operates in the Palestinian refugee camps in the territories. [AVI BE.]

UNITED STATES LITERATURE (see **15**:1564; **Dc./17**:590). As in the preceding decennial this article covers creativity of a "non-scientific" nature, e.g., poetry, drama, literary criticism, belles lettres, historical novels, and journalism. A limited number of representative titles is listed in each category. The list is by no means exhaustive or judgmental. No translations or reprints are included.

The 1980s witnessed a publishing explosion under the imprimatur of Orthodox Judaism. This mirrors a unique socio-religious development in American Judaism. Next in line, quantitatively are works on the Holocaust, both fiction and non-fiction.

The following selection is listed alphabetically by author's name:

Yaacov Agam in *Art and Judaism* (1985) reports on discussions with Bernard Mandelbaum highlighting the significance of their respective points of view. George K. Anderson's *Legend of the Wandering Jew* (1981) presents an historical and literary analysis of the stereotypical tale. Feminine images of biblical literary tradition are depicted by Nehama Aschkenazy in *Eve's Journey* (1986). Linda Beyer in *The Blessing and the Curse* (1988) focuses attention on the problem of restlessness associated with being an adopted child. Gina Barkhorden-Nahi in *Cry of the Peacock* (1991) portrays Jewish history in Iran in the past two centuries, including the period of Khomeini's revolution, against the background of fortunes and misfortunes of one family. Alan L. Berger in *Crisis and Covenant* (1985) discusses Holocaust themes in American Jewish fiction. An unusual study is offered by Jakub Blum and Vera Rich in *The Image of the Jew in Soviet Literature: The Post-Stalin period* (1985). Philip V. Bohlman in *The Land Where Two Streams Flow* (1989) examines German-Jewish contributions to the musical culture of Israel. New observations on art and literature

To three possessions thou shouldst look · Acquire a field, a friend, a book.
November 7th to December 7th, 1985
Jewish Book Month
JWB Jewish Book Council
15 East 26th Street · New York, N.Y. 10010-1579 · (212)532-4949

Poster for Jewish Book Month, 1985, drawn by Maurice Sendak (Courtesy Jewish Book Council, N.Y.)

of the Holocaust are offered by Randolph Braham in *Reflections of the Holocaust on Art and Literature* (1990). Themes of intertwined relationships between Jewish and Arab women are dealt with in Roger Clever's novel *Daughters of Jerusalem* (1986).

Susan Compton in *Marc Chagall — My Life, My Dreams 1922–1940* (1990) explores the artist's etchings created in that period comparing them with some of his later works on identical themes. Matt Cohen's novel *The Spanish Doctor* (1985) depicts a Marrano wandering through the madness of medieval anti-Semitic Europe finally finding peace in his home as a Jew in Kiev. Modern-day Israel with its restless atmosphere of politics, survivors' complexes, and fear of war, is depicted by Blanch d'Apulget in the novel *Winter in Jerusalem* (1986). *The Monological Jew* by L. S. Dembo (1988) is a study in literary criticism. Henry Denker's novel *Payment in Full* (1991) deals with diverse religious heritages articulating specific aspects in each of them. Unlike the often-heard prophecies of demise, Wayne D. Dosic predicts in *The Best is Yet to Come: Renewing American Judaism* (1988) a process of the strengthening of American Judaism through blending with American culture. *The Seventh Sanctuary* by David Easterman (1987) is a tale about searching for a murderer intent upon the destruction of Israel and the simultaneous restoration of the Nazi Reich. The National Critics Book Circle singled out Stanley Elkin's *The Rabbi of Lud* (1987) for its unusual humorous characteristics. Themes of pride in her Jewish heritage overweigh considerations of fame in Julie Ellis' novel *The Only Sin* (1986). Over 800 films with Jewish characters and themes are reviewed by Patricia Erens in *The Jew in American Cinema* (1985). Lynn Fried in *House Around* (1986) copes with the depressing reality caused by the realization that her parents are insensitive to interracial conflicts in South Africa. Cynthia Ozick's works and ideals are analyzed by Lawrence S. Friedman in *Understanding Cynthia Ozick* (1991). Samuel S. Friedman sees in *The Oberammergau Passion Play* a source of unabating anti-Semitism. Lester Goldberg's lyrical novel *In Siberia It Is Very Cold* (1987) tells the tale of a refugee from Zamosc, Poland, surviving the rigors of far-off Asiatic Russia.

The unsupportive environment to maintain a Jewish home in Galveston, Texas, at the beginning of the 20th century, is vividly described by Gloria Goldberg in *West to Eden* (1987). Social and religious turmoil emerge in Alex J. Goldman's *The Rabbi is a Lady* (1987) when the congregation becomes aware of the leadership talents of the rabbi's widow. Robert Greenfield's *Temple* (1983), a highly acclaimed novel and winner of an award by the National Jewish Book Council, described a Harvard Graduate School "dropout." A *Mother's Secret* by Carolyn Haddad (1985) explores the depth of "mother's love" utilizing a Jewish partisan's trust during World War II that a villager would shelter her daughter. Roberta Kaleshofsky offers a glimpse in *Bodmin 1349* (1988) of the murderous pogroms against Jews by their Christian neighbors following the Black Death. Frederick Karl depicts in *Franz Kafka, Representative Man* (1991) the historical, cultural, and artistic world from which Kafka arose. Charles S. Liebman and Steven M. Cohen explore in *Two Worlds of Israeli and American Experiences* (1990) how Israelis and American Jews differ in their conceptions of Judaism. Curt Leviant presents in *The Man Who Thought He Was the Messiah* (1990) a fictional version of the life of Rabbi Naḥman of Bratslav. Sol Liptzin in *Biblical Themes in World Literature* (1984) studies biblical motifs that stimulated the creative imagination of renowned writers.

Daphne Markin reflects in *Enchantment* (1986) the spirit of the 1950s regarding the love/hate relationships in a wealthy German-Jewish Orthodox family in Manhattan's Upper East Side. Gabriella Mantner chronicles in *Lovers and Fugitives* (1986) the courageous flight of a pair of escapees from Nazi persecution in Rotterdam. Jacob Neusner in *The Public Side of Learning the Political Consequence of Scholarship in the Context of Judaism* (1985) views the study of Judaism within the framework of the study of religion. Chaim Potok's *Davita's Harp* (1984) reflects tendencies to obliterate boundaries within the American Jewish community — the heroine (Davita), herself the daughter of a gentile leftist journalist married to a woman who cannot erase from her memory her ḥasidic upbringing, flirts with Christianity, but then turns to Orthodox Judaism.

The theme of endurance during the Nazi rule over Eastern Europe is utilized by Elio Romano in a *Generation of Wrath: A Story of Embattlement* (1986). Paul Romsey's *Contemporary Religious Poetry* (1987) includes materials dealing with Jewish themes. David Raphael's novel *The Alhambra Decree* (1989) chronicles events which led to the expulsion of some 150,000 Jews from Segovia, Spain, in 1492. A study of Jews and art and Jewish artists is offered by Harold Rosenberg in *Art and Other Serious Matters* (1985). Philip Roth deals with

The *Heritage Mosaic* which portrays the essence of American-Jewish experience from 1654 to the present, Mt. Sinai Memorial Park, Los Angeles (Courtesy Mt. Sinai Memorial Park, L.A.)

a number of problems in *Counterlife* (1987) ranging from English anti-Semitism to Israeli militancy and ethnic abrasiveness. Moshe Safdie sketches in *Jerusalem: The Future of the Past* (1989) a projection of architectural problems while building something true to the present as well as the past. Sandra Schor focuses attention on Baruch Spinoza in her novel *The Great Letter E* (1990). June Flaum-Singer elaborates in *The Markoff Woman* (1986) the saga of the descendant of a Russian immigrant to America who "makes it" in the world of commerce but is plagued by inner hollowness until he returns to his religious heritage. Bodie Thoeme's *The Return to Zion* (1987) is the final novel of the trilogy "the Zion chronicle," about the founding of the State of Israel. Eric Werner offers a comprehensive study in *The Sacred Bridge, vol. II* (1985) of the relationship between liturgy and music in Synagogue and Church during the first millennium. Melvin Wilk's *Jewish Presence in T. S. Eliot and Franz Kafka* (1986) traces Eliot's anti-Semitism and Kafka's search for religious dimensions in their respective works.

[S.FA.]

UNITED STATES OF AMERICA
(see **15**:1585; **Dc./17**:592)
1980–1992 Key Events and Trends.

Jewish Community Studies. During the 1980s, observers of American Jewish life were engaged in an escalating debate over whether the proverbial glass was half full or half empty. Optimists saw a Jewish community which was the most materially secure in history, fully integrated into the surrounding society, and well represented in all branches of American science, art, academia, government, and commerce. Internally, the Jewish community supported an extensive and sophisticated network of local, national and international organizations that were active in a myriad of social welfare, cultural, educational, and political causes.

In contrast, critics pointed to an unprecedented rise in the rate of intermarriage, an ominously low Jewish birth rate, the migration of younger professionals away from Jewish population centers, and increasing Jewish cultural illiteracy. More than half of the American Jewish adult population was now too young to carry any personal recollections of the Holocaust era or the birth of the state of Israel. Many were drawn to other social and humanitarian causes and viewed events within the Jewish community as irrelevant to their lives. Viewed from this perspective, it appeared that American Jewish communal life was fractured and its future lay in jeopardy.

American Modernity and Jewish Identity (1983), by Queen's College sociologist Steven Cohen, sought to present a fairly representative scenario of American Jewish communal life for the times. Cohen's analysis and conclusions were based on previously collected survey data taken mainly from the Boston area. His general conclusions confirmed some commonly held perceptions, namely, that the American Jewish community was well educated, solidly middle-class (or higher), upwardly and geographically mobile. Other trends which Cohen identified were less positive. Among these was evidence that American Jews were marrying later than their parents' generation and at an average age which exceeded the national population. This was considered one reason for the drop of Jewish fertility to a level below that of comparably aged Americans. Jewish divorce rates had increased, but appeared to be less than half of those of white Protestants. The rate of intermarriage was higher but remained much below the rate of other white ethnic groups. The overall result, said Cohen, was an increase in the number of Jewish singles, childless, intermarrieds, and divorcees, referred to by social scientists as "alternative" households.

Charles Silberman's *A Certain People: American Jews and Their Lives Today* (1985), was an astute but subjective analysis of collected anecdotes and observations. Silberman delivered a "good news" palliative, an upbeat response to those who were concerned about the future of Jewish life in America. American Jews, said Silberman, having successfully been absorbed into the American mainstream where anti-Semitism is no longer a serious problem, could finally be open about their ethnicity. Intermarriage was not necessarily a problem as many non-Jewish spouses ultimately convert, thereby adding to the Jewish population. His optimism on behalf of Jewish life in America reflected the surge in national pride and confidence shared by many Americans during the Reagan era.

Cohen's generally positive message and Silberman's outright exuberant prognostication were strengthened by the conclusions drawn by Brown University sociologist and demographer Calvin Goldscheider. Goldscheider argued in *Jewish Continuity and Change: Emerging Patterns in America* (1986) that there was sufficient empirical evidence to show that the American Jews were not disappearing as a result of assimilation. Rather, through a process of adaptation to modernity, the Jewish community was in the process of transforming itself. Although significantly different from the immigrant generation, and even different from the American Jewish community of forty and fifty years earlier, the present Jewish community has succeeded in maintaining a viable social and religious network based on family, friends, and institutions. "As a community, Jews," says Goldscheider, "are surviving in America, even as some individuals enter and leave the community."

In spite of such reassurance, by 1988 the contradictory trends and tensions that characterized American Jewish life provided the inspiration for the title of Leonard Fein's "Where Are We?" In this essay, the founder and former editor of *Moment* magazine offered his own analysis of contemporary American Jewry. One hundred years after the Jewish mass immigration from Eastern Europe, the American Jewish community reflected an agglomerate of contradictory religious beliefs and practices (or the lack of), a vested interest in its solidly middle class status, unresolved emotions over the Holocaust and Israel, and uncertainty about its long term prospects for survival. According to Fein, with the exception of mainly Orthodox religious circles, political liberalism, which he defined as a commitment to social justice and pluralism, remained the one identifiable social value of Jewish community life.

In spite of the many complex issues challenging Jewish survival, Fein remained optimistic. He saw a commitment to liberalism as not only a valid strategy for survival, but even the preferred one in America's democratic and open society.

The new abundance of research, articles and, books on American Jewish life was itself a phenomenon which represented this period. It was, historically speaking, the first fruits of the growth of Jewish studies programs at American universities during the previous decade. With the aid of more powerful computers and improvements in social science methodology increasingly accurate information about the Jewish community became available. About 50 Jewish communities undertook local surveys during the 1980s.

But as Goldstein pointed out (*American Jewish Year Book* [AJYB] 1992) comparing the results of these surveys did not yield an accurate picture of American Jewish life. "The (different) surveys," he noted, "... varied considerably in scope and quality: They... relied on different questionnaires, varying sampling designs and coverage of the Jewish population, and diverse tabulation plans. The absence of standardized methods and definitions (including who was to be counted as a Jew) made it difficult and sometimes impossible to compare findings across communities."

A view of the new library of the Jewish Theological Seminary in New York City on its dedication day (Courtesy the Movement for Masorti Judaism in Israel, Jerusalem)

Additional demographic, social, and attitudinal data was gathered throughout these years in national surveys undertaken by academic and communal institutions. Prominent among these was the Cohen Center for Modern Jewish Studies at Brandeis University and the American Jewish Committee. The latter institution produced a series of studies on American Jews under the direction of Steven M. Cohen.

The rapidly growing body of local and national survey data contributed to the creation in 1986 of the North American Jewish Data Bank. This new institution was a joint project of the Council of Jewish Federations and the Center for Jewish Studies of the Graduate School and the University Center of the City University of New York.

SURVIVAL VERSUS ASSIMILATION. The chances for Jewish survival in the shape of ongoing acculturation was strongly debated between two camps. One included such social scientists as Steven M. Cohen, Paul Ritterband, Calvin Goldscheider, Fred Massarik, Gary Tobin, Leonard Fein and author Charles Silberman. These "transformationalists," as this group became known, posited that American Jews were not abandoning Judaism or the Jewish community, but were transforming the concepts associated with Jewish practice and affiliation. They saw Judaism and the Jewish community as being inclusive rather than exclusive in responding to the challenges of modernity.

This view was rejected by the "assimilationists." Belonging to this camp were sociologists Charles Liebman, Marshall Sklare, Sidney Goldstein, Hebrew University demographers U. O. Schmelz and Sergio DellaPergola, and such senior communal professionals as Steven Bayme, Donald Feldstein, and Rabbi Arthur Hertzberg. They interpreted current trends as signifying an ongoing process of assimilation, i.e., the eventual integration beyond recognition of Jews into the general society, a process which, assuming similar ongoing social and economic conditions, they felt was likely to continue.

INTERMARRIAGE. The single most cited indicator of this process was the rate of intermarriage. By the beginning of the 1980s the national rate of intermarriage estimated to have been around 30 percent, was becoming a serious concern within the Jewish community. In under ten years it emerged as a full blown crisis (see pages 57–64).

Studies showed that intermarriage was more common both among younger Jews marrying for the first time and among divorcees who had married for a second or third time. A Council of Jewish Federations/North American Jewish Data Bank report indicated that for the years 1982–1987 the percentage of intermarriage among American Jews was 14 percent for first marriages and 40 percent for second marriages. In all studies on the subject, a significant difference was found between men and women in every age group with Jewish men constantly demonstrating a higher rate of intermarriage.

Coupled with gender, denomination was also found to play a role among Jews who had intermarried. Studies showed the intermarriage rate among Orthodox Jews to be negligible. The estimated intermarriage rate among Conservative Jews was about 10 percent and among Reform Jews it was 30 percent. Those calling themselves secular Jews, humanist Jews, or "just Jews," had the highest rate, over 50 percent. The longer a Jewish family had been in America, the greater the chance that the youngest generation of that family would intermarry.

The 1990 Council of Jewish Federations (CJF) National Population Survey, the most comprehensive study of American Jewry undertaken since 1971, revealed not only that one-third of all American Jews were presently married to non-Jews, but among those who had married since 1985, the intermarriage rate had reached an unprecedented 52 percent.

The 1990 CJF survey also reported that the American Jewish community had lost more members (210,000) through conversion than it has gained (185,000). The Cohen Center for Modern Jewish Studies at Brandeis University reported that only about one of every four marriages between a Jew and a born non-Jew resulted in the non-Jewish partner's conversion to Judaism. While there was little evidence of Jews converting to another religion, the majority of marriages in the United States between Jews and non-Jews did not result in all-Jewish households (Tobin 1991).

One of the reasons cited for the significant increase in mixed, or non-conversionary, marriages was the relaxation of social barriers between ethnic and religious groups among younger Americans. New attitudes, in turn, lead to greater acceptance of the multi-religious home. The openness to mixed-marriage was further facilitated by the ease in finding rabbis willing to sacralize the matrimony of a Jew and a non-Jew. This growing practice was investigated in 1987 in a survey of the Reform rabbinate which found that 50.4 percent of the rabbis who responded to the survey acknowledged officiating at intermarriages, a figure 9 percent higher than the results from a 1972 survey. An additional 32 percent who did not perform intermarriages would, however, refer a couple to a colleague who does, leaving only 18 percent that did not officiate or refer. While most of the rabbis performed intermarriage only upon the fulfillment of certain conditions by the bride and groom, others imposed no conditions at all. As the response rate to the survey was only 39 percent of the total reform rabbinate, the actual number of American Reform rabbis who had or would be willing to officiate at mixed marriages remained uncertain. Those who did, however, were in violation of a 1973 policy statement of the Central Conference of American [Reform] Rabbis stating that rabbis who officiate at mixed intermarriages "do so contrary to the clear guidelines of their rabbinic organization."

Although a small percentage of Conservative rabbis were known to perform mixed marriages, the movement's Rabbinical Assembly strongly opposed the practice. Conservative rabbis who officiated at such ceremonies risked expulsion from the Assembly.

MARRIAGE AND FAMILY. Concern over the high rate of intermarriage was compounded by evidence of the growing number of Jews who had either never married or had not begun a family by the time they had reached their mid-thirties. The 1983 National Survey of American Jews (1983 AJYB) estimated that 38 percent of the adult Jewish population of the United States was single. Twenty-one percent reported never having been married. Although the figure was not published, it is likely that many of these were people over 30 years of age. By 1990, according to the CJF survey, 49.5 percent of Jewish males and 50 percent of Jewish females between the ages of 25–34 had never married. For comparison, in 1957 29 percent of Jewish males and 9 percent of Jewish females in this age range had never married, according to the U.S. Bureau of the Census survey entitled "Religion Reported by the Civilian Population." In 1970/71, the National Jewish Population Survey found that only 17 percent of Jewish males and 10 percent of Jewish females had never married. Among Jewish women, all studies indicated the chance of being single was greatest for those with graduate degrees, especially after age 30.

The growing phenomenon of single Jews served as an impetus for the proliferation of Jewish dating services throughout the country. The venerable tradition of Jewish matchmaking was transformed during the 1980s into a nationwide industry. Some services, established mainly in large urban areas, were operated on a private commercial basis. Others were run under the non-profit auspices of community agencies such as B'nai B'rith, the Jewish Community Centers, or a local synagogue. Two synagogues in particular, the Orthodox Lincoln Square in New York and the Conservative Adas Israel in Washington, D.C., developed well-known and successful programs for Jewish singles. Advice columns for Jewish singles proliferated, and Jewish matchmaking and dating services were advertised frequently in Jewish newspapers and periodicals.

Speculation abounded about the future size of the Jewish community. "Assimilationists" argued that the American Jewish community could soon lose the ability to biologically replace itself. To counter these fears, "transformationalists" argued that American Jewish women were openly following the trend of American women in general who were registering a sharp increase in marriage and fertility between the ages 30–39. This, they argued, combined with an appreciable number of converts to Judaism, would contribute to the stabilization and subsequent growth of the Jewish population, assuming the American Jewish community maintained the minimum replacement average of 2.1 children per couple. However, the 1990 CJF survey indicated below replacement level birth rates of .87 for women between the ages 25–34 and 1.57 for women between the ages 35–44. The average number of people in a Jewish household during the 1980s fell to 2.7, smaller than the national median of 2.9.

The 1990 CJF survey also indicated that 16.4 percent of all ever married men and 18.2 percent of all ever married women had ended at least one marriage in divorce. Figures were higher for middle-aged men aged 45–64 years, 22 percent, as for Jewish males who classified themselves as secular, 24.5 percent, compared to those who classified themselves as Jews by religion, 13.6 percent. Middle-aged Jewish women also divorced more frequently, 18 percent for those aged 35–44, as for women who defined themselves as secular Jews, 27.2 percent, rather than Jewish by religion, 16.3 percent. While divorce had become more frequent among American Jews than in previous generations, comparative data revealed it to be less common than among the general population.

GEOGRAPHIC DISPERSION AND MOBILITY. While the largest concentration of Jews continued to reside in the Northeast (43.5 percent), the trend in population movement during the 1980s continued to be away from the Northeast and Midwest (11.3 percent) to the South (21.8 percent) and West (23.4 percent). By comparison, in 1970 the National Jewish Population Survey had found 64 percent of the Jewish population living in the Northeast, 17 percent in the Midwest, and only 19 percent, combined, in the South and West.

Kosmin, Ritterband, and Scheckner (AJYB 1986) noted the greater distribution of American Jews among smaller urban areas than in the past. In comparison to 1936 when 90 percent of the Jewish population was dispersed over 17 urban areas, this same percentage was now spread over thirty areas. The migration was characterized by Jews who had moved from the largest Northeastern and Midwestern cities, such as New York, Philadelphia and Boston, to smaller urban areas in the South and West such as Atlanta and Phoenix. As a result, during this 50-year period, the Jewish population in the New York metropolitan area had decreased from about 2.6 million to 2.2 million. Chicago's Jewish population decreased from 378,000 to about 250,000. By the mid-1980s the Jewish communities of Philadelphia, Pittsburgh, Cleveland, Detroit, and St. Louis had all declined.

In contrast, by the 1980s there were six Jewish communities west of the Rocky Mountains whose populations had grown to over 100,000. Los Angeles, with an estimated 604,000 Jews was now the second largest Jewish community in the United States, followed by Miami/Ft. Lauderdale metropolitan region, with an estimated 367,000 Jews.

Figures from the 1990 CJF survey indicated that from May 1985 to the summer of 1990, some 700,000 respondents, or 23.5 percent of the American Jewish population had migrated to at least one new out of state residence. Many of the migrating Jewish families and Jewish singles sought a residential area that included or was in proximity to a synagogue, Jewish school, or a Jewish community center. However, nothing comparable to the highly concentrated Jewish neighborhoods or post-World War II suburbs were being recreated. Furthermore, while three-quarters of all Jews could be found living in metropolitan areas, about 25 percent now lived in non-metropolitan areas where access to Jewish communal institutions, if available, was dependent upon an automobile. Eight percent of American Jews now resided in smaller non-metropolitan areas of less than 150,000 people. (AJYB 1992).

Population. The 1982 American Jewish Yearbook estimated the Jewish population of the U.S. to be slightly over 5.9 million, an increase of some 200,000 over the adjusted baseline figure of 5.7 million published in 1970. Its 1987 mid-decade Jewish population estimate was 5,814,000. End of the decade figures indicated that the number representing the country's "core Jewish population," i.e., those who reported themselves Jews by religion (born Jews or converted) or as secular Jews (born Jewish who report no current religion) had dropped to 5,515,000.

Demographic surveys had their critics. Gary Tobin argued that all national Jewish population figures prior to the 1990 CJF survey were inherently inaccurate since they either consisted of a composite of non-standardized and therefore noncomparable data, or the applied survey methodology, for example, using distinctive Jewish names, did not garner a truly representative sample. It is therefore possible, he argued, that the core Jewish population of the United States, if defined in broader terms, was significantly larger. But the release of the 1990 CJF survey strengthened the suspicion that the American Jewish population was in fact becoming smaller.

Jewish Education. In 1987 Liebman charged that most of what passed for American Jewish education, at least at the supplementary school level was "not about the Jewish past, the Jewish tradition, or Jewish culture (but rather) preparation for bar or bat mitzvah (and) learning to be a proud Jew." Among the few objective sources of information on Jewish

Kindergarten students of the Conservative Solomon Schechter Day School of Raritan Valley, East Brunswick, N.J., on a field trip teaching the children about autumn, Sukkot, and Thanksgiving (By permission of the school)

education nationwide was the 1981 National Survey of Jews (AJYB 1983). The survey showed that nine percent of the children of the adult respondents were then receiving bar/bat mitzvah lessons, 18 percent were enrolled in Sunday School, 40 percent were enrolled in Hebrew School, and seven percent were attending a yeshivah or day school. In total, 74 percent of Jewish children were the recipients of some form of Jewish education.

Additional findings on Jewish education for the 1980s were reported by Sylvia Barack Fishman of the Cohen Center for Modern Jewish Studies at Brandeis University. On the basis of data collected in Federation-sponsored population studies from 18 cities throughout the United States, Fishman estimated the percentage of American Jews receiving formal Jewish education to be far higher than at any other time in the past. Her analysis indicated that at least three-quarters of all children ages six to thirteen in Eastern and Midwestern cities were receiving some type of formal Jewish education. The figure for Southwestern cities was reported to be about 60 percent. After age 13, however, the percentage of students enrolled in any type of formal Jewish education dropped to about 25. After age 18 the figures fell even lower, depending on the city.

The 1990 National Jewish Population Survey reported that 3,350,000 of those surveyed were estimated to have received some form of Jewish education at some point in their lives. Overall, fewer women than men were the recipients of formal Jewish education. Among adult Jewish respondents between the ages of 18–44, for example, 52 percent of males and 44 percent females had more than five years of formal Jewish education. The survey reported the median years of Jewish education for this age group to have been 6.2 for males and 4.6 for females.

In spite of the availability of adult or continuing Jewish education classes that were available in synagogues, community centers, and Jewish colleges around the country, outside of the Orthodox community Jewish education remained primarily a part-time activity associated with Jewish childhood. Deborah Lipstadt (1989) stated in an article that dealt with the policy implications of adult Jewish education, "It is clear that the Jewish and Judaic content of (educational efforts undertaken by Jewish fundraising and political action organizations) is weak and often nil. Where it is present, it is often expressed in the most simple, if not simplistic, of fashions."

The quality of American Jewish education varied greatly from one communal context to the next. Some communities made Jewish education a local priority and supported the effort with the necessary funding and other resources, but the variety of settings resulted in the lack of a standardized terminology used to assess the range and quality of programs. For example, Sunday school and day school programs reflected two completely different philosophies and levels of Jewish education. Nonetheless, some surveys considered the two settings equally since both could technically be defined as "formal" institutions. Ongoing and comprehensive nationwide survey data were lacking in this area.

An attempt to improve the quality of Jewish education nationally came in 1981 when the Federation movement established the Jewish Education Service of North America (JESNA). JESNA was founded "to improve the quality and strengthen the impact of Jewish education by providing leadership and a broad range of services and informational resources locally, throughout North America, and in relationships with Israeli and world educational institutions."

In spite of certain advances in the coordination of Jewish educational activities in the United States during the 1980s, due mainly to the efforts of JESNA and other organizations, there was a clear impression by the end of the decade that Jewish education as a nationwide communal enterprise was not succeeding. Jewish education had become the victim of a vicious cycle of insufficient funding, insufficient talent, and insufficient leadership. In an attempt to remedy this situation, a private, interdenominational and non-partisan body consisting of noted Jewish educators and top philanthropists calling itself the Commission of Jewish Education in North America was created in 1988. Unofficially it was known as the Mandel Commission, having been spearheaded by community leader Morton L. Mandel of Cleveland. After two years the commission produced a major report, "A Time to Act," which analyzed the current condition of Jewish education in North America and offered a concrete plan of action whose goal was to "significantly improve the effectiveness of Jewish education (within) a coalition of community institutions, supplemented with continental institutions and resources." It planned to establish a body which would develop nationwide standards and curricula for quality Jewish education and assist local communities to make available the necessary funds to support high quality programs.

Religious Observance. The results of various surveys offered observers, at best, an imperfect picture of American Jewish religious life. The difficulties associated with measuring religious practices was in part a reflection of the ambiguous terms used on surveys. For example, synagogue affiliation or membership, a standard survey item, need not have reflected attendance at religious services. Similarly, it was difficult to draw inferences about religiosity based on other religious practices, such as participation in a Passover *seder* or the observance of dietary laws, since many of these practices meant different things to different respondents.

The following figures compare responses to five religious observance survey items which appeared in national surveys undertaken in 1981 (AJYB 1983) and 1990 (CJF):

	1981	1990
1. Attend a Passover Seder	77%	86%
2. Light Ḥanukkah Candles	67%	77%
3. Belong to a Synagogue	51%	41%
4. Light Sabbath Candles	22%	44%
5. Maintain Dietary Laws	15%	17%

This shows that, in general, infrequently practiced activities were more likely to be adhered to than those involving more regular participation.

Jewish Identity. Jewish identity, a more abstract concept than religious observance, was also evaluated on the basis of surveys.

The following nine-year comparison of three standard survey items (sources: AJYB 1983 and 1990 CJF) suggests certain trends.

	1981	1990
1. Most/All Friends Jewish	61%	45%
2. Contribution to UJA/Federation	49%	45%
3. Have visited Israel	37%	31%

Although these items do not define the total parameters of Jewish identity, it is significant that responses to all of these items in the 1990 survey had fallen to below 50%.

Results such as these, combined with additional information from the 1990 CJF survey which indicated that only 28 percent of all intermarried couples were raising their children as Jews and over 70 percent were raising their children with no religion or as Christians, intensified expressions of pessimism. Feldstein, for one, noted that "research on non-conversionary marriages suggests that most, including many who are raised to consider themselves Jewish, ultimately are lost to the Jewish community."

In spite of these findings, transformationalists remained optimistic. Goldscheider maintained that there was "increasing empirical support for the view that intermarriages do not automatically result in numerical losses to the Jewish community and may in the majority of cases represent gains, quantitatively and qualitatively." He noted that in 85 percent of American Jewish households children receive some exposure to Jewish education, which if true, was a higher percentage than in previous generations.

The most profound analysis of the affects of intermarriage on Jewish identity came in a report by Peter Y. Medding, Gary Tobin, Sylvia Barack Fishman, and Mordechai Rimor, "Intermarriage and American Jews Today: New Findings and Policy Implications, A Summary Report," published by the Cohen Center for Modern Jewish Studies at Brandeis University in 1990. The report was based on data collected in eight different Jewish communities across the United States between 1985 and 1988. The analysis divided intermarriage, or outmarriage, into conversionary marriages — between a born Jew and a born non-Jew who converts to

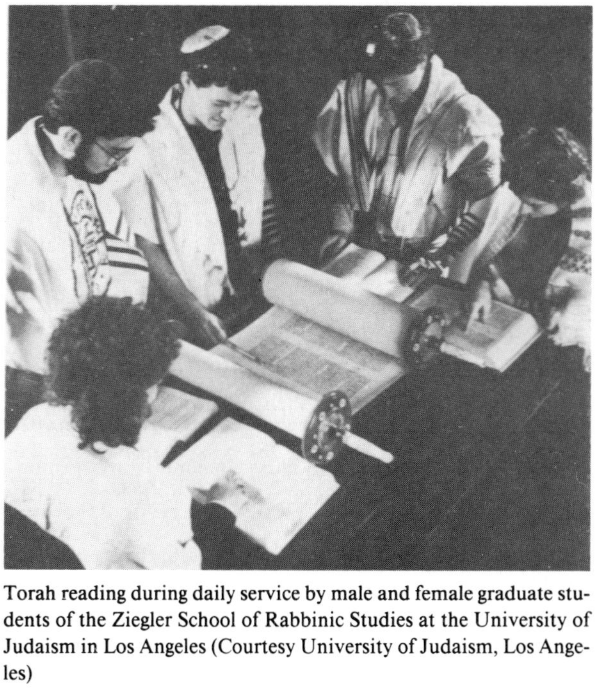

Torah reading during daily service by male and female graduate students of the Ziegler School of Rabbinic Studies at the University of Judaism in Los Angeles (Courtesy University of Judaism, Los Angeles)

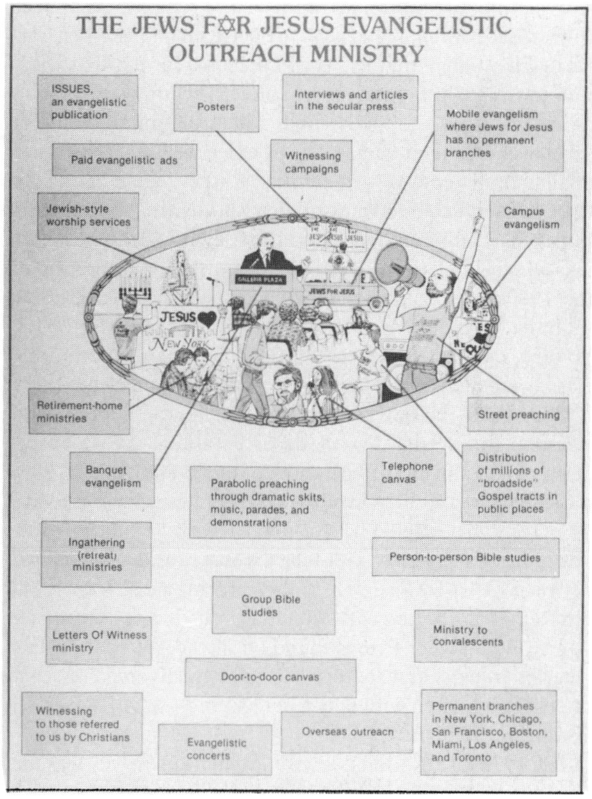

Jews for Jesus material on outreach strategy

Judaism, and mixed marriages — between a born Jew and a born non-Jew who does not convert to Judaism. (1992 AJYB)

The different consequences arising from conversionary and mixed marriages were found to be significant; the report stated that "Jewish identification fared well overall in conversionary marriages. However, conversionary marriages did not fare so consistently well in developing an unambiguous Jewish identity. Here, denominational differences were decisive. While very few Conservative conversionary marriages resulted in dual-identity households, nearly a third of Reform conversionary marriages did so." This the researchers attributed to the differing standards and requirements characteristic of conversionary marriages.

In contrast to conversionary marriages, it was clear from the data that Jewish identification does not fare well in mixed marriages and that "the level of Jewish identification among the overwhelming majority of mixed-marriages is low." Tobin reported (1991), "All measures of communal involvement — belonging to a synagogue, attendance at a synagogue, ritual observance, membership in Jewish organizations, contributions to Jewish philanthropies and support for Israel — are considerably lower among mixed marrieds than among conversionary marriages or marriages between two born Jews."

"Furthermore," he noted there, "mixed marriage families are far less likely to enroll their children in Jewish education than households headed by conversionary or intermarried couples."

Medding et al. (1992) investigated the role of Jewish education in preventing intermarriage. They reported that a "comparison of those with more than six years of Jewish education and those with less or none at all confirms that Jewish education is clearly associated with higher rates of intermarriage and lower rates of mixed marriage." However, the best chance of Jewish education serving as an effective deterrent to intermarriage was when the exposure was long term, formal, and intensive.

Regarding the future, Medding et al. predicted that "over time, choices will have to be made between being either Jewish or Christian or neither. The low level of Jewish identification in (mixed marriage) households to begin with, the pull of the majority, and the strength and attraction of common secular and general values do not augur well for the choice of an unambiguous Jewish identity. Rather than meeting the hope of being able to transmit Jewish identity, mixed marriages may prove to be terminal for Jewish identity."

OTHER SIGNS OF ACCULTURATION. By the beginning of the 1980s the postponement of marriage, high geographic mobility, a preference for small families, and a growing divorce rate, traits which typified the American middle-class, were also all characteristic of American Jewish life.

The 1970 National Jewish Population Survey had reported an overall Jewish divorce rate of five percent. National data from the beginning of the 1980s (AJYB 1983) indicated the "all ages ever divorced" rate to have risen to 14 percent. The 1990 CJF National Jewish Population Survey indicated a further rise in the divorce rate, distinguishing between "Jews by Religion," nine percent, and "Born Jews/No Religion," 14 percent. Percentages also varied from city to city, with higher figures found on the West Coast. In Los Angeles 14 percent were reported as being divorced or separated, as compared with only 5 percent in Boston, Baltimore, and Minneapolis.

The 1990 CJF National Jewish Population Survey was the first national Jewish survey to ask divorcees whether they had obtained a *get* (a Jewish writ of divorce). According to the results, the vast majority of divorced American Jews do not obtain a *get*. Of 800,000 cases (including divorces from mixed marriages not requiring a *get*), only about 113,000, or slightly over 14 percent, included a *get*.

A major finding of the 1990 CJF survey was that only 17 percent of all households containing a "core Jew" (a born Jew or a convert) reflected the stereotyped nuclear family consisting of two Jewish parents and children. Thus, the "alternative household," referring variously to a single parent household, a non-married, including same sex couple raising children, a couple that has chosen to remain childless, or a remarried couple raising the offspring of previous marriages together as siblings, was becoming more normative as American Jews continue marrying later, divorcing more frequently, and having fewer children.

Another indication of increasing acculturation was the growth in the number of reported cases of Jews involved in gambling, alcoholism, drug abuse, and domestic violence, such as incest and rape. The rise in public awareness to these problems could be attributed either to a true increase in the number of incidents or more assiduous documentation by professionals and community officials.

Estimates were that between five and ten percent of American Jews could be classified as alcoholics. A smaller percent suffered from drug addiction. The origins of these problems appeared to be unrelated to background, profession, or position in the community. As the seriousness of alcohol and drug addiction within the Jewish community became better appreciated, Jewish support groups were established as an alternative to the Christian-oriented Alcoholics Anonymous.

Cases of domestic violence in the Jewish community, although relatively atypical, became reported more frequently. In 1988 B'nai B'rith women began sponsoring events in chapters across the country geared toward heightening awareness of domestic violence within the Jewish community. BBW chapters also sponsored the establishment of *kasher* safe-houses for women across the country.

Social workers reported the tendency of some rabbis to dismiss reports of such violence with their congregations because of the difficulty they had conceptualizing this phenomenon within a Jewish household. Nationally, the problem was estimated to effect from one quarter to one third of the community. Reported incidents involved physical, emotional, and sexual abuse as well as neglect of spouses, children, and older parents. Until the 1980s little was written about the occurence of incest among Jewish families. As a result of greater openness and support for victims, the reporting of incidents became more frequent. Occurrences involving Jewish families were found to be without any relationship to socio-economic or denominational background.

Cults. It was reported that Jews represented a disproportional percentage of the estimated 8,000,000 Americans in cults and Christian missionary groups, such as Hare Krishna and Jews for Jesus. Among certain cult groups, Jewish involvement ran as high as 50 percent. The primary target group was teens and young adults, aged 15–30, who felt alienated from family, community, or school, and knew little of their own religion. Lonely and unsatisfied with their lives, these individuals were particularly susceptible to the advances of cult recruiters and Christian missionaries.

An Era of Ideological Diversity. Two major ideological debates underscored developments within American Jewish communal life during this era. One, a purely parochial issue, centered around the role of religious pluralism in American Jewish life. The other was, in effect, a political conflict that was waged in print, at the ballot box, and through various forms of activism, between Jewish liberals and conservatives who took sides over a variety of social, economic, and foreign policy issues, many having little or no bearing upon the fate or welfare of the Jewish community.

RELIGIOUS IDEOLOGY. The polarization of American Judaism's denominational groups was a major communal issue during the 1980s, reaching its most contentious point around the middle of the decade. According to Rabbi Haskel Lookstein, a moderate Orthodox spokesman and president of the New York Board of Rabbis, the controversy reached a stage where many religious leaders were unable to speak to each other civilly. What pretended to be the "developing schism" was likened to the 18th-century dispute between Polish Ḥasidim and Mitnaggedim.

One factor contributing to the wider publicity received by what was essentially an internal community debate was that "decisions regarding patrilineal descent, the conversion of the unchurched, the (rabbinic) ordination of women, the off-limits of non-Orthodox synagogues (were) communicated to other Jewish religious movements through the Op-Ed section of the *New York Times*" (Schulweis 1985).

A deeper reason, perhaps, was that by the 1980s Orthodoxy in America had undergone a process of revitalization that had been completely unanticipated. Instead of disappearing in the face of ongoing modernization and technology, its numbers had grown as a result of a high internal birth rate and its success in recruiting new members from outside the Orthodox community. Its growth resulted in greater resources, new and bigger institutions, and subsequently more influence and greater assertiveness within the wider Jewish community. American Orthodoxy's new confidence was bolstered by its ties to the Orthodox establishment in the state of Israel.

Traditional American Orthodoxy, in contrast to the modern, or moderate, Orthodoxy associated with New York's Yeshiva University, was openly committed to reinstituting the type of religious Jewish community life that had flourished in Europe until the eve of World War II. Its leaders reviled American society's emphasis on individualism and pluralism. They recognized as legitimate only their own interpretation of Judaism, which was based on the strict rigid interpretation of *halakhah* (Jewish religious law).

The historic 1983 decision by the Reform movement's Central Conference of American Rabbis to accept the child of a Jewish father and non-Jewish mother as Jewish without need of conversion; its religious outreach program to families of mixed religions or the unchurched; the decision by the Jewish Theological Seminary in 1983 to ordain Conservative women rabbis; and the announcement in 1987 to graduate women as Conservative cantors all served to exacerbate existing tensions with the Orthodox community.

Although united with Reform Judaism over the legitimacy of religious pluralism, the Conservative movement's understanding of *halakhah* forced it to reject the Reform position on patrilineal descent. The Rabbinical Assembly's Committee on Jewish Law and Standards voted in April 1983, 18 to 1, to reaffirm the view that "according to Judaism, both historic and contemporary, the Jewishness of a child is based solely on the affirmed Jewishness of the mother." This policy was reconfirmed by the 600 delegates attending the 84th annual Rabbinical Assembly convention in May 1984.

The decision by the Reform movement to recognize patrilineal descent was so controversial as to prompt the appearance of Rabbi Alexander Shapiro, president of the Conservative Rabbinical Assembly, at the 96th annual meeting of the Central Conference of American Rabbis in June 1985. Addressing his Reform colleagues, the Conservative leader cautioned that "if patrilinealism remains in place, then Conservative rabbis might have to question the Jewish status of someone from a sister movement," resulting in "a cleavage in Jewish life which would threaten the survival of the Jewish people."

Orthodox spokesmen were more outspoken. Lookstein characterized the Reform movement's adoption of patrilineal descent as "a wedge... that fosters polarization, anger, resentment, bitterness, and divisiveness." Nevertheless, Lookstein and his modern Orthodox colleagues were prepared to enter into a dialogue with representatives from the other movements. Traditional Orthodox leaders were not and did not hesitate to strongly denounce what they viewed as the continuing erosion of Jewish life in America. At the 63rd national convention held in 1986, leaders of America's Agudat Israel and its Council of Torah Sages strongly attacked Reform and Conservative Judaism, refusing to sanction any form of dialogue with any of its representatives.

This increasingly palpable schism was the theme of the March 1986 conference sponsored by the national Jewish Center for Learning and Leadership (CLAL) which was entitled "Will There Be One Jewish People by the Year 2000?"

From left to right: CLAL president Rabbi Irving Greenberg, Rabbi Gerson D. Cohen, Rabbi Alexander Schindler, and Elie Wiesel after the opening session of the first Critical Issues Conference (Courtesy CLAL, New York)

The founder and president of CLAL, Rabbi Irving Greenberg, a spokesman for liberal Orthodoxy, predicted the irreconcilable bifurcation of the Jewish community in the not too distant future unless a way could be found to reconcile denominational differences over matters of conversion, patrilineal descent, and divorce. The suggestion to establish a joint *bet din* (rabbinic court) to handle these issues, whose members would be chosen on the basis of scholarship and religious observance and not on the basis of denominational affiliation, was discussed but never developed. By the end of 1992, although the gap between the denominations remained the same, the vociferous tone of the conflict had diminished as the Jewish community seemed to adjust to the new status quo.

POLITICAL IDEOLOGY. A perceived change in the general political attitudes and activities among a larger percent of American Jews was another key topic during this period. The discussion arose in light of evidence of increasing Jewish support for conservative political interests. Some commentators questioned whether the American Jewish community was reneging on its longstanding commitment to liberal values and support for the Democratic Party.

The idea that American Jews were becoming more politically conservative had its roots in Jewish voting patterns beginning as far back as the 1972 presidential election in which liberal Democrat George McGovern challenged incumbent Republican Richard Nixon. At the time a small percent of Jewish voters broke traditional Jewish voting patterns but mainly on selected issues. These changes related to affirmative action and job quotas, issues which many Jews felt represented a form of reverse discrimination.

A comparison of results from the Gallup Religion Poll indicates that between 1966 and 1976 the number of Jewish Democrats had dropped from 64 percent to 56 percent, while the number of Jewish Republicans had remained approximately the same, around 9 percent. A Gallup poll from 1986 reveals that the number of Jewish Democrats had reached 50 percent while the number of Jewish Republicans had doubled to 16 percent. (Other Jewish respondents presumably were either undecided or not willing to declare their party affiliation.) By 1990 it appears that discontent with the Bush administration helped return the number of Jewish Democrats to just under 60%, although the number of Jewish Republican voters remained at 15%.

Some people viewed the American Jewish community's steadfast support for Israel as evidence of its parochial and increasingly conservative interests. This support was repeatedly demonstrated in public opinion polls. It was proffered even in the face of charges from critics that Israel was guilty, *inter alia*, of a series of human rights violations in the administered territories, had engaged in secret nuclear testing and weapons sales with the apartheid government of South Africa, and had played a key role in the Iran-contra (Irangate) affair. Certain ideologues of the left, Jewish and non-Jewish, argued that there was an intrinsic conflict between being liberal and supporting Israel. But Cohen (1983 AJYB) found no empirical correlation between identification with liberal causes and either personal concern for or travel to Israel among respondents that he polled.

The majority of American Jews remained loyal to their liberal heritage, particularly the Democratic voting patterns handed down by previous generations. Nevertheless, a conservative minority which was active, articulate and sufficiently funded, proved to be a group to be reckoned with. Fein (1988) characterized this group as "a new voice in Jewish life... the neo-conservatives, and there is no gainsaying that they have dramatically altered the nature of Jewish political debate. They press upon the Jews a new form of Jewish particularism that is not easily denied; they represent themselves as uniquely willing to ask of public policy whether it's good for the Jews and as uniquely able to answer that question properly." The most popular forum for Jewish neo-conservative ideas remained the pages of *Commentary* magazine edited by Norman Podhoretz.

Irving Kristol, another leading neo-conservative publisher and author, contended that the conservative domestic and foreign policies of the political right were consistent with both Jewish and American ideals. "There are," wrote Kristol in the pages of *Moment* magazine (October 1988) "really only two issues of public policy that have a significant bearing on the American Jewish condition today. One is of the United State's policy toward Israel. Neo-conservatives tend to believe, with good reason, that it is important for the United States to be strong militarily and to be willing to 'protect' military force when needed to defend a friendly nation. If the United States is not strong, and is reluctant to use its strength, the survival of Israel is at risk. But also at risk is the survival of other democracies — and perhaps, in the long run, of American democracy itself. So we are talking about a 'Jewish interest' that is also an 'American interest,' and one that is consistent with both Jewish and American ideals."

"The other public policy issue that affects American Jews," said Kristol, "is affirmative action directed at racial and ethnic minorities, as currently interpreted, i.e., effectively in terms of quotas. This does have harmful effects on Jews who wish to enter universities or professional schools, and in general restricts employment possibilities for Jews. But the main objection to affirmative action is that the racial and ethnic quotas it generates are leading to the fractionating of American society. Such a society would violate traditional American ideas, and would surely be harmful to the American Jewish community."

The neo-conservativism within the Jewish community, no matter how articulately formed, remained a minority view. The liberalism associated with the Roosevelt–Kennedy–Humphrey branch of the Democratic party was too much a part of the American Jewish ethos.

Because of the continued concentration of Jewish voters in large urban areas, the effect of the Jewish vote in general elections remained disproportionate to its size in the body politic (Lipstadt, Pruitt, Woocher 1984). This explained the attention drawn by even minor political shifts within the American Jewish community. Such was the case with rumors that beginning with Richard Nixon, and especially under Ronald Reagan, the Republican Party had managed to sway a large percentage of the Jewish electorate. In fact, according to most analyses, the American Jewish community gave only 34–37 percent of its vote to Ronald Reagan in 1980.

Jewish liberal instincts found their outlet in 1986 with the birth of *Tikkun*. Founded and edited by 'sixties activist Michael Lerner, *Tikkun* was a reaction, in Lerner's words, to the "over-materialism and lack of spirituality in Jewish life." Pragmatically, it challenged the conservative interests of the Jewish establishment symbolized by *Commentary*. Like Breira in the 1970s and later the New Jewish Agenda, *Tikkun* adopted the mandate of formulating a progressive political agenda for the American Jewish community.

It gained immediate prominence because of the noted intellectuals, Jewish and non-Jewish, whose articles and interviews it published and because of the outspoken dovish opinions of its editor, especially with regard to Israel's treatment of the Palestinians in the Administered Territories. For example, in the March/April 1989 issue, *Tikkun*'s gloss on the text of the Passover *Haggadah* included the statement "This year the Jewish people itself has become the symbol of oppression to another people: the Palestinians."

Other left of center political Jewish action groups also adapted Jewish symbols to their cause. In 1989, Passover *seder* services commemorating the fight against the AIDS virus were held in many cities and *seder* ceremonies to which the homeless, both Jews and non-Jews, were invited were held in Miami, San Francisco, and St. Louis.

On virtually all the key social issues throughout the decade, which included protection of the environment, guaranteeing the rights of homosexuals, support for the Equal Rights Amendment, nuclear freeze, handgun control, federal spending for social programs, particularly abortion counseling, and opposition to prayer in public schools, American Jews as a whole, in public opinion surveys and at the ballot box, overwhelmingly and consistently supported the liberal position. A series of surveys demonstrated the positive relationship between youth and education and liberalism, i.e., the younger and better educated the respondent, the higher was his score on the survey's liberal public opinion index. Contrary to popular assumptions, young Jewish leaders were not turning to the right in anything approaching large numbers. The majority remained both Democrats and liberals on a broad range of social and economic issues.

Social research uncovered an interesting relationship between religious observance and an individual's general political outlook. According to Cohen's survey (1983), Jews whose ritual behavior was minimal to moderate tended to be the most liberal, while those who were either very observant or totally non-observant were generally the most conservative. In attempting to account for this seeming paradox, Cohen explained that whereas traditional Jews placed parochial interests ahead of more universal ones, the political conservatism of highly acculturated Jews was probably the result of the latter having abandoned the liberal orientation of Jewish community life.

Church-State Issues. The image of the Reagan White House as a bastion of Republican, white, Christian values encouraged political assertiveness among fundamentalist church groups. This resulted in an unprecedented effort on the part of national Christian fundamentalist organizations to align themselves with the conservative New Right political movement in attempting to influence both the electoral and legislative processes.

In 1980 and 1984, the Christian Right offered its endorsement to congressional candidates who had gone on record as being opposed to abortion and the proposed Equal Rights Amendment. Groups such as the Moral Majority fought hard to defeat all liberal candidates for federal and state office, especially incumbents. While running for re-election in 1980, President Reagan officially welcomed the involvement of the Christian Right in American politics.

The difficulty the Jewish community had with these groups went beyond their opposition to its own positions on most social issues. Rather, politically active Christian evangelicals, or "New Christians," sought to introduce Christian religious symbols and practices into the American public domain. This was seen as attempt to emphasize the Christian character of America. Examples of issues that reached the federal level include: government support for religious schools through tuition-tax credits or vouchers, government aid for remedial teaching programs and lunch programs; prayer, meditation, Bible classes or the distribution of religious literature in public schools or on public school property; equal access to school premises during after school hours by both non-sectarian and religious organizations; and the display on public property at Christmas of the nativity scene. Of these four issues, the federal courts denied the first two, government funding and public school prayer, but allowed for equal access and the erecting of religious symbols under certain circumstances.

While most of the organized Jewish community strongly opposed these efforts, certain Orthodox circles found common cause with Christian fundamentalists, Catholic, and other groups that sought a more liberal interpretation of the laws separating church and state. Orthodox families who were burdened by the high cost of sending children to private Jewish schools favored the idea of tuition tax credits as well as federal or state aid for specialized programs. Lubavich Ḥasidim mirrored the efforts of Christian groups to build creche scenes by erecting large *menorot* and *sukkot* booths in city parks and public squares.

In 1984 the U.S. Supreme Court ruled to allow the display of public nativity scenes on public property. In 1985 a similar ruling was offered with regard to privately sponsored displays. These decisions were strongly criticized by the organized Jewish community as having shown favoritism to Christianity over other religions. In an attempt to emphasize equality in their opposition to all such practices, Jewish organizations in some cities openly opposed the efforts of local Lubavich groups to erect *menorot* and *sukkot*.

For different reasons, some Christian-oriented groups also opposed these Ḥabad activities. In 1987, the Ḥabad (Lubavich) House of Cincinnati sought a federal ruling over its right to place an 18–foot-high, electrically lit *menorah* in the city's Fountain Square. In 1990, the Ḥabad House won a federal court order allowing the *menorah*. In response, the local Ku Klux Klan, under the protection of a separate court ruling, erected a 10–foot-high cross which stood for 10 days within 200 feet of the *menorah*.

Black-Jewish Relations. Relations at the community level between blacks and Jews over the last decade were troubled. This was reflected in reports by the press. Surveys also indicated that anti-Semitism among blacks, particularly on college campuses was up, and a handful of black leaders gained notoriety for their anti-Israel and anti-Jewish sentiments. Less frequently reported were examples of cooperation taking place among black and Jewish leaders in Congress, in city halls, and in inter-communal dialogues around the country. Certain experts in the area of community relations, such as Murray Friedman of the American Jewish Committee staff and a member of the federal Civil Rights Commission during the Reagan era, conceded that "the black-Jewish alliance of the civil rights days is simply gone." He called for a "normalization" of relations between blacks and Jews within the present context because "we cannot go back to the strategies of the 1960s."

Various surveys from this period reflected a growing resentment of Jews by blacks, especially among younger blacks on college campuses. Anti-Jewish sentiments were accompanied by anti-Israel and pro-Palestinian attitudes. During fall 1992 an Anti-Defamation League poll showed that 37 percent of blacks, in contrast to 17 percent of whites, fell into the "most anti-Semitic" category, i.e., those who answered "Yes" to six out of 11 possible Jewish stereotypes. Similar polls over the years showed that blacks, in fact, share mixed positive and negative attitudes towards Jews.

Undoubtedly, some of the outstanding issues between the two communities were rooted in the past. But the issues themselves were current. For example, prominent black leader the Rev. Jesse Jackson had made himself anathema to many American Jews in 1979, the year he embraced PLO Chairman Yasser Arafat in front of the press, called for the establishment of an independent Palestinian state and criticized the Jewish community for the dismissal of American UN Ambassador Andrew Young by President Jimmy Carter after his unauthorized contact with Yasser Arafat.

During the 1980s Jackson continued to be critical of Israel for its relationship with South Africa, and called Zionism a "kind of poisonous weed that is choking Judaism," while he continued to support Palestinian demands for an independent state. However, the nadir of Jackson's relationship with American Jews came in 1984 when in a private conversation with a black *Washington Post* reporter, Jackson referred to Jews as "Hymies" and to New York as "Hymietown." The Jewish community, aghast at the candidate's remark, subsequently received an apology by Jackson during a speech made at a synagogue. But Jackson still refused to condemn the openly anti-Semitic public statements of Nation of Islam leader Louis Farrakhan.

A 1988 survey following Jackson's failed bid to win the Democratic presidential nomination showed that 59 percent of American Jews continued to regard him as an anti-Semite. By the beginning of the 1990s, Jackson had made attempts to improve his relationship with the Jewish community, initially by condemning anti-Semitism at the 1992 World Jewish Congress on anti-Semitism in Brussels and later by spearheading efforts of black-Jewish cooperation, speaking at synagogues and to rabbinical groups.

Black-Jewish relations were also strained by the vituperative statements of Farrakhan. In addition to a remark threatening the Jewish community made in response to alleged death threats received by Jackson, Farrakhan, in a March 1984 radio broadcast declared Hitler a "great man," and in a June broadcast referred to Judaism as a "gutter religion." He also accused Jewish doctors of injecting the AIDS virus into black babies. Within the black community, Farrakhan was criticized by the NAACP, the Urban League, and many church groups. While Jackson acknowledged Farrakhan's remarks to have been "reprehensible and morally indefensible," he never condemned Farrakhan directly for having made them. At a gathering before 40,000 followers in Atlanta in October 1992, Farrakhan denied that he had anything for which to apologize to Jews, saying that blacks have many historical grievances against them.

A third black personality to have stirred controversy with his statements about Jews was Afro-centrist Professor Leonard Jeffries, founding chairman of the black studies department at the City College of New York. During a 1991 speech he presented at a black culture festival in Albany in which he defended New York State's "multi-cultural" education reform plan, Jeffries attacked Jews in particular for opposing the plan. Among his most controversial statements about Jews at that time, and reiterated on subsequent occasions, were (1) that "rich Jews" had played an important role in establishing the 17th-century African slave trade and that (2) Jewish producers and directors of Russian background had over the years, in partnership with Italian Mafia figures, purposely cast blacks in demeaning and degrading roles in Hollywood films. Although he remained a tenured professor, Jeffries was removed as department head in March 1992 for having made these statements.

An eruption broke out in the Crown Heights section of Brooklyn in 1991. On the night of August 19, a station wagon driven by an aide to Rabbi Menachem Schneerson, the Lubavicher rebbe, careened out of control and crashed into a Crown Heights sidewalk, killing a seven-year-old black boy and badly injuring a black girl.

The driver of the vehicle was immediately set upon by angry black bystanders when he stepped out of the station wagon to try and offer assistance. He was severely beaten and robbed before police reached the scene. A Jewish-run ambulance service, Hatzolah, arrived and was directed by the police to remove the driver and his passengers, who had become the object of the gathering crowd's anger. The riled group interpreted this as an act of racism, although a city ambulance had arrived on the scene minutes later to tend to the two black children.

The crowd broke up into smaller groups which ran in different directions throwing rocks and bottles at people, cars, and homes. One of these frenzied groups came upon 29–

year-old Yankel Rosenbaum, an ultra-Orthodox Jew from Australia who had come to New York to conduct research at the YIVO Institute. He was beaten and stabbed to death. Arrested for Rosenbaum's murder and found carrying a knife and three blood-stained dollar bills, was 17-year-old Lemrick Nelson, Jr. In November 1992, in spite of pathologists having found traces of DNA that matched Rosenbaum's, Lemrick was acquitted by a mostly black and Latino jury.

These incidents were followed by three days and four nights of rioting by blacks in Crown Heights, a community variously estimated to include 12,000 to 25,000 mostly Hasidic Jews and 100,000 to 180,000 blacks. The New York Police Department and the city's first black mayor David Dinkins were criticized for not being able to control the riots in Crown Heights or of purposely reacting with restraint in order to appease the extremists within the black community. The "Crown Heights Pogrom," as this episode became known, acted as a catalyst for additional rioting by blacks in other large cities around the country over the next few days. It also initiated further attempts at inter-community dialogue between well-intending black and Jewish leaders.

In contrast to the disruptions and acrimony of the Crown Heights riots and other displays of black-Jewish enmity during this period, there were examples of cooperation and constructive relations between the two communities. Unfortunately, these cases drew less media attention than instances involving violence. Among these were Project CURE, a grassroots youth dialogue group that was established in the wake of the Crown Heights episode. Established at the instigation of the New York Mayor's office and funded partly by the municipality and partly by private donations and emphasized dialogue and joint activities designed to break down mutual stereotypes and help prevent further violence.

Other mainly black-Jewish groups were Baltimore's BLEWS, formed in 1978 to provide a meeting ground for black and Jewish politicians, clergy and organizational leaders, Washington, D.C.'s project YACHAD, a non-profit group dedicated to mobilizing resources to finance and build low-income housing, and the New York-based Jewish Fund for Justice, founded in 1984, which had given out over $1.4 million in grants intended to help combat poverty and inequality.

Involvement in Other Causes. Many American Jews continued to be active on behalf of social and political causes which, some argued, were only at best indirectly related to the interests of the Jewish community. These included support for the civil rights of homosexuals, assistance for the victims of the AIDS virus and support for medical research to find a cure for the disease, abortion rights, the struggle against apartheid in South Africa and militant regimes around the globe, nuclear freeze, protecting the environment, the feminist movement, support for the homeless, and putting an end to worldwide poverty and hunger. While many Jews comfortably opted for membership in social and humanitarian organizations at large, some felt the need to establish alternative organizations comprised solely of Jewish membership since they viewed their commitment to these causes as an expression of their Jewish identity.

Specific examples of the latter included: (1) the Jewish Fund for Justice, which provided grants to fight poverty in America, (2) the American Jewish World Service, which funded environmental development programs in the Third World, (3) Mazon, a Jewish response to world hunger, and (4) the National Jewish AIDS Project, an educational body created to raise the consciousness of Jewish communal leaders and organizations about the AIDS virus and its victims. By the end of the decade, approximately 20 gay and lesbian congregations existed around the country.

Political Involvement. The key political challenge to the Jewish community during the 1980s was how it could continue to promote its liberal social agenda and still maintain a fruitful working relationship with three successive Republican administrations. To achieve this, the Jewish leadership took full advantage of the American democratic process. In spite of not having supported their candidacies, the organized Jewish community knew it could call upon Reagan and Bush, respectively, for cooperation and support in matters of mutual interest. These included the security of the state of Israel and support for human rights, particularly the right of Jews and others to emigrate from the Soviet Union, Ethiopia, and Syria.

The method most effectively developed by the Jewish community for this purpose was political lobbying. This was the era of PACs, or political action committees. PACs were local or regional versions of the long-established and highly proficient American-Israel Public Affairs Committee, AIPAC. PACs were created to raise money and provide endorsements for local candidates whose positions on Israel and Soviet Jewry were met with approval by the Jewish community. These groups also offered an opportunity to those who wished to play an active, albeit behind the scenes, role in local and national politics. PAC activists often traveled to Washington, D.C., for private meetings with senators, congressmen, key congressional staff members, and other political power brokers.

Critics, both within and outside of the Jewish community, pointed to the fact that most PAC support was seemingly rendered without regard for issues other than Israel's security and human rights. Still, it was difficult to deny the results rendered by organized lobbying. Following the model created by PACs, most national Jewish organizations, as well as some of the larger community federations, established offices in Washington, D.C. Their professional staffs conferred with members of Congress and representatives of the administration over positions taken by the Jewish community that covered a range of domestic and foreign issues.

Jewish political involvement was also expressed in the increasing number of Jewish elected officials. As publicly elected officials these men, and an increasing number of women, represented all the electorate. But as Jews they could generally be depended on to represent the official position of the Jewish community on important issues. Whereas in the 97th Congress in 1980 there was a total of 28 Jewish congressmen and 5 Jewish senators, by the 103rd Congress in 1992 this had grown to 33 Jewish congressmen out of a total of 435, or 7.5 percent, including four women, and 10 out of 100 Jewish senators, i.e., 10 percent, among them two women. This increase was less significant for the amount of influence it implied than the degree to which it demonstrated how little the American voting public paid to a candidate's religion. For example, in 1992, two Jewish senators were

Madeline Kunin, former governor of Vermont

elected from Wisconsin, whose Jewish residents constituted approximately 0.7 percent of the state's population, and from California, whose Jewish community represented about only 3.2 percent of the state. States that elected a Jewish member to the House of Representatives included New Mexico and Vermont where Jews were only 0.4 percent and 0.9 percent, respectively, of the general population.

According to a 1992 University of Michigan study, American Jews remained an active political force, since about 90 percent of the Jewish population was spread among only 12 states, namely, New York, New Jersey, Massachusetts, Pennsylvania, Illinois, California, Florida, Maryland, Connecticut, Ohio, Texas, and Michigan. But the voter apathy which came to characterize the general American population had its effect on the number of American Jewish voters which declined from 92 percent in 1952 to 67 percent at the time of the study. As a result, the Jewish community stood at risk of losing the high-voter-turnout edge that had been the source of its national political influence.

Anti-Semitism and Terrorism. Events during the 1980s seemed to indicate that anti-Semitism in America was operating at two levels. Discriminatory or social anti-Semitism decreased in comparison to previous decades. This type of anti-Semitism was based on discriminatory practices in the workplace, in schools, especially colleges and universities, at country clubs and in upper-class communities. In July 1981, a survey conducted on behalf of the American Jewish Committee reported that anti-Semitism of this nature had in fact declined significantly over a 17–year period.

The success of Jews within American academia, at one time a domain known for restrictions against Jews and other ethnic minorities, was equally impressive. In more recent years, Jews have served as the presidents of four Ivy League universities, Dartmouth, Pennsylvania and Columbia, as well as at the University of Chicago, the University of Michigan, the University of Indiana, Brooklyn College and Bard College. By 1993 Richard Levin, the most recently appointed, Harold T. Shapiro, appointed in 1988, and Neil Rudenstine, appointed in 1991, had become the presidents of the American academic pantheon, Yale, Princeton and Harvard, respectively. Most of the above-mentioned schools at one time in this century had maintained a strict quota on Jewish student enrollment. For many, all of this was indisputable proof that previously unbreachable social barriers in America had finally been torn down.

Such achievements notwithstanding, anti-Semitism in America had not disappeared. In 1987, after a five-year downward trend, the Anti-Defamation League's annual "Audit of Anti-Semitic Incidents" reported an increase in isolated incidents of anti-Semitic vandalism. This other level of anti-Semitic expression threatened both physical property and human lives. The latter threat was realized in the 1984 machine-gun slaying of Denver radio talk show host Alan Berg by a white supremacist organization calling itself The Order. However, most anti-Semitic acts in this category were expressed through vandalism and damage to property, including swastika daubings on synagogues, Jewish homes, storefronts, and Jewish cemetery headstones, the slashing of automobile tires, the breaking of windows, threatening telephone calls, arson, and bombings. By the end of the decade, the ADL reported 1,432 such incidents annually, the highest in its 11 years of monitoring. Not until 1992 did the ADL report an 8 percent drop in anti-Semitic incidents, the first decline in six years. A report issued by the Anti-Defamation League stated that 20 percent of American adults are "hardcore" anti-Semites and an additional 39 percent "mildly" anti-Semitic, a group equaling approximately 100 million Americans.

From approximately the middle of the decade additional attention was paid by the media to groups whose statements and activities threatened the sense of well-being and security of American Jews, blacks, and other minorities. These included certain Christian fundamentalist groups, racist organizations such as neo-Nazis groups, skinhead gangs, the Aryan Nation, and The Order. Anti-Jewish statements or activities disguised as politically legitimate anti-Israel expressions originated in either (1) politically far left circles, (2) the Arab-American community, or (3) Black Muslim groups.

Anti-Jewish signs on a commercial vehicle in a Los Angeles suburb (From the David Geffen Collection, Jerusalem)

Election campaigns focused the country's attention on two formerly relatively unknown personalities, Lyndon LaRouche and David Duke. LaRouche was a local left-wing politician in the 1970s and 1980s who changed his world outlook and ran three times as a marginal right-wing presidential candidate, a purveyor of Communist and anti-Semitic conspiracy theories. In 1986, two LaRouche followers, without having revealed their ties to his party, entered and won the Democratic primary election as nominees for lieutenant governor and secretary of state in Illinois. They, along with LaRouche candidates in other states, lost heavily in the final elections, but their few successes stirred great controversy. In 1989, LaRouche was sentenced to 15 years in federal prison for fraud and tax evasion.

David Duke was a former grand wizard of the Knights of the Ku Klux Klan and the leader of the National Association for the Advancement of White People. In 1988, Duke ran as a presidential candidate on the slate of the neo-Nazi Populist Party. At the beginning of the following year he narrowly won a seat in the Louisiana state legislature. In December, he announced his intention to run as a Republican for the U.S. Senate. Although he had avoided making any overt racial or anti-Semitic statements during his statewide campaign, he was strongly denounced by both the Republican Party and President George Bush. In October 1990 he faced Democratic incumbent Senator J. Bennett Johnston and captured 43.5 percent of the total ballot, including 55 percent of the white vote. Although Duke lost to Johnston, his relative popularity among Southern white voters and others raised considerable concern among Jews and non-Jews alike.

To the surprise of many observers, the well-publicized Wall St. "insider" scandals of 1986, among whose key figures were extremely wealthy Jewish businessmen, did not result in an appreciable rise in anti-Semitic or anti-Israel feelings among the American public. The principle figures included Ivan Boesky and Michael Milken, both of whom received prison sentences.

Nor was there any general rise in anti-Semitism attributable to the Jonathan Pollard affair. This dramatic real-life spy episode, which stunned the American Jewish community, and had direct, albeit short-term, implications for U.S.-Israel diplomatic relations, went almost unnoticed by most Americans. It served as the most dramatic and poignant example to date of the dual loyalty issue to which the organized American Jewish community is sensitive. Pollard, who served as a civilian intelligence analyst for the U.S. Navy, was arrested by the FBI on November 21, 1985, together with his wife and charged with providing a contact at the Israeli Embassy in Washington with classified security information involving "scientific, technical and military" data, specifically intelligence information on Arab and Soviet weapons development, over the course of a year and a half in exchange for $45,000 and assorted personal amenities.

In June 1986, Pollard and his wife pleaded guilty to all charges, with the understanding that their plea-bargain and the cooperation they extended the United States Justice Department would result in a reduced sentence. Nevertheless, in March 1987 Pollard received a life-time term in a U.S. federal prison and his wife was sentenced to five years in a U.S. federal prison as an accessory.

Pollard's spying and the punishment he received aroused widespread and heated debate, but this controversy was mainly limited to Jewish circles. Almost no one denied that Pollard was guilty of the crime with which he was charged, but the sentences were criticized by many as being unjustifiably harsh. The information Pollard passed on to Israel did not jeopardize American security and furthermore, "friendly spying" was a practice also engaged in by the United States. Major Jewish groups in addition to numerous rabbis from all denominations joined in a campaign to win his pardon.

Neither did the 1986 Irangate, or Iran-Contra, Affair result in any perceptible increase in anti-Semitism. The possibility arose from the role Israel played in this U.S. government scandal. In response to a secret request from the Reagan administration, Israel's government under then Prime Minister Shimon Peres supplied American made-arms to Iran. The profit from the sale was diverted through a Swiss bank account belonging to Contra rebels fighting the leftist Nicaraguan government. Israel officially denied handling the funds for this covert operation that was illegal according to U.S. federal law.

Marilyn Klinghoffer being led off the *Achille Lauro* after hostages were released in Alexandria, Egypt, harbor, October 10, 1985 (AFP Photo International by Mike Nelson)

American Jews remained relatively sheltered throughout the 1980s from acts of international terror related to the conflicts in the Middle East, but there were two dramatic exceptions. The first was the hijacking in October 1985 by members of the Palestine Liberation Front of the Italian pleasure ship *Achille Lauro* traveling between the ports of Alexandria and Ashdod. During the episode the terrorists, who were led by PLO faction head Mohammed Abu al-Abbas, killed a 69-year-old disabled American Jewish tourist, Leon Klinghoffer, who was shot and thrown overboard along with his wheelchair. Although apprehended by U.S. Navy jets over international waters in an attempt to escape and then handed over to Italy, Abu al-Abbas was subsequently released by Italian authorities on the pretense of insufficient evidence. The remaining four hijackers were eventually convicted and sentenced.

The second exception was the assassination of Rabbi Meir Kahane on American soil. Kahane was the most controversial Jewish figure of the past two decades. Founder of the American Jewish vigilante group the Jewish Defense League (JDL), he emigrated in 1975 to Israel where he established the extreme right-wing political party Kach and succeeded in being elected to Israel's parliament, the Knesset, serving from 1984 to 1988.

On November 5, 1990, Kahane was shot dead at close range inside a Manhattan hotel minutes after addressing an audience. Arrested for the shooting was Egyptian-born El Sayyid A-Nosair, who was seen holding a gun in the presence of Kahane moments before the shooting. A jury later acquitted him on charges of murder, but convicted him on the lesser charge of carrying and concealing an unauthorized weapon.

The Holocaust: Memorialization, Revisionism, and Nazi War Criminals in the U.S. Memorialization efforts on the part of American Jewry developed into a major activity and social psychological phenomenon. Faced with the reality of Holocaust survivors succumbing to natural attrition and aided by the retrospective vision of two generations, American Jews focused considerable resources, including time, money and skills, on producing an unprecedented number of Holocaust projects to serve as testaments and memorials for posterity. This was expressed in everything from the creation of artwork, books, films, events and conferences for survivors and their children, school curricula and tours to Eastern Europe to visit the sites of former Jewish communities and Nazi death camps. By the beginning of the 1990s the Holocaust museum became the most sophisticated and ultimate expression of this trend.

During the 1980s a number of Jewish communities, among them Baltimore, Chicago, Miami, New York, Pittsburgh, San Francisco, and St. Louis, dedicated monuments or established small museums and educational centers as a focus for Holocaust memorial events. The two major efforts were the Beit HaShoah—Museum of Tolerance in Los Angeles and the United States Holocaust Memorial Museum in Washington, D.C.

A major mid-decade controversy erupted over President Ronald Reagan's May 1985 visit to the military cemetery in Bitburg, West Germany. The visit was planned to commemorate the 40th anniversary of Nazi Germany's surrender and to symbolize the spirit of reconciliation between the United States and Germany. The controversy, which provoked an international response, lay in the fact that among the 2,000 dead soldiers interred were 47 members of the Nazi Waffen SS. Furthermore, at the time the President's itinerary was

Freedom Sunday for Soviet Jews, Washington, D.C., December 6, 1987 (Courtesy National Conference on Soviet Jewry; photo Twin Lens Photo, Silver Spring, MD)

first announced, it included no visit to Bergen-Belsen, a nearby concentration camp. In spite of growing criticism and pressure, Reagan proceeded with his planned visit to the cemetery where he layed a wreath. He, however, also visited the site of Bergen-Belsen where in his speech he addressed the feelings of Holocaust survivors.

Holocaust Revisionism succeeded in drawing increased attention during the 1980s. The most active revisionist organization in the United States during this period was the California-based Institute for Historical Review, founded in 1978 by Willis Carto, a known anti-Semite. Other known Holocaust revisionists operating in the United States included Arthur Butz, professor of computer science at Northwestern University and author of *The Hoax of the Twentieth Century*, David McCalden, a co-founder of the I.H.R., Bradley Smith, publisher of *Prima Facie*, a racist and anti-Semitic monthly newsletter, and Charles Weber, professor of German at the University of Tulsa and author of *The Holocaust: 120 Questions and Answers.*

As early as 1949, the Jewish community had been aware of the presence of Nazi war criminals in the United States. However, interest in the subject remained generally low until the mid–1970s and the beginning of the 1980s. As a result of document research and field investigations performed by the Office of Special Investigations (OSI), established in 1979 as a special unit within the Criminal Division of the U.S. Justice Department, it was revealed that in the years following World War II over 1,000 Nazi war criminals or collaborators had found refuge in the United States. Many were actually brought to the United States through the efforts of the U.S. State Department, the intelligence branches of the Army, Navy, and Air Force, the F.B.I., and the C.I.A., having been recruited to serve as agents and consultants in anti-Communist operations during the late 1940s and the 1950s.

By the beginning of 1980, the OSI had collected documentation on 413 war criminals residing in the United States. Of those, the OSI filed 37 court briefs by 1984. Among the cases to have been reported by the press during this period were Valerian Trifa, a Romanian, who was expelled by the United States in 1983 and made his way to Portugal where he died; Feodor Fedorenko, a Pole, who was deported to the Soviet Union in 1984 and executed in 1987; Andrija Artukovic, a Croatian, who was extradited to Yugoslavia in 1986 and sentenced to death; and Karl Linnas, an Estonian, deported to the U.S.S.R. in April 1987 where he died three months later in a hospital. The only case of an accused war criminal being stripped of his naturalized American citizenship and being extradited to Israel was that of Ukrainian born John Demjanjuk (see DEMJANJUK TRIAL).

Soviet Jewry. An historic demonstration on behalf of Soviet Jewry was held in Washington, D.C., during the first week of December 1987. This mass rally, co-sponsored by some 50 national Jewish organizations and 300 local Jewish federations from throughout North America, brought over 200,000 demonstrators together on the eve of the Reagan-Gorbachev summit. It also marked a rare display in organizational unity. The Soviet Jewry movement in the United States had been split for years between the more moderate National Conference on Soviet Jewry, on the one hand, and the more confrontational Union of Councils for Soviet Jews and the Student Struggle for Soviet Jewry on the other.

Upon the advent of *glasnost* in the late 1980s, Soviet Jewish emigration figures soon began to climb. The American Jewish community now found itself confronted by two major issues, one ideological, but with very pragmatic implications, the other material.

As the emigration of Soviet Jews continued, the American Jewish community found itself in a confrontation with the State of Israel over the emigres' destination. The United States was willing to accept a fixed number of Soviet Jewish immigrants as refugees and was by far the emigres' most popular destination. But Israel argued that its willingness to accept unconditionally all emigrating Soviet Jews belied their refugee status. Israel wanted cooperating authorities to direct virtually all emigrating Soviet Jews to its shores. During the first year of the Soviet Union's more liberal emigration policy, the monthly dropout rate, a figure that referred to those Soviet Jewish emigrants who changed their destination from Israel to another country (usually the United States) while in transit, often reached over 90 percent.

Most American Jews supported the policy of "freedom of choice." The Union of Councils for Soviet Jews and the Student Struggle for Soviet Jewry criticized Israeli pressure on American Jewish organizations and the United States. The National Conference on Soviet Jewry and other major Jewish organizations, while upholding the principle of "freedom of choice," accepted a dual track compromise whereby the large backlog of Jews already holding Israeli visas would emigrate to Israel through Romania, while those as yet without visas and seeking to emigrate to the United States would have to apply for an American visa in Moscow.

The number of Soviet Jews who applied for and received exit visas grew significantly. In September 1988, as a result of the new dimensions of Soviet Jewish emigration, the United States became more selective in awarding refugee status to applicants. This status was now meted out on a more selective basis, so that by August 1989, nearly one quarter of all applicants for U.S. immigrant visas were being refused. In July 1989 the United States announced that its immigration budget for Eastern European refugees was exhausted and temporarily stopped processing visa applications for the thousands of Soviet Jews who were by now languishing in transit centers in Ladispoli, near Rome, and in Vienna.

In the fall, following negotiations with American Jewish groups, the Bush administration announced that it was fixing a new annual immigration quota for Soviet Jews at 43,000 with priority extended to those with immediate, or first-degree, family members already residing in the United States. It was also allocating $75 million to resettlement programs. As a result of this new policy, which also involved closing down the transit centers and requiring applicants to apply for immigrant visas in Moscow, the majority of Soviet emigrés gave up trying to seek entry to the United States.

Even with the new, more stringent quota on Soviet Jewish immigration, the American Jewish community was faced with the huge task of resettling tens of thousands of new arrivals. In the last quarter of 1989 18,000 Soviet Jews arrived in the United States. The funds set aside by the U.S. government for total Soviet resettlement were insufficient. In order to insure that the Soviet Jews coming to the United States were provided with all the means and opportunities for successful resettlement, defined to mean their material resettlement as well as their religious, cultural, and educational integration into the Jewish community, the Council of Jewish Federations and the United Jewish Appeal launched a $75 million voluntary campaign called "Passage to Freedom," but its national goal was never reached. By the end of the year, only about two-fifths of the money had been collected.

The combination of stricter American immigration laws and the difficulties involved in resettling Soviet Jews locally gradually influenced American Jewish leadership to heed the government of Israel's calls for receiving the bulk of emigrés. In January 1990 the UJA and CJF announced "Operation Exodus," a $420 million campaign, whose goal was to bring directly to Israel and resettle the overwhelming majority of Soviet Jews seeking to emigrate. "Operation Exodus" was a financial success and 95 percent of the goal was reached within ten months, the majority pledged by the biggest givers in the largest Jewish communities. "Exodus II," the worldwide campaign in 1991 to raise an additional $1.3 billion, was launched when the number of Soviet Jews coming to Israel turned out to be more than double the original estimate. From the results of the "Exodus II" campaign, it became clear that the desire of American Jewry lay in assisting the emigrating Soviet Jews resettle in Israel.

By the end of 1990 it was reported that over 181,000 Jews had left the Soviet Union. In response to this new situation, President Bush, in December 1990, waived key agricultural restrictions of the Jackson-Vanik Amendment, which since 1974 stood as a symbol of American Jewish opposition to the Soviet Union's disregard for human rights.

American Jews played an active role in bringing Ethiopian Jewry to Israel. The major airlifts in 1984–85 and 1991 were largely made possible by behind-the-scenes diplomacy by the U.S. government and through funds raised by the U.S. Jewish community. The American Association for Ethiopian Jews was established in 1969 and the North American Conference on Ethiopian Jewry in 1982. The objectives of these activist groups included raising the awareness of Jews and the world to the condition of the Jews of Ethiopia and visiting Jewish communities in Ethiopia to demonstrate solidarity and to provide material assistance. The subsequent cost of resettling the Ethiopian Jews in Israel was absorbed into the UJA's Operation Exodus campaign.

These humanitarian activities on behalf of Soviet and Ethiopian Jews were representative of the efforts by American Jews on behalf of distressed Jewish communities worldwide. The International Coalition for the Revival of the Jews of Yemen, based in New York, was established in 1989 to

The cover of a dual-language, Russian-English, manual for Russian Jews new to the Atlanta area developed by the Jewish Family and Children's Bureau in conjunction with the Resettlement Committee of the Social Service Advisory Board and the Jewish Vocational Service, agencies of the Atlanta Jewish Federation (From the David Geffen Collection, Jerusalem)

offer assistance to Yemen's remaining Jews. The Syrian Jewish community of Brooklyn continued its own efforts to secure the emigration of kinsmen remaining in the Jewish centers of Damascus, Aleppo, and Kamishly. Other organizations, such as the American Jewish Joint Distribution Committee, continued their contacts with these communities or remained otherwise involved on their behalf.

Activities on Behalf of and Attitudes towards Israel. The 1980s were a period in which the relationship between American Jews and Israel underwent measurable change, characterized by the disenchantment on the part of many American Jews with Israel's image. For some American Jews it led to a willingness to publicly criticize Israel for adopting policies and actions perceived to be detrimental to itself or the Jewish people.

Many identify the ascendency of Menaḥem Begin and his rightwing Likkud-led coalition government in June 1977 as the beginning of this change. Begin's ideology and rhetoric, especially his desire for settling "Greater Israel," were viewed by many American Jews as being jingoistic and provocative. Begin's successor, Yiẓḥak Shamir bore the same political ideology.

Immediately following the 1967 Six-Day War, the State of Israel took on the role, in sociologist Charles Liebman's words, of "the religion of American Jews." Leonard Fein characterized Israel as the "center" and "purpose" of Jewish life, "a mythic place, a land of heroes and of miracles." This veneration found expression in unparalleled volunteer fundraising and political action. But after nearly a decade of unflagging admiration and support, the aura surrounding the State of Israel began to dim.

Issues and events which led to this change included: the Likkud government's extensive settlement program in the administered territories in contradiction to the policy of successive American administrations; Israel's bombing of Iraq's atomic reactor in June 1981; the extension of Israeli law to the Golan Heights in December 1981; the bombing of Beirut and Israel's indirect role in the Sabra and Shatilla refugee camp massacres during the 1982 Lebanon War; the sale of arms to Iran prior to the Irangate scandal; Israel's military and commercial ties to South Africa's apartheid government; the still unresolved and highly charged Who is a Jew? issue as one facet of Israel's completely un-American mix of religion and state; and Israel's role as portrayed in the media during the Palestinian uprising, or *intifada*. Certain American Jewish intellectuals were among the most critical of Israel's policies and actions.

In 1987, American Jews sought and acquired a change in the composition and the operation of the Jewish Agency. As a result of strong protests over the operation of the Agency, especially the allocation of authority along Israeli political party lines and the disproportionate funding of Orthodox institutions at the expense of Conservative and Reform programs, American Jewish leaders succeeded in establishing a higher level of accountability for Agency expenditures and passed two resolutions barring Agency support for non-Zionist (ultra-Orthodox) institutions and for schools that refused to recognize Ethiopian immigrants as Jews.

Especially upsetting from the point of view of American Jews, and the only issue to have brought about a direct confrontation between the American Jewish community and the government of Israel, was the revival of the "Who is a Jew?" controversy. Although the roots of the argument lay in internal Israeli political developments going back to the beginning of the state, a string of events reignited the crisis at the end of 1988 and brought about the direct involvement of American Jewish leaders. The two contenders for the Israel premiership, Yiẓḥak Shamir and Shimon Peres, after the general elections were angling for the support of ultra-religious parties who stipulated the condition that Israeli law would be changed to recognize as Jews only those who underwent conversion under the auspices of an Orthodox rabbi in accordance with traditional Jewish law, *halakhah*.

Employing a Washington, D.C.-style lobbying effort, American Jews flew to Israel and met personally with government ministers, members of the Knesset, academicians, heads of industry, and the arts. The professional and lay heads of federations and other major American Jewish organizations came to state emphatically that any change in Israeli law would bring about the spiritual and possibly the physical alienation of American Jews from the State of Israel. In exchange for other concessions, the religious parties demanding this amendment agreed not to insist on their demand. A new government led by the Likkud party was formed and the "Who is a Jew?" law was not amended.

In a controversial March 1987 Op-Ed article that appeared in *The Washington Post* American Jewish scholar Jacob Neusner wrote "It's time to say that America is a better place to be a Jew than Jerusalem." In addition to concern over the general instability of the region and Israel's external and internal political dilemmas, Neusner was disappointed that the Jewish State had not proven to be the world center of Jewish spirituality, scholarship, art or literature. The Jewish community in the United States, he felt, had equal claim to that title.

The psychological gap between American and Israeli Jews was experienced in both directions, particularly during the 1991 Gulf War. While American Jews identified with the threat posed to Israel to the point of experiencing personal anguish, Israelis reported feeling abandoned by American Jews. As noted in *The Jerusalem Report* (February 27, 1992): "From August 1990, when Iraq invaded Kuwait... through March 1991, Israel lost a full 500,000 tourists, as compared to the year before... most of the drop was among American Jewish visitors; tourism from Europe and Christian America remained more or less stable."

The American Jewish community maintained its own complement of activists and organizations which reflected Israel's political spectrum. American Friends for Peace Now and the *Tikkun* group constituted the left-wing American Jewish opponents of American Friends of Gush Emunim and those within the *Commentary* circle. But neither the group of critical intellectuals of the left nor the "Greater Israel" zealots of the right represented the views held by the majority of American Jews. In spite of certain misgivings and criticisms in response to seemingly harsh Israeli actions reported by the press, throughout this period the majority of American Jews constituted a steadfast and loyal block that strongly identified with the State of Israel. This was demonstrated in a decade long series of opinion surveys carried out by Steven Cohen for the American Jewish Committee.

American Jewish conservatives who previously had censured any public dissent on Israel which emanated from the Jewish community, now felt obligated to voice their concerns over the policies of the Rabin government. *Commentary* editor Norman Podhoretz and *N.Y. Times* columnist A.M. Rosenthal were chief among those who abandoned their former objections to publicly criticizing Israel.

Organizational Life. The American Jewish community of the 1980s was, in a certain sense, the sum of its organizational matrix. Conflicts over religious or political matters found expression through organizational disputes. One example of the former was the refusal of Orthodox members to approve admission of the Reconstructionist movement to the multi-denominational Synagogue Council of America in 1986. An example of the latter was the October 1988 episode in which the executive professionals of the American Jewish Congress, the American Jewish Committee, and the Anti-

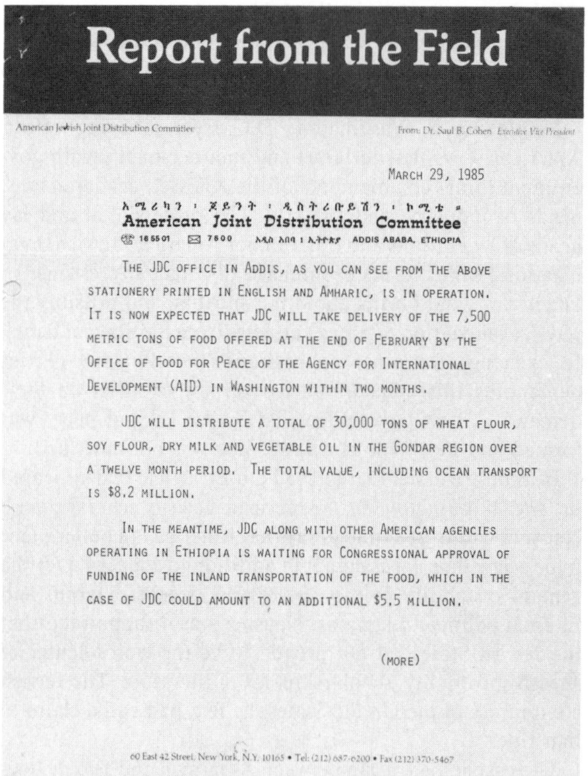

Report from the Field

American Jewish Joint Distribution Committee

From: Dr. Saul B. Cohen Executive Vice President

MARCH 29, 1985

American Joint Distribution Committee

165501 7600 ADDIS ABABA, ETHIOPIA

THE JDC OFFICE IN ADDIS, AS YOU CAN SEE FROM THE ABOVE STATIONERY PRINTED IN ENGLISH AND AMHARIC, IS IN OPERATION. IT IS NOW EXPECTED THAT JDC WILL TAKE DELIVERY OF THE 7,500 METRIC TONS OF FOOD OFFERED AT THE END OF FEBRUARY BY THE OFFICE OF FOOD FOR PEACE OF THE AGENCY FOR INTERNATIONAL DEVELOPMENT (AID) IN WASHINGTON WITHIN TWO MONTHS.

JDC WILL DISTRIBUTE A TOTAL OF 30,000 TONS OF WHEAT FLOUR, SOY FLOUR, DRY MILK AND VEGETABLE OIL IN THE GONDAR REGION OVER A TWELVE MONTH PERIOD. THE TOTAL VALUE, INCLUDING OCEAN TRANSPORT IS $8.2 MILLION.

IN THE MEANTIME, JDC ALONG WITH OTHER AMERICAN AGENCIES OPERATING IN ETHIOPIA IS WAITING FOR CONGRESSIONAL APPROVAL OF FUNDING OF THE INLAND TRANSPORTATION OF THE FOOD, WHICH IN THE CASE OF JDC COULD AMOUNT TO AN ADDITIONAL $5.5 MILLION.

(MORE)

60 East 42 Street, New York, N.Y. 10165 • Tel: (212) 687-6200 • Fax (212) 370-5467

A 1985 newsletter, *Report from the Field*, with Amharic and English-headed stationery telling of the JDC operation in Addis Ababa, Ethiopia

Defamation League considered establishing an alternative lobbying organization to AIPAC which the leadership of these three organizations felt had gone beyond "the consensus of the organized Jewish community," i.e., had become a rubber-stamp of the Shamir government.

During the 1980s, these three organizations, originally established to combat anti-Semitism in the United States and educate against prejudice and discrimination, became more vocal and active with regard to the Middle-East peace process.

The American Jewish Congress organized fact-finding missions to the Middle-East to meet with Arab heads of state and became identified with the policies of Shimon Peres and the Labor party. Both the American Jewish Committee and the Union of American Hebrew Congregations tended to be critical of Israel's handling of the *intifada*. The ADL remained generally supportive of Israel's actions, both with regard to the peace process and the Palestinian uprising.

Ironically, it was the Zionist organizations in the United States which maintained the lowest profile on Middle-East issues. The purpose served by these organizations and their operation was critically examined by Charles Hoffman in *The Smoke Screen: Israel, Philanthropy and American Jews* (1989), who wrote that "Not prepared to transmit the message to the bulk of American Jewry that *aliyah* is the collective obligation of all Jews," the various Zionist organizations remained preoccupied mainly with fundraising, public relations, publications and informal educational programs for American Jewish youth. Many community leaders, among them Menachem Rosensaft, himself a past president of the Labor Zionist Alliance, came to question the present relevance of the Zionist organizations given the reality of the State and the activities carried out on its behalf by so many other American Jewish organizations.

The Washington, D.C.-based American Israel Public Affairs Committee (AIPAC) remained one of the best known and most effective American Jewish voluntary organizations. *The New York Times* called AIPAC "The most powerful, best-run and effective foreign policy interest group in Washington." As a result, AIPAC was constantly under scrutiny by opponents for evidence of "dual loyalty."

Two blows befell AIPAC towards the end of 1992. In August, Prime Minister Yiẓhak Rabin, at a closed-door meeting in Washington, severely criticized the leadership of AIPAC for its strategy of lobbying the American executive branch, which he declared to be Israel's diplomatic prerogative, and also, for being too antagonistic and confrontational in its relations with Israel's critics and opponents. In November 1992 AIPAC's president, David Steiner, was forced to resign after he admitted to making secretly recorded statements about his personal influence at the White House.

Further solidifying their role as the "central address of the Jewish community" during these years were the local Jewish federations. Requiring only a generally affordable contribution in return for membership, the over 190 federations in North America (including Canada) claimed to represent the broadest based constituency within the American Jewish community. Their considerable concentration of community resources allowed them to allocate support to a wide range of both domestic and overseas Jewish causes, and via the United Jewish Appeal (UJA), especially to Israel. Any national institution as large and powerful as the Jewish federation system was bound to engender criticism. Although they proved their ability to respond to various emergencies—such as providing $2 million in emergency relief to the Jewish communities in the Miami area devastated in August 1992 by Hurricane Andrew, federations were charged with exploiting crises affecting the Jewish people in order to meet predetermined fundraising goals. Other criticism included an overemphasis on the amassing of dollars at

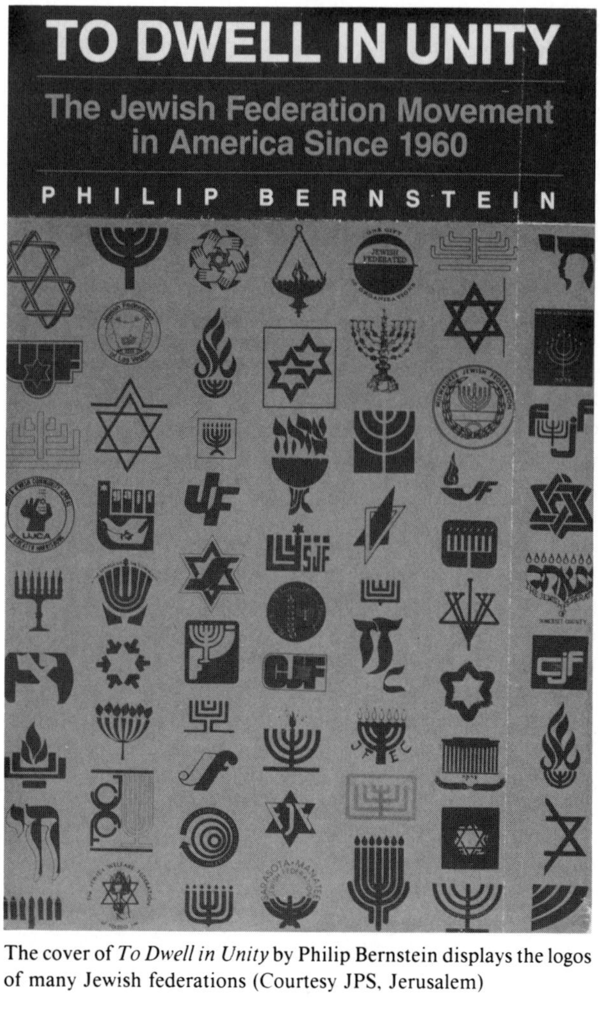

The cover of *To Dwell in Unity* by Philip Bernstein displays the logos of many Jewish federations (Courtesy JPS, Jerusalem)

the expense of demanding greater Jewish knowledge and education among its leadership. A third criticism was leveled at its centralized control of resources and dependency upon political consensus. More recent criticism focused on the high salaries and generous benefits enjoyed by high-ranking federation executives.

In November 1992 the national Council of Jewish Federations, at its annual General Assembly, approved a new governance proposal that created a 500–member Board of Delegates based on proportional representation and a form of community taxation based on the "fair share" principle of collective responsibility. The CJF also created the National Funding Councils, which were intended to more equitably govern local federation grants to national Jewish organizations.

The oldest national Jewish organization in the United States, B'nai B'rith, continued to experience membership shrinkage during the 1980s. In 1989 it was reported that the organization's membership had dropped to about 136,000, from around 200,000 in 1969. Among the reasons offered to explain B'nai B'rith's problems were its difficulty in defining its purpose, its image of being primarily a social organization, and the preference of busy two-career families for giving donations to volunteering.

Other mainstream Jewish organizations suffered a similar decline in membership roles during these years. The growing involvement of professional Jewish women in the workplace during the 1980s made it more difficult for organizations like Hadassah, ORT and Na'amat (formerly Pioneer Women), to recruit new members. Synagogues were threatened with decline in membership in light of evidence indicating that third and fourth generation American Jews were even less likely to join a synagogue than their parents or grandparents. The exception to this trend was the increased, albeit still very limited popularity in the alternative synagogue, or *ḥavurah* movement. Originally established outside the synagogue establishment, by the 1980s both the Reform and Conservative movements were fostering and supporting various forms of local *ḥavurot*.

A few national Jewish organizations experienced significant growth and development. The most successful was the Los Angeles-based Simon Wiesenthal Center. By the end of 1992, it reported approximately 385,000 contributors, an annual budget of about $12 million, and a professional staff of 100. Another organization which grew in popularity toward the end of this era was American Friends of Peace Now (it became Americans for Peace Now in 1989). Throughout most of the 1980s, American Friends of Peace Now was on "the margins of American Jewish life" (*Baltimore Jewish Times*, September 25, 1992), but its credibility was firmly established with the ascendancy of the Labor-led coalition government in Israel after the June 1992 election. It reported 10,000 members divided among 21 chapters throughout the United States, and was accepted for membership in the Conference of Presidents of Major American Jewish Organizations.

Fundraising remained the core activity of American Jewish organizational life. The largest annual fundraising campaign in the American Jewish community remained the local federation-UJA drive which divided collected funds between local charities and Israel. In more recent years, the national trend has been to decrease the proportion sent to Israel. Thus, in 1983, National UJA received approximately 48 percent of the combined federation campaign, domestic needs received 29 percent, and the remaining 23 percent went to other overseas causes. By comparison, in 1991 the National UJA received 40 percent, 36 percent was retained for local agencies, and 24 percent was allocated overseas."

The New Israel Fund, an alternative philanthropy, established in 1979, emphasized support for groups "working to protect civil and human rights, to improve the status of women, to bridge social and economic gaps, to further Jewish-Arab coexistence, and to foster pluralism and tolerance" in Israel. In 1989 it distributed about $6.5 million to some 150 Israeli non-profit oranizations. Another symbol of alternative giving was the Abraham Fund Directory, published in 1992, which listed nearly 300 organizations to which American Jews could make direct, tax-deductible contributions.

The influx of nearly a half-million new immigrants to Israel at the end of the decade led to the involvement of a few American Jewish communities in Israel's economic development. In addition to charitable donations used to support immigrant absorption, social welfare, and education in Israel, the Jewish Agency requested federations to support new economic ventures in Israel, especially among new immigrants. The goals of this effort were to increase employment opportunities and to improve Israel's exports, particularly in the area of high technology. A few communities, among them Baltimore, New York, and Atlanta, became involved in this new area. Most federations declined, citing the potential dangers involved in combining philanthropy and business.

The Chronicle of Philanthropy ranked the United Jewish Appeal first in fundraising contributions in 1992, "more than any other non-profit organization." The $668.1 million reported was not based on total income because government grants and other earning (such as income from endowments and investments) were not included.

However, the 1990 CJF Jewish Population Survey indicated that "younger Jews are much less devoted to Israel than older Jews." But while Israel is not the center of Jewish life for most American Jews, it remains the focus for Jewish communal fundraising.

The death of billionaire Baltimorian Harry Weinberg in November 1991 resulted in the largest Jewish-oriented foundation in the world. With assets of $762.8 million, it ranked as the 22nd largest foundation in the United States. A quarter of its annual grants were reserved for Jewish groups, another 25 percent for non-Jewish causes, and the remaining 50 percent was not earmarked for any particular group.

Poverty Among Jews. At the other end of the economic spectrum were American Jews living below the poverty line. In the early 1980s it was estimated that approximately 250,000 Jews in New York City were living on annual incomes of less than $3,500. In Chicago, where the estimated number of poor Jews was thought to be around 35,000, the Jewish Federation during the mid–1980s created Project Ezra, an umbrella project that coordinated the skills and resources of its various agencies. While the majority of the Jewish poor were elderly, many were former corporate executives and professionals who fell victims to the weakened economy.

Jewish Life on College Campuses. By the end of the decade, more than half of all American Jews under the age of 65 were college graduates. A disproportionate number of Jewish college graduates went on to graduate studies in pursuit of a professional career. It was estimated that some 85 percent of young Jews were active at colleges and universities either as students, teachers, or researchers.

The Jewish college students of the 1980s benefited from a plethora of Judaica courses, Judaica degree programs, and Judaica departments on campuses throughout the United States. The 1986 Jewish Directory and Almanac, edited by Ivan L. Tillem, listed the names of hundreds of American colleges and universities in 44 states (and Canada), the estimated size of each school's Jewish student enrollment, the number of Judaica courses that are taught, the Judaica degree programs that are offered, as well as facilities available for *kasher* dining.

But Jewish students on North American campuses faced two major problems, anti-Semitism and assimilation. Jewish students were confronted by well-organized anti-Israel campus protests, at times accompanied by obvious anti-Semitic expressions. Jewish student leaders present at the November 1990 General Assembly of the Council of Jewish Federations in San Francisco complained that, in their effort to remain "politically correct," university administrators on many campuses often prevented Jewish students from protesting against anti-Israel and anti-Semitic black, pro-Palestinian, and Third World student groups.

A report by the ADL revealed that anti-Semitic incidents on American campuses doubled in the years 1988–1992, spurred by messages of racial hate from Louis Farrakhan and other speakers popular with black students. The ADL report compared the 1988 total of 54 campus-based anti-Semitic incidents with the 1992 total of 114 which were reported at 60 colleges and universities. These incidents ranged from verbal and written threats, to vandalism and assault, including a bullet fired into the windows of the University of Arizona Hillel House in 1988.

Arts and Letters. There was an upsurge in activity in all the arts within the Jewish community in recent years as evidenced by the productions by Jewish theater groups across the country, such as San Francisco's A Traveling Jewish Theater, the appearance of Jewish art festivals in major cities, and the Martin Steinberg Center for the Arts, an American Jewish Congress affiliate.

Two forms of Jewish music, choral and *klezmer*, contributed to the cultural revival of the period. The former was best represented by the Zamir Chorale. Originally founded in New York in 1960 under the direction of Stanley Sperber, by the 1980s there were similar organizations in Boston, Washington, D.C., Connecticut and Chicago, and Los Angeles. The proliferation of Jewish choirs was sufficient for the creation of the American Hebrew Choral Festival whose annual performances drew capacity audiences.

Klezmer music, a form of popular Jewish music based largely on the wedding melodies used in Eastern Europe and songs from the Yiddish Theater, experienced a remarkable revival in the United States after having become virtually extinct. The rise of *klezmer* bands began in the 1970s but experienced the greatest growth during the 1980s. Virtually every major American city became home to at least one *klezmer* ensemble.

Handcrafted Judaica developed into a major form of Jewish artistic expression. Jewish ritual objects and symbols such as the *ḥanukkiah* (Ḥanukkah *menorah*), the wine goblet, the *mezuzah*, the spice box, and the prayer shawl, found new forms of expression in various media, including wood, metal, precious metals, fabrics, plastic, and glass. The marriage contract, the *ketubbah*, was developed into a sophisticated form of artwork. The legal text was hand-written calligraphy on genuine parchment and embellished with Jewish themes.

Unprecedented growth also took place in the area of Jewish children's literature. American children's literature has been enriched and changed by the infusion of well-produced creative fiction and non-fiction for Jewish audiences.

An increasing number of American Jewish museums receive "more significant assistance from the federal state and local arts and humanities agencies... than they receive from Jewish community sources or from private patronage" (Tom Freudenheim, *Moment*, Oct. 1989). (See MUSEUMS, p. 287). [AR.J.GE.]

UNIVERSITY OF JUDAISM, institution for Jewish education located in Los Angeles, affiliated with the *Jewish Theological Seminary of America. The University of Judaism was established in 1947, initially to serve as a teachers' college and school where the adults could further their Jewish education. Initially a branch of the Seminary, it now has an independent board and is responsible for its own fundraising, while remaining affiliated to the parent school. The university has grown to include four degree-granting schools, a wide range of adult education courses, and outreach programs which encompass Jewish communities in the Western United States and Canada.

Class session in the Beit Midrash of the University of Judaism, Los Angeles, 1987 (Courtesy University of Judaism, Los Angeles)

Lee College, established in 1982, is an undergraduate liberal arts college which combines the study of Jewish and Western civilizations with professional career preparation. All students are required to take a year of Hebrew language. The David Lieber School of Graduate Studies offers a number of programs including an M.B.A. degree which is unique in stressing the not-for-profit sector and management programs in which the student can specialize in general or Jewish community organizations. The school also offers an M.A. in education, Jewish studies, and rabbinical literature.

The Fingerhut School of Education aims at preparing Jewish education professionals for teaching, administration, research, and curriculum design. The University of Judaism operates the Clejan Educational Resources Center which has advanced audiovisual and computer equipment, with access from anywhere in the United States.

The Graduate School of Judaica is intended primarily for students who intend to enter the rabbinate and the course of study parallels the first two years of rabbinical school of the Jewish Theological Seminary of America.

The university has a number of programs to meet the social and cultural needs of the Jewish community and offers extension courses attended by over 1,000 adults weekly. The Elderhostel program brings together 90 adults over the age of 60 for live-in education programs of a week to ten days, meeting 18 hours per week. The university also sponsors home study groups which meet monthly and has a year-round conference center in Ojai, California; the site is used by Camp Ramah in the summers. The Wagner Program for Human Services, with 150 participants, prepares adults in a two-year program to become trained paraprofessional volunteers to work in the Jewish community.

The university is located in the Santa Monica Mountains and includes academic and administration buildings, an auditorium, a residence hall and apartment complex. [ED.]

UZBEKISTAN (see **16**:39), one of the independent republics of the CIS. In 1979 it had 99,900 Jews and in 1989–94,900, including 151,400 in Tashkent. A large proportion of Jews in the republic are Central Asian (Bukharan) Jews who mainly live in Samarkand, Tashkent, and Bukhara and speak the Jewish dialect of Tadzhik. They have preserved their identity more than the local Ashkenazi Jews. The Jewish birth rate in 1988–89 was 13.4 per 1,000 and the mortality rate — 10.9 per 1,000.

Emigration in 1989 was recorded at 4,358 Jews (with 2,379 from Tashkent, 218 from Fergana province, and 772 from Samarkand province). Immigration to Israel in 1990 totaled 20,192, with 9,786 from Tashkent. Emigration rose from Fergana province and Andizhan in the wake of the violent ethnic conflicts there. After the pogrom against Jews and Armenians in Andizhan in May 1990 emigration from that province jumped to 2,202. In 1991, 13,515 Jews went from Uzbekistan to Israel, including 7,179 from Tashkent and 1,220 from Andizhan.

Tashkent has a Jewish culture center (its chairman is Roman Rabich). The monthly newspaper *Shofar* in Russian and Tadzhik has been published in Samarkand since 1992. Two Jews were elected to the Supreme Soviet of the republic in 1990.

An air route from Tashkent to Israel via Varna was inaugurated in June 1991. The Jewish Agency has been operating openly since January 1992. Diplomatic relations were established between independent Uzbekistan and Israel in 1992. [MI.BE.]

UZIEL, BARUCH (1900–1977), educator, lawyer, folklorist, and politician. Born and educated in Salonika, Uziel helped to found the youth organization "Machzikei Ivrit" whose goal was to spread the Hebrew language in the spirit of the Haskalah. In his home, he published the first Hebrew newspaper in Salonika, *Ha-Teḥiyyah.* Sent to Palestine in 1913 to study teaching, he was caught there by World War I and as a Greek citizen was exiled in 1917 to Syria by the Turkish authorities. After the British conquered Palestine, he returned to continue his studies and remained in the country. He was among the organizers of the Sephardi faction in the Va'ad Le'umi. He taught in various places and also graduated in law and became involved in politics.

Uziel always maintained a close connection with Salonika and in the 1920s, helped the *aliyah* of Salonikan fishermen to Acre and later organized the immigration of Salonikan stevedores to Haifa port. He also helped to lay the foundations for research into Sephardi folklore, in particular from Salonika. He wrote stories about Judeo-Spanish life in Salonika, eventually published in *Be-sha'arei Saloniki, Novelot (1973).*

He initiated the founding of the "Haifa-Saloniki" committee, which eventually received the name Va'adat ha-Yam ("the sea committee"). This committee together with the Va'ad le-ma'an Haifa ("the committee for Haifa") organized and brought 300 Jewish Salonikan seamen and their families to Haifa. As secretary of Va'ad ha-Yam he coordinated their immigration and absorption and served as a liaison between the committee and the relevant bodies in Greece and Ereẓ Israel.

In 1931 he was elected a member of the executive of Maccabi in Palestine and was in charge of the department of culture and propaganda. He served as president of the Association of Greek Immigrants and after World War II went to Greece in order to release property confiscated by the Nazis in the Holocaust.

In 1959 he wrote *Berit ha-Periferiyyah — Haẓa'ah le-Mediniyyut Yisraelit* proposing non-Arabic people of the Middle East ally with Israel to curb Arab imperialism.

Active in the General Zionist party, he was elected to the Fifth Knesset in 1961 and was head of the Knesset Education Committee. He was re-elected to the Sixth Knesset.

Uziel was the chief editor of *Guinzah Saloniki* (1961) and edited the Salonika commemorative memorial book *Saloniki Ir ve-Em be-Yisrael* (1967). [YI.K.]

V

VARMUS, HAROLD ELIOT (1939–), microbiologist and educator, Nobel Prize winner. Born in Oceanside, New York, Varmus studied at Amherst (B.A.), Harvard (M.A.), and Columbia University from which he received his M.D. degreee in 1966. He joined the University of California San Francisco department of microbiology in 1970 and became a professor in 1979. The recipient of several awards in recognition of the contribution of his research to science, such as the Lasker Foundation Award in 1982 and the Armand Hammer Cancer prize in 1985, he was a Nobel laureate in medicine in 1989 along with J. Michael Bishop for their joint research in the 1970s. They determined that growth-regulating genes normally found in almost every animal cell could suffer subtle alterations which resulted in uncontrolled cancer growth. The changes in the cell resulted from mutations or from exposure to chemical carcinogens. The genes studied were called oncogenes. The researchers' work provided the material needed to determine whether cancer was caused by viruses or through internal changes in the gene of normal cells, a long-debated based issue. [ED.]

VATICAN (see **16:**731; **Dc./17:**611). **Relations with Israel.** The State of Israel was not mentioned in papal documents before the 1980s but in 1980 Pope John Paul II made the first public papal reference to the State saying that "the Jewish people after tragic experiences connected with the extermination of so many of its sons and daughters, driven by the desire for security, set up the State of Israel." His Good Friday apostolic letter in 1984 was devoted to "the fate of the Holy City, Jerusalem" and reaffirmed the claims of the Church made over the previous dozen years for an internationally guaranteed statute for Jerusalem and the Holy Places (which after the Six-Day War had replaced the demand for the territorial internationalization of Jerusalem). The statement mentioned the Jewish and Muslim attachment to the city. Of especial significance was the statement: "For the Jewish people who live in the State of Israel and preserve in that land such precious testimonies to their history and faith, we must ask for the desired security and the due tranquillity that is the prerogative of every nation and condition of life and of progress for every society." These sympathetic remarks, according to Vatican officials, were to be seen as a statement of *de facto* recognition of the State of Israel although they were not pursued further through any diplomatic channel. In the following years Pope John Paul II made a number of references to Israel along these lines, usually balanced with an "evenhanded" reference to the plight of the Palestinians.

Members of Vatican-Jewish (IJCIC) Liaison Committee being shown a model of the Holocaust Museum, Washington, D.C., 1992; second from left, Edgar Bronfman, and then Cardinal Cassidy and Monsignor Fumigalli (Courtesy Geoffrey Wigoder, Jerusalem)

Upbeat statements were made by a number of high Catholic personalities known for their devotion to fostering Jewish-Catholic understanding. Thus Cardinal Martini of Milan said "The hope that emerges from the Holocaust is the Messianic promise of the land, of a reconciled land of Jerusalem, the city of peace, of a future world of messianic *Shalom*," while Cardinal Willebrands, at the time head of the Vatican's commission of religious relations with the Jews stated "To carry the memory of many millions of deaths is a terrible burden; to have a place under the sun where to live in peace and security is a form of hope." A number of national Bishops' Conferences spoke out on the link between the land of Israel and the Jewish people. Already in 1975 the U.S. bishops recognized the Jewish tie to the land of Israel and called on Christians to understand this link, while a 1984 document of the Brazilian bishops on relations with the Jews stated, *inter alia*, "God gave the ancient land of Canaan in which the Jews lived to Abraham and his descendants. We must recognize the rights of the Jews to a calm political existence in their country of origin, without letting that create injustice or violence for other peoples. For the Jewish people, these rights became reality in the State of Israel."

Relations with Israel underwent a severe strain in 1982 when the pope received Yassir Arafat. The event was aggravated by the prominent role placed by Archbishop Hilarion Capucci (see **Dc./17**:612) in organizing the event. Capucci had been caught redhanded gunrunning for the PLO and to secure his release from Israel prison, the Vatican had undertaken that he would be kept out of Middle East politics but it was not long before he was again involved. The Arafat reception led the International Jewish Committee for Interreligious Consultations (IJCIC) to suspend its relations with the Vatican for almost a year, and these were only resumed on a promise that it would be received in the Vatican Secretariat of State to discuss Vatican–Israel relations. The group was received by Monsignor (later Cardinal) Silvestrini who put forward four problems that would have to be resolved before the Holy See would be able to establish diplomatic relations with Israel: these were the occupation of Lebanon (where Israel troops still remained after the 1982 Lebanon War), the Palestinian refugees, the West Bank, and the status of Jerusalem. These conditions were later repeated on various occasions. (The previous claim that the nonfinality of Israel's borders was also a factor was not stressed and seldom mentioned subsequently.) At a 1987 IJCIC–Vatican meeting, suspicions of Jewish participants that theological motivations were also a factor impeding the establishment of relations were emphatically denied by the Vatican participants who agreed to state this explicitly in the official communiqué.

The third Vatican document on Judaism and the Jews — "The Common Bond" or "Notes on the Correct Way to present the Jews...in the Roman Catholic Church" issued in 1985 contained a section on Israel, being the first official Vatican document to allude to the State. Recognition was given to the continuing Jewish attachment to the land and its meaning for Jews but at the same time it warned against attributing any Christian religious significance to the link with the land. It also stated "The existence of the State of Israel and its political options should be envisaged not in a perspective which is itself religious but in their reference to the common principles of international law." While welcoming the overall inclusion of the subject, Jewish circles were critical of the wording, noting its opaqueness and ambiguities.

Throughout the 1980s, contacts were maintained between Israel and the Vatican. Israeli leaders were received by the pope while a special diplomat charged with Vatican relations was accredited to Israel's Rome embassy. There were also contacts between the Catholic hierarchy in Israel and the Foreign Ministry although the Catholics were not accredited to the State of Israel. The new Latin patriarch appointed in 1988 was Monsignor Sabbah, the first native Palestinian to hold the position. Israelis felt that many of his pronouncements and action reflected Palestinian sympathies.

The Vatican has always maintained a keen interest in establishing its influence in the Holy Land. At the end of World War I it fought for the Palestine Mandate to be granted to a Catholic power, while in 1948 it lobbied intensively for the internationalization of Jerusalem. The start of the peace process in 1991 caused concern to the Vatican inasmuch as major changes were a possibility and it was not a party to the negotiations. Moreover, the establishment of relations with Israel by such countries as Russia, India, and China left the Holy See's position exceptional. As to its fears of retribution in Arab lands in the event of ties with Israel, the fact that the Arab states themselves were sitting with Israel mitigated this fear. Consequently in July 1992 delegations of the Holy See and Israel met in the Vatican and set up "a bilateral permanent working commission to meet regularly to study and define together issues of mutual interest, and in view of normalizing relations," Vatican spokesmen subsequently added the hope that the negotiations would lead to the establishment of diplomatic relations. The Vatican in this way put aside the main issues it had been insisting on and the negotiations continued throughout 1992 and into 1993 dealing with issues affecting the Church in Israel (e.g., the tax status of Catholic institutions). Finally an agreement was reached and a document of mutual recognition was signed in December 1993.

See also JEWISH-CHRISTIAN RELATIONS. [G.W.]

VORST, LOUIS J. (1903–1987), chief rabbi of Rotterdam, Holland. The son of a diamond worker, Vorst entered the Amsterdam Rabbinical and Teachers' Seminar in 1914 and obtained the degree of *"maggid"* in 1924. He taught at Jewish elementary schools in Amsterdam and in 1927 became head of Jewish studies at the new Jewish post-elementary school

Rabbi Louis J. Vorst
(Courtesy S. Vorst)

there. In 1931 he was invited by Chief Rabbi A. B. N. Davids of Rotterdam to head Jewish education in that city. When Chief Rabbi Davids died in Bergen-Belsen in 1945, Vorst, who had survived although seriously weakened, returned after the liberation to Rotterdam where he took over most of the duties of Chief Rabbi Davids as well as resuming his own duties. He was given the personal title of rabbi, although he had not obtained the rabbinical diploma entitling him to become a chief rabbi. In 1959 he passed the rabbinical examination at the Amsterdam Ashkenazi Seminar and was then appointed chief rabbi of the Rotterdam District. He retired in 1971 and went to live in Israel. On his retirement he was made a Commander in the Order of the Netherlands Lion.

On his promotion to the position of chief rabbi the Jewish

Congregation of Rotterdam in September 1959 published a volume of essays *(Opstellen)* in his honor. [H.Bo.]

W

WACHTLER, SOL (1930–), U.S. jurist, chief judge of the New York State Court of Appeals. He was born in Brooklyn, New York, in 1930, and received his B.A. degree cum laude and his law degree from Washington and Lee University. He was in private law practice in Jamaica, Long Island, until his appointment as a justice of the New York Supreme Court in 1968; later in that year he was elected to a full term in the court. In 1972 he was elected to the New York State Court of Appeals, the state's highest court, and in January 1985 the governor appointed him chief judge of the court. In this position he supervised a system that included some three thousand judges and about twelve thousand non-judicial personnel.

As chief judge of the Court of Appeals, Judge Wachtler said that he has set for himself two chief missions: namely, to achieve collegiality for the court, so that it may speak with "one voice" and win for itself again the reputation it enjoyed under the leadership of Benjamin N. *Cardozo; and to streamline and modernize the administration of the state's judicial system. [M.R.K.]

WALDHEIM AFFAIR. The "Waldheim Affair" is the term conventionally applied to the controversy surrounding the disclosure of the previously unknown past of Kurt Waldheim, former Secretary General of the United Nations, which arose during his campaign for the Austrian presidency in 1986. The affair not only focused international attention on Waldheim personally, but also raised broader questions relating to the history of anti-Semitism in Austria and the role Austrians' played in the Nazi dictatorship and the "Final Solution." A concomitant of the Waldheim affair was the reemergence in Austrian political culture of the appeal to anti-Semitic prejudice for political ends. Employing a coded idiom more appropriate to "post-Auschwitz" political debate, the Waldheim camp (principally the Christian democratic Austrian People's Party [ÖVP], which had nominated him) helped construct a hostile image of Jews *("Feindbild")* which served both to deflect criticism of Waldheim's credibility and to explain the international "campaign" against him. The central assumption of this *"Feindbild"* was that Waldheim and Austria were under attack from an international Jewish conspiracy.

Kurt Waldheim had enjoyed an exceptionally successful career in the Austrian foreign service after World War II. Taken on as secretary to Foreign Minister Karl Gruber in 1946, Waldheim served in various posts abroad and in Vienna, including two stints as Austrian representative to the UN and was appointed foreign minister in January 1968 by Chancellor Josef Klaus (ÖVP). His term as minister ended in March 1970, when the Socialists (SPÖ) under Bruno Kreisky won the parliamentary elections. Shortly thereafter, Waldheim returned to New York as Austria's ambassador to the UN. In January 1971, he was again in Vienna temporarily to run as the ÖVP candidate for president, which in Austria is a largely ceremonial post for which elections are held every six years. Though he made a very respectable showing, Waldheim lost to the incumbent Socialist Franz Jonas and afterwards returned to his post in New York. On December 22, 1971, Waldheim was elected Secretary General of the UN, and reelected to a second term in 1976. His bid for a third term, however, failed, and in March 1982, Waldheim, described by one journalist as "the most successful Austrian diplomat since Metternich," finally came home to Austria.

Waldheim's international prominence and personal ambition left few in doubt that he would run for the Austrian presidency in 1986, but it was unclear whether as the candidate of the ÖVP, or as a consensus candidate of the two major parties. The ÖVP hoped to draw maximum political advantage from Waldheim's candidacy for itself, without identifying him so closely with it that it would endanger either Waldheim's election as president or the hoped-for attendant political "turn." Then chairman Alois Mock pushed through Waldheim's nomination by the ÖVP as a "non-partisan" candidate in March 1985, more than a year prior to the elections, very early by traditional Austrian standards. The SPÖ, also conscious of Waldheim's electoral appeal, had not ruled out a joint candidacy until confronted with the ÖVP's fait accompli. One month later, the SPÖ presented Kurt Steyrer, then minister for health and environment, as its standard bearer. Two minor candidates, Freda Meissner-Blau from the Greens, and Otto Scrinzi, former FPÖ member of parliament and representative of the (German) nationalist far right in Austria, also entered the race.

The relatively uneventful early phase of the campaign, in which Kurt Waldheim was the clear front runner, ended abruptly in March 1986. Indeed, the Waldheim affair may be properly said to date from March 3, 1986, when the Austrian weekly *Profil* published documents first revealing details of Waldheim's unknown past. *Profil*'s disclosures were followed on March 4 by nearly identical revelations by the *World Jewish Congress (WJC), and the *New York Times (NYT).* Waldheim had always denied any affiliation with the Nazis of any kind, and, in both his public statements and in the relevant passages in his memoirs, had claimed that his military service ended in the winter of 1941–42, with his wounding on the eastern front. The evidence made public by *Profil*, the WJC, and the *NYT* suggested on the contrary that the former secretary general had been a member of the Nazi Student Union and that he had also belonged to a mounted riding unit of the *Sturmabteilung*, or S.A., while attending the Consular Academy in Vienna between 1937 and 1939. Other documents revealed that Waldheim had been declared fit for duty in 1942, after his wound had healed. By the end of March 1942, Waldheim had been assigned to Army High Command 12 (which became Army Group E in January 1943), then based on Thessalonika (Salonica), and remained attached to it until the war's end. Army Group E, commanded by Alexander Löhr, was known for its involvement in the deportations of Jews from Greece and for the savagery of its military operations against Yugoslav partisans and their suspected civilian supporters.

For his part, Waldheim denied membership in any Nazi organization and offered evidence suggesting his ideological hostility to Nazism. He conceded having served in Army Group E, but denied participation of any kind in atrocities committed by units under Löhr's command, and claimed to have known nothing of the deportation of the Jews of Thessalonika.

The more general strategy pursued by Waldheim and his supporters was to brand the disclosures as part of a "defamation campaign" designed to inhibit his chances in the presidential election. Waldheim's argument ran along the following lines: The accusations of the WJC and the *NYT* represent a continuation of a slander campaign which the SPÖ had been waging against him for some time. The Socialists or their accomplices had fed documents to the WJC and the *NYT* in order to damage Waldheim's international reputation, his main advantage over Steyrer. Such allegations were all the less credible, since Waldheim had been cleared by the Austrian secret service at the time he entered the diplomatic service 40 years previously. Moreover, during his candidacy for UN secretary general, the CIA, the KGB, and the Israelis all investigated him and would not have allowed his election had there been anything in the least incriminating against him. He had not mentioned his tour of duty in the Balkans in his memoirs, Waldheim claimed, because he had had such a minor function and also because his injury on the eastern front had represented a major caesura in his life. He knew nothing of Jewish deportations and had had nothing to do with other atrocities. But if Waldheim were to be blamed for such things, then truly every Wehrmacht soldier would also come under suspicion.

Although the Waldheim affair became an international media extravaganza, the principal source of documents relating to Waldheim's past, as well as his most vocal critic, was the WJC, an organization based in New York whose primary activities involve campaigning to defend threatened Jewish communities throughout the world and lobbying for what it perceives as the common interests of Jews. The series of press releases and disclosures of documents (24 between March 4 and July 8, date of the second round of the Austrian presidential election) by the WJC set the pace and largely the terms for the debate on Waldheim in the United States. In the early phase of the controversy, the WJC published evidence relating to Waldheim's membership in the S.A. and Nazi Student Union, which it believed amounted to proof of his "Nazi past." The material on Waldheim's wartime past the WJC first presented was patchy and inconclusive, but over the next several months it made public dozens of additional documents which helped complete the picture of Waldheim's various duties in the Balkans.

On March 22, the WJC published a copy of the Central Registry of War Criminals and Security Suspects (CROWCASS), a list compiled by the U.S. Army of persons suspected of war crimes, showing that Waldheim had been sought by Yugoslavia after the war for, among other things, murder. The basis for the CROWCASS listing was a file of the United Nations War Crimes Commission (UNWCC), and this latter file was in turn based on a dossier prepared by the Yugoslav authorities and submitted to the UNWCC shortly before it concluded its deliberations in 1948.

With the publication of the Yugoslav file, known as the *Odluka*, or "Decision," the debate on Waldheim's past acquired a far more serious dimension: allegations of war crimes had been leveled against Waldheim by the Yugoslav War Crimes Commission and these had been reviewed and endorsed by the UNWCC. The WJC's subsequent disclosures as well as the discussion on Waldheim's past in general were heavily influenced by this new discovery.

On March 25, 1986, the WJC presented the findings of Robert E. Herzstein, the historian it had commissioned to look into Waldheim's past. Herzstein had discovered that Waldheim had served as a staff officer in the military intelligence department of Army Group E and had been assigned to the Battle Group West Bosnia, whose troops were responsible for the slaughter of thousands of Yugoslavs in the Kozara mountains in 1942. Waldheim had also received an award for valor (the King Zvonimir medal) from the puppet Croatian government at the end of this campaign.

The WJC continued to offer documents it felt corroborated the findings in the *Odluka*, and pressed U.S. Attorney General Edwin Meese to place Waldheim's name on the so-called "watch list" of undesirable aliens, effectively barring him from entering the U.S. In the international media, calls for the publication of Waldheim's UN file were coupled with more intensive efforts to find a "smoking gun."

The issues involving Waldheim's possible criminality were in any event never self-evident. The possibilities for inferring something opprobrious about Waldheim's service in the Wehrmacht from his previously concealed "Nazi past" were legion, while the publication of the CROWCASS and the Yugoslav *Odluka* transformed vague intimations about his military duties into concrete juridical suspicion.

Embarrassing, if not necessarily inculpatory, documents were surfacing daily, but there were few around who could reliably interpret what they meant. Moreover, merely keeping track of Waldheim's whereabouts in the Balkans was difficult: he had served in seven different posts in at least 10 locations in present-day Yugoslavia, Albania, and Greece. The issue of Waldheim's possible war criminality was also complicated by ignorance about the practice of the Nuremberg Tribunal. On the one hand, much of what the Wehrmacht did to Yugoslav partisans was gruesome but "legal." On the other hand, the conditions under which an officer of Waldheim's rank and position could even incur criminal liability were narrowly circumscribed. Categories of guilt, complicity, responsibility, etc., easily elided, while the suspicious background to the compilation of the *Odluka*, which undermined if not vitiated the charges made in it, only became known later.

In Austria itself, Waldheim and his supporters continued to portray all new claims about his wartime role as slander, and Waldheim as the victim of a coordinated international "defamation campaign," initiated by socialists, led by the World Jewish Congress and promoted by the international press, particularly the *New York Times*. In the course of the election campaign, the WJC became the main object of abuse, and the abundant political invective arrayed by politicians of the ÖVP against it as scapegoat helped promote and legitimate anti-Semitic prejudice in public discourse to an extent unseen since 1945. Waldheim also attempted to identify his own fate with that of his generation and country by claiming that he, like thousands of other Austrians, had merely done his "duty" under Nazi Germany, an appeal which struck a responsive note among many Austrian voters.

In the election on May 4, 1986, Waldheim polled 49.7% of the votes, just short of the majority needed to win. During the six weeks leading up to the second round, the Socialists emphasized their candidate's ability to reconcile a divided nation, but to no avail. Waldheim won the second round handily: his 53.9% of the votes was the largest of its kind (i.e., when not running against an incumbent) in the Second Republic.

Whatever actually determined Austrian voting behavior is open to a great deal of speculation, but the result was almost certainly not affected in any significant way by a negative backlash against the Waldheim camp's anti-Semitic wager. At the same time, the election does not appear reducible to a moral referendum on Waldheim or his past, for it is doubtful either that Austrian voters conceived the election in such ethico-political terms or that their votes reflected their respective moral choices. Dissatisfaction with government policies or the desire to deliver a protest vote for any one of several reasons seem to have motivated voters at least as much as a reflexive national spite or even anti-Semitic prejudice. What cannot be doubted is that Waldheim's diminished credibility and his perceived trivialization of Nazi atrocities (in the eyes of his critics, if not his supporters) did not cost him the election.

Contrary to Waldheim's expectations, interest in the unanswered questions about his past did not disappear after his election. Waldheim received no official invitations from any country in western Europe, and some official government visitors to Austria even avoided traveling to Vienna, as protocol would otherwise have required them to pay a courtesy call on the Austrian president. Some prominent private individuals, such as political scientist Ralf Dahrendorf, also boycotted events where Waldheim would have been present. In April 1987, the U.S. Department of Justice announced that it was placing Waldheim on the watch list, further reinforcing his pariah status.

Since Waldheim's election, three independent research efforts, a commission of seven historians established at the request of the Austrian government, a panel of five international jurists engaged by British and U.S. television production companies, and a commission of the British Ministry of Defense, have illuminated Waldheim's wartime career in great detail, and none found anything in Waldheim's behavior which could implicate him personally in any criminal activity. Waldheim himself considered these judgments a complete vindication, and he and his supporters found the stigma which still attached to him incomprehensible.

Waldheim's diplomatic isolation was broken initially by the pope, who received Waldheim officially in June 1987, and Waldheim subsequently visited a few Arab countries, some of whose papers had defended Waldheim against ostensible Zionist attacks. Though in April 1990 the U.S. Justice Department confirmed its decision to bar Waldheim, an indication of a possible thaw in attitudes towards Waldheim came the following July, when presidents Richard von Weizsäcker of Germany and Vaclav Havel of Czechoslovakia publicly met Waldheim at the Salzburg Festival, where Havel gave the ceremonial address in which he, albeit, indirectly attacked Waldheim by speaking of those who distort their memoirs.

In Austria itself, President Waldheim did not become the kind of integrative figure he had wished. Waldheim was initially an irritation and embarrassment to many, and was even forced by opponents in the government into remaining silent at the official commemoration of jubilee of the Austrian *Anschluss* in March 1988. During the second half of his term, which ended in 1992, on the other hand, Waldheim's treatment in the press suggested that increasing numbers of Austrians had accepted Waldheim as president, even though he would never be accorded the respect and affection his predecessors had enjoyed.

More broadly conceived, the Waldheim affair symbolizes the post-war unwillingness or inability adequately to confront the complications of the Nazi abomination. It remains to be seen whether current infelicitous images of Austria's Nazi past will be supplanted by the more prosaic Trapp family pendant, or whether the Waldheim affair becomes the occasion for a more general effort on all sides to come to terms with the past. If so, then Waldheim may indeed be said to have performed an important function.

Bibliography: R. Mitten. *The Waldheim Phenomenon in Austria. The Politics of Antisemitic Prejudice* (1991); R. Wodak, P. Nowak, J. Pelikan, R. de Cillia, H. Gruber, and R. Mitten, *'Wir sind alle unschuldige Täter!' Studien zum Nachkriegsantisemitismus* (1990); R. Scheide, K. Gruber, and F. Trauttmansdorff (eds.), *Kurt Waldheim's Wartime Years. A Documentation* (1987); H. Born, *Für die Richtigkeit. Kurt Waldheim* (1987); H. Czernin, "Waldheims Balkanjahre." Seven-part series on Waldheim's Balkan year; *Profil* Numbers 49–52 (1987), 1–4 (1988); J. L. Collins, Jr., H. Fleischer, G. Fleming, H. R. Kurz, M. Messerschmidt, J. Vanwelkenhuyzen, and J. L. Wallach, *Der Bericht der internationalen Historikerkommission* Vienna: Supplement to *Profil* 7 (February 15, 1988); R. E. Herzstein, *Waldheim. The Missing Years* (1988); M. Palumbo, *The Waldheim Files: Myth and Reality* (1988). [RI.MI.]

WEINBERG, HARRY (1908–1990), U.S. philanthropist. Born in Galicia, Weinberg went to the U.S.A. as a young man. He grew up in Baltimore in absolute poverty but by the age of 40 he was a millionaire and by the time he was 50, he was a billionaire. He lived in Hawaii for the last 20 years of his life.

With all his money, he never indulged himself. In the 1950s after purchasing the Scranton, Pennsylvania, bus lines, he lived in a rented, second-floor apartment even though he could have bought the entire block the house stood on.

Weinberg was known for working seven days a week and his main interest appeared to be in acquiring as much as he could. His chief hobby was charity. He gave annual grants to yeshivot and Orthodox synagogues in Baltimore, even though he was not Orthodox. He donated $3 million to the Honolulu congregation for its building and an endowment fund. He aided the Associated Jewish Community Federation of Baltimore in many ways. He also gave funds to many non-Jewish institutions.

He established two foundations. The first, the Harry and Jeanette Weinberg Foundation, had assets at his death of almost $1 billion and was the 11th largest private foundation in the U.S.A. The other foundation, the Harry Weinberg Foundation, was worth $90 million and was devoted solely to the benefit of the Associated Jewish Community Federation in Baltimore.

The larger foundation disburses $45 million annually. Its charter stipulates that 25% of its disbursements go to organizations that primarily benefit Jews and 25% to organizations that primarily benefit non-Jews. The remaining 50% will go to any groups — Jewish or non-Jewish — deemed worth by the foundation's trustees. There are no geographical limitations on disbursements, and it was intended that both Israel's and Baltimore's homeless would benefit. [M.D.G.]

WEINGREEN, JACOB (1908–), Hebrew and Bible scholar. Born in Manchester, he graduated from Trinity College, Dublin where he became professor of Hebrew in 1939. During the period immediately following World War II, he served as director of education in the Displaced Persons' Camp in Bergen-Belsen.

Jacob Weingreen (Courtesy Asher Benson, Dublin)

Weingreen's best-known publication, *A Practical Grammar for Classical Hebrew* was published in 1939 and remains in general use 50 years later. A French edition, *Hébreu Biblique* appeared in 1984. His other works have included *Classical Hebrew Composition* (1957), *From Bible to Mishna — The Continuity of Tradition* (1976), and *Introduction to the Critical Study of the Text of the Hebrew Bible* (1982). His writings, as well as his teaching, have been distinguished by their lucidity.

He received many honors and was president of the Society for Old Testament Studies, Great Britain and Ireland (1961), of the British Association of Jewish Studies (1976), and governor of the *Irish Times* Trust from 1974.

An abiding interest in archeology led to his foundation of what, on his retirement, was named the Weingreen Museum of Biblical Antiquities in Trinity College, Dublin. His contention that the Book of Deuteronomy is not, as widely believed, one of the main sources of the Pentateuch because it bears the characteristic of a mishnah caused a stir among biblical scholars [ASH.B.]

WEXNER, LESLIE H. (1937–), U.S. industrialist and philanthropist. Born in Dayton, Ohio, Wexner moved to Columbus, Ohio, when he was a teenager. After graduating from Ohio State University, he worked briefly in his father's shop for women's clothes. In 1963 his own merchandising career began when he borrowed $10,000 and opened the first "The Limited" store in Columbus, Ohio. "The Limited" has grown to over 3,600 stores throughout the United States, but Wexner has maintained his corporate headquarters in Columbus. In recent assessments by *Forbes* magazine, his wealth has been estimated at between $1.3 and $2.6 billion.

Leslie H. Wexner (From the David Geffen Collection, Jerusalem)

The Wexner Foundation which has assets of $80 million, was established by Wexner in 1984. His first major step in the Jewish field was the creation of the Wexner Heritage program to provide potential American Jewish lay leaders with a two-year intensive Jewish study program. By the end of 1990, 300 American Jews from 20 cities had participated in the program.

In 1988 the foundation introduced a Fellowship Program for rabbinical students as well as graduate students in Jewish education programs and in Jewish communal service programs, to complement which an institutional grants program was created to aid academic institutions of all types to build programs for Jewish professionals.

Also in 1988, the Wexner-Israel Fellowship Program was created. Annually 10 outstanding Israeli civil servants up to age 45 are chosen to study for a master's degree at Harvard's Kennedy School of Government. The goal of the program is to provide Israel's next generation of leaders with advanced public management training. [M.D.G.]

WHITE, THEODORE H. ("Teddy"; 1915–1986), U.S. journalist and author. White was born in Boston, Massachusetts. He studied at Harvard University, graduating in 1938. His grandfather was a rabbi from Pinsk who spent his last days

Theodore H. White (Courtesy Ms. Heyden White; photo Carl Mydans)

in pious devotion at the Western Wall in Jerusalem. In his autobiography *In Search of History* (1978) White refers to his Jewish and Hebrew education. "What I learned, then, from age 10 to age 14, when I went on to evening courses at the Hebrew College of Boston was the Bible. . . ." "We learned it, absorbed it, thought in it, until the ancient Hebrew became a working rhythm in the mind, until it became a second language. Memory was the foundation of learning at the Hebrew school, and the memory cut grooves on young minds that even decades cannot erase. Even now, when a biblical phrase runs through my mind, I am trapped and annoyed unless I convert it into Hebrew — whereupon the memory retrieves it from Boston, Mass., where little Jewish-American boys were forced to learn of nomads and peasants of three thousand years ago, forced to learn of spotted lambs, of the searing summer and of the saving rains (Yoreh and Malkosh)." In later years, he used to make his own Haggadah for Passover written on special cards and assigning the parts to his children. In his youth Teddy White helped to organize the student Zionist activists on the New England campuses in the Avukah (Torch) Society. He helped organize a boycott of German goods in Boston. White was "lured" however to other interests which he defined as Harvard and history.

A year after graduating from Harvard, Teddy White was *Time* magazine's war correspondent in China and by 1945, at the age of 30, he was Time Bureau Chief. His first book (with Annalee Jacoby) was *Thunder Out of China* (1946). Between 1948 and 1953 White was in Europe and wrote *Fire in the Ashes* (1953). Returning to the U.S. White became a national political correspondent for *The Reporter* magazine, then for *Colliers*, and then for *Life*. He also published two novels (*The Mountain Road* [1958] on the evacuation of Chinese and American armed forces and *The View from the Fortieth Floor* [1960] on his 1950s stint at *Collier's* magazine) and one play and wrote several television documentaries.

White achieved his greatest acclaim as the author of a series of books called *The Making of the President* for 1960, 1964, 1968, and 1972 elections, for which he won the Pulitzer prize, and a wrap-up volume called *America in Search of Itself*, published in 1982. He had planned a 1976 "Making of the President" book, but the Watergate scandal led him to write *Breach of Faith* instead. [SHI.AR.]

WIESEL, ELIE (see **16**:507; **Dc./17**:618). Additional works by Wiesel are *Le Testament d'un poète juif assassiné* (1980); *The Testament*, (1981); *Five Biblical Portraits* (1981); and *Ecstasy and Sadness; Further Tales of the Hasidic Masters* (1982). Wiesel was the recipient of the Nobel Peace Prize in 1986 in recognition of his unceasing efforts on behalf of human dignity.

WILENTZ, ROBERT N. (1927–), U.S. jurist. Born in Perth Amboy, New Jersey, Wilentz attended Princeton University, received his B.A. degree from Harvard, and his law degree from Columbia. He joined his father's law firm in Perth Amboy and practiced from 1952 to 1979. He was elected to the New Jersey legislature in 1966 and served until 1969. He was in the U.S. Navy in World War II. In 1979 he was appointed chief justice of the N.J. Supreme Court for a seven-year term, and his appointment was made permanent in 1986. Under his administration the New Jersey Supreme Court achieved a reputation for not being reluctant to move creatively towards adjudication in areas previously untouched by judicial action.

David Wilentz, father of the chief justice, was attorney general of New Jersey, who prosecuted Bruno Richard Hauptmann in 1932 for the kidnap-murder of the twenty-month-old son of Charles A. Lindbergh. [M.R.K.]

WORLD ZIONIST ORGANIZATION. See JEWISH AGENCY.

Y

YAD IZHAK BEN-ZVI, Israel research institute. Yad Izhak Ben-Zvi was established in 1963 by a decision of the Israel government. During the first years of its existence its main activities were focused on gathering and consolidating the archives of Izhak and Rahel *Ben-Zvi and the publication of the writings of Izhak Ben-Zvi.

In 1969 the Knesset adopted a law determining the aims of the Yad, which was charged with advancing research about the history of the Land of Israel and the dissemination of information about it and its various settlements and the heritage of the Jewish communities of Muslim lands. In 1972 the Yad moved to its permanent headquarters in the building which had served as the residence of the President of Israel in Jerusalem.

Through its two research institutes Yad Ben-Zvi carries out its activities in its two main spheres of interest: study of the Land of Israel and its settlements and research into Jewish communities in Muslim lands. Its Institute for History of Jewish Settlement in the Land of Israel initiates studies carried out directly by the Institute or through research grants; publishes the results of research; and organizes scientific conferences. The policy of the Institute is determined by an academic council, which consists of senior Israeli researchers from the various universities. The Institute is responsible for two periodicals which deal with the history of the Land of Israel: *Shalem*, which appears twice a year, and *Cathedra*, a quarterly. The Institute maintains centers in common with each of the five Israeli universities, each center being headed by a senior researcher at that particular institution.

The Ben-Zvi Institute for the Study of Jewish Communities in the East (Makhon Ben-Zvi) is a joint project of Yad Izhak Ben-Zvi and the Hebrew University of Jerusalem. It was founded in 1949 by Izhak Ben-Zvi and deals with the history, literature, language, and material and spiritual culture of Jewish communities in the Middle East from the Middle Ages to modern times. In addition to two regular publications — *Sefunot*, an annual, and *Pe'amim*, a quarterly — it has published numerous books.

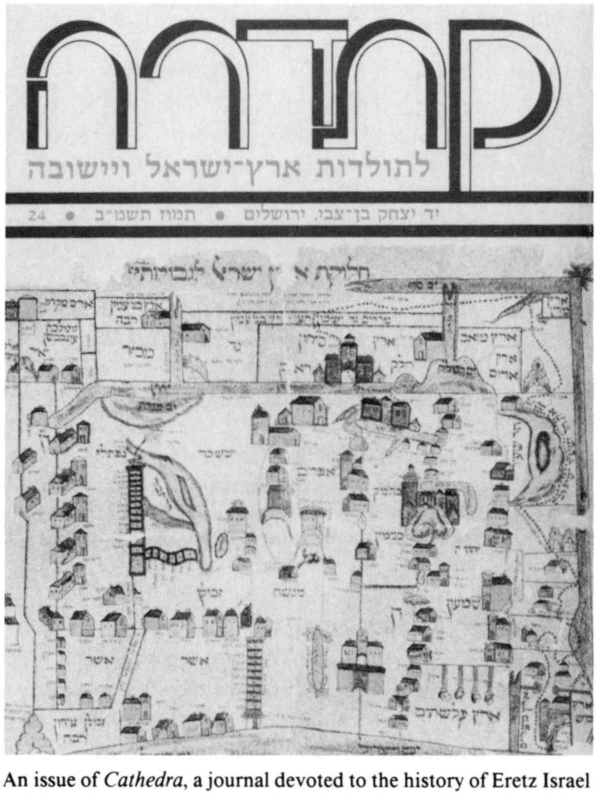

An issue of *Cathedra*, a journal devoted to the history of Eretz Israel and its *yishuv* (Jewish settlement), published by Yad Izhak Ben-Zvi

The Yad also runs the Raḥel Yanait-Ben-Zvi Center for Jerusalem Studies for Youth (established 1972), where each year more than 30,000 students learn of Jerusalem and its environs. The Center publishes books and pamphlets for teachers and high school students.

The Yad's publishing division produces studies as well as source material on the Jewish settlement in the Land of Israel from the time of the Bible to the establishment of the state. The Yad also has an archive and a library. It conducts discussions, tours, and study days for the general public and for teachers devoted to aspects of the history of the Land of Israel.

Yad Izhak Ben-Zvi is a public institution headed by a public council which meets three times a year. [D.B.-S.]

YIDDISH LITERATURE. Yiddish literature continued to age in the 1980s. Almosty all its writers were born before the destruction of the Yiddish heartland in Eastern Europe. Readers also aged and decreased. The Yiddish press diminished. The most prestigious daily, the New York *Forverts (*Jewish Daily Forward)* was converted in 1982 to a weekly after eighty-five years of existence. The repertoire of ever fewer theatrical performances consisted of older plays and nostalgic musicals. Novelists, except in Israel, preferred as subject matter the longed-for, destroyed world of yesteryear. Aging survivors of ghettos, Nazi concentration camps, and Soviet gulags published memoirs and narratives of their experiences or participated in *Yizkor* books about perished Jewish communities.

Heroic efforts were made to slow down the decline of Yiddish creativity. Grants, prizes, and awards for Yiddish books multiplied. The World Council for Yiddish and Jewish Culture looked back in 1986 on a decade of support for Yiddish writers, publishers, and journals. Its bilingual annual, *Gesher — Brikn*, has featured since 1983 translations of Hebrew works into Yiddish and of Yiddish works into Hebrew. Its monthly organ, *Yiddish Welt*, has coordinated since 1985 worldwide Yiddish activities.

In New York, the *Biographical Lexicon of Modern Yiddish Literature*, initiated 1954 by CYCO — the Central Yiddish Culture Organization — was completed in 1981. By then, none of the early editors and administrators, Samuel Niger, Jacob Shatzky, Moshe Starkman, Jacob Pat, and Chaim Bass, was alive. However, the editors of the final volume, Berl Cohen, Israel Knox, and Elias Schulman, succeeded in enlisting 32 writers from all continents for the project, whose eight volumes encompassed biographies, evaluations, and bibliographies of more than 7,000 Yiddish writers of the 19th and 20th centuries.

In Buenos Aires, Shmuel Rozhansky completed in 1984 the editing of the 100 volumes of *Masterpieces of Yiddish Literature.* The first volume, in 1957, dealt with the pioneer of Yiddish poetry and drama Solomon *Ettinger. The 100th volume bore the symbolic title *Tsu Neiem Lebn* ("Toward A New Life") and consisted of poems, tales, and essays which could serve to counteract the prophets of the doom of Yiddish.

In Tel Aviv, the literary quarterly *Die Goldene Keyt*, edited by Abraham Sutzkever since its founding in 1949, attracted Yiddish writers from all continents. The *Yerushalaimer Almanakh*, a literary quarterly edited by Yosef Kerler in Israel's capital, and *Bei Sikh*, a parallel periodical edited by Y. J. Yanosovitch in Tel Aviv, were at first organs of Yiddish writers who had streamed into Israel from Soviet Russia in the 1970s but gradually expanded to include other writers.

In Israel, multivolumed prose epics of superb quality were still being created, such as Mordecai Tsanin's *Artapanos* series, begun in 1967 and completed in 1985, and Elie

Schechtman's *Erev* ("On the Eve"), begun in Kiev in 1965 and continued in Jerusalem, where its seven parts were combined in a single volume of 1,222 pages in 1983. The former work spans 2,000 years of the Eternal Jew's wanderings and tribulations in exile until his homecoming to the reestablished Jewish state. The latter recounts the travails and undying hopes of Russian Jewry from the pogrom-ridden Czarist era to the present. Schechtman also completed by 1986 the first three books of the autobiographic novel *Ringer Oif Der Neshome* ("Rings about the Soul").

Israel increasingly became the theme of its poets. Their verses mirrored its landscape, reflected its reality, and sang of its hopes for the regeneration of the Jewish people. Pioneering poets who began in Mandated Palestine and who continued to publish lyric volumes of excellent quality included Joseph Papiernikov, I. H. Biletzky, J. Z. Shargel and Hillel Shargel. Many poets flocked to Israel after the Holocaust. Prominent among them were Moshe Jungman, Shlomo Worsoger, Freed Weininger, Nachman Rapp, Y. J. Yanosovitch, Bunim Heller, Shlomo Shenhud, Rivka Basman, Hadassah Rubin, and Assia.

When the gates of Soviet Russia were opened in 1971, an influx of Yiddish writers went to Jerusalem, including Yosef Kerler, Ziame Telesin, Rochel Boymvol, and Meir Kharats. Along with David Sfard, poet and essayist who had been forced to leave Poland in 1969, Ephraim Shidletsky, and Nachman Rapp, they sought to make Jerusalem a Yiddish center rivaling Tel Aviv. If they did not succeed to wrest to themselves the hegemony over Yiddish, it was because the Tel Aviv area harbored the main publishers of Yiddish books, the Yiddish newspapers *Letzte Neies* and *Israel Stimme*, and congenial meeting places for writers: the Sholem Aleichem House, the Liessin House, the Leivick House, the Sholem Asch House. Worldwide recognition came to Abraham Sutzkever, Tel Aviv's most influential Yiddish poet, on his 70th birth year 1983. He became the most frequently translated Yiddish lyricist and the subject for a profound study by David Wolpe in 1985. Increased fame also came to Isaiah Spiegel, novelist of the Lodz ghetto and of Auschwitz, poet, and essayist with deep insight into literary phenomena and personalities. In Tel Aviv were active Meir Yellin, novelist of the Kovno ghetto; Abraham Karpinowitch, whose tales resurrected Vilna's streets and denizens; Hirsh Osherowitch, whose biblical poems, unpublishable in Russia, appeared in 1981; the literary critics Eliezer Podriachek and David Stokfish; Joseph Luden, novelist, poet, and art critic; Ḥayyim Maltinski, whose poems appeared shortly before his death in 1986; and the poet Chaim Seltzer.

In earlier decades, Jerusalem's university had the only chair in Yiddish studies. Its first occupant Dov Sadan was succeeded by Chone Shmeruk. By the mid-1980s, however, the universities of Tel Aviv, Haifa and Beersheba, and Bar-Ilan University had also introduced courses in Yiddish language, literature, and folklore.

In the Diaspora, European, American and South African universities inaugurated Yiddish courses and published studies in Yiddish, but literary creativity waned. In Russia, only writers grouped around *Sovetish Heymland*, edited by Aaron Vergelis, could be published. In other Eastern European countries, only Romania produced significant literary works. Seven volumes of *Bucarester Shriftn* were completed between 1978 and 1984. Of this annual's editors, I. Caro's short stories (1980), Chaim Goldenstein's novel (1982) and Wolf Tambour's novel (1982) followed by his shorter narratives (185) attracted attention.

In Central Europe, Leizer Aichenrand maintained a lonely Yiddish vigil in Switzerland, where his last poems appeared in 1984, shortly before his death.

In Western Europe, Yiddish creativity in France was impoverished by the death in 1981 of Moshe Shulsteyn and Benjamin Shlevin, but the Paris newspaper *Unzer Vort* continued to appear. In 1980, Moshe Waldman published his poems of four decades and Menucha Ram her short stories *Shteyner* ("Stones"). In 1983 the novelist I. Finer completed his fictional trilogy *Tsvai Mishpokhes* ("Two Families") and Rivke Lopé the second volume of her essays on literary personalities. In England, the death in 1983 of Joseph Leftwich and A. N. Stencl, and in 1984 of Jacob Meitlis removed three strong pillars of Yiddish literature and scholarship and led to the discontinuance of *Loshn un Lebn*, which Stencl had founded and edited since 1940.

In South Africa, the *Yiddishe Zeitung*, edited by Levi Shalit, ceased publication in 1985 but *Dorem Afrike*, edited by Zalman Levi, continued as the literary organ of the Yiddish writers. David Fram's poems *A Shvalb Oifn Dakh* ("A Swallow On the Roof") appeared in 1983 and David Wolpe's collected essays in 1984.

In Australia, *Melbourner Bleter* served as the sole literary organ for its few Yiddish writers. Itzhak Kahn won wider recognition with his essays and Sheva Glas-Wiener with her ghetto tales.

In Canada, C. L. Fuchs edited in 1980 a literary lexicon encompassing 422 Canadian writers in Yiddish and Hebrew. Peretz Miranski published his newest harvest of lyrics in 1983; Isaac Goldkorn verse-epigrams in 1981 and poetic fables in 1984; M. M. Shaffir his autumnal lyric booklets in 1983 and 1984; Jacob Zipper his last essays in 1983; Yehuda Elberg his carefully constructed novels and stories; and Sholem Shtern challenging essays and finely chiselled lyrics.

In the United States, the popularity of the sole Yiddish literature Nobel laureate I. Bashevis-Singer remained undimmed and the prestige of Yiddish in academic circles rose to new heights, but original creativity lagged behind former decades. The periodicals *Zukunft* and *Yiddishe Kultur* still attracted writers and readers. Shlome Schwartz continued with poetic collections in 1981 and 1984; Shea Tenenbaum with impressionistic tales, essays, and reminiscences in 1981 and 1984; Shmuel Izban with short stories in 1980; Itche Goldberg with selected essays in 1981; Martin Birnbaum with poems and songs in 1981; Y. E. Ronnch with his last poems in 1981; and Chaim Bass with his last essays in 1980.

The waning of Yiddish literary creativity, however, became more evident with each year as writers aged and passed away with no successors in sight. [S.L.]

YOUNG, STUART (1934–1986), British public servant. The son of a North London flour merchant, Young entered accountancy at 17, and at 23 was senior partner of his own firm, specializing in corporate finance. He entered British public life as appeals chairman of European Architectural Heritage Year 1975, subsequently becoming a member of the Historic Buildings Council, a trustee of the National Gallery, and a leader of the Architectural Heritage Fund. In 1983 he became the youngest chairman of the governors of the British Broadcasting Corporation. Appointed with a view to the use of his accountancy skills for the internal reorganization of the B.B.C., he became a champion of its independence from government. An active Zionist from 1950, Young volunteered his services in the 1967 Six-Day War, took a leading part in the raising of funds for Israel, and became president of the Joint Israel Appeal in Britain. Among many other communal appointments, he planned the reorganization of Anglo-Jewish welfare services as chairman of the Central Council for Jewish Social Service.

Bibliography: *The Times* (Aug. 30, 1986); *Jewish Chronicle* (Sept. 5, 1986). [V.D.L.]

YUGOSLAVIA (see **16**:868; **Dc./17**:361). The violent breakup of Yugoslavia which began in 1991 and the bloody civil war that accompanied it had far-reaching and traumatic effects on the 5,000 to 6,000 Jews who lived in the country.

Yugoslavia was a loose federation of six republics: Serbia, Croatia, Slovenia, Bosnia-Herzegovina, Macedonia, and Montenegro. By the end of 1992, Slovenia and Croatia were independent states; civil war still raged in Bosnia-Herzegovina and the status of Macedonia was unclear. Serbia and Montenegro alone made up a rump Yugoslavia.

Until the division of the country, Yugoslav Jews had belonged to communities joined in autonomous republic-wide organizations which in turn were members of a nation-wide Federation based in Belgrade.

Most Jews were concentrated in the capital cities of three of the republics: Zagreb, capital of Croatia, with about 1,200 Jews, Sarajevo, capital of Bosnia-Herzegovina, with about 1,000, and Belgrade, capital of Serbia and also the federal capital, with about 1,500 Jews. The remaining Jews lived in much smaller scattered communities, mostly in Croatia and Serbia's Vojvodina province. Fewer than 100 Jews lived in Slovenia, and only 100 in Macedonia.

There was little overt anti-Semitism, and the rate of intermarriage was high. Through the 1980's participation grew in wide-ranging programs and activities run by the Federation and the individual communities (with the help of international Jewish philantropic organizations). These included a summer camp on the Adriatic Sea, annual Maccabi sports competitions, old-age care facilities, women's and youth groups and educational programs including religion classes, Hebrew classes, and the first Jewish kindergarten in Yugoslavia in more than a decade, which opened in Zagreb, the most active community, in 1989. Yugoslavia had only one rabbi — Belgrade-based Cadik Danon — but by the late 1980s one young man was in Israel studying to become a rabbi, and several others were training as cantors or lay leaders for religious services.

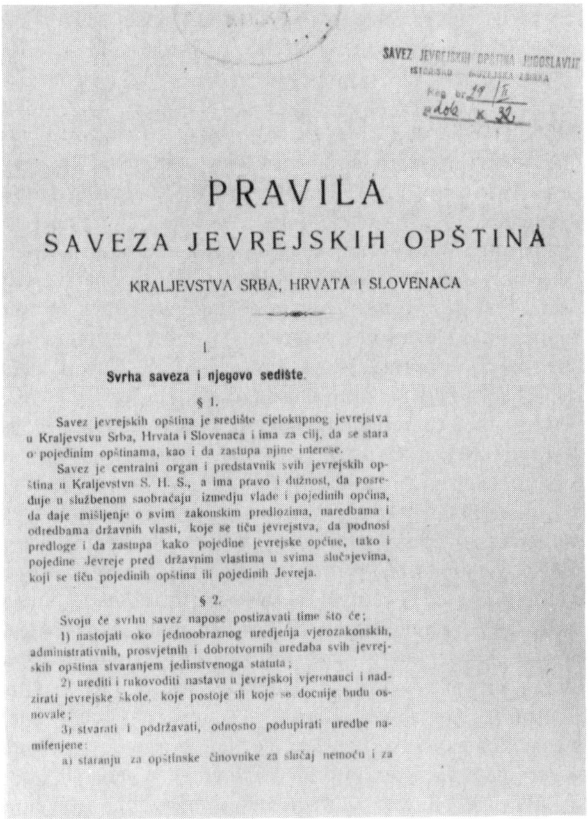

PRAVILA

SAVEZA JEVREJSKIH OPŠTINA

KRALJEVSTVA SRBA, HRVATA I SLOVENACA

I.

Svrha saveza i njegovo sedište.

§ 1.

Savez jevrejskih opština je središte cjelokupnog jevrejstva u Kraljevstvu Srba, Hrvata i Slovenaca i ima za cilj, da se stara o pojedinim opštinama, kao i da zastupa njine interese.

Savez je centralni organ i predstavnik svih jevrejskih opština u Kraljevstvn S. H. S., a ima pravo i dužnost, da posreduje u službenom saobraćaju izmedju vlade i pojedinih općina, da daje mišljenje o svim zakonskim predlozima, naredbama i odredbama državnih vlasti, koje se tiču jevrejstva, da podnosi predloge i da zastupa kako pojedine jevrejske općine, tako i pojedine Jevreje pred državnim vlastima u svima slučajevima, koji se tiču pojedinih opština ili pojedinih Jevreja.

§ 2.

Svoju će svrhu savez napose postizavati time što će;

1) nastojati oko jednoobraznog uredjenja vjerozakonskih, administrativnih, prosvjetnih i dobrotvornih uredaba svih jevrejskih opština stvaranjem jedinstvenoga statuta;

2) urediti i rukovoditi nastavu u jevrejskoj vjeronauci i nadzirati jevrejske škole, koje postoje ili koje se docnije budu osnovale;

3) stvarati i podržavati, odnosno podupirati uredbe namijenjene:

a) staranju za opštinske činovnike za slučaj nemoću i za

Rules of the Jewish (Israelite) religious communities of the Kingdom of Serbs, Croats, and Slovenes, 1919 (From catalogue to "Jews in Yugoslavia" exhibition)

Stobi, remains of a synagogue, 3rd–4th cent., and of a Byzantine church, 5th cent. (From catalogue to "Jews in Yugoslavia" exhibition)

Although Yugoslavia had not restored diplomatic relations with Israel broken after the Six-Day War in 1967, commercial and cultural ties as well as cooperation in the areas of sports and tourism burgeoned during the 1980s. Slovenia's Adria Airlines established direct flights to and from Israel in 1989. Yugoslavia's Jews also maintained close ties with various international Jewish organizations, and by the late 1980s Yugoslav government officials also met with Jewish and Israeli representatives. At a meeting in New York in July 1987, Yugoslav leader Lazar Mojsov told World Jewish Congress president Edgar Bronfman that he would "work toward better relations with the Jewish world as a whole and with the State of Israel."

A landmark cultural event was a major exhibition on the Jews of Yugoslavia which opened in Zagreb in April 1988 and then was shown elsewhere in the country, attracting tens of thousands of visitors, before going on to the United States and Israel. Belgrade's first Holocaust memorial (aside from memorials in the Jewish cemetery) was dedicated in 1990; it was by the Jewish sculptor Nandor Glid.

The mounting separatism and ethnic tensions that came to the fore in the late 1980s had their effect on the Jewish communities. Some Jews felt that Serbian overtures to Israel including the formation in 1989 of a Servian-Jewish friendship society and the twinning of various Serbian-Israeli cities were mainly aimed at courting world Jewry to give support to Serbia in its opposition to any decentralization of the state. A leader of the tiny Jewish community in Slovenia warned of possible anti-Semitism after a youth magazine published *Protocols of the Elders of Zion* in 1990. In Zagreb, Jewish leaders at the end of 1990 expressed concern that Croatian nationalism might prompt a resurgence of anti-Semitism, but later threw support behind the Croatian government when it seceded from Yugoslavia and became embroiled in civil war.

When the civil war broke out following Slovenian and Croatian secession in the summer of 1991, the status of Jewish communities again became a political issue. Serbs and Croats attempted to discredit each other with accusations of anti-Semitism. In early 1992 Klara Mandic, a founder of the Serbian-Jewish Friendship Society, visited the United States and in a series of lectures and articles charged the Croatian government of Franjo Tudjman with reviving fascism and anti-Semitism and planning "genocide" against Serbs in Croatia. Nenad Porges, president of the Zagreb Jewish Community, countered by accusing Serbs of anti-Semitism and expressing support for the Tudjman government.

The civil war led to great suffering and destruction, particularly after fighting spread from Croatia to Bosnia-Herzegovina. Jews had to flee their homes along with hundreds of thousands of other citizens, and Jewish monuments and property were damaged or destroyed along with countless other buildings. Among them, the medieval synagogue in Dubrovnik was damaged by bombs; the Jewish community center in Osijek was hit by shelling; and Serbian fighters used the ancient Jewish cemetery overlooking Sarajevo as a position from which to fire onto the city. In Zagreb, terrorist bombs in August 1991 wrecked the Jewish community offices and prayer hall and also damaged the Jewish cemetery.

Starting in April 1992, the American Jewish Joint Distribution Committee carried out daring air and overland evacuations of almost the entire Jewish population of Sarajevo.

Almost from the beginning of the civil strife, communications between Zagreb, Sarajevo, and Belgrade were difficult or cut altogether. Local Jewish communities became fully autonomous and ultimately independent as the former Yugoslav republics became independent. In Zagreb, gala celebrations in September 1992 marked the reopening of the Jewish community center and prayer hall after a full-scale restoration, partially funded by local authorities, following a terrorist bombing of the year before. [R.E.G.]

Z

ZAFRANI, HAIM (1922–), Jewish scholar, writer, educator, and historian. Haim Zafrani was born in Mogador, Morocco, where from 1939 to 1962 he taught in schools and became general supervisor of Arabic in the schools of Morocco. He was also the representative of the Alliance Israélite Universelle in the country. In 1962 he moved to France where he held the chair in Hebrew at the École Nationale des Langues Orientales Vivantes in Paris from 1962 to 1966 and worked at the Centre National de la Recherche Scientifique (C.N.R.S.), also in Paris, from 1966 to 1969. From 1975 he held the chair in Hebrew at the University of Paris VIII, where he was chairman of the department of Hebrew language and Jewish civilization from its establishment in October 1969.

Zafrani's studies include the preparation of a critical edition and French translation of the Bible. This is part of a group project involving researchers from Paris, Jerusalem, Tel Aviv, Morocco, and Egypt.

Zafrani has also studied and conducted research into the kabbalistic texts and mystical traditions of the Jews of the Maghreb. He has published ten books and many articles on Hebrew, Judeo-Arabic, and Judeo-Berber liguistics, and on Jewish thought in the Muslim West and in Islamic countries. Among his works are *Mille ans de vie juive au Maroc* (1982) and *Kabbale, vie mystique et magie* (1986), *Poésie juive en Terre d'Islam* (1977; translated into Hebrew), *Littératures dialectales et populaire juives in Occident Musulman.*

[GI.KO.]

ZELDOVICH, YAKOV BORISOVICH (1914–), Soviet theoretical physicist. Zeldovich was born in Minsk. From 1931 he worked at the Institute of Chemical Physics of the Academy of Science of the U.S.S.R. (A.S. U.S.S.R.), and from 1964 at the Academy's Institute of Applied Mathematics. In 1958 he was made a member of the Academy of Sciences. Professor at the University of Moscow from 1966, he was one of the founders of contemporary theories of combustion, detonation, and shock waves and the author of a number of works on the theory of the last stages of the evolution of stars and galaxies which involved the theory of general relativity and the theory of gravitational collapse. He has also proposed a number of experiments and methods for verifying cosmological theories. Zeldovich was awarded a Lenin Prize, four Stalin Prizes, and three times hailed as a Hero of Socialist Labor. [S.J.E.R.]

ZEMLYACHKA (Zalkind), ROZALIYA SAMOYLOVNA (other Party pseudonyms — Samoylova, Demon and Osipov; 1876–1947), Soviet government and Party official. Born in Kiev, daughter of a merchant, she became a member of the Social-Democratic Party in 1896. In 1901 she was a representative of the newspaper *Iskra* in Odessa and Yekaterinoslav. After the Party split of 1903, Zemlyachka became a member of the Bolshevik Central Committee and in 1905 secretary of the Moscow committee of the Russian Social Democratic Workers Party, working in the Party's military organization.

She was arrested on a number of occasions. In 1909 she was secretary of the Baku Party organization and then spent some time abroad. In 1915–16 Zemlyachka was a member of the Moscow bureau of the Central Committee of the Bolshevik Party. During the February Revolution of 1917 she was secretary of the Moscow Committee of the Bolsheviks and participated in the armed seizure of power. From 1918 to 1920 she headed the political departments of the 8th and 13th armies and was the first woman in Soviet Russia to be awarded a medal (that of the Combat Red Banner). From 1920 to 1926 she occupied various Party posts, including, from Nov. 1920, that of secretary of the provincial Party committee in the Crimea where together with B. *Kun, she carried out a policy of mass terror. From 1926 she was a member, deputy chairman, and then chairman of state and Party control organs. She was distinguished for her merciless attitude in regard to Party purges and sanctioned repressions. From 1939 to 1943, in addition to serving in other capacities, she was deputy chairman of the Council of Peoples' Commissars of the U.S.S.R. [MA.KI./S.J.E.R.]

ZIMBABWE (see **14:**148; **Dc./17:**526). Due to the incidence of the civil war which raged in the former colony of Rhodesia from 1976 until the culmination of the Lancaster House Conference at the end of 1979, the Jewish community of Zimbabwe shrank from a total of 7,000 to around 1,200 in December 1987. Moreover, available statistics have established that this is not merely an aging, but rather an aged community, since some two-thirds of those remaining are now over the normal retirement age of 65. Nevertheless, remarkably all the institutions developed during the heyday between the Federation of Rhodesia and Nyasaland in 1953 and the onset of civil strife in 1976/7 continue not only to exist, but in most cases are viable and even thriving.

Almost all the Jews of Zimbabwe are to be found in the two main cities of Harare and Bulawayo, the ratio of the respective populations being roughly 2:1. The former midlands communities of Gweru, Kwe Kwe, and Kadoma no longer exist, there being less than 20 Jews left in all three centers, none of them children. A marked measure of communal discipline prevails nowadays, due largely to the fact that the Central African Jewish Board of Deputies has finally been recognized as the supreme authoritative body by both the government agencies and the community in general.

Bulawayo enjoyed the services of a rabbi throughout 1986/7. As Rabbi Avnit (who hails from Israel) is also a *shoḥet* (ritual slaughterer), the whole community has been able to enjoy a regular supply of *kasher* meat, after lapses dur-

CENTRAL AFRICAN
ZIONIST DIGEST
(Registered at the G.P.O. as a Newspaper)
The official organ of THE C.A. ZIONIST ORGANISATION, published monthly
P.O. Box 1162 BULAWAYO Phone 67383
CHESHVAN, 5752 — OCTOBER, 1991 Volume 34, No. 7

Jerusalem, Friday, October 18

MIDDLE EAST PEACE CONFERENCE SET FOR OCTOBER 30 IN MADRID.

Jerusalem, Friday, October 18

THE SOVIET UNION RESTORES FULL DIPLOMATIC TIES WITH ISRAEL.

ON his eighth week-long trip to the Middle East region, the U.S. Secretary of State James Baker, on Friday October 18, announced in Jerusalem, that invitations were extended to Israel and her Arab neighbours, i.e. Syria, Egypt, Lebanon, Jordan and to the Palestinians, to attend a Middle East Peace Conference, sponsored jointly by the United States and the Soviet Union, to be held in Madrid, Spain, on Wednesday October 30.

The President of the United States George Bush and the President of the Soviet Union Mikhail Gorbachev, are scheduled to be present at the opening session and to address Conference, which is expected to last for three days, to be followed by face-to-face talks between Israel and the Arab States and the Palestinians.

"The negotiating process that we are seeking to launch with this invitation, holds the hope of a new era in the Middle East," Baker told a news conference in Jerusalem.

Baker, who arrived in the Middle East on Sunday October 13, held talks with Egyptian President Hosni Mubarak, Syrian President Assad, Jordanian King Hussein, Israel's Prime Minister Yitzhak Shamir and the Palestinian representatives.

The Arab delegations to participate are Egypt, Syria, Lebanon and a joint Jordan/Palestinian delegation.

Premier Shamir, was not able at the time to give a direct answer of 'yes' for Israel to participate in the Conference without prior approval of his cabinet, which he said, is to be convened on Sunday October 20, but he told Baker, that he would recommend the acceptance of the invitation.

Just prior to Baker's announcement on the invitations to the Conference, the Soviet Foreign Minister Boris Pankin, who was also in Jerusalem on that day, after a meeting with Israel's Foreign Minister David Levy, announced that the Soviet Union is to re-establish full diplomatic relations with Israel, with immediate effect, afer a break of some 24 years.

It took James Baker, some eight months of diplomacy — since the end of the Gulf War, and hard bargaining which entailed eight trips to the region, until he was now able to issue the invitation to the parties concerned, to participate in the proposed conference.

On his return home, Baker stopped over for some hours in Madrid, for talks with the Spanish Prime Minister Felipe Gonzalez, on the arrangements for the Conference to be held in Madrid on October 30.

עם ישראל חי

STOP PRESS: After a seven-hour-long heated debate, the Israel Cabinet at its meeting held on Sunday October 20, approved the recommendation by Prime Minister Shamir, to accept the invitation of participating in the Middle East Peace Conference, sponsored jointly by the United States and the Soviet Union, to be held in Madrid on October 30. Sixteen ministers voted in favour, and the three who voted against, were, Ariel Sharon, Minister of Housing, Yuval Ne'eman, Minister of Science and Technology and Rehavam Ze'evi, Minister-without Portfolio.

The *Central African Zionist Digest*, a monthly publication of the C.A. Zionist Organization

ing the previous four years. At the end of the 1980s Harare was without professional spiritual leadership.

The policy of "reconciliation" advocated by the prime minister, the Hon. Robert G. Mugabe, at the time of independence in April 1980 has been strictly honored by the regime. There has been little, if any, evidence of classical anti-Semitism, except for one small broadcasting incident which was promptly dealt with by the minister of information after intervention by the Board of Deputies. Nonetheless, the ceaseless activities of the P.L.O. "embassy" in Zimbabwe, coupled with the fact that it has been recognized by the government which has officially declared its policy as "anti-Israel" and "anti-Zionist," have irked members of the community and given them a disturbing sense of unease. It is felt that the future of a once proud and vital Jewish entity is in jeopardy. [G.Ros/I.J.A.]

ZIONIST CONGRESSES (16:1164). The 30th–32nd World Zionist Congresses, all convened within the decade under review, exhibit several noteworthy trends. The meetings have become progressively less ideological, of shorter duration, attended by more delegates who represent more world Jewish organizations — and have been increasingly democratic. Yet the World Zionist Organization has less status in the Jewish world than in previous periods and has lost substantial power to its offspring, the Jewish Agency.

In 1982, the 30th Congress had 656 accredited representatives; two congresses later, 721 delegates were accredited to the congress. The 32nd Congress was also the first at which an incumbent chairman of the World Zionist Executive, running for a second term, was challenged by another candidate.

The 30th Zionist Congress met December 7–17, 1982. Even before it opened there were numerous appeals to the Zionist High Court protesting alleged infringements of democratic practices during elections. The High Court felt it had no recourse but to disqualify all representatives of Zionist parties and groupings in the U.S. Meeting in extraordinary session three days before the congress opened, the Zionist General Council decided to make an unprecedented exception and passed a resolution which empowered the High Court itself to apportion mandates on a one-time basis. The court reluctantly complied. In a judgment against a previous attempt by the Zionist General Council to bypass holding elections for the congress, Dr. Moshe Landau wrote, "This is not petty legalistic quibbling... when Zionism is attacked and slandered on all sides by the enemies of the Jewish people, it is doubly important that Zionism zealously guard its image as a movement which maintains its own democratic principles."

Worldwide, five election districts held direct elections, indirect elections were conducted in four, but 16 districts opted for a system of mutually agreed lists instead of elections.

The 31st Congress, December 6–11, 1987, was on the whole a democratically elected congress, boasting a considerable number of first-time delegates. The American Zionist Federation conducted a nationwide election by mail, supervised by the independent American Arbitration Association, in which 183,000 valid votes were cast. However in electoral districts outside the U.S., only 40,000 people actually voted in elections.

The major groups represented at the congress, by size of representation, were Likkud, Labor Zionist Movement, Confederation of United Zionists, Mizrachi, Arzenu (Reform), Mapam, Mercaz (Conservative), Tzomet and Teḥiyyah. The results showed major gains for the relatively new Zionist organizations of the Reform and Conservative movements, which ate into the traditional base of support held by Hadassah and the Zionist Organization of America. For the first time since 1948, the balance of power in negotiations to form a coalition was held by a bloc representing the Diaspora, composed of the Confederation, Arzenu, and Mercaz. These groups joined with Labor and Mapam to form a majority.

Simcha Dinitz, of Labor, was elected chairman of the World Zionist Organization Executive; Meir Shitreet, of Ḥerut, was elected treasurer.

The issue of religious pluralism in Israel was a major focus of concern at the 31st Congress due to the increased presence of the Reform and Conservative movements. The congress passed a resolution which called for the "complete equality of rights to all streams of the Jewish religion and [for] granting their rabbis the legal right to perform all life cycle events and other rabbinic functions". This decision was the cause of much agitation in the ranks of the Mizrachi delegation as well as among Orthodox delegates in other groups.

The 32nd Zionist Congress, July 26–30, 1992, was the tenth to be held in Jerusalem since the establishment of the

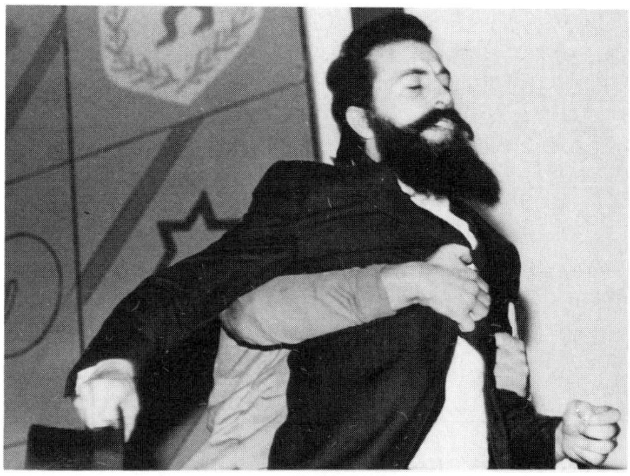

Man dressed as Theodor Herzl being forcibly removed from 31st Zionist Congress, December 7, 1987 (GPO, Jerusalem)

State. There were ten plenary sessions, four of which were of a cultural and festive nature. Consequently the work of the congress, traditionally marked by earnest debate, was mainly conducted in the committees which submitted their resolutions for ratification at the closing plenary.

The resolutions fell into two categories, declarative and practical. Since the Resolutions Committee which processes the decisions of the various committees before they can be put to a vote at the plenary does not permit any operational resolution which has a budgetary component attached to it, most of the resolutions tend to be declarative.

Simcha Dinitz was re-elected Chairman by a majority of almost 80 percent. A precedent of sorts was established when the losing candidate's faction (Arzenu) was excluded from the Executive which customarily is a wall-to-wall coalition rather than a majority cabinet.

On the whole changes that have occurred in the WZO since the 31st Congress both reflect and are caused by a younger, Israeli-born leadership which tends to be less ideological and more pragmatic.

Simcha Dinitz and Meir Shitreet overlooked the legacy to revitalize contemporary Zionist ideology by reformulating some of its tenets mandated to them by Arye Dulzin in his last years in office. Dinitz chose to operate primarily in the Jewish Agency field abandoning the ideological thrust of the Herẓliyyah Process of 1983. At a meeting held at the home of the president of Israel in 1990, called to discuss "The WZO, Changes in Ideology and Status," Dinitz said, "In essence the crisis confronting the Zionist movement is not ideological but functional. Whereas the WZO is somewhat shabby, dusty, oversensitive, and not terribly efficient, the Jewish Agency is business-like, healthful, robust, and efficient. It is also more ruthless."

Four matters of vital Zionist importance failed to be substantively addressed by the 32nd Congress. These were the diminished standing of Zionist Federations throughout the world; the options regarding partnership with the fundraisers in the Jewish Agency: unification or dissolution; the change in the thrust of the Settlement Department — once the flagbearer of Zionist pioneering — to a Jewish Agency department of urban and rural welfare; and finally, the transfer of increasingly large segments of *aliyah* and absorption work to government care.

Looming in the background of the 32nd Congress was the notion that, in reality, the World Zionist Organization had outlived its mandate. There were some who felt that since the WZO had failed to come to terms with essential aspects central to itself, a courageous discussion was called for and that the 33rd Zionist Congress, which will also be the centenary conclave since the first World Zionist Congress was convened in Basle, could be an appropriate occasion.

[AM.H.]

Necrology

ADLER, STELLA, d. 1992, **2**:271; **15**:1077
ADMON, YEDIDYAH, d. 1981, **2**:292
AGRANAT, SHIMON, d. 1992, **2**:373
AGUS, IRVING A., d. 1984, **2**:434
AGUS, JACOB BERNARD, d. 1986, **2**:435
AKZIN, BENJAMIN, d. 1985, **2**:504
ALFRINK, BERNHARDUS JOHANNES, d. 1987, **2**:607
ALMOGI, YOSEF AHARON, d. 1991, **2**:662
ALTMANN, ALEXANDER, d. 1987, **2**:779
AMIR, ANDA, d. 1981, **2**:848
ARDON, MORDECAI, d. 1992, **3**:401
ARLEN, HAROLD, d. 1986, **12**:681
ARONOW, DONALD, d. 1987, **15**:312
ARONSON, DAVID, d. 1988, **3**:494
ASCH, MOSES, d. 1986, **13**:1618
ASHBEL, DOV, d. 1989, **1**:27; **3**:695
ASHENHEIM, NEVILLE, d. 1984, **3**:699
ASHTOR, ELIAHU, d. 1984, **3**:737
ASIMOV, ISAAC, d. 1992, **3**:748
ASSAF, MICHAEL, d. 1983, **10**:309
ASTOR, ALEXANDER, d. 1988, **3**:839
AUB, MAX, d. 1972, **3**:838
AUSUBEL, NATHAN, d. 1986, **3**:907
AVIGAD, NAHMAN, d. 1992, **3**:961
AVRUTICK, ABRAHAM N., d. 1982, **7**:1360
AXELROD, NATAN, d. 1987, **12**:460

BAMBERGER, FRITZ, d. 1984, **4**:151
BAND, MAX, d. 1974, **4**:158
BARAM, MOSHE, d. 1986, **Dc./17**:171
BARON, SALO WITTMAYER, d. 1989, **1**:28, **4**:253
BAR-YOSEF, YEHOSHUA, d. 1992, **4**:286
BASHEVIS SINGER, ISAAC, d. 1991, **4**:293
BASS, ALFIE, d. 1987, **15**:1054
BASS, HYMAN B., d. 1983, **4**:313
BATSHAW, HARRY, d. 1984, **4**:327
BEGIN, MENAHEM, d. 1992, **4**:392; **Dc./17**:175
BEIN, ALEXANDER, d. 1988, **4**:401
BEN-AMI, OVED, d. 1988, **4**:460
BEN-AMOTZ, DAHN, d. 1989, **4**:462
BENDER, MORRIS BORIS, d. 1983, **4**:477
BENEDEK, THERESE F., d. 1977, **4**:481
BEN-HAIM, PAUL, d. 1984, **4**:517
BENTOV (GUTGELD), MORDEKHAI, d. 1985, **4**:555
BENTWICH, JOSEPH D., d. 1982, **4**:557
BEN-YEHUDAH, BARUKH, d. 1990, **4**:569
BEN-ZION, d. 1987, **4**:574
BERENDSOHN, WALTER, d. 1984, **Dc./17**:183
BERGNER, ELIZABETH, d. 1986, **4**:617
BERKOVITS, ELIEZER, d. 1992, **4**:633
BERLIN, IRVING, d. 1989, **4**:657
BERLINGER, ELIEZER, d. 1985, **16**:37
BERMAN, JACOB, d. 1984, **4**:666
BERMAN, MORTON MAYER, d. 1986, **4**:667
BERNARDI, HERSCHEL, d. 1986, **15**:1078
BERNAYS, PAUL ISAAC, d. 1977, **4**:674
BERNBACH, WILIAM, d. 1982, **4**:674
BERNSTEIN, LEONARD, d. 1990, **4**:686
BERNSTEIN, PHILIP SIDNEY, d. 1985, **4**:688
BESICOVITCH, ABRAM SAMOILOVITCH, d. 1970, **4**:703
BESSIS, ALBERT, d. 1972, **4**:709
BETTELHEIM, BRUNO, d. 1990, **4**:776
BICKERMAN, ELIAS JOSEPH, d. 1981, **4**:978
BILETZKI, ISRAEL HAYYIM, d. 1992, **4**:995
BIN-GORION, IMMANUEL, d. 1987, **4**:595
BIRNBAUM, PHILIP, d. 1988, **4**:1042
BIRNBAUM, SOLOMON, d. 1989, **4**:1042
BLANK, SHELDON HAAS, d. 1989, **4**:1072
BLANKFORT, MICHAEL S., d. 1982, **15**:1579
BLAU JOSEPH LEON, d. 1986, **4**:1075
BLOCH, FELIX, d. 1983, **4**:1099
BLOCK, MOSES RUDOLPH, d. 1985, **Dc./17**:193
BLOOMINGDALE, ALFRED S., d. 1982, **4**:1134
BLUME, PETER, d. 1992, **4**:1139
BLUMENKRANTZ, BERNHARD, d. 1989, **1**:28, **4**:1141
BOHM, DAVID, d. 1992, **4**:1182
BOKSER, BEN-ZION, d. 1984, **4**:1184
BOLOTOWSKY, ILYA, d. 1981, **3**:597
BORGES, JORGE LUIS 1986, **15**:255
BRAUDE, MAX, d. 1982, **4**:1315
BRAUDE, WILLIAM GORDON, d. 1088, **4**:1315
BRAUN, FELIX, d. 1973, **4**:1318
BREUER, MARCEL, d. 1979, **Dc./17**:197
BRICKMAN, WILLIAM IW., d. 1986, **1**:28

BRILLING, BERNHARD, d. 1987, **4**:1375
BRONFMAN, GERALD, d. 1986, **4**:1405
BRUCE, FREDERICK FYVIE, d. 1990, **1**:28
BRUNSCHVIG, ROBERT, d. 1990, **4**:1420
BUHLER, CHARLOTTE, d. 1974, **4**:1468
BULOFF, JOSEPH, d. 1985, **4**:1497
BUNSHAFT, GORDON, d. 1990, **4**:1507
BURNS, ARTHUR FRANK, d. 1987, **4**:1530
BURROWS, ABE, d. 1985, **15**:1079
BURSTEIN, PESACH, d. 1986, **4**:1531

CARNOVSKY, MORRIS, d. 1992, **15**:1080
CASPER, BERNARD, d. 1988, **5**:228
CASTEL, MOSHE ELAZAR, d. 1991, **5**:236
CHAGALL, MARC, d. 1985, **5**:318
CHAVEL, CHARLES (DOV) BER, d. 1982, **5**:366
CHODOROV, EDWARD, d. 1988, **15**:1080
CHURGIN, YAAKOV YEHOSHUA, d. 1990, **5**:558
CLURMAN, HAROLD, d. 1980, **5**:619
COHEN, BENJAMIN VICTOR, d. 1983, **5**:667
COHEN, GERSON, d. 1991, **16**:1266; **Dc./17**:211
COHEN, JOHN MICHAEL, d. 1989, **6**:785, 787
COHEN, MARCEL, d. 1974, **5**:681
COHEN, NAT, d. 1988, **15**:311
COHEN, SIR REX ARTHUR LOUIS, d. 1988, **5**:661
COHEN, RUTH LOUISA, d. 1991, **5**:685
COHEN, WILBUR JOSEPH, d. 1987, **5**:686
COMAY, MICHAEL SAUL, d. 1987, **5**:758
COOPER, IRVING, d. 1985, **11**:1201
COPLAND, AARON, d. 1990, **5**:954
COURANT, RICHARD, d. 1972, **5**:1003
CROHN, BURRILL BERNARD, d. 1983, **5**:1125
CROWN, HENRY, d. 1990, **5**:1130
CUKOR, GEORGE, d. 1983, **12**:465
CUNNINGHAM, SIR ALAN G., d. 1983, **8**:470

DAGHANI, ARNOLD, d. 1985, **3**:575
DAHLBERG, EDWARD, d. 1977, 5:1224
DALVEN, RAE, d. 1992, **1**:129
DANIN, EZRA, d. 1984, **5**:1295
DASSAULT, MARCEL, d. 1985, **5**:1310
D'AVIGDOR-GOLDSMID, JAMES ARTHUR, d. 1987, **5**:1368
DESCHIN, JACOB, d. 1983, **13**:486
DIEZ MACHO, ALEJANDRO, d. 1985, **6**:45
DON-YAHIA, SHABBETAI, d. 1981, **6**:170
DORATI, ANTAL, d. 1988, **Dc./17**:223
DRAPKIN, ISRAEL, d. 1990, **6**:208
DUBINSKY, DAVID, d. 1982, **6**:246
DUBNOW-ERLICH, SOPHIA, d. 1986, **6**:844
DUJOVNE, LEON, d. 1984, **6**:265
DUKER, ABRAHAM GORDON, d. 1987, **6**:266
DULZIN, ARYE LEIB, d. 1989, **Dc./17**:224
DUPONT-SOMMER, ANDRÉ, d. 1983, **6**:275
DU PRÉ, JACQUELINE, d. 1987, **Dc./17**:477

EISENBERG, AZRIEL LOUIS, d. 1985, **5**:451
ELATH, ELIAHU, d. 1990, **6**:570
ELHANANI, ARYEH, d. 1985, **Dc./17**:232
EMANUEL, ISAAC SAMUEL, d. 1972, **6**:726
EPSTEIN, JUDITH, d. 1988, **6**:833
ETTINGER, SAMUEL, d. 1988, **Dc./17**:240

FAJANS, CASIMIR, d. 1975, **6**:1139
FAJANS, ISAAC, d. 1985, **16**:358
FALK, LEON, Jr., d. 1988, **6**:1155
FEINBERG, ABRAHAM L., d. 1986, **6**:1211
FEINBERG, CHARLES E., d. 1988, **5**:311; 1572
FEINBERG, NATHAN, d. 1988, **6**:1212
FEINSTEIN, MOSES, d. 1986, **6**:1213
FEITELSON, DINAH, d. 1992, **Dc./17**:245
FELDMAN, MORTON, d. 1987, **Dc./17**:246
FIELDS, JACK, d. 1987, **12**:1376; **15**:305
FINKEL, JOSHUA, d. 1983, **6**:1291
FINKELSTEIN, LOUIS, d. 1991, **6**:1293
FOREMAN, CARL, d. 1984, **12**:467
FORTAS, ABE, d. 1982, **6**:1441
FORTES, MEYER, d. 1983, **6**:1442
FRAENKEL, JOSEF, d. 1987, **1**:30
FRAENKEL, OSMOND K., d. 1983, **10**:1508
FRANCK, ISAAC, d. 1985, **16**:358
FRANKENSTEIN, CARL, d. 1990, **7**:82
FRANKFURTER, DAVID, d. 1982, **7**:94
FRANZBLAU, ABRAHAM NORMAN, d. 1982, **7**:109
FREEHOF, SOLOMON BENNETT, d. 1990, **7**:121
FREIER, RECHA, d. 1984, **7**:134
FREIMAN, LAWRENCE, d. 1987, **7**:135
FRENKEL, IZHAK YEDIDIAH, d. 1986, **Dc./17**:255
FREUD, ANNA, d. 1982, **7**:160
FREUND, PAUL ARTHUR, d. 1992, **7**:168
FRIED, MORTON HERBERT, d. 1986, **7**:171
FRIEDMAN, THEODORE, d. 1992, **7**:189
FRISCH, LEO, d. 1984, **12**:37
FRISCH, OTTO ROBERT, d. 1979, **7**:198
FRYE, PETER, d. 1991, **12**:1343

GALILI, ISRAEL, d. 1986, **7**:270
GAMORAN, ISRAEL, d. 1984, **5**:451
GAMZU, HAYYIM, d. 1982, **7**:308
GASTER, THEODOR HERZL, d. 1992, **7**:333
GELBER, LIONEL, d. 1989, **7**:363
GELBER, MARVIN, d. 1990, **7**:363
GELBRUN, ARTUR, d. 1985, **12**:690
GERSHWIN, IRA, d. 1983, **7**:518
GERSON-KIWI, EDITH (ESTHER), d. 1992, **7**:519
GILDESGAME, PIERRE, d. 1981, **11**:665
GILELES, EMIL, d. 1985, **7**:572
GINSBERG, HAROLD LOUIS, d. 1990, **1**:30; **7**:580
GINSBURG, DAVID, d. 1988, **5**:382
GINZBURG, NATALIA, d. 1991, **7**:586
GLATZER, NAHUM NORBERT, d. 1990, **7**:616
GLUCK, MAXWELL, d. 1984, **Dc./17**:561
GLUCKMAN, HENRY, d. 1987, **7**:625
GODDARD, PAULETTE, d. 1990, **12**:468
GODOWSKY, LEOPOLD, d. 1983, **7**:687
GOITEIN, SHLOMO DOV, d. 1985, **7**:694

Goldberg, Alexander, d. 1985, **7**:698
Goldberg, Arthur Joseph, d. 1990, **7**:698
Goldberg, Nathan, d. 1979, **15**:68
Goldmann, Nahum, d. 1982, **7**:723
Goldsmith, Raymond William, d. 1988, **7**:737
Goldstein, Israel, d. 1986, **7**:747
Goldstein, Nathaniel, d. 1981, **12**:1127
Goldstein, Reuben, d. 1984, **15**:306
Goldstein, Sidney, d. 1989, **7**:749
Golomb, Abraham, d. 1982, **7**:763
Goodman, Benny, d. 1986, **7**:779
Goodman, Percival, d. 1989, **7**:782
Gordis, Robert, d. 1992, **7**:789
Grade, Chaim, d. 1982, **7**:843
Graubart, David, d. 1984, **5**:415
Greenberg, Hank, d. 1986, **7**:904
Greene, Lorne, d. 1987, **15**:1083
Gross, Chaim, d. 1991, **7**:933
Grossman, Ladislav, d. 1981, **5**:1209
Grunwald, Kurt, d. 1990, **7**:951
Guggenheim, Marguerite (Peggy), d. 1979, **7**:967
Gunzburg, Niko, d. 1984, **7**:979
Guttman, Louis, d. 1987, **7**:992

Haas, Willy, d. 1973, **7**:1010
Haber, Samuel L., d. 1984, **7**:1022
Haber, William, d. 1988, **12**:1485
Hacohen, David, d. 1984, **7**:1038
Hager, Hayyim, d. 1979, **16**:199
Halkin, Abraham Solomon, d. 1990, **1**:31; **7**:1191
Halkin, Simon, d. 1987, **7**:1192
Halper, Albert, d. 1984, **7**:1202
Halpern, Benjamin, d. 1990, **7**:1203
Halpern, Harry, d. 1981, **12**:1119
Hanft, Benjamin, d. 1985, **13**:1363
Harman, Avraham, d. 1992, **7**:1344
Hart, Herbert Lionel Adolphus, d. 1992, **7**:1356
Hauser, Emill, d. 1978, **12**:692
Hausner, Gideon, d. 1990, **7**:1479
Hazan, Ya'akov, d. 1992, **7**:1523
Heifetz, Jascha, d. 1987, **8**:260
Held, Moshe, d. 1984, **16**:1508
Hellman, Lillian Florence, d. 1984, **8**:315
Herbstein, Joseph, d. 1983, **8**:343
Herman, Woody, d. 1987, **12**:1122
Hiller, Kurt, d. 1972, **8**:491
Him, George, d. 1982, **3**:602
Hobson, Laura Z., d. 1986, **15**:1581
Hoffman, Isidore B., d. 1981, **8**:808
Hofstadter, Robert, d. 1990, **8**:813
Hook, Sidney, d. 1989, **8**:969
Horovitz, Vladimir, 1989, **8**:983
Houseman, John, d. 1988, **15**:1085
Hyman, Cecil, d. 1981, **8**:1143
Hyman, Herbert, d. 1985, **15**:68

Ikor, Roger, d. 1986, **8**:1244
Indelman, Elhanan, d. 1983, **5**:457

Jabes, Edmond, d. 1991, **7**:150
Jacobs, James ("Jimmy"), d. 1988, **15**:310
Jacobson, Sydney, d. 1988, **9**:1242
Jacoby, Oswald, d. 1984, **9**:1245
Jaffe, Benjamin, d. 1986, **9**:1263
Jaffe, Sam, d. 1984, **12**:468
Jakobson, Roman, d. 1982, **9**:1271
James, Harry, d. 1983, **12**:694
Janco, Marcel, d. 1984, **9**:1275
Jankelevitch, Vladimir, d. 1985, **9**:1276
Janner, Barnett, Lord, d. 1982, **9**:1276
Janowitz, Morris, d. 1988, **9**:1278
Javits, Jacob Koppel, d. 1986, **9**:1302
Jessel, Richard Frederick, d. 1988, **10**:6
Jones, Hans, d. 1993, **10**:181
Jung, Leo, d. 1987, **10**:471

Kagan, Rachel, d. 1982, **16**:594
Kahn, Richard Ferdinand, Lord, d. 1989, **10**:692
Kaldor, Nicholas, d. 1986, **10**:704
Kamenetzky, Jacob, d. 1986, **10**:726
Kantorovich, Leonid, d. 1986, **Dc./17**:434
Kapitza, Peter Leonidovich, d. 1984, **10**:747
Kaplan, Joseph, d. 1991, **10**:750
Kaplan, Mordecai Menahem, d. 1983, **10**:751
Kasher, Menahem, d. 1983, **10**:807
Kassil, Lev Abramovich, d. 1970, **10**:813
Katz, Katriel, d. 1988, **16**:697
Katz, Sholom, d. 1982, **7**:1548
Kaufman, Benjamin, d. 1981, **11**:1552
Kaverin, Benjamin Aleksandrovich, d. 1990, **10**:851
Kaye, Danny, d. 1987, **10**:853
Kaye, Nora, d. 1987, **10**:854
Kelman, Wolfe, d. 1990, **10**:901
Kenaani, David, d. 1982, **10**:905
Kipnis, Levin, d. 1990, **10**:1038
Kirsanov, Semyon Isaacovich, d. 1972, **10**:1049
Kisch, Guido, d. 1986, **10**:1062
Klarman, Yosef, d. 1985, **Dc./17**:438
Klatzkin, Raphael, d. 1987, **16**:212
Klein, Ernest, d. 1984, **Dc./17**:348
Klein, Julius, d. 1984, **10**:1100
Klopfer, Donald, d. 1986, **13**:1371
Knopf, Alfred A., d. 1984, **10**:1116
Koestler, Arthur, d. 1983, **10**:1132
Kogan, Leonid Borissovich, d. 1982, **10**:1134
Kohs, Samuel Calmin, d. 1984, **10**:1148
Kol, Moshe, d. 1989, **10**:1158
Komroff, Manuel, d. 1974, **15**:1582
Kook, Zevi Yehudah, d. 1982, **10**:1187
Kormendi, Ferenc, d. 1972, **10**:1205
Kormis, Frederick, d. 1986, **Dc./17**:441
Korn, Rachel, d. 1982, **10**:1205
Koussevitsky, David, d. 1985, **10**:1227
Kramer, Samuel Noah, d. 1990, **10**:1238
Krasna, Norman, d. 1984, **12**:469
Krasner, Lee, d. 1984, **3**:604

KREISKY, BRUNO, d. 1990, **10**:1254
KRESSEL, GETZEL, d. 1986, **10**:1260
KROOK (KRANK), DOROTHEA, d. 1989, **Dc./17**:442
KRULEWITCH, MELVIN LEVIN, d. 1978, **11**:1574
KUZNETS, SIMON, d. 1985, **10**:1306

LACRETELLE, JACQUES DE, d. 1985, **10**:1342
LAND, EDWIN, d. 1991, **10**:1384
LANDA, ABRAM, d. 1989, **10**:1384
LASKI, MARGHANITA, d. 1988, **10**:1438
LASKIN, BORA, d. 1984, **10**:1439
LAWSON, JOHN HOWARD, d. 1977, **15**:1582
LEFTWICH, JOSEPH, d. 1983, **10**:1564
LEHRMAN, SIMON MAURICE, d. 1988, **5**:450
LENGYEL, EMIL, d. 1985, **10**:313
LERNER, ABBA PETACHJA, d. 1982, **11**:41
LERNER, ALAN JAY, d. 1986, **11**:42
LERNER, MAX, d. 1992, **11**:43
LE ROY, MERVYN, d. 1987, **12**:470
LESLIE, ROBERT L., d. 1987, **11**:47
LEVENE, HARRY, d. 1988, **15**:306
LEVI, PRIMO, d. 1987, **11**:85
LEVINE, JOSEPH E., d. 1987, **12**:470
LEVINTHAL, ISRAEL HERBERT, d. 1982, **11**:121
LEVISKY, FERNANDO, d. 1982, **15**:255
LEVY, PAUL, d. 1971, **11**:160
LEWENTHAL, RAYMOND, d. 1988, **Dc./17**:479
LICHTWITZ, HANS (URI NAOR), d. 1988, **13**:1026; **14**:1120
LIEBERMAN, SAUL, d. 1983, **11**:218
LIPMAN, VIVIAN DAVID, d. 1990, **Dc./17**:453
LIPMANN, FRITZ ALBERT, d. 1986, **11**:282
LIPSKY, ELEAZAR, d. 1993, **11**:296
LIPTON, SEYMOUR, d. 1986, **11**:297
LISHANSKY, BATYA, d. 1992, **3**:605
LIVINGSTONE, MARY, d. 1983, **15**:1078
LOCKER, MALKE, d. 1990, **11**:421
LOCKSPEISER, SIR BEN, d. 1990, **11**:422
LOEBL, EUGEN, d. 1987, **11**:441
LOEWE, FREDERICK, d. 1988, **12**:698
LOEWENSTAM, AYALA, d. 1987, **1**:33
LONDON, ARTHUR, d. 1986, **11**:482
LOTHAR, ERNST, d. 1974, **11**:509
LOURIE, ARTHUR, d. 1966, **12**:698
LYONS, EUGENE, d. 1984, **10**:313

MACHLUP, FRITZ, d. 1983, **11**:669
MAGNIN, EDGAR F., 1984, **11**:718
MAISELS, MOSES HAYYIM, d. 1984, **11**:793
MALAMUD, BERNARD, d. 1986, **11**:819
MALAVSKY, SAMUEL, d. 1985, **7**:1549
MALTZ, ALBERT, d. 1985, **11**:833
MANCROFT, STORMONT, d. 1987, **11**:861
MANDEL, ARNOLD, d. 1987, **11**:863
MANN, DANIEL, d. 1991, **12**:451, 471
MANN, FREDERIC RAND, d. 1987, **11**:880
MARKUS, RIXI, d. 1992, **5**:169
MARSHALL, JAMES, d. 1986, **11**:1062
MATAS, ROY, d. 1986, **16**:551
MEDAN, MEIR, d. 1989, **1**:34
MENDES-FRANCE, PIERRE, d. 1982, **11**:1345
MENKES, ZYGMUNT, d. 1986, **11**:1354
MEYER, ERNST HERMANN, d. 1988, **12**:700
MEYERHOFF, JOSEPH, d. 1985, **11**:1468
MICHAELSON, ISAAC CHESAR, d. 1982, **11**:1492
MIKES, GEORGE, d. 1988, **6**:789
MILLER, LOUIS, d. 1988, **1**:34; **11**:1581
MILLER, RAY, d. 1987, **15**:306
MILSTEIN, NATHAN, d. 1992, **11**:1587
MITIN, MARK BORISOVICH, d. 1987, **12**:160
MIZLER, HARRY, d. 1990, **15**:306
MOCATTA, SIR ALAN ABRAHAM, d. 1990, **12**:198
MOCH, JULES SALVADOR, d. 1985, **12**:199
MOMIGLIANO, ARNALDO DANTE, d. 1987, **12**:235
MONTAGU, EWEN EDWARD, d. 1985, **12**:264
MONTOR, HENRY, d. 1982, **12**:281
MORAVIA, ALBERTO, d. 1990, **12**:305

NACHMANSON, DAVID, d. 1983, **4**:1032
NAGEL, ERNEST, d. 1985, **12**:757
NAROT, JOSEPH, d. 1980, **12**:832
NATHAN, ROBERT, d. 1985, **12**:856
NAUMBERG, MARGARET, d. 1983, **12**:895
NEHER, ANDRÉ, d. 1988, **12**:939
NEMEROV, HOWARD, d. 1991, **15**:1578, 1583
NEUMANN, ROBERT, d. 1975, **12**:1013
NEVELSON, LOUISE, d. 1988, **3**:606

OLAN, LEVI A., d. 1984, **16**:633
OLLENDORF, FRANZ, d. 1981, **12**:1368
OLSHAN, ISAAC, d. 1983, **12**:1371
OMER, HILLEL, d. 1990, **12**:1389
ORLINSKY, HARRY MEYER, d. 1992, **12**:1471
ORMANDY, EUGENE, d. 1985, **12**:702

PACIFICI, ALFONSO, d. 1983, **13**:5
PAGEL, WALTER, d. 1983, **13**:13
PALEY, WILLIAM SAMUEL, d. 1989, **13**:41
PASTERNAK, JOSEPH, d. 1991, **12**:449, 472
PATAI, EDITH, d. 1976, **13**:178
PEDERSEN, JOHANNES, d. 1951, **13**:210
PEERCE, JAN, d. 1984, **13**:211
PERELMAN, CHAIM, d. 1983, **13**:275
PERLZWEIG, MAURICE L., d. 1985, **13**:298
PETUCHOWSKI, JAKOB JOSEF, d. 1991, **13**:349
PEVSNER, SIR NIKOLAUS, d. 1983, **13**:350
PFEFFER, LEO, d. 1993, **13**:355
PHILLIPS, LAZARUS, d. 1987, **13**:406
PICON, MOLLY, d. 1992, **13**:501
PINCHERELE, MARC, d. 1974, **12**:702
PODOLOFF, MAURICE, d. 1985, **15**:304
POLIER, JUSTINE WISE, d. 1987, **16**:568
POLOTSKY, HANS JACOB, d. 1991, **13**:837
POPKIN, ZELDA, d. 1983, **15**:1573
POPPER, HANS, d. 1988, **11**:1202
POSTAN, MICHAEL MOISSEYY, d. 1981, **13**:931
PRAWER, JOSHUA, d. 1990, **13**:978

PREMINGER, OTTO LUDWIG, d. 1986, **13**:1014
PRINZ, JOACHIM, d. 1988, **13**:1116

QUASTEL, JUDAH HIRSCH, d. 1987, **13**:1420

RABI, ISIDOR ISAAC, d. 1988, **13**:1469
RABINOWITZ, LOUIS ISAAC, d. 1984, **13**:1477
RACHMILEWITZ, MOSHE, d. 1985, **13**:1493
RAMBERT, DAME MARIE, d. 1982, **13**:1539
RAPAPORT, NATHAN, d. 1987, **3**:608
RAUH, JOSEPH L., d. 1992, **13**:1575
REPETUR, BERL, d. 1989, **5**:1455
RESHEVSKY, SAMUEL, d. 1992, **14**:82
REVIV, HANOCH, d. 1990, **1**:36
RIBALOW, HAROLD URIEL, d. 1982, **14**:150
RICKOVER, HYMAN GEORGE, d. 1986, **14**:164
RIEGELMAN, HAROLD, d. 1982, **14**:165
RIMALT, ELIMELEKH, d. 1988, **8**:1379; **9**:680
RITZ, HARRY, d. 1986, **12**:473
RITZ, JIMMY, d. 1985, **12**:473
ROGERS, BERNARD, d. 1968, **12**:704
ROKEAH, DAVID, d. 1985, **14**:226
ROMANO, EMANUEL, d. 1985, **7**:619
ROSE, LEONARD, d. 1984, **Dc./17**:480
ROSEN, SHELOMO, d. 1985, **Dc./17**:528
ROSENAU, HELEN, d. 1984, **3**:650
ROSENBERG, ANNA M., d. 1983, **14**:276
ROSENBERG, STUART, d. 1990, **1**:36, **14**:279
ROSENSOHN, ETTA LASKER, d. 1966, **14**:290
ROSENSTEIN, ARTHUR, d. 1985, **13**:484
ROSENSTOCK, JOSEPH, d. 1985, **10**:463
ROTHENSTEIN, SIR JOHN, d. 1992, **14**:334
ROTHSCHILD, ALAIN DE, d. 1982, **14**:340
ROTHSCHILD, DOROTHY DE, d. 1988, **14**:1255
ROTHSCHILD, NATHANIEL MAYER VICTOR, LORD, d. 1990, **14**:347
ROTHSCHILD, PHILLIPE DE, d. 1988, **15**:318
ROUTTENBERG, MAX JONAH, d. 1987, **14**:354
RUBINSTEIN, ARTUR, d. 1982, **14**:374
RUDERMAN, JACOB ISAAC, d. 1987, **14**:379
RUDIN, JACOB PHILIP, d. 1982, **14**:379
RUDNICKI, ADOLF, d. 1990, **14**:380
RUZHIN, ISAAC (FRIEDMAN) OF BUHUSI, d. 1992, **14**:531
RYSKIND, MORRIE, d. 1985, **15**:1059

SACHER, MICHAEL, d. 1986, **14**:592
SACKHEIM, MAXWELL B., d. 1982, **2**:318
SADAN, DOV, d. 1989, **14**:618
SALMON, SIR CYRIL BARNET, d. 1991, **14**:688
SALMON, GEOFFREY, d. 1990, **14**:688
SAMBURSKY, SAMUEL, d. 1990, **14**:766
SANDAUER, ARTUR, d. 1989, **14**:765
SASSOON, SOLOMON DAVID, d. 1985, **14**:899
SCHACHT, AL(EXANDER), d. 1984, **15**:301
SCHEIBER, ALEXANDER, d. 1985, **14**:951
SCHIFF, DOROTHY, d. 1989, **14**:960
SCHIFF, JOHN M., d. 1987, **15**:312
SCHNEIDER, ALAN (ABRAM LEONIDOVICH), d. 1984, **15**:1090
SCHNEIDER, ALEXANDER, d. 1993, **12**:706
SCHNEIDER, ISIDOR, d. 1977, **15**:1574, 1583
SCHOCKEN, GERSHOM, b. 1912, d. 1990, **14**:987
SCHOLEM, GERSHOM GERHARD, d. 1982, **14**:991
SCHONFELD, HUGH, d. 1988, **Dc./17**:547
SCHONFELD, SOLOMON, d. 1984, **14**:994
SCHOTZ, BENNO, d. 1984, **14**:999
SCHUMAN, WILLIAM, d. 1985, **14**:1008
SCHWARTZ, ARTHUR, d. 1984, **15**:1059
SEELIGMAN, ISAAC LEO, d. 1982, **14**:1097
SEGAL, HENRY C., d. 1985, **2**:821
SEGAL, SAMUEL, LORD, d. 1985, **14**:1108
SEGHERS, ANNA, d. 1983, **14**:1110
SEGRÈ, EMILIO GINO, d. 1989, **14**:1113
SELIGSON, JULIUS, d. 1987, **15**:314
SERKIN, RUDOLF, d. 1991, **12**:707
SHALEV, YITZHAK, d. 1992, **14**:1266
SHALOM, SHIN, d. 1990, **14**:1271
SHALON, RAHEL, d. 1988, **8**:1433
SHAMRI, ARIE, d. 1978, **14**:1293
SHANKMAN, JACOB KESTIN, d. 1986, **14**:1294
SHAPIRO, HARRY LIONEL, d. 1990, **14**:303
SHARF, ZE'EV, d. 1984, **14**:1308
SHARON, ARYEH, d. 1984, **14**:1316
SHAW, IRWIN, d. 1984, **14**:1322
SHAW, SIR SEBAG, d. 1982, **10**:1495
SHEAR, MURRAY JACOB, d. 1983, **5**:87
SHINNAR, FELIX, d. 1985, **14**:72
SHINWELL, EMANUEL, d. 1986, **14**:1409
SHKLOVSKI, JOSEPH S., d. 1985, **3**:807
SHUSTER, ZACHARIAH, d. 1986, **5**:543
SIEGEL, IDA, d. 1982, **15**:1264
SIEGEL, SEYMOUR, d. 1988, **Dc./17**:556
SIEGEMEISTER, ELIE, d. 1991, **14**:1512
SIGNORET, SIMONE, d. 1985, **12**:474
SILKIN, JOHN, d. 1987, **14**:1540
SILKIN, SAMUEL, d. 1988, **14**:1540
SILVERS, PHIL, d. 1985, **15**:1091
SISKIND, AARON, d. 1991, **14**:1622
SKLARE, MARSHALL, d. 1992, **14**:1647
SKOLSKY, SIDNEY, d. 1983, **10**:307
SLOTKI, ISRAEL WOLF, d. 1988, **14**:1677
SMOLI, ELIEZER, d. 1970, **15**:12
SOFAER, ABRAHAM, d. 1988, **15**:1091
SOLOVEITCHIK, JOSEPH DOV, d. 1993, **15**:132
SONNEBORN, RUDOLF G., d. 1986, **15**:154
SONNTAG, JACOB, d. 1984, **6**:790
SOYER, RAPHAEL, d. 1987, **15**:216
SPERBER, MANNES, d. 1984, **15**:261
SPEWACK, BELLA, d. 1990, **15**:262
SPIEGEL, SAMUEL P., d. 1985, **12**:474
SPIEGEL, SHALOM, d. 1984, **15**:272
STEINBERG, MARTIN R., d. 1983, **11**:1210
STEINMAN, ELIEZER, d. 1970, **15**:372
STEMBER, CHARLES, d. 1982, **15**:68
STENCL, ABRAHAM NAHUM, d. 1983, **15**:379

STERN, CURT, d. 1981, **4**:1031
STERN, MAX, d. 1982, **15**:390
STONE, I. F., d. 1989, **10**:317
STONE, IRVING, d. 1984, **15**:1584
STONE, JULIUS, d. 1985, **15**:413
STRASBERG, LEE, d. 1982, **15**:421
STROOCK, ALAN, d. 1985, **15**:441
STUTSCHEWSKY, JOACHIM, d. 1982, **15**:461
SULZBERGER, MARION, d. 1983, **11**:1201
SUSSKIND, DAVID, d. 1987, **15**:1091
SZERYING, HENRYK, d. 1988, **12**:710
SYRKIN, MARIE, d. 1989, **15**:650

TABIB, MORDEKHAI, d. 1979, **15**:690
TALPIR, GABRIEL JOSEPH, d. 1990, **15**:779
TAMIR, SHMUEL, d. 1987, **Dc./17**:575
TAMMUZ, BENJAMIN, d. 1989, **15**:789
TANENBAUM, MARC, d. 1992, **13**:1253
TANENBAUM, SIDNEY, d. 1988, **15**:303
TARTAKOWER, ARIEH, d. 1982, **15**:826
TEDESCHI, GAD, d. 1992, **15**:897
TISCHLER, MAX, d. 1989, **5**:388
TISHBY, ISAIAH, d. 1992, **15**:1153
TOPOLSKI, FELIX, d. 1989, **Dc./17**:583
TOUBIN, ISAAC, d. 1986, **2**:819
TOV, MOSHE, d. 1989, **10**:1455
TRIOLET, ELSA, d. 1970, **15**:1396
TSUR, JACOB, d. 1990, **15**:1417
TUCHMAN, BARBARA WERTHEIM, d. 1989, **15**:1421
TURKOW, JONAS, d. 1988, **15**:1464
TURKOW, MARK, d. 1983, **15**:1464
TWORKOV, JACK, d. 1982, **3**:612

URI, AVIVA, d. 1989, **3**:612
URIS, HAROLD, d. 1982, **16**:9

VEINER, HARRY, d. 1992, **16**:85
VINEBERG, ARTHUR, d. 1988, **11**:1202
VISHNIAC, ROMAN, d. 1990, **16**:166
VOLTERRA, EDOARDO, d. 1984, **16**:221

WALLENSTEIN, ALFRED, d. 1982, **12**:713
WARBURG, EDWARD MORTIMER, d. 1992, **16**:285
WECHSLER, JAMES A., d. 1983, **10**:318
WEICHMANN, HERBERT, d. 1983, **16**:373
WEINER, LAZAR, d. 1982, **12**:713
WEINTRAUB, PHILIP (MICKEY), d. 1986, **15**:301
WEISS, PETER, d. 1982, **16**:415
WEISS-ROSMARIN, TRUDE, d. 1989, **16**:419
WELENSKY, SIR ROY, d. 1991, **16**:442
WELTSCH, ROBERT, d. 1982, **16**:447
WERNER, ERIC, d. 1988, **16**:452
WILLEN, JOSEPH, d. 1985, **16**:516
WINNICK, HENRY ZVI, d. 1982, **16**:549
WINTERNITZ, EMANUEL, d. 1983, **12**:714
WISCHNITZER, RACHEL, b. 1885, d. 1989, **16**:555
WISE, GEORGE SCHNEIWEIS, d. 1987, **16**:563
WISE, JAMES WATERMAN, d. 1983, **16**:568
WISEMAN, ADELE, d. 1992, **5**:116
WOLFSOHN, SIR ISAAC, d. 1991, **16**:619
WOLMAN, ABEL, d. 1989, **Dc./17**:620
WYZANKSI, CHARLES EWARD, Jr., d. 1986, **16**:682

YAARI (WALD), MEIR, d. 1987, **16**:691
YAARI, YEHUDAH, d. 1982, **16**:692
YADIN, YIGAEL, d. 1984, **16**:984
YALAN-STEKELIS, MIRIAM, d. 1984, **16**:694
YESHURUN, AVOT, d. 1992, **16**:773

ZARCHIN, ALEXANDER, d. 1988, **16**:935
ZARETZKI, JOSEPH, d. 1981, **12**:1127
ZARITZKY, YOSSEF, d. 1985, **16**:938
ZASLOFSKY, MAX, d. 1985, **15**:303
ZEFIRA, BRACHAH, b. 1911, d. 1990, **16**:968
ZIMBALIST, EFREM, d. 1985, **16**:1024
ZIMMERMAN, CHARLES SASCHA, d. 1983, **16**:1025
ZIPPER, YA'AKOV, d. 1983, **Dc./17**:638
ZMORA, YISRAEL, d. 1983, **16**:1190
ZOHARY, MICHAEL, d. 1983, **16**:1215
ZOLTY, BEZALEL, d. 1982, **Dc./17**:639
ZUCKERMAN, PAUL, d. 1986, **Dc./17**:1986

Glossary

Asterisked terms have separate entries in the Encyclopaedia.

Actions Committee, early name of the Zionist General Council, the supreme institution of the World Zionist Organization in the interim between Congresses. The Zionist Executive's name was then the "Small Actions Committee."

***Adar,** twelfth month of the Jewish religious year, sixth of the civil, approximating to February–March.

***Aggadah,** name given to those sections of Talmud and Midrash containing homiletic expositions of the Bible, stories, legends, folklore. anecdotes, or maxims. In contradistinction to **halakhah.*

***Agunah,** woman unable to remarry according to Jewish law, because of desertion by her husband or inability to accept presumption of death.

Aḥaronim, later rabbinic authorities. In contradistinction to **rishonim* ("early ones"). See **Dc./17:**134.

Ahavah, liturgical poem inserted in the second benediction of the morning prayer *(*Ahavah Rabbah)* of the festivals and/or special Sabbaths.

Aktion (Ger.), operation involving the mass assembly, deportation, and murder of Jews by the Nazis during the *Holocaust.

***Aliyah,** (1) being called to Reading of the Law in synagogue; (2) immigration to Ereẓ Israel; (3) one of the waves of immigration to Ereẓ Israel from the early 1880s.

***Amidah,** main prayer recited at all services; also known as *Shemoneh Esreh* and *Tefillah.*

***Amora** (pl. **amoraim**), title given to the Jewish scholars in Ereẓ Israel and Babylonia in the third to sixth centuries who were responsible for the **Gemara.*

Aravah, the *willow; one of the *Four Species used on *Sukkot ("festival of Tabernacles") together with the **etrog, hadas,* and **lulav.*

***Arvit,** evening prayer.

Asarah be-Tevet, fast on the 10th of Tevet commemorating the commencement of the siege of Jerusalem by Nebuchadnezzar.

Asefat ha-Nivḥarim, representative assembly elected by Jews in Palestine during the period of the British Mandate (1920–48).

***Ashkenaz,** name applied generally in medieval rabbinical literature to Germany.

***Ashkenazi** (pl. **Ashkenazim**), German or West-, Central-, or East-European Jew(s), as contrasted with *Sephardi(m).

***Av,** fifth month of the Jewish religious year, eleventh of the civil, approximating to July–August.

***Av bet din,** vice-president of the supreme court *(bet din ha-gadol)* in Jerusalem during the Second Temple period; later, title given to communal rabbis as heads of the religious courts (see **bet din*).

***Badḥan,** jester, particularly at traditional Jewish weddings in Eastern Europe.

***Bakkashah** (Heb. "supplication"), type of petitionary prayer, mainly recited in the Sephardi rite on Rosh Ha-Shanah and the Day of Atonement.

Bar, "son of . . ."; frequently appearing in personal names.

***Baraita** (pl. **baraitot**), statement of **tanna* not found in *Mishnah.

***Bar mitzvah,** ceremony marking the initiation of a boy at the age of 13 into the Jewish religious community.

Ben, "son of . . ."; frequently appearing in personal names.

Berakhah (pl. **berakhot**), *benediction, blessing; formula of praise and thanksgiving.

***Bet din** (pl. **battei din**), rabbinic court of law.

***Bet ha-midrash,** school for higher rabbinic learning; often attached to or serving as a synagogue.

***Bilu,** first modern movement for pioneering and agricultural settlement in Ereẓ Israel, founded in 1882 at Kharkov, Russia.

***Bund,** Jewish socialist party founded in Vilna in 1897, supporting Jewish national rights; Yiddishist, and anti-Zionist.

Cohen (pl. **Cohanim**), see Kohen

Community settlement *(yishuv kehillati),* a settlement to average 1,000–2,000 inhabitants, organized as a cooperative society imposing on its members duties on the community's behalf, but leaving them free in the choice of occupation, in the structure of their homes, etc.

***Conservative Judaism,** trend in Judaism developed in the United States in the 20th century which, while opposing extreme changes in traditional observances, permits certain modifications of *halakhah* in response to the changing needs of the Jewish people.

***Consistory** (Fr. *consistoire*), governing body of a Jewish communal district in France and certain other countries.

***Conservo(s),** term applied in Spain and Portugal to converted Jew(s), and sometimes more loosely to their descendants.

***Crypto-Jew,** term applied to a person who although observing outwardly Christianity (or some other religion) was at heart a Jew and maintained Jewish observances as far as possible (see Converso; Marrano; New Christian; Jadīd al-Islām).

***Dayyan,** member of rabbinic court.

Decisor, equivalent to the Hebrew *posek,* the rabbi who gives the decision *(halakhah)* in Jewish law or practice.

***Devekut,** "devotion"; attachment or adhesion to God; communion with God.

***Diaspora,** Jews living in the "dispersion" outside Ereẓ Israel; area of Jewish settlement outside Ereẓ Israel. (Cf. *galut.*)

Din, a law (both secular and religious), legal decision, or lawsuit.

Divan, diwan, collection of poems, especially in Hebrew, Arabic, or Persian.

Dunam, unit of land area (1,000 sq. m., c. 1/4 acre), used in Israel.

Einsatzgruppen, mobile units of Nazi S.S. and S.D.; in U.S.S.R. and Serbia, mobile killing units.

***Ein-Sof,** "without end"; "the infinite"; hidden, impersonal aspect of God; also used as a Divine Name.

***Elul,** sixth month of the Jewish religious calendar, 12th of the civil, precedes the High Holiday season in the fall.

Endloesung, see *Final Solution.

Ereẓ Israel, Land of Israel; Palestine.

***Eruv,** technical term for rabbinical provision permitting the alleviation of certain restrictions.

***Etrog,** citron; one of the *Four Species used on *Sukkot together with the **lulav, hadas,* and *aravah.*

Even ha-Ezer, see Shulḥan Arukh.
***Exilarch,** lay head of Jewish community in Babylonia (see also *resh galuta*), and elsewhere.
***Final Solution** (Ger. *Endloesung*), in Nazi terminology, the Nazi-planned mass murder and total annihilation of the Jews.
***Gabbai,** official of a Jewish congregation; originally a charity collector.
***Galut,** "exile"; the condition of the Jewish people in dispersion. (Cf. Diaspora.)
***Gaon** (pl. **geonim**), head of academy in post-talmudic period, especially in Babylonia.
Gaonate, office of *gaon.
***Gemara,** traditions, discussions, and rulings of the **amoraim*, commencing on and supplementing the *Mishnah, and forming part of the Babylonian and Palestinian talmuds (see Talmud).
***Gematria,** interpretation of Hebrew word according to the numerical value of its letters.
General Government, territory in Poland administered by a German civilian governor-general with headquarters in Cracow after the German occupation in World War II.
***Genizah,** depository for sacred books. The best known was discovered in the synagogue of Fostat (old Cairo).
Get, bill of *divorce.
***Ge'ullah,** hymn inserted after the **Shema* into the benediction of the morning prayer of the festivals and special Sabbaths.
***Gilgul,** metempsychosis; transmigration of souls.
***Golem,** automaton, especially in human form, created by magical means and endowed with life.
Green line, popular designation for the 1949 armistice demarcation lines in Israel, dividing the territory under Israeli rule until 1967 from those added as a result of the Six-Day War.
***Ḥabad,** initials of *ḥokhmah, binah, da'at*: "wisdom, understanding, knowledge"; ḥasidic movement founded in Belorussia by *Shneur Zalman of Lyady.
Hadas, *myrtle; one of the *Four Species used on Sukkot together with the **etrog*, **lulav*, and *aravah*.
***Haftarah** (pl. **haftarot**), designation of the portion from the prophetical books of the Bible recited after the synagogue reading from the Pentateuch on Sabbaths and holidays.
***Haganah,** clandestine Jewish organization for armed self-defense in Ereẓ Israel under the British Mandate, which eventually evolved into a people's militia and became the basis for the Israel army.
***Haggadah,** ritual recited on *Passover eve at the *seder* table.
Haham, title of chief rabbi of the Spanish and Portuguese congregation in London, England.
***Ḥakham,** title of rabbi of *Sephardi congregation.
***Ḥakham bashi,** title in the 15th century and modern times of the chief rabbi in the Ottoman Empire, residing in Constantinople (Istanbul), also applied to principal rabbis in provincial towns.
Hakhsharah ("preparation"), organized training in the Diaspora of pioneers for agricultural settlement in Ereẓ Israel.
***Halakhah** (pl. **halakhot**), an accepted decision in rabbinic law. Also refers to those parts of the *Talmud concerned with legal matters. In contradistinction to **aggadah*.
Ḥaliẓah, biblically prescribed ceremony (Deut. 25:9–10) performed when a man refuses to marry his brother's childless widow, enabling her to remarry.
***Hallel,** term referring to Psalm 113–18 in liturgical use.
***Ḥalukkah,** system of financing the maintenance of Jewish communities in the holy cities of Ereẓ Israel by collections made abroad, mainly in the pre-Zionist era (see *kolel*).
Ḥalutz (pl. **ḥalutzim**), pioneer, esp. in agriculture, in Ereẓ Israel.
Ḥalutziyyut, pioneering.
***Ḥanukkah,** eight-day celebration commemorating the victory of *Judah Maccabee over the Syrian king *Antiochus Epiphanes and the subsequent rededication of the Temple.
Ḥasid, adherent of *Ḥasidism.
Ḥasidei Ashkenaz, medieval pietist movement among the Jews of Germany
***Ḥasidism,** (1) religious revivalist movement of popular mysticism among Jews of Germany in the Middle Ages; (2) religious movement founded by *Israel ben Eliezer Ba'al Shem Tov in the first half of the 18th century;
***Haskalah,** "Enlightenment"; movement for spreading modern European culture among Jews c. 1750–1880. See *maskil*.
***Havdalah,** ceremony marking the end of Sabbath or festival.
***Ḥazzan,** precentor who intones the liturgy and leads the prayers in synagogue; in earlier times a synagogue official.
***Ḥeder** (lit. "room"), school for teaching children Jewish religious observance.
Heikhalot, "palaces"; tradition in Jewish mysticism centering on mystical journeys through the heavenly spheres and palaces to the Divine Chariot (see Merkabah).
***Ḥerem,** excommunication, imposed by rabbinical authorities for purposes of religious and/or communal discipline; originally, in biblical times, that which was separated from common use either because it was an abomination or because it was consecrated to God.
Ḥeshvan, see Marḥeshvan.
***Hevra kaddisha,** title applied to charitable confraternity (**ḥevrah*), now generally limited to associations for burial of the dead.
***Ḥibbat Zion,** see Ḥovevei Zion.
***Histadrut** (abbr. for Heb. **Ha-Histadrut ha-Kelalit shel ha-Ovedim ha-Ivriyyim be-Ereẓ Israel**). Ereẓ Israel Jewish Labor Federation, founded in 1920; subsequently renamed Histadrut ha-Ovedim be-Ereẓ Israel.
***Holocaust,** the organized mass persecution and annihilation of European Jewry by the Nazis (1933–1945).
***Hoshana Rabba,** the seventh day of *Sukkot on which special observances are held.
Ḥoshen Mishpat, see Shulḥan Arukh.
Ḥovevei Zion, federation of *Ḥibbat Zion, early (pre-*Herzl) Zionist movement in Russia.
Illui, outstanding scholar or genius, especially a young prodigy in talmudic learning.
***Iyyar,** second month of the Jewish religious year, eighth of the civil, approximating to April–May.
I.Ẓ.L. (initials of Heb. ***Irgun Ẓeva'i Le'ummi**; "National Military Organization"), underground Jewish organization in Ereẓ Israel founded in 1931, which engaged from 1937 in retaliatory acts against Arab attacks and later against the British mandatory authorities.
***Jadīd al-Islām** (Ar.), a person practicing the Jewish religion in secret although outwardly observing Islam.
***Jewish Legion,** Jewish units in British army during WWI.
***Jihād** (Ar.), in Muslim religious law, holy war waged against infidels.
Judenrat (Ger. "Jewish council"), council set up in Jewish communities and ghettos under the Nazis to execute their instructions.
***Judenrein** (Ger. "clean of Jews"), in Nazi terminology the condition of a locality from which all Jews had been eliminated.
***Kabbalah,** the Jewish mystical tradition:
Kabbalah iyyunit, speculative Kabbalah;
Kabbalah ma'asit, practical Kabbalah;
Kabbalah nevu'it, prophetic Kabbalah.
Kabbalist, student of Kabbalah.
***Kaddish,** liturgical doxology.
Kahal, Jewish congregation; among Ashkenazim, *kehillah*.
***Kalām** (Ar.), science of Muslim theology; adherents of the Kalām are called *mutakallimūn*.
***Karaite,** member of a Jewish sect originating in the eighth century which rejected rabbinic (*Rabbanite) Judaism and claimed to accept only Scripture as authoritative.
***Kasher,** ritually permissible food.
Kashrut, Jewish *dietary laws.
***Kavvanah,** "intention"; term denoting the spiritual concentration accompanying prayer and the performance of ritual or of a commandment.
***Kedushah,** main addition to the third blessing in the reader's repetition of the *Amidah* in which the public responds to the precentor's introduction.
Kefar, village; first part of the name of many settlements in Israel.
Kehillah, congregation; see *kahal*.
Kelippah (pl. **kelippot**), "husk(s); mystical term denoting force(s) of evil.
***Keneset Yisrael,** comprehensive communal organization of the Jews in Palestine during the British Mandate.
Keri, variants in the masoretic (*masorah) text of the Bible between the spelling *(ketiv)* and its pronunciation *(keri)*.

***Kerovah** (pl. **kerovot**), poem(s) incorporated into the **Amidah.*
Ketiv, see *keri.*
***Ketubbah,** marriage contract, stipulating husband's obligations to wife.
Kevuẓah, small commune of pioneers constituting an agricultural settlement in Ereẓ Israel (evolved later into *kibbutz).
***Kibbutz** (pl. **kibbutzim**), larger-size commune constituting a settlement in Ereẓ Israel based mainly on agriculture but engaging also in industry.
***Kiddush,** prayer of sanctification, recited over wine or bread on eve of Sabbaths and festivals.
***Kiddush ha-Shem,** term connoting martyrdom or act of strict integrity in support of Judaic principles.
***Nuremberg Laws,** Nazi laws excluding Jews from German citizenship, and imposing other restrictions.
Oleh, Olim,immigrant(s) to Ereẓ Israel (see **Aliyah*).
***Omer,** first sheaf cut during the barley harvest, offered in the Temple on the second day of Passover.
Omer, Counting of (Heb. *Sefirat ha-Omer*), 49 days counted from the day on which the *omer* was first offered in the Temple (according to the rabbis the 16th of Nisan, i.e., the second day of Passover) until the festival of Shavuot; now a period of semi-mourning.
Oraḥ Ḥayyim, see Shulḥan Arukh.
***Orthodoxy** (Orthodox Judaism), modern term for the strictly traditional sector of Jewry.
***Pale of Settlement,** 25 provinces of czarist Russia where Jews were pemitted permanent residence.
***Palmaḥ** (abbr. for Heb. *peluggot maḥaẓ;* "shock companies"), striking arm of the *Haganah.
***Pardes,** medieval biblical exegesis giving the literal, allegorical, homiletical, and esoteric interpretations.
***Parnas,** chief synagogue functionary, originally vested with both religious and administrative functions; subsequently an elected lay leader.
Partition plan(s), proposals for dividing Ereẓ Israel into autonomous areas.
Paytan, composer of **piyyut* (liturgical poetry).
***Peel Commission,** British Royal appointed by the British government in 1936 to inquire into the Palestine problem and make recommendations for its solution.
Pesaḥ, *Passover.
***Pilpul,** in talmudic and rabbinic literature, a sharp dialectic used particularly by talmudists in Poland from the 16th century.
***Pinkas,** community register or minute-book.
***Piyyut** (pl. **piyyutim**), Hebrew liturgical poetry.
***Pizmon,** poem with refrain.
Posek (pl. ***posekim**), decisor; codifier or rabbinic scholar who pronounces decisions in disputes and on questions of Jewish law.
***Prosbul,** legal method of overcoming the cancellation of debts with the advent of the *sabbatical year.
***Purim,** festival held on Adar 14 or 15 in commemoration of the delivery of the Jews of Persia in the time of *Esther.
Rabban, honorific title higher than that of rabbi, applied to heads of the *Sanhedrin in mishnaic times.
***Rabbanite,** adherent of rabbinic Judaism. In contradistinction to *Karaite.
Reb, rebbe, Yiddish form for rabbi, applied generally to a teacher or ḥasidic rabbi.
***Reconstructionism,** trend in Jewish thought originating in the United States.
***Reform Judaism,** trend in Judaism advocating modification of *Orthodoxy in conformity with the exigencies of contemporary life and thought.
Resh galuta, lay head of Babylonian Jewry (see Exilarch).
Responsum (pl. ***responsa**), written opinion *(teshuvah)* given to question *(she'elah)* on aspects of Jewish law by qualified authorities; pl. collecton of such queries and opinions in book form *(she'elot u-teshuvot).*
***Rishonim,** older rabbinical authorities. Distinguished from later authorities *(aḥaronim).*
***Rishon le-Zion,** title given to Sephardi chief rabbi of Ereẓ Israel.
***Rosh Ha-Shanah,** two-day holiday (one day in biblical and early mishnaic times) at the beginning of the month of *Tishri (September–October), traditionally the New Year.
Rosh Ḥodesh, *New Moon, marking the beginning of the Hebrew month.
Rosh Yeshivah, see *Yeshivah.
***R.S.H.A.** (initials of Ger. *Reichssicherheitshauptamt;* "Reich Security Main Office"), the central security department of the German Reich, formed in 1939, and combining the security police (Gestapo and Kripo) and the S.D.
***Sanhedrin,** the assembly of ordained scholars which functioned both as a supreme court and as a legislature before 70 C.E. In modern times the name was given to the body of representative Jews convoked by Napoleon in 1807.
***Savora** (pl. **savoraim**), name given to the Babylonian scholars of the period between the **amoraim* and the **geonim,* approximately 500–700 C.E.
S.D. (initials of Ger. *Sicherheitsdienst:* "security service"), security service of the *S.S. formed in 1932 as the sole intelligence organization of the Nazi party.
Seder, ceremony observed in the Jewish home on the first night of Passover (outside Ereẓ Israel first two nights), when the **Haggadah* is recited.
***Sefer Torah,** manuscript scroll of the Pentateuch for public reading in synagogue.
***Sefirot, the ten,** the ten "Numbers"; mystical term denoting the ten spheres or emanations through which the Divine manifests itself; elements of the world; dimensions, primordial numbers.
Selektion (Ger.), (1) in ghettos and other Jewish settlements, the drawing up by Nazis of lists of deportees; (2) separation of incoming victims to concentration camps into two categories – those destined for immediate killing and those to be sent for forced labor.
Seliḥah (pl. ***seliḥot**), penitential prayer.
***Semikhah,** ordination conferring the title "rabbi" and permission to give decisions in matters of ritual and law.
Sephardi (pl. ***Sephardim**), Jew(s) of Spain and Portugal and their descendants, wherever resident, as contrasted with *Ashkenazi(m).
Shabbatean, adherent of the pseudo-messiah *Shabbetai Ẓevi (17th century).
Shaddai, name of God found frequently in the Bible and commonly translated "Almighty."
***Shaḥarit,** morning service.
Shali'aḥ (pl. **sheliḥim**), in Jewish law, messenger, agent; in modern times, an emissary from Ereẓ Israel to Jewish communities or organizations abroad for purposes of fund-raising, organizing pioneer immigrants, education, etc.
Shalmonit, poetic meter introduced by the liturgical poet *Solomon ha-Bavli.
***Shammash,** synagogue beadle.
***Shavuot,** Pentecost; Festival of Weeks; second of the three annual pilgrim festivals, commemorating the receiving of the Torah at Mt. Sinai.
***Sheḥitah,** ritual slaughtering of animals.
***Shekhinah,** Divine Presence.
Shelishit, poem with three-line stanzas.
***Sheluḥei Ereẓ Israel** (or **shadarim**), emissaries from Ereẓ Israel.
***Shema** ([Yisrael]; "hear . . . [O Israel]," Deut. 6:4), Judaism's confession of faith, proclaiming the absolute unity of God.
Shemini Aẓeret, final festal day (in the Diaspora, final two days) at the conclusion of *Sukkot.
Shemittah, *Sabbatical year.
Sheniyyah, poem with two-line stanzas.
***Shephelah,** southern part of the coastal plain of Ereẓ Israel.
***Shevat,** eleventh month of the Jewish religious year, fifth of the civil, approximating to January–February.
***Shi'ur Komah,** Hebrew mystical work (c. eighth century) containing a physical description of God's dimensions; term denoting enormous spacial measurement used in speculations concerning the body of the **Shekhinah.*
Shivah, the "seven days" of *mourning following burial of a relative.
***Shofar,** horn of the ram (or any other ritually clean animal excepting the cow) sounded for the memorial blowing on *Rosh Ha-Shanah, and other occasions.
Shoḥet, person qualified to perform **sheḥitah.*
Shomer, *Ha-Shomer, organization of Jewish workers in Ereẓ Israel founded in 1909 to defend Jewish settlements.
***Shtadlan,** Jewish repesentative or negotiator with access to dignitiaries of state, active at royal courts, etc.

***Shtetl,** Jewish small-town community in Eastern Europe.

***Shulḥan Arukh,** Joseph *Caro's code of Jewish law in four parts:
Oraḥ Ḥayyim, laws relating to prayers, Sabbath, festivals, and fasts;
Yoreh De'ah, dietary laws, etc.;
Even ha-Ezer, laws dealing with women, marriage, etc.;
Ḥoshen Mishpat, civil, criminal law, court procedure, etc.

Siddur, among Ashkenazim, the volume containing the daily prayers (in distinction to the **maḥzor* containing those for the festivals).

***Simḥat Torah,** holiday marking the completion in the synagogue of the annual cycle of reading the Pentateuch; in Ereẓ Israel observed on Shemini Aẓeret (outside Ereẓ Israel on the following day).

***Sinai Campaign,** brief campaign in October–November 1956 when Israel army reacted to Egyptian terrorist attacks and blockade by occupying the Sinai peninsula.

Sitra ahra, "the other side" (of God); left side; the demoniac and satanic powers.

***Sivan,** third month of the Jewish religious year, ninth of the civil approximating to May–June.

***Six-Day War,** rapid war in June 1967 when Israel reacted to Arab threats and blockade by defeating the Egyptian, Jordanian, and Syrian armies.

***S.S.** (initials of Ger. *Schutzstaffel*: "protection detachment"), Nazi formation established in 1925 which later became the "elite" organization of the Nazi Party and carried out central tasks in the "Final Solution."

***Status quo ante** community, community in Hungary retaining the status it had held before the convention of the General Jewish Congress there in1868 and the resultant split in Hungarian Jewry.

***Sukkah,** booth or tabernacle erected for *Sukkot when, for seven days, religious Jews "dwell" or at least eat in the *sukkah* (Lev. 23:42).

***Sukkot,** festival of Tabernacles; last of the three pilgrim festivals, beginninng on the 15th of Tishri.

Sūra (Ar.), chapter of the Koran.

Ta'anit Esther (Fast of *Esther), fast on the 13th of Adar, the day preceding Purim.

Takkanah (pl. ***takkanot**), regulation supplementing the law of the Torah; regulations governing the internal life of communities and congregations.

***Tallit (gadol),** four-cornered prayer shawl with fringes *(ẓiẓit)* at each corner.

***Tallit katan,** garment with fringes *(ẓiẓit)* appended, worn by observant male Jews under their outer garments.

***Talmud,** "teaching"; compendium of discussions on the Mishnah by generations of scholars and jurists in many academies over a perod of several centuries. The Jerusalem (or Palestinian) Talmud mainly contains the discussions of the Palestinian sages. The Babylonian Talmud incorporates the parallel discussion in the Babylonian academies.

Talmud torah, term generally applied to Jewish religious (and ultimately to talmudic) study; also to traditional Jewish religious public schools.

***Tammuz,** fourth month of the Jewish religious year, tenth of the civil, approximating to June–July.

Tanna (pl. ***tannaim**), rabbinic teacher of mishnaic period.

***Targum,** Aramaic translation of the Bible.

***Tefillin,** phylacteries, small leather cases containing passages from Scripture and affixed on the forehead and arm by male Jews during the recital of morning prayers.

Tell (Ar. "mound," "hillock"), ancient mound in the Middle East composed of remains of successive settlements.

***Terefah,** food that is not **kasher*, owing to a defect in the animal.

***Territorialism,** 20th-century movement supporting the creation of an autonomous territory for Jewish mass-settlement outside Ereẓ Israel.

***Tevet,** tenth month of the Jewish religious year, fourth of the civil, approximating to December–January.

Tikkun ("restitution," "reintegration"), (1) order of service for certain occasions, mostly recited at night; (2) mystical term denoting restoration of the right order and true unity after the spiritual "catastrophe" which occurred in the cosmos.

Tishah be-Av, Ninth of *Av, fast day commemorating the destruction of the First and Second Temples.

***Tishri,** seventh month of the Jewish religious year, first of the civil, approximating to September–October.

Tokheḥah reproof sections of the Pentateuch (Lev. 26 and Deut. 28); poem of reproof.

***Torah,** Pentateuch or the Pentateuchal scroll for reading in the synagogue; entire body of traditional Jewish teaching and literature.

Tosafist, talmudic glossator, mainly French (12–14th centuries), bringing additions to the commentary by *Rashi.

***Tosafot,** glosses supplies by tosafist.

***Tosefta,** a collection of teachings and traditions of the *tannaim*, closely related to the Mishnah.

Tradent, person who hands down a talmudic statement in the name of his teacher or other earlier authority.

***Tu bi-Shevat,** the 15th day of Shevat, the New Year for trees; date marking a dividing line for fruit tithing; in modern Israel celebrated as arbor day.

***Uganda Scheme,** plan suggested by the British government in 1903 to establish an autonomous Jewish settlement area in East Africa.

***Va'ad Le'ummi,** the national council of the Jewish community in Ereẓ Israel during the period of the British *Mandate (1920–1048).

***Wannsee Conference,** Nazi conference held on Jan. 20, 1942, at which the planned annihilation of European Jewry was endorsed.

Waqf (Ar.), (1) a Muslim charitable pious foundation; (2) state lands and other property passed to the Muslim community for public welfare.

War of Independence, war of 1947–49 when the Jews of Israel fought off Arab invading armies and ensured the establishment of the new State.

***White Paper(s),** report(s) issued by British government, frequently statements of policy, as issued in connection with Palestine during the *Mandate period.

***Wissenschaft des Judentums** (Ger. "Science of Judaism"), movement in Europe beginning in the 19th century for scientific study of Jewish history, religion, and literature.

Yad Vashem, Isael official authority for commemorating the *Holocaust in the Nazi era and Jewish resistance and heroism at that time.

Yeshivah (pl. ***yeshivot**), Jewish traditional academy devoted primarily to study of rabbinic literature; *rosh yeshivah*, head of the yeshivah.

YHWH, the letters of the holy name of God, the Tetragrammaton.

Yibbum, see levirate marriage.

Yiḥud, "union"; mystical term for intention which causes the union of God with the **Shekhinah*.

Yishuv, settlement; more specifically, the Jewish community of Ereẓ Israel in the pre-State period. The pre-Zionist community is generally designated the "old yishuv" and the community evolving from 1880, the "new yishuv."

Yom Kippur, Yom ha-Kippurim, *Day of Atonement, solemn fast day observed on the 10th of Tishri.

Yoreh De'ah, see Shulḥan Arukh.

Yoẓer, hymns inserted in the first benediction *(Yoẓer Or)* of the morning **Shema*.

***Ẓaddik,** person outstanding for his faith and piety; especially a ḥasidic rabbi or leader.

Ẓimẓum, "contraction"; mystical term denoting the process whereby God withdraws or contracts within Himself so leaving a primordial vacuum in which creation can take place; primordial exile or self-limitation of God.

***Zionist Commission (1918),** commission appointed in 1918 by the British government to advise the British military authorities in Palestine on the implementation of the *Balfour Declaration.

Ẓiyyonei Zion, the organized opposition to Herzl in connection with the *Uganda Scheme.

***Ẓiẓit,** fringes attached to the **tallit* and **tallit katan*.

***Zohar,** mystical commentary on the Pentateuch; main textbook of *Kabbalah.

Zulat, hymn inserted after the **Shema* in the morning service.

Index

A

Aarhus (tn. Den.) 138
AARON BEN ELIJAH (**2**:10)
- Karaism 258ff
Abadi, Lillian 355
Aba-Sava (stlmt., Rus.) 289
ABBAS, MOSES JUDAH (**2**:39)
- poetry 310
Abecassi, Nuno Kruz 316
Abeles, Sir Peter 110
ABELLA (fam.) 97
Abella Irving 97, 128
Abella, Rosalie, Silberman 97, 128
Aberbach, David 181
Aberbech, M. 360
ABILEAH, ARIE 293
Abingdon Press (publ. house, U.S.A.) 319
Abkhazia 160, 211
Abrabanel (fam.) 342
Abraham Ben Simḥah ha-Sefaradi 267
Abrahams, Florence 130
Abrahams, Robert 130
Abrahamson, Maurice
- *illus:*
- - Terenure Synagogue 188
Abram, Ido 298
ABRAMSON, SHRAGA (**2**:172)
- geonic literature 157ff
- poetry 312
Abravanel (fam.) *see* Abrabanel
ABSE, DANNIE (**2**:176)
- English literature 146
Abu Ali Alḥusain Ibn Abdalla Ibn Sina 310
ABULAFIA, TODROS BEN JUDAH HA-LEVI (**2**:195)
- poetry 312
Abu-Lashin, Johar 352
Abu Mazen (PLO member) 334
Abu Nidal (terrorist group) 196
Achille Lauro (It. ship) 245, 378
- *illus:*
- - Marilyn Klinghoffer led off 378
ACIP, *see* Conseil d'Administration de l'Association Culturelle de Paris
ACRE (**2**:221)
- archaeological excavations 101
- Karaites 257
- Muslim court 228
- population 200
Adam, Yekutiel 287
Adamovich, Yehuda 287
Addis Ababa 119, 212
ADELAIDE (**2**:259)
- Jewish community 111
Adler, Abraham 175
ADLER, CYRUS (**2**:272)
- Conservative Judaism 134
Adler, Elhanan 313
ADLER, ISRAEL (**12**:680; **Dc./17**:472)
- ḥazzanut 175
- Hebrew mss 313
Adler, Jacques 113
Adler, Margarete 302
Adler, Ya'akov 310
ADOPTION (**2**:298)
- legislation 217ff
ADVERTISING (**2**:316)
- Israel smoking law 215
Aelion, Moshe 168
Afanasev, Yurii 338
AFENDOPOLO, CALEB BEN ELIJAH (**2**:325)
- Karaism 258
Afida Ha-Kohen, Shelomo 258
Afn Shvel (pub., U.S.A.) 317
AFRICA (**2**:330)
- French possessions 149
- Ibiza and Formentera 184
- Israel relations 206, 209
African Christian-Jewish Consultation 252
Afrikanerwearstandsbeweging (mvmt., S.A.) 347
AGAM, YAACOV (**2**:342)
- U.S. literature 365
AGE AND THE AGED (**2**:343)
- Denmark 138
- Ireland 187ff
- Netherlands 296
- Romania 328
- Russia 328
- *illus:*
- - Rishon le-Ziyyon Geriatric Center 199
AGMON, SHMUEL 243
AGNON, SHMUEL YOSEF (**2**:367; **Dc./17**:133)
- Hebrew Literature 180ff
Agoos, Jeff 349
AGUDAT ISRAEL (**2**:421)
- American Judaism 373
- Argentina 107
- Politics 195, 223
- Russia 331
Aguinis, Marcos 106
AḤAD HA-AM (**2**:490)
- Hebrew literature 181
AḤA OF SHABḤA (**2**:449)
- geonic literature 158
Aharoni, Zvi 176
AHARONOV, YAKIR 242
Aharonson, Shlomo 236
Aichenrand, Leizer 392
AIDS 148, 149, 275, 374
Aini, Lea 178
AIPAC, *see* American-Israel Public Affairs Committee
ALASKA (**2**:513) 97
ALBAHARI, DAVID 97
ALBANIA (**2**:522)
- Jewish immigration to Israel, 166, 210, 212
- Waldheim, Kurt 388
ALBANY (**12**:524)
- Black-Jewish relations 375
ALBECK, ḤANOKH (**2**:528)
- Cairo *Genizah* 155
ALBECK, SHALOM (**2**:527)
- Talmud research 360
Albek, Bruria 240
ALBERTA (**2**:530)
- Jewish community 127
Alcoholism 337, 372
Alcott, Amy 350
Alekseev, Vadim 351
ALEPPO (**2**:562)
- Jewish community 355, 381
Alexander, Phillip 145
Alexander, Sharon 240
Alexei I (emp., Byz.) 267
Alfonsin, Raúl 105, 170
Algaba, Jacob di 309
Algamil Yosef 258
ALGAZI, ISAAC BEN SOLOMON (**2**:608)
- *Ḥazzanut* 175
Algemeine Journal (newsp., U.S.A.) 316
ALGERIA (**2**:612)
- Arab boycott 122
- Gulf War 208
- Iranian propaganda 187
- Islamic fundamentalism 197
- Palestinian National Council 205, 306
- PLO 305, 306
Alhanati, Daniel 167
AL-ḤARIZI, JUDAH BEN SOLOMON (**2**:627)
- poetry 313
AL-JAMA (**2**:635)
- Ibiza 184
Allalalouf, Edgar 168
Alldis, John 233
Allen, Jim 144
ALLEN, WOODY (**15**:1077; **Dc./17**:140)
- Lasser, Louise 283
Allgemeine Wochenzeitung der Juden in Deutschland 161
ALLIANCE ISRAÉLITE UNIVERSELLE (**2**:648)
- France 150
- *illus:*
- - "Juifs & Citoyens" exhibit catalogue 151
Allnut, Yair 349
ALLON, YIGAL (**2**:655; **Dc./17**:140)
- settlement plan 213
Allony, Nehemia 157, 159, 259, 309
Alma Ata (city, Kazakhstan) 260
Almagor, Gila 240
Almog, Ruth 163, 177
AL-MUKAMMIS, DAVID IBN (**2**:671)
- Karaite philosopher 259
ALONI, SHULAMIT (**Dc./17**:140)
- Greece 166
ALPERT, HERB 292
Alpha Publishing (publ. house, U.S.A.) 319
ALSACE (**2**:751)
- Jewish Community 149, 152
Alsina Trias, T. 310
ALTBAUER, MOSHE (**1**:27)
- Israel Prize 242
ALTER ROBERT B. 98
ALTERMAN, NATHAN (**2**:773; **Dc./17**:140)
- Hebrew literature 180ff
Alterman Blay, Eva 123
Altman, Paul 129
ALTMAN, SIDNEY 98
Altmann, Klaus, *see* BARBIE, NIKOLAUS
Altshul, Bill 111
Alvarez, Al 146
Alzado, Llye 350
Amanah (stlmt. mvmt.) 171, 213
- *illus:*
- - settlement map 171
Amar, Moshe 238
AMERICA-ISRAEL CULTURAL FOUNDATION (**2**:816)
- art 236
American Association for Ethiopian Jews 380
American Hebrew Choral Festival 384
AMERICAN ISRAELITE (**2**:821)
- press 317
American-Israel Public Affairs Committee 376, 382
AMERICAN JEWISH COMMITTEE (**2**:822)
- American Jews 368
- anti-Semitism survey 377
- Jewish-Christian relations 251
- press 317
American Jewish Congress 381
AMERICAN JEWISH JOINT DISTRIBUTION COMMITTEE (**2**:827)
- India 185
- Komzet 263
- Poland 314
- Romania 327
- Syrian jews 381
- Yugoslavia 394
- *illus:*
- - Ethiopian immigrants in kindergarten 231

American Jewish World Service 376
AMERICAN SEPHARDI FEDERATION 98
AMERSFOORT (2:832)
- Jewish community 295
AMIA (orgn., Arg.) 105
AMICHAI, YEHUDA (2:838)
- Hebrew literature 179ff
- Israel Prize 240
Aminoah, N. 358
AMIR, AHARON (2:848)
- Hebrew literature, 176, 180
Amir, Eldad 352
AMIRAN, RUTH (2:849)
- Israel prize 240
Amit, Mikhal 234
Amital, Yehudah 307
Amos, Stanley 350
AMRAM BEN SHESHNA (2:891; **Dc./17**:141)
- *siddur* 159
AMSTERDAM (2:895)
- Jewish community 294ff
- Jewish Historical Museum 290
- liturgical traditions 175
- museum 298
- *illus:*
- - Maimonides Jewish Lyceum 295
- - 350th anniversary celebrations 295
Anagnostaki, Maoli 169
ANAN BEN DAVID (2:919)
- Karaism 259
Anani, Nabil 238
Anchorage (city, Alsk.) 97
ANCONA (2:941)
- Jewish community 244ff
Anderson George K. 365
Anderson, Olaf 259
Andizhan (city, Uzbekistan) 337, 385
Andreeva, Nina 337
Anisimov, Elijah 286
ANISIMOV, ILYA SHERBATOVICH (3:23)
- Mountain Jews 286
Anne Frank Gymnasium (Hung.) 184
A-Nosair, El Sayyid 378
Anspach, Henryt 302
Anspach, Paul 302
Antall, Jozef 183ff
ANTIPATRIS (3:78)
- archaeological excavations 103
ANTI-SEMITISM (3:87) 98
- Argentina 105ff
- Australia 109, 112
- Austria 113, 387
- Belarus 117
- Belgium 117
- Brazil 124
- Canada 126
- Czechoslovakia 136
- England 143
- France 149ff, 152
- Germany 162
- Germany, East 164
- Greece 166ff
- Hungary 183
- IJA 186
- India 185
- Iran 186
- Ireland 188
- Italy 245
- Jewish-Christian Relations 251
- New Zealand 299
- Poland 314
- Romania 327
- Russia 211, 329ff, 337ff
- South Africa 346
- Switzerland 355
- United Nations 364
- United States 375, 377
- U.S. campuses 384
- Yugoslavia 393
- *illus:*
- - Leningrad Jewish cemetery demonstration 331
Antisemitism World Report 186
ANTSCHEL, PAUL, *see* CELAN, PAUL
ANTWERP (3:167)
- Jewish community 117
Apartheid 346, 376
APPELFELD, AHARON (3:222)
- Anglo-Jewish writers circle 146
- Hebrew literature 177
- Israel prize 240
- *illus:*
- - *Mesillat Barzel* cover 177
Apulget, Blanch D' 366
Arab boycott, *see* BOYCOTT, ARAB
ARAB LEAGUE (3:242)
- Arab boycott 121
ARAB WORLD (**Dc./17**:143)
- administered territories 203ff
- anti-Semitism 100
- Arab boycott 121
- France 149
- Gulf War 208
- Hungary terrorist attack 184
- India 185
- *intifada* and Palestinian conflict 191
- Iran 186
- Israeli settlements 213
- Israel-Lebanon War 189
- Italy 244
- Jewish population 212
- PLO 305ff
- politics in Israel 194
- Reform Judaism 324
- Russian arms 197
- Russian immigration to Israel 211
- Russian Jews 334
- South Africa 347
- Turkey 362
- United Nations 364
- Vatican 386
- Waldheim Affair 389
ARAD (city, Isr.; 3:243)
- archaeological excavations 101ff
- art museum 236
ARAD (city, Transyl.; 3:250)
- Jewish community 328
Arad, Yael 302, 350, 352
Arafat, Yasser 144, 196, 203ff, 254, 305ff, 346, 365, 375, 386
Arbatova, Mia 236
ARCHAEOLOGY (3:303; **Dc./17**:155) 100
- museums 287
- Orthodox demonstrations 224
- *illus:* text
ARCHITECTURE AND ARCHITECTS (3:336)
- archaeological excavations 100ff
ARCHIVES (3:366;/ **Dc./17**:162)
-*ḥazzanut* 175
- museums 288
ARENS, MOSHE 104
- politics 193
- Pollard Affair 315
- U.S. relations 208
- *illus:*
- - efforts on behalf of refuseniks 332
Arfa, M. 312
ARGENTINA (3:408; **Dc./17**:162) 105
- *aliyah* to Israel 199
- anti-Semitism 99
- Conservative Judaism 134
- Iranian terrorist attack 187
- Klarsfeld, Beate 261
- Sephardi conference 342
- Yiddish Literature 391
- *illus:* text
Argentinian Association for a Secular and Humanistic Judaism 107
ARGOV, ALEXANDER (SASCHA) 241
Argov, Shelomo 196
Aridor, Yoram 190
Ariel (tn., Isr.) 172
Arieli, Y. 359
Arieli-Orloff, L. A. 178, 180
ARIZONA (3:449)
- anti-Semitics incidents 384
- crypto-Jews 342
Arlon (tn., Belg.) 117
ARMENIA (3:472)
- Azerbaijan war 115
- Jerusalem patriarchate 227
- Jewish population 328
Arndt, Judy 111
ARNHEM (3:485)
- Jewish community 295
Arnon, Yehudit 235
Arom, Z. 357
Aron, Yossi 111
Aronow, Don 351
Arouch, Salomon 168
Arpali, Boaz 180ff
ART (3:499)
- Israel 236
- Italy 245
Artom, Emanuele 246
Artscroll (publ. house, U.S.A.) 318
Artukovic, Andrija 379
Artzenu (Ref. orgn.) 323, 395
Aruba (Isl.) 130
Aryan Nation (U.S.) 377
ARZA, *see* Association of Reform Zionists of America
Asael, Lili 167
Ascension Church (Jer.) 233
Aschenbach, Ernst 261
Aschkenazy, Nehama 365
ASF, *see* AMERICAN SEPHARDI FEDERATION
ASHDOD (3:695)
- coal stockpile 221
- Karaites 259
- population 214
Asher, Barry 350
ASHKELON (3:713)
- population 200
- power plant 220
- *illus:*
- - Peres in supermarket 218
ASHKENAZ (3:719)
- Cairo *Genizah* 156
- France 149
- Netherlands 294ff
- Russia 329
- Turkey 363
- Uzbekistan 385
Ashkenazi, Albert 168
ASHKENAZI, JOSEPH BEN SHALOM (**10**:236)
- Talmud research 359
Ashkenazi, Yehuda 298
ASNER, EDWARD 282
Asociación Internacional des Escritores Judios en Lengua Hispana y Portuguese 342
Assabi, Ady 345
Assad, Ḥafez 226, 356
ASSEO, DAVID (3:765)
- Turkey 362
ASSIMILATION (3:770; **Dc./17**:165)
- Czechoslovakia 136
- Estonia 147
- Greece 166
- Hungary 183
- Russia 330ff
- U.S. campuses 384
- U.S. Jews 368
Assis, M. 359
Association Football 349, 353
Association of Activists and Friends of Jewish Culture (Rus.) 334
Association of Jewish Public Organizations of Ukraine 364
Association of Jews from the Commonwealth of Independent States 110
Association of Reform Zionists of America 323
Astafev, Victor 337
ASTRAKHAN (3:786)
ATHENS (3:815)
- Jewish community 167
- museum 290
ATHLIT (3:821)
- archaeological excavations 103
ATLANTA (3:824)
- migration of Jews 369
Atra Kadisha (orgn., Isr.) 224
Attal, R. 312
ATTALI, JACQUES 108
Atzmon, Ẓvi 180
AUCKLAND (3:839)
- Jewish community 299
AUERBACH, CARL, A. 108
Auerbach, Philipp 161
Aufbau (period., U.S.A.) 317
AUGSBURG (3:849)
- museum 290
Augusta Victoria (Jer.) 233
AUSCHWITZ (3:854)
- convent controversy 108, 314
- Greek Jewry 168
- Holocaust denial 100
- Jewish-Christian relations 252
AUSCHWITZ CONVENT 108
- Belgium protests 118
- Catholic-Jewish relations 314
- *illus:*
- - WIZO demonstration against Carmelite convent 251
Aus der Funten, Ferdinand H. 296
Austin, Jack 128
AUSTRALIA (3:877; **Dc./17**:165) 109
- *aliyah* to Israel 212
- anti-Semitism 99
- CAJE 131
- ḥavurah movement 174
- IPO concert 232
- Israel coal imports 221
- Israel relations 209
- Los Angeles 273
- Russian emigrants 338
- Yiddish literature 392
Australian Jewish News 113
AUSTRIA (3:887; **Dc./17**:167) 113
- anti-Semitism 98
- Brunner, Alois 125
- *ḥazzanut* 175
- museums 290
- Waldheim affair 387
- *illus:*
- - Cantor Adler receives medal 175
Austrian Cultural Institute 176
Automobile racing 349
AVENARY, ḤANOCH (**12**:681; **Dc./17**:472)
- *ḥazzanut* 175
Averbuch, Ilan 236
- *illus:*
- - "Fata Morgana" 237
AVIDAN, DAVID (**Dc./17**:168)
- Hebrew literature 179
Avigur-Rotem, Gabriela 178
Avilov, Nikolai 302
AVINERI, SHLOMO, 114
Aviv (newsp., Belor.) 117
Avi-Zimra, Mandil 310
Avner, Yehuda 112, 187
Avnit, Rabbi 394
AVOT (3:983)
- Cairo *Genizah* 156
AVRECH, YESHAYAHU 241
Ayali, M. 358
Ayalon, Leah 180
Azaria, Shabetai 167
AZERBAIJAN (3:1005) 114
- Jewish population 328
- Komzet 264
- Mountain Jews 284
AZHAROT, AZHARAH (3:1007)
- Cairo *Genizah* 233
- prayerbooks 159
Azi, Assad 238
Aziz (newsp., Azerbaijan) 115
Azoulai, Ariella 238

B

BA'ALEI TESHUVAH (**Dc./17**:169)
- Los Angeles 274
- Russia 331
- South Africa 345
BABI YAR (4:27)
- 50th anniversary of mass murder 364
- Jewish public meetings 331, 334
BACALL, LAUREN 282
BACCHI, ROBERTO (4:53)
- Israel Prize 240
Bach, Johann Sebastian 232
Bacon , Hirsch Leib 175
Bacon, Isaac 175, 181
BADEN (4:59)
- Jewish community 355
BADINTER, ROBERT 115
BAER YITZḤAK (Fritz; 4:82)
- poetry 312
Bagdanovka (stlmt., Rus.) 287
Bahat, Avner 175
Bahrein 122
Bakala, Nikou 169
Baker, James 208ff, 356

Baker, Kenneth 143
BAKKASHAH (**4**:116)
- geonic literature 159
Bakri, Mukhammed 239
BAKSHI-DORON, ELIAHU 115
BAKU (**4**:119)
- Jewish community 115, 335
- Mountain Jews 284ff
Balaban, Avraham 180
Balabanoff, Nicholas 182
Balearic Islands *see* IBIZA and FORMENTERA
Balenki, Valeri 350
BALIN, MARTY 292
Ballybough (Ire.) 188
Baltic States 209
BALTIMORE (**4**:145)
- Black-Jewish relations 376
- Catholic-Jewish Liaison Committee 252
- divorce rate 372
- Holocaust memorial 378
BAMBERGER, BERNARD JACOB (**4**:150)
- Reform Judaism 322
Bamberger, J.D. 357
Banai, Porez-Dror 179
Bancroft, Anne 282
BANIAS (**4**:162)
- archaeolgical excavations 103
Banitt, M. 313
Bank of Israel 219
Bansard, Jean-Pierre 150
Barabash, Uri 239
Barack Fishman, Sylvia 368ff
BARAK, EHUD 115
- IDF 197
BARASH, ASHER (**4**:200)
- Hebrew literature 181
BARABADOS (**4**:205)
- Jewish community 129
- *illus:*
- - stamp series 129
BARBIE, NIKOLAUS ("KLAUS"), TRIAL OF 115
- Klarsfeld, Beate and Serge 261
- trial 152
Barcelona (city, Venez.) 128
Barcus, Basil 350
Bar-El, Yehudit 181
BARENBOIM, DANIEL (**4**:220; **Dc./17**:472)
- Israel cultural life 234
Barkat Taisin 238
Barkhorden-Nahi, Gina 365
Bar-Lev, Jenifer 238
BAR MITZVAH, BAT MITZVAH (**4**:243)
- Reform Judaism 322
- United States 370
Barnea, Ezra 175
Barneeveld (Neth.) 297
BARON, DEVORAH (**4**:252)
- Hebrew literature 181
Barranquilla (city, Colom.) 128, 130
BARRENNESS AND FERTILITY (**4**:256)
- Russia 328
Barshai, Avinoam 181
Barta, Istvan 302
Bartana, Ortsion 181
Bar-Tikvah, Benjamin 310
Barton, Harris 350
BARTOV, HANOCH (**4**:265; **Dc./17**:172)
- Hebrew literature 176ff
Bartrop, Paul R. 113
Barvitsioti, Taki 169
Bar-Yosef, Hamutal 181
Bar-Yosef, Yitzhak 178
Barzel, Hillel 180
Baseball 349
BASHEVIS-SINGER, ISAAC (**4**:293; **Dc./17**:173)
- Yiddish literature 392
BASHYAZI, ELIJAH (**4**:297)
- Karaite philosophy 259
BAṢIR, JOSEPH AL- (**4**:301)
Karaite philosophy 259
Basketball 349, 352
BASKIN, LEONARD (**4**:303)
- Reform Judaism 322
BASLE (**4**:303)
- Jewish community 354
- museum 291
- *illus:*
- - Jewish Museum 291
Basman, Rivka 392
Bass, Chaim 391, 392
Basser, Russell 351
Bat-Shahar, Hanna 177ff
BATSHEVA AND BAT-DOR DANCE COMPANIES (**4**:327)
- dance in Israel 234, 242
- Ordman, Jeannette 302
BAT YAM (**4**:328)
- art museum 236
- cantorial training school 174
- Karaites 257
- population 200
Baudouin (k., Belg.) 118
Bauer, Seth 302, 351
BAUER, YEHUDA 116
Bauman, Shaul 238
Bayme, Steven 368
Beaglehole, Ann 299
Beal, Doug 351
Beatrix, Queen (Neth.) 297
- *illus:*
- - 350th anniversary of Amsterdam Ashkenazi Congregation 295
Beatty, Warren 239
Beauvoir, Simone de 270
Becker, Fritz 246
BECKER, GARY STANLEY 116
Bedford, Robert 168
Beek (Neth.) 297
Beem, Hartog 298
Be'er, Haim 177, 181
Beerman, Leonard 275
BEERSHEBA (**4**:383; **Dc./17**:174)
- archaeological excavations 101
- Karaites 257
- Muslim court 228
- population 200, 214
- Reform Judaism 321
BE'ER YA'AKOV (**4**:386)
- Mountain Jews 286
Begin, Binyamin Ze'ev 193
BEGIN, MENAHEM (**4**:392; **Dc./17**:175)
- American Jews 381
- Lebanon War 189ff, 207
- politics 195
- resignation 193
- Safire, William 340
Begun, Iosif 331ff
Begun, Vladimir 330
Behrman House (publ., U.S.A.) 318
BEIN, ALEXANDER (**4**:401)
- Israel Prize 241
BEINART, HAIM 116
- Israel Prize 243
BEIRUT (**4**:402)
- Lebanon War 189ff, 196
Bei Sikh (period., Isr.) 391
Beit-Arie, M. 313
Beit Sahour (vill.) 227
Beit Yatir (stlmt., Isr.) 221
Beizer, Mikhail 332
Bejerano, Maya 179
BELARUS (Belorussia; **4**:443) 117
- Israel relations 209
- Jewish population 328
- Komzet 263
Belém (city, Braz.) 123
Belenki, Valeri 302
BELFAST (**4**:415)
- Jewish community 188
BELGIUM (**4**:416; **Dc./17**:176) 117
- anti-Semitism 98
- Auschwitz convent 108
- museum 292
- Pres. Herzog's visit 209
- Sephardim 342
- solar energy 222
- World Conference for Soviet Jewry 333
BELGRADE (**4**:426)
- Jewish community 393
- museum 290
Belinfante, Judith 296
Belize 130
Belize City 130
Belkin, Debbi 349
BELKIN, SAMUEL (**4**:437)
- Orthodoxy, Modern 304
BELLOW, SAUL (**4**:441; **Dc./17**:177)
- Norwegian book 301
BELMONTE (**4**:442)
- crypto-Jews 316
Belogorsk, *see* KARASUBAZAR
Belo Horizonte (city, Braz.) 123
Belorussia, *see* BELARUS
Belov, Vasillii 337
Ben-Ardot, Solon 167
Benayahu ben Hoshayahu 102
Benaya-Seri, Dan 177
Ben-David, Arnon 238
BEN-DAVID, JOSEPH 118
Ben-David, Mishka 181
Ben-David, Zadok 236
Ben-Dor Niv, Orna 240
BENE-BERAK (**4**:479)
- population 200
BENEI AKIVA (**4**:490)
- Russia 335
- South Africa 347
BENE ISRAEL (**4**:493; **Dc./17**:178)
- India 185
BEN-GURION UNIVERSITY OF THE NEGEV (**Dc./17**:181)
- solar energy research 221
- *illus:*
- - new immigrant scientists 232
BEN-HAIM, PAUL (**4**:517; **Dc./17**:473)
- obituary 234
Ben Hayyim, Z. 359
Ben-Hinnom, Valley of, *see* GEHINNOM
Benichou, Fabrice 350
Benima, Tamarah 298
BENJAMIN, JUDAH PHILIP (**4**:528)
- Evans' biography 147
BENKOW, JO (Josef Elias) 118
- Norwegian literature 300
Benmaior, Leon 168
Ben-Menahem, N. 311
Ben-Mordechai, Isaac 180
Ben Nahoom, Jonathan 178
Ben-Ner, Yitzhak 177
Benninga, Carina 302, 350
Ben-Nun, Tova 327
Ben-Ozer, Yuval 233
BEN-PORAT, MIRIAM 243
Ben-Porat, Ziva 181
Ben-Sasson, M. 158
Ben-Shammai, Haggai 259
Ben-Shemen, S. 357
Ben-Shushan, J. 357
Bensuli, Joseph 309
BENVENISTI, DAVID (**Dc./17**:183)
- Israel Prize 240
Ben Yaakov, Bareket 239
Benyamini, Daniel 234
BEN-YIZHAK, AVRAHAM (**4**:570)
- Hebrew literature 180
BEN-ZVI, IZHAK (**4**:577)
- Yad Izhak Ben-Zvi 391
BEN-ZVI, RAHEL (**4**:581)
- Yad Izhak Ben-Zvi 391
Ben-Zvi Institute (Isr.), *see* YAD BEN-ZVI
Berama, Israel 178
Berati, Yianni 169
Bercuson, David J. 128
BERDYCZEWSKI, MICHA JOSEF (**4**:592)
- Hebrew literature 178, 180ff
BERECHIAH BEN NATRONAI HA-NAKDAN (**4**:596)
- poetry 309
Berendt, Rozsa T. 184
Berenson, Senda 349
Berg, Alan 377
BERGEL, BERND 293
BERGEN BELSEN (**4**:610)
- Reagan visit 379
- *illus:*
- - Israel Pres. Herzog reciting *kaddish* 163
Berger, Alan L. 365
Berger, Istevan 184
Berger, Jay 351
Berger, Mark 302, 350
Berger, Max 114
Bergman, Avraham, *see* BIRAN, AVRAHAM
Bergmann-Pohl, Sabine 163
BERGNER, YOSSL (**4**:618)
- art 237
Bering, Vitus 97
BERKOFF, STEVEN 119
- English literature 146
Berland, Robert 302, 350
Berlianu, Victor 327
BERLIN (**4**:639; **Dc./17**:185)
- Jewish community 161
- museum 290
- synagogue 175
- *illus:*
- - Juedische Lebenwseiten Exhibition 162
Berlinger, Eliezer 295, 298
Berman, L. 358
BERMANT, CHAIM ICYK (**6**:787)
- English literature 146
BERNE (**4**:675)
- Jewish community 354
- *illus:*
- - Holocaust memorial 355
- - synagogue 355
Bernheim, Alfred 239
Bernius, Frieder 234
Bernshtein, Ori 179
Bernstein, Kenny 349
BERNSTEIN, LEONARD (**4**:686; **Dc./17**:185)
- Israel visit 234
Bernstein, Thomas 351
BERTINI, K. AHARON (**4**:697)
- Hebrew literature 179, 180
BERTINORO, OBADIAH BEN ABRAHAM YARE (**4**:698)
- Talmud research 357
BERTONOFF, DEBORAH (**4**:699)
- Israel Prize 243
Besen, Marc 110
Besser, Yaakov 179ff
BETA ISRAEL (**6**:1143; **Dc./17**:245) 119
- airlift to Israel 191, 206, 210, 212, 224
- American Jews 380
- Reform Judaism 321
- *illus:*
- - Ashkelon absorption center 224
- - call for re-unification with *fallash moura* 212
- - caravans 215
- - childcare worker in kindergarten 231
BETAR (**4**:714)
- Russia 334
- South Africa 347
Bet Aryeh (stlmt., Isr.) 171
Be-Terem (journ., Isr.) 173
Bet Gan (vill. Er. Isr.) 164
BET GUVRIN (**4**:731)
- archaeological excavations 103
BETH HATEFUTSOTH (**Dc./17**:187)
- Center for Jewish Music 176
- Czech exhibition 135
Bethge, Eberhard 254
- 500th anniversary of expulsion of Jews from Spain 341
BETHLEHEM (**4**:741)
- Basilica of the Nativity 227
- educational facilities 227
Bet Shamai Publications (publ. house, U.S.A.) 319
BET(H)-SHEAN (**4**:757)
- archaeological excavations 101
- education system 230
- Israel Festival 233
- *illus:*
- - caldarium in the thermae 104
Bevis Marks (syn., Lond.) 145
Beyer, Linda 365
Bezalel Art (publ. house, U.S.A.) 319
Bezek (co., Isr.) 216
BEZEM, NAPHTALI (**3**:597)
- art 237
BIALIK, HAYYIM NAHMAN (**4**:795)
- Hebrew literature 180ff
- poetry 312
BIBLE (**4**:814)
- Cairo *Genizah* 155
- geonic literature 157
- Krimchak 268
- Orthodoxy, Modern 304
- Reform Judaism 322
- *illus:*
- - contest for Jewish youth, France 150

- - *Daniel, Book of* 158
Biblio Press (publ. house, U.S.A.) 319
BIEL (**4**:981)
- Jewish community 355
Bietenhard, H. 360
BIGAMY AND POLYGAMY (**4**:985)
- Krimchaks 268
- Mountain Jews 285
BILETZKY, I.H. (**4**:995)
- Yiddish Literature 392
Binet, A. 357
Bin-Nun, Yoel 172
Biondini, Alejandro 106
BIRAN, AVRAHAM 120
Biran, Yoav 187
Birdwood, Dowager Lady 144
Birkenau (concen. camp) 109, 314
Birnbaum, Martin 392
BIROBIDZHAN (**4**:1044)
- 50th anniversary celebrations 330
- Jewish Autonomous Oblast 333
- Komzet 263
Birobidzhaner Shtern (news., Rus.) 336
Biron, Avner 232
Bishkek (city, Kyrgyztan) 270
Bishop, J. Michael 385
Bitburg cemetery (Ger.) 378
Bitzaron (period., U.S.A.) 318
Blackman, Ph. 357
Blaiavsky, Alexander 259
Blakeney, Michael 113
Blanke Bevrydingsbeweging (mvmt., S.A.) 347
Blatter, Janet 128
Blau, J. 155, 312
Blau, Joshua (**4**:1075)
- Israel Prize 241
BLAU, PETER 120
Blau, Yankel 364
BLEUSTEIN-BLANCHET, MARCEL 121
BLEWS (Black-J. gr., U.S.) 376
Blidstein, G. J. 312
Bloch Publishing (publ. house, U.S.A.) 319
Blonski, Jan 253
BLOOD-AVENGER (**4**:1116)
- Mountain Jews 285
BLOOD LIBEL (**4**:1120)
- Italy 246
- Mountain Jews 286
Bloom, Gilad 351
Blubstein, Rachel *see* RAHEL
Blum, Jakub 365
Blum, Walter 350
Blumberg, Judy 350
Blumenfeld, Theodore (Tuvia) 328
Blumenthal, David R. 259
Blumenthal, Hans 175
B'NAI B'RITH (**4**:1144; **Dc./17**:194)
- anti-Semitism 127
- black anti-Semitism 375
- 500th anniversary of expulsion of Jews from Spain 341
- Jewish-Christian relations 251
- Klutznick Museum 288
- Russia 335
- U.S. membership 383
BOARD OF DEPUTIES OF BRITISH JEWS (**4**:1150)
- Auschwitz convent controversy 109
- England 145
BOBRUISK (**4**:1155)
- Jewish community 117, 335
BOEHM, YOHANAN 293
- music in Israel 233, 234
Boeken, Nico 298
Boesky, Ivan 377
BOGALE, YONA 121
Bogart, Humphrey 282
BOGORAD, LAWRENCE 121
Bohe, Felix 359
Bohlman, Philip V. 365
Bokser, B.M. 360
BOLIVIA (**4**:1187)
- Barbie, Klaus 116
- Klarsfeld, Beate and Serge 261
Bolle, Godfried ("Freedy") 298
BOLOGNA (**4**:1190)
- Jewish community 244
BOMBAY (**4**:1192)
- Jewish community 185
Bonder, Nilton 124
BONDI, ARON (**5**:380)
- Israel Prize 241
Bonfils, R. 309
Books (**4**:1220)
- publishing 318
BOONE, RICHARD 282
BORISOV (**4**:1250)
- cemetery desevrated 117
Bornstein-Markovetsky, Leah 167
Borodin, Igor 337
Borodow, Andrew 351
Bosley, K. 312
Bosnia-Herzegovina (rep., Yug.) 187, 393
BOSTON (**4**:1264)
- divorce rate 372
- Jewish choirs 384
- migration of Jews 370
Botha, P.W. 346
BOTVINNIK, MIKHAIL (**4**:1272)
- Kasparov, Gary 259
Bovin, Alexander 334
Bowling 350
Boxing 320, 350, 352
BOYCOTT, ARAB (**4**:1282) 121
- administered areas 204
- England 144
- *intifada* 191
- Japan 209, 248
Boymvol, Rochel 392
Brabant (reg., Belg.) 117
Braham, Randolph 366
Brailovskii, Victor 333
BRANDEIS, LOUIS DEMBITZ (**4**:295; **Dc./17**:196)
- Friendly, Henry Jacob 153
BRANDEIS UNIVERSITY (**4**:1300)
- American Jews 368
Brandsdorfer, Y. 359
Brasilia (city, Braz.) 123
BRATISLAVA (**4**:1309)
- Jewish community 135
Braunstein, Amit 234
Braverman, Naḥum 274
Bravin, Nick 350
Braybrooke, Marcus 254
BRAZIL (**4**:1322; **Dc./17**:196) 123
- Catholic Church and Israel 386
- Jewish-Christian relations 254
- Sephardi conference 342
Breda prison (Neth.) 296
BRENNER, JOSEPH ḤAYYIM (**4**:1347; **Dc./17**:197)
- Hebrew literature 178, 181
BRESLAU (**4**:1353)
- Jewish community 313
Brett, Lily 112
BRIGHTON (**4**:1373)
- Jewish community 143
Brink, Siegfried Ten 298
Brinker, Menaḥem 181
Brinner, William 259
BRISBANE (**4**:1376)
- Jewish community 111
Briscoe, Ben 187
BRITISH COLUMBIA (**14**:1380)
- Jewish community 127
British National Party 143
Brittan, Leon 143
Brobart (tn., Neth.) 295
Brockman, Shimshon 352
Brockway, Allan 255
Brodersohn, Mario 105
BRODSKI, YOSIF (**4**:1395; **Dc./17**:197) 124
- Nobel Prize 299
Brodsky, Vladimir
- *illus:*
- - efforts on behalf of refusniks 332
BRODY, HEINRICH (Ḥayyim; **4**:1399)
- poetry 312
Brody, Robert 158
BRONFMAN, EDGAR MILES 124
- anti-Semitism in Austria 113
- Czechoslovakia 135
- Jewish-Christian relations 252
- Yugoslavia 393
Bronfman, Saidye 124
Bronstein, Herbert 322
BROOKNER, ANITA 124
- English literature 146
BROOKS, MEL 282
Brown, Larry 349
BROWN, MICHAEL STUART 125
- Goldstein, Joseph Leonard 165
BRUNNER, ALOIS 125
- Klarsfeld, Serge 261
- Koretz, Zvi 265ff
BRUNSWICK (**4**:1421)
- museum 290
BRUSSELS (**4**:1422)
- Jewish community 117
- museum 292
- Sephardim 342
- World Conference for Soviet Jewry 333
Bubis, Ignatz 161
Buchanan, Pat 99
BUCHAREST (**4**:1438)
- Jewish community 327
- *aliyah* transit point 339
Buchwald, Martyn, *see* BALIN, MARTY
BUDAPEST (**4**:1448)
- *aliyah* transit point 339
- Jewish community 184
- museum 292
BUENOS AIRES (**4**:1461)
- Conservative Judaism 134
- Iranian terrorist attack 187
- Jewish community 105ff
- Sephardi conference 341
- Spanish and Portuguese literature 348
- Yiddish literature 391
- *illus:*
- - memorial service for IDF soldiers 105
Bufalino, Brenda 235
BUFFALO (**4**:1465)
- museum 289
Bught (Neth.) 297
Bujnah, Musa 310
Bukantz, Jeff 350
BUKHARA (**4**:1470)
- 1989 census 329
- Tadzhikistan 356
- Uzbekistan 384
Bukaee, Rafi 239
BULAWAYO (**4**:1479)
- Jewish community 394
Bulgach, Pablo 351
Bulka, Reuven 128
Buna (labor camp) 320
BUND (**4**:1497)
- press 316
Bunte, W. 357
Buren, Paul van 254
Bures, Susan 113
BURG, YOSEF (**4**:1510; **Dc./17**:200)
- politics 195
Burgin, Elise 351
BURIAL (**4**:1515)
- Reform Judiasm 322
Bush, George 209, 364
- "Jewish vote" 373
- Soviet Jews 380
Butalah, Kamal 238
Butrus-Ghali, Dr. 364
Butz, Arthur 100, 379
Buynak (vill., Rus.) 284
Buynaksk (tn., Rus.) 284
Buzaglo, Chaim 240
BYZANTINE EMPIRE (**4**:1549)
- Krimchaks 267
- Mountain Jews 284

C

CABUL (**5**:2)
- archaeological excavations 102
CAESAREA (**5**:6)
- archaeological excavations 103
CAHN, SAMMY 125
CAIRO (**5**:25)
- Karaites 258
CAJE, *see* COALITION FOR THE ADVANCEMENT OF JEWISH EDUCATION 131
CALABRIA (**5**:33)
- excavations 245
CALCUTTA (**5**:39)
- Jewish community 185
CALIFORNIA (**5**:56)
- Jewish elected officials 377
- Jewish political force 377
- Karaites 258
- Los Angeles 273
- solar eneregy 222
- Iranian Jews 186
Calmat, Alain 350
CAMBRIDGE (**5**:69)
- Cairo *Genizah* 155
- *illus:*
- - *Genizah* mss being repaired 155
Cameran Singers (Isr.) 233
Camhi, Morris 168
Camp David Agreement 206
- United Nations 365
Camp Ramah (U.S.) 133, 384
CANADA (**5**:102; **Dc./17**:201) 125
- anti-Semitism 98, 100
- Arab boycott 122
- cantors convention 175
- Israel Sinfonietta tour 232
- Jewish Book Month 250
- Pres. Herzog's visit 209
- Russian emigrants 338
- Syrian Jewry 356
- Yiddish literature 392
CANADIAN JEWISH CONGRESS (**5**:113)
- anti-Semitism 127
- *illus:*
- - rally in support of Anatoly Sharansky 127
Canoeing 350
Canterbury (city, N.Z.) 299
CANTILLATION (**5**:128)
- *ḥazzanut* 175
Cantors Assembly of the United States 175
Cape Haitien (Haiti) 130
CAPERNAUM (**5**:136)
- archaeological excavations 104
- St. Peter's house 227
CAPE TOWN (**5**:139)
- Jewish community 345
Caplan, Leslie 112
Capucci, Hilarion 386
Caracciolo, Nicola 245
Cardozo, Abraham Lopes 175
CARIBBEAN JEWISH COMMUNITIES (**16**:473) 128
- 500th anniversary of expulsion of Jews from Spain 342
Carlebach, Julius 163
Carmel College (Austr.) 111
Carmi, Ilan 168
Carmi, Udi 350
Carmilly-Weinberger, Moshe 184
Caro, I. 392
CARPENTRAS (**5**:203)
- anti-Semitism 98, 106, 152
Carpi, D. 313
Cartago (city, Costa Rica) 128
CARTER, JIMMY (**Dc./17**:204)
- Black-Jewish relations 375
Carto, Willis 379
CARTOONISTS (**5**:215)
- Feiffer, Jules 198
- Tim 361
Carucci, Beniamino 246
Cashdan, E. 358
Casioperra (Surinam) 129
Cassidy, Edward 252
Cassuto, M.D. 309
Cassuto, Nathan 245
Cassuto, Sherri 351
Castel (fam.) 342
Castel-Bloom, Orly 178
Castoria, Beri *see* Nahmias, Beri
Castro, Emilio 253
Castro, Federico Pe'rez 310
Castro, Fidel 130
CATACOMBS (**5**:249)
- Italy 245
Catane, M. 358
Cathedra (journ. Isr.) 391
CAUCASUS (**5**:257)
- Gery 164
- Komzet 264

- Mountain Jews 284
Cavalla (tn., Gr.) 166
Ceasescu, Nicolai 327
Cech, Thomas 98
CELAN, PAUL 130
Celibidache, Sergiu 234
CEMETERY (**5**:271)
- anti-Semitic desecration 98, 106, 113, 117, 124, 147, 152
- Berne 355
- Caribbean Jewish communities 129
- Germany 162
- Germany, East 164
- India 185
- Ireland 188
- Netherlands 295
- Russia 331, 337
- South Africa 346
- *illus:*
- - Buenos Aires memorial service for IDF soldiers 105
- - Leningrad demonstration against anti-Semitism 331
CENSORHIP (**5**:276)
- legislation 216ff
CENTRAL CONFERENCE OF AMERICAN RABBIS (**5**:285)
- American Judaism 373
- mixed marriages 368ff
- Reform Judaism 320ff
Central Council of Jews in Germany 161
Central Registry of War Criminals and Security Suspects 388
Central Yiddish Cultural Organization 250, 391
Centre Chrétien des Etudes Juives (Jer.) 227
CEREMONIAL OBJECTS (**5**:288)
- museums 287ff
- United States 384
Chaim (journ., Rus.) 336
Chania (tn. Crete) 167
CHANNEL ISLANDS (**5**:334)
- Nazi war crimes 144
Chapichev, Ya.I. 269
Chaplin, Saul 125
Charalambous, Marino 169
CHARITY (**5**:338)
- French appeal 149
- ḥavurah movement 174
Charleroi (tn., Belg.) 117
Charlotte Amalie (city, St. Thomas) 129
Charmley, John 144
CHARPAK, GEORGES 131
Chavurah, *see* HAVURAH
Chavurat Shalom (mvmt., U.S.A.) 174
Cheliabinsk (tn., Rus.) 334
CHELMNO (**5**:374)
- Demjanjuk, Iwan 137
Chelouche, David 120
Cherecheanu (anti-Sem., Rum.) 327
Cheris, Elaine 350
Chernick, M.L.
- Talmud research 358
CHERNOVTSY (**5**:393)
- Jewish community 335
CHICAGO (**5**:410)
- Holocaust memorial 378
- Jewish choir 384
- Jewish population 369
- Karaites 258
- poverty among Jews 383
- Spertus Museum 288
Chiesa, Bruno 259
CHILDREN'S LITERATURE (HEBREW) (**5**:429; **Dc./17**:205)
- United States 384
CHILE (**5**:461; **Dc./17**:207)
- Conservative Judaism 135
- Klarsfeld, Beate 261
CHINA (**5**:470; **Dc./17**:208)
- Arab arms race 198
- Israel relations 206, 209
- Kaufman, Avrham Yosifovich 260
Chirac, Jacques 149
Chlenov, Mikhail 331, 334
CHMIELNICKI, BOGDAN (**5**:480)
- Ukrainian hero 364
CHOIRS (**5**:486)
- Bucharest 328
- United States 384
Christian Friends of Israel (Jap.) 248
CHRISTIANITY (**5**:505)
- anti-Semitism 99
- *falas moura* 119
- Gery 164
- Israel-Lebanon War 189ff
- Jewish books 319
- Jewish-Christian relation 251
- missionary groups in U.S. 372
Christian-Jewish Relations (jrnl.) 186
Christianopoulo, Dino 169
CHUFUT-KALE (**5**:536)
- Krimchaks 267
CHURCH, CATHOLIC (**5**:536)
- Auschwitz convent 108
- Caribbean Jewish communities 129
- Czechoslovakian anti-Semitism 136
- Israel 226ff
- Italy 244, 146
- Jewish-Christian relations 251ff
- Poland 314
- Vatican 385
Churchill, Randolph 164
CHURCHILL, SIR WINSTON LEONARD SPENCER (**5**:555)
- biography 164
Church of the Creator (mvmt., S.A.) 347
Church of the Redeemer (Jer.) 232
CIA 387
CINCINNATI (**5**:562)
- Ḥabad *menorah* 375
- press 317
CIRCUMCISION (**5**:567)
- Russia 331
- Russian *olim* 225
- Reform Judaism 322
Citizens' Rights and Peace Movement (Isr.) 195
Ciudadela (Arg.) 106
CIVIL MARRIAGW (**5**:595)
- Greece 166
Civil Rights Movement (U.S.A.) 323
CJE, *see* European Jewish Congress
CLAL 131
- American Judaism 373
Clark, Alan 144
Clark, Joe 126
Claus, Prince
- *illus:*
- - 350th anniversary of Amsterdam Ashkenazi Congregation 295
CLEVELAND (**5**:606)
- Jewish community 369
- Temple Museum 289
Clever, Roger 366
Clinton, Bill
- Arab boycott 122
CLUNY (**5**:619)
- museum 292
COALITION FOR THE ADVANCEMENT OF JEWISH EDUCATION 131
COCHIN (**5**:621)
- synagogues 185
Coevorden (Neth.) 297
Cohen, A. 360
COHEN, ARTHUR A. 132
Cohen, Benny 150
Cohen, Berl
- Yiddish literature 391
Cohen, Edwina, *see* Currie, Edwina
Cohen, Eli 240
Cohen, Erik 151
Cohen-Gan, Pinchas 237ff
COHEN, GERSON D. (**16**:1266; **Dc./17**:211)
- Conservative Judaism 133
Cohen, H.G. 313
Cohen, Howard *see* COSELL, HOWARD
COHEN, SIR JOHN EDWARD (**5**:679)
- Porter, Sir Leslie 315
Cohen, Martin A. 259
Cohen, Matt 366
Cohen, N. 358
Cohen, R. 357
Cohen, Scott 351
Cohen, Shimon 232
Cohen, Solomon 168
COHEN, STANLEY 132
Cohen, Steven M.
- U.S. Jewish communal life 367
- U.S. literature 366
Cohen Stuart, G.H. 298
Cohen Y. (J.) 357
Cohen Yehuda 234
Cohn, Al 349
COINS AND CURRENCY (**5**:695)
- archaeological excavations 103
Colaḥan, C.A. 311
Collective Israel Actie 298
Colligan, Sumi E. 258
Collor de Mello, Fernando 123
COLOGNE (**5**:738)
- Jewish community 162
- museum 290
COLOMBIA (**5**:744)
- Israel coal imports 221
- Israel soccer team 353
- Jewish community 128ff
Colón (city, Pan.) 128
Colonia Mauricio (stlmt., Arg.) 106
Coloquio (journ. Arg.) 107
COLUMBUS, CHRISTOPHER (**5**:756)
- Sephardim 342
Columbus Platform (Ref. Judaism, U.S.A.) 322
COMMANDMENTS, THE 613 (**5**:760)
- Gery 164
- Orthodoxy, Modern 304
Commentary (mag., U.S.A.) 317, 374
Committee of Rabbis for Human Rights 307
Committee of 35 (orgn., Eng.) 332
Common-law wife 217
Commonwealth Jewish Council 185
Commonwealth of Independent States 211
COMMUNISM (**5**:792)
- anti-Semitism 99
- Hungarian Jewish community 184
- Israel Party 194, 202ff
- Jewish responsibility 314
- Romania 327
Compton, Susan 366
Comunidades (newsp., Arg.) 107
Confederation of United Zionists 395
CONFERENCE OF PRESIDENTS OF MAJOR AMERICAN JEWISH ORGANIZATIONS (**5**:871; **Dc./17**:211)
- Americans for Peace Now 383
Conference on Security and Co-operation in Europe 100
CONNECTICUT (**5**:897)
- Jewish political force 377
Conseil d'Administration de l'Association Culturelle de Paris (orgn., Fr.) 150
Conseil Representatif des Institutions Juives de France 150
CONSERVATIVE JUDAISM (**5**:901) 132
- American Judaism 373
- Argentina 107
- *ḥazzanut* 175
- Law of Return 226
- publishing 318
- U.S. intermarriage rates 368
- Ẓionist Congress (31st) 395
CONSISTORY (**5**:907)
- France 150
- *illus:*
- - "Juifs & Citoyens" exhibit catalogue 151
Controversia (journ., Arg.) 107
Conversion, Forced
- Ibiza and Formentera 184
COPENHAGEN (**5**:952)
- Jewish community 137
- museum 291
- *illus:*
- - Sukkah in kindergarten 138
- - synagogue 138
Corach, Carlos 106
CORFU (**5**:970)
- Jewish community 166, 167, 169
Corinaldi, Michael 258
Cork (tn., Ire.) 188
Cornblit, Joey 350
Coro (city, Venez.) 128, 130
COSELL, HOWARD 135
Cossiga, Francesco 244
COSTA RICA (**5**:989)
- Jewish community 128ff
Cotler, Irwin 128
Cotti, Flavio 355
Council of American Jewish Museums 289
COUNCIL OF JEWISH FEDERATIONS (**5**:993) 380
Counterpoint (mag., Isr.) 172
Covent Garden Opera House (Lonc 188
CRACOW (**5**:1026)
- Jewish community 313ff
- museum 292
CRETE (**5**:1088)
- Cairo *Genizah* 156
- Chania synagogue 167
Cretzianu, Alexander 182
CRIF *see* Conseil Representatif des Institutions Juives de France
CRIMEA (**5**:1103)
- Komzet 263
- Krimchaks 266
Crimea, *see* also KRIMCHAKS
Croatia (rep., Yug.) 393
CROLL, DAVID ARNOLD (**5**:1126
- Canada 128
Croner, Helga 255
CRYPTO-JEWS (**5**:1145)
- Sephardim 342
CRYSTAL, BILLY 282
Csak, Ibolya 302
Csurka, Istvan 99, 183
CUBA (**5**:1146; **Dc./17**:213)
- Jewish community 130
Cullman, Joseph, III 351
Curaçao (isl., Neth. Antilles) 128ff
Curitiba (city, Braz.) 123
Currie, Edwina 143
Curtis, Tony 240
Cuyk (Neth.) 297
CZECHOSLOVAKIA (**5**:188; **Dc./17**:213) 135
- *aliyah* transit point 339
- Israel relations 209
- Jewish-Christian relations 253
- museum 292
- Pres. Herzog's visit 209
- Soviet Jews 211

D

Dadashevs (fam. Rus.) 285
Dadiani, Lionel 330, 338
Dagan, Elisha 238
Dages, Willy 296
Daghestan (reg., Rus.) 264, 284
Dahrendorf, Ralf 389
DAIA (**5**:1225)
- Argentina 106
DALLAS (**5**:1229)
- Holocaust Memorial Center 289
DALVEN, RACHEL (RAE) (**1**:29) 167
DAMAGES (**5**:1233)
- legislation against dogs 218
DAMARI, SHOSHANA (**12**:687)
- Israel Prize 242
DAMASCUS (**5**:1237)
- Israel-Lebanon War 189ff
- Jewish community 355, 381
DAN (**5**:1259)
- archaeological excavations 101ff
- *illus:*
- - triple-arched gate 101
DAN, JOSEPH 136
Dana, J. 309
Daneels, Cardinal 109
DANIEL, JEAN 136
DANIEL BEN MOSES AL-QŪMISI (**5**:1292)
- Karaite philosophy 259
Danisov, Andre 352
Danon, Cadik 393
Dar, Gidi 240
Darousheh, Abd al-Wahab 203

Dasheskii, Vladislav 331
David, Hanna 311
David, Nurit 238
David, Y. 309ff
Davids, A.B.N. 386
Davidson, Gisella 313
Davidson, Y. 159
Davis, Al 350
Davis, William H. 182
DAWIDOWICZ, LUCY 137
Dayan, Assi 240
Day schools, Jewish 134
DAYYAN (**5**:1390)
– Supreme Court decision 217
DEAD SEA SCROLLS (**5**:1396)
– Karaites 259
Deakin (city, Austr.) 111
DEBRECEN (**5**:1434)
– Jewish community 184
Decourtray, Cardinal 109
De Gaulle, Charles 361
Degel ha-Torah (polit. Party, Isr.) 223
Deir al-Sultan (monastery, Jer.) 227
Delek (oil co., Isr.) 221
DellaPergola, Sergio 105, 368
Delvalle, Eric 129
DEMALACH, YOEL 241
Dembo, L.S. 366
Demirel (P.M., Turk.) 342
DEMJANJUK TRIAL 137
Demjanuk, John (Iwan) 137, 379
Democratic Front for Peace and Equality (Isr.) 194
Democratic List (polit. party, Isr.) 203
Democratic Party (U.S.) 373
DEMOGRAPHY (**5**:1493)
– Alaska 97
– Argentina 105
– Australia 109
– Azerbaijan 114
– Belarus 117
– Belgium 117
– Brazil 123
– Canada 127
– Czechoslovakia 135
– Denmark 138
– England 142
– Estonia 147
– France 149
– Georgia 160
– Germany 161
– Germany, East 163
– India 185
– Iran 186ff
– Ireland 187
– Israel, State of 172, 198
– Italy 244
– Japan 247
– Kazakhstan 260
– Kyrgyzstan 270
– Latvia 270
– Lithuania 272
– Los Angeles 273
– Moldova 281
– Netherlands 294
– Norway 299
– Poland 313
– Portugal 316
– Romania 327
– Russia 328ff
– South Africa 344
– Switzerland 355
– Syria 355
– Tadzhikistan 356
– Turkey 363
– Ukraine 364
– U.S.A. 369
– Uzbekistan 384
– Yugoslavia 393
– Zimbabwe 394
Denekamp (Neth.) 297
Denker, Henry 366
DENMARK (**5**:1536; **Dc./17**:221) 137
– museum 291
DENVER (**5**:1542)
– museum 289
– *illus:*
– – *Intermountain Jewish News, The* 316
DERBENT (**5**:1550)
– Mountain Jews 284
Derderian, Yegishe 227
Deri, Arieh 195
DERRIDA, JACQUES 138
DERSHOWITZ, ALAN M. 139
Deschenes, Jules 127
Desert Sculpture Park (Isr.) 236
DETROIT (**5**:1566)
– Jewish community 369
Deutsch, Ayala-Helga 175
Deutsch, Judah (Robert) 184
Deutsch, Tomas 351
De Vinney, Timothy 167
DIAMOND, NEIL 292
DIASPORA (**6**:8)
– Reform Judaism 323
Dictionaries
– Mishnah 357
– Russian-Jewish (Yiddish) 330
DIDYMOTEIKHON (**6**:24)
– Jewish community 166
DIMITROVSKY, H.Z. (**6**:49; **Dc./17**:222)
– Talmud research 358
DININ, SAMUEL (**6**:57)
– Los Angeles 275
DINITZ, SIMCHA (**Dc./17**:222)
– Russian Jewry 334
– Zionist Congresses 395ff
Dinkins, David 376
DINUR, BENZION (**6**:57)
– poetry 312
Diodoros I 226
DISCRIMINATION (**6**:67)
– anti-Semitism 100
– labor law 218
– Reform Judaism 324
– Russian Jews 329
– United States 377
Dishon, Yehudit 310
Diski, Jenny 147
DIVORCE (**6**:122)
– Canada 128
– Israel 202
– U.S.A. 367ff
DNEPROPETROVSK (**6**:141)
– Jewish community 364
– pogrom 337
DOCTOROW, EDGAR LAWRENCE 139
Doesburg (Neth.) 297
DOG (**6**:152)
– legislation 218
Dolan, Zipora 178
DOLGIN, SIMON ARTHUR (**Dc./17**:223)
– Los Angeles 275
Doman, Istvan 184
Dome of the Rock 203
DOMINICAN REPUBLIC (**6**:160)
– Jewish community 128, 130
Doncaster (Austr.) 110
DONETSK (**6**:167)
– Jewish associations 334
– Jewish community 364
Donner, Batia 236
DONSKOY, MARK SEMENOVICH 140
Donsky, S. 359
Doppelt, Frederick A. 322
DOR (**6**:172)
– archaeological excavations 102ff
Dor, Moshe 179ff
Dorchin, Yaacov 236
Dordrecht (Neth.) 297
Doria, Ch. 312
Dorman, Menachem 181
Dorner, Dalia 137
DOROHOI (**6**:175)
– Jewish community 328
Doron, Aviva 309, 311ff
Doros (tn., Crimea) 267
Dorot (orgn., U.S.A.) 174
Dosic, Wayne D. 366
DOTHAN, MOSHE 140
DOTHAN, TRUDE 140
Doubleday (publ. house, U.S.A.) 318
Dragunskii, David 329
Drahobych (tn., Ukr.) 364
DRANCY (**6**:207)
– Brunner, Alois 125
DREIFUSS, RUTH 140
– Bundesrat 355
DRESDEN (**6**:211)
– Jewish community 163
Dresner, Julius 246
Drielsma, Appie 297
Drobles, Matityahu 171
Dror (youth mvmt.) 334
Drory, Rina 312
Druckman, Chaim 171
Drugs 216, 330, 372
Druk, Mircea 281
Dubb, Allie A. 344
Dubin, Charles 128
DUBLIN (**6**:248)
– Jewish community 187ff
– museum 291
– Weingreen Museum 389
– *illus:*
– – Jewish Museum 187
– – Terenure Synagogue 188
DUBROVNIK (**6**:257)
– medieval synagogue 394
Dubrovsky, Svetlana 238
Dudley, Jane 235
Duis, Thomas 233
Duke, David 99, 377
DULZIN, ARYE (**Dc./17**:224)
– Zionist ideology 396
DUNASH BEN LABRAT (**6**:270)
– poetry 310, 313
DUNEDIN (**6**:273)
– Jewish community 299
Dushanbe (tn., Tadzhikistan) 356
Dutch Resistance Museum 295
DVIR (**6**:325)
– Hebrew literature 178
Dweik, Taleb 238
DWORKIN, RONALD 141
DYEING (**6**:327)
– Ibiza and Formentera 184
Dyman, Menahem, *see* HARAN, MENAHEM
Dzhankoysk (reg., Rus.) 263

E

Easterman, David 366
East European Jewish Affairs (journ., Eng.) 186
Ebal, Mount. (Er. Isr.) 102
EBAN, ABBA (**6**:343; **Dc./17**:227)
– Pollard Affair 315
Ecology 215
Edelman, Brad 350
Edelshtein, Iulii 331
– *illus:*
– – arrival in Israel 335
EDUCATION (**6**:381)
– Argentina 105, 108
– Austria 114
– Belgium 117
– CAJE 131
– Canada 128
– Conservative Judaism 133
– England 145
– France 151
– Greece 167
– Hungary 183ff
– Iran 186
– Ireland 188
– Netherlands 295
– New Zealand 299
– publishing in U.S.A. 318
– Russia 330
– South Africa 345
– Syria 355
– Turkey 363
– U.S.A. 369
– *illus:*
– – *Gate of Mitzvah* 322
Edwin Mellen Press (publ. House, U.S.A.) 319
EFIMOV, BORIS EFIMOVICH 263
Efrat (tn., Isr.) 172
Efrat, Benni 238
EGYPT (**6**:479; **Dc./17**:229)
– anti-Semitism 100
– Argentinian missile project 107
– Cairo *Genizah* 156
– Iranian propaganda 187
– Islamic fundamentalism 197
– Israel oil imports 221
– Israel relations 206
– Karaites 258
– PLO 305
– United Nations 365
Egyseg (journ., Hung.) 184
Ehrenfeld, Asher (Georg) 327
EHRLICH, ABEL (**12**:688; **Dc./17**:473)
– music prize 234
Ehrlich, Baruch 259
Ehrlich, Marcello 234
EICHMANN, ADOLF OTTO (**6**:517)
– Brunner, Alois 125
Edelman, Adolf 338
EINSTEIN, ALBERT (**6**:535; **Dc./17**:231)
– Russian anti-Semitism 337
Ein Zik (site, Isr.) 101
Eisenberg, Paul Chaim 113
– *illus:*
– – Cantor Adler's award 175
EISENSTADT (**6**:546)
– Jewish cemetery descrated 114
– museum 290
– *illus:*
– – Jewish Museum 113
Eitan, Lior 234
Eitan, Rafael (Mossad agent) 315
EITAN, RAPHAEL ("Raful"; **Dc./17**:232)
– IDF 196
– *illus:*
– – greets Rabbi Pinḥasi 194
EITINGER, LEO S. (**6**:558)
– Norwegian literature 300
EL AL (**6**:560; **Dc./17**:232)
– Amsterdam aircraft disaster 298
ELATH (**6**:566)
– free trade zone law 215
ELAZAR, DANIEL J. 141
– Canada 128
Elazar, David H. 141
Elberg, Yehuda 392
Elbeze, D. 358
Elbilia, Gilles 350
Elburg (Neth.) 297
ELEAZAR BEN JACOB HA-BAVLI (**6**:590)
– poetry 309
Elek, Ilona 302
ELIAHU, MORDECHAI 141
– chief rabbinate 224
ELIAV, ARIE (Lova) 242
– U.S. literature 318
Eliezer, N. 357
ELION, GERTRUDE BELL 141
Elisha, Ron 112
Elishah ben Samuel (paytan, Rus.) 284
Elizur, J. 359
Elizur, S. 309ff
Elizur-Epstein, b. 358
Elkann, Jean-Paul 150
ELKIN, STANLEY 142
– U.S. literature 366
Ellis, Julie 366
Elon Moreh (stlmt., Isr.) 221
Emancipation
– France, bicentennial celebrations 152
Emanuel (tn., Isr.) 172
Emmanuel, Taamrat 121
Encyclopaedia Talmudica 358
Engel, E. 313
ENGLAND (**6**:747; **Dc./17**:234) 142
– *aliyah* to Israel 212
– anti-Semitism 98, 100
– Arab boycott 122
– Auschwitz convent controversy 109
– Conservative Judaism 135
– Falklands War 105
– ḥavurah movement 174
– *ḥazzanut* 175
– Institute of Jewish Afairs 185ff
– Iranian Jews 186
– Jewish-Christian relations 252
– museums 291
– Pres. Herzog's visit 209
– Reform Judaism 324
– struggle for Soviet Jewry 332
– Waldheim affair 389
– Yiddish literature 392
– *illus:*
– – anti-Semitic propaganda 100

Englander, Tibor (Samuel) 183
ENGLISH LITERATURE (**6**:773; **Dc./17**:237) 145
Engonopoulo, Niko 169
ENTEBBE RAID (**Dc./17**:238)
- Shomron, Dan 344
EPSTEIN, JACOB NAHUM (**6**:830)
- geonic literature 157ff
- Talmud research 357
Epstein, Zipporah 360
Equestrian 350
Erder, Yoram 259
Erens, Patricia 366
ERFURT (**6**:837)
- Jewish community 163
ERLIK, DAVID 243
Eruv (leg. device) 144
Espionage
- Pollard affair 99, 314, 377
- Sharansky exchange 333
Essas, Eliahu 331
Estaban, Fenando Diaz 311
ESTONIA (**6**:916) 147
- anti-Semitism 338
- Jewish population 328
ETHICS (**6**:933)
- geonic literature 157
ETHIOPIA (**6**:943)
- airlift of Jews to bIsrael 191, 199, 210
- Beta Israel 119, 206
- U.S. struggle for release of Jews 376
Et La'asot (journ., Isr.) 134
ETTINGER, SOLOMON (**6**:954)
- Yiddish literature 391
Etzioni, Moshe 229
Europa (newsp., Rum.) 327
European Economic Community
- France 149
- Israel relations 209
- Italy 245
- Likkud opposition to peace concept 207
European Jewish Congress 150
European Parliament 149, 333
European Soccer Federation 352
EUTHANASIA (**6**:978)
- legislation 218
EVANS, ELI 147
Evans, Gareth 112
EVENARI, MICHAEL (**6**:983)
- Israel Prize 241
EVEN-OR, MARY 293
- necrology 234
Everac, Paul 327
Evers, Hans 298
Evers, S. 295
Evosges (vill., Fr.) 116
Evseev, Evgeni 330
EXPULSIONS (**6**:1069)
- 500th anniversary of Spain 341
EZRA, DEREK, LORD 147
Ezyon bloc 172

F

Fabian, Hans-Erich 161
FABIUS, LAURENT147
- AIDS scandal 149
Fairbanks (city, Alsk.) 97
FAITLOVITCH, JACQUES (**6**:1137)
- Bogale, Yona 121
Falashas, *see* BETA ISRAEL
Falas(h) moura (Chr. Beta Israel) 119, 212, 225
FALK, PETER 282
Falklands War 99, 105
FAMILY (**6**:1164)
- Falashas 120
- ḥavurah movement 174
- Mountain Jews 285
Farandaouri, Maria 233
Farrakhan, Louis 99, 375, 384
Fassbind, Alfred 175
Fatkh-Ali-Khan 285
Faurisson, Robert 100, 144
FBI 315
Federation CJA (Can.) 128
Federation of Jewish Men's Club (U.S.) 134
Federation of Jewish Welfare Organizations (L.A.) 277
Federation of Romanian Jewish Communities 327
Fedorenko, Feodor 379
Fefer, Joelle 351
Feierstein, Ricardo 348
FEIFFER, JULES 148
Fein, David 236
Fein, Leonard 367
Feinberg, Kai 300
FEINBRUN-DOTHAN, NAOMI 243
Feingold, Ben-Ami 181
FEINSTEIN, ELAINE 148
- English literature 145
Feintuch, J.Z. 358
FELDER, GEDALIA (**Dc./17**:246)
- Canada 128
Feldheim (publ. house, U.S.A.) 319
Feldman, Y. 309ff
Feldman, Yael 181
Feldmann, Fabio 123
Feldmayer, Peter 184
Feldstein, Donald 368ff
Feliks, J. 357
Felipe (Pr., Sp.) 168
Fencing 350
FEODOSIYA (**6**:1224)
- Krimchaks 266
FERDINAND AND ISABELLA (**6**:1228)
- beatification 254
Fergana (prov., Uzbek.) 385
Fernandes, Rene 129
FERRARA (**6**:1231)
- Jewish community 244
Fertility 198
FESTIVALS (**6**:1237)
- ḥavurah movement 174
- Reform Judaism 322
- Russia 331ff, 335
FEUERSTEIN, REUVEN (**13**:1346)
- Israel Prize 244
Fichman, David Mironovich, *see* KNUT, DOVID
FICHMANN, JACOB (**6**:1258)
- Hebrew literature 180
Fields, Harvey 275
FINAL SOLUTION (**6**:1278)
- Austria 387
- Brunner, Alois 125
Finer, I. 392
Finestein, Israel 145
Fink, Berny 236
Fink, Janis, *see* IAN, JANIS
FINKELSTEIN, LOUIS (**6**:1293; **Dc./17**:247)
- Conservative Judaism 134
- Talmud research 359
FINKIELKRAUT, ALAIN 148
FINLAND (**6**:1295)
- *aliyah* transit point 338
- Estonian community 147
FINNISTON, SIR HAROLD MONTAGUE (Monty) 149
Finta, Imre 127
F.L.P.E., *see* Fonds d'Investissement Pour l'Education
Fischer, Franz 296
Fischer, Georg, *see* BRUNNER, ALOIS
Fischer, Yona 237
Fish, Jon 351
Fish, Morris 128
Fishman, Sylvia Barack 368ff
FITERMAN, CHARLES 149
Fiterman, Jacobo 106
Flanders (reg., Belg.) 117
Flaum-Singer, June 367
Flax, Ken 351
Fleischer, Bruce 350
Fleischer, Ezra 309ff
FLORENCE (**6**:1358)
- museum 290
FLORIDA (**6**:1361)
- 500th anniversary of expulsion of Jews from Spain 341
- Jewish political force 377
- press 317
F.N. (polit. party, Fr.) *see* National Front
Fogel, David 180
FOGELBERG, DAN 292
FOLKLORE (**6**:1374)
- Krimchaks 269
Fonda, Jane 301
Fonds d'Investissement Pour l'Education 151
Fonds Social Juif Unifié 150
Football (American) 350
Formentera (Balearic Isl.) *see* IBIZA and FORMENTERA
Fort Lauderdale 369
Forverts, see JEWISH DAILY FORWARD
Foster, Lawrence 232
Foster City (U.S.A.) 258
Fountain, Ian 233
Fradkin, Daniel 232
Fraenkel, J. 360
Fram, David 392
FRANCE (**7**:7; **Dc./17**:248) 149
- *aliyah* to Israel 212
- anti-Semitism 98
- Arab boycott 122
- Barbie trial 115
- Brunner, Alois 125
- Conservative Judaism 135
- Iranian Jews 186
- Israel Sonfonietta tour 232
- museum 292
- Pres. Herzog's visit 209
- Sephardim 342
- Syrian Jews, plight of 356
- Yiddish literature 392
- *illus:* text
- - Paris Museum of Jewish Art 291
FRANCO, AVRAHAM 152
Franco, Hillel 169
FRANK, ANNE (**7**:52; **Dc./17**:250)
- Holocaust denial 100
- *illus:*
- - anti-Semitic doggerel 99
Frank, Irit 240
Frank, John 300
Frankel, Y.
- Talmud research 360
FRANKFORT ON THE MAIN (**7**:83)
- Jewish community 161ff
- museum 290
- *illus:*
- - Rothschild Palais 161
Franzos, J. 359
Freehling, Allen 275
FREEHOF, SOLOMON BENNETT (**7**:121)
- Reform Judaism 323ff
Freiheits Partei (polit. party, Aus.) 98
FRENCH LITERATURE (**7**:138; **Dc./17**:250)
- French Jewry 152
FRENKEL, IZḤAK YEDIDIAH (**Dc./17**:255)
- Recanati, Abraham Samuel 320
Frenkel, Rachel 180
Frey, Gerhard 162
FRIBOURG (**7**:170)
- Jewish community 355
Fridland, Mikhail Yefeimovich, *see* KOL'TSOV, MIKHAIL
Fried, Lynn 366
FRIEDAN, BETTY 153
Friedberg, John 350
Friedberg, Paul 350
FRIEDENBERG, SAMUEL (**7**:175)
- JTS museum 288
FRIEDKIN, WILLIAM 282
Friedlander, Eitan 352
FRIEDLANDER, SAUL (**7**:182)
- Israel Prize 240
FRIEDMAN, DANIEL 243
Friedman, Harry G. 288
FRIEDMAN, JEROME ISAAC 153
Friedman, Lawrence S. 366
Friedman, Murray 375
Friedman, Rosemary 146
Friedman, Samuel S. 366
FRIENDLY, HENRY JACOB 153
FRISCHMANN, DAVID (**7**:198)
- Hebrew literature 178, 181
Frith, Benjamin 233
Frizis, Mordechai 168
FROMAN, DOV 243
FROMAN, IAN 242
Front National (polit. party, Fr.) 98
Frosh, Sidney 145
Fruchtman, M. 309
Frum, Barbara 128
Frunze, *see* Bishkek
F.S.J.U., *see* Fonds Social Juif Unifié
Fuchs, C.L. 392
Fuchs, Esther 181
Fuks, Rena 298
Fumagalli, Pierfrancesco 245
Fundacion Tzedaka (Arg.) 108
Funès, Louis de 305
Fuxon-Heyman, Sarah 234

G

Gabbai, Eliyahu 310
Gabel, Andrew 350
GABIROL, SOLOMON BEN JUDAH, IBN (**7**:235)
- Cairo *Genizah* 156
Gal, Fedor 136
GALILEE (**17**:265)
- Arabs 203
- archaeological excavations 101
- Gery 164
- Lebanon War 189, 196, 206
- legislation 216
- new settlements 213
- Russian immigrants 211
- wind energy 221
- *illus:*
- - aerial view of *mizpim* 214
Galilee Soloists Chamber Ensemble 232
Galinski, Heinz 161ff
Galsky, Desider 135
GAMALA (**7**:295)
- archaeological excavations 103
GAMBLING (**7**:299)
- American Jews 372
Gamsakhurdiia, Zviad 160
GAMUS GALLEGOS, PAULINA 154
Gandel, John 110
Gandhi, Indira 262
Gandhi, Rajiv 185
Gans, Isaac 154
GANS, MOZES ("Max") H. 154, 298
Ganshtakovka (stlmt., Rus.) 287
Ganuz, Y. 313
Gaon, Izzika 237
GAON, SOLOMON (**7**:325)
- Spanish prize 168
Garbuz, Yair 237
GARFUNKLE, ART 292
Gass, Adolfo 105
Gavison, Shabi 240
Gaylord, Mitch 302, 350
Gayssot Law (Fr.) 152
GAZA STRIP (**7**:343)
- *intifada* 191ff, 203
- new settlements 213
GDANSK (**7**:346)
- *ḥazzanut* 175
- JTS musuem 288
Gecas, Antony 143
Gechtman, Gideon 236
GEFFEN, DAVID 292
GEHINNOM (**7**:357)
- archaeological excavations 102
GEKHT, SEMEN GRIGOREVICH 154
Geldman, Mordechai 179
GELFAND, EVGENIY ALEKSANDROVICH GNEDIN 154
GELFOND (Gelfand), ALEXANDER LAZAREVICH (Israel) 154
Geller, Max 352
Gemaryahu ben Shaphan 102
Gemayel, Amin 190
Gemayel, Basheer 189ff, 196
GENEVA (**7**:402)
- Jewish community 354
- Sephardim 342

GENIZAH (7:404; **Dc./17**:259) 155
- geonic literature 158
- Greek Jewry 168
- poetry, medieval 309ff
- Talmud research 357ff
GENOA (7:407)
- Jewish community 244
- Krimchaks 267ff
Genscher, Hans-Dietrich 163
GEONIC LITERATURE 157
George, St. 337
George II (Gr.)
- *illus:*
-- Rabbi Koretz and 264
GEORGIA (7:423; CIS rep.) 160
- Jewish population 328
- Komzet 264
Gerber, I. 286
GERIZIM, MOUNT (7:436)
- archaeological excavations 103
GERMANY (7:457; **Dc./17**:261) 161
- anti-Semitism 98, 100
- Arab boycott 122
- Israel Sinfonietta tour 232
- Jewish-Christian relations 253
- museums 290
- Poetry, Hebrew 313
- Soviet Jews 211, 339
Germany, East (G.D.R.) 163, 175
GERONDI, ZERAHIAH BEN ISAAC HA-LEVI (7:509)
- poetry 309
Gersh, Joe 112
Gershenson, Oscar 233
GERSHOM BEN JUDAH ME'OR HA-GOLAH (7:511)
- poetry 313
Gershuni, Moshe 238
GERSON-KIWI, EDITH (7:519)
- obituary 234
Gerstein, Dudu 238
Gertz, Nurith 181
GERY (Rus. gp.) 164
Gesher (seminar program, Isr.) 231
Getter, Tamar 238
Geva, Avital 238
Geva, Tsibi 238
GHENT (7:541)
- Jewish community 117
GHETTO (7:542)
- Ibiza and Formentera 185
Gil, Moshe 156, 259
Gilad, Ya'acov 240
Gilat, Y.D. 360
Gilbert, Brad 302, 351
GILBERT, MARTIN 164
- Soviet Jewry, struggle for 333
GILBOA, AMIR (7:569)
- Hebrew literature 179ff
- Israel Prize 240
GILBOA, JACOB (**Dc./17**:473)
- music prize 234
Gilboa, Menucha 180
Gilboa, Moshe 166
GILEAD, ZERUBAVEL (7:572)
- Hebrew literature 179
Gillman, Sid 350
GINNOSAR (7:578)
- archaeological excavations 103
Ginsberg, Brian 350
Ginton, Ellen 237ff
GINZBERG, LOUIS (7:584)
- geonic letters 159
- Talmud research 358
Girsch, Pesi 239
Gish, Lillian 239
Gitlin, Michael 238
GLASGOW (7:602)
- Jewish community 143
- *Jewish Echo* closes down 145
Glasnost (freedom of cultural life) 333, 337
Glas-Wiener, Sheva 392
Glazer, J. 298
Glemp, Cardinal 109
Gklickstein, Shlomo 351
Glid, Nandor 393
Glikman, J. 357
Gluckman, Ann 299
GLUECK, NELSON (7:627)
- Hebrew Union College 321
GNEDIN-GELFAND, EVGENIY ALEKSANDROVICH, *see* GELFAND, EVGENIY ALEXSANDROVICH GNEDIN
GNESSIN,URI NISSAN (7:634)
- Hebrew literature 181
Goffin, Gerry 292
GOITEIN, SHLOMO DOV (7:694)
- Cairo *Genizah* 156
- poetry 311
Gokavitzki, J. 358
Gold, Alan 128
GOLD, PHILIP 165
Goldberg, A. 357
Goldberg, Gloria 366
Goldberg, Itche 392
Goldberg, Lester 366
Goldbloom, Victor 128
GOLDBLUM, NATHAN 242
Goldemberg, José 123
Goldenberg, Jo 152
Goldene Keyt, Die (journ., Isr.) 391
Goldenstein, Chaim 392
GOLDIN, JUDAH (7:718)
- Talmud research 359
Goldkorn, Isaac 392
Goldman, Alex J. 366
Goldscheider, Calvin 367
Goldschmidt, D. 159, 309, 313
GOLDSCHMIDT, LAZARUS (7:729)
- Talmud research 358
Goldshten, Isai 161
GOLDSTEIN, FANNY (7:745)
- Jewish Book Council 250
Goldstein, Joseph (au.) 181
GOLDSTEIN, JOSEPH LEONARD 165
- Brown, Michael Stuart 125
Goldstein, Limor 240
Goldstein, Margie 350
Goldstein, Naomi, *see* FRIEDAN, BETTY
GOLDSTEIN, SIDNEY (7:749)
- American Jews 368
- demography 161
Goldstein, Zvi 238
Golf 188, 350
Golinkin, Noah 134
Golombeck, Isaac 236
Golvan, Colin 113
Goma-Mazod (tn., Iraq) 156
GOMEL (7:767)
- Jewish community 117
Gondar (reg. Eth.) 119
Gonen, Rika 239
Gonz, Arpad 183ff
Gonzalez, Felipe 298
Goodblatt, Avrum 168
Goodman, Susan 238
Goodside, Grace, *see* PALEY, GRACE
Gorbachev, Mikhail 123, 210, 330, 334, 343, 351
- *illus:*
-- with Henry Sobel 124
Gorckhavskya, Maria 350
GORDIMER, NADINE (7:786; **12**:786) 165
- Nobel Prize 299
GORDIS, ROBERT (7:789)
- Conservative Judaism 133
Gordish, D.M. 360
GORDON, JUDAH LEIB (7:797)
- Hebrew literature 181
GORDON, MICHAEL 282
GOREN, SHLOMO (7:808; **Dc./17**:269)
- Talmud research 359
GORKI (7:810)
- Jewish community 734
GORKI, MAXIM (7:810)
- Gelfond, A.L. 155
Gornichem (Neth.) 297
GORNICK, VIVIAN 165
Gorodetskii, Lev 334
Gorokhovskaya, Maria 302
GOSHEN-GOTTSTEIN, MOSHE 242
GOTTLIEB, ALLAN (7:820)
- Canada 128
Gottfried, Brian 351
GOTTSCHALK, ALFRED (**Dc./17**:270)
- H.U.C. 321
- Los Angeles 275
Gottstein, Jacob 97
Goudsmit, R. 298
GOULD, MILTON S. 165
Gourgey, Percy S. 185
GOURI, HAIM (7:832; **Dc./17**:170)
- Hebrew literature 179
- Israel Prize 242
Gouttman, Rodney 113
Govrin Nurit 181
Grabb, Jim 351
Gradstein, Rabbi 185
GRAEBE, HERMANN FRIEDRICH 166
GRAETZ, HEINRICH (7:845)
- Schorsch, Ismar 344
Graff, Michael 113
Graham, Marthaa 302
Granick, Sam 121
GRAY, HERBERT (7:862; **Dc./17**:179)
- Canadian politics 128
GRAYZEL, SOLOMON (7:863)
- Jewish Book Council 250
GREECE (7:687; **Dc./17**:279) 166
- Brunner, Alois 125
- museum 290
- Sephardim 342
- Waldheim, Kurt 387
GREEK LITERATURE, MODERN (7:898) 169
Greek Orthodox Church (Isr.) 227
Green, W.A. 360
Green, Warren P. 259
Greenbaum, A. 157
Greenbaum, Dan 302, 351
GREENBERG, HENRY BENJAMIN (Hank; 7:904)
- baseball 349
GREENBERG, IRVING (7:904)
- CLAL 131
- American Judaism 373
GREENBERG, MOSHE 169
GREENBERG, SIMON (7:906)
- Los Angeles 276
Greenberg, Steve 349
GREENBERG, URI ẒEVI (7:906; **Dc./17**:280)
- Hebrew literature 180
GREENFIELD, JONAS CARL 170
Greenfield, Robert 366
GRENOBLE (7:922)
- Jewish community 149
Grief, Gidon 168
GRINSPUN, BERNARDO 170
- Argentina 105
Grodzinski (bakery, Eng.) 145
GRONINGEN (7:931)
- synagogue 290
GROSSMAN, DAVID 170
- Germany 165
- Hebrew literature 176, 178
- U.S. literature 318
Grossman, Larry 128
Grossman, Vasili 337
Grosz, Paul 114
GROZNY (7:940)
- Mountain Jews 284
Gruber, Karl 387
Grubman, Michael 238
GRUENING, ERNEST HENRY (7:947)
- Alaska 97
Grunzweig, Emil 217
Guarda (tn., port.) 316
Gulf War, *see* Persian Gulf War
Gur-Arieh, Eli 238
GUREVICH, MIKHAIL IOSIFOVICH 170
GUSH EMUNIM (**Dc./17**:281) 171
- American Friends 381
- new settlements 213ff
- peace movements 307
- politics 195, 223ff
Gutman, Amos 239ff
GUTTMAN, ISRAEL 172
GVATI, CHAIM 240
Gweru (tn., Zimbabwe) 394
Gyarmati, Dezso 302
Gymnastics 350
GYÖR (7:999)
- Hungary 184

H

HAARLEM (7:1008)
- Jewish community 296
Haas, P.J. 357
ḤABAD (7:1013)
- Argentina 107
- Australia 110
- Brazil 123
- France 150ff
- Hungary 184
- Italy 244
- Los Angeles 274
- Netherlands 295
- New Zealand 299
- politics in Israel 223
- press 316
- Russia 331ff
- South Africa 345
- U.S. displays 375
HABERMANN, ABRAHAM MEIR (7:1024)
- poetry 309ff
HABIBI, EMIL 244
Hadany, Israel 236
HADASSAH (7:1041)
- U.S. membership 383
- Zionist Congress (31st) 395
Hadassah Magazine (period., U.S.A.) 318
HADASSI, JUDAH (7:1046)
- Karaite philosophy 259
Haddad, Carolyn 366
ḤADERAH (7:1047)
- power station 220
Hadomi, Lea 181
HAGGADAH, PASSOVER (7:1079)
- Reform Judaism 322
- *illus:*
-- India (1875) 185
-- Russian-Hebrew 225
HAGGAHOT (7:1104)
- Talmud research 357
HAGUE, THE (7:1123)
- Jewish community 294ff
- Jewish Historical Museum 290
Haguel, Daniel 168
HAI BEN SHERIRA (7:1130)
- Cairo *Genizah* 156
- geonic literaqture 157
- poetry 309
Haider, Jörg 114
HAIFA (7:1133)
- Gulf War 208
- Muslim court 228
- population 200, 214
- Reform Judaism 321
Haifa Symphony Orchestra 232, 234
HAITI (7:1141)
- Jewish community 130
Hajj (Musl. pilgrimage) 229
Hakim, Danny 351
Ḥakkak, Balfour 310
Ḥakkak, Herzl 310
Hakkerts, Sara 238
HALAKHAH (7:1156)
- geonic literature 157
- *ḥazzanut* 175
- Orthodoxy, Modern 303
- Reform Judaism 323
- U.S. religious life 373
HALAKHOT GEDOLOT (7:1167)
- new edition 158
HALAKHOT KEẒUVOT (7:1170)
- geonic literature 158
HALAKHOT PESUKOT (7:1171)
- Yehudai Gaon 158
Halamisch, M. 359
Halegua, Moshe 167
Halerstadt, Eva 298
Halevi, Dr. 264
Halevi, Yosef 181
Ḥalfi, Avraham 180
Halivni, D. 358
HALKIN, SIMON (7:1192; **Dc./17**:287)
- Hebrew literature 179, 181
Hallevi, Haim 257
Hallo, Joe 168

HALPER, BENZION (**7**:1202)
– geonic literature 158
Halperin, Hagit 181
Hamas (Isl. orgn.) 186, 191ff, 197, 203, 206, 306
HAMBURG (**7**:1225)
– Jewish community 161
Hamburger, Viktor 271
HAMEIRI, AVIGDOR (**7**:1231)
– Hebrew literature 178, 181
Hameiri, Israel 178
Hamelburg, S. 357
HAMLISCH, MARVIN 282
HAMMAT-GADER (**7**:1241)
– archaeological excavations 103, 104
HAMMER, ARMAND 172
HAMMER, ZEVULUN (**Dc./17**:287)
– education minister 230
Hamzi, Alberto 175
HANANEL BEN HUSHI'EL (**7**:1252)
– Cairo *Genizah* 155
Hanaton (kib., Isr.) 134
Handeli, Yaakov 168
Hanukaevs (fam., Rus.) 285
HANUKKAH (**7**:1280)
– Habad in France 150
– Karaites 257
HAPOEL (**7**:1319)
– Israel 353
Haran, Menahem 173
Harare (city, Zimbabwe) 394
HARARI, HAYYIM 242
HARARI, OVADIAH 241
Harari Commission (Isr.) 231
HARBIN (**7**:1331)
– Kaufman, Avraham Yosifovich 260
Hardy, René 115
Hare Krishna (cult) 372
Hareven, Shulamith 176, 177
Har he-Halutz (observation outpost, Isr.) 322
HARMAN (HERMAN), ABRAHAM (**7**:1344)
– Public Council for Soviet Jewry 332
Harmenberg, Johan 302
Harpenas, G. 159, 358
HARRIS, BARBARA 282
Harris, Charles 351
Harris, Cyril 345
HARTMAN, DAVID 173
Hartt, Stanley 128
HA-SHOMER HA-ZAIR (**7**:1372)
– Russia 334
Hasida, Y. 309
Hassan Bey Mosque (Jaffa) 228
Hassan II (k., Mor.) 207
HATOKAI, ALDIN 241
Hatzi, Dimitri 169
Hauptmann, Bruno Richard 390
Havazelet, H. 158
Havazelet, M. 359
Havel, Vaclav 135, 389
HAVURAH (mvmt., U.S.A.) 174
– Los Angeles 274
Hawke, Bob 112
Hayde, A. van der 359
Hayden, Bill 111
Hayman, D. 359
Hayoun, M.R. 358
Hazan, Ephraim 309ff
HAZAN, YA'AKOV (**7**:1523)
– Israel Prize 242
HAZAZ, HAYYIM (**7**:1524; **Dc./17**:289)
– Hebrew literature 181
HA-ZORE'A (**7**:1540)
– archaeological excavations 101
HAZZAN (**7**:1542; **Dc./17**:289) 174
– U.S. women 373
– *illus:* text
– – Archipova synagogue, Moscow 336
HEBREW GRAMMAR (**8**:77; **Dc./17**:292)
– French schools 151
– geonic literature 157, 159
– Russia 330ff
– Syria 356
HEBREW LITERATURE, MODERN (**8**:175; **Dc./17**:295) 176
Hebrew Publishing (publ. house, U.S.A.) 319
HEBREW UNION COLLEGE–JEWISH INSTITUTE OF RELIGION (HUC-JIR; **8**:216; **Dc./17**:300)
– *hazzanut* 176
– Los Angeles 275
– Reform Judaism 321
– Skirball Museum 288
HEBREW UNIVERSITY OF JERUSALEM (**8**:219; **Dc./17**:300)
– Yiddish studies 392
HEBRON (**8**:226)
– Jewish underground attack on Muslim college 203
HECHT, REUBEN (**Dc./17**:301)
– Israel Prize 242
Hecker, Zvi 236
Heerlen (tn., Neth.) 295
HEFER, HAYIM (**8**:241)
– Israel Prize 240
Hefetz, Yaacov 236
Heffner, Avraham 240
HEIDELBERG (**8**:256)
– College for Jewish Studies 163
Heilbrunn, Philip 111
Heinemann, J. 313
HEINEMANN, YIZHAK (**8**:277)
– poetry 309ff
Heintz, A.L. 295
HELFMAN, ELHANAN 243
HELLER, BUNIM (**8**:307)
– Yiddish literature 392
Heller, Dov 236
Heller, Rachel 238
Helsinki Accords 333
Hemley, Cecil 132
HENDEL, IDA (**12**:692)
– *illus:*
– – Huberman Gala Concert 233
HENDEL, JUDITH (**8**:323)
– Hebrew literature 177
Henefeld, Nadav 349
Henrietta Szold (refugee ship) 320
Henrix, Hans Hermann 255
HENRY, BUCK 282
Heppner, Dorothy 128
Herlitz, Esther 233
Hermon, Shalom 236
HERODIUM (**8**:388)
– archaeological excavations 103
Herscher, Uri D. 276
Herschler, M. 357
Herschman, Mordechai 176
Hershberg, Israel 238
HERSHEY, BARBARA 283
HERSTIK, NAPHTALI (**Dc./17**:290)
– *hazzanut* 175
HERTZBERG, ARTHUR (**8**:398; **Dc./17**:302)
– American Jews 368
HERUT MOVEMENT (**8**:400)
– politics in Israel 193
Herzberg, Abel J. 298
HERZLIYYAH (**8**:421)
– art museum 236
Herzog, Aura 182
HERZOG, CHAIM (**8**:424; **Dc./17**:303) 181
– Argentina visit 107
– Australia visit 111
– Canada visit 126
– Denmark visit 137
– 500th anniversary of expulsion of Jews from Spain 342
– France visit 152
– Germany visit 163
– Hungary visit 184
– Ireland 187
– Poland visit 314
– United Nations 364
– world tour 209
– *illus:*
– – addressing Canadian Parliament 126
– – family exhibit 187
– – King Taufa'ahau Topou IV of Tonga with 210
– – Pres. De Klerk of south Africa 346
– – Pres. Mobutu of Zaire 209
– – reciting *kaddish* in Bergen-Belsen 163
HERZOG, ISAAC (**8**:422)
– Herzog, Chaim 181
Herzog, Sarah, 181
Herzstein, Barbara, *see* HERSHEY, BARBARA
Heskes, Irene 176
Hess, Walter 128
Hidden Children Conference 296
Hier, Marvin 274
Hilaly, Taj al- 112
Hilberg, Raul 182
HILDESHEIMER, AZRIEL (**8**:476)
– geonic literature 158
Hildesheimer, N.Z. 158
Himmelreich, Alfonse 239
Hirsch, John 128
HIRSCH, JUDD 360
Hirsch, Richard 323
HIRSCHMANN, IRA ARTHUR 182
Hirshberg, Jehoash 259
Hirshman, M.G. 359
HISTADRUT (**8**:534)
– Arab representatives 202
– economy and inflation 191ff
– Likkud attitude 193
– National Health Service 194
HISTADRUT IVRIT OF AMERICA (**8**:542)
– Jewish Book Council 250
Histadrut Morim (teachers' union, Isr.) 229
HISTORIOGRAPHY (**8**:551)
– Hebrew literature 180
HIWI AL-BALKHI (**8**:792)
– Cairo *genizah* 155
– geonic literature 159
Hizbollah (Isl. orgn.) 186
Hoban, Russell 146
Hobart (city, Austr.) 111
Hoch, Jan Ludvik, *see* MAXWELL, ROBERT
Hockey, Field 350
Hoffman, Charles 382
Hoffman, Louise 113
Hoffman, Yoel 177ff
Hoffmann, Sh. 360
HOHENEMS (**8**:815)
– Sulzer, Salomon 175
Holl, Hartmut 233
Holman, Marshall 350
HOLOCAUST (**8**:828)
– anti-Semitism and denial 100, 144
– Auschwitz convent controversy 108
– Australian War Crimes Act 112
– Barbie trial 115
– Belgium 118
– Brunner, Alois 125
– Canada 126
– CLAL 131
– Czechlovakian victims 136
– English literature 147
– France 152
– Greek Jewry 166ff
– Greek literature 169
– Israel legislation 216
– Jewish-Christian relations 251
– Karaites 259
– Klarsfeld, Beate and Serge 261
– Krimchaks 266
– Memorial Foundation For Jewish Culture 280
– Mountain Jews 287
– museums 289, 328
– Netherlands 296
– Norwegian literature 301
– Polish responsibility 314
– Romania 328
– Russian anti-Zionists 330
– Russian Jews 334
– Swiss memorial 355
– U.S. literature 318; 365
– U.S. memorialization 378
– Waldheim's Nazi activities 113
– Yugoslavia 393
– *illus:*
– – Berne cemetery 355
– – 40th anniversary of French Jews' deportation 151
Holocaust and Genocide Studies (journ., Isr.) 116
Holocaust and Heroism Day (Rus.) 334
HOLON (**8**:918)
– population 200
– Reform Judaism 321
Holtzman, Avner 181
HOLY PLACES (**8**:920)
– Christian 227
Holy Sepulcher, Church of the (Jer.) 227
Holzman, William (Red.) 349
HOMOSEXUALITY (**8**:961)
– Netherlands 296
– Reform Judaism 324
– United States 376
Honecker, Erich 164
Hopkins S. 309
Horodisch, Abraham 298
HOROVITZ, ISRAEL 182
Horowitz, Ch. 358
Horowitz, Jacob 180
Horowitz, Winowa, *see* RYDER, WINONA
Horse racing 350
Horthy, Miklos 278
Horvat Alim (site, Isr.) 104
Horvat Rosh Zayit (site, Isr.) 102
HOSPITALS (**8**:1033)
– Christians in Israel 228
– Iran 187
Howard, Michael 143
Howe, Sir Geoffrey 144
Hoyerswerda (tn., Ger.) 162
Hozerim bi-teshuvah ("returners to religion"), *see* BA'ALEI TESHUVAH
Hurdlicka, Alfred 113
HUBERMAN, BRONISLAW (**8**:1055)
– Huberman gala concert 232
– *illus:*
– – musicians participating 233
Humphrey, Judith 168
HUNGARY (**8**:1078; **Dc./17**:317) 18:
– anti-Semitism 99
– Conservative Judaism 135
– *hazzanut* 175
– Israeli orchestra tours 222
– Israel relations 209, 234
– Jewish-Christian relations 253
– Lutz, Carl 278
– museum 292
– Romanian ethnic tension 327
– Soviet Jews 211, 339
Hunter Publishing (publ. house, U.S.A.) 319
Hurd, Douglas 144
Hurgin, Jacob 178
HUROK, SOLOMON (**8**:1113)
– Dershowitz' defense of Siegel 139
Hurvitz, Ya'ir 179ff
HUSSEIN (**8**:1131)
– Arafat agreement 203
– Israel relations 207ff
Hussein, Saddam 144, 186, 197, 202, 205, 208
Hypnosis 215

I

IAN, JANIS 292
Iantovskii, Semen 332
Ibgi, Moshe 240
IBIZA and FORMENTERA (Baleari Isl.) 184
IBN EZRA, ABRAHAM (**8**:1163)
– Cairo *Genizah* 156
– poetry 309ff
IBN EZRA, ISAAC (**8**:1170)
– poetry 309
IBN EZRA, MOSES (**8**:1170)
– poetry 309
IBN GHAYYAT, ISAAC (**8**:1175)
– poetry 309
IBN ZABARA, JOSEPH BEN MEIR (**8**:1211)
– poetry 311
Ice skating 350
'Id ad-Adha (Musl. feast) 229
'Id al-Fitr (Musl. fest) 229
IHUD HABONIM (**8**:1240)
– South Africa 347
IJA, *see* INSTITUTE OF JEWISH AFFAIRS
Ikonicoff, Moises 106
Iliescu (pres., Rum.) 328

Il'inka (vill., Rus.) 164
ILLINOIS (**8**:1254)
– Jewish political force 377
IMBER, NAPHTALI HERZ (**8**:1290)
– Hebrew literature 181
Imberman, Shmuel 240
Immanuel College (Eng.) 145
INBAL, ELIAHU (**Dc./17**:473)
– Israel cultural life 234
INBAL DANCE THEATER (**8**:1309)
– dance in Israel 235
INCEST (**8**:1316)
– American Jews 372
INDEPENDENCE DAY, ISRAEL (**8**:1344)
– India 185
– Russian celebrations 331
– *illus:*
– – Conservative Prayer 134
INDIA (**8**:1349; **Dc./17**:319) 185
– Israel relations 206, 209
– *illus:* text
INDIANAPOLIS (**8**:1362)
– 500th anniversary of expulsion of Jews from Spain 341
Indo-Israel Friendship League 185
INQUISITION (**8**:1380)
– Ibiza and Formentera 184
Institute for Historical Review (U.S.) 379
Institute for Jewish Experience 131
INSTITUTE OF JEWISH AFFAIRS 185
– Jewish writers' circle 146
Intermarriage, *see* MIXED MARRIAGE
International Association of Lawyers 333
International Catholic-Jewish Liaison Committee 251
International Christian Embassy 227
International Coalition for the Revival of the Jews of Yemen 380
International Council of Christians and Jews 188
International Council of Jewish Women 188
International Harp Contest (Jer.) 233
International Jewish Committee on Interreligious Consultations 251, 386
Intifada
– Administered Territories 203
– beginning of 191
– Canadian public opinion 126
– economy of Israel 219
– IDF 196ff
– Iranian press 187
– Israeli Arabs 202
– Palestinian nationalism 189
– PLO 306
– *illus:*
– – Bir Zeit University students 204
– – PLO poster 205
– – rioting in Nablus *Casbah* 191
IONNINA (**8**:1435)
– Greek literature 169
– Jewish community 166
– *illus:*
– – birth amulet 166
Ioannou, Georgos 167, 169
IRAN (**8**:1439; **Dc./17**:321) 186
– anti-Semitism 100
– Israel, threat to 197, 208
– Jewish community 212
– Klarsfeld, Serge 261
– Los Angeles 273
– Mountain Jews 284
– terrorist attack on Istanbul synagogue 362
"Irangate" 186, 378
IRAQ (**8**:1444)
– Arab boycott 122
– Argentinian missile project 107
– England 144
– German aid 163
– Gulf War 197, 205
– Iran war 186, 197, 208
– PLO 306
Iraqi-Iranian War 186, 208
IRELAND (**8**:1464; **Dc./17**:322) 187
– museum 291
Ireland–Israel Economic and Business Association 188
Irgun Morim (teachers' union, Isr.) 229
Irish Council of Christians and Jews 188
Irish Genealogical Congress 188
Irish–Israel Friendship Association 188
Irving, David 100, 127, 144
Isaac ben Solomon al-Ahdab 309
Isaac-Polachek, Nurit 238
ISAACS, JEREMY 188
ISAACSON, JOSÉ 188
ISAIAH (**9**:44)
– Saadiah Gaon's commentary 155
Isenberg, Shirley 185
ISFAHAN (**9**:77)
– Jewish community 186
Ish-Shalom, Michael 312
ISLAM (**9**:92)
– fundamentalism and anti-Semitism 100
– Iranian revolution 186
– Mountain Jews 284
– Netherlands synagogue 295
– Islamic Jihad 203
Islamic Movement (Isr.) 203
Islamic Resistance Movement, *see* Ḥamas
"Islamic Revolution" 186
ISRAEL, LAND OF
PREHISTORY (**Dc./17**:323)
– archaeological excavations 100ff
ISRAEL, STATE OF
AGRICULTURE (**9**:773; **Dc./17**:367)
– labor force 201
– Palestinian workers 192
ALIYAH AND ABSORPTION (**9**:515; **Dc./17**:345) 210
– Argentina 199
– Azerbaijan 115
– Belarus 117
– Beta Israel 119, 206, 224, 231, 249, 380
– Caribbean Jewish communities 129
– economy 219
– Estonia 147
– Ethiopia 191, 199, 219, 226
– Georgia 160
– Gery 164
– Hungary 183ff
– India 185
– Kazakhstan 260
– Kyrgyzstan 270
– Lithuania 272
– Moldova 281
– Latvia 270
– population growth 198
– Romania 327
– Russia 189, 195, 198ff, 206, 214, 219, 224, 226, 231, 249, 328ff, 338, 379ff
– Tadzhikistan 356
– Ukraine 364
– U.S.A. 199
– Uzbekistan 385
– *illus:*
– – Ashkelon transit center 119
– – Edelshtein with family 335
ARAB POPULATION (**9**:1021; **Dc./17**:342) 202
– fertility rate 198
– Muslims 228
– politics 194
BANKING (**9**:824; **Dc./17**:375)
– stock market crash 190, 218
– Supreme Court decision re stock exchange crisis 218
– *illus:*
– – stock market crash 191
CENTRAL GOVERNMENT (**Dc./17**:331) 192
CIVIL SERVICE (**9**:623)
– Arab employees 204
– politization 192
CULTURAL LIFE (**9**:996; **Dc./17**:397) 232
– Art (**9**:1009; **Dc./17**:402) 236
– Dance (**9**:1006; **Dc./17**:400) 234
– Motion Pictures (**12**:460) 239
– Music (**9**:1006; **Dc./17**:397) 232
– Russian immigrants 211
– Yiddish literature 391
DEFENSE FORCES (**9**:681; **Dc./17**:337) 196
– Arab village leagues 203
– *intifada* 191
– Israel Prize to *yeshivot* hesder 243
– Lebanon War 100, 189ff, 206ff
– politics 195
– Russian immigrants 212
– yeshivah students' deferment 224, 230
– *illus:*
– – Buenos Aires memorial service 105
– – convoy withdrawal from Lebanon 207
– – HUC rabbinical students 321
– – youngsters in Nablus provoke soldiers 198
ECONOMIC AFFAIRS (**6**:697; **Dc./17**:364) 218
– Arab boycott 121
– education 229
– Russia 334
– Russian immigrants 212
– stock market crash 190
EDUCATION (**9**:928; **Dc./17**:389) 229
– Christian schools 227
– *Ḥaredi* schools 224
– Labor Party changes 194
ENERGY RESOURCES (**9**:790; **Dc./17**:365) 220
– Electricity (**9**:790) 220
– Oil and Gas (**9**:793) 220ff
FOREIGN RELATIONS AND INTERNATIONAL AFFAIRS (**9**:421; **Dc./17**:331) 206
– Argentina 107
– Australia 111
– Austria 114
– Belarus 117
– Belgium 118
– Canada 126
– Czechoslovakia 135
– England 144
– Ethiopia 119
– France 152
– Germany 163
– Greece 166
– Hungary 184
– India 185
– Iran 186
– Ireland 187
– Italy 245
– Japan 248
– Netherlands 297
– Poland 314
– Portugal 316
– Romania 328
– Russia 334, 339
– South Africa 346ff
– Uzbekistan 385
– Vatican 251, 385
– *illus:*
– – Pres De Klerk of South Africa 346
– – Pres. Mitterrand addressing Knesset 152
FOREIGN TRADE (**9**:759)
– Arab boycott 122
– Germany 163
– India 185
– Japan 248
– Romania 328
GENERAL SURVEY (**9**:404; **Dc./17**:326) 189
– American Jews 373, 381
– Demjanjuk trial 137
– former Soviet citizens visit Russia 333
– Ḥavurah movement 174
– Iranian Jews' attitude 186
– Jews in Japan 247
– migrants to Los Angeles 273
– PLO 306
– Pollard Affair 315, 378
– Russian anti-Semitism 99
– struggle for Soviet Jewry 332
– United Nations 367ff
– U.S. Black-Jewish relations 375
– *illus:*
– – struggle for refuseniks 332
HEALTH SERVICES (**9**:982; **Dc./17**:390)
– legislation 216
– Likkud attitude 193
HOUSING (**9**:562)
– Beta Israel 119
– legislation 216
– Palestinian workers 192
– regional and settlement planning 214
INDUSTRY (**9**:815; **Dc./17**:374)
– labor force 201
LABOR (**9**:848; **Dc./17**:386) 201
– economy 219
– Ethiopian immigrants 120
– legislation 216
LEGAL AND JUDICIAL SYSTEM (**9**:628; **Dc./17**:361)
– Demanjuk trial 137
– Kakh barred from elections 194
– Petroleum Law 223
– Shari'a Law 229
– "Sports Law" 353
– Supreme Court 192
– Yad Izhak Ben-Zvi law 391
NEW SETTLEMENT (**9**:546; **Dc./17**:349) 213
– Gush Emunim 171
– *illus:*
– – advertisement 211
POLICE (**9**:655)
– criminal register law 215
– ministry 192
POLITICAL LIFE AND PARTIES (**9**:656; **Dc./17**:334) 193
– Arab population 202ff
– basic law 215
– Gush Emunim 171
– National Unity Government 190
– peace movements, religious 307
– Soviet Jewry, struggle for 333
POPULATION (**9**:472; **Dc./17**:338) 198
– Arabs 202
– Christians 226
– Jerusalem 248
– Judea, Samaria and Gaza Strip 213
– Karaites 257
– Muslims 228
– regional and settlement planning 214
– Russian immigrants 211
REGIONAL AND SETTLEMENT PLANNING (**9**:546; **Dc./17**:349) 214
RELIGIOUS LIFE
– Christians (**9**:910; **Dc./17**:393) 226
– – fertility rate 198
– Druze (**9**:924; **Dc./17**:397)
– – fertility rate 198
– Jews (**9**:887; **Dc./17**:390) 223
– – Beta Israel 120
– – Conservative Judaism 134
– – *Ḥazzanut* 174ff
– – median age 328
– – Mountain Jews 286
– – political parties 193
– – Reform Judaism 321
– – Sephardim 342
– Karaites 257
– Muslims (**9**:918; **Dc./17**:395) 228
– – fertility rate 198
SPORTS (**15**:294; **Dc./17**:563) 351
– judo 350
STATE COMPTROLLER (**9**:617)
– Ben-Porat's critical reports 192
– criticism of IDF in Gulf War 197
– legislation 216
– parties' election expenses 195
TAXATION (**9**:749)
– Eilat free trade zone law 215
TOURISM (**9**:845)
– Belgium 118
– Christian pilgrims 327
– Gulf War 381
– Hungary 184
– Italy 245
– Poland 314
– Romania 328
– Russia 333ff
TRANSPORTATION (**9**:831)
– Arab workers 204
– direct flights from Russia 334, 339
– Slovenia air flights 393
– Tashkent, air route 385
YOUTH MOVEMENT (**9**:976)
– Conservative Judaism 134
Israel Antiquities Authority 104
Israel Ballet 235
ISRAEL BEN SAMUEL HA-KOHEN (**9**:1059)

- prayerbooks 159
Israel Camerata String Orchestra 232
ISRAEL CHAMBER ORCHESTRA (**Dc./17**:409)
- cultural life 232, 234
Israel Chemicals Corporation 221
Israel Committee Netherlands 298
Israel Council of Progressive Rabbis 324
Israel Electric Corporation 220
ISRAEL EXPLORATION SOCIETY (**9**:1060)
- Israel Prize 242
Israel Festival 174, 233ff
ISRAELI, SHAUL 244
Israelites (movmt., S.A.) 347
ISRAEL LABOR PARTY (**9**:1068)
- Government of National Unity 192
- Leadership struggle 193
- *illus:*
- - television ad 194
Israel Museum (Jer.) 326
Israel National Opera 234
Israelovici, Leonardo 246
ISRAEL PHILHARMONIC ORCHESTRA (**9**:1072)
- jubilee celebrations 232, 234
ISRAEL PRIZE (**Dc./17**:410) 240
- Music 234
Israel Sinfonietta 232, 234
Israel Stimme (Newsp., Isr.) 392
Israel Symphony Orchestra Rishon le-Zion 232, 234
ISTANBUL (**9**:1086)
- Jewish community 362ff
- Karaites 258
- Sephardim 342
Itai, Avner 233
ITALY (**9**:1115; **Dc./17**:411) 244
- anti-Semitism 98
- Arab boycott 122
- Iranian Jews 186
- Israel Sinfonietta tour 232
- Jewish-Christian relations 251ff
- Krimchaks 268
- love poems 312
- Maccabi Tel Aviv 352
- museums 290
- Rhodian Holocaust survivors 168
- *illus:*
- - demonstration of behalf of Syrian Jewry 356
Itzhaki, M. 309ff
Itzhakovich-Yiẕhaki, Jacob 286
Iukhneva, Natalia 338
Ivanov, Iurii 330
Ivan III (grand duke, Moscow) 268
Ivory Coast (Rep., Afr.) 209
"Iwan the Terrible", *see* DEMJANJUK TRIAL
IZBAN, SHMUEL (**9**:1158)
- Yiddish literature 392
Izieu (vill., Fr.) 116
IZMIR (**9**:1162)
- Jewish community 363

J

Jabbar, 'Abd al- 259
Jackson, Jesse 99, 375
JACOB, JACK FREDERICK RAPHAEL (**Dc./17**:415)
- India 185
Jacob, Walter 323
Jacob from Goma-Mazod 156
Jacobi, Joe 350
Jacobi, Joseph 302
Jacobs, Gary (Kid) 350
JACOBS, LOUIS (**9**:1236)
- Conservative Judaism 135
- Talmud research 358
Jacobs, S. 295
JACOBSON, DAN (**9**:1239; **Dc./17**:415)
- English literature 146
JACOBSON, HOWARD 247
- English literature 145ff
Jacoby, Emil 277
Jaffe, Eli 174
Jai Alai 350
Jaite, Martin 351
JAKOBOVITS, IMMANUEL (**9**:1270; **Dc./17**:416)
- England 145
JAMAICA (**9**:1272; **Dc./17**:416)
- Jewish community 129
James I (K., Aragon) 184
JAMMER, MOSHE 241
Janner, Greville 144
JAPAN (**9**:1280; **Dc./17**:416) 247
- anti-Semitism 100
- Arab boycott 122
- Israel relations 209
JAPHETH BEN ALI HA-LEVI (**9**:1286)
- Karaite exegesis 259
Jarden, D. 309
Jaroslavsky, Cesar 105
Jason Aronson (publ. house, U.S.A.) 319
JASSY (**9**:1293)
- Jewish community 327
Jebel Ta'amur (site, Isr.) 101
Jeffries, Leonard 375
Jehiel Ben Ḥarosh 309
JERICHO (**9**:1365)
- archaeological excavation 102
Jerne, Niels 280
JERUSALEM (**9**:1378; **Dc./17**:417) 248
- archaeological excavations 101
- cantors convention 175
- Christian community 226ff
- *Ḥazzanut* 174
- Holland Village 296
- immigrant musicians 232
- *intifada* 203, 205
- Iraqi-Iranian War 186
- Israel Labor Party 194
- Karaites 257
- Mountain Jews 286
- municipal elections 223
- Muslim court 228
- population 200, 214
- Reagan Plan 189
- Reform Judaism 321
- Sabbath desecration 224
- Sephardim 342
- UN resolution 297
- U.S. opposition to Israel sovereignty 209
- Vatican attitude 385
- Zionist Congress (32nd) 395
- *illus:*
- - Fourth Misgav Yerushalayim Sephardi Studies Conference (1992) 342
- - Ketef Hinnom burial cave 102
- - Pres. De Klerk 346
- - Priestly Blessing plaque 103
- - Ramadan prayers on Temple Mount 228
- - secular Jews demonstrate for movies on Sabbath 224
- - Via Dolorosa 226
Jerusalem National Film and Television School 240
Jerusalem Oratorio Choir 233
JERUSALEM POST (**9**:1594)
- U.S. readership 317
Jerusalem Prize 188
Jerusalem Symphony Orchestra 232
Jerusalem Temple Institute 223
JESHUA BEN JUDAH (**10**:3)
- Karaite philosophy 259
Jeszensky, Geza 184
JEWISH AGENCY (**10**:26) 249
- American jews 381
- France 151
- Hungary 183ff
- immigrant absorption 191, 210ff
- Romania 327
- Russia 334ff
- Zionist Congress 395
Jewish Blind Society (Eng.) 145
JEWISH BOOK COUNCIL 250
- JWB and 294
- publishing 318
Jewish Braille Review (period, U.S.A.) 318
Jewish Care (Eng.) 145
JEWISH-CHRISTIAN RELATIONS (**Dc./17**:421; **Dc./17**:421) 251
- Auschwitz convent 109
- Brazil 123
- Netherlands 297
- New Zealand 299
- Poland 314
- Switzerland 355
- *illus:*
- - Polish Archbishop and U.S. Rabbi lead interfaith memorial service at Birkenau 314
- - East German colloquim 163
JEWISH CHRONICLE (**10**:40)
- university chairs 145
JEWISH COLONIZATION SOCIETY (**10**:44)
- Komzet 263
Jewish Community Centers Association of North America, *see* NATIONAL JEWISH WELFARE BOARD
Jewish Council for Community Relations (Eng.) 143
Jewish Culture Association of Ukraine 364
Jewish Culture Organization (Hung.) 184
Jewish Currents (period., U.S.A.) 318
JEWISH DAILY FORWARD (**10**:49) 255
- press 316
- weekly 391
Jewish Defense League 378
Jewish Echo (newsp., Scot.) 145
Jewish Education Service of North. America 370
Jewish Federation of Greater Toronto 128
Jewish Fund for Justice (U.S.) 376
Jewish Guardian (period., U.S.A.) 318
Jewish Historical and Ethnographic Commission (Rus.) 331
Jewish Historical Institute (Pol.) 312
Jewish Historical Society of Oregon (publ. house, U.S.A.) 319
Jewish Music Council (U.S.) 294
JEWISH PUBLICATION SOCIETY OF AMERICA (**10**:80)
- publishing 319
Jewish Religious Youth Union (Ind.) 185
Jewish Representative Council of Ireland 188
Jewish Theater (Pol.) 313
JEWISH THEOLOGICAL SEMINARY (**10**:95; **Dc./17**:425)
- American Judaism 373
- Conservative Judaism 133
- *Ḥazzanut* 176
- Jewish Museum 287
- University of Judaism 276, 384
- *illus:*
- - men and women at prayer 133
- - new library 368
Jewish Welfare Board (Eng.) 145
JEWS' COLLEGE (**10**:98; **Dc./17**:425)
- new accommodations 145
Jews for Jesus (mvmt.) 345, 372
- *illus:*
- - material on outreach strategy 371
Jibril, Aḥmad 203
JIHĀD (**10**:103)
- Mountain Jews 285
Joden Savane (loc., Surinam) 129
JOEL, BILLY 292
JOHANNESBURG (**10**:155)
- Jewish community 345
John Paul II (pope) 113, 123, 246, 251, 385, 389
Johnston, J. Bennett 377
JOHN XXIII (**10**:159)
- Hirschmann, Ira Arthur 182
Jonas, Franz 387
Jones, Kathy 351
JONG, ERICA 255
Joods, Maatschappelijk Werk (orgn., Neth.) 294
JORDAN (river; **10**:190)
- Israel Labor Party 194
JORDAN, HASHEMITE KINGDOM OF (**10**:198)
- Administered Territories 204
- Arab boycott 122
- Arab village leagues 203
- Gulf War 205
- Iranian propaganda 187
- Israeli Muslims' hajj 229
- Israel Labor Party 194
- Israel-Lebanon War 189
- PLO 305ff
JOSEPH BEN TANHUM YERUSHALMI (**10**:237)
- poetry 310
JOSHUA BEN ABRAHAM MAIMUNI (**10**:277)
- Cairo *Genizah* 156
Joshua, Operation 119
JOSIPOVICI, GABRIEL 255
- English literature 146
JOURNALISM (**10**:303)
- legislation 217
Juan Carlos (K., Sp.) 342
Judah ben Benjamin 309
Judah ben Shemariah 155
JUDAH HALEVI (**10**:355)
- Cairo *Genizah* 156
- poetry 309
Judaica Press (publ. house, U.S.A.) 319
JUDAISM (**10**:383)
- American Jews 368
- Gery sect 164
- Jewish-Christian relations 251ff
- Orthodoxy, Modern 303ff
- Russia 333, 335
- Vatican relations 386
Judaismo Laico (journ., Arg.) 107
JUDAIZERS (**10**:397)
- Gery 164
JUDEA (**10**:403)
- Arab population 203
- new settlements 213
JUDEO-PERSIAN (**10**:429; **Dc./17**:428)
- Cairo *Genizah* 156
JUDEO-TAT (**10**:441)
- Mountain Jews 284
- textbook by Levi Natranova 285
- *Vata Sovetimu* 336
Juderiá, *see* GHETTO
Judo 350, 352
Jueva Presencia (newsp., Arg.) 108
Juhud-Kata (Rus.) 284
Juliana (Q. Mother, Neth.) 296ff
Juneau (city, Alsk.) 97
Jung (co., Ger.) 166
Jungman, Moshe 392
Just, Meir 295
JWB, *see* NATIONAL JEWISH WELFARE BOARD

K

KABAKOFF, JACOB (**10**:487)
- Hebrew literature 181
KABRI (**10**:657)
- archaeological excavations 101
Kach, *see* Kakh
Kadari, Yehuda 175
Kaddum (stlmt., Isr.) 171
KADISHMAN, MENASHE (**Dc./17**:431)
- art 237
Kadoma (tn., Zimbabwe) 394
Kaffa, *see* FEODOSIYA
KAFKA, FRANZ (**10**:672)
- Prague museum 136
Kaftantzi, George 169
Kagan, Zipora 180
Kahana, Jeffrey 233
KAHANA, KALMAN (**10**:681; **Dc./17**:431)
- geonic literature 157
- Talmud research 357
KAHANA-CARMON, AMALIA (**Dc./17**:432)
- Hebrew literature 177, 180
Kahana-Gueler, Dina 236
Kahan Commission 190, 196
- *illus:*

-- opponents 190
Kahana, Meir 378
KAHLER, ERICH 255
Kahn, Itzhak 392
KAHN, JEAN 256
- CRIF 150
Kakh (polit. party, Isr.) 194, 378
Kaleshofsky, Roberta 366
KALININDORF (**10**:76)
- Komzet 263
KALLIR, ELEAZAR (**10**:713)
- Cairo *Genizah* 156
- poetry 309
Kallodopoulos, Alexandros 165
Kallos, Gary 351
Kalms, Stanley 145
Kaminsky, Melvin, *see* BROOKS, MEL
Kamishly (tn., Syr.) 355, 381
Kampanelli, Iakavou 169
KAMPELMAN, MAX M. 256
KANETI, SELIM 257
KANIEVSKY, JACOB ISRAEL 257
Kanievsky, Miriam 257
Kaniewski, S.J.C. 359
Kaniuk, Yoram 163, 177
Kanjewski, C. 359
Kann, Nitsa 180
Kanner, Dan 351
Kanovich, Grigorii (activist, Rus.) 331
KANOVICH, GRIGORY 257
- Lithuania 272
- Russia 330
Kanter, Sh. 360
Kanter, Zvika 236, 238
Kaplan, Abraham 176
Kaplan, Enrique 106
KAPLAN, MORDECAI M. (**10**:751)
- Conservative Judaism 134
- University of Judaism 276
Kaplan, Robert 128
Kappah, J. 159
Kara, Y. 358
Karaevano, Mikhail 331
Karagatsi, M. 169
KARAITES (**10**:762) 257
- Krimchaks 266ff
Karajan, Herbert van 163
KARASUBAZAR (**10**:786)
- Krimchaks 266
Karate 351
Karavan, Dani 236
Kar-Ben Copies (publ. house, U.S.A.) 319
Kardos, Peter 184
KARELITZ, AVRAHAM YESHAYAHU (**10**:787, **Dc./17**:435)
- Kanievsky, Jacob Israel 257
Karelli, Zoe 169
Karl, Frederick 366
KARMI'EL (**10**:799)
- dance festival 235
KARNI, YEHUDA (**10**:801)
- Hebrew literature 180
Karpati, Karoly 302
KARPINOWITCH, ABRAHAM (**10**:803)
- Yiddish literature 392
Karpov, Anatoly 259
Kartun-Blum, Ruth 179, 181
KASHER (**10**:806)
- *kashrut* law 215
KASHER, MENAHEM MENDEL (**10**:807; **Dc./17**:435)
- Orthodoxy, Modern 304
Kasovsky, M. 358
KASPAROV, GARY 259
Kasparov, Kim 259
Katchko, Adolf 176
Katif (loc., Isr.) 221
KATZ, ELIHU 242
Katz, Robert 300
Katz, Shlomo 176
KATZ, SHMUEL (**Dc./17**:436)
- Hebrew literature 181
KATZENELSON, ITZHAK (**10**:830)
- Hebrew literature 180
KATZIR, EPHRAIM (**10**:816; (**Dc./17**:436)
- U.S.S.R. visit 332
Katzir, Judith 178
KATZNELSON, SHULAMIT 241
KAUFMAN, AVRAHAM YOSIFOVICH 260
Kaufman, Samuel H. 165
KAUFMANN, DAVID (**10**:842)
- Cairo *Genizah* 156
Kavafi, K.P. 169
KAZAKHSTAN (rep., CIS) 260
- Iran 187
- Israel relations 209
- Jewish population 328
Kazantakis, Nikos 169
Kazantzi, Toli 169
KAZYONNY RAVVIN (**10**:860)
- Mountain Jews 286
Keating, Paul 112
Kedar, Zvi 112
KEDESH-NAPHTALI (**10**:665)
- archaeological excavations 103
Kedumim (stlmt., Isr.) 171
- *illus:*
-- spring 1982 213
Keegstra, James 126
Keeve, Damon 351
KEFAR HASIDIM (**10**:885)
- *illus:*
-- Computer Project and Girls' Town 231
KEFAR SAVA (**10**:891)
- population 214
Kehat, Amira 313
KELAL YISRAEL (**10**:898)
- Reform Judaism 323
Keller, Ricky 176
Kelman-Ezrachi, Naama 226
Kenai (tn., Alsk.) 97
Kenan, Amos 176, 318
Kenaz, Joshua 177ff
Kendal, Henry 153
Keneally, Thomas 113, 147
KENYA (**10**:910)
- Jewish-Christian relations 252
KERCH (**10**:911)
- Krimchaks 266ff
Kerem, Yitzchak 167, 168
KEREN HA-YESOD (**10**:914; **Dc./17**:436)
- Jewish Agency 250
Kerler, Yosef 391
KERMANSHAH (**10**:918)
- Jewish community 186
KEROVAH (**10**:920)
- Cairo *Genizah* 156
Kesler, M. 357
Kestenbaum, Eliezer 357
Ketchikan (tn., Alsk.) 97
K.G.B. 330ff, 387
Khan Hussein 284
Khanukayev, Sergei 232
Kharats, Meir 392
KHARKOV (**10**:939)
- Jewish community 364
- Zionist organization 334
Khasbulatov, Ruslan 334
Khashakhar (newsp., Est.) 147, 336
KHAZARS (**10**:944)
- Krimchaks 267
- Mountain Jews 284
KHERSON (**10**:953)
- Krimchaks 267
Khirbat Shua (site, Isr.) 104
Khirbet Beit Loya (site, Isr.) 104
Kholmianskii, Alexander 331ff
Khomeini, Ayotolah
- Iranian Jews 186
KHOURI, MAKRAM 241
Khrushchev, Nikita 340
Khuzistan (reg., Iran) 186
Kibbutz Chamber Orchestra 232, 234
Kibbutz Contemporary Dance Company 235
KIBBUTZ MOVEMENT (**10**:963)
- Israel Labor Party 194
- population 201
- Reform Judaism 322
KIEL, YEHUDA 244
Kiesinger, Kurt 261
KIEV (**10**:991)
- Babi Yar meeting 331
- Jewish community 364
KIMHI, DOV (**10**:1004)
- Hebrew literature 178
Kimmel, Betsy 351
KING, CAROLE 292
King David Schools (S.A.) 345
Kingston (city, Jam.) 129
Kiraly, Isabella B. 183
Kirghizia, *see* KYRGYZSTAN
Kirill, Archbishop 254
KIRIMI, ABRAHAM (**10**:1046)
- Krimchaks 267
KIRKISANI, JACOB AL- (**10**:1047)
- Karaite philosophy 259
KIROVOGRAD (**10**:1049)
- Jewish community 364
Kirschner, Allon 351
KIRSZENSTEIN-SZEWINSKA, IRENA 260
- sports 351
KIRYAT GAT (**10**:1055)
- Karaites 257
KIRYAT ONO (**10**:1056)
- Reform Judaism 321
KIRYAT SHEMONAH (**10**:1057)
- terrorist attack in army camp 203
KIS, DANILO (Daniel) 260
Kiselev, Evgenii 338
KISHINEV (**10**:1063)
- Jewish community 281, 335
Kislovodsk (tn., Rus.) 287
KISSINGER, HENRY ALFRED (**10**:1076; **Dc./17**:438)
- U.S. World Cup '94 349
Kister, M.J. 312
Kiviat, Abel 351
Klapholz, Y.J. 360
KLARSFELD, BEATE AUGUSTE 261
- Barbie, Klaus 116
KLARSFELD, SERGE 261
- Barbie, Klaus 116
- Vichy census 152
Klasmer, Gabi 236, 238
Klaus, Josef 387
Klein, Carole, *see* KING, CAROLE
Klein, Larry 351
KLEIN, THEODORE (Theo) 261
- CRIF 150
Kleinman, Lazar 136
Klerk, F.W. de 346
Klestil, Thomas 114
Klezmer music 384
Klimovsky, Gregorio 105, 107
Klinghoffer, Leon 245, 378
KLUG, AARON 262
KNESSET (**10**:1112)
- Arab members 202
- Eleventh 193
- Gush Emunim 171
- laws passed 215
- Orthodox parties 223
- "Righteous Gentiles" tribute 228
- Sports Law 353
- Tenth 192
- Twelfth 192ff
- Yad Izhak Ben-Zvi 391
- *illus:*
-- Ethiopian immigrants demonstrate 120
-- Pres. Mitterrand addressing 152
Knokke (tn., Belg.) 117
Knoll, Yishai 234
KNOPFLER, MARK 293
Knox, Israel
- Yiddish literature 391
Knut, Adriana (Sarah) 262
KNUT, DOVID 262
KOBE (**10**:1118)
- Jewish community 247
KODER, SHABDAI SAMUEL 262
Koehler, George 280
KOENIGSBERG (**10**:1128)
- *Hazzanut* 175
Kogan, Evgenii 147
Kogan, Itzhak 332
Kohav Ya'ir (stlmt., Isr.) 214
Kohl, Helmut 122, 163
Kohn, Jacob 274ff
Kohn, Rachel 113
Kohnstamm, Mrs. H. 298
Koifman, Evgenii 330
Kokantzi, Nikou 169
Kokkalidou-Nahmia, Nino 169
Kokos, Khozya 268
Kolbe, Maximilian 254
Kol Demama (dance co., Isr.) 234
KOLLEK, THEODORE (**10**:1163)
- Austria 114
- Israel Prize 242
- sports stadium 248
- *illus:*
-- Spitz, Mark, with 349
-- with general secretary of ICCJ 227
Kollender, Rachel 259
KOLODIN, IRVING 262
Kolodizki, S. 359
Koltai, Leslie 277
KOL'TSOV, MIKHAIL 262
Kommisar, Jacob 300
KOMZET 263
KONIG, LEA 241
König, Michael 114
KOOK, ABRAHAM ISAAC (**10**:1182)
- Orthodoxy, Modern 304
- Talmud research 357
Kopelowitz, Lionel 145
Koppelson, Arnold 168
KOPS, BERNARD (**10**:1190)
- English literature 146
Kopuit, Maurits 298
KOPYTMAN, MARK RUVIMOVICH 264
Korchnoi, Viktor 259
KORCZAK-MARLA, ROZKA 264
Korea, North 198
Korea, South 209
Koren, E. 313
Koren, Yeshayahu 177
KORETZ, ZVI 264
- Greece 168
Korneev, Lev 330
Korotych, Vitalii 338
Kosharovskii, Iulii 335
Kosher Directory (period., U.S.A.) 31
KOSICE (**10**:1215)
- Jewish community 135
KOSINSKI, JERZY 205
Kosman, Admiel 180
Kostantini, Moisis 168
Kostick, Gavin 147
Kotalla, Joseph 296
KOUCHNER, BERNARD 265
Koussevitzky, David 176
KOVNER, ABBA (**10**:1229; **Dc./17**:442)
- Hebrew literature 179ff
Kozhinov, Vadim 337
Krakowski, Shmuel 172
Kramer, Ivan 235
Krasilschikov, Y.A. 359
Krasnov, Yevgeniy 351, 352
Krasnoyarsk (tn., Rus.) 335
KRASUCKI, HENRI 266
Kraus, David 183ff
Krauss, Hans-Joachim 254
Krausz, Moshe (Miklos) 278
Kravchuk (pres., Ukr.) 364
KREISKY, BRUNO (**10**:1254; **Dc./17**:442)
- Waldheim Affair 387
KRESSEL, GETZEL (**10**:1260)
- Hebrew literature 181
Kreuzlingen (tn., Switz.) 355
Krichevskii, Ilya 338
Krickstein, Aaron 351
KRIEGEL, ANNIE 266
- Trigano, Shmouel 362
Kriegsman, Cheryl 351
Kriens (tn., Switz.) 355
KRIMCHAKS 266
- Komzet 264
- 1989 census 329
Kriss, Grigory 302
Kristol, Irving 374
Kritz, Reuven 180ff
Kronitz, Leon 128
Krupnick, E. 360
Krupnik, Igor 331
Krupp, M. 357
Ktav (publ. house, U.S.A.) 319
KUBA (**10**:1283)
- Mountain Jews 284
Kuhnen, Michael 162
Ku Klux Klan 375
Kulakov, A. 337
KUN, BÉLA (**10**:1290) 269
Kunin, Baruch Shlomo 274
KUNIN, MADELEINE 269
Kunzel, Beate Auguste, *see* KLARSFELD, BEATE AUGUSTI
Kupferman, Moshe 237
Kuppat Holim 194

KURDISTAN (**10**:1295)
- Talmud research 359
KUSHNER, ALEKSANDER SEMENOVICH 269
Kutler, Dan 351
Kutschmann, Walter 106
Kuwait 122, 205ff, 306
Kwe Kwe (tn., Zimbabwe) 394
Kyoto (city, Jap.) 247
KYRGYZSTAN (state, CIS) 270
- Israel relations 209
- Jewish population 328

L

Labor Zionist Movement 395
LA CHAUX-DE-FONDS (**10**:1332)
- Jewish community 355
LADINO (**10**:1342; **Dc./17**:445)
- Turkey 363
Ladispoli (transit camp, It.) 339, 380
Lafer, Celso 123
Laish (bib. city), *see* DAN
LAJSA, *see* Latinoamerican Jewish Studies Association
Lambrinou, Yianni 169
Lamm, Maurice 275
Landau, Dov 181
LANDAU, MOSHE 243
- Zionism 395
Land Day 202
Landesman, Georg (Joshua) 183ff
LANG, JACK 270
Lange, David 299
Lange, Nicholas 168
Langlamet, Marie-Pierre 233
LANZMANN, CLAUDE 270
Laor, Dan 181
Laor, Yitzhac 179
Lapin, Daniel 274
LARISSA (**10**:1430)
- Jewish community 167
La Rouche, Lyndon 377
Lasker, Daniel J. 259
LASKIN, BORA (**10**:1439; **Dc./17**:446)
- Canada 128
LASSER, LOUISE 283
LATIN AMERICA (**10**:1448; **Dc./17**:446)
- anti-Semitism 99
- Conservative Judaism 134
- 500th anniversary of expulsion of Jews from Spain 341
- Israel relations 209
- Jewish-Christian relations 254
- Sephardim 342
- Spanish and Portuguese literature 347
Latinoamerican Jewish Studies Association 107
LATVIA (**10**:1462) 270
- Jewish community 335, 338
- Jewish population 328
LAU, ISRAEL MEIR 271
Lau, Moshe Ḥayyim 271
Lau, Naftali 271
Lauder Foundation 184
Laurence, Margaret 128
LAUSANNE (**10**:1471)
- Jewish community 354
LAUTERBACH, JACOB ZALLEL (**10**:1473)
- Reform Judaism 323
Lavi, Alberto 167
Lavie, Amos 240
Lavie, Raffi 238
LAW OF RETURN (**10**:1485)
- American Jews 381
- non-Orthodox movements 226
- Reform Judaism 321, 323
Lazar, Osias 328
LEAR, NORMAN 283
LEBANON (**10**:1542)
- Arab boycott 122
- Dutch Unifil troops 297
- "Irangate" affair 186
- Irish UN troops 188
- Israeli invasion 100, 162, 166, 186, 189ff, 196ff, 202, 206ff, 218
- Klarsfeld, Beate and Serge 261
- PLO 305
- UNIFIL 365
- *illus:*
- - IDF convoy withdrawal 207
- - Saad Haddad with forces 189
Lebow, Fred 351
LEDERMAN, LEON MAX 271
- Schwartz, Melvin 341
- Steinberger, Jack 353
Lee College (U.S.) 384
LEEDS (**10**:1560)
- Jewish community 143
Leeuwarden (Neth.) 297
Lefkowitz, David 176
LEFTWICH, JOSEPH (**10**:1564)
- Yiddish literature 392
Leibler, Isi 110,112
- *illus:*
- - with Malcolm Fraser 110
Leibler, Mark 112
Lein, Evgenii 331
LEIPZIG (**10**:1590)
- Jewish community 163
Lendhardt, P. 358
LENIN, VLADIMIR ILYICH (**11**:13)
- Hammer, Armand 173
LENINGRAD (**11**:14)
- Denmark 138
- Jewish community 328, 337
- "refuseniks" 333
- *illus:*
- - demonstration against anti-Semitism 331
- - "Refuseniks" 330
Leningradskii Evreskii Almanakh (newsp., Rus.) 331, 336
Lenowitz, H. 312
Leo Baeck Institute 176
Leopold, David 97
Le Pen, M. 143
Lerer, Oded 237
Leskli, Ḥezi 180
Lestrange, Gisèle de 130
Lerman, Antony 186
Lerner, Michael 374
Lerner, Tillie, *see* OLSEN, TILLIE
Lesbianism 324
Lete, Olmo 310
Letzte Neies (newsp., Isr.) 392
Leuchter, Fred 100, 144
Levi, Zalman 392
Levi, Errikos 168
Levi, Itamar 178
LEVI, PRIMO (**11**:85; **Dc./17**:449)
- Italy 244
- Norwegian books 301
Leviant, Curt 366
LEVI-MONTALCINI, RITA 271
- Cohen, Stanley 132
- Italy 244
LEVIN, A. LEO 271
Levin, B.M. 158
Levin, Dov 137, 335
Levin, I. 309ff
Levin, Neil 176
Levin, Joseph A. 176
Levin, Richard 377
Levin, Robert 300
Levine, Stephen 299
Levinger, J.S. 309
Levinger, Moshe 171, 172
LEVINSON, BARRY 283
LEVITA, ELIJAH (**11**:132)
- liturgical hymns 159
LEVI-TANNAI, SARA (**Dc./17**:450)
- dance in Israel 235
Levitas, Ilya 364
LEVITZKI, ALEXANDER 242
Levy, Abraham 342
LEVY, DAVID 272
- Likkud leadership 193
Levy, Gerry 112
Levy, Marv 350
Levy, Moshe 196ff
Levy, Pamela 238
Levy, Rebecca 168
LEWANDOWSKI, LOUIS (**11**:167)
- *Ḥazzanut* 175
LEWIN, BENJAMIN MANASSEH (**11**:169)
- geonic literature 157
Lewis, Stephen 128
Leyden (city, Neth.) 297
L'Heureux-Dire, Claire 97
Liberman, Serge 112
Liberalno-Demokraticheskaii Partiia (orgn., Rus.) 337
LIBRARIES (**11**:190)
- France 150
LIBRARY, JEWISH NATIONAL AND UNIVERSITY (**11**:197)
- Cairo *Genizah* 155
LIBYA (**11**:198; **Dc./17**:452)
- Arab boycott 122
- Gulf War 208
Lichten, Joseph 246
Lieber, David 276
Lieberman, Nancy 302
LIEBERMAN, SAUL (**11**:218; **Dc./17**:452)
- Talmud research 359
Liebermann, P. 358
Liebman, Charles
- American Jew 368
- U.S. literature 366
Liebrecht, Savyon 178
LIÈGE (**11**:226)
- Jewish community 117
Lifshits, Vladimir 330ff
Lightstone, J.N. 360
LIKKUD (**Dc./17**:453)
- american jews 381
- Government of National Unity 192
- Gush Emunim 171
- leadership struggle 193ff
- "Peace for Peace" concept 207
- settlements 213
- Zionist Congress (31st) 395
Lilith (period., U.S.A.) 318
Limburg (prov., Neth.) 295
LIMERICK (**11**:251)
- Jewish cemetery 188
Lindbergh, Charles A. 390
Lindenbaum, Shalom 180
Linder, Amnon 319
Linnas, Karl 379
Lipsker, Avidov 180
Lipski, Sam 113
Lipstadt, Deborah 370
Lipstein, Rachel 169
LIPTZIN, SOL (**11**:299)
- U.S. literature 366
LISBON (**11**:299)
- Jewish community 316
Lischka, Kurt 261
LISHANSKY, BATYA (**3**:605)
- Israel Prize 241
Liss, A. 357
LISSAK, MOSHE 244
List, Albert A. 287
List, Vera 287
LITHUANIA (**11**:361) 272
- Jewish culture 330
- Jewish population 328, 337ff
- Mountain Jews 286
LITURGY (**11**:392)
- geonic literature 157, 159
- poetry 313
- Sephardim 342
LITVINOFF, EMANUEL (**11**:405)
- English literature 145
LIVERPOOL (**11**:409)
- Jewish schools 145
Lockwood Wilfrid 259
LODZ (**11**:425)
- Jewish community 313
Loewinger, D.S. 313
Logunov, A. 337
LOḤAMEI HA-GETTA'OT (**11**:462)
- Salonikan Jewry 167
Löhr, Alexander 113, 387
Lohrmann, Klaus 114
LONDON (**11**:469)
- IJA 186
- Jewish community 143, 145
- museums 291
Long, Tracy 351
Lookstein, Haskel 372
Loosdrecht (Neth.) 297
Lope, Rivke 392
Lorch, Stephen 111
LOS ANGELES (**11**:497) 272
- Conservative Judaism 134
- divorce rate 372
- Holocaust museum 378
- Jewish choir 384
- Jewish community 369
- Reform Judaism 322
- Simon Wiesenthal Center 383
- Skirball Museum 288
- University of Judaism 384
- *illus:*
- - anti-Jewish signs 377
- - emergency conference on Soviet Jewry 329
- - *Jewish Calendar, The* 318
- - memorial plaque for Israeli athletes murdered at Munich Olympics 350
- - Torah reading at University of Judaism 371
Lotan (kib., Isr.) 322
LOTMAN, LIDIYA MIKHAYLOVNA 278
LOTMAN, YURI MIKHAILOVICH 278
LOUISIANA (**11**:517)
- Duke runs for Senate 377
Loussac, Zachary 97
Louther, William 236
Loutraki (tn., Gr.) 167
Louvish, Simon 145
Lovinger, Joseph 167
Lovy, Tamas 184
Lowenstein, David 351
Lubofsky, Ronald 111
LUCCA (**11**:549)
- Jewish community 244
Luden, Joseph 392
Lugano (tn., Switz.) 354
Luge (Toboggan) 351
Luitjens, Jacob 127
Lurie, Bob 349
Lustiger, Cardinal 109
LUTZ, CARL (Charles) 278
LUXEMBURG, ROSA (**11**:592)
- Gelfond, Alexander Lazarevich 15
Luz, La (newsp., Arg.) 107
Luz (co., Isr.) 221ff
Luz, Zvi 180ff
LUZKI, SIMḤAH ISAAC (**11**:595)
- Karaism 258
Luzzato, A. 313
LUZZATTO, SAMUEL DAVID (**11**:604)
- poetry 312
LVOV (**11**:608)
- Jewish community 335, 364
LYDDA (**11**:619)
- waqf property 228
LYONS (**11**:623)
- Barbie trial 115
- Jewish community 149
- Touvier, Paul 152
Lyons, Sir Jack 143
Lyosov, Sergei 338

M

Maaleh Gilboa (kib., Isr.) 221
MAARIV (newsp.; **11**:639)
- U.S. sales 316
Maastricht (tn., Neth.) 295
Maastricht treaty 149
MACCABI (**15**:294; **Dc./17**:457)
- Romania 327
- Russia 334
- Tel Aviv basketball team 352
- Turkish sportsmen 363
- Yugoslavia 393
MACCABIAH (**11**:662)
- quadrennial 353
McCalden, David 379
Macedonia (rep., Yug.) 393
McGovern, George 373
MacGregor, Lord 144
Macharski, Cardinal 108
Machzikei Ivrit (y. orgn., Gr.) 385
Mc Nabb, Lawrence 236
Madison Books (publ. house, U.S.A. 319

Madrid peace conference 206, 209, 306, 356
Magarik, Aleksei 330ff
MAGDEBURG (**11**:685)
- Jewish community 163
Magid, Isidore 110
Magidson, Victor 338
Maginim (y. mvmt., S.A.) 347
MAGNES, JUDAH LEON (**11**:716)
- memorial museum 288
MAHANAIM (**11**:724)
- Mountain Jews 286
Mahanaim (orgn., Rus.) 335
Maharashta (state, Ind.) 185
Mahutan, Hava 236
MAHZOR (**11**:731)
- Reform Judaism 322
MAIMONIDES (**11**:754)
- Cairo *Genizah* 155
- 850th anniversary of death 251
- Karaite philosophy 259
Maiziere, Lothar de 162
Major, John 122, 143, 144
MAJORCA (**11**:795)
- Ibiza and Formentera 184
Makhachkalah (tn., Rus.) 284
Makhon Ben-Zvi, *see* Ben-Zvi Institute
Makhoul, Bashir 238
Maksymiuk, Jerzy 232, 234
MAKUYA (**Dc./17**:458)
- Israel support 248
Malachi, Zevi 309ff
Malah, Raphael, *see* Shawat, Fradji
MALAMAT, ABRAHAM 279
MALOVANY, JOSEPH (**Dc./17**:291)
- *Hazzanut* 175
- Norway 300
- *illus:*
- - Archipova synagogue, Moscow 336
Malovsky, Samuel 176
Maltinski, Hayyim 392
MAMET, DAVID 361
Manahat (site, Isr.) 101
Manaus (city, Braz.) 123
MANCHESTER (**11**:858)
- Jewish community 143, 145
- museum 291
Mandel, Morton L. 370
Mandela, Nelson 346
MANDELBAUM, BERNARD (**16**:1401)
- U.S. literature 365
Mandelbaum, D. 359
Mandic, Klara 393
Mangup (tn., Crimea), *see* Doros
MANILOW, BARRY 293
MANITOBA (**11**:879)
- Arab boycott 122
- Jewish community 127
Mann, Erica, *see* JONG, ERICA
MANN, JACOB (**11**:881)
- geonic letters 159
Manoogian, Torkom 227
Mansdorf, Amos 351, 353
Mansour, Sliman 238
Mantner, Gabriella 366
MANTUA (**11**:895)
- Jewish community 244
Manufacturers' Association (Isr.) 191
Maor, Chaim 238
MAPAM (**11**:914)
- politics 195
- Zionist Congress (31st) 395
Mar-Chaim, Josef 234
Marchais, Georges 149
MARCUS, RUDOLPH ARTHUR 279
MARGALIOT, MORDECAI (**11**:956)
- Cairo *Genizah* 155
- geonic literature 158
Margrethe II (q., Den.) 137
Margriet, Princess (Neth.) 297
Marilus, I.M. 327
Markin, Daphne 366
Markman, Hillel 235
Marko, Ivan 235
Markoglou, Prodromo 169
MARKOWITZ, HARRY M. 279
Markovitz, Sandra, *see* HARRIS, BARBARA
Markus Weiner Publishing (publ. house, U.S.A.) 319
Marom, Shlomo 184
MARRIAGE (**11**:1025)
- Falashas 120, 225
- Iran 186
- Krimchaks 268
- legislation 217
- Reform Judaism 323
- Supreme Court decision re Reform rabbis 217
- U.S.A. 367
Marrus, Michael 128
Marseilles (**11**:1055)
- Jewish community 149
Martini, Cardinal 245, 386
Martinique (isl.) 130
Martynov, Ivan 330
MARX, KARL (Ger. publ.; **10**:314)
- Germany 161
Marx, Michael 112
MARYLAND (**11**:1076)
- Jewish Historical Society 289
- Jewish political force 377
Masada College (Austral.) 111
Massa Carrara (loc., It.) 246
MASSACHUSETTS (**11**:1111)
- Jewish political force 377
Massarik, Fred 368
Matalon, Ronit 178
Mathis, Edith 233
MATSAS, JOSEPH 279
Matsas, Nestoros 168, 169
Matsas, Yosef 167
Mattathias ben Samuel Ha-Kohen 284
MATTHAU, WALTER 283
Mattiyahu, Margalit 168
Matzad (polit. pty., Isr.) 171
Mauro, Pesce 359
MAUTHAUSEN (**11**:1136)
- Dutch Jews 297
MAXWELL, ROBERT 280
- England 143
Mayer, Daniel 136
Mayer, Helene 302
Mayer, Uri 232
MAZLI'AH (**11**:1153)
- Karaites 257
Mazon (orgn., U.S.) 376
Mazor, Yair 181
Mazower, Mark 168
Mazsihkisz (orgn., Hung.) 184
MAZURSKY, PAUL 283
Mecca (city, Saudi Arabia) 229
Medding, Peter Y. 371
MEDICAL ETHICS, JEWISH (**Dc./17**:462)
- Reform Judaism 323
MEDINA (**11**:1211)
- Israeli Muslims 229
MEDINI, HAYYIM HEZEKIAH (**11**:1216)
- Krimchaks 268
- *illus:*
- - *Sedei Hemed* 269
Medved, Michael 274
Megamot (journ., Arg.) 107
Meged, Mati 176
MEGED, AHARON (**11**:1221)
- Germany 163
- Hebrew literature 176
Mehta, Zubin
- *illus:*
- - Huberman Gala Concert 233
Meier, Levi 318
Meimad (party, Isr.) 223, 307
Meiri, Dalia 236
Meiseles, I. 309
Meissner-Blau, Freda 387
Meitlis, Jacob 392
Meizlish, M. 358
MELAMED, EZRA ZION (**11**:1275)
- geonic literature 157
- Israel Prize 241
- Talmud research 358
MELBOURNE (**11**:1277)
- Jewish community 110ff
Melbourne Chronicle (journ., Austr.) 112
Melbourner Bleter (newsp., Austr.) 392
Melchior, Michael 300
Melitz Center for Jewish-Zionist Education 227
Mellor, David 144
MEMORIAL FOUNDATION FOR JEWISH CULTURE 280
- Russian Jews 335
Menachem, Jak 168
MENAHEM BEN JACOB IBN SARUQ (**11**:1305)
- poetry 310ff
Menasche, Albert 167
MENDELE MOKHER SEFORIM (**11**:1317)
- Hebrew literature 178
Mendelevich, Yosef 332
- *illus:*
- - Israeli efforts on behalf of refuseniks 332
Mendelsohn, Oskar 300
Mendelson, Sol 176
Menem, Carlos E. 106ff
Mengly-Girei (Crimean Khan) 268
Mensch Makers Press (publ. House, U.S.A.) 319
MENTAL ILLNESS (**11**:1372)
- homosexuality 324
Mercaz 395
Meretsky, Irving 302
Merez (polit. pty., Isr.) 194
Meridor, Dan 193
Merkaz ha-Rav yeshivah (Jer.) 224, 342
Merten, Max 169, 265
MESSIAH (**11**:1407)
- Reform Judaism 322
METALS AND MINING (**11**:1428)
- archaeological excavations 101
Metar (stlmt., Isr.) 214
METULLAH (**11**:1449)
- energy conservation facility 223
MEXICO (**11**:1453)
- Conservative Judaism 134
- crypto-Jews 342
- Israel oil imports 221
- Los Angeles 273
Mexico City (Mex.) 342
Meyer, Marshall 105, 134
Meyers, Norman 350
Meyuhas (fam.) 342
Mezah, Dudu 238
MIAMI (**11**:1477)
- American Sephardi Federation 98
- Holocaust memorial 378
- Hurricane Andrew devastates 382
- Jewish community 369
- *seder* ceremonies 374
- Sephardim 342
Micah Publications (publ. house U.S.A.) 319
MICHIGAN (**11**:1498)
- Jewish political force 377
MIDLER, BETTE 293
MIDRASH (**11**:1507)
- Cairo *Genizah* 155
- research 357ff
- Talmud research 359
Mielnik, Tamara 236
Mielziner, M. 358
MIGRATION (**16**:1518)
- Iran 186
Mikoyan, Ar. I. 170
MIKVEH (**11**:1534)
- Budapest 184
- Ireland 188
MILAN (**11**:1545)
- Jewish community 244ff
Milano, Paolo 246
Mila Publishing House (Arg.) 107
Milch, Klara 302
Miles, Anthony 260
MILITARY SERVICE (**11**:1550)
- Alaska 97
- Greece 168
- Iran 186
- South Africa 346
- U.S. personnel in Japan 247
Milken, Michael 377
Miller, Ann 351
Miller, Avi 236
Miller, Marvin 349
Miller, Merton 279
Miller, Philip E. 259
Miller, Shoshana 226
- *illus:*
- - demonstration 225
Milligan, Lord 143
Milnitzky, Benno 124
MILSTEIN, CESAR 280
Milton, Sybil 128
MINHAG (**12**:4)
- geonic literature 158
MINNEAPOLIS (**12**:35)
- divorce rate 372
MINSK (**12**:51)
- Jewish community 117, 334ff
Mintz, Alan 181
Mintz, Shlomo 232
- *illus:*
- - Huberman Gala Concert 233
Miranski, Peretz 392
Mirivili, Strati 169
Miron, Dan 180ff
MIRSKY, AARON (**12**:85)
- poetry 310, 312
Mirvis, Ephraim 187
- *illus:*
- - Presidential visit to Terenure Synagogue 188
MISHNAH (**12**:93)
- Cairo *Genizah* 155
- geonic literature 157
- research 357ff
Mishori, Gilad 234
MISKOLC (**12**:153)
- Jewish community 184
Mitelberg, Louis, *see* TIM
Mitropoulou, Kostoulas 169
Mitsotakis, Constantinos 166ff
Mitterrand, François 98, 108, 122, 147, 149ff
- *illus:*
- - meeting Chief Rabbi Sirat 150
MITZVAH (**12**:162)
- Reform Judaism 322
MIXED MARRIAGE, INTERMARRIAGE (**12**:164)
- Australia 110
- Canada 128
- Caribbean Jewish communities 129
- Czechoslovakia 136
- France 149
- Greece 166
- Hungary 183
- Iran 186
- Italy 244
- Karaites 258
- Reform Judaism 323
- Romania 327ff
- Russia 328
- Switzerland 355
- Turkey 363
- Ukraine 364
- U.S.A. 57, 367
- Yugoslavia 393
MIZPEH RAMON (**12**:174)
- Desert Sculpture Park 236
MIZRACHI (mvmt.) (**12**:175)
- Zionist congress 395
Mizrachi, Motti 236ff
MNOUCHKINE, ALEXANDRE 281
MNOUCHKINE, ARIANE 281
MOATI SERGE 281
Mock, Alois 387
MODAI, YITZHAK (**Dc./17**:469)
- economic policy 191ff
MODIANO, PATRICK 281
Modigliani, Enrico 245
MODIGLIANI, FRANCO 281
Moellin (city, Ger.)
- Pogrom acts 162
Mo'ezet Yesha (orgn., Er. Isr.) 171, 172
MOGILEV (**12**:214)
- Jewish community 117
Moisesville (tn., arg.) 106
Moissis, Raphael 168
Mojsov, Lazar 393
Moldavi, M. 313
MOLDOVA (Moldavia) 281
- Jewish community 211
- Jewish population 328
Moledet (polit. party, Isr.) 194
Molho, Rena 168
Molotov, *see* GELFORD, ALEXANDER LAZAREVICH
Moment (mag., U.S.A.) 317
MOMIGLIANO, ARNALDO DANTE (**12**:235)
- necrology 246
Monash (city, Austral.) 111
MONGOLIA (**12**:256)
- Israel relations 209
Mongols 267, 284

Mons (tn., Belg.) 117
Montagu, Ivor 351
Montenegro (rep.; Yug.) 393
Monterey Park (city, U.S.) 273
MONTEVIDEO (**12**:278)
– *illus:*
– – demonstration on behalf of Soviet Jewry 332
MONTPELLIER (**12**:282)
– Jewish community 149
MONTREAL (**12**:283)
– Jewish community 126ff
Mordon, Ida 167
Moreau, Jeanne 239
Moretti, Isabelle 233
Morgan, Mal 112
Moriah, Avner 238
Mormons (rel. sect) 228
MOROCCO (**12**:326; **Dc./17**:471)
– Arab boycott 122
– CAJE 131
– Islamic fundamentalism 197
– Jewish community 212
– Klarsfeld, Beate 261
– migrants to the Netherlands 295
Mortality 198
Mosaic Religious Association (Pol.) 313
Mosco, Maisie 146
Moscovitz, L. 359
MOSCOW (**12**:359)
– anti-Semitism 337
– direct flights to Israel 334
– *ḥazzanut* 175
– Hebrew instruction center 331
– Jewish community 328ff
– "refuseniks" 333
– *illus:*
– – Archipova synagogue 336
"Moses, Operation" 119
MOSES BEN JACOB OF KIEV (**12**:420)
– Krimchaks 268
MOSHAV (**12**:435)
– Israel Labor Party 194
– population 201
MOSHINSKY, ELIJAH 282
– Australia 112
Moskovich, Wolf 259
Mossad (Isr. intelligence orgn.) 189
Mossenson, David 113
Mosseri, Claude 313
MOSSINSOHN, YIGAL (**12**:442)
– Hebrew literature 178
MOTION PICTURES (**12**:463) 282
– Australian Jewish Film Festival 112
– Greek Jewry 168
– Israel 239
– Russia 338
– Sephardim 342
Motorboat racing 351
Moulin, Jean 116
MOUNTAIN JEWS (**12**:478) 284
– Komzet 264
– 1989 census 329
Mount Scopus College (Austr.) 111
Moustakis, Marcos 168
Movitch, Miriam 167
Moynihan, Daniel Patrick 364
Mubarak, Husni 205ff
Mugabe, Robert G. 395
Mulder, Dirk C. 298
Muller, Moshe 238
Mulroney, Brian 126
– *illus:*
– – Israel Pres. Herzog addressing Canadian Parliament 126
Mundo Israelita (newsp., Arg.) 107
Munk, E. 358
Muradoy, Gershon 286
Murphy, Richard 204
Musaph, Herman 298
Musatti, Cesare 246
Musée d'Art et d'Histoire du Judaïsme
– *illus:*
– – "Juifs & Citoyens" exhibit catalogue 151
Museum of Israeli Art (Ramat Gan) 236
MUSEUMS (**12**:538) 287
– Australia 113
– Belgium 118
– Christians 228
– England 145
– Germany 163
– Greece 167
– Ireland 187, 389
– Netherlands 296, 298
– State Jewish Museum, Prague 135
– Turkey 363
– United States 185, 287, 328, 342, 378ff
– Vilna 272
– *illus:*
– – Austria 113
– – Greek museum 166
– – Irish Jewish Museum, Dublin 187
MUSIC (**12**:554)
– *ḥazzanut* 174ff
– Karaites 259
– United States 384
– *illus:*
– – music concert, Poland 313
MUSIC, POPULAR (**12**:554) 292
MUSICIANS (**12**:679; **Dc./17**:472) 293
Muslim Brotherhood 306
Mussner, Franz 254
Muszynski, Henrik 253
Muti, Riccardo 233

N

Na-aman, Michal 238
Na'amat 383
Nachmann, Werner 161
Nadich, J. 360
NADIR SHAR (**12**:755)
– Mountain Jews 284
Nagid, Chaim 178
Nagler, Alexander 340
Nagler, Neville 145
Nagorny-Karabakh 115
NAḤAL (**12**:768)
– Israel Prize 241
Naḥal Nissana (site, Isr.) 101
Naḥal Rephaim (site, Isr.) 101
– *illus:*
– – remains of houses 101
NAHARIYYAH (**12**:769)
– Reform Judaism 321
Nahmias, Beri 168
Nahon, G. 312
Nahon, Marco 167
NAJARA, ISRAEL (**12**:798)
– poetry 310, 313
Nalchik (city, Rus.) 284
NAPLES (**12**:822)
– Jewish community 244
Naqdi, Gershon Lalah ben Moses 284
Nar, Albertos 168
NARKISS, BEZALEL 294
Natan, H. 359
National Coal Supply Company (Isr.) 221
National Conference on Soviet Jewry 332, 379, 380
NATIONAL FOUNDATION FOR JEWISH CULTURE (**12**:871)
– museums 289
National Front (polit. pty, Eng.) 143
National Front (F.N.; polit. pty., Fr.) 149
Nationalist Socialist Irish Workers' Party 188
National Jewish AIDS Project 376
National Jewish Archive of Broadcasting 289
National Jewish Bibliographic Center (It.) 245
National Jewish Center for Learning and Leadership, *see* CLAL
National Jewish Population Survey (U.S.) 372
NATIONAL JEWISH WELFARE BOARD (**12**:872) 294
– Jewish Book Council 250
Nationalnodemokraticheskaia partiia 337
NATIONAL RELIGIOUS PARTY (**12**:884)
– peace movements 307
– politics 195, 223
National Salvation Front 99
NATIONAL SOCIALISM (**12**:882)
– Austria 387
– Ibiza and Formentera 185
– Waldheim Affair 387ff
Nation of Islam Movement, (U.S.) 99, 375
Nativity, Basilica of the (Isr.) 227
NATRA SERGIU (**Dc./17**:484)
– music prize 234
NATRONAI BAR HILAI (**12**:886)
– prayer book 159
Navagon (Ind.) 185
Naveh, Hannah 181
Navon, David 244
NAVON, ITZHAK (**Dc./17**:484)
– education minister 230
– 500th anniversary of expulsion of Jews from Spain 342
– Israel-Lebanon War 190
Navot, Amnon 178
NAZARETH (**12**:899)
– Christian medical services 228
– Muslim court 228
Naẓerat Illit (tn., Isr.) 321
Nea Church (Jer.) 104
Nederlands Israelitisch Kerkgenootschap (orgn., Neth.) 294
NEGEV (**12**:925)
– archaeological excavations 101
– electricity plant 221
– new settlements 213
– population 214
– solar energy 221
NEGRO-JEWISH RELATIONS IN THE U.S. (**12**:932)
– anti-Semitism 99
– community relations 375
NEHAMA, JOSEPH 294
Nekudah (mag., Isr.) 172
Nelson, Lemrick, Jr. 376
NEMOY, LEON (**12**:947)
– Karaites 258
NEO-FASCISM (**12**:951)
– anti-Semitsm 99
NEOLOGY (**12**:952)
– Hungary 184
NEO-NAZISM (**12**:954; **Dc./17**:486)
– anti-Semitism 98ff
– Austria 114
– Estonia 147
– France 152
– Germany 162
– Greece 167
– United States 377
NETANYAH (**12**:969)
– population 200, 214
– Reform Judaism 321
– *illus:*
– – absorption center 224
– – Russian musicians 232
Netanyahu, Binyamin 193ff
NETHANEL BEN MOSES HA-LEVI (**12**:972)
– Cairo *Genizah* 156
NETHERLANDS, THE (**12**:793; **Dc./17**:488) 294
– Arab boycott 122
– Barbie, Klaus 115
– Caribbean Jewish communities 129
– Jewish Historical Museum 290
– liturgical traditions 175
– *Memorbook* 154
– Pres. Herzog's visit 209
NETHERLANDS ANTILLES (**12**:993; **Dc./17**:492)
– Jewish community 130
Netivot Shalom (rel. gp., Isr.) 172, 223, 307
Neue Kronen Zeitung (newsp., Aus.) 113
NEUFELD, HENRY 241
Neuman, Ernest 327
Neuman, Isaak 164
– *illus:*
– – E. Berlin Jewish-Christian colloquium 163
Neumann, Paul 351
NEUSNER, JACOB (**12**:1015)
– Talmud research 357
– U.S. literature 366
Neustein, Joshua 238
Neveh Ilan 240
Neveh Noy (site, Isr.) 101
Nevis (isl., W. Indies) 130
New Israel Fund 383
New Israel Opera 232
NEW JERSEY (**12**:1027)
– Jewish political force 377
NEWLEY, ANTHONY 283
Newman, Ed 350
NEWMAN, PETER C. 299
NEWMAN, RANDI 293
NEW MEXICO (**12**:1037)
– Jewish elected officials 377
NEWSPAPERS, HEBREW (**12**:1044)
– US.A. 316
Newton (city, Mass.) 289
New Traditions (mag., U.S.A.) 174
NEW YORK CITY (**12**:1062)
– American Sephardi Federation 98
– anti-Semitism 99
– book fair 318
– Crown Heights incident 375
– Ḥavurah 174
– *ḥazzanut* 176
– Holocaust memorial 378
– Iranian terrorist attack 187
– Jewish Museum 185
– Karaites 258
– migration of Jews 369
– museum 287ff
– poverty among Jews 383
– press 316
– Reform Judaism 322
– Sephardim 342
– Soviet Jewry, struggle for 333
– Syrian Jews 356
– Syrian Jewish community 381
– Yiddish literature 391
– Zamir Chorale 384
– *illus:*
– – JTS library 368
NEW YORK STATE (**12**:1125)
– Jewish political force 377
NEW ZEALAND (**12**:1127; **Dc./17**:165) 299
– anti-Semitism 99
– Israel relations 209
– Jewish-Christian relations 253
NICARAGUA (**12**:1135)
– Iran-Contra affair 378
NICE (**12**:1135)
– Jewish community 149
NICHOLAS I (**12**:1137)
– Mountain Jews 285
Nieuw Israelitisch Weekblad (newsp., Neth.) 154
NIGER, SAMUEL (**12**:1154)
– Yiddish literature 391
Nigheal, Gedalya 181
Nikel, Lea 237
Nikolaidi, I.A. 169
Nini, Y. 309
Ninio, Moshe 238
Nisanov, Ezekiel 286
Nisanov, Judah 286
Nisanov, Ẓevi 286
Nissim, Isaac 359
Nissim-Oghly, Sharbat, *see* ANISIMOIV, ILYA SHERBATOVICH
Nitzan, Shlomo 176, 178
Niv, Orna 168
Nivollet-Montgriffen (vill., Fr.) 116
NIXON, RICHARD MILHAUS (**Dc./17**:493)
– "Jewish vote" 373
– Safire, William 340
No'am (school network, Isr.) 134, 23
NOBEL PRIZE (**12**:1201; (**Dc./17**:493) 299
Noe, B. 357
Nono, Shelomo ben Shabbetai 257
Norris, Chuck 240
North American Conference on Ethiopian Jewry 380
NORWAY (**12**:122; **Dc./17**:494) 299
– Israel oil imports 221
– museum 291
Nosenko, Vladimir 338
Novak, David 255
Novo-Zlatopol (reg., Ukr.) 263
NOY, DOV 301

NUDEL, IDA 301
- U.S. congress 332
Nudler, Mikhail 331
Nueva Sion (newsp., Arg.) 107
Nyasaland 394

O

OAKLAND (**12**:1294)
- museum 288
Obadja Ben Isa 357
Oberammergau (vill., Ger.) 254
Oberlander, Baruch 184
ODESSA (**12**:1319)
- Jewish community 335, 364
OFAKIM (**12**:1334)
- Karaites 257
Ofek, Abraham 237
OFEK, URIEL (**12**:1334; **Dc./17**:497)
- Hebrew literature 180
Offer, Ofra 178
Ofrah (stlmt., Isr.) 171, 172
Ofrat, Gideon 237
OHIO (**12**:1343)
- Jewish political force 377
Ojai (Calif.) 384
Okinawa (city, Jap.) 247
Olmert, Ehud 193, 249
O'Loughlin, Chris 350
OLSEN, TILLIE 301
OLYMPIC GAMES (**12**:1375; **Dc./17**:498) 302
- Israel athletes 352
Oman 122
OMAR, COVENANT OF (**12**:1378)
- Mountain Jews 286
OMER, HILLEL (**12**:1389)
- Hebrew literature 179
ONTARIO (**12**:1407)
- Arab boycott 122
- Jewish population 127
Operation Desert Storm 149
"Operation Exodus" 380
"Operation Moses" 210, 212, 224
"Operation Solomon" 119m 199, 210, 212, 225
- *illus:*
- - World Zionist Press Service folder 249
Oppenheimer, A. 358
Or, Amir 180
ORAL LAW (**12**:1439)
- Orthodoxy, Modern 304
Orange County (Calif.) 273
Order, The (orgn., U.S.) 377
ORDMAN, JEANETTE 302
- Bar-Dor Dance Company 235
Organization of Radical Intellectual Jews in Iran 186
Orgel Lester, Judy 239
Orion, Ezra 236
Ormann, G.J. 358
ORPAZ, YIZHAK (**Dc./17**:499)
- Hebrew literature 177
ORT (**12**:1481)
- Argentina 108
- Komzet 263
- U.S. membership 383
Orth, Elisabeth 114
ORTHODOXY (**12**:1491) 303
- Australia 111
- England 142
- France 150
- Gerry 164
- *hazzanut* 175
- Hungary 184
- Israel 223
- Israel political parties 193
- Los Angeles 274ff
- publishing 318
- Russia 331ff
- South Africa 345
- Switzerland 355
- United States 372ff
- U.S. intermarriage rate 368
- U.S. literature 365
Or Yossef (orgn., Fr.) 151
Osaka (city, Jap.) 247
Osetia 160
Osherowitch, Hirsh 392
OSIJEK (**12**:1498)
- Yugoslavia 394
OSLO (**12**:1499)
- Jewish community 300
Osmos, Marco 167
Ostend (tn., Belg.) 117
Ostrow, Ruth 110
OTTAWA (**12**:1521)
- multilateral peace talks 126
Otzar Ha-Torah (orgn., Fr.) 151
Ouaknin, M.A. 360
Oud-Beyerland (Neth.) 297
Ouderamstel (tn., Neth.) 296
Ouderkerk-on-the Amstel (vill., Neth.) 296
OURY, GERARD 305
Owens, Jesse 351
OXFORD (**12**:1534)
- Cairo *Genizah* 155
OZ, AMOS (**Dc./17**:500)
- Frankfurt Book Fair award 163
- Hebrew literature 176ff, 180
- Russian translations 338
Ozal, Turgut 342, 362
OZICK, CYNTHIA (**Dc./17**:500)
- U.S. literature 366
Ozida, Samuel di 357
Oz VeShalom (rel. gp., Isr.) 172, 307

P

Pacifi, R. 360
PADEH, BARUCH 241
PADUA (**13**:8)
- Jewish community 244
Pagis, Dan 179ff, 309
Palamas, Kostas 169
PALESTINE LIBERATION ORGANIZATION (PLO) 305
- Argentina 107
- Canada 126
- Denmark 138
- England 144
- France 152
- Iran 186
- Ireland 187
- Israeli Arabs 202ff
- Israel recognition of 33
- Israel Supreme Court decision 217
- Lebanon 189, 196ff, 206ff
- Likkud's attitude 193
- Netherlands 296ff
- New Zealand 299
- Russian Jews 334, 339
- Tunisia 190
- United Nations 365
- Vatican relations 386
- Zimbabwe 395
- *illus:*
- - *intifada* poster 205
PALEY, GRACE 307
Palma de Mallorca (city, Majorca) 184
Palm Beach Jewish World (newsp., Florida) 317
PALTOI BAR ABBAYE (**13**:50)
- geonic literature 157
PAMA (co., Isr.) 221
Pamyat (orgn., Rus.) 211, 337
PANAMA (**13**:53; **Dc./17**:501)
- Jewish community 128
Panama City 128
Panova, Galina 236
Panthikapei, *see* KERCH
Papadiamantis, Alexander 169
Papagiotopoulou, I.M. 169
Papandreou, Andreas 166
Papastratis, Sotiris 167
PAPIERNIKOV, JOSEPH (**13**:67)
- Yiddish literature 392
Papirofsky, Joseph, *see* PAPP, JOSEPH
PAPO, IZIDOR JOSEF 307
Papoulias, Karolas 166
PAPP, JOSEPH 361
PARAGUAY (**13**:85)
- Klarsfeld, Beate 261
Paramaribo (city, Surinam) 129
- *illus:*
- - Zedek ve-Shalom synagogue 129
PARDO, DAVID (**13**:93)
- Talmud research 359
PARIS (**13**:103)
- Jewish community 149
- museum 292
- *illus:*
- - 40th anniversary of French Jews' deportation 151
- - Museum of Jewish Art 291
Paritskii, Alexander 333
Parnes, Anthony 143
PARTISANS (**13**:140)
- Waldheim Affair 388
Parvus, *see* GELFOND, ALEXANDER LAZAREVICH
Pascall, Julia 147
PASSOVER (**13**:163)
- *hazzanut* 175
- Israel legislation 216
- U.S. *seder* ceremonies 374
- *illus:*
- - *Haggadah*, India 185
- - *Haggadah*, Russian-Hebrew 225
Pasternak, Velvel 176
PAT, JACOB (**13**:177)
- Yiddish literature 391
Paterson, David 145
Patriot (orgn., Rus.) 336
Patterns of Prejudice (journ., Eng.) 186
Pawlawski, Michael 127
Pawlikowski, John 254
Paxton, Robert 128
Paz (oil co., Isr.) 221
Paz-Gal (co., Isr.) 222
Paz-Pimat (co., Isr.) 222
PEACE MOVEMENTS, RELIGIOUS 307
PEACE NOW (**Dc./17**:502)
- American friends 381, 383
- Canadian friends 126
- Gush Emunim 172
- Italian protesters 245
- Netherlands 296
Peace Today (orgn., Rus.) 334
PEARLMAN, MOSHE 307
Peartree (pub. house, U.S.A.) 319
Peck, A.J. 357
PECS (**13**:203)
- Hungary 184
Peled Commission 231
Peles, Josef 234
PELLEG, FRANK (**13**:220)
- special concert 232
PENAL LAW (**13**:222)
- Israel law 216
Penderecki, Krzysztyof 232
PENN, ALEXANDER (**13**:228)
- Hebrew literature 181
PENNSYLVANIA (**13**:229)
- Jewish political force 377
Penso, Alain 168
Perahia, Murray 167
PEREC, GEORGES 308
PERES, SHIMON (**13**:278; **Dc./17**:503) 308
- American Jewish Congress 382
- Austrian visit 114
- Government of National Unity 191ff, 207ff
- Iran relations 186, 378
- Japan visit 248
- leadership struggle 193ff
- Netherlands 298
- Pollard Affair 315
- Shamir, Yizhak 342
- ultra-religious parties 381
- *illus:*
- - Ashkelon supermarket 218
- - Hammer, Armand, and 173
- - with Margaret Thatcher 144
Perestroika (rebuilding) 330ff, 333, 337
Peretz, David 308
Peretz, Nissan 238
Peretz, Yitzhak 225
Perez, Jung 320
Perkiss, Shahar 351
Perl, Nestor 106
Perla, Y.Y.F. 158
Perlasca, Giorgio 246
Perry-Amitai, Lily 178
Persian Gulf War
- American Jews 381
- Arab world 205
- Argentinian participation 107
- Australia 112
- France 149
- Germany 163
- Israel 191, 196ff, 202, 208ff, 211, 23
- Italy 245
- Netherlands 297
- *illus:*
- - Tel Aviv Scud attack 208
PERTH (**13**:321)
- Jewish commmunity 110ff
PETAH TIKVAH (**13**:336)
- art museum 236
- cantorial training school 175
- population 200, 214
Petersburg (tn., Alsk.) 97
PETLYURA, SIMON (**13**:340)
- Ukrainian Hero 364
Petrovsk Port, *see* Makhachkalah
PETUCHOWSKI, JAKOB JOSEF (**13**:349)
- poetry 309
PHILADELPHIA (**13**:368)
- migration of Jews 369
- museum 289
PHILANTHROPY (**13**:376)
- United States 383
PHILLIPS, LAZARUS (**13**:406)
- Canada 128
PHILOSOPHY, JEWISH (**13**:421; **Dc./17**:503)
- Conservative Judaism 133
- geonic literature 157
- Orthodoxy, Modern 304
PHOENIX (**13**:481)
- migration of Jews 369
- Plotkin Judaica Museum 289
PHOTOGRAPHY (**13**:483)
- Israel 236, 238
Picciotto Fargain, Liliana 245
Pikul, Valentin 330
PILCH, JUDAH 308
PILGRIMAGE (**13**:510)
- Christian 227
- Muslim 229
Pincas, Israel 179
Pincus, Jacob 350
Pinerua Ordaz, Luis 154
Pines, S. 312
Pinhasi, Rabbi
- *illus:*
- - Raphael Eitan greets 194
Pinhasov, Asaf 286
Pinner, Hayyim 145
PINTER, HAROLD (**13**:551
- English literature 146
Piracy 184
PIRKOI BEN BABOI (**13**:560)
- letters 159
PISA (**13**:561)
- Jewish community 244
PITTSBURGH (**13**:568)
- Holocaust memorial 378
- Jewish community 369
PITTSBURGH PLATFORM (**13**:57
- Reform Judaism 322
PIYYUT (**13**:573)
- Cairo *Genizah* 155
- poetry, medieval Hebrew 309ff
Plaut, Joshua 168
PLAUT, W. GUNTHER (**13**:631)
- Reform Judaism 322
Plaza, Antonio 106
PLO, *see* PALESTINE LIBERATIO ORGANIZATION
PLOESTI (city, Rum.)
- Jewish community 327
PODHORETZ, NORMAN (**13**:667)
- *Commentary* 374
Podriachek, Eliezer 392
Podvoloschiska, Julius, *see* Dresner, Julius
POETRY (**13**:670)
- Hebrew literature 178ff
POETRY, MEDIEVAL HEBREW (**13**:681; **Dc./17**:510) 309
POGROMS (**13**:694)
- Russia 330, 337
- Ukraine 364

- Uzbekistan 385
Poincaré, Henri 337
POLAND (**13**:709; **Dc./17**:511) 313
- *aliyah* transit point 339
- anti-Semitism 100
- Auschwitz convent 108
- Germany, East 163
- *hazzanut* 175
- immigration to Denmark 138
- Israel cultural life 232
- Israel relations 209, 234
- Jewish-Christian relations 253
- Karaites 258
- museum 292
- Pres. Herzog's visit 209
- Soviet Jews 211, 339
- Yiddish literature 392
Polgar, Isaac 309
Poliakoff, Stephen 146
Polikar, Yehuda 168, 240
POLISH, DAVID (**13**:797)
- Reform Judaism 322
Politi, Kosma 169
POLITICS (**13**:805)
- American Jews 373
- England 143
- France 147, 149
- Hungary 184
- Iran 186
- Ireland 187
- Israel 245
- Italy 245
- Russia 334
- Switzerland 355
POLLACK, ISRAEL 243
Pollard, Jonathan Jay 99, 314
POLLARD AFFAIR 314
- American Jewish community 377
Polo, Water 351
Polonskii, Pinkhas 331
Polonsky, Lester 97
Polyukovich, Ivan 112
PONARY (**13**:847)
- Holocaust memorial 272
POONA (**13**:850)
- Jewish community 185
POOR, PROVISION FOR THE (**13**:850)
- Krimchaks 269
- U.S. 374, 383
Popular Front for the Liberation of Palestine 203
Porat, Hanan 171
Porath, Yehoshua 181
Porges, Nenad 393
PORT ELIZABETH (**13**:909)
- Jewish community 345
Porter, J. 315
PORTER, SIR LESLIE 315
PORTER, SHIRLEY 315
Porto (tn., Port.) 316
PORTO ALEGRE (**13**:914)
- Jewish community 123
Porton, G. 360
PORTUGAL (**13**:925; **Dc./17**:512) 316
- museum 291
PORUSH, ISRAEL (**Dc./17**:513)
- Australia 111
POTOCK, CHAIM (**15**:1579; **Dc./17**:513)
- Norwegian book 301
- U.S. literature 366
POTTERY (**13**:936)
- archaeological excavations 101
- *illus:*
- - Ketef Hinnom 102
POVERTY (**13**:944)
- France 149
PRAGUE (**13**:964)
- Jewish community 135
- museum 292
- *illus:*
- - Altneuschul 136
- - banner of Franz Kafka 135
Praisman, Leonid 332
Pratelli, D. 360
Pratt, Richard 110
PRAYER (**13**:978)
- *hazzanut* 175
- poetry 312
- Reform Judaism 322
PRAYER BOOKS (**13**:985)
- Conservative Judaism 134
- geonic literature 157, 159
- Reform Judaism 322
- *illus:*
- - Conservative *Sim Shalom* 134
PREIL, GABRIEL JOSHUA (**13**:1013; **Dc./17**:514)
- Hebrew literature 179, 181
PRESS (**13**:1023; **Dc./17**:514) 316
- Russia 336
- Yiddish press 391
Presse, Di (newsp., Arg.) 107
Presse, Die (newsp., Aus.) 113
Pressman, Jacob 274
Preston, Rosalind 145
PRETORIA (**13**:1058)
- Jewish community 345
Price, Charles 110
PRIESTLY BLESSING (**13**:1060)
- archaeological excavations 102
- *illus:*
- - Jerusalem plaque 103
Primor, Sigal 236, 239
PRINCE, HAROLD 361
Prins, Ralph 297
Proceedings (period., U.S.A.) 318
Progressive List for Peace (polit. party, Isr.) 203
Pro Israel (newsp., Gr.) 320
Project Ezra (U.S.) 174, 383
PROPERTY (**13**:1146)
- mortgage law 216
PROSELYTES (**13**:1182)
- Beta Israel 224
- Interior Ministry decision 226
- Supreme Court decision 211
- Reform Judaism 321
- Russia 331
- U.S. Jews 371ff
PROTESTANTS (**13**:1247)
- Jewish-Christian relations 252
PRYWES, MOSHE (**Dc./17**:514)
- Israel Prize 243
Public Council for Soviet Jewry 332
PUBLISHING (**13**:1364) 318
- Russia 330
PUERTO RICO (**16**:1555)
- Jerwish community 130
Puker Rivo, Sharon 176
PURIM (**13**:390)
- *illus:*
- - Moscow kindergarten party 329
PURIMSHPIL (**13**:1396)
- Russia 330ff
PURITY AND IMPURITY, RITUAL (**13**:1405)
- Hungary 184
Pyatigorsk (tn., Rus.) 287

Q

Qaitagh (tn., Rus.) 285
Qamishli
- Jewish community 355, 381
Qaraqaitagh (khanate) 284)
Qasr al-Yahud (loc., Isr.) 227
Qatar 122
Qessotch (priests) 120
Quartet Books (publ. house, U.S.A.) 319
QUEBEC (**13**:1422)
- Jewish community 125ff

R

Raab, Esther 180
Raalte (Neth.) 297
Raanan, O. 309
RA'ANANNAH (**13**:1438)
- Reform Judaism 321
Raananaah Symphonette Orchestra 232, 234
RABBANITES (**13**:1444)
- Karaites 258
- Krimchaks 266
RABBATH-AMMAN (**13**:1444)
- PLO office 203
RABBI, RABBINATE (**13**:1445)
- Mountain Jews 286
- Reform Judaism 321
- Russia 331
- U.S. women 373
RABBINICAL ASSEMBLY (**13**:1460)
- Conservative Judaism 134
- American Judaism 373
RABBINICAL SEMINARIES (**13**:1463)
- Budapest 184
Rabbinic Conference of the Union of Liberal & Progressive Synagogues 324
Rabel, Khalil 238
Rabich, Roman 385
Rabicovitch, Shelomoh 241
Rabim (youth orgn.) 334
Rabin, Ozer 180
RABIN, YIZHAK (**13**:1471; **Dc./17**:517) 319
- Administered Territories 205
- AIPAC criticism 382
- Arab boycott 122
- defense ministry 197
- Government of National Unity 192, 207
- leadership struggle 193
- Pollard Affair 315
- primary elections 194
Rabinov, Yehoshua 179
Rabinovich, Noam 236
Rabinovitz, Israel 238
Rabinowitz, A.S. 359
Rabinowitz, Z.M. 309
RACE, THEORY OF (**12**:1483)
- anti-Semitism 98
- France 149, 152
- Germany 162
- Israel law 216
- Russian anti-Zionists 330
- Zionism 334, 338, 364
RACHEL (**13**:1516)
- Hebrew literature 180
Rachum, Stephanie 237
Raices Judaismo Contemporaneo (journ., Arg.) 107
Raj, Tamas 184
Rajzman, Bernard 302, 351
Rakita, Mark 302
Rallis (P.M., Gr.) 265
Ram, Menucha 392
Ramadan 186, 229
Ramah camps (U.S.) 133, 275, 335
Ramat Aviv (sub., Tel Aviv) 321, 342
RAMAT GAN (**13**:1530)
- art museum 236
- population 200
- Reform Judaism 321
RAMAT HA-GOLAN (**13**:1531)
- archaeological excavations 100
- Israeli politics 194
- new settlements 213
- UNDOF 365
- wind energy 221
Ramat ha-Sharon (tn., Isr.) 321
RAMLEH (**13**:1540)
- dance company 235
- Karaites 257
- waqf property 228
Ramras-Rauch, Gila 180
RAMSES III (**13**:1545)
- Bet Shean excavations 101
Rand, Shuli 240
Random House (pub., U.S.A.) 318
Rannen (mosh., Isr.) 257
Rantzer, Philip 238
RAPE (**13**:1548)
- American Jews 372
Raphael, David 366
RAPHAEL, FREDERIC (**13**:1550)
- English literature 146
Raphael, Shmuel 168
Rapp, Nachman 392
Rappaport, Talia 237
Rasm, el-Kabash (site, Isr.) 100
Rasputin, Valentin 337
Ratisbonne monastery (Jer.) 227
RATOSH, YONATHAN (**13**:1573)
- Hebrew literature 181
Rattok, Lily 180, 181
Ratzaby, Y. 310
Rauca, Albert Helmut 127
RAVIKOVITCH, DALIA (**13**:1584)
- Hebrew literature 179
RAYNE, MAX, LORD 319
RAZON, JACKO 320
- Greece 168
REAGAN, RONALD (**Dc./17**:520)
- Bitburg controversy 378
- Iran-Contra affair 378
- Israel-Lebanon War 189
- Jewish electorate 374
- Middle East peace plan 305
- Soviet Jewry, struggle for 332
RECANATI (fam.) (**13**:1607) 320
RECANATI, ABRAHAM SAMUEL 320
Recanati, David 168
Recanati, Yehudah Leib (Leon) 320
RECIFE (**13**:1613)
- Jewish community 123
RECONSTRUCTIONISM (**13**:1615; **Dc./17**:521)
- Conservative Judaism 133
- Synagogue Council of America 381
Reder, Walter 113
Reeb, David 238
REFORM JUDAISM (**14**:23) 320
- American Judaism 373ff
- Australia 111
- England 142, 145
- *hazzanut* 175
- India 185
- Ireland 187
- Law of Return 226
- Los Angeles 274ff
- Netherlands 295
- publishing 318
- Russia 335
- South Africa 345
- Supreme Court decision on marriages 217
- Switzerland 355
- U.S. intermarriage rates 368
- Zionist Congress (31st) 395
"Refuseniks" (gr., Rus.) 329, 333, 34[illegible]
- *illus:*
- - Israeli efforts on behalf of 332
- - Leningrad apartment 330
Regev, Uri 322
Rehovot Chamber Orchestra 232
Reich, Seymour
- *illus:*
- - Pope John Paul II 385
Reichert, V.E. 309
Reichmann (fam.) 128, 183
Reimann, Viktor 113
Reiner, Carl 282, 283
REINER, ROB 283
Reisman, Bernard 174
Reistetter, Stephen 127
Reitman, Dorothy 128
Renanot Institute (Jer.) 175
Rendsburg (tn., Ger.) 290
Rendtorff, Rolf 255
Rennan, Paul 234
REPARATIONS, GERMAN (**14**:72)
- Greek Holocaust survivors 168
- IJA 186
Republican Party (U.S.) 373
Republikaner Partei (polit. party, Ger.) 98
Republikanskaia Narodnaia partiia Rossii (orgn., Rus.) 337
RESNICK, JUDITH 325
RESPONSA (**14**:83; **Dc./17**:524)
- Conservative Judaism 134
- geonic literature 157, 159
- *hazzanut* 175
- Reform Judaism 322, 324
RESURRECTION (**14**:96)
- Orthodoxy, Modern 303
"Returners to religion", *see Hozerim bi-teshuvah*
Reuvain, Shlomo 167
REUVENI, AHARON (**14**:113)
- Hebrew literature 178, 181
REVEL, BERNARD (**14**:116; **Dc./17**:526)
- Orthodoxy, Modern 304

REVELATION (**14**:117)
- Orthodoxy, Modern 303
REVISTA CULTULUI MOZAIC (period., Rum.; **14**:132)
- Romania 328
- Reykjavik 333
Rezan, Maria 168
RHODES (**14**:145)
- Jewish community 169
- Yad Vashem memorial 167
Rhodesia, *see* ZIMBABWE
RICH, ADRIENNE 325
Rich, Vera 365
RICHMOND (**14**:160)
- museum 289
RICHTER, BURTON 325
Rico, Aldo 106
Riddles 311
RIEGNER, GERHART 325
- Jewish-Christian relations 252
Riemer, Chaim 328
RIFKIND, MALCOLM 325
- secretary of state for defense 143
RIGA (**14**:172)
- Jewish community 270
- Jewish social and cultural life 334
- Rumbula forest meeting 331
Rigert, David 302
RIGHTEOUS OF THE NATIONS (**14**:184)
- Greece 166
- Italy 246
- Knesset tribute 228
- *illus:*
- - Graebe, Herman F. 166
Riklis, Eran 240
Rimmer, Itzu 236
Rimon, Meir 234
Rimon, Yuval 236
Rimor, Mordechai 371
RIO DE JANEIRO (**14**:190)
- Jewish community 123
- Sephardi conference 342
Rio Grande do Sul (state, Braz.) 124
RISHON LE-ZION (**14**:193)
- population 200
- Reform Judaism 321
- *illus:*
- - geriatric center 199
Riskin, Shlomo 131
Ritterband, Paul
- U.S.A. 368
Rivlin, A.E. 358
Rivlin, Bracha 167
Robel, Yaakov 105
ROBINSON, JACOB (**14**:207)
- IJA 186
Robinson, Mary 188
- *illus:*
- - Terenure Synagogue visit 188
Robinson, Nehemia 186
Robinson, Nick
- *illus:*
- - Tenerure Synagogue visit 188
Rocard, Michel 265
RODAN, MENDI (**Dc./17**:474)
- music in Israel 232
RODENSKY, SHEMUEL 241
Rodina (orgn., Rus.) 337
Roermond (tn., Neth.) 295
Rogatlikoy (stlmt., Rus.) 269
Roitman, David (7:1550)
- *ḥazzanut* 176
ROKEAḤ, DAVID (**14**:226)
- Hebrew literature 179
Rokeaḥ, Z.E. 313
Roland, Joan 185
Roller Skating 351
Roloff, Elisabeth 232
Romanenko, Alexander 330, 333
Romania, *see* RUMANIA
Romania Mare (newsp., Rum.) 327
Romano, Elio 366
Romanov (fam., Rus.) 173
Romberg, Oswaldo 237
ROME (**14**:240)
- Jewish community 244ff
- museum 291
- pope's visit to synagogue 252
Romero, E. 309
Romhany, Laszlo 183
Romsey, Paul 366
RONLY-RIKLIS, SHALOM (**Dc./17**:475)
- Israel cultural life 232
Ronnch, Y.E.
- Yiddish literature 392
Ronson, Gerald 143
Rosen, Al 349
Rosen, David 187
Rosen, Mel 351
ROSEN, MOSES (**14**:270)
- Romania 327
Rosenbaum, Shmuel 112
Rosenbaum, Yankel 376
Rosenberg, A.Y. 357
Rosenberg, Harold 366
ROSENBERG, LOUIS (**14**:279)
- Canada 128
ROSENBERG, STUART E. (**14**:279)
- Canada 128
ROSENBLATT, (Yossele) JOSEPH (**14**:282)
- *ḥazzanut* 176
Rosenfeld, Harry 97
ROSENFELD, SHALOM 241
Rosenha Judaica (news., Braz.) 123
Rosenkranz, Shmuel 112
Rosen-Moked, T. 309
Rosensaft, Hadassah (Bimko) 161
ROSENSAFT, JOSEF (**14**:290)
- Germany 161
Rosensaft, Menachem 382
Rosenson, Y. 358
Rosenthal, A.M. 381
Rosenthal, D. 357, 359
Rosenthal, E.S. 358
Rosenthal, Odeda 299
ROSENZWEIG, FRANZ (**14**:299)
- poetry 312
Ross, Malcolm 126
Ross, Wendy 299
Rossi (Rus. orgn.) 371
Rostock (tn., Ger.) 162
Rotem, Mordecai 321
Roth, Mark 350
ROTH, PHILIP (**14**:330) 326
- U.S. literature 366
Roth, Stephen J. 186
Rothenberg, Alan 349
Rothenberg, J. 312
Rothman, M.L. 97
ROTHSCHILD, BATHSHEVA DE (**14**:340)
- Israel Prize 242
- Ordman, Jeannette 302
Rothschild, David de 150
Rothschild, Edouard Alphonse de 302
Rothschild, Evelyn 326
ROTHSCHILD, NATHANIEL CHARLES JACOB, LORD 326
Rothschild, Nathaniel Mayer 326
ROTTERDAM (**14**:349)
- Jewish community 294ff
ROULEAU, ERIC (Elie Rafoul) 326
Rowing 351
Rozenshtein, Grigorii 331ff
Rozhansky, Shmuel 391
RSFSR, *see* RUSSIA
Rua, Fernando de la 107
RUBENS, BERNICE 326
- English literature 145ff
Rubin, David 145
RUBIN, HADASSAH (**14**:370)
- Yiddish literature 392
Rubin, Sam 350
Rubin Academy of Music and Dance (Jer.) 234
RUBINSTEIN, ARTHUR (**14**:374; **Dc./17**:480, 531)
- 100th birthday festivities 232
Rubinstein, Hilary L. 113
Rubinstein, W.D. 113
Rubruquis, Wilhelm 284
Rudakov, Alexander 238
Rudenstine, Neil 377
RUEBNER, TUVIA (**14**:382)
- Hebrew literature 179ff
Rueti (tn., Switz.) 175
RUMANIA (Romania; **14**:386; **Dc./17**:531) 327
- *aliyah* transit station 380
- anti-Semitism 99ff
- *ḥazzanut* 175
- Pres. Herzog's visit 209
- Soviet Jews 211
- Yiddish literature 392
Rumbula forest (Riga) 331
RUSSIA (**14**:433; **Dc./17**:533) 328
- anti-Semitism 99, 211, 337
- Arab States 197
- Australia, migrants to 110
- Demjanjuk trial 137
- Denmark 138
- Dutch Solidarity Committee 298
- Germany, East 163
- Germany, emigration to 151
- Gery sect 164
- Hammer, Armand 172
- *ḥazzanut* 175
- immigration to Israel 192, 195, 198ff, 210
- IPO tour 232
- Israel-Arab peace talks 209
- Israel-Lebanon War 189
- Israel relations 209, 234
- Israel sport 351
- Jewish emigrants in Hungarian transit center 184
- Karaites 258
- Komzet 263
- Krimchaks 268ff
- Los Angeles 273
- Mountain Jews 284
- New Zealand 299
- Orthodox Church 254
- Ramah camps 135
- Salonikan archives 168
- Transmigrants in Italy 266
- United Nations 367ff
- U.S. struggle for release of Jews 376, 379ff
- Yiddish 392
- Yiddish literature 392
- *illus:* text
- - Jews deplane in Israel 210
Russian-Orthodox Church 331
Russkii Nationalno-Patrioticheskii Tsentr (orgn., Rus.) 337
Rutland, Suzanne 113
Rutskoi, Alexandeer 334
RYTDER, WINONA 283

S

SAADIAH (Ben Joseph) GAON (**14**:543)
- Cairo *Genizah* 155
- geonic literature 157ff
- *illus:*
- - *Daniel, Book of* 158
Saban, Giacomo 252
Sabar, Y. 359
Sabatello, Fausto 246
Sabato, Ernesto 105
Sabbaḥ, Michel Asad 226
Sabbah, Monsignor 386
Sabbatarians, *see* Subbotniki
SABBATH (**14**:557)
- ḥavurah movement 174
- public desecration in Israel 224
- Reform Judaism 322
SABBATICAL YEAR AND JUBILEE (**14**:574)
- chief rabbinate decision 224
Sabra and Shatilla (ref. camps, Leb.) 190, 196, 207
Sabyrov, Shamil 302
Sachs, Aryeh 179
SACHS, MICHAEL (**14**:595)
- poetry 312
SACHSENHAUSEN ORANIENBERG (**14**:597)
- desecration 162
SACKS, JONATHAN HENRY 339
- Australia visit 111
- chief rabbi, England 145
SADAI, YIZḤAK (**Dc./17**:475)
- music prize 234
SADAN, DOV (**14**:618)
- Hebrew literature 181
- poetry 312
- Yiddish 392
Sadan-Loebenstein, Nili 181
Sadat, Jehan 123
SADAT, MUHAMMED ANWAR AL- (**Dc./17**:541)
- Israel relations 206
SADEH, PINḤAS (**14**:623)
- Hebrew literature 179
Sadik, Yusuf 258
Sadosky, Manuel 106
Saenz-Badillos, Angel 309, 312
SAFDIE, MOSHE (3:365)
- HUC extension 236
- U.S. literature 367
- University of Judaism 276
Safieh, Afif 297
SAFIRE, WILLIAM 339
Safrai, Channah 298
Safrai, Sh. 360
Safrai, Z. 358
Safran, J. 360
Sagine-Rejto, Ildiko 302
Said ben Babshad 310
Sa'id Yona 241
St. Eustatius (isl., Antilles) 128, 130
ST. GALL (**14**:660)
- Jewish community 354
St. Genis-Laval (vill., Fr.) 116
St. John's Hospice (Jer.) 226
ST. LOUIS (**14**:662)
- Holocaust memorial 378
- Jewish community 369
- *seder* ceremonies 374
St. Maarte (isl., Neth. Antilles) 130
St. Rambert-en-Bugey (vill., Fr.) 116
St. Thomas Island 129
SALK, JONAS EDWARD (**14**:686)
- Goldblum, Nathan 242
Salmon, Y. 312
SALMON BEN JEROHAM (**14**:689)
- Karaites 259
Salomon, Albert 340
SALOMON, CHARLOTTE (**14**:694) 340
Salomon, Doron 232
Salomon-Lindberg, Paula 340
SALONIKA (**14**:699; **Dc./17**:543)
- Brunner, Alois 125
- Greek literature 169
- Recanati, Abraham 320
- Sephardim 342
- Waldheim, Kurt 387
- Yad Vashem memorial 167
- *illus:*
- - Rabbi Koretz and King George II 265
Salper, J. 358
SALT TRADE AND INDUSTRY (**14**:712)
- Ibiza and Formentera 184
SALTMAN, AVROM 240
Salutskii, Anatolii 334
Salvador (city, Braz.) 123
Salvador, Prinz Luis 185
Salzberger, Gabi 239
Salzer, J. 358
Salzmann, Laurence 341
SAMARIA (**14**:723)
- Arab population 203
- new settlements 213
Samarkand 384
Samid, Alberto 107
Samkush (Samkersh; tn., Crimea) 267
Samuel, Robert 321
SAMUEL BEN HOPHNI (**14**:807)
- geonic literature 157ff
SAMUEL HA-NAGID (**14**:816)
- poetry 309
Samuels, Diane 147
San Christobel (Ibiza) 185
Sanders, Joseph 294
SAN FRANCISCO (**14**:833)
- General Assembly of the Council of Jewish Federations 384
- Holocaust memorial 378
- Karaites 258
- museum 289
- *seder* ceremonies 374
San José (city, Costa Rica) 128
San Marino (city, U.S.) 273
SANTOB DE CARRION (**14**:849)
- poetry 309
Santo Domingo (Dominican Rep.) 128, 130
SÃO PAULO (**14**:850)
- Jewish community 123
- Sephardi conference 342

- *illus:*
- - dedication of Maimonides Square 123
Saperstein, David 323
Saporta y Beja, Enrique 167
SARAJEVO (**14**:869)
- Jewish community 393
- museum 290
SARATOV (**14**:873)
- Gery 164
Sarhi, Ron 233
Sarkany, Miklos 302
SARNA, NAHUM 340
Sarney, José 123
SARTABA (**14**:889)
- archaeological excavations 103
Sartre, Jean Paul 270
Satmar (ḥas. dyn.) 316
SÁTORALJAÚJHELY (**14**:906)
- *illus:*
- - Holocaust survivor 183
Saudi Arabia 122, 197, 208, 229
Saunders, Ernest 143
Scalfaro, Oscar Luigi 245
Schach, Eliezer 223
Schall, Noah 176
Schaverin (caterer, Eng.) 145
Schechtman, Elie 391
- Scheer, Eva 300
SCHEIBER, ALEXANDER (**1**:36; **14**:951)
- Cairo *Genizah* 155
- Karaites 259
- poetry 309
SCHECHTER, SOLOMON (**14**:948)
- Zionism 134
Scheinblum, Monte 350
Scheindlin, R.P. 309ff
Scheininger, Les 128
Schenker, Zoltan 302
Scheuer, Richard 321
Schildbret, Lucy, *see* DAWIDOWICZ, LUCY
SCHINDLER, ALEXANDER M. (**Dc./17**:545)
- Reform Judaism 323
SCHINDLER, OSKAR (**Dc./17**:546)
- Keneally's book 147
Schipansky, I. 158, 358
SCHIRMAN, JEFIM (**14**:968)
- poetry 309
SCHISGAL, MURRAY 361
Schjon, Frank, Lord 341
SCHLESWIG-HOLSTEIN (**14**:973)
- museum 290
Schmelz, U.O. 105
- American Jews 368
Schmelzer, M.H. 309
SCHMIDT, JOSEPH (**14**:979)
- *ḥazzanut* 175
SCHNEERSOHN, MENAḤEM MENDEL (**Dc./17**:546)
- Israel politics 223
- Orthodoxy, Modern 304
Schoenfield, Al 351
Schoneveld, Jacob J. 298
Schoon, Simon 298
Schor, Sandra 367
Schorr, Renen 240
SCHORSCH, ISMAR 134, 341
Schreir, Peter 233
Schulman, Elias 391
Schulweis, Harold 274
SCHULZ, BRUNO (**14**:1008)
- Grossman, David 170
Schutz, David 177
Schwamberger, Joseph 106
SCHWARTZ, NELVIN 341
- Steinberg, Jack 353
Schwartz, Moshe 312
Schwartz, Shlome 392
SCHWARZBARD, SHALOM (**14**:1027)
- Ukraine 364
Schwarzbaum, H. 309
Schwebel, Ivan 238
Schwarzwald, O. 357
Schweitzer, Josef 184
Scientific Liaison Unit (Isr.) 315
Scliar, Moacyr 123
SCOUTING (**14**:1037)
- Ireland 188
Scriabin 262
SCRIBE (**14**:1041)
- Talmud research 357
Scrinzi, Otto 387
SCULPTURE (**14**:1059)
- in Israel 236ff
SEATTLE (**14**:1082)
- American Sephardi Federation 98
SEDEH BOKER (**14**:1089)
- solar energy research 221ff
SEDOT YAM (**14**:1094)
- archaeological excavations 104
Seedna Ali Mosque 228
Segal, E. 357
SEGAL, GEORGE 283
Segal, Hugh 128
SEGAL, URI (**Dc./17**:475)
- Israel cultural life 232
Segre, Augusto 246
SEGRE, EMILIO GINO (**16**:1113)
- necrology 246
Seineldin, Mohamed Ali 106
SEIXAS, MOSES MENDES (**14**:1117)
- Washington, George 288
Sela, Joel 352
Self, Will 147
Selig, Alan (Bud) 349
Selinger, Arbital 304, 351
Selinger, Arie 351
Sella, Aviem 315
Sellers, Peter (**14**:1136)
- *Being There* 265
Seltzer, Chaim 392
SEMIKHAH (**14**:1140)
- Conservative Judaism 133
Semanario Israelita (newsp., Arg.) 108
Semel, Nava 178
Semenovich, Yakov, *see* KANOVICH, GRIGORY
Seminario Rabbinico Latin Americano 134
SENED, ALEXANDER (**14**:1159)
- Hebrew literature 176
Sened, Yonat 176
Seow, C.L. 319
SEPHARDIM (**14**:1164) 341
- American Sephardi Federation 98
- education 230
- England 142
- France 149
- Netherlands 295
- politics 223
- Shas 195
- Turkey 363
- *illus:*
- - Danish stamp 138
SEPPHORIS (**14**:1177)
- archaeological excavations 104
Seras, Andrew 351
Serbia (rep., Yug.) 187, 393
Sered (camp, Slov.) 125
Seroussi, Edwin 175
SEVASTOPOL (**14**:1198)
- Krimchaks 266
SEX (**14**:1206)
- prisoner's rights to home leave 217
Sfard, David 392
SHAANAN, AVRAHAM (**14**:1211)
- Hebrew literature 180
Shabetai, Elie 167
Shabiba (Arab youth group) 204
Shabtai, Jacob 177
Shafarevich, Igor 337
SHAFFER, PETER (**14**:1256; **Dc./17**:552)
- English literature 146
Shaffir, M.M. 392
SHAḤAM, NATHAN (**14**:1257)
- Hebrew literature 176ff
Shaḥar, David 176
Shai, Hadassah 310
Shakdiel, Leah 226
Shaked, Gershon 180ff
Shaked, Malka 181
Shaked, S. 312
Shakhnovskii, Vladimir 331
Shalem (period, Isr.) 391
Shalev, Avner 178
Shalev, Meir 178
SHALEV, YITZHAK (**14**:1266)
- Hebrew literature 179
Shalev, Zruyah 180
Shalit, Levi 392
Shallon, David 232
Shalom (newsp., Turk.) 363
SHALOM, SHIN (**14**:1271; **Dc./17**:553)
- Hebrew literature 179ff
SHALOM ALEICHEM (**14**:1272)
- 125th anniversary celebrations 330
Shalom Hartman Institute for Advanced Studies 227
Shalom Magazine (period., Braz.) 123
Shalom Noticia (newsp., Braz.) 123
Shambadal, Lior 232
Shamiakin, I. 330
Shamil (rebel, Rus.) 285
Shamir, Michal 238
SHAMIR, MOSHE (**14**:1289)
- Hebrew literature 176, 178, 181
- Israel Prize 242
SHAMIR, YIZḤAK (**Dc./17**:553) 342
- American Jews 381
- Government of National Unity 192ff
- Greece 166
- Lebanon War 197, 207
- Pollard Affair 315
- succession struggle 193ff
Shamir, Ziva 181
Shamtoniya (city, Iraq) 156
Shapira, Arieh 234
Shapira, Sarit 238
Shapiro, Alexander 133, 373
SHAPIRO, AVRAHAM 342
- Israel Chief Rabbi 224, 295
SHAPIRO, BERNARD J. 343
Shapiro, Harold T. 377
Sharansky, Avital (Natalya) 343
SHARANSKY, NATAN (Anatoly) 343
- Gilbert, Martin 164
- U.S. Congress 332
- *illus:*
- - efforts on behalf of refuseniks 332
Sharett, Rina 235
Shargel, Hillel 392
Shargel, J.Z. 392
Shari'a courts (Musl.) 228ff
SHARON, ARIEL ("ARIK"; **Dc./17**:554)
- Gould, Milton S. 165
- Gush Emunim 171
- Lebanon war 189ff
- Likkud leadership 193
- settlement campaigns 203
Sharon, Yosef 179ff
Sharovsky, Yeruham 232
Sharpe, William 279
Sharrif, Abu Bassam 144
Shas (polit. party, Isr.) 195, 223
Shatilla, *see* Sabra and Shatilla
Shatter, Alan 187
SHATZKY, JACOB (**14**:1318)
- Yiddish literature 391
Shavit, Uzi 181
Shavit, Zohar 181
Shaw, Steven 131
Shawat, Fradji 309
Shay, H. 357
Shcharansky, Anatoly, *see* SHARANSKY NATAN
SHECHEM (**14**:1330)
- archaeological excavations 103
- *illus:*
- - rioting in *Casbah* 191
- - young children provoke IDF soldiers 198
Sheer, Gorby 351
SHEḤITAH (**14**:1337)
- Karaites 257ff
- Romania 328
- Russia 331
Sheinfeld, Ilan 179ff
Shemakha (tn., Rus.) 284
SHEMER, NAOMI (**12**:707)
- Israel Prize 241
SHEMI, YEḤIEL (**14**:1376)
- Israel Prize 241
- sculpture 236
Shenfeld, Ruth 181
Shenhar, Aliza 181
Shenhud, Shlomo 392
Shepatin, Giselle 351
SHEPETOVKA (**14**:1379)
- Jewish community 364
SHER, ANTHONY 344
SHERIFF, NOAM (**12**:708; **Dc./17**:554)
- music in Israel 232
SHERIRA BEN ḤANINA GAON (**14**:1381)
- geonic literature 157ff
Shevardnadze, Eduard 160
- *illus:*
- - with Israel PM Shamir 342
Shidletsky, Ephraim 392
Shi'ism (Isl. sect) 186, 197
Shikmim (site, Isr.) 101
SHILOAH, SILOAM (**14**:1399)
- archaeological excavations 101
SHILOH (**14**:1401)
- archaeological excavations 102
Shiloni, J. 359
Shimoni, Yuval 178
Shinan, A. 313, 359
Shinhar Commission (Isr.) 231
Shinui (polit. party, Isr.) 195
Shirai, Mitsuko 233
SHIRAZ (**14**:1415)
- Jewish community 186
- Shitreet, Meir 395
Shkolnik, Leonid 336
Shlevin, Benjamin 392
Shlisky, Joseph 176
SHMERUK, CHONE (**14**:1426)
- Yiddish 392
Shmuessen Mit Kinder Un Yugent (period., U.S.A.) 318
Shnaider, Mikhail 331ff
Shofar (newsp., Uzbek.) 385
SHOFMAN, GERSHON (**14**:1448)
- Hebrew literature 181
Shoham, Haim 181
SHOMRON, DAN 344
- defense forces 197
Shooting 351
Shorashim (mosh., Isr.) 134
SHORE, DINAH (**15**:1091)
- Sports 350
Short, Nigel 260
Shoshana, A. 359
Shtern, Sholem 392
Shuberoff, Oscar 106
Shulsteyn, Moshe 392
Shultz, George 190, 207
Shunari, Jonathan 259
Shuni (site, Isr.) 104
Shur, Yekutiel 234
Shva, Shlomo 181
SIBERIA (**14**:1486)
- Gery 164
SICK, VISITING THE (**14**:1496)
- ḥavurah movement 174
Sidon, Karol 136
Siegel, Sheldon 139
SIGHET (**14**:1523)
- *illus:*
- - home of Elie Wiesel 327
Silberman, Charles 367
Silberman, Jerry, *see* WILDER, GENE
Silberman, Rosalie, *see* Abella, Rosalie Silberman
Silman, Y. 311
Silver, Vivienne 239
Silverman, Rachel 351
Silverstone, Jack 128
Silvestrini, Cardinal 386
SIMEON BAR ISAAC (**14**:1551)
- Cairo *Genizah* 155
SIMEON BEN MEGAS HA-KOHEN (**14**:1561)
- poetry 309
Simeon ha-Darshan 359
SIMFEROPOL (**14**:1560)
- Krimchaks 266
- *illus:*
- - Bazaar 268
Simon, Murray E. 176
SIMON, PAUL 293
Simon, Uriel 259
SINAI (**14**:1593)
- Gush Emunim 171
- Multinational Forces 365
SINCLAIR, CLIVE 344
- English literature 145ff
SINGAPORE (**14**:1608)
- Pres. Herzog's visit 209
Singer, Guenter 162
Singh, Gyani Zail 185
SIRAT, RENE SAMUEL (**Dc./17**:557)

- France 150
- *illus:*
- - meeting Pres. Mitterrand 150
SITRUK, JOSEPH 344
- France 150
Sivan, Aryeh 179
Skiing 351
Skinheads 98, 112, 124, 162, 183, 314, 377
Skirbal, Henry 323
SKLARE, MARSHALL (**14**:1647)
- American Jews 368
SLAVE TRADE (**14**:1660)
- Krimchaks 267
Slobin, Mark 176
SLOVAKIA (**14**:1678)
- Jewish community 135
Slovenia (rep., Yug.) 393
Smadga, Shay Oren 350, 352
Smilevitch, E. 360
Smirnov-Ostashvili 338
Smislov, Vasili 259
Smith, Bessie 148
Smith, Bradley 379
Smoking 215
SMOLENSK (**15**:6)
- Komzet 264
Smorgon (fam.) 110
Smuggling 184
Snir, Lea 179
Sobel, Henry 123
- *illus:*
- - with Mikhail Gorbachev 124
SOBIBOR (**15**:21)
- Demjanjuk trial 137
Sobol, Mordecai 174
Social and Cultural Association (Pol.) 313
Socialist International 194
SOCIEDAD HEBRAICA ARGENTINA (**15**:52)
- dance troupe 105
Society for the Study of the Jews of Greece 168
Socolof, Joseph 350
Soetendorp, Avraham 298
Sogdia (tn., Crimea), *see* Sudak
Soius russikh ofitserov (orgn., Rus.) 337
Sokolow, Moshe 155, 259, 360
Solar energy 221
- *illus:*
- - Sedeh Boker 222
Solelim (y. mvmt., Isr.) 134
Solkhat (city, Crimea), *see* Stariy Krym
Solodar, Caesar 330
Solomon, Harold 351
Solomon, Norman 253
Solomos, Dionysios 169
SOLOVEITCHIK, JOSEPH DOV (**15**:1321; **Dc./17**:557)
- Orthodoxy, Modern 303
SOLOW, ROBERT MERTON 344
Soltes, Mordecai 250
Solzhenitsyn, A. 155
Somek, Roni 179
Somerville (tn., U.S.A.) 174
Sommer, Yossi 240
SONDHEIM, STEPHEN 361
Sonol (oil co., Isr.) 221
SOPRON (**15**:161)
- museum 292
Soragna (tn., It.) 291
Sorin, Julian 328
Sosnowski, Saul 347
Sosúa (vill., Dominican Rep.) 130
Souissa, Albert 177
Sourrille, Juan 106
SOUTH AFRICA (**15**:184; **Dc./17**:588) 344
- *aliyah* to Israel 212
- anti-Semitism 99
- Australia, migrants to 110
- Israel coal imports 221
- Los Angeles 273
- New Zealand 299
- U.S. Jews against apartheid 376
- Yiddish literature 392
- Yiddish studies 392
South African Jewish Board of Deputies 345
South African Zionist Federation 345
Souza, Ernst de 129
SOVETISH HEYMLAND (**15**:215)
- Jewish Historical and Ethnographic Commission 331
- Russia 336
- Yiddish writers 392
Soviet Jewry Education and Information Center 332
Soviet Public Anti-Zionist Committee 329
SPAIN (**15**:245; **Dc./17**:559)
- Caribbean Jewish community 129
- 5ooth anniversary of expulsion of Jews 341
- French Jewry 152
- Ibiza and Formentera 184
- Ibn Ezra symposium 312
- Italy 245
- museum 291
- Pres. Herzog's visit 209
SPANISH AND PORTUGUESE LITERATURE (**15**:254; **Dc./17**:559) 347
- Talmud research 357
Spanish Civil War 185
Spector, Norman 128
Spector, Shmuel 259
SPERBER, DANIEL 244
- Talmud research 357
Sperber, Stanley 384
SPIEGEL, ISAIAH (**15**:271)
- Yiddish literature 392
SPIEGEL, NATHAN 243
SPIELBERG, STEVEN 283
Spiliakos, Dimitri 166
SPITZ, MARK 348
- Sports 351
Spivakoff, Vladimir 234
SPORTS (**15**:291; **Dc./17**:563) 349
- legislation 216
- Turkey 363
SPORTS IN ISRAEL (**9**:1019; **Dc./17**:563) 351
Sri Lanka 209
Stalindorf (reg., Ukr.) 263
Stamps
- *ḥazzanut* 175
- Iran 186
- Sulzer, Salomon 175
- Surinam 129
- *illus:*
- - Barbados synagogue 129
- - Denmark Sephardi Jews 138
Stanislawski, Michael 181
Stantsiya Zima (vill., Rus.) 164
Stariy Krym (city, Crimea) 267
Starki, Yianni 169
Starkman, Moshe 391
Stavroulakis, Nikos 167
- *illus:*
- - working on 19th-cent. amulet 166
STEG, ADOLPHE 353
- A.I.U. leader 150
STEIN, EDITH (**15**:350)
- beatification of 254
Steinberg, M. 118
Steinberg Center for the arts (U.S.) 384
STEINBERGER, JACK 353
- Schwartz, Melvin 341
Steiner, David 382
STEINER, GEORGE (**6**:790) 353
- Anglo-Jewish writers circles 146
STEINHARDT, LAURENCE ADOLF (**15**:369)
- Hirschmann, Ira Arthur 182
STEINSALTZ, ADIN 354
- Israel Prize 242
- Russian yeshivah 335
- Talmud research 358
"Steipler, The", *see* KANIEVSKY, JACOB ISRAEL
Stemberger, G. 360
STENCL, A.N. (**15**:397)
- Yiddish literature 392
STERLING, SIR JEFFREY (MAURICE) 354
Stern, David 349
STERN, ISAAC (**15**:386; **Dc./17**:566)
- *illus:*
- - Huberman Gala Concert 233
Stern, Max 234
STERN, MOSHE (**Dc./17**:291)
- *ḥazzanut* 175
STERNBERG, SIR SIGMUND 354
Steyrer, Kurt 387
STOCK EXCHANGE, TEL AVIV (**9**:829)
- crisis 218
- *illus:*
- - stock market crash 191
Stokfish, David 392
Stoleru, Lionel 152
STONE, OLIVER 283
STRACK, H. (**15**:418)
- Talmud research 358
STRASBOURG (**15**:422)
- Jewish community 149
Stratford College (Ire.) 188
STRAUSS, ARYEH LUDWIG (**15**:433)
- poetry 312
STRAUSS-KAHN, DOMINIQUE 354
STREICHMANN, YEHEZKIEL (**3**:611)
- Israel Prize 243
Strikes (Isr.) 229
Stroganov, A. 269
Stroumsa, Sarah 259
Strumza, Jacques 168
Stubrin, Marcelo 105
Student Struggle for Soviet Jewry 332, 379, 380
STUDY (**15**:453)
- ḥavurah movement 174
- Reform Judaism 322
- Russia 331
STUTTGART (**15**:462)
- Jewish community 161
Subbotniki (Rus. sect) 164
SUCCESSION (**15**:475)
- common-law wife 217
Sudak (tn., Crimea) 267
Sudan 119, 212, 305
Suessmuth, Rita 163
SUKKOT (**15**:495)
- ḥavurah movement 174
- *illus:*
- - Copenhagen kindergarten 138
SULZBERGER, MAYER (**15**:509)
- museums 287
SULZER, SALOMON (**15**:510)
- memorial day 175
Summers, Judith 146
Surfing 351
SURINAM (**15**:529)
- Jewish commmunty 128ff
- *illus:*
- - Zedek ve-Shalom Synagogue, Paramaribo 129
Surkhan-Khan 284
SUTZKEVER, ABRAHAM (**15**:538)
- Israel Prize 241
- Yiddish literature 391, 392
SUZMAN, JANET 354
Svyatoslav (pr., Rus.) 267
Swed, Elie 355
Swed, Selim 355
SWEDEN (**15**:545; **Dc./17**:567)
- Conservative Judaism 135
Swimming 351
SWITZERLAND (**15**:559; **Dc./17**:568) 354
- museum 291
- Schmidt Archive 175
- Sephardim 342
- Yiddish literature 392
- *illus:*
- - Jewish Museum, Basle 291
SYDNEY (**15**:564)
- Jewish community 110ff
SYNAGOGUE (**15**:579)
- archaeological excavations 103
- Caribbean islands 129
- Central and East European 65
- Conservative Judaism 132, 133
- Czechoslovakia 136
- Denmark 137, 138
- England 142
- 500th anniversary of expulsion of Jews from Spain 341
- France 152
- Germany 162, 290
- Germany, East 164
- *ḥazzanut* 174ff
- Hungary 292
- Ibiza and Formentera 185
- India 185
- Ireland 187
- Italy 245
- Netherlands 290, 295
- Russia 335
- South Africa 345
- Turkey 362
- Ukraine 364
- U.S. membership 383
- Yugoslavia 394
- *illus:*
- - Barbados 129
- - Berne, Switzerland 355
- - Copenhagen, Denmark 138
- - Dublin Terenure Synagogue 188
- - Karaite, Turkey 258
- - Paramaribo, Surinam 129
- - Moscow 336
- - Salonika 265
- - 350th anniversary of Amsterdam Ashkenazi Congregation 295
SYNAGOGUE COUNCIL OF AMERICA (**15**:630)
- Jewish-Christian relations 251
Synagogue Light (period., U.S.A.) 31;
SYRIA (**15**:636; **Dc./17**:569) 355
- American Jews 381
- Arab boycott 122
- British relations 144
- Brunner, Alois 125
- emigration of Jews 210
- Gulf War 208
- Islamic fundamentalism 197
- Israel-Lebanon War 189ff, 196ff, 207
- Jordanian relations 207
- Klarsfeld, Beate 261
- PLO 305ff
Szeged (city, Hung.) 184
Sznajder, Andrew 351
Szombat (journ., Hung.) 184
Szyszman, Simon 258

T

Taba 207
TABGHA (**15**:688)
- Church of the Multiplication of the Loaves and Fishes 217
TABIB, MORDEKHAI (**15**:690)
- Hebrew literature 181
Table tennis 351
Tadjikistan 211
- *aliyah* to Israel 211
- Jewish population 328
TADMOR, HAYIM 356
Tadzhik (J. Dialect) 384
TADZHIKISTAN 356
Tagliacozzo, Sergio 246
Tagriberdi (hist., Egy.) 284
Taiar, Israel, *see* Iantovskii, Semen
Taibeh (tn., Isr.) 228
TAKKANOT (**15**:712)
- geonic literature 157ff
Tal, Mikhal 234
Tal, Zvi 137
Talgram, Itai 232
TALLINN (**15**:742)
- Jewish community 147, 334
Talmage, Frank 128
Talmi, Yoav 232
TALMON, SHEMARYAHU 356
Talmon, Zvi 175
TALMUD, BABYLONIAN (**15**:755)
- Cairo *Genizah* 155
- geonic literature 157
- research 357ff
TALMUD, JERUSALEM (**15**:772)
- research 358ff
TALMUD, RECENT RESEARCH (**Dc./17**:571) 357
Talmud torah (school system, Isr.) 230
TALPIR, GABRIEL JOSEPH (**15**:779)
- Hebrew literature 179
Tamami, Giuliano 259
Taman (port, Crimea) 266ff
Tamar, Issachar 359
Tamar Dance Company 235
Tambour, Wolf 392

Tambov (tn., Rus.) 164
TAMMUZ, BENJAMIN (**15**:789)
- Hebrew literature 176, 178
Tanenbaum, Joseph 128
Tan-Pai, Yehoshua 179
Targarona, Judit 312
TARIF, AMIN 243
Tarki (stlmt., Rus.) 286
Tarnopolskii, Yurii 333
Tartakover, David 237
TARTU (**15**:827)
- cemetery desecrated 147
TASHKENT (**15**:828)
- Jewish associations 334
- Jewish community 384
TASMANIA (**15**:830)
- Jewish community 109ff
Tatars 267
Taviani (hist.) 342
TAXATION (**15**:837)
- Italian Jews 244
Taylor, Mervyn 187
TAYLOR, SIR PETER MURRAY 360
Taylor, Richard 153
TCHERNICHOWSKY, SAUL (**15**:877)
- Hebrew literature 180
TCHERNOWITZ-AVIDAR, YEMIMAH (**15**:885)
- Israel Prize 241
Tefen (indus. zone, Isr.) 236
TEHERAN (**15**:905)
- Jewish community 186
Teḥiyyah (polit. party, Isr.) 171ff, 194, 213, 395
Teitelbaum, Avi 184
Teitelbaum, David 164
TEL AVIV (**15**:916)
- Cantorial training school 175
- Buenos Aires "twin" city 107
- dance center 235
- Gulf War 208
- Krimchaks 266
- Maccabi basketball team 352
- Mountain Jews 287
- Muslim court 228
- population 200, 214
- Reform Judaism 321
- Salonikan immigrants 320
- sculptures 236
- women elect chief rabbi 226
- Yiddish literature 391
- *illus:*
- - Scud attack 208
- - west to east view 201
Tel Aviv Museum of Art 236
Tel Aviv String Quartet 232
Tel Aviv Symphony Orchestra 232
TEL AVIV UNIVERSITY (**15**:925)
- *ḥazzanut* 175
- Sephardim 342
Telesin, Ziame 392
TELEVISION AND RADIO (**15**:927) 282
- Argentina 108
- Australia 112
- Belgium 118
- Brazil 123
- Ireland 188
- Isaacs, Jeremy 188
- Israel law 216
- Israel Prize 241
- "Jerusalem in Spain" series 342
- Russia 335
- South Africa 345
- *illus:*
- - Labor Party election ad 194
TEL ḤAI (**15**:931)
- art 236
Tells
- Dan 120
- Amal 101
- Aphek 101
- Arad 101
- Mikne 102
- Yenoam 101
Telscher, Eliot 351
Temir-Khan-Shurah, *see* Buynaksk
TEMPLE MOUNT (**15**:988)
- Arabs killed in incident 248
- *intifada* 205
- messianic groups 223
- *illus:*
- - Ramadan prayers 228
"Temple Mount Faithful" (group, Isr.) 206, 223
Tenenbaum, Shea 392
Tennis 351, 353
Tenuah ha-Masortit (Isr.), *see* CONSERVATIVE JUDAISM
TERKEL, STUDS (Louis) 360
TEXAS (**15**:1034; **Dc./17**:582)
- Jewish political force 377
Thatcher, Margaret 143, 332
- *illus:*
- - with Shimon Peres 144
THEATER (**15**:1077) 360
- controversial play banned 217
- Russian "refusal" activists 331
- United States 384
THEODOR, JULIUS (**15**:1100)
- Cairo *Genizah* 155
Theotoka, Georgou 169
THERESIENSTADT (**15**:1112)
- memorial museum 136
Thoeme, Bodie 367
Thomas, D.M. 147
TIBBON, JUDAH BEN SAUL IBN (**15**:1129)
- geonic literature 159
Ticho House (Jer.) 232
TIFLIS (**15**:1138)
- Georgia 160
- Gery 164
- Jewish community 335ff
Tigre (reg., Eth.) 119
Tikkun (mag., U.S.A.) 317, 374, 381
Tillem, Ivan L. 383
TIM 361
TIMISOARA (**15**:1143)
- Jewish community 327
Timman, Jan 259
Timopeyeva, Nina 235
Ting, Samuel 325
Tishchenko, Sergei 338
TISO, JOSEF (**15**:1155)
- Slovakia 136
Tmutarakan, *see* Samkush
Toaff, Elio 246, 252
Tobago (isl., W. Indies) 130
Tobi, Yosef 311
Tobin, Gary 368ff
Toboggan, *see* Luge
TOKYO (**15**:1192)
- Jewish community 247
TOLEDANO (fam; **15**:1193)
- reunion in Spain 342
TOLEDO (**15**:1198)
- museum 291
Tolkovsky, Zvi 239
TOMAR (**15**:1213)
- museum 291
Tomassi, Giorgia 233
TOMBS AND TOMBSTONES (**15**:1215)
- archaeological excavations 101
- Krimchaks 267
Tomson, Shaun 351
TORAH (**15**:1235)
- Orthodoxy, Modern 303ff
TORONTO
- cantors' convention 175
- Jewish community 126ff
- Syrian Jewry 356
Torres, Dara 302, 351
TOSEFTA (**15**:1283)
- Talmud research 359
Touati, Ch. 312
TOULOUSE (**15**:1286)
- Jewish community 149
Touvier, Paul 152
Townsend, J.T. 360
Track and field 351
TRANSPLANTS (**15**:1337)
- Orthodoxy, Modern 304
TRANSYLVANIA (**15**:1341)
- Jewish community 327
Trawniki (concen. camp) 137
Treason 218
TREBLINKA (**15**:1365)
- Demjanjuk trial 137
Treinin, Avner 179
Trevisan Semi, Emanuela 258
TRIESTE (**15**:1392)
- Jewish community 244
Trifa, Valerian 379
TRIGANO, SHMOUEL 362
- France 150
TRIKKALA (**15**:1395)
- Jewish community 167
Trinidad 130
TRIPOLI (Leb.; **15**:1396)
- PLO 305
TROKI, ISAAC (**15**:1403)
- Karaism 258
Trondheim (city, Nor.) 291, 300
Troper, Harold 97, 128
Trotsky, Leon 330
Tsanin, Mordecai 391
Tsokos, Constantinos 166
Tsur, Reuven 181, 309
Tsur-Rotenstreich Committee (Isr.) 315
Tucacas (city, Venez.) 128
Tuchersfeld (vill., Ger.) 290
TUCSON (**15**:1423)
- Sephardi studies 342
Tudjman, Franjo 393
Tukan, Boris 259
Tulsa (city, U.S.) 289
TUMARKIN, IGAEL (**15**:1429)
- art 237
TUNISIA (**15**:1430; **Dc./17**:587)
- Arab boycott 122
- Phoenix Museum 289
- PLO 196ff, 204, 297, 305
TURIN (**15**:1453)
- Jewish community 244
TURKEY (**15**:1456; **Dc./17**:587) 362
- 500th anniversary of the expulsion of Jews from Spain 341
- Jewish community 212
- Karaites 258
- love poems 312
- Mountain Jews 284
- *illus:*
- - Karaite synagogue 258
Turkmenia (rep., C.I.S.) 328
Twenthe (tn., Neth.) 295
TYKOCINSKI, HAYYIM (**15**:1476)
- geonic literature 158
Tzadok, Arnon 239
Tzalla, Kimona 169
Tzioba, Friksou 169
TZOMET 395
Tzori, Hillel 234
Tzur, Yaakov 167

U

Uj Elet (newsp., Hung.) 184
UKRAINE (**15**:1513) 364
- Israel relations 209
- Jewish Population 328
- Komzet 263
- pogroms 337
Ulkumen, Salahattin 167
Ullman, Micha 237
Ulmann, Liv 301
ULPAN (**15**:1525)
- new immigrants 231
Umm al-Fahm (vill., Isr.) 203
- *illus:*
- - school building 202
Union for Traditional Conservative Judaism 133
UNION OF AMERICAN HEBREW CONGREGATIONS (**15**:1536)
- criticism of Israel's handling *intifada* 382
- Los Angeles 275
- publishing 318
- Reform Judaism 320ff
Union of Councils for Soviet Jewry 332, 379, 380
Union of Italian Jewish Communities 244
Union of Soviet Writers 330
United Arab Emirates 122
United Communal Fund (S.A.) 345
UNITED JEWISH APPEAL (**15**:1540)
- Jewish Agency 250
- Soviet Jews campaign 380
UNITED NATIONS (**15**:1543) 364
- anti-Israel resolutions 100, 107, 209, 297, 334, 338
- Arafat, Yasser 205
- Iran 186
- Irish troops in Lebanon 188
- Israel Arab peace negotiations 209
- Netherlands 297
- PLO 306
- Syrian Jews 356
- Ukraine 364
- Waldheim Affair 387
UNRWA 365
UNTSO 365
UNITED STATES LITERATURE (**15**:1564; **Dc./17**:590) 365
- writers' symposium 145
UNITED STATES OF AMERICA (**15**:1585; **Dc./17**:592) 367
- American Sephardi Federation 98
- anti-Semitism 98, 100
- Arab boycott 122
- Barbie, Klaus 116
- CAJE 131
- CLAL 131
- Conservative Judaism 132
- Demjanjuk trial 137
- 500th anniversary of expulsion of Jews from Spain 341
- Gulf War 197
- ḥavurah movement 174
- *ḥazzanut* 175
- "Irangate" 186
- Iranian Jews 186
- Iran terrorist attack 187
- Israel coal imports 221
- Israel economy 219
- Israeli settlements 213
- Israel-Lebanon War 189ff, 196, 206
- Israel relations 206
- Israel Sinfonietta tour 232
- Jewish Book Council 250
- Jewish-Christian relations 253
- Jews in Japan 247
- Jewish population 198
- Karaites 258
- Krimchaks 266
- Los Angeles 272
- median age of Jews 328
- museums 287
- National Jewish Welfare Board 294
- N.Y. Jewish Museum 185
- P.L.O., recognition of 191, 204ff, 306
- Pollard Affair 314
- Pres. Herzog's visit 209
- press 316
- publishing 318
- Reform Judaism 322
- Russian Jews 210, 332ff, 338
- solar energy plants 222
- South Africa 347
- Soviet citizens visit Russia 333
- Soviet Summit Conference, Reykjavik 333
- Syrian Jews, plight of 356
- United Nations 364
- Waldheim Affair 388
- Yiddish literature 392
- Zionist Congresses 395
- *illus:*
- - emergency conference on Soviet Jewry 329
- - JTS students at prayer 133
UNITED SYNAGOGUE (**15**:1672)
- financial crisis 145
UNITED SYNAGOGUE OF AMERICA (**15**:1673)
- Conservative Judaism 134
United Synagogue Youth (U.S.) 133
Universalism 322
UNIVERSITIES (**15**:1674)
- American Jews 383
- Australia 111
- Belgium 118
- Brazil 123
- England 145
- France 151
- Germany 163
- Japan 248
- Poland 314
- United States 377
- Yiddish studies 392
UNIVERSITY OF JUDAISM (U.S.A.) 384
- Conservative Judaism 134

- Los Angeles 274
- *illus:*
- - Torah reading 371
Uno, Sousuke 248
Unzer Vort (newsp., Fr.) 392
URBACH, EPHRAIM ELIMELECH (**16:**4)
- Talmud research 358
Uri, Aviva 238
URIS, LEON (**16:**10)
- U.S. literature 318
URUGUAY (**16:**10)
- Klarsfeld, Beate 261
- *illus:*
- - demonstration of behalf of Soviet Jewry 332
U.S.S.R., *see* RUSSIA
Utevskii, Lev 331
UTRECHT (**16:**36)
- Jewish community 295
UZBEKISTAN (**16:**39) 384
- Jewish population 328
- Komzet 264
- pogrom 337
UZIEL, BARUCH 385

V

Vafopoulou, G.Th. 169
Vahl Davis, Graham de 112
VAJDA, GEORGES (**16:**52)
- Karaites 258
- poetry 309
Valdez (tn., Alsk.) 97
Valle Rodriguez, Carlos del 310
Van Dam, Hendrik George 161
Vanunu case 218
Vardi, Yair 235
VARMUS, HAROLD ELIOT 385
Varna 385
Varon, Miri 178
Vasilev, Dimitrii 337
Vasilikou, Vasili 169
Vasserman, Grigorii 332
VATICAN (**16:**731; **Dc./17:**611) 385
- Auschwitz convent controversy 109
- Israel relations 228
- Italian Jewish community 245
- Jewish-Christian relations 246, 251
Vega, Louis Alvarez 299
Venezi, Ilia 169
VENICE (**16:**94)
- Jewish community 244ff
- museum 290
Venlo (tn., Neth) 295
VERGELIS, AARON (**16:**111)
- Yiddish 392
VERMONT (**16:**112)
- Jewish elected officials 377
Vèrtes, Arpad 184
Vevey 355
Viareggio (tn., It.) 244
Victoria (state, Austr.) 109ff
VIENNA (**16:**122)
- *aliyah* transit center 380
- *ḥazzanut* 175
- Institute of Jewish Studies 290
- Jewish community 113
Vietnam 209
Vietnam War 323
VILNA (**16:**138)
- Jewish community 272
- Ponari meeting 331
VILNAY, ZEV (**16:**151)
- Israel Prize 240
VINNITSA (**16:**159)
- Jewish community 364
Vinokurov, Eduoard 302
Virgin, Tomb of the (Jer.) 227
VIRGIN ISLANDS (**16:**164; **Dc./17:**614)
- Jewish community 129
VITAL, SAMUEL (**16:**176)
- poetry 310
Viterbo, Boldo 246
Viticulture 285
Vitsen, N. 284
Vitta, Edoardo 246
Vlamms Blok (polit. party, Belg.) 98
Vlasov, Andrei 137
VOGEL, DAVID (**16:**202)
- Hebrew literature 178
Volpin, Yitzhak 117
Volvovskii, Leonid (Arye) 330ff
VORONEZH (**16:**224)
- Gery 164
VORST, LOUIS J. 386
Voz Judia, La (newsp., Arg.) 108
Vranitzky, Franz 113, 114
Vzgliad (newsp., Rus.) 336

W

Wachsman, Daniel 239ff
WACHTLER, SOL 387
Wadi Qelt 103
Wagner, Gottfried 163
Wagner, Heinrich 112
WAHL, ISAAK 244
Wahrhaftig, S. 358
Waldegrave, William 144
Waldheim, Kurt 113, 168, 246, 254, 261, 387
- United Nations 365
WALDHEIM AFFAIR 387
Waldman, Eliezer 171
Waldman, Moshe 392
Walesa, Lech 109, 314
Wallach, Yona 179
Wallenstein, Meir 310
Waller, Harold M. 128
Wallonia (reg., Belg.) 117
Walqayit (reg., Eth.) 119
Waltham (city, Mass.) 289
Wandering You Press (publ. house, U.S.A.) 319
WANNSEE CONFERENCE (**16:**264)
- Holocaust commemorative center 163
Waqf (Musl. rel. trust) 228
Warburg, Frieda Schiff 287
WAR CRIMES TRIALS (**16:**288)
- Australia 112
- Barbie, Nikolaus 116
- Canada 127
- Demjanjuk trial 137
- England 143
- IJA 186
- Klarsfeld, Beate and Serge 261
- United States 379
- Waldheim, Kurt 365
WARHAFTIG, ZERAḤ (**16:**30)
- Israel Prize 241
WARSAW (**16:**333)
- Jewish community 313ff
- *illus:*
- - deputy defense minister addressing U.S. rabbis 314
Warsaw Ghetto 334
WASHINGTON, D.C. (**16:**356)
- Black-Jewish project 376
- Fabrengen 174
- Holocaust Memorial Museum 289, 328, 378
- Jewish choirs 384
- Klutznick Museum 288
- PAC's 376
- press 317
- *illus:*
- - *Moment: The Magazine of Jewish Culture and Opinion* 317
WASHINGTON, GEORGE (**16:**359)
- Seixas, Moses 288
WASSERMAN, DALE 361
Wasserman, Rabbi (Rum.) 328
Watanabe 122
Waterloo (tn., Belg.) 117
WAYNE, JOHNNY (**15:**1093)
- Canada 128
Wayne State University Press 319
Weber, Charles 379
Weesp (Neth.) 297
Weidberg, Ron 234
Weightlifting 351ff
WEINBERG, HARRY 389
- philanthropic foundation 383
Weinberg, Wilhelm 161
Weinberger, L.J. 309
Weiner, Gerald 128
Weinfeld, J.Sh. 359
Weinfeld, Moshe 356
Weinfeld, Yocheved 238
WEINGREEN, JACOB 389
Weininger, Freed 392
Weisfish, N.M. 358
Weiss, Abner 275
Weiss, Abraham 109
Weiss, Daniella 171, 172
Weiss, Hillel 181
WEISS, MEIR 243
Weissensee (tn., Ger.) 164
WEITZ, RA'ANAN (**Dc./17:**616)
- Israel Prize 243
WEIZMANN INSTITUTE OF SCIENCE (**16:**438)
- solar energy research 221
Weizsaecker, Richard von 163, 389
Weldon, Fay 148
WELLER, MICHAEL361
Wellington (city, N.Z.) 299
Wener, Luck 351
Werner, Eric 367
WERSES, SAMUEL 242
- Hebrew literature 181
Wertheimer, A.J. 359
WERTHEIMER, SAMSON (**16:**457)
- Austrian Jewish museum 290
WERTHEIMER, STEF 243
WESKER, ARNOLD (**16:**460)
- English literature 146
West Bloomfield (Mich.) 289
WESTERBORK (**16:**466)
- memorial 296
WESTERN WALL (**16:**467)
- *intifada* 206
- Women of the Wall 226
Wexler, Paul 259
WEXNER, LESLIE H. 390
WHITE, THEODORE H. ("Teddy") 390
Wieder, Naphtali 259
WIESEL, ELIE (**16:**507; **Dc./17:**618) 390
- Austria 114
- CLAL 131
- Nobel Prize 299
- Norwegian books 301
- *illus:*
- - former home in Sighet 327
Wieseltier, Meir 179
WIESENTHAL, SIMON (**Dc./17:**618)
- Austrian anti-Semitism 113
- Norwegian book 301
Wiesenthal Center (L.A., U.S.A.) 274, 289
Wigoder, Geoffrey 254
WILCHEK, MEIR 243
WILDER, GENE 284
WILENSKY, MOSHE (**Dc./17:**476)
- Israel Prize 234, 241
Wilentz, David 390
WILENTZ, ROBERT N. 390
Wilk, Melvin 367
Willebrands, Johannes 252, 386
Wilsker, Arye 156, 309
Wind energy 221
Wine, Hubert
- *illus:*
- - Terenure Synagogue 188
Wingate Institute (Isr.) 242
Winterthur (Switz.) 355
WISCONSIN (**16:**555)
- Jewish elected officials 377
Wiseman, Shloime 128
WISLICENY, DIETER (**16:**569)
- Brunner, Alois 125
- Koretz, Zvi 265
Wisse, Ruth 128
Witchel, John 351
WITTENBERG, YIZḤAK (**16:**591)
- Korczak-Marla, Rozka 264
WIZO (**16:**593)
- Ireland 188
Wohlberg, Max 176
Wolf, Alfred 275
Wolfe, Ray 128
Wolff, Hayley 351
Wolfsohn, Alfred 340
Wolfson, Ron 134
Wollheim, Norbert 161
Wolpe, David 392
Wolpe, Michael 234
WOMAN (**16:**623)
- Conservative Judaism 133
- equal opportunity in labor law 216
- equal rights in U.S.A. 153
- Israel labor law 216
- Jewish education in U.S. 370
- rabbis in Israel 226
- Reform Judaism 322ff
- teachers' strike 229
- U.S. rabbis and cantors 373
- *illus:*
- - cantor, U.S.A. 176
Women of the Wall (group, Isr.) 226
Women's League for Conservative Judaism 134
World Apartheid Movement (S.A.) 347
World Conference for Soviet Jewry 333
World Council for Yiddish and Jewish Culture 391
World Council of Churches 252
WORLD JEWISH CONGRESS (**16:**637)
- anti-Semitism 375
- Austria 113
- Belgium 117
- European Jewish Congress 150
- Germany 162
- Hungary 183
- Institute of Jewish Affairs 146, 186
- Jewish-Christian relations 251
- Latin American Prize 188
- Reform Judaism 324
- Russia 335
- Turkey 362
- Waldheim Affair 387
WORLD SEPHARDI FEDERATION (**Dc./17:**620)
- American Sephardi Federation 98
World Union for Progressive Judaism 321
World Zionist Organization, *see* JEWISH AGENCY
WORMS (**16:**643)
- Rashi House 290
Worsoger, Shlomo 392
Wrestling 351
Wybran, Joseph 117

X

Xenophobia 152

Y

YAARI, MENAḤEM 241
YACHAD (Black-J. gr., U.S.) 376
Yachting 351ff
Yad Harav Herzog (Jer.) 357ff
YADIN, YIGAEL (**16:**694; **Dc./17:**625)
- archaeological excavations 101
- Israel Prize 243
- Greek Jewry 167
- Greek Righteous Gentiles 166
YAD IZHAK BEN-ZVI 391
- Israel Prize 241
Yahalom, Y. 309ff
Yahel (kib., Isr.) 322
Yakovlev, Alexander 338
YALKUT SHIMONI (**16:**707)
- Talmud research 359
Yammit
- *illus:*
- - aerial view 206, 207
Yampolsky, Berta 235
Yaniv, Shlomo 181
YANNAI (**16:**712)
- poetry 309
Yanosovitch, Y.J. 391, 392
Yaoz-Kest, Itamar 180

YASKI, AVRAHAM 240
Yassif, E. 309, 312
Yatha, Dimitri 169
YAVETS, ZVI 243
Yavneh School (Hung.) 184
Yedaya, Oded 238
YEDIOTH AHRONOTH (newsp.; **16:**727)
- U.S. sales 316
YEHOSHUA, AVRAHAM B. (**16:**730)
- Hebrew literature 176ff
- Norwegian books 301
- U.S. books 318
YEHUDAI BEN NAHMAN (**16:**731)
- geonic literature 158
Yehuda Publishing House (Arg.) 108
YEIVIN, ISRAEL 242
Yellin, Meir 392
Yeltsin, Boris 337ff
YEMEN (**16:**739)
- American Jews 380
- Arab boycott 122
- emigration of Jews 210
- Gulf War 208
- love poems 312
- PLO 305
YEROḤAM (**16:**759)
- woman elected to religious council 226
Yerushalaimer Almanakh (journ., Isr.) 391
Yerushalmi, David ben Moses 257
YESHIVA UNIVERSITY (**16:**760; **Dc./17:**627)
- American Orthodoxy 372
- 500th anniversary of expulsion of Jews from Spain 342
- museum 288
YESHIVOT (**16:**762)
- Israel 224, 230
- Israel Prize to *yeshivot hesder* 243
YESHURUN, AVOT (**16:**773)
- Hebrew literature 179
- Israel Prize 244
Yeshurun, Itzhak "Zeppel" 239
YESUD HA-MA'ALAH (**16:**773)
- archaeological excavations 104, 120
- Gery 164
YEVPATORIA (**16:**778)
- Komzet 263
Yid, Der (newsp., U.S.A.) 316
Yiddishe Kultur (period, U.S.) 392
Yiddishe Zeitung (newsp., S.A.) 392
YIDDISH LANGUAGE (**16:**789)
- Cairo *Genizah* 156
- press 316, 336
- Russia 329
YIDDISH LITERATURE (**16:**798; **Dc./17:**627) 391
- Cairo *Genizah* 156
Yiddish Welt (journ.) 391
Yiftahel (site, Isr.) 101
Yishai, Roglit 234
Yisrael Shelanu (newsp., U.S.A.) 316
YIVO (**16:**837; **Dc./17:**629)
- Jewish book council 250
YIVO Annual (period., U.S.A.) 318
YIZHAR, S. (**16:**840)
- Hebrew literature 176, 178
Yodfat (kib., Isr.) 221
Yoma, Zulema 107
YOM KIPPUR WAR (**Dc./17:**58)
- Israel-Lebanon War 189
Yonassi, Yitzchak 352
Yonathan, Nathan 180
YORK (**16:**840)
- Clifford's Tower massacre anniversary 145
YOSE BEN YOSE (**16:**856)
- poetry 310
YOSEF, OVADIAH (**16:**857; **Dc./17:**631)
- Falashas 120
- Shas 195, 224
Yoshino, Naoko 233
YOTVATAH (**16:**859)
- archaeological excavations 104
Young, Andrew 375
Young, Lord 143
YOUNG, STUART 392
YOUTH ALIYAH (**16:**861)
- Jewish Agency 249
Yuchvitz, Boris 238
YUGOSLAVIA (**16:**868; **Dc./17:**361) 393
- anti-Semitism 99
- immigration to Israel 212
- Iranian propaganda 187
- Maccabi Tel Aviv 352
- museums 290
- Waldheim, Kurt 387
Yuhas, Dan 234
YURTNER, YEHOSHUA 240
Yuval Ensemble (Isr.) 174
Yuval Trio 232

Z

Zaandam (Neth.) 297
Zable, Arnold 112
Zablud, Robert 112
ZACH, NATHAN (**16:**903)
- Hebrew literature 179
ZACUTO, MOSES BEN MORDECAI (**16:**906)
- poetry 311
ẒADDIK, JOSEPH BEN JACOB IBN (**16:**911)
- poetry 309
ZAFRANI, HAIM 394
- Hebrew poetry 309
ZAGREB (**16:**917)
- Jewish community 393
Zaire (state, Afr.) 209
- *illus:*
- - Pres. Mobutu in Israel 209
Zak, Gershon 241
Zak, Y. 358
Zakynthos (tn., Gr.) 166
Zalkind, Rozaliya Samoylovna, *see* ZEMLYACHKA, ROZALIYA SOMOYLOVNA
Zalmona, Yigal 237
Zalmonovitch, Shemaryahu, *see* TALMON, SHEMARYAHU
Zamir Chorale (U.S.) 384
ZECHARIAH BEN SOLOMON-ROFE (**16:**960)
- Talmud research 359
Zeilinger, Leonid 332
Zeini, A.R. 358
ZELDA (MISHKOVSKY; **Dc./17:**636)
- Hebrew literature 179
Zeldin, Isaiah 274
ZELDOVICH, YAKOV BORISOVICH 394
Zêlichenok, Roald 330ff
Zelman, Leon 114
Zemach, Ada 181, 309, 312
Zemer, Moshe 321
ZEMLYACHKA (Zalkind), ROZALIYA SAMOYLOVNA 394
ZENTRALWOHLFAHRTSTELLE DER DEUTSCHEN JUDEN (**16:**993)
- Germany 161
ZEVI, BRUNO (**16:**1004)
- Italy 245
Zevi, Tullia 244
Zhirinovskii, Vladimir 337
ZHITOMIR (**16:**1011)
- Jewish community 364
Zilberg, Samuil 334
Zilk, Helmut 113, 114
ZIMBABWE (**14:**148; **Dc./17:**526) 394
Zimmerman, Akiva 175
Zimriyyah (Isr.) 233
Zinger, Jacob 183ff
Zinger, Oedon 184
Zinger, Victor 302
Zingeris, Emanuel 272
ZION (mt., Jer.; **16:**1030)
- Cenacle refurbished 227
"Zion, Prisoners of" 331ff
ZIONISM (**16:**1031)
- anti-Semitism 99, 144, 334, 364
- Arab boycott 122
- Conservative Judaism 134
- Gush Emunim 171
- Hungary 183
- India 185
- Jewish Agency 249
- Mountain Jews 286
- Netherlands 296
- press 316
- Reform Judaism 320ff
- Romania 327
- Russia 329ff
- South Africa 347
- U.S. Negro-Jewish relations 375
ZIONIST CONGRESSES (**16:**1164; **Dc./17:**638) 395
- Reform Judaism 323
- Zionist Federation of Russia 335
ZIONIST ORGANIZATION OF AMERICA (**16:**1178)
- Zionist Congress (31st) 395
ZIPPER, JACOB (**Dc./17:**638)
- Yiddish literature 392
Zisels, Yosef (Iosif) 334, 364
Ziv, Pinḥas 313
Ziv, T.R. 360
Zogratakis, Georgos 167
ZOHAR, MIRIAM 241
Zoltai, Gustav 183ff
Ẓomet (polit. pty., Isr.) 194
Zuccotti, Susan 245
Zucker, Dedi
- *illus:*
- - efforts on behalf of refuseniks 332
Zuckerman, Buck Henry, *see* HENRY, BUCK
ZUCKERMAN, PINCHAS (**Dc./17:**476)
- *illus:*
- - Huberman Gala Concert 233
Zuesse, Evan 113
Zundel, Ernst 100, 126
Zukunft (period. U.S.) 392
Zur, Menahem 234
Zur, Reuven 312
ZURICH (**16:**1241)
- Jewish community 354
Zwick, Judith Halevi 181
Zwicky, Fay 112
Zwolle (Neth.) 297

Come ye and let us go up to the mountain of the Lord
of His ways and we will walk in His paths for out of Zi
Jerusa